September 1–3, 2014
Gothenburg, Sweden

Association for
Computing Machinery

Advancing Computing as a Science & Profession

ICFP'14

Proceedings of the 2014 ACM SIGPLAN

International Conference on Functional Programming

Sponsored by:

ACM SIGPLAN

Supported by:

Jane Street, Google, Microsoft Research, Mozilla, ORACLE LABS, Standard Chartered, Bloomberg, Credit Suisse, Cyberpoint, Erlang Solutions, Facebook, Galois, Klarna AB, LexiFi, Twitter, alephcloud, IntelliFactory, Opera Software, QuviQ, & Systor Vest

Association for
Computing Machinery

Advancing Computing as a Science & Profession

The Association for Computing Machinery
2 Penn Plaza, Suite 701
New York, New York 10121-0701

Notice to Past Authors of ACM-Published Articles
ACM intends to create a complete electronic archive of all articles and/or other material previously published by ACM. If you have written a work that has been previously published by ACM in any journal or conference proceedings prior to 1978, or any SIG Newsletter at any time, and you do NOT want this work to appear in the ACM Digital Library, please inform permissions@acm.org, stating the title of the work, the author(s), and where and when published.

ISBN: 978-1-4503-2873-9 (Digital)

ISBN: 978-1-4503-3265-1 (Print)

Additional copies may be ordered prepaid from:

ACM Order Department
PO Box 30777
New York, NY 10087-0777, USA

Phone: 1-800-342-6626 (USA and Canada)
+1-212-626-0500 (Global)
Fax: +1-212-944-1318
E-mail: acmhelp@acm.org
Hours of Operation: 8:30 am – 4:30 pm ET

Printed in the USA

Chairs' Welcome

It is our great pleasure to welcome you to Gothenburg for the 19th ACM SIGPLAN International Conference on Functional Programming: ICFP 2014.

This year's conference continues its tradition as a forum for researchers, developers, and students to discuss the latest work on the design, implementation, principles, and use of functional programming. The conference covers the entire spectrum, from theory to practice.

This year's call for papers attracted 97 submissions: 85 regular research papers, 9 functional pearls and 3 experience reports. Out of these, the program committee accepted 28 papers, two of which are functional pearls and another two are experience reports. In addition to these papers, the technical program includes three invited keynotes: "Using Formal Methods to Enable More Secure Vehicles: DARPA's HACMS Program" by Kathleen Fisher, "Behavioral Software Contracts" by Robby Findler, and "Depending on Types" by Stephanie Weirich. All three keynote presentations address topics that are currently of high relevance and are presented by leading researchers in these areas.

As usual, the main conference is complemented by a range of affiliated events as well as the ICFP Programming Contest, whose results are announced during the conference. This year, ICFP comes with eleven affiliated events covering a wide range of specialist topics, from functional art and music to high-performance computing. Moreover, the tutorials, talks, and BoFs under the umbrella of the Commercial Users of Functional Programming (CUFP) workshop focus on the application of functional programming in modern software development and industrial practice.

With the increasing popularity of functional programming, ICFP is steadily growing and its success depends on an ever larger number of researchers, developers, and volunteers: the authors of research papers who entrust their precious work to ICFP, the many reviewers who generously donate their time, the participants in the programming competition, and the steadily growing list of organisers and volunteers whose work enables ICFP. We like to specifically acknowledge the excellent work of the local organisers, Björn von Sydow and his team as well as Annabel Satin; Anil Madhavapeddy, who liaised with our industrial sponsors; Tom Schrijvers and Sam Tobin-Hochstadt for overseeing the organisation of the workshops; David Van Horn for spreading the word about ICFP; and, last but not least, Duncan Coutts and Nicolas Wu for shouldering the challenging task of organising the programming contest.

We are indebted to our sponsors who made it possible to keep registration cost reasonable and who kindly supported students who would not have been able to attend the conference without financial aid. Their generosity helps our community to grow and thrive.

We hope that you enjoy, as a conference attendee or reader of the proceedings, the conference and affiliated events and benefit from the wide array of technical work.

Johan Jeuring
ICFP'14 General Chair
Universiteit Utrecht, The Netherlands

Manuel M. T. Chakravarty
ICFP'14 Program Chair
University of New South Wales, Australia

Table of Contents

Session 6: Contracts & Scheme

Session 7: Tools Used in Anger

Session 8: Type Systems

Session 9: Incremental Computing

Keynote 3

Session 10: Homotopy Type Theory

Session 11: Abstract Interpretation

Session 12: Depending on Types

Session 13: Domain Specific Languages II

Session 14: Abstract Machines

ICFP 2014 Organization

General Chair: Johan Jeuring *(Universiteit Utrecht, The Netherlands)*

Program Chair: Manuel M. T. Chakravarty *(University of New South Wales, Australia)*

Workshop Co-Chairs: Tom Schrijvers *(Ghent University, Belgium)*
Sam Tobin-Hochstadt *(Indiana University, USA)*

Programming Contest Co-Chairs: Duncan Coutts *(Well Typed LLP, UK)*
Nicolas Wu *(University of Oxford, UK)*

Local Arrangements Chair: Björn von Sydow *(Chalmers University of Technology, Sweden)*

Industrial Relations Chair: Anil Madhavapeddy *(University of Cambridge, UK)*

Publicity Chair: David Van Horn *(University of Maryland, USA)*

Student Research Competition Chair: Meng Wang *(Chalmers University of Technology, Sweden)*

Video Chair: Malcolm Wallace *(Standard Chartered Bank, UK)*
Iavor Diatchki *(Galois, USA)*

Student Volunteer Captains: Ramona Enache *(Chalmers University of Technology, Sweden)*
Nick Smallbone *(Chalmers University of Technology, Sweden)*

Steering Committee: Manuel Chakravarty *(University of New South Wales, Australia)*
Robby Findler *(Northwestern University, USA)*
Kathleen Fisher *(Tufts University, USA)*
Jeremy Gibbons *(University of Oxford, UK)*
John Jeuring *(Universiteit Utrecht, The Netherlands)*
Gabriele Keller *(University of New South Wales, Australia)*
John Launchbury *(Galois, USA)*
Yaron Minsky *(Jane St Capital, USA)*
Greg Morrisett *(Harvard University, USA)*
John Reppy *(University of Chicago, USA)*
Michael Sperber *(Active Group, Germany)*
Peter Thiemann *(Universität Freiburg, Germany)*
Tarmo Uustalu *(Institute of Cybernetics, Estonia)*
David Van Horn *(University of Maryland, USA)*
Jan Vitek *(Purdue University, USA)*

Program Committee: Edwin Brady *(University of St Andrews, UK)*
Derek Dreyer *(MPI-SWS, Germany)*
Ralf Hinze *(University of Oxford, UK)*
Zhenjiang Hu *(National Institute of Informatics, Japan)*
Patricia Johann *(Appalachian State University, USA)*
Ken Friis Larsen *(University of Copenhagen, Denmark)*
Yukiyoshi Kameyama *(University of Tsukuba, Japan)*
Anil Madhavapeddy *(University of Cambridge, UK)*
Geoffrey Mainland *(Drexel University, USA)*
David Mazières *(Stanford University, USA)*
Jay McCarthy *(Brigham Young University, USA)*
Matthew Might *(University of Utah, USA)*
Ulf Norell *(Chalmers University of Technology, Sweden)*
Tiark Rompf *(Oracle Labs and EPFL, USA & Switzerland)*
Chung-chieh Shan *(Indiana University, USA)*
Mary Sheeran *(Chalmers University of Technology, Sweden)*
Matt Sottile *(Galois, USA)*
Don Syme *(Microsoft Research, UK)*
Jesse Tov *(Harvard University, UK)*

Additional reviewers: Nada Amin
Kazuyuki Asada
Aslan Askarov
Robert Atkey
Michael Ballantyne
Dariusz Biernacki
Pierre Boutillier
Ana Bove
Kevin Brown
William Byrd
Jacques Carette
Stephen Chang
James Cheney
Adam Chlipala
John Clements
Russ Cox
Alcino Cunha
Jason Dagit
David Darais
Jan de Muijnck-Hughes
Stephen Dolan
Joshua Dunfield
Martin Dybdal
Peter Dybjer
Christopher Earl
Martin Elsman
Kento Emoto
Jay Fenwick
Andrzej Filinski
Robby Findler
Sebastian Fischer
Deepak Garg
Thomas Gazagnaire
Kimball Germane
Andy Gill
Thomas Gilray
Adam Gundry
Troels Henriksen
Soichiro Hidaka
Geoffrey Hulette
Atsushi Igarashi
Mauro Jaskelioff
Manohar Jonnalagedda
Vojin Jovanovic
Ohad Kammar
Hiroyuki Kato
Shin-Ya Katsumata
Peter Kessler

Additional reviewers (continued):

Scott Kilpatrick
Daniel King
Oleg Kiselyov
Hsiang-Shang Ko
Daniel Licata
Chuan-Kai Lin
Ben Lippmeier
José Pedro Magalhães
Gregory Malecha
Kazutaka Matsuda
Conor Mcbride
Jan Midtgaard
Torben Mogensen
Shin-Cheng Mu
Prashanth Mundkur
Keisuke Nakano
Georg Neis
Dominic Orchard
Hugo Pacheco
Sungwoo Park
Anders Persson
Maciej Piróg
Jérémy Planul
Marc Pouzet
Prabhakar Ragde
Isao Sasano
Alan Schmitt
Gerardo Schneider
Tom Schrijvers
Christopher Schwaab
Ilya Sergey
David Sheets
Satnam Singh
Franck Slama
Deian Stefan
Sandro Stucki
Kohei Suenaga
Eijiro Sumii
Josef Svenningsson
Nikihil Swamy
David Swasey
Matus Tejiscak
Tachio Terauchi
David Terei
Kanae Tsushima
Hiroshi Unno
David Van Horn
Meng Wang
Leo White
Nicolas Wu
Jeremy Yallop
Edward Yang
Beta Ziliani

ICFP'14 Sponsor & Partners

Sponsor:

SIGPLAN

Partners:

Platinum partner

Jane Street

Gold partners

Google

Microsoft Research

mozilla

Oracle Labs

Standard Chartered

Silver partners

Bloomberg

Credit Suisse Quantitative Strategies

cyberpoint

Erlang Solutions

galois

Klarna

LexiFi

Bronze partners

alephcloud

IntelliFactory

OPERA software

QuviQ

Systor Vest

Using Formal Methods to Enable More Secure Vehicles

DARPA's HACMS Program

Kathleen Fisher
Tufts University
kathleen.fisher@tufts.edu

Abstract

Networked embedded systems are ubiquitous in modern society. Examples include SCADA systems that manage physical infrastructure, medical devices such as pacemakers and insulin pumps, and vehicles such as airplanes and automobiles. Such devices are connected to networks for a variety of compelling reasons, including the ability to access diagnostic information conveniently, perform software updates, provide innovative features, and lower costs. Researchers and hackers have shown that these kinds of networked embedded systems are vulnerable to remote attacks and that such attacks can cause physical damage and can be hidden from monitors [1–4].

DARPA launched the HACMS program to create technology to make such systems dramatically harder to attack successfully. Specifically, HACMS is pursuing a clean-slate, formal methods-based approach to the creation of high-assurance vehicles, where high assurance is defined to mean functionally correct and satisfying appropriate safety and security properties. Specific technologies include program synthesis, domain-specific languages, and theorem provers used as program development environments. Targeted software includes operating system components such as hypervisors, micro kernels, file systems, and device drivers as well as control systems such as autopilots and adaptive cruise controls. Program researchers are leveraging existing high-assurance software including NICTA's seL4 microkernel and INRIA's CompCert compiler.

Although the HACMS project is less than halfway done, the program has already achieved some remarkable success. At program kick-off, a Red Team easily hijacked the baseline open-source quadcopter that HACMS researchers are using as a research platform. At the end of eighteen months, the Red Team was not able to hijack the newly-minted SMACCMCopter running high-assurance HACMS code, despite being given six weeks and full access to the source code of the copter. An expert in penetration testing called the SMACCMCopter "the most secure UAV on the planet".

In this talk, I will describe the HACMS program: its motivation, the underlying technologies, current results, and future directions.

Categories and Subject Descriptors D.2.4 [Software/Program Verification]: Formal Methods; D.4.7 [Software/Organization and Design]: Real-time systems and embedded systems

Keywords High Assurance Software; Formal Methods; Cyber-Physical Systems; HACMS

References

[1] W. Burleson, S. S. Clark, B. Ransford, and K. Fu. Design challenges for secure implantable medical devices. In Proceedings of the 49th Annual Design Automation Conference, DAC'12, pages12–17, New York, NY, USA, 2012. ACM.ISBN978-1-4503-1199-1. URL http://doi.acm.org/10.1145/2228360.2228364.

[2] S. Checkoway, D. McCoy, B. Kantor, D. Anderson, H. Shacham, S. Savage, K. Koscher, A. Czeskis, F. Roesner, and T. Kohno. Comprehensive experimental analyses of automotive attack surfaces. In Proceedings of the 20th USENIX Conference on Security, SEC'11, Berkeley, CA, USA, 2011. USENIX Association. URL http://dl.acm.org/citation.cfm?id=2028067.2028073.

[3] K. Munro. SCADA – A critical situation. Network Security, 2008 (1):4 – 6, 2008. ISSN 1353-4858. URL http://www.sciencedirect.com/science/article/pii/S1353485808700059.

[4] Teso, Hugo. Aircraft hacking: Practical aero series. http://conference.hitb.org/hitbsecconf2013ams/hugo-teso/,2013.

ICFP'14, September 1–6, 2014, Gothenburg, Sweden.

ACM 978-1-4503-2873-9/14/09.
http://dx.doi.org/10.1145/2628136.2628165

Building Embedded Systems with Embedded DSLs

(Experience Report)

Patrick C. Hickey Lee Pike Trevor Elliott James Bielman John Launchbury

Galois, Inc.

{pat, leepike, trevor, jamesjb, john}@galois.com

Abstract

We report on our experiences in synthesizing a fully-featured autopilot from embedded domain-specific languages (EDSLs) hosted in Haskell. The autopilot is approximately 50k lines of C code generated from 10k lines of EDSL code and includes control laws, mode logic, encrypted communications system, and device drivers. The autopilot was built in less than two engineer years. This is the story of how EDSLs provided the productivity and safety gains to do large-scale low-level embedded programming and lessons we learned in doing so.

Categories and Subject Descriptors D.3.2 [*Language Classifications*]: Applicative (functional) languages

Keywords Embedded Domain Specific Languages; Embedded Systems

1. Introduction

Embedded programming involves the lowest levels of abstraction. Most development is in low-level languages, like C or assembly, and programs interact intimately with the hardware. Embedded domain-specific languages (EDSLs) are in some sense at the other end of the software spectrum: they are often embedded (in a different sense of the word!) in high-level programming languages such as Haskell or ML, and are used to lift the programmer's abstraction level.

That said, there is no reason in-principle why EDSLs cannot be used for embedded programming; this report is about our experience in building new EDSLs for embedded programming and the benefits and difficulties in using them. Our experiences are based on building an autopilot system called SMACCMPilot using our EDSLs. The breadth and scope of the project sets it apart. The autopilot software is a complete embedded system that includes not just the core flight control algorithms, but also device drivers, encrypted network stack, mode logic, and concurrency and task management. As far as we know, it is one of the largest (open-source) embedded systems projects developed using the EDSL approach.

Our story is a largely positive one: we developed the Ivory and Tower languages and their (EDSL) compilers from scratch in approximately 14 engineer-months. Then, we used them to build the SMACCMPilot hardware support and application in another 22 engineer-months. We achieved a dramatic increase in productivity as well as code quality. By construction, the generated C excludes large classes of errors and undefined behaviors.

Our goal in this paper is to summarize some of our lessons-learned. While we use specific examples, the lessons apply more generally to large embedded-system design in EDSLs. Our target audience includes both researchers developing new EDSLs for low-level programming as well as practitioners considering using EDSLs.

All of the EDSLs described herein, as well as SMACCMPilot itself, are open-source software. Further documentation and links to the sources are available at `smaccmpilot.org`.

ICFP'14, September 1–6, 2014, Gothenburg, Sweden.

ACM 978-1-4503-2873-9/14/09…$15.00.
http://dx.doi.org/10.1145/2628136.2628146

2. Ivory: Safe C Programming

At face value, our approach sounds audacious if not ludicrous: faced with a deadline for developing a new high-assurance autopilot system in one-and-a-half years, start by designing a new programming language and compiler from the ground up.

Of course, developing an EDSL is not the same as developing a stand-alone compiler. Much of the typical compiler tool-chain, such as the front-end parser/lexer, is provided for free by the host language. It took approximately 6 engineer-months to create the first EDSL language and compiler, which totals about 6k lines of Haskell code.

The language we developed for generating safe embedded C code is called *Ivory*. Ivory compiles to restricted C code suitable for embedded programming. Ivory shares the goal of other "safe-C" languages and compilers like Cyclone [9] and Rust [16]. Our main motivation for not using those languages is our desire for an EDSL providing convenient, Turing-complete, type-safe macro-language (Haskell) to improve our productivity.

There have also been some "safe-C" EDSLs including Atom [8], Copilot [13], and Feldspar [2]. The most significant difference between these languages and Ivory is that they are focused on pure computations (e.g., Feldspar is a DSL for digital signal processing), and do not provide convenient support for defining in-memory data-structures and manipulating memory. Ivory is designed to be a EDSL that can be used for writing safe memory-manipulating embedded C.

Ivory also makes contributions from a programming language perspective, namely in its expressiveness and type-safety. We overview each, then present a small example, to give the reader a feel for the language.

Expressiveness Regarding the expressiveness, Ivory has a variety of useful features, including:

- *Memory-areas*: the ability to allocate stack-based memory and manipulate both local and global memory areas [4].

- *Product types*: C structs with well-typed accessors.
- *FFI*: typed interfaces for calling arbitrary C functions.
- *Bit-fields*: support for typed manipulation of bit-fields and registers [5].

We built Ivory with some limitations to simplify generating safe C programs. Ivory does not support heap-based dynamic memory allocation (but global variables can be defined). C arrays are fixed-length. There is no pointer arithmetic. Pointers are non-nullable. Union types are not supported. Unsafe casts are not supported: casts must be to a strictly more expressive type (e.g., from an unsigned 8-bit integer to an unsigned 16-bit integer) or a default value must be provided for when the cast is not valid. The most common unsafe C cast is not possible: no void-pointer type exists in Ivory.

In Ivory, these have not been limiting factors, particularly because of the power of using Haskell as a macro system. For example, while arrays must be of fixed size at C compile-time, we can define a single *Haskell* function that is polymorphic in the array size that becomes instantiated at a particular size at each use site.

Type-checking Ivory's domain-specific type checking focuses on guaranteeing memory safety and helping programmers reason about their programs' nonfunctional behaviors more easily.

In addition, Ivory programs have an *effects* type associated with them, implemented as a parameter to the Ivory monad. There are three kinds of effects tracked:

- *Allocation effects*: whether a program performs (stack-based) memory allocation as well as whether pointers point into global or stack memory.
- *Return effects*: whether a program contains a `return` statement.
- *Break effects*: whether a program contains a `break` statement.

Allocation effects allow memory allocation to be restricted and tracked at the type level. For example, from a program's type alone, we can determine whether it allocates memory on the stack, making stack usage easier to track. More importantly for memory-safety, allocation effects also ensure Ivory programs contain no dangling pointers: it is a type error to return a pointer to locally-allocated memory.

Return and break statements fundamentally affect control-flow and can result in unexpected behavior by breaking out of the current block or returning from a function. For example, in a top-level while loop implementing an real-time operating system task, there should be no break or return statements; we can enforce this with the type system. Tracking these effects is novel, we believe, and particularly important in the context of an EDSL in which programs are generated and manipulated heavily in the host language.

In an EDSL, we have at least two options for type checking: (1) write a domain-specific type-checker *in* Haskell (relying on Haskell's type-system just for macro-language type-checking), or (2) embed the domain-specific type checker into Haskell's type system.

We were motivated to pursue option (2) because it allows us to discover problems sooner in the development cycle. In the case of option (1), we only find out about problems in the program's AST during code generation. Option (2) ensures that all macro and library code is typed correctly, independent of its use in the generated code. We discuss the issues of finding errors early on in more detail in Section 5.

When we began developing Ivory, our hypothesis was that recent type-system extensions to the Glasgow Haskell Compiler (GHC) make it feasible to embed the invariants necessary to ensure memory-safe C programming into the type-system [12]. From a practical standpoint, Ivory demonstrates just how far the type-

```
[ivory|
struct fooStruct
  { bar :: Stored Uint8
  ; baz :: Array 10 (Stored Sint16)
  }
|]

setBaz :: Def ([Ref Global (Struct "fooStruct"), Sint16] :-> ())
setBaz = proc "setBaz" $ \ref val -> body (prgm ref val)

prgm :: Ref Global (Struct "fooStruct") -> Sint16 -> Ivory eff ()
prgm ref val = arrayMap $ \ix ->
                 store ((ref ~> baz) ! ix) val
```

```
// foo_source.c
#include "foo_module.h"

void setBaz(struct fooStruct* n_var0, int16_t n_var1) {
  for ( int32_t n_ix0 = (int32_t) 0
      ; n_ix0 <= (int32_t) 9
      ; n_ix0++ ) {
      n_var0->baz[n_ix0] = n_var1;
  }
}

// foo_module.h
struct fooStruct {
    uint8_t bar;
    int16_t baz[10U];
};

void setBaz(struct fooStruct* n_var0, int16_t n_var1);
```

Figure 1. Example Ivory module definition

system has come, allowing us to replicate the type safety of compilers like Cyclone, etc.

We do not have space to adequately describe Ivory's type system; we leave that to a forthcoming paper. Here we will note that the embedding depends on the use of data kinds [20], type families [18], and rank-2 polymorphism [10].

Ivory example We present a small example of Ivory code. The example omits many features of the language, but should give the reader a feeling for it.

Consider Figure 1, in which an Ivory program is shown, as well as the corresponding generated C sources and headers (making a few syntactic changes to the C for readability, not relevant to the example).

First, we define a struct (or product type) using a quasiquoter that is part of the Ivory language. The Ivory code generated by Template Haskell [19] constructs a struct definition containing two fields consisting of an unsigned byte and an array of 10 signed 16-bit integers. Template Haskell also constructs a new type-level literal, `fooStruct`, that is unique to the defined struct. The `Stored` type constructor signifies that the value is allocated in-memory [4]. The `Array` type constructor takes a type-level natural number as a parameter (available as a Glasgow Haskell Compiler extension) to fix the size of an array.

A procedure, corresponding to a C function, has a type of the form

```
Def (params :-> out)
```

where `params` are the procedure's parameter types and `out` is its return type. The procedure `setBaz` takes two arguments and its return type is unit, corresponding to the `void` type in C. The types of the procedure's arguments are types in a type-level list: the first argument is a *reference*, a non-null pointer by construction, to a struct, and the second argument is a signed 16-bit integer. The `Ref` type constructor takes a *scope* type and a memory-area type.

The scope type denotes either stack-allocated scope, or global (and statically allocated) scope. In the example, we expect the reference to be to a global.

Procedures are defined with the `proc` operator that takes a string, corresponding to the name of the function that will be generated in C, and a function from the procedures arguments to its body. The body of the function is an Ivory program that sets each element in the `baz` field of the struct with the value `val` passed to it, leaving the `bar` field unchanged.

Following [4], Ivory guarantees memory-safe array access in the type system since array lengths are statically known. Ivory provides an `arrayMap` operator that applies a function to each valid index into the array. The function applied in this case is a `store` operation that takes a reference to a memory area, a value, and stores the value in the area. It is a type-error if the value's type and memory-area's type do not match.

The operation (`ref ~> baz`) takes the struct reference and returns a reference to the `baz` field. The bang (`!`) operator takes a reference to an array, an index, and returns a reference to the value at that index. The safety of indexing is maintained since the operator has the type

```
(!) :: Ref s (Array len area) -> Ix len -> Ref s area
```

tying the length of the array to the maximum index. For example, an index type (`Ix 10`) supports index values from 0 to 9.

The example only shows a small part of Ivory's language and does not exhibit some of its additional features to prevent unsafe programs. For example, if `setBaz` had allocated stack memory and created a reference to it, then tried to return the reference (creating a dangling pointer), it would result in a type error.

Additionally, for application-specific properties that cannot be type-checked, Ivory permits the insertion of assertions, assumptions on arguments, and requirements on return values. Ivory also automatically inserts checks for arithmetic underflow/overflow and division-by-zero. All these checks are useful during testing and we have used them to assist with static analysis and model-checking the generated C.

3. Tower: from Functions to Architectures

In many embedded systems, programmers produce an entire system of software that interacts with multiple input and output peripherals concurrently using a real-time operating system (RTOS). Typical RTOSes provide just a few low-level locking and signaling primitives for scheduling. Since microcontrollers do not have the virtual memory managment units (MMUs) found on larger processors, the RTOS kernel cannot protect any system memory against badly behaved user code. These restrictions put significant burden on programmers: they must ensure all tasks, and all communication between tasks, are implemented correctly.

During our initial development of SMACCMPilot, we found ourselves generating high-quality C functions from Ivory, which guarantees memory-safety of the generated code. But whenever we needed "glue code" to implement inter-process communication, initialize data-structures, read the system clock, lock the processor, etc., we were forced to abandon our well-typed world and tediously use C directly via Ivory's foreign function interface. Furthermore, the hand-written C is OS-specific, meaning it would have to be rewritten for any OS port.

Extending Ivory The hand-written glue code was ruining both our productivity and our assurance story. We wanted a language to describe the structure of the glue code that would generate it for us. Our key insight was that such an EDSL could be built as a macro over Ivory, using Ivory's code-generation facilities, without losing anything.

From these ideas, the Tower EDSL was born. Tower is an extension to the Ivory language that is designed to deal with the specific concerns of multithreaded software architectures. Tower still allows the programmer to use all the low-level power of Ivory for general programming, but uses a separate language for describing tasks and the connections between them. It took about 4 engineer-months and 3k lines of Haskell code to build Tower. This is one of the great productivity features of working with EDSLs: if we discover the language we built is difficult, tricky, or unsafe for solving a particular problem, we can extend that language with a library without modifying the compiler.

In Tower, one specifies tasks and communication channels, and the Tower compiler generates correct Ivory implementations, as well as architecture description artifacts. Tower hides the dangerous low-level scheduling primitives from the user, and keeps type information for channels (i.e., the datatype of the channel message), expressed as Ivory types, in the Haskell type system.

Tower allows the programmer to describe a static graph of channels and tasks. For the intended use case in high assurance systems, a static configuration of channels and tasks simplifies reasoning about memory requirements and permits the system to be analyzed for schedulability.

Multiple interpreters In the Tower front end, the programmer specifies a system that can be compiled to multiple artifacts.

Tower is designed to support different operating systems via a swappable backend. Since all code that touches operating system primitives is generated by Tower, it is easy for the user to specify a system and compile it for different operating systems. Tower supports both the open-soure FreeRTOS [7] as well as the formally-verified eChronos RTOS [6] developed by NICTA.

Tower also has a backend which generates a system description in the Architecture Analysis and Design Language (AADL) [17]. We also built a backend for the Graphviz language to generate graphs of tasks and channels. These output formats make it possible to visualize, analyze, and automatically check properties about the system.

Tower example In Figure 2, we sketch a small Tower example that is representative of a device driver that blinks an LED. Small simplifications to Tower have been made in the code, eliding details relating to code generation and backend selection.

In the first column of the figure, the communication architecture is defined in the `Tower` monad. The program initializes a unidirectional channel between two tasks as well as the tasks themselves. A channel, or queue, consists of transmit (`tx`) and receive (`rx`) endpoints, respectively. The `blinkTask` task is an RTOS task that will send output to the `lightswitch` RTOS task via an RTOS-mediated channel. The `lightswitch` task toggles the LED based on the incoming Boolean values. (In the third column, a graph of the tower program is shown, generated from the Tower compiler's Graphviz dot output, showing the architectural structure of the two tasks as well as the queue between them.)

To conserve space, we only define `blinkTask`. The second column contains the definition of `blinkTask`, defined in the `Task` monad. The `blinkTask` task takes a channel source and returns a task. The task first initializes an *emitter* for the channel then creates a reference to allocated memory that is private to the task. Every 100 milliseconds, an Ivory action is taken. In this case, the action is to call Ivory function `blinkFromTime` that is executed whenever the task is enabled (we elide the implementation of `blinkFromTime` in this example). The boolean value `res` is then emitted on the channel.

```
blinkTower :: Tower ()
blinkTower = do
  (tx,rx) <- channel
  task "blink" (blinkTask tx)
  task "lightswitch" $
    onChannel rx $
      \lit -> do
        ifte_ lit (turnOn light)
                  (turnOff light)
```

```
blinkTask :: ChannelSource (Stored IBool)
          -> Task ()
blinkTask chan = do
  tx  <- withChannelEmitter chan
  res <- taskLocal
  onPeriod period $ \now -> do
    res <- call blinkFromTime now
    emit_ tx res
  where period = Milliseconds 100
```

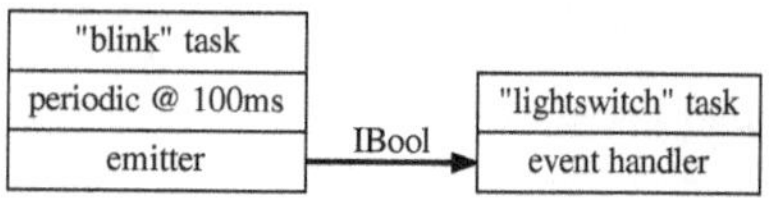

Figure 2. Tower (Col. 2), Task (Column. 1), Graphviz output (Col. 3)

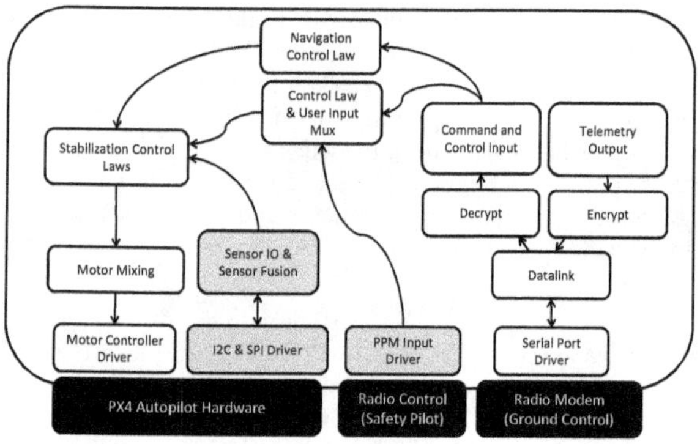

Figure 3. Simplified diagram of SMACCMPilot software architecture. Tasks written in Ivory are shown as white boxes, tasks implemented in legacy C++ code are gray boxes, channels are arrows, hardware components are black boxes.

4. SMACCMPilot: a High-Assurance Autopilot

Our main use for Ivory and Tower thus far has been in building a robust autopilot. The result is SMACCMPilot, an open-source (BSD licensed) autopilot system for quadcopter unmanned air vehicles (UAVs). It is a complete embedded system that includes low-level IO peripheral drivers, an encrypted communication protocol stack, and several layers of control systems.

SMACCMPilot runs on open source flight controller hardware from the PX4 Autopilot project [15]. The hardware platform is a custom printed circuit board with an ARM Cortex M4 microcontroller and the accelerometer, magnetometer, gyroscope, and barometer sensors used to determine the orientation and altitude of the vehicle.

A simplified software architecture of SMACCMPilot is shown in Figure 3. The flight control software is primarily responsible for reading the sensors, estimating the vehicle's attitude and position using sensor fusion, calculating control outputs, and sending motor power commands to the motor controllers. Higher level controllers manage navigation, and an encrypted command, control, and telemetry link interprets ground station instructions and sends system state to the operator.

The result is a reasonably complex piece of embedded software. SMACCMPilot has 30 tasks connected by 47 channels, and 57 globally shared state variables. Most of those shared state variables are controller tuning parameters, which can be modified by commands sent over the telemetry link.

SMACCMPilot was developed alongside the Ivory/Tower tools. The complete system took approximately 22 engineer-months to develop. The low level drivers for the system were written first in C, then transliterated to Ivory as the language became mature enough to support them. We built a stack for command, control, and telemetry, encapsulated in an encrypted packet protocol. A few components from the ArduPilot open source project, the biggest of which is a 10kloc C++ library for inertial sensor fusion, are still used inside SMACCMPilot. We plan to replace the remaining C++ code with Ivory implementations in the future.

Complexity comparison The SMACCMPilot application code is 10kloc of Ivory, the board support code is 3kloc of Ivory (and Tower), and the telemetry link binary packing and unpacking code is a machine-generated 10kloc of Ivory code. When compiled, the complete application is 48kloc of generated C code, and depends on some external C libraries to implement the operating system (4kloc) and other functions, such as sensor fusion. This is comparable to existing open source flight controller systems.

We can compare this to two systems which have a similar feature set and run on similar hardware to SMACCMPilot. The ArduPilot project [1] and the PX4 project are popular open source autopilots. Both implement all of the low level drivers to support similar (or identical) microcontroller based flight controller boards, comparable control laws, and implement the same MAVLink telemetry protocol. We do note that the APM and PX4 projects have more high level autonomous capabilities than SMACCMPilot has at this time.

The ArduPilot project is over 60kloc of C++, runs in three pseudo-threads, and supports at least four distinct autopilot hardware platforms. The PX4 Autopilot software stack has 25kloc of C/C++ application code, 25kloc of C/C++ platform support code, and depends on the large (50kloc+) NuttX operating system.

5. Lessons Learned

In this section, we discuss some of the benefits and challenges of using EDSLs for embedded programming, focusing on those that were surprising to us, despite our teams' previous experience in functional programming and embedded development.

Our experience using Ivory and Tower to build SMACCMPilot has been an extreme lesson in "eating our own dog-food". We had multiple developers writing the compilers and using them to build applications concurrently. We learned a few lessons that are relevant to any compiler development but particularly relevant to EDSL development.

Type-checking for embedded programming Build times are non-trivial for large software systems. At the time of writing, a fresh build of SMACCMPilot and associated test programs is over seven minutes of real time (and 12 minutes of CPU time since we have a multi-threaded build system). One reason the build time is so large is that it requires Cabal (the Haskell package manager) to discover library dependencies and install packages, compile the Haskell sources, and then compile the C sources. As well, some sources are compiled multiple times for different targets on multiple operating systems.

Then, to execute the software on the embedded device, we have to write the software to the device's memory via a JTAG programmer or a serial bootloader, which takes on the order of ten seconds.

All this is to say that the end-to-end debug cycle might mean testing a small number of changes to Ivory or Tower per hour. Clearly, the debug cycle in embedded development particularly motivates us to make fewer bugs and to discover them early.

During development, it became apparent how useful Haskell type-checking is for embedded programming. As described in Section 2, we have embedded Ivory's type system in Haskell's. Thus, domain-specific type-errors are caught during Haskell type-checking. Type-checking, and other static warnings reported by GHC, are nearly instantaneous since it can be done on a module-by-module basis. The type system tracks the global or stack frame provenance of references, as well as structure accessors and array indices, to ensure all well-typed Ivory programs generate memory-safe C. The upshot is that Ivory programs that would generate unsafe C programs are caught immediately.

In addition, we have found it useful to detect potential bugs even if the C compiler might also detect them. To take one example, consider unused variable declarations. While a C compiler can detect this, perhaps late in the compilation phase, we discover these warnings nearly instantaneously during type checking. Moreover, the more preprocessing we can do in Haskell, the more potential errors we may find, and with a better relation to the EDSL source.

However, not every property of interest in embedded programming can be conveniently embedded in the Haskell type system with GHC extensions. For example, integer overflows checks are not practical to embed.

Moreover, GHC's type error reporting can be unwieldy. Ivory users would benefit from domain-specific error reporting which could, for example, describe type errors in the vocabulary of Ivory, rather than burden the user to interpret the way the Ivory language types are embedded into Haskell types. For example, passing the wrong number of arguments to an Ivory function in a procedure call is reported as a type error when using functional dependencies, whereas a mismatch between the type of a procedure and the number of arguments provided in its declaration is reported as a kind error. The errors reported are of the particular type-level implementation given for Ivory types. Haskell does not yet have good facilities for type-level programming abstraction.

Type-safe system plumbing Adding many new features to SMACCMPilot is easy. In fact, the most tedious part is writing the business logic in Tower, where we define a new task, and then plumb values representing communication channels through the code. There is nothing conceptually difficult in doing so—it is similar to any monadic interface for specifying a graph. When changes cross Haskell function boundaries, we must modify the arguments to the Haskell function that generates the Tower task (or modifying the fields of a data-type if channels have been grouped together). Channels are typed, so type-checking detects most plausible inter-task communication errors.

Stepping back, the idea that plumbing arguments to Haskell functions is the hardest part of embedded development is amazing. We are not dealing with bugs in low-level OS interfaces, we are not making timing or resource contention errors in communication, we are not dealing with type-errors like you might find in raw C (where data might be cast to `void*` or `char[]`).

Because plumbing is so easy, it encourages us to improve modularity in the system. Defining a new RTOS task is easy, so we might as well modularize functionality to improve isolation and security. For example, in the ground station communication subsystem, encryption and decryption are each executed in isolated tasks, simplifying the architectural analysis of the system. As we noted in Section 4, our system is significantly more modular than other autopilots.

Faking a module system In Ivory and Tower, top-level functions and structures are packaged into a Haskell data structure to provide to the Ivory compiler. The onus is on the programmer to package up all the necessary components.

On one hand, the approach provides the programmer control over how to modularize the generated C code, deciding which definitions to put in a C source or header file. On the other hand, we have found it to be verbose, tedious, and error-prone. Generally, we want the C files to have similar structure to the Haskell modules in which Ivory programs are written. From that respect, the Ivory module system simply duplicates the Haskell module system.

Worse is when the programmer forgets to package a definition. The error only becomes apparent at C *link* time, near the end of a long build process. Missing definitions have plagued our builds.

We could move symbol resolution up the build cycle to the C-code generation phase. Ideally, we would move it up the build cycle even further. We are currently exploring the use of Template Haskell to generate Ivory modules at compile-time to assist the programmer.

Control your compiler If we were writing our application in a typical compiled language, even a high-level one, and found a compiler bug, we would perhaps file a bug report with the developers... and wait. If we had access to the sources, we might try making a change, but doing so risks introducing new bugs or at the least, forking the compiler. Most likely, the compiler would not change, and we would either make some *ad-hoc* work-around or introduce regression tests to make sure that the specific bug found is not hit again. Such a situation is notorious in embedded cross-compilers that usually have a small support team and are themselves many revisions behind the main compiler tool-chain.

But with an EDSL the situation is different. With a small code-base implementing the compiler, it is easy to write new passes or inspect passes for errors. Rebuilding the compiler takes seconds.

More generally, we have a different mindset programming in an EDSL: if a class of bug occurs a few times—whether caused in the compiler or not—we change the language/compiler to eliminate it (or at least to automatically insert assertions to check for it). Instead of a growing test-suite, we have a growing set of checks in the compiler, to help eliminate both our bugs and the bugs in *all* future Ivory programs.

We claim that Ivory code compiles to memory-safe C code. However, a formal proof of these claims, or more generally, a proof that the semantics of Ivory programs are implemented by the generated C code, is work-in-progress. However, a small number of primitives and simple compiler facilitates inspection and testing. In all, this is less assurance than is given by fully verified toolchains, such as CompCert [11]. Other approaches more specific to bringing assurance to EDSL compilers could be borrowed as well [14].

Everything is a library With an EDSL, and particularly a Turing-complete macro language, everything is a library. The distinction between language developers and users becomes ambiguous. As an extreme example, one can think of Tower as "just" a library for Ivory. A small example is defining a conditional operator in terms of Ivory's if-then-else primitive as shown in Figure 4. All types above were introduced in Section 2. With the `cond_` operator, we can replace nested if-then-else statements as shown in the figure with more convenient conditionals, without modifying the language.

Because macros are so easy to define and natural in EDSL development, our biggest challenge has been ensuring developers on our team put useful ones in a standard library, to be shared.

```
data Cond eff a =
  Cond IBool (Ivory eff a)

(==>) :: IBool -> Ivory eff a
      -> Cond eff a
(==>) = Cond

cond_ :: [Cond eff ()]
      -> Ivory eff ()
cond_ [] = return ()
cond_ ((Cond b f):cs) =
  ifte_ b f (cond_ cs)
```

```
cond_
  [ x >? 100 ==> ret 10
  , x >? 50  ==> ret 5
  , true     ==> ret 0 ]

ifte_ (x >? 100)
 (ret 10)
 (ifte_ (x >? 50)
   (ret 5)
     (ret 0))
```

Figure 4. Conditional Ivory macro.

Semantics To take advantage of legacy cross-compilers, we are forced to generate C code from our EDSL. A large focus in designing Ivory is to allow expressive but well-defined programs. We believe Ivory cannot produce memory-unsafe C programs. However, undefined C programs can be generated from Ivory; for example, signed integer overflow and division-by-zero are undefined. Guaranteeing programs are free from these behaviors is decidable (the arithmetic is on fixed-width integer types), but intractable to prove automatically.

To assist the programmer, the Ivory compiler automatically inserts predicates into the generated code to check for overflow, division-by-zero, etc. The user defines the behavior of the program if a check fails. For example, during testing, we define the checks to insert a breakpoint for use with a debugger. Another option may be to do nothing and rely on the semantics provided by the C compiler. Still another option might be to trap to a user-defined exception-handler. Currently, SMACCMPilot contains approximately 2500 compiler-inserted non-trivial checks that cannot be constant-folded away. In the future, we hope to *prove* these checks never fail.

Early in the development process, we used the CBMC model checker [3] to partially verify the assertions in the generated C code. However, as our application grew, we ran into three problems. First, a naive application of whole program model checking did not scale to our application size. Second, many assertions depend on user-provided preconditions (e.g. on inputs from hardware devices). Third, some assertions were undecidable (e.g. non-linear arithmetic).

There are two other semantics categories to consider: defined behavior and implementation-defined behavior. In Ivory, we attempt to eliminate almost all implementation-defined behaviors. For example, only fixed-width size types, like `uint8_t` or `int32_t`, can be generated. Implementation-defined sizes, like `int` or `char` are not used. We have found these to be dangerous: programmers might assume properties about the size of a type that do not hold in a non-standard architecture (e.g., that an `int` is at least 32 bits or that `char` is unsigned; both are implementation-defined). Such assumptions are particularly dangerous when porting code between different embedded platforms. Indeed, when we ported portions of ArduPilot, initially built for an 8-bit AVR architecture to a 32-bit ARM, we found these sorts of implicit assumptions.

Finally, even defined behavior is not necessarily intuitive behavior. For example, in C, the defined behavior for arithmetic on values that have a size-type smaller than `int` is to implicitly promote them to `int`s before performing the arithmetic.

For example, given

```
uint8_t a = 10;
uint8_t b = 250;
bool    x = a-b > 0;
bool    y = (uint8_t)(a-b) > 0;
```

x evaluates to 0 and y to 1, provided that

```
sizeof(uint8_t) < sizeof(int)
```

This behavior is worrisome to the embedded programmer because, across various embedded processors and C compilers, integer sizes are often defined differently.

In Ivory, arithmetic is at the size of the operands, which we believe is more intuitive. We force the generated C to respect this semantics by inserting casts into expressions. So the Ivory expression `a-b` results in the C expression `(uint8_t) (a-b)`.

6. Conclusions

We have described our use of the Ivory and Tower EDSLs for building a large embedded system.

Many of the advantages of EDSLs for embedded programming relate to type-checking in Haskell. Of course, some bugs cannot be caught statically. For the most part, once type-checking is complete, we are confident that the bug is a logical bug. We do not spend our time chasing segmentation faults or strange undefined or compiler-dependent behaviors but rather focus on the bugs that result from our misunderstanding of the application, not the programming environment.

What is next? In the next few years, SMACCMPilot will continue to grow. It, along with the Ivory & Tower tools, are open source, in the hope of engaging a broader community. We will add new hardware, new sensors, and new controllers so that it is not only one of the highest-assurance autopilots in existence but is competitive with others in terms of functionality.

In addition, we are looking to improve the usability of Ivory and Tower. For example, we are working to integrate verification tools more closely into the language. We have also begun to define quasiquoters for the languages so that C programmers might feel more at home with the language but power (Haskell) users can still enjoy the benefits of EDSL programming.

In short, we believe EDSLs can be brought down from the ivory tower (pun intended) to the grungy world of embedded programming.

Acknowledgments

This work is supported by DARPA under contract no. FA8750-12-9-0169. Opinions expressed herein are our own. A number of people have provided input and advice; we particularly thank Kathleen Fisher, Iavor Diatchki, and Andrew Tridgell. Joe Kiniry and Adam Foltzer, and the anonymous reviewers provided helpful comments on earlier drafts of the paper.

References

[1] APM Project. APM multiplatform autopilot suite. Website `http://ardupilot.com/`. Retrieved Feb. 2014.

[2] E. Axelsson, K. Claessen, M. Sheeran, J. Svenningsson, D. Engdal, and A. Persson. The design and implementation of Feldspar - an embedded language for digital signal processing. In *Implementation and Application of Functional Languages*, volume 6647 of *LNCS*, pages 121–136. Springer, 2011.

[3] E. Clarke, D. Kroening, and F. Lerda. A tool for checking ANSI-C programs. In *Tools and Algorithms for the Construction and Analysis of Systems (TACAS)*, LNCS, pages 168–176. Springer, 2004.

[4] I. S. Diatchki and M. P. Jones. Strongly typed memory areas programming systems-level data structures in a functional language. In *Proceedings of the ACM SIGPLAN Workshop on Haskell*, pages 72–83. ACM, 2006.

[5] I. S. Diatchki, M. P. Jones, and R. Leslie. High-level views on low-level representations. In *Intl. Conference on Functional Programming*, pages 168–179. ACM, 2005.

[6] eChronos. eChronos. Website `http://ssrg.nicta.com.au/projects/TS/echronos`. Retrieved Feb. 2014.

[7] FreeRTOS. FreeRTOS. Website `http://freertos.org/`. Retrieved Feb. 2014.

[8] T. Hawkins. Controlling hybrid vehicles with Haskell. Presentation. *Commercial Users of Functional Programming* (CUFP), 2008. Available at `http://cufp.galois.com/2008/schedule.html`.

[9] T. Jim, J. G. Morrisett, D. Grossman, M. W. Hicks, J. Cheney, and Y. Wang. Cyclone: A safe dialect of C. In *USENIX Conference*, Berkeley, CA, USA, 2002. USENIX.

[10] J. Launchbury and S. L. Peyton Jones. Lazy functional state threads. pages 24–35, June 1994.

[11] X. Leroy. Formal verification of a realistic compiler. *Communications of the ACM*, 52(7):107–115, 2009.

[12] S. Lindley and C. McBride. Hasochism: The pleasure and pain of dependently typed haskell programming. In *Symposium on Haskell*, pages 81–92. ACM, 2013.

[13] L. Pike, A. Goodloe, R. Morisset, and S. Niller. Copilot: A hard real-time runtime monitor. In *Runtime Verification (RV)*, volume 6418, pages 345–359. Springer, 2010.

[14] L. Pike, N. Wegmann, S. Niller, and A. Goodloe. Experience report: a do-it-yourself high-assurance compiler. In *Proceedings of the Intl. Conference on Functional Programming (ICFP)*. ACM, September 2012.

[15] Pixhawk. PX4 autopilot project. Website `http://pixhawk.org/`. Retrieved Feb. 2014.

[16] Rust. Rust. Website `http://www.rust-lang.org/`. Retrieved Feb. 2014.

[17] SAE-AS5506. *Architecture Analysis and Design Language*. SAE, Nov 2004.

[18] T. Schrijvers, S. Peyton Jones, M. Chakravarty, and M. Sulzmann. Type checking with open type functions. *Intl. Conference on Functional Programming*, pages 51–62, Sept. 2008. ISSN 0362-1340.

[19] T. Sheard and S. P. Jones. Template meta-programming for haskell. *SIGPLAN Notices*, 37(12):60–75, Dec. 2002.

[20] B. A. Yorgey, S. Weirich, J. Cretin, S. Peyton Jones, D. Vytiniotis, and J. P. Magalhães. Giving haskell a promotion. In *Workshop on Types in Language Design and Implementation*, pages 53–66. ACM, 2012.

Concurrent NetCore: From Policies to Pipelines

Cole Schlesinger
Princeton University
35 Olden St.
Princeton, NJ 08540
cschlesi@cs.princeton.edu

Michael Greenberg
Princeton University
35 Olden St.
Princeton, NJ 08540
mg19@cs.princeton.edu

David Walker
Princeton University
35 Olden St.
Princeton, NJ 08540
dpw@cs.princeton.edu

Abstract

In a Software-Defined Network (SDN), a central, computationally powerful *controller* manages a set of distributed, computationally simple *switches*. The controller computes a policy describing how each switch should route packets and *populates* packet-processing tables on each switch with rules to enact the routing policy. As network conditions change, the controller continues to add and remove rules from switches to adjust the policy as needed.

Recently, the SDN landscape has begun to change as several proposals for new, reconfigurable switching architectures, such as RMT [5] and FlexPipe [14] have emerged. These platforms provide switch programmers with many, flexible tables for storing packet-processing rules, and they offer programmers control over the packet fields that each table can analyze and act on. These reconfigurable switch architectures support a richer SDN model in which a switch *configuration* phase precedes the rule population phase [4]. In the configuration phase, the controller sends the switch a graph describing the layout and capabilities of the packet processing tables it will require during the population phase. Armed with this foreknowledge, the switch can allocate its hardware (or software) resources more efficiently.

We present a new, typed language, called Concurrent NetCore, for specifying routing policies *and* graphs of packet-processing tables. Concurrent NetCore includes features for specifying sequential, conditional and concurrent control-flow between packet-processing tables. We develop a fine-grained operational model for the language and prove this model coincides with a higher-level denotational model when programs are well-typed. We also prove several additional properties of well-typed programs, including strong normalization and determinism. To illustrate the utility of the language, we develop linguistic models of both the RMT and FlexPipe architectures and we give a multi-pass compilation algorithm that translates graphs and routing policies to the RMT model.

Categories and Subject Descriptors D.3.2 [*Programming Languages*]: Language Classifications—Specialized application languages

General Terms Design, Languages, Theory

ICFP '14, September 1–6, 2014, Gothenburg, Sweden.

ACM 978-1-4503-2873-9/14/09...$15.00.
http://dx.doi.org/10.1145/2628136.2628157

Keywords Software-defined networking; network programming languages; OpenFlow; Frenetic

1. Introduction

Over the past several years, a new networking technology known as *Software-Defined Networking* (SDN) has emerged as a viable competitor to traditional networking infrastructure. In a software-defined network, a logically centralized *controller* machine (or cluster of machines) manages a distributed collection of *switches*. The controller is a general-purpose server whose primary job is to decide how to route packets through the network while avoiding congestion, managing security, handling failures, monitoring load, and informing network operators of problems. The switches, on the other hand, are specialized hardware devices with limited computational facilities. In general, a switch implements a collection of simple rules that match bit patterns in the incoming packets, and based on those bit patterns, drop packets, modify their fields, forward the packets on to other switches, or send the packet to the controller for additional, more general analysis and processing. The switch itself does not decide what rules to implement—that job lies with the controller, which sends messages to the switches to install and uninstall the packet-forwarding rules needed to achieve its higher-level, network-wide objectives. SDN is distinguished from traditional networks by its centralized, programmatic control. In contrast, traditional networks rely on distributed algorithms implemented by the switches, and network administrators manually configure each switch in the hope of inducing behavior that conforms to a global (and often poorly specified) network policy.

SDN has had a tremendous impact in the networking community, both for industry and academia. Google has adoped SDN to manage its internal backbone, which transmits all its intra-datacenter traffic—making it one of the largest networks in the world [9], and many other major companies are following Google's lead. Indeed, the board of the Open Networking Foundation (ONF)—the main body responsible for defining SDN standards, such as OpenFlow [10]—includes the owners of most of the largest networks in the world (Google, Facebook, Microsoft, etc) and its corporate membership numbers over a hundred. On the academic side, hundreds of participants have attended the newly-formed HotSDN workshop, and several tracks of top networking conferences, such as NSDI and SIGCOMM, are dedicated to research in SDN. But at its heart, management of Software-Defined Networks is an important new programming problem that calls for a variety of new, high-level, declarative, domain-specific programming languages, as well as innovation in compiler design and implementation.

OpenFlow 1.0: successes and failures. The OpenFlow protocol is a popular protocol for communication between the controller and switches. The first version, OpenFlow 1.0 [10], supported a simple abstraction: Each switch is a *single* table of packet-forwarding rules. Each such rule can match on one or more of twelve standard packet fields (source MAC, destination MAC, source IP, destination IP, VLAN, *etc.*) and then execute a series of actions, such as dropping the packet, modifying a field, or forwarding it out a port. A controller can issue commands to install and uninstall rules in the table and to query statistics associated with each rule (*e.g.*, the number of packets or bytes processed).

The single table abstraction was chosen for the first version of OpenFlow because it was a "least common denominator" interface that many existing switches could support with little change. It worked, and OpenFlow switches from several hardware vendors, including Broadcom and Intel, hit the market quickly. The simplicity of the OpenFlow 1.0 interface also made it a relatively easy compilation target for a wave of newly-designed, high-level SDN programming languages, such as Frenetic [7], Procera [15], Maple [16], FlowLog [13] and others.

Unfortunately, while the simplicity of the OpenFlow 1.0 interface is extremely appealing, hardware vendors have been unable to devise implementations that make efficient use of switch resources. Packet processing hardware in most modern ASICs is not, in fact, implemented as a single match-action table, but rather as a collection of tables. These tables are often aligned in sequence, so the effects of packet processing by one table can be observed by later tables, or in parallel, so non-conflicting actions may be executed concurrently to reduce packet-processing latency.

Each table within a switch will typically match on a fixed subset of a packet's fields and will be responsible for implementing some subset of the chip's overall packet-forwarding functionality. Moreover, different tables may be implemented using different kinds of memory with different properties. For example, some tables might be built with SRAM and only capable of *exact matches* on certain fields—that is, comparing fields against a single, concrete bit sequence (eg. 1010001010). Other tables may use TCAM and be capable of *ternary wildcard matches*, where packets are compared to a string containing concrete bits and wildcards (*e.g.* 10?1??1001?) and the wildcards match either 0 or 1. TCAM is substantially more expensive and power-hungry than SRAM. Hence, TCAM tables tend to be smaller than SRAM. For instance, the Broadcom Trident has an L2 table with SRAM capable of holding ~100K entries and a forwarding table with TCAM capable of holding ~4K entries [6].

In addition to building fixed-pipeline ASICs, switch hardware vendors are also developing more programmable hardware pipelines. For example, the RMT design [5] offers a programmable parser to extract data from packets in arbitrary application-driven ways, and a pipeline of 32 physical match-action tables. Each physical table in this pipeline may be configured for use in different ways: (1) As a wide table, matching many bits at a time, but containing fewer rows, (2) as a narrower table, matching fewer bits in each packet but containing more rows, (3) as multiple parallel tables acting concurrently on a packet, or (4) combined with other physical tables in sequence to form a single, multi-step logical table. Intel's FlexPipe architecture [14] also contains a programmable front end, but rather than organizing tables in a sequential pipeline, FlexPipe contains a collection of parallel tables to allow concurrent packet processing, a shorter pipeline and reduced packet-processing latency.

In theory, these multi-table hardware platforms could be programmed through the single-table OpenFlow 1.0 interface. However, doing so has several disadvantages:

- The single OpenFlow 1.0 interface serves as a bottleneck in the compilation process: Merging rules from separate tables into a single table can lead to an explosion in the number of rules required to represent the same function as one might represent via a set of tables.

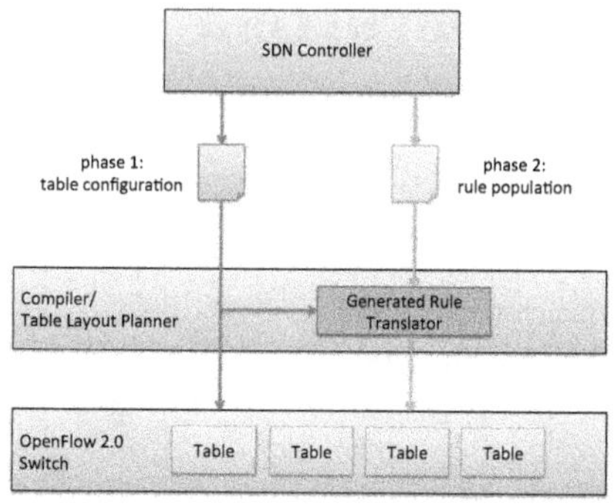

Figure 1. Architecture of an OpenFlow 2.0 System

- Once squeezed into a single table, the structure of the rule set is lost. Recovering that structure and determining how to split rules across tables is a non-trivial task, especially when the rules appear dynamically (without advance notice concerning their possible structure) at the switch.
- Newer, more flexible chips such as RMT, FlexPipe or NetFPGAs have a configuration stage, wherein one plans the configuration of tables and how to allocate different kinds of memory. The current OpenFlow protocol does not support configuration-time planning.

Towards OpenFlow 2.0. As a result of the deficiencies of the first generation of OpenFlow protocols, a group of researchers have begun to define an architecture for the next generation of OpenFlow protocols [4] (See Figure 1). In this proposal, switch configuration is divided into two phases: table configuration and table population.

During the table configuration phase, the SDN controller describes the *abstract* set of tables it requires for its high-level routing policy. When describing these tables, it specifies the packet fields read and written by each table, and the sorts of patterns (either exact match or prefix match) that will be used. In addition, the table configuration describes the topology of the abstract tables—the order they appear in sequence (or in parallel) and the conditions necessary for executing the rules within a table.

We call the tables communicated from controller to switch *abstract*, because they do not necessarily correspond directly to the *concrete* physical tables implemented by the switch hardware. In order to bridge the gap between abstract and concrete tables, a compiler will attempt to find a mapping between what is requested by the controller and what is present in hardware. In the process of determining this mapping, the compiler will generate a function capable of translating sets of *abstract rules* (also called an *abstract policy*) supplied by the controller, and targeted at the abstract tables, into *concrete rules/policy* implementable directly on the concrete tables available in hardware. After the table configuration phase, and during the table population phase, the rule translator is used to transform abstract rules into concrete ones.

The configuration phase happens on a human time scale: a network administrator writes a policy and a controller program and runs the compiler to configure the switches and SDN controllers on her network appropriately. Rule population, on the other hand, happens on the time scale of network activity: a controller's algorithm may install, e.g., new firewall or NAT rules after observing a single packet—concrete examples of these and other rule installations can be found in Section 2.

Contributions of this paper. The central contribution of this paper is the design of a new language for programming OpenFlow

2.0 switches. This compiler intermediate language is capable of specifying high-level switch policies as well as concrete, low-level switch architectures. We call the language *Concurrent NetCore* (or CNC, for short), as it is inspired by past work on NetCore [7, 11] and NetKAT [3].[1] Like NetCore and NetKAT, Concurrent NetCore consists of a small number of primitive operations for specifying packet processing, plus combinators for constructing more complex packet processors from simpler ones. Concurrent NetCore introduces the following new features.

- *Table specifications*: Table specifications act as "holes" in an otherwise fully-formed switch policy. These tables can be filled in (*i.e.,* populated) later. Policies with tables serve as the phase-1 configurations in the OpenFlow 2.0 architecture. Ordinary, hole-free policies populate those holes later in the switch-configuration process.
- *Concurrent composition*: Whereas NetCore and NetKAT have a form of "parallel composition," which copies a packet and performs different actions on different copies, CNC also provides a new *concurrent* composition operator that allows two policies to act simultaneously on the same packet. We use concurrent composition along with other features of CNC to model the RMT and Intel FlexPipe packet-processing pipelines.
- *Type System*: Unlike past network programming languages, CNC is equipped with a simple domain-specific type system. These types perform two functions: (1) they determine the kinds of policies that may populate a table (which fields may be read or written, for instance), and thereby guarantee that well-typed policies can be compiled to the targeted table, and (2) they prevent interference between concurrently executing policies, thereby ensuring that the overall semantics of a CNC program is deterministic.

The key technical results of the paper include the following:

- *Semantics for Concurrent NetCore*: We define a small-step operational semantics for CNC that captures the intricate interactions between (nested) concurrent and parallel policies. In order to properly describe interacting concurrent actions, this semantics is structured entirely differently from the denotational models previously defined for related languages.
- *Metatheory of Concurrent NetCore*: The metatheory includes a type system and its proof of soundness, as well as several auxiliary properties of the system, such as confluence and normalization of all well-typed policies. We derive reasoning principles relating the small-step CNC semantics to a NetKAT-like denotational model.
- *Multipass compilation algorithm*: We show how to compile high-level *abstract* configurations into the constrained lower-level *concrete* configuration of the RMT pipeline [5]. In doing so, we show how to produce *policy transformation functions* that will map abstract policy updates into concrete policy updates. We have proven many of our compilation passes correct using reasoning principles derived from our semantics. We offer this compilation as a proof of concept of "transformations within CNC" as a compilation strategy; we believe that many of our algorithms and transformations will be reusable when targeting other platforms.

A technical appendix is available that includes a full presentation of the compilation algorithm, theorems, and proofs [1].

[1] Because we focus on programming individual switches in this paper, our language does not contain Kleene Star, which is more useful for specifying paths across a network than policies on a single switch. Hence, our language is a Net*Core* as opposed to a Net*KAT*.

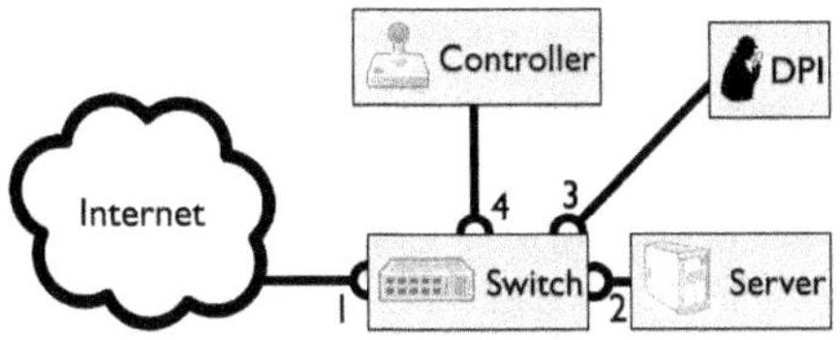

Figure 2. A simple network.

The following section introduces CNC in greater detail through a series of examples, while Section 3 presents a formal semantics for CNC, and Section 4 describes its metatheory. The models of both the RMT and Intel FlexPipe architectures are described in Section 5, followed by our compilation algorithm in Section 6. Section 7 describes related work, and we conclude in Section 8.

2. CNC by example

In this section, we introduce CNC through a series of examples, starting with user policies that define high-level packet processing, and then showing how CNC can model low-level switching hardware. Because CNC can model both ends of the spectrum, it can serve as a common intermediate language within an OpenFlow 2.0 compilation system. Section 6 will illustrate this idea via algorithms that demonstrate how to transform our high-level user policies into components for placement in RMT tables.

2.1 Simple switch policies

Consider the picture in Figure 2. This picture presents several devices, a switch, a controller, a server and a DPI[2] box, as well as a link to "the internet." The switch has four ports (labelled 1, 2, 3, 4 in the picture) that connect it to the other devices and to the internet. Our goal is to write a *policy* for the switch to specify how it forwards packets in and out of its ports.

In general, we model packets as records with a number of fields which map to values drawn from a finite set. Our examples typically use an idealized collection of fields such as src (the packet's source IP address), in (the port the packet arrives on), and out (the port a packet should leave on). [3] Switch policies are functions that map packets to sets of packets. For example, a policy that drops all packets will map any packet to the empty set of packets. A policy that forwards packets from the internet (port 1) to the server (port 2) will map packets with in field 1 to a packet with out 2. A policy that forwards packets from the internet to both the DPI box and the server will map packets with in $= 1$ to a pair of packets with out $= 2$ and out $= 3$.

We build our policies out of a collection of primitive operations and policy combinators. The simplest primitive filters packets based on the contents of a single field. For example, when applied to a packet pk, the test src $=$ 10.0.0.1 returns $\{pk\}$ when pk's src field is 10.0.0.1 and returns the empty set of packets otherwise. Using such tests as well as standard boolean connectives *and* (;), *or* (+) and *not* ($\neg$), one can easily build up a function on packets that implements a firewall (either dropping each packet or returning it unchanged). For example, we might want to implement the following firewall w on the switch in Figure 2. It admits ssh or $http$ traffic on port 1, but blocks all other traffic arriving on port 1. All

[2] DPI is *deep packet inspection*, a form of network security monitoring that inspects not just packet headers but their payloads as well.

[3] Using in and out fields to designate ingress and egress ports rather than a single port field that indicates where the packet is "right now" deviates slightly from past presentations of NetCore and NetKAT, but more faithfully models our hardware targets.

traffic on ports other than 1 is allowed.

$$w \quad = \quad \mathsf{in} = 1; (\mathsf{typ} = ssh + \mathsf{typ} = http) + \neg(\mathsf{in} = 1)$$

In order to make changes to packets, we use the assignment primitive $f \leftarrow value$. Complex policies may perform the actions of a set of simpler policies in series using the sequential composition operator $(p_1; p_2)$. Alternatively, a policy may copy a packet and perform both p_1 and p_2 on the separate copies, taking the union of their results $(p_1 + p_2)$. We have reused the symbols ";" and "+" (conjunction and disjunction) here as it turns out their semantics as logical predicates coincides with their semantics as policy combinators (the boolean algebra is a sub-algebra of the policy algebra).

As an example, to define a static routing policy r for our switch, we might write the following policy.

$$r \quad = \quad \mathsf{in} = 1; \mathsf{out} \leftarrow 2 + \mathsf{in} = 2; \mathsf{out} \leftarrow 1$$

The policy above has the effect of routing packets from port 1 to port 2 and from port 2 to port 1. In more detail, it first copies the incoming packet (+). Then, in the first branch, it tests whether the input port is 1; if not, the packet is dropped; if so, the out field is assigned 2. The second branch is dual, forwarding packets from port 2 to port 1. The guards on each branch guarantee that the 'copying' is purely notional; in general, one codes the conditional statement if a then p_1 else p_2 as $a; p_1 + \neg a; p_2$.

The above features are not new—they are present in NetCore [11, 12] and NetKAT [3]. However, in order to serve as a configuration language for OpenFlow 2.0, we require a couple of additional features, as well as the development of a simple type system for policies. First, the policies so far are completely static. They offer no room for populating new packet-processing rules at run time. To admit this kind of dynamic extension of static policies, we add *typed table variables*, which we write $(x : \tau)$. For example, we write $(x : (\{\mathsf{typ}, \mathsf{src}\}, \{\mathsf{out}\}))$ to indicate that the controller may later install new rules in place of x, and any such rules will only read from the typ and src header fields and write to the out field. The controller could use this table to dynamically install rules that forward selected subsets of packets to the DPI box for additional scrutiny. The typing information informs the switch of the kind of memory it needs to reserve for the table x (in this case, memory wide enough to be able to hold patterns capable of matching on both the typ and src fields). We model rule population as a set of *table bindings* b, i.e., a closing substitution.

A second key extension is concurrency, written $p_1 \,||\, p_2$. In order to reduce packet-processing latency within a switch, one may which to execute p_1 and p_2 concurrently on the *same* packet (rather than making copies). The latter is only legal provided there is no interference between subpolicies p_1 and p_2. In CNC, interference is prevented through the use of a simple type system. This type system prevents concurrent writes and ensures determinism of the overall packet-processing policy language.

As an example, consider the following policy p, which assembles each of the components described earlier. This policy checks for compliance with the firewall w while concurrently implementing a routing policy. The routing policy statically routes all packets to the server (this is the role of r) while dynamically selecting those packets to send to the DPI box (this is the role of x).

$$\begin{aligned} m &= (x : (\{\mathsf{typ}, \mathsf{src}\}, \{\mathsf{out}\})) \\ p &= w \,||\, (r + m) \end{aligned}$$

In essence, we have a form of *speculative execution* here. The policy $r + m$ is speculatively copying the packet and modifying it's out field while the firewall decides whether to drop it. If the firewall ultimately decides to drop the packet, then the results of routing and monitoring are thrown away. If the firewall allows the packet, then we have already computed how many copies of the packet are going out which ports. This kind of speculative execution is safe and deterministic when policies are well-typed.

2.2 Modeling programmable hardware architectures

In addition to providing network administrators with a language for defining policies, our language of network policies aptly describes the hardware layout of switches' packet-processing pipelines. In this guise, table variables represent TCAM or SRAM tables, and combinators describe how these hardware tables are connected. The key benefit to devising a shared language for describing both user-level programs and hardware configurations is that we can define compilation as a semantics-preserving policy translation problem, and compiler correctness as a simple theorem about equivalence of input and output policies defined in a common language. Below, we demonstrate how to model key elements of the RMT [5] and FlexPipe [14] architectures. Both chips offer differently architectured fixed pipelines connecting reconfigurable tables.

RMT. In RMT (as well as in FlexPipe), multicast is treated specially: the act of copying and buffering multiple packets during a multicast while processing packets as quickly as they come in ("at line rate") is the most difficult element of chip design.

The RMT multicast stage consists of a set of queues, one per output port. Earlier tables in the pipeline indicate the ports on which a packet should be multicast by setting bits in a metavariable bitmap we call out_i. The multicast stage consists of a sum, where each summand corresponds to a queue on a particular output port—when the ith out bit is set, the summand tags the packet with a unique identifier and sets its output port out to i accordingly.

$$\begin{aligned} \mathsf{multicast} \quad &= \quad (out_1 = 1; f_{\mathsf{tag}} \leftarrow v_1; \mathsf{out} \leftarrow 1) \\ &+ \quad (out_2 = 2; f_{\mathsf{tag}} \leftarrow v_2; \mathsf{out} \leftarrow 2) \\ &+ \quad \ldots \end{aligned}$$

In addition to the multicast processor, the RMT architecture provides thirty-two physical tables, which may be divided into sequences in the ingress and egress pipelines. Overall, the RMT pipeline consists of the ingress pipeline, followed by the multicast stage, followed by the egress pipeline.

$$\begin{aligned} \mathsf{pipeline} \quad = \quad & (x_1 : \tau_1); \ldots; (x_k : \tau_k); \\ & \mathsf{multicast}; \\ & (x_{k+1} : \tau_{k+1}); \ldots; (x_{32} : \tau_{32}) \end{aligned}$$

FlexPipe. The FlexPipe architecture makes use of concurrency by arranging its pipeline into a diamond shape. Each point of the diamond is built from two tables in sequence, with incoming packets first processed by the first pair, then concurrently by the next two pairs, and finally by the last pair. This built-in concurrency optimizes for common networking tasks, such as checking packets against an access control list while simultaneously calculating routing behavior.

$$\begin{aligned} \mathsf{pair}_i \quad &= \quad (x_{i,1} : \tau_{i,1}); (x_{i,2} : \tau_{i,2}) \\ \mathsf{diamond} \quad &= \quad \mathsf{pair}_1; (\mathsf{pair}_2 \,||\, \mathsf{pair}_3); \mathsf{pair}_4 \end{aligned}$$

The FlexPipe multicast stage occurs after the diamond pipeline and, like the RMT multicast stage, relies on metadata set in the ingress pipeline to determine multicast. FlexPipe can make up to five copies ("mirrors") of the packet that can be independently modified, but each copy can be copied again to any output port, so long as no further modifications are required.

$$\begin{aligned} \mathsf{multicast} \quad &= \quad \mathsf{mirror}; \mathsf{egress}; \mathsf{flood} \\ \mathsf{pipeline} \quad &= \quad \mathsf{diamond}; \mathsf{multicast} \end{aligned}$$

We present models of both RMT and FlexPipe (including mirror, egress and flood) in greater detail in Section 5.

Fields	$f \in \mathsf{F} ::= f_1 \mid \cdots \mid f_k$	
Packets	$pk \in \mathsf{PK} ::= \mathsf{F} \rightharpoonup \mathsf{Val}$	
Variables	$x, y \in \mathsf{Var}$	
Types	$\tau \in \mathcal{P}(\mathsf{R}) \times \mathcal{P}(\mathsf{W})$	
Predicates	$a, b ::= \mathsf{id}$	*Identity (True)*
	$\mid \mathsf{drop}$	*Drop (False)*
	$\mid f = v$	*Match*
	$\mid \neg a$	*Negation*
	$\mid a + b$	*Disjunction*
	$\mid a; b$	*Conjunction*
Policies	$p, q ::= a$	*Filter*
	$\mid f \leftarrow v$	*Modification*
	$\mid (x : \tau)$	*Table variable*
	$\mid p + q$	*Parallel composition*
	$\mid p; q$	*Sequential composition*
	$\mid p \;{}_{W_p}\|\|_{W_q}\; q$	*Concurrent composition*
States	$\sigma ::= \langle p, \delta \rangle$	
Packet trees	$\delta ::= \langle \mathsf{PK}, \mathsf{W} \rangle$	*Leaves*
	$\mid \langle \mathsf{par}\ \delta_1\ \delta_2 \rangle$	*Parallel processing*
	$\mid \langle \mathsf{not}_{\mathsf{PK}}\ \delta \rangle$	*Pending negation*
	$\mid \langle \mathsf{con}_{\mathsf{W}}\ \delta_1\ \delta_2 \rangle$	*Concurrent processing*

Figure 3. Packets, types, and predicate/policy syntax

3. Concurrent NetCore

We define the syntax of Concurrent NetCore in Figure 3. The language is broken into two levels: predicates and policies. Predicates, written with the metavariables a and b, simply filter packets without modifying or copying them. Policies, written with the metavariables p and q, can (concurrently) modify and duplicate packets. Every predicate is a policy—a read-only one. Both policies and predicates are interpreted using a *set semantics*, much like NetKAT [3]. Policies are interpreted as functions from sets of packets to sets of packets, while predicates have two interpretations: as functions from sets of packets to sets of packets, but also as Boolean propositions selecting a subset of packets. A *packet*, written with the metavariable pk, is finite partial function from *fields* to *values*. We fix a set of fields F, from which we draw individual fields f. We will occasionally refer to sets of fields using the metavariables R and W when they denote sets of readable or writable fields, respectively. We do not have a concrete treatment for values $v \in \mathsf{Val}$, though Val must be finite and support a straightforward notion of equality. One could model both equality and TCAM-style wildcard matching, but for simplicity's sake, we stick with equality only.

As explained in Section 2, the policies of Concurrent NetCore include the predicates as well as primitives for field modification, tables $(x : \tau)$, sequential composition (;), parallel composition (+), and concurrency (||). One difference from our informal presentation earlier is that concurrent composition $p \;{}_{W_p}\|\|_{W_q}\; q$ formally requires a pair of write sets W_p and W_q where W_p denotes the set of fields that p may write and W_q denotes the set of fields that q may write. Our operational semantics in Section 3.1 will in fact get *stuck* if p and q have a race condition, *e.g.*, have read/write dependencies.

Table variables $(x : \tau)$ are holes in a policy to be filled in by the controller with an initial policy, which the controller updates as the switch processes packets. The type $\tau = (\mathsf{R}, \mathsf{W})$ constrains the fields that the table may read from (R) and write to (W). For example, the rules that populate the table $(x : (\{\mathsf{src}, \mathsf{typ}\}, \{\mathsf{dst}\}))$ can only ever read from the `src` and `typ` fields and can only ever write to the `dst` fields. In practice, this means that the controller can substitute in for x any policy matching its type (or with a more restrictive type).

A note on packet field dependences. Packet formats often have complex dependencies, e.g., if the Ethertype field is `0x800`, then the Ethernet header is followed by an IP protocol header. Switches handle attempts to match or modify a missing field at run time, although the specific behavior varies by target architecture. In the RMT chip, for instance, there is a valid bit indicating the presence (or absence) of each possible field. In OpenFlow 1.0 architectures, matching against a missing field always succeeds. In both cases, writing to a missing field is treated as a non-operation. Hence, we assume that each packet arriving at each switch contains fields $f_1, \ldots, f_k$, although in practice the value associated with each field (which we treat abstractly) may be a distinguished "not present" value.

3.1 Small-step operational semantics

We give a small-step semantics for *closed* policies, *i.e.*, policies where table variables have been instantiated with concrete policies.

Just like the switches we are modeling, our policies actually work on packets one at a time: switches take an input packet and produce a (possibly empty) set of (potentially modified) output packets. As a technical convenience, our operational semantics generalizes this, modeling policies as taking a *set* of packets to a set of packets. Making this theoretically expedient choice—as we will show in Lemma 3—doesn't compromise our model's adequacy.

While other variants of NetCore/NetKAT use a denotational semantics, we use a completely new small-step, operational semantics in order to capture the interleavings of concurrent reads and writes of various fields of a packet. The interaction between (nested) concurrent processing of shared fields and packet-copying parallelism is quite intricate and hence deserves a faithful, fine-grained operational model. In Section 4, we define a type system that guarantees the strong normalization of all concurrent executions, and show that despite the concurrency, we can in fact use a NetKAT-esque set-theoretic denotational semantics to reason about policies at a higher level of abstraction if we so choose.

Using PK to range over sets of packets, we define the states σ for the small-step operational semantics $\sigma \to \sigma'$ in Figure 3. These states $\sigma = \langle p, \delta \rangle$ are pairs of a policy p and a packet tree δ. Packet trees represent the state of packet processing: which packets, or packet components, are the different branches of the parallel and concurrent compositions working on? When processing a negation, from what set of packets will we take the complement?

The leaves of packet trees are of the form $\langle \mathsf{PK}, \mathsf{W} \rangle$, where PK is a set of packets and W is a set of fields indicating the current *write permission*. The write permission indicates which fields may be written; other fields present in the packets $pk \in \mathsf{PK}$ may be read but not written. Packet processing is done when we reach a terminal state, $\langle \mathsf{id}, \langle \mathsf{PK}, \mathsf{W} \rangle \rangle$.

There are three kinds of packet tree branches. The packet tree branch $\langle \mathsf{par}\ \delta_1\ \delta_2 \rangle$ represents a parallel composition $p + q$ where p is operating on δ_1 and q is operating on δ_2. The packet tree branch $\langle \mathsf{not}_{\mathsf{PK}}\ \delta \rangle$ represents a negation $\neg a$ where a is running on δ—when a terminates with some set of packets PK', we will compute $\mathsf{PK} \setminus \mathsf{PK}'$, i.e., those packets *not* satisfying a. The packet tree branch $\langle \mathsf{con}_{\mathsf{W}}\ \delta_1\ \delta_2 \rangle$ represents a concurrent composition $p \;{}_{W_p}\|\|_{W_q}\; q$ where p works on δ_1 with write permission W_p and q works on δ_2 with write permission W_q. We also store W, the write permission before concurrent processing, so we can restore it when p and q are done processing.

We write $\sigma \to \sigma'$ to mean that the state σ performs a step of packet processing and transitions to the state σ'. Packet processing modifies the packets in a state and/or reduces the term. The step relation relies on several auxiliary operators on packets and packet sets. We read $pk[f := v]$ as, "update packet pk's f field with the value v;" and $pk \setminus \mathsf{F}$ as, "packet pk without the fields in F;" and

$\mathsf{PK} \setminus \mathsf{F}$ as, "those packets in PK without the fields in F," which lifts $pk \setminus \mathsf{F}$ to sets of packets. Finally, we pronounce $\times$ as "cross product." Notice that $\mathsf{PK} \setminus \mathsf{F}$ only produces the empty set when PK is itself empty—if every packet $pk \in \mathsf{PK}$ has only fields in F, then $\mathsf{PK} \setminus \mathsf{F} = \{\bot\}$, the set containing the empty packet. Such a packet set is not entirely trivial, as there remains one policy decision to be made about such a set of packets: drop (using drop) or forward (using id)? On the other hand, $\emptyset \times \mathsf{PK} = \mathsf{PK} \times \emptyset = \emptyset$.

With these definitions to hand, we define the step relation in Figure 4. The following invariants of evaluation and well-typed policies may be of use while reading through Figure 4 the following.

- Policy evaluation begins with a leaf $\langle \mathsf{PK}, \mathsf{W}\rangle$ and ends with a leaf $\langle \mathsf{PK}', \mathsf{W}\rangle$ with the same write permissions W.
- Policies may modify the values of existing fields within packets, but they cannot introduce new packets nor new fields—policies given the empty set of packets produce the empty set of packets.

The first few rules are straightforward. The (DROP) rule drops all its input packets, yielding $\emptyset$. In (MATCH), a match $\langle f = v, \langle \mathsf{PK}, \mathsf{W}\rangle\rangle$ filters PK, producing those packets which have f set to v. In (MODIFY), a modification $\langle f \leftarrow v, \langle \mathsf{PK}, \mathsf{W}\rangle\rangle$ updates packets with the new value v. Both (MATCH) and (MODIFY) can get stuck: the former if f is not defined for some packet, and the latter if the necessary write permission ($f \in \mathsf{W}$) is missing.

Sequential processing for $p; q$ is simpler: we run p to completion (SEQL), and then we run q on the resulting packets (SEQR). A special packet tree branch is not necessary, because q runs on any and all output that p produces. Intuitively, this is the correct behavior with regard to drop: if p drops all packets, then q will run on no packets, and will therefore produce no packets.

The parallel composition $p + q$ is processed on $\langle \mathsf{PK}, \mathsf{W}\rangle$ in stages, like all of the remaining rules. First, (PARENTER) introduces new packet tree branch, $\langle \mathsf{par}\ \langle \mathsf{PK}, \mathsf{W}\rangle\ \langle \mathsf{PK}, \mathsf{W}\rangle\rangle$, duplicating the original packets: one copy for p and one for q. PARL and PARR step p and q in parallel, each modifying its local packet tree. When both p and q reach a terminal state, PAREXIT takes the union of their results. Note that PAREXIT produces the identity policy, id, in addition to combining the results of executing p and q, and we restore the initial write permissions W. As with NetKAT, $p + q$ has a set semantics, rather than bag semantics. If p and q produce an identical packet pk, only one copy of pk will appear in the result.

Negation $\neg a$, like parallel composition, uses a special packet tree branch (not)—in this case, to keep a copy of the original packets. Running $\neg a$ on PK, we first save a copy of PK in the packet tree $\langle \mathsf{not}_{\mathsf{PK}}\ \langle \mathsf{PK}, \mathsf{W}\rangle\rangle$ (NOTENTER), preserving the write permissions. We then run a on the copied packets (NOTINNER). When a finishes with some PK_a, we look back at our original packets and return the saved packets *not* in PK_a (NOTEXIT).

Concurrent composition is the most complicated of all our policies. To run the concurrent composition $p\ {}_{\mathsf{W}_p}||_{\mathsf{W}_q}\ q$ on packets PK with write permissions W, we first construct an appropriate packet tree (CONENTER). We split the packets based on two sets of fields: those written by p, W_p, and those written by q, W_q. We also store the original write permissions W—a technicality necessary for the metatheory, since in well typed programs $\mathsf{W} = \mathsf{W}_p \cup \mathsf{W}_q$ (see (CON) in the typing rules in Figure 5, Section 4). The sub-policies p and q run on restricted views of PK, where each side can (a) read and write its own fields, and (b) read fields *not written by the other.* To achieve (a), we split W between the two. To achieve (b), we remove certain fields from each side: the sub-policy p will process $\mathsf{PK} \setminus \mathsf{W}_q$ under its own write permission W_p (CONL), while the sub-policy q will process $\mathsf{PK} \setminus \mathsf{W}_p$ under its own write permission W_q (CONR). Note that it is possible to write bad sets of fields for W_p and W_q in three ways: by overlapping, with W_p and W_q sharing fields (stuck in (CONENTER)); by dishonesty, where p tries to write to a field not in W_p (stuck later in (MODIFY)); and by mistake, with p reading from a field in W_q (stuck later in (MATCH)). While evaluation derivations of such erroneous programs will get stuck, our type system rules out such programs (Lemma 1). When both sides have terminated, we have sets of packets PK_P and PK_q, the result of p and q processing fragments of packets and concurrently writing to separate fields. We must then reconstruct a set of complete packets from these fragments. In (CONEXIT), the cross product operator $\times$ merges the writes from PK_p and PK_q. We take every possible pair of packets pk_p and pk_q from PK_p and PK_q and construct a packet with fields derived from those two packets. (It is this behavior that leads us to call it the 'cross product'.) In the merged packet pk, there are three ways to include a field:

1. We set $pk.f$ to be $pk_p.f$ when $f \notin \mathsf{Dom}\left(pk_q\right)$. That is, f is in W_p and may have been written by p.
2. We set $pk.f$ to be $pk_q.f$ when $f \notin \mathsf{Dom}\left(pk_p\right)$. Here, $f \in \mathsf{W}_q$, and q may have written to it.
3. We set $pk.f$ to $pk_p.f$, which is equal to $pk_q.f$. For a f to be found in both packets, it must be that $f \notin \mathsf{W}_p \cup \mathsf{W}_q$—that is, f was not written at all.

This accounts for each field in the new packet pk, but do we have the right number of packets? If p ran a parallel composition, it may have duplicated packets; if q ran drop, it may have no packets at all. One guiding intuition is that well typed concurrent compositions $p\,||\,q$ should be equivalent to $p; q$ and $q; p$. (In fact, *all* interleavings of well typed concurrent compositions should be equivalent, but sequential composition already gives us a semantics for the 'one side first' strategy.) The metatheory in Section 4 is the ultimate argument, but we can give some intuition by example:

- Suppose that $\mathsf{PK} = \{pk\}$ and that $p = f_1 \leftarrow v_1$ and $q = f_2 \leftarrow v_2$ update separate fields. In this case $\mathsf{PK}_p = \{(pk \setminus \{f_2\})[f_1 := v_1]\}$ and $\mathsf{PK}_q = \{(pk \setminus \{f_1\})[f_2 := v_2]\}$. Taking $\mathsf{PK}_p \times \mathsf{PK}_q$ yields a set containing a single packet pk', where $pk'(f_1) = v_1$ and $pk'(f_2) = v_2$, but $pk'(f) = pk(f)$ for all other—just as if we ran $p; q$ or $q; p$.
- Suppose that $p = \mathsf{id}$ and $q = \mathsf{drop}$. When we take $\mathsf{PK}_p \times \mathsf{PK}_q$, there are no packets at all in PK_q, and so there is no output. This is equivalent to running id; drop or drop; id.
- Suppose that $p = f_1 \leftarrow v_1 + f_1 \leftarrow v_1'$ and $q = f_2 \leftarrow v_2$. Running $p\ {}_{\{f_1\}}||_{\{f_2\}}\ q$ on PK will yield

$$\begin{array}{rcl} \mathsf{PK}_p & = & \{pk[f_1 := v_1] \mid pk \in \mathsf{PK} \setminus \{f_2\}\} \cup \\ & & \{pk[f_1 := v_1'] \mid pk \in \mathsf{PK} \setminus \{f_2\}\} \\ \mathsf{PK}_q & = & \{pk[f_2 := v_2] \mid pk \in \mathsf{PK} \setminus \{f_1\}\} \\ \mathsf{PK}_p \times \mathsf{PK}_q & = & \{pk[f_2 := v_2][f_1 := v_1] \mid pk \in \mathsf{PK}\} \cup \\ & & \{pk[f_2 := v_2][f_1 := v_1'] \mid pk \in \mathsf{PK}\} \end{array}$$

  Which is the same as running $p; q$ or $q; p$.

We should note that $p\ {}_{\mathsf{W}_p}||_{\mathsf{W}_q}\ q$ is *not* the same as $p; q$ when W_p and W_q are incorrect, e.g., when p tries to write a field $f \notin \mathsf{W}_p$, or when q tries to read a field $f \in \mathsf{W}_p$. Sequential composition may succeed where concurrent composition gets stuck!

3.2 Modeling the SDN controller

The operational semantics is defined on *closed* policies—that is, policies without table variables. At configuration time, the controller installs a (possibly open) policy on each switch, which tells the switch how to arrange its packet processing pipeline. Next, at population time, the controller will send messages to the switch instructing it to replace each abstract table variable with a concrete (closed) policy, after which packet processing proceeds as described by the operational semantics from Figure 4.

Packet operations

$$pk[f := v] = \lambda f' . \begin{cases} v & f = f' \\ pk(f') & \text{otherwise} \end{cases} \qquad pk \setminus \mathsf{F} = \lambda f . \begin{cases} \bot & f \in \mathsf{F} \\ pk(f) & \text{otherwise} \end{cases} \qquad \mathsf{PK} \setminus \mathsf{F} = \{pk \setminus \mathsf{F} \mid pk \in \mathsf{PK}\}$$

$$pk_1 \times pk_2 = \lambda f . \begin{cases} pk_1(f) & \text{when } f \notin \mathsf{Dom}\,(pk_2) \\ pk_2(f) & \text{when } f \notin \mathsf{Dom}\,(pk_1) \\ pk_1(f) & \text{when } pk_1(f) = pk_2(f) \end{cases} \qquad \mathsf{PK}_1 \times \mathsf{PK}_2 = \{\, pk_1 \times pk_2 | \, pk_1 \in \mathsf{PK}_1, pk_2 \in \mathsf{PK}_2\}$$

Reduction relation

$\boxed{\sigma_1 \to \sigma_2}$

$$\frac{}{\langle \mathsf{drop}, \langle \mathsf{PK}, \mathsf{W}\rangle\rangle \to \langle \mathsf{id}, \langle \emptyset, \mathsf{W}\rangle\rangle}\ \textsc{Drop} \qquad \frac{}{\langle f = v, \langle \mathsf{PK}, \mathsf{W}\rangle\rangle \to \langle \mathsf{id}, \langle \{pk \in \mathsf{PK} \mid pk(f) = v\}, \mathsf{W}\rangle\rangle}\ \textsc{Match}$$

$$\frac{f \in \mathsf{W}}{\langle f \leftarrow v, \langle \mathsf{PK}, \mathsf{W}\rangle\rangle \to \langle \mathsf{id}, \langle \{pk[f := v] \mid pk \in \mathsf{PK}\}, \mathsf{W}\rangle\rangle}\ \textsc{Modify} \qquad \frac{\langle p, \delta\rangle \to \langle p', \delta'\rangle}{\langle p; q, \delta\rangle \to \langle p'; q, \delta'\rangle}\ \textsc{SeqL} \qquad \frac{}{\langle \mathsf{id}; q, \delta\rangle \to \langle q, \delta\rangle}\ \textsc{SeqR}$$

$$\frac{}{\langle p + q, \langle \mathsf{PK}, \mathsf{W}\rangle\rangle \to \langle p + q, \langle \mathsf{par}\ \langle \mathsf{PK}, \mathsf{W}\rangle\ \langle \mathsf{PK}, \mathsf{W}\rangle\rangle\rangle}\ \textsc{ParEnter} \qquad \frac{\langle p, \delta_p\rangle \to \langle p', \delta_p'\rangle}{\langle p + q, \langle \mathsf{par}\ \delta_p\ \delta_q\rangle\rangle \to \langle p' + q, \langle \mathsf{par}\ \delta_p'\ \delta_q\rangle\rangle}\ \textsc{ParL}$$

$$\frac{\langle q, \delta_q\rangle \to \langle q', \delta_q'\rangle}{\langle p + q, \langle \mathsf{par}\ \delta_p\ \delta_q\rangle\rangle \to \langle p + q', \langle \mathsf{par}\ \delta_p\ \delta_q'\rangle\rangle}\ \textsc{ParR} \qquad \frac{}{\langle \mathsf{id} + \mathsf{id}, \langle \mathsf{par}\ \langle \mathsf{PK}_p, \mathsf{W}\rangle\ \langle \mathsf{PK}_q, \mathsf{W}\rangle\rangle\rangle \to \langle \mathsf{id}, \langle \mathsf{PK}_p \cup \mathsf{PK}_q, \mathsf{W}\rangle\rangle}\ \textsc{ParExit}$$

$$\frac{}{\langle \neg a, \langle PK, \mathsf{W}\rangle\rangle \to \langle a, \langle \mathsf{not}_{\mathsf{PK}}\ \langle \mathsf{PK}, \mathsf{W}\rangle\rangle\rangle}\ \textsc{NotEnter} \qquad \frac{\langle a, \delta\rangle \to \langle a', \delta'\rangle}{\langle a, \langle \mathsf{not}_{\mathsf{PK}}\ \delta\rangle\rangle \to \langle a', \langle \mathsf{not}_{\mathsf{PK}}\ \delta'\rangle\rangle}\ \textsc{NotInner}$$

$$\frac{}{\langle \mathsf{id}, \langle \mathsf{not}_{\mathsf{PK}}\ \langle \mathsf{PK}_a, \mathsf{W}\rangle\rangle\rangle \to \langle \mathsf{id}, \langle \mathsf{PK} \setminus \mathsf{PK}_a, \mathsf{W}\rangle\rangle}\ \textsc{NotExit}$$

$$\frac{\mathsf{W}_p \cap \mathsf{W}_q = \emptyset \qquad \mathsf{W}_p \cup \mathsf{W}_q \subseteq \mathsf{W}}{\langle p\ {}_{\mathsf{W}_p}||_{\mathsf{W}_q}\ q, \langle \mathsf{PK}, \mathsf{W}\rangle\rangle \to \langle p\ {}_{\mathsf{W}_p}||_{\mathsf{W}_q}\ q, \langle \mathsf{con}_{\mathsf{W}}\ \langle \mathsf{PK} \setminus \mathsf{W}_q, \mathsf{W}_p\rangle\ \langle \mathsf{PK} \setminus \mathsf{W}_p, \mathsf{W}_q\rangle\rangle\rangle}\ \textsc{ConEnter}$$

$$\frac{\langle p, \delta_p\rangle \to \langle p', \delta_p'\rangle}{\langle p\ {}_{\mathsf{W}_p}||_{\mathsf{W}_q}\ q, \langle \mathsf{con}_{\mathsf{W}}\ \delta_p\ \delta_q\rangle\rangle \to \langle p'\ {}_{\mathsf{W}_p}||_{\mathsf{W}_q}\ q, \langle \mathsf{con}_{\mathsf{W}}\ \delta_p'\ \delta_q\rangle\rangle}\ \textsc{ConL} \qquad \frac{\langle q, \delta_q\rangle \to \langle q', \delta_q'\rangle}{\langle p\ {}_{\mathsf{W}_p}||_{\mathsf{W}_q}\ q, \langle \mathsf{con}_{\mathsf{W}}\ \delta_p\ \delta_q\rangle\rangle \to \langle p\ {}_{\mathsf{W}_p}||_{\mathsf{W}_q}\ q', \langle \mathsf{con}_{\mathsf{W}}\ \delta_p\ \delta_q'\rangle\rangle}\ \textsc{ConR}$$

$$\frac{}{\langle \mathsf{id}\ {}_{\mathsf{W}_p}||_{\mathsf{W}_q}\ \mathsf{id}, \langle \mathsf{con}_{\mathsf{W}}\ \langle \mathsf{PK}_p, \mathsf{W}_p\rangle\ \langle \mathsf{PK}_q, \mathsf{W}_q\rangle\rangle\rangle \to \langle \mathsf{id}, \langle \mathsf{PK}_p \times \mathsf{PK}_q, \mathsf{W}\rangle\rangle}\ \textsc{ConExit}$$

Figure 4. Concurrent NetCore operational semantics

Definition 1. *Population-time updates and closing functions.*

Popluation-time updates $b \in \mathsf{Var} \rightharpoonup \mathsf{Policy}$
Closing functions $T_b \in \mathsf{Policy} \to \mathsf{Policy}$

We model population-time updates as partial functions mapping table variables to closed policies. The function $T_b\ (p)$ structurally recurses through a policy p, replacing each table variable x with $b(x)$. That is, the policy p is a configuration-time specification, and $T_b\ (p)$ is an instance of that specification populated according to the update function b. Population-time updates and closing functions will play a large role in Section 6, when we present a compilation algorithm for transforming a policy (and subsequent updates) to fit on a fixed target architecture.

4. Metatheory

The operational semantics of Section 3.1/Figure 4 defines the behavior of policies on packets. A number of things can cause the operational semantics to get stuck, which is how we model errors:

1. Unsubstituted variables—they have no corresponding rule.
2. Reads of non-existent fields—(MATCH) can't apply if there are packets $pk \in \mathsf{PK}$ such that $f \notin \mathsf{Dom}\,(pk)$, as might happen if CONENTER were to split packets incorrectly.
3. Writes to fields without write permission—(MODIFY) only allows writes to a field f if $f \in \mathsf{W}$.
4. Race conditions—concurrency splits the packet tree based on the write permissions of its subpolicies, and incorrect annotations can lead to stuckness via being unable to apply (CONENTER), which requires that $\mathsf{W}_p \cap \mathsf{W}_q = \emptyset$, or via getting stuck on (2) or (3) later in the evaluation due to the reduced fields and permissions each concurrent sub-policy runs with.

We define a type system in Figure 5, with the aim that well typed programs won't get stuck—a property we show in our proof of normalization, Lemma 1. First, we define entirely standard typing contexts, Γ. We will only run policies typed in the empty environment, i.e., with all of their tables filled in. Before offering typing rules for policies, we define well formedness of types and typing of packet sets. A type $\tau = (\mathsf{R}, \mathsf{W})$ is well formed if R and W are subsets of a globally fixed set of fields F and if $\mathsf{R} \cap \mathsf{W}$ is empty. A set of packets PK conforms to a type $\tau = (\mathsf{R}, \mathsf{W})$ if every packet $pk \in \mathsf{PK}$ has *at least* those fields in $\mathsf{R} \cup \mathsf{W}$.

The policies id and drop can both be typed at any well formed type, by (ID) and (DROP), respectively. Table variables $(x : \tau)$ are typed at their annotations, τ. The matching policy $f = v$ is well typed at τ when f is readable or writable (MATCH). Similarly, $f \leftarrow v$ is well typed at τ when f is writable in τ (MODIFY).

$$\Gamma ::= \cdot \mid \Gamma, (x : \tau)$$

$$(\mathsf{R}_1, \mathsf{W}_1) \cup (\mathsf{R}_2, \mathsf{W}_2) = ((\mathsf{R}_1 \setminus \mathsf{W}_2) \cup (\mathsf{R}_2 \setminus \mathsf{W}_1), \mathsf{W}_1 \cup \mathsf{W}_2)$$

$\boxed{\vdash \tau}$ $\boxed{\vdash \mathsf{PK} : \tau}$

$$\frac{\mathsf{R}, \mathsf{W} \subseteq \mathsf{F} \qquad \mathsf{R} \cap \mathsf{W} = \emptyset}{\vdash (\mathsf{R}, \mathsf{W})} \qquad \frac{\forall pk \in \mathsf{PK}.\ \mathsf{R} \cup \mathsf{W} \subseteq \mathsf{Dom}\,(pk)}{\vdash \mathsf{PK} : (\mathsf{R}, \mathsf{W})}$$

$\boxed{\Gamma \vdash p : \tau}$

$$\frac{\vdash \tau}{\Gamma \vdash \mathsf{id} : \tau}\textsc{Id} \qquad \frac{\vdash \tau}{\Gamma \vdash \mathsf{drop} : \tau}\textsc{Drop} \qquad \frac{(x : \tau) \in \Gamma \qquad \vdash \tau}{\Gamma \vdash x : \tau}\textsc{Var}$$

$$\frac{\vdash (\mathsf{R}, \mathsf{W}) \qquad f \in \mathsf{R} \cup \mathsf{W}}{\Gamma \vdash f = v : (\mathsf{R}, \mathsf{W})}\textsc{Match} \qquad \frac{\vdash (\mathsf{R}, \mathsf{W}) \qquad f \in \mathsf{W}}{\Gamma \vdash f \leftarrow v : (\mathsf{R}, \mathsf{W})}\textsc{Modify}$$

$$\frac{\Gamma \vdash a : (\mathsf{R}, \emptyset)}{\Gamma \vdash \neg a : (\mathsf{R}, \mathsf{W})}\textsc{Not} \qquad \frac{\Gamma \vdash p : \tau_1 \qquad \Gamma \vdash q : \tau_2}{\Gamma \vdash p + q : (\tau_1 \cup \tau_2)}\textsc{Par}$$

$$\frac{\Gamma \vdash p : \tau_1 \qquad \Gamma \vdash q : \tau_2}{\Gamma \vdash p; q : (\tau_1 \cup \tau_2)}\textsc{Seq}$$

$$\frac{\begin{array}{c}\Gamma \vdash p : (\mathsf{R}_p, \mathsf{W}_p) \qquad \Gamma \vdash q : (\mathsf{R}_q, \mathsf{W}_q) \\ \mathsf{W}_p \cap \mathsf{W}_q = \emptyset \qquad \mathsf{W}_p \cap \mathsf{R}_q = \emptyset \qquad \mathsf{R}_p \cap \mathsf{W}_q = \emptyset\end{array}}{\Gamma \vdash p\ {}_{\mathsf{W}_p}||_{\mathsf{W}_q}\ q : ((\mathsf{R}_p, \mathsf{W}_p) \cup (\mathsf{R}_q, \mathsf{W}_q))}\textsc{Con}$$

Figure 5. Concurrent NetCore typing rules

Negations $\neg a$ are well typed at $\tau = (\mathsf{R}, \mathsf{W})$ by (NOT) when a is well typed at the read-only version of τ, i.e., $(\mathsf{R}, \emptyset)$. We restrict the type to being read-only to reflect the fact that (a) only predicates can be negated, and (b) predicates never modify fields.

If p is well typed at τ_1 and q is well typed at τ_2, then their parallel composition $p + q$ is well typed at $\tau_1 \cup \tau_2$. Union on types is defined in Figure 4 as taking the highest privileges possible: the writable fields of $\tau_1 \cup \tau_2$ are those that were writable in either τ_1 or τ_2; the readable fields of the union are those fields that were readable in one or both types but weren't writable in either type. We give their sequential composition the same type.

Concurrent composition has the most complicated type—we must add (conservative) conditions to prevent races. Suppose $\Gamma \vdash p : (\mathsf{R}_p, \mathsf{W}_p)$ and $\Gamma \vdash q : (\mathsf{R}_q, \mathsf{W}_q)$. We require that:

- There are no write-write dependencies between p and q ($\mathsf{W}_p \cap \mathsf{W}_q = \emptyset$; a requirement of (CONENTER).
- There are no read-write or write-read dependencies between p and q ($\mathsf{W}_p \cap R_q = \emptyset$ and $\mathsf{R}_p \cap \mathsf{W}_q = \emptyset$). This guarantees that (MATCH) won't get stuck trying to read a field that isn't present.

If these conditions hold, then we say the concurrent composition is well typed: $\Gamma \vdash p\ {}_{W_p}||_{W_q}\ q : (\mathsf{R}_p, \mathsf{W}_p) \cup (\mathsf{R}_q, \mathsf{W}_q)$. Note that this means that the W stored in the con packet tree will be $\mathsf{W}_p \cup \mathsf{W}_q$, and well typed programs meet the $\mathsf{W}_p \cup \mathsf{W}_q \subseteq \mathsf{W}$ requirement of (CONENTER) exactly. These conditions are conservative—some concurrent compositions with overlapping reads and writes are race-free. We use this condition for a simple reason: switches make similar disjointness restrictions on concurrent tables.

Two metatheorems yield a strong result about our calculus: strong normalization. We first prove well typed policies are normalizing when run on well typed leaves $\langle \mathsf{PK}, \mathsf{W} \rangle$—they reduce to the terminal state $\langle \mathsf{id}, \langle \mathsf{PK}', \mathsf{W} \rangle \rangle$ with some other, well typed set of packets PK' and the same write permissions W.

Lemma 1 (Normalization). *If*

$\vdash \tau = (\mathsf{R}, \mathsf{W})$ *and* $\vdash \mathsf{PK} : \tau$ *and* $\cdot \vdash p : \tau$

then $\langle p, \langle \mathsf{PK}, \mathsf{W} \rangle \rangle \rightarrow^* \langle \mathsf{id}, \langle \mathsf{PK}', \mathsf{W} \rangle \rangle$ *such that*

1. $\vdash \mathsf{PK}' : \tau$, *and*
2. $\mathsf{PK}' \setminus \mathsf{W} \subseteq \mathsf{PK} \setminus \mathsf{W}$.

Proof. By induction on the policy p, leaving τ general. The only difficulty is showing that (CONEXIT) can always successfully merge the results of well typed concurrency, which can be seen by a careful analysis of the cross product, using part (2) of the IH to show that fields not in the write permission W are "read-only". □

Next we show that our calculus is confluent—even for ill typed terms. This result may be surprising at first, but observe that concurrency is the only potential hitch for confluence. A concurrent composition with an annotation that conflicts with the reads and writes of its sub-policies will get stuck before ever running (CONEXIT). Even ill typed programs will be confluent—they just might not be confluent at terminal states. We can imagine an alternative semantics, where concurrency really worked on shared state—in that formulation, only well typed programs would be confluent.

Lemma 2 (Confluence). *If* $\sigma \rightarrow^* \sigma_1$ *and* $\sigma \rightarrow^* \sigma_2$ *then there exists* σ' *such that* $\sigma_1 \rightarrow^* \sigma'$ *and* $\sigma_2 \rightarrow^* \sigma'$.

Proof. By induction on the derivation of $\sigma \rightarrow^* \sigma_1$, proving the (stronger) single-step diamond property first. □

Normalization and confluence yield *strong normalization*. Even though our small-step operational semantics is nondeterministic, well typed policies terminate deterministically. We can in fact do one better: our small-step semantics (without concurrency) coincides exactly with the denotational semantics of NetKAT [3], though we (a) do away with histories, and (b) make the quantification in the definition of sequencing explicit. Since our policies are 'switch-local', we omit Kleene star.

Lemma 3 (Adequacy). *If* $\cdot \vdash p : \tau = (\mathsf{R}, \mathsf{W})$ *with no concurrency, then for all packets* $\vdash \mathsf{PK} : \tau$, *if* $\langle p, \langle \mathsf{PK}, \mathsf{W} \rangle \rangle \rightarrow^* \langle \mathsf{id}, \langle \mathsf{PK}', \mathsf{W} \rangle \rangle$ *then* $\mathsf{PK}' = \bigcup_{pk \in \mathsf{PK}} [\![p]\!]\, pk$, *where:*

$$\begin{array}{rcl}
[\![p]\!] & \in & \mathsf{PK} \rightarrow \mathcal{P}(\mathsf{PK}) \\
[\![\mathsf{id}]\!]\, pk & = & \{pk\} \\
[\![\mathsf{drop}]\!]\, pk & = & \emptyset \\
[\![f = v]\!]\, pk & = & \begin{cases} \{pk\} & pk(f) = v \\ \emptyset & \textit{otherwise} \end{cases} \\
[\![f \leftarrow v]\!]\, pk & = & \{pk[f := v]\} \\
[\![\neg a]\!]\, pk & = & \{pk\} \setminus ([\![a]\!]\, pk) \\
[\![p + q]\!]\, pk & = & [\![p]\!]\, pk \cup [\![q]\!]\, pk \\
[\![p; q]\!]\, pk & = & \bigcup_{pk' \in [\![p]\!] pk} [\![q]\!]\, pk'
\end{array}$$

Proof. By induction on $\cdot \vdash p : \tau$. □

The set-based reasoning principles offered by the denotational semantics are quite powerful. We can in fact characterize the behavior of *well typed* concurrent compositions as:

$$\begin{array}{rcll}
[\![p\ {}_{W_p}||_{W_q}\ q]\!] & \triangleq & [\![p; q]\!] & \text{(Lemma 5)} \\
& = & [\![q; p]\!] & \text{(Lemma 4)}
\end{array}$$

Lemma 4 (Concurrency commutes). *If* $\vdash \mathsf{PK} : \tau$ *then*

$$\begin{array}{l}
\vdash p\ {}_{\mathsf{W}_p}||_{\mathsf{W}_q}\ q : \tau \textit{ and } \langle p\ {}_{\mathsf{W}_p}||_{\mathsf{W}_q}\ q, \mathsf{PK} \rangle \rightarrow^* \langle \mathsf{id}, \mathsf{PK}' \rangle \\
\iff \vdash q\ {}_{\mathsf{W}_q}||_{\mathsf{W}_p}\ p : \tau \textit{ and } \langle q\ {}_{\mathsf{W}_q}||_{\mathsf{W}_p}\ p, \mathsf{PK} \rangle \rightarrow^* \langle \mathsf{id}, \mathsf{PK}' \rangle.
\end{array}$$

Proof. We reorder the congruence steps so that whenever we use CONL in one derivation, we use CONR in the other, and vice versa. Confluence (Lemma 2) proves the end results equal. □

Lemma 5 (Concurrency serializes). *If* $\vdash p \; _{\mathsf{W}_p}||_{\mathsf{W}_q} \; q : (\mathsf{R}, \mathsf{W})$ *and* $\vdash \mathsf{PK} : \tau$ *then* $\langle p \; _{\mathsf{W}_p}||_{\mathsf{W}_q} \; q, \langle \mathsf{PK}, \mathsf{W} \rangle \rangle \rightarrow^* \langle \mathsf{id}, \langle \mathsf{PK}', \mathsf{W} \rangle \rangle$ *iff* $\langle p; q, \langle \mathsf{PK}, \mathsf{W} \rangle \rangle \rightarrow^* \langle \mathsf{id}, \langle \mathsf{PK}', \mathsf{W} \rangle \rangle$.

Proof. Rewriting derivations by confluence (Lemma 2) to run p using (CONL/SEQL) and then q (nesting in CONR under concurrency). We rely on auxiliary lemmas relating, for all p, p's behavior on $PK \setminus \mathsf{W}_q$ and on PK (when $\mathsf{R}_p \cap \mathsf{W}_q = \mathsf{W}_p \cap W_q = \emptyset$). □

5. Modeling RMT and FlexPipe architectures

In addition to serving programmers at a user level, our language of network policies can model the hardware layout of a switch's packet-processing pipeline. When we interpret Concurrent NetCore policies as pipelines, table variables represent TCAM or SRAM tables, and combinators describe how tables are connected.

Figure 6 presents models for the RMT and FlexPipe architectures at a finer level of detail than in Section 2.2. Both the RMT and FlexPipe architectures share some physical characteristics, including the physical layout of hardware tables. These physical tables are built from SRAM or TCAM memory and hold rules that match on packet header fields and, depending on the results of the match, modify the packet header. Each table has a fixed amount of memory, but it can be reconfigured, in the same way the height and width of a rectangle can vary as the area remains constant. The width of a table is determined by the number of bits it matches on from the packet header, and the height determines the number of rules it can hold. Hence, knowing in advance that the controller will only ever install rules that match on the src is valuable information, as it allows more rules to be installed. Although both chips support complex operations—such as adding and removing fields, arithmetic, checksums, and field encryption—we only model rewriting the value of header fields.

Physical tables are so-called match/action tables: the table comprises an ordered list of rules matching some fields on the header of a packet. The table selects a matching rule and executes its corresponding action. We model physical tables in the pipeline as table variables, so we must be careful that our compiler only substitutes in policies that look like rules in a match/action table. In an implementation of a compiler from Concurrent NetCore to a switch, we would have to actually translate the rule-like policies to the switch-specific rule population instructions. In our model and the proofs of correctness, we treat policies of the form

$$\mathsf{matches}; \mathsf{crossbar}; \mathsf{actions}$$

as rules (the translation to syntactically correct OpenFlow rules is straightforward enough at this point). The matches policy matches some fields and selects actions to perform; the crossbar policy collects the actions selected, and then the actions policy runs them. (We elaborate on these phases below.) We believe that this is an adequate model, since it would not be hard to translate CNC policies in this form to rules for a particular switch. Our model requires that run-time updates to physical tables be of the form above; i.e., the binding $b(x : \tau)$ (Definition 1) has a rule-like tripartite structure.

If statements. Before examining each physical table stage in detail, it is worth noting that the multicast combinator also serves as a form of disjunction. For example, consider the policy $a; p + \neg a; q$. The packet splits into two copies, but the predicates on the left- and right-hand sides of $+$ are disjoint—at least one copy will always be dropped. Hence, this particular form never actually produces multiple packet copies. It is useful to know syntactically that no multicast happens—as we will see, it turns out that physical table stages contain sequences of nested if statements. We write (if a then p else q) for $(a; p + \neg a; q)$.

Physical tables. Each variable mapped to a physical table by the binding $b(x : \tau)$ comprises three stages. The *match* stage is first. A single match (match_i) sets the metadata field act_i based on a subset of fields drawn from the packet header. These fields implicitly determine the width of the match. The metadata field act_i holds an action identifier A_{jk}, a stand-in for the slightly more structured action languages of the RMT and FlexPipe chips. By convention, the j index of action identifiers groups updates to the same fields. For example, $A_{11} \dots A_{1k}$ might correspond to updating the src field, $A_{21} \dots A_{2j}$ the dst field, and so on. By construction, action selection is written to a metadata field act_i that is unique to that match, allowing for the match stage to execute multiple matches concurrently. Once the act_i fields are set, the physical table has a *crossbar* that combines the metadata fields and selects the actions to execute—which we model with metadata fields $\mathsf{do}_{A_{jk}}$, one for each A_{jk}. Each field $\mathsf{do}_{A_{jk}}$ is consumed by an *action* stage, which runs the corresponding actions on the packet. Each action_f stage tests for actions denoting updates to field f, which allows actions to execute concurrently.

As an example, suppose we would like to compile the routing and firewall policies $(r \parallel w)$ from Figure 2 as a single physical table.

$$\begin{array}{rcl} r & = & \mathsf{in} = 1; \mathsf{out} \leftarrow 2 + \mathsf{in} = 2; \mathsf{out} \leftarrow 1 \\ w & = & \mathsf{in} = 1; (\mathsf{typ} = ssh + \mathsf{typ} = http) + \neg(\mathsf{in} = 1) \end{array}$$

First, let's fix four concrete action values—we'll say that a value of 11 means "modify the out field to 1" ($\mathsf{out} \leftarrow 1$); a value of 12 means "modify the out field to 2" ($\mathsf{out} \leftarrow 2$); a value of 31 means "do nothing" (id); and a value of 41 means "drop the packet" (drop). We begin by defining two concurrent match stages, one each for r and w.

$$\begin{array}{rcl} \mathsf{match}_r & = & \mathsf{if\ in} = 1 \mathsf{\ then\ act}_r \leftarrow 12 \\ & & \mathsf{else\ if\ in} = 2 \mathsf{\ then\ act}_r \leftarrow 11 \\ & & \mathsf{else\ act}_r \leftarrow 41 \\ \mathsf{match}_w & = & \mathsf{if\ in} = 1; \mathsf{typ} = ssh \mathsf{\ then\ act}_w \leftarrow 31 \\ & & \mathsf{else\ if\ in} = 1; \mathsf{typ} = http \mathsf{\ then\ act}_w \leftarrow 31 \\ & & \mathsf{else\ if\ in} = 1 \mathsf{\ then\ act}_w \leftarrow 41 \\ & & \mathsf{else\ act}_w \leftarrow 31 \\ \mathsf{matches} & = & \mathsf{match}_r \parallel \mathsf{match}_w \end{array}$$

The match_r construct mirrors the structure of r, but rather than directly modifying the out field directly, it assigns an action identifier to the act_r metadata field. Encoding w is slightly more complex, thanks to the presence of disjunction (+) and negation. But it follows a similar pattern: In addition to converting w to a sequence of nested if statements, match_w assigns an action identifier to the act_w metadata field in place of taking an action directly. The matches stage is made up of match_r and match_w composed concurrently.

The crossbar stage collects the action values assigned in the matches stage in order to communicate them to the actions stage, where modifications to the packet header fields occur.

$$\begin{array}{rcl} \mathsf{crossbar} & = & \mathsf{if\ act}_r = 11 + \mathsf{act}_w = 11 \mathsf{\ then\ do}_{11} \leftarrow 1 \\ & & \mathsf{else\ if\ act}_r = 12 + \mathsf{act}_w = 12 \mathsf{\ then\ do}_{12} \leftarrow 1 \\ & & \mathsf{else\ if\ act}_r = 31 + \mathsf{act}_w = 31 \mathsf{\ then\ do}_{31} \leftarrow 1 \\ & & \mathsf{else\ if\ act}_r = 41 + \mathsf{act}_w = 41 \mathsf{\ then\ do}_{41} \leftarrow 1 \\ & & \mathsf{else\ drop} \end{array}$$

The actions stage consumes the output of the crossbar in order to effect modifications to the header fields. Actions on the same field are grouped; in this case, modifications to the out field are handled by $\mathsf{action}_{\mathsf{out}}$. This allows each action group to be executed concurrently, because they operate on different fields by construc-

Physical tables

$$
\begin{array}{rcl}
\mathsf{match}_i & = & \mathsf{if}\ f_{11} = v_{11}; \ldots ; f_{1n} = v_{1n} \\
& & \mathsf{then\ act}_i \leftarrow A_{j1} \\
& & \mathsf{else\ if}\ f_{21} = v_{21}; \ldots ; f_{2m} = v_{2m} \\
& & \mathsf{then\ act}_i \leftarrow A_{k2} \\
& & \mathsf{else}\ \ldots \\
\mathsf{matches} & = & \mathsf{match}_1 \mid\mid \mathsf{match}_2 \mid\mid \ldots \\
\mathsf{crossbar} & = & \mathsf{if\ act}_1 = A_{11} + \mathsf{act}_2 = A_{11} + \ldots \\
& & \mathsf{then\ do}_{A_{11}} \leftarrow 1 \\
& & \mathsf{else\ if\ act}_1 = A_{21} + \mathsf{act}_2 = A_{21} + \ldots \\
& & \mathsf{then\ do}_{A_{21}} \leftarrow 1 \\
& & \mathsf{else}\ \ldots \\
\mathsf{action}_j & = & \mathsf{if\ do}_{A_{j1}} = 1\ \text{then perform}\ A_{j1}\text{'s writes} \\
& & \mathsf{else\ if\ do}_{A_{j2}} = 1\ \text{then perform}\ A_{j2}\text{'s writes} \\
& & \ldots \\
\mathsf{actions} & = & \mathsf{action}_1 \mid\mid \mathsf{action}_2 \mid\mid \ldots \\
\mathsf{physical} & = & x : \tau \\
T_b\ (\mathsf{physical}) & = & \mathsf{matches; crossbar; actions}
\end{array}
$$

RMT model

$$
\begin{array}{rcl}
\mathsf{multicast} & = & (out_1 = 1; f_{\mathsf{tag}} \leftarrow v_1; \mathsf{out} \leftarrow 1) \\
& + & (out_2 = 2; f_{\mathsf{tag}} \leftarrow v_2; \mathsf{out} \leftarrow 2) \\
& + & \ldots \\
\mathsf{pipeline} & = & \mathsf{physical}_1; \ldots ; \mathsf{physical}_k; \mathsf{multicast}; \\
& & \mathsf{physical}_{k+1}; \ldots ; \mathsf{physical}_{32} \\
& & \text{where } k \leq 16
\end{array}
$$

FlexPipe model

$$
\begin{array}{rcl}
\mathsf{mirror} & = & m = 0 + \sum_i m_i = 1; m \leftarrow i \\
\mathsf{egress} & = & \mathsf{if}\ f_{11} = v_{11}; \ldots ; f_{1n} = v_{1n} \\
& & \mathsf{then}\ f'_{11} \leftarrow v'_{11}; \ldots ; f'_{1n} \leftarrow v'_{1n} \\
& & \mathsf{else\ if}\ f_{21} = v_{21}; \ldots ; f_{2m} = v_{2m} \\
& & \mathsf{then}\ f'_{21} \leftarrow v'_{21}; \ldots ; f'_{2n} \leftarrow v'_{2n} \\
& & \mathsf{else}\ \ldots \\
\mathsf{flood} & = & \sum_i out_i = 1; \mathsf{out} \leftarrow i \\
\mathsf{pair} & = & \mathsf{physical}_1; \mathsf{physical}_2 \\
\mathsf{diamond} & = & \mathsf{pair}_1; (\mathsf{pair}_2 \mid\mid \mathsf{pair}_3); \mathsf{pair}_4 \\
\mathsf{pipeline} & = & \mathsf{diamond; mirror; egress; flood}
\end{array}
$$

Figure 6. Modeling RMT and Intel FlexPipe.

tion.

$$
\begin{array}{rcl}
\mathsf{action}_{\mathsf{out}} & = & \mathsf{if\ do}_{11} = 1\ \mathsf{then\ out} \leftarrow 1 \\
& & \mathsf{else\ if\ do}_{12} = 1\ \mathsf{then\ out} \leftarrow 2 \\
& & \mathsf{else\ id} \\
\mathsf{action}_{\mathsf{id}} & = & \mathsf{if\ do}_{31} = 1\ \mathsf{then\ id} \\
& & \mathsf{else\ id} \\
\mathsf{action}_{\mathsf{drop}} & = & \mathsf{if\ do}_{41} = 1\ \mathsf{then\ drop} \\
& & \mathsf{else\ id} \\
\mathsf{actions} & = & \mathsf{action}_{\mathsf{out}} \mid\mid \mathsf{action}_{\mathsf{id}} \mid\mid \mathsf{action}_{\mathsf{drop}}
\end{array}
$$

Separating tables into three stages may seem excessive, but suppose r also modified the typ field. In this case, $r \mid\mid w$ is no longer well typed (because r writes to typ while w reads from it), but we may still extract concurrency from $w; r$: By splitting reading and writing into separate phases, the match stage for applying the access control policy (match_w) can run concurrently with the match determining the output port (match_r) with little change from the example above. Concurrent processing like this is a key feature of both the RMT and FlexPipe architectures.

RMT. The RMT chip provides a thirty-two table pipeline divided into ingress and egress stages, which are separated by a multicast stage. As a packet arrives, tables in the ingress pipeline act upon it before it reaches the multicast stage. To indicate that the packet should be duplicated, ingress tables mark a set of metadata fields corresponding to output ports on the switch. The multicast stage maintains a set of queues, one per output port. The chip enqueues a copy of the packet (really a copy of the packet's header and a pointer to the packet's body) into those queues selected by the metadata, optionally marking each copy with a distinct tag. Finally, tables in the egress pipeline process each copy of the packet.

We model the multicast stage as the parallel composition of sequences of tests on header and metadata fields followed by the assignment of a unique value tag and an output port, where each summand corresponds to a queue in the RMT architecture. We model the ingress and egress pipelines as sequences of tables, where each of the thirty-two tables may be assigned to one pipeline or the other, but not both. The RMT architecture makes it possible to divide a single physical table into pieces and assign each piece to a different pipeline. We leave modeling this as future work.

FlexPipe. While physical tables have built-in concurrency within match and action stages, the FlexPipe architecture also makes use of concurrency between physical tables. The ingress pipeline is arranged in a diamond shape. Each point of the diamond is built from two tables in sequence, with incoming packets first processed by the first pair, then concurrently by the next two pairs, and finally by the last pair. This built-in concurrency is optimized for common networking tasks, such as checking packets against an access control list while simultaneously calculating routing behavior—as in our firewall example of Figure 2.

The FlexPipe architecture breaks multicast into two stages separated by a single egress stage. The mirror stage makes up to four additional copies of the packet. Each copy sets a unique identifier to a metadata field m and writes to a bitmap out corresponding to the ports on which this copy will eventually be emitted—this allows for up to five potentially modified packets to be emitted from each port for each input packet. The egress stage matches on the metadata field m and various other fields to determine which modifications should be applied to the packet, and then applies those corresponding updates. Finally, the flood stage emits a copy of each mirrored packet on the ports set in its out bitmap.

6. Compilation

Compilation consists of several passes, each of which addresses a discrepancy between the expressivity of the high-level policy and the physical restrictions of the hardware model. In this section, we target the RMT architecture.

- **Multicast consolidation** transforms a policy with arbitrary occurrences of multicast ($+$) into a pipelined policy wherein multicast occurs at just a single stage.
- **Field extraction** moves modifications of a given field to an earlier stage of a pipelined policy.
- **Table fitting** partitions a pipelined policy into a sequence of tables, possibly combining multiple policy fragments into a single table.

Each pass takes a well-typed policy as input and produces an equivalent, refactored policy as well as a *binding transformer* as output.

Definition 2 (Binding transformer). *A binding transformer θ is an operator on table bindings b.*

$$\theta \in (\mathsf{Var} \rightharpoonup \mathsf{Policy}) \to \mathsf{Var} \rightharpoonup \mathsf{Policy}$$

Binding transformers play the role of the "generated rule translator" from Figure 1. In other words, during the switch population phase, the controller will issue table bindings b—essentially, closing substitutions, see Definition 1—in terms of the original policy, pre-compilation. It is the binding transformer θ's job to transform these table bindings so that they can be applied sensibly to the post-compilation pipeline configured on the switch.

6.1 Multicast consolidation

There are two important differences between the kind of multicast that Concurrent NetCore offers and the kind supported by the RMT pipeline. First, multicast may not occur arbitrarily in the RMT pipeline; rather, there is a fixed multicast stage sandwiched between two pipelines. Second, the multicast stage must know the destination output port of each packet copy *at the time the packet is copied.* We use *multicast consolidation* to rewrite a high-level policy into a form with a distinct multicast stage. The next section describes how we use *field extraction* to extract potential modifications to a given field from a subpolicy—which we will use to isolate writes to the output port to the multicast stage.

Informally, multicast consolidation works as follows. Suppose a policy p contains two instances of parallel composition, along with subpolicies q, r, and s that do not contain parallel composition.

$$p = q + r + s$$

Multicast consolidation rewrites p into two stages: the *consolidation* stage makes three copies of the packet and sets a fresh metadata field unique to each packet.

$$p_c = f_1 \leftarrow 1 + f_2 \leftarrow 1 + f_3 \leftarrow 1$$

Next, the *egress* stage replaces the original occurrences of multicast in p with a sequence of tests on the new metadata fields.

$$\begin{aligned} p_e = \;& \text{if } f_1 = 1 \text{ then } q \text{ else id};\\ & \text{if } f_2 = 1 \text{ then } r \text{ else id};\\ & \text{if } f_3 = 1 \text{ then } s \text{ else id} \end{aligned}$$

The consolidation and egress stages are composed sequentially. By convention, fresh metadata fields are initialized to zero. Hence, $p_c; p_e$ acts equivalently to p, producing at most three packets: one processed by q, another by r, and a third by s.

To capture this formally, we define syntactically restricted forms for the consolidation and egress stages that model consolidated packet duplication and tagging. The consolidation form is similar to the multicast stage presented in Figure 6 but slightly higher-level, in that it may contain table variables and additional field modifications—later compilation phases will factor these out.

Definition 3 (Multicast consolidation stages).

$$\begin{array}{llcl} \textit{consolidation sequence } s & & ::= & \Pi_i f_i \leftarrow 1 \mid (x : \tau); \Pi_i f_i \leftarrow 1 \\ \textit{consolidation stage } m & \in \mathsf{M} & ::= & \sum_i a_i; s_i \\ \textit{egress stage } n & \in \mathsf{N} & ::= & \text{id} \mid x : \tau \mid n; r \\ & & \mid & n; \text{if } \Pi_i f_i = 1 \text{ then } r \text{ else id} \end{array}$$

A *consolidation stage* is the sum of zero or more predicated *consolidation sequences*, each of which assigns to a set of fields (used for tagging each packet copy for later processing). We use the product notation $\Pi_i f_i \leftarrow v_i$ to stand for a sequence of field modifications $f_1 \leftarrow v_1; \ldots; f_n \leftarrow v_n$. Sequences may optionally begin with tables, which allows for multicast to be increased or decreased at run time.

An *egress stage* consists of a sequence of smaller policies. The sequence may begin with a table, which allows the egress stage to grow or shrink at population time; otherwise, it begins with id. Each remaining subpolicy takes one of two forms. Either it is drawn from the fragment of CNC that does not contain multicast, which we represent with the metavariable r, or it may be a multicast-free fragment embedded within an if statement that tests some subset of the metadata fields set in the consolidation stage. Intuitively, r alone represents a part of the original policy to be applied to all multicast copies of the packet, whereas an if statement selectively applies the policy it wraps to some copies of the packet, leaving others untouched.

Definition 4 (Multicast consolidation).

$$\mathsf{pipeline} \;::\; (\mathsf{Var} \to \mathsf{Nat}) \to \mathsf{Policy} \to (\mathsf{M} \times \mathsf{N} \times \Theta)$$

Given an arbitrary policy p, the function pipeline $s\ p$ factors the policy into a consolidation stage m followed by an egress stage n. The argument s is a user-supplied hint mapping each table to the number of copies it may make of a packet. The pipeline function is syntax-directed and presented in its entirety in the technical appendix; we highlight two interesting cases here. As one might expect, the bulk of the work takes place in the multicast case:

$$\begin{aligned} &\text{pipeline } s\ (p + q) = \\ &\quad \text{let } f = \text{a fresh metadata field in} \\ &\quad \text{let } (\textstyle\sum_i m_i), n_1, \theta_1 = \text{pipeline } s\ p \text{ in} \\ &\quad \text{let } (\textstyle\sum_j m_j), n_2, \theta_2 = \text{pipeline } s\ q \text{ in} \\ &\quad \text{let } n_3, \theta_3 = \text{qualify}(f = 0, n_1) \text{ in} \\ &\quad \text{let } n_4, \theta_4 = \text{qualify}(f = 1, n_2) \text{ in} \\ &\quad ((\textstyle\sum_i m_i; f \leftarrow 0) + (\textstyle\sum_j m_j; f \leftarrow 1), n_3; n_4, \\ &\qquad \theta_1 \circ \theta_2 \circ \theta_3 \circ \theta_4) \end{aligned}$$

Given a policy $p + q$, our strategy is as follows. First, recursively consolidate p and q. Then, pick a fresh field f that neither p nor q use. For each summand in the consolidation stage produced from p, set f to 0, and assign 1 to f in summands produced from q. Finally, predicate each egress pipeline from p with $f = 0$ and from q with $f = 1$—the qualify function transforms if a then n else id into an egress pipeline n' with the predicate a conjoined to the guard in each subseqent if statement. Finally, note that by construction, θ functions extend the domain of table bindings to accommodate new table variables. Hence, we can simply compose the θ functions produced by recursive compilation.

Table variables are the other tricky case—we must use the s argument to see how much more multicast has been reserved, deferring some of the multicast consolidation to rewrites that will occur during the population phase.

$$\begin{aligned} &\text{pipeline } s\ (x : \tau) = \\ &\quad \text{let } fs = s(x) \text{ fresh metadata fields in} \\ &\quad \text{let } t_m = y : (\{\}, fs) \text{ in} \\ &\quad \text{let } t_n = z : (\tau.1 \cup fs, \tau.2) \text{ in} \\ &\quad \text{let } \theta' = (\lambda b, w.\text{let } m, n, \theta = \text{pipeline } s\ (b\ x) \text{ in} \\ &\qquad \text{if } w = y \text{ then } m \text{ else if } w = z \text{ then } n \text{ else } T_{\theta\ b}\ w) \text{ in} \\ &\quad (t_m, t_n, \theta') \end{aligned}$$

Applied to a table variable, the pipeline function produces a θ function that, in turn, compiles all future table updates—using the s map to preallocate metadata fields for future updates. A key property of table updates is that they produce closed terms—hence, invoking pipeline inside θ on the updated table $b\ x$ runs no risk of divergence.

Example. As a brief example, let's look at how multicast consolidation will work on the $r + m$ fragment of the example policy from Section 2. Recall that m contains a table variable—which may introduce more multicast later. The compiler relies on a hint, s, that pre-allocates metadata fields corresponding to the amount of multicast that future updates may contain. Let $fs = s\ x$ be a set of such fields. The policy produced by pipeline $s\ (r+m)$ will be

$$(f \leftarrow 0 + y : (\{\mathsf{typ}, \mathsf{src}\}, fs); f \leftarrow 1);$$
$$(\mathsf{if}\ f = 0\ \mathsf{then}\ r\ \mathsf{else\ id});$$
$$(\mathsf{if}\ f = 1\ \mathsf{then}\ z : (\{\mathsf{typ}, \mathsf{src}\} \cup fs, \{\mathsf{out}\})\ \mathsf{else\ id}),$$

and the binding transformer θ will be

$$(\lambda b, w.\mathsf{let}\ q, r, \theta' = \mathsf{pipeline}\ s\ (T_b\ x)\ \mathsf{in}$$
$$\mathsf{if}\ w = y\ \mathsf{then}\ q\ \mathsf{else\ if}\ w = z\ \mathsf{then}\ r\ \mathsf{else}\ T_b\ w).$$

We introduce a fresh metadata field f to consolidate multicast in a single stage and tag each packet copy, and the remainder of the policy uses the tag to determine whether to apply r or m to each fragment. Because m contains a table variable x, we also add new tables y and z to handle any multicast that m may contain in the future—and we produce a function θ to ensure this.

Suppose an update arrives to x in as part of a table binding, b. Applying $\theta\ b$ to the compiled policy will consolidate any multicast present in b and install appropriate policies in y and z. Since $T_b\ x$ produces a closed policy, θ' is always the identity function.

Proof of semantic preservation. Finally, we prove that the original policy is equivalent to the compiled policy for all table updates. We use z to model the fact that metadata is initially assigned a value of 0 when the packet arrives at the switch, and that metadata is not observable once the packet has left the switch. The proof proceeds by induction on the structure of the policy p.

Lemma 6 (Multicast consolidation preserves semantics). *Let fs be the metadata fields used to tag multicast packets, and let* $z = \Pi_{f \in fs} f \leftarrow 0$. *If* $\vdash p : \tau$ *and* $m, n, \theta = \mathsf{pipeline}\ s\ p$, *then* $T_b\ (z; p; z) \equiv T_{\theta\ b}\ (z; m; n; z)$.

Proof. By induction on the structure of p, relying on Lemmas 4 and 5 and the axioms of NetKAT [3] to establish equivalence. □

6.2 Field extraction

The RMT architecture also requires that the output port of each packet be set during the multicast stage. Field extraction examines a policy to determine all the conditions under which a given field modification may take place, and then rewrites the policy so that modifications to that field happen first. For example, suppose we wish to extract modifications to the field f from this policy.

$$\mathsf{if}\ b\ \mathsf{then}\ f \leftarrow v_1; p\ \mathsf{else}\ f \leftarrow v_2; q$$

Either f is set to v_1 or v_2, and the predicate b determines which occurs. Using a fresh field f', we can rewrite this policy.

$$(b; f \leftarrow v_1; f' \leftarrow 0 + \neg b; f \leftarrow v_2; f' \leftarrow 1); \mathsf{if}\ f' = 0\ \mathsf{then}\ p\ \mathsf{else}\ q$$

Introducing f' is necessary because b may depend on the value of f. For example, suppose b is $f = v_3$. The clause $f' = 0$ in the if statement ensures that p is executed if f was set to v_1.

We define a *modification stage* as a sum of all the conditions leading to a given field being modified, coupled with the modification. The function $\mathsf{ext}_f\ p$ splits a policy p into a modification stage for the field f followed by the remainder of the policy.

Definition 5 (Modification stage).

modification sequence	s	$::=$	$\Pi_i f_i \leftarrow v_i$
		$\mid$	$(x : \tau); \Pi_i f_i \leftarrow v_i$
modification sum	$e \in \mathsf{E}$	$::=$	$\sum_j a_j; s_j$

Definition 6 (Field extraction).

$$\mathsf{ext}_f \quad :: \quad \mathsf{Policy} \rightarrow (\mathsf{E} \times \mathsf{Policy} \times \Theta)$$

The interesting case lies in extracting modification conditions from within an if statement.

$$\begin{aligned}
&\mathsf{ext}_f\ (\mathsf{if}\ b\ \mathsf{then}\ p\ \mathsf{else}\ q) = \\
&\quad \mathsf{let}\ f' = \text{a fresh metadata field in} \\
&\quad \mathsf{let}\ (\textstyle\sum_i a_{1i}; m_{1i}), p_1, \theta_1 = \mathsf{ext}_f\ p\ \mathsf{in} \\
&\quad \mathsf{let}\ (\textstyle\sum_j a_{2j}; m_{2j}), q_2, \theta_2 = \mathsf{ext}_f\ q\ \mathsf{in} \\
&\quad \mathsf{let}\ e = \textstyle\sum_i b; a_{1i}; m_{1i}; f' \leftarrow 0 + \\
&\qquad\qquad \textstyle\sum_j \neg b; a_{2j}; m_{2j}; f' \leftarrow 1\ \mathsf{in} \\
&\quad (e, \mathsf{if}\ f' = 0\ \mathsf{then}\ p_1\ \mathsf{else}\ q_2, \theta_2 \circ \theta_1)
\end{aligned}$$

In this case, we begin by recursively extracting any modifications from the branches of the if statement. We then sequence the predicate b with the conditions produced from the true branch and $\neg b$ with those from the false branch. However, modifications m_{1i} (from the recursive call $\mathsf{ext}_f\ p$) or m_{2j} (from the recursive call $\mathsf{ext}_f\ q$) might affect the predicate b. We therefore save b's pre-modification value in a fresh field f'. After we've run the modification sums from p and q, we produce a conditional that now tests f', which holds the original result of the predicate b.

As with multicast consolidation, we show that when metadata has been zeroed at the beginning and end of the policy, the interpretation of the original and compiled forms are equivalent for all table updates.

Lemma 7 (Field extraction preserves semantics). *Let fs be the metadata fields used to tag field extraction, and let* $z = \Pi_{f \in fs} f \leftarrow 0$. *If* $\vdash r : \tau$ *and* $e, r', \theta = $ *pipeline* $s\ r$, *then* $T_b\ (z; r; z) \equiv T_{\theta\ b}\ (z; e; r'; z)$.

Proof. By induction on the structure of p, relying on Lemmas 4 and 5 and the axioms of NetKAT [3] to establish equivalence. □

Composing multicast consolidation with field extraction (on the out field) produces two large summations. The next step is to factor the summations and group summands by output port. It is unclear whether/how the RMT architecture supports emitting multiple copies of a packet out the same output port, and so we reject programs of that shape here—we stick to a set semantics, though we can simulate a bag semantics with metadata fields. Now, valid policies consist of a single large summation of tests followed by modifications, ending with modification of the out field.

$$\sum_i \Pi_j f_{ij} = v_{ij}; \Pi_k f_{ik} \leftarrow v_{ik}; \mathsf{out} \leftarrow i$$

A final transformation splits this summation into a sequence of three smaller summations, of which the middle aligns precisely with the multicast stage of the RMT pipeline.

$$(\textstyle\sum_i \Pi_j f_{ij} = v_{ij}; out_i \leftarrow 1);$$
$$(\textstyle\sum_i out_i = 1; f_{\mathsf{tag}} \leftarrow i; \mathsf{out} \leftarrow i);$$
$$(\textstyle\sum_i f_{\mathsf{tag}} = i; \Pi_k f_{ik} \leftarrow v_{ik})$$

We have not yet proved that this transformation is semantics preserving, although we expect that doing so is straightforward. The next section presents techniques for compiling these, and other policies, to physical table format.

6.3 Table fitting

At this stage of the compilation process, every occurrence of parallel composition has been consolidated to a single multicast stage, appropriate for deployment to the RMT's multicast stage. What remains are table variables, predicates, field modifications, and if statements joined by sequential and concurrent combinators. Two tasks remain to match the policy with the architecture model. First, predicates, field modifications, and if statements must be replaced by table variables. A binding transformer will reinstate these policy fragments into the tables at population time. Second, the table variables in the user policy must be fitted to the table variables in the architecture model.

Both steps depend on a second compilation algorithm to compile a table-free user policy to a single physical table. With a few small modifications, we can adapt the compilation algorithm described in [3] for compiling policies to a physical table format. We call this *single table* compilation.

$$\textsf{single\_table} :: \textsf{Policy} \rightarrow \textsf{Policy}$$

The resulting policy fits the shape of the matches; crossbar; actions table format described in Figure 6. The extension to the algorithm described in [3] is straightforward, and we defer a complete presentation to a technical report.

Table insertion. At configuration time, the RMT switch consists solely of tables arranged via sequential and concurrent composition. Non-table elements in the user policy are fixed—i.e., the topology of tables cannot at population time (when the switch is "running")—but they cannot be installed directly on the switch at configuration time. Rather, they must be replaced by table variables, and then reinstalled at population time by a binding transformation. As a small example, consider the policy $\textsf{typ} = \textit{http}; x : \tau$. No matter which policies are installed into x at population time, they will always be preceded by the filter on the typ field. Hence, we can produce a new policy with a fresh table variable, $y : (\{\}, \{\textsf{typ}\}); x : \tau$, and a binding transformation

$$(\lambda b, w.\textsf{if } w = y \textsf{ then typ} = \textit{http} \textsf{ else } T_b\ w).$$

Definition 7 (Table insertion).

$$\begin{array}{lcl}
\textsf{insert_table}\ p; q & = & \textsf{let}\ p', \theta_p = \textsf{insert_table}\ p\ \textsf{in} \\
 & & \textsf{let}\ q', \theta_q = \textsf{insert_table}\ q\ \textsf{in} \\
 & & (p'; q', \theta_p \circ \theta_q) \\
\textsf{insert_table}\ p \mid\mid q & = & \textsf{let}\ p', \theta_p = \textsf{insert_table}\ p\ \textsf{in} \\
 & & \textsf{let}\ q', \theta_q = \textsf{insert_table}\ q\ \textsf{in} \\
 & & (p' \mid\mid q', \theta_p \circ \theta_q) \\
\textsf{insert_table}\ p & = & (x : \tau, (\lambda b, w. \\
 & & \quad \textsf{if}\ w = x\ \textsf{then single_table}\ (T_b\ p) \\
 & & \quad \textsf{else}\ T_b\ w))
\end{array}$$

After completing this step, the transformed user policy consists of table variables and sequential and concurrent combinators. We don't define a case for parallel composition because all of the multicast has already been consolidated.

Table fitting. Single-table compilation comes with a cost—the number of rules in the compiled table grows exponentially with the number of sequential combinators in the original policy. However, thanks to the concurrency inherent within physical tables, the policy $p \mid\mid q$ does not incur any overhead when installed in a single table. This leads to a choice. Suppose we have a policy $(p; (q \mid\mid r)) : \tau$ that we would like to compile to a sequence of two tables, $(x_1 : \tau); (x_2 : \tau)$. Recall that concurrency is commutative (Lemma 4) and equivalent to sequential composition (Lemma 5). Hence, there are four ways we might compile this policy.

In the first case, p is compiled to x_1 and $q \mid\mid r$ to x_2. The cost of p (written $|p|$) refers to the number of TCAM or SRAM rows the compiled policy fills. The cost of placing q and r in the same table is $|q| + |r|$. In the next, the division is $p; q$ and r, and here, the cost of placing p and q in the same table is multiplicative in their sizes. Similarly, $p; r$ might be placed in x_1 and q in x_2 at the cost $|p| * |r| + |q|$. Finally, the RMT chip has the capability to join its physical stages together to emulate a single, larger "logical stage." That capability provides a final option, which is to compile p, q, and r to a single table (paying the largest overhead of $|p| * |q| * |r|$). If p, q, and r are of equal size, then the first option is most efficient. But when p is small and x_1 has space remaining, it may make sense to pay the cost of compiling $p; q$ or $p; r$ to x_1. The RMT "logical table" feature is suitable for cases in which p, q, or r are too large to fit in a single physical table. The RMT chip has a limited number of bits a table can match and the number of rules it can hold—each match stage stage has sixteen blocks of 40b by 2048 entry TCAM memory and eight 80b by 1024 entry SRAM blocks—so deciding how to partition a policy into tables matters.

Since there are many choices about how to fit a collection of tables, we have defined a dynamic programming algorithm to search for the best one. The goal of the algorithm is to fit a well-typed policy, without parallel composition, into as few tables as possible.

Definition 8 (TCAM cost measurement).

$$\begin{array}{lcl}
\textsf{table_cost} & \in & \textsf{Var} \rightarrow \mathbb{N} \\
\textsf{height}\ x & = & \textsf{table_cost}\ x \\
\textsf{height}\ p; q & = & \textsf{height}\ p * \textsf{height}\ q \\
\textsf{height}\ p \mid\mid q & = & \textsf{height}\ p + \textsf{height}\ q \\
\textsf{blocks}\ p & = & \lceil(\textsf{width}\ p)/40\rceil * \lceil(\textsf{height}\ p)/2048\rceil
\end{array}$$

As input, the algorithm relies on a user-supplied annotation predicting the maximum size of each user table at population time, written table_cost x. We also rely on several utility functions. The width of a policy (width p) returns the number of bits it matches, while the height (height p) uses the user-supplied annotation to gauge the number of entries that will ever be installed into the policy at population time. Together, they calculate the number of TCAM blocks necessary to implement a policy (blocks p). Similar measurements exist for compiling to SRAM, but we focus on TCAM here.

As input, the algorithm also takes a policy containing only sequences of tables. The policy AST is a tree with combinators at the nodes and tables at the leaves. We need to flatten this tree into the RMT pipeline. To do so, we must consider different groupings of the tree's fringe. For convenience, let t_{ij} represent an in-order numbering of the leaves of the abstract syntax tree, starting with t_{11} as the leftmost leaf. For example, given a policy $(x : \tau_x); (y : \tau_y); (z : \tau_z)$, then t_{23} would be $(y : \tau_y); (z : \tau_z)$.

```
input : A sequence of t_{1n}
input : table_cost
let m[1...n, 1...n] and s[1...n-1, 2...n] be new
  tables;
for i = 1 to n do
 | m[i, i] = ⌈(blocks t_i)/16⌉;
end
for l = 2 to n do
    for i = 1 to n - l + 1 do
        j = i + l - 1;
        m[i, j] = ∞;
        for k = i to j - 1 do
            q =
              min(m[i, k] + m[k + 1, j], ⌈blocks t_{ij}/16⌉);
            if q < m[i, j] then
                m[i, j] = q;
                s[i, j] = k;
            end
        end
    end
end
return m and s
```

Algorithm 1: Table fitting.

The algorithm proceeds by building a table m, where each cell $m[i, j]$ holds the smallest number of tables into which the sequence t_{ij} can fit. The crux of the algorithm lies on line 10. Given a sequence t_{ij} for which the optimal fit for each subsequence has been computed, either the entire sequence may be compiled to a single logical table that can be deployed across $\lceil \text{blocks}\, t_{ij}/16 \rceil$ physical tables, or there exists a partitioning t_{ik}, t_{kj} where both subsequences fit into sets of tables, and so the entire sequence fits into the sum of the size of the sets. The algorithm contains three nested loops iterating over t_{1n}, giving it a complexity on the order of $\mathcal{O}(n^3)$, where n is size of the policy AST's fringe. The table s records the best partition chosen at each step, from which we can reconstruct the sets of subsequences to compile to each table.

It remains to convert a user policy with concurrent and sequential composition to one without concurrent composition. We apply a brute-force approach. For each concurrent operator $p \,||\, q$, produce two sequences, $p; q$ and $q; p$. Apply Algorithm 1 to each, and select the smallest result. There are on the order of $\mathcal{O}(2^m)$ sequences, where m is the number of concurrency operators, and so this final determinization step runs in $\mathcal{O}(2^m n^3)$. Fortunately, in our experience, policies tend to have on the order of tens of tables, although the tables themselves may hold many more rules.

7. Related work

NetCore [7, 11, 12] is a simple compositional language for specifying static data plane forwarding policy. NetKAT [3] extended NetCore with Kleene star, and a sound and complete equational theory for reasoning about networks. Concurrent NetCore shares a common core with NetCore (and NetKAT), but adds table specifications, concurrency, and a type system. These additions necessitate a new approach to the semantics—the denotational techniques used for NetCore and NetKAT do not extend easily to models of concurrency. Moreover, these new features make it possible to express controller requirements as well as next generation switch hardware features. We have focused on specifying the properties of individual switches here, so Kleene star is unnecessary, but it would be interesting to investigate adding it in the future to facilitate reasoning about networks of multi-table switches.

Concurrent Kleene Algebra (CKA) [8] is a related calculus that latter offers four composition operators: sequential composition, alternation, disjoint parallel composition and fine-grained concurrent composition. One key difference between NetCore/KAT and CKA (as well as other interpretations of Kleene algebra we are aware of) is that NetCore interprets "alternation" (disjunction) in a non-standard way as "copying parallel" composition. This leads to new and interesting interactions with our concurrent composition, which is most similar to CKA's disjoint parallel composition. Concurrent NetCore also has a type system and interpretation specialized to network programming, while CKA is presented at an extremely high level of abstraction.

Bossart *et al.* [4] recently proposed an architecture for programming OpenFlow 2.0 switches, which we follow in this paper. Bossart's configuration language includes components for programming the packet parser as well as the match-action packet processing. We focus on just the match-action processing here, but provide a formal semantics and metatheoretic analysis of our work, whereas they provide no semantics. We also consider concurrent and parallel composition, which they do not. Another important inspiration is the ONF's ongoing work on typed table patterns [2].

8. Conclusion

Concurrent NetCore offers at once (a) a language for specifying routing policies and (b) packet-processing pipelines. It's novel operational semantics and type system recover strong reasoning principles. As such, it is an excellent intermediate language for compiling routing policies—since CNC can express both high-level policies and low-level pipelines, a multipass compiler can use the same reasoning principles throughout.

Acknowledgments

This work stemmed from many stimulating discussions with Nick Feamster, Muhammad Shahbaz, and Jennifer Rexford. We would also like to thank Pat Bossart, Dan Daly, Glen Gibb, Nick McKeown, Dan Talayco, Amin Vahdat, and George Varghese for conversations on this topic. This work is supported in part by the NSF under grants CNS-1111520, and SHF-1016937, the ONR under award N00014-12-1-0757, and a Google Research Award. Any opinions, ndings, and conclusions or recommendations expressed in this material are those of the authors and do not necessarily reect the views of the NSF or Google.

References

[1] Concurrent netcore: From policies to pipelines. See http://tinyurl.com/k2z81z5.

[2] Openflow forwarding abstractions working group charter, April 2013. See http://goo.gl/TtLtw0.

[3] Carolyn Jane Anderson, Nate Foster, Arjun Guha, Jean-Baptiste Jeannin, Dexter Kozen, Cole Schlesinger, and David Walker. NetKAT: Semantic foundations for networks. In *POPL*, January 2014.

[4] Pat Bosshart, Dan Daly, Martin Izzard, Nick McKeown, Jennifer Rexford, Dan Talayco, Amin Vahdat, George Varghese, and David Walker. Programming protocol-independent packet processors. See http://arxiv.org/abs/1312.1719, December 2013.

[5] Pat Bosshart, Glen Gibb, Hun-Seok Kim, George Varghese, Nick McKeown, Martin Izzard, Fernando A. Mujica, and Mark Horowitz. Forwarding metamorphosis: fast programmable match-action processing in hardware for SDN. In *SIGCOMM*, pages 99–110, 2013.

[6] Broadcom BCM56846 StrataXGS 10/40 GbE switch. See http://www.broadcom.com/products/features/BCM56846.php, 2014.

[7] Nate Foster, Rob Harrison, Michael J. Freedman, Christopher Monsanto, Jennifer Rexford, Alec Story, and David Walker. Frenetic: A network programming language. In *ICFP*, September 2011.

[8] C. A. R. Hoare, Bernhard M oller, Georg Struth, and Ian Wehrman. Concurrent kleene algebra. In *CONCUR*, pages 399–414, 2009.

[9] Sushant Jain, Alok Kumar, Subhasree Mandal, Joon Ong, Leon Poutievski, Arjun Singh, Subbaiah Venkata, Jim Wanderer, Junlan Zhou, Min Zhu, Jonathan Zolla, Urs Hölzle, Stephen Stuart, and Amin Vahdat. B4: Experience with a globally-deployed software defined WAN. In *SIGCOMM*, 2013.

[10] Nick McKeown, Tom Anderson, Hari Balakrishnan, Guru Parulkar, Larry Peterson, Jennifer Rexford, Scott Shenker, and Jonathan Turner. OpenFlow: Enabling innovation in campus networks. *SIGCOMM Computing Communications Review*, 38(2):69–74, 2008.

[11] Christopher Monsanto, Nate Foster, Rob Harrison, and David Walker. A compiler and run-time system for network programming languages. In *POPL*, January 2012.

[12] Christopher Monsanto, Joshua Reich, Nate Foster, Jennifer Rexford, and David Walker. Composing software-defined networks. In *NSDI*, April 2013.

[13] Tim Nelson, Arjun Guha, Daniel J. Dougherty, Kathi Fisler, and Shriram Krishnamurthi. A balance of power: Expressive, analyzable controller programming. In *HotSDN*, 2013.

[14] Recep Ozdag. Intel Ethernet Switch FM6000 Series - software defined networking. See goo.gl/AnvOvX, 2012.

[15] Andreas Voellmy, Hyojoon Kim, and Nick Feamster. Procera: A language for high-level reactive network control. In *HotSDN*, pages 43–48, 2012.

[16] Andreas Voellmy, Junchang Wang, Y. Richard Yang, Bryan Ford, and Paul Hudak. Maple: Simplifying SDN programming using algorithmic policies. In *SIGCOMM*, 2013.

SeLINQ: Tracking Information across Application-Database Boundaries

Daniel Schoepe   Daniel Hedin   Andrei Sabelfeld

Chalmers University of Technology, Gothenburg, Sweden

Abstract

The root cause for *confidentiality* and *integrity* attacks against computing systems is insecure *information flow*. The complexity of modern systems poses a major challenge to secure *end-to-end* information flow, ensuring that the insecurity of a single component does not render the entire system insecure. While information flow in a variety of languages and settings has been thoroughly studied in isolation, the problem of tracking information across component boundaries has been largely out of reach of the work so far. This is unsatisfactory because tracking information across component boundaries is necessary for end-to-end security.

This paper proposes a framework for uniform tracking of information flow through both the application and the underlying database. Key enabler of the uniform treatment is recent work by Cheney et al., which studies database manipulation via an embedded language-integrated query language (with Microsoft's LINQ on the backend). Because both the host language and the embedded query languages are functional F#-like languages, we are able to leverage information-flow enforcement for functional languages to obtain information-flow control for databases "for free", synergize it with information-flow control for applications and thus guarantee security across application-database boundaries. We develop the formal results in the form of a security type system that includes a treatment of algebraic data types and pattern matching, and establish its soundness. On the practical side, we implement the framework and demonstrate its usefulness in a case study with a realistic movie rental database.

Categories and Subject Descriptors D.4.6 [*Operating Systems*]: Security and Protection—information-flow controls

Keywords end-to-end security, information flow, static analysis, language-integrated queries

1. Introduction

Increasingly, we trust interconnected software on desktops, laptops, tablets, and smart phones to manipulate a wide range of sensitive information such as medical, commercial, and location information. This trust can be justified only if the software is designed, constructed, monitored, and audited to be robust and secure.

Securing heterogeneous systems *Heterogeneity* is a major roadblock in the path of software security. Modern computing systems are built with a large number of components, often run on different platforms and written in multiple programming languages.

ICFP '14, September 1–6, 2014, Gothenburg, Sweden.

ACM 978-1-4503-2873-9 /14/09... $15.00.
http://dx.doi.org/10.1145/2628136.2628151

It is not surprising that systems often break at component boundaries. The OWASP Top 10 project identifies ten most critical web application security risks [2]. The top of the list is dominated by attacks across component boundaries: injection attacks (with SQL injection as prime example) are number 1 on the list; cross-site scripting attacks are number 3. In both, untrusted data bypasses inter-component filtering, which leads executing malicious commands (commonly in SQL or JavaScript) to compromise *confidentiality* and *integrity*.

In the face of complexity and heterogeneity of today's systems, it is vital to ensure *end-to-end security* [45], overarching component boundaries.

Information-flow control The root cause for confidentiality and integrity attacks against computing systems is insecure *information flow*. For confidentiality, this implies a possibility of leaking information from sensitive sources to attacker-observable sinks. For integrity, this implies a possibility of data from untrusted sources to compromise data on trusted sinks.

Enforcing secure information flow is more involved than enforcing safety properties like tracking units of measure [33] or taint tracking [47]. This is due to the fact that there are two different types of information flows. The first type of flow, the *explicit* flows, originates from the explicit propagation of values, via, e.g., parameter passing. Tracking this kind of flows is similar to tracking units of measure or taint tracking. The second type of flows, the *implicit* [25] flows, corresponds to flows via the control flow. Consider

```
l = if (h) then true else false
```

Depending on the value of h, either the *then* branch or the *else* branch of the conditional is chosen to be evaluated to give the final result. In the above program, this has the effect of leaking the Boolean value of h into l, constituting an implicit flow from h to l. A different machinery is needed to track this kind of flows, which distinguishes enforcement of secure information flow from enforcement of safety properties [51].

A large, extensively surveyed [13, 29, 30, 41], body of work has studied information-flow control. However, with a few recent exceptions (discussed in Section 6), the problem of information flow for different components has largely been explored in isolation. This is unsatisfactory because tracking information across component boundaries is necessary for end-to-end security.

Motivated by the above, this paper focuses on information-flow control for systems with database components.

Database integration Programs commonly access databases via libraries that connect and interact with the database. If we take SQL as an example, querying is typically done by constructing a query string that is passed to the database as illustrated below.

```
let query  = "SELECT Name FROM People";
let result = SqlCommand(query, db).execute();
```

The problem with this approach is that the queries are constructed at runtime without any guarantees on the query. In general it is hard to verify that the constructed queries are meaningful let alone decide information flow properties for the queries. The created string could be an invalid query or even the result of an SQL injection. Further, the returned information is by necessity encoded in a generic way, which makes it both inefficient and error prone to work with. Instead, it is attractive to integrate database query mechanism into the language as facilitated, e.g, by Google's Web Toolkit [4], Ruby on Rails [11], and Microsoft's LINQ [5].

In functional setting, an elegant approach to provide language-integrated query is to use meta-programming based on quotations and antiquotations. This is the approach taken by Cheney et al. [16]. The goal is to provide access to SQL databases in F# (with Microsoft's LINQ on the backend). F# provides quotation via `<@ @>`, which creates a typed representation of a given F# expression e. Assuming that e has type t, then `<@` e `@>` is a value of type $\textbf{Expr}\langle t \rangle$. Antiquotes `(% )` provide a way to splice in typed quoted values into other quoted expressions. This approach capitalizes on the flexible meta-programming capabilities of F# [50]. With this framework we can express the above query in F# in the following way.

```
let query =
<@ for p in (% db).People do
     yield p.Name
@>
let result = run query
```

From the type of the spliced in database, `db`, the type system of F# is able to determine the type of `query` to $\textbf{Expr}\langle\textbf{list string}\rangle$. In turn `query` is given to `run` which, when run, executes the query resulting in a list of **strings**. The typing of the program is compile time, whereas the creation and execution of the actual query is runtime. At runtime the quoted expression is parsed by the F# runtime and the typed result is passed to `run` for normalization and evaluation. This produces and performs the actual SQL query. Note how antiquotation is used to splice in the database allowing the construction of multiple queries using the same database connection.

Contributions This paper puts homogeneous meta-programming to work to develop information-flow type systems for heterogeneous systems. In particular we present an information-flow type system for a subset of F# with database queries. The presented development is an instance of a general method that allows for the reuse of existing type systems to create information flow type systems that seamlessly spans language boundaries. Thus, the method is not limited to database queries.

Because both the host language and the embedded query languages are F#-like subsets, we are able to leverage information-flow enforcement for functional languages to obtain information-flow control for databases "for free". The simplicity of the resulting type system and the relatively small modifications needed is evidence for the success of the approach.

In a nutshell, the paper contains the following main contribution:

(i) We leverage homogeneous meta-programming to provide information-flow security for a subset of F# including database access via the essence of query processing in Microsoft LINQ, as it is expressed in F#.

In addition, the paper contains further contributions:

(ii) We develop the formal results in the form of a security type system and show that it enforces the security condition of *noninterference* [28] (Section 2).

(iii) We develop an analysis to treat algebraic data types and pattern matching, establish its soundness, and implement it as a part of our prototype (Section 4).

(iv) We present an implementation of the type checker and a translator from our language to executable F# code (Section 3).

(v) We demonstrate the usefulness of our framework by a case study with a realistic movie rental database (Section 5).

The full soundness proof and the code of the framework and case study are available online[1].

2. Framework

This section presents a simple functional language with support for product types, records, lists, quoted expressions and antiquotations, the security type system, and shows that the type system enforces information-flow security with respect to a small-step semantics.

Recall that the fundamental idea is that, since the information-flow of the database interaction is fully described in the quoted language, the type systems is able to enforce information-flow security for the database interactions for free.

2.1 Language

The language is based on the one used by Cheney et al. [16] with the addition of security levels to the type system.

Figure 1 shows the syntax of security levels, types, and terms. We write $\overline{x}$ to denote a sequence of entities x. For example, $\overline{f : t}$ is a shorthand for a sequence $f_1 : t_1, f_2 : t_2, \ldots, f_n : t_n$ of typings of record fields.

$$\ell ::= \mathtt{L} \mid \mathtt{H}$$

$$b ::= \textbf{int}^\ell \mid \textbf{string}^\ell \mid \textbf{bool}^\ell$$

$$t ::= b \mid t \to t \mid t * t \mid \{\overline{f : t}\} \mid (t\ \textbf{list})^\ell \mid \textbf{Expr}\langle t \rangle$$

$$T ::= (\{\overline{f : b}\})\ \textbf{list}^\ell$$

$$\Gamma, \Delta ::= \cdot \mid \Gamma, x : t$$

$$\begin{array}{rl} e ::= & c \mid x \mid op(\overline{e}) \mid \textbf{lift}\ e \mid \textbf{fun}(x) \to e \mid \textbf{rec}\ f(x) \to e \mid (e, e) \\ \mid & \textbf{fst}\ e \mid \textbf{snd}\ e \mid \{\overline{f = e}\} \mid e.f \mid \textbf{yield}\ e \mid [] \\ \mid & e\ @\ e \mid \textbf{for}\ x\ \textbf{in}\ e\ \textbf{do}\ e \mid \textbf{exists}\ e \mid \textbf{if}\ e\ \textbf{then}\ e \mid \textbf{run}\ e \\ \mid & \texttt{<@}\ e\ \texttt{@>} \mid (\texttt{\%}\ e\ ) \mid \textbf{database}(x) \end{array}$$

Figure 1. Syntax of language and types

We remark on some of the interesting constructs: c denotes built-in constants, such as integers and booleans. op denotes built-in operators, such as addition and logical connectives. **lift** e lifts an expression of type t to type $\textbf{Expr}\langle t \rangle$. **for** x **in** e_1 **do** e_2 is used to express list comprehensions where x is bound successively to elements in e_1 when evaluating e_2. The results of evaluating e_2 for each element are then concatenated. **run** e denotes running a quoted expression e. This involves generating an SQL query based on the quoted term. e_1 @ e_2 denotes concatenation of e_1 and e_2. Section 2.2 provides further details. **exists** e evaluates to **true** if and only if the expression e does not evaluate to the empty list. This can be used to check if the result of a query is empty. Similarly, **if** e_1 **then** e_2 evaluates to e_2 if e_1 evaluates to a non-empty list and to [] otherwise. **yield** e denotes a singleton list consisting of expression e. `<@` e `@>` denotes a quoted expression e. The language allows only closed quoted terms, since this simplifies the semantics of the language and is still able to express all the desired concepts. Quoted functions can be expressed by abstracting in the quoted term as opposed to abstracting on the level of the host language. `(%` e `)` denotes antiquotation of the expression e, and allows splicing of quoted expressions into quoted expressions in a type-safe way.

Security type language The security type language is defined by annotating a standard type language for a functional fragment with

[1] `http://www.cse.chalmers.se/~schoepe/selinq/`

quotations with security levels ℓ. Without loss of generality the security levels are taken from the two-element security lattice consisting of a level L for non-confidential information and a level H for confidential information. Information-flow integrity policies can be expressed dually [14]. The types are split into base types (b), which can occur as types of columns in tables (T), and general types (t) which include function types, lists, and quoted expressions.

As is common, we consider a database to be a collection of tables. Each table consists of at least one named column, each of which is equipped with a fixed security level annotated type. The security levels on types for database columns express which columns contain confidential data and which columns do not.

To express security policies for databases, each database is given a type signature. Such a type signature describes tables as lists of records. Each record field corresponds to a column in the sense that the field name matches the name of the column in the database. A column is specified as confidential or public by using a suitable type for the corresponding field in the record. The ordering of elements in a list used to represent table contents is irrelevant.

To illustrate the addition of security levels to the type system in the case of databases, consider an example, adapted from Cheney et al. [16], involving a database of people and couples, `PeopleDB`. In this scenario, we assume that the names of people are confidential, while the age is not, which leads to the following type for `PeopleDB`.

```
PeopleDB :
  { People :
    { Id : int^L; Name : string^H; Age : int^L } list^L
  ; Couples :
    { Person1 : int^L ; Person2 : int^L } list^L
  }
```

Now consider the situation where we want to query the database for couples where one partner is more than 10 years older than the other partner. This can be done by iterating once over all couples in the database and then iterating twice over all people in the database. For each couple and pair of persons, one then checks if they are part of the couple that is being considered and checks if the age difference is higher than 10. If that is the case, the name of the first partner along with the age difference is returned as part of the result, which is a list of records consisting of a name and the age difference.

```
let db = <@ database "PeopleDB" @>

type ResultType = {name : string^H ; diff : int^L}

let differences : Expr < ResultType list ^ L > =
  <@ for c in (% db).Couples do
     for p1 in (% db).People do
     for p2 in (% db).People do
     if (c.Person1 = p1.Id) &&
        (c.Person2 = p2.Id) &&
        (abs (p1.Age - p2.Age) > 10) then
     yield ({ name = p1.Name
            ; diff = p1.Age - p2.Age })
  @>

let main = run differences
```

As can be seen in the above program the information-flow policy for this program is specified by giving a type annotation to the quoted expression that generates the query, i.e., a type annotation for `differences`. In particular, the name components of the result are typed confidential, while the age differences are public. This matches the policy specified for the database contents, in which the names of people are confidential while their ages are not. The type system ensures that the result type of `differences` is in fact compatible with the policy specified for the database. Changing the security annotation of the `name` field from secret to public as follow results in a type error.

```
// No longer well-typed:
type ResultType = {name : string^L ; diff : int^L}
```

2.2 Operational Semantics

We denote evaluation of an expression e using database data in Ω to another expression e' by $e \longrightarrow_\Omega e'$. Ω is a function that maps database names to the actual content of the database it refers to, and δ is a mapping that maps operators to their corresponding semantics. Σ maps constants and databases to their respective types.

We assume that Ω is consistent with the typing for databases given in Σ: for each database $\Omega(db)$ is assumed to be a value of type $\Sigma(db)$.

The evaluation rules in Figures 2, 3, 4, and 5 follow [16]. Let $\longrightarrow_\Omega^*$ be the reflexive-transitive closure of $\longrightarrow_\Omega$. Evaluation and normalization of the quoted language is denoted by $eval_\Omega(norm(e))$. This evaluation entails generating database queries that can be executed by actual database servers. In particular, higher-order features such as nested records or function applications need to be evaluated to obtain computations that can be expressed in SQL. Figure 6 shows the syntax. The semantics is call-by-value with left-to-right evaluation of terms. This is formalized using evaluation contexts $\mathcal{E}$. Quotation contexts $\mathcal{Q}$ are used to ensure that there are no antiquotations left of the hole.

We denote substitution of free occurrences of a variable x in expression e with another expression e' by $e[x \mapsto e']$.

$$
\begin{aligned}
V ::=\ & c \mid \mathbf{fun}(x) \to e \mid \mathbf{rec}\ f(x) \to e \mid (V, V) \mid \{\overline{f = V}\} \\
\mid\ & [] \mid \mathbf{yield}\ V\ @\ \ldots\ @\ \mathbf{yield}\ V \mid \texttt{<@}\ Q\ \texttt{@>}
\end{aligned}
$$

$$
\begin{aligned}
Q ::=\ & c \mid op(\overline{Q}) \mid \mathbf{lift}\ Q \mid x \mid \mathbf{fun}(x) \to Q \mid Q\ Q \mid (Q, Q) \\
\mid\ & \{\overline{f = Q}\} \mid Q.f \mid \mathbf{yield}\ Q \mid [] \mid Q\ @\ Q \mid \mathbf{for}\ x\ \mathbf{in}\ Q\ \mathbf{do}\ Q \\
\mid\ & \mathbf{exists}\ Q \mid \mathbf{if}\ Q\ \mathbf{then}\ Q \mid \mathbf{database}(db)
\end{aligned}
$$

$$
\begin{aligned}
\mathcal{E} ::=\ & [] \mid op(\overline{V}, \mathcal{E}, \overline{M}) \mid \mathbf{lift}\ \mathcal{E} \mid \mathcal{E}\ e \mid V\ \mathcal{E} \mid (\mathcal{E}, e) \mid (V, \mathcal{E}) \\
\mid\ & \{\overline{f = V}, f' = \mathcal{E}, \overline{f = e}\} \mid \mathcal{E}.f \mid \mathbf{yield}\ \mathcal{E} \mid \mathcal{E}\ @\ e \mid V\ @\ \mathcal{E} \\
\mid\ & \mathbf{for}\ x\ \mathbf{in}\ \mathcal{E}\ \mathbf{do}\ e \mid \mathbf{exists}\ \mathcal{E} \mid \mathbf{if}\ \mathcal{E}\ \mathbf{then}\ e \mid \mathbf{run}\ \mathcal{E} \\
\mid\ & \texttt{<@}\ \mathcal{Q}[(\%\ \mathcal{E}\ )]\ \texttt{@>}
\end{aligned}
$$

$$
\begin{aligned}
\mathcal{Q} ::=\ & [] \mid op(\overline{Q}, \mathcal{Q}, \overline{e}) \mid \mathbf{fun}(x) \to \mathcal{Q} \mid \mathbf{lift}\ \mathcal{Q} \mid \mathcal{Q}\ e \mid V\ \mathcal{Q} \\
\mid\ & (\mathcal{Q}, e) \mid (Q, \mathcal{Q}) \mid \{\overline{f = Q}, f' = \mathcal{Q}, \overline{f = e}\} \mid \mathcal{Q}.f \\
\mid\ & \mathbf{yield}\ \mathcal{Q} \mid \mathcal{Q}\ @\ e \mid V\ @\ \mathcal{Q} \mid \mathbf{for}\ x\ \mathbf{in}\ \mathcal{Q}\ \mathbf{do}\ e \mid \mathbf{for}\ x\ \mathbf{in}\ Q\ \mathbf{do}\ \mathcal{Q} \\
\mid\ & \mathbf{exists}\ \mathcal{Q} \mid \mathbf{if}\ \mathcal{Q}\ \mathbf{then}\ e \mid \mathbf{if}\ Q\ \mathbf{then}\ \mathcal{Q} \mid \mathbf{run}\ \mathcal{Q}
\end{aligned}
$$

Figure 2. Values and evaluation contexts

2.3 Security Condition

The goal of the type system is to enforce a notion of noninterference for functional language. Noninterference formalizes computational independence between secrets and non-secrets, guaranteeing that no information about the former can be inferred from the latter. More precisely, this is expressed as the preservation of an equivalence relation under pairwise execution; given two inputs that are equal in the components that are visible to an attacker, evaluation should result in two output values that also coincide in the components that can be observed by the attacker.

To that end this section introduces a notion of low-equivalence denoted by $\sim$ that demands that parts of values with types that are annotated with L are equal, while placing no demands on the secret counterparts. More formally, we introduce a family of equivalence relations on values parametrized by types.

$$
\begin{aligned}
op(\overline{V}) &\longrightarrow \delta(op, \overline{V})\\
(\textbf{fun}(x) \to N)\ V &\longrightarrow N[x \mapsto V]\\
(\textbf{rec}\ f(x) \to N)\ V &\longrightarrow M[f \mapsto \textbf{rec}\ f(x) \to N, x \mapsto V]\\
\textbf{fst}\ (V_1, V_2) &\longrightarrow V_1\\
\textbf{snd}\ (V_1, V_2) &\longrightarrow V_2\\
\{\overline{f = V}\}.f_i &\longrightarrow V_i\\
\textbf{if true then}\ M &\longrightarrow M\\
\textbf{if false then}\ M &\longrightarrow []\\
\textbf{for}\ x\ \textbf{in yield}\ V\ \textbf{do}\ M &\longrightarrow M[x \mapsto V]\\
\textbf{for}\ x\ \textbf{in}\ []\ \textbf{do}\ N &\longrightarrow []\\
\textbf{for}\ x\ \textbf{in}\ L\ @\ M\ \textbf{do}\ N &\longrightarrow (\textbf{for}\ x\ \textbf{in}\ L\ \textbf{do}\ N)\ @\ (\textbf{for}\ x\ \textbf{in}\ M\ \textbf{do}\ N)\\
\textbf{exists}\ [] &\longrightarrow \textbf{false}\\
\textbf{exists}\ [\overline{V}] &\longrightarrow \textbf{true}, \qquad |\overline{V}| > 0\\
\textbf{run}\ Q &\longrightarrow eval(norm(Q))\\
\textbf{lift}\ c &\longrightarrow \texttt{<@}\ c\ \texttt{@>}\\
\texttt{<@}\ \mathcal{Q}[(\texttt{\%}\ \texttt{<@}\ Q\ \texttt{@>}\ )]\ \texttt{@>} &\longrightarrow \texttt{<@}\ \mathcal{Q}[Q]\ \texttt{@>}
\end{aligned}
$$

$$
\frac{M \longrightarrow N}{\mathcal{E}[M] \longrightarrow \mathcal{E}[N]}
$$

Figure 3. Evaluation rules for host language

$$
\begin{aligned}
(\textbf{fun}(x) \to R)\ Q &\rightsquigarrow R[x \mapsto Q]\\
\{\overline{f = Q}\}.f_i &\rightsquigarrow Q_i\\
\textbf{for}\ x\ \textbf{in yield}\ Q\ \textbf{do}\ R &\rightsquigarrow R[x \mapsto Q]\\
\textbf{for}\ y\ \textbf{in}\ (\textbf{for}\ x\ \textbf{in}\ P\ \textbf{do}\ Q)\ \textbf{do}\ R &\rightsquigarrow \textbf{for}\ x\ \textbf{in}\ P\ \textbf{do}\ (\textbf{for}\ y\ \textbf{in}\ Q\ \textbf{do}\ R)\\
\textbf{for}\ x\ \textbf{in}\ (\textbf{if}\ P\ \textbf{then}\ Q)\ \textbf{do}\ R &\rightsquigarrow \textbf{if}\ P\ \textbf{then}\ (\textbf{for}\ x\ \textbf{in}\ Q\ \textbf{do}\ R)\\
\textbf{for}\ x\ \textbf{in}\ []\ \textbf{do}\ N &\rightsquigarrow []\\
\textbf{for}\ x\ \textbf{in}\ (P\ @\ Q)\ \textbf{do}\ R &\rightsquigarrow\\
&\quad (\textbf{for}\ x\ \textbf{in}\ P\ \textbf{do}\ R)\ @\ (\textbf{for}\ x\ \textbf{in}\ Q\ \textbf{do}\ R)\\
\textbf{if true then}\ Q &\rightsquigarrow Q\\
\textbf{if false then}\ Q &\rightsquigarrow []
\end{aligned}
$$

Figure 4. Symbolic reduction phase

$$
\begin{aligned}
\textbf{for}\ x\ \textbf{in}\ P\ \textbf{do}\ (Q\ @\ R) &\hookrightarrow\\
&\quad (\textbf{for}\ x\ \textbf{in}\ P\ \textbf{do}\ Q)\ @\ (\textbf{for}\ x\ \textbf{in}\ P\ \textbf{do}\ R)\\
\textbf{for}\ x\ \textbf{in}\ P\ \textbf{do}\ [] &\hookrightarrow []\\
\textbf{if}\ P\ \textbf{then}\ (Q\ @\ R) &\hookrightarrow (\textbf{if}\ P\ \textbf{then}\ Q)\ @\ (\textbf{if}\ P\ \textbf{then}\ R)\\
\textbf{if}\ P\ \textbf{then}\ [] &\hookrightarrow []\\
\textbf{if}\ P\ \textbf{then}\ (\textbf{if}\ Q\ \textbf{then}\ R) &\hookrightarrow \textbf{if}\ P\ \texttt{\&\&}\ Q\ \textbf{then}\ R\\
\textbf{if}\ P\ \textbf{then}\ (\textbf{for}\ x\ \textbf{in}\ Q\ \textbf{do}\ R) &\hookrightarrow \textbf{for}\ x\ \textbf{in}\ Q\ \textbf{do}\ (\textbf{if}\ P\ \textbf{then}\ R)
\end{aligned}
$$

Figure 5. Ad-hoc reduction phase

Definition 1 ($\sim_t$). *The family of equivalence relations $\sim_t$ is defined inductively by the rules in figure 7.*

$$
\begin{aligned}
S &::= [] \mid X \mid X\ @\ X\\
X &::= \textbf{database}(db) \mid \textbf{yield}\ Y \mid \textbf{if}\ Z\ \textbf{then yield}\ Y\\
&\mid\ \textbf{for}\ x\ \textbf{in database}(db).f\ \textbf{do}\ X\\
Y &::= x \mid \{\overline{f = Z}\}\\
Z &::= c \mid x.f \mid op(\overline{X}) \mid \textbf{exists}\ S
\end{aligned}
$$

Figure 6. Normalized terms

$$
\frac{\ell = \mathrm{L} \Rightarrow i = i'}{i \sim_{\textbf{int}^\ell} i'} \qquad
\frac{\ell = \mathrm{L} \Rightarrow s = s'}{s \sim_{\textbf{string}^\ell} s'} \qquad
\frac{\ell = \mathrm{L} \Rightarrow b = b'}{b \sim_{\textbf{bool}^\ell} b'}
$$

$$
\frac{\begin{array}{c}\forall v_1, v_2, v_1', v_2', \Omega_1, \Omega_2.(\Omega_1 \sim_\Sigma \Omega_2 \wedge v_1 \sim_t v_2 \wedge\\ e_1[x \mapsto v_1] \overset{*}{\longrightarrow}_{\Omega_1} v_1' \wedge e_2[x \mapsto v_2] \overset{*}{\longrightarrow}_{\Omega_2} v_2') \Rightarrow\\ v_1' \sim_{t'} v_2'\end{array}}{\textbf{fun}(x) \to e_1 \sim_{t \to t'} \textbf{fun}(x) \to e_2}
$$

$$
\frac{\begin{array}{c}\forall v_1, v_2, v_1', v_2', \Omega_1, \Omega_2.\\ \Omega_1 \sim_\Sigma \Omega_2 \wedge v_1 \sim_t v_2 \wedge\\ e_1[f \mapsto \textbf{rec}\ f(x) \to e_1, x \mapsto v_1] \overset{*}{\longrightarrow}_{\Omega_1} v_1' \wedge\\ e_2[f \mapsto \textbf{rec}\ f(x) \to e_2, x \mapsto v_2] \overset{*}{\longrightarrow}_{\Omega_2} v_2' \Rightarrow\\ v_1' \sim_{t'} v_2'\end{array}}{\textbf{rec}\ f(x) \to e_1 \sim_{t \to t'} \textbf{rec}\ f(x) \to e_2}
$$

$$
\frac{v_1 \sim_{t_1} v_1' \qquad v_2 \sim_{t_2} v_2'}{(v_1, v_2) \sim_{t_1 * t_2} (v_1', v_2')} \qquad
\frac{\overline{v \sim_t w}}{\{\overline{f = v}\} \sim_{\{\overline{f:t}\}} \{\overline{f = w}\}}
$$

$$
\frac{\ell = \mathrm{L} \Rightarrow (|[\overline{v}]| = |[\overline{w}]| \wedge \overline{v \sim_t w})}{[\overline{v}] \sim_{(t\ \textbf{list})^\ell} [\overline{w}]}
$$

$$
\frac{\begin{array}{c}\forall \Omega_1, \Omega_2.\Omega_1 \sim \Omega_2 \Rightarrow\\ eval_{\Omega_1}(norm(e_1)) \sim_t eval_{\Omega_2}(norm(e_2))\end{array}}{e_1 \sim_{\textbf{Expr}\langle t\rangle} e_2}
$$

Figure 7. Introduction rules for $\sim_t$

When the type is evident from the context, we omit the subscript on $\sim$. Moreover, we also write $\sim$ for sequences of values.

To present the relations in a more concise manner, we combine the cases for different security levels using implication in the premises; e.g. equality on base types is only required if the security level is L.

Base types are compared using ordinary equality if the values are considered public. In the case of function types and quoted expressions, $\sim_t$ corresponds to noninterference for the bodies of the functions.

Records are related by $\sim$ if they contain the same fields, and each field's contents are also related by $\sim$. Two lists are required to have the same length if the list type is annotated with L, but their contents may differ based on the element type.

To illustrate this, consider two lists of integers $l_1 = \textbf{yield}\ 1\ @\ []$ and $l_2 = \textbf{yield}\ 2\ @\ []$. If the lists are typed with the type $t = (\textbf{int}^{\mathrm{H}}\ \textbf{list})^{\mathrm{L}}$, the length of the list is considered public, while the contents are confidential. If in contrast the type is $t' = (\textbf{int}^{\mathrm{L}}\ \textbf{list})^{\mathrm{L}}$, neither the contents nor the length of the list is confidential. Hence $l_1 \sim_t l_2$ holds while $l_1 \sim_{t'} l_2$ does not.

For simplicity, $\sim_t$ is stated from the point of view of an observer on level L. $\sim_t$ can be generalized for an arbitrary lattice by parametrizing it with the level of the observer. Instead of checking if the level annotation on the type is equal to H, one then checks if it is higher than the level of the observer.

Let Ω be a mapping from database names to database contents. We define low-equivalence for database mappings structurally in the following way.

Definition 2 ($\sim_\Sigma$). *$\Omega_1 \sim_\Sigma \Omega_2$ holds if and only if for all databases db it holds that $\Omega_1(db) \sim_{\Sigma(db)} \Omega_2(db)$*

With this we are ready to define the top-level notion of security, based on *noninterference* [28]. Since the family of low-equivalence relations is parametrized by types the definition is done with respect to the initial database type and the final result type.

Definition 3 ($NI(e_1, e_2)_{\Sigma,t}$). *Two expression e_1 and e_2 are non-interfering with respect to the database type Σ and the exit type t if for all Ω_1, Ω_2, v_1 and v_2 such that $\Omega_1 \sim_\Sigma \Omega_2$, and $e_i \longrightarrow^*_{\Omega_i} v_i$ for $i \in \{1, 2\}$ it holds that*

$$v_1 \sim_t v_2$$

In particular for any given closed expression e, $NI(e, e)_{\Sigma,t}$ should be read as e is secure with respect to the security policy expressed by Σ and t, i.e., no secret parts of the database as defined by Σ is able to influence the public parts of the returned value as defined by t.

As common [1, 38, 48] in this setting, noninterference is *termination-insensitive* [41, 52] in the sense that leaks via the observation of (non)termination are ignored.

2.4 Type System

Figure 8 presents the typing rules for the host language. Typing judgments are of the form $\Gamma \vdash e : t$ where Γ is a typing context mapping variables to types, e is an expression, and t is a type. It denotes that expression e has type t in context Γ. $\ell \sqcup \ell'$ denotes the join of levels ℓ and ℓ', i.e., $\ell \sqcup \ell' = \mathtt{H}$ iff $\mathtt{H} \in \{\ell, \ell'\}$, and $\ell \sqcup \ell' = \mathtt{L}$ otherwise.

Figure 9 presents the typing rules for the quoted language. Typing judgments in the quoted language have the form $\Gamma; \Delta \vdash e : t$, where Γ is the typing context for the host language and Δ is the typing context for the quoted language.

Most types contain a level annotation ℓ that denotes whether or not the "structure" of the value is confidential. In the case of base types such **int** or **string**, this means that their values are confidential or not. In the case of $(t\ \textbf{list})^\ell$, the level ℓ indicates whether or not the length of the list is confidential. If $\ell = \mathtt{H}$, the entire list value is considered a secret, but if the $\ell = \mathtt{L}$, the length of the list may be disclosed to a public observer. However, the elements of the list may or may not be confidential depending on the level of the elements given by the type t.

Record types, functions, and quoted expression types do not carry an explicit level annotation, since their security level is contained in sub-components of the type.

In the case of records, it suffices to annotate the type of each field, since the structure of a record can not be modified dynamically. The confidentiality of a function is contained in the level annotation on the result type. The intuition is that, in the absence of side effects, the only way for a function to disclose information is via its result. For types for quoted expressions, i.e., types of the form $\textbf{Expr}\langle t\rangle$, the level annotation is already contained in t.

We assume that types for operators, constants, and databases are given by the mapping Σ. Moreover, we also assume that each query only uses a single database.

The typing rules for expressions in the host language and expressions in the quoted language are nearly identical with a few exceptions:

- Recursion is only allowed in the host language.
- Quotations are only allowed in the host language.
- Expressions of the form $\textbf{database}(x)$ are only allowed in the quoted language.
- Antiquotations are only allowed in the quoted language.

$$\textsc{Const}\ \frac{\Sigma(c) = t}{\Gamma \vdash c : t^\ell} \qquad \textsc{Var}\ \frac{x : t \in \Gamma}{\Gamma \vdash x : t} \qquad \textsc{Lift}\ \frac{\Gamma \vdash e : t}{\Gamma \vdash \textbf{lift}\ e : \textbf{Expr}\langle t\rangle}$$

$$\textsc{Fun}\ \frac{\Gamma, x : t \vdash e : t'}{\Gamma \vdash \textbf{fun}(x) \to e : (t \to t')} \qquad \textsc{Rec}\ \frac{\Gamma, x : t, f : t \to t' \vdash e : t'}{\Gamma \vdash \textbf{rec}\ f(x) \to e : t \to t'}$$

$$\textsc{Apply}\ \frac{\Gamma \vdash e_1 : t \to t' \qquad \Gamma \vdash e_2 : t}{\Gamma \vdash e_1\ e_2 : t'} \qquad \textsc{Op}\ \frac{\Sigma(op) = \bar{t} \to t \qquad \overline{\Gamma \vdash e : t^\ell}}{\Gamma \vdash op(\bar{e}) : t^{\bigsqcup \ell_i}}$$

$$\textsc{Pair}\ \frac{\Gamma \vdash e_1 : t_1 \qquad \Gamma \vdash e_2 : t_2}{\Gamma \vdash (e_1, e_2) : t_1 * t_2} \qquad \textsc{Fst}\ \frac{\Gamma \vdash e : t_1 * t_2}{\Gamma \vdash \textbf{fst}\ e : t_1}$$

$$\textsc{Snd}\ \frac{\Gamma \vdash e : t_1 * t_2}{\Gamma \vdash \textbf{snd}\ e : t_2} \qquad \textsc{Record}\ \frac{\overline{\Gamma \vdash M : t}}{\Gamma \vdash \{\overline{f = M}\} : \{\overline{f : t}\}}$$

$$\textsc{Project}\ \frac{\Gamma \vdash L : \{\overline{f : t}\}}{\Gamma \vdash L.f_i : t_i} \qquad \textsc{Yield}\ \frac{\Gamma \vdash M : t}{\Gamma \vdash \textbf{yield}\ M : (t\ \textbf{list})^\ell} \qquad \textsc{Nil}\ \frac{}{\Gamma \vdash [\,] : (t\ \textbf{list})^\ell}$$

$$\textsc{Union}\ \frac{\Gamma \vdash M : (t\ \textbf{list})^\ell \qquad \Gamma \vdash N : (t\ \textbf{list})^{\ell'}}{\Gamma \vdash N \mathbin{@} M : (t\ \textbf{list})^{\ell \sqcup \ell'}}$$

$$\textsc{For}\ \frac{\Gamma \vdash M : (t\ \textbf{list})^\ell \qquad \Gamma, x : t \vdash N : (t'\ \textbf{list})^{\ell'}}{\Gamma \vdash \textbf{for}\ x\ \textbf{in}\ M\ \textbf{do}\ N : (t'\ \textbf{list})^{\ell \sqcup \ell'}}$$

$$\textsc{Exists}\ \frac{\Gamma \vdash M : (t\ \textbf{list})^\ell}{\Gamma \vdash \textbf{exists}\ M : \textbf{bool}^\ell} \qquad \textsc{If}\ \frac{\Gamma \vdash L : \textbf{bool}^\ell \qquad \Gamma \vdash M : (t\ \textbf{list})^{\ell'}}{\Gamma \vdash \textbf{if}\ L\ \textbf{then}\ M : (t\ \textbf{list})^{\ell \sqcup \ell'}}$$

$$\textsc{Run}\ \frac{\Gamma \vdash M : \textbf{Expr}\langle t\rangle}{\Gamma \vdash \textbf{run}\ M : t} \qquad \textsc{Quote}\ \frac{\Gamma; \cdot \vdash M : t}{\Gamma \vdash \texttt{<@}\ M\ \texttt{@>} : \textbf{Expr}\langle t\rangle}$$

$$\textsc{Sub}\ \frac{\ell \leq \ell' \qquad \Gamma \vdash M : t^\ell}{\Gamma \vdash M : t^{\ell'}}$$

Figure 8. Type system for host language

When lists are constructed using **yield** and [] they can be assigned an arbitrary level. Expressions of the form $e_1 \mathbin{@} e_2$ reveal information about the structure of both lists and hence their security levels are combined in the result type. Similarly, **exists** only reveals information about the structure of the list, but nothing about the contents. Therefore, the security level of list contents is discarded and only the security level of the list itself is present in the result type.

$$\textsc{ConstQ}\quad \frac{\Sigma(c) = t}{\Gamma;\Delta \vdash c : t^{\ell}} \qquad \textsc{FunQ}\quad \frac{\Gamma;\Delta, x : t \vdash e : t'}{\Gamma;\Delta \vdash \mathbf{fun}(x) \to e : t \to t'}$$

$$\textsc{VarQ}\quad \frac{x : t \in \Delta}{\Gamma;\Delta \vdash x : t} \qquad \textsc{ApplyQ}\quad \frac{\Gamma;\Delta \vdash e_1 : t \to t' \qquad \Gamma;\Delta \vdash e_2 : t}{\Gamma;\Delta \vdash e_1\, e_2 : t'}$$

$$\textsc{OpQ}\quad \frac{\Sigma(op) = \overline{t} \to t \qquad \overline{\Gamma;\Delta \vdash M : t^{\ell}}}{\Gamma;\Delta \vdash op(\overline{M}) : t^{\bigsqcup \ell_i}}$$

$$\textsc{PairQ}\quad \frac{\Gamma;\Delta \vdash e_1 : t_1 \qquad \Gamma;\Delta \vdash e_2 : t_2}{\Gamma;\Delta \vdash (e_1, e_2) : t_1 * t_2} \qquad \textsc{FstQ}\quad \frac{\Gamma;\Delta \vdash e : t_1 * t_2}{\Gamma;\Delta \vdash \mathbf{fst}\, e : t_1}$$

$$\textsc{SndQ}\quad \frac{\Gamma;\Delta \vdash e : t_1 * t_2}{\Gamma;\Delta \vdash \mathbf{snd}\, e : t_2} \qquad \textsc{RecordQ}\quad \frac{\overline{\Gamma;\Delta \vdash M : t}}{\Gamma;\Delta \vdash \{\overline{f = M}\} : \{\overline{f : t}\}}$$

$$\textsc{ProjectQ}\quad \frac{\Gamma;\Delta \vdash L : \{\overline{f : t}\}}{\Gamma;\Delta \vdash L.f_i : t_i} \qquad \textsc{YieldQ}\quad \frac{\Gamma;\Delta \vdash M : t}{\Gamma;\Delta \vdash \mathbf{yield}\, M : (t\ \mathbf{list})^{\ell}}$$

$$\textsc{NilQ}\quad \frac{}{\Gamma;\Delta \vdash [\,] : (t\ \mathbf{list})^{\ell}} \qquad \textsc{ExistsQ}\quad \frac{\Gamma;\Delta \vdash M : (t\ \mathbf{list})^{\ell}}{\Gamma;\Delta \vdash \mathbf{exists}\, M : \mathbf{bool}^{\ell}}$$

$$\textsc{IfQ}\quad \frac{\Gamma;\Delta \vdash L : \mathbf{bool}^{\ell} \qquad \Gamma;\Delta \vdash M : (t\ \mathbf{list})^{\ell'}}{\Gamma;\Delta \vdash \mathbf{if}\, L\, \mathbf{then}\, M : (t\ \mathbf{list})^{\ell \sqcup \ell'}}$$

$$\textsc{UnionQ}\quad \frac{\Gamma;\Delta \vdash M : (t\ \mathbf{list})^{\ell} \qquad \Gamma;\Delta \vdash N : (t\ \mathbf{list})^{\ell'}}{\Gamma;\Delta \vdash N\ @\ M : (t\ \mathbf{list})^{\ell \sqcup \ell'}}$$

$$\textsc{ForQ}\quad \frac{\Gamma;\Delta \vdash M : (t\ \mathbf{list})^{\ell} \qquad \Gamma;\Delta, x : t \vdash N : (t'\ \mathbf{list})^{\ell'}}{\Gamma;\Delta \vdash \mathbf{for}\, x\, \mathbf{in}\, M\, \mathbf{do}\, N : (t'\ \mathbf{list})^{\ell \sqcup \ell'}}$$

$$\textsc{SubQ}\quad \frac{\ell \le \ell' \qquad \Gamma;\Delta \vdash M : t^{\ell}}{\Gamma;\Delta \vdash M : t^{\ell'}} \qquad \textsc{DatabaseQ}\quad \frac{\Sigma(db) = \{\overline{f : t}\}}{\Gamma;\Delta \vdash \mathbf{database}(db) : \{\overline{f : t}\}}$$

$$\textsc{Antiquote}\quad \frac{\Gamma \vdash e : \mathbf{Expr}\langle t \rangle}{\Gamma;\Delta \vdash (\%\, e\,) : t}$$

Figure 9. Typing rules for quoted language

Note that the rule QUOTE ensures that its arguments are typed in an empty context for quoted expressions. This expresses that only closed quoted terms are allowed in this language. Running a quoted expression e of type $\mathbf{Expr}\langle t \rangle$ using **run** e results in a an expression of type t (rule RUN).

Expressions of the for **database**(db) get their type from the mapping Σ. The rule ANTIQUOTE allows to reference entities defined in the host language from within a quoted expression. The argument of an antiquotation must itself be a quoted expression.

The rules SUB and SUBQ allows raising the security level of an expression. $\ell \le \ell'$ holds if and only if $\ell = \mathtt{L} \vee \ell = \ell' = \mathtt{H}$.

To illustrate the type system further, we explain the typing rule FOR rule in greater detail. Recall that **for** expressions are used to denote list comprehensions. The typing rule assigns the resulting list the join of the security level of both sub-expressions. The following two examples demonstrate why this is required.

Consider the following program that uses a **for** expression to leak the structure of the lists xs and ys. We assume xs to have type $(t\ \mathbf{list})^{\ell}$ for some type t and level ℓ, whereas ys has type $(t'\ \mathbf{list})^{\ell'}$.

```
for x in xs do ys
```

Since the resulting lists for each element of xs will be concatenated, the resulting list will have length $|xs| \times |ys|$ where $|a|$ denotes the length of a. If either xs or ys contains only one element, the length of the other list is revealed through the result. To account for this information flow, the resulting list will be typed with level $\ell \sqcup \ell'$.

2.5 Soundness Result

As explained above, the soundness result is stated in terms of noninterference, i.e., as the preservation of a low-equivalence relation under pairwise execution. If we start out in any two low-equivalent environments then the result of running a well-typed program will be low-equivalent with respect to the type of the program.

Assuming that the typing of the execution environment corresponds to the capabilities of the attacker, noninterference guarantees that all information readable by the attacker is independent of confidential information. To make the connection between the database policy Σ and the type system explicit we write $\Sigma \vdash e : t$ even though Σ was kept implicit in the type rules in Figures 8 and 9.

Theorem 1 (Typing soundness). *If* $\Sigma \vdash e : t$, *then* $NI(e, e)_{\Sigma,t}$.

Proof of theorem 1. Immediate from Lemma 1 by expanding the definition of NI since e is a closed term. □

Lemma 1 (Typing soundness (generalized)). *If* $\overline{x : t} \vdash e : t$, $e[\overline{x} \mapsto \overline{v_1}] \longrightarrow^*_{\Omega_1} v_1'$, $e[\overline{x} \mapsto \overline{v_2}] \longrightarrow^*_{\Omega_2} v_2'$, $\Omega_1 \sim_{\Sigma} \Omega_2$ *and* $\overline{v_1} \sim \overline{v_2}$, *then* $v_1' \sim_t v_2'$.

Proof. Mutual induction over the typing derivation $\Gamma \vdash e : t$ and analogous statement for the quoted language. The full proof can be found in the full version of the paper. □

3. Implementation

Since F# contains an abundance of features not relevant to the current development we implement the language presented in Section 2, rather than attempting to enrich the F# implementation with security types. Our implementation compiles programs in this language to executable F# code. Given that the presented language is a subset of F#, the compilation consists mainly of removing level annotations in types in the program and establishing a connection to the database server.

This allows reusing the F# infrastructure for language-integrated query, as well as the improvements to this mechanism [16].

To simplify writing programs in the presented language, we implement a type inference algorithm supporting polymorphism for both levels and types. The basic approach that is used is based on constraint generation and unification [23]. For efficiency reasons the implementation is based on equality constraints, even though full inference would require inequality constraints. Interpreting inequality constraints as equality constraints introduces inaccuracies that prevents the types of some programs to be inferred properly.

However, since constraints are only generated in case they cannot be shown to be satisfied at the point of introduction it is always possible to resolve any such inaccuracies by providing type information in the form of type annotations. In practice, the type inference allows us to leave out many type annotations as witnessed by the examples in this paper.

The type-checker and compiler are implemented in Haskell, using the *BNFC* tool [3] for generating parsing and lexing code. The resulting binary takes a program in the language presented in Section 2.1 and produces F# code as output if the program is well-typed. If the program is not well-typed an error message detailing the reason for the type-checking failure is produced.

To illustrate the compilation, consider the output of the compiler for the example from Section 2.1 that queries the database for couples where the age difference between partners is greater than 10 years.

```
// import statements omitted

let ConnectionString_PeopleDB =
  "Data Source=.\MyInstance;Initial "\
  "Catalog=PeopleDB;Integrated Security=SSPI"
type dbSchema_PeopleDB =
  SqlDataConnection<ConnectionString_PeopleDB>
let db_PeopleDB = dbSchema_PeopleDB.GetDataContext()
let db = <@ db_PeopleDB @>
type ResultType = {name : string; diff : int; }
let differences : Expr<ResultType IQueryable> =
 <@ query { for c in (%db).Couples do
            for p1 in (%db).People do
            for p2 in (%db).People do
            if (c.Person1 = p1.Id) &&
               (c.Person2 = p2.Id) &&
               (abs (p1.Age - p2.Age) > 10) then
            yield { name = p1.Name
                  ; diff = p1.Age - p2.Age } }
 @>
let main = PLinq.Query.qquery
  { for x in (%differences) do yield x }
main
```

The above code example first imports all necessary libraries as well as the implementation of the supplementary concepts [16]. The subsequent part handles establishing a connection to the database server running on the same machine. The compiler generates a separate connection to the server for each database that is used by the program. Type synonyms and function definitions are compiled in a straight-forward way. The main difference is that all security levels have been removed from any types in the program.

For technical reasons, F# does not support query generation for quoted list expressions and therefore the compiler translates occurrences of the **list** type to **IQueryable** instead. Moreover, we translate expressions of the form **run** e into calls to a function `testPLinqQ` from the implementation accompanying [16]. This function takes a quoted expression, translates it into an SQL query, executes it and then returns the results.

Since our approach is purely static, and all security type information is erased during compilation, performance is unaffected, compared to ordinary F# code. Additionally, by reusing the results from Cheney et al. [16], we are able to benefit from the optimizations to F#'s LINQ mechanism presented there. Cheney et al. include a performance evaluation that is also valid for this implementation.

The code for the implementation is available online. The URL is given in Section 1.

4. Algebraic Data Types

We extend the language presented so far with algebraic data types and information-flow control for them.

This enriches the language with a way to express parametrized recursive data types that subsumes tuples and records. The addition is a proper extension to the language; neither tuples nor records can be recursive or parametrized in our language. We argue that introducing algebraic data types is a natural development due to their expressiveness and easy deconstruction via pattern matching. Encoding algebraic data types in an extended notion of records would both require extensions to the existing constructs that are similar to the extension needed to add algebraic data type and the result would be significantly less elegant.

Algebraic data types allow for the definition of new data types by composing existing data types. An algebraic data type consists of one or more constructors that can contain another type as their argument, including recursive occurrences of the defined data type. Pattern-matching is used deconstruct values in an algebraic data type by matching against the different constructors and parameters. The data contained in the parameters of a value in the data type can be extracted by giving a variable in the pattern.

Syntax Without loss of generality, consider an algebraic data type T with type argument α, which can be a product of several type variables. Constructors $C_1, \ldots, C_l$ have the form C_i of t_i where t_i is the argument of the constructor. Constructors with no arguments can be considered to take a value of unit type as an argument. For clarity, we only match on the outermost constructor of a single expression at a time. To track information flow, a security level annotation is then added to the type T. The expressions and values are extended as follows:

$$e ::= \ldots \mid C_i\ e \mid \textbf{match}\ e\ \textbf{with}\ C_1\ x_1 \rightarrow e_1\ ;\ \ldots\ ;\ C_k\ x_k \rightarrow e_k$$

$$\begin{aligned}\mathcal{E} ::=&\ C_1\ \mathcal{E} \mid \ldots \mid C_k\ \mathcal{E}\\ \mid&\ \textbf{match}\ \mathcal{E}\ \textbf{with}\ C_1\ x \rightarrow e;\ \ldots\ ;\ C_k\ x \rightarrow e\end{aligned}$$

$$\begin{aligned}\mathcal{Q} ::=&\ C_1\ \mathcal{Q} \mid \ldots \mid C_l\ \mathcal{Q}\\ \mid&\ \textbf{match}\ \mathcal{Q}\ \textbf{with}\ C_1\ x \rightarrow e;\ \ldots\ ;\ C_k\ x \rightarrow e\end{aligned}$$

$$V ::= \ldots \mid C_i\ V$$

Semantics The semantics is extended with the following rules for evaluation of constructors and pattern matching.

$$\begin{aligned}(\textbf{match}\ C_i\ v\ \textbf{with}&\\ &\mid C_1\ x_1 \rightarrow e_1\\ &\mid \ldots\\ &\mid C_k\ x_k \rightarrow e_k) \longrightarrow e_i[x_i \mapsto v]\end{aligned}$$

These rules correspond to the usual semantics of algebraic data types in other functional languages. Constructors with values as arguments are themselves values and cannot be evaluated further. If a constructor argument is not a value, it is evaluated. **match** expressions evaluate the expression that is being matched on first, and then evaluate the appropriate branch while binding the argument to the constructor to a name.

Type system To support algebraic data types in the type system, we use two rule schemas which generate several typing rules for each algebraic data type in the program. For each algebraic data type with l constructors, one rule for **match** expressions is added and l typing rules for the constructors.

The rule schema for constructors takes into account that type arguments to constructors might contain the type that is being defined. In that case their level annotations need to be combined to keep the structure of the value confidential. $T^{\ell} \in t_i$ holds for all components of t_i of the for $\alpha\ T^{\ell}$.

In the case of **match** expressions, the structure of the algebraic data type is used to decide which branch to evaluate. To track this flow of information, the type of the branches needs to be upgraded to the level annotation of the algebraic data type. For this, we define an upgrade function $upg(t, \ell)$ which denotes upgrading the type t to have at least level ℓ in its outermost components.

Definition 4 (Upgrade function)**.** *$upg(t, \ell)$ is defined by recursion on the structure of t.*

$$\begin{aligned}
upg(\textbf{\textit{int}}^{\ell}, \ell') &= \textbf{\textit{int}}^{\ell \sqcup \ell'} \\
upg(\textbf{\textit{bool}}^{\ell}, \ell') &= \textbf{\textit{bool}}^{\ell \sqcup \ell'} \\
upg(\textbf{\textit{string}}^{\ell}, \ell') &= \textbf{\textit{string}}^{\ell \sqcup \ell'} \\
upg(t \rightarrow t', \ell') &= t \rightarrow upg(t', \ell') \\
upg(t_1 * t_2, \ell') &= upg(t_1, \ell') * upg(t_2, \ell') \\
upg(\{\overline{f : t}\}, \ell') &= \{\overline{f : upg(t, \ell')}\} \\
upg((t\ \textbf{\textit{list}})^{\ell}, \ell') &= (t\ \textbf{\textit{list}})^{\ell \sqcup \ell'} \\
upg(\textbf{\textit{Expr}}\langle t \rangle, \ell') &= \textbf{\textit{Expr}}\langle upg(t, \ell') \rangle \\
upg((\alpha\ T)^{\ell}, \ell') &= (\alpha\ T)^{\ell \sqcup \ell'}
\end{aligned}$$

CONSTR

$$\frac{e : t_i}{\Gamma \vdash C_i\ e : T^{\bigsqcup_{T^{\ell} \in t_i} \ell}}$$

MATCH

$$\frac{\Gamma \vdash e : (\alpha\ T)^{\ell} \qquad \forall 1 \leq i \leq l. \Gamma, x_i : t_i \vdash e_i : t}{\Gamma \vdash (\textbf{match}\ e\ \textbf{with} \mid C_1\ x_1 \rightarrow e_1 \mid \ldots \mid C_k\ x_k \rightarrow e_k) : upg(t, \ell)}$$

In the rule CONSTR, $\bigsqcup_{T^{\ell} \in t_i} \ell$ denotes the join of all levels on occurrences of T in the type t_i. This ensures that the level annotation on the resulting value is not lower than its components. For instance, the constructor rule for the node constructor of a binary tree type will require the structure of the constructed tree to be at least as confidential as the structure of the two sub-trees.

To be able to extend the soundness result for the type system to algebraic data types, the family of equivalence relations $\sim$ also needs to be extended for each algebraic data type. In doing so, we follow the intuition given for $\sim$ in the base language. The level annotation ℓ on $(\alpha\ T)^{\ell}$ corresponds to the confidentiality of the *structure* of the type, i.e. which constructor a value consists of. If ℓ is high, we consider the entire value, including components, to be confidential.

It should be pointed out that the rule schemas assume that the defined algebraic data types are well-formed, i.e.,

- recursive occurrences of the defined type must have the same type argument α, and
- the only type variables that can occur in arguments to constructors must be type variables in α.

Soundness The low-equivalence relation is extended to the values of algebraic data types. As for the built-in list data type, if $\ell = \mathrm{L}$, arguments to constructors may or may not be confidential, depending on their level annotations.

$$\frac{\ell = \mathrm{L} \Rightarrow (i = j \wedge v_1 \sim_{t_i} v_2)}{C_i\ v_1 \sim_{\alpha\ T^{\ell}} C_j\ v_2}$$

We prove the same soundness theorem as for the base language in this extended setting.

Theorem 2. *If $\vdash e : t$, $\Omega_1 \sim_{\Sigma} \Omega_2$, $e \longrightarrow^{*}_{\Omega_1} v_1$ and $e \longrightarrow^{*}_{\Omega_2} v_2$, then $v_1 \sim_t v_2$.*

Proof. Extension of proof for Lemma 1 for the new typing rules that are induced by algebraic data types. □

Note that while the theorem statement is the same, the set of types and expressions is now potentially larger, since it is extended in accordance with the algebraic data types defined in e.

Example: lists One common use for algebraic data types is to define recursive structures such as list. To demonstrate that our extension is capable of supporting such use cases, consider the following user-defined list data type:

```
type 'a MyList =
  | Nil
  | Cons of ('a, 'a MyList)
```

Instantiating the above rule schemas for the user-defined list type **MyList** yields the following three type rules; two for the constructors, and one for the matching.

$$\frac{}{\Gamma \vdash \textbf{Nil} : {'a}\ \textbf{MyList}^{\ell}} \qquad \frac{\Gamma \vdash e_1 : {'a} \qquad \Gamma \vdash e_2 : {'a}\ \textbf{MyList}^{\ell}}{\Gamma \vdash \textbf{Cons}\ (e_1, e_2) : {'a}\ \textbf{MyList}^{\ell}}$$

$$\frac{\begin{array}{c}\Gamma \vdash e : {'a}\ \textbf{MyList}^{\ell} \\ \Gamma \vdash e_1 : t \qquad \Gamma, x : ({'a}, {'a}\ \textbf{MyList}^{\ell}) \vdash e_2 : t\end{array}}{\Gamma \vdash \textbf{match}\ e\ \textbf{with} \mid \textbf{Nil} \rightarrow e_1 \mid \textbf{Cons}\ x \rightarrow e_2 : upg(t, \ell)}$$

The generated rules match the intuitions given for the rest of the type system. Since **match** expressions information about the results of the branches (which have level ℓ') as well as the structure of the list (i.e. level ℓ) that the expression matches on, the level of the resulting list is $\ell \sqcup \ell'$. Moreover, the type system allows us to define corresponding functions for the **yield**, **exists**, **@**, and **for** constructs that are built into the language. The inferred type of each definition is given as a comment. Since the implementation sometimes generates extraneous type variables in inferred types that have no effect on generality, we give slightly simplified but equivalent types here.

```
// t → (t MyList)^ℓ
let yield' =
  fun x -> Cons (x, Nil)

// (t MyList)^ℓ → bool^ℓ
let exists' = fun xs -> match xs with
  | Nil -> False
  | Cons xs' -> True

// (t MyList)^ℓ → (t MyList)^ℓ → (t MyList)^ℓ
let rec union' = fun xs -> fun ys -> match xs with
  | Nil -> ys
  | Cons xs' -> Cons (fst xs', union' (snd xs') ys)

// (t1 MyList)^ℓ1 → (t1 → (t2 MyList)^(ℓ1⊔ℓ2))
// → (t2 MyList)^(ℓ1⊔ℓ2)
let rec for' =
  fun xs -> fun f -> match xs with
  | Nil -> Nil
  | Cons xs' -> union' (f (fst xs'))
                       (for' (snd xs') f)
```

Note that the types of these functions correspond roughly to the typing rules given for the built-in constructs. However, in the case of `union'` and `for'`, the type is slightly more restrictive than the typing rule, due to the way recursion is type-checked. However, these restrictions only affect the type of arguments and may only require lifting an argument expression to a higher security level.

Example: trees To further illustrate algebraic data types in the context of information flow, we discuss another common use, namely tree structures. We define an algebraic data type for binary trees:

```
type 'a BinTree =
  | Leaf
  | Node of (('a BinTree * 'a) * 'a BinTree)
```

In the same manner as for the user-defined list type, this will result in one rule for **match** expressions and two rules for the constructors:

$$\frac{}{\Gamma \vdash \textbf{Leaf} : ('a\ \textbf{BinTree})^{\ell}}$$

$$\frac{\Gamma \vdash e : ((('a\ \textbf{BinTree})^{\ell_1} * 'a) * ('a\ \textbf{BinTree})^{\ell_2})}{\Gamma \vdash \textbf{Node}\ e : ('a\ \textbf{BinTree})^{\ell_1 \sqcup \ell_2}}$$

$$\frac{\Gamma \vdash e : ('a\ \textbf{BinTree})^{\ell_1 \sqcup \ell_2} \qquad \Gamma \vdash e_1 : t \qquad \Gamma, x : ((('a\ \textbf{BinTree})^{\ell_1} * 'a) * ('a\ \textbf{BinTree})^{\ell_2}) \vdash e_2 : t}{\Gamma \vdash \textbf{match}\ e\ \textbf{with} \mid \textbf{Leaf} \to e_1 \mid \textbf{Node}\ x \to e_2 : upg(t, \ell_1 \sqcup \ell_2)}$$

The two typing rules for the constructors ensure that confidentiality of the tree structure is propagated correctly from the subtrees that are passed to the **Node** constructor. This construction is analogous to typing rules for lists in that the structure of the tree might be public while the tree elements might be confidential.

To illustrate the last point, consider a tree where the structure of the tree is not confidential while its elements are secrets:

```
let privTree : (int^H BinTree)^L =
  Node ((Leaf, (5 : int^H)),
        Node ((Leaf, (6 : int^H)), Leaf))
```

Since only the content at the leaves is considered private, counting the number of leaves of this tree can be typed with L:

```
let rec countLeaves =
  fun t -> match t with
    | Leaf -> 1
    | Node x -> countLeaves (fst (fst x)) +
                1 +
                countLeaves (snd x)

let result : int^L = countLeaves privTree
```

In contrast, trying to add all the integers in this tree and annotating the result with a low type will not type-check, since the computation involves more than merely the structure of the tree:

```
let rec sumElements =
  fun t -> match t with
    | Leaf -> 1
    | Node x -> sumElements (fst (fst x)) +
                snd (fst x) +
                sumElements (snd x)

// this is not well-typed:
let result' : int^L = sumElements privTree
```

5. Case Study: Movie Rental Database

In this section we exemplify the type system on a realistic example, a database to keep track of customer records by a movie rental chain, depicted in Figure 10. The example data and database schema [10] are courtesy of `postgresqltutorial.com` with permission to use their sample database in this work. The database contains information about approx. 16000 rentals, 600 customers, and 1000 movies. We use an existing sample database to demonstrate that our technique is applicable for database schemas that were not designed with information flow security in mind.

We first introduce a security policy for the database and consider various interesting queries that can be performed. Using the same setting, we illustrate the use of algebraic data types.

5.1 Basic Queries

The database keeps track of various information related to the movie rentals. Each rental is associated with a film, a customer, and a payment. The payments contain payment information and identifies the staff and the customer involved in the transaction. For both staff and customers address information is stored.

A reasonable security policy for such a database is to consider the names and exact addresses of customers and staff as confidential, while the rest of the data is considered public. In particular, the city of customers and the payment information are not considered confidential. The former is not a problem unless the city uniquely identifies a person and the latter does not contain any sensitive information. This security policy allows for querying the database for various interesting statistical information without disclosing confidential information about the customers.

Consider, for instance, the following example, which collects all rental ids for a given city.

```
let db = <@ database "Rentals" @>

let findCityId =
  <@ fun city -> for c in (%db).City do
                 if c.City1 = city then
                 yield c.City_id @>

let cityRentals : Expr<string^L -> int^L list^L> =
  <@ fun city -> for cid in (%findCityId) city do
                 for r in (%db).Rental do
                 for cu in (%db).Customer do
                 for a in (%db).Address do
                 if a.City_id = cid &&
                    cu.Address_id = a.Address_id &&
                    r.Customer_id = cu.Customer_id
                 then yield r.Rental_id @>
```

First in the example is the function `findCityId` that collects the city ids for a city of a given name. This function is used in `cityRentals` to look for rentals by customers living in that city. Note that while customer data is used, the type system ensures that only non-sensitive data affects the computation of the result. The rental ids can easily be used to produce interesting statistics about the relative popularity of films for different cities.

In contrast, trying to find all customers who rented a particular movie while forces the result to be secret, since the names of the customers are confidential. Thus, the following program is rejected by the type checker:

```
let rentalsForMovieTitle =
  <@ fun title -> for f in (%db).Film do
                  for r in (%db).Rental do
                  for i in (%db).Inventory do
                  if f.Title = title &&
                     r.Inventory_id = i.Inventory_id &&
                     i.Film_id = f.Film_id
                  then yield r @>

let customersWhoRented
      : Expr< string^L -> string^L list^L > =
  <@ fun title ->
      for r in (%rentalsForMovieTitle) title do
```

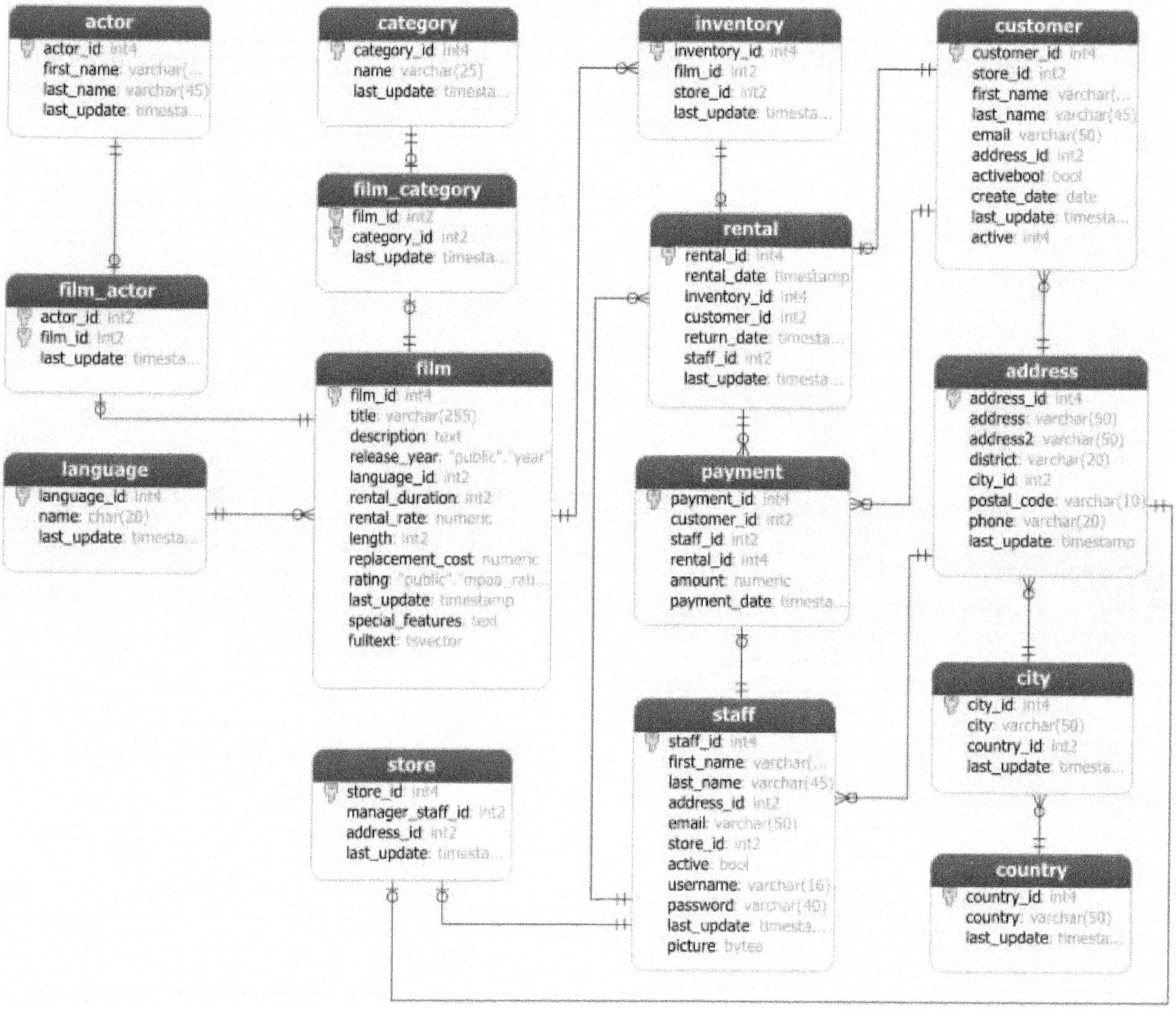

Figure 10. E-R diagram of movie rental database (image courtesy of `postgresqltutorial.com`)

```
   for c in (%db).Customer do
   if c.Customer_id = r.Customer_id
   then yield c.Last_name @>
```

The reason for the (correct) type error is that first and last names of customers are typed as $\textbf{string}^H$ while the function `customersWhoRented` attempts to return a list containing elements of type $\textbf{string}^L$. Changing the security annotation to reflect this makes the type system accept the program.

More complicated queries can be handled with the same ease as the simpler above examples. Consider, for instance, the following query that finds all movies that were rented at least twice by the same customer:

```
let moviesRentedTwice : Expr< int^L list^L > =
 <@ for r1 in (%db).Rental do
   for r2 in (%db).Rental do
   for i in (%db).Inventory do
   for f in (%db).Film do
   for c in (%db).Customer do
   if not (r1.Rental_id = r2.Rental_id) &&
      r1.Inventory_id = i.Inventory_id &&
      r2.Inventory_id = i.Inventory_id &&
      i.Film_id = f.Film_id &&
      r1.Customer_id = c.Customer_id &&
      r2.Customer_id = c.Customer_id
   then yield f.Film_id @>
```

Thus, the above examples illustrate the power of the method clearly. By giving a security policy for the contents of the database we are able to track information flow in advanced queries in term of the information flow of the quoted language. Not only does this allow us to establish security information flow in programs that interact with databases, it does so in a way that is intuitively simple to understand; an additional benefit of expressing the database interaction in a homogeneous way is that it makes the information flow in the interaction more immediate.

5.2 Algebraic Data Types

To demonstrate the usefulness of information-flow tracking for algebraic data types discussed in Section 4 in a more practical setting, we will now consider an example demonstrating information-flow tracking from values stored in the database in conjunction with user-defined algebraic data types.

One plausible scenario for the use of such a database is to aggregate some information about the customer in order to make predictions about which movies he would be interested in. For instance, one might want to determine a user's favorite category along with the movies he watched in that category. To that end, we can introduce the following algebraic data type that encodes a category along with a list of movie ids. (We only consider two categories for simplicity.):

```
type Category =
  | Action of (int^L list^L)
  | Scifi of (int^L list^L) ;;
```

Moreover, this information could be part of a larger record that stores information about a customer, where some information might be confidential and should not be used when the program output can be observed by the attacker. As an example, we consider a program that produces records of the following form:

```
type UserInfo =
  { uid : int^L
  ; firstName : string^H
  ; lastName : string^H
  ; favoriteCategory : Category^L
  } ;;
```

With this type, information about the favorite movie genre of a user can be used for prediction purposes, while the actual *name* of the customer cannot be retrieved without the resulting program being typed as H.

The following code produces a list of categories along with movie ids that a user, identified by their id, has rented:

```
let filmsByCustomer =
  <@ fun uid ->
     for r in (%db).Rental do
     for i in (%db).Inventory do
     for f in (%db).Film do
     if r.Customer_id = uid &&
        r.Inventory_id = i.Inventory_id &&
        i.Film_id = f.Film_id
     then yield f.Film_id @> ;;

let filmCategories =
  <@ fun fid ->
     for c in (%db).Category do
     for cf in (%db).Film_category do
     if cf.Film_id = fid &&
        cf.Category_id = c.Category_id
     then yield c.Name @> ;;

let userMovieInfo =
  <@ fun uid ->
     for fid in (%filmsByCustomer) uid do
     for cname in (%filmCategories) fid do
     yield { catname = cname ; fid = fid } @> ;;
```

Since the LINQ framework in F# does not allow producing values of user-defined algebraic data types from within a query, we first need to produce a record that contains the list of categories and movie ids returned by `userMovieInfo`.

```
let compileStats : Expr< UserInfo list^L > =
  <@ for cust in (%db).Customer do
     yield { uid = cust.Customer_id
           ; firstName = cust.First_name
           ; lastName = cust.Last_name
           ; movieCategories =
             (%userMovieInfo) cust.Customer_id } @>
```

To turn the information in the `movieCategories` field into an element of the defined algebraic data type, the following code counts the given list of movie data and then produces a value of type **Category** depending on which category occurs more often. (This is intentionally not written in a functional style to avoid having to introduce many additional auxiliary functions commonly found in functional languages.) The code then constructs a new record with the `movieCategories` replaced by the users favorite category.

Note that this computation now takes place in the host language, and security levels from the query result are propagated to these functions.

```
let updateCount =
  fun minfo -> fun statsrec ->
    { actionMovies =
        if' (minfo.catname = "action")
            (yield minfo.fid) [] @
        statsrec.actionMovies
    ; scifiMovies =
        if' (minfo.catname = "scifi")
            (yield minfo.fid) [] @
        statsrec.scifiMovies }

let emptyCounts = { actionMovies = [] ; scifiMovies = [] }

let countCategories =
  fun catList -> fold catList updateCount emptyCounts

let favoriteUserCategory =
  fun minfos ->
  let statsrec = countCategories minfos
  in (if' (length statsrec.actionMovies >
           length statsrec.scifiMovies)
          (Action (statsrec.actionMovies))
          (Scifi (statsrec.scifiMovies)))

let stats = map (fun x ->
  { uid = x.uid
  ; firstName = x.firstName
  ; lastName = x.lastName
  ; favoriteCategory =
    favoriteUserCategory (x.movieCategories) })
  (run compileStats)

let getCategories : Category^L list^L =
  map (fun x -> favoriteUserCategory
                  (x.movieCategories))
      (run compileStats)
```

The type system then correctly infers that the computation of the category does in fact not depend on confidential information about the user, while the name and email fields of the resulting records do. `if'` works like the built-in **if** construct except that it can produce values that are not lists and also requires an expression for the else case.

Moreover, attempting to find the favorite category of one particular user, identified by name, and typing the result with L will be prevented by the type checker. Concretely, an example such as the following, will be rejected by the type checker:

```
let attack : Category^L list^L =
  for x in getCategories do
  if x.firstName = "John" && x.lastName = "Doe"
  then yield x.favoriteCategory
```

6. Related Work

Until recently, little work has been done on bridging information-flow controls for applications [13, 29, 30, 41] and databases they manipulate. While mainstream database management systems such as PostgreSQL [7], SQLSever [8], and MySQL [6] include protection mechanisms at the level of table and columns, as is, these mechanisms are decoupled from applications.

Below, we focus on the work that shares our motivation of integrating the security mechanisms of the application and database, with the goal of tracking information flow.

WebSSARI by Huang et al. [32] is a tool that combines static analysis with instrumented runtime checks. The focus is on PHP applications that interact with an SQL database. The system succeeds at discovering a number vulnerabilities in PHP applications. Given its complexity, its soundness is only considered informally.

Li and Zdancewic [35] present an imperative security-typed language suitable for web scripting and a general architecture that includes a data storage, access control, and presentation layers. The focus is on suitable labels for confidentiality and integrity policies as well as the possibilities of safe label downgrading [44]. No soundness results for the type system are reported.

A line of work has originated from, or influenced by, from Links by Cooper et al. [21], a strongly-typed multi-tier functional language for the web. Links supports higher-order queries. On the other hand, Links comes with a non-standard database backend, making its interoperability non-trivial.

DIFCA-J by Yoshihama et al. [53] is an architecture for dynamic information-flow tracking in Java. The architecture covers database queries as performed by Java programs via Java DataBase Connectivity (JDBC) APIs.

Baltopoulos and Gordon [12] study secure compilation by augmenting the Links compiler with encryption and authentication of data stored on the client. Source-level reasoning is formalized by a type-and-effect system for a concurrent λ-calculus. Refinement types are used to guarantee that integrity properties of source code are preserved by compilation.

SELinks by Corcoran et al. [22] also builds on Links. With the Fable type system by Swamy et al. [49] at the core, the authors study the propagation of labels, as described by user-defined functions, through database queries. Fable's flexibility accommodates a variety of policies, including dynamic information-flow control, provenance, and general safety policies based on security automata.

DBTaint by Davis and Chen [24] shows how to enhance database data types with one-bit taint information and instantiate with two example languages in the web context: Perl and Java.

Chlipala's UrFlow [18] offers a static information-flow analysis as part of the Ur/Web domain-specific language for the development of web applications. Policies can be defined in terms of SQL queries. User-dependent policies are expressed in terms of the users' runtime knowledge.

Caires et al. [15] are interested in type-based access control in data-centric systems. They apply refinement types to express permission-based security, including cases when policies dynamically depend on the state of the database. This line of work leads to information-flow analysis by Lourenço and Caires [37]. This analysis is presented as a type system with value-indexed security labels for λ-calculus with data manipulation primitives. The type system is shown to enforce noninterference.

Hails by Giffin et al. [27] is a web framework for building web applications with mandatory access control. Hails supports a number of independently such useful design pattern as privilege separation, trustworthy user input, partial Lourenço and Caires [37] update, delete, and privilege delegation.

IFDB by Schultz and Liskov [46] proposes a database management system with decentralized information-flow control. IFDB is implemented by modifying PostgreSQL as well as modifying application environments in PHP and Python. The underlying model is the Query by Label model that provides abstractions for managing information flows in a relational database. This powerful model includes confidentiality and integrity labels, and models decentralization and declassification.

LabelFlow by Chinis et al. [17] dynamically tracks information flow in PHP. It is designed to deal with legacy applications, and so it transparently extends the underlying database schema to associate information-flow labels with every row.

The SLam calculus by Heintze and Riecke [31] pioneers information-flow control in a functional setting. The security type system treats a simple language with first-class functions, based on the λ-calculus. This is the first illustration of how noninterference can be enforced in the functional setting. Our security type system adopts as the starting point the security type system by Pottier and Simonet [40], which they have developed for a core of ML, and which serves as the base for the Flow Caml tool [48]. Compared to that work, our system includes the formalization and implementation of algebraic data types and pattern matching. Experiments with Flow Caml indicate support for algebraic data types but without evidence of soundness [40].

The tools like SIF [19], SWIFT [20], and Fabric [36] allow the programmer to enforce powerful policies for confidentiality and integrity in web applications. The programmer labels data resources in the source program with fine-grained policies using Jif [38], an extension of Java with security types. The source program is compiled against these policies into a web application where the policies are tracked by a combination of compile-time and run-time enforcement. The ability to enforce fine-grained policies is an attractive feature. At the same time, SIF and SWIFT do not provide database support. Fabric supports persistent storage while leaving interoperability with databases for future work.

A final note on related work is that care has to be taken when setting security policies for sensitive databases. Narayanan and Shmatikov's widely publicized work [39] demonstrates how to de-anonymize data from Netflix' database (where names were "anonymized" by replacing them with random numbers) using publicly available external information from sources as the Internet Movie Database [9].

7. Conclusion

We have presented a uniform security framework for information-flow control in a functional language with language-integrated queries (with Microsoft's LINQ on the backend). Because both the host language and the embedded query languages are both functional F#-like languages, we are able leverage information-flow enforcement for functional languages to obtain information-flow control for databases "for free", synergize it with information-flow control for applications, and thus guarantee security across application-database boundaries . We have developed a security type system with a novel treatment of algebraic data types and pattern matching, and established its soundness. We have implemented the framework and demonstrated its usefulness in a case study with a realistic movie rental database.

A natural direction for future work includes support of declassification [44] policies. This will enable more fine-grained labels and richer scenarios with intended information release. The functional setting allows for particularly smooth integration of policies of *what* [34, 35, 43] is released, where we can express aggregates through *escape hatches* [42], as represented by functions with no side effects. We believe that enriching the model with these policies will also open up for direct connections to the *database inference* [26] problem, much studied in the area of databases.

Acknowledgments

Thanks are due to Phil Wadler whose talk on language-integrated queries at Chalmers was an excellent inspiration for this work. This work was funded by the European Community under the ProSecuToR and WebSand projects and the Swedish research agencies SSF and VR.

References

[1] SPARKAda Examinar. Software release. `http://www.praxis-his.com/sparkada/`.

[2] OWASP Top 10: Ten Most Critical Web Application Security Risks. `https://www.owasp.org/index.php/Top_10_2013-Top_10/`, 2013. Accessed: 2014-02-20.

[3] BNF Converter. `http://bnfc.digitalgrammars.com/`, 2014. Accessed: 2014-02-20.

[4] Google Web Toolkit. `http://www.gwtproject.org/`, 2014. Accessed: 2014-02-20.

[5] LINQ (Language-Integrated Query). `http://msdn.microsoft.com/en-us/library/bb397926.aspx`, 2014. Accessed: 2014-02-20.

[6] Privileges Provided by MySQL. `https://dev.mysql.com/doc/refman/5.1/en/privileges-provided.html`, 2014. Accessed: 2014-02-20.

[7] Database Roles and Privileges. `http://www.postgresql.org/docs/9.0/static/user-manag.html`, 2014. Accessed: 2014-02-20.

[8] Authorization and Permissions in SQL Server. `http://msdn.microsoft.com/en-us/library/bb669084(v=vs.110).aspx`, 2014. Accessed: 2014-02-20.

[9] Internet Movie Database. `http://www.imdb.com/`, 2014. Accessed: 2014-02-20.

[10] PostgreSQL sample database. `http://www.postgresqltutorial.com/postgresql-sample-database/`, 2014. Accessed: 2014-02-20.

[11] Ruby on Rails. `http://rubyonrails.org/`, 2014. Accessed: 2014-02-20.

[12] I. G. Baltopoulos and A. D. Gordon. Secure compilation of a multi-tier web language. In *TLDI*, pages 27–38, 2009.

[13] N. Bielova. Survey on JavaScript security policies and their enforcement mechanisms in a web browser. *J. Log. Algebr. Program.*, pages 243–262, 2013.

[14] A. Birgisson, A. Russo, and A. Sabelfeld. Unifying Facets of Information Integrity. In *ICISS*, pages 48–65, 2010.

[15] L. Caires, J. A. Pérez, J. a. C. Seco, H. T. Vieira, and L. Ferrão. Type-Based Access Control in Data-Centric Systems. In *ESOP*, pages 136–155, 2011.

[16] J. Cheney, S. Lindley, and P. Wadler. A practical theory of language-integrated query. In *ICFP*, pages 403–416. ACM, 2013.

[17] G. Chinis, P. Pratikakis, S. Ioannidis, and E. Athanasopoulos. Practical information flow for legacy web applications. In *ICOOOLPS*, pages 17–28, 2013.

[18] A. Chlipala. Static Checking of Dynamically-Varying Security Policies in Database-Backed Applications. In *OSDI*, pages 105–118, 2010.

[19] S. Chong, K. Vikram, and A. C. Myers. SIF: Enforcing Confidentiality and Integrity in Web Applications. In *Proc. USENIX Security Symposium*, pages 1–16, Aug. 2007.

[20] S. Chong, J. Liu, A. C. Myers, X. Qi, K. Vikram, L. Zheng, and X. Zheng. Building secure web applications with automatic partitioning. *Commun. ACM*, 52(2):79–87, 2009. .

[21] E. Cooper, S. Lindley, P. Wadler, and J. Yallop. Links: Web Programming Without Tiers. In *FMCO*, pages 266–296, 2006.

[22] B. J. Corcoran, N. Swamy, and M. W. Hicks. Cross-tier, label-based security enforcement for web applications. In *SIGMOD Conference*, pages 269–282, 2009.

[23] L. Damas and R. Milner. Principal type-schemes for functional programs. In *POPL*, pages 207–212. ACM, 1982.

[24] B. Davis and H. Chen. DBTaint: Cross-application Information Flow Tracking via Databases. In *WebApps*, pages 12–12. USENIX Association, 2010.

[25] D. E. Denning and P. J. Denning. Certification of Programs for Secure Information Flow. *Comm. of the ACM*, 20(7):504–513, July 1977.

[26] J. Domingo-Ferrer, editor. *Inference Control in Statistical Databases, From Theory to Practice*, volume 2316 of *LNCS*, 2002. Springer.

[27] D. B. Giffin, A. Levy, D. Stefan, D. Terei, D. Mazières, J. C. Mitchell, and A. Russo. Hails: Protecting Data Privacy in Untrusted Web Applications. In *OSDI*, pages 47–60, 2012.

[28] J. A. Goguen and J. Meseguer. Security Policies and Security Models. In *Proc. IEEE SP*, pages 11–20, Apr. 1982.

[29] G. L. Guernic. *Confidentiality Enforcement Using Dynamic Information Flow Analyses*. PhD thesis, Kansas State University, 2007.

[30] D. Hedin and A. Sabelfeld. A perspective on information-flow control. *Proc. of the 2011 Marktoberdorf Summer School. IOS Press*, 2011.

[31] N. Heintze and J. G. Riecke. The SLam Calculus: Programming with Secrecy and Integrity. In *POPL*, pages 365–377, 1998.

[32] Y.-W. Huang, F. Yu, C. Hang, C.-H. Tsai, D.-T. Lee, and S.-Y. Kuo. Securing web application code by static analysis and runtime protection. In *WWW*, pages 40–52, 2004.

[33] A. Kennedy. Types for Units-of-Measure: Theory and Practice. In Z. Horváth, R. Plasmeijer, and V. Zsók, editors, *CEFP*, volume 6299 of *Lecture Notes in Computer Science*, pages 268–305. Springer, 2009. ISBN 978-3-642-17684-5. URL `http://dblp.uni-trier.de/db/conf/cefp/cefp2009.html#Kennedy09`.

[34] P. Li and S. Zdancewic. Downgrading policies and relaxed noninterference. In *POPL*, pages 158–170, 2005.

[35] P. Li and S. Zdancewic. Practical Information-flow Control in Web-Based Information Systems. In *CSFW*, 2005. .

[36] J. Liu, M. D. George, K. Vikram, X. Qi, L. Waye, and A. C. Myers. Fabric: a platform for secure distributed computation and storage. In *SOSP*, pages 321–334, 2009.

[37] L. Lourenço and L. Caires. Information Flow Analysis for Valued-Indexed Data Security Compartments. In *TGC*, 2013.

[38] A. C. Myers, L. Zheng, S. Zdancewic, S. Chong, and N. Nystrom. Jif: Java Information Flow. Software release. Located at `http://www.cs.cornell.edu/jif`, July 2001.

[39] A. Narayanan and V. Shmatikov. Robust De-anonymization of Large Sparse Datasets. In *IEEE Symp. on Security and Privacy*, 2008.

[40] F. Pottier and V. Simonet. Information flow inference for ML. In *POPL*, pages 319–330. ACM, 2002.

[41] A. Sabelfeld and A. C. Myers. Language-based information-flow security. *IEEE Journal on Selected Areas in Communications*, pages 5–19, 2003.

[42] A. Sabelfeld and A. C. Myers. A Model for Delimited Information Release. In *ISSS*, volume 3233 of *LNCS*, pages 174–191, 2003.

[43] A. Sabelfeld and D. Sands. A Per Model of Secure Information Flow in Sequential Programs. *Higher Order and Symbolic Computation*, 14 (1):59–91, Mar. 2001.

[44] A. Sabelfeld and D. Sands. Declassification: Dimensions and Principles. *J. Computer Security*, 17(5):517–548, Jan. 2009.

[45] J. H. Saltzer, D. P. Reed, and D. D. Clark. End-To-End Arguments in System Design. *ACM Trans. Comput. Syst.*, pages 277–288, 1984.

[46] D. A. Schultz and B. Liskov. IFDB: decentralized information flow control for databases. In *EuroSys*, pages 43–56, 2013.

[47] E. J. Schwartz, T. Avgerinos, and D. Brumley. All You Ever Wanted to Know About Dynamic Taint Analysis and Forward Symbolic Execution (but Might Have Been Afraid to Ask). In *Proceedings of the 2010 IEEE Symposium on Security and Privacy*, SP '10, pages 317–331, Washington, DC, USA, 2010. IEEE Computer Society. ISBN 978-0-7695-4035-1. . URL `http://dx.doi.org/10.1109/SP.2010.26`.

[48] V. Simonet. The Flow Caml system. Software release. Located at `http://cristal.inria.fr/~simonet/soft/flowcaml`, 2003.

[49] N. Swamy, B. J. Corcoran, and M. Hicks. Fable: A Language for Enforcing User-defined Security Policies. In *IEEE Symp. on Security and Privacy*, 2008.

[50] D. Syme. Leveraging .NET Meta-programming Components from F#: Integrated Queries and Interoperable Heterogeneous Execution. In *Workshop on ML*, pages 43–54. ACM, 2006. .

[51] D. Volpano. Safety versus Secrecy. In *Proc. Symp. on Static Analysis*, volume 1694 of *LNCS*, pages 303–311. Springer-Verlag, Sept. 1999.

[52] D. Volpano, G. Smith, and C. Irvine. A Sound Type System for Secure Flow Analysis. *J. Computer Security*, 4(3):167–187, 1996.

[53] S. Yoshihama, T. Yoshizawa, Y. Watanabe, M. Kudo, and K. Oyanagi. Dynamic Information Flow Control Architecture for Web Applications. In *ESORICS*, pages 267–282, 2007.

Type-Based Parametric Analysis of Program Families

Sheng Chen
Oregon State University
chensh@eecs.oregonstate.edu

Martin Erwig
Oregon State University
erwig@eecs.oregonstate.edu

Abstract

Previous research on static analysis for program families has focused on lifting analyses for single, plain programs to program families by employing idiosyncratic representations. The lifting effort typically involves a significant amount of work for proving the correctness of the lifted algorithm and demonstrating its scalability. In this paper, we propose a parameterized static analysis framework for program families that can automatically lift a class of type-based static analyses for plain programs to program families. The framework consists of a parametric logical specification and a parametric variational constraint solver. We prove that a lifted algorithm is correct provided that the underlying analysis algorithm is correct. An evaluation of our framework has revealed an error in a previous manually lifted analysis. Moreover, performance tests indicate that the overhead incurred by the general framework is bounded by a factor of 2.

Categories and Subject Descriptors F.3.3 [*Logics and Meanings of Programs*]: Studies of Program Constructs–Functional constructs,Type structure; D.3.2 [*Programming Languages*]: Language Classifications–Applicative (functional) languages

General Terms Languages, Theory

Keywords Variational types, constraint-based type system, static-analysis lifting, program families, choice calculus

1. Introduction

Software increasingly includes some form of variation. This can range from something as simple as having a few configuration options represented by `#ifdef` annotations to fully-fledged software product lines (SPLs) [13]. Each such variational program effectively encodes a (potentialy huge) number of programs and is thus also often called a *program family* [31].

Ensuring static properties of program families is challenging because the brute-force approach of generating and analyzing each individual program is generally infeasible due to the sheer number of programs a program family may encode.[1] Thus, the design of scalable analysis algorithms for program families has been the subject of much research, such as the variationalization of parsing [19, 23], type checking [1, 10, 17, 22, 24], dataflow analysis [5, 25], model checking [2, 11, 12, 14] and theorem proving [16, 41].

Most of these approaces employ some form of "lifting" strategy to extend a traditional analysis algorithm to deal with variational code. For instance, the variability-aware module system [24] is the result of lifting the module system introduced by Cardelli [6], the variational type inference [10] is the result of lifting the algorithm $\mathcal{W}$ [15], and the variability-aware dataflow analysis [5] is a lifted version of the traditional intraprocedural dataflow analysis [28]. All these approaches follow a similar pattern that typically involves the following steps.

(1) Add variability to data structures used in the traditional analysis. For example, variational types are represented as sets of plain types [1], value sets for dataflow analysis are extended to functions from features to values [5], or in variational type inference [9, 10], types, unifiers, and typing environment are all made variational using an explicit choice representation [18]. A similar representation has been adopted in [24, 25].

(2) Adapt analysis rules to deal with variational data structures. This applies in the obvious way to all data structure extensions mentioned in (1). Some approaches require additional machinery. For example, in [10], a type equivalence relation is required to make comparisons with choice types less rigid, and for the model checking approach described in [11, 12], the nodes and edges of transition systems are annotated with features, leading to feature transition systems.

(3) Prove that variation elimination commutes with the analysis, that is, a selection made from a program family and its analysis result should result in a plain program p and a result r such that running the traditional analysis on p would produce r. For example, the work on type checking [22] and type inference [9, 10] presented such proof. A similar proof was absent for the dataflow analysis [5], but was later presented in [4].

(4) A performance evaluation that demonstrates the efficiency gain of the lifted analysis over the brute-force approach.

This commonality indicates a general mechanism to systematically lift traditional static analyses to make them work for program families, avoiding the tedious steps of adding variability, performing proofs, and evaluating performance. So far, however, such a method is not available. The only attempt at something similar was recently made by Bodden et al. [3]. However, their approach only works for dataflow analyses formulated in the IFDS framework [35].

In this paper, we propose a type-based framework for automatically lifting plain-program static analyses to program families. Our method is applicable if (a) the analysis to be lifted can be expressed as a type system and (b) the program family is expressed using annotations (such as `#ifdef` CPP commands).

We have formalized our framework based on type analysis because it is both popular [30] and expressive [27]. Specifically, fol-

[1] For example, MySQL contains some 900 macros. Assuming these are pair-wise independent binary macros, the encoded number of program variants is close to the number of atoms in the universe to the 4th power.

ICFP'14, September 1–6, 2014, Gothenburg, Sweden.

ACM 978-1-4503-2873-9/14/09...$15.00.
http://dx.doi.org/10.1145/2628136.2628155.

lowing the spirit of HM(X) [29], a parameterized Hindley-Milner type system, we design VHM(X), an extension of HM(X) with variational constructs and an annotation model, allowing a richer set of information to be tracked during type checking. The success and scope of the HM(X) has been demonstrated with a wide range of program analyses, such as overloading [39], conditional constraints [32], or flow inference [33]. It has also been extended by abstract polymorphic data types [37] and guarded algebraic data types [38].

1.1 A Simple Example: Control Flow Analysis

As one example, we consider a type-based 0CFA (context-insensitive control flow analysis), discussed by Palsberg [30], that answers the question "what is the potential set of functions an expression may be evaluated to?" Consider, for example, the following expression introduced in [30].

$$f = ((\lambda^1 h.\lambda^2 x.h\,x)\ (\lambda^3 y.y))\ (\lambda^4 z.z)$$

The type-based 0CFA developed in [21] computes $\lambda z.z$, written as $\{4\}$, as the analysis result for f, meaning that f will evaluate to the abstraction labeled by 4.

Now consider the following, related program family that is obtained by creating a choice named D between $\lambda^3 y.y$ and $\lambda^5 w.\lambda^6 y.y$.

$$e = ((\lambda^1 h.\lambda^2 x.h\,x)\ D\langle(\lambda^3 y.y), (\lambda^5 w.\lambda^6 y.y)\rangle)\ (\lambda^4 z.z)$$

Choice expressions such as $D\langle e_1, e_2\rangle$ denote variation points in the program. They require that one of the alternatives e_1 and e_2 be selected to obtain a plain program from the program family. By selecting the first alternative of D in e, we obtain f. If we instead select the second alternative, we obtain the following expression g.

$$g = ((\lambda^1 h.\lambda^2 x.h\,x)\ (\lambda^5 w.\lambda^6 y.y))\ (\lambda^4 z.z)$$

For g, 0CFA produces the result $\{6\}$. This means that for the program family e we obtain the variational result $D\langle\{4\},\{6\}\rangle$, which reflects the fact that the result of the analysis depends on the selection made for D. For the first alternative, we get the result $\{4\}$, and for the second alternative, we get $\{6\}$.

Since the brute-force approach of generating all variants and running the analysis on each variant separately doesn't scale, a 0CFA for program families has to work with the variation representation (choices, as shown, or other) directly.

Now instead of having to go through the four steps sketched above over and over again, for each new program analysis, we would rather develop a method that, given a suitable representation of a single-program analysis, would generate a provably correct program-family version of that analysis automatically.

1.2 Contributions, Perspectives, and Previous Work

This work is related to the HM(X) system developed by Odersky et al. [29] and our variational type inference algorithm [10], but extends both significantly.

We extend HM(X) in two ways. First, we make expressions, types, constraints, and also typing systems *variational*, which allows us to deal with program *families*. Second, types and also derivations are extended with annotations, which allow us to encode more type-based analyses in the framework.

There are also two major differences compared to our variational type inference [10]. First, this paper develops an analysis lifting framework while the previous work was about a type inference algorithm for variational programs. The machinery developed in this paper is more general, and the variational type inference algorithm can be expressed as an instance of the lifting framework. Second, from a technical point of view, the need for a general variational constraint solving algorithm has provided a more fundamental understanding of the problem domain. Specifically, the variational constraint solving algorithm developed here, while being more general, is also significantly simpler than our previous variational unification algorithm [10] when instantiated with the Robinson algorithm [36].

This paper presents a systematic approach to automatically lift program analyses to families of functional (and other) programs. Our work is based on a variation representation that we briefly review in Section 2. The paper then makes the following contributions.

- We introduce the idea of an automated analysis lifting framework in the form of HM(X) in Section 3.
- We present a parameterized type system that declaratively specifies the computation of analyses in Section 4. We show that the variational analysis is sound provided the underlying analysis is sound.
- In Section 5 we develop a constraint-based inference system for the type system, which is both sound and complete with respect to the type system.
- In Section 6 we construct a variational constraint solver that is parameterized by domain-specific constraint solvers. We prove that the variational constraint solver is sound/most general provided the underlying solver is sound/most general.
- In Section 7 we evaluate a prototype implementation by comparing it with manually lifted static analyses. The evaluation has revealed an error in one such manually lifted analysis, and has indicated that the runtime overhead of our approach is bounded by a factor of 2.

Beyond the theoretical lifting framework, this paper has another important impact on programming language research. With the ability to lift a class of analyses, our framework makes what we call "property-guided product derivation" feasible. In current practice, selection of programs from program families is solely based on features and functional properties. However, in many cases it would be useful to have additional selection criteria available. For example, selecting programs based on different side effects, different sets of exceptions, different kinds of security policies, and so on. Our framework enables users to express such additional non-functional requirements as part of the program selection process.

2. Variation Representation

In this paper, we focus on the static analyses for so-called "annotative" program families, that is, program families that are obtained by directly annotating program parts that vary, for example, using CPP directives. For concreteness, we use binary choices as provided by the choice calculus [18] to represent variation. The choice calculus can be viewed as a restricted, yet more disciplined version of the C preprocessor.

The main construct of the choice calculus is a named *choice* to represent alternatives in programs (and other artifacts). For the work in this paper we can assume that all choice names are globally scoped and that each choice has exactly two alternatives. For example, the expression $A\langle$`succ`, `odd`$\rangle$ `1` represents the two *plain* expressions `succ 1` and `odd 1`. The name A is called a *dimension*.

Choices can be eliminated through a *selection* operation, which applies a *selector* s, given by a dimension D and an index i, to an expression and replaces each of its choices named D by its ith alternative. For lambda calculus with binary choices, selection is

Term variables	x, y, z	Annotation variables	β
Type variables	α	Type constructors	T
Choices	A, B, D	Program locations	l
Constraints	C		

Expressions	e	$::=$	$x \mid \lambda^l x.e \mid e\ e \mid \textbf{let}\ x = e\ \textbf{in}\ e \mid D\langle e, e\rangle$
Monotypes	τ	$::=$	$\alpha^\varphi \mid \tau \to^\varphi \tau$
Variational types	ϕ	$::=$	$\tau \mid D\langle \phi, \phi\rangle \mid \phi \to^\varphi \phi \mid T^\varphi\ \overline{\phi}$
Constraints	C	$::\supset$	$true \mid \phi \equiv \phi \mid \varphi \leq \varphi \mid D\langle C, C\rangle \mid C \wedge C \mid \exists \alpha.C$
Type schemas	σ	$::=$	$\forall \overline{\alpha}\overline{\beta}[C].\phi$
Annotations	φ	$::\supset$	$\varnothing \mid \{l\} \mid \beta \mid \varphi \cup \varphi \mid D\langle \varphi, \varphi\rangle$
Selectors	s	$::=$	$D.i$
Type environments	Γ	$::=$	$\varnothing \mid \Gamma, x \mapsto \sigma$
Substitutions	θ	$::=$	$\varnothing \mid \theta, \alpha \mapsto \phi$

Figure 1. Syntax of expressions, types, constraints, etc.

defined as follows.

$$\lfloor x \rfloor_s = x$$
$$\lfloor \lambda x.e \rfloor_s = \lambda x.\lfloor e \rfloor_s$$
$$\lfloor e_1\ e_2 \rfloor_s = \lfloor e_1 \rfloor_s\ \lfloor e_2 \rfloor_s$$
$$\lfloor D\langle e_1, e_2\rangle \rfloor_s = \begin{cases} \lfloor e_1 \rfloor_s & \text{if } s = D.1 \\ \lfloor e_2 \rfloor_s & \text{if } s = D.2 \\ D\langle \lfloor e_1 \rfloor_s, \lfloor e_2 \rfloor_s\rangle & \text{otherwise} \end{cases}$$

The selection operation essentially traverses the AST and replaces choices along the way; it thus extends naturally to other language constructs.

For example, selecting $A.1$ from the expression $e = A\langle\texttt{succ},\texttt{odd}\rangle\ \texttt{1}$ results in the expression $\lfloor e \rfloor_{A.1} = \texttt{succ 1}$. Selection synchronizes choices in the same dimension. For example, the expression $A\langle\texttt{succ},\texttt{odd}\rangle\ A\langle\texttt{1},\texttt{True}\rangle$ represents two expressions, `succ 1` and `odd True`, which can be obtained by one selection. In contrast, we need two selections, one in A and one in B, to eliminate the choices in the expression $A\langle\texttt{succ},\texttt{odd}\rangle\ B\langle\texttt{1},\texttt{True}\rangle$. Since the dimensions A and B are independent of one another, the choices represents four plain expressions.

Note that the choice representation is generic and can be used with any object language. It can thus represent variation in programs, types, and other software artifacts and data structures.

In the case of globally scoped choices, the semantics of a variational expression e can be expressed as a mapping from sets of selectors to plain expressions. A formal definition can be found in [10]. For illustration, here is a simple example.

$$[\![A\langle\texttt{succ}, B\langle\texttt{odd},\texttt{even}\rangle\rangle\ \texttt{1}]\!] =$$
$$\{\{A.1\} \mapsto \texttt{succ 1}, \{A.2, B.1\} \mapsto \texttt{odd 1}, \{A.2, B.2\} \mapsto \texttt{even 1}\}$$

3. VHM(X) Syntax

We present the core syntax for VHM(X) in Section 3.1 and explain how to extend the syntax to encode static analyses in Section 3.2.

3.1 Core Syntax

We consider a parameterized type system over basic lambda calculus plus let-polymorphism and choice constructs. Figure 1 presents the syntax of various concepts used throughout this paper. The definition of expressions is conventional, except for the choice construct (see Section 2). We also attach a label l to lambda abstractions to track information about abstractions during type checking. In addition, we may make use of constants, such as `succ` and `even`, which have to appear in the initial type environment.

Another important extension of the HM(X) framework [29] is the addition of annotations (φ) to types. An annotation is a set representing information of interest for a specific analysis. Thus, the definition of φ is partly unspecified, and we adopt the notation $::\supset$ from [29] to indicate this fact. However, labels are always available as annotations, as is clear from the definition of φ. The distributive nature of choices [18] allows us to view $D\langle\varphi_1,\varphi_2\rangle \cup \varphi$ as $D\langle\varphi_1 \cup \varphi, \varphi_2 \cup \varphi\rangle$. (The case for $\varphi \cup D\langle\varphi_1,\varphi_2\rangle$ is symmetric.) This equivalence can be employed to normalize annotations such that choice constructs will not be nested within sets.

The definition of monotypes is fairly simple. However, types can carry annotations (φ). Later we will see that monotypes are the only types that are allowed to appear in the type part of a type schema. More complicated type definitions will become part of the constraints that will be discussed shortly. This design decision is motivated by Sulzmann et al. [40], who observed that in the presence of non-regular equational theories type inference may fail to compute principal types even with the help of a most general unification algorithm. They proposed as a solution to push complicated type definitions into constraints. This is what we adopt in this paper.

The definition of variational types ϕ differs from conventional type definitions in two aspects. First, we include choice types $D\langle\phi,\phi\rangle$ to represent variation in types. Second, since different instances of VHM(X) involve different type representations, we allow each instance of VHM(X) to supply extra type definitions, through the use of annotated type constructors of the form $T^\varphi\ \overline{\phi}$. Type constructors can take an arbitrary number of arguments, including 0, in which case they represent primitive types, such as `bool` and `int`. Like monotypes, variational types are also annotated.

The definition for constraints C is also open. However, we assume that the following constraints are always defined.

(i) *true* denotes a constraint that is always satisfied.

(ii) The constraint $\phi_1 \equiv \phi_2$ represents a type equivalence requirement between two types ϕ_1 and ϕ_2.

(iii) The constraint $\varphi_1 \leq \varphi_2$ imposes a partial order on annotations.

(iv) The constraint $D\langle C_1, C_2\rangle$ allows a variation in constraints.

(v) The constraints $C_1 \wedge C_2$ and $\exists\alpha.C$ have the same meaning as in first-order logic.

Each instance of VHM(X) may extend the definition of constraints.

A type schema, written as $\forall\overline{\alpha}\overline{\beta}[C].\tau$, consists of a constraint and a monotype. Note that it is polymorphic both over types and annotations. The constraint part C places a requirement on types and annotations that may be substituted for $\overline{\alpha}$ and $\overline{\beta}$ in τ: Only types and annotations that satisfy C can be used. Type schemas are considered equivalent modulo bound variable renaming.

We use θ to range over substitutions. We write $FV(C)$ for the set of free variables in C (where the $\exists$ quantifier is the only binding symbol in constraints). We also use $FV(\sigma)$ to denote the set of free variables in σ and extend its definition to type environments Γ in the usual way. The application of substitution to constraints, type schemas, and type environment, written as $\theta(C)$, $\theta(\sigma)$, and $\theta(\Gamma)$, respectively, is also defined in the usual way.

Note that the definition of ϕ and C allows us to shift complex conditions from types to constraints. For example, the expression $A\langle\texttt{succ},\texttt{odd}\rangle$ has the type $A\langle\texttt{int} \to \texttt{int}, \texttt{int} \to \texttt{bool}\rangle$, which we can also express by saying that $A\langle\texttt{succ},\texttt{odd}\rangle$ has the type α under the constraint $\alpha \equiv A\langle\texttt{int} \to \texttt{int}, \texttt{int} \to \texttt{bool}\rangle$.

3.2 Syntax Extensions

To instantiate VHM(X) for a specific analysis, the following information must be supplied.

- A type definition to extend ϕ, given as a type signature $\mathscr{T}$.
- An annotation definition $\mathscr{A}$ that extends φ.
- A constraint definition $\mathscr{C}$ to extend C.

These components prepare the framework for the addition of the analysis proper, which has to be provided as an extension of the type system and will be discussed in Section 4.3.

The extensibility of VHM(X) through the components $\mathscr{T}$, $\mathscr{A}$, and $\mathscr{C}$ offers much flexibility and allows a wide variety of analyses to be instantiated. In many instances, however, only a part of these components is needed, and VHM(X) can retain most of its default behavior.

As an example, consider the 0CFA. Section 1.1. The only annotations will be the labels for abstractions, which are already part of VHM(X). We thus have $\mathscr{A} = \varnothing$. Similarly, all the types and constraints for 0CFA are already present, that is, $\mathscr{T} = \mathscr{C} = \varnothing$.

For another example, consider exception analysis which tries to determine statically what kind of exceptions may be raised during the evaluation of an expression (see, for example, [28]). To instantiate VHM(X), we extend the type definition by a set of nullary exception type constructors, that is, we define $\mathscr{T} = \{EX_1, \ldots, EX_n\}$. In addition, we extend the definition of annotation with types, that is, $\varphi ::= \cdots \mid \{\phi\}$, so that exception types can be type annotations. Finally, the constraint definition $\mathscr{C}$ is extended by a predicate $Ex\ \phi$ to denote that ϕ is an exception type.

4. VHM(X) Type System

In this section we present the logical specification of the VHM(X) framework. We begin with the entailment relation in Section 4.1, which is followed by a discussion of typing rules for reasoning about programs in Section 4.2. We then show how to instantiate the logical part of VHM(X) to encode new static analyses in Section 4.3. Finally, we investigate the property of VHM(X) by comparing it to HM(X) in Section 4.4.

4.1 Constraint Entailment

The exact interpretation of constraints depends, in general, on the analysis that is being implemented. However, we require constraints to always satisfy the entailment relation defined in Figure 2. Intuitively, $C_1 \Vdash C_2$ means that the constraint C_1 is more restrictive than C_2. The top part of Figure 2 presents the relation with regard to the definition of constraints, and the bottom part defines entailment with regard to type equivalence constraints in particular.

Rule C1 expresses the monotonicity of constraints, where we use the notation $C_1 \supseteq C_2$ to denote that C_1 is more constrained than C_2 by interpreting the connective $\wedge$ as set union $\cup$ and each primitive constraint C as $\{C\}$. The rule can also be understood by viewing the constraints in a set as a conjunction, which means the set with more constraints is more restrictive. Rule C2 states transitivity, and rule C3 requires entailment to be preserved over substitution. Rules C4 and C5 deal with existential quantification. Since quantifying a constraint with $\exists$ hides part of the constraint, it becomes less restrictive [29]. Rules C6 to C8 handle choices between constraints. The validity of these rules can be seen by considering the rules that result when making an arbitrary selection for the choice D. The purpose of rule C9 is to allow the decomposition of choices into two constraints. Again, we can verify the validity of this rule by eliminating the variation in this rule, which results in two rules, with each can be verified by the rule C1. This rule offers many opportunities for optimization.

$$\text{C1}\ \frac{C_1 \supseteq C_2}{C_1 \Vdash C_2} \qquad \text{C2}\ \frac{C_1 \Vdash C_2 \qquad C_2 \Vdash C_3}{C_1 \Vdash C_3} \qquad \text{C3}\ \frac{C_1 \Vdash C_2}{\theta(C_1) \Vdash \theta(C_2)}$$

$$\text{C4}\ \ C \Vdash \exists\alpha.C \qquad \text{C5}\ \frac{C_1 \Vdash C_2}{\exists\alpha.C_1 \Vdash \exists\alpha.C_2} \qquad \text{C6}\ \frac{C \Vdash C_1 \qquad C \Vdash C_2}{C \Vdash D\langle C_1, C_2\rangle}$$

$$\text{C7}\ \frac{C_1 \Vdash C \qquad C_2 \Vdash C}{D\langle C_1, C_2\rangle \Vdash C} \qquad \text{C8}\ \frac{C_1 \Vdash C_2 \qquad C_3 \Vdash C_4}{D\langle C_1, C_3\rangle \Vdash D\langle C_2, C_4\rangle}$$

$$\text{C9}\quad D\langle C_1, true\rangle \wedge D\langle true, C_2\rangle \Vdash D\langle C_1, C_2\rangle$$

$$\text{E1}\quad \phi_1 \equiv \phi_2 \Vdash \phi_2 \equiv \phi_1 \qquad \text{E2}\quad \phi_1 \equiv \phi_2 \wedge \phi_2 \equiv \phi_3 \Vdash \phi_1 \equiv \phi_3$$

$$\text{E3}\quad \Vdash \phi \equiv \phi \qquad \text{E4}\quad \phi_1 \equiv \phi_2 \Vdash \phi[\phi_1] \equiv \phi[\phi_2]$$

$$\text{E5}\quad \Vdash D\langle \phi, \phi\rangle \equiv \phi \qquad \text{E6}\quad \Vdash D\langle \phi_1, \phi_2\rangle \equiv D\langle \lfloor\phi_1\rfloor_{D.1}, \lfloor\phi_2\rfloor_{D.2}\rangle$$

$$\text{E7}\quad C \Vdash D\langle T^{\varphi_1}\ \overline{\phi_1}, T^{\varphi_2}\ \overline{\phi_2}\rangle \equiv T^{D\langle\varphi_1,\varphi_2\rangle}\ \overline{D\langle\phi_1, \phi_2\rangle}$$

$$\text{A1}\ \frac{\varphi_1 \subseteq \varphi_2}{C \Vdash \varphi_1 \leq \varphi_2}$$

Figure 2. Entailment relation of constraints

For the entailment of type equivalence constraints, rules E1 to E3 express that type equivalence is reflexive, symmetric, and transitive. Rule E4 states that the type equivalence relation is a congruence, where $\phi[]$ denotes a type term with a hole (context) into which we can plug a type. Rules E5 and E6 express two fundamental invariances of choice types. Rule E7 allows the annotations attached to a type constructor T that occurs in both alternatives of a choice D to be extracted and combined with T. This rule is valid because selection commutes with term construction, that is, $\lfloor T\ \phi\rfloor_s = T\ \lfloor\phi\rfloor_s$, a fact that follows immediately from the definition of selection (see Section 2). The importance of this rule lies in the fact that it allows us to represent variational types succinctly. For instance, we can push the choice into the term and factor

$$D\langle(\alpha \xrightarrow{\{1\}} \alpha) \xrightarrow{\{2\}} \alpha \xrightarrow{\{1\}} \alpha, (\alpha \xrightarrow{\{1\}} \alpha) \xrightarrow{\{3\}} \alpha \xrightarrow{\{1\}} \alpha\rangle$$

into $(\alpha \xrightarrow{\{1\}} \alpha) \xrightarrow{D\langle\{2\},\{3\}\rangle} \alpha \xrightarrow{\{1\}} \alpha$.

Finally, we add the rule A1 for the partial order relation $\leq$ for annotations. Together with the rules C6 through C8, we define a partial ordering on variational annotations. Specific instances may extend the definition of $\leq$.

4.2 Typing Rules

The idea of type-based static analysis is to attach annotations to types and typing derivations and aggregate the information along the typing process [28]. Different analyses introduce their own specific annotations and relations between annotations that have to be integrated into the generic typing framework. To facilitate this flexibility, we parameterize the syntax-directed typing rules by a family of constraints, defining one particular constraint relationship R_e for each kind of expression e. The arity of R_e varies for different constructors of e; as a general rule of thumb, R_e needs enough parameters to relate the annotations obtained from the premises of a typing rule to the annotation provided in its conclusion. The premises of each syntax-directed typing rule can thus be partitioned into two parts: (i) a specification of the relation between types and (ii) a specification of the relation between labels and annotations (ex-

$$\frac{\Gamma(x) = \forall\overline{\alpha}\overline{\beta}[C].\tau^{\varphi_1} \quad C' \Vdash C \quad C' \Vdash R_x\ \varphi_1\ \varphi_2}{C';\Gamma \vdash x : \tau^{\varphi_1}/\varphi_2}\ \text{VAR}$$

$$\frac{C;\Gamma,(x,\tau) \vdash e : \tau'/\varphi_1 \quad C \Vdash R_\lambda\ l\ \varphi_1\ \varphi_2\ \varphi_3}{C;\Gamma \vdash \lambda^l x.e : \tau \xrightarrow{\varphi_2} \tau'/\varphi_3}\ \text{ABS}$$

$$\frac{C;\Gamma \vdash e_1 : \tau_1/\varphi_1 \quad C;\Gamma \vdash e_2 : \tau_2/\varphi_2 \quad C \Vdash \tau_1 \equiv \tau_2 \xrightarrow{\varphi_3} \tau \quad C \Vdash R_{App}\ \varphi_1\ \varphi_2\ \varphi_3\ \varphi_4}{C;\Gamma \vdash e_1\ e_2 : \tau/\varphi_4}\ \text{APP}$$

$$\frac{C;\Gamma \vdash e : \sigma/\varphi_1 \quad C;\Gamma,(x,\sigma) \vdash e' : \tau/\varphi_2 \quad C \Vdash R_{Let}\ \varphi_1\ \varphi_2\ \varphi_3}{C;\Gamma \vdash \textbf{let}\ x = e\ \textbf{in}\ e' : \tau/\varphi_3}\ \text{LET}$$

$$\frac{C_1;\Gamma \vdash e_1 : \tau_1/\varphi_1 \quad C_2;\Gamma \vdash e_2 : \tau_2/\varphi_2 \quad D\langle C_1,C_2\rangle \Vdash D\langle \tau_1,\tau_2\rangle \equiv \tau}{D\langle C_1,C_2\rangle;\Gamma \vdash D\langle e_1,e_2\rangle : \tau/D\langle \varphi_1,\varphi_2\rangle}\ \text{CHOICE}$$

$$\frac{C;\Gamma \vdash e : \tau/\varphi \quad C \Vdash \tau \preceq \tau'}{C;\Gamma \vdash e : \tau'/\varphi}\ \text{SUB} \qquad \frac{C';\Gamma \vdash e : \tau/\varphi \quad C \Vdash C'}{C;\Gamma \vdash e : \tau/\varphi}\ \text{WEAKEN}$$

$$\frac{C_1 \wedge C_2;\Gamma \vdash e : \tau/\varphi \quad \overline{\alpha}\overline{\beta} \# FV(C_1) \cup FV(\Gamma)}{C_1 \wedge \exists\overline{\alpha}\overline{\beta}.C_2;\Gamma \vdash e : \forall\overline{\alpha}\overline{\beta}[C_2].\tau/\varphi}\ \text{GEN}$$

$$\frac{C;\Gamma \vdash e : \sigma/\varphi \quad \overline{\alpha}\overline{\beta} \# FV(\sigma) \cup FV(\Gamma)}{\exists\overline{\alpha}\overline{\beta}.C;\Gamma \vdash e : \sigma/\varphi}\ \text{SIMPLE}$$

Figure 3. Typing rules for VHM(X)

pressed by R_e). The family of constraints R_e has to be instantiated by each specific analysis instance. Whenever the second part is not needed, it can be simply turned off by using the constraint *true* as instantiation.

The typing judgment of VHM(X) has the form $C;\Gamma \vdash e : \sigma/\varphi$, which computes the type schema σ for the expression e under the typing assumptions in Γ and the constraint C that expresses the assumptions about free type variables in Γ and σ. In addition, an annotation φ is maintained by the typing relation. This annotation links the annotation constraints to the typing process and ensures that the information computed within the annotations is available as results in the type derivation. Figure 3 presents the rules for assigning types and annotations to expressions. The syntax-directed rules are shown in the upper half, and the remaining rules are collected at the bottom.

The rule VAR allows us to instantiate a type schema $\forall\overline{\alpha}\overline{\beta}[C].\tau$ with any constraint C' as long as it entails C and the parameterized constraint $R_x\ \varphi_1\ \varphi_2$ is satisfied (which expresses the relationship between the stored and returned annotation for a variable).

The rule ABS extends the traditional rule by a premise that demands the relationship R_λ hold between the annotations of the abstraction's body (φ_1), the function type (φ_2), and the whole derivation (φ_3). Note that usually φ_2 collects interesting information about the evaluation of the abstraction while φ_3 collects the information about defining the abstraction [28]. For example, in case of exception analysis (Section 4.3), the constraint is instantiated as $R_\lambda\ l\ \varphi_1\ \varphi_2\ \varphi_3 = \varphi_1 \leq \varphi_2 \wedge \varphi_2 \leq \varphi_1 \wedge \varphi_3 \leq \varnothing \wedge \varnothing \leq \varphi_3$, and denotes that the potential exceptions that may be raised in an abstraction are those that may be raised by evaluating the body e. Moreover, there is no exception raised for defining an abstraction.

The rule APP is more subtle. For an application $e_1\ e_2$ to be well typed, we use a more relaxed relation than requiring the argument type of e_1 to match the type of e_2. We require instead that the type of e_1 be *equivalent* to a function type whose argument type is the type of e_2. This relaxation effectively deals with the fact that choices in type expressions increase the compatibility between types. For example, the expression `odd` $D\langle$`1,2`$\rangle$ should be considered type correct even though the argument type of `odd` (which is `int`) is *not* equal to the type of $D\langle$`1,2`$\rangle$ (which is $D\langle$`int,int`$\rangle$).

The rule LET for introducing let-polymorphism simply aggregates the annotations obtained from the typing of the subexpressions [40].

The typing for a choice expression is obtained by combining the result for its alternatives. Specifically, we pack corresponding constraints and result types into the choice that we are typing, as expressed by the rule CHOICE.

Similar to the HM(X) framework, we use a subsumption relation to allow a type to be interpreted as some other type, as captured in rule SUB. The semantics of this relation is left unspecified, which thus allows different instances of VHM(X) to specify their interpretations as needed for their particular purposes. For example, in typing Haskell, it should be instantiated to the syntactical equality relation. On the other hand, subsumption can be interpreted as a subtyping relation when subtyping is involved. In any case, we require the relation to satisfy the standard partial ordering axioms, the contra-variance rule for function types, plus the following rules for choice types.

$$\frac{C \Vdash \phi_1 \preceq \phi \quad C \Vdash \phi_2 \preceq \phi}{C \Vdash D\langle \phi_1,\phi_2\rangle \preceq \phi} \qquad \frac{C \Vdash \phi \preceq \phi_1 \quad C \Vdash \phi \preceq \phi_2}{C \Vdash \phi \preceq D\langle \phi_1,\phi_2\rangle}$$

$$\frac{C \Vdash \phi_1 \preceq \phi_2 \quad C \Vdash \phi_3 \preceq \phi_4}{C \Vdash D\langle \phi_1,\phi_3\rangle \preceq D\langle \phi_2,\phi_4\rangle}$$

The rule GEN borrowed from [40], introduces a type schema for a typing judgment. The essential idea is that the constraint is split into two parts, one part (C_2) constrains the free variables in the result type τ and the type environment Γ, while the other (C_1) doesn't. As a result, only C_2 appears as the constraint for the result type schema. (We write $S_1 \# S_2$ to express that two sets S_1 and S_2 are disjoint.) Many rules exist for generalization, but this rule has many advantages over previous ones [29]. The novel part is that $\exists\alpha.C_2$ remains in the left-hand side of the judgment, whose goal is to ensure that the constraint C_2 must be satisfiable. In other words, to generalize a type, the generalized type must at least have one instance. Further details motivating the use of $\exists\alpha.C_2$ were presented in [29].

The rule SIMPLE allows us to hide type variables and simplifies the constraint part of a typing judgment. For example, in the judgment `Eq` $\alpha_1;\Gamma \vdash e : \alpha_2 \rightarrow$ `bool`$/\varnothing$, the constraint is not needed, and we can thus transform it into $\exists\alpha_1$.`Eq` $\alpha_1;\Gamma \vdash e : \alpha_2 \rightarrow$ `bool`$/\varnothing$. We don't simply drop the constraint `Eq` α_1, because we want to maintain the fact that the constraint `Eq` α_1 must be satisfiable. The rule WEAKEN allows us to strengthen the constraint in a typing judgment while deriving the same result.

We don't have an instantiation rule to eliminate type schemas because the polymorphism is introduced through the let expressions and as a result, we only need to instantiate variable references, which is already realized in VAR.

4.2.1 Constraint Optimization

We observe that in GEN constraints are moved from the assumption into type schemas whereas in VAR constraints are moved in the opposite order, which means that when a variable is referenced repeatedly, the constraint from the type schema will be copied many times. Since it is important to keep the constraints to a manageable size, rules like the seemingly complicated GEN are needed to split constraints in premises into two parts and move as little as possible to the resulting type schema. Achieving high performance is a main goal of the VHM(X) framework. The entailment relation defined in Figure 2 and the rule WEAKEN offer many opportunities to optimize the representation of constraints. As an example consider the following judgement.

$$D\langle C, \texttt{Eq}\ \alpha\rangle; \Gamma \vdash \texttt{elem x} : [\alpha] \rightarrow \texttt{bool}/\varnothing$$

We assume that $\alpha \notin FV(C)$ and that C is a large, complicated constraint. Generalizing this judgment directly with GEN will not leave much room for optimization since the whole constraint $D\langle C, \texttt{Eq}\ \alpha\rangle$ will be copied to the result type schema. However, since C doesn't constrain α, it shouldn't be moved to the type schema. We can achieve a better result by first applying the WEAKEN rule and then using rule C9 from Figure 2. As a result, we first obtain the following judgment.

$$D\langle C, true\rangle \wedge D\langle true, \texttt{Eq}\ \alpha\rangle; \Gamma \vdash \texttt{elem x} : [\alpha] \rightarrow \texttt{bool}/\varnothing$$

When we now apply the rule GEN, we obtain the following judgement instead, which preserves the meaning: When the first alternative of the constraint is selected, the type variable α is not constrained and can be instantiated with any type.

$$D\langle C, true\rangle \wedge \exists\alpha.D\langle true, \texttt{Eq}\ \alpha\rangle; \Gamma \vdash$$
$$\texttt{elem x} : \forall\alpha[D\langle true, \texttt{Eq}\ \alpha\rangle].\alpha \rightarrow \texttt{bool}/\varnothing$$

4.3 Typing Extensions

To encode a specific analysis, the entailment $\Vdash$ relation among constraints may be extended, which includes an extension of $\equiv$ and $\leq$ as well. Moreover, two components of the typing rules have to be instantiated: the subsumption relation $\preceq$ and the constraint relation $\mathscr{R}$ between annotations that is used in the syntax-directed typing rules. $\mathscr{R}$ consists of four constraint relationships R_x, R_λ, R_{Let}, and R_{App}. Finally, types for extended expression constants have to be provided through the initial environment Γ_0.

For 0CFA, no extension for $\Vdash$, $\equiv$ and $\leq$ is needed. Also, the subsumption relation is interpreted as the type equivalence relation $\equiv$. For $\mathscr{R}$, we get $R_x\ \varphi_1\ \varphi_2 = R_{App}\ \varphi_1\ \varphi_2\ \varphi_3\ \varphi_4 = R_{Let}\ \varphi_1\ \varphi_2\ \varphi_3 = true$, which says that for these cases the constraint always holds. For the ABS rule we have $R_\lambda\ l\ \varphi_1\ \varphi_2\ \varphi_3 = \{l\} \leq \varphi_2$, which records each abstraction in its resulting function type.

As an example, consider again the expression e shown in Section 1.1. We first rewrite it as $e = (e_1\ D\langle e_2, e_3\rangle)\ e_4$. Based on the typing rules in Figure 3, we can conduct a 0CFA for e. We use the following constraint C.

$$C = \alpha_2 \equiv \alpha \xrightarrow{\{4\}} \alpha \wedge \alpha_3 \equiv \alpha_1 \xrightarrow{\{6\}} \alpha_1 \wedge \alpha_4 \equiv D\langle \alpha_2, \alpha_3\rangle$$

With C the following judgments are derivable.

$$C; \Gamma \vdash e_1 : (\alpha_2 \xrightarrow{D\langle\{3\},\{5\}\rangle} \alpha_4) \xrightarrow{\{1\}} \alpha_2 \xrightarrow{\{2\}} \alpha_4/\varnothing$$
$$C; \Gamma \vdash D\langle e_2, e_3\rangle : \alpha_2 \xrightarrow{D\langle\{3\},\{5\}\rangle} \alpha_4/\varnothing$$
$$C; \Gamma \vdash e_4 : \alpha_2/\varnothing$$

Now we can apply rule APP twice and obtain the judgment $C; \Gamma \vdash e : \alpha_4/\varnothing$. Based on the annotations for α_4, the result of 0CFA for e is $D\langle\{4\},\{6\}\rangle$, which is the same result we obtained in Section 1.1.

As another example consider instantiating VHM(X) for type inference of lambda calculus with let polymorphism. There is no extension needed here for $\equiv$, $\leq$ and $\Vdash$. We let $\preceq$ be type equality, which means that no extension is needed for $\preceq$. Moreover, since type inference doesn't involve the handling of annotations, we can define each constraint in $\mathscr{R}$ to be *true*.

For the exception analysis, we have to extend the type system as follows. First, for each exception type EX_i, the relation $\Vdash Ex\ EX_i$ is added to convey the fact that EX_i is an exception type. No extensions are needed for $\leq$ and $\equiv$. Next, each constraint that appears in the typing rules (Figure 3) has to be instantiated as follows [28] (we use $\varphi_1 =_\varphi \varphi_2$ to denote $\varphi_1 \leq \varphi_2 \wedge \varphi_2 \leq \varphi_1$).

$$R_x\ \varphi_1\ \varphi_2 = \varphi_2 =_\varphi \varnothing$$
$$R_\lambda\ l\ \varphi_1\ \varphi_2\ \varphi_3 = \varphi_2 =_\varphi \varphi_1 \wedge \varphi_3 =_\varphi \varnothing$$
$$R_{App}\ \varphi_1\ \varphi_2\ \varphi_3\ \varphi_4 = \varphi_4 =_\varphi \varphi_1 \cup \varphi_2 \cup \varphi_3$$
$$R_{Let}\ \varphi_1\ \varphi_2\ \varphi_3 = \varphi_3 =_\varphi \varphi_1 \cup \varphi_2$$

No extension for $\preceq$ is required. The initial type environment should be as follows.

$$\begin{aligned}\Gamma_0 = \{&(ex_i, EX_i),\\ &(\texttt{raise}, \forall\alpha_1\alpha_2[Ex\ \alpha_1].\alpha_1 \xrightarrow{\{\alpha_1\}} \alpha_2),\\ &(\texttt{handle}, \forall\alpha_1\alpha_2\beta_1\beta_2\beta_3[Ex\ \alpha_1 \wedge \beta_3 = \beta_2\backslash\{\alpha_1\}].\\ &\quad \alpha_1 \rightarrow \alpha_2^{\beta_1} \xrightarrow{\beta_1} \alpha_2^{\beta_2} \xrightarrow{\beta_3} \alpha_2)\}\end{aligned}$$

4.4 Properties

The most important property of VHM(X) is its correctness, that is, by running a lifted analysis on a program family we obtain a synchronized family of analysis results such that the original analysis would yield for any particular program, obtained through a selection with a decision δ, the same result that is obtained from the result family also by selection with δ.

The first step in establishing this result is to show that selection preserves the typing relation provided that the entailment relation is preserved over selection when the instantiated $\mathscr{R}$ constraints are involved. For example, if $C \Vdash R_\lambda\ l\ \varphi_1\ \varphi_2\ \varphi_3$, then $\lfloor C\rfloor_s \Vdash \lfloor R_\lambda\ l\ \varphi_1\ \varphi_2\ \varphi_3\rfloor_s$ must hold. Moreover, we require that for each type constructor T, the relation $\Vdash \lfloor T^\varphi\ \overline{\phi}\rfloor_s \equiv T^{\lfloor\varphi\rfloor_s}\ \overline{\lfloor\phi\rfloor_s}$ holds.

LEMMA 1. *If* $C; \Gamma \vdash e : \sigma/\varphi$, *then* $\lfloor C\rfloor_s; \lfloor\Gamma\rfloor_s \vdash \lfloor e\rfloor_s : \lfloor\sigma\rfloor_s/\lfloor\varphi\rfloor_s$.

PROOF The proof is by an induction over the typing derivation. Note that for each typing rule in Figure 3, the typing relation is preserved over selection.

We show one proof case for the CHOICE rule, which is established by induction over the structure of s. We show the case $s = D.1$. (The case for $s = D.2$ is analogous, and the case when s is neither $D.1$ nor $D.2$ follows by induction from the definition of selection defined in Section 2.)

Given $C_1; \Gamma \vdash e_1 : \tau_1/\varphi_1$ and $C_2; \Gamma \vdash e_2 : \tau_2/\varphi_2$, the induction hypotheses are that

$$\lfloor C_1\rfloor_{D.1}; \lfloor\Gamma\rfloor_{D.1} \vdash \lfloor e_1\rfloor_{D.1} : \lfloor\tau_1\rfloor_{D.1}/\lfloor\varphi_1\rfloor_{D.1} \quad (1)$$

and $\lfloor C_2\rfloor_{D.1}; \lfloor\Gamma\rfloor_{D.1} \vdash \lfloor e_2\rfloor_{D.1} : \lfloor\tau_2\rfloor_{D.1}/\lfloor\varphi_2\rfloor_{D.1}$. We have to show $\lfloor D\langle C_1, C_2\rangle\rfloor_{D.1}; \lfloor\Gamma\rfloor_{D.1} \vdash \lfloor D\langle e_1, e_2\rangle\rfloor_{D.1} : \lfloor\tau\rfloor_{D.1}/\lfloor D\langle\varphi_1, \varphi_2\rangle\rfloor_{D.1}$, which, by definition of selection, can be simplified to the following.

$$\lfloor C_1\rfloor_{D.1}; \lfloor\Gamma\rfloor_{D.1} \vdash \lfloor e_1\rfloor_{D.1} : \lfloor\tau\rfloor_{D.1}/\lfloor\varphi_1\rfloor_{D.1} \quad (2)$$

The additional hypothesis $D\langle C_1, C_2\rangle \Vdash D\langle\tau_1, \tau_2\rangle \equiv \tau$, together with Lemma 2, gives us that $\lfloor D\langle C_1, C_2\rangle\rfloor_{D.1} \Vdash \lfloor D\langle\tau_1, \tau_2\rangle \equiv \tau\rfloor_{D.1}$, which can be simplified to

$$\lfloor C_1\rfloor_{D.1} \Vdash \lfloor\tau_1\rfloor_{D.1} \equiv \lfloor\tau\rfloor_{D.1} \quad (3)$$

The result (2) we want to prove follows from (1) and (3). □

LEMMA 2. *If* $C_1 \Vdash C_2$, *then* $\lfloor C_1\rfloor_s \Vdash \lfloor C_2\rfloor_s$.

$$\text{I-VAR}\ \frac{\Gamma(x) = \forall\overline{\alpha}\overline{\beta}[C].\tau^{\varphi_1} \qquad \alpha_1 \text{ new} \qquad \beta_1 \text{ new}}{\exists\overline{\alpha}\overline{\beta}.(C \wedge R_x\ \varphi_1\ \beta_1 \wedge \alpha_1 \equiv \tau^{\varphi_1});\Gamma \vdash_I x : \alpha_1/\beta_1}$$

$$\text{I-ABS}\ \frac{C;\Gamma,(x,\alpha_1) \vdash_I e : \alpha_2/\beta_1 \qquad \alpha_3 \text{ new} \qquad \beta_2,\beta_3 \text{ new}}{\exists\alpha_1\alpha_2\beta_1.(C \wedge R_\lambda\ l\ \beta_1\ \beta_2\ \beta_3 \wedge \alpha_3 \equiv \alpha_1 \xrightarrow{\beta_2} \alpha_2);\Gamma \vdash_I \lambda^l x.e : \alpha_3/\beta_3}$$

$$\text{I-APP}\ \frac{C_1;\Gamma \vdash_I e_1 : \alpha_1/\beta_1 \qquad C_2;\Gamma \vdash_I e_2 : \alpha_2/\beta_2 \qquad \alpha_3 \text{ new} \qquad \beta_3,\beta_4 \text{ new}}{\exists\alpha_1\alpha_2\beta_1\beta_2.(C_1 \wedge C_2 \wedge R_{App}\ \beta_1\ \beta_2\ \beta_3\ \beta_4 \wedge \alpha_1 \preceq \alpha_2 \xrightarrow{\beta_3} \alpha_3);\Gamma \vdash_I e_1\ e_2 : \alpha_3/\beta_4}$$

$$\text{I-LET}\ \frac{C_1;\Gamma \vdash_I e : \alpha/\beta \qquad C_2;\Gamma,(x,\forall\alpha\beta[C_1].\alpha) \vdash_I e' : \alpha_1/\beta_1 \qquad \beta_2 \text{ new}}{(\exists\alpha\beta\beta_1.(C_1 \wedge R_{Let}\ \beta\ \beta_1\ \beta_2)) \wedge C_2;\Gamma \vdash_I \textbf{let}\ x = e\ \textbf{in}\ e' : \alpha_1/\beta_2}$$

$$\text{I-EQU}\ \frac{C_1;\Gamma \vdash_I e : \alpha/\beta \qquad C_1 \Vdash C_2 \qquad C_2 \Vdash C_1}{C_2;\Gamma \vdash_I e : \alpha/\beta}$$

$$\text{I-CHC}\ \frac{C_1;\Gamma \vdash_I e_1 : \alpha_1/\beta_1 \qquad C_2;\Gamma \vdash_I e_2 : \alpha_2/\beta_2 \qquad \alpha_3 \text{ new} \qquad \beta_3 \text{ new}}{\exists\alpha_1\alpha_2\beta_1\beta_2.(D\langle C_1,C_2\rangle \wedge D\langle\alpha_1,\alpha_2\rangle \equiv \alpha_3 \wedge \beta_3 = D\langle\beta_1,\beta_2\rangle);\Gamma \vdash_I D\langle e_1,e_2\rangle : \alpha_3/\beta_3}$$

Figure 4. Type inference for VHM(X)

PROOF By induction over the structure of C. □

Note that the reverse of Lemma 1 also holds. In expressing this result we use the notation $\Gamma_1 \uplus_D \Gamma_2$ to denote an environment Γ_3, for which $\lfloor\Gamma_3(x)\rfloor_{D.1} = \Gamma_1(x)$ and $\lfloor\Gamma_3(x)\rfloor_{D.2} = \Gamma_2(x)$ (for any variable x).

LEMMA 3. *If* $C_1;\Gamma_1 \vdash e_1 : \sigma_1/\varphi_1$ *and* $C_2;\Gamma_2 \vdash e_2 : \sigma_2/\varphi_2$, *then* $D\langle C_1,C_2\rangle;\Gamma_1 \uplus_D \Gamma_2 \vdash D\langle e_1,e_2\rangle : \sigma_3/D\langle\varphi_1,\varphi_2\rangle$ *is derivable and* $\lfloor\sigma_3\rfloor_{D.1} = \sigma_1$ *and* $\lfloor\sigma_3\rfloor_{D.2} = \sigma_2$.

PROOF Proof by contradiction with the help of Lemma 1. □

Based on Lemma 1, we can now state the following projection theorem. Any analysis for a plain program (that was selected from a program family) can be obtained from the corresponding family of results produced by the lifted analysis for the program family. We use δ to range over *complete* decisions, which are sets of selectors that eliminate all the choices in C, Γ, σ and φ.

THEOREM 1 (Projection). *Given* $C;\Gamma \vdash e : \sigma/\varphi$, *then* $\forall(\delta,e') \in [\![e]\!]$, $\lfloor C\rfloor_\delta;\lfloor\Gamma\rfloor_\delta \vdash e' : \sigma'/\varphi'$, *where* $\sigma' = [\![\sigma']\!](\delta)$ *and* $\varphi' = [\![\varphi]\!](\delta)$.

PROOF The proof is based on an induction over the structures of C, Γ, σ and φ, with the help of Lemma 1. □

Finally, we observe that, disregarding annotations, VHM(X) and HM(X) compute the same result in the absence of choices. Using $\vdash^{HM}$ to denote the typing relation of HM(X) [40], we have the following result.

LEMMA 4. *Given* C, Γ *and* e *plain, if* $C;\Gamma \vdash e : \sigma/\varphi$, *then* $C;\Gamma \vdash^{HM} e : \sigma'$, *where* σ' *can be obtained by eliminating annotations from* σ.

PROOF The proof can be established through an induction over the typing derivation based on the typing rules in Figure 3 and the rules in [40]. Moreover, observe that in absence of variation constructs, the $\equiv$ relation degenerates to type equality and the subsumption relation $\preceq$ introduced in Section 4.2 degenerates to the same subsumption relation as in [40]. □

5. Parametric Type Inference

In the specification of type-based analysis, constraints C serve as an input. However, in implementing the analysis, we need to dynamically generate and solve constraints. In this section, we discuss constraint generation; constraint solving will follow in Section 6.

In Figure 4 we present the inference rules for the judgment $C;\Gamma \vdash_I e : \alpha/\beta$, where Γ and e are the input and C, α, and β are the output. The presentation is an adaptation and extension of the type inference rules for HM(X) [40] to accommodate the handling of annotations and choices and uses the parametric constraints $\mathscr{R}$ introduced in Section 4.2.

The inference rules are derived from the corresponding typing rules (Figure 3) by moving the constraints in the premise to the left-hand side of the judgment in the conclusion. The rules gather constraints from subexpressions and add them to those of their parents to ensure correctness, that is, no conditions will be ignored. The minimality of constraints and thus the genrality of the inferred result follow from the fact that each rule only integrates constraints that are required for the particular construct under consideration.

For example, in I-VAR, the conclusion can be read as "when the constraint C is satisfied, x can have any type". Note that τ^{φ_1} may contain reference to $\overline{\alpha}\overline{\beta}$, which is why the constraint $\alpha_1 \equiv \tau^{\beta_1}$ appears inside the quantification $\exists\overline{\alpha}\overline{\beta}$. To consider another example, in rule I-APP the constraints from subexpressions, C_1 and C_2, the constraint for annotations $R_{App}\ \beta_1\ \beta_2\ \beta_3\ \beta_4$, and the constraint between the types of e_1, e_2, and the result type of the application $e_1\ e_2$, are simply collected in the constraint of the conclusion. The rules follow a similar pattern as the typing rules in Figure 3.

Note that there is only one non-syntax directed rule, I-EQU, which can be applied any time. The purpose of this rule is to keep the size of the constraint as small as possible by employing the relationships defined in Figure 2.

Given the inference rules in Figure 4, we can generate the following constraint C_1 for the expression $e_1 = \lambda^1 h.\lambda^2 x.h\ x$, which is a part of the expression e introduced in Section 1.1. The expression e_1 then has the type α_7 under the constraint C_1.

$$\begin{aligned} C_1 = &\exists\alpha_1\alpha_2\alpha_3\alpha_4\alpha_5\alpha_6(\alpha_1 \equiv \alpha_3 \wedge \alpha_2 \equiv \alpha_4 \wedge \alpha_3 \equiv \alpha_4 \xrightarrow{\beta_1} \alpha_5 \wedge \\ &\{2\} \le \beta_2 \wedge \alpha_6 \equiv \alpha_2 \xrightarrow{\beta_2} \alpha_5 \wedge \{1\} \le \beta_3 \wedge \alpha_7 \equiv \alpha_1 \xrightarrow{\beta_3} \alpha_6) \end{aligned}$$

The constraints for other parts of the expression e can be generated similarly and are omitted here.

We now investigate the relation between type inference rules in Figure 4 and specification rules defined in 3. First, type inference is sound, as stated in the following theorem.

THEOREM 2. *If* $C;\Gamma \vdash_I e : \alpha/\beta$, *then* $C;\Gamma \vdash e : \alpha/\beta$.

PROOF The proof is based on an induction over the structure of the expression e. □

Also, type inference is complete and principal and least constrained in the sense that the constraint generated by the relation $\vdash_I$ is minimal while satisfying the typing judgment discussed in Sec-

$\mathcal{V} : C \times \theta \to C \times \theta$

(a) $\mathcal{V}(\exists\alpha\beta.C,\theta) = (C_1, \theta_1 \backslash \{\alpha,\beta\})$ when $\{\alpha,\beta\}\ \#\ vars(\theta)$
where $(C_1,\theta_1) = \mathcal{V}(C,\theta)$

(b) $\mathcal{V}(D\langle C_1,C_2\rangle,\theta) = (D\langle C_3,C_4\rangle, \theta_3 \sqcup_D \theta_4)$
where $(C_3,\theta_3) = \mathcal{V}(C_1,\theta)$
$(C_4,\theta_4) = \mathcal{V}(C_2,\theta)$

(c) $\mathcal{V}(D\langle C,C\rangle,\theta) = \mathcal{V}(C,\theta)$

(d) $\mathcal{V}(C_1 \wedge C_2,\theta) = (C_3 \wedge C_4, \theta_4)$ when C_1 or C_2 not plain
where $(C_3,\theta_3) = \mathcal{V}(C_1,\theta)$
$(C_4,\theta_4) = \mathcal{V}(\theta_3(C_2),\theta_3)$

(e) $\mathcal{V}(D\langle\phi_1,\phi_2\rangle \equiv D\langle\phi_3,\phi_4\rangle,\theta) = \mathcal{V}(D\langle\phi_1 \equiv \phi_3, \phi_2 \equiv \phi_4\rangle,\theta)$

(f) $\mathcal{V}^{\star}(D\langle\phi_1,\phi_2\rangle \equiv \phi_3,\theta) = \mathcal{V}(D\langle\phi_1 \equiv \phi_3, \phi_2 \equiv \phi_3\rangle,\theta)$

(g) $\mathcal{V}^{\star}(\alpha \equiv \phi,\theta) = (true, \{(\alpha,\phi)\} \circ \theta)$ when $\alpha \notin FV(\phi)$

(h) $\mathcal{V}(\phi_1 \equiv \phi_2,\theta) =$ when $D \in dims(\phi_1,\phi_2)$
$\mathcal{V}(D\langle\lfloor\phi_1\rfloor_{D.1} \equiv \lfloor\phi_2\rfloor_{D.1}, \lfloor\phi_1\rfloor_{D.2} \equiv \lfloor\phi_2\rfloor_{D.2}\rangle,\theta)$

(i) $\mathcal{V}(\phi_1 \equiv \phi_2,\theta) = \mathcal{U}(\phi_1 \equiv \phi_2,\theta)$ when ϕ_1 and ϕ_2 plain

(j) $\mathcal{V}(P,\theta) = \mathcal{U}(P,\theta)$ when P analysis specific

Figure 5. Variational constraint solving

tion 4.2. We express this result in the following theorem, where we extend the definition of $\preceq$ to type schemas in the theorem, following a standard definition in [29].

THEOREM 3. *Given* $C;\Gamma \vdash e : \sigma/\varphi$, *then* $C';\Gamma \vdash_I e : \alpha/\beta$ *such that* $C \Vdash \exists\alpha\beta.C'$, $C \Vdash \forall\alpha\beta[C'].\alpha \preceq \sigma$ *and* $C \Vdash \beta \leq \varphi$.

PROOF The proof is based on an induction of the derivation tree of $C;\Gamma \vdash e : \sigma/\varphi$. □

6. Variational Constraint Solving

To compute an analysis result, we need to solve the constraints generated in the type inference phase. Since different analyses will introduce quite different constraints, there will be no single constraint solving algorithm that solves all generated constraints. Therefore, our algorithm will defer to an application-specific solver $\mathcal{U}$ to handle constraints that are specific to a particular analysis. $\mathcal{U}$ has to be provided by the implementor of the static analysis, but there is potential for the reuse of one solver for different analyses.

6.1 A Constraint Solving Algorithm

We say a constraint is *primitive* if it doesn't contain choices or existential quantification. In this section, we will use P to range over primitive constraints.

We assume that $\mathcal{U}$ can be applied to a given set of constraints C_1 and a given substitution θ_1 and returns a residual constraint C_2 together with substitution θ_2. We require that $\theta_2(C_2) = C_2$ and $C_2 \Vdash \theta_2(C_1)$. Note that constraint solving also involves the manipulation of mappings from β to φ. These can be treated like substitutions and are thus stored in θ as well.

Based on $\mathcal{U}$, we build a variational constraint solving algorithm $\mathcal{V}$, shown in Figure 5, which solves the core constraints defined in Figure 1. The signature of $\mathcal{V}$ is the same as that for $\mathcal{U}$. In the following we will briefly discuss the different cases. When none of the cases and conditions apply, the constraint solver fails, which indicates that the analysis for the particular program family cannot produce a result. It would be nice if VHM(X) could produce partial results in the presence of unsolvable constraints for some program variants. We can envision a corresponding extension following the approach presented in [9].

Case (a) deals with existential constraints $\exists\alpha\beta.C$, which can be solved by solving C and then removing the mappings for α and β from the result substitution (indicated in Figure 5 by using the notation $\theta_1 \backslash \{\alpha,\beta\}$). The condition $\{\alpha,\beta\}\ \#\ vars(\theta)$ ensures that the mappings for α and β will not be removed in θ, where $vars(\theta)$ compute the domain of θ and all free variables in θ. Thus, to make this rule applicable, we may have to first rename the bound variables α and β. Note that when C is unsatisfiable, then so is $\exists\alpha\beta.C$. Note also that our rule to solve existential constraints is simpler than the one given in [40] because our constraints are only based on boolean algebra and not cylindric algebra.

Case (b) shows that solving a variational constraints $D\langle C_1,C_2\rangle$ requires solving each alternative. The potentially different residual constraints are then combined again in a choice. The potentially differing substitutions are combined with the operation $\sqcup$, which is defined as follows.

$$\theta_1 \sqcup_D \theta_2(\alpha) = \begin{cases} D\langle\theta_1(\alpha),\theta_2(\alpha)\rangle & \alpha \in dom(\theta_1) \wedge \alpha \in dom(\theta_2) \\ D\langle\theta_1(\alpha),\alpha_1\rangle & \alpha \in dom(\theta_1) \wedge \alpha_1 \text{ fresh} \\ D\langle\alpha_1,\theta_2(\alpha)\rangle & \alpha \in dom(\theta_2) \wedge \alpha_1 \text{ fresh} \\ \alpha & \text{otherwise} \end{cases}$$

The reason for generating fresh type variables is to reflect the fact that an alternative of a choice might not have been constrained. For example, when $\alpha \notin dom(\theta_2)$, the second alternative will be replaced with a fresh type variable, which allows the second alternative to have any type.

Case (c) allows us to save work when constraints of two alternatives of a choice are the same, and case (d) deals with constraints of the form $C_1 \wedge C_2$, where either C_1 or C_2 is not plain. (Otherwise, the constraints should be dealt with by $\mathcal{U}$.) A conjunction is solved in sequence by threading updated substitutions.

The next group of cases (e) through (i) deals with type equivalence constraints of the form $\phi_1 \equiv \phi_2$. Case (e) handles choices in the same dimension, which reduces to solving the equivalence constraint between the corresponding alternatives. In case (f) one side is a choice while the other side is not (or a choice in a different dimension). In these cases, both alternatives of D are required to be equivalent with the type on the other side. The $\star$ attached to $\mathcal{V}$ in this case (and the next) indicates that there is a dual case that can be handled correspondingly, where the two arguments to $\equiv$ are swapped. Rule (g) deals with the case that one side is a type variable α, which succeeds by extending the substitution.

The situation becomes a little more complicated when the two types are of different form and contain choices, which is addressed by the rule (h). The general idea is to eliminate choices in the types so that they become simpler, which may lead to other rules being applicable. We achieve this by making selections into the types and and create a choice constraint. (The function *dims* determines the set of dimension names contained in types and expressions.)

A potentially more efficient strategy is to inspect the structures of the types and take the appropriate actions. For example, if the constraint is of the form $T^{\varphi_1}\ \overline{\phi_1} \equiv T^{\varphi_2}\ \overline{\phi_2}$, we can instead solve the constraints $\varphi_1 = \varphi_2 \wedge \overline{\phi_1 \equiv \phi_2}$. However, this works only when the constructor T forms a free algebra, that is, has no associated equational theory; it fails, for example, when T is commutative.

For unifying two plain types, we dispatch the task to the underlying solver $\mathcal{U}$, as expressed in rule (i). Solving the constraints between two annotations of the form $\varphi_1 \leq \varphi_2$ is similar to solving the type equivalence constraint and will not be repeated here.

Finally, when a constraint is domain specific, it is solved by the underlying solver $\mathcal{U}$, as shown in case (j).

With the constraint solving algorithm, we derive the following solution θ_1 for the constraint C_1 generated in Section 5.

$$\theta_1 = \{\alpha_7 \mapsto (\alpha_4 \xrightarrow{\beta_1} \alpha_5) \xrightarrow{\{1\}} \alpha_4 \xrightarrow{\{2\}} \alpha_5, \beta_2 \mapsto \{2\}, \beta_3 \mapsto \{1\}\}$$

Note that $\theta_1(\alpha_7)$ is also the inferred type for the expression e_1 ($\lambda^1 h.\lambda^2 x.h\ x$). With a little extra work, we can generate and solve constraints for the other parts of the expression e (introduced in Section 1.1) and verify that the inference result is the same as the result presented in Section 4.3 for e.

6.2 Relation to Variational Unification

Even though the variational constraint solving algorithm presented in Figure 5 is more general than the variational unification algorithm developed in [10], it is also simpler. We will use the following example to illustrate the differences. Note that in [10] we use the notation $\equiv^?$, instead of $\equiv$, to denote a unification problem.

$$A\langle \texttt{Int}, \alpha \rangle \equiv A\langle \alpha, \texttt{Bool} \rangle$$

The variational unification algorithm presented in [10] consists of three steps:

(a) qualify the unification problem by attaching to each type variable a path of selectors for enclosing choices,

(b) solve the qualified unification problem with a unifier for the qualified problem, and

(c) complete the unifier obtained in step (b) to a unifier for the original unification problem.

In the given example, we get for step (a) the following unification problem.

$$A\langle \texttt{Int}, \alpha_{A.2} \rangle \equiv A\langle \alpha_{A.1}, \texttt{Bool} \rangle$$

We then obtain the following qualified unifier for step (b).

$$\{\alpha_{A.1} \mapsto \texttt{Int}, \alpha_{A.2} \mapsto \texttt{Bool}\}$$

Finally, step (c) yields the completed unifier $\{\alpha \mapsto A\langle \texttt{Int}, \texttt{Bool} \rangle\}$. The decomposition of the algorithm into three steps poses a big challenge to both the implementation and the correctness proof of the algorithm.

Our constraint solving algorithm in Figure 5 simplifies the previous algorithm through the use of *context splitting* (cases (e) and (f)) and *context merging* (through the operation $\theta_1 \sqcup_D \theta_2$). Following this idea, we derive for the problem $\texttt{Int} \equiv \alpha$ the solution $\theta_3 = \{\alpha \mapsto \texttt{Int}\}$ in the context of the first alternative of A and $\theta_4 = \{\alpha \mapsto \texttt{Bool}\}$ in the context of the second alternative of A. The operation $\theta_3 \sqcup_D \theta_4$ produces the expected solution $\{\alpha \mapsto A\langle \texttt{Int}, \texttt{Bool} \rangle\}$.

The constraint solving algorithm in Figure 5 has the time complexity $O(mn)$ when it is instantiated with Robinson's unification algorithm, where m and n are the size of the left and right constraint, respectively. This is the same as the time complexity of step (b) of the previous variational unification algorithm. The implementation of the new algorithm, however, is much simpler. Moreover, proving the properties of the algorithm is also easier. We'll do this next.

6.3 Properties

The solver $\mathscr{V}$ inherits desirable properties of $\mathscr{U}$. For example, $\mathscr{V}$ is sound and principal provided that $\mathscr{U}$ is. We say (C_1, θ_1) is principal for (C, θ) if $C_1 \Vdash \theta_1(C)$ and for any other (C_2, θ_2) such that $C_2 \Vdash \theta_2(C)$ implies $\theta_1 \sqsubseteq \theta_2$ and $C_2 \Vdash \theta_2(C_1)$. Here $\theta_1 \sqsubseteq \theta_2$ holds if there is some θ_3 such that $\theta_2 = \theta_3 \circ \theta_1$. The definition is similar for the case of primitive constraints.

THEOREM 4 (Soundness of $\mathscr{V}$).
If $(P', \theta'_p) = \mathscr{U}(P, \theta_p)$ *implies* $P' \Vdash \theta'_p(P)$ *and* $\theta'_p(P') = P'$, *then* $(C', \theta') = \mathscr{V}(C, \theta)$ *implies* $C' \Vdash \theta'(C)$ *and* $\theta'(C') = C'$.

THEOREM 5 (Principality of $\mathscr{V}$).
If $(P', \theta'_p) = \mathscr{U}(P, \theta_p)$ *implies* (P', θ'_p) *is principal for* (P, θ_p), *then* $(C', \theta') = \mathscr{V}(C, \theta)$ *implies* (C', θ') *is principal for* (C, θ).

PROOF The proof for both theorems is based on the induction over the structures of constraints C. □

Thus the solver $\mathscr{V}$ has the same capability as $\mathscr{U}$. For example, if $\mathscr{U}$ is the Robinson unification algorithm, then $\mathscr{V}$ is a variational unification algorithm as developed in [10]. If $\mathscr{U}$ is the $\mathscr{U}_{\text{CFA}}$ algorithm [28] for 0CFA analysis, then $\mathscr{V}$ is the solver for variational 0CFA analysis.

We conjecture that $\mathscr{V}$ and $\mathscr{U}$ are in the same complexity class. For example, when $\mathscr{U}$ is decidable, then so is $\mathscr{V}$. Also, when $\mathscr{U}$ is semi-decidable, then so is $\mathscr{V}$. We leave this for future work.

```
-- Module F1                              -- Module F2
class A extends Object {                  class A extends Object {
    D mc(Object a) {                          F mc(Object a) {
        return new D() ;                          return new F() ;
    }                                         }
    C ma(C e) {                               E ma(E e) {
        return new C() ;                          return new E() ;
    }                                         }
}                                         }

class C extends Object {}                 class E extends Object {}
class D extends C {}                      class F extends E {}

-- Module F3, which requires exactly either F1 or F2
Object test2 = (new A()).ma ((new A()).mc(new Object())) ;


-- Output of FFJPL
*** Exception: Type error: Method invocation:
new A().ma(new A().mc(new Object())) is not well-formed!


-- Output of VHMX(X)
The SPL is well typed.
```

Figure 6. Discrepancy between FFJPL and VHM(X).

7. Evaluation

Does our framework make true on its promise to increase the accuracy of analysis lifting under an acceptable amount of overhead? We address this question in the following two subsections.

7.1 Reliability of Analysis Lifting

To evaluate the accuracy of VHM(X), we could compare its output with our previously developed variational type inference. However, it might be more informative if the evaluation is conducted by comparing VHM(X) with tools developed by other researchers. Since most variability-aware analyses have been done for imperative languages, we have choosen the FFJPL (Feature Featherweight Java Product Lines) system[2] developed by Apel et al. [1] as our evaluation counterpart. Another advantage of using FFJPL is that it demonstrates that our lifting framework is not tied to the specific calculus presented in this paper. Thus we have adopted our framework to Featherweight Java (FJ) and refer to this version as VFJ(X).

The idea of FFJPL is to allow each module to define new classes, extend, or refine classes defined in another module. Each FFJPL program consists of a set of modules and a feature model, which describes how modules may be combined together. To derive a particular program, decisions about which modules to select have to be made. All selected modules constitute the product.

For example, Figure 6 presents a small FFJPL program, which consists of three modules `F1`, `F2`, and `F3`. The feature model (not shown here) requires that the presence of `F3` requires exactly one of `F1` or `F2`. In both modules `F1` and `F2`, we define a class `A` with the same methods `mc` and `ma`. However, note that their signatures are different in different modules. Module `F3` contains a single statement for creating new objects. This product line contains 2 valid products, one consisting of modules `F1` and `F3`, and the other

[2] http://www.fosd.de/ffj

consisting of modules F2 and F3. It is easy to check that each product is well typed. According to the completeness theorem in [1], a product line is well typed if all valid products are well typed. Thus, the product line in Figure 6 should be well typed.

However, while our VFJ(TC) (VFJ(X) instantiated to type checking) correctly reports that the product line is well typed, FFJPL reports, incorrectly, a type error. We have not attempted to debug their type system or implementation. The important lesson here is that the general lifting framework VFJ(TC) gets it right while the hand-crafted analysis is erroneous.

Of course, this anecdotal piece of evidence does not prove the superiority of VFJ(X) or VHM(X) in general, but it is a reflection of the fact that the stratified approach that requires fewer definitions and much less implementation effort is more likely to be correct.[3]

For illustration, we present the typing rule for method invocations in both systems.

T-INVK-FFJPL

$$\frac{\Gamma \vdash t_0 : \overline{E} \dashv \Phi \qquad \forall E \in \overline{E}: validref(\Phi, E.m) \qquad \Gamma \vdash \overline{t} : \overline{\overline{G}} \dashv \Phi \qquad mtype(\Phi, m, \overline{last(E)}) = \overline{\overline{\overline{H}}} \to F \qquad \forall \overline{G} \in \overline{\overline{G}}, \forall \overline{H} \in \overline{\overline{\overline{H}}}: \overline{G} <: \overline{H}}{\Gamma \vdash t_0.m(\overline{t}) : F_{11}, \ldots, F_{n1}, \ldots, F_{1m}, \ldots, F_{nm} \vdash \Phi}$$

T-INVK-VFFJX

$$\frac{\begin{array}{c} C;\Gamma \vdash t_0 : E \dashv \Phi/\varphi_1 \\ validrefc(\Phi, E.m) \qquad C;\Gamma \vdash \overline{t} : G \dashv \Phi/\varphi_2 \\ G = G_1 \times \cdots \times G_n \qquad mtypec(\Phi, m, lastc(E)) = H \to^{\varphi_3} F \\ C \Vdash G \preceq H \dashv \Phi \qquad C \Vdash R_{Invk}\ \varphi_1\ \varphi_2\ \varphi_3\ \varphi_4 \end{array}}{C;\Gamma \vdash t_0.m(\overline{t}) : F \dashv \Phi/\varphi_4}$$

The rule T-INVK-FFJPL is a reproduction of the T-INVK$_{PL}$ rule in [1] except for renaming B, C, and D to F, G, and H, respectively, to avoid notational conflicts. The typing relation $\Gamma \vdash t : \overline{E} \dashv \Phi$ says that when feature Φ is chosen (similar to the notion about applying a selector to an expression), the expression t can have any potential mutually exclusive class type in $\overline{E}$. An expression can have more than one type because the same expression can have different types when different modules are selected.

We will not analyze each part of this rule. However, a notable difference is how types are represented. While FFJPL uses a flat list to represent a set of alternative types, VFJ(X) uses nested choice types to represent alternative types.

The bottom line is this. An important merit of the lifting framework is that the correctness of a variational analysis depends only on the easier to establish correctness of a single analysis (and its correct embedding in the framework).

7.2 Framework Runtime Overhead

We would like to know the overhead incurred by the general machineries of the lifting framework over manually lifted variational analysis algorithms. To this end, we have implemented VHM(X) and VFJ(X) (mentioned in Section 7.1) in Haskell and compared three instantiations with hand-crafted analyses.

First, we compared the FFJPL implementation with VFJ(TC) for 5 product lines (1 came with the FFJPL implementation and four others were created by us). The running time of VFJ(TC) is at most 32% slower than the FFJPL implementation.

Due to the limited number of available FFJPL product lines, we also compared the performance of VHM(X) with our own previously developed variational type inference algorithm for Variational Lambda Calculus (VLC) [10] and a manually created variational control-flow analysis algorithm.

[3] The definition of FFJPL is given in 26 rules, while the VFJ(X) extension requires only 6 rules. Moreover, the FFJPL implementation of the typing rules takes 250 LOC, while the VFJ(X) extension takes 30 LOC.

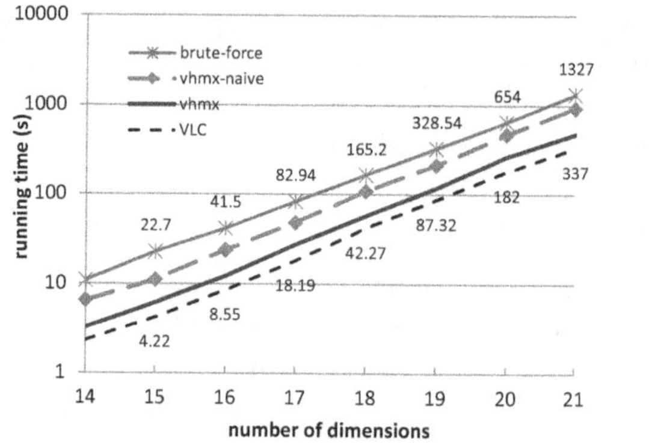

Figure 7. Efficiency comparison between VHM(X) and VLC

For the definition of VHM(TyInf), that is, VHM(X) instantiated for type inference, no extensions for $\mathscr{T}$, $\mathscr{A}$, $\mathscr{C}$ and $\preceq$ are needed; each element of $\mathscr{R}$ is set to *true*, and $\mathscr{U}$ is the Robinson unification algorithm [36]. To instantiate VHM(X) to VHM(TyInf), 9 LOC of Haskell are needed (to declare the class instance to specify $\mathscr{R}$). On the other hand, VLC has over 220 LOC of Haskell. (Here, we exclude the code for the Robinson unification algorithm that is common to both implementations.)

We show the performance for the two analyses in Figure 7. All times have been measured on a laptop with a 2.8 GHz dual core processor and 3GB memory running GHC 7.0.2 on Windows XP. We reuse the test cases from [10] that represent the worst-case performance for VLC. The X-axis denotes the number of dimensions. For these cases VLC doesn't do much better than the brute-force approach of generating and checking each variant individually. This is because there is no sharing in the expressions. For example, the expression with 21 dimensions essentially represents 2^{21} different variants by using a lot of abstractions.

The graph labeled "vhmx-naive" represents the performance of the most conservative strategy for solving type equivalence constraints using rule (h) from Figure 5. When two types are non-plain and the root of the types are not choices, the constraint is solved by splitting it into two constraints. Although this ensures correctness, it misses an opportunity for sharing. For example, given the constraint $\texttt{int} \to \texttt{bool} \equiv \texttt{int} \to D\langle \texttt{bool}, \alpha \rangle$, using (h), this will leads to two subproblems $\texttt{int} \to \texttt{bool} \equiv \texttt{int} \to \texttt{bool}$ and $\texttt{int} \to \texttt{bool} \equiv \texttt{int} \to \alpha$.

An alternative, more aggressive approach exploits the fact that two function types are equivalent if their corresponding argument and return types are equivalent. This means that we can decompose the above constraint into subproblems $\texttt{int} \equiv \texttt{int}$ and $\texttt{bool} \equiv D\langle \texttt{bool}, \alpha \rangle$, which are more efficient to solve. The graph labeled "vhmx" in Figure 7 shows the performance of an implementation of VHM(X) that employs this strategy.

We can observe that for the "vhmx" implementation the slowdown of VHM(X) over VLC is bounded by a factor of 2. This is also the case for non-worst-case expressions that offer more opportunities for sharing.

In Figure 8, we show another performance comparison between VHM(X), VLC, and the brute-force approach. The expressions used for Figure 8 are created from the expression used in Figure 7 whose number of dimensions is 21 by expanding the expressions by adding choice alternatives. Note that we only show part of the brute-force curve because the running time of it grows exponentially fast in the size of expressions, and showing its whole curve will make the difference between "vhmx" and VLC indiscernible. Again we observe that the running time of "vhmx" is within a factor of 2 of VLC, demonstrating that the price we pay for the flexibil-

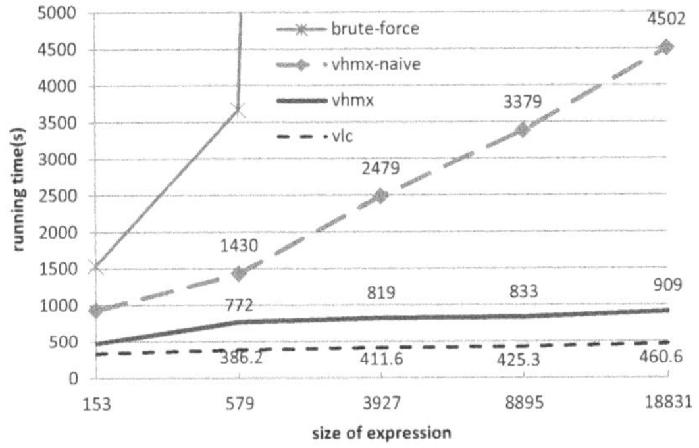

Figure 8. Efficiency comparison between VHM(X) and VLC against expression sizes.

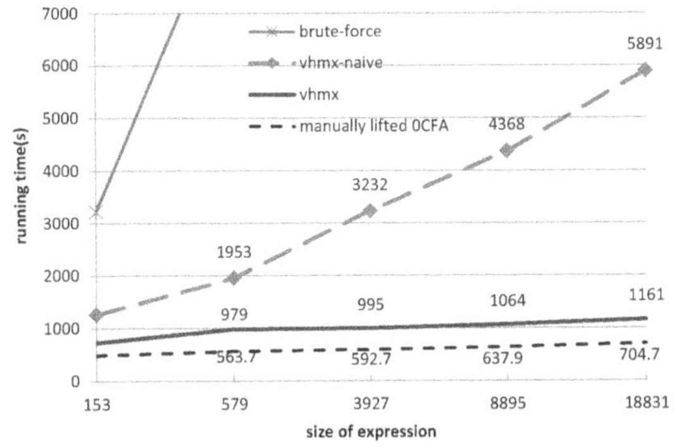

Figure 9. Efficiency comparison between VHM(X) and manually created 0CFA for variational programs

ity is acceptable. An interesting phenomenon in Figure 8 is that there is a more conspicuous discrepancy between the performance of "vhmx" and "vhmx-naive" than in Figure 7. One potential reason for this is that there are more opportunities for sharing for the expressions in Figure 8 than for those in Figure 7, and while "vhmx" takes the full advantage of these opportunities, "vhmx-naive" fails to do so.

Finally, we have also compared the performance of VHM(0CFA) and a manually lifted 0CFA. For this analysis no extension for $\mathscr{T}$, $\mathscr{A}$, $\mathscr{C}$ and $\preceq$ are needed. For $\mathscr{R}$, we only need $R_x\ l\ \varphi_1\ \varphi_2\ \varphi_3 = \{l\} \leq \varphi_2$ as discussed in Section 4.2. For $\mathscr{U}$, we use the unification algorithm presented in [28]. Again, instantiating VHM(X) for VHM(0CFA) requires 9 LOC whereas the hand-written 0CFA requires over 240 LOC in Haskell.

Figure 9 shows the running times of the brute-force approach that generates each program variant and applies 0CFA to each variant separately, VHM(0CFA) and the manually lifted 0CFA. Note that, like in Figure 8, we can't show the whole curve of the brute-force approach. To give a sense of the complexity, it takes the brute-force approach about 10 days to finish the case when the size is 18831. We observe that the slowdown of VHM(0CFA) over the manually created variational 0CFA is bounded by 1.73.

One possible reason for the smaller overhead for VHM(0CFA) compared to VHM(TyInf) is that more of the infrastructure of VHM(X) is used in 0CFA than in type inference. We conjecture that the overhead will be even lower for more complicated analyses, but we leave this question for future work to verify.

8. Related Work

The idea of this paper is inspired by the work of HM(X) [29, 40] and recent numerous efforts to verify properties of software product lines [1, 2, 5, 10–12, 14, 17, 22, 24, 25]. In this section, we compare VHM(X) with the most closely related work.

HM(X) and extensions Odersky et al. [29] formalized an extensible constraint-based type inference framework for Hindley-Milner-style type systems. Later, Sulzmann et al. [40] reformulated and improved the HM(X) framework by shifting the type descriptions from a type language to a constraint language.

We have built VHM(X) on the constraint-based HM(X) framework [40] and have extended it by adding labels to abstractions and annotations to types. The computation of annotations is expressed through relations between annotations attached to types and typing derivations, which are supplied as arguments for correspondingly parameterized syntax-directed typing rules. As a result, VHM(X) can encode more static analyses than HM(X). Second, and most importantly, we have introduced choices to all components of static analyses (types, constraints, and annotations), which allows us to lift static analyses to variational programs.

Type-based static analysis Type-based analysis, together with dataflow analysis, constraint-based analysis and abstract interpretation, are the main static analysis approaches [28].

Several type-based static analysis frameworks have been proposed. For example, the framework developed by Hankin and Métayer [20] is based on untyped lambda calculus and allows users to extend type as well as expression definitions. The biggest difference to VHM(X) is the way in which analyses are encoded. In VHM(X), we use type annotations whereas in their system this is done by interpreting types as specific sets of values (which requires users to also specify mappings from types to sets of values when encoding a static analysis). This makes it impossible to attach information to typing derivations, making the encoding of side-effect analysis and exception analysis close to impossible.

Instead of building an extensible analysis framework, Prose [34] took another approach by formalizing static analyses in a variant of System F [42]. The expressiveness of System F, together with the extensions, makes the proposed approach very expressive: some static analyses can be directly encoded without any extension needed from users. However, there are also some drawbacks. First, the problem of type checking System F is undecidable [42], which makes encoded static analyses undecidable as well. Second, the extraction of useful information is program specific and not analysis specific, that is, even for the same analysis different information has to be supplied to derive the analysis results for different programs. For example, to find dead expressions in a program, users first have to find the substitution such that the most general derivation tree for the program is preserved, which is not a simple task. Finally, with the limitation to two universes $\perp$ and $\top$, some static analyses are hard to embed. For example, it is not clear how to formalize effect and exception analysis.

The most important difference between VHM(X) and other frameworks is that instead of encoding analyses for single programs, VHM(X) lifts static analyses to program families.

Analyses for program families The software product line community has developed numerous variability-aware static analysis approaches (see citations above). A crucial difference to VHM(X) is that VHM(X) is a generic framework that can be instantiated to different analyses.

The main idea of variability-aware analysis is to take special actions when encountering variation constructs so that a whole program family can be checked directly. Liebig et al. [25] discussed that the principle for variability-aware analysis is to keep variability local and follow the ideas of late splitting and early joining. For example, when typing the expression `id` $D\langle$`succ,odd`$\rangle$ `3`, late splitting means we shouldn't separate the typing before we encounter the choice $D\langle$`succ,odd`$\rangle$. Thus, `id` should only be type checked once. Similarly, early joining ensures `3` is also only checked once. In [10] we have identified that *sharing* and *reduction* are the main factors for improving performance in variational type inference. Sharing corresponds to the principle of keeping variability local. Reduction means to replace a choice whose alternatives have the same type with either alternative. In this paper, we have exploited the idea of sharing and reduction to make VHM(X) efficient.

Bodden [3] has described the automatic lifting of static analyses to variational programs. His approach applies to dataflow analyses that are based on the IFDS framework [35]. However, a formal relation between the lifted analyses and the original analyses is not given. In contrast, analyses that are lifted within the VHM(X) framework provably retain their correctness for program families.

Choice types The concept of named choices was introduced in [18] as a basis for a unified and principled representation for software variations. This choice representation has facilitated a method for variational type inference [9, 10]. The idea of choice types was also adopted by Kästner et al. [24] to implement an efficient type checker for C programs with compilation macros and by Liebig et al. [25, 26] for implementing scalable type checking and dataflow analysis. Recently, we have successfully employed choice types for providing better feedback when type inference fails [7, 8].

9. Conclusions

Observing a growing need for static analyses for program families, we have developed the framework VHM(X) that supports the automatic generation of such analyses from single-program analyses. The two major advantages of our approach are the ability to reuse much of the computation infrastructure for new analyses and a correctness assurance (lifted analyses work correctly if the original analyses do). The presented framework helps to separate the concerns of static analysis and program variability, that is, any new program analysis can first be developed for the single-program case and then automatically lifted to work on program families.

Acknowledgments

This work is supported by the National Science Foundation under the grants CCF-1219165 and IIS-1314384.

References

[1] S. Apel, C. Kästner, A. Größlinger, and C. Lengauer. Type Safety for Feature-Oriented Product Lines. *Automated Software Engineering*, 17(3):251–300, 2010.

[2] S. Apel, A. von Rhein, P. Wendler, A. Größlinger, and D. Beyer. Strategies for Product-Line Verification: Case Studies and Experiments. In *IEEE Int. Conf. on Software Engineering*, pages 482–491, 2013.

[3] E. Bodden, T. Tolêdo, M. Ribeiro, C. Brabrand, P. Borba, and M. Mezini. SPLLIFT: Statically Analyzing Software Product Lines in Minutes Instead of Years. In *ACM SIGPLAN Conf. on Programming Language Design and Implementation*, pages 355–364, 2013.

[4] C. Brabrand, M. Ribeiro, T. Toldo, J. Winther, and P. Borba. Intraprocedural dataflow analysis for software product lines. In *Transactions on Aspect-Oriented Software Development X*, pages 73–108. 2013.

[5] C. Brabrand, M. Ribeiro, T. Tolêdo, and P. Borba. Intraprocedural Dataflow Analysis for Software Product Lines. In *Int. Conf. on Aspect-Oriented Software Development*, pages 13–24, 2012.

[6] L. Cardelli. Program fragments, linking, and modularization. In *ACM SIGPLAN-SIGACT Symp. on Principles of Programming Languages*, pages 266–277, 1997.

[7] S. Chen and M. Erwig. Counter-Factual Typing for Debugging Type Errors. In *ACM SIGPLAN-SIGACT Symp. on Principles of Programming Languages*, pages 583–594, 2014.

[8] S. Chen and M. Erwig. Guided Type Debugging. In *Int. Symp. on Functional and Logic Programming*, LNCS 8475, pages 35–51, 2014.

[9] S. Chen, M. Erwig, and E. Walkingshaw. An Error-Tolerant Type System for Variational Lambda Calculus. In *ACM Int. Conf. on Functional Programming*, pages 29–40, 2012.

[10] S. Chen, M. Erwig, and E. Walkingshaw. Extending Type Inference to Variational Programs. *ACM Trans. on Programming Languages and Systems*, 36(1):1:1–1:54, 2014.

[11] A. Classen, P. Heymans, P.-Y. Schobbens, and A. Legay. Symbolic Model Checking of Software Product Lines. In *IEEE Int. Conf. on Software Engineering*, pages 321–330, 2011.

[12] A. Classen, P. Heymans, P.-Y. Schobbens, A. Legay, and J.-F. Raskin. Model Checking Lots of Systems: Efficient Verification of Temporal Properties in Software Product Lines. In *IEEE Int. Conf. on Software Engineering*, pages 335–344, 2010.

[13] P. C. Clements and L. M. Northrop. *Software Product Lines: Practices and Patterns*. Addison-Wesley, Boston, 2001.

[14] M. Cordy, A. Classen, G. Perrouin, P.-Y. Schobbens, P. Heymans, and A. Legay. Simulation-based Abstractions for Software Product-Line Model Checking. In *IEEE Int. Conf. on Software Engineering*, pages 672–682, 2012.

[15] L. Damas and R. Milner. Principal Type Schemes for Functional Programming Languages. In *ACM Symp. on Principles of Programming Languages*, pages 207–208, 1982.

[16] B. Delaware, W. Cook, and D. Batory. Product lines of theorems. In *ACM SIGPLAN Int. Conf. on Object-Oriented Programming, Systems, Languages, and Applications*, pages 595–608, 2011.

[17] B. Delaware, W. R. Cook, and D. Batory. Fitting the Pieces Together: A Machine-Checked Model of Safe Composition. In *ACM SIGSOFT Int. Symp. on the Foundations of Software Engineering*, pages 243–252, 2009.

[18] M. Erwig and E. Walkingshaw. The Choice Calculus: A Representation for Software Variation. *ACM Trans. on Software Engineering and Methodology*, 21(1):6:1–6:27, 2011.

[19] P. Gazzillo and R. Grimm. SuperC: Parsing all of C by Taming the Preprocessor. In *ACM SIGPLAN Conf. on Programming Language Design and Implementation*, pages 323–334, 2012.

[20] C. Hankin and D. Métayer. A type-based framework for program analysis. In *Static Analysis Symposium*, LNCS 864, pages 380–394. 1994.

[21] N. Heintze. Control-flow analysis and type systems. In *Static Analysis Symposium*, LNCS 983, pages 189–206. 1995.

[22] C. Kästner, S. Apel, T. Thüm, and G. Saake. Type Checking Annotation-Based Product Lines. *ACM Trans. on Software Engineering and Methodology*, 21(3):14:1–14:39, 2012.

[23] C. Kästner, P. G. Giarrusso, T. Rendel, S. Erdweg, K. Ostermann, and T. Berger. Variability-aware parsing in the presence of lexical macros and conditional compilation. In *ACM SIGPLAN Int. Conf. on Object-Oriented Programming, Systems, Languages, and Applications*, pages 805–824, 10 2011.

[24] C. Kästner, K. Ostermann, and S. Erdweg. A Variability-Aware Module System. In *ACM SIGPLAN Int. Conf. on Object-Oriented Programming, Systems, Languages, and Applications*, pages 773–792, 2012.

[25] J. Liebig, A. von Rhein, C. Kästner, S. Apel, J. Dörre, and C. Lengauer. Large-Scale Variability-Aware Type Checking and Dataflow Analysis. Technical Report MIP-1212, Fakultät für Informatik und Mathematik, Universität Passau, 2012.

[26] J. Liebig, A. von Rhein, C. Kästner, S. Apel, J. Dörre, and C. Lengauer. Scalable analysis of variable software. In *Foundations of Software Engineering*, pages 81–91, 2013.

[27] M. Naik and J. Palsberg. A type system equivalent to a model checker. *ACM Trans. on Programming Languages and Systems*, 30(5):29:1–29:24, 2008.

[28] F. Nielson, H. R. Nielson, and C. Hankin. *Principles of program analysis*. Springer, 1999.

[29] M. Odersky, M. Sulzmann, and M. Wehr. Type Inference with Constrained Types. *Theory and Practice of Object Systems*, 5(1):35–55, 1999.

[30] J. Palsberg. Type-based analysis and applications. In *ACM SIGPLAN-SIGSOFT Workshop on Program Analysis for Software Tools and Engineering*, pages 20–27, 2001.

[31] D. L. Parnas. On the design and development of program families. *IEEE Trans. on Software Engineering*, 2(1):1–9, 1976.

[32] F. Pottier. A versatile constraint-based type inference system. *Nordic J. of Computing*, 7(4):312–347, Dec. 2000.

[33] F. Pottier and V. Simonet. Information flow inference for ML. *ACM Trans. on Programming Languages and Systems*, 25(1):117–158, 2003.

[34] F. Prost. A Formalization of Static Analyses in System F. In *Automated Deduction CADE-16*, pages 252–266. 1999.

[35] T. Reps, S. Horwitz, and M. Sagiv. Precise interprocedural dataflow analysis via graph reachability. In *ACM SIGPLAN-SIGACT Symp. on Principles of Programming Languages*, pages 49–61, 1995.

[36] J. A. Robinson. A machine-oriented logic based on the resolution principle. *Journal of the ACM*, 12(1):23–41, Jan. 1965.

[37] V. Simonet. An extension of HM(X) with bounded existential and universal data-types. In *ACM SIGPLAN Int. Conf. on Functional Programming*, pages 39–50, 2003.

[38] V. Simonet and F. Pottier. A constraint-based approach to guarded algebraic data types. *ACM Trans. on Programming Languages and Systems*, 29(1):1–38, 2007.

[39] P. J. Stuckey and M. Sulzmann. A theory of overloading. In *ACM SIGPLAN Int. Conf. on Functional Programming*, pages 167–178, 2002.

[40] M. Sulzmann, M. Müller, and C. Zenger. Hindley/Milner style type systems in constraint form. Research Report ACRC-99-009, University of South Australia, School of Computer and Information Science, 1999.

[41] T. Thüm, I. Schaefer, S. Apel, and M. Hentschel. Family-based deductive verification of software product lines. In *International Conference on Generative Programming and Component Engineering*, pages 11–20, 2012.

[42] J. B. Wells. Typability and Type Checking in System F Are Equivalent and Undecidable. *Annals of Pure and Applied Logic*, 98:111–156, 1998.

Romeo: a System For More Flexible Binding-Safe Programming

Paul Stansifer Mitchell Wand
Northeastern University
{pauls,wand}@ccs.neu.edu

Abstract

Current languages for safely manipulating values with names only support term languages with simple binding syntax. As a result, no tools exist to safely manipulate code written in those languages for which name problems are the most challenging. We address this problem with Romeo, a language that respects α-equivalence on its values, and which has access to a rich specification language for binding, inspired by attribute grammars. Our work has the complex-binding support of David Herman's λ_m, but is a full-fledged binding-safe language like Pure FreshML.

Categories and Subject Descriptors D.3.1 [*Formal Definitions and Theory*]

Keywords languages; binding; alpha-equivalence; macros

1. Introduction

Manipulating terms with binding information has traditionally posed a serious problem to metaprogrammers. In a survey of 9 DSL implementations, 8 were found to be prone to variable capture [4].

Building a system that does not suffer from this problem is difficult, because a name in isolation is meaningless; only its relationship with other names imbues a name with meaning. On the other hand, the meaninglessness of names inspires a motto for what it means to manipulate names correctly: a system is correct if α-conversion of input values results in outputs that are identical up to α-conversion [8].

Systems with this property have been created, allowing for programming with names but without insidious name problems. However, these systems generally support only term languages with simple binding structure [5, 12]. Our work is an extension of David Herman's macro system that supports complex binding structure [7], but as a full-fledged binding-safe language inspired by Pure FreshML [13].

1.1 Motivation

For example, consider the following Scheme term, exhibiting a complex binding structure:

ICFP'14, September 1–6, 2014, Gothenburg, Sweden.

ACM 978-1-4503-2873-9/14/09...$15.00.
http://dx.doi.org/10.1145/2628136.2628162

```
(let* ((a 1)
       (b (+ a a))
       (c (* b 5)))
  (display c))
```

In Scheme, the `let*` syntactic form is defined to bind the names it introduces not only in the body, but also in the right hand side of each subsequent arm. Thus, this example has no free names, and the value of `c` is 10. Formally expressing these properties is the job of binding specifications, such as those in Nominal Isabelle [17], Ott [16], and Cαml [12].

If we want to programmatically manipulate source code while respecting its binding structure, we must add to our system a notion of α-equivalence. Only then can the correctness motto of preservation of α-equivalence be well-defined. We would like our notion of α-equivalence to be as compositional as possible, even though a pair of α-equivalent may decompose into pairs of subterms which are not α-equivalent. For example, our expression above is α-equivalent to the following:

```
(let* ((d 1)
       (d (+ d d))
       (d (* d 5)))
  (display d))
```

This is despite the fact that `(display d)` is clearly not α-equivalent to `(display c)`. The standard solution is to observe that they *are* α-equivalent after performing a substitution determined by examining the binders. This is our solution as well, but in order to model forms like `let*`, we must allow binders to be "exported" up from subforms (and sub-subforms, etc.) in a well-defined way. We say such binders are "buried." Furthermore, such a buried binder may be referred to inside the form that exports it, causing it to participate in multiple binding relationships at different levels.

It is instructive to contrast our work to another system capable of handling complex binding structure, the Dybvig algorithm [3] used in many Scheme implementations. In this algorithm, names are dynamically marked to indicate which macro evaluation they originated from, in order to prevent errors caused by coincidental name collision. We will discuss the limitations of this approach in section 7.4.

An improvement upon this is David Herman's λ_m-calculus [7], a macro system that uses binding specifications to guarantee that α-equivalent inputs will expand to α-equivalent outputs. However, its macros can be defined only in terms of pattern-matching. Pattern-matching systems are a natural way to define simple macros, but they lack the power to define more intricate macros, which are often the macros that benefit the most from access to complex binding constructs.

$$
\begin{array}{lll}
\textit{CoreExpr} ::= \text{RAtom} & (\textit{variable reference}) & \text{var} \\
\quad | \; \text{Prod}(\textit{CoreExpr}, \textit{CoreExpr}) & (\textit{application}) & \text{app} \\
\quad | \; \text{Prod}(\text{BAtom}, \textit{CoreExpr}{\downarrow}0) & (\textit{abstraction}) & \text{lam} \\
\textit{Expr} ::= \text{RAtom} & (\textit{variable reference}) & \text{var} \\
\quad | \; \text{Prod}(\textit{Expr}, \textit{Expr}) & (\textit{application}) & \text{app} \\
\quad | \; \text{Prod}(\text{BAtom}, \textit{Expr}{\downarrow}0) & (\textit{abstraction}) & \text{lam} \\
\quad | \; \text{Prod}(\textit{LetStarClauses}, \textit{Expr}{\downarrow}0) & (\textit{sequential let}) & \text{let-star} \\
\textit{LetStarClauses} ::= \text{Prod}() & (\textit{no clauses}) & \text{lsc-none} \\
\quad | \; \text{Prod}^{\Uparrow(1 \triangleright 0)}(\text{Prod}^{\Uparrow 0}(\text{BAtom}, \textit{Expr}), \textit{LetStarClauses}{\downarrow}0) & (\textit{clause, and more clauses}) & \text{lsc-none} \\
\end{array}
$$

Figure 1. Example types for two lambda calculi, one of which has the `let*` form. (The names from the right-hand column are used to identify injections and as the variables for cases in Figure 2.)

```
1   (define-fn (convert e:Expr) : CoreExpr
2     (case e
3       (var ⇒ (inj_var var))
4       (app ⇒ (open app (e1,e2) (inj_app (prod convert(e1),convert(e2)))))
5       (lam ⇒ (open lam (bv,e-body) (inj_lam (prod bv,convert(e-body)↓0))))
6       (let-star ⇒
7         (open let-star (lsc,e-body)
8           (case lsc
9             (lsc-none ⇒ convert(e-body))
10            (lsc-some ⇒
11              (open lsc-some (bv,val-expr,lsc-rest)
12                (let e-rest be convert((inj_let-star (prod lsc-rest,e-body↓0)))
13                  in (inj_app (prod (inj_lam (prod bv,e-rest↓0)),convert(val-expr)))))))))))
```

Figure 2. A Romeo-L function to expand away `let*`

Our system is more flexible and can even operate outside the context of macro expansion altogether: we provide a full-fledged programming language for manipulating terms.

1.2 Example

As an example, we define in Figure 1 some types in our system, and in Figure 2 we define a function (using those types) that translates expressions from the lambda calculus augmented with a `let*` construct into the plain lambda calculus. We will discuss the meaning of the types in section 2.1, the behavior of the code in section 4.3, the way Romeo preserves α-equivalence for it in section 5.1, and the static guarantees that Romeo provides in section 6.3.

1.3 Contributions

Our primary contribution is an extension of David Herman's system for binding-safety in a pattern-matching macro system [7] to cover macros defined by procedures, and thus general meta-programming for terms with bindings. Our language is inspired by Pure FreshML [13].

Our system has the following features:

- Values in Romeo are "plain old data": atoms arranged in abstract syntax trees without binding information. Types provide the missing binding information.

- Romeo has an execution semantics which ensures that instead of a name "escaping" the context in which it is defined, a FAULT is produced.

- We prove a theorem guaranteeing that, in any execution, the dynamic environment can be replaced by one with α-equivalent values, and that execution will proceed to a value α-equivalent to what it otherwise would have.

- We provide a deduction system with which the programmer can establish that escape (and thus, FAULT) will never occur.

2. Binding language

2.1 Overview of binding types

Values in our system are plain old data, that is, S-expressions or something similar. We use binding types to specify the binding properties of these terms. Binding types augment a traditional context-free grammar with a single attribute (in the style of an attribute grammar) that represents the flow of bindings from one subterm to another.

In Figure 1, the type definition of *CoreExpr* looks like a traditional grammar for the lambda calculus, with one major difference: the notation *CoreExpr*$\downarrow$0 indicates that the binder "exported" by the child in position 0 (the BAtom, which exports the name in that position) is to be in scope in the *CoreExpr* body of the lambda. To facilitate the connecting of binders to references, the type for names that bind, BAtom, is made distinct from the type of names that reference binders, RAtom.

Our system observes the convention that all names bound in a particular value are bound in all subvalues, unless overridden by a new binding for the same name. It is possible to imagine a system in which old names are removable (e.g., a construct (unbind x e), in which the name x is not a valid reference in e, even if it was outside that construct), but this does not appear to be a feature that users are clamoring for. (But see the end-of-scope operator described by Hendriks and van Oostrom [6].)

A way to define the exports of a wide product is required when the binders are exported longer distances up the tree. Consider `let*`, in *Expr*. The "sequential let" line indicates that the binders exported by *LetStarClauses* are in scope in the body of the `let*` ex-

$$
\begin{array}{lll}
\textit{Expr} ::= \ldots & & (\textit{same as before}) \\
\quad | \ \mathrm{Prod}(\mathrm{BAtom}, \mathrm{BAtom}, \textit{Expr}{\downarrow}0 \uplus 1, \mathrm{BAtom}, \textit{Expr}{\downarrow}0 \uplus 3) & & (\textit{event handler})
\end{array}
$$

Figure 3. Typed production rule for event handler

pression. The grammar for *LetStarClauses* says that a set of `let*`-clauses is either empty or a pair consisting of a single clause and the rest of the clauses. In the second production for *LetStarClauses*, the $\mathrm{Prod}^{\Uparrow 0}(\mathrm{BAtom}, \textit{Expr})$ indicates that the first clause exports the binder from its position 0 (that is, the BAtom). However, this name is not in scope in the *Expr*. The *LetStarClauses*$\downarrow$0 indicates that the names exported from the first clause are in scope in the remainder of the clauses.

The $\Uparrow (1 \rhd 0)$ indicates that the entire set of clauses exports all the binders exported by either the first clause or the rest of the clauses, and that names in the rest of the clauses override those from the first clause. If we had wanted to specify that all the binders in a `let*` must be distinct, then we could have written $\Uparrow (1 \uplus 0)$, which behaves like $\Uparrow (1 \rhd 0)$, except that duplicated atoms are an error.

Thus we have an attribute grammar with a single attribute, whose values are sets of names representing bindings. These sets are synthesized from binders and inherited by other terms until they flow to references.

Our notations $\downarrow$, $\Uparrow$, $\rhd$, and $\uplus$ form an algebra of attributes; the tractability of this algebra is a key to many of our results. We call the terms in this language *binding combinators*.

2.1.1 Example: multiple, partially-shared bindings

For another example, imagine constructing a pair of event handlers, one of which handles mouse events and one of which handles keyboard events, but both of which need to know what GUI element is focused. This new form, defined in Figure 3, binds three atoms (the BAtoms, which are in positions 0, 1, and 3), one of which is bound in both subexpressions, and two of which are bound in only one of them. Here is a possible use of this new form:

```
(handler gui-elt
         mouse-evt (deal-with gui-elt mouse-evt)
         kbd-evt (tag gui-elt (text-of kbd-evt)))
```

And here is an α-equivalent, but harder-to-read, version:

```
(handler a
         b (deal-with a b)
         b (tag a (text-of b)))
```

The scope of the first `b` is the `(deal-with ...)`, and the scope of the second one is the `(tag ...)`.

Regardless of whether they have the same names, the meanings of the two events must not be conflated, but the GUI element must not be differentiated. For this reason, the operations our system performs on products must handle binding by first identifying what names are exported by each child (e.g. a BAtom or a Prod with a non-empty $\Uparrow$), and then determining which names are imported by which children. The latter is the responsibility of the $\downarrow$ operator.

Our goal of supporting realistic concrete syntax is particularly relevant here. The `handler` statement could be implemented as a function that gets called with a lambda (binding `gui-elt`) that returns a pair of lambdas (binding the `-evts`), at the cost of some inconvenience for the programmer. If the only binding construct in a language were lambda, an "off-the-shelf" nominal logic system would suffice as a basis for Romeo. However, programmer convenience is precisely the point of metaprogramming systems.

2.2 Binding types, in more detail

In this section, we introduce our actual language of binding types and the metalanguage we use to describe them.

$$
\begin{array}{ll}
a \in \textit{Atom} & \tau \in \textit{Type} ::= \mathrm{BAtom} \\
v \in \textit{Value} ::= a & \quad | \ \mathrm{RAtom} \\
\quad | \ \mathbf{inj0}(v) & \quad | \ \tau + \tau \\
\quad | \ \mathbf{inj1}(v) & \quad | \ \mathrm{Prod}_i^{\Uparrow\beta}(\tau_i{\downarrow}\beta_i) \\
\quad | \ \mathbf{prod}_i(v_i) & \quad | \ \mu X.\tau \\
 & \quad | \ X
\end{array}
$$

Values are either atoms, left- or right- injections of values (to model sum types), or tuples of values. We write $\mathbf{prod}_i(v_i)$ for the tuple $(v_0, \ldots, v_n)$, for some n. We will use notation like this for sequence comprehensions throughout our presentation.

The basic types are BAtom (for binders) and RAtom (for references). These types tell us how to interpret atoms. By convention, BAtoms export themselves and RAtoms export nothing.

Tuples are interpreted by Prod types. The wide product type $\mathrm{Prod}^{\Uparrow\beta_{\mathrm{ex}}}(\tau_0{\downarrow}\beta_0, \ldots, \tau_n{\downarrow}\beta_n)$, which we denote by the comprehension $\mathrm{Prod}_i^{\Uparrow\beta_{\mathrm{ex}}}(\tau_i{\downarrow}\beta_i)$, tells us how to interpret the value $\mathbf{prod}_i(v_i)$. The term β_i, constructed in our algebra of attributes, combines (some of) the binders exported by $v_0, \ldots, v_n$ to determine the local names bound in v_i. Again, by convention, these names override those inherited from outside ("above") $\mathbf{prod}_i(v_i)$. The binding combinator β_{ex}, similarly constructed in our algebra of attributes, combines the binders exported by $v_0, \ldots, v_n$ to determine the names exported as binders by the tuple $\mathbf{prod}_i(v_i)$.

To sidestep issues of parsing, we have sum types and injections. A value $\mathbf{inj0}(v)$ (resp. $\mathbf{inj1}(v)$) is interpreted by the type $\tau_0 + \tau_1$ so that v is interpreted by τ_0 (resp. τ_1).

Last, we have recursive types $\mu X.\tau$, where τ must be productive; to interpret a value v according to $\mu X.\tau$ is to interpret it according to $\tau[\mu X.\tau/X]$.

2.3 The algebra of binding combinators

Binding combinators are terms built from the following grammar:

$$
\begin{array}{l}
i, \ell \in \mathbb{N} \\
\beta \in \textit{Beta} ::= \varnothing \\
\quad | \ \beta \uplus \beta \\
\quad | \ \beta \rhd \beta \\
\quad | \ \ell
\end{array}
$$

As discussed above, we use binding combinators to collect names from the sets exported by the subterms of a sequence $\mathbf{prod}_i(v_i)$. We will need to interpret these combinators over both sets of names and substitutions (finite maps from names to names). As before, we make liberal use of comprehensions: we write $[\![\beta]\!]\,(A_i)_i$ for $[\![\beta]\!]\,(A_0, \ldots, A_n)$, etc. The interpretation is as follows:

$$
\begin{array}{l}
[\![\_]\!]\,(\_) : \textit{Beta} \times \overline{\textit{AtomSet}} \to \textit{AtomSet} \\
[\![\varnothing]\!]\,(A_i)_i \triangleq \varnothing \\
[\![\ell]\!]\,(A_i)_i \triangleq A_\ell \\
[\![\beta \rhd \beta']\!]\,(A_i)_i \triangleq [\![\beta]\!]\,(A_i)_i \cup [\![\beta']\!]\,(A_i)_i \\
[\![\beta \uplus \beta']\!]\,(A_i)_i \triangleq [\![\beta]\!]\,(A_i)_i \uplus [\![\beta']\!]\,(A_i)_i
\end{array}
$$

Here and elsewhere, we write $\overline{X}$ to mean a sequence of Xs.

A substitution σ is a partial function from atoms to atoms. For the purposes of manipulating them, we represent substitutions as a set of ordered pairs of atoms. Our substitutions are naïve, which is to say that they ignore binding structure and simply affect all names. We interpret β's on substitutions as follows:

$$
\begin{aligned}
[\![\_]\!]\,(\_) &: \mathit{Beta} \times \overline{\mathit{Subst}} \to \mathit{Subst}\\
[\![\varnothing]\!]\,(\sigma_i)_i &\triangleq \varnothing\\
[\![\ell]\!]\,(\sigma_i)_i &\triangleq \sigma_\ell\\
[\![\beta \rhd \beta']\!]\,(\sigma_i)_i &\triangleq [\![\beta]\!]\,(\sigma_i)_i \rhd [\![\beta']\!]\,(\sigma_i)_i\\
[\![\beta \uplus \beta']\!]\,(\sigma_i)_i &\triangleq [\![\beta]\!]\,(\sigma_i)_i \uplus [\![\beta']\!]\,(\sigma_i)_i
\end{aligned}
$$

In this definition, $\uplus$ is disjoint union, undefined if the sets are not disjoint, and $\sigma \rhd \sigma'$ is defined as follows:

$$
\sigma \rhd \sigma' \triangleq \sigma \cup \left\{ \langle a_{\mathrm{d}}, a_{\mathrm{r}} \rangle \;\middle|\; \begin{array}{l} \langle a_{\mathrm{d}}, a_{\mathrm{r}} \rangle \in \sigma' \\ a_{\mathrm{d}} \notin \mathrm{dom}(\sigma) \end{array} \right\}
$$

Using $[\![\beta]\!]\,(A_i)_i$, we can compute the binders exported from any value. We call these the *free binders* of the value. As suggested above, the free binders of a value are determined using the type.

$$
\begin{aligned}
\mathrm{fb}\Big(\mathrm{Prod}_i^{\Uparrow\beta_{\mathrm{exp}}}(\tau_i{\downarrow}\beta_i), \mathbf{prod}_i(v_i)\Big) &::= [\![\beta_{\mathrm{exp}}]\!]\,(\mathrm{fb}(\tau_i, v_i))_i\\
\mathrm{fb}(\tau_0 + \tau_1, \mathbf{inj0}(v)) &::= \mathrm{fb}(\tau_0, v)\\
\mathrm{fb}(\tau_0 + \tau_1, \mathbf{inj1}(v)) &::= \mathrm{fb}(\tau_1, v)\\
\mathrm{fb}(\mu X.\tau, v) &::= \mathrm{fb}(\tau[\mu X.\tau/X], v)\\
\mathrm{fb}(\mathrm{BAtom}, a) &::= \{a\}\\
\mathrm{fb}(\mathrm{RAtom}, a) &::= \varnothing
\end{aligned}
$$

There are several other useful quantities that we can compute using these combinators. First is the set of free references of a term:

$$
\begin{aligned}
\mathrm{fr}\Big(\mathrm{Prod}_i^{\Uparrow\beta_{\mathrm{exp}}}(\tau_i{\downarrow}\beta_i), \mathbf{prod}_i(v_i)\Big) &::= \bigcup_i \begin{pmatrix} \mathrm{fr}(\tau_i, v_i) \\ \smallsetminus [\![\beta_i]\!]\,(\mathrm{fb}(\tau_j, v_j))_j \end{pmatrix}\\
\mathrm{fr}(\tau_0 + \tau_1, \mathbf{inj0}(v)) &::= \mathrm{fr}(\tau_0, v)\\
\mathrm{fr}(\tau_0 + \tau_1, \mathbf{inj1}(v)) &::= \mathrm{fr}(\tau_1, v)\\
\mathrm{fr}(\mu X.\tau, v) &::= \mathrm{fr}(\tau[\mu X.\tau/X], v)\\
\mathrm{fr}(\mathrm{BAtom}, a) &::= \varnothing\\
\mathrm{fr}(\mathrm{RAtom}, a) &::= \{a\}
\end{aligned}
$$

Next is the set of free atoms of a term, which is just the union of the free binders and the free references:

$$
\mathrm{fa}(\tau, v) ::= \mathrm{fr}(\tau, v) \cup \mathrm{fb}(\tau, v)
$$

Last is the set of exposable atoms, which are those non-free names that will become free when the value in question is broken into subterms. These are the atoms which are on their "last chance" for renaming before they become free. This set, only defined on products, is equal to the union of the binders exported by each term in a sequence, less the terms that are exported to the outside:

$$
\begin{aligned}
&\mathrm{xa}\Big(\mathrm{Prod}_i^{\Uparrow\beta_{\mathrm{exp}}}(\tau_i{\downarrow}\beta_i), \mathbf{prod}_i(v_i)\Big)\\
&::= \Big(\bigcup_i \mathrm{fb}(\tau_i, v_i)\Big) \smallsetminus \mathrm{fb}\Big(\mathrm{Prod}_j^{\Uparrow\beta_{\mathrm{exp}}}(\tau_j{\downarrow}\beta_j), \mathbf{prod}_j(v_j)\Big)
\end{aligned}
$$

It is also useful to know the support of a binding combinator β:

$$
\begin{aligned}
\_ \,\hat{\in}\, \_ &\subseteq \mathbb{N} \times \mathit{Beta}\\
\ell \,\hat{\notin}\, \varnothing &\triangleq \text{false}\\
\ell \,\hat{\in}\, \ell' &\triangleq \ell = \ell'\\
\ell \,\hat{\in}\, \beta \rhd \beta' &\triangleq \ell \,\hat{\in}\, \beta \text{ or } \ell \,\hat{\in}\, \beta'\\
\ell \,\hat{\in}\, \beta \uplus \beta' &\triangleq \ell \,\hat{\in}\, \beta \text{ or } \ell \,\hat{\in}\, \beta'
\end{aligned}
$$

3. Alpha-equivalence

Our next task is to go from a binding type to a notion of α-equivalence on values described by that type. Because our binding types allow for buried binders (i.e., binders that may be an arbitrary depth from the form that binds them) to be exported, we define two values to be α-equivalent if both

- they export identical bindings, and
- local (non-exported) bindings can be renamed along with the names that reference them to make the terms identical.

We use $=_{\mathrm{B}}$ (pronounced "binder-equivalent") for the first relation and $=_{\mathrm{R}}$ (pronounced "reference-equivalent") for the second.

$$
\_ =_\alpha \_ : \_ \subseteq \mathit{Value} \times \mathit{Value} \times \mathit{Type}
$$

$$
\frac{v =_{\mathrm{B}} v' : \tau \qquad v =_{\mathrm{R}} v' : \tau}{v =_\alpha v' : \tau}\ \alpha\mathrm{EQ}
$$

3.1 Binder equivalence

Two values are $=_{\mathrm{B}}$ iff their exported (free) binders in the same positions are identical (references are irrelevant). Note that Bα-PROD examines only the subterms that are in the support of β_{ex}, because non-exported binders are the responsibility of $=_{\mathrm{R}}$.

Here and throughout, we omit the rules for injections and fixed points, which are trivial.

$$
\_ =_{\mathrm{B}} \_ : \_ \subseteq \mathit{Value} \times \mathit{Value} \times \mathit{Type}
$$

$$
\frac{}{a =_{\mathrm{B}} a : \mathrm{BAtom}}\ \mathrm{B}\alpha\text{-BATOM} \qquad \frac{}{a =_{\mathrm{B}} a' : \mathrm{RAtom}}\ \mathrm{B}\alpha\text{-RATOM}
$$

$$
\frac{\forall i \,\hat{\in}\, \beta_{\mathrm{ex}}.\ v_i =_{\mathrm{B}} v_i' : \tau_i}{\mathbf{prod}_i(v_i) =_{\mathrm{B}} \mathbf{prod}_i(v_i') : \mathrm{Prod}_i^{\Uparrow\beta_{\mathrm{ex}}}(\tau_i{\downarrow}\beta_i)}\ \mathrm{B}\alpha\text{-PROD}
$$

3.2 Reference equivalence

Calculating $=_{\mathrm{R}}$ is analogous to the conventional notion of α-equivalence, except that we need to extract and rename the bindings that are buried in subterms.

3.2.1 Joining the binders

We begin with the $\bowtie$ operator (pronounced "join"). It walks through both values in lockstep, collecting pairs of corresponding binding atoms and assigning a common fresh atom for each. The result is a pair of injective substitutions whose domains are equal to the set of free binders of the values being joined.

At a product, we do the following on each side: we first walk through each subterm, recursively generating substitutions for each binding exported by any of the subterms, making sure that there is no overlap between the fresh names (i.e. the ranges of the substitutions) assigned in different subterms. The substitutions for the subterms are then combined by β_{ex} to produce a substitution for the exported binders of the product term. These two substitutions (the last two terms of the $\bowtie$ relation) are the output of this relation.

We define $\#$ to be the disjointness operator over names, sets of names, and values. It is naïve, meaning that it entirely ignores binding structure. Therefore, $a \# \lambda b.b$ is true, but $a \# \lambda a.a$ is false.

$$
\_ \bowtie \_ : \_ \to \_ \bowtie \_ \subseteq \mathit{Value} \times \mathit{Value} \times \mathit{Type} \times \mathit{Subst} \times \mathit{Subst}
$$

$$
\frac{}{a \bowtie a' : \mathrm{BAtom} \to \{\langle a, a_{\mathrm{fresh}} \rangle\} \bowtie \{\langle a', a_{\mathrm{fresh}} \rangle\}}\ \mathrm{J\text{-}BATOM}
$$

$$
\frac{}{a \bowtie a' : \mathrm{RAtom} \to \varnothing \bowtie \varnothing}\ \mathrm{J\text{-}RATOM}
$$

$$
\frac{\begin{array}{cc} \forall i.\ v_i \bowtie v_i' : \tau \to \sigma_i \bowtie \sigma_i' & \forall i \neq j.\ \mathrm{rng}(\sigma_i) \# \mathrm{rng}(\sigma_j) \\ \sigma = [\![\beta_{\mathrm{ex}}]\!]\,(\sigma_i)_i & \sigma' = [\![\beta_{\mathrm{ex}}]\!]\,(\sigma_i')_i \end{array}}{\mathbf{prod}_i(v_i) \bowtie \mathbf{prod}_i(v_i') : \mathrm{Prod}_i^{\Uparrow\beta_{\mathrm{ex}}}(\tau_i{\downarrow}\beta_i) \to \sigma \bowtie \sigma'}\ \mathrm{J\text{-}PROD}
$$

For example, consider the two `let*` expressions we have previously discussed:

```
(let* ((a 1)              (let* ((d 1)
       (b (+ a a))                (d (+ d d))
       (c (* b 5)))               (d (* d 5)))
  (display c))              (display d))
```

The results of $\bowtie$ on their children in position 1 (the `display` expressions) are $\varnothing$ and $\varnothing$, because neither one has any free binders. Position 0 corresponds to the *LetStarClauses*, and is more interesting. $\bowtie$ will nondeterministically generate three names, which we will choose to be *aa*, *bb*, and *cc*. Then, we will have $\sigma_0 = \{\langle \mathtt{a}, \mathtt{aa}\rangle, \langle \mathtt{b}, \mathtt{bb}\rangle, \langle \mathtt{c}, \mathtt{cc}\rangle\}$ and $\sigma'_0 = \{\langle \mathtt{d}, \mathtt{cc}\rangle\}$. The different ranges of these substitutions indicate that some names (the ones called `a` and `b` in the left-hand value) cannot be referred to at all by references on the right-hand side, due to shadowing.

A more complete derivation of this is shown in Figure 4. The first step is straightforward: `c` and `d` are unified with each other, and the resulting substitutions are merged with the empty substitution. In the next step, `b` and `d` are unified, but the substitution in position 1 (which produced `cc`) takes precedence over the new definition of `d`. Finally, a similar process completes generating the substitutions corresponding to the free binders in each *LetStarClauses*.

3.2.2 Comparison by substitution

Now we can write the rules for $=_R$. At RAtom, the atoms being compared are necessarily free and must be identical in order to be reference-equal. Symmetrically to $=_B$, any two atoms are $=_R$ at BAtom.

At a product, the information from $\bowtie$ is used by $=_R$ to make the subterms comparable without requiring context. This is done as follows: For each pair of subterms v_i, v'_i, we use $\bowtie$ to generate a pair of substitutions σ_i, σ'_i that rename the binders exported by v_i, v'_i to be identical. We then apply these renamings to the subterms, as directed by β_i.

Applying these substitutions to each pair of subterms (resulting in the new values $[\![\beta_i]\!]\,(\sigma_j)_j(v_i)$ and $[\![\beta_i]\!]\,(\sigma'_j)_j(v'_i)$) allows us to examine each pair of children in isolation. Note that this substitution is naïve (that is, it disregards types and therefore binding). Even though we are only interested in the substitution's effect on free references, this naïvete is acceptable because, first, $=_R$ does not examine free binders, and second, (broadly speaking) the substitution of un-free names is harmless (this principle is illustrated by Lemma 3.2).

Because our substitutions are naïve, we require that each substitution's range be disjoint from the values being examined. Without this requirement, we would have `(let* ((x 7)) x)` $=_R$ `(let* ((y 7)) a)` : *Expr*, witnessed by $\sigma_0 = \{\langle \mathtt{x}, \mathtt{a}\rangle\}$ and $\sigma'_0 = \{\langle \mathtt{y}, \mathtt{a}\rangle\}$.

$$\_ =_R \_ : \_ \subseteq \mathit{Value} \times \mathit{Value} \times \mathit{Type}$$

$$\frac{}{a =_R a' : \text{BAtom}}\ \text{R}\alpha\text{-BATOM} \qquad \frac{}{a =_R a : \text{RAtom}}\ \text{R}\alpha\text{-RATOM}$$

$$\frac{\begin{array}{c}\forall i.\ v_i \bowtie v'_i : \tau_i \rightarrow \sigma_i \bowtie \sigma'_i \\ \forall i,j.\ \text{rng}(\sigma_i), \text{rng}(\sigma'_i) \# v_j, v'_j \\ \forall i \neq j.\ \text{rng}(\sigma_i) \# \text{rng}(\sigma_j) \\ \forall i.\ [\![\beta_i]\!]\,(\sigma_j)_j(v_i) =_R [\![\beta_i]\!]\,(\sigma'_j)_j(v'_i) : \tau_i\end{array}}{\mathbf{prod}_i(v_i) =_R \mathbf{prod}_i(v'_i) : \text{Prod}_{\tau \downarrow \beta}(\beta_{ex})}\ \text{R}\alpha\text{-PROD}$$

In our ongoing `let*` example, the appropriate substitution is a no-op on the *LetStarClauses*, which import nothing. Recursive application of $=_R$ will discover their shared binding structure and compare them as equal. On the other hand, the expression bodies will be both transformed into `(display cc)`, which lacks binding structure, and is naïvely equal to itself. So, the two expressions are $=_R$. (They are also trivially $=_B$, and therefore $=_\alpha$.) A complete derivation of their reference-equivalence, including analyzing the *LetStarClauses* themselves, is available at `http://hdl.handle.net/2047/d20005012`.

An example that better demonstrates the complexities of renaming is the event handler example from section 2.1.1. The result of invoking $\bowtie$ on each pair of children, in order to compare the two versions for α-equivalence, is in Figure 5.

All of the β's, except β_2 and β_4, are $\varnothing$. β_2 is $0 \uplus 1$ and β_4 is $0 \uplus 3$. The result of performing those substitutions is shown in Figure 6, establishing the relationship between `mouse-evt` and the first `b` and the relationship between `kbd-evt` and the second `b`.

3.3 Lemmas

The following lemmas establish that $=_\alpha$ has behavior consistent with an α-equivalence. Each follows from analogous lemmas about $=_B$ and $=_R$ (where fb and fr replace fa, if applicable).

Lemma 3.1. *$=_\alpha$ is an equivalence relation.*

Lemma 3.2 (Unfree atoms can be renamed). *Suppose σ is injective and* $\text{rng}(\sigma) \# v$ *and* $\text{dom}(\sigma) \# \text{fa}(\tau, v), \text{rng}(\sigma)$. *Then* $\sigma(v) =_\alpha v : \tau$.

Lemma 3.3 (Good substitutions preserve α-equivalence). *Suppose σ is injective and* $\text{rng}(\sigma) \# v, v'$ *and* $\text{dom}(\sigma) \# \text{rng}(\sigma)$. *Then* $v =_\alpha v' : \tau \Rightarrow \sigma(v) =_\alpha \sigma(v') : \tau$.

Lemma 3.4 (Free atoms are the same for α-equivalent values). $v =_\alpha v' : \tau \Rightarrow \text{fa}(\tau, v) = \text{fa}(\tau, v')$

4. Romeo

Romeo is a first-order, typed, side-effect-free language whose values are abstract syntax trees. It uses types to direct the interpretation of these trees as syntax trees with binding, and to direct the execution of expressions in a way that respects that binding structure. There are three parts to this:

- First, the execution semantics ensures that whenever the program causes a name to escape the context in which it is defined, a FAULT is produced.
- Second, we provide theorems guaranteeing that at any point in execution, the dynamic environment could be replaced by one with α-equivalent values, and execution would still proceed to a value α-equivalent to what it otherwise would have. Furthermore, execution is deterministic up to α: that is, the nondeterministic choices that are made (e.g. for fresh identifiers) do not change the α-equivalence class of the result.
- Last, we provide a deduction system to generate proof obligations which, if satisfied, guarantee that escape (and thus, FAULT) will never occur.

The syntax of Romeo is given as follows:

$$\begin{array}{rcl}
p \in \mathit{Prog} & ::= & \mathit{fD} \ldots\ e : \tau \\
\mathit{fD} \in \mathit{FnDef} & ::= & (\mathbf{define\text{-}fn}\ (f\ x : \tau \ldots\ \mathbf{pre}\ C) : \tau\ e\ \mathbf{post}\ C) \\
e \in \mathit{Expr} & ::= & (f\ x \ldots) \\
& | & (\mathbf{fresh}\ x\ \mathbf{in}\ e) \\
& | & (\mathbf{let}\ x\ \mathbf{where}\ C\ \mathbf{be}\ e\ \mathbf{in}\ e) \\
& | & (\mathbf{case}\ x\ (x\ e)\ (x\ e)) \\
& | & (\mathbf{open}\ x\ (x \ldots)\ e) \\
& | & (\mathbf{if}\ x\ \mathbf{equals}\ x\ e\ e) \\
& | & e^{\text{qlit}} \\
e^{\text{qlit}} \in \mathit{QuasiLit} & ::= & x \\
& | & (\mathbf{ref}\ x) \\
& | & (\mathbf{inj}_0\ e^{\text{qlit}}\ \tau) \\
& | & (\mathbf{inj}_1\ \tau\ e^{\text{qlit}}) \\
& | & (\mathbf{prod}_i^{\Uparrow\beta}\ e_i^{\text{qlit}} \downarrow \beta_i)
\end{array}$$

Here C ranges over a language of invariants from which the proof obligations for static safety are constructed. Romeo's operational semantics does not refer to these invariants. This sublanguage is discussed in Section 6.

$$\begin{array}{ll} & v_{0,1,1} \triangleq \texttt{((c (* b 5)))} \text{ and } v'_{0,1,1} \triangleq \texttt{((d (* d 5)))} \\ \text{Define:} & v_{0,1} \triangleq \texttt{((b (+ a a)) (c (* b 5)))} \text{ and } v'_{0,1} \triangleq \texttt{((d (+ d d)) (d (* d 5)))} \\ & v_0 \triangleq \texttt{((a 1) (b (+ a a)) (c (* b 5)))} \text{ and } v'_0 \triangleq \texttt{((d 1) (d (+ d d)) (d (* d 5)))} \end{array}$$

(3.1)	$\texttt{c} \bowtie \texttt{d} : \text{BAtom} \to \{\langle \texttt{c}, \texttt{cc}\rangle\} \bowtie \{\langle \texttt{d}, \texttt{cc}\rangle\}$	J-BATOM
(3.2)	$\texttt{(* b 5)} \bowtie \texttt{(* d 5)} : \mathit{Expr} \to \varnothing \bowtie \varnothing$	no free bindings
(3.3)	$\texttt{(c (* b 5))} \bowtie \texttt{(d (* d 5))} : \text{Prod}^{\Uparrow 0}(\text{BAtom}, \mathit{Expr}) \to \{\langle \texttt{c}, \texttt{cc}\rangle\} \bowtie \{\langle \texttt{d}, \texttt{cc}\rangle\}$	J-PROD, 3.1 and 3.2
(3.4)	$v_{0,1,1} \bowtie v'_{0,1,1} : \mathit{LetStarClauses} \to \{\langle \texttt{c}, \texttt{cc}\rangle\} \bowtie \{\langle \texttt{d}, \texttt{cc}\rangle\}$	J-PROD, 3.3
(3.5)	$\texttt{b} \bowtie \texttt{d} : \text{BAtom} \to \{\langle \texttt{b}, \texttt{bb}\rangle\} \bowtie \{\langle \texttt{d}, \texttt{bb}\rangle\}$	J-BATOM
(3.6)	$\texttt{(+ a a)} \bowtie \texttt{(+ d d)} : \mathit{Expr} \to \varnothing \bowtie \varnothing$	no free bindings
(3.7)	$\texttt{(b (+ a a))} \bowtie \texttt{(d (+ d d))} : \text{Prod}^{\Uparrow 0}(\text{BAtom}, \mathit{Expr}) \to \{\langle \texttt{b}, \texttt{bb}\rangle\} \bowtie \{\langle \texttt{d}, \texttt{bb}\rangle\}$	J-PROD, 3.5 and 3.6
(3.8)	$[\![1 \rhd 0]\!] \left(\{\langle \texttt{d}, \texttt{cc}\rangle\}, \{\langle \texttt{d}, \texttt{bb}\rangle\}\right) = \{\langle \texttt{d}, \texttt{cc}\rangle\}$	def. of $[\![]\!]$
(3.9)	$v_{0,1} \bowtie v'_{0,1} : \mathit{LetStarClauses} \to \{\langle \texttt{b}, \texttt{bb}\rangle, \langle \texttt{c}, \texttt{cc}\rangle\} \bowtie \{\langle \texttt{d}, \texttt{cc}\rangle\}$	J-PROD, 3.4, 3.7, and 3.8
(3.10)	$\texttt{a} \bowtie \texttt{d} : \text{BAtom} \to \{\langle \texttt{a}, \texttt{aa}\rangle\} \bowtie \{\langle \texttt{d}, \texttt{aa}\rangle\}$	J-BATOM
(3.11)	$\texttt{1} \bowtie \texttt{1} : \mathit{Expr} \to \varnothing \bowtie \varnothing$	no free bindings
(3.12)	$\texttt{(a 1)} \bowtie \texttt{(d 1)} : \text{Prod}^{\Uparrow 0}(\text{BAtom}, \mathit{Expr}) \to \{\langle \texttt{a}, \texttt{aa}\rangle\} \bowtie \{\langle \texttt{d}, \texttt{aa}\rangle\}$	J-PROD, 3.10 and 3.11
(3.13)	$[\![1 \rhd 0]\!] \left(\{\langle \texttt{d}, \texttt{cc}\rangle\}, \{\langle \texttt{d}, \texttt{aa}\rangle\}\right) = \{\langle \texttt{d}, \texttt{cc}\rangle\}$	by def. of $[\![]\!]$
(3.14)	$v_0 \bowtie v'_0 : \mathit{LetStarClauses} \to \{\langle \texttt{a}, \texttt{aa}\rangle, \langle \texttt{b}, \texttt{bb}\rangle, \langle \texttt{c}, \texttt{cc}\rangle\} \bowtie \{\langle \texttt{d}, \texttt{cc}\rangle\}$	J-PROD, 3.12, 3.9, and 3.13

Figure 4. Example derivation of $\bowtie$ for *LetStarClauses*

j	$v_j \quad v'_j$			$\sigma_j \quad \sigma'_j$
0	`gui-elt` $\bowtie$ `a`	: BAtom	$\to$	$\{\langle \texttt{gui-elt}, \texttt{gg}\rangle\} \bowtie \{\langle \texttt{a}, \texttt{gg}\rangle\}$
1	`mouse-evt` $\bowtie$ `b`	: BAtom	$\to$	$\{\langle \texttt{mouse-evt}, \texttt{mm}\rangle\} \bowtie \{\langle \texttt{b}, \texttt{mm}\rangle\}$
2	`(deal-with gui-elt mouse-evt)` $\bowtie$ `(deal-with a b)`	: *Expr*	$\to$	$\varnothing \bowtie \varnothing$
3	`kbd-evt` $\bowtie$ `b`	: BAtom	$\to$	$\{\langle \texttt{kbd-evt}, \texttt{kk}\rangle\} \bowtie \{\langle \texttt{b}, \texttt{kk}\rangle\}$
4	`(tag gui-elt (text-of kbd-evt))` $\bowtie$ `(tag a (text-of b))`	: *Expr*	$\to$	$\varnothing \bowtie \varnothing$

Figure 5. Substitutions generated for the handler example

$$\begin{array}{ll} [\![0 \uplus 1]\!] \, (\sigma_j)_j(\texttt{(deal-with gui-elt mouse-evt)}) & = \texttt{(deal-with gg mm)} \\ [\![0 \uplus 1]\!] \, (\sigma'_j)_j(\texttt{(deal-with a b)}) & = \texttt{(deal-with gg mm)} \\ [\![0 \uplus 3]\!] \, (\sigma_j)_j(\texttt{(apply-tag gui-elt (text-of kbd-evt))}) & = \texttt{(apply-tag gg (text-of kk))} \\ [\![0 \uplus 3]\!] \, (\sigma'_j)_j(\texttt{(apply-tag a (text-of b))}) & = \texttt{(apply-tag gg (text-of kk))} \end{array}$$

Figure 6. Result of substitution in the handler example

Typechecking is largely straightforward. In the body of **open**, the variables $x \ldots$ are given the types of the subterms of the scrutinee x, and in the body of **fresh**, x is bound to a new name at the type BAtom. In order to use that name as a reference, the **ref** form takes an argument of type BAtom and returns it as a RAtom.

We annotate injections with the types of the arm-not-taken, and product constructors with their binding structure. This allows us to write a function typeof(Γ, e) whose definition is routine.

4.1 Operational Semantics

We define Romeo's execution in big-step style.

We begin with auxiliary definitions that we will need:

$$\begin{array}{rcl} w \in \mathit{Result} & ::= & v \mid \text{FAULT} \\ \rho \in \mathit{ValEnv} & ::= & \epsilon \\ & \mid & \rho[z \to v] \\ \Gamma \in \mathit{TypeEnv} & ::= & \epsilon \\ & \mid & \Gamma, z{:}\tau \end{array}$$

$$\text{fa}_{\text{env}}(\Gamma, \rho) = \bigcup_{x \in \text{dom}(\Gamma)} \text{fa}(\Gamma(x), \rho(x))$$

The form of the execution judgment is:

$$\Gamma \vdash_{\text{exc}} \langle e, \rho \rangle \overset{k}{\Longrightarrow} w$$

The k argument indicates the number of execution steps taken to produce the result in question.

Observe that some execution rules depend on the type environment Γ. This is because the binding structures of values are represented in their types (τ), but not in their runtime representations (v). Therefore, type erasure is not possible — the meaning of values (and thus the behavior of those rules) depends on type information.

We can now give the rules for execution in Romeo. Rules that introduce names come in two forms, -OK, and -ESCAPE. In each case, the only difference is that FAULT occurs in the -ESCAPE case. A fault indicates that a name has escaped the scope that created it (E-FRESH-$\star$) or exposed it (E-OPEN-$\star$). Much of the rest of the machinery in those rules is about ensuring that newly introduced names do not collide with each other or with names in the environment.

4.2 Execution rules

We begin with the rules for evaluating **fresh** expressions. The rules require that the new name not occur in the environment ρ. Our determinacy theorems (Theorems 5.1 and 5.2) guarantee that the choice of the new name will not affect the result (up to α-equivalence). We have two versions of the rule: FRESH-ESCAPE which returns FAULT when the new name appears in the result of executing the body e, and FRESH-OK, which returns w when that is not the case.

During the execution of e, x is treated as a BAtom. It is convertable to a RAtom by the expression (**ref** x).

The hypothesis $\tau = \mathrm{typeof}((\Gamma, x{:}\mathrm{BAtom}), e)$ is needed to synthesize the type τ in order to determine the free atoms of the result, in order to determine whether to produce FAULT or not. Determining the type, of course, is entirely static and could be precomputed once rather than at each evaluation.

$$\frac{\begin{array}{c}\tau = \mathrm{typeof}((\Gamma, x{:}\mathrm{BAtom}), e)\\ a \notin \mathrm{fa}_{\mathrm{env}}(\Gamma, \rho)\\ \Gamma, x{:}\mathrm{BAtom} \vdash_{\mathrm{exe}} \langle e, \rho[x \to a]\rangle \overset{k}{\Longrightarrow} w\\ w = \mathrm{FAULT} \vee a \notin \mathrm{fa}(\tau, w)\end{array}}{\Gamma \vdash_{\mathrm{exe}} \langle(\mathbf{fresh}\ x\ \mathbf{in}\ e), \rho\rangle \overset{k+1}{\Longrightarrow} w}\ \textsc{E-Fresh-Ok}$$

$$\frac{\begin{array}{c}\tau = \mathrm{typeof}((\Gamma, x{:}\mathrm{BAtom}), e)\\ a \notin \mathrm{fa}_{\mathrm{env}}(\Gamma, \rho)\\ \Gamma, x{:}\mathrm{BAtom} \vdash_{\mathrm{exe}} \langle e, \rho[x \to a]\rangle \overset{k}{\Longrightarrow} w\\ w \neq \mathrm{FAULT} \wedge a \in \mathrm{fa}(\tau, w)\end{array}}{\Gamma \vdash_{\mathrm{exe}} \langle(\mathbf{fresh}\ x\ \mathbf{in}\ e), \rho\rangle \overset{k+1}{\Longrightarrow} \mathrm{FAULT}}\ \textsc{E-Fresh-Escape}$$

The next pair of rules deals with destructuring a product. Given a value $\rho(x) = \mathbf{prod}(v_{\mathrm{obj},0}, \ldots, v_{\mathrm{obj},n})$, the **open** expression chooses an α-variant $\mathbf{prod}(v_0, \ldots, v_n)$ and binds the resulting pieces to the variables x_i. In order to determine α-equivalence, the type τ is needed. In this way, types control the run-time behavior of Romeo programs. The names in the α-variant must be distinct both from names in the environment ρ and from each other (to the extent that they are not actually related by binding). This is taken care of by a subsidiary judgment $\vdash_{\text{suff-disj}}$. See section 4.2.2 for a more detailed discussion.

As with **fresh**, we have two rules which branch on whether any of the new names appear in the result of the body e. We test for escaped names by comparing the free atoms in the result with the exportable atoms of the renamed input. This suffices for safety because the only atoms that can become free are those that are exportable.

$$\frac{\begin{array}{c}\rho(x_{\mathrm{obj}}) =_\alpha \mathbf{prod}_i(v_i) : \tau_{\mathrm{obj}} \qquad \Gamma \vdash_{\mathrm{type}} x_{\mathrm{obj}} : \tau_{\mathrm{obj}}\\ \tau_{\mathrm{obj}} = \mathrm{Prod}_i^{\Uparrow\beta_{\mathrm{exp}}}(\tau_i{\downarrow}\beta_i) \qquad \tau = \mathrm{typeof}(\Gamma, e)\\ \mathrm{fa}_{\mathrm{env}}(\Gamma, \rho) \vdash_{\text{suff-disj}} \mathbf{prod}_i(v_i){:}\tau_{\mathrm{obj}}\\ \Gamma, (x_i{:}\tau_i)_i \vdash_{\mathrm{exe}} \langle e, \rho[x_i \to v_i]_i\rangle \overset{k}{\Longrightarrow} w\\ w = \mathrm{FAULT} \vee \mathrm{xa}(\tau_{\mathrm{obj}}, \mathbf{prod}_i(v_i)) \mathbin{\#} \mathrm{fa}(\tau, w)\end{array}}{\Gamma \vdash_{\mathrm{exe}} \langle(\mathbf{open}\ x_{\mathrm{obj}}\ ((x_i)_i)\ e), \rho\rangle \overset{k+1}{\Longrightarrow} w}\ \textsc{E-Open-Ok}$$

$$\frac{\begin{array}{c}\rho(x_{\mathrm{obj}}) =_\alpha \mathbf{prod}_i(v_i) : \tau_{\mathrm{obj}} \qquad \Gamma \vdash_{\mathrm{type}} x_{\mathrm{obj}} : \tau_{\mathrm{obj}}\\ \tau_{\mathrm{obj}} = \mathrm{Prod}_i^{\Uparrow\beta_{\mathrm{exp}}}(\tau_i{\downarrow}\beta_i) \qquad \tau = \mathrm{typeof}(\Gamma, e)\\ \mathrm{fa}_{\mathrm{env}}(\Gamma, \rho) \vdash_{\text{suff-disj}} \mathbf{prod}_i(v_i){:}\tau_{\mathrm{obj}}\\ \Gamma, (x_i{:}\tau_i)_i \vdash_{\mathrm{exe}} \langle e, \rho[x_i \to v_i]_i\rangle \overset{k}{\Longrightarrow} w\\ w \neq \mathrm{FAULT} \wedge \neg(\mathrm{xa}(\tau_{\mathrm{obj}}, \mathbf{prod}_i(v_i)) \mathbin{\#} \mathrm{fa}(\tau, w))\end{array}}{\Gamma \vdash_{\mathrm{exe}} \langle(\mathbf{open}\ x_{\mathrm{obj}}\ ((x_i)_i)\ e), \rho\rangle \overset{k+1}{\Longrightarrow} \mathrm{FAULT}}\ \textsc{E-Open-Escape}$$

To simplify the deduction system, we require variables in some places where expressions would be more natural (like function arguments or x_{obj} in **open**). As a result, programs are written in (roughly) A-normal form, naming intermediate results with **let**. There are two evaluation rules for **let**, depending on whether calculating e_{val} faults. As noted avove, the constraint C is ignored at run-time.

$$\frac{\begin{array}{c}\Gamma \vdash_{\mathrm{exe}} \langle e_{\mathrm{val}}, \rho\rangle \overset{k_{\mathrm{val}}}{\Longrightarrow} v_{\mathrm{val}} \qquad \tau_{\mathrm{val}} = \mathrm{typeof}(\Gamma, e_{\mathrm{val}})\\ \Gamma, x{:}\tau_{\mathrm{val}} \vdash_{\mathrm{exe}} \langle e_{\mathrm{body}}, \rho[x \to v_{\mathrm{val}}]\rangle \overset{k_{\mathrm{body}}}{\Longrightarrow} w\end{array}}{\Gamma \vdash_{\mathrm{exe}} \langle(\mathbf{let}\ x\ \mathbf{where}\ C\ \mathbf{be}\ e_{\mathrm{val}}\ \mathbf{in}\ e_{\mathrm{body}}), \rho\rangle \overset{k_{\mathrm{val}}+k_{\mathrm{body}}+1}{\Longrightarrow} w}\ \textsc{E-Let}$$

$$\frac{\Gamma \vdash_{\mathrm{exe}} \langle e_{\mathrm{val}}, \rho\rangle \overset{k}{\Longrightarrow} \mathrm{FAULT}}{\Gamma \vdash_{\mathrm{exe}} \langle(\mathbf{let}\ x\ \mathbf{where}\ C\ \mathbf{be}\ e_{\mathrm{val}}\ \mathbf{in}\ e_{\mathrm{body}}), \rho\rangle \overset{k+1}{\Longrightarrow} \mathrm{FAULT}}\ \textsc{E-Let-Fail}$$

As in Pure FreshML [13], we assume that our expressions are evaluated in a context of function definitions, so that from a function name we can retrieve the function's formals and body. Since this context is constant throughout an execution, it is elided in the evaluation judgment.

$$\frac{\begin{array}{c}\mathrm{body}(f) = e \qquad \mathrm{formals}(f) = (x_{\mathrm{formal},i}{:}\tau_{\mathrm{formal},i})_i\\ (x_{\mathrm{formal},i}{:}\tau_{\mathrm{formal},i})_i \vdash_{\mathrm{exe}} \langle e, [[x_{\mathrm{formal},i} \to \rho_i(x_{\mathrm{actual},i})]_i]\rangle \overset{k}{\Longrightarrow} w\end{array}}{\Gamma \vdash_{\mathrm{exe}} \langle(f\ (x_{\mathrm{actual},i})_i), \rho\rangle \overset{k+1}{\Longrightarrow} w}\ \textsc{E-Call}$$

The remainder of the rules are routine. For simplicity's sake, the equality test construct works only on atoms.

$$\frac{\begin{array}{c}\rho(x_{\mathrm{obj}}) = \mathbf{inj0}(v_0) \qquad \Gamma(x_{\mathrm{obj}}) = \tau_0 + \tau_1\\ \Gamma, x_0{:}\tau_0 \vdash_{\mathrm{exe}} \langle e_0, \rho[x_0 \to v_0]\rangle \overset{k}{\Longrightarrow} w\end{array}}{\Gamma \vdash_{\mathrm{exe}} \langle(\mathbf{case}\ x_{\mathrm{obj}}\ (x_0\ e_0)\ (x_1\ e_1)), \rho\rangle \overset{k+1}{\Longrightarrow} w}\ \textsc{E-Case-Left}$$

$$\frac{\begin{array}{c}\rho(x_{\mathrm{obj}}) = \mathbf{inj1}(v_1) \qquad \Gamma(x_{\mathrm{obj}}) = \tau_0 + \tau_1\\ \Gamma, x_1{:}\tau_1 \vdash_{\mathrm{exe}} \langle e_1, \rho[x_1 \to v_1]\rangle \overset{k}{\Longrightarrow} w\end{array}}{\Gamma \vdash_{\mathrm{exe}} \langle(\mathbf{case}\ x\ (x_0\ e_0)\ (x_1\ e_1)), \rho\rangle \overset{k+1}{\Longrightarrow} w}\ \textsc{E-Case-Right}$$

$$\frac{\begin{array}{c}\rho(x_{\mathrm{l}}) = a \qquad \rho(x_{\mathrm{r}}) = b \qquad a = b\\ \Gamma \vdash_{\mathrm{exe}} \langle e_0, \rho\rangle \overset{k}{\Longrightarrow} w\end{array}}{\Gamma \vdash_{\mathrm{exe}} \langle(\mathbf{if}\ x_{\mathrm{l}}\ \mathbf{equals}\ x_{\mathrm{r}}\ e_0\ e_1), \rho\rangle \overset{k+1}{\Longrightarrow} w}\ \textsc{E-If-Yes}$$

$$\frac{\begin{array}{c}\rho(x_{\mathrm{l}}) = a \qquad \rho(x_{\mathrm{r}}) = b \qquad a \neq b\\ \Gamma \vdash_{\mathrm{exe}} \langle e_1, \rho\rangle \overset{k}{\Longrightarrow} w\end{array}}{\Gamma \vdash_{\mathrm{exe}} \langle(\mathbf{if}\ x_{\mathrm{l}}\ \mathbf{equals}\ x_{\mathrm{r}}\ e_0\ e_1), \rho\rangle \overset{k+1}{\Longrightarrow} w}\ \textsc{E-If-No}$$

The E-PROG rule initiates evaluation of a program. It is notionally responsible for setting up the (non-notated) function context.

$$\frac{\epsilon \vdash_{\mathrm{exe}} \langle e, \epsilon\rangle \overset{k}{\Longrightarrow} v}{\vdash_{\mathrm{exe}} fD \ldots\ e \overset{k+1}{\Longrightarrow} v}\ \textsc{E-Prog}$$

4.2.1 Quasi-Literals

The last language component is a category called *quasi-literals*, so called because they look like literal syntax for object-level syntax objects, except that they contain variable references (which denote values), not literal atoms. Of course, those variables may refer to atom values generated by **fresh**. Quasi-literals also contain some type information to avoid the need for type inference.

$$\frac{v = [\![e^{\mathrm{qlit}}]\!]_\rho}{\Gamma \vdash_{\mathrm{exe}} \langle e^{\mathrm{qlit}}, \rho\rangle \overset{1}{\Longrightarrow} v}\ \textsc{E-QLit}$$

Their evaluation is specified by the following rules:

$$\llbracket \_ \rrbracket_{\_} : \mathit{QuasiLit} \times \mathit{ValEnv} \to \mathit{Value}$$
$$\llbracket x \rrbracket_\rho = \rho(x)$$
$$\llbracket (\textbf{ref}\ x) \rrbracket_\rho = \rho(x)$$
$$\llbracket (\textbf{inj}_0\ e^{\text{qlit}}\ \tau) \rrbracket_\rho = \textbf{inj0}(\llbracket e^{\text{qlit}} \rrbracket_\rho)$$
$$\llbracket (\textbf{inj}_1\ \tau\ e^{\text{qlit}}) \rrbracket_\rho = \textbf{inj1}(\llbracket e^{\text{qlit}} \rrbracket_\rho)$$
$$\llbracket \left(\textbf{prod}_i^{\Uparrow\beta_{\text{exp}}}\ e_i^{\text{qlit}} \downarrow \beta_i\right) \rrbracket_\rho = \textbf{prod}_i(\llbracket e_i^{\text{qlit}} \rrbracket_\rho)$$

4.2.2 Sufficient Disjointness

The requirement that evaluation be insensitive to α-equivalent inputs leads to strong requirements on the way that **open** destructures values. Consider the `let*` example above:

```
(let* ((a 1)              (let* ((d 1)
       (b (+ a a))               (d (+ d d))
       (c (* b 5)))              (d (* d 5)))
  (display c))             (display d)
```

These are α-equivalent, but if they were destructured without renaming, we would have $d = d = d$, even though $a \neq b \neq c$, violating our goal of being indifferent to α-conversion[1]. Therefore, we need to freshen each d to a distinct new name, e.g.

```
((aa 1)
 (bb (+ aa aa))
 (cc (* bb 5)))
```

The rule to ensure this is that, before destructuring, we must α-convert values such that the resulting renamed binders are disjoint from each other and from any names that appear in the environment. This gives rise to the hypothesis

$$\text{fa}_{\text{env}}(\Gamma, \rho) \vdash_{\text{suff-disj}} \textbf{prod}_i(v_i) : \tau_{\text{obj}}$$

in the E-OPEN-$\star$ rules. The $\vdash_{\text{suff-disj}}$ judgment here checks that binders exported by $\textbf{prod}_i(v_i)$'s non-exported subterms are distinct from each other, and that the exposable atoms are disjoint from the free atoms in the environment.

To check the first part of that, we define the judgment

$$\vdash_{\text{bndrs-disj}} v : \tau,$$

which checks that the exported binders in v (as determined by the type τ) are disjoint from each other.

$$\frac{}{\vdash_{\text{bndrs-disj}} a : \text{BAtom}}\ \text{BD-BATOM}$$

$$\frac{}{\vdash_{\text{bndrs-disj}} a : \text{RAtom}}\ \text{BD-RATOM}$$

$$\frac{\forall i,j \in \beta_{\text{ex}}.\ i \neq j \Rightarrow \text{fb}(\tau_i, v_i) \# \text{fb}(\tau_j, v_j) \qquad \forall i \in \beta_{\text{ex}}.\ \vdash_{\text{bndrs-disj}} v_i : \tau_i}{\vdash_{\text{bndrs-disj}} \textbf{prod}_i(v_i) : \text{Prod}_i^{\Uparrow\beta_{\text{ex}}}(\tau_i \downarrow \beta_i)}\ \text{BD-PROD}$$

We can now define $\vdash_{\text{suff-disj}}$:

$$\frac{\forall i \notin \beta_{\text{ex}}.\ \vdash_{\text{bndrs-disj}} v_i : \tau_i \qquad \forall i,j \notin \beta_{\text{ex}}.\ i \neq j \Rightarrow \text{fb}(\tau_i, v_i) \# \text{fb}(\tau_j, v_j) \qquad \text{xa}\left(\textbf{prod}_i(v_i), \text{Prod}_i^{\Uparrow\beta_{\text{ex}}}(\tau_i \downarrow \beta_i)\right) \# A}{A \vdash_{\text{suff-disj}} \textbf{prod}_i(v_i) : \text{Prod}_i^{\Uparrow\beta_{\text{ex}}}(\tau_i \downarrow \beta_i)}\ \text{SUFF-DISJ}$$

[1] In order to compare them, of course, the *LetStarClauses* would need to be destructured further. For simplicity, we consider the "last chance" for renaming to be the outermost level to which a name is exported, even if it is shadowed at that point.

4.3 Example

For an example, we write code that translates between two languages: from the lambda calculus augmented with a `let*` construct into the plain lambda calculus.

Our code, in Figure 2, mentions types defined in Figure 1. It is written in Romeo-L [10], which is a friendlier front-end to Romeo. For our purposes, the important differences are that the arguments to function calls and the scrutinees of **open** and **case** may be arbitrary expressions (not just variable references), and that Romeo-L can infer the strongest possible constraint C for **let**, so we may omit it. Furthermore, it will turn out (see section 6) that we need no pre- or post-condition from *convert* to show the absence of FAULT, so those constraints are also omitted.

Additionally, we have chosen to use more readable n-way sum types. This means that our **case** construct can branch 4 ways depending on whether the *Expr* it examines is a variable reference, an application, a lambda abstraction, or a let-star statement, and that injections take (as a subscript) a description of the choice that they are constructing.

Lines 3–5 are straightforward traversal of the existing *Expr* forms that are already forms in the core language (but, since their subterms might not be, they still need to be converted by recursively invoking *convert*).

Lines 6–11 destructure `let*` forms and handle the trivial case, where the `let*` does not have any arms. Line 12 recursively converts the body and all but the first arm of the `let*`, calling the result *e-rest*. Finally, line 13 constructs a beta-redex in the object language to bind the first arm's name to its value expression in *e-rest*.

5. Romeo respects α-equivalence

We are now ready to prove our main theorem: that Romeo respects α-equivalence. This is stronger than the corresponding result for Pure Fresh ML [13], which claims only that fresh names do not escape (see section 7.2 for a discussion).

Romeo is nondeterministic in its choice of names in the E-FRESH-$\star$ and E-OPEN-$\star$ rules. This complicates the definition of respecting α-equivalence. We show two results: first, that if two α-equivalent environments both terminate, then their results are α-equivalent, and second, if one of two α-equivalent environments yields a result, then the other one must yield at least one α-equivalent result as well.

For each of these theorems, the vast majority of the complexity is contained in the cases for E-FRESH-$\star$ and E-OPEN-$\star$ cases.

Since we must account for faulting, we extend the definition of α-equivalence to assert that FAULT $=_\alpha$ FAULT.

Complete proofs of all the theorems and lemmas we mention in this paper are available at `http://hdl.handle.net/2047/d20005013`.

Theorem 5.1 (Determinism up to α-equivalence, termination-insensitive version)**.**

$$\begin{array}{ll} \text{If} & \tau = \text{typeof}(\Gamma, e) \\ & \text{and } \rho =_\alpha \rho' : \Gamma \\ & \text{and } \Gamma \vdash_{\text{exe}} \langle e, \rho \rangle \overset{k}{\Longrightarrow} w \\ & \text{and } \Gamma \vdash_{\text{exe}} \langle e, \rho' \rangle \overset{k'}{\Longrightarrow} w' \\ \text{then} & w =_\alpha w' : \tau \end{array}$$

Proof. (Sketch) The major problem in the proof is that the two executions will potentially generate different fresh names in E-FRESH-$\star$ and E-OPEN-$\star$. Hence, even if the environments start out α-equivalent, they will not stay α-equivalent. For example, a **fresh** statement nondeterministically introduces a new free name into the environment. Therefore we must generalize our induction hypothesis to account for the ways in which ρ and ρ' diverge from α-equivalence.

We account for this divergence by introducing two injective substitutions to unify the names introduce by the two executions. So our induction hypothesis says that if $\sigma \circ \rho =_\alpha \sigma' \circ \rho' : \Gamma$ for a pair of injective substitutions σ and σ', then the results will be α-equivalent, modulo the same transformation (i.e. $\sigma(w) =_\alpha \sigma'(w') : \tau$).

Consider the case of E-FRESH-$\star$. As we enter the scope of the new name it generates, σ and σ' are extended to map the new names to a common fresh name, for the sake of the induction hypothesis.

When we exit from the scope, the induction hypothesis tells us that the results (of the inductive evaluation) are equivalent modulo the *extended* substitutions. The results of this evaluation step are either the same as those of the inductive step, or FAULT. We first show that the *original* substitutions suffice to α-equate those two values, and then that one side faults if and only if the other side does.

The E-OPEN-$\star$ case proceeds with a similar structure. However, in this case, we are not generating a single pair of new names, but unpacking a pair of values, which potentially contain many names. The crucial lemma to handle this states that, given two α-equivalent (and $\vdash_{\text{suff-disj}}$) values, breaking them apart into their children results in pairs of values which are pairwise α-equivalent modulo a *single* pair of substitutions. In other words, the subterms of a sufficiently disjoint value can all be placed into the same environment without losing any binding information (which would happen if there were any name collisions). After the induction hypothesis, E-OPEN-$\star$ proceeds like E-FRESH-$\star$.

The E-IF-$\star$ case, though simple, is crucial, because it shows that our induction hypothesis is strong enough to guarantee that a comparison between two names in ρ will always have the same result as a comparison between two names in ρ'. In particular, the injectivity of the substitutions that make ρ and ρ' α-equivalent is necessary. □

This theorem leaves open the possibility that some α-variant of ρ might result in an environment ρ' that cannot yield a result. The following theorem says that if one α-variant terminates (either with a value or FAULT), then every α-variant can terminate (and, by Theorem 5.1, when it does, the value will be α-equivalent to the result of the original). [2]

Theorem 5.2 (α-equivalent environments have equivalent termination behavior).

$$\begin{array}{ll} \text{If} & \tau = \text{typeof}(\Gamma, e) \\ & \text{and } \rho =_\alpha \rho' : \Gamma \\ & \text{and } \Gamma \vdash_{\text{exe}} \langle e, \rho \rangle \stackrel{k}{\Longrightarrow} w \\ \text{then} & \exists w'. \Gamma \vdash_{\text{exe}} \langle e, \rho' \rangle \stackrel{k}{\Longrightarrow} w' \text{ and } w =_\alpha w' : \tau \end{array}$$

Proof. (Sketch) For every choice of fresh name in the original computation, choose the same name in the other one. This preserves α-equivalence of ρ and ρ' for the induction hypothesis. □

5.1 Example

Consider again the example in Figure 2. Suppose that we had implemented a normal `let` construct (where the arms do *not* bind names from previous arms), with the type:

$$\begin{array}{rl} \textit{LetClauses} ::= & \text{Prod}() \\ | & \text{Prod}^{\Uparrow 1 \rhd 0}(\text{Prod}^{\Uparrow 0}(\text{BAtom}, \textit{Expr}), \textit{LetClauses}) \end{array}$$

[2] Since we are using big-step semantics, we cannot talk directly about non-termination.

The only difference, besides the name, is that the recursive *LetClauses* does not have a $\downarrow 0$. If we had wanted to change the code in Figure 2 to expand ordinary `lets` instead, the above change to the type of *Expr* is sufficient, and the otherwise identical code would respect *LetClause*'s binding behavior! This is a consequence of Theorem 5.1, which ensures that programs cannot observe anything about names except their binding structure, as defined by their binding specifications.

6. Checking Binding Safety Statically

This section describes the Romeo deduction system. The purpose of this deduction system is to generate constraints (proof obligations) which, if satisfied, guarantee that escape, and therefore FAULT, will never occur (see Theorem 6.1).

The proof system's judgment is of the form $\Gamma \vdash_{\text{proof}} \{H\}\, e\, \{P\}$. Like the execution semantics, it is type-dependent, and for a similar reason: types control which atoms will be bound or free, and thus whether operations are valid or not.

We use H, P, and C to range over constraints. Typically, H, the hypothesis, contains facts (about the atoms in the environment) that are true by construction. P, the postcondition, contains predicates that describe the connection between atoms in the environment and atoms in the output. C is used for general constraints, and for the constraints in **let** statements.

The obligations emitted by the deduction system must be satisfied by showing them true for all ρ compatible with Γ; in practice, we do this with an SMT Solver (for example, Romeo-L [10] uses Z3 [9]).

We begin by giving the syntax of constraints.

$$\begin{array}{rcl} z \in \textit{ConstrSetVar} & ::= & x \\ & | & \cdot \\ s \in \textit{SetDesc} & ::= & \varnothing \\ & | & s \cup s \\ & | & s \cap s \\ & | & \textit{sf}(z) \\ & | & \mathcal{F}_e(\Gamma) \\ \textit{sf} \in \textit{SetFn} & ::= & \mathcal{F} \mid \mathcal{F}_r \mid \mathcal{F}_b \mid \mathcal{X} \\ H, P, C \in \textit{Constraint} & ::= & C \wedge C \\ & | & s = s \\ & | & s \neq s \\ & | & s \mathbin{\#} s \\ & | & s \subseteq s \\ & | & z =_{\text{val}} e^{\text{qlit}} \\ & | & \textbf{true} \end{array}$$

Formulas are constructed from variables z, which range over program variables, and $\cdot$, which refers to the output value of the current expression. Set-valued terms are constructed from the free names ($\mathcal{F}$), free references ($\mathcal{F}_r$), free binders ($\mathcal{F}_b$), and exposable names ($\mathcal{X}$) of values, the free names of environments ($\mathcal{F}_e$), and then by the standard set constructors. Atomic formulas denote equality, inequality, etc., of sets, plus equality of values. Last, constraints are conjunctions of atomic formulas.

We use quasi-literals to describe values with variable interpolation. Because the type environment Γ is present, the type annotations of quasi-literals are redundant, but for economy of abstraction, we elected to reuse an existing concept instead of creating a new one.

In general, our rules are patterned after those in Pottier [13], using the type information in Γ to collect information about values. This subsumes Pottier's Δ. Most rules discharge their proof obligations by delegating them to proof obligations on subexpressions. The base cases of this recursion are P-CALL and P-QLIT, which describe proof obligations of the form $\Gamma \vDash H \Rightarrow P$. P-QLIT has only one obligation, which is to ensure that the result it produces

$$\frac{\mathrm{typeof}\left(\Gamma, e^{\mathrm{qlit}}\right) = \tau \qquad \Gamma, \cdot{:}\tau \vDash H \wedge \left(\cdot =_{\mathrm{val}} e^{\mathrm{qlit}}\right) \Rightarrow P}{\Gamma \vdash_{\mathrm{proof}} \{H\}\ e^{\mathrm{qlit}}\ \{P\}}\ \textsc{P-QLit}$$

$$\frac{\begin{array}{ccc} \mathrm{rettype}(f) = \tau & \mathrm{formals}(f) = (x_{\mathrm{formal},i})_i & \mathrm{argtype}(f) = (\tau_{\mathrm{formal},i})_i \\ \Gamma \vDash H \Rightarrow \mathrm{pre}(f)\,[x_{\mathrm{actual},i}/x_{\mathrm{formal},i}]_i & \multicolumn{2}{c}{\Gamma, \cdot{:}\tau \vDash H \wedge \mathcal{F}(\cdot) \subseteq \mathcal{F}_{\mathrm{e}}\left((x_{\mathrm{actual},i}{:}\tau_{\mathrm{formal},i})_i\right) \wedge \mathrm{post}(f)\,[x_{\mathrm{actual},i}/x_{\mathrm{formal},i}]_i \Rightarrow P} \end{array}}{\Gamma \vdash_{\mathrm{proof}} \{H\}\ \left(f\ (x_{\mathrm{actual},i})_i\right)\ \{P\}}\ \textsc{P-Call}$$

$$\frac{x \text{ fresh for } \Gamma, H, P \qquad \Gamma, x{:}\mathrm{BAtom} \vdash_{\mathrm{proof}} \{H \wedge \mathcal{F}(x) \# \mathcal{F}_{\mathrm{e}}(\Gamma)\}\ e\ \{P \wedge \mathcal{F}(x) \# \mathcal{F}(\cdot)\}}{\Gamma \vdash_{\mathrm{proof}} \{H\}\ (\textbf{fresh}\ x\ \textbf{in}\ e)\ \{P\}}\ \textsc{P-Fresh}$$

$$\frac{\begin{array}{c} \forall i.\ x_i \text{ is fresh for } \Gamma, H, P \\ \Gamma(x_{\mathrm{obj}}) = \mathrm{Prod}_i^{\Uparrow\beta_e}(\tau_i{\downarrow}\beta_i) \qquad \Gamma, (x_i{:}\tau_i)_i \vdash_{\mathrm{proof}} \left\{H \wedge \mathcal{X}(x_{\mathrm{obj}}) \# \mathcal{F}_{\mathrm{e}}(\Gamma) \wedge x_{\mathrm{obj}} =_{\mathrm{val}} \left(\textbf{prod}_i^{\Uparrow\beta_e}\ x_i{\downarrow}\beta_i\right)\right\}\ e\ \{P \wedge \mathcal{X}(x_{\mathrm{obj}}) \# \mathcal{F}(\cdot)\} \end{array}}{\Gamma \vdash_{\mathrm{proof}} \{H\}\ \left(\textbf{open}\ x_{\mathrm{obj}}\ \left((x_i)_i\right)\ e\right)\ \{P\}}\ \textsc{P-Open}$$

$$\frac{\begin{array}{c} x \text{ fresh for } \Gamma, H, P, C \\ \Gamma \vdash_{\mathrm{proof}} \{H\}\ e_{\mathrm{val}}\ \{C\} \qquad \mathrm{typeof}(\Gamma, e_{\mathrm{val}}) = \tau_{\mathrm{val}} \qquad \Gamma, x{:}\tau_{\mathrm{val}} \vdash_{\mathrm{proof}} \{H \wedge C[x/\cdot] \wedge \mathcal{F}(x) \subseteq \mathcal{F}_{\mathrm{e}}(\Gamma)\}\ e_{\mathrm{body}}\ \{P\} \end{array}}{\Gamma \vdash_{\mathrm{proof}} \{H\}\ (\textbf{let}\ x\ \textbf{where}\ C\ \textbf{be}\ e_{\mathrm{val}}\ \textbf{in}\ e_{\mathrm{body}})\ \{P\}}\ \textsc{P-Let}$$

$$\frac{\Gamma(x) = \tau_0 + \tau_1 \qquad \Gamma, x_0{:}\tau_0 \vdash_{\mathrm{proof}} \{H \wedge x =_{\mathrm{val}} (\textbf{inj}_0\ x_0\ \tau_1)\}\ e_0\ \{P\} \qquad \Gamma, x_1{:}\tau_1 \vdash_{\mathrm{proof}} \{H \wedge x =_{\mathrm{val}} (\textbf{inj}_1\ \tau_0\ x_1)\}\ e_1\ \{P\}}{\Gamma \vdash_{\mathrm{proof}} \{H\}\ (\textbf{case}\ x\ (x_0\ e_0)\ (x_1\ e_1))\ \{P\}}\ \textsc{P-Case}$$

$$\frac{\Gamma \vdash_{\mathrm{proof}} \{H \wedge \mathcal{F}(x_0) = \mathcal{F}(x_1)\}\ e_0\ \{P\} \qquad \Gamma \vdash_{\mathrm{proof}} \{H \wedge \mathcal{F}(x_0) \# \mathcal{F}(x_1)\}\ e_1\ \{P\}}{\Gamma \vdash_{\mathrm{proof}} \{H\}\ (\textbf{if}\ x_0\ \textbf{equals}\ x_1\ e_0\ e_1)\ \{P\}}\ \textsc{P-IfEq}$$

$$\frac{(x_i{:}\tau_i)_i \vdash_{\mathrm{proof}} \{C_0\}\ e\ \{C_1\}}{\vdash_{\mathrm{proof}} \left(\textbf{define-fn}\left(f\ (x_i{:}\tau_i)_i\ \textbf{pre}\ C_0\right) : \tau_0\ e\ \textbf{post}\ C_1\right)\ \mathrm{ok}}\ \textsc{P-FnDef} \qquad \frac{\forall i.\ \vdash fD_i\ \mathrm{ok} \qquad \epsilon \vdash_{\mathrm{proof}} \{\textbf{true}\}\ e\ \{\textbf{true}\}}{\vdash_{\mathrm{proof}} (fD_i)_i\ e\ \mathrm{ok}}\ \textsc{P-Prog}$$

Figure 7. Verification rules for the deduction system

obeys whatever constraints were imposed in P, given that the environment satisfies the assumptions in H. P-CALL has two obligations; first, that the invoked function's precondition is true (given H), and second that the resulting value satisfies the constraints in P (given H and the postcondition of the function).

As one might expect, the key rules are P-FRESH and P-OPEN, whose definitions are closely connected to E-FRESH-OK and E-OPEN-OK.

Proving the theorems in Section 5 required our language to have two important properties: that (a) no name can escape the context that exposed it, except as a bound name, and (b) no name is exposed twice from two different binding relationships at the same time (thereby revealing equality of two names that are not related by binding). For the purposes of dynamically respecting α-equivalence, property (a) was enforced by detecting such a situation and emitting FAULT instead, and property (b) was established by the constraints imposed on the names exposed in E-FRESH-$\star$ and E-OPEN-$\star$.

Now, for the purposes of the deduction system, property (a) appears in the postcondition of both P-FRESH and P-OPEN, as an obligation to prove that the exposed free names are disjoint from the free names of the result value (spelled '$\cdot$'), because the purpose of the deduction system is to prevent FAULTs. On the other hand, property (b) is a guarantee provided by the language dynamics, and therefore appears in the hypothesis of both rules, saying that the exposed names are guaranteed to be disjoint from the environment so far.

The rules P-OPEN and P-CASE each add additional information to their hypotheses. This information conveys the relationship between the atoms in the scrutinee (x_{obj} and x_0 respectively) and the atoms in its component(s). In the P-CASE case, even though the underlying values are different, their sets of free atoms (and free binders and exposable atoms, etc.) are identical, so for the logic's purposes, they are equivalent.

6.1 Odds and ends

In the **let** expression, the body subexpression has the same result as the expression as a whole, but the value subexpression does not. Therefore, in P-LET, the condition C (whose $\cdot$ refers to the value subexpression) must be adjusted for use as a hypothesis for the body subexpression. Fortunately, the name x refers to the value subexpression in question, so a simple $[x/\cdot]$ substitution suffices. H may be used unchanged by both subexpressions because it will contain no references to $\cdot$.[3]

A similar issue occurs in P-CALL. The pre- and post-conditions of the function (not to be confused with the expression's postcondition P) are expressed relative to the formal parameters, which are meaningless out of context. Because the actual arguments to a function invocation are all required to be variable references (rather than allowing them to be whole subexpressions), the solution is again simple: a simultaneous substitution from the formals to the actuals suffices to make the pre- and post-conditions meaningful in the caller's context.

Shadowing amongst Romeo program variables is incompatible with the deduction system, because obligations must be able to refer to (and distinguish) everything in Γ by name. This gives rise to the requirement that certain x's be fresh for Γ, H, and P; this requirement is easily satisfied by a simple renaming pass prior to type and proof checking.

P-CALL's body hypothesis contains a term representing extra information as a consequence of Lemma 6.1, which states that the

[3] This is different from the strategy used in Pure FreshML [13], in which postconditions are functions that produce predicates.

free atoms in the result of any expression are a subset of the the free atoms in the environment in which it is evaluated. A similar term appears in the hypothesis for P-LET's body subexpression.The proofs of Lemmas 6.1 and 6.1, and the definition of the typesystem (including $\Gamma \vdash_{\text{type-env}} \rho$), can be found at `http://hdl.handle.net/2047/d20005013`.

Lemma 6.1 (No names made up).

$$\begin{array}{ll} \text{If} & \tau = \text{typeof}(\Gamma, e) \\ & \text{and } \Gamma \vdash_{\text{type-env}} \rho \\ & \text{and } \Gamma \vdash_{\text{exe}} \langle e, \rho \rangle \stackrel{k}{\Longrightarrow} v \\ \text{then} & \text{fa}(\tau, v) \subseteq \text{fa}_{\text{env}}(\Gamma, \rho) \end{array}$$

Proof. By induction on k. □

Finally, in P-IFEQ, the result of the comparison can be expressed in our predicate language; in the branch in which the two atoms are equal, we note that their free atom sets (known to be singletons) are equal, and in the other branch, we note that their free atoms sets are disjoint.

6.2 Soundness of the Deduction System

The soundness of the deduction system is expressed in the following theorem.

Theorem 6.1 (Soundness of the deduction system).

$$\begin{array}{ll} \text{If} & \tau = \text{typeof}(\Gamma, e) \\ & \text{and } \Gamma \vdash_{\text{type-env}} \rho \\ & \text{and } \Gamma \vdash_{\text{proof}} \{H\}\ e\ \{P\} \\ & \text{and } \Gamma \vdash_{\text{exe}} \langle e, \rho \rangle \stackrel{k}{\Longrightarrow} w \\ \text{then} & w \neq \text{FAULT and } \Gamma, \cdot{:}\tau; \rho[\cdot \to w] \models H \Rightarrow P \end{array}$$

Proof. By induction on k. □

Observe that the theorem is unusually strong: it says that if there is *any* solution to the proof obligations, then the program is non-faulting for *any* suitably-typed environment ρ. This depends on the fact that the generation of proof obligations is deterministic (given pre- and post-conditions for the functions in the system).

6.3 Example

The Romeo-L code in Figure 2 contains a number of **open**s, each of which potentially can produce a FAULT. However, our deduction shows that FAULT will never happen. A complete derivation is too large to include here, but we will informally look at two examples.

First, on line 5, we are opening up a lambda abstraction. This "exposes" the lambda's binder (binding it to the variable *bv*). Fortunately, $(\textbf{inj}_{\text{lambda}}\ (\textbf{prod}\ bv, convert(e\text{-}body) \downarrow 0))$, the body of the **open**, has no free names from its left-hand child and binds *bv* in its right-hand child, so (regardless of the output of *convert*) the exposed name from *bv* is not free in the result.

Second, on line 7, we open up the whole `let*` form, exposing all of the names that *lsc* exports. We must show that those names do not escape this context. When *lsc-some* is destructured, we know from its type that *bv* and *lsc-rest*, together, export that same set of names.

The value returned from the **open** is an application, constructed on line 13. Its left-hand-side is a lambda, which binds *bv* in *e-rest*. Therefore, we need to show that the names exported by *lsc-rest* are bound in *e-rest*. Fortunately, *e-rest* is a `let*` construct (line 12), defined to bind the names exported by *lsc-rest* in *e-body*, which is exactly what we needed. Therefore, the left-hand side of the the function application constructed by *convert* contains no free references that could cause a FAULT.

Now, we look at the right-hand-side of that application, which we generate by calling *convert*(*val-expr*). By Lemma 6.1, we know that *convert* produces a value whose free names are a subset of its argument. How do we know what names are free in *val-expr*? We know that, as an expression, it exports nothing, and so has no free binders. Any free references in it would have also been free in *lsc-some* (because it binds no names in the scope of its value expression), and therefore free in *let-star* itself. But *let-star* is part of the environment in which it was opened (on line 7), so, by the freshness of newly-exposed names, the names we are worried about must be fresh for *val-expr*.

A similar argument can be used to verify the safety of the other **open**s. In this example, the programmer didn't need to supply any constraints to justify the function calls. In general, constraints are necessary for the same reasons as in Pure FreshML [13], and the same examples apply.

7. Related work

7.1 Statically Specified Binding in Template Macros

The work of Herman and Wand [7, 8] introduced the idea of a static binding specification for a template or pattern-matching macro system (like Scheme's `syntax-rules`). Herman defined a language for binding specifications, and gave an algorithm for deciding whether a pattern-and-template macro was consistent with its binding specification. In practice, however, the complex macros in a language like Scheme are often not expressible in a pattern-matching system. Romeo provides a path for extending this macro system to a procedurally-based one, like Scheme's `syntax-case`.

Although our binding annotation system is very similar in power to Herman's, we have made some changes in representation. The most noticeable is that where Herman and Wand use addresses into binary trees of values, we use indices into wide products.

7.2 Pure FreshML

The second source for this work is Pure FreshML [13]. Both Pure FreshML and Romeo are first-order, side-effect-free languages in which a runtime system ensures that introduced names do not escape their scope, and both provide a proof system that generates proof obligations which, if true, guarantee statically that no faults will occur. One important difference, important for our intended application of macro-expanders, is that Romeo manipulates plain S-expression-like data, guided by types, whereas Pure FreshML saves type information in values. Our presentation of the language and semantics are somewhat different: for example, we have separate constructs for destructuring products (**open**) and destructuring sum types (**case**).

The system in [13] leaves the actual language of binding specifications underdetermined. All the formal development is done in a simple system, roughly equivalent to the λ-calculus, but one of the key examples, normalization by evaluation, is done using the more expressive system of Cαml [12]. Still, both of these systems are too weak to express complex binding constructs. For example, neither can express the natural syntax of the `let*` construct.

Also, our language provides stronger guarantees than does Pure Fresh ML. The primary claim in [13] is that no fresh name escapes its scope. This is much weaker than respecting α-equivalence. Consider a boolean-valued function that tests its arguments for syntactic (not α-) equivalence and returns a boolean. This function would not violate the no-escape condition, but of course it violates α-equivalence. We conjecture that Pure FreshML does respect α-equivalence, but we have not attempted to prove this.

7.3 Ott

Ott [16] is a system for metaprogramming that accepts binding specifications with a syntax and semantics similar to ours. However, Ott's goals are significantly different. Instead of providing a complete, name-aware programming system, Ott generates code for use in a theorem-prover, including definitions of types and a capture-avoiding substitution function. Ott supports a number of theorem-provers and a number of representations for the terms in them. Additionally, it can export boilerplate code for OCaml.

Ott's binding specifications are strictly more expressive than ours: effectively, they allow for a single value to export multiple sets of names (these sets are designated by "auxiliary functions"), which can be bound separately.

In order to support theorem-provers, Ott includes a definition for α-equivalence between its "concrete abstract syntax trees" (the equivalent of our values v). Their definition is based on a partial equivalence relation which relates two tree positions in a term if they are connected by binding (i.e., they would have to be renamed together). From this intra-tree relation, it is fairly straightforward to extract a notion of α-equivalence: two trees are α-equivalent if both (1) their free names match, and (2) the partial equivalence relations representing their bound names are identical. It is not clear whether this definition would lead to simpler proofs of Theorems like 5.1 and 5.2.

7.4 Hygienic Macro Systems in Scheme

The goals of our work have a great deal in common with the goals of hygienic macro systems, like those used in Scheme. There are two major problems in dealing with hygienic macro systems in Scheme. The first is that there is not yet a widely-accepted, formal, implementation-independent definition for the property of being hygienic. The algorithm described by Dybvig [3], which is the basis for hygienic macro expansion in Scheme, seems "correct" in the sense that it tends to behave consistently with the intuition of its users. But there is no specification against which it can be proved correct. The closest things to a specification, given by Clinger [2] and Dybvig [3], are phrased in terms of the bindings inserted or introduced by the macro. However, given a macro definition (say, in template style), there is no obvious way to tell what those bindings should be without reference to the expansion algorithm. So this specification remains circular. The use of static binding specifications (introduced for this purpose in [7]) provides a more rigorous basis for hygiene.

Secondly, the Dybvig algorithm offers no *static* guarantees. If the designer makes a mistake, it will only be discovered after the macro is expanded (and probably after it is used, perhaps by an innocent end-user). By contrast, our system offers a static guarantee: if the macro definition binds a name incorrectly, the error will be detected at macro-definition time by the deduction system, not as a runtime fault.

Even simple macros can cause unexpected results in traditionally-hygienic systems. Suppose we want a macro that translates

```
(lazy-let ((x (long-calculation)))
  ... x ...)
```

into

```
(let ((x (delay (long-calculation))))
  ... (force x) ...)
```

If the body of the `lazy-let` contains a macro invocation like `(my-macro1 x x)` how is the expander for `lazy-let` to know whether either of the `x`'s refers to the `x` in the declaration of the `lazy-let`? In the absence of a binding specification for `my-macro1`, the only solution is to expand the macros bottom-up, which is undesirable for other reasons. If we had a binding specification for `my-macro1`, we could perform this transformation without reference to the expansion of `my-macro1`.

7.5 Binding in Theorem-Proving Systems

Ever since the POPLMark Challenge [1], there has been a large interest in coding terms with bindings in various proof assistants [11][14][17]. These works have differing goals than ours; they are primarily concerned with proving facts about programs, while we are aiming at a usable meta-programming system. They also generally depend on representing abstract syntax trees in a pre-existing theorem-proving framework like Coq or Agda, whereas we are concerned with the complications of concrete syntax (even in an S-expression based language). We observe that Pouillard and Pottier [15] call a function "well-behaved" iff it preserves α-equivalence, and judge a type system to be satisfactory only if the functions definable in the system are well-behaved.

7.6 Extensions to Romeo

As we have described it, writing programs in Romeo is tedious. Programs must be written in an ANF-like style. For example, the arguments to function calls must be variables and not more complicated expressions.

A second problem is that we have not yet described how the truth of $\Gamma \models H \Rightarrow P$ is to be determined, and, if it fails, how the programmer is supposed to figure out how to fix it.

These problems are addressed in Muehlboeck's master's thesis [10], which presents a more usable front-end for Romeo, called Romeo-L. Romeo-L programs are written in a more natural dialect, and are automatically translated into the core Romeo we have described here. This translation introduces **let** expressions to avoid the need to program in A-normal form, and for each **let** it infers the strongest possible constraint C. Therefore the user need only supply constraints for function definitions. In practice, this means a vastly reduced annotation burden.

Romeo-L also includes a connection to the Z3 SMT solver [9], which is able to check statements of the form $\Gamma \models H \Rightarrow P$, completing the automated checking of the deduction system. Furthermore, it can translate counterexamples provided by Z3 into sets of names, so that the user can understand them, and it can explain how they violate a constraint either written by the user, or implicit in the rules for **fresh** or **open**. We hope to report on this in a separate paper.

Acknowledgments

We would like to thank Fabian Muehlboeck for his work in testing and validating Romeo, and J. Ian Johnson for his contributions to early versions of the binding system. We would also like to thank the anonymous reviewers for their comments to improve this paper.

This material is based on research sponsored by the Defense Advanced Research Projects Agency and the Air Force Research Laboratory. Any opinions, findings, conclusions or recommendations expressed herein are those of the authors, and do not necessarily reflect those of the US Government, DARPA, or the Air Force.

References

[1] B. E. Aydemir et al. Mechanized metatheory for the masses: The PoplMark challenge. In *Proceedings of the 18th International Conference on Theorem Proving in Higher Order Logics*, TPHOLs'05, pages 50–65, Berlin, Heidelberg, 2005. Springer-Verlag. ISBN 3-540-28372-2, 978-3-540-28372-0. URL `http://dx.doi.org/10.1007/11541868_4`.

[2] W. Clinger and J. Rees. Macros that work. In *Proceedings of the 18th ACM SIGPLAN-SIGACT Symposium on Principles*

of Programming Languages, POPL '91, pages 155–162, New York, NY, USA, 1991. ACM. ISBN 0-89791-419-8. URL http://doi.acm.org/10.1145/99583.99607.

[3] R. K. Dybvig, R. Hieb, and C. Bruggeman. Syntactic abstraction in scheme. *Lisp Symb. Comput.*, 5(4):295–326, Dec. 1992. ISSN 0892-4635. URL http://dx.doi.org/10.1007/BF01806308.

[4] S. Erdweg, T. van der Storm, and Y. Dai. Capture-avoiding and hygienic program transformations. In *Proceedings of the 28th European Conference on Object-Oriented Programming*. To appear.

[5] S. E. Ganz, A. Sabry, and W. Taha. Macros as multi-stage computations: type-safe, generative, binding macros in MacroML. *ACM SIGPLAN Notices*, 36(10):74–74–85–85, Oct. 2001. ISSN 0362-1340. URL http://portal.acm.org/citation.cfm?id=507669.507646.

[6] D. Hendriks and V. van Oostrom. Adbmal. In F. Baader, editor, *Automated Deduction – CADE-19*, volume 2741 of *Lecture Notes in Computer Science*, pages 136–150. Springer Berlin Heidelberg, 2003. ISBN 978-3-540-40559-7. URL http://dx.doi.org/10.1007/978-3-540-45085-6_11.

[7] D. Herman. *A Theory of Typed Hygienic Macros*. Ph.D. thesis, Northeastern University, 2010. URL http://www.ccs.neu.edu/home/dherman/research/papers/dissertation.pdf

[8] D. Herman and M. Wand. A theory of hygienic macros. In *Proceedings of the Theory and Practice of Software, 17th European Conference on Programming Languages and Systems*, ESOP'08/ETAPS'08, pages 48–62, Berlin, Heidelberg, 2008. Springer-Verlag. URL http://dx.doi.org/10.1007/978-3-540-78739-6_4.

[9] L. D. Moura and N. Bjørner. Z3: An efficient SMT solver. *Tools and Algorithms for the Construction and Analysis of Systems SE - 24*, 4963:337–340, 2008. URL http://dx.doi.org/10.1007/978-3-540-78800-3_24.

[10] F. Muehlboeck. *Checking Binding Hygiene Statically*. Master's thesis, Northeastern University, 2013. URL http://hdl.handle.net/2047/d20003134.

[11] R. Pollack, M. Sato, and W. Ricciotti. A canonical locally named representation of binding. *J. Autom. Reason.*, 49(2):185–207, Aug. 2012. ISSN 0168-7433. URL http://dx.doi.org/10.1007/s10817-011-9229-y.

[12] F. Pottier. An overview of Cαml. *Electronic Notes in Theoretical Computer Science*, 148(2):27–52, 2006. URL http://www.sciencedirect.com/science/article/pii/S1571066106001253.

[13] F. Pottier. Static name control for FreshML. In *Proceedings of the 22nd Annual IEEE Symposium on Logic in Computer Science*, LICS '07, pages 356–365, Washington, DC, USA, 2007. IEEE Computer Society. ISBN 0-7695-2908-9. URL http://dx.doi.org/10.1109/LICS.2007.44.

[14] N. Pouillard and F. Pottier. A fresh look at programming with names and binders. In *Proceedings of the 15th ACM SIGPLAN International Conference on Functional Programming*, ICFP '10, pages 217–228, New York, NY, USA, 2010. ACM. ISBN 978-1-60558-794-3. URL http://doi.acm.org/10.1145/1863543.1863575.

[15] N. Pouillard and F. Pottier. A unified treatment of syntax with binders. *Journal of Functional Programming*, 22(4–5):614–704, Sept. 2012. URL http://dx.doi.org/10.1017/S0956796812000251.

[16] P. Sewell et al. Ott: Effective tool support for the working semanticist. *J. Funct. Program.*, 20(1):71–122, Jan. 2010. ISSN 0956-7968. URL http://dx.doi.org/10.1017/S0956796809990293.

[17] C. Urban. Nominal techniques in Isabelle/HOL. *J. Autom. Reason.*, 40(4):327–356, May 2008. ISSN 0168-7433. URL http://dx.doi.org/10.1007/s10817-008-9097-2.

Maximal Sharing in the Lambda Calculus with letrec[1]

Clemens Grabmayer
Dept. of Computer Science, VU University Amsterdam
de Boelelaan 1081a, 1081 HV Amsterdam
c.a.grabmayer@vu.nl

Jan Rochel
Dept. of Computing Sciences, Utrecht University
Princetonplein 5, 3584 CC Utrecht, The Netherlands
jan@rochel.info

Abstract

Increasing sharing in programs is desirable to compactify the code, and to avoid duplication of reduction work at run-time, thereby speeding up execution. We show how a maximal degree of sharing can be obtained for programs expressed as terms in the lambda calculus with letrec. We introduce a notion of 'maximal compactness' for $\lambda_{\mathsf{letrec}}$-terms among all terms with the same infinite unfolding. Instead of defined purely syntactically, this notion is based on a graph semantics. $\lambda_{\mathsf{letrec}}$-terms are interpreted as first-order term graphs so that unfolding equivalence between terms is preserved and reflected through bisimilarity of the term graph interpretations. Compactness of the term graphs can then be compared via functional bisimulation.

We describe practical and efficient methods for the following two problems: transforming a $\lambda_{\mathsf{letrec}}$-term into a maximally compact form; and deciding whether two $\lambda_{\mathsf{letrec}}$-terms are unfolding-equivalent. The transformation of a $\lambda_{\mathsf{letrec}}$-term L into maximally compact form L_0 proceeds in three steps: (i) translate L into its term graph $G = [\![L]\!]$; (ii) compute the maximally shared form of G as its bisimulation collapse G_0; (iii) read back a $\lambda_{\mathsf{letrec}}$-term L_0 from the term graph G_0 with the property $[\![L_0]\!] = G_0$. Then L_0 represents a maximally shared term graph, and it has the same unfolding as L.

The procedure for deciding whether two given $\lambda_{\mathsf{letrec}}$-terms L_1 and L_2 are unfolding-equivalent computes their term graph interpretations $[\![L_1]\!]$ and $[\![L_2]\!]$, and checks whether these are bisimilar.

For illustration, we also provide a readily usable implementation.

Categories and Subject Descriptors D.3.3 [*Language constructs and features*]: Recursion; F.3.3 [*Studies of Programming Constructs*]: Functional constructs

General Terms functional programming, compiler optimisation

Keywords Lambda Calculus with letrec; unfolding semantics; subterm sharing; maximal sharing; higher-order term graphs

1. Introduction

Explicit sharing in pure functional programming languages is typically expressed by means of the letrec-construct, which facilitates cyclic definitions. The λ-calculus with letrec, $\lambda_{\mathsf{letrec}}$ forms a syntactic core of these languages, and it can be viewed as their abstraction. As such $\lambda_{\mathsf{letrec}}$ is well-suited as a test bed for developing program transformations in functional programming languages. This certainly holds for the transformation presented here that has a strong conceptual motivation, is justified by a form of semantic reasoning, and is best described first for an expressive, yet minimal language.

1.1 Expressing sharing and infinite λ-terms

For the programmer the letrec-construct offers the possibility to write a program compactly by utilising subterm sharing. letrec-expressions bind subterms to variables; these variables then denote occurrences of the respective subterms and can be used anywhere inside of the letrec-expression. In this way, instead of repeating a subterm multiple times, a single definition can be given that is referenced from multiple positions.

We will denote the construct letrec here by let as in Haskell.

Example 1.1. Consider the λ-term $(\lambda x.\, x)\,(\lambda x.\, x)$ with two occurrences of the subterm $\lambda x.\, x$. These occurrences can be shared with as result the $\lambda_{\mathsf{letrec}}$-term ($\mathsf{let}\ id = \lambda x.\, x\ \mathsf{in}\ id\, id$).

As let-bindings permit definitions with cyclic dependencies, terms in $\lambda_{\mathsf{letrec}}$ are able to finitely denote infinite λ-terms (for short: λ^{∞}-terms). The λ^{∞}-term M represented by a $\lambda_{\mathsf{letrec}}$-term L can be obtained by a typically infinite process in which the let-bindings in L are unfolded continually with M as result in the limit. Then we say that M is the *infinite unfolding* of L, or that M is the denotation of L in the *unfolding semantics*, indicated symbolically by $M = [\![L]\!]_{\lambda^{\infty}}$.

Example 1.2. For the $\lambda_{\mathsf{letrec}}$-terms L and P and the λ^{∞}-term M:

$$L := \lambda f.\, \mathsf{let}\ r = f\, r\ \mathsf{in}\ r \qquad M := \lambda f.\, f\,(f\,(\ldots))$$
$$P := \lambda f.\, \mathsf{let}\ r = f\,(f\, r)\ \mathsf{in}\ r$$

it holds that both L and P (which represent fixed-point combinators) have M as their infinite unfolding: $[\![L]\!]_{\lambda^{\infty}} = [\![P]\!]_{\lambda^{\infty}} = M$.

L and P in this example are 'unfolding-equivalent'. Note that L represents M in a more compact way than P. It is intuitively clear that there is no $\lambda_{\mathsf{letrec}}$-term that represents M more compactly than L. So L can be called a 'maximally shared form' of P (and of M).

We address, and efficiently solve, the problems of computing the maximally shared form of a $\lambda_{\mathsf{letrec}}$-term, and of determining whether two $\lambda_{\mathsf{letrec}}$-terms are unfolding-equivalent. Note that these notions are based on the static unfolding semantics. We *do not consider* any dynamic semantics based on evaluation by β-reduction or otherwise.

1.2 Recognising potential for sharing

A general risk for compilers of functional programs is "[to construct] multiple instances of the same expression, rather than sharing a single copy of them. This wastes space because each instance occupies separate storage, and it wastes time because the instances will be reduced separately. This waste can be arbitrarily large, [...]"

[1] This work was supported by NWO in the framework of the project *Realising Optimal Sharing (ROS)*, project number 612.000.935.

ICFP '14, September 1–6, 2014, Gothenburg, Sweden.
Copyright is held by the owner/author(s). Publication rights licensed to ACM.
ACM 978-1-4503-2873-9 /14/09...$15.00.
http://dx.doi.org/10.1145/2628136.2628148

([28, p.243]). Therefore practical compilers increase sharing, and do so typically for supercombinator translations of programs (such as fully-lazy lambda-lifting). Thereby two goals are addressed: to increase sharing based on a syntactical analysis of the 'static' form of the program; and to prevent splits into too many supercombinators when an anticipation of the program's 'dynamic' behaviour is able to conclude that no sharing at run-time will be gained.

A well-known method for the 'static' part is common subexpression elimination (CSE) [6]. For the 'dynamic' part, a predictive syntactic program analysis has been proposed for fine-tuning sharing of partial applications in supercombinator translations [10].

We focus primarily on the 'static' aspect of introducing sharing. We provide a conceptual solution that substantially extends CSE. But instead of maximising sharing for a supercombinator translation of a program, we carry out the optimisation on the program itself (the $\lambda_{\mathsf{letrec}}$-term). And instead of applying a purely syntactical program analysis, we use a term graph semantics for $\lambda_{\mathsf{letrec}}$-terms.

1.3 Approach based on a term graph semantics

We develop a combination of techniques for realising maximal sharing in $\lambda_{\mathsf{letrec}}$-terms. For this we proceed in four steps: $\lambda_{\mathsf{letrec}}$-terms are interpreted as higher-order term graphs; the higher-order term graphs are implemented as first-order term graphs; maximally compact versions of such term graphs can be computed by standard algorithms; $\lambda_{\mathsf{letrec}}$-terms that represent compacted term graphs (or in fact arbitrary ones) can be retrieved by a 'readback' operation.

In more detail, the four essential ingredients are the following:

(1) A *semantics* $[\![\cdot]\!]_{\mathcal{H}}$ for interpreting $\lambda_{\mathsf{letrec}}$-terms as *higher-order term graphs*, which are first-order term graphs enriched with a feature for describing binding and scopes. We call this specific kind of higher-order term graphs 'λ-ho-term-graphs'.

The variable binding structure is recorded in this term graph concept because it must be respected by any addition of sharing. The term graph interpretation adequately represents sharing as expressed by a $\lambda_{\mathsf{letrec}}$-term. It is not injective: a λ-ho-term-graph typically is the interpretation of various $\lambda_{\mathsf{letrec}}$-terms. Different degrees of sharing as expressed by $\lambda_{\mathsf{letrec}}$-terms can be compared via the λ-ho-term-graph interpretations by a sharing preorder, which is defined as the existence of a homomorphism (functional bisimulation).

While comparing higher-order term graphs via this preorder is computable in principle, standard algorithms do not apply. Therefore efficient solvability of the compactification problem and the comparison problem is, from the outset, not guaranteed. For this reason we devise a first-order implementation of λ-ho-term-graphs:

(2) An *interpretation* $\mathcal{HT}$ of λ-ho-term-graphs into a specific kind of *first-order term graphs*, which we call 'λ-term-graphs'. It preserves and reflects the sharing preorder.

$\mathcal{HT}$ reduces bisimilarity between λ-ho-term-graphs (higher-order) to bisimilarity between λ-term-graphs (first-order), and facilitates:

(3) The use of standard methods for *checking* bisimilarity and for computing the bisimulation *collapse* of λ-term-graphs. Via $\mathcal{HT}$ also the analogous problems for λ-ho-term-graphs can be solved.

Term graphs can be represented as deterministic process graphs (labelled transition systems), and even as deterministic finite-state automata (DFAs). That is why it is possible to apply efficient algorithms for state minimisation and language equivalence of DFAs.

Finally, an operation to return from term graphs to $\lambda_{\mathsf{letrec}}$-terms:

(4) A *readback* function rb from λ-term-graphs to $\lambda_{\mathsf{letrec}}$-terms that, for every λ-term-graph G, computes a $\lambda_{\mathsf{letrec}}$-term L from the set of $\lambda_{\mathsf{letrec}}$-terms that have G as their interpretation via $[\![\cdot]\!]_{\mathcal{H}}$ and $\mathcal{HT}$ (i.e. a $\lambda_{\mathsf{letrec}}$-term for which it holds that $\mathcal{HT}([\![L]\!]_{\mathcal{H}}) = G$).

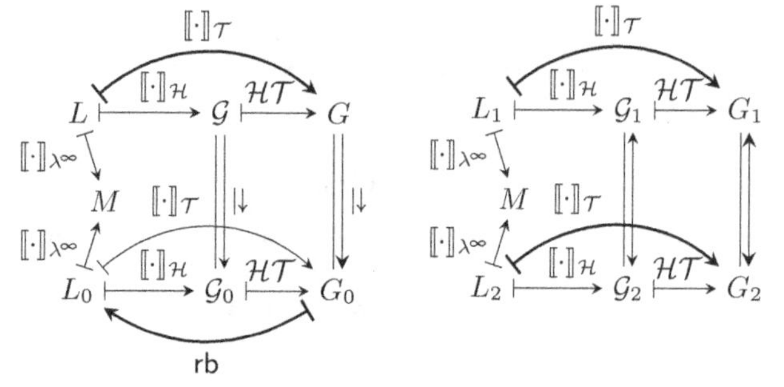

Figure 1. Component-step build-up of the methods for computing a maximally shared form L_0 of a $\lambda_{\mathsf{letrec}}$-term L (left), deciding unfolding equivalence of $\lambda_{\mathsf{letrec}}$-terms L_1 and L_2 via bisimilarity $\leftrightarrows$ (right).

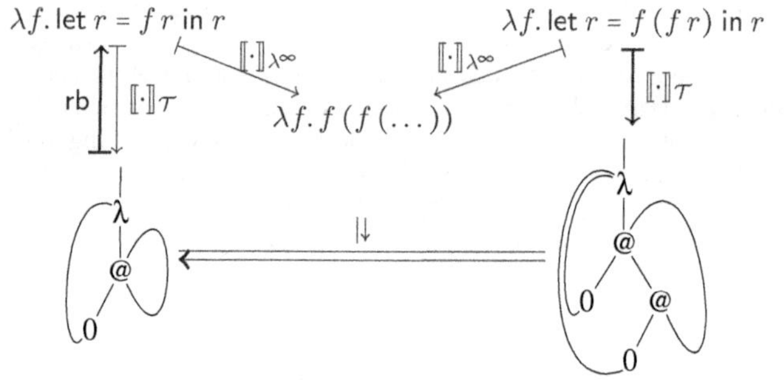

Figure 2. Computing a maximally compact version of the term P from Ex. 1.2 (right) by using composition of term graph semantics $[\![\cdot]\!]_{\mathcal{T}}$, collapse $|\!\downarrow$, and readback rb, yielding the term L (left).

1.4 Methods and their correctness

On the basis of the concepts above we develop efficient methods for introducing maximal sharing, and for checking unfolding equivalence, of $\lambda_{\mathsf{letrec}}$-terms, as sketched below.

In describing these methods, we use the following notation:

$\mathcal{H}$: class of λ-ho-term-graphs, the image of the semantics $[\![\cdot]\!]_{\mathcal{H}}$;
$\mathcal{T}$: class of λ-term-graphs, the image of the interpretation $\mathcal{HT}$;
$[\![\cdot]\!]_{\mathcal{T}} := \mathcal{HT} \circ [\![\cdot]\!]_{\mathcal{H}}$: first-order term graph semantics for $\lambda_{\mathsf{letrec}}$-terms;
$|\!\downarrow$: bisimulation collapse on $\mathcal{H}$ and $\mathcal{T}$;
rb : readback mapping from λ-term-graphs to $\lambda_{\mathsf{letrec}}$-terms.

We obtain the following methods (for illustrations, see Fig. 1):

- *Maximal sharing*: for a given $\lambda_{\mathsf{letrec}}$-term, a maximally shared form can be obtained by collapsing its first-order term graph interpretation, and then reading back the collapse: $\mathsf{rb} \circ |\!\downarrow \circ [\![\cdot]\!]_{\mathcal{T}}$
- *Unfolding equivalence*: for given $\lambda_{\mathsf{letrec}}$-terms L and P, it can be decided whether $[\![L]\!]_{\lambda^\infty} = [\![P]\!]_{\lambda^\infty}$ by checking whether their term graph interpretations $[\![L]\!]_{\mathcal{T}}$ and $[\![P]\!]_{\mathcal{T}}$ are bisimilar.

See Fig. 2 for an illustration of the application of the maximal sharing method to the $\lambda_{\mathsf{letrec}}$-terms L and P from Ex. 1.2.

The correctness of these methods hinges on the fact that the term graph translation and the readback satisfy the following properties:

(P1) $\lambda_{\mathsf{letrec}}$-terms L and P have the same infinite unfolding if and only if the term graphs $[\![L]\!]_{\mathcal{T}}$ and $[\![P]\!]_{\mathcal{T}}$ are bisimilar.

(P2) The class $\mathcal{T}$ of λ-term-graphs is closed under homomorphism.

(P3) The readback rb is a right inverse of $[\![\cdot]\!]_{\mathcal{T}}$ up to isomorphism $\simeq$, that is, for all term graphs $G \in \mathcal{T}$ it holds: $([\![\cdot]\!]_{\mathcal{T}} \circ \mathsf{rb})(G) \simeq G$.

Note: (P2) and (P3) will be established only for a subclass $\mathcal{T}_{\text{eag}}$ of $\mathcal{T}$. Furthermore, practicality of these methods depends on the property:

(P4) Translation $[\![\cdot]\!]_{\mathcal{T}}$ and readback rb are efficiently computable.

1.5 Overview of the development

In the Preliminaries (Section 2) we fix basic notions and notations for first-order term graphs. λ_{letrec}-terms and their unfolding semantics are defined in Section 3. In Section 4 we develop the concept of 'λ-ho-term-graph', which gives rise to the class $\mathcal{H}$, and the higher-order term graph semantics $[\![\cdot]\!]_{\mathcal{H}}$ for λ_{letrec}-terms.

In Section 5 we develop the concept of first-order 'λ-term-graph' in the class $\mathcal{T}$, and define the interpretation $\mathcal{HT}$ of λ-ho-term-graphs into λ-term-graphs as a mapping from $\mathcal{H}$ to $\mathcal{T}$. This induces the first-order term graph semantics $[\![\cdot]\!]_{\mathcal{T}} := \mathcal{HT} \circ [\![\cdot]\!]_{\mathcal{H}}$, for which we also provide a direct inductive definition.

In Section 6 we define the readback rb with the desired property as a function from λ-term-graphs to λ_{letrec}-terms. Subsequently in Section 7 we report on the complexity of the described methods, individually, and in total for the methods described in Subsection 1.4.

In Section 8 we link to our implementation of the presented methods. Finally in Section 9 we explain easy modifications, describe possible extensions, and sketch potential practical applications.

1.6 Applications and scalability

While our contribution is at first a conceptual one, it holds the promise for a number of practical applications:

- Increasing the efficiency of the execution of programs by transforming them into their maximally shared form at compile-time.
- Increasing the efficiency of the execution of programs by repeatedly compactifying the program at run time.
- Improving systems for recognising program equivalence.
- Providing feedback to the programmer, along the lines: 'This code has identical fragments and can be written more compactly.'

These and a number of other potential applications are discussed in more detail in Section 9.

The presented methods scale well to larger inputs, due to the quadratic bound on their runtime complexity (see Section 7).

1.7 Relationship with other concepts of sharing

The maximal sharing method is targeted at increasing 'static' sharing in the sense that a program is transformed at compile time into a version with a higher degree of sharing. It is not (at least not a priori) a method for 'dynamic' sharing, i.e. for an evaluator that maintains a certain degree of sharing at run time, such as graph rewrite mechanisms for fully-lazy [31] or optimal evaluation [1] of the λ-calculus. However, we envisage run-time collapsing of the program's graph interpretation integrated with the evaluator (see Section 9).

The term 'maximal sharing' stems from work on the ATERM library [5]. It describes a technique for minimising memory usage when representing a set of terms in a first-order term rewrite system (TRS). The terms are kept in an aggregate directed acyclic graph by which their syntax trees are shared as much as possible. Thereby terms are created only if they are entirely new; otherwise they are referenced by pointers to roots of sub-dags. Our use of the expression 'maximal sharing' is inspired by that work, but our results generalise that approach in the following ways:

- Instead of first-order terms we consider terms in a higher-order language with the letrec-construct for expressing sharing.
- Since letrec typically defines cyclic sharing dependencies, we interpret terms as cyclic graphs instead of just dags.
- We are interested in increasing sharing by bisimulation collapse instead of by identifying isomorphic sub-dags.

ATERM only checks for equality of subexpressions. Therefore it only introduces horizontal sharing and implements a form of *common subexpression elimination (CSE)* [28, p. 241]. Our approach is stronger than CSE: while Ex. 1.1 can be handled by CSE, this is not the case for Ex. 1.2. In contrast to CSE, our approach increases also vertical and twisted sharing.[2]

1.8 Contribution of this paper in context

Blom introduces *higher-order term graphs* [4], which are extensions of first-order term graphs by adding a scope function that assigns a set of vertices, its *scope*, to every abstraction vertex.

In the paper [12] we introduced, for interpreting λ_{letrec}-terms, a modification of Blom's higher-order term graphs (the λ-ho-term-graphsof the class $\mathcal{H}$) in which scopes are represented by means of 'abstraction prefix functions'. We also investigated first-order term graphs with scope-delimiter vertices. In particular, we examined which specific class of first-order λ-term-graphs can faithfully represent higher-order λ-ho-term-graphs in such a way that compactification of the latter can be realised through bisimulation collapse of the former (this led to the λ-term-graphs of the class $\mathcal{T}$).

Whereas in the paper [12] we exclusively focused on the graph formalisms, and investigated them in their own right, here we connect the results obtained there to the language λ_{letrec} for expressing sharing and cyclicity. Since the methods presented here are based on the graph formalisms, and rely on their properties for correctness, we recapitulate the concepts and the relevant results in Sec. 4 and 5.

The translation $[\![\cdot]\!]_{\mathcal{T}}$ of λ_{letrec}-terms into first-order term graphs was inspired by related representations that use scope delimiters to indicate end of scopes. Such representations are generalisations of a de Bruijn index notation for λ-terms [8] in which the de Bruijn indexes are numerals of the form $\mathsf{S}(\ldots(\mathsf{S}(\mathsf{0}))\ldots)$. In the generalised form, due to Patterson and Bird [3], the symbol S can occur anywhere between a variable occurrence and its binding abstraction. The idea to view S as a scope delimiter was employed by Hendriks and van Oostrom, who defined an end-of-scope symbol ⅄ [17]. It is also crucial for Lambdascope-graphs (interaction nets) on which van Oostrom defines an optimal evaluator for the λ-calculus [26].

In the report [11], and in the paper [13] we used a closely related higher-order rewrite system in order to precisely characterise those λ^{∞}-terms that can be expressed by (in the sense that they arise as infinite unfoldings of) finite terms in λ_{letrec}, and respectively, in λ_{μ}.

2. Preliminaries

By $\mathbb{N}$ we denote the natural numbers including zero. For words w over an alphabet A, the length of w is denoted by $|w|$.

Let Σ be a TRS-signature [30] with arity function $ar : \Sigma \to \mathbb{N}$. A *term graph over* Σ (or a Σ*-term-graph*) is a tuple $\langle V, lab, args, r\rangle$ where: V is a set of *vertices*, $lab : V \to \Sigma$ the *(vertex) label function*, $args : V \to V^*$ the *argument function* that maps every vertex v to the word $args(v)$ consisting of the $ar(lab(v))$ successor vertices of v (hence $|args(v)| = ar(lab(v))$), and r, the *root*, is a vertex in V. Term graphs may have infinitely many vertices.

Let G be a term graph over signature Σ. As useful notation for picking out an arbitrary vertex, or the i-th vertex, from among the ordered successors of a vertex v in G, we define for each $i \in \mathbb{N}$ the indexed edge relation $\rightarrowtail_i \subseteq V \times V$, and additionally the (not indexed) edge relation $\rightarrowtail \subseteq V \times V$, by stipulating for all $w, w' \in V$:

$$w \rightarrowtail_i w' \;:\Leftrightarrow\; \exists w_0, \ldots, w_n \in V.\; args(w) = w_0 \cdots w_n \wedge w' = w_i$$
$$w \rightarrowtail w' \;:\Leftrightarrow\; \exists i \in \mathbb{N}.\; w \rightarrowtail_i w'$$

A *path* in G is described by $w_0 \rightarrowtail_{k_1} w_1 \rightarrowtail_{k_2} \cdots \rightarrowtail_{k_n} w_n$, where $w_0, w_1, \ldots, w_n \in V$ and $n, k_1, k_2, \ldots, k_n \in \mathbb{N}$. An *access path* of a

[2] For definitions of horizontal, vertical, and twisted sharing we refer to [4].

vertex w of G is a path that starts at the root of G, ends in w, and does not visit any vertex twice. Access paths need not be unique. A term graph is *root-connected* if every vertex has an access path.

Note: By a 'term graph' we will, from now on, always mean a root-connected term graph.

Let $G_1 = \langle V_1, lab_1, args_1, r_1 \rangle$, $G_2 = \langle V_2, lab_2, args_2, r_2 \rangle$ be term graphs over signature Σ, in the sequel.

A *bisimulation* between G_1 and G_2 is a relation $R \subseteq V_1 \times V_2$ such that the following conditions hold, for all $\langle w, w' \rangle \in R$:

$$\left.\begin{array}{lr} \langle r_1, r_2 \rangle \in R & \text{(roots)} \\ lab_1(w) = lab_2(w') & \text{(labels)} \\ \langle args_1(w), args_2(w') \rangle \in R^* & \text{(arguments)} \end{array}\right\} \quad (1)$$

where the extension $R^* \subseteq V_1^* \times V_2^*$ of R to a relation between words over V_1 and words over V_2 is defined as:

$$\begin{aligned} R^* := \{ \langle w_1 \cdots w_k, w'_1 \cdots w'_k \rangle \mid \\ w_1, \dots, w_k \in V_1, w'_1, \dots, w'_k \in V_2, \\ \text{for } k \in \mathbb{N} \text{ such that } \langle w_i, w'_i \rangle \in R \text{ for all } 1 \le i \le k \}. \end{aligned}$$

We write $G_1 \leftrightarrows G_2$ if there is a bisimulation between G_1 and G_2, and we say, in this case, that G_1 and G_2 are *bisimilar*. Bisimilarity $\leftrightarrows$ is an equivalence relation on term graphs.

A *functional bisimulation* from G_1 to G_2 is a bisimulation that is the graph of a function from V_1 to V_2. An alternative characterisation of this concept is that of *homomorphism* from G_1 to G_2: a morphism from the structure G_1 to the structure G_2, that is, a function $h : V_1 \to V_2$ such that, for all $v \in V_1$ it holds:

$$\left.\begin{array}{lr} h(r_1) = r_2 & \text{(roots)} \\ lab_1(v) = lab_2(h(v)) & \text{(labels)} \\ h^*(args_1(v)) = args_2(h(v)) & \text{(arguments)} \end{array}\right\} \quad (2)$$

where h^* is the homomorphic extension $h^* : V_1^* \to V_2^*, v_1 \cdots v_n \mapsto h(v_1) \cdots h(v_n)$ of h to words over V_1. We write $G_1 \rightrightarrows G_2$ if there is a functional bisimulation (a homomorphism) from G_1 to G_2. An *isomorphism* between G_1 and G_2 is a bijective homomorphism $i : V_1 \to V_2$ from G_1 to G_2. If there is an isomorphism between G_1 and G_2, we write $G_1 \simeq G_2$, and say that G_1 and G_2 are *isomorphic*.

Let $f \in \Sigma$. An *f-homomorphism* between G_1 and G_2 is a homomorphism h between G_1 and G_2 that shares only vertices with the label f: $h(w_1) = h(w_2) \Rightarrow lab_1(w_1) = lab_1(w_2) = f$ holds for all $w_1, w_2 \in V_1$. If this is the case, we write $G_1 \rightrightarrows^f G_2$. An *$f$-bisimulation* between G_1 and G_2 is a bisimulation between G_1 and G_2 such that its restriction to vertices with labels different from f is a bijective function. We use $\leftrightarrows^f$ to indicate *f-bisimilarity*.

The relation $\rightrightarrows$ is a preorder, the *sharing preorder* on the class of term graphs over a given signature Σ. It induces a partial order on the isomorphism equivalence classes of term graphs over Σ.

Let $G = \langle V, lab, args, r \rangle$ be a term graph. A *bisimulation collapse* of G is a maximal element in the class $\{G' \mid G \rightrightarrows G'\}$ up to $\simeq$, that is, a term graph G'_0 with $G \rightrightarrows G'_0$ such that if $G'_0 \rightrightarrows G''_0$ for some term graph G''_0, then $G''_0 \simeq G'_0$. The *canonical bisimulation collapse* $G{\mid\downarrow}$ of G is defined as the root-connected part of the 'factor term graph' $G/_R$ of G with respect to the largest bisimulation R between G and G (the largest 'self-bisimulation' on G), which is an equivalence relation on V. The *factor term graph $G/_\sim$* of G with respect to an equivalence relation $\sim$ on V is defined as $G/_\sim := \langle V/_\sim, lab/_\sim, args/_\sim, [r]_\sim \rangle$ where $V/_\sim$ is the set of $\sim$-equivalence classes of vertices in V, $[r]_\sim$ is the $\sim$-equivalence class of r, and $lab/_\sim$ and $args/_\sim$ are the mappings on $V/_\sim$ that are induced by lab and $args$, respectively. Every two bisimulation collapses of G are isomorphic. This justifies the common abbreviation of saying that 'the bisimulation collapse' of G is unique up to isomorphism.

3. Unfolding Semantics of $\lambda_{\mathsf{letrec}}$-terms

Informally, we regard *$\lambda_{\mathsf{letrec}}$-terms* as being defined by the following grammar:

$$\begin{array}{rcll} L & ::= & \lambda x. L & (\textit{abstraction}) \\ & \mid & L\, L & (\textit{application}) \\ & \mid & x & (\textit{variable}) \\ & \mid & \mathsf{let}\ B\ \mathsf{in}\ L & (\textit{letrec}) \\ B & ::= & f_1 = L, \dots, f_n = L & (\textit{equations}) \\ & & (f_1, \dots, f_n \in \mathcal{R} \text{ all distinct}) & \end{array}$$

Formally, we consider $\lambda_{\mathsf{letrec}}$-terms to be defined correspondingly as terms in the formalism of Combinatory Reduction Systems (CRS) [30]. CRSs are a higher-order term rewriting framework tailor-made for formalising and manipulating expressions in higher-order languages (i.e. languages with binding constructs like λ-abstractions and let-bindings). They provide a sound basis for defining our language and for reasoning with letrec-expressions. By formalising a system of unfolding rules as a CRS we conveniently externalise issues like name capturing and α-renaming, which otherwise would have to be handled by a calculus of explicit substitution. Also, we can lean on the rewriting theory of CRSs for the proofs.

As CRS-signature we use $\Sigma_{\lambda_{\mathsf{letrec}}} = \Sigma_\lambda \cup \{\mathsf{let}_n, \mathsf{rec\text{-}in}_n \mid n \in \mathbb{N}\}$, with $\Sigma_\lambda = \{\mathsf{abs}, \mathsf{app}\}$, where the unary symbol abs and the binary symbol app represent λ-abstraction and application, respectively; the symbols let_n of arity one, and $\mathsf{rec\text{-}in}_n$ of arity $n+1$ together formalise let-expressions with n bindings. By $|L|$ we denote the size (the number of symbols) of a $\lambda_{\mathsf{letrec}}$-term L. By $Ter(\lambda_{\mathsf{letrec}})$ we denote the set of CRS-terms over $\Sigma_{\lambda_{\mathsf{letrec}}}$. For readability, we rely on the informal first-order notation.

Infinite λ-terms are formalised as iCRS-terms (terms in an infinitary CRS [22]) over Σ_λ, forming the set $Ter(\lambda^\infty)$. Informally, infinite λ-terms are generated co-inductively by the alternatives (*abstraction*), (*application*), and (*variable*) of the grammar above.

In order to formally define the infinite unfolding of $\lambda_{\mathsf{letrec}}$-terms we utilise a CRS whose rewrite rules formalise unfolding steps [11]. Every $\lambda_{\mathsf{letrec}}$-term L that represents an infinite λ-term M can be rewritten by a typically infinite rewrite sequence that converges to M in the limit. However, not every $\lambda_{\mathsf{letrec}}$-term represents an λ^∞-term. For instance the $\lambda_{\mathsf{letrec}}$-term $Q = \lambda x. \mathsf{let}\ f = f\ \mathsf{in}\ f\, x$ with a meaningless let-binding for f does not unfold to a λ^∞-term. Therefore we introduce a constant symbol $\bullet$, called 'black hole', for expressing meaningless bindings, in order to define the unfolding operation as a total function. The unfolding semantics of Q will then be $\lambda x. \bullet\, x$. So we extend the signature Σ_λ to $\Sigma_{\lambda_\bullet}$ including $\bullet$, and denote the set of infinite λ-terms over Σ_λ by $Ter(\lambda_\bullet^\infty)$. Similarly, the rules below are defined for terms in $Ter(\lambda_{\mathsf{letrec},\bullet})$ based on signature $\Sigma_{\lambda_{\mathsf{letrec},\bullet}}$ that extends $\Sigma_{\lambda_{\mathsf{letrec}}}$ by the blackhole constant.

Definition 3.1 (unfolding CRS for $\lambda_{\mathsf{letrec}}$-terms)**.** The rules:

$$\begin{array}{ll} (@) & \mathsf{let}\ B\ \mathsf{in}\ L_0\, L_1 \to (\mathsf{let}\ B\ \mathsf{in}\ L_0)\,(\mathsf{let}\ B\ \mathsf{in}\ L_1) \\ (\lambda) & \mathsf{let}\ B\ \mathsf{in}\ \lambda x. L_0 \to \lambda x. \mathsf{let}\ B\ \mathsf{in}\ L_0 \\ (\mathsf{let\_in}) & \mathsf{let}\ B_0\ \mathsf{in}\ \mathsf{let}\ B_1\ \mathsf{in}\ L \to \mathsf{let}\ B_0, B_1\ \mathsf{in}\ L \\ (\mathsf{let\text{-}rec}) & \mathsf{let}\ B_1,\ f = L,\ B_2\ \mathsf{in}\ f \to \mathsf{let}\ B_1,\ f = L,\ B_2\ \mathsf{in}\ L \\ (\mathsf{gc}) & \mathsf{let}\ f_1 = L_1, \dots, f_n = L_n\ \mathsf{in}\ P \to P \\ & \qquad \text{(if } f_1, \dots, f_n \text{ do not occur in } P\text{)} \\ (\mathsf{tighten}) & \mathsf{let}\ B_1,\ f = g,\ B_2\ \mathsf{in}\ L \\ & \qquad \to \mathsf{let}\ B_1[f := g],\ B_2[f := g]\ \mathsf{in}\ L[f := g] \\ & \qquad \text{(where } g \text{ with } g \ne f \text{ a recursion variable in } B_1 \text{ or } B_2\text{)} \\ (\bullet) & \mathsf{let}\ B_1,\ f = f,\ B_2\ \mathsf{in}\ L \to \mathsf{let}\ B_1,\ f = \bullet,\ B_2\ \mathsf{in}\ L \end{array}$$

define, in informal notation, the *unfolding CRS* for $\lambda_{\mathsf{letrec}}$-terms with rewrite relation $\to_{\mathsf{unf}}$. Here is the CRS-notation for two of the rules:

$(\lambda)\quad \mathsf{let}_n([\vec{f}]\,\mathsf{rec\text{-}in}_n(X_1(\vec{f}),\ldots,X_n(\vec{f}),\mathsf{abs}([x]\,Z(\vec{f},x))))$
$\qquad\to\ \mathsf{abs}([x]\,\mathsf{let}_n([\vec{f}]\,\mathsf{rec\text{-}in}_n(X_1(\vec{f}),\ldots,X_n(\vec{f}),Z(\vec{f},x))))$

$(\mathsf{let\_in})\quad \mathsf{let}_n([\vec{f}]\,\mathsf{rec\text{-}in}_n(\vec{X}(\vec{f}),\mathsf{let}_m([\vec{g}]\,\mathsf{rec\text{-}in}_m(\vec{Y}(\vec{f},\vec{g}))),Z(\vec{f},\vec{g})))$
$\qquad\to\ \mathsf{let}_{n+m}([\vec{f}\vec{g}]\,\mathsf{rec\text{-}in}_{n+m}(\vec{X}(\vec{f}),\vec{Y}(\vec{f},\vec{g}),Z(\vec{f},\vec{g})))$

Example 3.2 (Unfolding derivation of L from Ex. 1.2).
$\lambda f.\,\mathsf{let}\ r = f\ r\ \mathsf{in}\ r \to_{\mathrm{unf}}^{(\text{let-rec})} \lambda f.\,\mathsf{let}\ r = f\ r\ \mathsf{in}\ f\ r \to_{\mathrm{unf}}^{(@)}$
$\lambda f.\,(\mathsf{let}\ r = f\ r\ \mathsf{in}\ f)\,(\mathsf{let}\ r = f\ r\ \mathsf{in}\ r) \to_{\mathrm{unf}}^{(\mathrm{gc})}$
$\lambda f.\,f\,(\mathsf{let}\ r = f\ r\ \mathsf{in}\ r) \to_{\mathrm{unf}}^{(\text{let-rec})} \ldots$

We say that a $\lambda_{\mathsf{letrec}}$-term L *unfolds to* an $\lambda^\infty_\bullet$-term M, or that L *expresses* M, if there is a (typically) infinite $\to_{\mathrm{unf}}$-rewrite sequence from L that converges to M, symbolically $L \twoheadrightarrow_{\mathrm{unf}} M$. Note that any such rewrite sequence is strongly convergent (the depth of the contracted redexes tends to infinity), because the resulting term does not contain any let-expressions.

Lemma 3.3. *Every $\lambda_{\mathsf{letrec}}$-term unfolds to precisely one $\lambda^\infty_\bullet$-term.*

Proof (Outline). Infinite normal forms of $\to_{\mathrm{unf}}$ are $\lambda^\infty_\bullet$-terms since: every occurrence of a let-expression in a $\lambda_{\mathsf{letrec},\bullet}$-term gives rise to a redex; and infinite $\lambda_{\mathsf{letrec},\bullet}$-terms without let-expressions are $\lambda^\infty_\bullet$-terms. Also, outermost-fair rewrite sequences in which the rules (tighten) and ($\bullet$) are applied eagerly are (strongly) convergent.

Unique infinite normalisation of $\to_{\mathrm{unf}}$ follows from finitary confluence of $\to_{\mathrm{unf}}$. In previous work [11] we proved confluence for the slightly simpler CRS without the final two rules, which together introduce black holes in terms with meaningless bindings. That confluence proof can be adapted by extending the argumentation to deal with the additional critical pairs. □

Definition 3.4. The *unfolding semantics* for $\lambda_{\mathsf{letrec}}$-terms is defined by the function $[\![\cdot]\!]_{\lambda^\infty_\bullet} : \mathit{Ter}(\lambda_{\mathsf{letrec}}) \to \mathit{Ter}(\lambda^\infty_\bullet)$, where $L \mapsto [\![L]\!]_{\lambda^\infty_\bullet} :=$ the infinite unfolding of L.

Remark 3.5 (Regular and strongly regular λ^∞-terms). λ^∞-terms that arise as infinite unfoldings of $\lambda_{\mathsf{letrec}}$-terms form a proper subclass of those λ^∞-terms that have a regular term structure [11]. λ^∞-terms that belong to this subclass are called 'strongly regular', and can be characterised by means of a decomposition rewrite system, and as those that contain only finite 'binding–capturing chains' [11, 13].

4. Lambda higher-order term graphs

In this section we motivate the use of higher-order term graphs as a semantics for $\lambda_{\mathsf{letrec}}$-terms; we introduce the class $\mathcal{H}$ of 'λ-ho-term-graphs' and define the semantics $[\![\cdot]\!]_{\mathcal{H}}$ for interpreting $\lambda_{\mathsf{letrec}}$-terms as λ-ho-term-graphs. Finally, we sketch a proof of the correctness of $[\![\cdot]\!]_{\mathcal{H}}$ with respect to unfolding equivalence (the property (P1)).

We start out from a natural interpretation of $\lambda_{\mathsf{letrec}}$-terms as first-order term graphs: occurrences of abstraction variables are resolved as edges pointing to the corresponding abstraction; occurrences of recursion variables as edges to the subgraph belonging to the respective binding. We therefore consider term graphs over the signature $\Sigma^\lambda_\bullet = \{@, \lambda, 0, \bullet\}$ with arities $ar(@) = 2$, $ar(\lambda) = 1$, $ar(0) = 1$, and $ar(\bullet) = 0$. These function symbols represent applications, λ-abstractions, abstraction variables, and black holes.

We will later define a subclass of these term graphs that excludes meaningless graphs. In line with the choice to regard all terms as higher-order terms (thus modulo α-conversion), we consider a nameless graph representation, so that α-equivalence of two terms can be recognised as their graph interpretations being isomorphic.

For a term graph G over $\Sigma^\lambda_\bullet$ with set V of vertices we will henceforth denote by $V(@)$, $V(\lambda)$, $V(0)$, and $V(\bullet)$ the sets of *application vertices*, *abstraction vertices*, *variable vertices*, and *blackhole vertices*, that is, those with label @, λ, 0, $\bullet$, respectively.

Example 4.1 (Natural first-order interpretation). The $\lambda_{\mathsf{letrec}}$-terms L and P in Ex. 1.2 can be represented as the term graphs in Fig. 2.

These two graphs are bisimilar, which suggests that L and P are unfolding-equivalent. Moreover, there is a functional bisimulation from the larger term graph to the smaller one, indicating that L expresses more sharing than P, or in other words: L is more compact. Also, there is no smaller term graph that is bisimilar to L and P. We conclude that L is a maximally shared form of P.

However, this translation is incorrect in the sense that bisimilarity does not in general guarantee unfolding equivalence, the desired property (P1). This is witnessed by the following counterexample.

Example 4.2 (Incorrectness of the natural first-order interpretation).

$$\begin{aligned} L_1 &= \mathsf{let}\ f = \lambda x.\,(\lambda y.\,f\ y)\ x\ \mathsf{in}\ f \\ L &= \mathsf{let}\ f = \lambda x.\,f\ x\ \mathsf{in}\ f \\ L_2 &= \mathsf{let}\ f = \lambda x.\,(\lambda y.\,f\ x)\ x\ \mathsf{in}\ f \end{aligned}$$

While $[\![L_1]\!]_{\lambda^\infty} = [\![L]\!]_{\lambda^\infty}$ and $[\![L]\!]_{\lambda^\infty} \neq [\![L_2]\!]_{\lambda^\infty}$, all of their term graphs G_1, G, G are bisimilar (please ignore the shading for now):

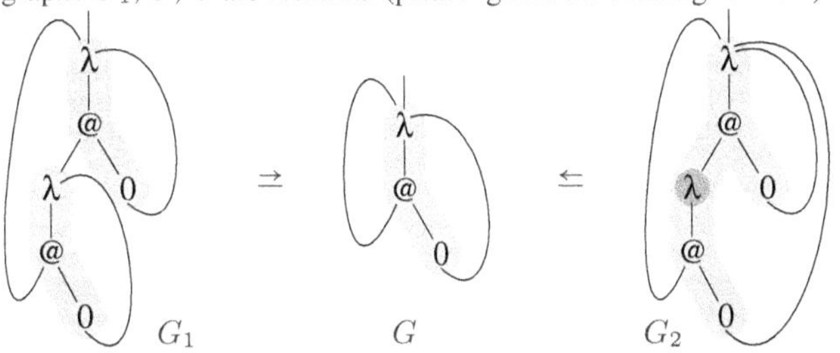

Consequently this interpretation lacks the necessary structure for correctly modelling compactification via bisimulation collapse.

We therefore impose additional structure on the term graphs. This is indicated by the shading in the picture above, and in the graphs throughout this paper. A shaded area depicts the *scope* of an abstraction: it comprises all positions between the abstraction and its bound variable occurrences as well as the scope of any abstraction on these positions. By this stipulation, scopes are properly nested.

Now note that the functional bisimulation on the right in the picture in Ex. 4.2 does *not* respect the scopes: The scope of the topmost abstraction vertex in the term graph G_2 interpreting L_2 contains another λ-abstraction; hence the image of this scope under the functional bisimulation cannot fit into, and is not contained in, the single scope in the term graph G of L. Also, the trivial scope of the vacuous abstraction in G_2 is not mapped to a scope in G. Thus the natural first-order interpretation is incorrect, in the sense that functional bisimulation does not preserve scopes on the first-order term graphs that are interpretations of $\lambda_{\mathsf{letrec}}$-terms.

To prevent that interpretations of not unfolding-equivalent terms like L_1 and L_2 in Ex. 4.2 become bisimilar, we enrich first-order term graphs by a formal concept of scope. More precisely, *abstraction prefixes* are added as vertex labels. They also serve the purpose of defining the subclass of meaningful term graphs over $\Sigma^\lambda_\bullet$ that sensibly represent cyclic λ-terms. In the enriched term graphs, each vertex v is annotated with a label $P(v)$, the *abstraction prefix* of v, which is a list of vertex names that identifies the abstraction vertices in whose scope v resides. Alternatively scopes can be represented by a scope function (as in [4]) that assigns to every abstraction vertex the set of vertices in its scope. In the article [12] we show that higher-order term graphs with scope functions correspond bijectively to those with abstraction prefix functions.

Abstraction prefixes can be determined by traversing over the graph and recording every binding encountered. When passing an abstraction vertex v while descending into the subgraph representing the body of the abstraction, one enters or opens the scope of v. This is recorded by appending v to the abstraction prefix of v's successor.

v is removed from the prefix at positions under which the abstraction variable is no longer used, but not before any other variable that was added to the prefix in the meantime has itself been removed. In other words, the abstraction prefix behaves like a stack. We call term graphs for representing $\lambda_{\mathsf{letrec}}$-terms that are equipped with abstraction-prefixes 'λ-higher-order term graphs' (λ-ho-term-graphs).

Example 4.3 (The λ-ho-term-graphs of the terms in Ex. 4.2).

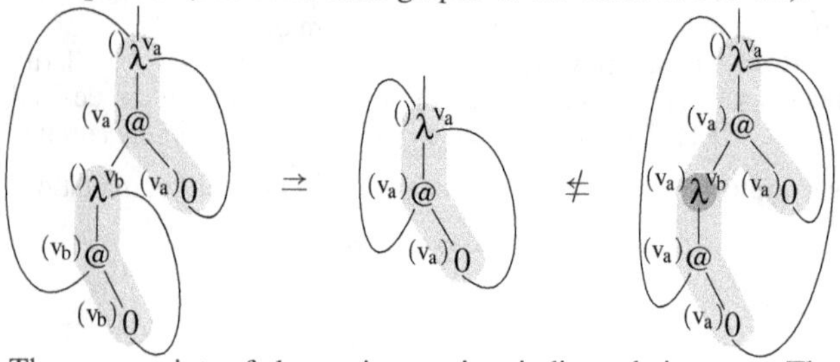

The superscripts of abstraction vertices indicate their names. The abstraction prefix of a vertex is annotated to its top left. Note that abstraction vertices themselves are not included in their own prefix.

We define λ-ho-term-graphs as term graphs over $\Sigma^{\lambda}_{\bullet}$ together with an abstraction-prefix function that assigns to each vertex an abstraction prefix. It has to respect certain correctness conditions restricting the λ-ho-term-graphs to exclude meaningless term graphs.

Definition 4.4 (correct abstraction-prefix function for term graphs over $\Sigma^{\lambda}_{\bullet}$). Let $G = \langle V, lab, args, r\rangle$ be a $\Sigma^{\lambda}_{\bullet}$-term-graph.

An *abstraction-prefix function* for G is a function $P : V \to V^*$ from vertices of G to words of vertices. Such a function is called *correct* if for all $w, w_0, w_1 \in V$ and $k \in \{0, 1\}$ it holds:

$$P(r) = \epsilon \qquad \text{(root)}$$

$$P(\bullet) = \epsilon \qquad \text{(black hole)}$$

$$w \in V(\lambda) \wedge w \rightarrowtail_0 w_0 \Rightarrow P(w_0) \leq P(w)w \qquad (\lambda)$$

$$w \in V(@) \wedge w \rightarrowtail_k w_k \Rightarrow P(w_k) \leq P(w) \qquad (@)$$

$$w \in V(0) \wedge w \rightarrowtail_0 w_0 \Rightarrow \begin{cases} w_0 \in V(\lambda) \\ \wedge\ P(w_0)w_0 = P(w) \end{cases} \qquad (0)$$

Here and later we denote by $\leq$ the 'is-prefix-of' relation.

Definition 4.5 (λ-ho-term-graph). A λ-*ho-term-graph* over $\Sigma^{\lambda}_{\bullet}$ is a five-tuple $\mathcal{G} = \langle V, lab, args, r, P\rangle$ where $G_{\mathcal{G}} = \langle V, lab, args, r\rangle$ is a term graph over $\Sigma^{\lambda}_{\bullet}$, called the term graph *underlying* $\mathcal{G}$, and P is a correct abstraction-prefix function for $G_{\mathcal{G}}$. The class of λ-ho-term-graphs over $\Sigma^{\lambda}_{\bullet}$ is denoted by $\mathcal{H}$.

Definition 4.6 (homomorphism, bisimulation for λ-ho-term-graphs). Let $\mathcal{G}_1 = \langle V_1, lab_1, args_1, r_1, P_1\rangle$ and $\mathcal{G}_2 = \langle V_2, lab_2, args_2, r_2, P_2\rangle$ be λ-ho-term-graphs over $\Sigma^{\lambda}_{\bullet}$.

A *bisimulation* between $\mathcal{G}_1$ and $\mathcal{G}_2$ is a relation $R \subseteq V_1 \times V_2$ that is a bisimulation between the term graphs $G_{\mathcal{G}_1}$ and $G_{\mathcal{G}_2}$ underlying $\mathcal{G}_1$ and $\mathcal{G}_2$, respectively, and for which also the following condition:

$$\langle P_1(w), P_2(w')\rangle \in R^* \qquad \text{(abstraction-prefix functions)} \quad (3)$$

(for R^* see p. 4 below (1)) is satisfied for all $w \in V_1$ and all $w' \in V_2$. If there is a such bisimulation between $\mathcal{G}_1$ and $\mathcal{G}_2$, then we say that $\mathcal{G}_1$ and $\mathcal{G}_2$ are *bisimilar*, and denote this fact by $\mathcal{G}_1 \leftrightarrows \mathcal{G}_2$.

A *homomorphism* (a *functional bisimulation*) from $\mathcal{G}_1$ to $\mathcal{G}_2$ is a morphism from the structure $\mathcal{G}_1$ to the structure $\mathcal{G}_2$, or more explicitly, it is a homomorphism $h : V_1 \to V_2$ from $G_{\mathcal{G}_1}$ to $G_{\mathcal{G}_2}$ that additionally satisfies, for all $w \in V_1$, the following condition:

$$h^*(P_1(w)) = P_2(h(w)) \qquad \text{(abstraction-prefix functions)} \quad (4)$$

where h^* is the homomorphic extension of h to words over V_1. We write $\mathcal{G}_1 \mathrel{\underline{\to}} \mathcal{G}_2$ if there is a homomorphism from $\mathcal{G}_1$ to $\mathcal{G}_2$.

4.1 Interpretation of $\lambda_{\mathsf{letrec}}$-terms as λ-ho-term-graphs

In order to interpret a $\lambda_{\mathsf{letrec}}$-term L as λ-ho-term-graph, the translation rules $\mathcal{R}$ from Fig. 3 are applied to a 'translation box' $\boxed{(*[])L}$. It contains L furnished with a prefix consisting of a dummy variable $*$, and an empty set $[]$ of binding equations. The translation process proceeds by induction on the syntactical structure of the prefixed $\lambda_{\mathsf{letrec}}$-expression's body. Ultimately, a term graph G over $\Sigma^{\lambda}_{\bullet}$ is produced, together with a correct abstraction-prefix function for G.

For reading the rules $\mathcal{R}$ in Fig. 3 correctly, observe the details as described here below. Illustrations of the translation process when applied to two $\lambda_{\mathsf{letrec}}$-terms used here can be found in Appendix A of the extended version [15] of this paper.

- A translation box $\boxed{(\vec{p})L}$ contains a prefixed, partially decomposed $\lambda_{\mathsf{letrec}}$-term L. The prefix contains a vector $\vec{p}$ of annotated λ-abstractions that have already been translated and whose scope typically extends into L. Every prefix abstraction is annotated with a set of binding equations that are defined at its level. There is special dummy variable denoted by $*$ at the left of the prefix that carries top-level function bindings, i.e. binding equations that are not defined under any enclosing λ-abstraction. The λ-rule strips off an abstraction from the body of the expression, and pushes the abstraction variable into the prefix, which initially contains an empty set of function bindings.
- Names of abstraction vertices are indicated to the right, and abstraction-prefixes to the left of the created vertices. In order to refer to the vertices in the prefix we use the following notation: $vs(\vec{p}) = v_1 \cdots v_n$ if $\vec{p} = *[B_0]\ x_1^{v_1}[B_1]\ \ldots\ x_n^{v_n}[B_n]$.
- Vertices drawn with dashed lines have been created in earlier translation steps, and are referenced by edges in the current step.
- In the S-rule, which takes care of closing scopes, $FV(L)$ stands for the set of free variables in L.
- The let-rule for translating let-expressions creates a box for the in-part as well as for each function binding. The translation of each of the bindings starts with an *indirection vertex*. These vertices guarantee the well-definedness of the process when it translates meaningless bindings such as $f = f$, or $g = h$, $h = g$, which would otherwise give rise to loops without vertices. The let-rule pushes the function bindings into the abstraction prefix, associating each function binding with one of the variables in the abstraction prefix. There is some freedom as to which variable a function binding is assigned to. This freedom is limited by scoping conditions that ensure that the prefixed term is a valid CRS-term: function bindings may only depend on variables and functions that occur further to the left in the prefix. The chosen association also directly determines the prefix lengths used in the translation boxes for the function bindings.
- Indirection vertices are eliminated by an erasure process at the end: Every indirection vertex that does not point to itself is removed, redirecting all incoming edges to the successor vertex. Finally every loop on a single indirection vertex is replaced by a *black hole* vertex that represents a meaningless binding. Abstraction prefixes for such black holes are defined to be empty.

Definition 4.7. We say that a term graph G over $\Sigma^{\lambda}_{\bullet}$ and an abstraction-prefix function P is $\mathcal{R}$-*generated from* a $\lambda_{\mathsf{letrec}}$-term L if G and P are obtained by applying the rules $\mathcal{R}$ from Fig. 3 to $\boxed{(*[])L}$.

Proposition 4.8. Let L be a $\lambda_{\mathsf{letrec}}$-term. Suppose that a term graph G over $\Sigma^{\lambda}_{\bullet}$, and an abstraction-prefix function P are $\mathcal{R}$-generated from L. Then P is a correct abstraction-prefix function for G, and consequently, G and P together form a λ-ho-term-graph in $\mathcal{H}$.

There are two sources of non-determinism in this translation: the S-rule for shortening prefixes can be applicable at the same time as other rules; also the let-rule does not fix the lengths $l_1, \ldots, l_k$ of the λ: $(\vec{p})\,\lambda x.\,L \implies (\vec{p}\,x^v[\,])\,L$ (vertex $(vs(\vec{p}))\,\lambda^v$)

@: $(\vec{p})\,L_0\,L_1 \implies (\vec{p})\,L_0 \quad (\vec{p})\,L_1$ (vertex $(vs(\vec{p}))\,@$)

f: $(\vec{p}\,x^v[\ldots,f^w=L,\ldots])\,f \implies$ $(vs(\vec{p})\,v)\,w$

0: $(x_0^{v_0}[B_0]\ \cdots\ x_n^{v_n}[B_n])\,x_n \implies (v_1\ldots v_n)\ 0$ (to λ^{v_n})

S: $(\vec{p}\,x^v[f_1^{v_1}=L_1,\ldots,f_n^{v_n}=L_n])\,L \ \underset{f_i\notin FV(L)}{\overset{x\notin FV(L)}{\implies}}\ (\vec{p})\,L$

let:
$$(x_0^{v_0}[B_0]\ \cdots\ x_n^{v_n}[B_n])\ \text{let } B \text{ in } L_0 \implies$$

$(v_1\ldots v_{l_1})\,w_1 \qquad (x_0^{v_0}[B_0']\ \cdots\ x_n^{v_n}[B_n'])\,L_0 \qquad (v_1\ldots v_{l_n})\,w_k$

$(B_i' = B_i, \{f_j^{w_j} = L_j \mid l_j = i,\ 1 \le j \le k\})$

$(x_0^{v_0}[B_0']\ \cdots\ x_{l_1}^{v_{l_1}}[B_{l_1}'])\,L_1 \quad \cdots \quad (x_0^{v_0}[B_0']\ \cdots\ x_{l_k}^{v_{l_k}}[B_{l_k}'])\,L_k$

$(B \text{ stands for } f_1 = L_1,\ldots,f_k = L_k)$

$l_1,\ldots,l_k \le n$ such that $\forall i,j \le k : l_i < l_j \Rightarrow \forall f = L \in B_{l_i}',\ g = P \in B_{l_j}' : g \notin FV(L)$

and $\forall i \le k\ \{y \mid y \text{ is required variable of } f_i\} \subseteq \{x_0,\ldots,x_{l_i}\}$

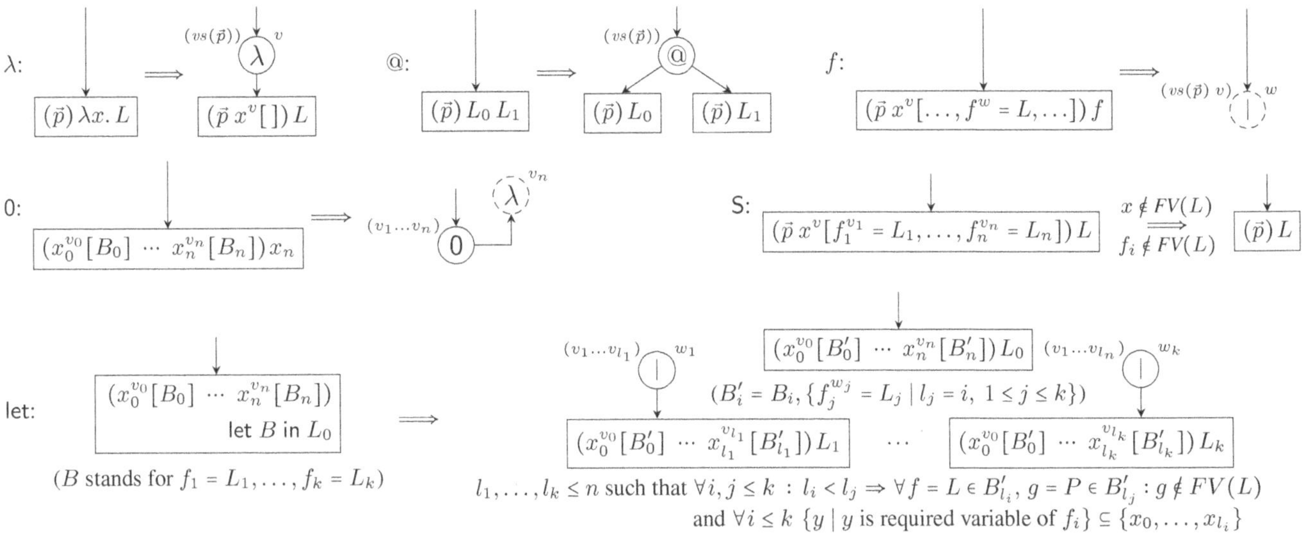

Figure 3. Translation rules $\mathcal{R}$ for interpreting λ_{letrec}-terms as λ-ho-term-graphs. See Section 4.1 for explanations.

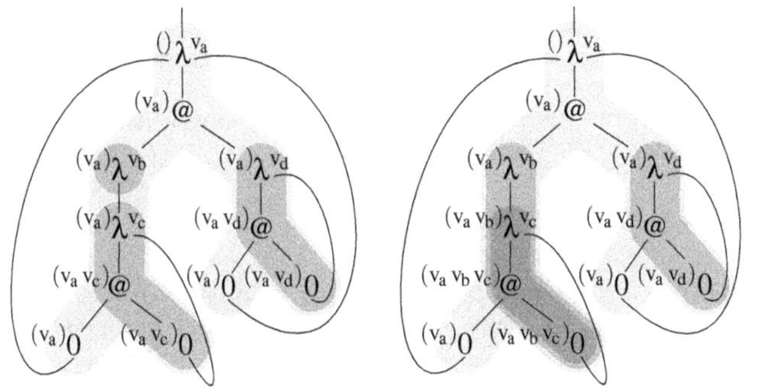

Figure 4. Translation of $\lambda a.\,(\lambda b.\,\lambda c.\,a\,c)\,(\lambda d.\,a\,d)$ with eager scope-closure (left), and with lazy scope-closure (right). While in the left term graph four vertices can be shared, with as result the translation of the term $\lambda a.\,\text{let } f = \lambda c.\,a\,c \text{ in } (\lambda b.\,f)\,f$, in the right term graph only a single variable occurrence can be shared.

abstraction prefixes for the translations of the binding equations, but admits various choices of prefixes that are shorter than the prefix of the left-hand side. Neither kind of non-determinism affects the term graph that is produced, but in general several abstraction-prefix functions, and thus different λ-ho-term-graphs, can be obtained.

4.2 Interpretation as eager-scope λ-ho-term-graphs

Of the different translations of a λ_{letrec}-term into λ-ho-term-graphs we are most interested in the one with the shortest possible abstraction prefixes. We say that such a term graph has 'eager scope-closure', or that it is 'eager-scope'. The reason for this choice is illustrated in Fig. 4: eager-scope closure allows for more sharing.

Definition 4.9 (eager scope). Let $\mathcal{G} = \langle V, lab, args, r, P \rangle$ be a λ-ho-term-graph. $\mathcal{G}$ is called *eager-scope* if for every $w \in V$ with $P(w) = pv$ for $p \in V^*$ and $v \in V$, there is a path $w = w_0 \twoheadrightarrow w_1 \twoheadrightarrow \cdots \twoheadrightarrow w_m \twoheadrightarrow_0 v$ in $\mathcal{G}$ from w to v with $P(w) \le P(w_i)$ for all $i \in \{1,\ldots,m\}$, and (this follows) $w_m \in V(0)$ and $v \in V(\lambda)$.

Hence if a λ-ho-term-graph is not eager-scope, then it contains a vertex w with abstraction-prefix $v_1 \ldots v_n$ from which v_n is only reachable, if at all, by leaving the scope of v_n. It can be shown that

in this case another abstraction-prefix function with shorter prefixes exists, and in which v_n has been removed from the prefix of w.

Proposition 4.10 (eager-scope = minimal scope; uniqueness of eager-scope λ-ho-term-graphs). Let $\mathcal{G}_i = \langle V, lab, args, r, P_i \rangle$ for $i \in \{1,2\}$ be λ-ho-term-graphs with the same underlying term graph. If $\mathcal{G}_1$ is eager-scope, then $|P_1(w)| \le |P_2(w))|$ for all $w \in V$. If, in addition, also $\mathcal{G}_2$ is eager-scope, then $P_1 = P_2$. Hence eager-scope λ-ho-term-graphs over the same underlying term graph are unique.

Also, we will call a translation process 'eager-scope' if it resolves the non-determinism in $\mathcal{R}$ in such a way that it always yields eager-scope λ-ho-term-graphs. In order to obtain an eager-scope translation we have to consider the following aspects.

Garbage removal. In the presence of *garbage*, unused function bindings, a translation cannot be eager-scope. Consider the term $\lambda x.\,\lambda y.\,\text{let } f = x \text{ in } y$. The expendable binding $f = x$ prevents the application of the S-rule, and hence the closure of the scope of λx, directly below λx. Therefore we will assume that *all unused function bindings are removed* prior to applying the rules $\mathcal{R}$. A λ_{letrec}-term without garbage will be called *garbage-free*.

Short enough prefix lengths in the let-rule. For obtaining an eager-scope translation, we will usually stipulate that the S-rule is applied eagerly, i.e. it is given precedence over the other rules. This is clearly necessary for keeping the abstraction prefixes minimal. But how do we choose the prefix lengths $l_1,\ldots,l_k$ in the let-rule? The prefix lengths l_i determine at which position a binding $f_i = L_i$ is inserted into the abstraction prefixes. Therefore l_i may not be chosen too short; otherwise a function f depending on a function g may end up to the right of g, and hence may be removed from the prefix by the S-rule prematurely, preventing completion of the translation. Yet simply choosing $l_i = n$ may prevent scopes from being minimal. For example, when translating the term $\lambda a.\,\lambda b.\,\text{let } f = a \text{ in } a\,a\,(f\,a)\,b$, it is crucial to allow shorter prefixes for the binding than for the in-part. As shown in Fig. 5 the graph on the left does not have eager scope-closure even if the S-rule is applied eagerly. Consequently the opportunity for sharing the lower application vertices is lost.

Required variable analysis. For choosing the prefixes in the let-rule correctly, the translation process must know for each function-binding which λ-variables are 'required' on the right-hand side of its definition. For this we use an analysis obtaining the required variables for positions in a λ_{letrec}-term as employed by algorithms for lambda-lifting [7, 21]. The term 'required variables' was coined

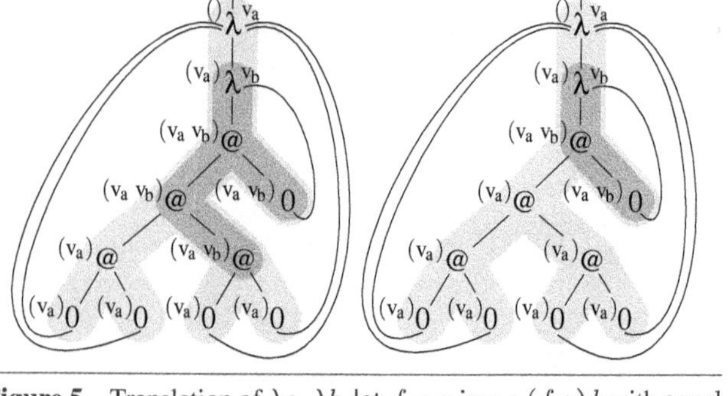

Figure 5. Translation of $\lambda a. \lambda b.$ let $f = a$ in $a\,a\,(f\,a)\,b$ with equal (left) and with minimal prefix lengths (right) in the let-rule.

by Morazán and Schultz [24]. A λ-variable x is called *required at a position* p in a $\lambda_{\mathsf{letrec}}$-term L if x is bound by an abstraction above p, and has a free occurrence in the complete unfolding of L below p (also recursion variables from above p are unfolded). The required variables at position p in L can be computed as those λ-variables with free occurrences that are reachable from p by a downwards traversal with the stipulations: on encountering a let-binding the in-part is entered; when encountering a recursion variable the traversal continues at the right-hand side of the corresponding function binding (even if it is defined above p).

With the result of the required variable analysis at hand, we now define properties of the translation process that can guarantee that the resulting λ-ho-term-graph is eager-scope.

Definition 4.11 (eager-scope and minimal-prefix generated)**.** Let L be a $\lambda_{\mathsf{letrec}}$-term, and let $\mathcal{G}$ be a λ-ho-term-graph.

We say that $\mathcal{G}$ is *eager-scope* $\mathcal{R}$-generated from L if $\mathcal{G}$ is $\mathcal{R}$-generated from L by a translation process with the following property: for every translation box reached during the process with label $(\vec{p}\,x^{v}[B])\,P$, where P is a subterm of L at position q, it holds that if x is not a required variable at q in L, then in the next translation step performed to this box either one of the rules f or let is applied, or the prefix is shortened by the S-rule.

We say that $\mathcal{G}$ is $\mathcal{R}$-generated *with minimal prefixes* from L if $\mathcal{G}$ is $\mathcal{R}$-generated from L by a translation process in which minimal prefix lengths are achieved by giving applications of the S-rule precedence over applications of all other rules, and by always choosing prefixes minimally in applications of the let-rule.

Proposition 4.12. Let $\mathcal{G}$ be a λ-ho-term-graph that is $\mathcal{R}$-generated from a garbage-free $\lambda_{\mathsf{letrec}}$-term L. The following statements hold:

(i) If $\mathcal{G}$ is eager-scope $\mathcal{R}$-generated from L, then $\mathcal{G}$ is eager-scope.
(ii) If $\mathcal{G}$ is $\mathcal{R}$-generated with minimal prefixes from L, then $\mathcal{G}$ is eager-scope $\mathcal{R}$-generated from L, hence by (i) $\mathcal{G}$ is eager-scope.

Definition 4.13. The semantics $[\![\cdot]\!]_{\mathcal{H}}$ of $\lambda_{\mathsf{letrec}}$-terms as λ-ho-term-graphs is defined as $[\![\cdot]\!]_{\mathcal{H}} : \mathit{Ter}(\lambda_{\mathsf{letrec}}) \to \mathcal{H},\ L \mapsto [\![L]\!]_{\mathcal{H}} :=$ the λ-ho-term-graph that is $\mathcal{R}$-generated with minimal prefixes from a garbage-free version L' of L.

Proposition 4.14. For every $\lambda_{\mathsf{letrec}}$-term L, $[\![L]\!]_{\mathcal{H}}$ is eager-scope.

4.3 Correctness of $[\![\cdot]\!]_{\mathcal{H}}$ with respect to unfolding semantics

In preparation of establishing the desired property (P1) in Sect. 5, we formulate, and outline the proof of, the fact that the semantics $[\![\cdot]\!]_{\mathcal{H}}$ is correct with respect to the unfolding semantics on $\lambda_{\mathsf{letrec}}$-terms.

Theorem 4.15. *$[\![L_1]\!]_{\lambda^\infty} = [\![L_2]\!]_{\lambda^\infty}$ if and only if $[\![L_1]\!]_{\mathcal{H}} \leftrightarrows [\![L_2]\!]_{\mathcal{H}}$, for all $\lambda_{\mathsf{letrec}}$-terms L_1 and L_2.*

Sketch of Proof. Central for the proof are λ-ho-term-graphs that have tree form and only contain variable backlinks, but no recursive backlinks. They form the class $\mathcal{H}_T \subsetneq \mathcal{H}$. Every $\mathcal{G} \in \mathcal{H}$ has a unique 'tree unfolding' $\mathit{Tree}(\mathcal{G}) \in \mathcal{H}_T$. We make use of the following statements. For all $L, L_1, L_2 \in \mathit{Ter}(\lambda_{\mathsf{letrec}})$, $M, M_1, M_2 \in \mathit{Ter}(\lambda^{\infty}_{\bullet})$, $\mathcal{G}, \mathcal{G}_1, \mathcal{G}_2 \in \mathcal{H}$, and $\mathcal{T}r, \mathcal{T}r_1, \mathcal{T}r_2 \in \mathcal{H}_T$ it can be shown that:

$$L_1 \to_{\mathrm{unf}} L_2 \;\Rightarrow\; [\![L_1]\!]_{\mathcal{H}} \leftharpoondown [\![L_2]\!]_{\mathcal{H}} \qquad (5)$$

$$L \twoheadrightarrow_{\mathrm{unf}} M \text{ (hence } [\![L]\!]_{\lambda^\infty} = M) \;\Rightarrow\; [\![L]\!]_{\mathcal{H}} \leftharpoondown [\![M]\!]_{\mathcal{H}} \qquad (6)$$

$$[\![M]\!]_{\mathcal{H}} \in \mathcal{H}_T \qquad (7)$$

$$[\![M_1]\!]_{\mathcal{H}} \simeq [\![M_2]\!]_{\mathcal{H}} \;\Rightarrow\; M_1 = M_2 \qquad (8)$$

$$\mathcal{G} \leftharpoondown \mathit{Tree}(\mathcal{G}) \qquad (9)$$

$$\mathcal{T}r_1 \leftrightarrows \mathcal{T}r_2 \;\Rightarrow\; \mathcal{T}r_1 \simeq \mathcal{T}r_2 \qquad (10)$$

$$\mathcal{G}_1 \leftrightarrows \mathcal{G}_2 \;\Rightarrow\; \mathit{Tree}(\mathcal{G}_1) \simeq \mathit{Tree}(\mathcal{G}_2) \qquad (11)$$

Hereby (5) is used for proving (6), and (9) with (10) for (11). Now for proving the theorem, let L_1 and L_2 be arbitrary $\lambda_{\mathsf{letrec}}$-terms.

"$\Rightarrow$": Suppose $[\![L_1]\!]_{\lambda^\infty} = [\![L_2]\!]_{\lambda^\infty}$. Let M be the infinite unfolding of L_1 and L_2, i.e., $[\![L_1]\!]_{\mathcal{H}} = M = [\![L_2]\!]_{\mathcal{H}}$. Then by (6) it follows $[\![L_1]\!]_{\mathcal{H}} \leftharpoondown [\![M]\!]_{\mathcal{H}} \rightharpoonup [\![L_2]\!]_{\mathcal{H}}$, and hence $[\![L_1]\!]_{\mathcal{H}} \leftrightarrows [\![L_2]\!]_{\mathcal{H}}$.

"$\Leftarrow$": Suppose $[\![L_1]\!]_{\mathcal{H}} \leftrightarrows [\![L_2]\!]_{\mathcal{H}}$. Then by (11) it follows that $\mathit{Tree}([\![L_1]\!]_{\mathcal{H}}) \simeq \mathit{Tree}([\![L_2]\!]_{\mathcal{H}})$. Let $M_1, M_2 \in \mathit{Ter}(\lambda^{\infty}_{\bullet})$ be the infinite unfoldings of L_1 and L_2, i.e. $M_1 = [\![L_1]\!]_{\lambda^\infty}$, and $M_2 = [\![L_2]\!]_{\lambda^\infty}$. Then (6) together with the assumption entails $[\![M_1]\!]_{\mathcal{H}} \leftrightarrows [\![M_2]\!]_{\mathcal{H}}$. Since $[\![M_1]\!]_{\mathcal{H}}, [\![M_2]\!]_{\mathcal{H}} \in \mathcal{H}_T$ by (7), it follows by (10) that $[\![M_1]\!]_{\mathcal{H}} \simeq [\![M_2]\!]_{\mathcal{H}}$. Finally, by using (8) we get $M_1 = M_2$, and hence $[\![L_1]\!]_{\lambda^\infty} = M_1 = M_2 = [\![L_2]\!]_{\lambda^\infty}$. □

5. Lambda term graphs

While modelling sharing expressed by $\lambda_{\mathsf{letrec}}$-terms through λ-ho-term-graphs facilitates comparisons via bisimilarity, it is not immediately clear how the compactification of λ-ho-term-graphs via the bisimulation collapse $|\!\downarrow$ for λ-ho-term-graphs (which has to respect scopes in the form of the abstraction-prefix functions) can be computed efficiently. We therefore develop an implementation as first-order term graphs, for which standard methods are available.

As witnessed by Ex. 4.2, the scoping information cannot just be discarded, as functional bisimilarity on the underlying term graphs does not faithfully implement functional bisimilarity on λ-ho-term-graphs. Therefore the scoping information has to be incorporated in the first-order interpretation, which we accomplish by extending $\Sigma^{\lambda}_{\bullet}$ with S-vertices, scope delimiters, that signify the end of scopes. When translating a λ-ho-term-graph into a first-order term graph, S-vertices are placed along those edges in the underlying term graph at which the abstraction prefix decreases in the λ-ho-term-graph.

Example 5.1 (Adding S-vertices)**.** Consider the terms in Ex. 4.2 and their λ-ho-term-graphs in Ex. 4.3. In the first-order interpretation below, the shading is just for illustration purposes; it is *not* part of the structure, and does *not directly* impair functional bisimulation.

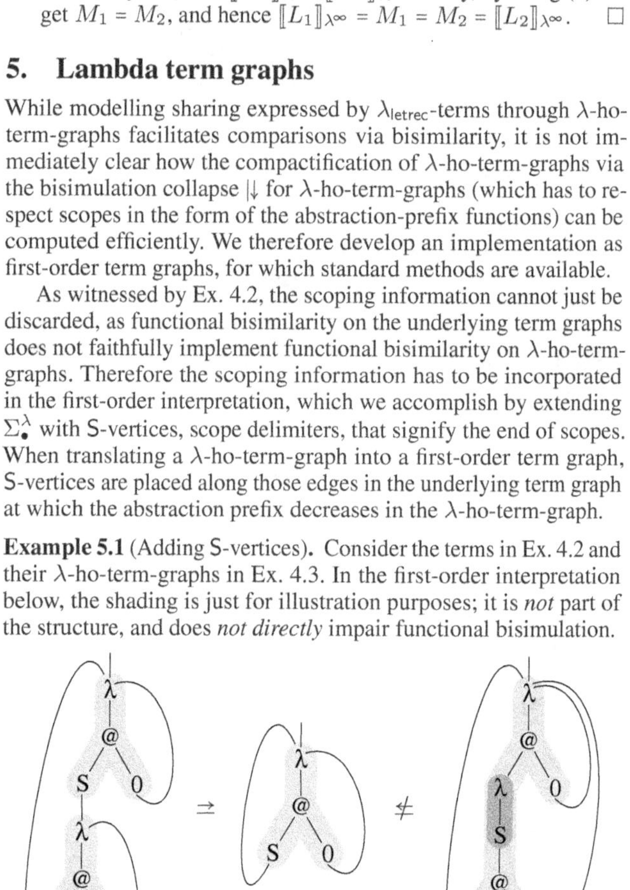

The addition of scope delimiters resolves the problem of Ex. 4.2. They adequately represent the scoping information.

As for λ-ho-term-graphs, we will define correctness conditions by means of an abstraction-prefix function. However, the current approach with unary delimiter vertices leads to a problem.

Example 5.2 (S-backlinks)**.** The term graph with scope delimiters on the left admits a functional bisimulation that fuses two S-vertices that close different scopes. We cannot hope to find a unique abstraction prefix for the resulting fused S-vertex. This is remedied on the right by using a variant representation that requires backlinks from each S-vertex to the abstraction vertex whose scope it closes. Then S-vertices can only be fused if the corresponding abstractions have already been merged. Hence in the presence of S-backlinks, as in the right illustration below, only the variable vertex can be shared.

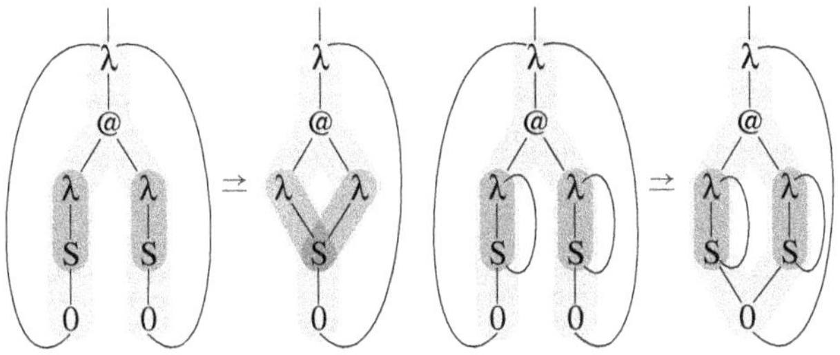

Therefore we consider term graphs over the extension $\Sigma^{\lambda}_{\mathsf{S},\bullet}$ of $\Sigma^{\lambda}_{\bullet}$ with a symbol S of arity 2; one edge targets the successor vertex, the other is a backlink. We give correctness conditions, similar as for λ-ho-term-graphs, and define the arising class of 'λ-term-graphs'.

Definition 5.3 (correct abstraction-prefix function for term graphs over $\Sigma^{\lambda}_{\mathsf{S},\bullet}$)**.** Let $G = \langle V, lab, args, r\rangle$ be a $\Sigma^{\lambda}_{\mathsf{S},\bullet}$-term-graph.

An *abstraction-prefix function* $P : V \to V^*$ on G is called *correct* if for all $w, w_0, w_1 \in V$ and $k \in \{0,1\}$ it holds:

$$P(r) = \epsilon \qquad \text{(root)}$$
$$P(\bullet) = \epsilon \qquad \text{(black hole)}$$
$$w \in V(\lambda) \wedge w \rightarrowtail_0 w_0 \Rightarrow P(w_0) = P(w)w \qquad (\lambda)$$
$$w \in V(@) \wedge w \rightarrowtail_k w_k \Rightarrow P(w_k) = P(w) \qquad (@)$$
$$w \in V(0) \wedge w \rightarrowtail_0 w_0 \Rightarrow \begin{cases} w_0 \in V(\lambda) \\ \wedge\ P(w_0)w_0 = P(w) \end{cases} \qquad (0)_1$$
$$w \in V(\mathsf{S}) \wedge w \rightarrowtail_0 w_0 \Rightarrow \begin{cases} P(w_0)v = P(w) \\ \text{for some } v \in V \end{cases} \qquad (\mathsf{S})_1$$
$$w \in V(\mathsf{S}) \wedge w \rightarrowtail_1 w_1 \Rightarrow \begin{cases} w_1 \in V(\lambda) \\ \wedge\ P(w_1)w_1 = P(w) \end{cases} \qquad (\mathsf{S})_2$$

While in λ-ho-term-graphs the abstraction prefix can shrink by several vertices along an edge (cf. Def. 4.4), here the situation is strictly regulated: the prefix can only shrink by one variable, and only along the outgoing edge of a delimiter vertex.

Proposition 5.4 (uniqueness of the abstraction prefix function)**.** Let G be a term graph over the signature $\Sigma^{\lambda}_{\mathsf{S},\bullet}$. If P_1 and P_2 are correct abstraction prefix functions of G, then $P_1 = P_2$.

Definition 5.5 (λ-term-graph)**.** A *λ-term-graph* is a term graph $G = \langle V, lab, args, r\rangle$ over $\Sigma^{\lambda}_{\mathsf{S},\bullet}$ that has a correct abstraction-prefix function (which is not a part of G). The class of λ-term-graphs is $\mathcal{T}$.

Definition 5.6 (eager scope)**.** A λ-term-graph G is called *eager-scope* if together with its abstraction-prefix function it meets the condition in Def. 4.9. $\mathcal{T}_{\text{eag}}$ denotes the class of eager-scope graphs.

5.1 Correspondence between λ-ho- and λ-term-graphs

The correspondences between λ-ho-term-graphs and λ-term-graphs:

$$\mathcal{HT} : \mathcal{H} \to \mathcal{T} \qquad\qquad \mathcal{TH} : \mathcal{T} \to \mathcal{H}$$

are defined as follows: For obtaining $\mathcal{HT}(\mathcal{G})$ for a $\mathcal{G} \in \mathcal{H}$, insert scope-delimiters wherever the prefix decreases, as illustrated in Fig. 6. For obtaining $\mathcal{TH}(G)$ for a $G \in \mathcal{T}$, retain the abstraction-prefix function, and remove every delimiter vertex from G, thereby connecting its incoming edge with its outgoing edge. For formal definitions and well-definedness of $\mathcal{TH}$ and $\mathcal{HT}$, see [12].

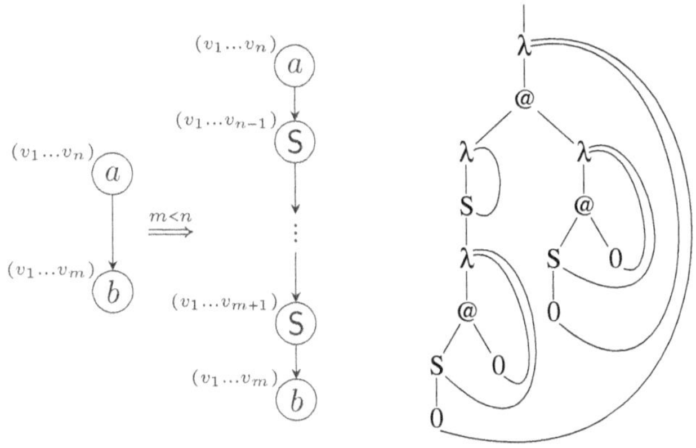

Figure 6. Left: definition of $\mathcal{HT}$ by inserting S-vertices, between edge-connected vertices of a λ-ho-term-graph. Right: interpretation $\mathcal{HT}(\mathcal{G})$ of the eager-scope λ-ho-term-graph $\mathcal{G}$ in Fig. 4.

Note that a λ-ho-term-graph may have multiple corresponding λ-term-graphs that differ only with respect to their 'degree' of S-sharing (the extent to which S-vertices occur shared). $\mathcal{HT}$ maps to a λ-term-graph with no sharing of S-vertices at all.

The proposition below guarantees the usefulness of the translation $\mathcal{HT}$ for implementing functional bisimulation on λ-ho-term-graphs. In particular, this is due to items (iii) and (iv). As formulated by item (i), $\mathcal{TH}$ is a retraction of $\mathcal{HT}$ (and $\mathcal{HT}$ a section of $\mathcal{TH}$). The converse is not the case, yet it holds up to S-sharing by item (ii). For the proof, we refer to our article [12].

Proposition 5.7 (correspondence with λ-ho-term-graphs)**.**

(i) $\mathcal{TH} \circ \mathcal{HT} = \text{id}_{\mathcal{H}}$.
(ii) $(\mathcal{HT} \circ \mathcal{TH})(G) \mathrel{\underline{\to}}^{\mathsf{S}} G$ holds for all $G \in \mathcal{T}$.
(iii) $\mathcal{TH}$ and $\mathcal{HT}$ preserve and reflect functional bisimulation $\mathrel{\underline{\to}}$ and bisimulation $\mathrel{\underline{\leftrightarrow}}$ on $\mathcal{H}$ and $\mathcal{T}$.
(iv) $\mathcal{TH}$ and $\mathcal{HT}$ preserve and reflect the property eager-scope.
(v) $\mathcal{T}$ is closed under $\mathrel{\underline{\to}}^{\mathsf{S}}$, $\mathrel{\underline{\leftarrow}}^{\mathsf{S}}$, and $\mathrel{\underline{\leftrightarrow}}^{\mathsf{S}}$.
(vi) $\mathcal{HT}$ and $\mathcal{TH}$ induce isomorphisms between $\mathcal{H}$ and $\mathcal{T}/_{\mathrel{\underline{\leftrightarrow}}^{\mathsf{S}}}$.

5.2 Closedness of $\mathcal{T}$ under functional bisimulation

While preservation of $\mathrel{\underline{\to}}$ by $\mathcal{HT}$ is necessary for its implementation via $\mathrel{\underline{\to}}$ on $\mathcal{T}$, the practicality of the interpretation $\mathcal{HT}$ also depends on the closedness of $\mathcal{T}$ under $\mathrel{\underline{\to}}$. Namely, if the bisimulation collapse $G = \mathcal{HT}(\mathcal{G})|\!\downarrow$ of the interpretation of some $\mathcal{G} \in \mathcal{H}$ were not contained in $\mathcal{T}$, then the converse interpretation $\mathcal{TH}$ could not be applied to G in order to obtain the bisimulation collapse of $\mathcal{G}$.

A subclass $\mathcal{K}$ of the term graphs over a signature Σ is called *closed under functional bisimulation* if, for all term graphs G, G' over Σ, whenever $G \in \mathcal{K}$ and $G \mathrel{\underline{\to}} G'$, then also $G' \in \mathcal{K}$.

Note that for obtaining this property the use of variable backlinks, and backlinks for delimiter vertices is crucial (cf. Ex. 5.2).

Yet the class $\mathcal{T}$ is actually not closed under $\mathrel{\underline{\to}}$: See Fig. 7 at the top for a homomorphism from a non-eager-scope λ-term-graph to a term graph over $\Sigma^{\lambda}_{\mathsf{S},\bullet}$ that is not a λ-term-graph (as suggested by the overlapping scopes). But the bisimulation collapse of an eager-scope version of this λ-term-graph is again a λ-term-graph (at the bottom). This motivates the following theorem, which is proved in the extended report of [12]. It justifies property (P2) with $\mathcal{T}_{\text{eag}}$ for $\mathcal{T}$.

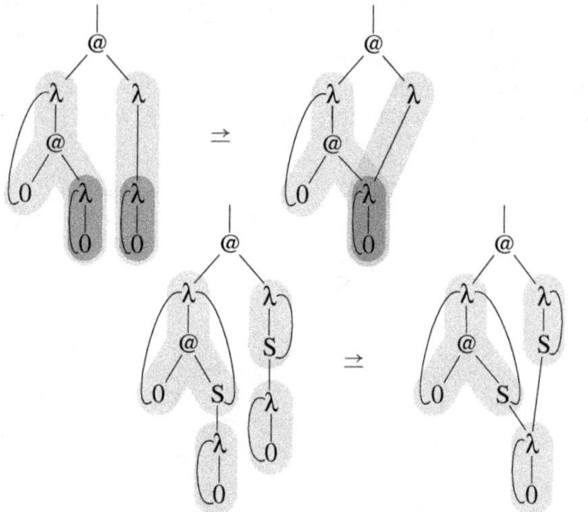

Figure 7. $\mathcal{T}$ is not closed under functional bisimulation, but $\mathcal{T}_{\text{eag}}$ is.

Theorem 5.8. *The class $\mathcal{T}_{\text{eag}}$ of eager-scope λ-term-graphs is closed under functional bisimulation $\rightharpoonup$.*

5.3 λ-term-graph semantics for λ_{letrec}-terms

We will consider in fact two interpretations of λ_{letrec}-terms as λ-term-graphs: first we define $[\![\cdot]\!]^{\text{min}}_{\mathcal{T}}$ as the composition of $[\![\cdot]\!]_{\mathcal{H}}$ and $\mathcal{HT}$; then we define the semantics $[\![\cdot]\!]_{\mathcal{T}}$ with more fine-grained S-sharing, which is necessary for defining a readback with the property (P3).

By composing the interpretation $\mathcal{HT}$ of λ-ho-term-graphs as λ-term-graphs with the λ-ho-term-graph semantics $[\![\cdot]\!]_{\mathcal{H}}$, a semantics of λ_{letrec}-terms as λ-term-graphs is obtained. There is, however, a more direct way to define this semantics: by using an adaptation of the translation rules $\mathcal{R}$ in Fig. 3, on which $[\![\cdot]\!]_{\mathcal{H}}$ is based. For this, let $\mathcal{R}_{\mathsf{S}}$ be the result of replacing the rule S in $\mathcal{R}$ by the version in Fig. 8. While applications of this variant of the S-rule also shorten the abstraction-prefix, they additionally produce a delimiter vertex.

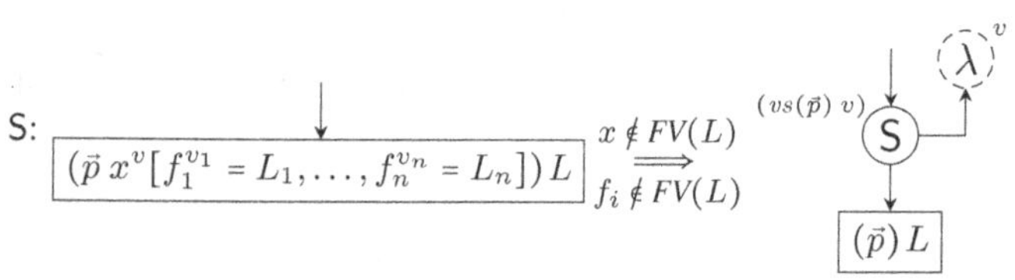

Figure 8. Delimiter-vertex producing version of the S-rule in Fig. 3

Here, at the end of the translation process, every loop on an indirection vertex with a prefix of length n is replaced by a chain of n S-vertices followed by a black hole vertex.Note that, while the system $\mathcal{R}_{\mathsf{S}}$ inherits all of the non-determinism of $\mathcal{R}$, the possible degrees of freedom have additional impact on the result, because now they also determine the precise degree of S-vertex sharing.

By analogous stipulations as in Def. 4.11 we define the conditions under which a λ-term-graph is called *eager-scope* $\mathcal{R}_{\mathsf{S}}$-generated, or $\mathcal{R}_{\mathsf{S}}$-generated *with minimal prefixes*, from a λ_{letrec}-term. For these notions, statements entirely analogous to Prop. 4.12 hold.

Definition 5.9. The *semantics* $[\![\cdot]\!]^{\text{min}}_{\mathcal{T}}$ for λ_{letrec}-terms as λ-term-graphs is defined as $[\![\cdot]\!]^{\text{min}}_{\mathcal{T}} : Ter(\lambda_{\text{letrec}}) \to \mathcal{T}_{\text{eag}}$, $L \mapsto [\![L]\!]^{\text{min}}_{\mathcal{T}} :=$ the λ-term-graph that is $\mathcal{R}_{\mathsf{S}}$-generated with minimal prefixes from a garbage-free version L' of L.

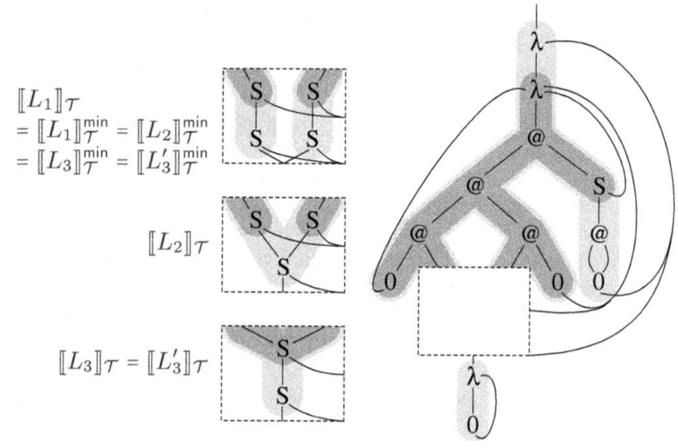

Figure 9. Translation of the λ_{letrec}-terms from Ex. 5.14 with the semantics $[\![\cdot]\!]^{\text{min}}_{\mathcal{T}}$ and $[\![\cdot]\!]_{\mathcal{T}}$. For legibility some backlinks are merged.

For an example, see Ex. 5.14 below. In $[\![\cdot]\!]^{\text{min}}_{\mathcal{T}}$, 'min' also indicates that λ-term-graphs obtained via this semantics exhibit minimal (in fact no) sharing (two or more incoming edges) of S-vertices. This is substantiated by the next proposition, in the light of the fact that $\mathcal{HT}$ does not create any shared S-vertices.

Proposition 5.10. $[\![\cdot]\!]^{\text{min}}_{\mathcal{T}} = \mathcal{HT} \circ [\![\cdot]\!]_{\mathcal{H}}$.

Hence $[\![\cdot]\!]^{\text{min}}_{\mathcal{T}}$ only yields λ-term-graphs without sharing of S-vertices, and therefore its image cannot be all of $\mathcal{T}_{\text{eag}}$. As a consequence, we cannot hope to define a readback function rb with respect to $[\![\cdot]\!]^{\text{min}}_{\mathcal{T}}$ that has the desired property (P3), because that requires that the image of the semantics is $\mathcal{T}_{\text{eag}}$ in its entirety.

Therefore we modify the definition of $[\![\cdot]\!]^{\text{min}}_{\mathcal{T}}$ to obtain a λ-term-graph semantics $[\![\cdot]\!]_{\mathcal{T}}$ with image $\text{im}([\![\cdot]\!]_{\mathcal{T}}) = \mathcal{T}_{\text{eag}}$. This is achieved by letting the let-binding-structure of the λ_{letrec}-term influence the degree of S-sharing as much as possible, while staying eager-scope.

We say that a λ-ho-term-graph $\mathcal{G}$ is *eager-scope $\mathcal{R}$-generated with maximal prefixes* from a λ_{letrec}-term L if $\mathcal{G}$ is $\mathcal{R}$-generated from L by a translation process in which in applications of the let-rule the prefixes are chosen maximally, but so that the eager-scope property of the process is not compromised. It can be shown that this condition fixes the prefix lengths per application of the let-rule.

Definition 5.11. The *semantics* $[\![\cdot]\!]_{\mathcal{T}}$ for λ_{letrec}-terms as λ-term-graphs is defined as $[\![\cdot]\!]_{\mathcal{T}} : Ter(\lambda_{\text{letrec}}) \to \mathcal{T}_{\text{eag}}$, $L \mapsto [\![L]\!]_{\mathcal{T}} :=$ the λ-term-graph that is eager-scope $\mathcal{R}_{\mathsf{S}}$-generated with maximal prefixes from a garbage-free version L' of L.

Proposition 5.12. $[\![L]\!]^{\text{min}}_{\mathcal{T}} \rightharpoonup^{\mathsf{S}} [\![L]\!]_{\mathcal{T}}$ holds for all λ_{letrec}-terms L.

Now due to this, and due to Prop. 5.7, (iii), the statement of Thm. 4.15 can be transferred to $\mathcal{T}$, yielding property (P1) for $[\![\cdot]\!]_{\mathcal{T}}$.

Theorem 5.13. *For all λ_{letrec}-terms L_1 and L_2 the following holds: $[\![L_1]\!]_{\lambda^\infty} = [\![L_2]\!]_{\lambda^\infty}$ if and only if $[\![L_1]\!]_{\mathcal{T}} \leftrightarrows [\![L_2]\!]_{\mathcal{T}}$.*

Example 5.14. Consider the following four λ_{letrec}-terms:

$L_1 = \text{let } I = \lambda z.\, z \text{ in } \lambda x.\, \lambda y.\, \text{let } f = x \text{ in } ((y\, I)\, (I\, y))\, (f\, f)$

$L_2 = \lambda x.\, \text{let } I = \lambda z.\, z \text{ in } \lambda y.\, \text{let } f = x \text{ in } ((y\, I)\, (I\, y))\, (f\, f)$

$L_3 = \lambda x.\, \lambda y.\, \text{let } I = \lambda z.\, z,\ f = x \text{ in } ((y\, I)\, (I\, y))\, (f\, f)$

$L'_3 = \lambda x.\, \text{let } I = \lambda z.\, z \text{ in } \lambda y.\, \text{let } f = x,\ g = I \text{ in } ((y\, g)\, (g\, y))\, (f\, f)$

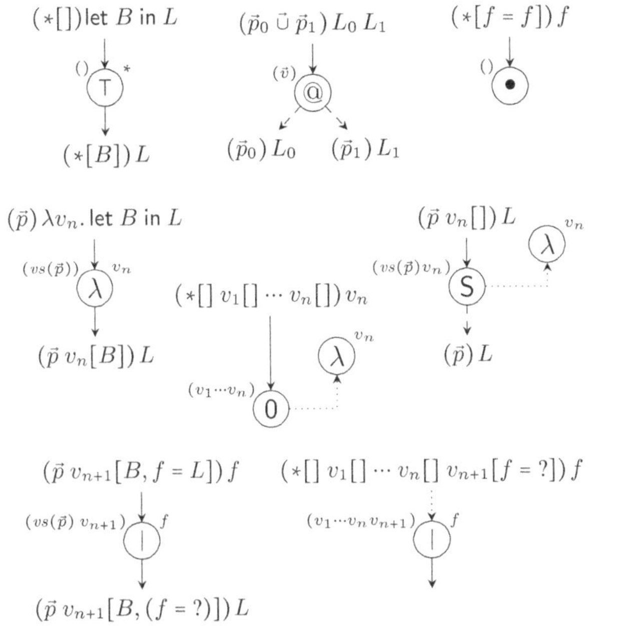

Figure 10. Readback synthesis rules for computing a representing λ_{letrec}-term from a λ-term-graph. The rules for $\top$- and λ-vertices have variants for B is empty. For explanations, see Def. 6.1, (Rb-5).

The three possible fillings of the dashed area in Fig. 9 depict the translations $[\![L_1]\!]_{\mathcal{T}}$, $[\![L_2]\!]_{\mathcal{T}}$, and $[\![L_3]\!]_{\mathcal{T}} = [\![L_3']\!]_{\mathcal{T}}$. The translations of the four terms with $[\![\cdot]\!]^{\text{min}}$ are identical:
$[\![L_1]\!]_{\mathcal{T}}^{\text{min}} = [\![L_2]\!]_{\mathcal{T}}^{\text{min}} = [\![L_3]\!]_{\mathcal{T}}^{\text{min}} = [\![L_3']\!]_{\mathcal{T}}^{\text{min}} = [\![L_1]\!]_{\mathcal{T}}$.

6. Readback of λ-term-graphs

In this section we describe how from a given λ-term-graph G a λ_{letrec}-term L that represents G (i.e. for which $[\![L]\!]_{\mathcal{T}} = G$ holds) can be 'read back'. For this purpose we define a process based on term synthesis rules. It defines a readback function from λ-term-graphs to λ_{letrec}-terms. We illustrate this process by an example, formulate its most important properties, and sketch the proof of (P3).

The idea underlying the definition of the readback procedure is the following: For a given λ-term-graph G, a spanning tree T for G (augmented with a dedicated root node) is constructed that severs cycles of G at (some) recursive bindings, and at variable and S-backlinks. Now the spanning tree T facilitates an inductive bottom-up (from the leafs upwards) synthesis process along T, which labels the edges of G (except for variable backlinks) with prefixed λ_{letrec}-terms. For this process we use local rules (see Fig. 10) that synthesise labels for incoming edges of a vertex from the labels of its outgoing edges. Eventually the readback of G is obtained as the label for the edge that singles out the root of term graph.

The design of the readback rules is based on a decision about where let-bindings are placed in the synthesised term. Namely there exists some freedom for these placements, as certain kind of shifts of let-expressions (let-floating steps [14]) preserve the λ-term-graph interpretation. Here, let-bindings will always be declared in a let-expression that is placed as high up in the term as possible: a binding arising from the term synthesised for a shared vertex w is placed in a let-expression that is created at the enclosing λ-abstraction of w (the leftmost vertex in the abstraction-prefix $P(w)$ of w).

Definition 6.1 (readback of λ-term-graphs)**.** Let $G \in \mathcal{T}$ be a λ-term-graph. The process of computing the readback of G (a λ_{letrec}-term) consists of the following five steps, starting on G:

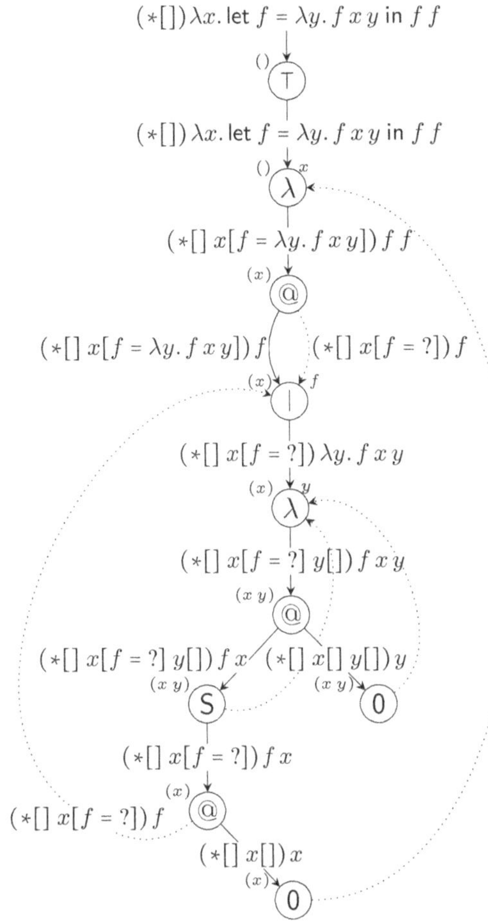

Figure 11. Example of the readback synthesis from a λ-term-graph.

(Rb-1) Determine the abstraction-prefix function P for G by performing a traversal over G, and associate with every vertex w of G its abstraction-prefix $P(w)$.

(Rb-2) Add a new vertex on top with label $\top$, arity 1, and empty abstraction prefix. Let G' be the resulting term graph, and P' its abstraction-prefix function.

(Rb-3) Introduce indirection vertices to organise sharing: For every vertex w of G' with two or more incoming non-variable-backlink edges, add an indirection vertex w_0, redirect the incoming edges of w that are not variable backlinks to w_0, and direct the outgoing edge from w_0 to w. In the resulting term graph G'' only indirection vertices are shared[3]; their names will be used. Extend P' to an abstraction-prefix function P'' for G'' so that every indirection vertex w_0 gets the prefix of its successor w.

(Rb-4) Construct a spanning tree T'' of G'' by using a depth-first search (DFS) on G''. Note that all variable backlinks and S-backlinks, and some of the recursive back-bindings, of G'', are not contained in T'', because they are back-edges of the DFS.

(Rb-5) Apply the readback synthesis rules from Fig. 10 to G'' with respect to T''. By this a complete labelling of the edges of G'' by prefixed λ_{letrec}-terms is constructed. The rules define how the labelling for an incoming edge (on top) of a vertex w is synthesised under the assumption of an already determined labelling of an outgoing edge of (and below) w. If the outgoing

[3] Incoming variable backlinks are not counted as sharing here.

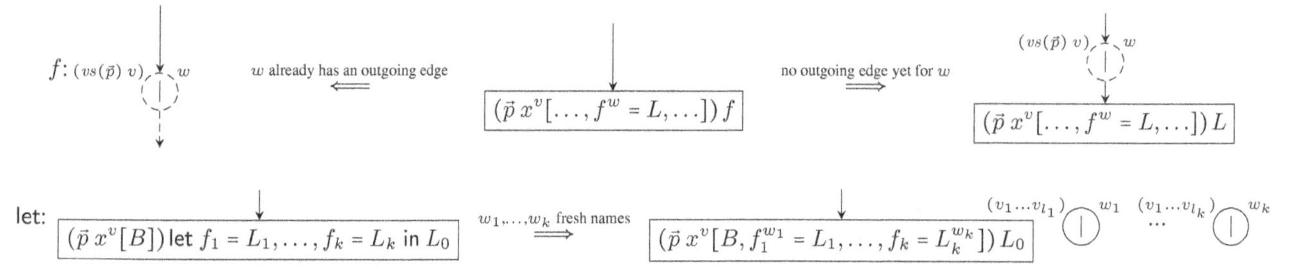

Figure 12. Modification of (two of) the translation rules in Fig. 3 for a variant definition of the λ-term-graph interpretation of λ_{letrec}-terms. Here the translation of a let-expression does not directly spawn translations for the binding equations, but the in-part has to be translated first.

edge in the rule does not carry a label, then the labelling of the incoming edge can happen regardless. Note that in these rules:

- full line (dotted line) edges indicate spanning tree (non-spanning tree) edges, broken line edges either of these sorts;
- abstraction prefixes of vertices are crucial for the 0-vertex, and the second indirection vertex rule, where the prefixes in the synthesised terms are created; in the other rules the prefix of the assumed term is used; for indicating a correspondence between a term's and a vertex's abstraction prefix we denote by $v(\vec{p})$ the word of vertices occurring in a term's prefix $\vec{p}$;
- the rule for indirection vertices with incoming non-spanning tree edge introduces an unfinished binding $f = ?$ for f; unfinished bindings are completed in the course of the process;
- the @-vertex rule applies only if $v(\vec{p}_0) = v(\vec{p}_1)$; the operation $\vec{\cup}$ used in the synthesised term's prefix builds the union per prefix variable of the pertaining bindings; if the prefixed terms $(\vec{p}_0)\, L_0$ and $(\vec{p}_1)\, L_1$ assumed in this rule contain a yet unfinished binding equation $f = ?$ and a completed equation $f = P$ at a λ-variable z, then the synthesised term contains the completed binding $f = P$ for f at z;
- not depicted in Fig. 10 are variants of ⊤- and λ-vertices rules for the cases with empty B: then no let-binding is introduced in the synthesised term, but the term from the in-part is used.

If this process yields the label $(*[])L$ for the (root-)edge pointing to the new top vertex of G'', where L is a λ_{letrec}-term, then we call L the *readback of* G.

Note that firing of the rules in step (Rb-5) of the readback process proceeds in bottom-up direction in the spanning tree, starting from the back-edges, with some room for parallelism concerning work in different subtrees. Furthermore observe that on all directed edges e (spanning tree edges or back edges) the rule applied to derive the edge label is uniquely determined by (is tied to) the label of the target vertex v of e, with the single exception of v being an indirection vertex. In that case one of the two indirection vertex rules applies, depending on whether e is a spanning-tree edge or a back-edge.

Proposition 6.2. Let G be a λ-term-graph. The process described in Def. 6.1 produces a complete edge labelling of the (modified) term graph, with label $(*[])L$ for the topmost edge, where L is a λ_{letrec}-term. Hence it yields L as the readback of G. Thus Def. 6.1 defines a function $\mathsf{rb} : \mathcal{T} \to \mathit{Ter}(\lambda_{\text{letrec}})$, the *readback function*.

Example 6.3. See Fig. 11 for the illustration of the synthesis of the readback from an example λ-term-graph. Full line edges are in the spanning tree, dotted line edges are not. Note that at the top vertex, no empty let-binding is created since the variant of the ⊤-vertex rule for empty binding groups is applied.

The following theorem validates property (P3), with $\mathcal{T}_{\text{eag}}$ for $\mathcal{T}$.

Theorem 6.4. *For all* $G \in \mathcal{T}_{\text{eag}}$*:* $([\![\cdot]\!]_{\mathcal{T}} \circ \mathsf{rb})(G) = [\![\mathsf{rb}(G)]\!]_{\mathcal{T}} \simeq G$, *i.e.,* rb *is a right-inverse of* $[\![\cdot]\!]_{\mathcal{T}}$, *and* $[\![\cdot]\!]_{\mathcal{T}}$ *a left-inverse of* rb, *up to* $\simeq$. *Hence* rb *is injective, and* $[\![\cdot]\!]_{\mathcal{T}}$ *is surjective, thus* $im([\![\cdot]\!]_{\mathcal{T}}) = \mathcal{T}_{\text{eag}}$.

Sketch of Proof. Graph translation steps can be linked with corresponding readback steps in order to establish that the former roughly reverse the latter. Roughly, because e.g. reversing a λ-readback step necessitates both a λ- and a let-translation step. (For illustrations of the stepwise reversal of readback steps through translation steps we refer to two figures in the extended version of this paper [15].) However, this correspondence holds only for a modification of the translation rules $\mathcal{R}_S$ from Fig. 3, Fig. 8 where the rules let (for let-expressions) and f (for occurrences of recursion variables) are replaced by the locally-operating versions in Fig. 12, and a rule for creating a top vertex is added. Now the translation of a let-expression does no longer directly spawn translations of the defined recursive bindings, but the bindings will only be translated later once their calls have been reached during the translation process of the in-part, or of the definitions of other already translated bindings. Note that in the let-rule in Fig. 12 function bindings are associated with the rightmost variable in the prefix, which corresponds to choosing $l_i = n$ in the let-rule in Fig. 3. While such a stipulation does not guarantee the eager-scope translation of every term, it actually does so for all λ_{letrec}-terms that are obtained by the readback (on these terms the translation so defined coincides with $[\![\cdot]\!]_{\mathcal{T}}$ from Def. 4.13).

The proof uses induction on access paths, and an invariant that relates the eager-scope property localised for a vertex v with the applicability of the S-rule to the readback term synthesised at v. □

7. Complexity analysis

Here we report on a complexity analysis for the individual operations from the previous sections, for the used standard algorithms, and overall, for compactification and unfolding equivalence.

In the lemma below, (ii) and (v) justify the property (P4) of our methods. Items (iii) and (iv) detail the complexity of standard methods when used for computing bisimulation collapse and bisimilarity of λ-term-graphs. Note that first-order term graphs can be modelled by deterministic process graphs, and hence by DFAs. Therefore bisimilarity of term graphs can be computed via language equivalence of corresponding DFAs [19] (in time $O(n\alpha(n))$ [25], where α is the quasi-constant *inverse Ackermann function*), and bisimulation collapse via state minimisation of DFAs (in time $O(n \log n)$) [18].

Lemma 7.1. *(i)* $\text{size}([\![L]\!]_{\mathcal{T}}) \in O(|L|^2)$ *for* $L \in \mathit{Ter}(\lambda_{\text{letrec}})$.
(ii) Translating $L \in \mathit{Ter}(\lambda_{\text{letrec}})$ *into* $[\![L]\!]_{\mathcal{T}} \in \mathcal{T}$ *takes time* $O(|L|^2)$.
(iii) Collapsing $G \in \mathcal{T}$ *to* $G{\downarrow\!\!\downarrow}$ *is in* $O(\text{size}(G) \log \text{size}(G))$.
(iv) Deciding bisimilarity of $G_1, G_2 \in \mathcal{T}$ *requires time* $O(n\alpha(n))$ *for* $n = \max\{\text{size}(G_1), \text{size}(G_2)\}$.
(v) Computing the readback $\mathsf{rb}(G)$ *for a given* $G \in \mathcal{T}$ *requires time* $O(n \log n)$, *for* $n = \text{size}(G)$.

Based on this lemma, and on further considerations, we obtain the following complexity statements for our methods.

Theorem 7.2. *(i) The computation, for a $\lambda_{\mathsf{letrec}}$-term L with $|L| = n$, of a maximally compactified form $(\mathsf{rb} \circ |\!\downarrow \circ [\![\cdot]\!]_{\mathcal{T}})(L)$ requires time $O(n^2 \log n)$. By using an* S*-unsharing operation* $\mathsf{unsh}_{\mathsf{S}}$*, a (typically smaller) $\lambda_{\mathsf{letrec}}$-term $(\mathsf{rb} \circ \mathsf{unsh}_{\mathsf{S}} \circ |\!\downarrow \circ [\![\cdot]\!]_{\mathcal{T}})(L)$ of size $O(n \log n)$ can be obtained, with the same time complexity.*

(ii) The decision of whether $\lambda_{\mathsf{letrec}}$-terms L_1 and L_2 are unfolding-equivalent requires time $O(n^2 \alpha(n))$ for $n = \max\{|L_1|, |L_2|\}$.

8. Implementation

We have implemented our methods in Haskell using the Utrecht University Attribute Grammar System. The implementation is available at `http://hackage.haskell.org/package/maxsharing/`. The output produced for the examples in this paper, and explanations can be found in the appendix of the extended version [15] of this paper.

9. Modifications, extensions and applications

We have described an adaptation of the bisimulation proof method for $\lambda_{\mathsf{letrec}}$-terms. Recognising unfolding equivalence and increasing sharing are reduced to problems involving first-order term graphs. The principal idea is to use the nested scope structure of higher-order terms for an interpretation by term graphs with scope delimiters.

We conclude by describing easy modifications, rather direct extensions, and finally, promising areas of application for our methods.

9.1 Modifications

Implicit sharing of λ-variables. Multiple occurrences of the same λ-variable in a $\lambda_{\mathsf{letrec}}$-term L are not shared (represented by a shared variable vertex) in the graph interpretation $[\![L]\!]_{\mathcal{H}}$. Consequently, our method compactifies the term $\lambda x. x\, x$ into $\lambda x. \mathsf{let}\ f = x\ \mathsf{in}\ f\, f$. Such explicit sharing of variables is excessive for many applications. It can be remedied easily, namely by unsharing variable vertices before applying the readback, or by preventing the readback from introducing let-bindings when only a variable vertex is shared.

Avoiding aliases produced by the readback. The readback function in Section 6 is sensitive to the degree of sharing of S-vertices in the given λ-term-graph: it maps two λ-term-graphs that only differ in what concerns sharing of S-vertices to different $\lambda_{\mathsf{letrec}}$-terms. Typically, for λ-term-graphs with maximal sharing of S-vertices this can produce let-bindings that are just 'aliases', such as g is alias for I in L_3' from Ex. 5.14. This can be avoided in two ways: by slightly adapting the readback function, or by performing maximal unsharing of S-vertices before applying the readback as defined.

Preventing disadvantageous sharing. Introducing sharing at compile-time can cause 'space leaks', i.e. a needlessly high memory footprint, at run-time, because 'a large data structure becomes shared [...], and therefore its space which before was reclaimed by garbage collection now cannot be reclaimed until its last reference is used' [9]. For this reason, realisations of CSE [6] restrict the locally operating rewrite rules employed for introducing sharing by suitable conditions that account for the type of potentially shared subexpressions, and their strictness in the program. For our global method of introducing sharing via the bisimulation collapse, a different approach is needed.

Here the bisimulation collapse can be restricted so that sharing is not introduced at vertices that should not be shared. More precisely, it can be prevented that any unshared vertex (in-degree one) from a pre-determined set of 'sharing-unfit' vertices would have a shared vertex (in-degree greater than one) as its image in the bisimulation collapse. This can be achieved by modifying the graph interpretation $[\![\cdot]\!]_{\mathcal{T}}$. Any set of sharing-unfit positions in L gives rise to a set of sharing-unfit vertices in $[\![L]\!]_{\mathcal{T}}$. In the modification of $[\![L]\!]_{\mathcal{T}}$, special back-links are added from every sharing-unfit vertex with in-degree one to its immediate successor. These back-links prevent that such a sharing-unfit vertex v can collapse with another vertex v' without that also the predecessors of v and v' would collapse as well.

A more general notion of readback. Condition (P3) is rather rigorous in that it imposes a sharing structure on $\lambda_{\mathsf{letrec}}$ that is specific to λ-term-graphs (degrees of S-sharing). For a weaker version of (P3) with $\leftrightarrow^{\mathsf{S}}$ in place of isomorphism, a readback does not have to be injective, and, independently of how much S-sharing a translation into λ-term-graphs introduces, a readback function always exists.

9.2 Extensions

Full functional languages. In order to support programming languages that are based on $\lambda_{\mathsf{letrec}}$ like Haskell, additional language constructs need to be supported. Such languages can typically be desugared into a core language, which comprises only a small subset of language constructs such as constructors, case statements, and primitives. These constructs can be represented in an extension of $\lambda_{\mathsf{letrec}}$ by additional function symbols. In conjunction with a desugarer our methods are applicable to full programming languages.

Other programming languages, and calculi with binding constructs. Most programming languages feature constructs for grouping definitions that are similar to letrec. We therefore expect that our methods can be adapted to many imperative languages in particular, and may turn out to be fruitful for optimising compilers. Our methods for achieving maximal sharing certainly generalise to theoretical frameworks, and calculi with binding constructs, such as the π-calculus [23], and higher-order rewrite systems (e.g. CRSs and HRSs, [30]) as used here for the formalisation of $\lambda_{\mathsf{letrec}}$.

Fully-lazy lambda-lifting. There is a close connection between our methods and fully-lazy lambda-lifting [20, 28]. In particular, the required-variable and scope analysis of a $\lambda_{\mathsf{letrec}}$-term L on which the λ-term-graph-translation $[\![L]\!]_{\mathcal{T}}$ is based is closely analogous to the one needed for extracting from L the supercombinators in the result $\hat{L}$ of fully-lazy lambda-lifting L. Moreover, the fully-lazy lambda-lifting transformation can even be implemented in a natural way on the basis of our methods. Namely as the composition $\mathsf{rb}_{LL} \circ [\![\cdot]\!]_{\mathcal{T}}$ of the translation $[\![\cdot]\!]_{\mathcal{T}}$ into λ-term-graphs, where rb_{LL} is a variant readback function that, for a given λ-term-graph, synthesises the system $\hat{L}$ of supercombinators, instead of the $\lambda_{\mathsf{letrec}}$-term $\mathsf{rb}(L)$.

Maximal sharing on supercombinator translations of $\lambda_{\mathsf{letrec}}$-terms. $\lambda_{\mathsf{letrec}}$-terms L correspond to supercombinator systems $\hat{L}$, the result of fully-lazy lambda-lifting L: the combinators in $\hat{L}$ correspond to 'extended scopes' [11] (or 'skeletons' [2]) in L, and supercombinator reduction steps on $\hat{L}$ correspond to weak β-reduction steps L. In the case of λ-calculus this has been established by Balabonski [2]. Via this correspondence the maximal-sharing method for $\lambda_{\mathsf{letrec}}$-terms can be lifted to obtain a maximal-sharing method systems of supercombinators obtained by fully-lazy lambda-lifting.

Non-eager scope-closure strategies. We focused on eager-scope translations, because they facilitate maximal sharing, and guarantee that interpretations of unfolding-equivalent $\lambda_{\mathsf{letrec}}$-terms are bisimilar. Yet every scope-closure strategy [11] induces a translation and its own notion of maximal sharing. For adapting our maximal sharing method it is necessary to modify the translation into first-order term graphs in such a way that the image class obtained is closed under homomorphism ($\mathcal{T}$ is not closed under $\rightarrow$, unlike its subclass $\mathcal{T}_{\mathrm{eag}}$). This can be achieved by using delimiter vertices also below variable vertices to close scopes that are still open [12, report].

Weaker notions of sharing. The presented methods deal with sharing as expressed by letrec that is horizontal, vertical, or twisted [4]. By contrast, the construct μ [4, 13] expresses only vertical, and the non-recursive let only horizontal, sharing. By restricting bisimulation, our methods can be adapted to the λ-calculus with μ, or with let.

Nested term graphs. The nested scope structure of a λ_{letrec}-term can also be represented by a nested structure of term graphs. The representation of a λ_{letrec}-term as a 'nested term graph' [16] starts with an ordinary term graph in which some of the vertices are labelled by 'nested' symbols that designate outermost bindings together with their scope. Any such vertex is additionally associated with a usual term graph that specifies the subterm context describing the scope, where any inner scopes are again expressed by nested symbols. The association between nested symbols and their term graph specifications is required to be tree-like. The implementation result developed here can be generalised to show that nested term graphs can be implemented faithfully by first-order term graphs [16].

9.3 Applications

Maximal sharing at run-time. Maximal sharing can be applied repeatedly at run-time in order to regain a maximally shared form, thereby speeding up evaluation. This is reminiscent of 'collapsed tree rewriting' [29] for evaluating first-order term graphs represented as maximally shared dags. Since the state of a program in the memory at run-time is typically represented as a supercombinator graph, compactification by bisimulation collapse can take place directly on that graph (see Sec. 9.2), no translation is needed. Compactification can be coupled with garbage collection as bisimulation collapse subsumes some of the work required for a mark and sweep garbage collector. However, a compromise needs to be found between the costs for the optimisation and the gained efficiency.

Additional prevention of disadvantageous sharing. While static analysis methods for preventing sharing that may be disadvantageous at run-time can be adapted from CSE to the maximal-sharing method (see Sec. 9.1), this has yet to be investigated for binding-time analysis [27] and a sharing analysis of partial applications [10].

Code improvement. In programming it is generally desirable to avoid duplication of code. As an extension of CSE, our method is able to detect code duplication. The bisimulation collapse of the term graph interpretation of a program can, together with the readback, provide guidance on how code can be refactored into a more compact form. This application requires some fine-tuning to avoid excessive behaviour like the explicit sharing of variable occurrences (see Sec. 9.1). Yet for this only lightweight additional machinery is needed, such as size constraints or annotations to restrict the bisimulation collapse.

Function equivalence. Recognising whether two programs implement the same function is undecidable. Still, this problem is tackled by proof assistants, and by automated theorem provers used in type-checkers of compilers for dependently-typed programming languages such as Agda. For such systems co-inductive proofs are more difficult to find than inductive ones, and require more effort by the user. Our method for deciding unfolding equivalence could help to develop new approaches to finding co-inductive proofs.

Acknowledgment We want to thank Vincent van Oostrom for extensive feedback on a draft, Doaitse Swierstra and Dimitri Hendriks for helpful comments, and Jeroen Keiren for a suggestion concerning restricting the bisimulation collapse. We also thank the anonymous reviewers for their comments, and a number of stimulating questions.

References

[1] A. Asperti and S. Guerrini. *The Optimal Implementation of Functional Programming Languages.* Cambridge University Press, 1998.

[2] T. Balabonski. A unified approach to fully lazy sharing. In *Proceedings of POPL '12*, pages 469–480, New York, NY, USA, 2012. ACM.

[3] R. S. Bird and R. Patterson. de Bruijn notation as a nested datatype. *Journal of Functional Programming*, 9(1):77–91, 1999.

[4] S. Blom. *Term Graph Rewriting – Syntax and Semantics.* PhD thesis, Vrije Universiteit Amsterdam, 2001.

[5] M. v. d. Brand and P. Klint. ATERMs for manipulation and exchange of structured data: It's all about sharing. *Information and Software Technology*, 49(1):55–64, 2007.

[6] O. Chitil. Common Subexpressions Are Uncommon in Lazy Functional Languages. In *Selected Papers from the 9th International Workshop IFL (IFL '97)*, pages 53–71, London, UK, UK, 1998. Springer-Verlag.

[7] O. Danvy and U. P. Schultz. Lambda-lifting in quadratic time. *Journal of Functional and Logic Programming*, 2004, 2004.

[8] N. G. de Bruijn. Lambda Calculus Notation with Nameless Dummies, a Tool for Automatic Formula Manipulation, with Applic. to the Church-Rosser Theorem. *Indagationes Mathematicae*, 34:381–392, 1972.

[9] A. L. de Medeiros Santos. *Compilation by Transformation in Non-Strict Functional Languages.* PhD thesis, University of Glasgow, 1995.

[10] B. Goldberg and P. Hudak. Detecting Sharing of Partial Applications in Functional Programs. Technical Report YALEU/DCS/RR-526, Department of Computer Science, Yale University, March 1987.

[11] C. Grabmayer and J. Rochel. Expressibility in the Lambda Calculus with Letrec. Technical report, arXiv, August 2012. arXiv:1208.2383.

[12] C. Grabmayer and J. Rochel. Term Graph Representations for Cyclic Lambda Terms. In *Proceedings of TERMGRAPH 2013*, number 110 in EPTCS, 2013. For an extended report see: arXiv:1308.1034.

[13] C. Grabmayer and J. Rochel. Expressibility in the Lambda Calculus with μ. In *Proceedings of RTA 2013*, 2013. Report: arXiv:1304.6284.

[14] C. Grabmayer and J. Rochel. Confluent Let-Floating. In *Proceedings of IWC 2013 (2nd International Workshop on Confluence)*, 2013.

[15] C. Grabmayer and J. Rochel. Maximal Sharing in the Lambda Calculus with letrec. Technical report, 2014. arXiv:1401.1460.

[16] C. Grabmayer and V. van Oostrom. Nested Term Graphs. Technical report, arXiv, May 2014. arXiv:1405.6380.

[17] D. Hendriks and V. van Oostrom. $\curlywedge$. In F. Baader, editor, *Proceedings CADE-19*, volume 2741 of *LNAI*, pages 136–150. Springer, 2003.

[18] J. Hopcroft. An $n \log n$ Algorithm for Minimizing States in a Finite Automata. Technical report, Stanford University, CA, USA, 1971.

[19] J. Hopcroft and R. Karp. A Linear Algorithm for Testing Equivalence of Finite Automata. Technical report, Cornell University, 1971.

[20] R. Hughes. Supercombinators: A new implementation method for applicative languages. In *LFP '82: Proceedings of the 1982 ACM symposium on LISP and functional programming*, pages 1–10, 1982.

[21] T. Johnsson. Lambda lifting: Transforming programs to recursive equations. In *FPCA*, pages 190–203, 1985.

[22] J. Ketema and J. G. Simonsen. Infinitary Combinatory Reduction Systems. *Information and Computation*, 209(6):893 – 926, 2011.

[23] R. Milner. *Communicating and mobile systems: the π-calculus.* Cambridge University Press, 1999.

[24] M. T. Morazán and U. P. Schultz. Optimal lambda lifting in quadratic time. In *Workshop IAFL 2007*, number 5083 in LNCS. Springer, 2008.

[25] D. A. Norton. Algorithms for Testing Equivalence of Finite Automata. Master's thesis, Dept. of Computer Science, Rochester Institute of Technology, 2009. `https://ritdml.rit.edu/handle/1850/8712`.

[26] V. v. Oostrom, K.-J. van de Looij, and M. Zwitserlood. Lambdascope. Extended Abstract, Workshop ALPS, Kyoto, April 10th 2004, 2004.

[27] J. Palsberg and M. Schwartzbach. Binding-time analysis: abstract interpretation versus type inference. In *Int. Conf. on Computer Languages, 1994*, pages 289–298, 1994.

[28] S. L. Peyton Jones. *The Implementation of Functional Programming Languages.* Prentice-Hall, Inc., 1987.

[29] D. Plump. *Evaluation of Functional Expressions by Hypergraph Rewriting.* PhD thesis, Universität Bremen, 1993.

[30] Terese. *Term Rewriting Systems*, volume 55 of *Cambridge Tracts in Theoretical Computer Science.* Cambridge University Press, 2003.

[31] C. P. Wadsworth. *Semantics and Pragmatics of the Lambda-Calculus.* PhD thesis, University of Oxford, 1971.

Practical and Effective Higher-Order Optimizations

Lars Bergstrom
Mozilla Research *
larsberg@mozilla.com

Matthew Fluet
Matthew Le
Rochester Institute of Technology
{mtf,ml9951}@cs.rit.edu

John Reppy
Nora Sandler
University of Chicago
{jhr,nlsandler}@cs.uchicago.edu

Abstract

Inlining is an optimization that replaces a call to a function with that function's body. This optimization not only reduces the overhead of a function call, but can expose additional optimization opportunities to the compiler, such as removing redundant operations or unused conditional branches. Another optimization, copy propagation, replaces a redundant copy of a still-live variable with the original. Copy propagation can reduce the total number of live variables, reducing register pressure and memory usage, and possibly eliminating redundant memory-to-memory copies. In practice, both of these optimizations are implemented in nearly every modern compiler.

These two optimizations are practical to implement and effective in first-order languages, but in languages with lexically-scoped first-class functions (aka, closures), these optimizations are not available to code programmed in a higher-order style. With higher-order functions, the analysis challenge has been that the environment at the call site must be the same as at the closure capture location, up to the free variables, or the meaning of the program may change. Olin Shivers' 1991 dissertation called this family of optimizations *Super-β* and he proposed one analysis technique, called *reflow*, to support these optimizations. Unfortunately, reflow has proven too expensive to implement in practice. Because these higher-order optimizations are not available in functional-language compilers, programmers studiously avoid uses of higher-order values that cannot be optimized (particularly in compiler benchmarks).

This paper provides the first practical and effective technique for Super-β (higher-order) inlining and copy propagation, which we call unchanged variable analysis. We show that this technique is practical by implementing it in the context of a real compiler for an ML-family language and showing that the required analyses have costs below 3% of the total compilation time. This technique's effectiveness is shown through a set of benchmarks and example programs, where this analysis exposes additional potential optimization sites.

* Portions of this work were performed while the author was at the University of Chicago.

ICFP '14, September 1–6, 2014, Gothenburg, Sweden.

http://dx.doi.org/10.1145/2628136.2628153

Categories and Subject Descriptors D.3.0 [*Programming Languages*]: General; D.3.2 [*Programming Languages*]: Language Classifications—Applicative (functional) languages; D.3.4 [*Programming Languages*]: Processors—Optimization

Keywords control-flow analysis, inlining, optimization

1. Introduction

All high level programming languages rely on compiler optimizations to transform a language that is convenient for software developers into one that runs efficiently on target hardware. Two such common compiler optimizations are copy propagation and function inlining. Copy propagation in a language like ML is a simple substitution. Given a program of the form:

```
let val x = y
in
    x*2+y
end
```

We want to propagate the definition of `x` to its uses, resulting in

```
let val x = y
in
    y*2+y
end
```

At this point, we can eliminate the now unused `x`, resulting in

```
y*2+y
```

This optimization can reduce the resource requirements (*i.e.*, register pressure) of a program, and it may open the possibility for further simplifications in later optimization phases.

Inlining replaces a lexically inferior application of a function with the body of that function by performing straightforward β-substitution. For example, given the program

```
let fun f x = 2*x
in
    f 3
end
```

inlining `f` and removing the unused definition results in

```
2*3
```

This optimization removes the cost of the function call and opens the possibility of further optimizations, such as constant folding. Inlining does require some care, however, since it can increase the program size, which can negatively affect the instruction cache performance, negating the benefits of eliminating call overhead. The importance of inlining for functional languages and techniques for providing predictable performance are well-covered in the context of GHC by Peyton Jones and Marlow [PM02].

Both copy propagation and function inlining have been well-studied and are widely implemented in modern compilers for both first-order and higher-order programming languages. In this paper, we are interested in the *higher-order* version of these optimizations, which are not used in practice because of the cost of the supporting analysis.

For example, consider the following iterative program:

```
let
  fun emit x = print (Int.toString x)
  fun fact i m k =
    if i=0 then k m
    else fact (i-1) (m*i) k
in
  fact 6 1 emit
end
```

Higher-order copy propagation would allow the compiler to propagate the function `emit` into the body of `fact`, resulting in the following program:

```
let
  fun emit x = print (Int.toString x)
  fun fact i m k =
    if i=0 then emit m
    else fact (i-1) (m*i) emit
in
  fact 6 1 emit
end
```

This transformation has replaced an indirect call to emit (via the variable `k`) with a direct call. Direct calls are typically faster than indirect calls,[1] and are amenable to function inlining. Furthermore, the parameter `k` can be eliminated using *useless variable elimination* [Shi91], which results in a smaller program that uses fewer resources:

```
let
  fun emit x = print (Int.toString x)
  fun fact i m =
    if i=0 then emit m
    else fact (i-1) (m*i)
in
  fact 6 1
end
```

Function inlining also has a similar higher-order counterpart (what Shivers calls Super-β). For example, in the following program, we can inline the body of `pr` at the call site inside `fact`, despite the fact that `pr` is not in scope in `fact`:

```
let
  val two = 2
  fun fact i m k =
    if i=0
    then k m
    else fact (i-1) (m*i) k
  fun pr x = print (Int.toString (x*two))
in
  fact 6 1 pr
end
```

Inlining `pr` produces

```
let
  val two = 2
  fun fact i m k =
    if i=0
    then print (Int.toString (m*two))
    else fact (i-1) (m*i) k
  fun pr x = print (Int.toString (x*two))
in
  fact 6 1 pr
end
```

This resulting program is now eligible for constant propagation and useless variable elimination.

[1] Direct calls to known functions can use specialized calling conventions that are more efficient and provide more predictability to hardware instruction-prefetch mechanisms.

While some compilers can reproduce similar results on trivial examples such as these, implementing either of these optimizations in their full generality requires an environment-aware analysis to prove their safety. In the case of copy propagation, we need to ensure that the variable being substituted has the same value at the point that it is being substituted as it did when it was passed in. Similarly, if we want to substitute the body of a function at its call site, we need to ensure that all of the free variables have the same values at the call site as they did at the point where the function was defined. Today, developers using higher-order languages often avoid writing programs that have non-trivial environment usage within code that is run in a loop unless they have special knowledge of either the compiler or additional annotations on library functions (*e.g.*, `map`) that will enable extra optimization.

This paper presents a new approach to control-flow analysis (CFA) that supports more optimization opportunities for higher-order programs than are possible in either type-directed optimizers, heuristics-based approaches, or by using library-method annotations. We use the example of *transducers* [SM06], a higher-order and compositional programming style, to further motivate these optimizations and to explain our novel analysis.

Our contributions are:

- A novel, practical environment analysis (Section 5) that provides a conservative approximation of when two occurrences of a variable will have the same binding.
- Timing results (Section 9) for the implementation of this analysis and related optimizations, showing that it requires less than 3% of overall compilation time.
- Performance results for several benchmarks, showing that even highly tuned programs still contain higher-order optimization opportunities.

Source code for our complete implementation and all the benchmarks described in this paper is available at: `http://smlnj-gforge.cs.uchicago.edu/projects/manticore/`.

2. Manticore

The techniques described in this paper have been developed as part of the Manticore project and are implemented in the compiler for *Parallel ML*, which is a parallel dialect of Standard ML [FRRS11]. In this section, we give an overview of the host compiler and intermediate representation upon which we perform our analysis and optimizations. The compiler is a whole-program compiler, reading in the files in the source code alongside the sources from the runtime library. As covered in more detail in an earlier paper [FFR+07], there are six distinct intermediate representations (IRs) in the Manticore compiler:

1. Parse tree — the product of the parser.
2. AST — an explicitly-typed abstract-syntax tree representation.
3. BOM — a direct style normalized λ-calculus.
4. CPS — a continuation-passing style λ-calculus.
5. CFG — a first-order control-flow graph representation.
6. MLTree — the expression tree representation used by the ML-RISC code generation framework [GGR94].

The work in this paper is performed on the CPS representation.

2.1 CPS

Continuation-passing style (CPS) is the final high-level representation used in the compiler before closure conversion generates a first-order representation suitable for code generation. Our CPS transformation is performed in the Danvy-Filinski style [DF92]. This representation is a good fit for a simple implementation of control-flow analysis because it transforms each function return into a call to another function. The uniformity of treating all control-flow as function invocations simplifies the implementation. As a point of contrast, we have also implemented control-flow analysis on the BOM direct-style representation to support optimization of message passing [RX07]. The BOM-based implementation is almost 10% larger in lines of code, despite lacking the optional features, user-visible controls, and optimizations described in this paper.

The primary datatypes and their constructors are shown in Figure 1. Key features of this representation are:

- Each expression has a program point associated with it, which serves as a unique label.
- It has been normalized so that every expression is bound to a variable.
- The `rhs` datatype, not shown here, contains only immediate primitive operations, such as arithmetic and allocation of heap objects.
- The CPS constraint is captured in the IR itself — `Apply` and `Throw` are non-recursive constructors, and there is no way to sequence an operation after them.

```
datatype exp = Exp of (ProgPt.ppt * term)
and term
  = Let of (var list * rhs * exp)
  | Fun of (lambda list * exp)
  | Cont of (lambda * exp)
  | If of (cond * exp * exp)
  | Switch of (var * (tag * exp) list * exp option)
  | Apply of (var * var list * var list)
  | Throw of (var * var list)
and lambda = FB of {
  f : var,
  params : var list,
  rets : var list,
  body : exp
}
and ...
```

Figure 1. Manticore CPS intermediate representation.

3. Control-Flow Analysis

This section provides a brief background on control-flow analysis (CFA) along with an overview of our specific implementation techniques to achieve both acceptable scalability and precision. A more general introduction to control-flow analysis, in particular the 0CFA style that we use, is available in the book by Nielson *et al.* [NNH99]. For a detailed comparison of modern approaches to control-flow analysis, see Midtgaard's comprehensive survey [Mid12].

In brief, while many others have implemented control-flow analysis in their compilers [Ser95, CJW00, AD98], our analysis is novel in its tracking of a wider range of values — including boolean values and tuples — and its lattice coarsening to balance performance and precision.

3.1 Overview

A control-flow analysis computes a finite map from all of the variables in a program to a conservative abstraction of the values that they can take on during the execution of the code. That is, it computes a finite map

$$\mathcal{V} : \texttt{VarID} \overset{\text{fin}}{\to} \texttt{value}$$

```
datatype value
  = TOP
  | TUPLE of value list
  | LAMBDAS of CPS.Var.Set.set
  | BOOL of bool
  | BOT
```

Figure 2. Abstract values.

where the `value` type is defined as a recursive datatype similar to that shown in Figure 2. The special $\top$ (`TOP`) and $\bot$ (`BOT`) elements indicate either all possible values or no known values, respectively. A `TUPLE` value handles both the cases of tuples and ML datatype representations, which by this point in the compiler have been desugared into either raw values or tagged tuples. The `LAMBDAS` value is used for a set of variable identifiers, all of which are guaranteed to be function identifiers. The `BOOL` value tracks the flow of literal boolean values through the program.

As an example, consider the following code:

```
let fun double (x) = x+x
    and apply (f, n) = f(n)
in
    apply (double, 2)
end
```

After running CFA on this example, we have

$$\begin{aligned} \mathcal{V}(\texttt{f}) &= \texttt{LAMBDAS}(\{\textit{double}\}) \\ \mathcal{V}(\texttt{n}) &= \top \\ \mathcal{V}(\texttt{x}) &= \top \end{aligned}$$

These results indicate that the variable `f` must be bound to the function `double`. This example and the `value` representation in Figure 2 do not track numeric values, which is why `n` and `x` are mapped to $\top$. We are planning to track a richer set of values, including datatype-specific values, in the future in order to enable optimizations beyond the ones discussed in this paper.

3.2 Implementation

Our CFA implementation is straightforward and similar in spirit to Serrano's [Ser95]. We start with an empty map and walk over the intermediate representation of the program. At each expression, we update $\mathcal{V}$ by merging the value-flow information until we reach a fixed point where the map no longer changes. The most interesting difference from Serrano's implementation is that we use our tracked boolean values to avoid merging control-flow information along arms of conditional expressions that can never be taken. In our experience, the key to reducing the runtime of control-flow analysis while still maintaining high precision lies in carefully choosing (and empirically tuning) the tracked abstraction of values.

3.2.1 Tuning the lattice

Each time we evaluate an expression whose result is bound to a variable, we need to update the map with a new abstract value that is the result of merging the old abstract value and the new value given by the analysis. In theory, if all that we care about in the analysis is the mapping of call sites to function identifiers, we could use a simple domain for the value map ($\mathcal{V}$) based on just the powerset of the function identifiers. Unfortunately, this domain is insufficiently precise in practice because of the presence of tuples and datatypes. Furthermore, SML treats all functions has having a single parameter, which means that function arguments are packed into tuples at call sites and then extracted in the function body. Thus, the domain of abstract values needs to support tracking of information as it moves into and out of more complicated data structures.

We build a lattice over these abstract values using the $\top$ and $\bot$ elements as usual, and treating values of TUPLE and LAMBDAS type as incomparable. When two LAMBDAS values are compared, the subset relationship provides an ordering. It is this ordering that allows us to incrementally merge flow information, up to a finite limit. The most interesting portion of our implementation is in the merging of two TUPLE values. In the trivial recursive solution, the analysis may fail to terminate because of the presence of recursive datatypes (*e.g.*, on each iteration over a function that calls the cons function, we will wrap another TUPLE value around the previous value). In practice for typical Standard ML programs, we have found that limiting the tracked depth to 5 and then mapping any further additions to $\top$ results in a good balance of performance and precision.

Note that unlike some other analyses, such as sub-zero CFA [AD98], we do not limit the maximum number of tracked functions per variable. Avoiding this restriction allows us to use the results of our analysis to support optimizations that can still be performed when multiple functions flow to the same call site (unlike inlining). Furthermore, we have found that reducing the number of tracked function variables has no measurable impact on the runtime of the analysis, but it removes many optimization opportunities (*e.g.*, calling convention optimization across a set of common functions).

4. The Environment Problem

All but the most trivial optimizations require program analysis to determine when they are safe to apply. Many optimizations that only require basic data-flow analysis when applied to first-order languages are not safe for higher-order languages when based on a typical CFA such as that described in Section 3. In that version of CFA, the abstraction of the environment is a single, global map that maps each variable to a single abstract value from the lattice. This restriction means that the CFA results alone do not allow us to reason separately about bindings to the same variable that occur along different control-flow paths of the program.

For example, this restriction impedes higher-order inlining. First-order inlining of functions (simple β-reduction) is always a semantically safe operation. But, in a higher-order language, inlining a call through a closure that encapsulates a function and its environment is only safe when the free variables are guaranteed to have the same bound value at the capture location and the inlining location, a property that Shivers called *environmental consonance* [Shi91]. For example, in the following code, if CFA determines that the function g is the only one ever bound to the parameter f, then the body of g may be inlined at the call site labeled 1.

```
val x = 3
fun g i = i + x
fun map f l =
  case l
   of h::t => (f h)¹::(map f t)
    | _ => []

val res = map g [1,2,3]
```

While some compilers handle this particular special-case, in which all the free variables of the function are bound at the top level, the resulting optimizers are fragile and even small changes to the program can hinder optimization, as shown in the following code:

```
fun wrapper x = let
  fun g i = i + x
  fun map f l =
    case l
     of h::t => (f h)¹::(map f t)
      | _ => []
in
  map g [1,2,3]
end
val res1 = wrapper 1
val res2 = wrapper 2
```

Performing the inlining operation is again safe, but the analysis required to guarantee that the value of x is always the same at both the body of the function wrapper and in the call location inside of map is beyond simple heuristics.

Copy propagation Higher-order copy propagation suffers from the same problem. In this case, instead of inlining the body of the function (*e.g.*, because it is too large), we are attempting to remove the creation of a closure by turning an indirect call through a variable into a direct call to a known function. In the following code, the function g is passed as an argument to map and called in its body.

```
fun map f l =
  case l
   of h::t => (f h)::(map f t)
    | _ => []

val res = map g [1,2,3]
```

When g is in scope at the call site inside map and either g has no free variables or we know that those free variables will always have the same values at both the capture point (when it is passed as an argument to map) and inlining location, we can substitute g, potentially removing a closure and enabling the compiler to optimize the call into a direct jump instead of an indirect jump through the function pointer stored in the closure record.

Interactions These optimizations are not only important because they remove indirect calls. Applying them can also enable unused and useless variable elimination, as illustrated in the code resulting from the removal of the useless variable f:

```
fun map l =
  case l
   of h::t => (g h)::(map t)
    | _ => []

val res = map [1,2,3]
```

4.1 A Challenging Example

While most of the higher-order examples to this point could have been handled by more simple lexical heuristics and careful ordering of compiler optimization passes, those heuristics must be careful not to optimize in unsafe locations. The following example illustrates the importance of reasoning about environments when performing higher-order inlining on functions with free variables. The function mk takes an integer and returns a pair of a function of type (int -> int) * int -> int and a function of type int -> int; note that both of the returned functions capture the variable i, the argument to mk.

```
fun mk i =
  let
    fun g j = j + i
    fun f (h : int -> int, k)=
      (h (k * i))¹
  in
    (f, g)
  end
val (f1, g1) = mk 1
val (f2, g2) = mk 2
val res = f1 (g2, 3)
```

First, the function mk is called with 1, in order to capture the variable i in the closures of f1 and g1. Next, the function mk is called with 2, again capturing the variable i (but with a different value) in the closures of f2 and g2. Finally, we call f1 with the pair (g2, 3).

At the call site labeled 1, a simple 0CFA can determine that only the function `g` will ever be called. Unfortunately, if we inline the body of `g` at that location, as shown in the example code below, the result value `res` will change from 5 to 4. The problem is that the binding of the variable `i` is not the same at the potential inline location as it was at its original capture location.

```
fun mk i =
  let
    fun g j = j + i
    fun f (h : int -> int, k) =
      ((k * i) + i)
  in
    (f, g)
  end
val (f1, g1) = mk 1
val (f2, g2) = mk 2
val res = f1 (g2, 3)
```

While this example is obviously contrived, this situation occurs regularly in idiomatic higher-order programs and the inability to handle the environment problem in general is a limit in most compilers, leading developers to avoid higher-order language features in performance-critical code.

This final example shows a slightly more complicated program that defeats simple heuristics but in which the techniques presented in this work can determine that inlining is safe.

```
let
  val y = m ()
  fun f _ = y
  fun g h = (h ())1
in
  g f
end
```

At the call site labeled 1, it is clearly safe to inline the body of the function `f`, since `y` has the same binding at the inline location as the capture location. Since it is not a trivial idiomatic example, however, it is not commonly handled even by compilers that perform CFA-based optimizations.

4.2 Reflow Analysis

A theoretical solution to this environment problem that enables a suite of additional optimizations is *reflow analysis* [Shi91]. This analysis requires re-running control-flow analysis from the potential inlining point and seeing if the variable bindings for all relevant free variables are uniquely bound with respect to that sub-flow. Unfortunately, this operation is potentially quite expensive (up to the same complexity as the original CFA, at *each* potential inlining site) and no compiler performs it in practice.

5. Unchanged Variable Analysis

The major contribution of this work is an *unchanged variable analysis*. Instead of performing reflow at each call site, we use a novel analysis that builds upon the approximate control-flow graph of the program given by a control-flow analysis to enable us to perform an inexpensive test at each call site. The optimizations from Section 4 are safe when the free variables of the target function are guaranteed to be the same at its closure creation point and at the target call site. In Shivers' reflow analysis [Shi91], this question was answered by checking whether a binding for a variable had changed between those two locations via a re-execution of control-flow analysis. Our analysis instead turns that question into one of graph reachability: in the approximate control-flow graph corresponding to the possible executions of this program, is there a path between those two locations through a rebinding of any of the free variables?

5.1 Building the approximate control-flow graph

The approximate control-flow graph is built in two steps. First, build a static control-flow graph for each function, ignoring function calls through variables, with vertices annotated with variable bindings and rebindings. Then, augment those individual function control-flow graphs with edges from the call sites through variables to the potential target functions, as determined by the control-flow analysis. Though we only discuss our implementation of 0CFA in this work, this alternative to reflow analysis also works with other control-flow analyses.

The variable bindings and rebindings in a program written in the continuation-passing style (CPS) representation defined in Figure 1 happen in two cases:

- At the definition of the variable, which is either a **`let`**-binding or as a parameter of a function.
- In the case when a free variable of a function was captured in a closure and this captured value is restored for the execution of that function.

We capture both of these conditions through labeled vertices in the graph for each function. One vertex is labeled with all of the free variables of the function, since those are the ones that will be rebound when the function is called through a closure. A second vertex is labeled with all of the parameters to the function, since they will also be bound when the function is called. Finally, any vertex corresponding to a **`let`**-binding in the control-flow graph will be labeled with the variable being bound.

Call sites are augmented using the results of the control-flow analysis described in Section 3. In the intermediate representation, all targets of call sites are variables. In the trivial case, that variable is the name of a function identifier, and we can simply add an edge from the call site to that function's entry point. Otherwise, that variable is of function type but can be bound to many possible functions. In that case, the control-flow analysis will provide one of three results:

- The value $\bot$, indicating that the call site can never be reached in any program execution. No changes are made to the program graph in this case.
- The value $\top$, indicating that any call site may be reached. In this case, we add an edge to a special vertex that represents any call site, whose optimization is discussed in Section 5.4.
- A set of function identifiers. Here, we add one edge from the call site per function, to that function's entry point.

At this point, the graph is complete and enables us to reformulate the safety property. We can now simply ask: does there exist a path between the closure capture location and the target call site in the graph that passes through a (re)binding location for any of the free variables of the function that we want to inline? If such a path exists, then any optimization that relies on the free variables maintaining their bindings between those locations may be unsafe.

For a program of size n (with $O(n)$ functions and $O(n)$ call sites), the approximate control-flow graph has $O(n)$ vertices and $O(n^2)$ edges. The worst-case quadratic number of edges corresponds to the situation where the control-flow analysis determines that every function in the program could be called from every callsite in the program. In practice, though, we expect the number of edges to be closer to linear in the size of the program, due to the fact that the utility of control-flow analysis is the ability to determine that only a small number of functions are called from each callsite. Hence, we will express the subsequent graph-algorithm complexities in terms of the number of vertices $|V|$ and the number of edges $|E|$ in the approximate control-flow graph. With the standard $O(n^3)$ 0CFA algorithm, constructing the approximate control-flow graph is $O(n^3) + O(|V| + |E|) = O(n^3)$. Note that running the control-flow analysis is required in order to both build the approximate control-flow graph and to identify candidate inlining opportunities.

5.2 Computing graph reachability quickly

This question about the existence of paths between vertices in the graph is a reachability problem. There are off-the-shelf $O(|V|^3)$ algorithms such as Warshall's algorithm for computing graph reachability [War62], but those are far too slow for practical use. On even small graphs of thousands of vertices, they take seconds to run.

Therefore, we use an approach that collapses the graph quickly into a map we can use for logarithmic-time queries of the reachability between two vertices. Our approach performs two steps. First, we take the potentially cyclic graph and reduce it into a set of strongly-connected components. Then, we use a bottom-up approach to compute reachability in the resulting DAG. All queries are then performed against the resulting map from source component to set of reachable components.

Strongly-connected components We use Tarjan's $O(|V| + |E|)$ algorithm for computing the strongly-connected components [Tar72], as implemented in Standard ML of New Jersey by Matthias Blume.[2] This produces a directed acyclic graph (DAG), with $O(|V|)$ vertices (each corresponding to a strongly-connected component) and $O(|E|)$ edges (each corresponding one or more edges between vertices in the approximate control-flow graph that belong to distinct strongly-connected components); the collection of strongly-connected components are produced in topological sorted order. It also produces a map from each vertex in the approximate control-flow graph to its strongly-connected component in the DAG. There are two interesting types of components for this algorithm: those that correspond to exactly one vertex (program point) in the approximate control-flow graph and those that correspond to more than one vertex (program point). In the single vertex case, control-flow from that program point cannot reach itself. In the multiple vertex case, control-flow from each program point *can* reach itself. This distinction is crucial when initializing the reachability map.

Reachability in a DAG We compute a map from each strongly-connected component to its set of reachable components by processing the DAG in reverse topological sorted order. For each strongly-connected component, we initialize the reachability map for that component according to its size and then we add each successor component and everything that the successor component can reach. A more detailed description is shown in Algorithm 1.

Algorithm 1 Compute DAG reachability for a graph DAG

```
for n ∈ Vertices(DAG) in reverse topological sorted order do
    if SCCSize(n) = 1 then
        R(n) ← {}        ▷ Program point in n cannot reach itself
    else
        R(n) ← {n}  ▷ Each program point in n can reach itself
    end if
    for s ∈ Succs(n) do
        R(n) ← R(n) ∪ {s} ∪ R(s)
    end for
end for
```

We use a red-black tree to represent the set of reachable components, where the ordering of two strongly-connected components is given by the ordering of their "root" (i.e., representative) vertices. Furthermore, the implementation provides an $O(|s_1| + |s_2|)$ union operation [Hin99], better than a naive $O(|s_1| \log |s_2|)$ union operation via singleton inserts. Thus, the above is an $O(|E| * |V|)$ algorithm, dominated by the $\mathsf{R}(n) \cup \{s\} \cup \mathsf{R}(s)$ that is executed once per edge.

[2] This implementation uses a red-black tree to maintain per-vertex information and so incurs a cost of $O(\log |V|)$ to access the successor vertex's information when handling an edge, leading to an overall running time of $O(|V| + |E| \log |V|)$.

5.3 Performing the safety check

Having built the approximate control-flow graph and computed the strongly-connected components and reachability map, we can efficiently check the safety of a candidate inlining opportunity. We maintain a map from each variable to its set of (re)binding locations (vertices in the approximate control-flow graph). Given a candidate inlining opportunity, with a function-binding location and a call-site location, we check whether there exists a path from the function-binding location to a (re)binding location of a free variable and from the re(binding) location to the call-site location. Each of these path-existence checks is an $O(\log |E|)$ operation, performed by an $O(1)$ map from the source and destination locations (vertices in the approximate control-flow graph) to their strongly-connected components and an $O(\log |E|)$ query of the destination component in the set of components reachable from the source component. In practice, each candidate inlining opportunity has a small number of free variables that are (re)bound at a small number of locations, leading to analysis times that are less than 3% of total compilation time (Section 9.3).

5.4 Handling imprecision

In a practical implementation, we also need to handle a variety of sources of imprecision. C foreign function calls, the entry and exit point of the generated binary itself (*i.e.*, the `main` function), and the limited lattice size all contribute to situations where a call site may be through a variable whose target is $\top$, or unknown. The obvious way to handle this situation when creating the graph is to add an edge from any call site labeled $\top$ to every possible function entry point. Unfortunately, that approach frequently connects the entire graph, preventing the compiler from proving that any variables remain unchanged through any non-trivial portions of the graph.

Instead, we take advantage of the fact that a call to an unknown function is really only a call to one of the functions that has unknown callers. We therefore add an edge from any call site labeled $\top$ to any function whose callers are not all known. These functions are identified during control-flow analysis, which in addition to computing the potential values that a variable can take on also tracks when a function is passed into a portion of the program that we cannot precisely analyze. Fortunately, that set of functions is small even for large programs, so the graph remains useful.

5.5 Limitations

While safe, this analysis necessarily is more limited than general formulations of higher-order inlining as shown by Shivers' kCFA framework (for $k > 0$) or Might's ΔCFA approach [Shi91, MS06]. Both of those analyses are able to distinguish environments created by different control-flow paths through the program. Our analysis collapses all different control-flow paths to each function, resulting in a potential loss of precision. For example, in the following program, our attempt to inline at the call site labeled 1 will fail.

```
let val y = 2
  fun f _ = y
  fun confounding _ = raise Fail ""
  fun g h = (h ())¹
  fun callsG b k = if b then g k else 0
  val bad = callsG false confounding
in
  callsG true f
end
```

After the first call to callsG, the function confounding is in the abstract possible set of functions that can be bound to the parameter k. Even though in the first call the boolean tracking avoids analyzing g and adding confounding to the list of possible values for h, when the second call comes through, the function f is added to the possible set of values for k and then *both* of those are added to the set of values that could be bound to h. Fundamentally, this problem is the one that stronger forms of control-flow analysis handle, though there are clearly heuristics that could be used to increase the precision in this specific case.

6. Safe example

In the introduction, we discussed an iterative version of the factorial function and pointed out that we might like to transform the argument that consumes the result of the computations to be either a direct call or inlined. A slightly modified version of that example appears below:

```
let
  fun fact i m k =
    if i = 0
    then k m
    else fact (i-1) (m*i) k
in
  fact 6 1 (fn i => h i)
end
```

In this example, the consuming function is an anonymous function that makes a call to another variable, h, which is free in this block. We would like to optimize this code by performing a higher-order inlining of that code to produce the following output:

```
let
  fun fact i m k =
    if i = 0
    then h m
    else fact (i-1) (m*i) k
in
  fact 6 1 (fn i => h i)
end
```

In order for that operation to be safe, though, we need to show two properties:

1. The variable h is in scope at the inlining location.
2. The variable h has the same binding at its inlining point as it did at the point where the closure would have captured it.

The first property is lexically immediate. In the rest of this section, we will demonstrate how unchanged variable analysis allows us to verify the second property.

6.1 Building the control-flow graph

The first step in unchanged variable analysis is construction of a control-flow graph. In order to make that graph easier to visualize, we have normalized the source code, broken bindings of arguments onto separate lines from bindings of function identifiers, and annotated the example with line numbers; the resulting program is given in Figure 3. The line numbers will be used in the rest of this section in the graph visualizations.

The static control-flow graph is shown with the solid lines in Figure 4. Note that this graph separates the actions of binding a variable of function type (such as fact in line 2) from the operation of actually running its body, which starts on line 3 of the listing with the binding of any free variables (in this case, none) and continues on line 4 with the binding of the parameters to arguments.

```
1  let
2      fun fact
3          (* FV: *)
4          i m k =
5        if i = 0
6        then let in  k m
7             end
8        else let val i' = i-1
9                 val m' = m*i
10            in  fact i' m' k
11            end
12       (* fi *)
13     fun clos
14         (* FV: h *)
15         i =
16       let in  h i
17       end
18 in  fact 6 1 clos
19 end
```

Figure 3. Normalized source code for a safe example.

After running CFA on the factorial example above, we determine the following:

$$
\begin{aligned}
\mathcal{V}(\texttt{fact}) &= \{\texttt{LAMBDAS}(\{\texttt{fact}\})\} \\
\mathcal{V}(\texttt{clos}) &= \{\texttt{LAMBDAS}(\{\texttt{clos}\})\} \\
\mathcal{V}(\texttt{k}) &= \{\texttt{LAMBDAS}(\{\texttt{clos}\})\} \\
\mathcal{V}(\texttt{i}) &= \{\top\} \\
\mathcal{V}(\texttt{i'}) &= \{\top\} \\
\mathcal{V}(\texttt{m}) &= \{\top\} \\
\mathcal{V}(\texttt{m'}) &= \{\top\} \\
\mathcal{V}(\texttt{j}) &= \{\top\} \\
\mathcal{V}(\texttt{h}) &= \{\top\}
\end{aligned}
$$

The only interesting values in this finite map are the binding of the variable k to the function value clos and the binding of the variable h to the unknown target $\top$. These binding allow us to annotate the graph with higher-order control-flow paths from line 6 to line 14 and from line 17 to line 7 (corresponding to the call of and return from clos at the call site k m on line 6) and from line 16 to $\top$ and from $\top$ to line 17 (corresponding to the call of and return from an unknown function at the call site h i on line 16). These higher-order control-flow paths are shown with dotted lines in Figure 4.

Finally, the non-singleton strongly-connected components for the control-flow graph are show with boxed subgraphs in Figure 4.

6.2 Performing the unchanged variable analysis

Now, we are at a point where we know that clos is the only function being called at line 6, making it a candidate for inlining. But, its free variables (h) were captured at line 13, so we now need to check the graph for the following property:

> Does there exist a path starting from vertex 13 and ending at vertex 6 that passes through any vertex that rebinds variable h?

In this example, that property trivially holds, as there are *no* vertices in this subgraph where h is rebound and so the inlining is safe.

7. Unsafe example

For a negative case, we revisit the unsafe example from Section 4, repeated here:

```
fun mk i =
  let
    fun g j = j + i
    fun f (h : int -> int, k)=
      (h (k * i))[1]
  in
```

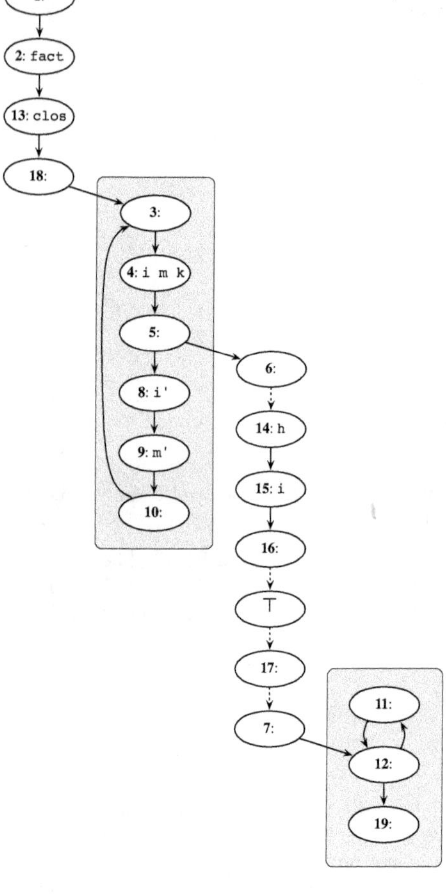

Figure 4. Control-flow graph for safe example.

```
    (f, g)
  end
val (f1, g1) = mk 1
val (f2, g2) = mk 2
val res = f1 (g2, 3)
```

In this example, control-flow analysis will determine that the function g is the only function that will be called at the call site labeled 1, making it a candidate for inlining. But, we need to determine whether or not it is safe to do so. That is, is i, the free variable of g, the same when h is invoked as when it was captured by g?

As in the safe example, the first step in our presentation is to normalize and annotate the example to aid in the visualization of the control-flow graph; the resulting program is given in Figure 5.

7.1 Building the control-flow graph

As in the previous section, we build a static control-flow graph (solid lines) and add higher-order control-flow paths (dotted lines) where control-flow analysis was able to determine the target of the call through a variable with function type. This graph is shown in Figure 6.

The interesting parts of the control-flow analysis results map are the following:

$$\begin{aligned}
\mathcal{V}(\texttt{f1}) &= \{\texttt{LAMBDAS}(\{\texttt{f}\})\} \\
\mathcal{V}(\texttt{g1}) &= \{\texttt{LAMBDAS}(\{\texttt{g}\})\} \\
\mathcal{V}(\texttt{f2}) &= \{\texttt{LAMBDAS}(\{\texttt{f}\})\} \\
\mathcal{V}(\texttt{g2}) &= \{\texttt{LAMBDAS}(\{\texttt{g}\})\} \\
\mathcal{V}(\texttt{h}) &= \{\texttt{LAMBDAS}(\{\texttt{g}\})\}
\end{aligned}$$

```
1   fun mk
2         (* FV: *)
3         i =
4     let
5         fun g
6               (* FV: i *)
7               j =
8             let val t1 = j + i
9             in  t1  end
10        fun f
11              (* FV: i *)
12              (h, k) =
13            let val t2 = k * i
14            in  h t2
15            end
16    in  (f, g)  end
17  val (f1, g1) = let in  mk 1
18                 end
19  val (f2, g2) = let in  mk 2
20                 end
21  val res = let in  f1 (g2, 3)
22            end
```

Figure 5. Normalized source code for an unsafe example.

These binding allow us to annotate the graph with higher-order control-flow paths from line 21 to line 11 and from line 15 to line 22 (corresponding to the call of and return from f at the call site f1 (g2, 3) on line 21) and from line 14 to line 6 and from line 9 to line 15 (corresponding to the call of and return from g at the call site h t2 on line 14).

7.2 Performing the unchanged variable analysis

Control-flow analysis has informed us that we should be able to inline the body of function g at line 14. But, we now need to check the graph for the following property:

> Does there exist a path starting from vertex 5 and ending at vertex 14 that passes through any vertex (in this case, vertices 3 and 11) that rebinds variable i?

Since there exists such a path in the graph (*e.g.*, $5 \to 10 \to 16 \to 20 \to 21 \to 11 \to 12 \to 13 \to 14$), this inlining is potentially (and actually!) unsafe, so it is disallowed under the unchanged variable condition tested in our system.

8. Example — Transducers

Transducers are program fragments that perform four tasks within an infinite loop: receive input, compute on that input, output a result, and loop back around. These fragments can then be composed together to form pipelined or stream processing programs which are used extensively in networks, graphics processing, and many other domains. Writing programs in this style gives developers modularity in the sense that when new functionality needs to be added, they can simply add a new transducer to the pipeline, eliminating the need to modify any substantial portion of existing code. Shivers and Might showed that if these transducers are implemented in a continuation-passing style, a number of standard optimizations, along with Super-β inlining, can effectively merge composed transducers into one loop that contains all the computation of the entire pipeline [SM06]. In this section, we show that unchanged variable analysis along with higher-order inlining is the first practical compiler implementation capable of performing these optimizations on transducers.

Figure 7 provides a library for building and composing transducers. Channels are used for passing information between transducers. Specifically, they are represented as continuations that take a value of type 'a and another chan. A dn_chan is used for outputting information to the next transducer and an up_chan is

```
(* Type for channels *)
  datatype ('a, 'b) chan = Chan of ('a * ('b, 'a) chan) cont

(* Types for the specific kinds of channels *)
  type 'a dn_chan = ('a, unit) chan
  type 'a up_chan   = (unit, 'a) chan

(* Source/Sink (first/last in the chain) *)
  type ('a, 'r) source = 'a dn_chan -> 'r
  type ('a, 'r) sink   = 'a up_chan -> 'r

(* transducer (middle in the chain) *)
  type ('a, 'b, 'r) transducer = 'a up_chan * 'b dn_chan -> 'r

(* change control upstream or downstream *)
  fun switch (x : 'a, Chan k : ('a, 'b) chan) : 'b * ('a, 'b) chan = callcc (fn k' => throw k (x, Chan k'))

(* Put value x on down channel dnC *)
  fun put (x : 'a, dnC : 'a dn_chan) : 'a dn_chan = (case switch (x, dnC) of ((), dnC') => dnC')

(* Get a value from up channel upC *)
  fun get (upC : 'a up_chan) : 'a * 'a up_chan = (case switch ((), upC) of (x, upC') => (x, upC'))

(* Compose sources, transducers, and sinks. *)
  fun sourceToTrans (source : ('a, 'r) source, trans : ('a, 'b, 'r) transducer) : ('b, 'r) source =
        fn (dnC : 'b dn_chan) => callcc (fn k =>
          source (case callcc (fn upK => throw k (trans (Chan upK, dnC))) of (_, upC') => upC'))


  fun transToSink (trans : ('a, 'b, 'r) transducer, sink : ('b, 'r) sink) : ('a, 'r) sink =
        fn (upC : 'a up_chan) => callcc (fn k =>
          trans (upC, case callcc (fn upK => throw k (sink (Chan upK))) of ((), dnC') => dnC'))

  fun sourceToSink (source : ('a, 'r) source, sink : ('a, 'r) sink) : 'r =
        callcc (fn k => source ( case callcc (fn upK => throw k (sink (Chan upK))) of ((), dnC) => dnC))
```

Figure 7. Transducer library code.

used for receiving information from the previous transducer. The `put` function throws to a `dn_chan`, giving it a value and its current continuation wrapped in a `chan`. When this continuation is invoked, it will return a new `dn_chan`. The `get` function throws to an `up_chan`, giving it a unit value and its current continuation wrapped in a `Chan` constructor. When this continuation is invoked, it will return the value being passed down to the transducer as well as a new `up_chan`.

8.1 Simple composition

A pipeline is composed of a source at the beginning, zero or more transducers in the middle, and a sink at the end. The `sourceToTrans` function is used to link a source to a transducer, yielding a new source. Similarly, the `transToSink` function is used to link a transducer to a sink, yielding a new sink. Linking a source to a sink with the `sourceToSink` function executes the transducer pipeline.

Figure 8 illustrates a simple stream of transducers, where the source infinitely loops, outputting the value 5 to the sink, which then prints this value each time. These two functions are then composed using the `sourceToSink` function. Ideally, we would like to generate code that merges these transducers together, yielding one tight loop that simply prints the value five in each iteration, rather than passing control back and forth between these two co-routines.

8.2 Optimization

In order to fuse these two co-routines, we need to be able to inline the calls to the co-routines, which requires Super-β analysis, as noted by Shivers and Might [SM06]. Running the analysis and inlining performed in this paper successfully fuses those co-routines and removes the creation of the closure across that boundary. For example, running the transducer shown in Figure 8 for 10,000 steps, we reduce the overall memory usage from 4.6M to 3.9M, for a savings of roughly 15%. The remaining memory usage is almost entirely in internal library calls due to the `print` function (which is not well-optimized in Manticore).

9. Evaluation

In this section, we show that this analysis is both practical and effective. In Section 9.3, we show that the compile-time cost of adding this analysis is under 3% of the total compilation time. Section 9.4 provides support that the optimizations provided by this analysis are both found and typically result in performance improvements in our benchmarks.

9.1 Experimental method

Our benchmark machine has two 8 core Intel Xeon E5-2687 processors running at 3.10 GHz. It has 64 GB of physical memory. This machine runs x86_64 Ubuntu Linux 12.04.3, kernel version 3.2.0-49. We ran each benchmark experiment 30 times, and speedups are based upon the median runtimes. Times are reported in seconds.

This work has been implemented, tested, and is part of the current Manticore compiler's default optimization suite.

9.2 Benchmarks

For our empirical evaluation, we use seven benchmark programs from our parallel benchmark suite and one synthetic transducer benchmark. Each benchmark is written in a pure, functional style.

The Barnes-Hut benchmark [BH86] is a classic N-body problem solver. Each iteration has two phases. In the first phase, a quadtree is constructed from a sequence of mass points. The second phase then uses this tree to accelerate the computation of the gravitational force on the bodies in the system. Our benchmark

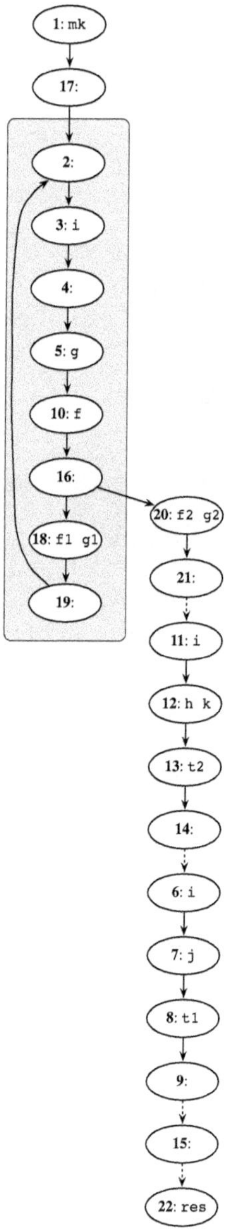

Figure 6. Control-flow graph for unsafe example.

```
(* Source *)
fun putFive (dnC : int dn_chan) =
      putFive (put (5, dnC))

(* Sink *)
fun printVal (upC : int up_chan) =
      let val (x, upC') = get upC
          val _ = print (Int.toString x)
      in  printVal upC'
      end

(* Run *)
val _ = sourceToSink (putFive, printVal)
```

Figure 8. Transducer example.

runs 20 iterations over 400,000 particles generated in a random Plummer distribution. Our version is a translation of a Haskell program [GHC].

The DMM benchmark performs dense-matrix by dense-matrix multiplication in which each matrix is 600×600.

The Raytracer benchmark renders a 2048×2048 image as a two-dimensional sequence, which is then written to a file. The original program was written in ID [Nik91] and is a simple ray tracer that does not use any acceleration data structures.

The Mandelbrot benchmark computes the Mandelbrot set, writing its output to an image file of size 4096×4096.

The Quickhull benchmark determines the convex hull of 12,000,000 points in the plane. Our code is based on the algorithm by Barber *et al.* [BDH96].

The Quicksort benchmark sorts a sequence of 10,000,000 integers in parallel. This code is based on the NESL version of the algorithm [Sca].

The SMVM benchmark performs a sparse-matrix by dense-vector multiplication. The matrix contains 3,005,788 elements, and the vector contains 10,000, and the multiplication is iterated 75 times.

In addition to the parallel benchmarks, the transducer benchmark is the sequential benchmark described in Section 8. For benchmarking purposes, we simulate running the transducer through 2,000,000 iterations.

9.3 Compilation performance

In Table 1, we have broken down the compilation time of the larger parallel benchmarks. While we have included the number of lines of code of the benchmarks, Manticore is a whole-program compiler, including the entire basis library. Therefore, in addition to the lines of code, we have also reported the number of expressions, where an expression is an individual term from the intermediate representation shown in Figure 1. By that stage in the compilation process, all unreferenced and dead code has been removed from the program.

The most important results are:

- Control-flow analysis is basically free.
- The unchanged variable analysis presented in this work (which represents the majority of the time spent in both the copy propagation and inlining passes) generally makes up 1-2% of the overall compilation time.
- Time spent in the C compiler, GCC, generating final object code is the longest single stage in our compiler.

9.4 Benchmark performance

Across our already tuned benchmark suite, we see several improvements and only one statistically significant slowdown, as shown in Table 2. It might seem strange that the number of inlinings is different for the sequential and parallel implementations of each benchmark, but this is due to the fact that the parallel implementations use more sophisticated runtime library functions, exposing more opportunities for optimization. The largest challenge with analyzing the results of this work is that for any tuned benchmark suite, the implementers will have already analyzed and removed most opportunities for improvement. When we investigated the usefulness of these optimizations on some programs we ported from a very highly tuned benchmark suite, the Computer Language Benchmark Game [CLB13], we could find zero opportunities for further optimization. So, the primary result that we have to show in this section for existing benchmarks is that this optimization, even performed using only a simple size-based heuristic, does not harm our tuned performance by more than 0.5% in the worst case (and within one standard deviation of the performance) and in some cases results in

Benchmark	Lines	Expressions	Total (s)	CFA (s)	Copy Prop. (s)	H-O Inline (s)	GCC (s)
Barnes-hut	334	17,400	8.79	0.042	0.175	0.198	2.56
Raytracer	501	12,800	6.54	0.019	0.112	0.124	2.64
Mandelbrot	85	9,900	5.06	0.013	0.091	0.098	1.70
Quickhull	196	15,200	7.67	0.039	0.182	0.177	2.05
Quicksort	74	11,900	5.49	0.022	0.111	0.122	1.11
SMVM	106	13,900	7.25	0.033	0.131	0.123	2.52

Table 1. Benchmark program sizes, both in source lines and total number of expressions in our whole-program compilation. Costs of the analyses and optimizations are also provided, in seconds.

gains of around 1%. This optimization can result in slowdowns, due to increasing the live range of variables and the resulting increase in register pressure.

In the one example program that has not already been tuned so far that there are no higher-order optimization opportunities within hot code — the transducer benchmark described in Section 8 — we see a speedup of 4.7% due to removing the need for a closure within an inner loop.

10. Related Work

The problem of detecting when two environments are the same with respect to some variables is not new. It was first given the name *environment consonance* in Shivers' Ph.D. thesis [Shi91]. He proposed checking this property by re-running control-flow analysis (CFA) incrementally — at cost polynomial in the program size — at each inlining point.

Might revisited the problem in the context of his Ph.D. thesis, and showed another form of analysis, ΔCFA, which more explicitly tracks environment representations and can check for safety without re-running the analysis at each inlining point [MS06]. Unfortunately, this approach also only works in theory — while its runtime is faster in practice than a full 1CFA (which is exponential), it is not scalable to large program intermediate representations. Might also worked on anodization, which is a more recent technique that identifies when a binding will only take on a single value, opening up the possibility of several optimizations similar to this one [Mig10].

Reps, Horowitz, and Sagiv were among the first to apply graph reachability to program analysis [RHS95], focusing on dataflow and spawning an entire field of program analyses for a variety of problems, such as pointer analysis and security. While they also present an algorithm for faster graph reachability, theirs is still polynomial time, which is far too slow for the number of vertices in our graphs. A different algorithm for graph reachability that has even better asymptotic performance than the one we present in Section 5.2 is also available [Nuu94], computing reachability at the same time that it computes the strongly-connected components. However, it relies on fast language implementation support for mutation, which is not the case in our compiler's host implementation system, Standard ML of New Jersey [AM91], so we use an algorithm that better supports the use of functional data structures.

Serrano's use of 0CFA in the Bigloo compiler is the most similar to our work here [Ser95]. It is not discussed in this paper, but we similarly use the results of CFA to optimize our closure generation. In that paper, he does not discuss the need to track function identifiers within data types (*e.g.*, lists in Scheme) or limit the depth of that tracking, both of which we have found crucial in ML programs where functions often are at least in tuples, due to the default calling convention. Bigloo does not perform inlining of functions with free variables.

Waddell and Dybvig use a significantly more interesting inlining heuristic in Chez Scheme, taking into account the potential impact of other optimizations to reduce the size of the resulting code, rather than just using a fixed threshold, as we do [WD97]. While they also will inline functions with free variables, they will only do so when either those variables can be eliminated or they know the binding at analysis time. Our approach differs from theirs in that we do not need to know the binding at analysis time and we support whole-program analysis, including all referenced library functions.

The Glasgow Haskell Compiler has an extremely sophisticated inliner that has been tuned for many years, using a variety of type-, annotation-, and heuristic-based techniques for improving the performance of programs through effective inlining [PM02]. However, even after inlining and final simplification, this compiler cannot inline the straightforward higher-order example in Section 6.

11. Conclusion

In this work, we have demonstrated the first *practical* and general approach to higher-order inlining and copy propagation. We hope that this work ushers in new interest and experimentation in environment-aware optimizations for higher-order languages.

11.1 Limitations

As with all optimizations, this analysis and optimization are fragile with respect to changes to the code being optimized. Making things even more unpredictable for the developer, the output of control-flow analysis can also be affected by non-local changes if those changes cause the analysis to hit performance cutoffs and default to conservative worst-case partial results. We believe that adopting monomorphization, as used in the MLton compiler [Wee06], would both increase the precision of the analysis' results and remove the largest sources of imprecision in control-flow analysis — large numbers of polymorphic uses of common combinators such as `map` and `fold`.

11.2 Future work

This work identifies opportunities for performing optimizations, but does not investigate the space of heuristics for when they are beneficial. We currently perform the copy propagation unconditionally and perform the higher-order inlining using the same simple code-growth metric that we use for standard inlining. But, these optimizations could introduce other negative impacts on some programs, as it might increase the live range of variables. Identification of these negative impacts and heuristics for avoiding them is left to future work.

We have also provided an implementation of an analysis that shows when free variables are unchanged along a control-flow path, but we have not generated a formal proof that these optimizations are correct.

Further, we have not investigated other optimizations, such as rematerialization, that were presented in some of Might's recent

Benchmark	Sequential Speedup	Sequential Copy Prop.	Sequential Inlined	16 Processors Speedup	16 Processors Copy Prop.	16 Processors Inlined
Barnes-hut	1.2%	12	11	0%	15	17
DMM	0.3%	3	11	0.8%	6	17
Mandelbrot	-0.3%	0	3	0.3%	3	9
Quickhull	0.3%	12	11	0.3%	15	17
Quicksort	1.5%	2	4	0%	5	9
Raytracer	-0.3%	0	3	-0.2%	3	9
SMVM	0.4%	2	14	-0.5%	5	21
Transducer	4.7%	1	3	*N/A*	*N/A*	*N/A*

Table 2. Performance results from copy propagation and higher-order inlining optimizations.

work on anodization [Mig10] and might have an analog in our framework.

Finally, our control-flow analysis needs further optimizations, both to improve its runtime and its precision. We have previously investigated Hudak's work on abstract reference counting [Hud86], which resulted in improvements in both runtime and precision,[3] but that implementation is not yet mature [Ber09].

Acknowledgments

David MacQueen, Matt Might, and David Van Horn all spent many hours discussing this problem with us, and without their valuable insights this work would likely have languished. One anonymous reviewer commented extensively on an earlier draft of this work, substantially improving its presentation.

This material is based upon work supported by the National Science Foundation under Grants CCF-0811389 and CCF-1010568, and upon work performed in part while John Reppy was serving at the National Science Foundation. The views and conclusions contained herein are those of the authors and should not be interpreted as necessarily representing the official policies or endorsements, either expressed or implied, of these organizations or the U.S. Government.

References

[AD98] Ashley, J. M. and R. K. Dybvig. A practical and flexible flow analysis for higher-order languages. *ACM TOPLAS*, **20**(4), July 1998, pp. 845–868.

[AM91] Appel, A. W. and D. B. MacQueen. Standard ML of New Jersey. In *PLIP '91*, vol. 528 of *LNCS*. Springer-Verlag, New York, NY, August 1991, pp. 1–26.

[BDH96] Barber, C. B., D. P. Dobkin, and H. Huhdanpaa. The quickhull algorithm for convex hulls. *ACM TOMS*, **22**(4), 1996, pp. 469–483.

[Ber09] Bergstrom, L. Arity raising and control-flow analysis in Manticore. Master's dissertation, University of Chicago, November 2009. Available from `http://manticore.cs.uchicago.edu`.

[BH86] Barnes, J. and P. Hut. A hierarchical $O(N \log N)$ force calculation algorithm. *Nature*, **324**, December 1986, pp. 446–449.

[CJW00] Cejtin, H., S. Jagannathan, and S. Weeks. Flow-directed closure conversion for typed languages. In *ESOP '00*. Springer-Verlag, 2000, pp. 56–71.

[CLB13] CLBG. The computer language benchmarks game, 2013. Available from `http://benchmarksgame.alioth.debian.org/`.

[DF92] Danvy, O. and A. Filinski. Representing control: A study of the CPS transformation. *MSCS*, **2**(4), 1992, pp. 361–391.

[3] Best results were achieved when using a `maxrc` of 1.

[FFR+07] Fluet, M., N. Ford, M. Rainey, J. Reppy, A. Shaw, and Y. Xiao. Status Report: The Manticore Project. In *ML '07*. ACM, October 2007, pp. 15–24.

[FRRS11] Fluet, M., M. Rainey, J. Reppy, and A. Shaw. Implicitly-threaded parallelism in Manticore. *JFP*, **20**(5–6), 2011, pp. 537–576.

[GGR94] George, L., F. Guillame, and J. Reppy. A portable and optimizing back end for the SML/NJ compiler. In *CC '94*, April 1994, pp. 83–97.

[GHC] GHC. Barnes Hut benchmark written in Haskell. Available from `http://darcs.haskell.org/packages/ndp/examples/barnesHut/`.

[Hin99] Hinze, R. Constructing red-black trees. In *WAAAPL'99: Workshop on Algorithmic Aspects of Advanced Programming Languages*, Paris, France, 1999. pp. 89–99.

[Hud86] Hudak, P. A semantic model of reference counting and its abstraction (detailed summary). In *LFP '86*, Cambridge, Massachusetts, USA, 1986. ACM, pp. 351–363.

[Mid12] Midtgaard, J. Control-flow analysis of functional programs. *ACM Comp. Surveys*, **44**(3), June 2012, pp. 10:1–10:33.

[Mig10] Might, M. Shape analysis in the absence of pointers and structure. In *VMCAI '10*, Madrid, Spain, 2010. Springer-Verlag, pp. 263–278.

[MS06] Might, M. and O. Shivers. Environment analysis via ΔCFA. In *POPL '06*, Charleston, South Carolina, USA, 2006. ACM, pp. 127–140.

[Nik91] Nikhil, R. S. *ID Language Reference Manual.* Laboratory for Computer Science, MIT, Cambridge, MA, July 1991.

[NNH99] Nielson, F., H. R. Nielson, and C. Hankin. *Principles of Program Analysis.* Springer-Verlag, New York, NY, 1999.

[Nuu94] Nuutila, E. An efficient transitive closure algorithm for cyclic digraphs. *IPL*, **52**, 1994.

[PM02] Peyton Jones, S. and S. Marlow. Secrets of the Glasgow Haskell Compiler inliner. *JFP*, **12**(5), July 2002.

[RHS95] Reps, T., S. Horwitz, and M. Sagiv. Precise interprocedural dataflow analysis via graph reachability. In *POPL '95*, San Francisco, 1995. ACM.

[RX07] Reppy, J. and Y. Xiao. Specialization of CML message-passing primitives. In *POPL '07*. ACM, January 2007, pp. 315–326.

[Sca] Scandal Project. A library of parallel algorithms written NESL. Available from `http://www.cs.cmu.edu/~scandal/nesl/algorithms.html`.

[Ser95] Serrano, M. Control flow analysis: a functional languages compilation paradigm. In *SAC '95*, Nashville, Tennessee, United States, 1995. ACM, pp. 118–122.

[Shi91] Shivers, O. *Control-flow analysis of higher-order languages.* Ph.D. dissertation, School of C.S., CMU, Pittsburgh, PA, May 1991.

[SM06] Shivers, O. and M. Might. Continuations and transducer composition. In *PLDI '06*, Ottawa, Ontario, Canada, 2006. ACM, pp. 295–307.

[Tar72] Tarjan, R. Depth-first search and linear graph algorithms. *SIAM JC*, **1**(2), 1972, pp. 146–160.

[War62] Warshall, S. A theorem on boolean matrices. *JACM*, **9**(1), January 1962.

[WD97] Waddell, O. and R. K. Dybvig. Fast and effective procedure inlining. In *SAS '97*, LNCS. Springer-Verlag, 1997, pp. 35–52.

[Wee06] Weeks, S. Whole program compilation in MLton. Invited talk at ML '06 Workshop, September 2006.

Worker/Wrapper/Makes it/Faster

Jennifer Hackett Graham Hutton
School of Computer Science, University of Nottingham
{jph,gmh}@cs.nott.ac.uk

Abstract

Much research in program optimization has focused on formal approaches to correctness: proving that the meaning of programs is preserved by the optimisation. Paradoxically, there has been comparatively little work on formal approaches to efficiency: proving that the performance of optimized programs is actually improved. This paper addresses this problem for a general-purpose optimization technique, the worker/wrapper transformation. In particular, we use the call-by-need variant of improvement theory to establish conditions under which the worker/wrapper transformation is formally guaranteed to preserve or improve the time performance of programs in lazy languages such as Haskell.

Categories and Subject Descriptors D.1.1 [*Programming Techniques*]: Applicative (Functional) Programming

Keywords general recursion; improvement

1. Introduction

To misquote Oscar Wilde [31], "functional programmers know the value of everything and the cost of nothing"[1]. More precisely, the functional approach to programming emphasises what programs *mean* in a denotational sense, rather than what programs *do* in terms of their operational behaviour. For many programming tasks this emphasis is entirely appropriate, allowing the programmer to focus on the high-level description of what is being computed rather than the low-level details of how this is realised. However, in the context of program optimisation both aspects play a central role, as the aim of optimisation is to improve the operational performance of programs while maintaining their denotational correctness.

A research paper on program optimisation therefore should justify both the correctness and performance aspects of the optimisation described. There is a whole spectrum of possible approaches to this, ranging from informal tests and benchmarks [19], to tool-based methods such as property-based testing [3] and space/time profiling [24], all the way up to formal mathematical proofs [17]. For correctness, it is now becoming standard to formally prove that an optimisation preserves the meaning of programs. For performance, however, the standard approach is to provide some form of empirical evidence that an optimisation improves the efficiency of programs, and there is little published work on formal proofs of improvement.

In this paper, we aim to go some way toward redressing this imbalance in the context of the *worker/wrapper transformation* [7], putting the denotational and operational aspects on an equally formal footing. The worker/wrapper transformation is a general purpose optimisation technique that has already been formally proved correct, as well as being realised in practice as an extension to the Glasgow Haskell Compiler [26]. In this paper we formally prove that this transformation is guaranteed to preserve or improve time performance with respect to an established operational theory. In other words, we show that the worker/wrapper transformation never makes programs slower. Specifically, the paper makes the following contributions:

- We show how Moran and Sands' work on *call-by-need improvement theory* [15] can be applied to formally justify that the worker/wrapper transformation for least fixed points preserves or improves time performance;
- We present preconditions that ensure the transformation improves performance in this manner, which come naturally from the preconditions that ensure correctness;
- We demonstrate the utility of the new theory by verifying that examples from previous worker/wrapper papers indeed exhibit a time improvement.

The use of *call-by-need* improvement theory means that our work applies to lazy functional languages such as Haskell. Traditionally, the operational beheaviour of lazy evaluation has been seen as difficult to reason about, but we show that with the right tools this need not be the case. To the best of our knowledge, this paper is the first time that a general purpose optimisation method for lazy languages has been formally proved to improve time performance.

Improvement theory does not seem to have attracted much attention in recent years, but we hope that this paper can help to generate more interest in this and other techniques for reasoning about lazy evaluation. Whereas in many papers calculations and proofs are often omitted or compressed for reasons of brevity, in this paper they are the central focus, so are presented in detail.

[1] The general form of this misquote is due to Alan Perlis, who originally said it of Lisp programmers.

ICFP '14, September 1–6, 2014, Gothenburg, Sweden.

ACM 978-1-4503-2873-9 /14/09...$15.00.
http://dx.doi.org/10.1145/2628136.2628142

2. Example: Fast Reverse

We shall begin with an example that motivates the rest of the paper: transforming the naïve list reverse function into the so-called "fast reverse" function. This transformation is an instance of the worker/wrapper transformation, and there is an intuitive, informal justification of why this is an optimisation. Here we give this non-rigorous explanation; the remainder of this paper will focus on building the tools to strengthen this to a rigorous argument.

We start with a naïve definition of the reverse function, which takes quadratic time to run as each append $+\!\!+$ takes time linear in the length of its left argument:

$$\begin{aligned} &reverse && :: [a] \to [a] \\ &reverse\,[\,] && = [\,] \\ &reverse\,(x : xs) && = reverse\;xs +\!\!+ [x] \end{aligned}$$

We can write a more efficient version by using a *worker* function *revcat* with a *wrapper* around it that simply applies the worker function with [ ] as the second argument:

$$\begin{aligned} &reverse' && :: [a] \to [a] \\ &reverse'\;xs && = revcat\;xs\,[\,] \end{aligned}$$

The specification for the worker *revcat* is as follows:

$$\begin{aligned} &revcat && :: [a] \to [a] \to [a] \\ &revcat\;xs\;ys && = reverse\;xs +\!\!+ ys \end{aligned}$$

From this specification we can calculate a new definition that does not depend on *reverse*. Because *reverse* is defined by cases, we will have one calculation for each case.

Case for [ ]:

$$\begin{aligned} & revcat\,[\,]\;ys \\ = & \quad \{\text{ specification of } revcat \} \\ & reverse\,[\,] +\!\!+ ys \\ = & \quad \{\text{ definition of } reverse \} \\ & [\,] +\!\!+ ys \\ = & \quad \{\text{ definition of } +\!\!+ \} \\ & ys \end{aligned}$$

Case for $(x : xs)$:

$$\begin{aligned} & revcat\,(x : xs)\;ys \\ = & \quad \{\text{ specification of } revcat \} \\ & reverse\,(x : xs) +\!\!+ ys \\ = & \quad \{\text{ definition of } reverse \} \\ & (reverse\;xs +\!\!+ [x]) +\!\!+ ys \\ = & \quad \{\text{ associativity of } +\!\!+ \} \\ & reverse\;xs +\!\!+ ([x] +\!\!+ ys) \\ = & \quad \{\text{ definition of } +\!\!+ \} \\ & reverse\;xs +\!\!+ (x : ys) \\ = & \quad \{\text{ specification of } revcat \} \\ & revcat\;xs\,(x : ys) \end{aligned}$$

Note the use of associativity of $+\!\!+$ in the third step, which is the only step not simply by definition or specification. Left-associated appends such as $(xs +\!\!+ ys) +\!\!+ zs$ are less time-efficient than the equivalent right-associated appends $xs +\!\!+ (ys +\!\!+ zs)$, as the former traverses *xs* twice. The intuition here is that the efficiency gain from this step in the proof carries over in some way to the rest of the proof, so that overall our calculated definition of *revcat* is more efficient than its original specification. The calculation gives us the following definition, which runs in linear time:

$$\begin{aligned} &reverse\;xs && = revcat\;xs\,[\,] \\ &revcat\,[\,]\;ys && = ys \\ &revcat\,(x : xs)\;ys && = revcat\;xs\,(x : ys) \end{aligned}$$

Unfortunately, there are a number of problems with this approach. Firstly, we calculated *revcat* using the *fold-unfold* style of program calculation [2]. This is an informal calculation, which fails to guarantee total correctness. Thus the resulting *reverse* function may fail in some cases where the original succeeded. Secondly, while we are applying the common pattern of factorising a program into a worker and a wrapper, the reasoning we use is ad-hoc and does not take advantage of this. We would like to abstract out this pattern to make future applications of this technique more straightforward. Finally, while intuitively we can see an efficiency gain from the use of associativity of $+\!\!+$, this is not a rigorous argument. Put simply, we need rigorous proofs of both *correctness* and *improvement* for our transformation.

3. Worker/Wrapper Transformation

The worker/wrapper transformation, as originally formulated by Gill and Hutton [7], allowed a function written using general recursion to be split into a recursive *worker* function and a *wrapper* function that allows the new definition to be used in the same contexts as the original. The usual application of this technique would be to write the worker to use a different type than the original program that supports more efficient operations, thus hopefully resulting in a more efficient program overall. Gill and Hutton gave conditions for the correctness of the transformation; here we present the more general theory and correctnesss conditions recently developed by Sculthorpe and Hutton [25].

3.1 The Fix Theory

The idea of the worker/wrapper transformation for fixed-points is as follows. Given a recursive program *prog* of some type A, we can write *prog* as some function f of itself:

$$\begin{aligned} &prog :: A \\ &prog = f\;prog \end{aligned}$$

We can rewrite this definition so that it is explicitly written using the well-known fixpoint operator fix:

$$\begin{aligned} &\mathrm{fix} && :: (a \to a) \to a \\ &\mathrm{fix}\,f && = f\,(\mathrm{fix}\,f) \end{aligned}$$

resulting in the following definition:

$$prog = \mathrm{fix}\,f$$

Next, we write functions $abs :: B \to A$ and $rep :: A \to B$ that allow us to convert from the original type A to some other type B that supports more efficient operations. We finish by constructing a new function $g : B \to B$ that allows us to rewrite our original definition of *prog* as follows:

$$prog = abs\,(\mathrm{fix}\;g)$$

Here *abs* is the *wrapper* function, while fix g is the *worker*. The pattern of the worker/wrapper transformation can be captured by a theorem that expresses necessary and sufficient conditions for its correctness [25]. This theorem has assumptions that express the required relationship between the functions *abs* and *rep*, and conditions that provide a specification for the function g in terms of *abs*, *rep* and f:

Theorem 1 (Worker/Wrapper Factorisation).
Given

$$\begin{array}{ll} abs : B \to A & f : A \to A \\ rep : A \to B & g : B \to B \end{array}$$

satisfying one of the assumptions

$$\begin{array}{ll} (A)\ abs \circ rep & = id_A \\ (B)\ abs \circ rep \circ f & = f \\ (C)\ \text{fix}\,(abs \circ rep \circ f) & = \text{fix}\, f \end{array}$$

and one of the conditions

$$\begin{array}{ll} (1)\ g = rep \circ f \circ abs & (1\beta)\ \text{fix}\, g = \text{fix}\,(rep \circ f \circ abs) \\ (2)\ g \circ rep = rep \circ f & (2\beta)\ \text{fix}\, g = rep\,(\text{fix}\, f) \\ (3)\ f \circ abs = abs \circ g & \end{array}$$

we have the factorisation

$$\text{fix}\, f = abs\,(\text{fix}\, g)$$

The different assumptions and conditions allow one to choose which will be easiest to verify.

3.2 Proving Fast Reverse Correct

Recall once again the naïve definition of *reverse*:

$$\begin{array}{ll} reverse & :: [a] \to [a] \\ reverse\,[\,] & = [\,] \\ reverse\,(x : xs) & = reverse\, xs +\!\!+ [x] \end{array}$$

As we mentioned before, this naïve implementation is inefficient due to the use of the append operation $+\!\!+$. We would like to use worker/wrapper factorisation to improve it. The first step is to rewrite the function using fix:

$$\begin{array}{ll} reverse & = \text{fix}\, rev \\ rev & :: ([a] \to [a]) \to ([a] \to [a]) \\ rev\, r\,[\,] & = [\,] \\ rev\, r\,(x : xs) & = r\, xs +\!\!+ [x] \end{array}$$

The next step in applying worker/wrapper is to select a new type to replace the original type $[a] \to [a]$, and to write *abs* and *rep* functions to perform the conversions. We can represent a list *xs* by its *difference list* $\lambda ys \to xs +\!\!+ ys$, as first demonstrated by Hughes [12]. Difference lists have the advantage that the usually costly operation of $+\!\!+$ can be implemented with function composition, typically leading to an increase of efficiency. We write the following functions to convert between the two representations:

$$\begin{array}{ll} \textbf{type}\ \mathit{DiffList}\ a = [a] \to [a] & \\ \mathit{toDiff} & :: [a] \to \mathit{DiffList}\ a \\ \mathit{toDiff}\ xs & = \lambda ys \to xs +\!\!+ ys \\ \mathit{fromDiff} & :: \mathit{DiffList}\ a \to [a] \\ \mathit{fromDiff}\ h & = h\,[\,] \end{array}$$

We have $\mathit{fromDiff} \circ \mathit{toDiff} = id$:

$$\begin{array}{ll} & \mathit{fromDiff}\,(\mathit{toDiff}\, xs) \\ = & \{\ \text{definition of}\ \mathit{toDiff}\ \} \\ & \mathit{fromDiff}\,(\lambda ys \to xs +\!\!+ ys) \\ = & \{\ \text{definition of}\ \mathit{fromDiff}\ \} \\ & (\lambda ys \to xs +\!\!+ ys)\,[\,] \\ = & \{\ \beta\text{-reduction}\ \} \\ & xs +\!\!+ [\,] \\ = & \{\ [\,]\ \text{is identity of}\ +\!\!+\ \} \\ & xs \end{array}$$

From these functions it is straightforward to create the actual *abs* and *rep* functions. These convert between the original function type $[a] \to [a]$ and a new function type $[a] \to \mathit{DiffList}\ a$ where the returned value is represented as a difference list, rather than a regular list:

$$\begin{array}{l} rep\ \ :: ([a] \to [a]) \to ([a] \to \mathit{DiffList}\ a) \\ rep\ h = \mathit{toDiff} \circ h \\ \\ abs\ \ :: ([a] \to \mathit{DiffList}\ a) \to ([a] \to [a]) \\ abs\ h = \mathit{fromDiff} \circ h \end{array}$$

Assumption (A) holds trivially:

$$\begin{array}{ll} & abs\,(rep\ h) \\ = & \{\ \text{definitions of}\ abs\ \text{and}\ rep\ \} \\ & \mathit{fromDiff} \circ \mathit{toDiff} \circ h \\ = & \{\ \mathit{fromDiff} \circ \mathit{toDiff} = id\ \} \\ & h \end{array}$$

Now we must verify that the definition of *revcat* that we calculated in the previous section

$$\begin{array}{ll} revcat\,[\,]\ ys & = ys \\ revcat\,(x : xs)\ ys & = revcat\ xs\,(x : ys) \end{array}$$

satisfies one of the worker/wrapper conditions. We first rewrite *revcat* as an explicit fixed point.

$$\begin{array}{ll} revcat & = \text{fix}\ rev' \\ rev'\ h\,[\,]\ ys & = ys \\ rev'\ h\,(x : xs)\ ys & = h\ xs\,(x : ys) \end{array}$$

We now verify condition (2), $rev' \circ rep = rep \circ rev$, which expands to $rev'\ (rep\ r)\ xs = rep\ (rev\ r)\ xs$. We calculate from the right-hand side, performing case analysis on *xs*. Firstly, we calculate for the case when *xs* is empty:

$$\begin{array}{ll} & rep\,(rev\ r)\,[\,] \\ = & \{\ \text{definition of}\ rep\ \} \\ & \mathit{toDiff}\,(rev\ r\,[\,]) \\ = & \{\ \text{definition of}\ rev\ \} \\ & \mathit{toDiff}\,[\,] \\ = & \{\ \text{definition of}\ \mathit{toDiff}\ \} \\ & \lambda ys \to [\,] +\!\!+ ys \\ = & \{\ [\,]\ \text{is identity of}\ +\!\!+\ \} \\ & \lambda ys \to ys \\ = & \{\ \text{definiton of}\ rev'\ \} \\ & rev'\ (rep\ r)\,[\,] \end{array}$$

and then for the case where *xs* is non-empty:

$$\begin{array}{ll} & rep\,(rev\ r)\,(x : xs) \\ = & \{\ \text{definition of}\ rep\ \} \\ & \mathit{toDiff}\,(rev\ r\,(x : xs)) \\ = & \{\ \text{definition of}\ rev\ \} \\ & \mathit{toDiff}\,(r\ xs +\!\!+ [x]) \\ = & \{\ \text{definition of}\ \mathit{toDiff}\ \} \\ & \lambda ys \to (r\ xs +\!\!+ [x]) +\!\!+ ys \\ = & \{\ \text{associativity and definition of}\ +\!\!+\ \} \\ & \lambda ys \to r\ xs +\!\!+ (x : ys) \\ = & \{\ \text{definition of}\ \mathit{toDiff}\ \} \\ & \lambda ys \to \mathit{toDiff}\,(r\ xs)\,(x : ys) \\ = & \{\ \text{definition of}\ rep\ \} \\ & \lambda ys \to rep\ r\ xs\,(x : ys) \\ = & \{\ \text{definition of}\ rev'\ \} \\ & rev'\ (rep\ r)\,(x : xs) \end{array}$$

For total correctness on infinite lists we must also verify the condition holds for the undefined value $\perp$:

$$
\begin{aligned}
& rep\,(rev\ r)\ \bot \\
= & \quad \{ \text{ definition of } rep \ \} \\
& toDiff\,(rev\ r\ \bot) \\
= & \quad \{ \ rev \text{ pattern matches on second argument } \} \\
& toDiff\ \bot \\
= & \quad \{ \text{ definition of } toDiff \ \} \\
& \lambda ys \to \bot +\!\!+\ ys \\
= & \quad \{ +\!\!+ \text{ strict in first argument } \} \\
& \lambda ys \to \bot \\
= & \quad \{ \ rev' \text{ pattern matches on second argument } \} \\
& rev'\ (rep\ r)\ \bot
\end{aligned}
$$

Now that we know our *rev′* satisfies condition (2), we have a new definition of *reverse*

$$reverse = abs\ revcat = fromDiff \circ revcat$$

which eta-expands as follows:

$$
\begin{aligned}
& reverse\ xs && = revcat\ xs\ [\,] \\
& revcat\ [\,]\ ys && = ys \\
& revcat\ (x : xs)\ ys && = revcat\ xs\ (x : ys)
\end{aligned}
$$

The end result is the same improved definition of *reverse* we had before. Thus the worker/wrapper theory has allowed us to formally verify the correctness of our earlier transformation. Furthermore, the use of a general theory has allowed us to avoid the need for induction which would usually be needed to reason about recursive definitions.

4. Improvement Theory

Thus far we have only reasoned about correctness. In order to develop a worker/wrapper theory that can prove *efficiency* properties, we need an operational theory of *program improvement*. More than just expressing extensional information, this should be based on intensional properties of resources that a program requires. For the purpose of this paper, the resource we shall consider is execution time.

We have two main design goals for our operational theory. Firstly, it ought to be based on the operational semantics of a realistic programming language, so that conclusions we draw from it are as applicable as possible. Secondly, it should be amenable to techniques such as (in)equational reasoning, as these are the techniques we used to apply the worker/wrapper correctness theory.

For the first goal, we use a language with similar syntax and semantics to GHC Core, except that arguments to functions are required to be atomic, as was the case in earlier versions of the language [20]. (Normalisation of the current version of GHC Core into this form is straightforward.) The language is call-by-need, reflecting the use of lazy evaluation in Haskell. The efficiency behaviour of call-by-need programs is notoriously counterintuitive. Our hope is that providing formal techniques for reasoning about call-by-need efficiency we will go some way toward easing this problem.

For the second goal, our theory must be based around relation R that is a preorder, as transitivity and reflexivity are necessary for inequational reasoning to be valid. Furthermore, to support reasoning in a compositional manner, it is essential to allow substitution. That is, given terms M and N, if $M\ R\ N$ then $\mathbb{C}[M]\ R\ \mathbb{C}[N]$ should also hold for any context $\mathbb{C}$. A relation R that satisfies both of these properties is called a *precongruence.*

A naïve approach to measuring execution time would be to simply count the number of steps taken to evaluate a term to some normal form, and consider that a term M is more efficient than a term N if its evaluation finishes in fewer steps. The resulting relation is clearly a preorder; however it is not a precongruence in a call-by-need setting, because meaningful computations can be done with terms that are not fully normalised. For example, just because M normalises and N does not, it does not follow that M is necessarily more efficient in *all* contexts.

The approach we use is due to Moran and Sands [15]. Rather than counting the steps taken to normalise a term, we compare the steps taken in *all* contexts, and only say that M is improved by N if for any context $\mathbb{C}$, the term $\mathbb{C}[M]$ requires no more evaluation steps than the term $\mathbb{C}[N]$. The result is a relation that is trivially a precongruence: it inherits transitivity and reflexivity from the numerical ordering $\leqslant$, and is substitutive by definition.

Improvement theory [23] was originally developed for call-by-name languages by Sands [21]. The remainder of this section presents the call-by-need time improvement theory due to Moran and Sands [15], which will provide the setting for our operational worker/wrapper theory. The essential difference between call-by-name and call-by-need is that the latter implements a *sharing* strategy, avoiding the repeated evaluation of terms that are used more than once.

4.1 Operational Semantics of the Core Language

We shall begin by presenting the operational model that forms the basis of this improvement theory. The semantics presented here are originally due to Sestoft [27].

We start from a set of variables *Var* and a set of constructors *Con*. We assume all constructors have a fixed arity. The grammar of terms is as follows:

$$
\begin{aligned}
x, y, z &\in Var \\
c &\in Con \\
M, N &::= x \\
&\mid \lambda x \to M \\
&\mid M\ x \\
&\mid \mathbf{let}\ \{\vec{x} = \vec{M}\}\ \mathbf{in}\ N \\
&\mid c\ \vec{x} \\
&\mid \mathbf{case}\ M\ \mathbf{of}\ \{c_i\ \vec{x_i} \to N_i\}
\end{aligned}
$$

We use $\vec{x} = \vec{M}$ as a shorthand for a list of bindings of the form $x = M$. Similarly, we use $c_i\ \vec{x_i} \to N_i$ as a shorthand for a list of cases of the form $c\ \vec{x} \to N$. All constructors are assumed to be saturated, that is, we assume that any $\vec{x}$ that is the operand of a constructor c has length equal to the arity of c. Literals are represented by constructors of arity 0. We treat α-equivalent terms as identical.

A term is a *value* if it is of the form $c\ \vec{x}$ or $\lambda x \to M$. In Haskell this is referred to as a *weak head normal form.* We shall use letters such as V, W to denote value terms.

Term contexts take the following form, with substitution defined in the obvious way.

$$
\begin{aligned}
\mathbb{C}, \mathbb{D} &::= [-] \\
&\mid x \\
&\mid \lambda x \to \mathbb{C} \\
&\mid \mathbb{C}\ x \\
&\mid \mathbf{let}\ \{\vec{x} = \vec{\mathbb{C}}\}\ \mathbf{in}\ \mathbb{D} \\
&\mid c\ \vec{x} \\
&\mid \mathbf{case}\ \mathbb{C}\ \mathbf{of}\ \{c_i\ \vec{x_i} \to \mathbb{D}_i\}
\end{aligned}
$$

A value context is a context that is either a lambda abstraction or a constructor applied to variables.

The restriction that the arguments of functions and constructors always be variables has the effect that all bindings

$$
\begin{array}{lll}
\langle \Gamma\,\{x = M\}, x, S\rangle & \to \langle \Gamma, M, \#x : S\rangle & \{\ \textsc{Lookup}\ \}\\
\langle \Gamma, V, \#x : S\rangle & \to \langle \Gamma\,\{x = V\}, V, S\rangle & \{\ \textsc{Update}\ \}\\
\langle \Gamma, M\ x, S\rangle & \to \langle \Gamma, M, x : S\rangle & \{\ \textsc{Unwind}\ \}\\
\langle \Gamma, \lambda x \to M, y : S\rangle & \to \langle \Gamma, M\ [y\,/\,x], S\rangle & \{\ \textsc{Subst}\ \}\\
\langle \Gamma, \mathbf{case}\ M\ \mathbf{of}\ \mathit{alts}, S\rangle & \to \langle \Gamma, M, \mathit{alts} : S\rangle & \{\ \textsc{Case}\ \}\\
\langle \Gamma, c_j\ \vec{y}, \{c_i\ \vec{x_i} \to N_i\} : S\rangle & \to \langle \Gamma, N_j\ [\vec{y}\,/\,\vec{x_j}], S\rangle & \{\ \textsc{Branch}\ \}\\
\langle \Gamma, \mathbf{let}\ \{\vec{x} = \vec{M}\}\ \mathbf{in}\ N, S\rangle & \to \langle \Gamma\,\{\vec{x} = \vec{M}\}, N, S\rangle & \{\ \textsc{Letrec}\ \}
\end{array}
$$

Figure 1. The call-by-need abstract machine

made during evaluation must have been created by a **let**. Sometimes we will use $M\ N$ (where N is not a variable) as a shorthand for $\mathbf{let}\ \{x = N\}\ \mathbf{in}\ M\ x$, where x is fresh. We use this shorthand for both terms and contexts.

An abstract machine for executing terms in the language maintains a state $\langle \Gamma, M, S\rangle$ consisting of: a heap Γ, given by a set of bindings from variables to terms; the term M currently being evaluated; the evaluation stack S, given by a list of tokens used by the abstract machine. The machine works by evaluating the current term to a value, and then decides what to do with the value based on the top of the stack. Bindings generated by **let** constructs are put on the heap, and only taken off when performing a LOOKUP. A LOOKUP executes by putting a token on the stack representing where the term was looked up, and then evaluating that term to value form before replacing it on the heap. In this way, each binding is only ever evaluated at most once. The semantics of the machine is given in Figure 1. Note that the LETREC rule assumes that $\vec{x}$ is disjoint from the domain of Γ; if not, we need only α-rename so that this is the case.

4.2 The Cost Model and Improvement Relations

Now that we have a semantics for our model, we must devise a *cost model* for this semantics. The natural way to do this for an operational semantics is to count steps taken to evaluate a given term. We use the notation $M{\downarrow}^n$ to mean the abstract machine progresses from the initial state $\langle \emptyset, M, \epsilon\rangle$ to some final state $\langle \Gamma, V, \epsilon\rangle$ with n occurences of the LOOKUP step. It is sufficient to count LOOKUP steps because the total number of steps is bounded by a linear function of the number of LOOKUP steps [15]. Furthermore, we use the notation $M{\downarrow}^{\leqslant n}$ to mean that $M{\downarrow}^m$ for some $m \leqslant n$.

From this, we can define our improvement relation. We say that "M is *improved* by N", written $M \mathrel{\underset{\sim}{\triangleright}} N$, if the following statement holds for all contexts $\mathbb{C}$:

$$\mathbb{C}[M]{\downarrow}^m \Longrightarrow \mathbb{C}[N]{\downarrow}^{\leqslant m}$$

In other words, a term M is improved by a term N if N takes no more steps to evaluate than M in all contexts. That this relation is a congruence follows immediately from the definition, and that it is a preorder follows from the fact that $\leqslant$ is itself a preorder. We sometimes write $M \mathrel{\underset{\sim}{\triangleleft}} N$ for $N \mathrel{\underset{\sim}{\triangleright}} M$. If both $M \mathrel{\underset{\sim}{\triangleright}} N$ and $M \mathrel{\underset{\sim}{\triangleleft}} N$, we write $M \mathrel{\underset{\sim}{\triangleleft\triangleright}} N$ and say that M and N are *cost-equivalent.*

For convenience, we define a "tick" operation on terms that adds exactly one unit of cost to a term:

$$\checkmark M \equiv \mathbf{let}\ \{x = M\}\ \mathbf{in}\ x \quad \{\text{ where } x \text{ is free in } M\ \}$$

This definition for $\checkmark M$ takes exactly two steps to evaluate to M: one to add the binding to the heap, and the other to look it up. Only one of these steps is a LOOKUP step, so the result is that the cost of evaluating the term is increased by exactly one. Using ticks allows us to annotate terms with individual units of cost, allowing us to use rules to "push" cost around a term, making the calculations more convenient. We could also define the tick operation by adding it to the grammar of terms and modifying the abstract machine and cost model accordingly, but this definition is equivalent. We have the following law: $\checkmark M \mathrel{\underset{\sim}{\triangleright}} M$.

The improvement relation $\mathrel{\underset{\sim}{\triangleright}}$ covers when one term is at least as efficient as another in all contexts, but this is a very strong statement. We use the notion of "weak improvement" when one term is at least as efficient as another within a constant factor. Specifically, we say M is weakly improved by N, written $M \mathrel{\underset{\approx}{\triangleright}} N$, if there exists a linear function $f(x) = kx + c$ (where $k, c \geqslant 0$) such that the following statement holds for all contexts $\mathbb{C}$:

$$\mathbb{C}[M]{\downarrow}^m \Longrightarrow \mathbb{C}[N]{\downarrow}^{\leqslant f(m)}$$

This can be read as "replacing M with N may make programs worse, but cannot make them *asymptotically* worse". We use symbols $\mathrel{\underset{\approx}{\triangleleft}}$ and $\mathrel{\underset{\approx}{\triangleleft\triangleright}}$ for inverse and equivalence analogously as for standard improvement.

Because weak improvement ignores constant factors, we have the following *tick introduction/elimination* law:

$$M \mathrel{\underset{\approx}{\triangleleft\triangleright}} \checkmark M$$

It follows from this that any improvement $M \mathrel{\underset{\sim}{\triangleright}} N$ can be *weakened* to a weak improvement $M' \mathrel{\underset{\approx}{\triangleright}} N'$ where M' and N' denote the terms M and N with all the ticks removed.

The last notation we define is *entailment*, which is used when we have a chain of improvements that all apply with respect to a particular set of definitions. Specifically, where $\Gamma = \{\vec{x} = \vec{V}\}$ is a list of bindings, we write:

$$\Gamma \vdash M_1 \mathrel{\underset{\sim}{\triangleright}} M_2 \mathrel{\underset{\sim}{\triangleright}} \ldots \mathrel{\underset{\sim}{\triangleright}} M_n$$

to mean:

$$\mathbf{let}\ \Gamma\ \mathbf{in}\ M_1 \mathrel{\underset{\sim}{\triangleright}} \mathbf{let}\ \Gamma\ \mathbf{in}\ M_2 \mathrel{\underset{\sim}{\triangleright}} \ldots \mathrel{\underset{\sim}{\triangleright}} \mathbf{let}\ \Gamma\ \mathbf{in}\ M_n$$

4.3 Selected Laws

We finish this section with a selection of laws taken from [15]. The first two are β-reduction rules. The following cost equivalence holds for function application:

$$(\lambda x \to M)\ y \mathrel{\underset{\sim}{\triangleleft\triangleright}} M\ [y\,/\,x]$$

This holds because the abstract machine evaluates the left-hand-side to the right-hand-side without performing any LOOKUPs, resulting the same heap and stack as before. Note that the substitution is variable-for-variable, as the grammar for our language requires that the argument to function application always be a variable.

In general, where a term M can be evaluated to a term M', we have the following relationships:

$$
\begin{array}{l}
M \mathrel{\underset{\sim}{\triangleright}} M' \\
M' \mathrel{\underset{\approx}{\triangleleft\triangleright}} M
\end{array}
$$

The latter fact may be non-obvious, but it holds because evaluating a term will produce a constant number of ticks, and tick-elimination is a weak cost-equivalence. In this manner we can see that partial evaluation by itself will never save more than a constant-factor of time.

The following cost equivalence allows us to substitute a variable for its binding. However, note that this is only valid for *values*, as bindings to other terms will be modified in the course of execution. We thus call this rule *value-β*.

$$\begin{array}{l}\textbf{let } \{x = V, \vec{y} = \vec{\mathbb{C}}[x]\} \textbf{ in } \mathbb{D}[x] \\ \mathrel{\underset{\sim}{\lhd\rhd}} \\ \textbf{let } \{x = V, \vec{y} = \vec{\mathbb{C}}[\checkmark V]\} \textbf{ in } \mathbb{D}[\checkmark V]\end{array}$$

The following law allows us to move let bindings in and out of a context when the binding is to a value. Note that we assume that x does not appear free in $\mathbb{C}$, which can be ensured by α-renaming, and that no free variables in V are captured in $\mathbb{C}$. We call this rule *value let-floating*.

$$\mathbb{C}[\textbf{let } \{x = V\} \textbf{ in } M] \mathrel{\underset{\sim}{\lhd\rhd}} \textbf{let } \{x = V\} \textbf{ in } \mathbb{C}[M]$$

We also have a *garbage collection* law allowing us to remove unused bindings. Assuming that x is not free in $\vec{N}$ or L, we have the following cost equivalence:

$$\textbf{let } \{x = M; \vec{y} = \vec{N}\} \textbf{ in } L \mathrel{\underset{\sim}{\lhd\rhd}} \textbf{let } \{\vec{y} = \vec{N}\} \textbf{ in } L$$

The final law we present here is the rule of *improvement induction*. The version that we present is stronger than the version in [15], but can be obtained by a simple modification of the proof given there. For any set of value bindings Γ and context $\mathbb{C}$, we have the following rule:

$$\frac{\Gamma \vdash M \mathrel{\underset{\sim}{\rhd}} \checkmark\mathbb{C}[M] \qquad \Gamma \vdash \checkmark\mathbb{C}[N] \mathrel{\underset{\sim}{\rhd}} N}{\Gamma \vdash M \mathrel{\underset{\sim}{\rhd}} N}$$

This allows us to prove an $M \mathrel{\underset{\sim}{\rhd}} N$ simply by finding a context $\mathbb{C}$ where we can "unfold" M to $\checkmark\mathbb{C}[M]$ and "fold" $\checkmark\mathbb{C}[N]$ to N. In other words, the following proof is valid:

$$\begin{array}{ll}\Gamma \vdash M & \\ \mathrel{\underset{\sim}{\rhd}} & \\ \quad \checkmark\mathbb{C}[M] & \\ \mathrel{\underset{\sim}{\rhd}} & \{ \text{hypothesis} \} \\ \quad \checkmark\mathbb{C}[N] & \\ \mathrel{\underset{\sim}{\rhd}} & \\ \quad N & \end{array}$$

In this way the technique is similar to proof principles such as guarded coinduction [4, 28].

As a corollary to this law, we have the following law for *cost-equivalence* improvement induction. For any set of value bindings Γ and context $\mathbb{C}$, we have:

$$\frac{\Gamma \vdash M \mathrel{\underset{\sim}{\lhd\rhd}} \checkmark\mathbb{C}[M] \qquad \Gamma \vdash \checkmark\mathbb{C}[N] \mathrel{\underset{\sim}{\lhd\rhd}} N}{\Gamma \vdash M \mathrel{\underset{\sim}{\lhd\rhd}} N}$$

The proof is simply to start from the assumptions and make two applications of improvement induction: first to prove $M \mathrel{\underset{\sim}{\rhd}} N$, and second to prove $N \mathrel{\underset{\sim}{\rhd}} M$.

5. Worker/Wrapper and Improvement

In this section, we prove a factorisation theorem for improvement theory analogous to the worker/wrapper factorisation theorem given in section 3.1. Before we do this, however, we must prove two preliminary results: a *rolling rule* and a *fusion rule*. Rolling and fusion are central to the worker/wrapper transformation [7, 13], so it is only natural that we would need versions of these to apply worker/wrapper transformation in this context.

5.1 Preliminary Results

The first rule we prove is the *rolling rule*, so named because of its similarity to the rolling rule for least-fixed points. In particular, for any pair of value contexts $\mathbb{F}$, $\mathbb{G}$, we have the following weak cost equivalence:

$$\textbf{let } \{x = \mathbb{F}[\mathbb{G}[x]]\} \textbf{ in } \mathbb{G}[x] \mathrel{\underset{\approx}{\lhd\rhd}} \textbf{let } \{x = \mathbb{G}[\mathbb{F}[x]]\} \textbf{ in } x$$

The proof begins with an application of cost-equivalence improvement induction. We let $\Gamma = \{x = \mathbb{F}[\checkmark\mathbb{G}[x]], y = \mathbb{G}[\checkmark\mathbb{F}[y]]\}$, $M = \checkmark\mathbb{G}[x]$, $N = y$, $\mathbb{C} = \mathbb{G}[\checkmark\mathbb{F}[-]]$. The premises of induction are proved as follows:

$$\begin{array}{ll}\Gamma \vdash M & \\ \equiv & \{ \text{definitions} \} \\ \quad \checkmark\mathbb{G}[x] & \\ \mathrel{\underset{\sim}{\lhd\rhd}} & \{ \text{value-}\beta \} \\ \quad \checkmark\mathbb{G}[\checkmark\mathbb{F}[\checkmark\mathbb{G}[x]]] & \\ \equiv & \{ \text{definitions} \} \\ \quad \checkmark\mathbb{C}[M] & \end{array}$$

and

$$\begin{array}{ll}\Gamma \vdash \checkmark\mathbb{C}[N] & \\ \equiv & \{ \text{definitions} \} \\ \quad \checkmark\mathbb{G}[\checkmark\mathbb{F}[y]] & \\ \mathrel{\underset{\sim}{\lhd\rhd}} & \{ \text{value-}\beta \} \\ \quad y & \\ \equiv & \{ \text{definitions} \} \\ \quad N & \end{array}$$

Thus we can conclude $\Gamma \vdash M \mathrel{\underset{\sim}{\lhd\rhd}} N$, or equivalently **let** Γ **in** $M \mathrel{\underset{\sim}{\lhd\rhd}}$ **let** Γ **in** N. We expand this out and apply garbage collection to remove the unused bindings:

$$\textbf{let } \{x = \mathbb{F}[\checkmark\mathbb{G}[x]]\} \textbf{ in} \checkmark\mathbb{G}[x] \mathrel{\underset{\sim}{\lhd\rhd}} \textbf{let } \{y = \mathbb{G}[\checkmark\mathbb{F}[y]]\} \textbf{ in } y$$

By applying α-renaming and weakening we obtain the desired result. The second rule we prove is *letrec-fusion*, analogous to fixed-point fusion. For any value contexts $\mathbb{F}$, $\mathbb{G}$, we have the following implication:

$$\begin{array}{l}\mathbb{H}[\checkmark\mathbb{F}[x]] \mathrel{\underset{\sim}{\rhd}} \mathbb{G}[\checkmark\mathbb{H}[x]] \\ \Rightarrow \\ \textbf{let } \{x = \mathbb{F}[x]\} \textbf{ in } \mathbb{H}[x] \mathrel{\underset{\sim}{\rhd}} \textbf{let } \{x = \mathbb{G}[x]\} \textbf{ in } x\end{array}$$

For the proof, we assume the premise and proceed by improvement induction. Let $\Gamma = \{x = \mathbb{F}[x], y = \mathbb{G}[y]\}$, $M = \checkmark\mathbb{H}[x]$, $N = y$, $\mathbb{C} = \mathbb{G}$. The premises are proved by:

$$\begin{array}{ll}\Gamma \vdash M & \\ \equiv & \{ \text{by definitions} \} \\ \quad \checkmark\mathbb{H}[x] & \\ \mathrel{\underset{\sim}{\lhd\rhd}} & \{ \text{value beta} \} \\ \quad \checkmark\mathbb{H}[\checkmark\mathbb{F}[x]] & \\ \mathrel{\underset{\sim}{\rhd}} & \{ \text{by assumption} \} \\ \quad \checkmark\mathbb{G}[\checkmark\mathbb{H}[x]] & \\ \equiv & \{ \text{definition} \} \\ \quad \checkmark\mathbb{C}[M] & \end{array}$$

and

$$\begin{array}{ll}\Gamma \vdash \checkmark\mathbb{C}[N] & \\ \equiv & \{ \text{by definitions} \} \\ \quad \checkmark\mathbb{G}[y] & \\ \mathrel{\underset{\sim}{\lhd\rhd}} & \{ \text{value beta} \} \\ \quad y & \\ \equiv & \{ \text{definition} \} \\ \quad N & \end{array}$$

Thus we conclude that $\Gamma \vdash M \gtrsim N$. Expanding and applying garbage collection, we obtain the following:

$$\textbf{let } \{x = \mathbb{F}[x]\} \textbf{ in} \checkmark \mathbb{H}[x] \gtrsim \textbf{let } y = \mathbb{G}[y] \textbf{ in } y$$

Again we obtain the desired result via weakening and α-renaming. As improvement induction is symmetrical, we can also prove the following dual fusion law, in which the improvement relations are reversed:

$$\mathbb{H}[\checkmark\mathbb{F}[x]] \lesssim \mathbb{G}[\checkmark\mathbb{H}[x]]$$
$$\Rightarrow$$
$$\textbf{let } \{x = \mathbb{F}[x]\} \textbf{ in } \mathbb{H}[x] \lessapprox \textbf{let } \{x = \mathbb{G}[x]\} \textbf{ in } x$$

For both the rolling and fusion rules, we first proved a version of the conclusion with normal improvement, and then weakened to weak improvement. We do this to avoid having to deal with ticks, and because the weaker version is strong enough for our purposes.

Moran and Sands also prove their own fusion law. This law requires that the context $\mathbb{H}$ satisfy a form of *strictness*. Specifically, For any value contexts $\mathbb{F}$, $\mathbb{G}$ and fresh variable x, we have the following implication:

$$\mathbb{H}[\mathbb{F}[x]] \gtrsim \mathbb{G}[\mathbb{H}[x]] \wedge \textit{strict}\,(\mathbb{H})$$
$$\Rightarrow$$
$$\textbf{let } \{x = \mathbb{F}[x]\} \textbf{ in } \mathbb{C}[\mathbb{H}[x]] \gtrsim \textbf{let } \{x = \mathbb{G}[x]\} \textbf{ in } \mathbb{C}[x]$$

This version of fusion has the advantage of having a stronger conclusion, but its strictness side-condition and lack of symmetry make it unsuitable for our purposes.

5.2 The Worker/Wrapper Improvement Theorem

Using the above set of rules, we can prove the following *worker/wrapper improvement* theorem, giving conditions under which a program factorisation is a time improvement:

Theorem 2 (Worker/Wrapper Improvement).

Given value contexts Abs, Rep, $\mathbb{F}$, $\mathbb{G}$ *for which* x *is free satisfying one of the assumptions*

$$(A)\ \mathsf{Abs}[\mathsf{Rep}[x]] \mathrel{\triangleleft\!\triangleright}_{\approx} x$$
$$(B)\ \mathsf{Abs}[\mathsf{Rep}[\mathbb{F}[x]]] \mathrel{\triangleleft\!\triangleright}_{\approx} \mathbb{F}[x]$$
$$(C)\ \textbf{let } x = \mathsf{Abs}[\mathsf{Rep}[\mathbb{F}[x]]] \textbf{ in } x \mathrel{\triangleleft\!\triangleright}_{\approx} \textbf{let } x = \mathbb{F}[x] \textbf{ in } x$$

and one of the conditions

$$(1)\ \mathbb{G}[x] \lessapprox \mathsf{Rep}[\mathbb{F}[\mathsf{Abs}[x]]]$$
$$(2)\ \mathbb{G}[\checkmark\mathsf{Rep}[x]] \lesssim \mathsf{Rep}[\checkmark\mathbb{F}[x]]$$
$$(3)\ \mathsf{Abs}[\checkmark\mathbb{G}[x]] \lesssim \mathbb{F}[\checkmark\mathsf{Abs}[x]]$$
$$(1\beta)\ \textbf{let } x = \mathbb{G}[x] \textbf{ in } x \lessapprox \textbf{let } x = \mathsf{Rep}[\mathbb{F}[\mathsf{Abs}[x]]] \textbf{ in } x$$
$$(2\beta)\ \textbf{let } x = \mathbb{G}[x] \textbf{ in } x \lessapprox \textbf{let } x = \mathbb{F}[x] \textbf{ in } \mathsf{Rep}[x]$$

we have the improvement

$$\textbf{let } x = \mathbb{F}[x] \textbf{ in } x \gtrapprox \textbf{let } x = \mathbb{G}[x] \textbf{ in } \mathsf{Abs}[x]$$

Given a recursive program **let** $x = \mathbb{F}[x]$ **in** x and *abstraction* and *representation* contexts Abs and Rep, this theorem gives us conditions we can use to derive a factorised program **let** $x = \mathbb{G}[x]$ **in** $\mathsf{Abs}[x]$. This factorised program will be at worst a constant factor slower than the original program, but can potentially be asymptotically faster. In other words, we have conditions that guarantee that such an optimisation is "safe" with respect to time performance.

The proof given in [25] for the original factorisation theorem centers on the use of the rolling and fusion rules. Because we have proven analogous rules in our setting, the proofs can be adapted fairly straightforwardly, simply by keeping the general form of the proofs and using the rules of improvement theory as structural rules that fit between the original steps. The details are as follows.

We begin by noting that $(A) \Rightarrow (B) \Rightarrow (C)$, as in the original case. The first implication $(A) \Rightarrow (B)$ no longer follows immediately, but the proof is simple. Leting y be a fresh variable, we reason as follows:

$$\begin{array}{ll}
 & \mathsf{Abs}[\mathsf{Rep}[\mathbb{F}[y]]] \\
\mathrel{\triangleleft\!\triangleright}_{\approx} & \{ \text{ garbage collection, value-}\beta \text{ } \} \\
 & \textbf{let } x = \mathbb{F}[y] \textbf{ in } \mathsf{Abs}[\mathsf{Rep}[x]] \\
\mathrel{\triangleleft\!\triangleright}_{\approx} & \{ (A) \} \\
 & \textbf{let } x = \mathbb{F}[y] \textbf{ in } x \\
\mathrel{\triangleleft\!\triangleright}_{\approx} & \{ \text{ value-}\beta\text{, garbage collection } \} \\
 & \mathbb{F}[y]
\end{array}$$

The final step is to observe that as both x and y are fresh, we can substitute one for the other and the relationship between the terms will remain the same. Hence, we can conclude (B).

As in the original theorem, we have that (1) implies (1β) by simple application of substitution, (2) implies (2β) by fusion and (3) implies the conclusion also by fusion. Under assumption (C), we have that (1β) and (2β) are equivalent. We show this by proving their right hand sides cost-equivalent, after which we can simply apply transitivity.

$$\begin{array}{ll}
 & \textbf{let } x = \mathbb{F}[x] \textbf{ in } \mathsf{Rep}[x] \\
\mathrel{\triangleleft\!\triangleright}_{\approx} & \{ \text{ value-}\beta \text{ } \} \\
 & \textbf{let } x = \mathbb{F}[x] \textbf{ in } \mathsf{Rep}[\mathbb{F}[x]] \\
\mathrel{\triangleleft\!\triangleright}_{\approx} & \{ \text{ value let-floating } \} \\
 & \mathsf{Rep}[\mathbb{F}[\textbf{let } x = \mathbb{F}[x] \textbf{ in } x]] \\
\mathrel{\triangleleft\!\triangleright}_{\approx} & \{ (C) \} \\
 & \mathsf{Rep}[\mathbb{F}[\textbf{let } x = \mathsf{Abs}[\mathsf{Rep}[\mathbb{F}[x]]] \textbf{ in } x]] \\
\mathrel{\triangleleft\!\triangleright}_{\approx} & \{ \text{ value let-floating } \} \\
 & \textbf{let } x = \mathsf{Abs}[\mathsf{Rep}[\mathbb{F}[x]]] \textbf{ in } \mathsf{Rep}[\mathbb{F}[x]] \\
\mathrel{\triangleleft\!\triangleright}_{\approx} & \{ \text{ rolling } \} \\
 & \textbf{let } x = \mathsf{Rep}[\mathbb{F}[\mathsf{Abs}[x]]] \textbf{ in } x
\end{array}$$

Finally, we must show that condition (1β) and assumption (C) together imply the conclusion. This follows exactly the same pattern of reasoning as the original proof, with the addition of two applications of value-let floating:

$$\begin{array}{ll}
 & \textbf{let } x = \mathbb{F}[x] \textbf{ in } x \\
\mathrel{\triangleleft\!\triangleright}_{\approx} & \{ (C) \} \\
 & \textbf{let } x = \mathsf{Abs}[\mathsf{Rep}[\mathbb{F}[x]]] \textbf{ in } x \\
\mathrel{\triangleleft\!\triangleright}_{\approx} & \{ \text{ rolling } \} \\
 & \textbf{let } x = \mathsf{Rep}[\mathbb{F}[\mathsf{Abs}[x]]] \textbf{ in } \mathsf{Abs}[x] \\
\mathrel{\triangleleft\!\triangleright}_{\approx} & \{ \text{ value let-floating } \} \\
 & \mathsf{Abs}[\textbf{let } x = \mathsf{Rep}[\mathbb{F}[\mathsf{Abs}[x]]] \textbf{ in } x] \\
\gtrapprox & \{ (1\beta) \} \\
 & \mathsf{Abs}[\textbf{let } x = \mathbb{G}[x] \textbf{ in } x] \\
\mathrel{\triangleleft\!\triangleright}_{\approx} & \{ \text{ value let-floating } \} \\
 & \textbf{let } x = \mathbb{G}[x] \textbf{ in } \mathsf{Abs}[x]
\end{array}$$

We conclude this section by discussing a few important points about the worker/wrapper improvement theorem and its applications. Firstly, we note that the condition (A) will never actually hold. To see this, we let Ω be a divergent term; that is, one that the abstract machine will never finish evaluating. By substituting into the context **let** $x = \Omega$ **in** $[-]$, we obtain the following cost-equivalence:

$$\textbf{let } x = \Omega \textbf{ in } \mathsf{Abs}[\mathsf{Rep}[x]] \mathrel{\triangleleft\!\triangleright}_{\approx} \textbf{let } x = \Omega \textbf{ in } x$$

This is clearly false, as the left-hand side will terminate almost immediately (as Abs is a value context), while the right-hand side will diverge. Thus we see that assumption (A) is impossible to satisfy. We leave it in the theorem for completeness of the analogy with the earlier theorem from section 3.1. In situations where (A) would have been used with the earlier theory, the weaker assumption (B) can always be used instead. As we will see later with the examples, frequently only very few properties of the context $\mathbb{F}$ will be used in the proof of (B). A *typed* improvement theory might allow these properties to be assumed of x instead, thus making (A) useful again.

Secondly, we note the restriction to value contexts. This is not actually a particularly severe restriction: for the common application of recursively-defined functions, it is fairly straightforward to ensure that all contexts be of the form $\lambda x \to \mathbb{C}$. For other applications it may be more difficult to find Abs and Rep contexts with the required relationship.

Finally, we note that only conditions (2) and (3) use normal improvement, with all other assumptions and conditions using the weaker version. This is because weak improvement is not strong enough to permit the use of fusion, which these conditions rely on. This makes these conditions harder to prove. However, when these conditions are used, their strength allows us to narrow down the source of any constant-factor slowdown that may take place.

6. Examples

6.1 Reversing a List

In this section we shall demonstrate the utility of our theory with two practical examples. We begin by revisiting the earlier example of reversing a list. In order to apply our theory, we must first write *reverse* as a recursive let:

$$\begin{aligned}
&reverse &&= \textbf{let}\ \{f = \mathsf{Revbody}\,[f]\}\ \textbf{in}\ f\\
&\mathsf{Revbody}[M] &&= \lambda xs \to \textbf{case}\ xs\ \textbf{of}\\
& && \quad [\,] \to [\,]\\
& && \quad (y : ys) \to M\ ys +\!\!+ [y]
\end{aligned}$$

The *abs* and *rep* functions from before give rise to to the following contexts:

$$\begin{aligned}
\mathsf{Abs}[M] &= \lambda xs \to M\ xs\ [\,]\\
\mathsf{Rep}[M] &= \lambda xs \to \lambda ys \to M\ xs +\!\!+ ys
\end{aligned}$$

We also require some extra theoretical machinery that we have yet to introduce. To start with, we must assume some rules about the append operation $+\!\!+$. The following associativity rules were proved by Moran and Sands [15].

$$\begin{aligned}
(xs +\!\!+ ys) +\!\!+ zs &\succsim xs +\!\!+ (ys +\!\!+ zs)\\
xs +\!\!+ (ys +\!\!+ zs) &\succsim (xs +\!\!+ ys) +\!\!+ zs
\end{aligned}$$

We assume the following identity improvement as well, which follows from theorems also proved in [15]:

$$[\,] +\!\!+ xs \succsim xs$$

We also require the notion of an *evaluation context*. An evaluation context is a context where evaluation is impossible unless the hole is filled, and have the following form:

$$\begin{aligned}
\mathbb{E} ::= &\ \mathbb{A}\\
&\mid \textbf{let}\ \{\vec{x} = \vec{M}\}\ \textbf{in}\ \mathbb{A}\\
&\mid \textbf{let}\ \{\vec{y} = \vec{M};\\
&\qquad x_0 = \mathbb{A}_0[x_1];\\
&\qquad x_1 = \mathbb{A}_1[x_2];\\
&\qquad \ldots\\
&\qquad x_n = \mathbb{A}_n\}\\
&\quad \textbf{in}\ \mathbb{A}[x_0]
\end{aligned}$$

$$\begin{aligned}
\mathbb{A} ::= &\ [-]\\
&\mid \mathbb{A}\ x\\
&\mid \textbf{case}\ \mathbb{A}\ \textbf{of}\ \{c_i\ \vec{x_i} \to M_i\}
\end{aligned}$$

Note that a context of this form must have exactly one hole. The usefulness of evaluation contexts is that they satisfy some special laws. We use the following in this example:

$$\begin{aligned}
&\mathbb{E}[\checkmark M]\\
\lessapprox\!\!\!\!\gtrapprox\ &\{\ \text{tick floating}\ \}\\
&\checkmark\mathbb{E}[M]
\end{aligned}$$

$$\begin{aligned}
&\mathbb{E}[\textbf{case}\ M\ \textbf{of}\ \{c_i\ \vec{x_i} \to N_i\}]\\
\lessapprox\!\!\!\!\gtrapprox\ &\{\ \text{case floating}\ \}\\
&\textbf{case}\ M\ \textbf{of}\ \{c_i\ \vec{x_i} \to \mathbb{E}[N_i]\}
\end{aligned}$$

$$\begin{aligned}
&\mathbb{E}[\textbf{let}\ \{\vec{x} = \vec{M}\}\ \textbf{in}\ N]\\
\lessapprox\!\!\!\!\gtrapprox\ &\{\ \text{let floating}\ \}\\
&\textbf{let}\ \{\vec{x} = \vec{M}\}\ \textbf{in}\ \mathbb{E}[N]
\end{aligned}$$

We conclude by noting that while the context $[-] +\!\!+ ys$ is not strictly speaking an evaluation context (as the hole is in the wrong place), it is cost-equivalent to an evaluation context and so also satisfies these laws. The proof is as follows:

$$\begin{aligned}
&[-] +\!\!+ ys\\
\equiv\ &\{\ \text{desugaring}\ \}\\
&(\textbf{let}\ \{xs = [-]\}\ \textbf{in}\ (+\!\!+)\ xs)\ ys\\
\lessapprox\!\!\!\!\gtrapprox\ &\{\ \text{let floating}\ [-]\ ys\ \}\\
&\textbf{let}\ \{xs = [-]\}\ \textbf{in}\ (+\!\!+)\ xs\ ys\\
\lessapprox\!\!\!\!\gtrapprox\ &\{\ \text{unfolding}\ +\!\!+\ \}\\
&\textbf{let}\ \{xs = [-]\}\ \textbf{in}\\
&\quad \checkmark\textbf{case}\ xs\ \textbf{of}\\
&\qquad [\,] \to ys\\
&\qquad (z : zs) \to \textbf{let}\ \{rs = (+\!\!+)\ zs\ ys\}\ \textbf{in}\ z : rs\\
\lessapprox\!\!\!\!\gtrapprox\ &\{\ \text{desugaring tick and collecting lets}\ \}\\
&\textbf{let}\ \{xs = [-];\\
&\quad r = \textbf{case}\ xs\ \textbf{of}\\
&\qquad [\,] \to ys\\
&\qquad (z : zs) \to \textbf{let}\ \{rs = (+\!\!+)\ zs\ ys\}\ \textbf{in}\ z : rs\\
&\quad \}\ \textbf{in}\ r
\end{aligned}$$

Now we can begin the example proper. We start by verifying that Abs and Rep satisfy one of the worker/wrapper assumptions. While earlier we used (A) for this example, the corresponding assumption for worker/wrapper improvement is unsatisfiable. Thus we instead verify assumption (B). The proof is fairly straightforward:

$$\begin{aligned}
&\mathsf{Abs}[\mathsf{Rep}[\mathsf{Revbody}[f]]]\\
\equiv\ &\{\ \text{definitions}\ \}\\
&\lambda xs \to (\lambda xs \to \lambda ys \to \mathsf{Revbody}[f]\ xs +\!\!+ ys)\ xs\ [\,]\\
\lessapprox\!\!\!\!\gtrapprox\ &\{\ \beta\text{-reduction}\ \}\\
&\lambda xs \to \mathsf{Revbody}[f]\ xs +\!\!+ [\,]\\
\equiv\ &\{\ \text{definition of Revbody}\ \}\\
&\lambda xs \to (\lambda xs \to \textbf{case}\ xs\ \textbf{of}\\
&\quad [\,] \to [\,]\\
&\quad (y : ys) \to f\ ys +\!\!+ [y])\ xs +\!\!+ [\,]\\
\lessapprox\!\!\!\!\gtrapprox\ &\{\ \beta\text{-reduction}\ \}\\
&\lambda xs \to (\textbf{case}\ xs\ \textbf{of}\\
&\quad [\,] \to [\,]\\
&\quad (y : ys) \to f\ ys +\!\!+ [y]) +\!\!+ [\,]\\
\lessapprox\!\!\!\!\gtrapprox\ &\{\ \text{case floating}\ [-] +\!\!+ [\,]\ \}\\
&\lambda xs \to \textbf{case}\ xs\ \textbf{of}\\
&\quad [\,] \to [\,] +\!\!+ [\,]\\
&\quad (y : ys) \to (f\ ys +\!\!+ [y]) +\!\!+ [\,]
\end{aligned}$$

$$
\begin{array}{l}
\underset{\approx}{\lhd\rhd} \quad \{ \text{ associativity is weak cost equivalence } \} \\
\lambda xs \to \textbf{case } xs \textbf{ of} \\
\quad [\,] \to [\,] +\!\!+ [\,] \\
\quad (y : ys) \to f\ ys +\!\!+ ([y] +\!\!+ [\,]) \\
\underset{\approx}{\lhd\rhd} \quad \{ \text{ evaluating } [\,] +\!\!+ [\,],\ [y] +\!\!+ [\,] \ \} \\
\lambda xs \to \textbf{case } xs \textbf{ of} \\
\quad [\,] \to [\,] \\
\quad (y : ys) \to f\ ys +\!\!+ [y] \\
\equiv \quad \{ \text{ definition of revbody } \} \\
\mathsf{Revbody}\ [f]
\end{array}
$$

As before, we use condition (2) to derive our $\mathbb{G}$. The derivation is somewhat more involved than before, requiring some care with the manipulation of ticks.

$$
\begin{array}{l}
\mathsf{Rep}[\checkmark \mathsf{Revbody}[f]] \\
\equiv \quad \{ \text{ definitions } \} \\
\lambda xs \to \lambda ys \to \\
\quad (\checkmark \lambda xs \to \quad \textbf{case } xs \textbf{ of} \\
\qquad\qquad [\,] \to [\,] \\
\qquad\qquad (z : zs) \to f\ zs +\!\!+ [z])\ xs +\!\!+ ys \\
\underset{\sim}{\lhd\rhd} \quad \{ \text{ float tick out of } [-]\ xs +\!\!+ ys \ \} \\
\lambda xs \to \lambda ys \to \\
\quad \checkmark((\lambda xs \to \quad \textbf{case } xs \textbf{ of} \\
\qquad\qquad [\,] \to [\,] \\
\qquad\qquad (z : zs) \to f\ zs +\!\!+ [z])\ xs +\!\!+ ys) \\
\underset{\sim}{\lhd\rhd} \quad \{ \ \beta\text{-reduction } \} \\
\lambda xs \to \lambda ys \to \checkmark((\textbf{case } xs \textbf{ of} \\
\qquad\qquad [\,] \to [\,] \\
\qquad\qquad (z : zs) \to f\ zs +\!\!+ [z]) +\!\!+ ys) \\
\underset{\sim}{\lhd\rhd} \quad \{ \text{ case floating } [-] +\!\!+ ys \ \} \\
\lambda xs \to \lambda ys \to \checkmark(\textbf{case } xs \textbf{ of} \\
\qquad\qquad [\,] \to [\,] +\!\!+ ys \\
\qquad\qquad (z : zs) \to (f\ zs +\!\!+ [z]) +\!\!+ ys) \\
\underset{\sim}{\rhd} \quad \{ \text{ associativity and identity of } +\!\!+ \ \} \\
\lambda xs \to \lambda ys \to \checkmark(\textbf{case } xs \textbf{ of} \\
\qquad\qquad [\,] \to ys \\
\qquad\qquad (z : zs) \to f\ zs +\!\!+ ([z] +\!\!+ ys)) \\
\underset{\sim}{\rhd} \quad \{ \text{ evaluating } [y] +\!\!+ ys \ \} \\
\lambda xs \to \lambda ys \to \checkmark(\textbf{case } xs \textbf{ of} \\
\qquad\qquad [\,] \to ys \\
\qquad\qquad (z : zs) \to f\ zs +\!\!+ (z : ys)) \\
\underset{\sim}{\lhd\rhd} \quad \{ \text{ case floating tick } (\star) \ \} \\
\lambda xs \to \lambda ys \to \textbf{case } xs \textbf{ of} \\
\qquad\qquad [\,] \to \checkmark ys \\
\qquad\qquad (z : zs) \to \checkmark(f\ zs +\!\!+ (z : ys)) \\
\underset{\sim}{\rhd} \quad \{ \text{ removing a tick } \} \\
\lambda xs \to \lambda ys \to \textbf{case } xs \textbf{ of} \\
\qquad\qquad [\,] \to ys \\
\qquad\qquad (z : zs) \to \checkmark(f\ zs +\!\!+ (z : ys)) \\
\underset{\sim}{\lhd\rhd} \quad \{ \text{ desugaring } \} \\
\lambda xs \to \lambda ys \to \textbf{case } xs \textbf{ of} \\
\qquad\qquad [\,] \to ys \\
\qquad\qquad (z : zs) \to \\
\qquad\qquad\quad \checkmark(\textbf{let } ws = (z : ys) \textbf{ in} \\
\qquad\qquad\qquad f\ zs +\!\!+ ws) \\
\underset{\sim}{\lhd\rhd} \quad \{ \ \beta\text{-expansion } \} \\
\lambda xs \to \lambda ys \to \textbf{case } xs \textbf{ of} \\
\qquad\qquad [\,] \to ys \\
\qquad\qquad (z : zs) \to \\
\qquad\qquad\quad \checkmark \textbf{let } ws = (z : ys) \textbf{ in} \\
\qquad\qquad\qquad (\lambda as \to \lambda bs \to f\ as +\!\!+ bs)\ zs\ ws \\
\underset{\sim}{\lhd\rhd} \quad \{ \text{ tick floating } [-]\ zs\ ws \ \} \\
\quad \lambda xs \to \lambda ys \to \textbf{case } xs \textbf{ of} \\
\qquad\qquad [\,] \to ys \\
\qquad\qquad (z : zs) \to \\
\qquad\qquad\quad \textbf{let } ws = (z : ys) \textbf{ in} \\
\qquad\qquad\qquad (\checkmark \lambda as \to \lambda bs \to f\ as +\!\!+ bs)\ zs\ ws \\
\equiv \quad \{ \text{ definition of } \mathsf{Rep} \ \} \\
\quad \lambda xs \to \lambda ys \to \textbf{case } xs \textbf{ of} \\
\qquad\qquad [\,] \to ys \\
\qquad\qquad (z : zs) \to \\
\qquad\qquad\quad \textbf{let } ws = (z : ys) \textbf{ in} \\
\qquad\qquad\qquad (\checkmark \mathsf{Rep}[f])\ zs\ ws \\
\equiv \quad \{ \text{ taking this as our definition of } \mathbb{G} \ \} \\
\quad \mathbb{G}[\checkmark \mathsf{Rep}[f]]
\end{array}
$$

The step marked $\star$ is valid because $\checkmark[-]$ is itself an evaluation context, being syntactic sugar for **let** $x = [-]$ **in** x. Thus we have derived a definition of $\mathbb{G}$, from which we create the following factorised program:

$$
\begin{array}{l}
reverse = \textbf{let } \{ rec = \mathbb{G}[rec] \} \textbf{ in } \mathsf{Abs}[rec] \\
\mathbb{G}[rec] \ = \lambda xs \to \lambda ys \to \textbf{case } xs \textbf{ of} \\
\qquad\qquad [\,] \to ys \\
\qquad\qquad (z : zs) \to \textbf{let } ws = (z : ys) \textbf{ in} \\
\qquad\qquad\quad rec\ zs\ ws
\end{array}
$$

Expanding this out, we obtain:

$$
\begin{array}{l}
reverse = \textbf{let } \{ rec = \\
\quad \lambda xs \to \lambda ys \to \textbf{case } xs \textbf{ of} \\
\qquad [\,] \to ys \\
\qquad (z : zs) \to \textbf{let } ws = (z : ys) \textbf{ in} \\
\qquad\quad rec\ zs\ ws \} \\
\qquad \textbf{in} \quad \lambda xs \to rec\ xs\ [\,]
\end{array}
$$

The result is an implementation of fast reverse as a recursive let. The calculations here have essentially the same structure as the correctness proofs, with the addition of some administrative steps to do with the manipulation of ticks.

To illustrate the performance gain, we have graphed the performance of the original *reverse* function against the optimised version in Figure 2. We used the Criterion benchmarking library [18] with a range of list lengths to compare the performance of the two functions The resulting graph shows a clear improvement from quadratic time to linear. We chose to use relatively small list lengths for our graphs, but the trend continues for larger values.

6.2 Tabulating a Function

Our second example is that of tabulating a function by producing a stream (infinite list) of results. Given a function f that takes a natural number as its argument, the *tabulate* function should produce the following result:

$$[f\,0, f\,1, f\,2, f\,3, \ldots$$

This function can be implemented in Haskell as follows:

$$tabulate\ f = f\,0 \ : \ tabulate\ (f \circ (+1))$$

This definition is inefficient, as it requires that the argument to f be recalculated for each element of the result stream. Essentially, this definition corresponds to the following calculation, involving a significant amount of repeated work:

$$[f\,0, f\,(0+1), f\,((0+1)+1), f\,(((0+1)+1)+1), \ldots$$

We wish to apply the worker/wrapper technique to improve the time performance of this program. The first step is to write it as a recursive let in our language:

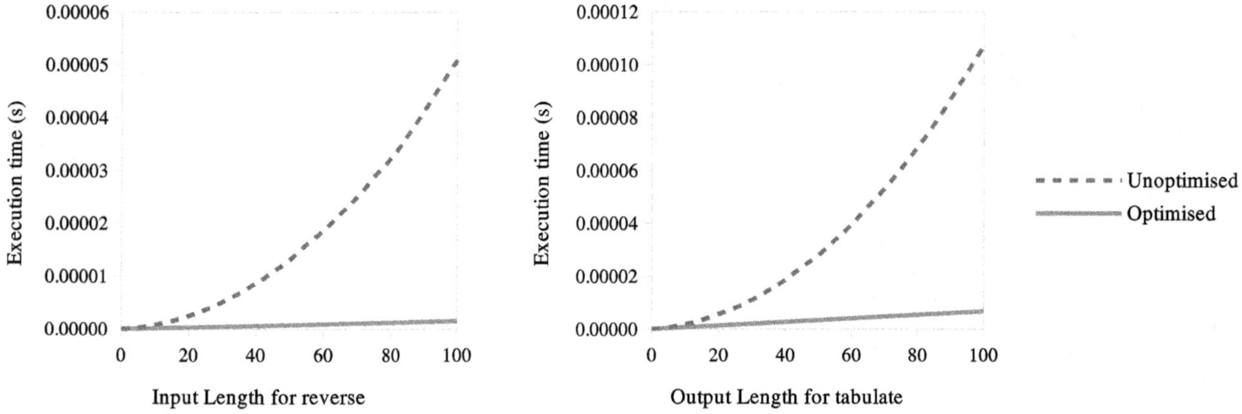

Figure 2. Performance comparisons of *reverse* and *tabulate*

$$
\begin{aligned}
&\mathit{tabulate} = \textbf{let}\ \{h = \mathbb{F}[h]\}\ \textbf{in}\ h\\
&\mathbb{F}[M] \quad = \lambda f \to \textbf{let}\ \{f' = \lambda x \to\\
&\qquad\qquad \textbf{let}\ \{x' = x + 1\}\ \textbf{in}\ f\,x'\}\\
&\qquad\qquad \textbf{in}\ f\,0\ :\ M\ f'
\end{aligned}
$$

Next, we must devise Abs and Rep contexts. In order to avoid the repeated work, we hope to derive a version of the *tabulate* function that takes an additional number argument telling it where to "start" from. The following Abs and Rep contexts convert between these two versions:

$$
\begin{aligned}
&\mathsf{Abs}[M] = \lambda f \to M\ 0\ f\\
&\mathsf{Rep}[M] = \lambda n \to \lambda f \to \textbf{let}\ \{f' = \lambda x \to\\
&\qquad\qquad\qquad\qquad \textbf{let}\ \{x' = x + n\}\\
&\qquad\qquad\qquad\qquad\quad \textbf{in}\ f\,x'\}\\
&\qquad\qquad\quad \textbf{in}\ M\ f'
\end{aligned}
$$

Once again, we must introduce some new rules before we can derive the factorised program. Firstly, we require the following two *variable substitution* rules from [15]:

$$
\begin{aligned}
&\textbf{let}\ \{x = y\}\ \textbf{in}\ \mathbb{C}\,[x] \underset{\sim}{\rhd} \textbf{let}\ \{x = y\}\ \textbf{in}\ \mathbb{C}\,[y]\\
&\textbf{let}\ \{x = y\}\ \textbf{in}\ \mathbb{C}\,[y] \underset{\approx}{\lhd\!\rhd} \textbf{let}\ \{x = y\}\ \textbf{in}\ \mathbb{C}\,[x]
\end{aligned}
$$

Next, we must use some properties of addition. Firstly, we have the following *identity* properties:

$$
\begin{aligned}
&x + 0 \underset{\sim}{\lhd\!\rhd} x\\
&0 + x \underset{\sim}{\lhd\!\rhd} x
\end{aligned}
$$

We also use the following property, combining associativity and commutativity. We shall refer to this as *associativity of* +. Where t is not free in $\mathbb{C}$, we have:

$$
\begin{aligned}
&\textbf{let}\ \{t = x + y\}\ \textbf{in}\\
&\quad \textbf{let}\ \{r = t + z\}\ \textbf{in}\ \mathbb{C}\,[r]\\
&\underset{\sim}{\lhd\!\rhd}\\
&\textbf{let}\ \{t = z + y\}\ \textbf{in}\\
&\quad \textbf{let}\ \{r = x + t\}\ \textbf{in}\ \mathbb{C}\,[r]
\end{aligned}
$$

Finally, we use the fact that sums may be floated out of arbitrary contexts. Where z does not occur in $\mathbb{C}$, we have:

$$
\mathbb{C}\,[\textbf{let}\ \{z = y + x\}\ \textbf{in}\ M] \underset{\sim}{\lhd\!\rhd} \textbf{let}\ \{z = y + x\}\ \textbf{in}\ \mathbb{C}\,[M]
$$

Now we can begin to apply worker/wrapper. Firstly, we verify that Abs and Rep satisfy assumption (B). Again, this is relatively straightforward:

$$
\begin{aligned}
&\mathsf{Abs}[\mathsf{Rep}[\mathbb{F}[h]]]\\
\equiv\ &\{\ \text{definitions}\ \}\\
&\lambda f \to (\lambda n \to \lambda f \to \textbf{let}\ \{f' = \lambda x \to\\
&\qquad\qquad\qquad\qquad \textbf{let}\ \{x' = x + n\}\\
&\qquad\qquad\qquad\qquad\quad \textbf{in}\ f\,x'\}\\
&\qquad\qquad \textbf{in}\ \mathbb{F}[h]\ f')\ 0\ f\\
\underset{\sim}{\lhd\!\rhd}\ &\{\ \beta\text{-reduction}\ \}\\
&\lambda f \to \textbf{let}\ \{f' = \lambda x \to\\
&\qquad\qquad \textbf{let}\ \{x' = x + 0\}\\
&\qquad\qquad\quad \textbf{in}\ f\,x'\}\\
&\quad \textbf{in}\ \mathbb{F}[h]\ f'\\
\underset{\approx}{\lhd\!\rhd}\ &\{\ x + 0 \underset{\sim}{\lhd\!\rhd} x\ \}\\
&\lambda f \to \textbf{let}\ \{f' = \lambda x \to\\
&\qquad\qquad \textbf{let}\ \{x' = x\}\\
&\qquad\qquad\quad \textbf{in}\ f\,x'\}\\
&\quad \textbf{in}\ \mathbb{F}[h]\ f'\\
\underset{\approx}{\lhd\!\rhd}\ &\{\ \text{variable substitution, garbage collection}\ \}\\
&\lambda f \to \textbf{let}\ \{f' = \lambda x \to f\,x\}\\
&\quad \textbf{in}\ \mathbb{F}[h]\ f'\\
\equiv\ &\{\ \text{defintion of}\ \mathbb{F}\ \}\\
&\lambda f \to \textbf{let}\ \{f' = \lambda x \to f\,x\}\\
&\quad \textbf{in}\ (\lambda f \to \textbf{let}\ \{f'' = \lambda x \to\\
&\qquad\qquad\qquad \textbf{let}\ \{x' = x + 1\}\ \textbf{in}\ f\,x\}\\
&\qquad\quad \textbf{in}\ f\,0\ :\ h\,f'')\ f'\\
\underset{\sim}{\lhd\!\rhd}\ &\{\ \beta\text{-reduction}\ \}\\
&\lambda f \to \textbf{let}\ \{f' = \lambda x \to f\,x\}\\
&\quad \textbf{in let}\ \{f'' = \lambda x \to\\
&\qquad \textbf{let}\ \{x' = x + 1\}\ \textbf{in}\ f'\ x'\}\\
&\qquad \textbf{in}\ f'\ 0\ :\ h\,f''\\
\underset{\approx}{\lhd\!\rhd}\ &\{\ \text{value-}\beta\ \text{on}\ f'\ \}\\
&\lambda f \to \textbf{let}\ \{f'' = \lambda x \to\\
&\quad \textbf{let}\ \{x' = x + 1\}\ \textbf{in}\ (\lambda x \to f\,x)\ x'\}\\
&\quad \textbf{in}\ (\lambda x \to f\,x)\ 0\ :\ h\,f''\\
\underset{\sim}{\lhd\!\rhd}\ &\{\ \beta\text{-reduction}\ \}\\
&\lambda f \to \textbf{let}\ \{f'' = \lambda x \to\\
&\quad \textbf{let}\ \{x' = x + 1\}\ \textbf{in}\ f\,x'\}\\
&\quad \textbf{in}\ f\,0\ :\ h\,f''
\end{aligned}
$$

$$
\begin{array}{l}
\equiv \quad \{ \text{ definition of } \mathbb{F} \ \} \\
\quad \mathbb{F}[h]
\end{array}
$$

Now we use condition (2) to derive the new definition of *tabulate*. This requires the use of a number of the properties that we presented earlier:

$$
\begin{array}{l}
\quad \mathsf{Rep}[\checkmark\mathbb{F}[h]] \\
\equiv \quad \{ \text{ definitions } \} \\
\quad \lambda n \to \lambda f \to \textbf{let } \{ f = \lambda x \to \\
\qquad\qquad\qquad\qquad \textbf{let } \{ x' = x + n \} \\
\qquad\qquad\qquad\qquad\quad \textbf{in } f\,x' \} \\
\qquad \textbf{in } (\hat{\ }\backslash f \to \textbf{let } \{ f'' = \lambda x \to \\
\qquad\qquad\qquad\qquad \textbf{let } \{ x'' = x + 1 \} \textbf{ in } f\,x'' \} \\
\qquad\quad \textbf{in } f\,0 : h\,f')\,f \\
\underset{\sim}{\lhd\!\rhd} \quad \{ \text{ tick floating } [-]\,f \ \} \\
\quad \lambda n \to \lambda f \to \textbf{let } \{ f = \lambda x \to \\
\qquad\qquad\qquad\qquad \textbf{let } \{ x' = x + n \} \\
\qquad\qquad\qquad\qquad\quad \textbf{in } f\,x' \} \\
\qquad \textbf{in} \checkmark (\lambda f \to \textbf{let } \{ f'' = \lambda x \to \\
\qquad\qquad\qquad\qquad \textbf{let } \{ x'' = x + 1 \} \textbf{ in } f\,x'' \} \\
\qquad\quad \textbf{in } f\,0 : h\,f')\,f \\
\underset{\sim}{\lhd\!\rhd} \quad \{ \ \beta\text{-reduction } \} \\
\quad \lambda n \to \lambda f \to \textbf{let } \{ f = \lambda x \to \\
\qquad\qquad\qquad\qquad \textbf{let } \{ x' = x + n \} \\
\qquad\qquad\qquad\qquad\quad \textbf{in } f\,x' \} \\
\qquad \textbf{in} \checkmark \textbf{let } \{ f'' = \lambda x \to \\
\qquad\quad \textbf{let } \{ x'' = x + 1 \} \textbf{ in } f\ x'' \} \\
\qquad\quad \textbf{in } f\ 0 : h\,f' \\
\underset{\sim}{\lhd\!\rhd} \quad \{ \text{ value-}\beta \text{ on } f\text{, garbage collection } \} \\
\quad \lambda n \to \lambda f \to \checkmark \textbf{let } \{ f' = \lambda x \to \\
\qquad\quad \textbf{let } \{ x' = x + 1 \} \textbf{ in} \\
\qquad\qquad (\checkmark \lambda x \to \\
\qquad\qquad\quad \textbf{let } \{ x'' = x + n \} \\
\qquad\qquad\qquad \textbf{in } f\,x'')\ x' \} \\
\qquad \textbf{in } (\checkmark \lambda x \to \textbf{let } \{ x'' = x + n \} \\
\qquad\quad \textbf{in } f\,x'')\ 0 : h\,f' \\
\underset{\sim}{\rhd} \quad \{ \text{ removing ticks, } \beta\text{-reduction } \} \\
\quad \lambda n \to \lambda f \to \checkmark \textbf{let } \{ f' = \lambda x \to \\
\qquad\quad \textbf{let } \{ x' = x + 1 \} \textbf{ in} \\
\qquad\qquad \textbf{let } \{ x'' = x' + n \} \\
\qquad\qquad\quad \textbf{in } f\,x'' \} \\
\qquad \textbf{in } (\textbf{let } \{ x'' = 0 + n \} \\
\qquad\quad \textbf{in } f\,x'') : h\,f' \\
\underset{\sim}{\lhd\!\rhd} \quad \{ \text{ associativity and identity of } + \ \} \\
\quad \lambda n \to \lambda f \to \checkmark \textbf{let } \{ f' = \lambda x \to \\
\qquad\quad \textbf{let } \{ n' = n + 1 \} \textbf{ in} \\
\qquad\qquad \textbf{let } \{ x'' = x + n' \} \\
\qquad\qquad\quad \textbf{in } f\,x'' \} \\
\qquad \textbf{in } (\textbf{let } \{ x'' = n \} \\
\qquad\quad \textbf{in } f\,x'') : h\,f' \\
\underset{\sim}{\rhd} \quad \{ \text{ variable substitution, garbage collection } \} \\
\quad \lambda n \to \lambda f \to \checkmark \textbf{let } \{ f' = \lambda x \to \\
\qquad\quad \textbf{let } \{ n' = n + 1 \} \textbf{ in} \\
\qquad\qquad \textbf{let } \{ x'' = x + n' \} \\
\qquad\qquad\quad \textbf{in } f\,x'' \} \\
\qquad \textbf{in } f\,n : h\,f' \\
\underset{\sim}{\lhd\!\rhd} \quad \{ \text{ value let-floating } \} \\
\quad \lambda n \to \lambda f \to f\,n : \\
\qquad \checkmark \textbf{let } \{ f' = \lambda x \to \\
\qquad\quad \textbf{let } \{ n' = n + 1 \} \textbf{ in} \\
\qquad\qquad \textbf{let } \{ x'' = x + n' \} \\
\qquad\qquad\quad \textbf{in } f\,x'' \} \\
\qquad\quad \textbf{in } h\,f' \\
\underset{\sim}{\lhd\!\rhd} \quad \{ \text{ sums float } \} \\
\quad \lambda n \to \lambda f \to f\,n : \\
\qquad \textbf{let } \{ n' = n + 1 \} \textbf{ in} \\
\qquad\quad \checkmark \textbf{let } \{ f' = \lambda x \to \\
\qquad\qquad \textbf{let } \{ x'' = x + n' \} \\
\qquad\quad \textbf{in } f\,x'' \} \\
\qquad\qquad \textbf{in } h\,f' \\
\underset{\sim}{\lhd\!\rhd} \quad \{ \ \beta\text{-expansion, tick floating } \} \\
\quad \lambda n \to \lambda f \to f\,n : \\
\qquad \textbf{let } \{ n' = n + 1 \} \textbf{ in} \\
\qquad (\checkmark \lambda n \to \lambda f \to \textbf{let } \{ f' = \lambda x \to \\
\qquad\qquad\qquad\qquad\qquad \textbf{let } \{ x' = x + n \} \\
\qquad\qquad\qquad\qquad\qquad\quad \textbf{in } f\,x' \} \\
\qquad\quad \textbf{in } h\,f')\ n'\ f \\
\equiv \quad \{ \text{ definition of } \mathsf{Rep} \ \} \\
\quad \lambda n \to \lambda f \to f\,n : \\
\qquad \textbf{let } \{ n' = n + 1 \} \textbf{ in} \\
\qquad (\checkmark \mathsf{Rep}[h])\ n'\ f \\
\equiv \quad \{ \text{ taking this as our definition of } \mathbb{G} \ \} \\
\quad \mathbb{G}[\checkmark \mathsf{Rep}[h]]
\end{array}
$$

Thus we have derived a definition of $\mathbb{G}$, from which we create the following factorised program:

$$
\begin{array}{ll}
\mathit{tabulate} & = \textbf{let } \{ h = \mathbb{G}[h] \} \textbf{ in } \mathsf{Abs}[h] \\
\mathbb{G}[M] & = \lambda n \to \lambda f \to f\,n : \textbf{let } \{ n' = n + 1 \} \textbf{ in } M\ n'\ f
\end{array}
$$

This is the same optimised *tabulate* function that was proved correct in [10], and the proofs here have a similar structure to the correctness proofs from that paper, except that we have now formalised that the new version of the *tabulate* function is indeed a time improvement of the original version. We note that the proof of (B) is complicated by the fact that η-reduction is not valid in this setting. In fact, if we assumed η-reduction then our proof of (B) here could be adapted into a proof of (A).

We demonstrate the performance gain in Figure 2, again based on Criterion benchmarks. This time, we keep the same input (in this case the function $\lambda n \to n * n$), but vary how many elements of the result stream we evaluate. Once again, we have an improvement from quadratic to linear performance, and the trend continues for larger values.

7. Related Work

We divide the related work into three sections. Firstly, we discuss various approaches to the operational semantics of lazy languages. Secondly, we discuss the history of improvement theory. Finally, we discuss other approaches that have been used to formally reason about efficiency.

7.1 Lazy Operational Semantics

The notion of call-by-need evaluation was first introduced in 1971 by Wadsworth [30]. However, the semantics most widely regarded as the definition of call-by-need is the natural semantics due to Launchbury [14], which was later used by Sestoft to derive the virtual machine semantics we use in this paper [27]. Ariola, Felleisen, Maraist, Odersky and Wadler presented a *call-by-need lambda calculus* [1], with operational semantics based on reductions between terms in the source language. This calculus supports an equational theory. However, Moran and Sands showed that this equational theory is subsumed by weak cost-equivalence [15].

7.2 Improvement Theory

Improvement theory was originally developed in 1991 by Sands [21], and applied in a call-by-name setting. In 1997 this was generalised to a wide class of call-by-name and call-by-value languages, also by Sands [22]. This theory was also applicable to a general class of *resources*, rather than just space and time. The theory for lazy languages was developed by Moran and Sands for time efficiency [15] and Gustavsson and Sands for space efficiency [8, 9]. Since the last of these papers was published in 2001, there does not seem to have been much work on improvement theory. We hope that this paper can help to regenerate interest in this topic.

7.3 Formal Reasoning About Efficiency

Okasaki [17] uses techniques of amortised cost analysis to reason about the asymptotic time complexity of lazy functional data structures. This is achieved by modifying analysis techniques such as the Banker's Method, where the notion of *credit* is used to spread out the notional cost of an expensive but infrequent operations over more frequent and cheaper operations. The key idea in Okasaki's work is to invert such techniques to use the notion of *debt*. This allows the analyses to deal with the persistence of data structures, where the same structure may exist in multiple versions at once. While credit may only be spent once, a single debt may be paid off multiple times (in different versions of the same structure) without risking bankruptcy. These techniques have been used to analyse the asymptotic performance of a number of functional data structures.

Sansom and Peyton Jones [24] give a presentation of the GHC profiler, which can be used to measure time as well as space usage of Haskell programs. In doing so, they give a formal cost semantics for GHC Core programs based around the notion of *cost centres*. Cost centres are a way of annotating expressions, so that the profiler can indicate which parts of the source program cost the most to execute. The cost semantics is used as a specification to develop a precise profiling framework, as well as to prove various properties about cost attribution and verify that certain program transformations do not affect the attribution of costs, though they may of course reduce cost overall. Cost centres are now widely-used in profiling Haskell programs.

Hope [11] applies a technique based on *instrumenting* an abstract machine with cost information to derive a cost semantics for call-by-value functional programs. More specifically, starting from a denotational semantics for the source language, one derives an abstract machine for this language using standard program transformation techniques, instruments this machine with cost information, and then reverses the derivation to arrive at an instrumented denotational semantics. This semantics can then be used to reason about the cost of programs in the high-level source language without reference to the details of the abstract machine. This approach was used to calculate the space and time cost of a range of programming examples, as well as to derive a new deforestation theorem for hylomorphisms.

8. Conclusion

In this paper, we have shown how improvement theory can be used to justify the worker/wrapper transformation as a program optimisation, by formally proving that, under certain natural conditions, the transformation is guaranteed to preserve or improve time performance. This guarantee is with respect to an established operational semantics for call-by-need evaluation. We then verified that two examples from previous worker/wrapper papers met the preconditions for this performance guarantee, demonstrating the use of our theory while also verifying the validity of the examples. This work appears to be the first time that rigorous performance guarantees have been given for a general purpose optimisation technique in a call-by-need setting.

8.1 Further Work

As well as for fixed points, worker/wrapper theories also exist for more structured recursion operators such as folds [13] and unfolds [10]. Though the theory we present here can be specialised to such operators, it may be beneficial to investigate this more closely, as doing so may reveal more interesting and subtle details yet to be uncovered.

As we mentioned earlier in this paper, a typed theory would be more useful, allowing more power when reasoning about programs. This would also match more closely with the original worker/wrapper theories, which were typed. The key barrier to this is that there is currently no typed improvement theory, so such a theory would have to be developed before the theory here could be made typed.

The theory we present here only applies to time efficiency. Gustavsson and Sands have developed an improvement theory for space [8, 9], so this would be an obvious next step for developing our theory. More generally, we could apply a technique such as that used by Sands [22] to develop a theory that applies to a large class of resources, and examine which assumptions must be made about the resources we consider for our theory to apply.

Assumptions (A), (B) and (C) are written as weak cost-equivalences, which limits the scope of our theory to cases where Abs and Rep are fairly simple. We would like to also be able to cover cases where the Abs and Rep contexts correspond to expensive operations, but the extra cost is made up for by the overall efficiency gain of the transformation. To cover such cases, we would require a richer version of improvement theory that is able to quantify *how much* better one program is than another.

As our examples show, the calculations required to derive an improved program can often be quite involved. The HERMIT system, devised by a team at the University of Kansas [6, 26], facilitates program transformations by providing an interactive interface for program transformation that verifies correctness. If improvement theory could be integrated into such a system, it would be significantly easier to apply our worker/wrapper improvement theory.

Finally, we are working on a general worker/wrapper theory that will apply to any operator with the property of *dinaturality* [5]. It is also interesting to consider whether such a general categorical approach can be applied to an operational theory. If this is the case, dinaturality may also provide the necessary machinery to *unify* the denotational (correctness) and operational (efficiency) theories, which as we have already observed in this paper are very similar in terms of their formulations and proofs. Voigtländer and Johann used parametricity to justify program transformations from a perspective of *observational approximation* [29]. It may be productive to investigate whether their techniques can be applied to a notion of improvement.

Acknowledgments

The authors would like to thank the reviewers as well as Neil Sculthorpe, for their helpful comments on this paper.

References

[1] Z. M. Ariola, M. Felleisen, J. Maraist, M. Odersky, and P. Wadler. The Call-by-Need Lambda Calculus. In *POPL '95*, pages 233–246. ACM, 1995.

[2] R. M. Burstall and J. Darlington. A Transformation System for Developing Recursive Programs. *Journal of the ACM*, 24 (1):44–67, 1977.

[3] K. Claessen and J. Hughes. QuickCheck: A Lightweight Tool for Random Testing of Haskell Programs. In *ICFP*. ACM, 2000.

[4] T. Coquand. Infinite Objects in Type Theory. In *TYPES '93*, volume 806 of *Lecture Notes in Computer Science*. Springer, 1993.

[5] E. Dubuc and R. Street. Dinatural Transformations. In *Lecture Notes in Mathematics*, volume 137 of *Lecture Notes in Mathematics*, pages 126–137. Springer Berlin Heidelberg, 1970.

[6] A. Farmer, A. Gill, E. Komp, and N. Sculthorpe. The HERMIT in the Machine: A Plugin for the Interactive Transformation of GHC Core Language Programs. In *Haskell Symposium (Haskell '12)*, pages 1–12. ACM, 2012.

[7] A. Gill and G. Hutton. The Worker/Wrapper Transformation. *Journal of Functional Programming*, 19(2), 2009.

[8] J. Gustavsson and D. Sands. A Foundation for Space-Safe Transformations of Call-by-Need Programs. *Electronic Notes on Theoretical Computer Science*, 26:69–86, 1999.

[9] J. Gustavsson and D. Sands. Possibilities and Limitations of Call-by-Need Space Improvement. In *ICFP*, pages 265–276. ACM, 2001.

[10] J. Hackett, G. Hutton, and M. Jaskelioff. The Under Performing Unfold: A New Approach to Optimising Corecursive Programs. 2013. To appear in the volume of selected papers from the 25th International Symposium on Implementation and Application of Functional Languages, Nijmegen, The Netherlands, August 2013.

[11] C. Hope. *A Functional Semantics for Space and Time*. PhD thesis, School of Computer Science, University of Nottingham, 2008.

[12] J. Hughes. A Novel Representation of Lists and its Application to the Function "reverse". *Information Processing Letters*, 22(3):141–144, 1986.

[13] G. Hutton, M. Jaskelioff, and A. Gill. Factorising Folds for Faster Functions. *Journal of Functional Programming Special Issue on Generic Programming*, 20(3&4), June 2010.

[14] J. Launchbury. A Natural Semantics for Lazy Evaluation. In *POPL '93*, pages 144–154. ACM, 1993.

[15] A. Moran and D. Sands. Improvement in a Lazy Context: An Operational Theory for Call-by-Need. Extended version of [16], available at `http://citeseerx.ist.psu.edu/viewdoc/download?doi=10.1.1.37.144&rep=rep1&type=pdf`.

[16] A. Moran and D. Sands. Improvement in a Lazy Context: An Operational Theory for Call-by-Need. In *POPL '99*, pages 43–56. ACM, 1999.

[17] C. Okasaki. *Purely Functional Data Structures*. Cambridge University Press, 1999.

[18] B. O'Sullivan. Criterion, A New Benchmarking Library for Haskell, 2009. URL `http://www.serpentine.com/blog/2009/09/29/criterion-a-new-benchmarking-library-for-haskell/`.

[19] W. Partain. The nofib Benchmark Suite of Haskell Programs. In *Glasgow Workshop on Functional Programming*, pages 195–202. Springer, 1992.

[20] S. L. Peyton Jones. Compiling Haskell by Program Transformation: A Report from the Trenches. In *ESOP*, pages 18–44. Springer, 1996.

[21] D. Sands. Operational Theories of Improvement in Functional Languages (Extended Abstract). In *Glasgow Workshop on Functional Programming*, 1991.

[22] D. Sands. From SOS Rules to Proof Principles: An Operational Metatheory for Functional Languages. In *POPL '97*, pages 428–441. ACM Press, 1997.

[23] D. Sands. Improvement Theory and its Applications. In *Higher Order Operational Techniques in Semantics, Publications of the Newton Institute*. Cambridge University Press, 1997.

[24] P. M. Sansom and S. L. Peyton Jones. Formally Based Profiling for Higher-Order Functional Languages. *ACM Transactions on Programming Languages and Systems*, 19(2), 1997.

[25] N. Sculthorpe and G. Hutton. Work It, Wrap It, Fix It, Fold It. *Journal of Functional Programming*, 2014.

[26] N. Sculthorpe, A. Farmer, and A. Gill. The HERMIT in the Tree: Mechanizing Program Transformations in the GHC Core Language. In *Proceedings of Implementation and Application of Functional Languages (IFL '12)*, volume 8241 of *Lecture Notes in Computer Science*, pages 86–103, 2013.

[27] P. Sestoft. Deriving a Lazy Abstract Machine. *Journal of Functional Programming*, 7(3):231–264, 1997.

[28] D. A. Turner. Elementary Strong Functional Programming. In *FPLE '95*, volume 1022 of *Lecture Notes in Computer Science*. Springer, 1995.

[29] J. Voigtländer and P. Johann. Selective Strictness and Parametricity in Structural Operational Semantics, Inequationally. *Theor. Comput. Sci.*, 388(1-3):290–318, 2007.

[30] C. P. Wadsworth. *Semantics and Pragmatics of the Lambda Calculus*. PhD thesis, Computing Laboratory, University of Oxford, 1971.

[31] O. Wilde. Lady Windermere's Fan, A Play About a Good Woman. First performed in 1892.

Compositional Semantics for Composable Continuations

From Abortive to Delimited Control

Paul Downen Zena M. Ariola
University of Oregon
{pdownen,ariola}@cs.uoregon.edu

Abstract

Parigot's $\lambda\mu$-calculus, a system for computational reasoning about classical proofs, serves as a foundation for control operations embodied by operators like Scheme's callcc. We demonstrate that the call-by-value theory of the $\lambda\mu$-calculus contains a latent theory of delimited control, and that a known variant of $\lambda\mu$ which unshackles the syntax yields a calculus of composable continuations from the existing constructs and rules for classical control. To relate to the various formulations of control effects, and to continuation-passing style, we use a form of compositional program transformations which preserves the underlying structure of equational theories, contexts, and substitution. Finally, we generalize the call-by-name and call-by-value theories of the $\lambda\mu$-calculus by giving a single parametric theory that encompasses both, allowing us to generate a call-by-need instance that defines a calculus of classical and delimited control with lazy evaluation and sharing.

Categories and Subject Descriptors F.3.3 [*Studies of Program Constructs*]: Control primitives

Keywords Delimited Control; Equational Theory; Program Transformation; Continuation-passing Style; Evaluation Strategy

1. Introduction

Many programming languages give the programmer the ability to manipulate the flow of control during execution. For example, exception handling mechanisms allow for a faulty execution path to be aborted up to the nearest recovery point, and the callcc operator, which first appeared in Scheme, gives access to the current control state in the program represented as a first-class function called a *continuation*. Griffin [16] observed that certain manipulations of control flow correspond to reasoning in classical logic: in the same way that intuitionistic logic corresponds to the λ-calculus, adding classical axioms corresponds to adding control operators like callcc. In order to extend the same high-level reasoning tools that apply to open programs in the pure λ-calculus, Sabry and Felleisen developed equational theories [14, 28, 29] for callcc that not only describe *operational* rules [18] that could be used in an evaluator, but also *observational* guarantees that the evaluator must fulfill. Of note, Sabry's [28] theory of callcc makes use of *continuation variables* that have special properties and can only be instantiated by callcc. As we will see, this not only greatly aids in reasoning about terms with free variables, but also helps in relating the equational and operational interpretations of callcc.

In another line of work, Parigot's [25] $\lambda\mu$-calculus gives a system for computing with classical proofs. As opposed to the previous theories based on the λ-calculus with additional primitive constants, the $\lambda\mu$-calculus begins with continuation variables integrated into its core, so that control abstractions and applications have the same status as ordinary function abstraction. In this sense, the $\lambda\mu$-calculus presents a native language of control. Both λ- and $\lambda\mu$-based approaches have their advantages: we have much more experience programming with the λ-calculus model and the $\lambda\mu$-calculus reveals insights into reasoning about control. Therefore, we aim to present both approaches side-by-side. Typically, a call-by-value version of the $\lambda\mu$-calculus has been related [3] to a different presentation of control based on Felleisen's [14] $\mathcal{C}$ operator, but here we show that it is indeed isomorphic to the call-by-value λ-calculus with the ordinary callcc operator.

However, callcc isn't the only effectful operation we are interested in — callcc alone is not capable of giving a direct-style representation of other effects like exception handling and mutable references. Instead, there is a variant of this *classical* mode of control, exemplified by the shift and reset operators [7], called *delimited control* or *composable continuations* because the reach of a control operator can be delimited in scope and continuations can be composed like ordinary functions. Filinski [15] showed that delimited control is vastly more powerful than classical control: delimited control operators can give a direct-style representation of any monadic effect in a call-by-value language. The call-by-value λ-calculus extended with the shift and reset operators [7] has been particularly well-studied, as they have a simple definition in terms of continuation composition and an equational theory due to Kameyama and Hasegawa [19].

Back in the setting of the $\lambda\mu$-calculus, a simple variant of the call-by-name calculus, attributed to de Groote [10], takes a more relaxed view of the syntax. Although these two calculi have been considered the same for typed programs, Saurin [31] discovered that in the untyped setting, de Groote's relaxed variant of the $\lambda\mu$-calculus, there called $\Lambda\mu$, enjoys a form of observational completeness — if two terms cannot be proven equal then they exhibit observably different behavior — which Parigot's original $\lambda\mu$-calculus does not have. Even more, Herbelin and Ghilezan [17] discovered that the call-by-name $\Lambda\mu$-calculus provides a theory for delimited control in a non-strict functional language: the syntactic relaxation gives rise to a native form of composable continuations with a call-by-name evaluation order.

Here, we show that the call-by-value interpretation of the $\lambda\mu$-calculus contains a latent theory of delimited control in strict func-

ICFP '14, September 1–6, 2014, Gothenburg, Sweden.

http://dx.doi.org/10.1145/2628136.2628147

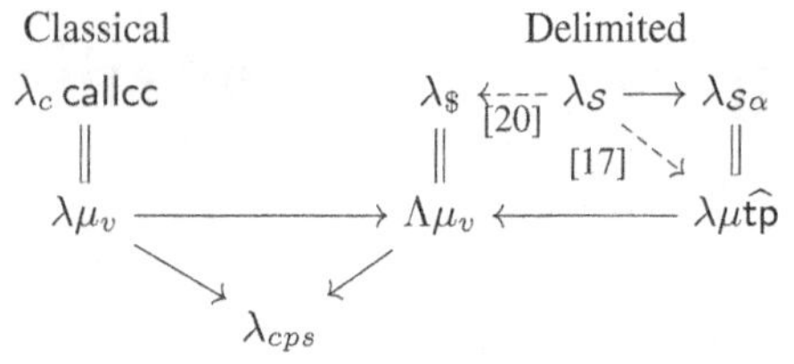

Figure 1. Correspondences of classical and delimited control.

$$V \in Value ::= x \mid \lambda x.M$$
$$M, N \in Term ::= V \mid M\ N$$
$$E \in EvalCxt ::= \Box \mid E\ M \mid V\ E$$

β_v	$(\lambda x.M)\ V = M\,\{V/x\}$
η_v	$\lambda x.V\ x = V$
β_Ω	$(\lambda x.E[x])\ M = E[M]$

Figure 2. The syntax and axioms of the pure λ_c-calculus.

tional languages as well. No new programming constructs are needed. No new rules are required. All we need to do is unshackle the syntactic restrictions on programs in the $\lambda\mu$-calculus. Key to this approach is the fact that the syntax of Parigot's $\lambda\mu$-calculus disallows programs from observing the result of invoking a continuation. Removing this restriction gives us an inherit interpretation of such programs from the existing theory, which turns out to be a delimited form of continuations. The call-by-value interpretation of the $\Lambda\mu$-calculus is particularly interesting because the role of the delimiter is more intricate than in the call-by-name setting, and has given rise to distinct control operators with different observational properties. In particular, we discover that the call-by-value $\Lambda\mu_v$-calculus is isomorphic to the call-by-value λ-calculus with the less-studied $\mathsf{shift_0}$ and $\mathsf{reset_0}$ delimited control operators, as described by Materzok's [20] $\lambda_\$$ theory. Therefore, the syntactic relaxation of the $\lambda\mu$-calculus gives us a canonical bridge from classical to delimited control in both the call-by-name and call-by-value settings.

The connections between the various control calculi are pictured in Figure 1, which contains both λ-based (λ_c callcc [28] for callcc, $\lambda_\$$ [20] for $\mathsf{shift_0}$, λ_S [19] for shift) and $\lambda\mu$-based ($\lambda\mu_v$ [17], $\Lambda\mu_v$, $\lambda\mu\widehat{\mathsf{tp}}$ [17]) approaches. The syntactic embedding from the more restricted $\lambda\mu_v$-calculus to the more relaxed $\Lambda\mu_v$-calculus provides the connection between the classical and delimited worlds, while maintaining soundness and completeness with respect to a typical *continuation-passing style* (CPS) transformation. We also spell out the connection with shift and reset, which can be embedded into $\mathsf{shift_0}$ [22] and the $\lambda\mu\widehat{\mathsf{tp}}$-calculus [17]. In particular, the connection with the $\Lambda\mu_v$-calculus suggests that, similar to Sabry's [28] theory of callcc, Kameyama and Hasegawa's [19] λ_S theory of shift can also benefit from the use of continuation variables (here called $\lambda_{S\alpha}$) to provide a more powerful tool for reasoning about open programs.

Along the way, we introduce a proof methodology for establishing an equational correspondence [29] between two theories that takes advantage of the typical *compositionality* and *hygiene* of program transformations in order to simplify the correspondence. In short, a general class of transformations preserves the basic structures of equality relations and substitution. Additionally, we connect the study of classical and delimited control in call-by-value and call-by-name languages by presenting a single *parametric* $\Lambda\mu$-calculus, similar to the parametric λ-calculus [27], that subsumes the equational theories for both evaluation strategies. The parametric calculus can serve as a bridge between the existing work on type systems and semantics for call-by-name $\Lambda\mu$-calculi and call-by-value control operators in the λ-calculus. We further exercise the parametric $\Lambda\mu$-calculus as a tool for studying evaluation strategies and control by deriving a call-by-need calculus with delimited control from the pure call-by-need λ-calculus [1].

In summary, our contributions are:

- We show that the call-by-value equational theory for the $\lambda\mu$-calculus that is sound and complete with respect to the usual CPS transformation remains sound and complete for the syntactically relaxed $\Lambda\mu$-calculus.
- We demonstrate a general technique of using compositional and hygienic program transformations to more easily relate the syntactic theories of different languages.
- We classify various call-by-value control effects, expressed by primitive control operators, by their correspondence with subsets of the $\Lambda\mu$-calculus: callcc corresponds with Parigot's original $\lambda\mu$-calculus, shift and reset correspond with a subset of $\Lambda\mu$ equal to Ariola *et al.*'s $\lambda\mu\widehat{\mathsf{tp}}$-calculus, and $\mathsf{shift_0}$ and $\mathsf{reset_0}$ correspond to the full $\Lambda\mu$-calculus.
- We generalize the call-by-name and call-by-value theories of the $\Lambda\mu$-calculus into a single parametric theory for control that can be instantiated by different evaluation strategies.
- We generate a strategy for the parametric theory of $\Lambda\mu$ that corresponds with Ariola and Felleisen's [1] call-by-need λ-calculus, thereby giving a theory of both classical and delimited control with lazy evaluation and sharing (memoization).

Next, we begin by reviewing ways to reason about callcc in the call-by-value λ-calculus and how Parigot's $\lambda\mu$-calculus provides a well-behaved syntactic restriction of first-class control operators.

2. Callcc and classical control

To understand control operators in a strict functional language, we first look to the flow of control in the pure, call-by-value λ_c-calculus [26], shown in Figure 2. The syntax of λ_c is the λ-calculus, which includes variables x, function abstractions $\lambda x.M$, and function calls $M\ N$. We can reason about the behavior of programs in this calculus by using the equational theory of Moggi's [23] computational λ-calculus, whose axioms are also given in Figure 2.[1] We can more specifically describe how to reduce a term to a value in terms of an operational semantics. Evaluation contexts E point out the current position of evaluation where we need to reduce the program, signified by the "hole" $\Box$, and are defined as usual for the pure call-by-value λ-calculus. We write $E[M]$ for plugging a term M into the context E by replacing the "hole" $\Box$ with M. In particular, evaluation contexts are defined so that the arguments to a function call are evaluated first and a function only receives a value, as described by the β_v axiom. Therefore, we can describe the operational semantics of the λ_c-calculus with the single rule:

$$E[(\lambda x.M)\ V] \mapsto E[M\,\{V/x\}]$$

It follows that β_v is an *operational* [18] rule, since it is used during evaluation, whereas η_v and β_Ω are instead *observational* properties that do not happen during evaluation, but also do not change the observable result of a program. Because the only operational step

[1] Note that the axioms must always be used in a way that is *hygienic*, so that they respect the static binding of variables given by the usual definitions of *free* and *bound* variables, and $M\,\{V/x\}$ stands for the usual capture-avoiding substitution of V for x in M. In the case of λ_c, x must not be free in V for η_v to hold, and x must not be free in E for β_Ω to hold. Similar such side conditions apply for the axioms in the other theories that follow.

$$
\begin{array}{lr}
C_{lift} & E[\mathsf{callcc}\ M] = \mathsf{callcc}(\lambda\alpha.E[M\ (\lambda x.\alpha(E[x]))]) \\
C_{abort} & E[\alpha\ M] = \alpha\ M \\
C_{current} & \mathsf{callcc}(\lambda\alpha.\alpha\ M) = \mathsf{callcc}(\lambda\alpha.M) \\
C_{elim} & \mathsf{callcc}(\lambda\alpha.M) = M
\end{array}
$$

Figure 3. The axioms of control in the λ_c callcc equational theory.

matches exactly the β_v axiom, it is straightforward to check that the equational theory is as strong as the operational semantics: if the operational semantics reaches a value so does the equational theory.

Languages like Scheme and SML/NJ allow programmers the ability to manipulate the control flow of their programs by giving them access to *continuations* — a representation of an evaluation context — as an object on par with first-class functions. One way to model such control effects in strict functional programming languages is to extend the λ_c-calculus with primitive operators that create or use continuations. The classic control operator to consider is callcc, first introduced in Scheme. Informally, when we call callcc in Scheme with a (higher-order) function h, the operator: (1) takes a snapshot of the current evaluation context, (2) wraps the evaluation context inside of a first-class function (the continuation) which jumps back to the currently active context when called, and (3) calls h with the continuation as its argument.

We can explain the behavior of first-class control more formally by extending the λ_c-calculus with callcc as a primitive function constant. To account for the continuation functions generated by callcc, we denote the continuation value captured in the context E as $[E]$, giving us the following operational steps:

$$
\begin{aligned}
E[(\lambda x.M)\ V] &\mapsto E[M\,\{V/x\}] \\
E[\mathsf{callcc}\ V] &\mapsto E[V\ [E]] \\
E[[E']\ V] &\mapsto E'[V]
\end{aligned}
$$

The second two rules explain how to evaluate callcc and continuations. To perform a call to callcc in an evaluation context E, wrap a copy of the context into the function $[E]$ and pass it along to the argument of callcc. To call $[E]$ at some later point during evaluation, "jump" out of the current evaluation context and restore the state of the program to E, plugging the argument into the hole of the context.

Example 1. To illustrate the behavior of callcc, consider the following term that captures its (empty) evaluation context and returns a function that, when given an input x, ends the program by "jumping" out of its calling context with the constant function $\lambda\_.x$.

$$
\begin{aligned}
\mathsf{callcc}(\lambda k.\lambda x.k\ (\lambda\_.x)) &\mapsto (\lambda k.\lambda x.k\ (\lambda\_.x))\ [\square] \\
&\mapsto \lambda x.[\square]\ (\lambda\_.x)
\end{aligned}
$$

If we use the function $\lambda x.[\square]\ (\lambda\_.x)$ in a larger program, we can see how the continuation $[\square]$ immediately ends the program and returns a constant function as the final result.

$$
\begin{aligned}
((\lambda x.[\square]\ (\lambda\_.x))\ 2) + 10 &\mapsto ([\square]\ (\lambda\_.2)) + 10 \\
&\mapsto \lambda\_.2
\end{aligned}
$$

End example 1.

Like with the pure calculus, we would like to also describe the behavior of callcc with an equational theory. However, because the operational steps for callcc and continuations manipulate their *entire* evaluation context, we cannot just apply them in an arbitrary sub-term of a program. This sort of issue is addressed by the equational theories for control developed by Felleisen and Sabry [14, 28, 29]. In particular, we will use Sabry's [28] theory of control, here called λ_c callcc, which extends the λ_c theory with the axioms of callcc shown in Figure 3. This theory extends the λ_c-calculus with the primitive function callcc and makes use of a distinguished set of *continuation variables*, α, β, *etc.* Continuation variables may only be introduced by the form $\mathsf{callcc}(\lambda\alpha.M)$, so that a term like $(\lambda\alpha.\alpha\ y)\ (\lambda x.x)$ is syntactically illegal. Note that this means there are two different syntactic forms that refer to callcc, either as an ordinary function application $\mathsf{callcc}\ (\lambda x.M)$ or the special form $\mathsf{callcc}(\lambda\alpha.M)$, which are equated by C_{lift}.

Unfortunately, unlike the case with the pure λ_c-calculus, it is no longer so clear how the equational theory relates to the operational semantics. In actuality, the equational theory is no longer as strong as the operational semantics. The program in Example 1 shows the problem, where there is no way to eliminate the top-most application of callcc in the term $\mathsf{callcc}(\lambda k.\lambda x.k\ (\lambda\_.x))$ so that it cannot be equated to a value. Therefore, for general terms there is a disconnect between the operational and equational accounts of callcc. However, is it possible that we can find some specific subset of "well-behaved" terms where the two semantics always coincide?

Example 2. Let's extend the term in Example 1 so that rather than returning its final result, it instead finishes by "jumping" to some continuation α. The operational interpretation of the term is similar to before, where we now supply α with a function that forms a constant function and jumps out of its calling context back to α.

$$
\begin{aligned}
\alpha\ (\mathsf{callcc}(\lambda k.\lambda x.k\ (\lambda\_.x))) &\mapsto \alpha\ ((\lambda k.\lambda x.k\ (\lambda\_.x))[\alpha\ \square]) \\
&\mapsto \alpha\ (\lambda x.[\alpha\ \square]\ (\lambda\_.x))
\end{aligned}
$$

If we use this function in a larger program, it behaves similarly to the function from Example 1, except that we now end the program by supplying a result to α rather than implicitly returning a value.

$$((\lambda x.[\alpha\ \square]\ (\lambda\_.x))\ 2) + 10 \mapsto\!\!\!\!\to \alpha\ (\lambda\_.2)$$

The equational theory in Figure 3 is capable of simulating this operational evaluation. In particular, the first step, which completely eliminates callcc, is achieved with the C_{lift}, C_{abort}, and C_{elim} axioms, resulting in a jump that passes a similar function to α. This sequence of steps is possible because we know that α will inevitably jump out of its calling context, so that any surrounding evaluation context is redundant garbage.

$$
\begin{aligned}
&\alpha\ (\mathsf{callcc}(\lambda k.\lambda x.k\ (\lambda b.lankx))) \\
&=_{C_{lift}} \mathsf{callcc}(\lambda\beta.\alpha\ ((\lambda k.\lambda x.k\ (\lambda\_.x))\ (\lambda y.\beta\ (\alpha\ y)))) \\
&=_{C_{abort}} \mathsf{callcc}(\lambda\beta.\alpha\ ((\lambda k.\lambda x.k\ (\lambda\_.x))\ (\lambda y.\alpha\ y))) \\
&=_{C_{elim}} \alpha\ ((\lambda k.\lambda x.k\ (\lambda\_.x))\ (\lambda y.\alpha\ y)) \\
&=_{\beta_v} \alpha\ (\lambda x.(\lambda y.\alpha\ y)\ (\lambda\_.x))
\end{aligned}
$$

Thus, calling a continuation variable like α serves as a marker that signifies the end of a usable evaluation context, and allows us to recognize the rest of the calling context as garbage and end the call to callcc early. The function that α receives behaves exactly like the one that was created by the operational semantics. For example, if we call it in the same context as before, we still end up with a jump that returns the constant function $\lambda\_.2$ to α.

$$
\begin{aligned}
((\lambda x.(\lambda y.\alpha\ y)\ (\lambda\_.x))\ 2) + 10 &=_{\beta_v} ((\lambda y.\alpha\ y)\ (\lambda\_.2)) + 10 \\
&=_{\beta_v} (\alpha\ (\lambda\_.2)) + 10 \\
&=_{C_{abort}} \alpha\ (\lambda\_.2)
\end{aligned}
$$

End example 2.

Example 2 shows how "jumps" are important for understanding callcc. By starting with a jump instead of a general term, we fix the mismatch between the operational semantics and equational theory. As it turns out [3], this concept is explicitly expressed by Parigot's $\lambda\mu$-calculus [25], in which jumps, referred to as *commands*, are given prominent status. A call-by-value version of the $\lambda\mu$-calculus is given in Figure 4, where we extend the syntax of the λ-calculus

$$V \in \mathit{Value} ::= x \mid \lambda x.M$$
$$M, N \in \mathit{Term} ::= V \mid M\ N \mid \mu\alpha.c$$
$$c \in \mathit{Command} ::= [\alpha]M$$
$$E \in \mathit{EvalCxt} ::= \Box \mid E\ M \mid V\ E$$

$$\mu_v \qquad [\alpha](E[\mu\beta.c]) = c\,\{[\alpha](E[M])/[\beta]M\}$$
$$\eta_\mu \qquad \mu\alpha.[\alpha]M = M$$
$$\beta_\mu \qquad (\lambda x.\mu\alpha.[\beta]M)\ N = \mu\alpha.[\beta](\lambda x.M)\ N$$

Figure 4. The syntax and axioms of control in the $\lambda\mu_v$-calculus.

with co-variables $\alpha, \beta, \ldots$ along with their abstraction $\mu\alpha.c$ and application $[\alpha]M$. Intuitively, the calculus can be viewed as imposing a syntactic restriction on the use of the callcc operator, where it must always be applied to a λ-abstraction whose body immediately jumps, as in callcc$(\lambda\alpha.\beta\ M)$.

The $\lambda\mu_v$ equational theory extends λ_c with the axioms of control given in Figure 4. Note that the axiom describing the behavior of a μ-abstraction makes use of *structural substitution* [2] to perform a pattern-matching substitution on terms, following the normal criteria for static scope and avoiding variable capture. The substitution $\{[\alpha]E[N]/[\beta]N\}$ replaces every command of the form $[\beta]N$, for an arbitrary term N, with $[\alpha]E[N]$. We can also describe the $\lambda\mu_v$-calculus in terms of an operational semantics, similar to λ_c and λ_c callcc. In particular, we always evaluate a command of the form $[\alpha]M$ according to the following two rules:

$$[\alpha]E[(\lambda x.M)\ V] \mapsto [\alpha]E[M\,\{V/x\}]$$
$$[\alpha]E[\mu\beta.c] \mapsto c\,\{[\alpha](E[M])/[\beta]M\}$$

Notice that the first rule is exactly the β_v axiom, as usual, and the second rule is exactly the μ_v axiom. Therefore, it is straightforward to show how the operational semantics and equational theory coincide. The μ_v axiom is the operational rule for implementing μ-abstractions, whereas η_μ and β_μ express observational properties of control.

Example 3. We can transcribe the λ_c callcc term from Example 2 into a command in the $\lambda\mu_v$-calculus by explicating some of the implicit behavior of the callcc operator. In particular, we need to explicitly say that we are returning a result to our current context, and state that invoking the bound co-variable will abort with the form $\mu\_.[\beta]M$. This gives us a command that produces a similar result as Example 2.

$$[\alpha]\mu\beta.[\beta](\lambda x.\mu\_.[\beta](\lambda\_.x)) \mapsto [\alpha](\lambda x.\mu\_.[\alpha](\lambda\_.x))$$

As before, when we call the function passed to α in a similar context, we see the similar result $[\alpha]\lambda\_.2$.

$$[\delta](((\lambda x.\mu\_.[\alpha](\lambda\_.x))\ 2) + 10) \mapsto [\delta]((\mu\_.[\alpha](\lambda\_.2)) + 10)$$
$$\mapsto [\alpha](\lambda\_.2)$$

The $\lambda\mu_v$ equational theory gives us the same result as the above: every operational step is an application of either the β_v or μ_v axioms. *End example* 3.

3. Compositional equational correspondence

We have mentioned that Parigot's $\lambda\mu$-calculus models the λ-calculus with callcc, but how can we relate the two equational theories? To answer this question, we will turn to Sabry and Felleisen's [29] concept of *equational correspondence*. In the general case, we have two equational theories — a theory Eq_S for equating programs in language L_S (for source) and a theory Eq_T for equating programs in language L_T (for target). We can say that Eq_S is in equational correspondence with Eq_T if and only if there are two translations, $\mathcal{T}^S$ from L_S to L_T and $\mathcal{S}^T$ from L_T back to L_S, that satisfy the following two criteria:[2]

(1) $\mathcal{T}^S$ and $\mathcal{S}^T$ are *inverses* up to Eq_S and Eq_T: $Eq_S \vdash \mathcal{S}^T[\![\mathcal{T}^S[\![M]\!]]\!] = M$ and $Eq_T \vdash \mathcal{T}^S[\![\mathcal{S}^T[\![P]\!]]\!] = P$.

(2) Eq_S and Eq_T are *sound* with respect to each other: $Eq_S \vdash M = N$ implies $Eq_T \vdash \mathcal{T}^S[\![M]\!] = \mathcal{T}^S[\![N]\!]$ and $Eq_T \vdash P = Q$ implies $Eq_S \vdash \mathcal{S}^T[\![P]\!] = \mathcal{S}^T[\![Q]\!]$.

Intuitively, criteria (1) guarantees that both languages are big enough to reflect each other, and criteria (2) guarantees that the translations preserve the intended semantics. When taken together, both criteria are enough to prove the additional property:

(3) Eq_S and Eq_T are *complete* with respect to each other: $Eq_T \vdash \mathcal{T}^S[\![M]\!] = \mathcal{T}^S[\![N]\!]$ implies $Eq_S \vdash M = N$ and $Eq_S \vdash \mathcal{S}^T[\![P]\!] = \mathcal{S}^T[\![Q]\!]$ implies $Eq_T \vdash P = Q$.

The *soundness and completeness* of a transformation is a weaker result than an equational correspondence: it expresses an embedding of the source language into the target such that the full source language corresponds to the image of the transformation. An equational correspondence adds the additional guarantee that the transformation covers the full target language, forming an isomorphism up to the two equational theories.

In order to establish an equational correspondence, we must surely show that the axioms of the two theories are inter-derivable. However, knowing that the axioms work out is not enough to show that every equation is preserved by the transformations — we also have to take care of the additional inference principles of the equational theories. Uses of reflexivity, transitivity, and symmetry in the two theories coincides for any pair of transformations. The biggest obstacle is *congruence*, the property that equality may be lifted into any context C so that $M = N$ implies $C[M] = C[N]$. However, we can guarantee that even congruence is preserved for a wide class of transformations. Therefore, we introduce a general proof methodology that takes advantage of typical properties of transformations to simplify establishing the correspondence.

Fortunately, many program transformations are *compositional*, meaning that the transformation of a term depends only on the transformation of its subterms. Compositionality of a transform, $[\![\_]\!]$, implies a form of context-free interpretation, so that for any context C in the source language, there exists a unique context in the target, denoted $[\![C]\!]$, such that $[\![C[M]]\!] \triangleq [\![C]\!][[\![M]\!]]$ for any M.[3] Crucially, there is a well-defined meaning for every context that can be given in isolation of both its input and its surrounding context. This property guarantees that the transformations respect congruence: if we apply the equation $Eq_S \vdash M = N$ inside a context C, then by congruence in the target language we also have that $Eq_T \vdash [\![C]\!][[\![M]\!]] = [\![C]\!][[\![N]\!]]$, where the transformation of C is not affected by the fact that we are plugging in a different term. Therefore, when working with an equational correspondence by compositional transformations, it is enough to show that the axioms of one theory are provable by the other — the other properties of equality follow.

[2] The notation $Eq_S \vdash M = N$ means that M and N are equated by Eq_S.

[3] We can plug one context into another, $C[C']$, in the obvious way by treating C' as a term. This means that contexts form a monoid with the empty context, $\Box$, as the identity element and plugging-in as the composition operation. Therefore, a compositional transformation can be seen as a monoid homomorphism that respects the compositional nature of contexts: $[\![\Box]\!] = \Box$ and $[\![C[C']]\!] = [\![C]\!][[\![C']\!]]$. In a language with different syntactic types, like $\lambda\mu_v$, contexts instead form a category and a compositional transformation is a functor between contexts in the source and target.

Proposition 1. *Compositional transformations preserve the structure of an equality relation: reflexivity, transitivity, symmetry, and congruence.*

Another obstacle that compositionality allows us to avoid is handling substitution. Since some axioms, like β_v, may rely on substitution, we end up having to show that substitution in the source and target language are compatible with one another. Since we are working with call-by-value languages that only allow substitution for a subset of terms, we would need a property of the form $[\![M]\!]\left\{[\![V]\!]^V/x\right\} = [\![M\{V/x\}]\!]$, where V is a value and $[\![V]\!]^V$ is the embedding of V into a target-level value.[4] First, we point out that ordinary capture-avoiding substitution can be implemented by an iterative procedure that replaces the free occurrences of the variable one by one. For example, when we are substituting V for x in a term M, we can identify a particular occurrence of the free variable x in $M = C[x]$ and replace x with V. If we can't find such an x then the substitution does nothing. Second, we also require that the transformation is *hygienic*, so that it does not capture or escape the static variables of its input. In other words, hygiene guarantees that C captures the variable x if and only if $[\![C]\!]$ does. Third, if source variables are values and are embedded directly into target variables, so that $[\![x]\!]^V \triangleq x$, then this procedure maps directly to the target language:

$$\begin{aligned}[\![C[x]]\!]\left\{[\![V]\!]^V/x\right\} &= [\![C]\!][[\![x]\!]^V]\left\{[\![V]\!]^V/x\right\}\\ &= [\![C]\!][[\![V]\!]^V]\left\{[\![V]\!]^V/x\right\} = [\![C[V]]\!]\left\{[\![V]\!]^V/x\right\}\end{aligned}$$

Structural substitution, which replaces one context with another, follows similarly.

Proposition 2. *Let $[\![\_]\!]$ be a hygienic, compositional transformation, and $[\![\_]\!]^V$ be the transformation of substitutable terms. If $[\![x]\!]^V \triangleq x$ then $[\![M]\!]\left\{[\![V]\!]^V/x\right\} \triangleq [\![M\{V/x\}]\!]$. Furthermore, $[\![M]\!]\{[\![C']\!]/[\![C]\!]\} \triangleq [\![M\{C'/C\}]\!]$.*

Therefore, in order to establish an equational correspondence with hygienic, compositional transformations, we only need to show that (1) the two transformations are inverses, and (2) the axioms of the two theories, which may rely on substitution, are inter-derivable. The rest of the correspondence follows generically from Propositions 1 and 2. Furthermore, one nice property about an equational correspondence, as well as soundness and completeness, is that it composes transitively [30]: if Eq_S is in equational correspondence with Eq_T and Eq_T is in equational correspondence with Eq_U, then Eq_S is also in equational correspondence with Eq_U. This fact lets us relate two theories in several steps by going through some intermediate languages.

4. Correspondence of $\lambda\mu_v$ and callcc

We can apply the proof technique described in Section 3 to formally relate the $\lambda\mu_v$-calculus to callcc in a call-by-value λ-calculus. First, we need to explain how to translate one language into the other in terms of two inverse, compositional transformations, spelling out the details of the transcription process used in Example 3. The interesting points of the syntactic translations are given in Figure 5, and the rest is defined homomorphically. With these two transformations, the equational correspondence follows straightforwardly from the outlined methodology. Compositionality and hygiene of the transformations is confirmed by observing that every clause in the grammars of $\lambda\mu_v$ and λ_c callcc is exactly defined by one clause in the transformation, that there are no additional parameters to the transformations, and that the transformations do not cause capture or escape of free static variables.

[4] Note that in a typical call-by-value language where values are implicitly included in general terms, we may have that the more general transformation $[\![V]\!]$ introduces a non-trivial context C, so that $[\![V]\!] \triangleq C[[\![V]\!]^V]$.

$$\begin{aligned}\mathcal{K}[\![\mu\alpha.c]\!] &\triangleq \mathsf{callcc}(\lambda\alpha.\mathcal{K}[\![c]\!])\\ \mathcal{K}[\![[\alpha]M]\!] &\triangleq \alpha\,\mathcal{K}[\![M]\!]\end{aligned}$$

$$\begin{aligned}\mathcal{K}^{-1}[\![\mathsf{callcc}]\!] &\triangleq \lambda h.\mu\alpha.[\alpha]h\;(\lambda x.\mu\_.[\alpha]x)\\ \mathcal{K}^{-1}[\![\mathsf{callcc}(\lambda\alpha.M)]\!] &\triangleq \mu\alpha.[\alpha]\mathcal{K}^{-1}[\![M]\!]\\ \mathcal{K}^{-1}[\![\alpha]\!] &\triangleq \lambda x.\mu\_.[\alpha]x\end{aligned}$$

Figure 5. The isomorphism between $\lambda\mu_v$ and λ_c callcc.

$$\begin{aligned}\mathcal{C}[\![x]\!]^V &\triangleq x\\ \mathcal{C}[\![\lambda x.M]\!]^V &\triangleq \lambda(x,\alpha).\mathcal{C}[\![M]\!]^M\;\alpha\\ \mathcal{C}[\![V]\!]^M &\triangleq \lambda\alpha.\alpha\,\mathcal{C}[\![V]\!]^V\\ \mathcal{C}[\![M\;N]\!]^M &\triangleq \lambda\alpha.\mathcal{C}[\![M]\!]^M\;\lambda x.\mathcal{C}[\![N]\!]^M\,\lambda y.x\;(y,\alpha)\\ \mathcal{C}[\![\mu\alpha.c]\!]^M &\triangleq \lambda\alpha.\mathcal{C}[\![c]\!]^c\\ \mathcal{C}[\![[\alpha]M]\!]^c &\triangleq \mathcal{C}[\![M]\!]^M\;\alpha\end{aligned}$$

Figure 6. CPS transformation $\mathcal{C}$ from $\lambda\mu_v$ to the λ-calculus.

Theorem 1. *λ_c callcc is in equational correspondence with $\lambda\mu_v$.*

Proof. The equational correspondence is formed by the $\mathcal{K}$ and $\mathcal{K}^{-1}$ transformations. Since the transformations are compositional and hygienic, we only need to show (1) that they are inverses of one another and (2) that the axioms of the two theories are inter-derivable. Criteria (1) follows by mutual induction on terms, values, *etc.* Criteria (2) follows by cases on the axioms. □

Crucially, the C_{abort} [28] axiom lets us recognize the abortive nature of continuations, even for free continuation variables. This lets us bridge the gap between Felleisen's [14] $\mathcal{C}$ operator and callcc. Intuitively, $\mathcal{C}(\lambda\alpha.M)$ may be encoded as $\mathsf{callcc}(\lambda\alpha.\mathtt{tp}\;M)$, where tp is a free continuation variable that stands for the "top-level." We then run a term M by explicitly marking the top-level of the program as in the jump $\mathtt{tp}\;M$. This same free tp co-variable also shows up in the correspondence [3] between $\mathcal{C}$ and $\lambda\mu_v$.

We can also use a similar methodology to verify that the equational theory of the $\lambda\mu_v$-calculus makes sense — that there are no equalities between programs that behave differently, or that we are not missing some crucial axiom that we would need to relate two similar programs. A now common technique for getting around this dilemma is to reduce the theory in question to another, more well-understood theory. This allows for the established understanding of the target theory to be reflected back to the source. In particular, it is typical to translate the language through a *continuation-passing style* (CPS) transformation into the λ-calculus (or a variant thereof), and to use the induced semantics that comes from the resulting λ-calculus terms as a definition of the semantics of the source language. The goal, then, is to establish an equational correspondence between the source language and the image of the CPS transformation in the target language.

Figure 6 gives a CPS transformation for terms, values, and commands of the $\lambda\mu_v$-calculus, based on Plotkin's [26] call-by-value CPS transformation. The CPS transformation is defined so that it does not depend on the evaluation strategy of the target λ-calculus

$$c \in \mathit{Command} ::= [q]M \qquad q \in \mathit{CoTerm} ::= \alpha \mid \tilde{\mu}x.c$$

$$\begin{array}{llll} \beta_v & (\lambda x.M)\,V = M\,\{V/x\} & \eta_v & \lambda x.V\,x = V \\ \mu_q & [q]\mu\alpha.c = c\,\{q/\alpha\} & \eta_\mu & \mu\alpha.[\alpha]M = M \\ \tilde{\mu}_v & [\tilde{\mu}x.c]V = c\,\{V/x\} & \eta_{\tilde{\mu}} & \tilde{\mu}x.[q]x = q \end{array}$$

$$\varsigma_v \quad E[M] = \mu\alpha.[\tilde{\mu}x.[\alpha]E[x]]M$$

Figure 7. The syntax and axioms of control in the $\lambda\mu\tilde{\mu}_v$-calculus.

$$\mathcal{C}[\![[q]M]\!]^c \triangleq \mathcal{C}[\![M]\!]^M\,\mathcal{C}[\![q]\!]^q \quad \mathcal{C}[\![\alpha]\!]^q \triangleq \alpha \quad \mathcal{C}[\![\tilde{\mu}x.c]\!]^q \triangleq \lambda x.\mathcal{C}[\![c]\!]^c$$

Figure 8. CPS transformation $\mathcal{C}$ for co-terms of $\lambda\mu\tilde{\mu}_v$.

— the argument to every function call is a value, so that the resulting term behaves the same according to both a call-by-name and call-by-value evaluation strategy. Intuitively, the transformation turns every term of the $\lambda\mu_v$-calculus into a function that accepts a continuation as a description of the entire future of the computation. The way to read the term $\mathcal{C}[\![M]\!]^M\ \alpha$ is "run M, and when it is done, the value it returns is passed to α." For instance, a value immediately returns, so the transformation of a value immediately calls the continuation and allows it to take over. The most complicated case is for function application $M\ N$, which can be read as: in a calling context α, first (1) run M and wait for it to return a value x, second (2) run N and wait for it to return a value y, and third (3) call x with y inside the original calling context α. Notice that the control constructs of $\lambda\mu_v$ translate directly to the concept of continuations used by the transformation: a μ-abstraction gives a name to the continuation and a command runs a term in a chosen continuation. Also note that, similar to the axioms of $\lambda\mu_v$, the CPS transformation must be hygienic and take care to respect the static binding of variables. For instance, in the transformation $\mathcal{C}[\![\lambda x.M]\!]^V \triangleq \lambda(x,\alpha).\mathcal{C}[\![M]\!]\ \alpha$, the x introduced by the λ-abstraction on the left must be the *same* x that is referenced by $\mathcal{C}[\![M]\!]$ on the right, but the α that is introduced must *not* be free in $\mathcal{C}[\![M]\!]$ to avoid unintentional variable capture.

There are some complications that arise when trying to form the equational correspondence between the $\lambda\mu_v$ and λ theories, which is typical when reasoning about CPS transformations. The primary issue is that we need to translate CPS terms back to the source calculus. For instance, if we see the CPS term $\alpha\ V$, we want to turn it into some command $[\alpha]V'$. However, for other cases, the reverse CPS transformation is not so obvious. Therefore, we introduce an intermediate calculus that is isomorphic to $\lambda\mu_v$, but is more closely connected with the CPS transformation. Borrowing syntax for the sequent calculus from Curien and Herbelin [6], we extend the $\lambda\mu_v$-calculus with $\tilde{\mu}$-abstractions as the opposite of μ-abstractions, giving us the $\lambda\mu\tilde{\mu}_v$-calculus in Figure 7. Note that this calculus no longer relies on structural substitution to capture an evaluation context, but instead first converts an evaluation context into a $\tilde{\mu}$-abstraction (by the ς_v axiom) as in the following example:

$$\begin{aligned} f\ (\mu\alpha.[\beta]\lambda x.\mu\_.[\alpha]x) &=_{\varsigma_v} \mu\alpha.'[\tilde{\mu}y.[\alpha'](f\ y)]\mu\alpha.[\beta]\lambda x.\mu\_.[\alpha]x \\ &=_{\mu_q} \mu\alpha.'[\beta]\lambda x.\mu\_.[\tilde{\mu}y.[\alpha'](f\ y)]x \\ &=_{\tilde{\mu}_v} \mu\alpha.'[\beta]\lambda x.\mu\_.[\alpha'](f\ x) \end{aligned}$$

Intuitively, the ς_v axiom recognizes the fact that evaluation contexts are *transformations* from inputs to outputs, and gives a name both to the input end, x, and the output end, α. In other words, an evaluation context is not only missing an input denoted by $\Box$, it is *also* missing an "output" that says what to do with the result. We also extend the CPS transformation as shown in Figure 8 to account for the new syntax, showing how the $\tilde{\mu}$-abstractions correspond exactly with λ-abstraction continuations. That way, it is relatively easy to translate a continuation of the form $\lambda x.M$ created by the CPS transformation back into the $\lambda\mu\tilde{\mu}_v$-calculus.

$$M^c ::= V^M\,V^q \mid V^q\,V^V \mid V^V\,(V^V, V^q) \quad V^M ::= \lambda\alpha.M^c$$
$$V^q ::= \alpha \mid \lambda x.M^c \quad V^V ::= x \mid \lambda(x,\alpha).M^c$$

Figure 9. The image of the CPS transformation of $\lambda\mu\tilde{\mu}_v$ by $\mathcal{C}$.

$$\begin{aligned} \mathcal{C}^{-1}[\![V^M\,V^q]\!]^c &\triangleq [\mathcal{C}^{-1}[\![V^q]\!]^q]\mathcal{C}^{-1}[\![V^M]\!]^M \\ \mathcal{C}^{-1}[\![V^q\,V^V]\!]^c &\triangleq [\mathcal{C}^{-1}[\![V^q]\!]^q]\mathcal{C}^{-1}[\![V^V]\!]^V \\ \mathcal{C}^{-1}[\![V^V\,(V'^V, V^q)]\!]^c &\triangleq [\mathcal{C}^{-1}[\![V^q]\!]^q]\mathcal{C}^{-1}[\![V^V]\!]^V\,\mathcal{C}^{-1}[\![V'^V]\!]^V \\ \mathcal{C}^{-1}[\![\lambda\alpha.M^c]\!]^M &\triangleq \mu\alpha.\mathcal{C}^{-1}[\![M^c]\!]^c \end{aligned}$$
$$\mathcal{C}^{-1}[\![\alpha]\!]^q \triangleq \alpha \qquad \mathcal{C}^{-1}[\![\lambda x.M^c]\!]^q \triangleq \tilde{\mu}x.\mathcal{C}^{-1}[\![M^c]\!]^c$$
$$\mathcal{C}^{-1}[\![x]\!]^V \triangleq x \quad \mathcal{C}^{-1}[\![\lambda(x,\alpha).M^c]\!]^V \triangleq \lambda x.\mu\alpha.\mathcal{C}^{-1}[\![M^c]\!]^c$$

Figure 10. The inverse of $\mathcal{C}$ on the image of $\lambda\mu\tilde{\mu}_v$.

The second issue is that the $\mathcal{C}$ transformation does not "reach" every program in the λ-calculus, even if we restrict ourselves to terms where function arguments are always values. Because of this fact, it is impossible to translate the entire λ-calculus back into the $\lambda\mu\tilde{\mu}_v$-calculus (or $\lambda\mu_v$-calculus) in a meaningful way. Therefore, we need to determine the *image* of the CPS transformation of $\lambda\mu\tilde{\mu}_v$ — that is, the smallest subset of the λ-calculus that includes the transformation of every $\lambda\mu\tilde{\mu}_v$ term and is closed under reduction. The general target of the transformation is the λ-calculus extended with pairs constructed as (M, N) and deconstructed by λ-abstractions of the form $\lambda(x,y).M$. For our purposes, we reason about CPS terms with the usual β and η axioms of the λ-calculus along with the following two rules for pairs:

$$\begin{array}{ll} \beta^\times & (\lambda(x,y).M)\,(N_1,N_2) = M\,\{N_1,N_2/x,y\} \\ \eta^\times & \lambda(x,y).M\,(x,y) = M \end{array}$$

The subset of this calculus reachable by the $\mathcal{C}$ transform is shown in Figure 9. Intuitively, M^c, V^M, V^q, and V^V are the image of commands, terms, co-terms and values of the $\lambda\mu\tilde{\mu}_v$-calculus, respectively. Notice that V^V is always a function deconstructing a pair, and all instances of $\lambda(x,y).M$ are in V^V, so that we only need to apply the $\eta^\times$ axiom to values in V^V.

We can now provide an inverse translation from this subset of the λ-calculus back to the $\lambda\mu\tilde{\mu}_v$-calculus, as shown in Figure 10. Note that sending a $\lambda\mu\tilde{\mu}_v$ term through both transformations changes the term. Most of the changes, for values and for functions, just introduce an extra η_μ expansion. The worst case is if we start with the application $M\ N$, where we end up with

$$\mathcal{C}^{-1}[\![\mathcal{C}[\![M\ N]\!]^M]\!]^M \triangleq \mu\alpha.[\tilde{\mu}x.[\tilde{\mu}y.[\alpha]x\ y]N']M'$$

This term is reminiscent of Sabry's [28] technique of *continuation-grabbing style*, where we write a CPS term in more abstract syntax as a way to relate to languages with control effects. In that light, we are relying on μ-abstractions to grab the continuation, on co-terms to represent continuations, and on commands to represent sending a continuation to a term.

With both transformations, it is now relatively straightforward to show the soundness and completeness of the $\lambda\mu\tilde{\mu}_v$ equational theory in terms of its CPS transformation using the methodology outlined in Section 3. We can check that the axioms of the two theories are provable with respect to the transformations. The β_v, μ_q, and $\tilde{\mu}_v$ axioms correspond with the various forms of β equality in the image of the CPS transformation, and the η_v, η_μ, and $\eta_{\tilde{\mu}}$ axioms correspond with the η equalities. The last axiom, ς_v, is necessary for proving that the $\mathcal{C}$ and $\mathcal{C}^{-1}$ transforms are inverses for function application, by simplifying the expanded term back down to the form $M\ N$.

Theorem 2. *The $\lambda\mu\tilde{\mu}_v$ equational theory is sound and complete with respect to the $\beta\eta$ theory of the λ-calculus with pairs.*

Proof. This follows from the fact that the $\mathcal{C}$ and $\mathcal{C}^{-1}$ transformations form an equational correspondence between $\lambda\mu\tilde{\mu}_v$ and the image of $\mathcal{C}$ in the λ-calculus. Criteria (1) holds by mutual induction on terms, values, *etc.* Criteria (2) holds by the fact that the transformations are compositional and hygienic and the axioms are interderivable. Criteria (3) for $\mathcal{C}$ follows from criteria (1) and (2). □

Additionally, we can show how the $\lambda\mu\tilde{\mu}_v$-calculus relates to the original $\lambda\mu_v$-calculus by the same methodology. Specifically, the $\tilde{\mu}$-abstractions can be considered syntactic sugar on top of the $\lambda\mu_v$-calculus, by using one free co-variable δ, which the $\lambda\mu\tilde{\mu}_v$ theory is able to erase

$$\lambda\mu\tilde{\mu}_v \vdash [\tilde{\mu}x.c]M =_{\varsigma_v,\mu_q,\beta_v} [\delta](\lambda x.\mu\_.c)\ M$$

so that we have not added anything essential that wasn't already in the $\lambda\mu_v$-calculus.[5] Therefore, we are justified in considering $\lambda\mu_v$ as the canonical calculus, and treating $\tilde{\mu}$-abstractions as syntactic sugar and the axioms of $\lambda\mu\tilde{\mu}_v$ in Figure 7 as derived equalities in the $\lambda\mu_v$ theory. By checking the axioms of $\lambda\mu\tilde{\mu}_v$ and $\lambda\mu_v$, we find that the two are in equational correspondence with one another.

Theorem 3. *$\lambda\mu_v$ is in equational correspondence with $\lambda\mu\tilde{\mu}_v$.*

Proof. The equational correspondence is formed by the compositional transformations that (a) inject $\lambda\mu_v$ terms into $\lambda\mu\tilde{\mu}_v$ unchanged, and (b) desugaring $\tilde{\mu}$-abstractions everywhere in a $\lambda\mu\tilde{\mu}_v$ term, by using a fresh co-variable δ. Criteria (1) and (2) follow from the same proof methodology as in Theorem 1. □

By putting everything together, as a corollary we get an alternate proof [28, 29] of the soundness and completeness of λ_c callcc with respect to its CPS transformation by factoring through $\lambda\mu_v$. Of note, the CPS transformation for callcc that we get out, after simplification, is the expected one:

$$\mathcal{C}[\![\mathcal{K}^{-1}[\![\mathsf{callcc}]\!]]\!]^V = \lambda(h,\alpha).h\ ((\lambda(x,\_).\alpha\ x),\alpha)$$

By comparing this CPS transformation of callcc with the encoding of callcc in the $\lambda\mu_v$-calculus, it shows how the $\lambda\mu_v$-calculus may be seen as a representation of control that is "closer" to the underlying CPS — and $\lambda\mu\tilde{\mu}_v$ is even closer still.

5. Relaxing the syntax

There is a variant of Parigot's $\lambda\mu$-calculus, originating from de Groote [10], which takes a more relaxed approach to the syntax of the calculus. In essence, the distinction between commands and terms is blurred, allowing them to mingle in new ways. Like the original $\lambda\mu$-calculus, this variant was originally studied as a typed calculus with a call-by-name interpretation. The command $[\alpha]M$, when considered as a term, can be given the type $\bot$ denoting falsehood. However, Saurin [31] showed that when considered in the untyped setting, this variant of the $\lambda\mu$-calculus, named the $\Lambda\mu$-calculus, enjoys certain properties that do not hold for Parigot's original presentation. In contrast to David and Py's [9] proof that the original $\lambda\mu$-calculus *does not* satisfy Böhm's theorem of separability, Saurin showed that the $\Lambda\mu$-calculus *does*. In other words, there are terms in the $\lambda\mu$-calculus which are equationally distinct but cannot be observably distinguished, whereas in the $\Lambda\mu$-calculus there is a reason for every inequality between terms — some context can tell them apart.[6] This suggests that in the untyped call-by-name setting, there is something missing from the $\lambda\mu$-calculus that is restored by relaxing the syntax.

$$V \in Value ::= x \mid \lambda x.M$$
$$M, N \in Term ::= V \mid M\ N \mid \mu\alpha.M \mid [\alpha]M$$
$$E \in EvalCxt ::= \Box \mid E\ M \mid V\ E$$

μ_v	$[\alpha](E[\mu\beta.M]) = M\{[\alpha](E[N])/[\beta]N\}$
η_μ	$\mu\alpha.[\alpha]M = M$
β_μ	$(\lambda x.\mu\alpha.[\beta]M)\ N = \mu\alpha.[\beta](\lambda x.M)\ N$

Figure 11. The $\Lambda\mu_v$-calculus.

$$\mathcal{C}[\![[q]M]\!]^M \triangleq \mathcal{C}[\![M]\!]^M\ \mathcal{C}[\![q]\!]^q$$
$$\mathcal{C}[\![\mu\alpha.M]\!]^M \triangleq \lambda\alpha.\mathcal{C}[\![M]\!]^M$$
$$\mathcal{C}[\![\tilde{\mu}x.M]\!]^q \triangleq \lambda x.\mathcal{C}[\![M]\!]^M$$

Figure 12. CPS transformation $\mathcal{C}$ for extra terms of $\Lambda\mu\tilde{\mu}_v$.

Here, we would like to ask the same question in the untyped call-by-value setting: is there something missing from the $\lambda\mu_v$-calculus that is restored by a more relaxed syntax? We begin by investigating a call-by-value variant of Saurin's $\Lambda\mu$-calculus. The call-by-value $\Lambda\mu_v$-calculus is shown in Figure 11, where the only change from $\lambda\mu_v$ is that in $\Lambda\mu_v$ terms and commands have been collapsed into the same syntactic type. This opens up the possibility to write new programs, like $\mu\alpha.\mu\beta.M$ and $\lambda x.[\alpha]x$, that were not legal in the $\lambda\mu_v$-calculus. However, it is important to stress that we are not adding anything *new* to the language — the only difference is that we allow the same constructs to be used in new contexts.

Because we are not adding anything new to the language, we don't need to add any new rules. Rather, we only lift the call-by-value equational theory $\lambda\mu_v$ into the relaxed setting by allowing the metavariables for terms and commands to stand in for more expressions, exactly the way we lifted the axioms of λ_c into the $\lambda\mu_v$-calculus. More specifically, the axioms of the $\Lambda\mu_v$ equational theory are the λ_c axioms plus the additional axioms of control in Figure 11. The $\Lambda\mu_v$ theory is a conservative extension of λ_c and $\lambda\mu_v$, where the only change is that the axioms of $\lambda\mu_v$ apply to more terms and in more contexts according to the conflation of terms and commands. For example, we now have the β_v equality $(\lambda x.[\alpha]x)\ V = [\alpha]V$ which was invalid in $\lambda\mu_v$, not because it wasn't a legal instance of β_v, but because $\lambda x.[\alpha]x$ was not a legal term. We also have the μ_v equality $[\alpha_1][\alpha_2]\mu\beta.M = [\alpha_1]M\{\alpha_2/\beta\}$ that occurs inside of a nested command, which could not be expressed in the syntax of $\lambda\mu_v$-calculus.

Likewise, we can apply the call-by-value CPS transformation $\mathcal{C}$ to the $\Lambda\mu_v$-calculus by lifting the transformation unchanged into the relaxed syntax. As before, we relate the CPS transformation to the intermediate language $\Lambda\mu\tilde{\mu}_v$, which extends co-terms with

[5] As a corollary, Theorem 2 implies that $\mathcal{C}$ in Figure 8 is the same as first desugaring away all $\tilde{\mu}$-abstractions and then taking the CPS transformation.

[6] More formally, for any two closed normal terms M and N that are not equated, there is a context C such that $C[M] = x$ and $C[N] = y$.

$$M ::= \lambda\alpha.M \mid M\, V^q \mid V^q\, V^V \mid V^V\, (V^V, V^q)$$
$$V^q ::= \alpha \mid \lambda x.M \quad V^V ::= x \mid \lambda(x,\alpha).M$$

Figure 13. The image of CPS transformation of $\Lambda\mu\tilde{\mu}_v$ by $\mathcal{C}$.

$$\mathcal{C}^{-1}[\![M\, V^q]\!]^M \triangleq [\mathcal{C}^{-1}[\![V^q]\!]^q]\mathcal{C}^{-1}[\![M]\!]^M$$
$$\mathcal{C}^{-1}[\![\lambda\alpha.M]\!]^M \triangleq \mu\alpha.\mathcal{C}^{-1}[\![M]\!]^M$$
$$\mathcal{C}^{-1}[\![\lambda x.M]\!]^q \triangleq \tilde{\mu}x.\mathcal{C}^{-1}[\![M]\!]^M$$
$$\mathcal{C}^{-1}[\![\lambda(x,\alpha).M]\!]^V \triangleq \lambda x.\mu\alpha.\mathcal{C}^{-1}[\![M]\!]^M$$

Figure 14. The inverse of $\mathcal{C}$ on the image of $\Lambda\mu\tilde{\mu}_v$.

$\tilde{\mu}$-abstractions, $\tilde{\mu}x.M$ and has the relaxed axioms

$$\mu_q \quad [q]\mu\alpha.M = M\,\{q/\alpha\} \qquad \tilde{\mu}_v \quad [\tilde{\mu}x.M]V = M\,\{V/x\}$$

in addition to those in Figure 7. The affected clauses of the transformation are shown in Figure 12, where a command may appear in a context previously reserved for terms, and vice versa for terms in contexts expecting commands. Again, the pattern of the CPS transformation is essentially the same. More specifically, $\mathcal{C}$ relates contexts in the $\Lambda\mu_v$-calculus to exactly the same contexts in the CPS λ-calculus: the transformation on terms still sends the context $\lambda x.\Box$ to $\lambda\alpha.\alpha\ (\lambda(x,\beta).\Box\ \beta)$, and still sends the context $\mu\alpha.\Box$ to $\lambda\alpha.\Box$. This is further evidence we have not changed our interpretation of the $\lambda\mu_v$ constructs, but are only using them in new ways.

It is interesting to observe the impact that the relaxed syntax of $\Lambda\mu_v$ has on the image of the CPS transformation. As seen in Figure 13, the previous distinction between the image of terms and commands is collapsed, as we may expect. But this collapse has opened up the possibilities of new terms in the CPS setting. More specifically, we may now have a sequence of applications, like $(\lambda\alpha.M)\ V_1^q\ V_2^q\ V_3^q$, which did not occur before. This shows us that the relaxed syntax of the $\Lambda\mu_v$-calculus has opened up the availability of more evaluation contexts in the resulting CPS terms, letting us supply a term with as many continuations as we want.

Extending our previous proof of the CPS soundness and completeness of $\lambda\mu\tilde{\mu}_v$ to cover $\Lambda\mu\tilde{\mu}_v$ is straightforward. The extension of the inverse CPS transformation of $\Lambda\mu\tilde{\mu}_v$ is shown in Figure 14. The $\mathcal{C}$ and $\mathcal{C}^{-1}$ transformations are still compositional and remain inverses, and the axioms of $\Lambda\mu\tilde{\mu}_v$ and the image of $\mathcal{C}$ are still mutually inter-derivable.

Theorem 4. *The $\Lambda\mu\tilde{\mu}_v$ equational theory is sound and complete with respect to the $\beta\eta$ theory of the λ-calculus with pairs.*

Proof. The $\mathcal{C}$ and $\mathcal{C}^{-1}$ transformations form an equational correspondence between $\Lambda\mu\tilde{\mu}_v$ and the image of $\mathcal{C}$ in the λ-calculus, as in the proof of Theorem 2. □

Additionally, $\Lambda\mu_v$ is in equational correspondence with $\Lambda\mu\tilde{\mu}_v$ in the same manner as $\lambda\mu_v$ and $\lambda\mu\tilde{\mu}_v$: we may desugar all $\tilde{\mu}$-abstractions using the same process as given in Section 4 for $\lambda\mu\tilde{\mu}_v$. As a corollary, we have soundness and completeness of $\Lambda\mu_v$ with respect to the λ-calculus with pairs by the $\mathcal{C}$ transformation.

Theorem 5. *$\Lambda\mu_v$ is in equational correspondence with $\Lambda\mu\tilde{\mu}_v$.*

Proof. The same as for Theorem 3, lifted into $\Lambda\mu\tilde{\mu}_v$. □

$\eta_{\widehat{tp}}$	$\mu\widehat{tp}.[\widehat{tp}]V = V$
$\mu_{\widehat{tp}}$	$[\widehat{tp}]\mu\widehat{tp}.c = c$
$\beta_{\widehat{tp}}$	$(\lambda x.\mu\widehat{tp}.[q]M)\ (\mu\widehat{tp}.c) = \mu\widehat{tp}.[q](\lambda x.M)\ (\mu\widehat{tp}.c)$

Figure 15. The axioms of $\widehat{tp}$ in the $\lambda\mu\widehat{tp}$ equational theory.

6. Shift and delimited control

So far, we have investigated the foundations of classical control — manipulations of control flow that are expressible by operators like callcc or Felleisen's [14] $\mathcal{C}$ operator. There is also another form of control effect referred to as *delimited* control. Intuitively, delimited control operators are different from callcc in two primary ways: (1) the evaluation context that is seen by the control operator is scoped by a *delimiter*, so that only a partial snapshot is taken of the program's control state, and (2) the continuation that is produced by the control operator does not jump somewhere else when called, but instead *returns* a result to its calling context. Because the continuations that come out of delimited control actually return something useful, so that the output of one may be fed to another, they are sometimes referred to as *composable continuations*. This additional compositional power — that we may isolate and run an effectful computation to see how it behaves, and that we may connect multiple continuations together — is essential for the expressive capabilities of delimited control.

Upon Saurin's [31] discovery of the observational completeness of $\Lambda\mu$ in the untyped call-by-name setting, Herbelin and Ghilezan [17] observed that the seemingly innocuous move from $\lambda\mu$ to $\Lambda\mu$ has a profound impact on the expressive power of the language. Whereas $\lambda\mu$ is a calculus for call-by-name classical control, $\Lambda\mu$ is a calculus for call-by-name *delimited* control. Indeed, even de Groote [10] and Ong and Stewart's [24] original analysis in call-by-name and call-by-value, respectively, relates typed $\Lambda\mu$-calculi to variants of Felleisen's [14] theory of control with a composable form of continuations that do not abort like in Felleisen's theory. Furthermore, Fujita [13] analyzes an alternative call-by-value theory for $\Lambda\mu$ with a CPS transformation that actually composes continuations much like the *continuation-composing style* transformation of the shift operator [8]. In essence, the type systems prevent programs from taking advantage of the extra expressibility that is latently present in the untyped calculi.

In his seminal work, Filinski [15] showed a different notion of completeness for delimited control in call-by-value functional languages: every computational effect that can be encoded as a monad can be directly expressed by delimited control operators. This property does not hold for classical control — for example, neither callcc nor $\mathcal{C}$ are able to express mutable references. So we see similar situations in call-by-name and call-by-value, where a delimited form of control is more complete than classical control. We have already seen some indications of delimited control hiding in callcc and $\lambda\mu_v$: a jump, $\alpha\ M$, marks the end of a usable context and a command, $[\alpha]M$, encapsulates a control effect. We will now see how the additional programs available in $\Lambda\mu_v$ let us express various forms of delimited control, and look for which one corresponds to the full $\Lambda\mu_v$-calculus.

6.1 The $\lambda\mu\widehat{tp}$-calculus

An obvious place to begin the search, since it is also based on Parigot's $\lambda\mu$-calculus, is with the $\lambda\mu\widehat{tp}$-calculus of Ariola *et al.* [4]. The $\lambda\mu\widehat{tp}$-calculus is a call-by-value language that extends $\lambda\mu_v$ with a single *dynamically bound* co-variable named $\widehat{tp}$, so that we have the new term $\mu\widehat{tp}.c$ and new command $[\widehat{tp}]M$. The intuition of the dynamic nature of $\widehat{tp}$ is that it corresponds to the dynamic

$$V \in \mathit{Value} ::= x \mid \lambda x.M$$
$$M, N \in \mathit{Term} ::= V \mid M\ N \mid \mu\alpha.c$$
$$c \in \mathit{Command} ::= [q]M \mid V \mid (\lambda x.c')\ c$$
$$q \in \mathit{CoTerm} ::= \alpha \mid \tilde{\mu}x.x$$

$$\mathcal{TP}^{-1}[\![\widehat{\mathsf{tp}}]\!] \triangleq \tilde{\mu}x.x$$
$$\mathcal{TP}^{-1}[\![\mu\widehat{\mathsf{tp}}.c]\!] \triangleq \mu\gamma.(\lambda x.[\gamma]x)\ \mathcal{TP}^{-1}[\![c]\!]$$

$$\mathcal{TP}[\![\tilde{\mu}x.x]\!]^q \triangleq \widehat{\mathsf{tp}}$$
$$\mathcal{TP}[\![V]\!]^c \triangleq [\widehat{\mathsf{tp}}]\mathcal{TP}[\![V]\!]^V$$
$$\mathcal{TP}[\![(\lambda x.c')\ c]\!]^c \triangleq [\widehat{\mathsf{tp}}](\lambda x.\mu\widehat{\mathsf{tp}}.\mathcal{TP}[\![c']\!])\ (\mu\widehat{\mathsf{tp}}.\mathcal{TP}[\![c]\!])$$

Figure 16. The embedding $\mathcal{TP}^{-1}$ of $\lambda\mu\widehat{\mathsf{tp}}$ into $\Lambda\mu_v$, the image of $\mathcal{TP}^{-1}$ in $\Lambda\mu_v$, and the translation back into $\lambda\mu\widehat{\mathsf{tp}}$.

scope of exception handling — the chosen handler is based on the call stack at run-time rather than lexical scope — and it is used to delimit the scope of μ-abstractions. Herbelin and Ghilezan [17] introduce an equational theory that is sound and complete with respect to the CPS transformation of $\lambda\mu\widehat{\mathsf{tp}}$, which includes all the axioms of $\lambda\mu_v$ along with the axioms of $\widehat{\mathsf{tp}}$ shown in Figure 15. Additionally, any of the $\lambda\mu_v$ axioms that mention a command of the form $[\alpha]M$ is extended to $[q]M$, where q is either α or $\widehat{\mathsf{tp}}$. Note that since $\widehat{\mathsf{tp}}$ is a dynamic variable, the $\eta_{\widehat{\mathsf{tp}}}$, $\mu_{\widehat{\mathsf{tp}}}$, and extended μ_v axioms are allowed to "capture" the $\widehat{\mathsf{tp}}$ variable which can happen when $\widehat{\mathsf{tp}}$ occurs "free" in V or α. Also notice that, unlike the usual situation, the $\eta_{\widehat{\mathsf{tp}}}$ rule is considered operational, allowing us to simplify terms like $\mu\widehat{\mathsf{tp}}.[\widehat{\mathsf{tp}}]5 = 5$. The $\mu_{\widehat{\mathsf{tp}}}$ rule, on the other hand, is purely an observational property that is never needed to evaluate a term in the $\lambda\mu\widehat{\mathsf{tp}}$-calculus.

The $\Lambda\mu_v$-calculus is large enough to express all of $\lambda\mu\widehat{\mathsf{tp}}$ without the use of dynamically scoped co-variables. For convenience, we will rely on $\tilde{\mu}$-abstractions as useful syntactic sugar (recall from Section 5 that $\Lambda\mu\tilde{\mu}_v$ and $\Lambda\mu_v$ are equivalent). One way to develop the embedding from $\lambda\mu\widehat{\mathsf{tp}}$ to $\Lambda\mu_v$ is to factor through the CPS transformations by first writing $\lambda\mu\widehat{\mathsf{tp}}$ in continuation-passing style, and then translating that term into the $\Lambda\mu_v$-calculus. The use of the dynamic co-variable $\widehat{\mathsf{tp}}$ in a command like $[\widehat{\mathsf{tp}}]M$, after some simplifications, is embedded as:

$$\mathcal{C}^{-1}[\![\mathcal{C}[\![\widehat{\mathsf{tp}}]\!]^q]\!]^q \triangleq \mathcal{C}^{-1}[\![\lambda x.\lambda\gamma.\gamma\ x]\!]^q =_{\eta_\mu} \tilde{\mu}x.x$$

That is to say, $\widehat{\mathsf{tp}}$ can be thought of as a (closed) co-term that, when given a value, just returns that value up to whoever is listening for the output of the command. Binding $\widehat{\mathsf{tp}}$ in a term like $\mu\widehat{\mathsf{tp}}.c$ is embedded as:

$$\begin{aligned}\mathcal{C}^{-1}[\![\mathcal{C}[\![\mu\widehat{\mathsf{tp}}.c]\!]^M]\!]^M &\triangleq \mathcal{C}^{-1}[\![\lambda\alpha.\lambda\gamma.\mathcal{C}[\![c]\!]^c\ \lambda x.\alpha\ x\ \gamma]\!]^M \\ &\triangleq \mu\alpha.\mu\gamma.[\tilde{\mu}x.[\gamma][\alpha]x]\mathcal{C}^{-1}[\![\mathcal{C}[\![c]\!]^c]\!]^M \\ &=_{\beta_v,\varsigma_v} \mu\alpha.(\lambda x.[\alpha]x)\ (\mathcal{C}^{-1}[\![\mathcal{C}[\![c]\!]^c]\!]^M)\end{aligned}$$

Thus, we can look at $\mu\widehat{\mathsf{tp}}.c$ in one of two ways. On the one hand, binding $\widehat{\mathsf{tp}}$ grabs the nearest two continuations (the second one, γ, is generally referred to as the *meta-continuation*) and then runs the command c in a meta-continuation made by composing the two. On the other hand, binding $\widehat{\mathsf{tp}}$ grabs the nearest continuation α, wraps it in a function, calls the function with c as an argument, and passes the value returned by c along to α. The embedding, $\mathcal{TP}^{-1}$, that translates the dynamic $\widehat{\mathsf{tp}}$ into $\Lambda\mu_v$ (using $\tilde{\mu}$-abstractions as syntactic sugar) is shown in Figure 16.

Example 4. Using the translation $\mathcal{TP}^{-1}$ into $\Lambda\mu_v$, we have an alternate interpretation of the dynamic $\widehat{\mathsf{tp}}$ co-variable that steps outside of the syntactic restrictions of $\lambda\mu\widehat{\mathsf{tp}}$. For example, the $\eta_{\widehat{\mathsf{tp}}}$ reduction of $\mu\widehat{\mathsf{tp}}.[\widehat{\mathsf{tp}}]z$ to z can be done in two separate steps. First, we concentrate on the command $[\widehat{\mathsf{tp}}]z$, and find out that it simplifies to the value z:

$$\mathcal{TP}^{-1}[\![[\widehat{\mathsf{tp}}]z]\!] \triangleq [\tilde{\mu}x.x]z =_{\tilde{\mu}_v} z$$

Therefore, the command $[\widehat{\mathsf{tp}}]z$ propagates z upward to give us $\mu\widehat{\mathsf{tp}}.[\widehat{\mathsf{tp}}]z = \mu\widehat{\mathsf{tp}}.z$. Next, the binding of $\widehat{\mathsf{tp}}$, when given the value z as its body, also propagates z upward:

$$\mathcal{TP}^{-1}[\![\mu\widehat{\mathsf{tp}}.z]\!] \triangleq \mu\gamma.(\lambda x.[\gamma]x)\ z =_{\beta_v} \mu\gamma.[\gamma]z =_{\eta_\mu} z$$

This lets us break down the reduction of $\widehat{\mathsf{tp}}$ into the two steps that propagate values upward: $\mu\widehat{\mathsf{tp}}.[\widehat{\mathsf{tp}}]z = \mu\widehat{\mathsf{tp}}.z = z$.

We can also explain the dynamic nature of $\widehat{\mathsf{tp}}$ by the fact that it signifies a *closed* co-term in the $\Lambda\mu_v$-calculus. For example, consider the following command which "captures" $\widehat{\mathsf{tp}}$ in terms of its embedding into $\Lambda\mu_v$:

$$\begin{aligned}&\mathcal{TP}^{-1}[\![[\widehat{\mathsf{tp}}]\mu\alpha.[\widehat{\mathsf{tp}}](\lambda x.\mu\widehat{\mathsf{tp}}.[\alpha]x)]\!] \\ &\triangleq [\tilde{\mu}y.y]\mu\alpha.[\tilde{\mu}z.z](\lambda x.\mu\gamma.(\lambda w.[\gamma]w)\ ([\alpha]x)) \\ &=_{\mu_v} [\tilde{\mu}z.z](\lambda x.\mu\gamma.(\lambda w.[\gamma]w)\ ([\tilde{\mu}y.y]x)) \\ &\triangleq \mathcal{TP}^{-1}[\![[\widehat{\mathsf{tp}}](\lambda x.\mu\widehat{\mathsf{tp}}.[\widehat{\mathsf{tp}}]x)]\!]\end{aligned}$$

The $\Lambda\mu_v$-calculus has no concept of dynamic variables, and yet the reduction gives the appearance of dynamic capture when viewed in the $\lambda\mu\widehat{\mathsf{tp}}$-calculus.

Finally, instead of interpreting $\mu\widehat{\mathsf{tp}}.c$ as a passive form that forces us to evaluate the underlying command c, we can give it a more active interpretation that re-arranges its evaluation context. For example, when we see the term $\mu\widehat{\mathsf{tp}}.[\beta]z$ in an evaluation context, we can use the call-by-value order of function calls to specify that $[\beta]z$ is to be evaluated first:

$$\begin{aligned}\mathcal{TP}^{-1}[\![[\alpha]((\mu\widehat{\mathsf{tp}}.[\beta]z) + 10)]\!] &\triangleq [\alpha]((\mu\gamma.(\lambda x.[\gamma]x)\ ([\beta]z)) + 10) \\ &=_{\mu_v} (\lambda x.[\alpha](x + 10))\ ([\beta]z)\end{aligned}$$

In general, the embedding of $\lambda\mu\widehat{\mathsf{tp}}$ into $\Lambda\mu_v$ gives us some derived equalities that are allowed by the more relaxed syntax:

$$[\widehat{\mathsf{tp}}]V = V \qquad \mu\widehat{\mathsf{tp}}.V = V$$
$$[q]E[\mu\widehat{\mathsf{tp}}.c] = (\lambda x.[q]E[x])\ c$$

End example 4.

As it turns out, the embedding of $\lambda\mu\widehat{\mathsf{tp}}$ does not cover the entire $\Lambda\mu_v$-calculus — there are some unreachable terms. However, we can still consider the image of $\lambda\mu\widehat{\mathsf{tp}}$ inside of $\Lambda\mu_v$, as shown in Figure 16, and give the correspondence between these two. Intuitively, the essential addition that $\widehat{\mathsf{tp}}$ gives us is the closed identity co-term, $\tilde{\mu}x.x$, and the ability to run a command and observe its result, $(\lambda x.c')\ c$.

Theorem 6. *The $\lambda\mu\widehat{\mathsf{tp}}$ equational theory is sound and complete with respect to the $\Lambda\mu_v$ equational theory.*

Proof. The compositional transformations $\mathcal{TP}$ and $\mathcal{TP}^{-1}$ form an equational correspondence between $\lambda\mu\widehat{\mathsf{tp}}$ and its image in $\Lambda\mu_v$. □

6.2 Shift and reset

One of the most well-studied presentations of delimited control is given by Danvy and Filinski's [7] shift and reset control operators. These operators were used by Filinski [15] to encode a direct representation of monadic effects, and have been given a sound and complete axiomatization by Kameyama and Hasegawa [19] with respect to their CPS transformations. Furthermore, the shift and

$$
\begin{array}{rr}
\mathsf{reset}_{value} & \langle V\rangle = V \\
\mathsf{reset}_{lift} & (\lambda x.\langle M\rangle)\,\langle N\rangle = \langle(\lambda x.M)\,\langle N\rangle\rangle \\
\mathcal{S}_{elim} & \mathcal{S}(\lambda\alpha.\alpha\, M) = M \\
\mathsf{reset}\,\mathcal{S} & \langle E[\mathcal{S}M]\rangle = \langle M\,(\lambda x.\langle E[x]\rangle)\rangle \\
\mathcal{S}\,\mathsf{reset} & \mathcal{S}(\lambda\alpha.\langle M\rangle) = \mathcal{S}(\lambda\alpha.M) \\
\mathcal{S}_{pure} & \langle\alpha\, V\rangle = \alpha\, V
\end{array}
$$

Figure 17. The axioms of shift ($\mathcal{S}$) and reset ($\langle M\rangle$) in $\lambda_{\mathcal{S}\alpha}$.

$$
\begin{aligned}
\mathcal{SR}[\![\mu\alpha.c]\!] &\triangleq \mathcal{S}(\lambda\alpha.\mathcal{SR}[\![c]\!]) \\
\mathcal{SR}[\![\mu\widehat{\mathsf{tp}}.c]\!] &\triangleq \mathcal{SR}[\![c]\!] \\
\mathcal{SR}[\![[q]M]\!] &\triangleq \langle\mathcal{SR}[\![q]\!]\ \mathcal{SR}[\![M]\!]\rangle \\
\mathcal{SR}[\![\alpha]\!] &\triangleq \alpha \\
\mathcal{SR}[\![\widehat{\mathsf{tp}}]\!] &\triangleq \lambda x.x
\end{aligned}
$$

$$
\begin{aligned}
\mathcal{SR}^{-1}[\![\mathcal{S}]\!] &\triangleq \lambda h.\mu\alpha.[\widehat{\mathsf{tp}}]h\,(\lambda x.\mu\widehat{\mathsf{tp}}.[\alpha]x) \\
\mathcal{SR}^{-1}[\![\mathcal{S}(\lambda\alpha.M)]\!] &\triangleq \mu\alpha.[\widehat{\mathsf{tp}}]\mathcal{SR}^{-1}[\![M]\!] \\
\mathcal{SR}^{-1}[\![\langle M\rangle]\!] &\triangleq \mu\widehat{\mathsf{tp}}.[\widehat{\mathsf{tp}}]\mathcal{SR}^{-1}[\![M]\!] \\
\mathcal{SR}^{-1}[\![\alpha]\!] &\triangleq \lambda x.\mu\widehat{\mathsf{tp}}.[\alpha]x
\end{aligned}
$$

Figure 18. The isomorphism between $\lambda_{\mathcal{S}\alpha}$ and $\lambda\mu\widehat{\mathsf{tp}}$.

reset operators, with Kameyama and Hasegawa's axiomatization, have been shown to correspond to the $\lambda\mu\widehat{\mathsf{tp}}$-calculus [4, 17]. Since the $\lambda\mu\widehat{\mathsf{tp}}$-calculus expresses only a subset of $\Lambda\mu_v$, it means that shift and reset is not the form of delimited control that corresponds to the full $\Lambda\mu_v$-calculus. However, for the sake of completeness, we still include shift and reset in our analysis.

Recall that for λ_c callcc, we gave a special status to continuation variables α that are introduced by a call to callcc, as in callcc$(\lambda\alpha.M)$, in the style of Sabry [28]. These special continuation variables correspond to a particular use of co-variables in the $\lambda\mu$-calculus, which allowed us to "abort" the current evaluation context when calling α. Although Kameyama and Hasegawa [19] do not consider continuation variables with special properties, they greatly ease local reasoning about open terms without explicit mention of their closing context. If we do, we may add a special rule for continuation variables which must be introduced by a shift, as in $\mathcal{S}(\lambda\alpha.M)$. In contrast to callcc, which creates functions that never return, the functions created by shift *always* return because they introduce a reset when called. Therefore, we may give the additional axiom that asserts that α is always a *pure* function that returns to its calling context, so a surrounding reset is unnecessary

$$\mathcal{S}_{pure} \qquad \langle\alpha\, V\rangle = \alpha\, V$$

which we add to Kameyama and Hasegawa's $\lambda_{\mathcal{S}}$-calculus to get the $\lambda_{\mathcal{S}\alpha}$-calculus shown in Figure 17. This axiom is supported by the embedding of continuation variables into $\lambda\mu\widehat{\mathsf{tp}}$ that reflects exactly the way that shift wraps up a continuation.

We strengthen the result of Herbelin and Ghilezan [17] and relate shift and reset to $\Lambda\mu_v$ through the $\lambda\mu\widehat{\mathsf{tp}}$-calculus. In particular, Kameyama and Hasegawa's [19] $\lambda_{\mathcal{S}}$ theory of shift and reset is sound and complete with respect to $\lambda_{\mathcal{S}\alpha}$, which is in equational correspondence with $\lambda\mu\widehat{\mathsf{tp}}$ by the compositional transformations in Figure 18. As a corollary, $\lambda_{\mathcal{S}}$ is sound and complete with respect to the $\Lambda\mu_v$-calculus.

Theorem 7. *The $\lambda_{\mathcal{S}}$ equational theory is sound and complete with respect to the $\lambda_{\mathcal{S}\alpha}$ equational theory, and $\lambda_{\mathcal{S}\alpha}$ is in equational correspondence with $\lambda\mu\widehat{\mathsf{tp}}$.*

Proof. There is a direct injection of $\lambda_{\mathcal{S}}$ into $\lambda_{\mathcal{S}\alpha}$ as well as a reverse embedding that forgets the special status of continuation variables. These compositional transformations form an equational correspondence between $\lambda_{\mathcal{S}}$ and the subset of $\lambda_{\mathcal{S}\alpha}$ terms that do not contain free occurrences of continuation variables. Furthermore, the compositional $\mathcal{SR}$ and $\mathcal{SR}^{-1}$ transformations form an equational correspondence between $\lambda_{\mathcal{S}\alpha}$ and $\lambda\mu\widehat{\mathsf{tp}}$. □

Example 5. Let us consider how continuations compose using shift and reset, $\lambda\mu\widehat{\mathsf{tp}}$, and $\Lambda\mu_v$, and how the reduction is simulated in each of the three calculi. For example, the term $\langle\mathcal{S}\,(\lambda k.k\,(k\,2)) + 10\rangle$ captures the evaluation context $\square + 10$ and applies it twice to the number 2, giving us 22 as the result. In terms of the $\lambda_{\mathcal{S}}$-calculus, we have the following reduction:

$$
\begin{aligned}
\langle\mathcal{S}\,(\lambda k.k\,(k\,2)) + 10\rangle &=_{\mathsf{reset}\,\mathcal{S}} \langle(\lambda k.k\,(k\,2))\,(\lambda x.\langle x+10\rangle)\rangle \\
&=_{\beta_v} \langle(\lambda x.\langle x+10\rangle)\,((\lambda x.\langle x+10\rangle)\,2)\rangle \\
&=_{\beta_v} \langle(\lambda x.\langle x+10\rangle)\,\langle 2+10\rangle\rangle \\
&=_{\mathsf{reset}_{value}} \langle(\lambda x.\langle x+10\rangle)\,12\rangle \\
&=_{\beta_v} \langle\langle 12+10\rangle\rangle \\
&=_{\mathsf{reset}_{value}} 22
\end{aligned}
$$

By translating the shift and reset operators into $\lambda\mu\widehat{\mathsf{tp}}$ using the $\mathcal{SR}^{-1}$ embedding, we get the simplified term

$$
\begin{aligned}
&\mathcal{SR}^{-1}[\![\langle\mathcal{S}\,(\lambda\alpha.\alpha\,(\alpha\,2)) + 10\rangle]\!] \\
&= \mu\widehat{\mathsf{tp}}.[\widehat{\mathsf{tp}}]((\mu\alpha.[\alpha](\mu\widehat{\mathsf{tp}}.[\alpha]2)) + 10)
\end{aligned}
$$

which also produces the answer 22:

$$
\begin{aligned}
&\mu\widehat{\mathsf{tp}}.[\widehat{\mathsf{tp}}]((\mu\alpha.[\alpha](\mu\widehat{\mathsf{tp}}.[\alpha]2)) + 10) \\
&=_{\mu_v} \mu\widehat{\mathsf{tp}}.[\widehat{\mathsf{tp}}]((\mu\widehat{\mathsf{tp}}.[\widehat{\mathsf{tp}}](2+10)) + 10) \\
&=_{\eta_{\widehat{\mathsf{tp}}}} \mu\widehat{\mathsf{tp}}.[\widehat{\mathsf{tp}}](12+10) \\
&=_{\eta_{\widehat{\mathsf{tp}}}} 22
\end{aligned}
$$

Again, we can translate the term into $\Lambda\mu_v$ using the $\mathcal{TP}^{-1}$ embedding to get the simplified term

$$
\begin{aligned}
&\mathcal{TP}^{-1}[\![\mu\widehat{\mathsf{tp}}.[\widehat{\mathsf{tp}}]((\mu\alpha.[\alpha](\mu\widehat{\mathsf{tp}}.[\alpha]2)) + 10)]\!] \\
&=_{\mu_v} \mu\gamma.(\lambda x.[\gamma]x)\,([\tilde{\mu}y.y]((\mu\alpha.(\lambda z.[\alpha]z)\,([\alpha]2)) + 10))
\end{aligned}
$$

which produces the same result:

$$
\begin{aligned}
&\mu\gamma.(\lambda x.[\gamma]x)\,([\tilde{\mu}y.y]((\mu\alpha.(\lambda z.[\alpha]z)\,([\alpha]2)) + 10)) \\
&=_{\mu_v} \mu\gamma.(\lambda x.[\gamma]x)\,((\lambda z.[\tilde{\mu}y.y](z+10))\,([\tilde{\mu}y.y](2+10))) \\
&=_{\tilde{\mu}_v,\beta_v} \mu\gamma.(\lambda x.[\gamma]x)\,([\tilde{\mu}y.y](12+10)) \\
&=_{\tilde{\mu}_v,\beta_v} \mu\gamma.[\gamma]22 \\
&=_{\eta_\mu} 22
\end{aligned}
$$

End example 5.

Observe that, like with callcc, the embeddings into $\lambda\mu\widehat{\mathsf{tp}}$ and $\Lambda\mu_v$ give the expected CPS transformation of shift and reset, up to currying. In particular, after the embeddings we attain a two-pass CPS transformation [8, 19] for shift and reset:

$$
\begin{aligned}
&\mathcal{C}[\![\mathcal{TP}^{-1}[\![\mathcal{SR}^{-1}[\![\mathcal{S}]\!]]\!]]\!]^V \\
&= \lambda(h,\alpha).h\,((\lambda(x,\beta).\lambda\gamma.\alpha\,x\,(\lambda y.\beta\,y\,\gamma)), (\lambda z.\lambda\gamma.'\gamma'\,z)) \\
&\mathcal{C}[\![\mathcal{TP}^{-1}[\![\mathcal{SR}^{-1}[\![\langle M\rangle]\!]]\!]]\!] \\
&= \lambda\alpha.\lambda\gamma.[\![M]\!]\,(\lambda x.\lambda\gamma.'\gamma'\,x)\,(\lambda y.\alpha\,y\,\gamma)
\end{aligned}
$$

Remark 1. Recall that in Section 5, we noted that the original typed interpretation of the de Groote [10]-style $\Lambda\mu$-calculus effectively

$$\begin{array}{ll} \beta_\$ & V\$\mathcal{S}_0(\lambda\alpha.M) = M\{V/\alpha\} \\ \eta_\$ & \mathcal{S}_0(\lambda\alpha.\alpha\$M) = M \\ \$_v & V\$V' = V\,V' \\ \$_E & V\$E[M] = (\lambda x.V\$E[x])\$M \end{array}$$

Figure 19. The axioms of shift₀ ($\mathcal{S}_0$) and $\$$ in $\lambda_\$$.

$$\begin{aligned} \mathcal{Z}[\![\mu\alpha.M]\!] &\triangleq \mathcal{S}_0(\lambda\alpha.\mathcal{Z}[\![M]\!]) \\ \mathcal{Z}[\![[q]M]\!] &\triangleq \mathcal{Z}[\![q]\!]\$\mathcal{Z}[\![M]\!] \\ \mathcal{Z}[\![\alpha]\!] &\triangleq \alpha \\ \mathcal{Z}[\![\tilde{\mu}x.M]\!] &\triangleq \lambda x.\mathcal{Z}[\![M]\!] \end{aligned}$$

$$\begin{aligned} \mathcal{Z}^{-1}[\![\mathcal{S}_0]\!] &\triangleq \lambda h.\mu\alpha.h\,(\lambda x.[\alpha]x) \\ \mathcal{Z}^{-1}[\![\mathcal{S}_0(\lambda\alpha.M)]\!] &\triangleq \mu\alpha.\mathcal{Z}^{-1}[\![M]\!] \\ \mathcal{Z}^{-1}[\![N\$M]\!] &\triangleq (\lambda k.[\tilde{\mu}x.k\,x]\mathcal{Z}^{-1}[\![M]\!])\;\mathcal{Z}^{-1}[\![N]\!] \\ \mathcal{Z}^{-1}[\![\alpha]\!] &\triangleq \lambda x.[\alpha]x \end{aligned}$$

Figure 20. The isomorphism between $\lambda_\$$ and $\Lambda\mu\tilde{\mu}_v$.

considers commands to have the type $\bot$. This typing would force x in both $[\tilde{\mu}x.x]M$ and $(\lambda x.c')\ c$ to always have the type $\bot$. Applying this typing regime to the $\lambda\mu\widehat{\mathsf{tp}}$-calculus, we would only allow $[\widehat{\mathsf{tp}}]M$ when M has type $\bot$, and likewise $\mu\widehat{\mathsf{tp}}.c$ would have type $\bot$. In other words, this type system severely restricts the new $\widehat{\mathsf{tp}}$ variable as there is no way to use it with interesting types like integers or booleans. This restriction gives an intuitive reason why de Groote's typing forces the $\Lambda\mu$-calculus to be equivalent in expressive power to Parigot's classical $\lambda\mu$-calculus, by enforcing the restriction in the types rather than in the syntax.

From another perspective, by embedding shift and reset into the $\Lambda\mu_v$-calculus, de Groote's typing would only allow $\langle M\rangle$ when M has the type $\bot$. Therefore, the classical type system restricts the use of the delimiter to terms that cannot return a result because they belong to a type with no values. However, there are extensions of the basic, classical type system for $\lambda\mu\widehat{\mathsf{tp}}$ [4] and $\lambda_{\mathcal{S}}$ [7] that allow for delimiters to return values with various types. In the approach taken here, the untyped semantics of the $\Lambda\mu_v$-calculus is already expressive enough to represent the dynamic behavior of delimited control. The difference between classical and delimited control is then a matter of choosing a less expressive, classical type system — like de Groote [10], Ong and Stewart [24], or Fujita [13] — or a more expressive, "delimited" one that allows programs like $([\tilde{\mu}x.x]1) + 2$ to be well-typed. *End remark* 1.

7. Correspondence of $\Lambda\mu_v$ and shift0

Having considered languages that only touch on a subset of the $\Lambda\mu_v$-calculus, we may wonder what language constructs express the full calculus. Next, we consider two other operators, now known as shift₀ and reset₀, that were introduced as variants of shift and reset by Danvy and Filinski [7], but have garnered relatively less attention. More recently, Materzok and Biernacki [20, 21] have investigated the static and dynamic semantics of shift₀ and reset₀. Intuitively, the difference between shift and shift₀ is that when shift captures its calling context, the surrounding reset delimiter is left in place, whereas when shift₀ captures its calling context the surrounding reset₀ delimiter is removed. For example, we have different equations for the two different operators:

$$\begin{aligned} \langle f\ (\mathcal{S}\ (\lambda k.M))\rangle &= \langle(\lambda k.M)\ (\lambda x.\langle f\ x\rangle)\rangle \\ \langle f\ (\mathcal{S}_0\ (\lambda k.M))\rangle_0 &= (\lambda k.M)\ (\lambda x.\langle f\ x\rangle_0) \end{aligned}$$

This seemingly minor alteration on the surrounding context makes all the difference. Indeed, Materzok [22] shows that shift₀ and reset₀ are not only powerful enough to encode shift and reset, they are able to represent an arbitrary hierarchy of nested shift and reset operators [8] with a dynamically growing and shrinking stack of continuations.

Example 6. We can view the difference between the shift and shift₀ operators by the influence they have over their delimited evaluation contexts. For example, the term $\mathcal{S}\ (\lambda k_1.\mathcal{S}\ (\lambda k_2.k_1\ (k_2\ 1)))$ appears to swap two surrounding evaluation contexts by capturing them locally as k_1 and k_2, respectively, and then applying them in the reverse order so that the nearest context k_1 sees the result of evaluating k_2 with 1. However, because shift leaves its surrounding reset delimiter intact, the second call to shift can only see the empty context. Therefore, the second shift effectively does nothing productive, and the net effect of the entire term is to yield 1. For example, if we evaluate the term using the $\lambda_{\mathcal{S}}$ theory in the context $\langle\langle\square \times 2\rangle + 10\rangle$, where the first evaluation context doubles its input and the second adds 10, then we get the same result as the simple numeric expression $(1 \times 2) + 10$:

$$\begin{aligned} &\langle\langle(\mathcal{S}\ (\lambda k_1.\mathcal{S}\ (\lambda k_2.k_1\ (k_2\ 1)))) \times 2\rangle + 10\rangle \\ &=_{\mathsf{reset}\ \mathcal{S},\beta_v} \langle\langle\mathcal{S}\ (\lambda k_2.(\lambda y.\langle y \times 2\rangle)\ (k_2\ 1))\rangle + 10\rangle \\ &=_{\mathsf{reset}\ \mathcal{S},\beta_v} \langle\langle(\lambda y.\langle y \times 2\rangle)\ ((\lambda x.\langle x\rangle)\ 1)\rangle + 10\rangle \\ &=_{\beta_v} \langle\langle(\lambda y.\langle y \times 2\rangle)\ \langle 1\rangle\rangle + 10\rangle \\ &=_{\beta_v,\mathsf{reset}_{value}} \langle\langle\langle 1 \times 2\rangle\rangle + 10\rangle \\ &=_{\mathsf{reset}_{value}} 12 \end{aligned}$$

Alternatively, consider the same term implemented with shift₀ in place of shift. The shift₀ operator removes its surrounding reset₀ delimiter after it is done, allowing the second call to shift₀ to capture some surrounding, possibly non-empty, evaluation context. Therefore, the net effect of the term is to swap the two nearest evaluation contexts, separated by reset₀, before yielding 1. Likewise, if we evaluate the term in the similar context $\langle\langle\square \times 2\rangle_0 + 10\rangle_0$ using Materzok's [20] $\lambda_{\mathcal{S}_0}$ theory for shift₀ and reset₀, we see that the program returns the result of $(1 + 10) \times 2$:

$$\begin{aligned} &\langle\langle(\mathcal{S}_0\ (\lambda k_1.\mathcal{S}_0\ (\lambda k_2.k_1\ (k_2\ 1)))) \times 2\rangle_0 + 10\rangle_0 \\ &=_{\langle\mathcal{S}_0\rangle,\beta_v} \langle(\mathcal{S}_0\ (\lambda k_2.(\lambda y.\langle y \times 2\rangle_0)\ (k_2\ 1))) + 10\rangle_0 \\ &=_{\langle\mathcal{S}_0\rangle,\beta_v} (\lambda y.\langle y \times 2\rangle_0)\ ((\lambda x.\langle x + 10\rangle_0)\ 1) \\ &=_{\beta_v} (\lambda y.\langle y \times 2\rangle_0)\ \langle 1 + 10\rangle_0 \\ &=_{\langle v\rangle,\beta_v} \langle 11 \times 2\rangle_0 \\ &=_{\langle v\rangle} 22 \end{aligned}$$

End example 6.

Materzok's [20] $\lambda_{\mathcal{S}_0}$ theory of shift₀ and reset₀ was developed in terms of another call-by-value λ-calculus which includes shift₀ and the delimiting form $M\$N$.[7] Intuitively, the term $V\$M$ surrounds M with a delimiter represented by V, where V is a function that describes how to resume if M evaluates to a value. If M is instead a call to shift₀, then V is captured along with the delimiter. The reset₀ delimiter comes out as the special case when we have $(\lambda x.x)\$M$, so that the delimiter immediately returns the value it's given. The axioms of the $\lambda_\$$-calculus are β_v, η_v and the additional axioms shown in Figure 19. The rules for $\lambda_\$$ already look quite similar to the rules for $\Lambda\mu\tilde{\mu}_v$, and in fact the two correspond. We give translations between $\Lambda\mu\tilde{\mu}_v$ and $\lambda_\$$ in Figure 20 which gives the exact correspondence between the two notions of delimited control.

[7] Additionally, $E\$M$ becomes another form of evaluation context.

$$M, N \in Term ::= x \mid \lambda x.M \mid M\ N \mid \mu\alpha.M \mid [\alpha]M$$
$$E \in EvalCxt ::= \Box \mid E\ M$$

β_n	$(\lambda x.M)\ N = M\{N/x\}$
η_n	$\lambda x.M\ x = M$
μ_n	$[\alpha]E[\mu\beta.M] = M\{[\alpha]E[N]/[\beta]N\}$
η_μ	$\mu\alpha.[\alpha]M = M$

Figure 21. The call-by-name $\Lambda\mu$-calculus.

$\beta_\mathcal{V}$	$(\lambda x.M)\ V = M\{V/x\}$
$\eta_\mathcal{V}$	$\lambda x.V\ x = V$
μ_E	$[\alpha]E[\mu\beta.M] = M\{[\alpha]E[N]/[\beta]N\}$
η_μ	$\mu\alpha.[\alpha]M = M$
$\beta_{E\Omega}$	$(\lambda x.E[x])\ M = E[M]$
β_μ	$(\lambda x.\mu\alpha.[\beta]M)\ N = \mu\alpha.[\beta](\lambda x.M)\ N$

Figure 22. A parametric equational theory for the $\Lambda\mu_\mathcal{S}$-calculus.

$$V \in Value_\mathcal{V} ::= x \mid \lambda x.M$$
$$E \in StrictCxt_\mathcal{V} ::= \Box \mid E\ M \mid V\ E$$
$$V \in Value_\mathcal{N} ::= M \qquad E \in StrictCxt_\mathcal{N} ::= \Box \mid E\ M$$

Figure 23. Call-by-value ($\mathcal{V}$) and call-by-name ($\mathcal{N}$) strategies.

In essence, the $V\$M$ delimiter corresponds to a command in $\Lambda\mu_v$ where V is converted into a co-term (*i.e.,* a continuation).

Theorem 8. *$\lambda_\$$ is in equational correspondence with $\Lambda\mu\tilde{\mu}_v$.*

Proof. The compositional $\mathcal{Z}$ and $\mathcal{Z}^{-1}$ transformations form an equational correspondence between $\lambda_\$$ and $\Lambda\mu\tilde{\mu}_v$. □

Remark 2. To illustrate the difference between shift/reset and shift₀/reset₀, we point out that reset₀ may be defined in the following equivalent ways:

$$\langle M\rangle_0 \triangleq (\lambda x.x)\$M \triangleq [\tilde{\mu}x.x]M \triangleq [\widehat{\mathsf{tp}}]M$$

Note that in the second two definitions, a command is being used in a place where we might normally expect a term in the $\lambda\mu_v$-calculus. This definition for the delimiter is observationally different from reset. For example, according to both $\lambda_\mathcal{S}$ and $\lambda\mu\widehat{\mathsf{tp}}$, the reset delimiter is idempotent:

$$\langle\langle M\rangle\rangle \triangleq \mu\widehat{\mathsf{tp}}.[\widehat{\mathsf{tp}}]\mu\widehat{\mathsf{tp}}.[\widehat{\mathsf{tp}}]M =_{\mu_{\widehat{\mathsf{tp}}}} \mu\widehat{\mathsf{tp}}.[\widehat{\mathsf{tp}}]M \triangleq \langle M\rangle$$

This equation makes sense because a reset forms a hard barrier that shift can never cross, so having more than one is redundant. However, the reset₀ delimiter is *not* idempotent:

$$\langle\langle M\rangle_0\rangle_0 \triangleq [\widehat{\mathsf{tp}}][\widehat{\mathsf{tp}}]M \neq [\widehat{\mathsf{tp}}]M \triangleq \langle M\rangle_0$$

This equation is impossible because multiple calls to shift₀ in a row can capture the evaluation context several layers out, effectively "digging" out of a series of nested reset₀s (see Example 6). For example, by instantiating the above M with $\mu\alpha.\mu\beta.(\lambda x.[\beta]x)$, we are able to differentiate between the contexts $[\widehat{\mathsf{tp}}][\widehat{\mathsf{tp}}]\Box$ and $[\widehat{\mathsf{tp}}]\Box$.[8] Note, however, that idempotency of reset is provable in $\Lambda\mu_v$ *regardless* of M, even if it does not come from $\lambda_\mathcal{S}$, so it is a property of $\Lambda\mu_v$ as a whole and not just the image of $\mathcal{SR}^{-1}$. In other words, this observational property of reset holds even with a program using shift₀ to "dig" out of nested reset₀ delimiters. It follows that not only are shift and shift₀ different control operators, reset and reset₀ are *different* delimiters, as shown by their different encodings and observational properties in the $\Lambda\mu_v$-calculus. Going the other way, Shan [33] shows how to operationally simulate shift₀ in terms of shift by directly representing [15] stacks of continuations. However, here we are not only concerned with the operational correctness of encodings, but also in preserving the other observational properties of the various control operators, like the idempotency of reset in $\lambda_\mathcal{S}$ or the $\eta_\$$ axiom from $\lambda_\$$. *End remark* 2.

8. A parametric approach to delimited control

Having determined a second interpretation of the $\Lambda\mu$-calculus, we can now start to examine the impact of evaluation strategies on delimited control effects by seeing how the call-by-value and call-by-name theories are related. Herbelin and Ghilezan [17] use the call-by-name equational theory shown in Figure 21 for analyzing the relationship between the relaxed $\Lambda\mu$-calculus and delimited control. Now, observe how the call-by-name axioms vary from the call-by-value axioms from Figures 2 and 11. On the one hand, in the call-by-name theory, the β rule for reducing function calls has been generalized so that the argument can be any term instead of a value, and likewise the η rule for eliminating a trivial λ-abstraction has been generalized for any term. On the other hand, the μ rule for capturing an evaluation context has been restricted, since call-by-name has a more restricted form of evaluation contexts: including only chains of applications like $\Box\ N_1\ N_2\ N_3$. Contrastingly, the η_μ rule is completely unchanged between the two theories.

At a higher level, consider what happens when we move from a call-by-name theory, like the original λ-calculus, to a call-by-value theory. We must restrict rules like β to only substitute the simpler subset of terms that we call "values" because it would be improper to substitute non-value terms — so by contrast every term in call-by-name is a "value" and subject to substitution. On the other hand, consider how to move from a call-by-value theory with control, like $\lambda\mu_v$ or $\lambda\,\mathsf{callcc}_v$, to a call-by-name theory. We must restrict rules like μ_v to avoid capturing certain contexts that are no longer "strict" and do not evaluate their inputs. For example, if we consider the $\lambda\mu$ term $(\lambda\_.M)\ (\mu\alpha.c)$, then the context $(\lambda\_.M)\ \Box$ is not strict — it never evaluates the term we plug into $\Box$ — so the correct move is to discard the argument $(\mu\alpha.c)$ instead of letting it capture its context.

Therefore, the differences between call-by-name and call-by-value can be summarized by the answers to two questions: "what terms are values?" and "what contexts are strict?" To further highlight the commonalities between the call-by-value and call-by-name theories of the $\Lambda\mu$-calculus, we present a unified *parametric* equational theory in Figure 22, similar to the parametric λ-calculus [27], but extended with control effects (both classical and delimited). In this theory, we state the basic axioms generically by assuming that there is some decision on what we mean by values V and evaluation contexts E, and leaving their precise definitions to be filled in later. More specifically, a definition for the sets of values and evaluation contexts is a definition of a *strategy* $\mathcal{S}$. We then recover our previous call-by-value and call-by-name equational theories by instantiating the parametric $\Lambda\mu_\mathcal{S}$-calculus with the appropriate strategies shown in Figure 23. As expected, the $\Lambda\mu_\mathcal{V}$ gives

[8] This is a dual to the usual concept of observational equivalence: rather than having a context to look at the differences between two terms, here we are using a term to look at the differences between two contexts.

$$V \in Value ::= \lambda x.M \quad M \in Term ::= V \mid x \mid M\ N$$
$$A \in Answer ::= B[V] \quad B \in BindCxt ::= \Box \mid (\lambda x.B)\ M$$
$$E \in EvalCxt ::= \Box \mid E\ M \mid (\lambda x.E[x])\ E \mid (\lambda x.E)\ M$$

$$\begin{array}{ll} deref & (\lambda x.E[x])\ V = (\lambda x.E[V])\ V \\ lift & (\lambda x.A)\ M\ N = (\lambda x.A\ N)\ M \\ assoc & (\lambda y.E[y])\ ((\lambda x.A)\ M) = (\lambda x.(\lambda y.E[y])\ A)\ M \end{array}$$

Figure 24. A call-by-need λ-calculus.

$$V \in Value_{\mathcal{AF}} ::= \lambda x.M$$
$$E \in EvalCxt_{\mathcal{AF}} ::= \Box \mid E\ M \mid (\lambda x.Q[x])\ E$$
$$Q \in Question ::= \Box \mid Q\ M \mid (\lambda x.Q[x])\ Q \mid (\lambda x.Q)\ M \mid [\alpha]Q \mid \mu\alpha.Q$$

Figure 25. A call-by-need ($\mathcal{AF}$) strategy.

us exactly the $\Lambda\mu_v$ theory, and in $\Lambda\mu_{\mathcal{N}}$ the $\beta_{E\Omega}$ and β_μ axioms fall out as derivable from the others, giving us the theory in Figure 21.

Call-by-need and delimited control: Having a parametric theory for the $\Lambda\mu$-calculus makes it easier to investigate the impact of a strategy on languages with classical or delimited control. For example, how might we fit call-by-need — a strategy for "more efficient" lazy evaluation that defers evaluating arguments to function calls until they are needed but remembers their value for future use — into the picture? To start, let's consider Ariola and Felleisen's [1] call-by-need λ-calculus, shown in Figure 24. We can see how the call-by-need λ-calculus defers and saves work by considering a possible evaluation trace for a term like $(\lambda x.M)\ N$:[9]

$$(\lambda x.\boxed{M})\ N = (\lambda x.E[x])\ \boxed{N} = \boxed{(\lambda x.E[x])\ V}$$
$$=_{deref} (\lambda x.E[V])\ V$$

However, life is not always so simple, since N may not evaluate exactly to a value V, but instead it might be a value surrounded by context of bindings, $B[V]$. To deal with this issue, the call-by-need λ-calculus has the axiom $assoc$ that moves the evaluation context $(\lambda x.E[x])\ \Box$ through the bindings until it reaches the value. Similarly, $lift$ brings an evaluation context like $\Box\ N$ to a value.

In order to turn this call-by-need λ-calculus into an instance of the parametric theory we need to figure out what is the correct definition for values and evaluation contexts. First, let's consider just the pure λ-calculus subset of the theory. The definition for values can be taken rather directly from Figure 24 which says that only λ-abstractions are values. This decision gives us a β_V rule that is a stronger version of $deref$ and can substitute a value into any context (recall the substitution procedure from Section 3). But what about the definition of evaluation contexts? The β_{Elift} rule, $E[(\lambda x.M)\ N] = (\lambda x.E[M])\ N$, that is derivable from $\beta_{E\Omega}$ (see [19] for deriving β_{lift} from β_Ω) can simulate $lift$ and $assoc$ assuming that both $\Box\ M$ and $(\lambda x.E[x])\ \Box$ are considered evaluation contexts. Therefore, our evaluation contexts should include at least these two cases.[10]

[9] The evaluation context has been highlighted by drawing a box that separates the term currently being evaluated from its surrounding context.

[10] We can already make some interesting comparisons between the three strategies by the way axioms for the pure λ-calculus are used: in $\mathcal{N}$, β_V is operational, η_V is observational, and $\beta_{E\Omega}$ is trivial; in $\mathcal{V}$, β_V is operational and η_V and $\beta_{E\Omega}$ are observational; in $\mathcal{AF}$, β_V and $\beta_{E\Omega}$ are operational and η_V is trivial.

Now, let's consider what happens when we take control effects into account. In particular, does it make sense for context $(\lambda x.E)\ M$ to be capturable by the μ_E rule? For example, what happens if we have a classical control effect inside the body of a function call? Because of the β_μ axiom, we could either pull out the μ-abstraction first or capture the binding context and copy it

$$[\alpha](\lambda x.\mu\beta.[\gamma]M)\ N =_{\beta_\mu,\mu_E} [\gamma](\lambda x.M\{\alpha/\beta\})\ N$$
$$=_{\mu_E} [\gamma]M\{[\alpha](\lambda x.N')\ N/[\beta]N'\}$$

leading to completely different sharing properties (whether there is one shared N or every β command gets a fresh copy of N) depending on which path you take. This same issue is raised in [5] on the interaction between bindings and control effects in call-by-need. Since the call-by-need λ-calculus is a calculus about sharing, non-deterministic sharing is undesirable, and we leave $(\lambda x.E)\ M$ out of our set of evaluation contexts. In a related question, what happens if we have an otherwise strict function whose body begins with a control effect, like $\lambda x.\mu\alpha.[\beta]x$? Should we be required to extract the μ-abstraction out of the function body before realizing the function was strict all along? Let's suppose that we call this function strict, since it will evaluate x in some evaluation context given by β, giving us the following step:

$$[\alpha](\lambda x.\mu\delta.[\beta]x)\ (\mu\gamma.M) =_{\mu_E} M\{[\alpha](\lambda x.\mu\delta.[\beta]x)\ N/[\gamma]N\}$$

These decisions give us the strategy for call-by-need shown in Figure 25, where the strict evaluation contexts are either a calling context, $E\ M$, or an application of a strict function that has some question about its argument, $(\lambda x.Q[x])\ E$. Also note that because the parametric $\Lambda\mu_{\mathcal{S}}$-calculus includes delimited control, this gives us a definition of the call-by-need evaluation strategy that works with delimited control effects. For example, in the terminology of the $\lambda\mu\widehat{\mathsf{tp}}$-calculus, we can derive the following equations by their embedding in the $\Lambda\mu_{\mathcal{AF}}$-calculus:

$$[\widehat{\mathsf{tp}}]\mu\alpha.M =_{\mu_E} M\{\widehat{\mathsf{tp}}/\alpha\} \qquad \mu\widehat{\mathsf{tp}}.[\widehat{\mathsf{tp}}]V =_{\beta_V,\mu_E,\eta_\mu} V$$

These equations are not terribly surprising, they are quite similar to the call-by-value axioms for $\widehat{\mathsf{tp}}$, but we were able to derive them completely from our decisions about what we mean by values and evaluation contexts. Of note, one difference with call-by-value is that $\mu\widehat{\mathsf{tp}}.[\widehat{\mathsf{tp}}]x$ does *not* reduce to x, because we said that x is not a value. However, it is relatively straightforward to come up with a call-by-need strategy with variables in the set of values, and to pull out the corresponding instance of the $\Lambda\mu_{\mathcal{S}}$ equational theory.

9. Conclusion

By now, we have seen how the core of classical control effects, as expressed by callcc in Scheme, naturally scales to the far more powerful world of delimited control. No new programming constructs or rules are required to explain delimited control — the characterization of classical control is enough. On the one hand, this conclusion may be rather surprising. After all, we know that delimited control operators like shift and reset are vastly more powerful than callcc. On the other hand, the conclusion should be reassuring. Compared to composable continuations, we have a relatively better understanding of callcc, so the fact that there are no new ingredients means that there is nothing extra that we have to explain. The theory that we get out for delimited control is the one that (1) arises canonically from a sub-language of classical control, (2) doesn't add any new programming constructs, and (3) applies the existing rules without change to a more flexible syntax.

Although they were introduced around the same time, presented side-by-side by Danvy and Filinski [7], the shift and reset formulation of delimited control receives more attention than the relatively neglected variants shift_0 and reset_0. For example, there was a ten-year lag between the developments of equational theories for shift and reset [19] and for shift_0 and reset_0 [20]. However, this analysis of composable continuations suggests that shift_0 is a more "primitive" control operator than shift, while still allowing for desirable and strong observational guarantees that hold for reset (like idempotency), and warrants more attention. On the one hand, Herbelin and Ghilezan [17] conjecture that the $\lambda\mu\widehat{\mathsf{tp}}$-calculus, and by extension the call-by-value λ-calculus with shift and reset, satisfy Böhm's theorem of separability. On the other hand, the close relationship with the call-by-value $\Lambda\mu_v$-calculus instead suggests beginning with separability of the shift_0 and reset_0 notion of composable continuations (or better yet shift_0 and \$), from which the others may follow.

The $\Lambda\mu$-calculus may also serve as a more general framework for understanding control effects in functional programming languages. For instance, although we focus on untyped semantics here, we can still consider type and effect systems for such languages. Materzok [20, 21] provides a type system for the call-by-value λ-calculus with the shift_0 operator, which may be translated to the call-by-value $\Lambda\mu_v$-calculus since the two are isomorphic. Additionally, Saurin [32] provides a type system for the call-by-name $\Lambda\mu$-calculus. It would be interesting to use the parametric $\Lambda\mu$-calculus as a common language to compare the two type systems, and to see the impact that evaluation strategy has on the static typing of programs using delimited control. This may suggest a generalized type and effect systems for static analysis of delimited control under both call-by-value and call-by-name evaluation strategies in the same vein as the parametric equational theory for the $\Lambda\mu$-calculus. Furthermore, in practice functional languages with delimited control allow for the use of multiple different prompts [12] for different purposes, like the ability to create exception handlers that catch only certain kinds of exceptions. The $\lambda\mu$-calculus has already [11] shed some light on this language feature, and the analysis of delimited control in the $\Lambda\mu$-calculus may provide more insight into a formulation that is practical yet easy to reason about with strong observational guarantees similar to shift and reset.

Acknowledgements

We would like to thank Matthew Might and the anonymous reviewers for their feedback and help in improving this paper. Paul Downen and Zena M. Ariola have been supported by NSF grant CCF-0917329.

References

[1] Z. M. Ariola and M. Felleisen. The call-by-need lambda calculus. *Journal of Functional Programmin*, 7(3):265–301, 1997.

[2] Z. M. Ariola and H. Herbelin. Control reduction theories: the benefit of structural substitution. *Journal of Functional Programming*, 18(3): 373–419, 2008.

[3] Z. M. Ariola, H. Herbelin, and A. Sabry. A proof-theoretic foundation of abortive continuations. *Higher-Order and Symbolic Computation*, 20(4):403–429, 2007.

[4] Z. M. Ariola, H. Herbelin, and A. Sabry. A type-theoretic foundation of delimited continuations. *Higher-Order and Symbolic Computation*, 22(3):233–273, 2009.

[5] Z. M. Ariola, P. Downen, H. Herbelin, K. Nakata, and A. Saurin. Classical call-by-need sequent calculi: The unity of semantic artifacts. In *FLOPS*, pages 32–46, 2012.

[6] P.-L. Curien and H. Herbelin. The duality of computation. In *ICFP*, pages 233–243, 2000.

[7] O. Danvy and A. Filinski. A functional abstraction of typed contexts. Technical Report 89/12, DIKU, University of Copenhagen, Copenhagen, Denmark, 1989.

[8] O. Danvy and A. Filinski. Abstracting control. In *LISP and Functional Programming*, pages 151–160, 1990.

[9] R. David and W. Py. Lambda-mu-calculus and Böhm's theorem. *Journal of Symbolic Logic*, 66(1):407–413, 2001.

[10] P. de Groote. On the relation between the $\lambda\mu$-calculus and the syntactic theory of sequential control. In *LPAR*, pages 31–43, 1994.

[11] P. Downen and Z. M. Ariola. Delimited control and computational effects. *Journal of Functional Programming*, 24(1):1–55, 2014.

[12] R. K. Dybvig, S. P. Jones, and A. Sabry. A monadic framework for delimited continuations. *Journal of Functional Programming*, 17(06): 687–730, 2007.

[13] K. etsu Fujita. Explicitly typed $\lambda\mu$-calculus for polymorphism and call-by-value. In *TLCA*, pages 162–176, 1999.

[14] M. Felleisen and R. Hieb. The revised report on the syntactic theories of sequential control and state. *Theoretical Computer Science*, 103(2): 235–271, 1992.

[15] A. Filinski. Representing monads. In *POPL*, pages 446–457, 1994.

[16] T. Griffin. A formulae-as-types notion of control. In *POPL*, pages 47–58, 1990.

[17] H. Herbelin and S. Ghilezan. An approach to call-by-name delimited continuations. In *POPL*, pages 383–394, 2008.

[18] H. Herbelin and S. Zimmermann. An operational account of call-by-value minimal and classical λ-calculus in "natural deduction" form. In *TLCA*, pages 142–156, 2009.

[19] Y. Kameyama and M. Hasegawa. A sound and complete axiomatization of delimited continuations. In *ICFP*, pages 177–188, 2003.

[20] M. Materzok. Axiomatizing subtyped delimited continuations. In *CSL*, pages 521–539, 2013.

[21] M. Materzok and D. Biernacki. Subtyping delimited continuations. In *ICFP*, pages 81–93, 2011.

[22] M. Materzok and D. Biernacki. A dynamic interpretation of the CPS hierarchy. In *APLAS*, pages 296–311, 2012.

[23] E. Moggi. Computational λ-calculus and monads. In *Logic in Computer Science*, 1989.

[24] C.-H. L. Ong and C. A. Stewart. A curry-howard foundation for functional computation with control. In *POPL*, pages 215–227, 1997.

[25] M. Parigot. Lambda-my-calculus: An algorithmic interpretation of classical natural deduction. In *LPAR*, pages 190–201, 1992.

[26] G. D. Plotkin. Call-by-name, call-by-value and the lambda-calculus. *Theoretical Computer Science*, 1(2):125–159, 1975.

[27] S. Ronchi Della Rocca and L. Paolini. *The Parametric Lambda Calculus: A Metamodel for Computation*. Texts in Theoretical Computer Science. An EATCS Series. Springer-Verlag, 2004.

[28] A. Sabry. Note on axiomatizing the semantics of control operators. Technical Report CIS-TR-96-03, Department of Computer and Information Science, University of Oregon, 1996.

[29] A. Sabry and M. Felleisen. Reasoning about programs in continuation-passing style. *Lisp and Symbolic Computation*, 6(3-4):289–360, 1993.

[30] A. Sabry and P. Wadler. A reflection on call-by-value. *ACM Transactions on Programming Languages and Systems*, 19(6):916–941, 1997.

[31] A. Saurin. Separation with streams in the $\lambda\mu$-calculus. In *LICS*, pages 356–365, 2005.

[32] A. Saurin. Typing streams in the $\Lambda\mu$-calculus. *ACM Transactions on Computational Logic*, 11(4), 2010.

[33] C. Shan. Shift to control. In *Workshop on Scheme and Functional Programming*, page 99, 2004.

Coeffects: A Calculus of Context-Dependent Computation

Tomas Petricek Dominic Orchard Alan Mycroft

Computer Laboratory, University of Cambridge

{firstname.lastname}@cl.cam.ac.uk

Abstract

The notion of *context* in functional languages no longer refers just to variables in scope. Context can capture additional properties of variables (usage patterns in linear logics; caching requirements in dataflow languages) as well as additional resources or properties of the execution environment (rebindable resources; platform version in a cross-platform application). The recently introduced notion of coeffects captures the latter, whole-context properties, but it failed to capture fine-grained per-variable properties.

We remedy this by developing a generalized coeffect system with annotations indexed by a coeffect *shape*. By instantiating a concrete shape, our system captures previously studied *flat* (whole-context) coeffects, but also *structural* (per-variable) coeffects, making coeffect analyses more useful. We show that the structural system enjoys desirable syntactic properties and we give a categorical semantics using extended notions of *indexed comonad*.

The examples presented in this paper are based on analysis of established language features (liveness, linear logics, dataflow, dynamic scoping) and we argue that such context-aware properties will also be useful for future development of languages for increasingly heterogeneous and distributed platforms.

Categories and Subject Descriptors D.3.1 [*Programming Languages*]: Formal Definitions and Theory

Keywords Context; Types; Coeffects; Indexed comonads

1. Introduction

Context is important for defining meaning – not just in natural languages, but also in logics and programming languages. The standard notion of context in programming is an environment providing values for free variables. An open term with free variables is context dependent – its meaning depends on the free-variable context. The simply-typed λ-calculus famously analyses such context usage. Other systems go further. For example, bounded linear logic tracks the number of times a variable is used [7].

In software engineering, "context" often encompasses more than just free-variable values. For example, in a distributed system, the context provides resources that may be available on a particular device (*e.g.*, a database on a server or a GPS sensor on a phone).

ICFP '14, September 1–6, 2014, Gothenburg, Sweden.

ACM 978-1-4503-2873-9/14/09...$15.00.

http://dx.doi.org/10.1145/2628136.2628160

In this paper, we develop a calculus for capturing various notions of context in programming. A key feature and contribution of the calculus is its *coeffect system* which provides a static analysis for contextual properties (coeffects). The system follows the style of type and effect systems, but captures a different class of properties. Another key contribution of the calculus is its semantics which can be smoothly instantiated for specific notions of context.

Coeffect systems were previously introduced as a generic analysis of context dependence which can be instantiated for various notions of context [15]. The formalization was restricted to tracking a class of *whole-context* properties where terms have just one coeffect. This limited the applications and precision of any analysis. For example, a whole-context liveness analysis marks the entire free-variable context as live (some variable may be used) or dead (no variable is used), but it cannot record liveness *per variable*.

We develop a more general system which captures both per-variable coeffects, which we call *structural*, and whole-context coeffects, which we call *flat*, and more. Our key contributions are:

- We present the *coeffect calculus* which augments the simply-typed λ-calculus with a general coeffect type system (Section 3). We demonstrate the two classes of flat (whole-context) and structural (fine-grained, per-variable) systems.
- We show practical examples, instantiating the calculus for structural systems capturing variable usage based on bounded linear logic, dataflow caching, and precise liveness analysis. We also instantiate the calculus to flat systems, building on and extending previous examples from [15].
- We discuss the syntactic properties of flat and structural variants of the coeffect calculus (Section 4). Notably, structural systems satisfy type preservation under both β-reduction and η-expansion, allowing their use with both call-by-name and call-by-value languages. This important property distinguishes structural coeffects from both effect systems and flat coeffects.
- We provide a denotational semantics, revisiting and extending the notion of *indexed comonads* to the structural setting (Section 5). We prove soundness by showing the correspondence between syntactic and semantic properties of coeffect systems.

Coeffects can be approached from multiple directions (Section 2.5) including syntactic (effect systems), semantic, and proof-theoretic. We emphasize the syntactic view, though we also outline a categorical semantics and note the interesting technical details.

2. Why coeffects matter

Coeffects are a way to describe notions of context that keep turning up in programming. To illustrate this, we overview three systems tracking contextual properties that motivate our general coeffect system. Two systems track per-variable properties (bounded linear logic and dataflow) and one tracks whole-context properties (implicit parameters). We start with some background and finish with a brief overview of the literature leading to coeffects.

2.1 Background, scalars and vectors

The λ-calculus is asymmetric – it maps a context with *multiple* variables to a *single* result. An expression with n free variables of types τ_i can be modelled by a function $\tau_1 \times \ldots \times \tau_n \rightarrow \tau$ with a product on the left, but a single value on the right. Effect systems attach effect annotations to the result τ. In coeffect systems, we attach coeffects to the context $\tau_1 \times \ldots \times \tau_n$ and we often (but not always) have one coeffect per variable. We call the overall coeffect a *vector* consisting of *scalar* coeffects. This asymmetry explains why coeffect systems are not trivially dual to effect systems.

It is useful to clarify how vectors are used in this paper. Suppose we have a set C of *scalars*. A vector R over C is a tuple $\langle r_1, \ldots, r_n \rangle$ of scalars. We use letters like R, S, T for vectors and r, s, t for scalars.[1] We also say that the *shape* of a vector $[R]$ (or more generally any container) is the set of *positions* in a vector. So, a vector of length n has shape $\{1, 2, \ldots, n\}$.

Just as in scalar-vector multiplication, we lift any binary operation $\bullet$ on scalars into a scalar-vector one: $s \bullet R = \langle s \bullet r_1, \ldots, s \bullet r_n \rangle$. Given two vectors R, S of the same shape, containing partially ordered scalars, we write $R \leq S$ for the pointwise extension of $\leq$ on scalars. Finally, the associative operation $\times$ concatenates vectors.

We note that an environment Γ containing n uniquely named, typed variables is also a vector, but we continue to write ',' for the product, so $\Gamma_1, x\!:\!\tau, \Gamma_2$ should be seen as $\Gamma_1 \times \langle x\!:\!\tau \rangle \times \Gamma_2$.

2.2 Bounded reuse

Bounded linear logic provides a modality that limits the number of times a proposition (variable) can be reused [7]. A type system corresponding to this logic can be used, for example, to restrict well-typed terms to polynomial-time algorithms. A proposition $!_k A$ means that A can be used at most k times. For uniformity with later notation, we write propositions A as τ. Our work attaches a vector of annotations to sets of assumptions, using the @ operator, *i.e.*, $\tau_1, \ldots, \tau_n @ \langle k_1, \ldots, k_n \rangle$, rather than writing bounds for each assumption as in $!_{k_1} A_1, \ldots, !_{k_n} A_n$.

Bounded linear logic includes explicit weakening and contraction rules that affect the multiplicity. Following the original logical style (but with our notation), these are written as:

$$(\text{weak})\frac{\Gamma @ R \vdash \tau}{\Gamma, \tau_0 @ R \times \langle 0 \rangle \vdash \tau} \qquad (\text{contr})\frac{\Gamma_1, \tau_0, \tau_0, \Gamma_2 @ R \times \langle s, t \rangle \times Q \vdash \tau}{\Gamma_1, \tau_0, \Gamma_2 @ R \times \langle s + t \rangle \times Q \vdash \tau}$$

The context $\Gamma @ R$ includes a *coeffect annotation* R which is a vector $\langle r_1, \ldots, r_n \rangle$ of the same length as Γ (a side-condition omitted for brevity). In weakening, unused propositions are annotated with 0 (no uses), while in contraction, multiple occurrences of a proposition are joined by adding the number of uses.

Bounded linear coeffects. The system in Figure 1 fleshes out the idea into a simple calculus. Variable access (*var*) has a singleton context with a singleton coeffect vector $\langle 1 \rangle$. Weakening (*weak*) extends the free-variable context with an unused variable and the coeffect with an associated scalar 0. Explicit contraction (*contr*) and exchange (*exch*) rules manipulate variables in the context and modify the annotations accordingly – adding the number of uses in contraction and switching vector elements in exchange.

For abstraction (*abs*), we know the number of uses of the parameter variable x and attach it to the function type $\tau_1 \xrightarrow{s} \tau_2$ as a *latent* coeffect. The remaining variables in Γ are annotated with the remaining coeffect vector R, specifying *immediate* coeffects.

Application (*app*) describes call-by-name evaluation. Applying a function that uses its parameter t-times to an argument that uses variables in Γ_2 S-times means that, in total, the variables in Γ_2 will be used $(t * S)$-times. Recall that $t * S$ is a scalar multiplication of a vector. Meanwhile, the variables in Γ_1 are used just R-times when reducing the expression e_1 to a function value.

Finally, the sub-coeffecting rule (*sub*) safely overapproximates the number of uses by the pointwise $\leq$ relation. We can view any variable as being used a greater number of times than it actually is.

[1] For better readability, the paper distinguishes different structures using colours. However ignoring the colour does not introduce any ambiguity.

$$(\text{var})\ \frac{}{x\!:\!\tau @ \langle 1 \rangle \vdash x : \tau} \qquad (\text{weak})\ \frac{\Gamma @ R \vdash e : \tau}{\Gamma, x\!:\!\tau_0 @ R \times \langle 0 \rangle \vdash e : \tau}$$

$$(\text{sub})\ \frac{\Gamma @ R \vdash e : \tau}{\Gamma @ R' \vdash e : \tau}\ (R \leq R') \qquad (\text{abs})\ \frac{\Gamma, x\!:\!\tau_1 @ R \times \langle s \rangle \vdash e : \tau_2}{\Gamma @ R \vdash \lambda x.e : \tau_1 \xrightarrow{s} \tau_2}$$

$$(\text{app})\ \frac{\Gamma_1 @ R \vdash e_1 : \tau_1 \xrightarrow{t} \tau_1 \quad \Gamma_2 @ S \vdash e_2 : \tau_2}{\Gamma_1, \Gamma_2 @ R \times (t * S) \vdash e_1\, e_2 : \tau_2}$$

$$(\text{contr})\ \frac{\Gamma_1, y\!:\!\tau_0, z\!:\!\tau_0, \Gamma_2 @ R \times \langle s, t \rangle \times Q \vdash e : \tau}{\Gamma_1, x\!:\!\tau_0, \Gamma_2 @ R \times \langle s + t \rangle \times Q \vdash e[z, y \leftarrow x] : \tau}$$

$$(\text{exch})\ \frac{\Gamma_1, x\!:\!\tau_1, y\!:\!\tau_2, \Gamma_2 @ R \times \langle s, t \rangle \times Q \vdash e : \tau}{\Gamma_1, y\!:\!\tau_2, x\!:\!\tau_1, \Gamma_2 @ R \times \langle t, s \rangle \times Q \vdash e : \tau}$$

Figure 1: Bounded reuse: Type & coeffect system in the λ-calculus

Example. To demonstrate, consider a term $(\lambda v.x{+}v{+}v)\ (x{+}y)$. According to the call-by-name intuition, the variable x is used three times – once directly inside the function and twice via the variable v after substitution. Similarly, y is used twice. Eliding the derivation of the function body's coeffect, abstraction yields:

$$(\text{abs})\ \frac{x\!:\!\mathbb{Z}, v : \mathbb{Z} @ \langle 1, 2 \rangle \vdash x + v + v : \mathbb{Z}}{x\!:\!\mathbb{Z} @ \langle 1 \rangle \vdash (\lambda v.x + v + v) : \mathbb{Z} \xrightarrow{2} \mathbb{Z}}$$

To avoid name clashes, we α-rename x to x' and later join x and x' using contraction. Assuming $(x' + y)$ is checked in a context that marks x' and y as used once, the application rule yields a judgment that is simplified as follows:

$$\frac{x\!:\!\mathbb{Z}, x'\!:\!\mathbb{Z}, y\!:\!\mathbb{Z} @ \langle 1 \rangle \times (2 * \langle 1, 1 \rangle) \vdash (\lambda v.x + v + v)\ (x' + y) : \mathbb{Z}}{(\text{contr})\ \dfrac{x\!:\!\mathbb{Z}, x'\!:\!\mathbb{Z}, y\!:\!\mathbb{Z} @ \langle 1, 2, 2 \rangle \vdash (\lambda v.x + v + v)\ (x' + y) : \mathbb{Z}}{x\!:\!\mathbb{Z}, y\!:\!\mathbb{Z} @ \langle 3, 2 \rangle \vdash (\lambda v.x + v + v)\ (x + y) : \mathbb{Z}}}$$

The first step performs scalar multiplication, producing the vector $\langle 1, 2, 2 \rangle$. In the second step, we use contraction to join variables x and x' from the function and argument terms respectively.

It is worth pointing out that reduction by substitution yields $x{+}(x{+}y){+}(x{+}y)$ which has the same coeffect as the original. We return to evaluation strategies in Section 4, and show that structural coeffect systems preserve types and coeffects under β-reduction.

2.3 Dataflow and data access

Dataflow languages, such as Lucid, describe computations over *streams* [20]. An expression is re-evaluated when new inputs are available (push) or when more output is demanded (pull). In causal dataflow, programs can access past values of a stream. We consider a language where **prev** e returns the previous value of e. In the language, **prev** (**prev** e) returns the second past value and so on.

An implementation of causal dataflow may cache past values of variables as an optimisation. The question is, how many past values should be cached? This can be approximated by a coeffect system.

Dataflow coeffects. The coeffect system for dataflow is similar to the one for bounded reuse, tracking a vector of natural numbers R as part of the context $\Gamma @ R$. Here, coeffects represent the maximal number of past values (*causality depth*) required for a variable.

$$\text{(contr)}\ \frac{\Gamma_1, y\!:\!\tau, z\!:\!\tau, \Gamma_2 @ R \times \langle s,t \rangle \times Q \vdash e : \tau}{\Gamma_1, x\!:\!\tau, \Gamma_2 @ R \times \langle \mathsf{max}(s,t) \rangle \times Q \vdash e[y,z \leftarrow x] : \tau}$$

$$\text{(app)}\ \frac{\Gamma_1 @ R \vdash e_1 : \tau_1 \xrightarrow{t} \tau_2 \quad \Gamma_2 @ S \vdash e_2 : \tau_1}{\Gamma_1, \Gamma_2 @ R \times (t+S) \vdash e_1\, e_2 : \tau_2}$$

$$\text{(var)}\ \frac{}{x\!:\!\tau @ \langle 0 \rangle \vdash x : \tau} \qquad \text{(prev)}\ \frac{\Gamma @ R \vdash e : \tau}{\Gamma @ 1 + R \vdash \textbf{prev}\ e : \tau}$$

Figure 2: Type and coeffect system for dataflow caching

Weakening, exchange, abstraction and sub-coeffecting are the same as in bounded linear coeffects, but the remaining rules differ. In Figure 2, accessed variables (*var*) are annotated with 0 meaning that no past value is required (only the current one). The (*prev*) rule crates caching requirements – it increments the number of required values for all variables used in e using scalar-vector addition.

Application and contraction have the same structure as before, but use different operators. If two variables are contracted, requiring s and t past values, then at most $\mathsf{max}(s,t)$ past values are needed (*contr*). That is, two caches are combined with the maximum of the two requirements, which satisfy the smaller requirements. In (*app*), the function requires t past values of its parameter. This means t past values of e_2 are needed which in turn requires S past values of its free variables Γ_2. Thus, we need $t+S$ past values of Γ_2 to perform the call (*e.g.*, we need $1+S$ values to get 1 past value of the input τ_1, $2+S$ values to get 2 past values of τ_1, *etc.*).

Example. As an example, consider a function $\lambda x.\textbf{prev}\ (y+x)$ applied to an argument $\textbf{prev}\ (\textbf{prev}\ y)$. The body of the function accesses the past value of two variables, one free and one bound:

$$\text{(abs)}\frac{y\!:\!\mathbb{Z}, x\!:\!\mathbb{Z} @ \langle 1,1 \rangle \vdash \textbf{prev}\ (y+x) : \mathbb{Z}}{y\!:\!\mathbb{Z} @ \langle 1 \rangle \vdash \lambda x.\textbf{prev}\ (y+x) : \mathbb{Z} \xrightarrow{1} \mathbb{Z}}$$

The expression always requires the previous value of y and adds it to a previous value of the parameter x. Evaluating the value of the argument $\textbf{prev}\ (\textbf{prev}\ y)$ requires two past values of y and so the overall requirement is 3 past values:

$$\text{(contr)}\ \dfrac{\text{(app)}\ \dfrac{y\!:\!\mathbb{Z} @ \langle 1 \rangle \vdash \lambda x. \ \ldots \quad y'\!:\!\mathbb{Z} @ \langle 2 \rangle \vdash (\textbf{prev}\ (\textbf{prev}\ y')) : \mathbb{Z}}{y\!:\!\mathbb{Z}, y'\!:\!\mathbb{Z} @ \langle 1,3 \rangle \vdash (\lambda x.\textbf{prev}\ (y+x))\ (\textbf{prev}\ (\textbf{prev}\ y')) : \mathbb{Z}}}{y\!:\!\mathbb{Z} @ \langle 3 \rangle \vdash (\lambda x.\textbf{prev}\ (y+x))\ (\textbf{prev}\ (\textbf{prev}\ y)) : \mathbb{Z}}$$

The derivation uses (*app*) to get requirements $\langle 1,3 \rangle$ and then (*contr*) to take the maximum, showing three past values are sufficient. Reducing the expression by substitution we get $\textbf{prev}\ (y + (\textbf{prev}\ (\textbf{prev}\ y)))$. Semantically, this performs stream lookups $y[1] + y[3]$ where the indices are the number of enclosing **prev**s.

We previously used dataflow as an example of coeffects [15], but tracked caching requirements on the whole context. The system outlined here is more powerful and practically useful, with finer-grained coeffects tracking per-variable caching requirements.

2.4 Implicit parameters

As our third example, we revisit Haskell implicit parameters [9] used in our earlier coeffect work [15]. Implicit parameters are variables that mix aspects of dynamic and lexical scoping. Implicit parameters are a distinct syntactic category to variables and we write them as $?\mathsf{p}$. For simplicity, we omit let-binding for implicit parameters and focus just on tracking requirements.

Implicit parameters coeffects. Implicit parameters are a whole-context coeffect not linked to ordinary variables. We keep track of sets of implicit parameters that are required by an expression (and their types). For example $\Gamma @ \{?\mathsf{p}_1 : \tau_1, \ldots, ?\mathsf{p}_n : \tau_n\}$ means that a context provides ordinary variables Γ and values for implicit parameters $?\mathsf{p}_i$. Unlike in the previous examples, we no longer need to distinguish between coeffects attached to variables (scalars) and coeffects attached to contexts (vectors), so we write r, s, t for both.

$$\text{(exch)}\ \frac{\Gamma_1, x\!:\!\tau_1, y : \tau_2, \Gamma_2 @ r \cup s \cup t \cup q \vdash e : \tau}{\Gamma_1, y\!:\!\tau_2, x : \tau_1, \Gamma_2 @ r \cup t \cup s \cup q \vdash e : \tau}$$

$$\text{(app)}\ \frac{\Gamma_1 @ r \vdash e_1 : \tau_1 \xrightarrow{t} \tau_1 \quad \Gamma_2 @ s \vdash e_2 : \tau_2}{\Gamma_1, \Gamma_2 @ r \cup t \cup s \vdash e_1\, e_2 : \tau_2}$$

$$\text{(param)}\ \frac{}{() @ \{?\mathsf{p} : \tau\} \vdash ?\mathsf{p} : \tau} \qquad \text{(abs)}\ \frac{\Gamma, x\!:\!\tau_1 @ r \cup s \vdash e : \tau_2}{\Gamma @ r \vdash \lambda x.e : \tau_1 \xrightarrow{s} \tau_2}$$

Figure 3: Type and coeffect system for implicit parameters

Despite the differences, the type system in Figure 3 follows the same structure as the earlier two examples. Context requirements are created when accessing an implicit parameter, in a system-specific rule (*param*). Structural rules (exchange, weaken, contract) do not affect the coeffects. For example, parameters are reordered in (*exch*), but this has no effect as set union $\cup$ is commutative.

In abstraction and application, the structural $\times$ operator (previously vector concatenation) becomes $\cup$. Sets of implicit parameters are not associated to individual variables and so they are unioned. The (*app*) rule uses $\cup$ to combine the implicit parameters required by the function with the requirements of the argument too.

We call this a *flat* coeffect system since coeffects have only one shape (there is no scalar/vector distinction). Other flat coeffect systems may use a richer structure [15]. In particular, the operations used in abstraction and application may differ (to accommodate over-approximation). We return to this in Section 3.5.

Example. Unlike structural (per-variable) coeffect systems, flat (whole-context) systems do not necessarily have principal coeffects. This arises from the (*abs*) rule which can freely split requirements between the function type and the declaring context. Consider a function $\lambda().?\mathsf{p}_1 + ?\mathsf{p}_2$. There are nine possible type and coeffect derivations, two of which are:

$$\emptyset @ \{\} \vdash \lambda().?\mathsf{p}_1 + ?\mathsf{p}_2 : \mathsf{unit} \xrightarrow{\{?\mathsf{p}_1:\mathbb{Z}, ?\mathsf{p}_2:\mathbb{Z}\}} \mathbb{Z}$$
$$\emptyset @ \{?\mathsf{p}_1 : \mathbb{Z}\} \vdash \lambda().?\mathsf{p}_1 + ?\mathsf{p}_2 : \mathsf{unit} \xrightarrow{\{?\mathsf{p}_2:\mathbb{Z}\}} \mathbb{Z}$$

In the first case, both parameters are dynamically scoped and have to be provided by the caller. In the second case, the parameter $?\mathsf{p}_1$ is available in the declaring scope and so it is (lexically) captured.

Although structural coeffects have more desirable syntactic properties, we aim to capture this non-principality too as it is practically useful – not only in Haskell's implicit parameters, but also in resource rebinding in distributed systems such as Acute [17].

2.5 Pathways to coeffects

This paper largely follows work on effect systems and their link to categorical semantics. We briefly review this and other directions leading to coeffects. An eager reader can return to this section later.

Effect systems. Effect systems [6] track effectful operations of computations such as memory access or lock usage [4]. They are written as judgments $\Gamma \vdash e : \tau \,\&\, \rho$ associating effects ρ with the result. Effect systems capture *output effects* where, as Tate puts it, *"all computations with [an] effect can be thunked as pure computations for a domain-specific notion of purity."* [18]. This thunking is typically a λ-abstraction. Given an effectful expression e, the function $\lambda x.e$ is an effect-free value that delays all effects:

$$\text{(abs)}\ \frac{\Gamma, x\!:\!\tau_1 \vdash e : \tau_2 \,\&\, \rho}{\Gamma \vdash \lambda x.e : \tau_1 \xrightarrow{\rho} \tau_2 \,\&\, \emptyset}$$

Coeffects do not follow this pattern. In contrast to effect systems, context requirements cannot be easily "thunked" as pure values. Lambda abstraction can split context requirements between *immediate* and *latent* requirements. This is akin to how lambda abstraction splits a free-variable context into the bound parameter (call site) and the remaining free variables (declaration site).

Categorical semantics. Moggi models effectful computations as functions of type $\tau_1 \rightarrow M\tau_2$ where M is a monad providing composition of effectful computations [10]. Wadler and Thiemann link effect systems to monads via annotated monads $\tau_1 \rightarrow M^{\rho}\tau_2$ [21], whose semantics has been provided by Katsumata [8].

Context-dependent computations require a different model. Uustalu and Vene use functions $C\tau_1 \rightarrow \tau_2$ where C is a *comonad* [19]. Our earlier work [15] used indexed comonads with denotations $C^r\tau_1 \rightarrow \tau_2$ adding annotations akin to Wadler and Thiemann. In Section 5 we extend indexed comonads to capture the general coeffect systems of this paper, in the style of Katsumata.

Language and meta-language. Moggi uses monads in two systems [10]. In the first system, a monad is used to model an effectful language itself – the semantics of a language uses a specific monad. In the second system, monads are added as type constructors, together with syntax corresponding to *unit* and *bind* operations.

For context dependence, Uustalu and Vene follow the first approach using comonads for their semantics [19]. Contextual-Modal Type Theory (CMTT) of Nanevski *et al.* [11] follows the latter approach, adding a comonad to the language via the $\Box$ modality of modal S4. We focus on concrete languages using the first approach. A "coeffect meta-language" is an interesting future work.

Sub-structural systems Sub-structural type systems restrict how a context is used. This is achieved by removing some of the structural typing rules (weakening, contraction, exchange). As the bounded linear logic example (Section 2.2) shows, our system can be viewed as a generalization of sub-structural type systems.

3. The coeffect calculus

The three calculi shown in the previous section track two kinds of contextual properties: bounded reuse and dataflow are structural (per-variable) systems, and implicit parameters and our earlier coeffect systems [15] are flat (whole-context) systems. This section presents our primary contribution: the general coeffect calculus.

The calculus is parameterised by an algebraic structure of coeffects. To capture both structural and flat systems, coeffect annotations are indexed by a *shape*. In flat systems, the shape is a singleton set $\{*\}$ and so annotations are *scalar* values. Structural systems use shapes matching the number of variables in a free-variable context $\{1, \ldots, n\}$ and so annotations are *vectors*. However, the coeffect calculus could also use shapes describing trees and other structures.

3.1 Understanding coeffects: syntax and semantics

The coeffect calculus provides both an analysis of context dependence (its coeffect system) and a semantics for context (see Section 5). These two features of the calculus provide different perspectives on coeffect annotations R in a judgment $\Gamma@R \vdash e : \tau$.

- Syntactically, coeffects model *contextual requirements* and may be overapproximated, so that more capabilities are required than necessary at runtime.
- Semantically, coeffects model *contextual capabilities* and behave like containers of capabilities, such that the semantics may throw away capabilities that will not be needed.

Thus there are two dual ways to understand coeffect annotations. Each perspective implies an alternate reading of the typing rules.

- As *contextual requirements*, the rules should be read top-down. The requirements of multiple sub-terms are *merged* and the requirements of a function body are *split* between immediate (declaration-site) and latent (call-site) coeffects.
- As *contextual capabilities*, the rules should be read bottom-up. The capabilities provided to a larger term are *split* between sub-terms; for functions, the capabilities of declaration-site and call-site are *merged* and passed to the body.

The reason for this asymmetry follows from the fact that context appears in a *negative position* in the model. In Section 5, the denotation of a judgment $\Gamma@R \vdash e : \tau$ is a function of the form $\mathsf{D}_R[\![\Gamma]\!] \rightarrow [\![\tau]\!]$ where $\mathsf{D}_R[\![\Gamma]\!]$ encodes the contextual capabilities used to evaluate a term. Similarly a function $\tau_1 \xrightarrow{s} \tau_2$ has a model of the form $\mathsf{D}_s[\![\tau_1]\!] \rightarrow [\![\tau_2]\!]$ with additional contextual capabilities attached to the input.

3.2 Structure of coeffects

We describe the algebraic structure of coeffects in three steps. First, we define a *coeffect scalar* structure which defines the basic building blocks of coeffect information; then we define *coeffect shapes* which determines how coeffect scalar values are related to the free-variable context. Finally, we define the *coeffect algebra* which consists of shape-indexed coeffect scalar values.

For example, in bounded reuse the coeffect scalar structure comprise natural numbers $\mathbb{N}$ with $+$ and $*$ operators. The shape for bounded reuse is the length of the free-variable context and so the coeffect annotation is a vector of matching length. Finally, the coeffect algebra specifies how vectors are concatenated and split in abstraction and application.

In the coeffect system of the calculus, contexts are annotated with shape-indexed coeffects (*e.g.*, vectors) as in $\Gamma@R \vdash e : \tau$. However, functions take just a single input parameter and so are annotated with scalar coeffect values as in $\sigma \xrightarrow{r} \tau$. From now on, we write σ for the *source* and τ for the *target* of function types.

Coeffect scalar. Coeffect scalar structures are equipped with two operations. In bounded reuse, those were $*$ for sequencing (in function application) and $+$ for context sharing (in contraction). Additional structure is needed for variable access and sub-coeffecting.

Definition 1. A *coeffect scalar* $(\mathcal{C}, \circledast, \oplus, \mathsf{use}, \mathsf{ign}, \leq)$ comprises a set $\mathcal{C}$ together with elements $\mathsf{use}, \mathsf{ign} \in \mathcal{C}$, relation $\leq$ and binary operations $\circledast, \oplus$ such that $(\mathcal{C}, \circledast, \mathsf{use})$ and $(\mathcal{C}, \oplus, \mathsf{ign})$ are monoids, $(\mathcal{C}, \leq)$ is a pre-order, and the following distributivity axioms hold:

$$(r \oplus s) \circledast t = (r \circledast t) \oplus (s \circledast t)$$
$$t \circledast (r \oplus s) = (t \circledast r) \oplus (t \circledast s)$$

The operation $\circledast$ must form a monoid with use to guarantee an underlying category in the semantics (Section 5). It models sequential composition with variable access (use) as the identity. The other element (ign) is used for variables that are not accessed. The operation $\oplus$ combines coeffects for contexts used in multiple places (contraction). The notation is inspired by the bounded reuse example, which uses coeffect scalar structure $(\mathbb{N}, *, +, 1, 0, \leq)$, but be aware that $\circledast$ and $\oplus$ are not always multiplication and addition.

Coeffect annotations R can be viewed as *containers* of scalar coeffects. For structural coeffects, the container is a vector, while for flat coeffects it is a trivial singleton container. The following definition takes inspiration from the work of Abbott *et al.* [1] which describes containers in terms of *shapes* and a set of *positions*.

Coeffect shapes. The coeffect system is parameterised by a set of shapes $\mathcal{S}$. A coeffect annotation is indexed by a shape $s \in \mathcal{S}$ calculated from the shape of the free-variable context Γ. The correspondence is not necessarily bijective. For example, flat coeffect systems have just a single shape $\mathcal{S} = \{\star\}$.

Thus, in the judgment $\Gamma @ R \vdash e : \tau$, the coeffect annotation R is drawn from the set of coeffect scalars $\mathcal{C}$ indexed by the shape of Γ. We write $s = [\Gamma]$ for the shape corresponding to Γ. We define shapes by a *set* of positions and so we can define $R \in s \to \mathcal{C}$ as a mapping from positions (defined by the shape) to scalar coeffects. We usually write this as the exponent $R \in \mathcal{C}^s$.

The set of shapes is equipped with an operation that combines shapes (when we combine variable contexts), an operation that computes shape from the free-variable contexts, and two special shapes in $\mathcal{S}$ representing empty context and singleton context.

Definition 2. A *coeffect shape* structure $(\mathcal{S}, [-], \diamond, \hat{0}, \hat{1})$ comprises a set $\mathcal{S}$ with a binary operation $\diamond$ on $\mathcal{S}$ for shape composition, a mapping from contexts to shapes $[\Gamma] \in \mathcal{S}$, and elements $\hat{0}, \hat{1} \in \mathcal{S}$ such that $(\mathcal{S}, \diamond, \hat{0})$ is a monoid and $[-]$ is partially specified on empty and singleton free-variable contexts by:

$$[\emptyset] = \hat{0} \qquad [v : \tau] = \hat{1}$$

This means that the elements $\hat{0}$ and $\hat{1}$ represent the shapes of empty and singleton free-variable contexts respectively. As said earlier, we use two kinds of shape structure:

- Structural coeffect shape is defined as $(\mathbb{N}, |-|, +, 0, 1)$. We treat numbers as sets $0 = \{\}, 1 = \{\emptyset\}, 2 = \{\emptyset, 1\}, 3 = \{\emptyset, 1, 2\} \ldots$ (so that a number is a set of positions). The shape mapping $|\Gamma|$ returns the number of variables in Γ. Empty and singleton contexts are annotated with 0 and 1, respectively, and shapes of combined contexts are added so that $|\Gamma_1, \Gamma_2| = |\Gamma_1| + |\Gamma_2|$. Therefore, a coeffect annotation is a *vector* $R \in \mathcal{C}^n$ and assigns a coeffect scalar $R(i) \in \mathcal{C}$ for each variable x_i in the context.
- Flat coeffect shape is defined as $(\{\star\}, \mathsf{star}, \diamond, \star, \star)$ where $\mathsf{star}(\Gamma) = \star$ and $\star \diamond \star = \star$ where $\star = \{\emptyset\}$. That is, there is a single shape $\star$ with a single position and all free-variable contexts have the same shape. Therefore, a coeffect annotation is drawn from $\mathcal{C}^\star$ which is isomorphic to $\mathcal{C}$ and so a coeffect scalar $r \in \mathcal{C}$ is associated with every free-variable context.

Using a shape with *no* positions reduces our system to the simply-typed λ-calculus with no context annotations. Trees can also be used to build a system akin to bunched typing [12].

Coeffect algebra. The coeffect calculus annotates judgments with shape-indexed, or *shaped*, coeffects. The *coeffect algebra* structure combines a coeffect scalar and coeffect shape structure to define shaped coeffects and operations for combining these. In Section 2, shaped coeffects were combined by the tensor $\times$ in structural examples and $\cup$ in the implicit parameters example. To capture the examples so far and those described previously [15], we distinguish two operators for combining shaped coeffects.

Definition 3. Given a coeffect scalar $(\mathcal{C}, \circledast, \oplus, \mathsf{use}, \mathsf{ign}, \leq)$ and a coeffect shape $(\mathcal{S}, [-], \diamond, \hat{0}, \hat{1})$ a *coeffect algebra* extends the two structures with $(\overline{\times}, \underline{\times}, \bot)$ where $\bot \in \mathcal{C}^{\hat{0}}$ is a coeffect annotation for the empty context and $\overline{\times}, \underline{\times}$ are families of operations that combine coeffect annotations indexed by shapes. That is $\forall n, m \in \mathcal{S}$:

$$\underline{\times}_{m,n}, \overline{\times}_{m,n} \; : \; \mathcal{C}^m \times \mathcal{C}^n \to \mathcal{C}^{m \diamond n}$$

A coeffect algebra induces the following two additional operations:

$$\begin{array}{lll} \langle - \rangle & : & \mathcal{C} \to \mathcal{C}^{\hat{1}} \\ \langle x \rangle & = & \lambda \hat{1}.x \end{array} \qquad \begin{array}{lll} \circledast_m & : & \mathcal{C} \times \mathcal{C}^m \to \mathcal{C}^m \\ r \circledast S & = & \lambda s.r \circledast (S(s)) \end{array}$$

$\langle - \rangle$ lifts a scalar coeffect to a shaped coeffect indexed by the singleton context shape. The $\circledast_m$ operation is a left multiplication of a vector by a scalar. As we always use lower-case for scalars and upper-case for vectors, using the same symbol is not ambiguous. We also tend to omit the subscript m and write just $\circledast$.

$\boxed{\Gamma @ R \vdash e : \tau}$

$$\text{(const)}\ \frac{}{() @ \bot \vdash c : \iota} \qquad \text{(var)}\ \frac{}{(x : \tau) @ \langle \mathsf{use} \rangle \vdash x : \tau}$$

$$\text{(abs)}\ \frac{\Gamma, x : \sigma @ R \,\overline{\times}\, \langle s \rangle \vdash e : \tau}{\Gamma @ R \vdash \lambda x.e : \sigma \xrightarrow{s} \tau}$$

$$\text{(app)}\ \frac{\Gamma_1 @ R \vdash e_1 : \sigma \xrightarrow{t} \tau \qquad \Gamma_2 @ S \vdash e_2 : \sigma}{\Gamma_1, \Gamma_2 @ R \,\underline{\times}\, (t \circledast S) \vdash e_1\, e_2 : \tau}$$

$$\text{(let)}\ \frac{\Gamma_1 @ S \vdash e_1 : \sigma \qquad \Gamma_2, x : \sigma @ R \,\overline{\times}\, \langle t \rangle \vdash e_2 : \tau}{\Gamma_1, \Gamma_2 @ R \,\underline{\times}\, (t \circledast S) \vdash \mathbf{let}\ x = e_1\ \mathbf{in}\ e_2 : \tau}$$

$$\text{(ctx)}\ \frac{\Gamma @ R \vdash e : \tau \qquad \Gamma' @ R' \rightsquigarrow \Gamma @ R, \theta}{\Gamma' @ R' \vdash \theta e : \tau}$$

$\boxed{\Gamma' @ R' \rightsquigarrow \Gamma @ R, \theta}$

$$\text{(weak)} \qquad \Gamma, x : \tau @ R \,\underline{\times}\, \langle \mathsf{ign} \rangle \rightsquigarrow \Gamma @ R, \emptyset$$

$$\text{(exch)} \quad \begin{array}{c} \Gamma_1, y : \sigma, x : \tau, \Gamma_2 @ R \,\underline{\times}\, \langle t \rangle \,\underline{\times}\, \langle s \rangle \,\underline{\times}\, Q \rightsquigarrow \\ \Gamma_1, x : \tau, y : \sigma, \Gamma_2 @ R \,\overline{\times}\, \langle s \rangle \,\overline{\times}\, \langle t \rangle \,\overline{\times}\, Q, \emptyset \end{array}$$

$$\text{(contr)} \quad \begin{array}{c} \Gamma_1, x : \tau, \Gamma_2 @ R \,\underline{\times}\, \langle s \oplus t \rangle \,\underline{\times}\, Q \rightsquigarrow \\ \Gamma_1, y : \tau, z : \tau, \Gamma_2 @ R \,\overline{\times}\, \langle s \rangle \,\overline{\times}\, \langle t \rangle \,\overline{\times}\, Q, [y, z \mapsto x] \end{array}$$

$$\text{(sub)} \quad \begin{array}{c} \Gamma_1, x : \tau, \Gamma_2 @ R \,\underline{\times}\, \langle s' \rangle \,\underline{\times}\, T \rightsquigarrow \\ \Gamma_1, x : \tau, \Gamma_2 @ R \,\overline{\times}\, \langle s \rangle \,\overline{\times}\, T, \emptyset \end{array} \qquad (s \leq s')$$

Figure 4: The general coeffect calculus

The operators $\underline{\times}$ and $\overline{\times}$ combine shaped coeffects associated with two contexts. For example, assume we have Γ_1 and Γ_2 with coeffects $R \in \mathcal{C}^m$ and $S \in \mathcal{C}^n$. In the structural system, the context shapes m, n denote the number of variables in the two contexts. The combined context Γ_1, Γ_2 has a shape $m \diamond n$ and the combined coeffects $R \,\overline{\times}\, S, R \,\underline{\times}\, S \in \mathcal{C}^{m \diamond n}$ are indexed by that shape.

For structural coeffect systems such as bounded reuse, both $\underline{\times}$ and $\overline{\times}$ are just the tensor product $\times$ of vectors. However, we need to distinguish them for flat coeffect systems discussed later.

The difference is explained by the semantics (Section 5), where $R \,\overline{\times}\, S$ is an annotation of the codomain of a morphism that merges the capabilities provided by two contexts (in the syntactic reading, splits the context requirements); $R \,\underline{\times}\, S$ is an annotation of the domain of a morphism that splits the capabilities of a single context into two parts (in the syntactic reading, merges their context requirements). Syntactically, this means that we always use $\overline{\times}$ in rule *premises* and $\underline{\times}$ in *conclusions*. For now, it suffices to use the bounded-reuse intuition and read the operations as tensor products.

The distinction between $\underline{\times}$ and $\overline{\times}$ provides flexibility to the calculus. For example, it is possible to instantiate the calculus such that structural rules are not permitted. In the case of flat and structural classes of system, different properties of $\underline{\times}$ and $\overline{\times}$ permit free use of structural rules. This is seen in the following sections.

3.3 General coeffect type system

In the previous section, we developed an algebraic structure capable of capturing different concrete context-dependent properties discussed in Section 2. Now, we use the structure to define the general coeffect calculus in Figure 4.

Coeffect annotations on free-variable contexts are shape-indexed, where for some shape $s \in \mathcal{S}$ then $R, S, T \in \mathcal{C}^s$. Function types are annotated with coeffects scalars $r, s, t \in \mathcal{C}$. The rules of Figure 4 manipulate coeffect annotations using the coeffect algebra operations ($\bar{\times}, \underline{\times}, \perp$) and the derived constructs $\langle - \rangle$ and $\circledast$. Free-variable contexts Γ are treated as vectors modulo duplicate use of variables – associativity is built-in. Variable order matters, but can be changed using the structural rules. Structural rules are expressed using a helper relation, written $\rightsquigarrow$.

Typing rules. Constants (*const*) and variables (*var*) annotate the context with special values. The empty unused context is annotated with $\perp \in \mathcal{C}^{\hat{0}}$ and the singleton context with $\langle \mathsf{use} \rangle \in \mathcal{C}^{\hat{1}}$. Note that the shapes $\hat{0}$, $\hat{1}$ match the shape of the variable contexts.

Lambda abstraction *splits* the context requirements using $\bar{\times}$ into a coeffect R and a coeffect $\langle s \rangle$ of a shape $\hat{1}$ (semantically, it *merges* capabilities provided by the declaration-site and call-site contexts). In structural systems such as bounded reuse, this identifies coeffect associated with the bound variable, because $\bar{\times}$ is not commutative.

The (*app*) rule follows the patterns seen earlier – it uses the scalar-vector multiplication ($t \circledast S$) of the coeffects S from the argument (associated with Γ_2) and the latent coeffect t of the function. Using the syntactic reading, it then *merges* context requirements for Γ_1 and Γ_2. In the dual semantic reading, it *splits* the provided context into two parts passed to the sub-expressions.

The typing of let-binding (*let*) corresponds to the typing of an expression $(\lambda x.e_2)\ e_1$. Syntactically, the context requirements are first split using $\bar{\times}$ and then re-combined using $\underline{\times}$.

Structural rules. The coeffect-annotated context can be transformed using structural rules that are not syntax-directed. These are captured by (*ctx*), which uses a helper relation representing context transformations $\Gamma'@R' \rightsquigarrow \Gamma@R, \theta$. The rule models that a context used in the rule conclusion $\Gamma'@R'$ can be transformed to a context required by the premise $\Gamma@R$ (using the semantic bottom-up reading). In the rule, θ is a variable substitution generated by the transformation, which is used in the (*contr*) rule.

Exchange and contraction decompose and reconstruct coeffect annotations using $\bar{\times}_{m,n}$ (in assumption) and $\underline{\times}_{m,n}$ (in conclusion). The shape subscripts are omitted, but we require the shapes to match using $m = [\Gamma_1]$ and $n = [\Gamma_2]$.

The (*weak*) rule drops an ignored variable annotated with $\langle \mathsf{ign} \rangle$ (compare with (*var*) annotated using $\langle \mathsf{use} \rangle$). The (*exch*) rule swaps variables/coeffects while (*contr*) combines coeffects using $\oplus$ to represent sharing of the context. Finally, (*sub*) represents sub-coeffecting and can be applied (pointwise) to any scalar coeffect.

3.4 Structural coeffects

The coeffect system uses a general notion of context shape, but it was designed with structural and flat systems in mind. The structural system is new in this paper and so we look at it first.

Recall the coeffect shapes that characterise structural systems: the shape is formed by natural numbers (with addition) modelling the number of variables in the context. The coeffect algebra is therefore formed by the free monoid (lists/vectors) over a coeffect scalar. This means that the system keeps a vector of coeffect scalar annotations – one for each variable. An empty context (*e.g.*, in the (*const*) rule) is annotated with a zero-length vector.

Definition 4. Given a coeffect scalar $(\mathcal{C}, \circledast, \oplus, \mathsf{use}, \mathsf{ign}, \leq)$ a *structural coeffect system* has:

- Coeffect shape $(\mathbb{N}, |-|, +, 0, 1)$ formed by natural numbers
- Coeffect algebra $(\times, \times, \langle\rangle)$ where $\times$ and $\langle\rangle$ are shape-indexed versions of the binary operation and the unit of a free monoid over $\mathcal{C}$. That is $\times : \mathcal{C}^n \times \mathcal{C}^m \rightarrow \mathcal{C}^{n+m}$ appends vectors (lists) and $\langle\rangle : \mathcal{C}^0$ represents empty vectors (lists).

The definition is valid since the shape operations form a monoid $(\mathbb{N}, +, 0)$ and $[-]$ (calculating the length of a list) is a monoid homomorphism from the free monoid to the monoid of shapes.

Examples. Defining a concrete structural coeffect system is easy, we just provide the coeffect scalar structure and the rest is free.

- To recreate the system for bounded reuse, we use coeffect scalars formed by $(\mathbb{N}, *, +, 1, 0, \leq)$. As in the system of Figure 1, *used* variables are therefore annotated with 1 and *unused* with 0. Contraction adds the number of uses via $+$ and application (sequencing) multiplies the uses.
- *Dataflow* uses natural numbers (of past values), but differently: $(\mathbb{N}, +, \mathsf{max}, 0, 0, \leq)$. Variables are initially annotated with 0 (and can be incremented using the **prev** keyword). Annotations of a shared variable are combined by taking maximum (of past values needed) and sequencing uses $+$.
- Another use of the system is to track *variable liveness*. The annotations are formed by $\mathcal{C} = \{\mathsf{D}, \mathsf{L}\}$ where L represents a *live* (used) variable and D represents a *dead* (unused) variable. The coeffect scalar structure is $(\mathcal{C}, \sqcap, \sqcup, \mathsf{L}, \mathsf{D}, \sqsubseteq)$ where $\mathsf{D} \sqsubseteq \mathsf{L}$.

  In sequential composition ($\sqcap$), a variable is live only if it is required by both of the computations ($\mathsf{L} \sqcap \mathsf{L} = \mathsf{L}$), otherwise it is marked as dead (D). A computation is not evaluated if its result is not needed. A shared variable ($\sqcup$) is live if either of the uses is live ($\mathsf{D} \sqcup \mathsf{D} = \mathsf{D}$, otherwise L).

Structural liveness is a practically useful, precise version of an example from our earlier work, which was a flat system overapproximating liveness of the entire context [15]. Since $\bar{\times} = \underline{\times} = \times$, structural rules (weaken, contract, exchange) are freely permitted, modifying the coeffects accordingly.

3.5 Flat coeffects

The same general coeffect system can be used to define systems that track whole-context coeffects as in the implicit parameters example (Section 2.4). Flat coeffect systems are characterised by a singleton set of shapes, such as $\{\star\}$. In this setting, the context annotations $\mathcal{C}^\star$ coincide with coeffect scalars $\mathcal{C}$.

In addition to the coeffect scalar structure, we also need to define $\underline{\times}$ and $\bar{\times}$. Our examples of flat coeffects use $\oplus$ (merging of scalar coeffects) for $\underline{\times}$ (merging of shaped coeffect annotations). However, the $\bar{\times}$ operation needs to be provided explicitly. Thus the general form of flat coeffect system is defined as follows.

Definition 5. Given a coeffect scalar $(\mathcal{C}, \circledast, \oplus, \mathsf{use}, \mathsf{ign}, \leq)$ and an operation $\wedge : \mathcal{C} \times \mathcal{C} \rightarrow \mathcal{C}$ such that $(r \wedge s) \leq (r \oplus s)$, we define:

- Flat coeffect shape $(\{\star\}, \mathit{const}\,\star, \diamond, \star, \star)$ where $\star \diamond \star = \star$
- Flat coeffect algebra $(\wedge, \oplus, \mathsf{ign})$, *i.e.*, the $\underline{\times} = \oplus$ and $\perp = \mathsf{ign}$ with the additional binary operation $\bar{\times} = \wedge$.

The additional axiom $(r \wedge s) \leq (r \oplus s)$ is required for β-equality in flat systems (see later Theorem 11, Section 4.2).

If $\bar{\times}$ is idempotent, then structural rules (weaken, contract, exchange) are freely permitted since any flat coeffect annotation r can be expanded to $r \bar{\times} r$. This property holds for all examples here, hence structural rules can always be applied.

If $\underline{\times}$ is also idempotent (as in all our examples), then exchange and contraction rules preserve the coeffects of the assumption in the conclusion. Otherwise $(r \wedge s) \leq (r \oplus s)$ means that exchange and contraction behave as the (*sub*) rule for subcoeffecting.

Examples. Implicit parameters are the prime example of a flat coeffect system, but other examples include rebindable resources [17] and Haskell type classes [13].

In the implicit parameters system (Section 2.4), coeffect scalars are sets of name-type pairs $\mathcal{C} = \mathcal{P}(\mathsf{Name} \times \mathsf{Type})$. Variables are annotated with $\emptyset$ and coeffects are combined or split (in the top-down reading for (*abs*)) using set union $\cup$. Thus, the coeffect scalar structure is $(\mathcal{P}(\mathsf{Name} \times \mathsf{Types}), \cup, \cup, \emptyset, \emptyset, \subseteq)$ with $\wedge = \cup$.

Remark 6. We previously described flat systems for liveness and dataflow [15]. Turning a structural system to a flat system requires finding $\wedge$ that underapproximates the capabilities of combined contexts. For dataflow, this is given by the min function, which satisfies the requirement because $\mathsf{min}(r, s) \leq \mathsf{max}(r, s)$.

In flat dataflow, we annotate the entire context with the maximal number of past elements required overall. We use the same coeffect scalars $(\mathbb{N}, +, \mathsf{max}, 0, 0, \leq)$ as in the structural version, but with $\wedge = \mathsf{min}$. Abstraction (which is the only rule using $\wedge$) becomes:

$$\text{(abs)}\ \frac{\Gamma, x : \sigma @ \mathsf{min}(r, s) \vdash e : \tau}{\Gamma @ r \vdash \lambda x.e : \sigma \xrightarrow{s} \tau}$$

Both the declaration-site and call-site must provide at least the number of past values required by the body. The overapproximation means both r and s can be greater than actually required. For dataflow, we could enforce that immediate and latent coeffects are identical, but that would require treating $\bar{\times}$ as a partial function.

4. Equational theory

Each of the concrete coeffect systems discussed in this paper has a different notion of context dependence, much like various effectful languages have different notions of effects (such as state or exceptions). However, there are common equational properties that hold for all (or some) of the systems we consider.

The equational theory in this section illuminates the axioms of coeffect algebra and the semantics of the calculus. We discuss syntactic substitution as it can form the basis for reduction in a concrete operational semantics. We consider structural and flat systems separately. This provides better insight into how the two systems work and differ. In particular, call-by-name evaluation is *coeffect preserving* for all structural, but only some flat systems.

The properties and proofs in this section are syntactic. In Section 5.5 we show that our denotational model of the coeffect calculus is sound with respect to the equational theory here.

We use standard syntactic substitution written as $e_1[x \leftarrow e_2]$, β-reduction and η-expansion, written as $\rightsquigarrow_\beta$ and $\rightsquigarrow_\eta$. Equality of terms e_1 and e_2, written as $\equiv$ is defined w.r.t their contexts, types and coeffects and is written $\Gamma @ R \vdash e_1 \equiv e_2 : \tau$.

4.1 Structural coeffect systems

For structural coeffect systems, recall that coeffects are vectors with $\underline{\times} = \bar{\times} = \times$ (vector concatenation) and $\perp = \langle\rangle$ (the empty vector), thus coeffect annotations comprise the free monoid over scalars. We first show substitution:

Lemma 7 (Substitution lemma). *In a structural coeffect calculus with a coeffect scalar structure* $(\mathcal{C}, \circledast, \oplus, \mathsf{use}, \mathsf{ign}, \leq)$*:*

$$\begin{array}{l}\Gamma @ S \vdash e_s : \sigma \ \ \wedge\ \ \Gamma_1, x : \sigma, \Gamma_2 @ R_1 \times \langle r\rangle \times R_2 \vdash e_r : \tau \\ \quad \Rightarrow\ \Gamma_1, \Gamma, \Gamma_2 @ R_1 \times (r \circledast S) \times R_2 \vdash e_r[x \leftarrow e_s] : \tau\end{array}$$

Proof. By induction over the derivation for e_r using the free monoid $(\mathcal{C}, \times, \langle\rangle)$ and coeffect scalar axioms (full proof [14]). □

Because of the vector (free monoid) structure, coeffects R_1, R_2, and $\langle r\rangle$ for the receiving term e_r are uniquely associated with Γ_1, Γ_2, and x respectively. Therefore, substituting e_s (which has coeffects S) for x introduces the context dependencies specified by S which are composed with the requirements r on x. Using the substitution lemma, we can demonstrate β-equality:

$$\frac{\dfrac{\Gamma_1, x : \sigma @ R \times \langle r\rangle \vdash e_1 : \tau}{\Gamma_1 @ R \vdash \lambda x.e_1 : \sigma \xrightarrow{r} \tau} \qquad \Gamma_2 @ S \vdash e_2 : \sigma}{\Gamma_1, \Gamma_2 @ R \times (r \circledast S) \vdash (\lambda x.e_1) e_2 \equiv e_1[x \leftarrow e_2] : \tau}$$

As a result, β-reduction preserves the type and coeffects of a term. This gives the following subject reduction property:

Theorem 8 (Subject reduction). *In a structural coeffect calculus, if* $\Gamma @ R \vdash e : \tau$ *and* $e \rightsquigarrow_\beta e'$ *then* $\Gamma @ R \vdash e' : \tau$.

Proof. Following from Lemma 7 and β-equality. □

Structural coeffect systems also exhibit η-equality, therefore satisfying both the *local soundness* and *local completeness* conditions of Pfenning and Davies [16]. This means that abstraction does not introduce too much, and application does not eliminate too much.

$$\frac{\dfrac{\Gamma @ R \vdash e : \sigma \xrightarrow{s} \tau \qquad x : \sigma @ \langle \mathsf{use}\rangle \vdash x : \sigma}{\Gamma, x : \sigma @ R \times (s \circledast \langle\mathsf{use}\rangle) \vdash e\, x : \tau}}{\Gamma @ R \vdash \lambda x.e\, x \equiv e : \sigma \xrightarrow{s} \tau}$$

The last step uses the equalities $s \circledast \langle\mathsf{use}\rangle = \langle s \circledast \mathsf{use}\rangle = \langle s\rangle$ arising from the monoid $(\mathcal{C}, \circledast, \mathsf{use})$ of the scalar coeffect structure.

This highlights another difference between coeffects and effects, as η-equality does not hold for many notions of effect. For example, in a language with output effects, $e = (\texttt{print "hi"}; (\lambda x.x))$ has different effects to its η-converted form $\lambda x.ex$ because the immediate effects of e are hidden by the purity of λ-abstraction. In the coeffect calculus, the *(abs)* rule allows immediate contextual requirements of e to "float outside" of the enclosing λ. Furthermore, the free monoid nature of $\times$ in structural coeffect systems allows the exact immediate requirements of $\lambda x.ex$ to match those of e.

4.2 Flat coeffect systems

The equational theory for flat coeffect systems is somewhat similar to effect systems where (co)effects are not linked to individual variables. In effectful languages, substituting an effectful computation for y in $\lambda x.y$ changes the latent effect associated with the function.

Similarly, for some of the flat coeffect systems, substituting a context-dependent computation for y in $\lambda x.y$ adds latent context requirements to the function type. However, this is not the case for *all* flat coeffect systems – for example, call-by-name reduction preserves types and coeffects for the implicit parameters system (which makes it a suitable model for Haskell). For other systems, we first briefly consider call-by-value reduction.

Call-by-value. The notion of *value* in coeffect systems differs from the usual syntactic understanding. As discussed earlier, a function $(\lambda x.e)$ is not necessarily a value in coeffect calculi, because it may not delay all context requirements of e. Thus a syntactic value v is a value if it has no immediate context requirements.

Definition 9. A syntactic value v is a *pure value* if $\Gamma @ \mathsf{Val} \vdash v : \tau$ where $\mathsf{Val} : \mathcal{C}^{[\Gamma]}$ is a coeffect indexed by the shape of Γ that always returns use. That is $\mathsf{Val} = \lambda n.\mathsf{use}$.

In call-by-value, the right-hand side of an application is evaluated to a pure value, which is then substituted for a variable. However, the discharging of coeffects prior to substitution is different for each coeffect system.

Recall that a flat coeffect system consists of coeffect scalars $(\mathcal{C}, \circledast, \oplus, \mathsf{use}, \mathsf{ign}, \leq)$ together with a binary operation $\wedge$ on $\mathcal{C}$ such that the coeffect algebra structure is $(\wedge, \oplus, \mathsf{ign})$.

Lemma 10 (Call-by-value substitution). *In a flat coeffect calculus with coeffect scalars* $(\mathcal{C}, \circledast, \oplus, \mathsf{use}, \mathsf{ign}, \leq)$ *and the* $\wedge$ *operator:*

$$\begin{array}{l}\Gamma @ \mathsf{VAL} \vdash e_s : \sigma \ \ \wedge\ \ \Gamma_1, x : \sigma, \Gamma_2 @ r \vdash e_r : \tau \\ \quad \Rightarrow\ \Gamma_1, \Gamma, \Gamma_2 @ r \vdash e_r[x \leftarrow e_s] : \tau\end{array}$$

Proof. By induction over the coeffect derivation, using the fact that both x and e_s are annotated with use. □

Lemma 10 holds for all flat coeffect systems, but it is weak. To use it, the operational semantics must provide a way of partially evaluating a term with requirements R to a value. Assuming a call-by-value reduction $\rightsquigarrow_{\mathsf{cbv}}$, using the above definition of value:

Theorem 11 (Call-by-value subject reduction). *In a flat coeffect calculus, if* $\Gamma @ r \vdash e : \tau$ *and* $e \rightsquigarrow_{\mathsf{cbv}} e'$ *then* $\Gamma @ r \vdash e' : \tau$.

Proof. A direct consequence of Lemma 10, using the flat coeffect system requirement $(r \wedge s) \leq (r \oplus s)$ to prove β-equality. □

Call-by-name. A term $(\lambda x.e_1)\ e_2$ can be β-reduced in the call-by-name strategy even if both sub-expressions have contextual requirements.

We call a flat coeffect algebra *top-pointed* if use (the coeffect of variable use) is the greatest (top) coeffect scalar $\mathcal{C}$ and *bottom-pointed* if it is the smallest (bottom) coeffect scalar with respect to the order $\leq$. Liveness analysis is an example of top-pointed coeffects as use $=$ L and D $\leq$ L.

Lemma 12 (Top-pointed substitution). *In a top-pointed flat coeffect calculus with* $(\mathcal{C}, \circledast, \oplus, \mathsf{use}, \mathsf{ign}, \leq)$ *and the* $\wedge$ *operator:*

$$\begin{aligned} &\Gamma @ s \vdash e_s : \sigma \quad \wedge \quad \Gamma_1, x : \sigma, \Gamma_2 @ r \vdash e_r : \tau \\ &\Rightarrow \quad \Gamma_1, \Gamma, \Gamma_2 @ r \vdash e_r[x \leftarrow e_s] : \tau \end{aligned}$$

Proof. Using sub-coeffecting ($s \leq \mathsf{use}$) and Lemma 10. □

As variables are annotated with the top element use, we can substitute a term e_s for any variable and use sub-coeffecting to get the original typing (because $s \leq \mathsf{use}$).

In a bottom-pointed coeffect system, substituting e for x increases the context requirements. However, if the system satisfies the condition that $\wedge = \circledast = \oplus$ then the context requirements arising from the substitution can be associated with the context Γ. As a result, substitution does not break soundness as in effect systems. The requirement $\wedge = \circledast = \oplus$ holds for our implicit parameters example (all three operators are set union) and allows the following substitution lemma:

Lemma 13 (Bottom-pointed substitution). *In a bottom-pointed flat coeffect calculus with* $(\mathcal{C}, \circledast, \oplus, \mathsf{use}, \mathsf{ign}, \leq)$ *and the* $\wedge$ *operator where* $\wedge = \circledast = \oplus$ *is idempotent and commutative:*

$$\begin{aligned} &\Gamma @ s \vdash e_s : \sigma \quad \wedge \quad \Gamma_1, x : \sigma, \Gamma_2 @ r \vdash e_r : \tau \\ &\Rightarrow \quad \Gamma_1, \Gamma, \Gamma_2 @ r \circledast s \vdash e_r[x \leftarrow e_s] : \tau \end{aligned}$$

Proof. By induction over $\vdash$, using the idempotent, commutative monoid structure to keep s with the free-variable context. □

The structural system is precise enough to keep distinct coeffects associated with each concrete variable. The flat variant described here is flexible enough to let us always re-associate new context requirements with the free-variable context.

The two substitution lemmas show that the call-by-name evaluation strategy can be used for certain coeffect calculi, including liveness and implicit parameters. Assuming $\rightsquigarrow_{\mathsf{cbn}}$ is the standard call-by-name reduction, the following theorem holds:

Theorem 14 (Call-by-name subject reduction). *In a flat coeffect system that satisfies the conditions for Lemma 12 or Lemma 13, if* $\Gamma @ r \vdash e : \tau$ *and* $e \rightsquigarrow_{\mathsf{cbn}} e'$ *then* $\Gamma @ r \vdash e' : \tau$.

Proof. Direct consequence of Lemma 12 or Lemma 13. □

5. Semantics

Coeffects provide a unified description of context dependence. In the previous sections, we used this to define a unified coeffect calculus. We now define a unified (categorical) semantics for the coeffect calculus. The semantics can be instantiated for different notions of context dependence and thus can model a wide range of context-aware languages (both for flat and structural systems).

We relate the semantics to the equational theory and show that it is sound with respect to term equality. For a variant of the flat system, a similar result has already been shown in the second author's PhD dissertation [13]. The semantics is introduced in pieces:

- Section 5.1 describes the signature (range and domain) of the interpretation $[\![-]\!]$, gives the interpretations for types and free-variable contexts (in flat and structural systems), and defines the signature of functors D which encode contexts.
- The first part of the semantics (Section 5.2) defines *sequential composition* of context-dependent computations via *indexed comonads* (introduced briefly in our previous work [15]) and the *indexed structural comonad* structure (new here).
- More structure is needed for the semantics of application and abstraction. Section 5.3 defines indexed monoidal operations for splitting and merging contexts. Concrete structures are given throughout for the semantics of the structural bounded reuse and flat implicit parameter systems.
- Section 5.4 puts the pieces together, defining the semantics of the coeffect calculus. The semantics is illustrated by executing an example bounded-reuse program (Example 26).
- Section 5.5 shows our semantics sound with respect to the syntactic equational theory of Section 4. This uses the derivation of the categorical structures for the semantics as *lax homomorphisms* between structure in a category of coeffect annotations $\mathbb{I}$ and the base category $\mathbb{C}$.

In this section, $\mathbb{C}, \mathbb{D}, \mathbb{I}$ range over categories. The objects of a category $\mathbb{C}$ are written $obj(\mathbb{C})$. The category of functors between $\mathbb{C}$ and $\mathbb{D}$ is written $[\mathbb{C}, \mathbb{D}]$. Exponential objects, representing function types in our model, are written in two ways, either B^A or $A \Rightarrow B$.

5.1 Interpreting contexts and judgments

The semantics is parameterised by a coeffect algebra, with scalar coeffects $(\mathcal{C}, \circledast, \oplus, \mathsf{use}, \mathsf{ign}, \leq)$, coeffect shape $(\mathcal{S}, [-], \diamond, \hat{0}, \hat{1})$, and $(\barwedge, \veebar, \bot)$. An interpretation $[\![-]\!]$ is given to types, free-variable contexts, and type and coeffect judgments, with a base Cartesian-closed category $\mathbb{C}$ for denotations and a category $\mathbb{I}$ of scalar coeffects, where $obj(\mathbb{I}) = \mathcal{C}$. Since $\mathbb{C}$ is Cartesian-closed, we use the λ-calculus as the syntax for giving concrete definitions in $\mathbb{C}$.

The interpretation $[\![-]\!]$ is parameterised by categorical structures which model a particular notion of context. The interpretation of free-variable contexts depends on shape, for which we give concrete definitions for flat and structural shapes.

Interpreting judgments. Type and coeffect judgments are interpreted (given denotations) as morphisms in $\mathbb{C}$, of the form:

$$[\![\Gamma @ R \vdash e : \tau]\!] : \mathsf{D}_R^{[\Gamma]} [\![\Gamma]\!] \rightarrow [\![\tau]\!]$$

The interpretation is a morphism from an interpretation of the context Γ to the interpretation of the result. The functor $\mathsf{D}_R^{[\Gamma]}$ over Γ encodes the semantic notion of context and is indexed by the free-variable context shape $[\Gamma]$ and coeffect annotation R.

The structure D can be thought of as a dependent product of functors D^n over possible shapes $n \in \mathcal{S}$

$$\mathsf{D} : \Pi_{n:\mathcal{S}}.\mathsf{D}^n \quad \text{where} \quad \mathsf{D}^n : \mathbb{I}^n \rightarrow [\mathbb{C}^n, \mathbb{C}]$$

For a fixed context shape n the functor $\mathsf{D}^n : \mathbb{I}^n \rightarrow [\mathbb{C}^n, \mathbb{C}]$ maps an n-indexed coeffect (think positions) to a functor from a context $\mathbb{C}^n$ to an object in $\mathbb{C}$. That is, given a coeffect annotation (matching the shape of the context), we get a functor $\in [\mathbb{C}^n, \mathbb{C}]$.

From a programming perspective, this functor defines a data structure that models the additional context provided to the program. The shape of this data structure depends on the coeffect annotation $\mathbb{I}^n$. For example, in bounded reuse, the annotation defines the number of values needed for each variable and the functor will be formed by lists of length matching the required number.

Types. Types are interpreted as objects of $\mathbb{C}$, that is $[\![\tau]\!] : obj(\mathbb{C})$ where function types have the interpretation as exponents:

$$[\![\sigma \xrightarrow{r} \tau]\!] = \mathsf{D}^{\hat{1}}_{\langle r \rangle}[\![\sigma]\!] \Rightarrow [\![\tau]\!]$$

The parameter of a function is wrapped by a functor $\mathsf{D}^{\hat{1}}_{\langle r \rangle}$ that defines a context with singleton shape $\hat{1}$, matching the single value that it contains. This interpretation is shared by all coeffect calculi.

Free-variable contexts. As described above, free-variable contexts Γ are given an interpretation as objects in $\mathbb{C}^{[\Gamma]}$. Thus, the interpretation of contexts is shape dependent.

We define $[\![-]\!]$ on free-variable contexts for structural and flat systems. For flat systems, there is only a single shape, so the interpretation is a product type inside the Cartesian-closed category $\mathbb{C}$. For structural systems, the shape matches the number of variables and so the model is a value in the product category $\mathbb{C} \times \ldots \times \mathbb{C}$.

Flat coeffects. Recall that $\mathcal{S} = \{\star\}$ and $[\Gamma] = \star$. Since the set of positions $\star$ is a singleton, then $\mathbb{C}^\star$ is isomorphic to $\mathbb{C}$. Therefore $[\![\Gamma]\!] : obj(\mathbb{C})$, which is defined as:

$$[\![x_1 : \tau_1, \ldots, x_n : \tau_n]\!] = [\![\tau_1]\!] \times \ldots \times [\![\tau_n]\!]$$

Denotations of typing judgments in a flat coeffect system are thus of the form (where $r \in \mathbb{I}$):

$$[\![x_1 : \tau_1, .., x_n : \tau_n @ r \vdash e : \tau]\!] : \mathsf{D}^\star_r([\![\tau_1]\!] \times ... \times [\![\tau_n]\!]) \to [\![\tau]\!]$$

Structural coeffects. Recall that $\mathcal{S} = \mathbb{N}$ and $[\Gamma] = |\Gamma|$ (number of free variables), thus $[\![\Gamma]\!] : obj(\mathbb{C}^{|\Gamma|})$. This is defined similarly to the above, but instead of using products in $\mathbb{C}$, we use the product of categories. Thus, denotations have the form:

$$[\![x_1 : \tau_1, \ldots, x_n : \tau_n @ R \vdash e : \tau]\!] : \mathsf{D}^n_R([\![\tau_1]\!], \ldots, [\![\tau_n]\!]) \to [\![\tau]\!]$$

where $|R| = n$ and we use commas (instead of $\times$) to denote the product of categories. This means that $\mathsf{D}^n : \mathbb{I}^n \to [\mathbb{C}^n, \mathbb{C}]$ is a functor between an n-length vector of coeffects indices and an n-ary endofunctor. Thus, the key difference between the flat and structural interpretations of free-variable contexts is that flat uses products of objects in $\mathbb{C}$ and the structural uses products of $\mathbb{C}$ in the category of categories.

Example 15 (Bounded reuse)**.** Recall bounded reuse has coeffect scalars $\mathcal{C} = \mathbb{N}$ and shapes $\mathcal{S} = \mathbb{N}$. We model contexts by replicating the value of each variable so there is a value for each use. This matches the model used by Girard *et al.* [7]. Contexts are described by $\mathsf{B} : \Pi_{n:\mathbb{N}}.(\mathbb{I}^n \to [\mathbb{C}^n, \mathbb{C}])$, where for $R = \langle r_1, \ldots, r_n \rangle$:

$$\mathsf{B}^n_R(A_1, \ldots, A_n) = A_1^{r_1} \times \ldots \times A_n^{r_n}$$
$$\mathsf{B}^n_R(f_1, \ldots, f_n) = \lambda \langle a_1, \ldots, a_n \rangle . \langle (f_1 \circ a_1), \ldots, (f_n \circ a_n) \rangle$$

Thus each object in the free-variable context A_i is exponentiated by its associated coeffect r_i. For the morphism mapping part, $f_i : A_i \to B_i$ and $a_i : {A_i}^{r_i}$, thus $(f_i \circ a_i) : {B_i}^{r_i}$. The exponent ${A_i}^{r_i}$ can be read as a product of r_i copies of A_i, *e.g.*:

$$\mathsf{B}^3_{1,0,2}(A, B, C) = A^1 \times B^0 \times C^2 = (A) \times 1 \times (C \times C)$$

Example 16 (Implicit parameters)**.** Recall the implicit parameter calculus with scalar coeffects as sets of names paired with types $\mathcal{C} = \mathcal{P}(\mathsf{Name} \times \mathsf{Types})$ and flat shape with singleton $\mathcal{S} = \{\star\}$.

Its contexts are defined by $\mathsf{I}^\star : \Pi_{n:\{\star\}}.(\mathbb{I}^n \to [\mathbf{Set}^n, \mathbf{Set}])$ which is equivalent to $\mathbb{I} \to [\mathbf{Set}, \mathbf{Set}]$ and defined as follows:

$$\mathsf{I}^\star_R A = A \times [\![R]\!] \qquad\qquad \mathsf{I}^\star_R f = \lambda(a, r).(f\ a, r)$$

The interpretation $[\![R]\!]$ maps a set of variable-type pairs to an object representing a set of variable-value pairs in $\mathbf{Set}$.

5.2 Sequential composition

Following the usual categorical semantics approach, we require a notion of sequential composition for our denotations. We show first a special case for $\mathsf{D}^{\hat{1}}$ (where $\mathbb{I}^{\hat{1}} = \mathbb{I}$ and $\mathbb{C}^{\hat{1}} = \mathbb{C}$) in both flat and structural systems[2] and thus $\mathsf{D}^{\hat{1}} : \mathbb{I} \to [\mathbb{C}, \mathbb{C}]$. Composition of morphisms $f : \mathsf{D}^{\hat{1}}_S A \to B$ and $g : \mathsf{D}^{\hat{1}}_R B \to C$ is defined by an *indexed comonad* (which we introduced previously [13, 15]).

Definition 17. An *indexed comonad* comprises a strict monoidal category $(\mathbb{I}, \bullet, I)$ and a functor $\mathsf{F} : \mathbb{I} \to [\mathbb{C}, \mathbb{C}]$ with two natural transformations (where we write $(\mathsf{F}\ R)\ A$ as $\mathsf{F}_R A$):

$$(\delta_{X,Y})_A : \mathsf{F}_{(X \bullet Y)} A \to \mathsf{F}_X(\mathsf{F}_Y A) \qquad\qquad (\varepsilon_I)_A : \mathsf{F}_I A \to A$$

where δ is called *comultiplication* and ε is called *counit*. We require indexed analogues of the usual comonad axioms (*cf.* [19]):

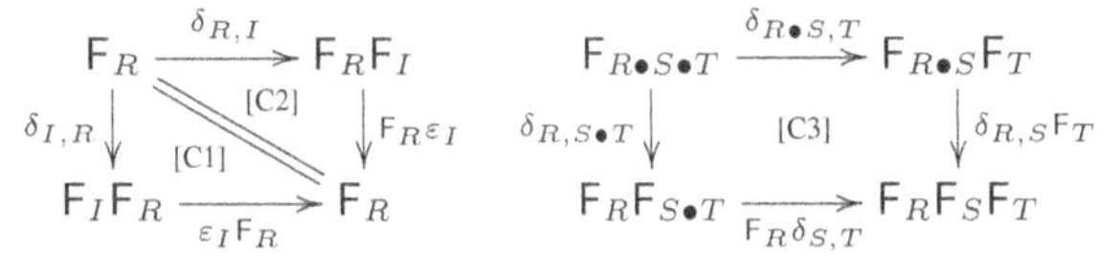

An indexed comonad $\mathsf{F} : \mathbb{I} \to [\mathbb{C}, \mathbb{C}]$ induces a notion of composition for all $f : \mathsf{F}_S A \to B$ and $g : \mathsf{F}_R B \to C$:

$$g \hat{\circ} f = g \circ \mathsf{F}_R f \circ \delta_{R,S}\ :\ \mathsf{F}_{R \bullet S} A \to C$$

with the identity $\hat{id}_A = (\varepsilon_I)_A : \mathsf{F}_I A \to A$ for all A. Thus indexed comonads induce a category which has the same objects as $\mathbb{C}$ and morphisms $\mathbb{C}_\mathsf{F}(A, B) = \bigcup_{R \in \mathbb{I}} \mathbb{C}(\mathsf{F}_R A, B)$. Note that an indexed comonad is not a family of (ordinary) comonads, because identity need only be defined for the functor F_I.

Therefore, if $\mathsf{D}^{\hat{1}}$ is an indexed comonad, there is a notion of composition for denotations with a single coeffect index.

Example 18 (Bounded reuse). $\mathsf{B}^{\hat{1}}_R$ (Example 15) has an indexed comonad structure, where the monoid $(\mathbb{N}, *, 1)$ from the coeffect scalar for bounded reuse induces a monoidal category structure on $\mathbb{I}$ (with $1 : \mathbb{I}$ and the bifunctor $* : \mathbb{I} \times \mathbb{I} \to \mathbb{I}$), with operations:

$$\varepsilon^{\hat{1}}_1 = \lambda \langle a_1 \rangle . a_1$$
$$\delta^{\hat{1}}_{R,S} = \lambda \langle a_1 ..., a_{RS} \rangle . \langle \langle a_1 ..., a_S \rangle, \langle a_{S+1}, ..., a_{S+S} \rangle, ..., \langle a_{(R-1)S+1}, ..., a_{RS} \rangle \rangle$$

Indexed comonads essentially model single-variable contexts. Counit here requires a single copy of the value from the context. Comultiplication splits R times S copies of a value into R copies of a context where each context contains just S copies of the value.

Remark 19. A semantics for dataflow coeffects is similar to bounded reuse with $\mathsf{D}^n_R(A_1, \ldots, A_n) = (A_1 \times A_1^{R_1}) \times ... \times (A_n \times {A_n}^{R_n})$, *i.e.*, each free-variable has an extra value representing the "current" value. A dataflow indexed comonad is similar to the above but with additive rather than multiplicative behaviour.

Example 20 (Implicit parameters)**.** For the coeffect scalar monoid $(\mathcal{P}(\mathsf{Name} \times \mathsf{Types}), \cup, \emptyset)$ of implicit parameters, I^* (Example 16) has an indexed comonad structure, with operations:

$$\varepsilon_\emptyset = \lambda(a, \emptyset).a \qquad\qquad \delta_{R,S} = \lambda(a, \gamma).((a, \gamma|_S), \gamma|_R)$$

where $\gamma|_R = \{(x, v) \mid (x, v) \in \gamma, (x, t) \in R\}$ filters incoming implicit parameters to those variable-value pairs where the variable is in the coeffect R.

[2] Since $\hat{1} = 1$ in structural and $\hat{1} \cong 1$ in flat, *i.e.*, $\star$ is isomorphic to 1.

These two examples (which are new here) provide composition for context-dependent computations indexed by coeffects in a flat calculus. For structural coeffects, we need to compose morphisms which have more than a single coeffect annotation. For this, we introduce the new notion of *structural indexed comonads*.

Definition 21. A *structural indexed comonad* comprises a functor $\mathsf{D} : \Pi_{n:\mathcal{S}}.(\mathbb{I}^n \rightarrow [\mathbb{C}^n, \mathbb{C}])$ where $(\mathbb{I}, \bullet, I)$ is a strict monoidal category, $\hat{1} \in \mathcal{S}$ which is terminal (*e.g.*, a singleton set), an indexed comonad over $\mathsf{D}^{\hat{1}} : \mathbb{I}^{\hat{1}} \rightarrow [\mathbb{C}^{\hat{1}}, \mathbb{C}]$ and a *structural comultiplication* natural transformation:

$$(\delta^n_{r,S})_{A^n} : \mathsf{D}^n_{r \bar{\bullet} S} A^n \rightarrow \mathsf{D}^{\hat{1}}_r \mathsf{D}^n_S A^n$$

where $A^n \in \mathbb{C}^n$, $r \in \mathbb{I}$, $S \in \mathbb{I}^n$ and $\bar{\bullet} : \mathbb{I} \times \mathbb{I}^n \rightarrow \mathbb{I}^n$ is the *monoid left action* that $\bullet$-lifts scalar coeffects to shaped coeffects (*i.e.*, the scalar-vector version of $\bullet$). Analogous laws to monoid left actions for unitality and associativity hold for structural comultiplication:

$$\begin{array}{ccc} \mathsf{D}^n_{I \bar{\bullet} R} & \xrightarrow{\delta^n_{I,R}} & \mathsf{D}^{\hat{1}}_I \mathsf{D}^n_R \\ & \overset{\text{[SC1]}}{\diagdown\!\!\diagdown} & \downarrow {\scriptstyle \varepsilon_I \mathsf{D}^n_R} \\ & & \mathsf{D}^n_R \end{array} \qquad \begin{array}{ccc} \mathsf{D}^n_{r \bar{\bullet}(s \bar{\bullet} T)} & \xrightarrow{\delta^n_{r \bullet s, T}} & \mathsf{D}^{\hat{1}}_{r \bullet s} \mathsf{D}^n_T \\ {\scriptstyle \delta^n_{r, s \bar{\bullet} T}} \downarrow & \text{[SC2]} & \downarrow {\scriptstyle \delta^{\hat{1}}_{r,s} \mathsf{D}^n_T} \\ \mathsf{D}^{\hat{1}}_r \mathsf{D}^n_{s \bar{\bullet} T} & \xrightarrow[\mathsf{D}^{\hat{1}}_r \delta^n_{s,T}]{} & \mathsf{D}^{\hat{1}}_r \mathsf{D}^{\hat{1}}_s \mathsf{D}^n_T \end{array} \qquad (1)$$

using axioms $I \bar{\bullet} R = R$ and $(r \bullet s) \bar{\bullet} T = r \bar{\bullet}(s \bar{\bullet} T)$ on coeffects respectively which are the monoid left action axioms for the scalar-vector application of $\bullet$. Note the use of indexed comonad comultiplication $\delta^{\hat{1}}$ for associativity [SC2].

Structural indexed comonads provide composition for morphisms $f : \mathsf{D}^n_S A^n \rightarrow B$ and singleton-shaped morphisms $g : \mathsf{D}^{\hat{1}}_r B \rightarrow C$:

$$g \hat{\circ} f = g \circ \mathsf{D}^{\hat{1}}_r f \circ \delta^n_{r,S} : \mathsf{D}^n_{r \bar{\bullet} S} A^n \rightarrow C$$

Note that this composition is asymmetric: the left morphism and right morphisms have different shapes. To compose morphisms which both have non-trivial context shapes requires additional structure for manipulating contexts (shown in the next section).

Example 22 (Bounded reuse)**.** $\mathsf{B} : \Pi_{n:\mathbb{N}}.(\mathbb{I}^n \rightarrow [\mathbb{C}^n, \mathbb{C}])$ has a structural indexed comonad structure with the indexed comonad $\mathsf{B}^{\hat{1}}$ (Example 18) and the following structural comultiplication:

$$\begin{array}{l} \delta^n_{r,S} = \lambda(\langle a^1_1, \ldots, a^1_{r*S_1} \rangle, \ldots, \langle a^n_1, \ldots a^n_{r*S_n} \rangle). \\ (\,(\,\langle a^1_1, \ldots, a^1_{S_1} \rangle, \qquad\qquad ..., \langle a^n_1, \ldots, a^n_{S_n} \rangle), \\ \;\;(\,\langle a^1_{(S_1+1)}, ..., a^1_{(S_1+1)+S_1} \rangle, ..., \langle a^n_{(S_n+1)}, \ldots, a^n_{(S_n+1)+S_n} \rangle), \\ \;\;\ldots \\ \;\;(\,\langle a^1_{(r-1)*s_1+1}, .., a^1_{r*S_1} \rangle, \quad ..., \langle a^n_{(r-1)*S_n+1}, ..., a^n_{r*S_n} \rangle)) \end{array}$$

The input is an n-variable context containing r times S_i copies of a^i for each variable. The output has r copies of a single n-variable context containing S_i copies of a^i for each variable. Thus, $\delta^n_{r,S}$ partitions the incoming context into r-sized contexts.

Note that in the case of the flat system, a structural indexed comonad collapses to a standard indexed comonad on $\mathsf{D}^{\hat{1}}$.

5.3 Splitting and merging contexts

Indexed comonads and structural indexed comonads give a semantics for sequential composition of contextual computations. However, this does not provide enough structure for a semantics of the full coeffect calculus. Core to the semantics of abstraction and application is the merging and splitting of contexts. Recall the free-variable contexts and coeffects in the *(abs)* and *(app)* rules:

$$\text{(app)}\frac{\Gamma_1 @ R \vdash e_1 ... \;\Gamma_2 @ S \vdash e_2 ...}{\Gamma_1, \Gamma_2 @ R \underline{\times} (t \circledast S) \vdash e_1 \, e_2 ...} \qquad \text{(abs)}\frac{\Gamma, x : \sigma @ R \overline{\times} \langle s \rangle \vdash e ...}{\Gamma @ R \vdash \lambda x.e : \sigma \xrightarrow{s} ...}$$

Reading *(app)* bottom-up, the context of the application is split into two contexts for each subterm e_1 and e_2. Reading *(abs)* bottom-up, the context of the abstraction is merged with the singleton context of the parameter. Capturing these notions in the denotational semantics requires some additional structure.

A (non-indexed) comonadic semantics for the λ-calculus requires a *monoidal comonad* with operation $\mathsf{m}_{A,B} : \mathsf{F}A \times \mathsf{F}B \rightarrow \mathsf{F}(A \times B)$ [19]. Previously, we defined a similar operation for the semantics of a flat coeffect system, with an indexed monoidal operation $\mathsf{m}^{R,S}_{A,B}$ for merging contexts. Dually, contexts were split with $\mathsf{n}^{R,S}_{A,B}$ [15]. We used two operations for combining and splitting the coeffect annotations, respectively. Here we generalize these to shape-indexed versions using $\overline{\times}$ and $\underline{\times}$.

Definition 23. A functor $\mathsf{D} : \Pi_{n:\mathcal{S}}.(\mathbb{I}^n \rightarrow [\mathbb{C}^n, \mathbb{C}])$ is an *indexed lax (semi)monoidal functor* and/or *colax (semi)monoidal functor* if it has the following natural transformations respectively:

$$\mathsf{m}^{n,m}_{R,S} : \mathsf{D}^n_R A \times \mathsf{D}^m_S B \rightarrow \mathsf{D}^{n \diamond m}_{R \overline{\times} S}(A \times B)$$
$$\mathsf{n}^{n,m}_{R,S} : \mathsf{D}^{n \diamond m}_{R \underline{\times} S}(A \times B) \rightarrow \mathsf{D}^n_R A \times \mathsf{D}^m_S B$$

satisfying associativity coherence conditions. In both, shape descriptions are combined by $\diamond$. The first operation models context merging and combines coeffects using $\overline{\times}$. The second models context splitting, with $\underline{\times}$ for the pre-split coeffect.

Example 24 (Bounded reuse)**.** For bounded reuse, B is an indexed lax and colax semimonoidal functor with the following operations:

$$\mathsf{m}^{n,m}_{R,S} = \lambda(\langle a_1, ..., a_n \rangle \times \langle b_1, ..., b_m \rangle).(\langle a_1, ..., a_n \rangle, \langle b_1, ..., b_m \rangle)$$
$$\mathsf{n}^{n,m}_{R,S} = \lambda(\langle a_1, ..., a_n \rangle, \langle b_1, ..., b_m \rangle).(\langle a_1, ..., a_n \rangle \times \langle b_1, ..., b_m \rangle)$$

Here $\mathsf{m}^{n,m}_{R,S}$ takes a pair of contexts and merges them simply by replacing the product in $\mathbb{C}$ which pairs the two arguments (written using $\times$) with products inside of B (written using tuple notation (x, y)). The operation $\mathsf{n}^{n,m}_{R,S}$ is the inverse.

Example 25 (Implicit parameters)**.** For implicit parameters, $\mathsf{I}^\star$ is an indexed lax and colax semimonoidal functor with operations:

$$\mathsf{m}^{\star,\star}_{R,S} = \lambda((a, \gamma_R), (b, \gamma_S)).((a, b), \gamma_R \cup \gamma_S)$$
$$\mathsf{n}^{\star,\star}_{R,S} = \lambda((a, b), \gamma).((a, \gamma|_R), (b, \gamma|_S))$$

As in Example 20, $\gamma|_R$ and $\gamma|_S$ restrict the set of implicit parameters γ to variable-value pairs for variables in R and S.

5.4 Putting it together

The semantics of the general coeffect calculus $[\![-]\!]$ is defined in Figure 5, using the structures described in the previous sections.

Core rules. The denotation in (*var*) maps a context of the singleton shape $\hat{1}$ containing just a single variable τ (with coeffect I) to a τ value using the counit operation.

The premise of (*abs*) takes a context of shape $n \diamond \hat{1}$ with coeffects $R \overline{\times} \langle s \rangle$ and a free-variables context consisting of Γ and an additional variable x. The denotation $g : \mathsf{D}^{n \diamond \hat{1}}_{R \overline{\times} \langle s \rangle} [\![\Gamma, x : \sigma]\!] \rightarrow [\![\tau]\!]$ is pre-composed with m, such that its context is obtained by merging the declaration-site context (Γ) and call-site context (σ):

$$g \circ \mathsf{m}^{n,\hat{1}}_{R,\langle s \rangle} : (\mathsf{D}^n_R [\![\Gamma]\!] \times \mathsf{D}^{\hat{1}}_{\langle s \rangle} [\![\sigma]\!]) \rightarrow [\![\tau]\!]$$

This is uncurried to give a denotation from a context to an exponential object representing the abstraction, where the singleton-shaped context becomes the source of the exponential.

The application rule (*app*) has two sub-expressions for the function and argument, with denotations requiring two distinct contexts:

$$g_1 : \mathsf{D}^n_R [\![\Gamma_1]\!] \rightarrow (\mathsf{D}^{\hat{1}}_{\langle t \rangle} [\![\sigma]\!] \Rightarrow [\![\tau]\!]) \qquad g_2 : \mathsf{D}^m_S [\![\Gamma_2]\!] \rightarrow [\![\sigma]\!]$$

$$\text{(var)}\ \frac{}{[\![x:\tau@\langle\mathsf{use}\rangle \vdash x:\tau]\!] = \varepsilon_I : \mathsf{D}^{\hat{1}}_I [\![x:\tau]\!] \to [\![\tau]\!]} \qquad \text{(abs)}\ \frac{[\![\Gamma, x{:}\sigma@R \bar{\times} \langle s\rangle \vdash e:\tau]\!] = g : \mathsf{D}^{n\diamond\hat{1}}_{R\bar{\times}\langle s\rangle}[\![\Gamma, x{:}\sigma]\!] \to [\![\tau]\!]}{[\![\Gamma@R \vdash \lambda x.e : \sigma \xrightarrow{s} \tau]\!] = \Lambda(g \circ \mathsf{m}^{n,\hat{1}}_{R,\langle s\rangle}) : \mathsf{D}^n_R[\![\Gamma]\!] \to (\mathsf{D}^{\hat{1}}_{\langle s\rangle}[\![\sigma]\!] \Rightarrow [\![\tau]\!])}$$

$$\text{(app)}\ \frac{[\![\Gamma_1@R \vdash e_1 : \sigma \xrightarrow{t} \tau]\!] = g_1 : \mathsf{D}^n_R[\![\Gamma_1]\!] \to (\mathsf{D}^{\hat{1}}_{\langle t\rangle}[\![\sigma]\!] \Rightarrow [\![\tau]\!]) \qquad [\![\Gamma_2@S \vdash e_2 : \sigma]\!] = g_2 : \mathsf{D}^m_S[\![\Gamma_2]\!] \to [\![\sigma]\!]}{[\![\Gamma_1, \Gamma_2@R \ltimes (t \circledast S) \vdash e_1\, e_2 : \tau]\!] = \Lambda^{-1} g_1 \circ (\mathsf{id} \times (\mathsf{D}^{\hat{1}}_{\langle t\rangle} g_2 \circ \delta^m_{t,S})) \circ \mathsf{n}^{n,m}_{R,t\circledast S} : \mathsf{D}^{n\diamond m}_{R\ltimes(t\circledast S)}[\![\Gamma_1,\Gamma_2]\!] \to [\![\tau]\!]}$$

$$\text{(ctx)}\ \frac{[\![\Gamma@R \vdash e:\tau]\!] = f : \mathsf{D}^n_R[\![\Gamma]\!] \to [\![\tau]\!] \qquad [\![\Gamma'@R' \rightsquigarrow \Gamma@R, \emptyset]\!] = c : \mathsf{D}^m_{R'}[\![\Gamma']\!] \to \mathsf{D}^n_R[\![\Gamma]\!]}{[\![\Gamma'@R' \vdash e:\tau]\!] = f \circ c : \mathsf{D}^m_{R'}[\![\Gamma']\!] \to [\![\tau]\!]}$$

$$\text{(weak)}\quad [\![\Gamma, x{:}\tau@R \ltimes \langle\mathsf{ign}\rangle \rightsquigarrow \Gamma@R, \emptyset]\!] = \pi_1 \circ \mathsf{n}^{n,\hat{1}}_{R,\langle\mathsf{ign}\rangle} : \mathsf{D}^{n\diamond\hat{1}}_{R\ltimes\langle\mathsf{ign}\rangle}([\![\Gamma]\!] \times [\![\sigma]\!]) \to \mathsf{D}^n_R[\![\Gamma]\!]$$

$$\text{(contr)}\quad [\![\Gamma_1, x{:}\tau, \Gamma_2@R \ltimes \langle s \oplus t\rangle \ltimes Q \rightsquigarrow \Gamma_1, y{:}\tau, z{:}\tau, \Gamma_2@R \bar{\times} \langle s\rangle \bar{\times} \langle t\rangle \bar{\times} Q, [y,z \mapsto x]]\!] = \mathsf{m}^{n,\hat{1},m}_{R,\langle s\oplus t\rangle,Q} \circ (\mathsf{id} \times \Delta_{s,t} \times \mathsf{id}) \circ \mathsf{n}^{n,\hat{1},\hat{1},m}_{R,\langle s\rangle,\langle t\rangle,Q}$$

$$\text{(exch)}\quad [\![\Gamma_1, y{:}\sigma, x{:}\tau, \Gamma_2@R \ltimes \langle t\rangle \ltimes \langle s\rangle \ltimes Q \rightsquigarrow \Gamma_1, x{:}\tau, y{:}\sigma, \Gamma_2@R \bar{\times} \langle s\rangle \bar{\times} \langle t\rangle \bar{\times} Q, \emptyset]\!] = \mathsf{m}^{n,\hat{1},\hat{1},m}_{R,\langle s\rangle,\langle t\rangle,Q} \circ (\mathsf{id} \times \mathsf{swap} \times \mathsf{id}) \circ \mathsf{n}^{n,\hat{1},\hat{1},m}_{R,\langle t\rangle,\langle s\rangle,Q}$$

where $\mathsf{swap} : A \times B \to B \times A$ **and** Λ, Λ^{-1} denote currying and uncurrying respectively

Figure 5: Denotational semantics for the coeffect calculus

The target of g_1 is an exponential object with singleton shape for the parameter of type σ. To evaluate g_1 and g_2, the semantics of (*app*) splits the incoming context over Γ_1, Γ_2 using n:

$$\mathsf{D}^{n\diamond m}_{R\ltimes(t\circledast S)}([\![\Gamma_1]\!] \times [\![\Gamma_2]\!]) \xrightarrow{\mathsf{n}^{n,m}_{R,t\circledast S}} \mathsf{D}^n_R[\![\Gamma_1]\!] \times \mathsf{D}^m_{t\circledast S}[\![\Gamma_2]\!]$$

Since e_2 computes the argument for function e_1, the denotation g_2 is sequentially composed with the parameter part of g_1. Thus, the structural indexed comonad (where $\bar{\bullet} = \circledast$) is used with g_2 to compute the correct context for the parameter of the function denotation g_1:

$$\mathsf{D}^m_{t\circledast S}[\![\Gamma_2]\!] \xrightarrow{\delta^m_{t,S}} \mathsf{D}^{\hat{1}}_{\langle t\rangle}\mathsf{D}^m_S[\![\Gamma_2]\!] \xrightarrow{\mathsf{D}^{\hat{1}}_{\langle t\rangle} g_2} \mathsf{D}^{\hat{1}}_{\langle t\rangle}[\![\sigma]\!]$$

This is composed with the previous equation by lifting to the right-component of the product:

$$\mathsf{D}^n_R[\![\Gamma_1]\!] \times \mathsf{D}^m_{t\circledast S}[\![\Gamma_2]\!] \xrightarrow{id \times (\mathsf{D}^{\hat{1}}_{\langle t\rangle} g_2 \circ \delta^m_{t,S})} \mathsf{D}^n_R[\![\Gamma_1]\!] \times \mathsf{D}^{\hat{1}}_{\langle t\rangle}[\![\sigma]\!]$$

This equation computes the calling context and parameter context for the function e_1, which is then composed with the uncurried g_1 denotation as shown in the (*app*) rule in Figure 5.

Structural rules. In Figure 5, (*ctx*) composes the denotation of an expression with a transformation c providing the semantic structural rules. The semantics of structural rules are defined by using $\mathsf{n}^{n,m}_{R,S}$ to split contexts, transforming the components, and merging the transformed contexts using $\mathsf{m}^{n,m}_{R,S}$. The (*contr*) rule uses an additional operation which duplicates a variable inside a context:

$$\Delta_{r,s} : \mathsf{D}^{\hat{1}}_{\langle r\oplus s\rangle} A \to \mathsf{D}^{\hat{1}\diamond\hat{1}}_{\langle r\rangle\bar{\times}\langle s\rangle}(A \times A)$$

Example 26. We demonstrate the semantics with a concrete example for the bounded reuse calculus. Consider the following term:

$$f : \mathbb{Z} \xrightarrow{2} \mathbb{Z}, x : \mathbb{Z}@\langle 2,4\rangle \vdash (\lambda z.z + z)\ (f\ x)$$

Let the denotation of the function body, prior to contraction, be $g = [\![x:\mathbb{Z}, y:\mathbb{Z}@\langle 1,1\rangle \vdash (+x)\,y : \mathbb{Z}]\!]$[3]. The example term's denotation is then constructed as follows:

$$[\![@\langle\rangle \vdash \lambda z.(+z)z : \mathbb{Z} \xrightarrow{2} \mathbb{Z}]\!] = \Lambda(g \circ \Delta_{1,1} \circ \mathsf{m}^{0,1}_{\langle\rangle,\langle 2\rangle}) \tag{2}$$

$$\begin{aligned} &[\![f : \mathbb{Z} \xrightarrow{2} \mathbb{Z}, x : \mathbb{Z}@\langle 1,2\rangle \vdash fx : \mathbb{Z}]\!] \\ &\quad = \Lambda^{-1}\varepsilon_1 \circ (id \times (\mathsf{D}\varepsilon_1 \circ \delta^1_{2,\langle 1\rangle})) \circ \mathsf{n}^{1,1}_{\langle 1\rangle,\langle 2\rangle} \\ &\quad = \Lambda^{-1}\varepsilon_1 \circ \mathsf{n}^{1,1}_{\langle 1\rangle,\langle 2\rangle} \qquad (3) \end{aligned}$$

$$\begin{aligned} &[\![f : \mathbb{Z} \xrightarrow{2} \mathbb{Z}, x : \mathbb{Z}@\langle 2,4\rangle \vdash (\lambda z.(+z)z)\ (fx) : \mathbb{Z}]\!] \\ &\quad = \Lambda^{-1}(2) \circ (id \times \mathsf{D}(3) \circ \delta^2_{2,\langle 2,1\rangle}) \circ \mathsf{n}^{0,2}_{\langle\rangle,\langle 4,2\rangle} \\ &\quad = g \circ \Delta_{1,1} \circ \mathsf{m}^{0,1}_{\langle\rangle,\langle 2\rangle} \circ (id \times \mathsf{D}(3) \circ \delta^2_{2,\langle 2,1\rangle}) \circ \mathsf{n}^{0,2}_{\langle\rangle,\langle 4,2\rangle} \qquad (4) \end{aligned}$$

where (3) and (4) are simplified. We "run" this semantics on an input, evaluating each step of the denotation as a function. We write context objects, *e.g.*, $\mathsf{D}^2_{\langle R,S\rangle}(A,B)$ as $\langle(a_1,...,a_R),(b_1,...,b_S)\rangle$ and products of contexts in $\mathbb{C}$, *e.g.*, $\mathsf{D}^n_R A \times \mathsf{D}^m_S B$, as $(a \times b)$.

$$\begin{aligned}
& \langle(f_1,f_2),(x_1,x_2,x_3,x_4)\rangle && : \mathsf{D}^2_{\langle 2,4\rangle}((\mathsf{D}^1_{\langle 2\rangle}\mathbb{Z} \Rightarrow \mathbb{Z}), \mathbb{Z}) \\
\xrightarrow{n^{0,2}_{\langle\rangle,\langle 2,4\rangle}}\ & \langle\rangle \times \langle(f_1,f_2),(x_1,x_2,x_3,x_4)\rangle && : \mathsf{D}^0_{\langle\rangle}1 \times \mathsf{D}^2_{\langle 2,4\rangle}(\textit{as above}) \\
\xrightarrow{id \times \delta^2_{2,\langle 1,2\rangle}}\ & \langle\rangle \times \langle\langle f_1,(x_1,x_2)\rangle, \langle f_2,(x_3,x_4)\rangle\rangle && \\
& && : \mathsf{D}^0_{\langle\rangle}1 \times \mathsf{D}^1_{\langle 2\rangle}\mathsf{D}^2_{\langle 2,1\rangle}((\mathsf{D}^1_{\langle 2\rangle}\mathbb{Z} \Rightarrow \mathbb{Z}), \mathbb{Z}) \\
\xrightarrow{id \times \mathsf{Dn}^{1,1}_{\langle 1\rangle,\langle 2\rangle}}\ & \langle\rangle \times \langle\langle f_1\rangle \times \langle x_1,x_2\rangle, \langle f_2\rangle \times \langle x_3,x_4\rangle\rangle && \\
& && : \mathsf{D}^0_{\langle\rangle}1 \times \mathsf{D}^1_{\langle 2\rangle}(\mathsf{D}^1_{\langle 1\rangle}(\mathsf{D}^1_{\langle 2\rangle}\mathbb{Z} \Rightarrow \mathbb{Z}) \times \mathsf{D}^1_{\langle 2\rangle}\mathbb{Z}) \\
\xrightarrow{id \times \mathsf{D}(\Lambda^{-1}\varepsilon_1)}\ & \langle\rangle \times \langle f_1\langle x_1,x_2\rangle, f_2\langle x_3,x_4\rangle\rangle && : \mathsf{D}^0_{\langle\rangle}1 \times \mathsf{D}^1_{\langle 2\rangle}\mathbb{Z} \\
\xrightarrow{\mathsf{m}^{0,1}_{\langle\rangle,\langle 1\rangle}}\ & \langle f_1\langle x_1,x_2\rangle, f_2\langle x_3,x_4\rangle\rangle && : \mathsf{D}^1_{\langle 2\rangle}\mathbb{Z} \\
\xrightarrow{\Delta_{1,1}}\ & \langle(f_1\langle x_1,x_2\rangle, f_2\langle x_3,x_4\rangle)\rangle && : \mathsf{D}^1_{\langle 1,1\rangle}(\mathbb{Z} \times \mathbb{Z}) \\
\xrightarrow{g}\ & [\![+]\!]\ \langle f_1\langle x_1,x_2\rangle\rangle\ \langle f_2\langle x_3,x_4\rangle\rangle && : \mathbb{Z}
\end{aligned}$$

5.5 Soundness, with respect to the equational theory

Our denotational semantics for the coeffect calculus is sound with respect to the equational theory of Section 4. That is:

Theorem 27 (Soundness).

$$\Gamma@R \vdash e \equiv e' : \tau \Rightarrow [\![\Gamma@R \vdash e : \tau]\!] \equiv [\![\Gamma@R \vdash e' : \tau]\!]$$

Proof of this follows from an interesting result which we first unpack: determining whether $[\![\Gamma@R \vdash e_1 : \tau]\!] \equiv [\![\Gamma@S \vdash e_2 : \tau]\!]$ follows from a proof (on coeffect annotations) that $R = S$.

[3] The full semantics has $[\![+]\!] : \mathsf{D}^0_{\langle\rangle}1 \to (\mathsf{D}^1_1\mathbb{Z} \Rightarrow (\mathsf{D}^1_1\mathbb{Z} \Rightarrow \mathbb{Z}))$ as primitive and uses double application $(+\,e_1)\,e_2$.

Lemma 28. *Every coeffect algebra axiom corresponds to an axiom of one of the categorical structures introduced here (indexed (structural) comonad or indexed (co)lax monoidal functor).*

For example, the monoid axiom $X \circledast \mathsf{use} = X$ for scalar coeffects corresponds to indexed comonad axiom $\mathsf{D}_X^{\hat{1}} \varepsilon_{\mathsf{use}} \circ \delta^{\hat{1}}_{X,\mathsf{use}} = id_{\mathsf{D}^{\hat{1}}_X}$ (which requires the monoid axiom to hold). This lemma follows from our derivation of the indexed categorical structures here. They are not derived *ad hoc* but systematically as (lax) *homomorphisms* (structure-preserving maps) between the structure of coeffect annotations in $\mathbb{I}$ and the structure of denotations in $\mathbb{C}$.

Proposition 29. *An indexed comonad on* D *witnesses that* D *is a* colax monoid homomorphism *between the (strict) monoidal categories* $(\mathbb{I}, \bullet, I)$ *and* $([\mathbb{C}, \mathbb{C}], \circ, 1_{\mathbb{C}})$ *(endofunctor composition).*

Unpacking this, a *monoid homomorphism* maps between the underlying sets of two monoids, preserving the monoid structure of one into the other, *i.e.*, given monoids $(X, \bullet, I)$ and $(Y, \otimes, E)$ then a monoid homomorphism is a mapping $F : X \to Y$ such that:

$$FX \otimes FY \equiv F(X \bullet Y) \qquad E \equiv FI \tag{5}$$

The axioms of each monoid are preserved trivially by these equalities, *e.g.*, $FX \equiv F(X \bullet I) \equiv FX \otimes FI \equiv FX \otimes E \equiv FX$. A homomorphism is *lax* if the above equalities (5) are instead morphisms (which we say *witness* the homomorphism) and *colax* if these morphisms go in the opposite direction. Thus, a colax monoid homomorphism is witnessed by:

$$\delta : FX \otimes FY \leftarrow F(X \bullet Y) \qquad \varepsilon : E \leftarrow FI$$

Note our choice of morphism names. F no longer preserves the monoid axioms *up to equality* but has axioms on δ and ε, *e.g.*, $F(X \bullet I) \xrightarrow{\delta} FX \otimes FI \xrightarrow{id \otimes \varepsilon} FX \otimes E$ equals $FX \xrightarrow{id} FX$.

Our indexed comonad definition is equivalent to D being a colax homomorphism between strict monoidal category $(X, \bullet, I)$ and the monoidal category of $\mathbb{C}$-endofunctors $(Y, \otimes, E) = ([\mathbb{C}, \mathbb{C}], \circ, 1_{\mathbb{C}})$, with endofunctor composition $\circ$ and the trivial endofunctor $1_{\mathbb{C}}$; monoids are now at the level of categories. The indexed comonads axioms are the axioms of the colax homomorphism. Equivalently, D is a *colax monoidal functor*.

A similar approach is taken to deriving the remaining structures below, though we give less detail for brevity.

Proposition 30. *A structural indexed comonad provides* $\delta^n_{R,S} : \mathsf{D}^{\hat{1}}_r \mathsf{D}^n_S A^n \leftarrow \mathsf{D}^n_{r \circledast S} A^n$ *which is a family of morphisms (indexed by shapes* n*) witnessing that* D *is a colax homomorphism between the following* monoid left-actions*:* $(\mathbb{I}^n, \circledast)$ *for* $(\mathbb{I}, \circledast, \mathsf{ign})$ *and* $(\mathbb{C}^n, \mathbb{C}], \hat{\circ})$ *for* $([\mathbb{C}, \mathbb{C}], \circ, 1_{\mathbb{C}})$*, defined:*

$$\begin{aligned}(r : \mathbb{I}) \circledast (\langle s_1, ..., s_n \rangle : \mathbb{I}^n) &= \langle r \circledast s_1, ..., r \circledast s_n \rangle : \mathbb{I}^n \\ (\mathsf{D}^{\hat{1}}_r : [\mathbb{C}, \mathbb{C}]) \;\hat{\circ}\; (\mathsf{D}^n_S : [\mathbb{C}^n, \mathbb{C}]) &= \mathsf{D}^{\hat{1}}_r \circ \mathsf{D}^n_S : [\mathbb{C}^n, \mathbb{C}]\end{aligned}$$

The axioms are the lax versions of the monoid left-action laws.

The lax and colax indexed monoidal operations $\mathsf{m}^{n,m}_{R,S}$ and $\mathsf{n}^{n,m}_{R,S}$ follow a similar derivation but as lax and colax monoid homomorphisms between composite monoids on coeffect annotations and shapes and $\times$ in $\mathbb{C}$. The details are elided here.

Returning to soundness, our semantics is therefore defined in terms of structures whose axioms correspond to axioms of the syntactic equational theory. Consequently, semantic proofs correspond to syntactic proofs, modulo naturality laws and product/exponent laws in $\mathbb{C}$. This result holds in the general coeffect calculus and semantics since every semantic structure has a unique corresponding structure on coeffect annotations (*i.e.*, $(\mathcal{C}, \circledast, \mathsf{use})$ for sequential composition of unary denotations, $(\mathcal{C}, \veebar)$ for splitting contexts, $(\mathcal{C}, \barwedge)$ for joining contexts).

Example 31. Section 4.1 showed η-equality for structural systems, which uses the properties (1) $\veebar = \barwedge = \times$ for structural systems and (2) $s \circledast \langle \mathsf{use} \rangle = \langle s \circledast \mathsf{use} \rangle = \langle s \rangle$. The semantics here is sound with respect to η-equality; the proof uses the corresponding axioms (1) $\mathsf{n}^{n,m}_{R,S} \circ \mathsf{m}^{n,m}_{R,S} = id$ and (2) $\varepsilon_{\mathsf{use}} \mathsf{D}^m_s \circ \delta^m_{\mathsf{use},s} = id$ (structural indexed comonad unit law [SC1], Definition 21).

The full semantic proofs of $\beta\eta$-equality then correspond to syntactic proofs on coeffect annotations. For brevity, we omit the full proofs here.

6. Related work

We expand on the overview of related work in Section 2.5.

Bounded reuse. The (*storage*) rule for bounded linear logic explains the contextual requirements induced by proposition reuse [7]:

$$(\text{storage})\frac{!_{\overline{Y}}\Gamma \vdash A}{!_{X\overline{Y}}\Gamma \vdash !_X A}$$

where $X\overline{Y} = \langle XY_1, .., XY_n \rangle$ is the scalar multiple of a vector. This rule is akin to the δ^n operation of structural indexed comonads, indeed, we can model it exactly using $\delta^n_{X,\overline{Y}}$ and the lifting $\mathsf{D}^{\hat{1}}_X$.

In BLL, the modality $!_X$ is a constructor and may appear both on the left- and right-hand sides of $\vdash$. In this paper, reuse bounds annotate typing rules, thus there is no constructor corresponding to bounded reuse in the language; reuse bounds are meta-level. Our choice to work at the meta-level means that the coeffect calculus provides a unified analysis and semantics to different notions of context; its term language is that of the standard λ-calculus.

Semantics. Previously we briefly introduced indexed comonads [15] without derivation. Here we derived indexed comonads as colax homomorphisms. This is dual to the *parametric effect monad* structure defined as a lax homomorphism [8]. Our semantics requires additional structure not needed for effects due to the asymmetry inherent in the λ-calculus.

The necessity modality $\Box$ in S4 logic corresponds to a comonad with lax monoidal functor structure $\mathsf{m} : \Box A \times \Box B \to \Box(A \times B)$. Bierman and de Paiva [2] defined a term language corresponding to a natural deduction S4, where contexts contain sequences of $\Box$-wrapped assumptions $x_1 : \Box A_1, \ldots x_n : \Box A_n$. Modelling these judgments does not require a context-splitting operation unlike in our approach, which uses the n operation of the form $\mathsf{n} : \Box(A \times B) \to \Box A \times \Box B$. Our approach can be thought of as having a single $\Box$ modality over the context which can represent both flat whole-context dependence and structural per-variable dependence.

Coeffect-like calculi Recent works have also developed coeffect systems, following related approaches. Brunel, Gaboardi, Mazza, and Zdancewic derive a kind of general structural coeffect system, taking inspiration from bounded linear logic [3]. Their work provides an operational semantics and proves soundness of its coeffect system with respect to the semantics. Their coeffect system provides a coeffect-indexed !-modality as a type constructor in the language, and explicit coeffect-inducing expressions for a particular notion of coeffect.

This differs to our approach where coeffects are implicit: they are not attached to a type constructor and can be introduced through variable use, *e.g.* the (*var*) rule. The coeffect systems of Brunel *et al.* allow "local coeffects", which we called structural (per-variable), but not "global coeffects" (flat or per-context). Our previous work provided just global/flat (per context) coeffects. Our new system here reconciles both kinds into one system.

There are a number of encouraging similarities in the approach of Brunel *et al.* Their semantics is similar (even isomorphic in some parts) to ours, defining an indexed comonad like structure in terms of a *positive action* $\bullet : \mathcal{S} \times \mathcal{A} \rightarrow \mathcal{A}$ on a monoidal category of coeffect annotations $\mathcal{S}$ (and base category $\mathcal{A}$) and an *exponential action* providing related operations to our indexed monoidal operations m and n.

There has been some other related bounded linear logic work, by Ghica and Smith, with "resource-aware types" annotated by a semiring of resource bounds [5]. This allows reuse bounds for BLL to be tracked, as well as other kinds of concurrency information. A categorical semantics is provided which is similar in style to that of Brunel *et al.* and which loosely resembles our indexed comonad approach (but does not require the additional indexed monoidal structures we used here). Included in their work, which this paper lacks, is a procedure for type-inference (using a decision procedure on semirings). Future work for us is to adopt a similar approach for inference of coeffects in our system.

Both the works of Brunel *et al.* and Ghica *et al.* use a semiring structure for annotations. Our scalar coeffect structure is similar: it is a semiring without commutativity of the $+$ operation (although all our examples here have a commutative $+$) and without the absorption law for multiplication (which only some of our systems have).

Future work is to unify the approaches of this paper and the coeffect systems of Brunel *et al.* and Ghica *et al.* Initial comparisons show several similarities, suggesting that unification is plausible.

7. Conclusions

In this paper, we looked at two forms of context-dependence analysis – *flat* coeffect systems that track whole-context requirements (such as implicit parameters, resources, or platform version) and *structural* coeffects that track per-variable requirements (such as usage or data access patterns). The newly introduced structural system makes applications such as liveness, bounded reuse, and dataflow analysis (from our earlier work) practically useful. With the move towards cross-platform systems running in diverse environments, analysing context dependence is vital for reasoning and compilation. The coeffect calculus provides a foundation for further study, similar to the type-and-effect discipline.

We presented the system together with its syntactic equational theory and categorical semantics. The equational theory is presented in order to explain how the systems work, but it also provides a basis for an operational semantics for concrete systems. Exploring these, and their connection to the denotational semantics, is further work.

Acknowledgments

Thanks are due to Marco Gaboardi, Dan Ghica, Marcelo Fiore, and Tarmo Uustalu for discussions on this work. We thank the anonymous reviewers for their comments and suggestions. This work was supported by CHESS.

References

[1] M. Abbott, T. Altenkirch, and N. Ghani. Containers: constructing strictly positive types. *Theor. Comput. Sci.*, 342(1):3–27, 2005.

[2] G. M. Bierman and V. C. de Paiva. On an intuitionistic modal logic. *Studia Logica*, 65(3):383–416, 2000.

[3] A. Brunel, M. Gaboardi, D. Mazza, and S. Zdancewic. A core quantitative coeffect calculus. In *Proceedings of ESOP*, volume 8410 of *Lecture Notes in Computer Science*, pages 351–370. Springer, 2014.

[4] C. Flanagan and S. Qadeer. A type and effect system for atomicity. In *Prooceedings of PLDI*, pages 338–349. ACM, 2003.

[5] D. R. Ghica and A. I. Smith. Bounded linear types in a resource semiring. In *Proceedings of ESOP*, volume 8410 of *Lecture Notes in Computer Science*, pages 331–350. Springer, 2014.

[6] D. K. Gifford and J. M. Lucassen. Integrating functional and imperative programming. In *Proceedings of Conference on LISP and func. prog.*, LFP '86, 1986. ISBN 0-89791-200-4.

[7] J.-Y. Girard, A. Scedrov, and P. J. Scott. Bounded linear logic: a modular approach to polynomial-time computability. *Theoretical computer science*, 97(1):1–66, 1992.

[8] S. Katsumata. Parametric effect monads and semantics of effect systems. In *Proceedings of POPL*, pages 633–646. ACM, 2014.

[9] J. Lewis, J. Launchbury, E. Meijer, and M. Shields. Implicit parameters: Dynamic scoping with static types. In *Proceedings of POPL*, page 118, 2000.

[10] E. Moggi. Notions of computation and monads. *Inf. Comput.*, 93(1), 1991. ISSN 0890-5401.

[11] A. Nanevski, F. Pfenning, and B. Pientka. Contextual modal type theory. *ACM Trans. Comput. Logic*, 9(3):23:1–23:49, June 2008.

[12] P. O'Hearn. On bunched typing. *J. Funct. Program.*, 13(4):747–796, July 2003. ISSN 0956-7968.

[13] D. Orchard. Programming contextual computations (PhD dissertation). Technical Report UCAM-CL-TR-854, University of Cambridge, Computer Laboratory, 2014. URL `http://www.cl.cam.ac.uk/techreports/UCAM-CL-TR-854.pdf`.

[14] T. Petricek. Context-aware programming languages (PhD thesis), 2014. Forthcoming.

[15] T. Petricek, D. A. Orchard, and A. Mycroft. Coeffects: Unified static analysis of context-dependence. In F. V. Fomin, R. Freivalds, M. Z. Kwiatkowska, and D. Peleg, editors, *ICALP (2)*, volume 7966 of *Lecture Notes in Computer Science*, pages 385–397. Springer, 2013.

[16] F. Pfenning and R. Davies. A judgmental reconstruction of modal logic. *Mathematical. Structures in Comp. Sci.*, 11(4):511–540, 2001.

[17] P. Sewell, J. J. Leifer, K. Wansbrough, F. Z. Nardelli, M. Allen-Williams, P. Habouzit, and V. Vafeiadis. Acute: High-level programming language design for distributed computation. *J. Funct. Program.*, 17(4-5):547–612, July 2007.

[18] R. Tate. The sequential semantics of producer effect systems. In *Proceedings of POPL 2013*, pages 15–26, 2013.

[19] T. Uustalu and V. Vene. Comonadic notions of computation. *Electron. Notes Theor. Comput. Sci.*, 203(5):263–284, 2008. .

[20] W. W. Wadge and E. A. Ashcroft. *LUCID, the dataflow programming language*. Academic Press Professional, Inc., San Diego, CA, USA, 1985. ISBN 0-12-729650-6.

[21] P. Wadler and P. Thiemann. The marriage of effects and monads. *ACM Trans. Comput. Logic*, 4:1–32, January 2003.

Behavioral Software Contracts

Robert Bruce Findler
Northwestern University & PLT
robby@eecs.northwestern.edu

Programmers embrace contracts. They can use the language they know and love to formulate logical assertions about the behavior of their programs. They can use the existing IDE infrastructure to log contracts, to test, to debug, and to profile their programs.

The keynote presents the challenges and rewards of supporting contracts in a modern, full-spectrum programming language. It covers technical challenges of contracts while demonstrating the non-technical motivation for contract system design choices and showing how contracts and contract research can serve practicing programmers.

The remainder of this article is a literature survey of contract research, with an emphasis on recent work about higher-order contracts and blame.

Early Contracts. Parnas (1972) suggested the use of logical assertions to describe software components. Meyer (1991; 1992) implemented the first full-fledged contract system and developed a matching software engineering philosophy, design by contract.

Findler and Felleisen (2002) introduced contracts to the functional programming world, generalizing them to higher-order languages, and introduced the ideas of blame and boundaries as independent concepts worthy of study.

Semantics. Findler and Felleisen used an operational model for contracts and did not define a notion of contract satisfaction. Blume and McAllester (2006) recognized this lack and responded with a quotient model, shedding light on the special status of the contract that does no checking. In parallel, Findler and Blume (2006) investigated contracts as Scott projections, thanks to a timely question from Bob Harper in 2002. Dimoulas and Felleisen (2011) countered from an observational equivalence perspective and pointed out that software engineering and formal methods naturally deal with different satisfaction relations.

Greenberg et al. (2010) studied dependent contracts, showing how there are natural variations hiding in Blume and McAllester's model. Dimoulas et al. (2011) designed a new combinator to monitor dependent contracts that assigns blame correctly when a dependent contract violates part of itself. Dimoulas et al. (2012) extended this model to introduce a notion of contract system completeness, i.e., a contract system that accounts for all possible violations.

Laziness. Contracts in lazy languages lead to complex and interesting semantic questions. As a hint at the complexity, consider a function that does not explore all of its argument, but where the unexplored part is rejected by the contract. Should this be a violation? Chitil et al. (2003) take the negative answer and show how to delay checks until the program observes the values that trigger the violation. Chitil and Huch (2006) later refine their technique to eliminate accidental sequentiality in the contract specification itself. Degen et al. (2012) tackle this question head on, showing that a contract system cannot report contract violations for all of the values that influence the program's final result without introducing unwanted strictness.

Features. Sophisticated language features demand sophisticated contract systems and more nuanced ways to assign blame.

Data structures require care to avoid excessive performance overhead (Findler et al. 2007).

Delimited and composable control operators provide new ways for values to flow and thus require special contract support (Takikawa et al. 2013).

Classes and object systems also lead to new concerns for contracts, from behavioral subtyping (Findler and Felleisen 2001; Findler et al. 2001) to support for first-class classes (Strickland and Felleisen 2010; Strickland et al. 2013).

ICFP '14, September 1–6, 2014, Gothenburg, Sweden.

ACM 978-1-4503-2873-9/14/09.
http://dx.doi.org/10.1145/2628136.2632855

Categories and Subject Descriptors D.3.3 [*Programming Languages*]: Language Constructs and Features; D.2.4 [*Software Engineering*]: Programming by contract

Keywords Contracts

Pragmatics. Strickland and Felleisen (2009) explore the crucial pragmatic question of how to draw boundaries between components.

A number of researchers have also explored parametric polymorphic contracts (Guha et al. 2007; Matthews and Ahmed 2008; Ahmed et al. 2011), using the idea that runtime sealing is the dynamic analog of polymorphic type checking.

Implementation. Herman et al. (2007) demonstrate how contract implementations break tail-recursion and design a virtual machine that recovers it.

Strickland et al. (2012) show how to add primitive interposition support to a runtime system that is strong enough to support contracts, but weak enough to avoid breaking guarantees of the underlying programming language.

Dimoulas et al. (2013) demonstrate how to give programmatic control for enabling and disabling contract checks to balance checking with performance.

Gradual Typing. The most active application of contracts is gradual typing (Flanagan 2006; Tobin-Hochstadt and Felleisen 2006; Siek and Taha 2006), which exploits dynamic contract checking so programmers can incrementally add types to untyped programs. Gronski and Flanagan (2007) clarified the relationship between gradual types and contracts.

Findler et al. (2004) gave an early instance of gradual typing, showing how structural and nominal OO type systems can coexist.

Gradual typing can be viewed as an interoperability problem, based on Matthews and Findler (2007)'s notion of a boundary. Tov and Pucella (2010) use this perspective to connect a language with an affine type systems to a simply-typed one using contracts that exploit mutable references to track how often resources are used.

Wadler and Findler (2009) and Dimoulas et al. (2012) refined the proof techniques for the Blame Theorem for gradually typed calculi, which ensures that either blame for a contract violation lies on the side with the weak type system or that the type is too strong.

References

A. Ahmed, R. B. Findler, J. Matthews, and P. Wadler. Blame for All. In *Proc. ACM Sym. Principles of Programming Languages*, 2011.

M. Blume and D. McAllester. Sound and Complete Models of Contracts. *J. Functional Programming* 16(4-5), 2006.

O. Chitil and F. Huch. A Pattern Logic for Prompt Lazy Assertions in Haskell. In *Proc. Implementation and Application of Functional Languages*, 2006.

O. Chitil, D. McNeill, and C. Runciman. Lazy Assertions. In *Proc. Implementation and Application of Functional Languages*, 2003.

M. Degen, P. Thiemann, and S. Wehr. The Interaction of Contracts and Laziness. In *Proc. Partial Evaluation and Program Manipulation*, 2012.

C. Dimoulas and M. Felleisen. On Contract Satisfaction in a Higher-Order World. *Trans. Programming Languages and Systems* 33(5), 2011.

C. Dimoulas, R. B. Findler, and M. Felleisen. Option Contracts. In *Proc. ACM Conf. Object-Oriented Programming, Systems, Languages and Applications*, 2013.

C. Dimoulas, R. B. Findler, C. Flanagan, and M. Felleisen. Correct Blame for Contracts: No More Scapegoating. In *Proc. ACM Sym. Principles of Programming Languages*, 2011.

C. Dimoulas, S. Tobin-Hochstadt, and M. Felleisen. Complete Monitors for Behavioral Contracts. In *Proc. Europ. Sym. on Programming*, 2012.

R. B. Findler and M. Blume. Contracts as Pairs of Projections. In *Proc. Sym. Functional and Logic Programming*, 2006.

R. B. Findler and M. Felleisen. Contract Soundness for Object-Oriented Languages. In *Proc. ACM Conf. Object-Oriented Programming, Systems, Languages and Applications*, 2001.

R. B. Findler and M. Felleisen. Contracts for Higher-order Functions. In *Proc. ACM Intl. Conf. Functional Programming*, 2002.

R. B. Findler, M. Flatt, and M. Felleisen. Semantic Casts: Contracts and Structural Subtyping in a Nominal World. In *Proc. Europ. Conf. Object-Oriented Programming*, 2004.

R. B. Findler, S. Guo, and A. Rogers. Lazy Contract Checking for Immutable Data Structures. In *Proc. Implementation and Application of Functional Languages*, 2007.

R. B. Findler, M. Latendresse, and M. Felleisen. Behavioral Contracts and Behavioral Subtyping. In *Proc. ACM Conf. Object-Oriented Programming, Systems, Languages and Applications*, 2001.

C. Flanagan. Hybrid Type Checking. In *Proc. ACM Sym. Principles of Programming Languages*, 2006.

M. Greenberg, B. C. Pierce, and S. Weirich. Contracts Made Manifest. In *Proc. ACM Sym. Principles of Programming Languages*, 2010.

J. Gronski and C. Flanagan. Unifying Hybrid Types and Contracts. In *Proc. Sym. Trends in Functional Programming*, 2007.

A. Guha, J. Matthews, R. B. Findler, and S. Krishnamurthi. Relationally-Parametric Polymorphic Contracts. In *Proc. Dynamic Languages Symposium*, 2007.

D. Herman, A. Tomb, and C. Flanagan. Space-Efficient Gradual Typing. In *Proc. Sym. Trends in Functional Programming*, 2007.

J. Matthews and A. Ahmed. Parametric Polymorphism Through Run-Time Sealing or, Theorems for Low, Low Prices! In *Proc. Europ. Sym. on Programming*, 2008.

J. Matthews and R. B. Findler. Operational Semantics for Multi-Language Programs. In *Proc. ACM Sym. Principles of Programming Languages*, 2007.

B. Meyer. *Eiffel: The Language*. Prentice Hall, 1991.

B. Meyer. Applying "Design by Contract". *IEEE Computer* 25(10), 1992.

D. L. Parnas. A Technique for Software Module Specification with Examples. *Communications of the ACM* 15(5), 1972.

J. G. Siek and W. Taha. Gradual Typing for Functional Languages. In *Proc. Scheme and Functional Programming*, 2006.

T. S. Strickland, C. Dimoulas, A. Takikawa, and M. Felleisen. Contracts for First-Class Classes. *Trans. Programming Languages and Systems* 35(3), 2013.

T. S. Strickland and M. Felleisen. Nested and Dynamic Contract Boundaries. In *Proc. Implementation and Application of Functional Languages*, 2009.

T. S. Strickland and M. Felleisen. Contracts for First-Class Classes. In *Proc. Dynamic Languages Symposium*, 2010.

T. S. Strickland, S. Tobin-Hochstadt, R. B. Findler, and M. Flatt. Chaperones and Impersonators: Run-Time Support for Reasonable Interposition. In *Proc. ACM Conf. Object-Oriented Programming, Systems, Languages and Applications*, 2012.

A. Takikawa, T. S. Strickland, and S. Tobin-Hochstadt. Constraining Delimited Control with Contracts. In *Proc. Europ. Sym. on Programming*, 2013.

S. Tobin-Hochstadt and M. Felleisen. Interlanguage Migration: from Scripts to Programs. In *Proc. Dynamic Languages Symposium*, 2006.

J. A. Tov and R. Pucella. Stateful Contracts for Affine Types. In *Proc. Europ. Sym. on Programming*, 2010.

P. Wadler and R. B. Findler. Well-typed Programs Can't Be Blamed. In *Proc. Europ. Sym. on Programming*, 2009.

Soft Contract Verification

Phúc C. Nguyễn
University of Maryland
pcn@cs.umd.edu

Sam Tobin-Hochstadt
Indiana University
samth@cs.indiana.edu

David Van Horn
University of Maryland
dvanhorn@cs.umd.edu

Abstract

Behavioral software contracts are a widely used mechanism for governing the flow of values between components. However, run-time monitoring and enforcement of contracts imposes significant overhead and delays discovery of faulty components to run-time.

To overcome these issues, we present *soft contract verification*, which aims to statically prove either complete or partial contract correctness of components, written in an untyped, higher-order language with first-class contracts. Our approach uses higher-order symbolic execution, leveraging contracts as a source of symbolic values including unknown behavioral values, and employs an updatable heap of contract invariants to reason about flow-sensitive facts. We prove the symbolic execution soundly approximates the dynamic semantics and that *verified programs can't be blamed.*

The approach is able to analyze first-class contracts, recursive data structures, unknown functions, and control-flow-sensitive refinements of values, which are all idiomatic in dynamic languages. It makes effective use of an off-the-shelf solver to decide problems without heavy encodings. The approach is competitive with a wide range of existing tools—including type systems, flow analyzers, and model checkers—on their own benchmarks.

Categories and Subject Descriptors D.2.4 [*Software Engineering*]: Software/Program Verification; D.3.1 [*Programming Languages*]: Formal Definitions and Theory

Keywords Higher-order contracts; symbolic execution

1. Static verification for dynamic languages

Contracts (Meyer 1991; Findler and Felleisen 2002) have become a prominent mechanism for specifying and enforcing invariants in dynamic languages (Disney 2013; Plosch 1997; Austin et al. 2011; Strickland et al. 2012; Hickey et al. 2013). They offer the expressivity and flexibility of programming in a dynamic language, while still giving strong guarantees about the interaction of components. However, there are two downsides: (1) contract monitoring is expensive, often prohibitively so, which causes programmers to write more lax specifications, compromising correctness for efficiency; and (2) contract violations are found only at run-time, which delays discovery of faulty components with the usual negative engineering consequences.

ICFP '14, September 1–6, 2014, Gothenburg, Sweden.
Copyright is held by the owner/author(s). Publication rights licensed to ACM.
ACM 978-1-4503-2873-9/14/09...$15.00.
http://dx.doi.org/10.1145/2628136.2628156

Static verification of contracts would empower programmers to state stronger properties, get immediate feedback on the correctness of their software, and avoid worries about run-time enforcement cost since, once verified, contracts could be removed. All-or-nothing approaches to verification of typed functional programs has seen significant advances in the recent work on static contract checking (Xu et al. 2009; Xu 2012; Vytiniotis et al. 2013), refinement type checking (Terauchi 2010; Zhu and Jagannathan 2013; Vazou et al. 2013, 2014), and model checking (Kobayashi 2009b; Kobayashi et al. 2010, 2011). However, the highly dynamic nature of untyped languages makes verification more difficult.

Programs in dynamic languages are often written in idioms that thwart even simple verification methods such as type inference. Moreover, contracts themselves are written within the host language in the same idiomatic style. This suggests that moving beyond all-or-nothing approaches to verification is necessary.

In previous work (Tobin-Hochstadt and Van Horn 2012), we proposed an approach to *soft contract verification*, which enables piecemeal and modular verification of contracts. This approach augments a standard reduction semantics for a functional language with contracts and modules by endowing it with a notion of "unknown" values refined by sets of contracts. Verification is carried out by executing programs on abstract values.

To demonstrate the essence of the idea, consider the following contrived, but illustrative example. Let `pos?` and `neg?` be predicates for positive and negative integers. Contracts can be arbitrary predicates, so these functions are also contracts. Consider the following contracted function (written in Lisp-like notation):

```
(f : pos? → neg?)          ; contract
(define (f x) (* x -1))  ; function
```

We can verify this program by (symbolically) running it on an "unknown" input. Checking the domain contract refines the input to be an unknown satisfying the set of contracts `{pos?}`. By embedding some basic facts about `pos?`, `neg?`, and `-1` into the reduction relation for `*`, we conclude `(* {pos?} -1)` $\longmapsto$ `{neg?}`, and voilà, we've shown once and for all `f` meets its contract obligations and cannot be blamed. We could therefore soundly eliminate any contract which blames `f`, in this case `neg?`.

This approach is simple and effective for many programs, but suffers from several shortcomings, which we solve in this paper:

Solver-aided reasoning: While embedding symbolic arithmetic knowledge for specific, known contracts works for simple examples, it fails to reason about arithmetic generally. Contracts often fail to verify because equivalent formulations of contracts are not hard-coded in the semantics of primitives. Many systems address this issue by incorporating an SMT solver. However, for a higher-order language, solver integration is often achieved by reasoning in a theory of uninterpreted functions or semantic embeddings (Knowles and Flanagan 2010; Rondon et al. 2008; Vytiniotis et al. 2013).

In this paper, we observe that higher-order contracts can be effectively verified using only a simple first-order solver. The key insight is that contracts delay higher-order checks and failures always occur with a first order witness. By relying on a (symbolic) semantic approach to carry out higher-order contract monitoring, we can use an SMT solver to reason about integers without the need for sophisticated encodings. (Examples in §2.3.)

Flow sensitive reasoning: Just as our semantic approach decomposes higher-order contracts into first-order properties, first-order contracts naturally decompose into conditionals. Our prior approach fails to reason effectively about conditionals, requiring contract checks to be built-in to the semantics. As a result, even simple programs with conditionals fail to verify:

```
(g : int? → neg?)
(define (g x) (if (pos? x) (f x) (f 8)))
```

This is because the true-branch call to `f` is `(f {int?})` by substitution, although we know from the guard that `x` satisfies `pos?`.

In this paper, we observe that flow-sensitivity can be achieved by replacing substitution with *heap-allocated* abstract values. These heap addresses are then refined as they flow through predicates and primitive operations, with no need for special handling of contracts (§2.2). As a result, the system is not only effective for contract verification, but can also handle safety verification for programs with no contracts at all.

First-class contracts: Pragmatic contract systems enable first-class contracts so new combinators can be written as functions that consume and produce contracts. But to the best of our knowledge, no verification system currently supports first class contracts (or refinements), and in most approaches it appears fundamentally difficult to incorporate such a notion.

Because we handle contracts (and all other features) by *execution*, first-class contracts pose no significant technical challenge and our system reasons about them effectively (§2.5).

Converging for non-tail recursion: Of course, simply executing programs has a fundamental drawback—it will fail to terminate in many cases, and when the inputs are unknown, execution will almost always diverge. Our prior work used a simple loop detection algorithm that handled only tail-recursive functions. As a result, even simple programs operating over inductive data timed out.

In this paper, we accelerate the convergence of programs by identifying and approximating regular accumulation of evaluation contexts, causing common recursive programs to converge on unknown values, while providing precise predictions (§2.4). As with the rest of our approach, this happens during execution and is therefore robust to complex, higher-order control flow.

Combining these techniques yields a system competitive with a diverse range of existing powerful static checkers, achieving many of their strengths in concert, while balancing the benefits of static contract verification with the flexibility of dynamic enforcement.

We have built a prototype soft verification engine, which we dub SCV, based on these ideas and used it to evaluate the approach (§4). Our evaluation demonstrates that the approach can verify properties typically reserved for approaches that rely on an underlying type system, while simultaneously accommodating the dynamism and idioms of untyped programming languages. We take examples from work on soft typing (Cartwright and Fagan 1991; Wright and Cartwright 1997), type systems for untyped languages (Tobin-Hochstadt and Felleisen 2010), static contract checking (Xu et al. 2009; Xu 2012), refinement type checking (Terauchi 2010), and model checking of higher-order functional languages (Kobayashi 2009b; Kobayashi et al. 2010, 2011).

SCV can prove all contract checks redundant for almost all of the examples taken from this broad array of existing program analysis and type checking work, and can handle many of the tricky higher-order verification problems demonstrated by other systems. In other words, our approach is competitive with type systems, model checkers, and soft typing systems on each of their chosen benchmarks—in contrast, work on higher-order model checking does not handle benchmarks aimed at soft typing or occurrence typing, and vice versa. In the cases where SCV does not prove the complete absence of contract errors, the vast majority of possible dynamic errors are ruled out, justifying numerous potential optimizations. Over this corpus of programs, 99% of the contract and run-time type checks are proved safe, and could be eliminated.

We also evaluate the verification of three small interactive video games which use first-class and dependent contracts pervasively. The results show the subsequent elimination of contract monitoring has a dramatic effect: from a factor speed up of 7 in one case, to three orders of magnitude in the others. In essence, these results show the games are infeasible without contract verification.

2. Worked examples

We now present the main ideas of our approach through a series of examples taken from work on other verification techniques, starting from the simplest and working up to a complex object encoding.

2.1 Higher-order symbolic reasoning

Consider the following simple function that transforms functions on even integers into functions on odd integers. It has been ascribed this specification as a contract, which can be monitored at run-time.

```
(e2o : (even? → even?) → (odd? → odd?))
(define (e2o f)
  (λ (n) (- (f (+ n 1)) 1)))
```

A contract monitors the flow of values between components. In this case, the contract monitors the interaction between the context and the `e2o` function. It is easy to confirm that `e2o` is correct with respect to the contract; `e2o` holds up its end of the agreement, and therefore cannot be blamed for any run-time failures that may arise. The informal reasoning goes like this: First assume `f` is an `even? → even?` function. When applied, we must ensure the argument is even (otherwise `e2o` is at fault), but may assume the result is even (otherwise the context is at fault). Next assume `n` is odd (otherwise the context is at fault) and ensure the result is odd (otherwise `e2o` is at fault). Since `(+ n 1)` is even when `n` is odd, `f` is applied to an even argument, producing an even result. Subtracting one therefore gives an odd result, as desired.

This kind of reasoning mimics the step-by-step computation of `e2o`, but rather than considering some particular inputs, it considers these inputs symbolically to verify all possible executions of `e2o`. We systematize this kind of reasoning by augmenting a standard reduction semantics for contracts with symbolic values that are refined by sets of contracts. At first approximation, the semantics includes reductions such as:

$$(+\ \{\texttt{odd?}\}\ 1) \longmapsto \{\texttt{even?}\}, \text{ and}$$
$$(\{\texttt{even?} \rightarrow \texttt{even?}\}\ \{\texttt{even?}\}) \longmapsto \{\texttt{even?}\}.$$

This kind of symbolic reasoning mimics a programmer's informal intuitions which employ contracts to refine unknown values and to verify components meet their specifications. If a component cannot be blamed in the symbolic semantics, we can safely conclude it cannot be blamed in general.

2.2 Flow sensitive reasoning

Programmers using untyped languages often use a mixture of type-based and flow-based reasoning to design programs. The analysis naturally takes advantage of type tests idiomatic in dynamic languages even when the tests are buried in complex expressions. The following function taken from work on occurrence typing (Tobin-Hochstadt and Felleisen 2010) can be proven safe using our symbolic semantics:

```
(f : (or/c int? str?) cons? → int?)
(define (f x p)
  (cond
    [(and (int? x) (int? (car p))) (+ x (car p))]
    [(int? (car p)) (+ (str-len x) (car p))]
    [else 0]))
```

Here, int?, str?, and cons? are type predicates for integers, strings, and pairs, respectively. The contract (or/c int? str?) uses the or/c contract combinator to construct a contract specifying a value is either an integer or a string.

A programmer would convince themselves this program was safe by using the control dominating predicates to refine the types of x and (car p) in each branch of the conditional.[1] Our symbolic semantics accommodates exactly this kind of reasoning in order to verify this example. However, there is a technical challenge here. A straightforward substitution-based semantics would not reflect the flow-sensitive facts. Focusing just on the first clause, a substitution model would give:

```
(cond
  [(and (int? {(or/c int? str?)}) (int? (car {cons?})))
   (+ {(or/c int? str?)} (car {cons?}))] ...)
```

At this point, it's too late to communicate the refinement of these sets implied by the test evaluating to true, so the semantics would report the contract on + potentially being violated because the first argument may be a string, and the second argument may be anything. We overcome this challenge by modelling symbolic values as heap-allocated sets of contracts. When predicates and data structure accessors are applied to heap addresses, we refine the corresponding sets to reflect what must be true. So the program is modelled as:

```
(cond
  [(and (int? L1) (int? (car L2)))
   (+ L1 (car L2))] ...)
where L1 ↦ {(or/c int? string?)}, L2 ↦ {cons?}
```

In the course of evaluating the test, we get to (int? L_1), the semantics conceptually forks the evaluator and refines the heap:

(int? L_1) $\longmapsto$ true, where $L_1 \mapsto$ {int?}
$\longmapsto$ false, where $L_1 \mapsto$ {string?}

Similar refinements to L_2 are communicated through the heap for (int? (car L_2)), thereby making (+ L_1 (car L_2)) safe. This simple idea is effective in achieving flow-based refinements. It naturally handles deeply nested and inter-procedural conditionals.

2.3 Incorporating an SMT solver

The techniques described so far are highly effective for reasoning about functions and many kinds of recursive data structures. However, effective reasoning about many kinds of base values, such as integers, requires sophisticated domain-specific knowledge. Rather than build such a tool ourselves, we defer to existing high-quality solvers for these domains. Unlike many solver-aided verification tools, however, we use the solver *only* for queries on base values, rather than attempting to encode a rich, higher-order language into one that is accepted by the solver.

[1] The call to str-len is safe because (and (int? x) (int? (car p))) being false and (int? (car p)) being true implies that (int? x) is false, which in turns implies x is a string as enforced by f's contract.

To demonstrate our approach, we take an example (intro3) from work on model checking higher-order programs (Kobayashi et al. 2010).

```
(>/c : int? → any → bool?)
(define (>/c lo) (λ (x) (and (int? x) (> x lo))))

(define (f x g) (g (+ x 1)))

(h : [x : int?] → [y : (>/c x)] → (>/c y))
(define (h x) ...) ; unknown definition

(main : int? → (>/c 0))
(define (main n) (if (≥ n 0) (f n (h n)) 1))
```

In this program, we define a contract combinator (>/c) that creates a check for an integer from a lower bound; a helper function f, which comes without a contract; and an *unknown* function h that given an integer x, returns a function mapping some number y that is greater than x to an answer greater than y—here h's specification is given, but not its implementation. (Note h's contract is dependent.) We verify main's correctness, which means it definitely returns a positive integer and does not violate h's contract.

According to its contract, main is passed an integer n. If n is negative, main returns 1, satisfying the contract. Otherwise the function applies f to n and (h n). Function h, by its contract, returns another function that requires a number greater than n. Examining f's definition, we see h (now bound to g) is eventually applied to (+ n 1). Let n_1 be the result of (+ n 1). And by h's contract, we know the answer is another integer greater than (+ n 1). Let us name this answer n_2. In order to verify that main satisfies contract (>/c 0), we need to verify that n_2 is a positive integer.

Once f returns, the heap contains several addresses with contracts:

n $\mapsto$ {int?, (≥/c 0)}
n_1 $\mapsto$ {int?, (=/c (+ n 1))}
n_2 $\mapsto$ {int?, (>/c n_1)}

We then translate this information to a query for an external solver:

```
n, n1, n2: INT;
ASSERT n ≥ 0;
ASSERT n1 = n + 1;
ASSERT n2 > n1;
QUERY n2 > 0;
```

Solvers such as CVC4 (Barrett et al. 2011) and Z3 (De Moura and Bjørner 2008) easily verify this implication, proving main's correctness.

Refinements such as (≥/c 0) are generated by *primitive* applications (≥ x 0), and queries are generated from translation of the heap, not arbitrary expressions. This has a few consequences. First, by the time we have value v satisfying predicate p on the heap, we know that p terminates successfully on v. Issues such as errors (from p itself) or divergence are handled elsewhere in other evaluation branches. Second, we only need to translate a small set of simple, well understood contracts—not arbitrary expressions. Evaluation naturally breaks down complex expressions, and properties are discovered even when they are buried in complex, higher-order functions. Given a translation for (>/c 0), the analysis automatically takes advantage of the solver even when the predicate contains > in a complex way, such as (λ (x) (or (> x 0) e) where e is an arbitrary expression. Predicates that lack translations to SMT only reduce precision, never soundness.

2.4 Converging for non-tail recursion

The techniques sketched above provide high precision in the examples considered, but simply executing programs on abstract values is unlikely to terminate in the presence of recursion. When an abstract value stands for an infinite set of concrete values, execution may proceed infinitely, building up an ever-growing evaluation context. To tackle this problem, we *summarize* this context to coalesce repeated structures and enable termination on many recursive programs. Although guaranteed termination is not our goal, the empirical results (§4) demonstrate that the method is effective in practice.

The following example program is taken from work on model checking of higher-order functional programs (Kobayashi et al. 2010), and demonstrates checking non-trivial safety properties on recursive functions. Note that no loop invariants need be provided by the user.

```
(main : (and/c int? ≥0?) → (and/c int? ≥0?))
(define (main n)
  (let ([l (make-list n)])
    (if (> n 0) (car (reverse l empty)) 0)))

(define (reverse l ac)
  (if (empty? l) ac
      (reverse (cdr l) (cons (car l) ac))))

(define (make-list n)
  (if (= n 0) empty
      (cons n (make-list (- n 1))))))
```

Again, we aim to verify both the specified contract for `main` as well as the preconditions for primitive operations such as `car`. Most significantly, we need to verify that `(reverse l empty)` produces a non-empty list (so that `car` succeeds) and that its first element is a positive integer. The local functions `reverse` and `make-list` do not come with a contract.

This problem is more challenging than the original OCaml version of the same program, due to the lack of types. This program represents a common idiom in dynamic languages: not all values are contracted, and there is no type system on which to piggy-back verification. In addition, programmers often rely on inter-procedural reasoning to justify their code's correctness, as here with `reverse`.

We verify `main` by applying it to an abstract (unknown) value n_1. The contract ensures that within the body, n_1 is a non-negative integer.

The integer n_1 is first passed to `make-list`. The comparison `(=` n_1 `0)` non-deterministically returns `true` and `false`, updating the information known about n_1 to be either `0` or `(>/c 0)` in each corresponding case. In the first case, `make-list` returns `empty`. In the second case, `make-list` proceeds to the recursive application `(make-list` n_2`)`, where n_2 is the abstract non-negative integer obtained from evaluating `(-` n_1 `1)`. However, `(make-list` n_2`)` is identical to the original call `(make-list` n_1`)` up to renaming, since both n_1 and n_2 are non-negative. Therefore, we pause here and use a summary of `make-list`'s result instead of continuing in an infinite loop.

Since we already know that `empty` is one possible result of `(make-list` n_1`)`, we use it as the result of `(make-list` n_2`)`. The application `(make-list` n_1`)` therefore produces the pair $\langle n_1, \texttt{empty}\rangle$, which is another answer for the original application. We could continue this process and plug this new result into the pending application `(make-list` n_2`)`. But by observing that the application produces a list of one positive integer when the recursive call produces `empty`, we approximate the new result $\langle n_1, \texttt{empty}\rangle$ to a non-empty list of positive integers, and then use this approximate answer as the result of the pending application `(make-list` n_2`)`. This then induces another result for `(make-list` n_1`)`, a list of two or more positive integers, but this is subsumed by the previous answer of non-empty integer list. We have now discovered *all* possible return values of `make-list` when applied to a non-negative integer: it maps `0` to `empty`, and positive integers to a non-empty list of positive integers.

Although our explanation made use of the order, the soundness of analyzing `make-list` does not depend on the order of exploring non-deterministic branches. Each recursive application with repeated arguments generates a waiting context, and each function return generates a new case to resume. There is an implicit worklist algorithm in the modified semantics (§3.8).

When `make-list` returns to `main`, we have two separate cases: either n_1 is 0 and `l` is `empty`, or n_1 is positive and `l` is non-empty. In the first case, `(>` n_1 `0)` is false and `main` returns `0`, satisfying the contract. Otherwise, `main` proceeds to reversing the list before taking its first element.

Using the same mechanism as with `make-list`, the analysis infers that `reverse` returns a non-empty list when either of its arguments (`l` or `acc`) is non-empty. In addition, `reverse` only receives arguments of proper lists, so all partial operations on `l` such as `car` and `cdr` are safe when `l` is not `empty`, without needing an explicit check. The function eventually returns a non-empty list of integers to `main`, justifying `main`'s call to the partial function `car`, producing a positive integer. Thus, `main` never has a run-time error in any context.

While this analysis makes use of the implementation of `make-list` and `reverse`, that does not imply that it is whole-program. Instead, it is *modular* in its use of unknown values abstracting arbitrary behavior. For example, `make-list` could instead be an abstract value represented by a contract that always produces lists of integers. The analysis would still succeed in proving all contracts safe except the use of `car` in `main`—this shows the flexibility available in choosing between precision and modularity. In addition, the analysis does not have to be perfectly precise to be useful. If it successfully verifies most contracts in a module, that already greatly improves confidence about the module's correctness and justifies the elimination of numerous expensive dynamic checks.

2.5 Putting it all together

The following example illustrates all aspects of our system. For this, we choose a simple encoding of classes as functions that produce objects, where objects are again functions that respond to messages named by symbols. We then verify the correctness of a *mixin*: a function from classes to classes. The `vec/c` contract enforces the interface of a 2D-vector class whose objects accept messages `'x`, `'y`, and `'add` for extracting components and vector addition.

```
(define vec/c
  ([msg : (one-of/c 'x 'y 'add)]
   → (match msg
       [(or 'x 'y) real?]
       ['add (vec/c → vec/c)])))
```

This definition demonstrates several powerful contract system features which we are able to handle:

- contracts are first-class values, as in the definition of `vec/c`,
- contracts may include arbitrary predicates, such as `real?`,
- contracts may be recursive, as in the contract for `'add`,
- function contracts may express *dependent* relationships between the domain and range—the contract of the result of method selection for `vec/c` depends on the method chosen.

Suppose we want to define a mixin that takes any class that satisfies the `vec/c` interface and produces another class with added vector operations such as `'len` for computing the vector's length. The `extend` function defines this mixin, and `ext-vec/c` specifies the new interface. We verify that `extend` violates no contracts and returns a class that respects specifications from `ext-vec/c`.

```
(extend : (real? real? → vec/c)
          → (real? real? → ext-vec/c))
(define (extend mk-vec)
  (λ (x y)
    (let ([vec (mk-vec x y)])
      (λ (m)
        (match m
          ['len
           (let ([x (vec 'x)] [y (vec 'y)])
             (sqrt (+ (* x x) (* y y))))]
          [_ (vec m)])))))

(define ext-vec/c
  ([msg : (one-of/c 'x 'y 'add 'len)]
   → (match msg
       [(or 'x 'y) real?]
       ['add (vec/c → vec/c)]
       ['len (and/c real? (≥/c 0))])))
```

To verify `extend`, we provide an arbitrary value, which is guaranteed by its contract to be a class matching `vec/c`. The mixin returns a new class whose objects understand messages `'x`, `'y`, `'add`, and `'len`. This new class defines method `'len` and relies on the underlying class to respond to `'x`, `'y`, and `'add`. Because the old class is constrained by contract `vec/c`, the new class will not violate its contract when responding to messages `'x`, `'y`, and `'add`.

For the `'len` message, the object in the new vector class extracts its components as abstract numbers `x` and `y`, according to interface `vec/c`. It then computes their squares and leaves the following information on the heap:

$$\begin{array}{lcl} \texttt{x}^2 & \mapsto & \{\texttt{real?}, \texttt{(=/c (* x x))}\} \\ \texttt{y}^2 & \mapsto & \{\texttt{real?}, \texttt{(=/c (* y y))}\} \\ \texttt{s} & \mapsto & \{\texttt{real?}, \texttt{(=/c (+ x}^2\ \texttt{y}^2\texttt{))}\} \end{array}$$

Solvers such as Z3 (De Moura and Bjørner 2008) can handle simple non-linear arithmetic and verify that the sum `s` is non-negative, thus the `sqrt` operation is safe. Execution proceeds to take the square root—now called `l`—and refines the heap with the following mapping:

$$\texttt{l} \ \mapsto\ \{\texttt{real?}, \texttt{(=/c (sqrt s))}\}$$

When the method returns, its result is checked by contract `ext-vec/c` to be a non-negative number. We again rely on the solver to prove that this is the case.

Therefore, `extend` is guaranteed to produce a new class that is correct with respect to interface `vec-ext/c`, justifying the elimination of expensive run-time checks. In a Racket program computing the length of 100000 random vectors, eliminating these contracts results in a 100-fold speed-up. While such dramatic results are unlikely in full programs, measurements of existing Racket programs suggests that 50% speedups are possible (Strickland et al. 2012).

3. A Symbolic Language with Contracts

In this section, we give a reduction system describing the core of our approach. Symbolic λ_C is a model of a language with first-class contracts and *symbolic values*. We first present the semantics, including handling of primitives and unknown functions. We then describe how the handling of primitive values integrates with external solvers. Finally, we show an abstraction of our symbolic system to accelerate convergence. For each abstraction, we relate concrete and symbolic programs and prove a soundness theorem.

At a high level, the key idea of our semantics is that abstract values behave non-deterministically in all possible ways that concrete values might behave. Furthmore, abstract values can be bounded by specifications in the form of contracts that limit these behaviors. As a result, an operational semantics for abstract values explores all the ways that the concrete program under consideration might be used.

Programs	p, q	$::=$	$\overrightarrow{m}\ e$
Modules	m	$::=$	(module $f\ u_c\ u$)
Expressions	e, c, d	$::=$	$v \mid x^\ell \mid e\, e^\ell \mid o\, \overrightarrow{e}^\ell \mid$ if $e\, e\, e \mid c \rightarrow \lambda x.d$
		$\mid$	$\texttt{mon}^{\ell,\ell}_{\ell}(c, e) \mid \texttt{blame}^{\ell}_{\ell} \mid \texttt{assume}(v, v)$
Pre-values	u	$::=$	$\lambda x.e \mid b \mid \langle v,v \rangle \mid v \rightarrow \lambda x.c \mid \bullet$
Values	v	$::=$	$a \mid u/\overrightarrow{v}$
Base values	b	$::=$	true $\mid$ false $\mid n \mid$ empty
Operations	o	$::=$	$o? \mid$ cons $\mid$ car $\mid$ cdr $\mid$ add1 $\mid + \mid =$
		$\mid$	...
Predicates	$o?$	$::=$	num? $\mid$ false? $\mid$ cons? $\mid$ empty?
		$\mid$	proc? $\mid$ dep?
Variables	x, f, ℓ	$\in$	*identifier*
Addresses	a	$\in$	*address*

Figure 1. Syntax of Symbolic λ_C

Given this operational semantics, we can then examine the results of evaluation to see if any results are errors blaming the components we wish to verify. If they do not, then our soundness theorem implies that there are no ways for the component to be blamed, regardless of what other parts of the program do. Thus, we have verified the component against its contract in all contexts. We make this notion precise in section 3.6.

3.1 Syntax of Symbolic λ_C

Our initial language models the functional core of many modern dynamic languages, extended with behavioral, first-class contracts, as well as symbolic values. The abstract syntax is shown in figure 1. Syntax needed only for symbolic execution is highlighted in gray; we discuss it after the syntax of concrete programs.

A program p is a sequence of module definitions followed by a top-level expression which may reference the modules. Each module m has a name f and exports a single value u with behavior enforced by contract u_c. (Generalizing to multiple-export modules is straightforward.)

Expressions include standard forms such as values, variable and module references, applications, and conditionals, as well as those for constructing and monitoring contracts. Contracts are first-class values and can be produced by arbitrary expressions. For clarity, when an expression plays the role of a contract, we use the metavariable c and d, rather than e. A *dependent* function contract ($c \rightarrow \lambda x.d$) monitors a function's argument with c and its result with the contract produced by applying $\lambda x.d$ to the argument.

A contract violation at run-time causes *blame*, an error with information about who violated the contract. We write $\texttt{blame}^{\ell}_{\ell''}$ to mean module ℓ is blamed for violating the contract from ℓ''. The form ($\texttt{mon}^{\ell,\ell'}_{\ell''}(c, e)$) monitors expression e with contract c, with ℓ being the positive party, ℓ' the negative party, and ℓ'' the source of the contract. The system blames the positive party if e produces a value violating c, and the negative one if e is misused by the *context* of the contract check. To make context information available at run-time, we annotate references and applications with labels indicating the module they appear in, or $\dagger$ for the top-level expression. For example, $x^\dagger$ denotes a reference to the name x from the top level, and $(\texttt{add1}\ x)^\ell$ denotes an addition inside module ℓ. When a module ℓ causes a primitive error, such as applying 5, we also write $\texttt{blame}^{\ell}_{\Lambda}$, indicating that it violates a contract with the language. We omit labels when they are irrelevant or can be inferred.

Pre-values u—extended to values below—include abstractions, base values, pairs of values, and dependent contracts with domain components evaluated. Base values include numbers, booleans, and the empty list. Primitive operations over values are standard, including predicates $o_?$ for dynamic testing of data types.

To reason about absent components, we equip λ_C with *unknown*, or *symbolic values*, which abstract over multiple concrete values exhibiting a range of behavior. An unknown value $\bullet$ stands for any value in the language. For soundness, execution must account for *all* possible concretizations of abstract values, and reduction becomes non-deterministic. As the program proceeds through tests and contract checks, more assumptions can be made about abstract values. To remember these assumptions, we take the *pre-values* and refine each with a set of contracts it is known to satisfy, written $u/\vec{v}$.

Finally, to track refinements of unknown values, we use heap addresses a as symbolic values and track them in a heap, which is a finite map from addresses to refined pre-values:

$$\text{Heaps} \quad \sigma ::= \overrightarrow{\langle a, u/\vec{v} \rangle}.$$

The heap σ maps addresses allocated for unknown values to refinements expressed as contracts; these refinements are updated during reduction and represent upper bounds on what they might be at runtime. Intuitively, any possible concrete execution can be obtained by substituting addresses with concrete values within bounds specified by the heap. We omit refinements when they are empty or irrelevant.

3.2 Semantics of Symbolic λ_C

We now turn to the reduction semantics for Symbolic λ_C, which combines standard rules for untyped languages with behavior for unknown values. Reduction is defined as a relation on states, parameterized by a module context:

$$\vec{m} \vdash \varsigma \longmapsto \varsigma'$$

States consist either of an expression paired with a heap, or blame:

$$\text{States} \quad \varsigma ::= (e, \sigma) \mid \mathtt{blame}^{\ell}_{\ell}.$$

We present the rules inline; a full version of all rules is given in the appendix of the the accompanying technical report (Nguyễn et al. 2014). In the inline presentation of rules, we systematically omit labels in contracts, these are presented in the full rules. We omit the module context whenever it is irrelevant.

3.2.1 Basic rules

Applications of primitives are interpreted by a δ relation, which maps operations, arguments and heaps to results and new heaps.

Apply-Primitive

$$\frac{\delta(\sigma, o\,\vec{v},) \ni \varsigma}{(o\ \vec{v}), \sigma \longmapsto \varsigma}$$

The use of a δ relation in reduction semantics is standard, but typically it is a function and is independent of the heap. We make δ dependent on the heap in order to use and update the current set of invariants; we make it a relation, since it may behave non-deterministically on unknown values. For example, in interpreting `(> • 5)`, the δ relation will produce two results: one `true`, with an updated heap to reflect the unknown value is `(>/c 5)`; the other `false`, with a heap reflecting the opposite. The δ relation is thus the hub of the verification system and a point of interaction with the SMT solver. It is described in more detail in section 3.3.

Applications of λ-abstractions follow standard β-reduction; applications of non-functions result in blame.

Apply-Function

$$\frac{}{((\lambda x.e)\ v), \sigma \longmapsto [v/x]e, \sigma}$$

Apply-Non-Function

$$\frac{\delta(\sigma, \mathtt{proc?}, v) \ni (\mathtt{false}, \sigma')}{(v\ v'), \sigma \longmapsto \mathtt{blame}, \sigma'}$$

Notice that the δ relation is employed to determine whether the value in operator position is a function using the `proc?` primitive. (Non-functions include concrete numbers and booleans as well as abstract values known to exclude functions; application of abstract values that may be functions is described in section 3.2.3.)

Conditionals follow a common treatment in untyped languages in which values other than `false` are considered true.

If-True

$$\frac{\delta(\sigma, \mathtt{false?}, v) \ni (\mathtt{false}, \sigma')}{\mathtt{if}\ v\ e_1\ e_2, \sigma \longmapsto e_1, \sigma'}$$

If-False

$$\frac{\delta(\sigma, \mathtt{false?}, v) \ni (\mathtt{true}, \sigma')}{\mathtt{if}\ v\ e_1\ e_2, \sigma \longmapsto e_2, \sigma'}$$

Just as in the case of *Apply-Non-Function*, the interpretation of conditionals uses the δ relation to determine whether `false?` holds, which takes into account all of the knowledge accumulated in σ and in either branch that is taken, updates the current knowledge to reflect whether `false?` of v holds. This is the mechanism by which control-flow based refinements are enabled.

The two rules for module references reflect the approach in which contracts are treated as *boundaries* between components (Dimoulas et al. 2011): a module self-reference incurs no contract check, while cross-module references are protected by the specified contract.

Module-Self-Reference

$$\frac{(\mathtt{module}\ f\ u_c\ u) \in \vec{m}}{\vec{m} \vdash f^{f}, \sigma \longmapsto u, \sigma}$$

Module-External-Reference

$$\frac{(\mathtt{module}\ f\ u_c\ u) \in \vec{m} \qquad f \neq \ell}{\vec{m} \vdash f^{\ell}, \sigma \longmapsto \mathtt{mon}(u_c, u), \sigma}$$

Finally, any state that is stuck with blame inside an evaluation context transitions to a final blame state that discards the surrounding context and heap.

Halt-Blame

$$\frac{}{\mathcal{E}[\mathtt{blame}], \sigma \longmapsto \mathtt{blame}}$$

Evaluation contexts as defined as follows:

$$\begin{aligned} \mathcal{E} ::= \ & [\,] \mid \mathcal{E}\ e \mid v\ \mathcal{E} \mid o\ \vec{v}\,\mathcal{E}\,\vec{e} \mid \mathtt{if}\ \mathcal{E}\ e\ e \\ \mid\ & \mathtt{mon}(\mathcal{E}, e) \mid \mathtt{mon}(v, \mathcal{E}) \mid \mathcal{E} \rightarrow \lambda x.e \end{aligned}$$

3.2.2 Contract monitoring

Contract monitoring follows existing operational semantics for contracts (Findler and Felleisen 2002), with extensions to handle and refine symbolic values.

There are several cases for checking a value against a contract. If the contract is not a function contract, we say it is *flat*, denoting a first-order property to be checked immediately. We thus expand the checking expression to a conditional.

Monitor-Flat-Contract

$$\frac{\delta(\sigma, \mathtt{dep?}, v_c) \ni (\mathtt{false}, \sigma') \qquad \sigma' \vdash v : v_c\,\mathbf{?}}{\mathtt{mon}(v_c, v), \sigma \longmapsto \mathtt{if}\ (v_c\ v)\ \mathtt{assume}(v, v_c)\ \mathtt{blame}, \sigma'}$$

Since contracts are first-class, they can also be abstract values; we rely on δ to determine whether a value is a flat contract by using (the negation of) the predicate for dependent contracts, `dep?`, instead of examining the syntax. This rule is standard except for the use of $\mathtt{assume}(v, v_c)$ and the $(\cdot \vdash \cdot : \cdot\,\mathbf{?})$ judgment. The $\mathtt{assume}(v, v_c)$ form, which would normally just be v, dynamically refines value v and the heap to indicate that v satisfies v_c; assume is discussed further in section 3.2.3. The judgment $\sigma' \vdash v : v_c\,\mathbf{?}$, which would normally just be omitted, indicates that the contract v_c cannot be statically judged to either pass or fail for v, which is why the predicate must be applied. This judgment and its closely related counterparts ($\cdot \vdash \cdot : \cdot$ ✓) and ($\cdot \vdash \cdot : \cdot$ ✗), which statically prove a value must or must not satisfy a given contract respectively, are discussed in section 3.4. If a flat contract can be statically proved or refuted, monitoring can be short-circuited.

Monitor-Proved

$$\frac{\delta(\sigma, \texttt{dep?}, v_c) \ni (\texttt{false}, \sigma') \quad \sigma' \vdash v : v_c \checkmark}{\texttt{mon}(v_c, v), \sigma \longmapsto v, \sigma'}$$

Monitor-Refuted

$$\frac{\delta(\sigma, \texttt{dep?}, v_c) \ni (\texttt{false}, \sigma') \quad \sigma' \vdash v : v_c \text{✗}}{\texttt{mon}(v_c, v), \sigma \longmapsto \texttt{blame}, \sigma'}$$

Monitoring a function contract against a function is interpreted the standard η-expansion of contracts.

Monitor-Function-Contract

$$\frac{\delta(\sigma, \texttt{proc?}, v) \ni (\texttt{true}, \sigma')}{\texttt{mon}(v_c \rightarrow \lambda x.d, v), \sigma \longmapsto \lambda x.\texttt{mon}(d, (v\ \texttt{mon}(v_c, x))), \sigma'}$$

Monitoring a function contract against a non-function results in an error.

Monitor-Non-Function

$$\frac{\delta(\sigma, \texttt{dep?}, v_c) \ni (\texttt{true}, \sigma_1) \quad \delta(\sigma_1, \texttt{proc?}, v) \ni (\texttt{false}, \sigma_2)}{\texttt{mon}(v_c, v), \sigma \longmapsto \texttt{blame}, \sigma_2}$$

When a dependent contract is represented by a address in the heap, we look up the address and use the result.

Monitor-Unknown-Function-Contract

$$\frac{\delta(\sigma, \texttt{dep?}, a) \ni (\texttt{true}, \sigma_1) \quad \delta(\sigma_1, \texttt{proc?}, v) \ni (\texttt{true}, \sigma_2) \quad \sigma_2(a) = v_c \rightarrow \lambda x.d}{\texttt{mon}(a, v), \sigma \longmapsto \lambda x.\texttt{mon}(d, v\ \texttt{mon}(v_c, x)), \sigma_2}$$

3.2.3 Handling unknown values

The final set of reduction rules concern unknown values and refinements.

Refine-Concrete

$$\frac{u \neq \bullet}{u, \sigma \longmapsto u/\emptyset, \sigma}$$

Refine-Unknown

$$\frac{a \notin dom(\sigma)}{\bullet, \sigma \longmapsto a, \sigma[a \mapsto \bullet/\emptyset]}$$

These two rules show reduction of pre-values, which initially have no refinement. If the pre-value is unknown, we additionally create a fresh address and add it to the heap.

The assume form uses the refine metafunction to update the heap of refinements to take into account the new information; see figure 2 for the definition of refine.

Assume

$$\frac{(\sigma', v') = \mathit{refine}(\sigma, v, v_c)}{\texttt{assume}(v, v_c), \sigma \longmapsto v', \sigma'}$$

Refinement is straightforward propagation of known contracts, including expanding values known to be pairs via cons? into pair values, and values known to be function contracts (via dep?) into function contract values.

Finally, we must handle application of unknown values. The first rule simply produces a new unknown value and heap address for the result of a call. If the unknown function came with a contract, this new unknown value will be refined by the contract via reduction.

Apply-Unknown

$$\frac{\delta(\sigma, \texttt{proc?}, a) \ni (\texttt{true}, \sigma')}{a\ v, \sigma \longmapsto a_a, \sigma'[a_a \mapsto \bullet]}$$

Havoc

$$\frac{\delta(\sigma, \texttt{proc?}, a) \ni (\texttt{true}, \sigma')}{a\ v, \sigma \longmapsto \texttt{havoc}\ v, \sigma'}$$

The second reduction rule for applying an unknown function, labeled *Havoc*, handles the possible dynamic behavior of the unknown function. A value passed to the unknown function may itself be a function with behavior, whose implementation we hope to verify. This function may further be invoked by the unknown function on unknown arguments. To simulate this, we assume *arbitrary* behavior from this unknown function and put the argument in a so-called demonic context implemented by the havoc operation, defined in a module added to every program; the definition is given below.

$$
\begin{array}{lll}
\mathit{refine}(\sigma, a, v) & = & (\sigma'[a \mapsto v'], a) \\
 & & \text{where } (\sigma', v') = \mathit{refine}(\sigma, \sigma(a), v) \\
\mathit{refine}(\sigma, \bullet/\vec{v}, \texttt{cons?}) & = & (\sigma[a_1 \mapsto \bullet][a_2 \mapsto \bullet], \langle a_1, a_2\rangle/\vec{v}) \\
 & & \text{where } a_1, a_2 \notin dom(\sigma) \\
\mathit{refine}(\sigma, \bullet/\vec{v}, \texttt{dep?}) & = & (\sigma[a \mapsto \bullet], a \rightarrow \lambda x.\bullet/\vec{v}) \\
 & & \text{where } a \notin dom(\sigma) \\
\mathit{refine}(\sigma, u/\vec{v}, v_i) & = & (\sigma, u/\vec{v} \cup \{v_i\})
\end{array}
$$

Figure 2. Refinement for Symbolic λ_C

```
(module havoc (any → λ_.false)
  (λx.amb({(havoc (x •)), (havoc (car x)), (havoc (cdr x))})))
```

$$
\begin{array}{lll}
\mathit{amb}(\{e\}) & = & e \\
\mathit{amb}(\{e, e_1, \ldots\}) & = & \texttt{if}\ \bullet\ e\ \mathit{amb}(\{e_1, \ldots\})
\end{array}
$$

The havoc function never produces useful results; its only purpose is to probe for all potential errors in the value provided. This context, and thus the havoc module, may be blamed for misuse of accessors and applications; we ignore these, as they represent potential failures in *omitted* portions of the program. Using havoc is key to soundness in modular higher-order static checking (Fähndrich and Logozzo 2011; Tobin-Hochstadt and Van Horn 2012); we discuss its role further in section 3.6. Intuitively, precise execution of properly contracted functions prevents havoc from destroying every analysis.

3.3 Primitive operations

Primitive operations are the primary place where unknown values in the heap are refined, in concert with successful contract checks. Figure 3 shows a representative excerpt of δ's definition; the full definition is given in the accompanying technical report.

The first three rules cover primitive predicate checks. Ambiguity never occurs for concrete values, and an abstract value may definitely prove or refute the predicate if the available information is enough for the conclusion. If the proof system cannot decide a definite result for the predicate check, δ conservatively includes *both* answers in the possible results and records assumptions chosen for each non-deterministic branch in the appropriate heap. The last three rules reveal possible refinements when applying partial functions such as add1, which fails when given non-numeric inputs. This mechanism, when combined with the SMT-aided proof system given below, is sufficient to provide the precision necessary to prove the absence of contract errors.

3.4 SMT-aided proof system

Contract checking and primitive operations rely on a proof system to statically relate values and contracts. We write $\sigma \vdash v : v_c$ ✓ to mean value v satisfies contract v_c, where all addresses in v are defined in σ. In other words, under any possible instantiation of the unknown values in v, it would satisfy v_c when checked according to the semantics. On the other hand, $\sigma \vdash v : v_c$ ✗ indicates that v definitely fails v_c. Finally, $\sigma \vdash v : v_c$ **?** is a conservative answer when information from the heap and refinement set is insufficient to draw a definite conclusion. The effectiveness of our analysis depends on the precision of this provability relation—increasing the number of contracts that can be related statically to values prunes spurious paths and eliminates impossible error cases.

$$\delta(\sigma, o?, v) \ni (\texttt{true}, \sigma) \quad \text{if } \sigma \vdash v : o? \checkmark$$
$$\delta(\sigma, o?, v) \ni (\texttt{false}, \sigma) \quad \text{if } \sigma \vdash v : o? \text{✗}$$
$$\delta(\sigma, o?, a) \supseteq \{(\texttt{true}, \sigma_t), (\texttt{false}, \sigma_f)\}$$
$$\text{if } \sigma \vdash a : o? \,\textbf{?} \text{ and } (\sigma_t, \_) = \mathit{refine}(\sigma, a, o?)$$
$$\text{and } (\sigma_f, \_) = \mathit{refine}(\sigma, a, \neg o?)$$
$$\ldots$$
$$\delta(\sigma, \texttt{add1}, n) \ni (n+1, \sigma)$$
$$\delta(\sigma, \texttt{add1}, v) \ni (a, \sigma'[a \mapsto \bullet/\texttt{num?}])$$
$$\text{where } \delta(\sigma, \texttt{num?}, v) \ni (\texttt{true}, \sigma'), v \neq n, \text{ and } a \notin \sigma'$$
$$\delta(\sigma, \texttt{add1}, v) \ni (\texttt{blame}_\Lambda, \sigma')$$
$$\text{where } \delta(\sigma, \texttt{num?}, v) \ni (\texttt{false}, \sigma')$$
$$\ldots$$

Figure 3. Selected primitive operations

3.4.1 Simple proof system

A simple proof system can be obtained which returns definite answers for concrete values, uses heap refinements, and handles negation of predicates and disjointness of data types.

$$\sigma \vdash n : \texttt{num?} \checkmark$$
$$\sigma \vdash n : o? \text{✗} \qquad \text{if } o? \in \{\texttt{cons?},\texttt{proc?},\text{etc.}\}$$
$$\sigma \vdash u/\vec{v} : v_i \checkmark \qquad \text{if } v_i \in \vec{v}$$
$$\sigma \vdash u/\vec{v} : o? \text{✗} \qquad \text{if } \neg o? \in \vec{v}$$
$$\sigma \vdash a : v \checkmark \qquad \text{if } \sigma \vdash \sigma(a) : v \checkmark$$
$$\sigma \vdash a : v \text{✗} \qquad \text{if } \sigma \vdash \sigma(a) : v \text{✗}$$
$$\sigma \vdash a : v\,\textbf{?} \qquad \text{if } \sigma \vdash \sigma(a) : v\,\textbf{?}$$
$$\ldots$$
$$\sigma \vdash v : v_c\,\textbf{?} \qquad \text{(conservative default)}$$

Notice that the proof system only needs to handle a small number of well-understood contracts. We rely on evaluation to naturally break down complex contracts into smaller ones and take care of subtle issues such as divergence and crashing. By the time we have $u/\vec{v}$, we can assume all contracts in $\vec{v}$ have terminated with success on u. With these simple and obvious rules, our system can already verify a significant number of interesting programs. With SMT solver integration, as described below, we can handle far more interesting constraints, including relations between numeric values, without requiring an encoding of the full language.

3.4.2 Integrating an SMT solver

We extend the simple provability relation by employing an external solver.

We first define the translation $\{\!\!\{\cdot\}\!\!\}_S$ from heaps and contract-value pairs into formulas in solver S:

$$\{\!\!\{\overrightarrow{(a,c)}\}\!\!\}_S = \bigwedge \overrightarrow{\{\!\!\{a : c\}\!\!\}_S}$$
$$\{\!\!\{a_1 : \texttt{(>/c } n\texttt{)}\}\!\!\}_S = \texttt{ASSERT } a_1 \texttt{ > } n$$
$$\{\!\!\{a_1 : \texttt{(>/c } a_2\texttt{)}\}\!\!\}_S = \texttt{ASSERT } a_1 \texttt{ > } a_2$$
$$\{\!\!\{a : \texttt{(=/c (+ } a_1\ a_2\texttt{))}\}\!\!\}_S = \texttt{ASSERT } a \texttt{ = } a_1 \texttt{ + } a_2$$
$$\ldots$$

The translation of a heap is the conjunction of all formulas generated from translatable refinements. The function is partial, and there are straightforward rules for translating specific pairs of $(a : c)$ where c are drawn from a small set of simple, well-understood contracts. This mechanism is enough for the system to verify many interesting programs because the analysis relies on evaluation to break down complex, higher-order predicates. Not having a translation for some contract c only reduces precision and does not affect soundness.

Next, the extension $(\vdash_S)$ is straightforward. The old relation $(\vdash)$ is refined by a solver S. Whenever the basic relation proves $\sigma \vdash v : c\,\textbf{?}$, we call out to the solver to try to either prove or refute the claim:

$$\frac{\{\!\!\{\sigma\}\!\!\}_S \wedge \neg\{\!\!\{v : c\}\!\!\}_S \text{ is unsat}}{\sigma \vdash_S v : c\checkmark} \qquad \frac{\{\!\!\{\sigma\}\!\!\}_S \wedge \{\!\!\{v : c\}\!\!\}_S \text{ is unsat}}{\sigma \vdash_S v : c\text{✗}}$$

The solver-aided relation uses refinements available on the heap to generate premises $\{\!\!\{\sigma\}\!\!\}_S$. Unsatisfiability of $\{\!\!\{\sigma\}\!\!\}_S \wedge \neg\{\!\!\{v : c\}\!\!\}_S$ is equivalent to validity of $\{\!\!\{\sigma\}\!\!\}_S \Rightarrow \{\!\!\{v : c\}\!\!\}_S$, hence value definitely satisfies contract c. Likewise, unsatisfiability of $\{\!\!\{\sigma\}\!\!\}_S \wedge \{\!\!\{v : c\}\!\!\}_S$ means v definitely refutes c. In any other case, we relate the value-contract pair to the conservative answer.

3.5 Program evaluation

We give a reachable-states semantics to programs: the initial program p is paired with an empty heap, and `eval` produces all states in the reflexive, transitive closure of the single-step reduction relation closed under evaluation contexts.

$$\texttt{eval} : p \to \mathcal{P}(\varsigma)$$
$$\texttt{eval}(\vec{m}e) = \{\varsigma \mid \vec{m} \vdash (e'; e), \emptyset \longmapsto\!\!\!\!\rightarrow \varsigma\}$$
$$\text{where } e' = \mathit{amb}(\{\texttt{true}, \overrightarrow{\texttt{havoc}f}\}),\ (\texttt{module } f\ v_c\ v) \in \vec{m}$$

Modules with unknown definitions, which we call *opaque*, complicate the definition of `eval`, since they may contain references to concrete modules. If only the main module is considered, an opaque module might misuse a concrete value in ways not visible to the system. We therefore apply `havoc` to each concrete module before evaluating the main expression.

3.6 Soundness

A program with unknown components is an abstraction of a fully-known program. Thus, the semantics of the abstracted program should approximate the semantics of any such concrete version. In particular, any behavior the concrete program exhibits should also be exhibited by the abstract approximation of that program.

However, we must be precise as to which behaviors are relevant. Suppose we have a single concrete module that links against a single opaque module. The semantics of this program should include all of the possible behaviors, both good and bad, of the known module assuming the opaque module always lives up to its contract. We exclude from consideration behaviors that cause the unknown module to be blamed, since it is of course impossible to verify an unknown program. In other words, we try to verify the parts of the program that are known, assuming arbitrary, but correct, behavior for the parts of the program that are unknown.

For this reason, the precise semantic account of blame is crucial. The demonic `havoc` context can introduce blame of both the known and unknown modules; since we can distinguish these parties, it is easy to ignore blame of the unknown context.

In the remainder of this section, we formally define the approximation relation and show that evaluation preserves the approximation, i.e. if program q is an approximation of program p (q is like p but with potentially more unknowns), then the evaluation of q is an approximation of the evaluation of p.

Approximation: We define two approximation relations: between modules and between pairs of expressions and heaps.

We write $\varsigma \sqsubseteq \varsigma'$ to mean "ς' approximates ς," or "ς refines ς'," which intuitively means ς' stands for a set of states including ς. For example, $(1, \{\}) \sqsubseteq (a, \{a \mapsto \bullet\})$.

One complication introduced by addresses is that a *single* address in the abstract program may accidentally approximate *multiple* distinct values in the concrete one. Such accidental approximations are not in general preserved by reduction, as in the following

$$\frac{(u/\vec{v},\sigma_1) \sqsubseteq^F (\sigma_2(a),\sigma_2) \quad F(a) = u/\vec{v}}{(u/\vec{v},\sigma_1) \sqsubseteq^F (a,\sigma_2)} \qquad \frac{(\sigma_1(a_1),\sigma_1) \sqsubseteq^F (\sigma_2(a_2),\sigma_2) \quad F(a_2) = a_1}{(a_1,\sigma_1) \sqsubseteq^F (a_2,\sigma_2)}$$

$$\frac{(u_1/\vec{v_1},\sigma_1) \sqsubseteq^F (u_2/\vec{v_2}),\sigma_2) \qquad (v_c,\sigma_1) \sqsubseteq^F (v_d,\sigma_2)}{(u_1/\vec{v_1} \cup \{v_c\},\sigma_1) \sqsubseteq^F (u_2/\vec{v_2} \cup \{v_d\},\sigma_2)}$$

$$\frac{}{(u,\sigma_1) \sqsubseteq^F (\bullet,\sigma_2)} \qquad \frac{(u_1/\vec{v_1},\sigma_1) \sqsubseteq^F (u_2/\vec{v_2},\sigma_2)}{(u_1/\vec{v_1} \cup v,\sigma_1) \sqsubseteq^F (u_2/\vec{v_2},\sigma_2)}$$

$$\frac{(\texttt{module}\ f\ u_c\ \bullet\ ) \in \vec{m} \qquad or \qquad f \in \{\dagger, \texttt{havoc}\}}{(\texttt{blame}^f_g,\sigma_1) \sqsubseteq^F_{\vec{m}} (e,\sigma_2)}$$

Figure 4. Selected Approximation Rules

example where $(e_1,\sigma_1) \sqsubseteq (e_2,\sigma_2)$:

$$\begin{array}{lcll} e_1 & = & \texttt{(if false 1 2)} & \sigma_1 = \{\} \\ e_2 & = & \texttt{(if } a\ a\ a\texttt{)} & \sigma_2 = \{a \mapsto \bullet\} \end{array}$$

The abstract program does not continue to approximate the concrete one in their next states:

$$\begin{array}{lcll} e_1 & \longmapsto & (2,\sigma_1') & \sigma_1' = \{\} \\ e_2 & \longmapsto & (a,\sigma_2') & \sigma_2' = \{a \mapsto \texttt{false}\} \end{array}$$

We therefore also define a "strong" version of the approximation relation, $\sqsubseteq^F$, where each address in the abstract program approximates exactly one value in the concrete program, and this consistency is witnessed by some function F from addresses to values. Then $e \sqsubseteq e'$ means that $\exists F.e \sqsubseteq^F e'$ Since no such function exists between e_1 and e_2 above, $e_1 \not\sqsubseteq^F e_2$ for any F, and therefore $e_1 \not\sqsubseteq e_2$.

Figure 4 shows the important cases in the definition of $\sqsubseteq^F$; we omit structurally recursive rules. All pre-values are approximated by $\bullet$, and unknown values with contracts approximate values that satisfy the same contracts. We extend the relation $\sqsubseteq^F_{\vec{m}}$ structurally to evaluation contexts $\mathcal{E}$, point-wise to sequences, and to sets of program states.

In the following example, $(e_1,\sigma_1) \sqsubseteq^F (e_2,\sigma_2)$, where $F = \{a_0 \mapsto \texttt{false}, a_1 \mapsto 1, a_2 \mapsto 2\}$:

$$\begin{array}{ll} e_1 = \texttt{(if false 1 2)} & \sigma_1 = \{\} \\ e_2 = \texttt{(if } a_1\ a_2\ a_3\texttt{)} & \sigma_2 = \{a_1 \mapsto \bullet, a_2 \mapsto \bullet, a_3 \mapsto \bullet\} \end{array}$$

Notice that F's domain is a superset of the domain of the heap σ_2. In addition, our soundness result does not consider additional errors that blame unknown modules or the `havoc` module, and therefore we parameterize the approximation relation $\sqsubseteq^F_{\vec{m}}$ with the module definitions $\vec{m}$ to select the opaque modules. We omit these parameters where they are easily inferred to ease notation.

With the definition of approximation in hand, we are now in a position to state the main soundness theorem for the system.

Theorem 1 (Soundness of Symbolic λ_C).
If $p \sqsubseteq^F_{\vec{m}} q$ where $q = \vec{m}e$ and $\varsigma \in eval(p)$, then there exists some $\varsigma' \in eval(q)$ such that $\varsigma \sqsubseteq^{F'}_{\vec{m}} \varsigma'$.

We defer all proofs to the technical report for space.

3.7 Verification and the blame theorem

We can now define verification as a simple corollary of soundness. First we defined when a module is *verified* by our approach.

Definition 1 (Verified module).
A module (`module` $f\ u_c\ u$) $\in p$ *is* verified in p *if* $u \neq \bullet$ *and* $eval(p) \not\ni \texttt{blame}^f$.

Now, by soundness, f is always safe.

Theorem 2 (Verified modules can't be blamed).
If a module named f is verified in p, then for any concrete program q for which p is an abstraction, $eval(q) \not\ni \texttt{blame}^f$.

3.8 Taming the infinite state space

A naive implementation of the above semantics will diverge for many programs. Consider the following example:

```
(define (fact n)
  (if (= n 0) 1 (* n (fact (- n 1)))))
(fact •)
```

Ignoring error cases, it eventually reduces non-deterministically to all of the following:

$$\begin{array}{r} 1 \text{ if } a_n \mapsto \texttt{0} \\ \texttt{(* } a_n \texttt{ 1)} \text{ if } a_n \not\mapsto \texttt{0}, a_{n-1} \mapsto \texttt{0} \\ \texttt{(* } a_n \texttt{ (* } a_{n-1} \texttt{ (fact } a_{n-1}\texttt{)))} \text{ if } a_n, a_{n-1} \not\mapsto \texttt{0} \end{array}$$

where a_{n-1} is a fresh address resulting from subtracting a_n by one. The process continues with a_{n-2}, a_{n-3}, etc. This behavior from the analysis happens because it attempts to approximate *all* possible concrete substitutions to abstract values. Although `fact` terminates for all concrete naturals, there are an infinite number of those: a_n can be `0`, `1`, `2`, and so on.

To enforce termination for all programs, we can resort to well-known techniques such as finite state or pushdown abstractions (Van Horn and Might 2012). But often those are overkill at the cost of precision. Consider the following program:

```
(let* ([id (λ (x) x)] [y (id 0)] [z (id 1)])
  (< y z))
```

where a monovariant flow analysis such as 0CFA (Shivers 1988) thinks `y` and `z` can be both `0` and `1`, and pushdown analysis thinks `y` is `0` and `z` is either `0` or `1`. For a concrete, straight-line program, such imprecision seems unsatisfactory. We therefore aim for an analysis that provides exact execution for non-recursive programs and retains enough invariants to verify interesting properties of recursive ones. The analysis quickly terminates for a majority of programming patterns with decent precision, although it is not guaranteed to terminate in the general case—see section 4 for empirical results.

One technical difficulty is that the semantics of contracts prevents us from using a recursive function's contract directly as a loop invariant, because contracts are only boundary-level enforcement. It is unsound to assume returned values of internal calls can be approximated by contracts, as in `f` below:

```
(f : nat? → nat?)
(define (f n) (if (= n 0) "" (str-len (f (- n 1)))))
```

If we assume the expression `(f (- n 1))` returns a number as specified in the contract, we will conclude `f` never returns, and is blamed either for violating its own contract by returning a string, or for applying `str-len` to a number. However, `f` returns `0` when applied to `1`. To soundly and precisely approximate this semantics in the absence of types, we recover data type invariants by execution.

Summarizing function results: To accelerate convergence, we modify the application rules as follows. At each application, we decide whether execution should step to the function's body or wait for known results from other branches. When an application `(f v)` reduces to a similar application, we plug in known results instead

$$\frac{\mathcal{E} \neq \mathcal{E}_1[(\mathtt{rt}_{\langle\sigma_0,\lambda x.e,v_0\rangle}\ \mathcal{E}_k)] \text{ for any } \mathcal{E}_1, \mathcal{E}_k, \sigma_0, v_0}{\langle\Xi, M, \mathcal{E}[((\lambda x.e)\ v)], \sigma\rangle \longmapsto \langle\Xi, M, \mathcal{E}[(\mathtt{rt}_{\langle\sigma,\lambda x.e,v\rangle}\ [v/x]e)], \sigma\rangle}$$

$$\frac{\overrightarrow{\langle a_o,a_n\rangle} = F \qquad \sigma' = \sigma\overrightarrow{[a_n \mapsto \sigma_0(a_0) \oplus \sigma(a_0)]}}{\langle\Xi, M, \mathcal{E}[(\mathtt{blur}_{\langle F,\sigma_0,v_0\rangle}\ v)], \sigma\rangle \longmapsto \langle\Xi, M, \mathcal{E}[v_0 \oplus v], \sigma'\rangle}$$

$$\frac{\mathcal{E} = \mathcal{E}_1[(\mathtt{rt}_{\langle\sigma_0,\lambda x.e,v_0\rangle}\ \mathcal{E}_k)] \text{ for some } \mathcal{E}_1, \mathcal{E}_k, \sigma_0, v_0 \qquad \langle\sigma,v\rangle \not\sqsubseteq \langle\sigma_0,v_0\rangle \qquad v_1 = v_0 \oplus v}{\langle\Xi, M, \mathcal{E}[((\lambda x.e)\ v)], \sigma\rangle \longmapsto \langle\Xi, M, \mathcal{E}[(\mathtt{rt}_{\langle\sigma,\lambda x.e,v_1\rangle}\ [v_1/x]e)], \sigma\rangle}$$

$$\frac{\begin{array}{c}\mathcal{E} = \mathcal{E}_1[(\mathtt{rt}_{\langle\sigma_0,v_f,v_0\rangle}\ \mathcal{E}_k)] \text{ for some } \mathcal{E}_1, \mathcal{E}_k, \sigma_0, v_0 \qquad \langle\sigma,v\rangle \sqsubseteq^F \langle\sigma_0,v_0\rangle \\ \Xi' = \Xi \sqcup [\langle\sigma_0, v_f, v_0\rangle \mapsto \langle F, \sigma, \mathcal{E}_1, \mathcal{E}_k\rangle] \qquad \langle v_a,\sigma_a\rangle \in M[\langle\sigma_0, v_f, v_0\rangle] \qquad \sigma' = \sigma\overrightarrow{[a_n \mapsto \sigma_a[a_o]]} \text{ where } \overrightarrow{\langle a_o,a_n\rangle} = F\end{array}}{\langle\Xi, M, \mathcal{E}[(v_f\ v)], \sigma\rangle \longmapsto \langle\Xi', M, \mathcal{E}_1[(\mathtt{rt}_{\langle\sigma_0,v_f,v_0\rangle}\ (\mathtt{blur}_{\langle F,\sigma_a,v_a\rangle}\ \mathcal{E}_k[v_a]))], \sigma'\rangle}$$

$$\frac{M' = M \sqcup [\langle\sigma_0, v_f, v_0\rangle \mapsto \langle v,\sigma\rangle]}{\langle\Xi, M, \mathcal{E}[(\mathtt{rt}_{\langle\sigma_0,v_f,v_0\rangle}\ v)], \sigma\rangle \longmapsto \langle\Xi, M', \mathcal{E}[v], \sigma\rangle}$$

$$\frac{M' = M \sqcup [\langle\sigma_0, v_f, v_0\rangle \mapsto \langle v,\sigma\rangle] \qquad \langle F, \sigma_k, \mathcal{E}_1, \mathcal{E}_k\rangle \in \Xi[\langle\sigma_0, v_f, v_0\rangle] \qquad \sigma'_k = \sigma_k\overrightarrow{[a_n \mapsto \sigma(a_o)]} \text{ where } \overrightarrow{\langle a_o,a_n\rangle} = F}{\langle\Xi, M, \mathcal{E}[(\mathtt{rt}_{\langle\sigma_0,v_f,v_0\rangle}\ v)], \sigma\rangle \longmapsto \langle\Xi, M', \mathcal{E}_1[(\mathtt{rt}_{\langle\sigma_0,v_f,v_0\rangle}\ (\mathtt{blur}_{\langle F,\sigma,v\rangle}\ \mathcal{E}_k[v]))], \sigma'_k\rangle}$$

Figure 5. Summarizing Semantics

Expressions	$e \mathrel{+}= (\mathtt{rt}_{\langle\sigma,v,v\rangle}\ e) \mid (\mathtt{blur}_{\langle F,\sigma,v\rangle}\ e)$
Values	$v \mathrel{+}= \mu x.\vec{v} \mid !x$
Evaluation contexts	$\mathcal{E} \mathrel{+}= (\mathtt{rt}_{\langle\sigma,v,v\rangle}\ \mathcal{E}) \mid (\mathtt{blur}_{\langle F,\sigma,v\rangle}\ \mathcal{E})$
Context memo tables	$\Xi ::= \overrightarrow{((\sigma,v,v),(F,\sigma,\mathcal{E},\mathcal{E}))}$
Value memo tables	$M ::= \overrightarrow{((\sigma,v,v),(v,\sigma))}$
Renamings	$F ::= \overrightarrow{\langle a,a\rangle}$

Figure 6. Syntax extensions for approximation

of executing `f`'s body again, avoiding the infinite loop. Correspondingly, when `(f v)` returns, we plug the new-found answer into contexts that need the result of `(f v)`. The execution continues until it has a set soundly describing the results of `(f v)`.

To track information about application results and waiting contexts, we augment the execution with two global tables M and Ξ as shown in figure 6. We borrow the choice of metavariable names from work on concrete summaries (Johnson and Van Horn 2014).

A value memo table M maps each application to known results and accompanying refinements. Intuitively, if $M(\sigma, v_f, v_x) \ni (v, \sigma')$ then in some execution branch, there is an application $(v_f\ v_x), \sigma \longmapsto\!\!\!\!\rightarrow (v, \sigma')$.

A context memo table Ξ maps each application to contexts waiting for its result. Intuitively, $\Xi(\sigma, v_f, v_x) \ni (F, \sigma', \mathcal{E}_1, \mathcal{E}_k)$ means during evaluation, some expression $\mathcal{E}_1[(\mathtt{rt}_{\langle\sigma,v_f,v_x\rangle}\ [\mathcal{E}_k[(v_f\, v_z)]])]$ with heap σ' is paused because applying $(v_f\ v_z)$ under assumptions in σ' is subsumed by applying $(v_f\ v_x)$ under assumptions in σ up to consistent address renaming specified by function F.

To keep track of function applications seen so far, we extend the language with the expression $(\mathtt{rt}_{\langle\sigma,v,v'\rangle}\ e)$, which marks e as being evaluated as the result of applying v to v', but otherwise behaves like e. The expression $(\mathtt{blur}_{\langle F,\sigma,v\rangle}\ e)$, whose detailed role is discussed below, approximates e under guidance from a "previous" value v.

Finally, we add recursive contracts $\mu x.\vec{v}$ and recursive references $!x$ for approximating inductive sets of values. For example, $\mu x.\{\mathtt{empty}, \langle\bullet/\mathtt{nat?}, !x\rangle\}$ approximates all finite lists of naturals.

A state in the approximating semantics with summarization consists of global tables Ξ, M, and a set S of explored states $\vec{\varsigma}$.

Reduction now relates tables Ξ, M, and a set of states $\vec{\varsigma}$ to new tables Ξ', M' and a new set of states $\vec{\varsigma}'$. We define a relation $\langle\Xi, M, \varsigma\rangle \longmapsto \langle\Xi, M, \varsigma\rangle$, and then lift this relation point-wise to sets of states. Figure 5 only shows rules that use the global tables or new expression forms.

In the first rule, if an application $((\lambda x.e)\ v)$ is not previously seen, execution proceeds as usual, evaluating expression e with x bound to v, but marking this expression using `rt`.

Second, if a previous application of $((\lambda x.e)\, v_0)$ results in application of the same function to a new argument v, we approximate the new argument before continuing. Taking advantage of knowledge of the previous argument, we guess the transition from the v_0 to v and heuristically emulate an arbitrary amount of such transformation using the $\oplus$ operator. For example, if v_0 is `empty` and v is $\langle \mathtt{1}, \mathtt{empty}\rangle$, we approximate the latter to $\mu x.\{\mathtt{empty}, \langle \mathtt{1}, !x\rangle\}$, denoting a list of `1`'s. If a different number is later prepended to the list, it is approximated to a list of numbers. The $\oplus$ operator should work well in common cases and not hinder convergence in the general case. Failure to give a good approximation to a value results in non-termination but does not affect soundness.

Third, when an application results in a similar one with potentially refined arguments, we avoid stepping into the function body and use known results from table M instead. In addition, we refine the current heap to make better use of assumptions about the particular "base case". We also remember the current context as one waiting for the result of such application. To speed up convergence, apart from feeding a new answer v_a to the context, we wrap the entire expression inside $(\mathtt{blur}_{\langle F,\sigma,v\rangle}\ [\ ])$ to approximate the future result.

The fourth rule in figure 5 shows reduction for returning from an application. Apart from the current context, the value is also returned to any known context waiting on the same application. Besides, the value is also remembered in table M. The resumption and refinement are analogous to the previous rule.

Finally, expression $(\mathtt{blur}_{\langle F,\sigma,v_0\rangle}\ v)$ approximates value v under guidance from the previous value v_0 and also approximates values on the heap from observation of the previous case. Overall, the approximating operator $\oplus$ occurs in three places: arguments of recursive applications, result of recursive applications, and abstract values on the heap when recursive applications return. Empirical results for our tool are presented in section 4.

Soundness of summarization: A system (Ξ, M, S) approximates a state ς if that state can be recovered from the system through approximation rules. The crucial rule, given below, states that if the system (Ξ, M, S) already approximates expression e and the application $(v_f\ v_x)$ is known to reduce to e, then (Ξ, M, S) is an approximation of $\mathcal{E}_k[e]$ where $\mathcal{E}_k$ is a waiting context for this application.

$$\frac{\begin{array}{c}(\mathtt{rt}_{\langle\_,v,\_\rangle}\,[\,])\notin\mathcal{E}_0\\ (v_x,\sigma)\sqsubseteq(v_z,\sigma') \qquad (v_y,\sigma)\sqsubseteq(v_z,\sigma')\\ \Xi(\sigma',v,v_z)\ni(F,\sigma',\mathcal{E}_0',\mathcal{E}_k') \qquad (\mathcal{E}_0,\sigma)\sqsubseteq(\mathcal{E}_0',\sigma')\\ (\mathcal{E}_k,\sigma)\sqsubseteq(\mathcal{E}_k',\sigma') \qquad (\mathcal{E}_0[(\mathtt{rt}_{\langle\sigma_1,v,v_y\rangle}\ e)],\sigma)\sqsubseteq(\Xi,M,S)\end{array}}{(\mathcal{E}_0[(\mathtt{rt}_{\langle\sigma_0,v,v_x\rangle}\ \mathcal{E}_k[(\mathtt{rt}_{\langle\sigma_1,v,v_y\rangle}\ e)])],\sigma)\sqsubseteq(\Xi,M,S)}$$

As a consequence, summarization properly handles repetition of waiting contexts, and gives results that approximate any number of recursive applications. We refer readers to the appendix of the accompanying technical report for the full definition of the approximation relation.

With this definition in hand, we can state the central lemma to establish the soundness of the revised semantics that uses summarization.

Lemma 1 (Soundness of summarization).
If $\varsigma \sqsubseteq (\Xi, M, S)$ *and* $\varsigma \longmapsto \varsigma'$, *then* $(\Xi, M, S) \longmapsto\!\!\!\!\!\rightarrow (\Xi', M', S')$ *such that* $\varsigma' \sqsubseteq (\Xi', M', S')$.

The proof is given in the accompanying technical report. With this lemma in place, it is straightforward to replay the proof of the soundness and blame theorems.

4. Implementation and evaluation

To validate our approach, we implemented a static contract checking tool, SCV, based on the semantics presented in section 3, along with a number of implementation extensions for increased precision and performance. We then applied SCV to a wide selection of programs drawn from the literature on verification of higher-order programs, and report on the results.

The source code for SCV and all benchmarks are available along with instructions on reproducing the results we report here:

`github.com/philnguyen/soft-contract`

In order to quantify the importance of the techniques presented in this paper, we also created a simpler tool which omits the key contributions of this work. This slimmed down system, which we refer to as "Simple" below, (a) does not call out to a solver, but relies on remembering seen contracts, (b) never refines the contracts associated with a heap address, but splits disjunctive contracts and unrolls recursive contracts, and (c) does not use our technique for summarizing repeated context. To enable a full comparison on all benchmarks, the Simple tool supports first-class contracts. This simpler system is extremely similar to that presented by our earlier work (Tobin-Hochstadt and Van Horn 2012), but works on all of our benchmarks.

Implementation extensions: SCV supports an extended language beyond that presented in section 3 in order to handle realistic programs. First, more base values and primitive operations are supported, such as strings and symbols (and their operations), although we do not yet use a solver to reason about values other than integers. Second, data structure definitions are allowed at the top-level. Each new data definition induces a corresponding (automatic) extension to the definition of `havoc` to deal with the new class of data. Third, modules have multiple named exports, to handle the examples presented in section 2, and can include local, non-exported, definitions. Fourth, functions can accept multiple arguments and can be defined to have variable-arity, as with `+`, which accepts arbitrarily many arguments. This introduces new possibilities of errors from arity mismatches. Fifth, a much more expressive contract language is implemented with `and/c`, `or/c`, `struct/c`, μ`/c` for conjunctive, disjunctive, data type, and recursive contracts, respectively. Sixth, we provide solver back-ends for both CVC4 (Barrett et al. 2011) and Z3 (De Moura and Bjørner 2008).

Evaluating on existing benchmarks: To evaluate the applicability of SCV to a wide variety of challenging higher-order contract checking problems, we collect examples from the following sources: programs that make use of control-flow-based typing from work on **occurrence typing** (Tobin-Hochstadt and Felleisen 2010), programs from work on **soft typing**, which uses flow analysis to check the preconditions of operations (Cartwright and Fagan 1991), programs with sophisticated specifications from work on model checking **higher-order recursion schemes** (Kobayashi et al. 2011), programs from work on inference of **dependent refinement types** (Terauchi 2010), and programs with rich contracts from our prior work on **higher-order symbolic execution** (Tobin-Hochstadt and Van Horn 2012). We also evaluate SCV on three interactive student video games built for a first-year programming course: **Snake**, **Tetris**, and **Zombie**. These programs were all originally written as sample solutions, following the style expected of students in the course. Of these, Zombie is the most interesting: it was originally an object-oriented program, translated using the encoding seen in section 2.5.

We present our results in summary form in table 1, grouping each of the above sets of benchmark programs; expanded forms of the tables are provided in the accompanying technical report. The table shows total line count (excluding blank lines and comments) and the number of static occurrences of contracts and primitives requiring dynamic checks such as function applications and primitive operations. These checks can be eliminated if we can show that they never fail; this has proven to produce significant speedups in practice, even without eliminating more expensive contract checks (Tobin-Hochstadt et al. 2011).

The table reports time (in milliseconds) and the number of false positives for SCV and our reduced system omitting the key contributions of this work (labeled "Simple"); "∞" indicates a timeout after 5 minutes.

A false positive is a contract violation reported by the analysis, but by human inspection, cannot happen. The programs we consider are all known not to have contract errors, and thus all potential errors are false positives.

In cases where a tool times out, we give an upper bound on the number of false positive error reports. For example, the Simple system times out on two of the higher-order recursion scheme programs, meaning that if it were to complete, it would report *at most* 94 false positives, counting all contract checks from the two programs on which it times out, and the measured false positives on the programs where it completes.

Execution times are measured on a Core i7 2.7GHz laptop with 8GB of RAM.

Discussion: First, SCV works on a benchmarks for a range of previous static analyzers, from type systems to model checking to program analysis.

Second, most programs are analyzed in a reasonable amount of time; the longest remaining analysis time is under 30 seconds. This demonstrates that although the termination acceleration method of section 3.8 is not fully general, it is effective for many programming patterns. For example, SCV terminates with good precision on `last`

Corpus	Lines	Checks	Simple Time (ms)	Simple False Pos.	SCV Time (ms)	SCV False Pos.
Occurrence Typing	115	142	155.8	15	8.9	0
Soft Typing	134	177	424.5	9	380.3	0
Higher-order Recursion Schemes	301	467	∞	≤ 94	3,253.8	4
Dependent Refinement Types	69	116	∞	≤ 66	193.0	1
Higher-order Symbolic Execution	236	319	∞	≤ 19	4,372.7	1
Student Video Games						
Snake	202	270	9,452.5	0	3.008.8	0
Tetris	308	351	∞	-	27,408.5	0
Zombie	249	393	∞	-	11,335.9	0

Table 1. Summary benchmark results. (See the accompanying technical report for detailed results.)

from Wright and Cartwright (1997), which hides recursion behind the Y combinator.

Third, across all benchmarks, over 99% (2329/2335) of the contract checks are statically verified, enabling the elimination both of small checks for primitive operations and expensive contracts; see below for timing results. This result emphasizes the value of static contract checking: gaining confidence about correctness from expensive contracts without actually incurring their cost.

Overall, our experiments show that our approach is able to discover and use invariants implied by conditional flows of control and contract checks. Obfuscations such as multiple layers of abstractions or complex chains of aliases do not impact precision (a common shortcoming of flow analysis).

Our approach does not yet give a way to prove deep structural properties expressed as dependent contracts such as "map over a list preserves the length" or "all elements in the result of filter satisfy the predicate", resulting in the false positives seen in table 1. However, it can already be used to verify many interesting programs because often safety questions depend only on knowledge of top-level constructors. Examples of these patterns appear in programs from Kobayashi et al. (2011) for programs such as `reverse` (see also §2.4), `nil`, and `mem`.

Finally, soft contract verification is more broadly applicable than the systems from which our benchmarks are drawn, which typically are successful only on their own benchmarks. For example, type systems such as occurrence typing (Tobin-Hochstadt and Felleisen 2010) cannot verify any non-trivial contracts, and most soft typing systems do not consider contracts at all. Systems based on higher-order model-checking (Kobayashi et al. 2011), and dependent refinement types (Terauchi 2010) assume a typed language; encoding our programs using large disjoint unions produces unverifiable results.

This broad applicability is why we are not able to directly compare SCV to these other systems across all benchmarks. Instead, the Simple system serves as a benchmark for a system which does not contain our primary contributions.

Contract optimization: We also report speedup results for the three most complex programs in our evaluation, which are interactive games designed for first-year programming courses (Snake, Tetris, and Zombie). For each, we recorded a trace of input and timer events while playing the game, and then used that trace to re-run the game (omitting all graphical rendering) both with the contracts that we verified, and with the contracts manually removed. Each game was run 100 times in both modes; the total time is presented below.

Program	Contracts On (ms)	Contracts Off (ms)
snake	475,799	59
tetris	1,127,591	186
zombie	12,413	1,721

The timing results are quite striking—speedup ranges from over 5x to over 5000x. This does not indicate, of course, that speedups of these magnitudes are achievable for real programs. Instead, it shows that programmers avoid the rich contracts we are able to verify, because of their unacceptable performance overhead. Soft contract verification therefore enables programmers to write these specifications without the run-time cost.

The difference in timing between Zombie and the other two games is intriguing because Zombie uses higher-order dependent contracts extensively, along the lines of `vec/c` from section 2.5, which intuitively should be more expensive. An investigation reveals that most of the cost comes from monitoring flat contracts, especially those that apply to data structures. For example, in Snake, disabling `posn/c`, a simple contract that checks for a `posn` struct with two numeric fields, cuts the run-time by a factor of 4. This contract is repeatedly applied to every such object in the game. In contrast, higher-order contracts, as in the object encodings used in Zombie, delay contracts and avoid this repeated checking.

5. Related work

In this section, we relate our work to four related strands of research: soft-typing, static contract verification, refinement types, and model checking of recursion schemes.

Soft typing: Verifying the preconditions of primitive operations can be seen as a weak form of contract verification and soft typing is a well studied approach to this kind of verification (Cartwright and Felleisen 1996). There are two predominant approaches to soft-typing: one is based on a generalization of Hindley-Milner type inference (Cartwright and Fagan 1991; Wright and Cartwright 1997; Aiken et al. 1994), which views an untyped program as being embedded in a typed one and attempts to safely eliminate coercions (Henglein 1994). The other is founded on set-based abstract interpretation of programs (Flanagan et al. 1996; Flanagan and Felleisen 1999). Both approaches have proved effective for statically checking preconditions of primitive operations, but the approach does not scale to checking pre- and post-conditions of arbitrary contracts. For example, Soft Scheme (Cartwright and Fagan 1991) is not path-sensitive and does not reason about arithmetic, thus it is unable to verify many of the occurrence-typing or higher-order recursion scheme examples considered in the evaluation.

Contract verification: Following in the set-based analysis tradition of soft-typing, there has been work extending set-based analysis to languages with contracts (Meunier et al. 2006). This work shares the overarching goal of this paper: to develop a static contract checking approach for components written in untyped languages with contracts. However the work fails to capture the control-flow-based type reasoning essential to analyzing untyped programs and is unsound (as discussed by Tobin-Hochstadt and Van Horn (2012)).

Moreover, the set-based formulation is complex and difficult to extend to features considered here.

Our prior work (Tobin-Hochstadt and Van Horn 2012), as discussed in the introduction, also performs soft contract verification, but with far less sophistication and success. As our empirical results show, the contributions of this paper are required to tackle the arithmetic relations, flow-sensitive reasoning, and complex recursion found in our benchmarks.

An alternative approach has been applied to checking contracts in Haskell and OCaml (Xu 2012; Xu et al. 2009), which is to inline monitors into a program following a transformation by Findler and Felleisen (2002) and then simplify the program, either using the compiler, or a specialized symbolic engine equipped with an SMT solver. The approach would be applicable to untyped languages except for the final step dubbed *logicization*, a type-based transformation of program expressions into first-order logic (FOL). A related approach used for Haskell is to use a denotational semantics that can be mapped into FOL, which is then model checked (Vytiniotis et al. 2013), but this approach is highly dependent on the type structure of a program. Further, these approaches assume a different semantics for contract checking that monitors recursive calls. This allows the use of contracts as inductive hypotheses in recursive calls. In contrast, our approach can naturally take advantage of this stricter semantics of contract checking and type systems, but can also accommodate the more common and flexible checking policy. Additionally, our approach does not rely on type information, the lack of which makes these approaches inapplicable to many of our benchmarks.

Contract verification in the setting of typed, first-order contracts is much more mature. A prominent example is the work on verifying C# contracts as part of the Code Contracts project (Fähndrich and Logozzo 2011).

Refinement type checking: Refinement types are an alternative approach to statically verifying pre- and post-conditions in a higher-order functional language. There are several approaches to checking type refinements; one is to restrict the computational power of refinements so that checking is decidable at type-checking time (Freeman and Pfenning 1991); another is allow unrestricted refinements as in contracts, but to use a solver to attempt to discharge refinements (Knowles and Flanagan 2010; Rondon et al. 2008; Vazou et al. 2013). In the latter approach, when a refinement cannot be discharged, some systems opt to reject the program (Rondon et al. 2008; Vazou et al. 2013), while others such as hybrid type-checking residualize a run-time check to enforce the refinement (Knowles and Flanagan 2010), similar to the way soft-typing residualizes primitive pre-condition checks. The end result of our approach most closely resembles that of hybrid checking, although the technique applies regardless of the type discipline and approaches the problem using different tools.

DJS (Chugh et al. 2012b,a) supports expressive refinement specification and verification for stateful JavaScript programs, including sophisticated dependent specifications which SCV cannot verify. However, most dependent properties require heavy annotations. Moreover, `null` inhabits every object type. Thus the approach cannot give the same guarantees about programs such as `reverse` (§2.4) without significantly more annotation burden. Additionally, it relies on whole program annotation, type-checking, and analysis.

Model checking higher-order recursion schemes: Much of the recent work on model checking of higher-order programs relies on the decidability of model checking trees generated by higher-order recursion schemes (HORS) (Ong 2006). A HORS is essentially a program in the simply-typed λ-calculus with recursion and finitely inhabited base types that generates (potentially infinite) trees. Program verification is accomplished by compiling a program to a HORS in which the generated tree represents program event sequences (Kobayashi 2009b; Kobayashi et al. 2010). This method is sound and complete for the simply typed λ-calculus with recursion and finite base types, but the gap between this language and realistic languages is significant. Subsequently, an untyped variant of HORS has been developed (Tsukada and Kobayashi 2010), which has applications to languages with more advanced type systems, but despite the name it does not lead to a model checking procedure for the untyped λ-calculus. A subclass of untyped HORS is the class of recursively typed recursion schemes, which has applications to typed object-oriented programs (Kobayashi and Igarashi 2013). In this setting, model checking is undecidable, but relatively complete with a certain recursive intersection type system (anything typable in this system can be verified). To cope with infinite data domains such as integers, counter-example guided abstraction refinement (CEGAR) techniques have been developed (Kobayashi et al. 2011). The complexity of model checking even for the simply typed case is n-EXPTIME hard (where n is the rank of the recursion scheme), but progress on decision procedures (Kobayashi and Ong 2009; Kobayashi 2009a) has lead to verification engines that can verify a number of "small but tricky higher-order functional programs in less than a second."

In comparison, the HORS approach can verify some specifications which SCV cannot, but in a simpler (typed) setting, whereas our lightweight method applies to richer languages. Our approach handles untyped higher-order programs with sophisticated language features and infinite data domains. Higher-order program invariants may be stated as behavioral contracts, while the HORS-based systems only support assertions on first order data. Our work is also able to verify programs with unknown external functions, not just unknown integer values, which is important for modular program verification, and we are able to verify many of the small but tricky programs considered in the HORS work.

6. Conclusions and perspective

We have presented a lightweight method and prototype implememtation for static contract checking using a non-standard reduction semantics that is capable of verifying higher-order modular programs with arbitrarily omitted components. Our tool, SCV, scales to realistic language features such as recursive data structures and modular programs, and verifies programs written in the idiomatic style of dynamic languages. The analysis proves the absence of run-time errors without excessive reliance on programmer help. With zero annotation, SCV already helps programmers find unjustified usage of partial functions with high precision and could even be modified to suggest inputs that break the program. With explicit contracts, programmers can enforce rich specifications to their programs and have those optimized away without incurring the significant run-time overhead entailed by dynamic enforcement.

While in this paper, we have addressed the problem of soft contract verification, the technical tools we have introduced apply beyond this application. For example, a run of SCV can be seen as a modular program analysis—it soundly predicts which functions are called at any call site. Moreover it can be composed with whole-program analysis techniques to derive modular analyses (Van Horn and Might 2010). A small modification to blur to cause it to pick a small set of concrete values would turn our system into a concolic execution engine (Larson and Austin 2003). Adding temporal contracts (Disney et al. 2011) to our system would produce a model checker for higher-order languages. This breadth of application follows directly from the semantics-based nature of our approach.

Acknowledgments

We thank Carl Friedrich Bolz, Jeffrey S. Foster, Michael Hicks, J. Ian Johnson, Lindsey Kuper, Aseem Rastogi, and Matthew Wilson for comments. We thank the anonymous reviewers of ICFP 2014 for their detailed reviews, which helped to improve the presentation and technical content of the paper. This material is based on research sponsored by the NSF under award 1218390, the NSA under the Science of Security program, and DARPA under the programs Automated Program Analysis for Cybersecurity (FA8750-12-2-0106). The U.S. Government is authorized to reproduce and distribute reprints for Governmental purposes notwithstanding any copyright notation thereon.

References

A. Aiken, E. L. Wimmers, and T. K. Lakshman. Soft typing with conditional types. POPL, 1994.

T. H. Austin, T. Disney, and C. Flanagan. Virtual values for language extension. OOPSLA, 2011.

C. Barrett, C. Conway, M. Deters, L. Hadarean, D. Jovanović, T. King, A. Reynolds, and C. Tinelli. CVC4. CAV. 2011.

R. Cartwright and M. Fagan. Soft typing. PLDI, 1991.

R. Cartwright and M. Felleisen. Program verification through soft typing. *ACM Comput. Surv.*, 1996.

R. Chugh, D. Herman, and R. Jhala. Dependent types for JavaScript. In *OOPSLA*, 2012a.

R. Chugh, P. M. Rondon, and R. Jhala. Nested refinements: A logic for duck typing. In *POPL*, 2012b.

L. De Moura and N. Bjørner. Z3: an efficient SMT solver. TACAS, 2008.

C. Dimoulas, R. B. Findler, C. Flanagan, and M. Felleisen. Correct blame for contracts: no more scapegoating. POPL, 2011.

T. Disney. contracts.coffee, July 2013. URL `http://disnetdev.com/contracts.coffee/`.

T. Disney, C. Flanagan, and J. McCarthy. Temporal higher-order contracts. ICFP, 2011.

M. Fähndrich and F. Logozzo. Static contract checking with abstract interpretation. FoVeOOS, 2011.

R. B. Findler and M. Felleisen. Contracts for higher-order functions. ICFP, 2002.

C. Flanagan and M. Felleisen. Componential set-based analysis. *ACM Trans. Program. Lang. Syst.*, 1999.

C. Flanagan, M. Flatt, S. Krishnamurthi, S. Weirich, and M. Felleisen. Catching bugs in the web of program invariants. PLDI, 1996.

T. Freeman and F. Pfenning. Refinement types for ML. PLDI, 1991.

F. Henglein. Dynamic typing: syntax and proof theory. *Science of Computer Programming*, 1994.

R. Hickey, M. Fogus, and contributors. core.contracts, July 2013. URL `https://github.com/clojure/core.contracts`.

J. I. Johnson and D. Van Horn. Abstracting abstract control. *CoRR*, 2014. URL `http://arxiv.org/abs/1305.3163`.

K. Knowles and C. Flanagan. Hybrid type checking. *ACM Trans. Program. Lang. Syst.*, 2010.

N. Kobayashi. Model-checking higher-order functions. PPDP, 2009a.

N. Kobayashi. Types and higher-order recursion schemes for verification of higher-order programs. POPL, 2009b.

N. Kobayashi and A. Igarashi. Model-Checking Higher-Order programs with recursive types. ESOP, 2013.

N. Kobayashi and C. H. L. Ong. A type system equivalent to the modal Mu-Calculus model checking of Higher-Order recursion schemes. LICS, 2009.

N. Kobayashi, N. Tabuchi, and H. Unno. Higher-order multi-parameter tree transducers and recursion schemes for program verification. POPL, 2010.

N. Kobayashi, R. Sato, and H. Unno. Predicate abstraction and CEGAR for higher-order model checking. PLDI, 2011.

E. Larson and T. Austin. High coverage detection of input-related security faults. USENIX Security, 2003.

P. Meunier, R. B. Findler, and M. Felleisen. Modular set-based analysis from contracts. In *POPL '06*, POPL, 2006.

B. Meyer. *Eiffel : The Language*. 1991.

P. C. Nguyễn, S. Tobin-Hochstadt, and D. Van Horn. Soft contract verification. *CoRR*, 2014. URL `http://arxiv.org/abs/1307.6239`.

C. H. L. Ong. On Model-Checking trees generated by Higher-Order recursion schemes. LICS, 2006.

R. Plosch. Design by contract for Python. 1997. APSEC/ICSC'97.

P. M. Rondon, M. Kawaguci, and R. Jhala. Liquid types. PLDI, 2008.

O. Shivers. Control flow analysis in Scheme. PLDI, 1988.

T. S. Strickland, S. Tobin-Hochstadt, R. B. Findler, and M. Flatt. Chaperones and impersonators: run-time support for reasonable interposition. OOPSLA, 2012.

T. Terauchi. Dependent types from counterexamples. POPL, 2010.

S. Tobin-Hochstadt and M. Felleisen. Logical types for untyped languages. ICFP, 2010.

S. Tobin-Hochstadt and D. Van Horn. Higher-order symbolic execution via contracts. OOPSLA, 2012.

S. Tobin-Hochstadt, V. St-Amour, R. Culpepper, M. Flatt, and M. Felleisen. Languages as libraries. PLDI, 2011.

T. Tsukada and N. Kobayashi. Untyped recursion schemes and infinite intersection types. FoSSaCS, 2010.

D. Van Horn and M. Might. Abstracting abstract machines. ICFP, 2010.

D. Van Horn and M. Might. Systematic abstraction of abstract machines. *Journal of Functional Programming*, 2012.

N. Vazou, P. Rondon, and R. Jhala. Abstract refinement types. ESOP, 2013.

N. Vazou, E. L. Seidel, R. Jhala, D. Vytiniotis, and S. Peyton-Jones. Refinement types for haskell. ICFP, 2014.

D. Vytiniotis, S. Peyton Jones, K. Claessen, and D. Rosén. HALO: Haskell to logic through denotational semantics. POPL, 2013.

A. K. Wright and R. Cartwright. A practical soft type system for Scheme. *ACM Trans. Program. Lang. Syst.*, 1997.

D. N. Xu. Hybrid contract checking via symbolic simplification. PEPM, 2012.

D. N. Xu, S. Peyton Jones, and S. Claessen. Static contract checking for Haskell. POPL, 2009.

H. Zhu and S. Jagannathan. Compositional and lightweight dependent type inference for ML. 2013.

On Teaching *How to Design Programs*

Observations from a Newcomer

Norman Ramsey
Department of Computer Science, Tufts University
nr@cs.tufts.edu

Abstract

This paper presents a personal, qualitative case study of a first course using *How to Design Programs* and its functional teaching languages. The paper reconceptualizes the book's six-step design process as an eight-step design process ending in a new "review and refactor" step. It recommends specific approaches to students' difficulties with function descriptions, function templates, data examples, and other parts of the design process. It connects the process to interactive "world programs." It recounts significant, informative missteps in course design and delivery. Finally, it identifies some unsolved teaching problems and some potential solutions.

Categories and Subject Descriptors D.1.1 [*Applicative (Functional) Programming*]; K.3.2 [*Computer and Information Science Education*]: Computer Science Education

Keywords Introductory programming course; Program by Design; How to Design Programs; Racket; Reflective practice

1. Introduction

This paper is about teaching introductory programming using the method called *Program by Design*, which is explained in the book called *How to Design Programs* (Felleisen et al. 2001). The method uses functional-programming principles, and the book uses functional languages derived from Scheme. The method has proven effective in different educational contexts at many levels (Felleisen et al. 2004b, 2009; Bieniusa et al. 2008; Bloch 2010; Schanzer, Fisler, and Krishnamurthi 2013).

How to Design Programs argues eloquently that everyone should learn to program. And the book keeps the promise implied by its title; my students really did learn. But knowing that students learned is not enough; a teacher needs to know what "learning to program" means. What exactly did my students learn to do? How did they learn it? In the jargon of the educator, what were the learning outcomes? While I have come to love lambdas and round parentheses and `cond` expressions, these are not the kinds of learning outcomes that teachers need to know about in order to ensure students' subsequent success in a *second* course. And although some valuable information is available from Bieniusa et al. (2008), from Crestani and Sperber (2010), and from Sperber and Crestani (2012), teachers need even more. This paper provides some.

ICFP '14, September 1–6, 2014, Gothenburg, Sweden.

ACM 978-1-4503-2873-9 /14/09... $15.00.
http://dx.doi.org/10.1145/2628136.2628137

The contributions of this paper are

- To articulate a refined, extended version of the design method presented in *How to Design Programs*, and to develop a view of the method, from a newcomer's perspective, that can help a teacher prepare and lead a class (Section 2)
- To identify, from observation, where students struggle with the method and what points can be emphasized to help them succeed (Section 3)
- To communicate what it's like for a functional programmer with no Scheme experience to work with the languages and tools (Section 4)
- To identify and learn from one beginner's mistakes (Section 5)
- To identify some open problems and sketch potential solutions (Section 6)

I have written the paper for people who wish to use functional programming to teach an introductory course. I assume experience with typeful functional programming at the level of Haskell, ML, or System F. I also assume that you have read something about LISP or Scheme (McCarthy 1960; Sussman and Steele 1975; Abelson and Sussman 1985), but not that you have actual experience with LISP, Scheme, or Racket—although beta readers who do have such experience report finding some value in the paper. I address questions like those we ask graduating PhD students: what parts were hard, and when I do it again, what I will do differently.

I address these questions using the "humanities" approach to educational research (Burkhardt and Schoenfeld 2003), in which authors reflect on their experience. Burkhardt and Schoenfeld write that "the test of quality is critical appraisal concerning plausibility, internal consistency and fit to prevailing wisdom. The key product of this approach is critical commentary." My reflections and commentary are informed by empirical observations in the classroom, but the paper is purely reflective, with no controlled experiments or quantitative measurements. Information bearing on my credibility as a reflective practitioner appears in Appendix A.

2. What is *Program by Design*?

If you teach a course in *Program by Design*, using *How to Design Programs*, you can expect these outcomes:

1. Your students will learn a step-by-step *design process*. The process is presented in six steps, but as explained below, I found it helpful to articulate eight steps.
2. Your students will learn to apply the process to design *functions* that consume increasingly sophisticated forms of data: strings, images, numbers and numeric intervals; enumerations; products; general sums (including sums of products); and lists, trees, or other sums of products whose definitions incorporate self-reference or mutual reference. Each form of data engenders a specialized instance of the design process: a *design recipe*.

3. With additional guidance, your students will learn to design interactive *programs* that are composed of many functions.

Your students can also pick up one or two techniques that don't fit neatly into the model of "process plus data equals recipe." Possibilities include using abstraction to eliminate duplicate or near-duplicate code; writing "generative" recursive functions; using higher-order functions on lists; using accumulating parameters; reasoning about costs; and programming with mutable state.

Your students can achieve these outcomes using either the complete, first edition of *How to Design Programs* or the incomplete second edition. (The choice is discussed in Web Appendix D.) With either edition, the key learning outcome is mastery of design recipes, and the distinctive aspect of the recipes is the design process.

2.1 Introduction to the (refined) design process

How to Design Programs presents the design process for functions in six steps:

1. Describe the data used by the function
2. Using a *signature*, *purpose statement*, and *header*, describe what the function does[1]
3. Show examples of what the function does
4. Write a *template* (definition with holes) for the function
5. Fill the template with code, completing the function
6. Test the function

But this six-step process supports only some of the skills the book teaches. The other skills primarily involve eliminating repetition and establishing a single point of truth, e.g., reducing multiple function definitions to a single function definition by abstracting over additional parameters, or eliminating repetitive case analysis and recursion by using higher-order functions. At first I found these skills hard to motivate, but after teaching them I realized they could fit into a new, seventh step of the design process:

7. Review and refactor the code

To call this seventh step "new" is not really fair; ideas that bear on reviewing and refactoring appear everywhere in *How to Design Programs*. What I have done is to *articulate* this step, which had been implicit and hidden.

The steps are presented sequentially, but in practice, they are richly interrelated. Early steps support multiple later steps, and later steps can trigger revisions in earlier steps. To help students use the design process mindfully, I taught them about the relationships shown in Figure 1. In the figure, as in class, I treat data description and data examples as separate steps numbered 1A and 1B, making eight steps in all. Separating data examples from data description makes the examples harder for students to forget, and it helps me bring out ways in which the description and development of functions parallel the description and exemplification of data.[2]

Students of *Program by Design* learn all steps of the design process immediately, using simple atomic data. They then learn to specialize the process for products, sums, sums of products, self-referential and mutually referential data (a.k.a. recursive types), functions as data, and finally mutable data.

[1] In the first edition, the signature is called a "contract."

[2] Sperber and Crestani (2012) also expand the design process into eight steps: they split function description into two steps (purpose statement and signature) and the function template into two steps ("skeleton" and template). They do not mention anything like "review and refactor."

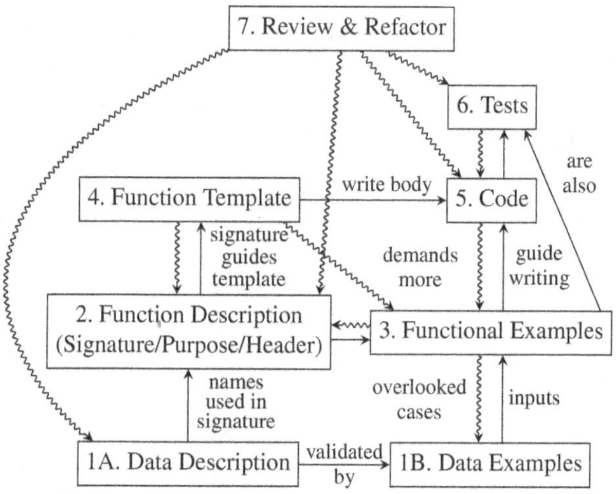

Figure 1. The revised, eight-step design process. Solid arrows show initial design; squiggly arrows show feedback.

2.2 Relating *Program by Design* to functional programming

Program by Design is not just a paper-and-pencil design method; it is supported by the DrRacket programming environment and by the Racket teaching languages: Beginning Student Language, Intermediate Student Language, and Advanced Student Language. The software and the languages are described in detail elsewhere (Findler et al. 2002; Felleisen et al. 2004a), but the languages are worth summarizing here: Beginning Student Language is a pure, eager, first-order, dynamically typed, functional language that has global definitions of functions and variables, structure (record) definitions, LISP's multiway conditionals, and language constructs for expressing unit tests. Intermediate Student Language adds nested definitions and `lambda`, making functions higher-order and first-class.[3] Advanced Student Language adds mutation and imperative I/O.

Is it functional programming? Well, the design method does not use equational reasoning or algebraic laws, ideas that some functional programmers deem essential (Bird and Wadler 1988). There are (at least at first) no higher-order functions, and the language is not lazy, which rules out the kinds of modularity that may make functional programming matter (Hughes 1989). And while testable equations are central, equational *properties* can be tested only if you can integrate add-on software that is documented in German (Crestani and Sperber 2010).

On the other hand, data are immutable. As a result, specifications of functions are simple and equational, and unit tests are simply equations. The Beginning and Intermediate languages are pure, so their evaluation can be explained (and debugged) using DrRacket's algebraic stepper. Function composition is encouraged. Control flow is expressed exclusively through a combination of function calls and conditionals. In particular, there are no loops; there are only recursive functions and higher-order list functions. And although there is no static type checking, your students will nevertheless learn to write parametric type definitions and polymorphic functions.

If your goal is to teach functional programming, this two-paragraph summary may tell you if *Program by Design* will meet your needs. Our institutional need, as detailed in Web Appendix C, was to teach beginning students how to solve problems using the computer; for us, functional programming is a means, not an end.

[3] Intermediate Student Language actually comes in two flavors: with and without `lambda`. I suggest that you use only the flavor that has `lambda`.

2.3 Understanding and teaching the design method

This section highlights aspects of *Program by Design* to which, in my first time teaching the method, I had to pay extra attention.

Data definitions use familiar types As Felleisen et al. (2004a) note, the syllabus is driven by *data definitions*. Data definitions are informal; a data definition is a comment that introduces a type and gives it a name.[4] The types are familiar: there are (immutable) base types, and new types can be formed using products, sums, arrows, and universal quantification. But types are extra-linguistic: although they are required in data definitions and function signatures, they appear only in comments and are not checked by the compiler.

A product type uses a *structure* like those found in Common Lisp (Steele 1990, Chapter 19). A structure, which is defined with `define-struct`, has named fields, and it comes with a *constructor function* for introduction and *selector functions* for elimination. It also comes with a *type predicate* that can identify a structure when it forms part of a sum. A structure definition alone, however, does not make a product type; that takes a data definition, which refers to the structure definition and also gives the type and meaning of each of the structure's fields.

A sum type is a matter of programming convention, documented in a data definition. Values automatically participate in sum types without explicit injection, so sums have no introduction form. The elimination form is the multiway conditional `cond`. The branches of the conditional use predicates that are consistent with the data definition of the sum type; these predicates typically include type predicates, from structure definitions or from base types.

Arrow types and polymorphic types resemble their counterparts in Haskell or ML. Arrows are introduced by `define` or `lambda` and are eliminated by function application. Polymorphism happens automatically without any extra notation.

Because the familiar foundations are in place, I found it easy to transplant ideas and techniques from Haskell and ML into the teaching languages from *How to Design Programs*. But the ideas and techniques have to be expressed a little differently, because the teaching languages lack some familiar conveniences: there are no anonymous tuple types; there is nothing corresponding to a value constructor; there is no `case` expression; and neither sums nor products can be eliminated using pattern matching.

Types guide code As suggested by Brooks (1975) and by Jackson (1975), the types of input data guide the shape of code. If a function f consumes a value of type τ, then f's body is typically designed around the elimination form(s) for type τ. In *How to Design Programs*, the body's design is called a *template*. The template for a sum uses `cond`; the template for a product uses the selector functions of the corresponding structure. (Values selected from a product are then "combined" by applying a function to them.)

Teaching types and code Words like "sum type" and "product type" are too mathematical for our beginning students, many of whom think they can't do math. To keep students comfortable enough to learn, I use Stephen Bloch's terminology: a definition of a product type is a *definition by parts*, and a definition of a sum type is a *definition by choices*. To avoid getting into the distinction between defining a name and using a type-formation rule, I also abuse terminology and talk about types that are "defined by name," like "image" and "number."

How to Design Programs made it easy for me to teach students to use the elimination forms for sums and products. It was not so easy to teach students to use named types. The "elimination form" for a named type is a function call, but what functions should students call? It depends on where the name comes from and what manner of type it refers to.

- If a type name refers to a base type (*atomic data*), then the right calls are to library functions or to helper functions written by the student. The student should look for a function whose signature says it consumes a value of the named type.
- If a type name refers to the data definition in which it appears, that definition is self-referential, and the right call is a *naturally recursive* call to the function being defined.
- If a type name refers to a data definition in a group of mutually referential definitions, then the design recipe calls for parallel development of a group of similar functions, one per data definition. The right call is to the function within the group that consumes data of the type referred to.
- Finally, if the type name refers to a data definition written by the student (or the instructor), then the right calls are to functions written by the student (or possibly the instructor). Again, the student should look for a function whose signature says it consumes a value of the named type. If no suitable function is available, I ask my students to create a *work order* for a new function and to put it on an *order list* (see the discussion of "wish lists" in Section 3.2 below).

This analysis suggests when and how to write a helper function and when and how to look for a library function.

Although the book pushed me, implicitly, to teach elimination forms, types can guide code in two other ways:

- In any function, you have available the inputs, the fields of any structure inputs, and the results of any natural recursions. You combine these values to compute the answer you want. But how? You could use the method of tables and examples described under Step 5 in Section 3.1 below, which relies on insight. Or you could use types.

  If you are designing a function f that is obligated to produce a result of type τ_r, you can treat τ_r as a "goal type," and you can ask if there is a function available, either defined or on your order list, that produces a result of that goal type τ_r. If you find such a function g of type $\tau_a \rightarrow \tau_r$, perhaps you already have a value of type τ_a, or perhaps you repeat the exercise with τ_a as the new goal type. Your goal-directed search produces, as candidate expressions, well-typed compositions of functions. It helps you by limiting what compositions you consider.
- Last, and rarely, you could design a function's template around the introduction form for the result type.

When I teach *Program by Design* again, I will make my students aware of this decision point in the construction of a function's template: should they use elimination forms, function composition, or an introduction form? They should use elimination forms usually, function composition sometimes, and an introduction form rarely.

A data-description pitfall Because a data definition is informal English, it can express invariants and other properties that are difficult to express in simple type systems based on System F—like the order invariant on a binary-search tree. Such expressive power is useful, but it also represents a potential pitfall. Because the role of a data definition is to guide the shape of code, good data definitions use the power of informal English only as a last resort. For example, I would never define a nonempty list of numbers as a list of numbers that contains at least one number. Such a definition is inferior because it expresses as a predicate (at least one) a property that should be structural (not empty). It leaves

[4] The first half of the book refers to a type as a "class of data." The word "type" is not introduced until functions are made first-class.

students with no guide to the structure of a *function* that consumes nonempty lists of numbers. A property such as "a nonempty list of numbers" or "a list of an even number of strings" should be expressed inductively as part of the structure of a data definition. For example,

```
;;  A *nonempty list of numbers* (lon+) is one of
;;     (cons n empty),    where n is a number
;;     (cons n ns),       where n is a number
;;                          and ns is a lon+
```

This data definition is the one to use for such functions as "minimum" or "maximum," which are defined only on nonempty lists—it tells a student exactly how to organize the functions.

Creativity and constraint The design process has a lot of steps, and the textbook has a lot of rules and prescriptions. Some steps call for students to get creative; others call for them to respect the rules and prescriptions. To help students succeed, I tried to be explicit about which were which.

- To look at the world or at a problem, and to capture its essential aspects in a data definition, is in my opinion the design step that requires the most creativity. It is also the most challenging. Because systematic design begins with data definition, and because I wanted my students to build on solid definitions, I rarely asked my students to create data definitions; instead, I provided most data definitions. To give students, safe, relatively easy opportunities to create their own data definitions, I recommend using "world programs" (Section 4.2 below).
- The other design step that requires creative problem solving is turning a function template into code. Because this step requires a less difficult, puzzle-solving style of creativity, I asked my students to turn templates into code all the time. To help them, I taught the method of tables and examples discussed under Step 5 in Section 3.1 below.
- The remaining steps of the design process reward order and method over creativity. Function signatures should mention only defined data and should be connected to words or relationships in the problem. Purpose statements must be written methodically and checked to be sure they are complete and comprehensive. Data examples should enumerate all possible shapes of data, and functional examples should also include examples of all shapes. Templates should be developed systematically using one of the three ways that types can guide code. Tests should come from functional examples; additional tests should be introduced only to help clarify function descriptions, to isolate bugs, or to prevent regressions.

Presenting functional abstraction and higher-order functions Both editions of *How to Design Programs* include sections on simplifying and generalizing code. In particular, the book shows how to combine two similar functions into one by abstracting over the parts that are different. Both the desire to simplify and the ability to abstract are essential for any working programmer, but they don't correspond to any step of the design process in the book, so I found them difficult to motivate. This difficulty will be resolved by making "review and refactor" an explicit, final step in the design process, as suggested above: simplification and abstraction will be two of a series of recommended refactorings.

What about standard higher-order functions on lists? Functions like `ormap` (a.k.a. `any` or `exists`), `andmap` (a.k.a. `all`), `map`, `filter`, and folds? I debated whether to teach them; in part, I feared that identifying common patterns of recursion would be too difficult, or that I could not offer enough practice time. Eventually, I decided to teach these functions because they are prominent in the book, and they are a functional programmer's power tools. To justify this decision, I concocted, with help from colleagues, a story about preparing for the future:

> Processing data in sequence is very common, and most languages provide features that help. You will see "loops" with keywords like "for", "while", or "repeat"; you may see "iterators"; and if you use a fashionable language like Python, you might even see fancy "list comprehensions."
>
> Why do such features matter? Because, if you are a principled software designer and you use a language that provides its own bricks, you use the bricks that are provided—you don't bake your own funny-shaped bricks out of raw clay. In other words, you must learn when and how to solve problems using built-in looping features.

I then explained that Intermediate Student Language provides these bricks in the form of general-purpose functions that implement "loops" for search, selection, and transformation. It even provides two very general-purpose functions that amount to "do something with each element": `foldl` works left-to-right, and `foldr` works right-to-left. My students learned to use these functions well enough, but I still don't fully understand how the functions fit into the steps of the design process.

3. Outcomes in the classroom; delivering a course

This section presents lessons I learned from teaching *Program by Design* at Tufts. Tufts is a private, American, Carnegie Research I university with very selective admissions. My course substituted for our usual first course in computing, which is required of all majors. Two-thirds of the students were in their first semester at university; most of the others were starting their third year. Most reported little or no prior experience with computer programming. Those who completed my course were eligible to continue to the second course in computing for majors, and most elected to do so.

My conclusions are drawn from observations in the classroom, in the laboratory, and of students' written work. I observed my students, my staff, and myself. For students, I address their learning about the design process and about some advanced topics. For myself, I confirm that my experiences are consistent with those published in the literature. Because my conclusions come from just a single case study, they are in no way definitive. But they should be informative enough to help both you and your students.

3.1 Where students struggle & where they don't (design steps)

Not all steps of the design process are equally easy to learn. Here I report on students' experience with seven of the eight design steps. (I conceived of the "review and refactor" step too late to teach it.)

Step 1A: Data definitions My students had little trouble learning to write monomorphic data definitions. What trouble they did have arose from compositionality: although the elements of a sum or product type can themselves be sum or product types, some students thought at first that the elements of a sum or product type had to be base types. Had I chosen better examples, my students could have avoided this misconception.

A few students had a more subtle problem: they wanted to nest sums and products more deeply than is wise. As is implicit in the examples in the textbook, defining a sum of products of named types is a good strategy and works well with the rest of the design method. But putting an additional sum or product under one of the nested products creates definitions that are harder to understand, and it militates against the effective use of helper functions.

Finally, late in the term, many students allowed their data definitions to get sloppy. Their most common fault was to conflate the name of a structure element with the name of its type.

Step 1B: Data examples A data definition is a kind of specification; like other specifications, it expresses what a programmer intends to model. So how do we tell if a data definition expresses the right intent? By writing *data examples*. Data examples also support problem-specific case analysis, e.g., which temperatures support deciduous trees? Or on a map, which hospitals lie in the local jurisdiction?

My students often forgot to write data examples. And initially, most of them struggled to write data examples that DrRacket would accept. The forgetting can be addressed, as suggested above, by teaching the construction of data examples as a discrete design step with its own number. The struggles with DrRacket should be addressed, in my opinion, by improving DrRacket so that it supports data examples as well as it currently supports *functional* examples. Let's look at that support.

For functional examples, each teaching language provides a syntactic form called `check-expect`. A `check-expect` may appear anywhere at top level; in particular, a `check-expect` that calls a function may appear before the definition of that function. Here is an example; the `check-expect` uses `swap` before its definition:

```
;; DATA DEFINITION: A (pairof X Y) is a structure
;;    (make-pair x y)
;; where x is an X and y is a Y
(define-struct pair (fst snd))

(check-expect
   (swap (make-pair 'fish 'fowl))
   (make-pair 'fowl 'fish))

;; swap : (pairof X Y) -> (pairof Y X)
;; return a pair that is equal to the given
;;   pair with the elements swapped
(define (swap p)
  (make-pair (pair-snd p) (pair-fst p)))
```

DrRacket accumulates uses of `check-expect` and related forms; waits until all functions, values, and structures have been defined; runs the accumulated uses in the context of the definitions; and finally rewards students by saying something like "All 16 tests passed!"

Data examples enjoy no comparable support:

- Data examples lack their own syntactic form; they are written either as top-level expressions or as right-hand sides of `define`.
- Data examples are not accumulated and summarized.
- Data examples win no rewards from DrRacket. In fact, when data examples are written as top-level expressions, DrRacket delivers light punishment: before reporting about tests, it sprays the values of those expressions to standard output. These values may distract from the values of other expressions that have more meaning or that have been placed in the code for use with Racket's algebraic stepper.
- A data example that incorporates a structure must appear *after* the relevant `define-struct`. This requirement confused and frustrated my students, who tripped over it repeatedly. Students expected data examples to be like function definitions and `check-expects`, both of which can refer to functions and structures before they are defined.[5]

[5] The definition of a *variable*, unlike the definition of a function, must also appear after any definitions to which it refers. But my students rarely defined variables and almost never defined a variable that depended on another variable. So if this similar restriction on variable definitions caused students any difficulty, I didn't see it.

My students eventually learned to place their data examples *after* all relevant definitions, but they deserve better. An idea of what "better" might look like appears in Section 6.1 below.

Step 2: Function descriptions A function description comprises a type signature, a *purpose statement*, and a *header*. The purpose statement is essentially Meyer's (1997) *contract* (precondition and postcondition), but it is informal and therefore not checkable by automated tools. The header names the parameters. Headers are easy, but for my students, learning to write good signatures and purpose statements was hard.

Students quickly learned the idea of signatures, but some students suffered from a misconception similar to their misconception about data definitions: that signatures could refer only to base types. With that misconception cleared up, students wrote signatures without difficulty, but like Crestani and Sperber's (2010) students, they wrote a lot of bad ones.

The worst kind of bad signature was imprecise because it contained ill-kinded types. Most often I saw a bare `list` (with no type parameter) or a bare `structure` (not identifying *which* structure). A less bad signature had a precise meaning that was inconsistent with the function it described, usually because it had the wrong number of parameters. Both kinds of bad signature could be ruled out by making signatures linguistic, as described by Crestani and Sperber. Unfortunately, because I did not find documentation on using Crestani and Sperber's signatures with the standard teaching languages, I can't confirm their experience.

Writing good purpose statements is very hard, even for students who are well past the beginning stages. I don't know of a royal road to writing purpose statements, but I do issue the following instructions, which relate purpose statements and function headers:

> Why is a function's header grouped with its signature and purpose statement? So you can use the *names* of the parameters in your purpose statement. Therefore, please make sure that your purpose statement refers to *each* parameter *by name*—and that it mentions the result.

The idea can be found in the textbook, but I needed to emphasize it. And checking purpose statements in a final "review and refactor" step of the design process is something even a raw beginner can do.

Steps 3 and 6: Functional examples and unit tests As noted above under Step 1B, functional examples are written using a special form called `check-expect`. This form, which is explained in the second edition of the textbook, shows two expressions that are expected to evaluate to equal values; a `check-expect` serves as both example and test. Even though we were using the first edition, I used `check-expect` for every functional example I presented.

My colleagues, my course staff, and I had worried that students would rebel against a mandated testing step for each function; students in our other classes almost never write unit tests, and they are seldom graded on any kind of testing. We needn't have worried. My students quickly learned to write functional examples and to reuse them as tests. All students learned to use tests, and most students grew to value them highly. My most vivid example comes from a hallway conversation about the differences between *Program by Design* and our standard first course, which is taught using C++. When I explained some of the limitations imposed by C++, one student was dumbfounded: "You mean they don't have `check-expect`?"

Although my students learned to use examples and tests routinely, not all students learned to use them well. For example, students were slow to learn that if a function consumes a value that is defined by choices (a sum type), they should write a functional example for each choice. (If there is no test for a given choice, DrRacket reports in Step 6 that code written for the choice is not tested, but by then it is too late for the missing functional example to play its role in guiding the construction of the code, as explained in Step 5 below.)

More subtle, and harder to learn, was the idea that functional examples should include a representative variety of *results*. The easiest context in which to introduce this idea is a function that returns a Boolean; there should be examples that return both `true` and `false`. Had I known that such functions might present difficulties, I could have forestalled a few instances in which students mistakenly wrote predicates that always returned `true`, for example.

Step 4: Templates Function templates were the most difficult part of the design process for my students to apply. My students weren't confused, and they didn't ask questions, but most of them consistently turned in code that, to an instructor, was obviously not derived from a legitimate template. Worse, students could not see for themselves that they had deviated from the template approach. Several deviations recurred frequently; I call them *confused conditionals* and *stubborn sums and structures*. I also describe *false choices*. To illustrate these deviations, I describe two students' implementations of `insert`, a function that inserts a key and value into a binary search tree. Such a tree is either `false` (the empty tree) or a `node` containing a key, a value, and left and right subtrees.

The good implementation follows the template approach. Function `insert` begins with the elimination construct for the sum: a conditional that asks `false?` and `node?`. The case for `node` selects the node's key and continues with a three-way conditional that compares the node's key with the input key. The conditional has three branches because the design recipe for ordered data partitions the input data into three subsets: a key in an ordered set must be less than, equal to, or greater than a search key. In the three-way conditional, two of the three branches contain naturally recursive calls to `insert`, passing the node's left and right subtrees, respectively.

The bad implementation also begins with the correct conditional. But its `node` case deviates from the template approach. It passes all inputs (including the node) to a helper function `change-value`, whose type is too general: `change-value` expects not a `node` but an arbitrary tree. And `change-value` doesn't use a template based on input data; instead, it calls a helper function `has-key?`, which tells if any node of the given tree contains the given key. Then `change-value` calls another helper function, either `update-value` or `add-node`. Finally, `add-node` contains a three-way conditional that asks if the input tree is `false` or if the given key is smaller or larger than the key in the node. Many things are wrong here; let's look first at the conditionals.

A conditional should either distinguish among alternatives in a sum type, like a `case` expression in Haskell or ML, or it should make some other single decision, like an `if` expression in Haskell or ML. The initial conditional in both implementations of `insert` acts like a `case` expression, distinguishing a node from an empty tree. Such conditionals are prescribed by the design recipe for sum types, and once that recipe is understood, they can be written quickly and easily. The second conditional in the good implementation of `insert` acts like nested `if` expressions, deciding how the input key relates to a node's key. As noted above, it is prescribed by a design recipe for ordered data. The conditional in `add-node` is a *confused conditional*: it mixes the discrimination of alternatives in the sum with discrimination among keys. Such conditionals are not prescribed by any design recipe, and they are usually hard to understand.

Now let's look at the types of the bad implementation's functions. Function `insert` discriminates between `node` and `false`, and it passes only a node to `change-value`. But `change-value` expects a tree, not a node. This tree is a *stubborn sum*—one that won't go away and is scrutinized repeatedly. Sure enough, trees are scrutinized by `insert`, `has-key?`, `update-value`, and `add-node`. That's four times as much scrutiny as the template (or the problem) calls for.

I've also seen *stubborn structures*. One example was in a function that takes a binary search tree keyed by number and returns the leaf whose key is closest to a given number. The template for a node structure should combine the node's key with computations on the node's left and right subtrees. But the example code examines the node's key, then calls a helper function with one subtree *and the node*. This node is a stubborn structure—instead of being abandoned once its elements have been selected, it is passed around, and multiple helper functions select elements from it, repeatedly.

Finally, a *false choice* is a conditional decision that ought not to be made, because one of the right-hand sides subsumes the others. A typical example consumes a list: the `empty?` choice handles empty lists, and the `cons?` choice, instead of using a natural recursion to handle the tail of the list, handles the whole list—and would work even if the list were empty. Another example is the conditional in the bad implementation of `insert`: if `insert` uses the helper function `change-value`, which can handle *any* tree, not just a node, then `insert` should not have a conditional. In yet another example, I saw conditionals with cases for a nonempty binary tree whose left or right subtree is empty—cases that are subsumed by the case for a general nonempty tree.

You can watch for these template problems, and you can warn students about them, but if students are to identify template problems independently, in their own code, I believe they need more support from DrRacket. Some ideas appear in Section 6.2 below.

Step 5: Coding As noted in Section 2.3 above, going from template to code sometimes requires creative puzzle solving. To help stimulate students' creativity, I have generalized a technique that is presented in the second edition of *How to Design Programs*, in the section on designing with self-referential data definitions.

The problem is to turn a template into code. The technique is to create one table of examples for each nontrivial case in the template's main conditional, or if the template does not begin with a conditional, one table for the whole template. The first column of the table is labeled *Wanted*, and it shows the value the function should return, which is taken from a functional example. Another column is needed for each application of a selector function and for each natural recursion. A labeled column for each input may also help, as may labeled columns for calls to helper functions.

Once the columns are set up, the student fills in a row for each functional example that meets the condition associated with the table. The *Wanted* column, the inputs, and the results of applying selector functions are filled in mechanically using the inputs from the functional example. Columns for natural recursions or for calls to helper functions are filled in using each called function's purpose statement. Here is an example of a table for the induction step of a recursive function that sums the first `n` natural numbers:

Wanted	`n`	`(sub1 n)`	`(sum-to (sub1 n))`
1	1	0	0
10	4	3	6
15	5	4	10

We hope the student sees that *Wanted* is `(+ n (sum-to (sub1 n)))`.

I found the table-of-examples technique so valuable that after two-thirds of the course, I devoted a full homework assignment to it and to remedial template writing. The next time I teach the course, I will ask students, on the very first assignment, to fill in tables of examples, using images and perhaps a few numbers.

3.2 Where students do & don't struggle (advanced topics)

Self-referential data and natural recursion I was wisely advised to start teaching recursion not with lists but with a richer recursive type. As my first example, I defined a particular binary tree: a *conspiracy* is either an empty conspiracy or a cell headed by a person and containing two recruits, each of which is also a conspiracy. To create a running example, I claimed a position at the root of a class-wide conspiracy, and I sent emails to two students asking them to recruit two classmates each, and to "give your [recruits] these instructions and ask them to recruit two more classmates into the conspiracy." Students seemed to enjoy the play-acting, and when the conspiracy was revealed at the blackboard, students were able to help me evaluate and then define such functions as the number of people in a conspiracy (population) or the number of steps needed to get a message to every conspirator (depth). Also, when the time came to explain the function template for self-referential data, I was able to draw an analogy between a recursive function call and the self-reference in my informal recruiting instructions.

After this successful introduction to recursion, I thought we were home free, but as I watched students tackle more ambitious problems, I observed a dispiriting phenomenon: many students tried to understand recursion by mentally inlining recursive calls, arbitrarily many times. Thinking about sequences of recursive calls abandons the template approach, makes students' heads hurt, and leads to hideous, broken code. In the future, I will insist even more often that when you call a function, you must *not* look at its definition, but only at its description—and in particular, at its purpose statement. It is only by trusting purpose statements that a programmer can build things that are big or recursive. I don't know if my students picked up bad habits elsewhere or if the desire to inline functions is innate, but now I do know I have to fight against it. And I know that if a student cannot write a crisp, clear purpose statement, that student is likely to struggle with recursive functions.

Generative recursion One of the contributions of *Program by Design* is to distinguish *natural* recursion, which amounts to structural induction, from *generative* recursion, which describes all other methods of dividing a problem into smaller subproblems (Felleisen et al. 2004a). Generative recursion provides opportunities for great homework problems, but I needed to give remedial homework on templates, and I had promised that students would do the language-classification project described in Section 5.1 below. So I assigned no generative-recursion homework. I was able to assess students' mastery of generative recursion only by observing them at work. In class, we tackled the construction of a 2D-tree from a list of points, and I set sorting a list of numbers as a quiz problem. In both problems, at least some students were able to identify which approaches were structural and which were generative. For example, given the standard structure in which a list is either `empty` or is made with `cons`, students correctly identified insertion sort as structural and selection sort as generative.

Local definitions and lambda expressions My students easily made the transition from Beginning Student Language to Intermediate Student Language, which adds local definitions and first-class, nested functions. They also easily absorbed `lambda`. Although `lambda` is officially an add-on, we went straight from Beginning Student Language to Intermediate Student Language *with* `lambda`; we never used Intermediate Student Language without `lambda`. And because my mandate was to teach programming and problem-solving, not functional programming, I did not dedicate any class time to `lambda`; I simply used it in examples in which I called higher-order list functions. To my surprise, in lab exercises designed to reinforce skills with higher-order functions, at least half the students chose to use `lambda`, without encouragement or instruction beyond what they had seen in class and read in the book.

Functional abstraction and higher-order functions Abstraction over differences includes abstraction over different *functions*, and abstracting over a function produces a higher-order function. I taught higher-order functions using a suggestion from Viera Proulx: present purpose statements for functions that answer similar questions. For example, "How many students in this class carry a MacBook?", "How many students in this class are freshmen?", and so on. My students swallowed the idea whole and were able to design, during class, a higher-order `how-many` function. And they sailed through a homework assignment in which they used abstraction to combine functions they had written previously.

My students also had little difficulty using standard higher-order functions on lists. They did so not only on small problems that emphasized standard list functions, but also on a large project for which they were instructed to avoid recursion when possible. A number of students were comfortable enough to complain about the names of `ormap` and `andmap`, which Haskell programmers know as `any` and `all`. Students did only one thing that disappointed me: many of them used a fold where a map or filter would be better. Correcting this fault would be an appropriate refactoring.

Parametric polymorphism As part of its story about abstraction, *How to Design Programs* introduces parametric polymorphism. Data definitions can abstract over type parameters, and function signatures can use universally quantified type variables.[6] My students' written work showed that most of them got the *idea* of a parametric data definition, but none of them learned to use the notation properly. And even granting some idiosyncratic notation, few of them wrote definitions that were clear and unambiguous.

To correct these problems, I would follow Crestani and Sperber (2010) in introducing a formal language for data definitions. And although I do not advocate static type checking, I do think my students would benefit from a static check that type expressions are well kinded—each type constructor should receive the expected number of type parameters.

My students had more problems with polymorphic function signatures. Most of them sometimes wrote signatures that were less polymorphic than their code, using a named type where a type variable would be permitted. Many of them also sometimes wrote signatures that were *more* polymorphic than their code, using a type variable where a named type was required. These problems would not have been detected by Crestani and Sperber's (2010) dynamic signature checker: the functions whose signatures aren't polymorphic enough aren't *used* at non-conforming types, and the functions whose signatures are too polymorphic won't be detected because a type variable does not trigger any dynamic checks.

Wish lists *How to Design Programs*, especially the first edition, emphasizes the design of functions over programs. But it does present one key tool for designing programs, which it calls the *wish list*. The wish list is a list of descriptions, each including a name, signature, and purpose statement, of functions that need to be written for the program to be complete.

Unfortunately, I never saw a student use a wish list effectively. And I often saw students use wish lists *ineffectively*: instead of being demanded by demonstrated needs, functions appeared on the wish list after a quick reading of a problem, without thought. The wish list turned into a fantasy list, containing anything a student might possibly wish for. Such lists result from muddy, wishful thinking about problems, not from systematic design.

[6] In the first edition, the universal quantifiers are implicit; in the second edition, fortunately, they are explicit. I have learned from many experiences not to ask undergraduate students to envision implicit universal quantifiers.

To fight against muddy, wishful thinking, in future courses I will avoid the term "wish list." I will instead refer to an "order list" and to "work orders." I will tell students that issuing a work order costs something, and they had better not order a function unless they're willing to pay for it. I look forward to seeing if the new words help.

3.3 Replicating others' experience

My classroom experience confirms what others have written about dynamic types, about lecturing, and about laboratories.

Dynamic types Findler et al. (2002) argue that the type systems of Haskell and ML are too sophisticated for beginning students, but that a first-order, monomorphic type system might be helpful for beginning students. Felleisen et al. (2004a) argue that dynamic typing is a benefit because students and teachers need not spend energy finding and explaining static type errors. (And when a type error occurs dynamically, it comes with an example!) My students' difficulty writing well-formed templates (Section 3.1) suggests that writing statically well-typed code might also be a challenge.

The compile-time checking provided by Haskell or ML would have ruled out many of the bad templates I observed—provided that sums and products were eliminated using case expressions and pattern matching, and that cases were checked for exhaustiveness. But as much as I love this compile-time checking, I have seen the difficulty that beginning students have writing proper templates, and I agree that compile-time checking is likely to be more of a barrier than a help. (Several colleagues report using hygienic macros to provide case expressions and pattern matching *without* compile-time checking. Such experiments sound intriguing.)

Live coding in the lecture theater Sperber and Crestani (2012) recommend that instructors teach design by solving problems using the full design process, with DrRacket, before a live audience of students. They caution against taking shortcuts. I found this method of teaching most effective during the second half of the course. I also found that a 75-minute lecture is too short for complete, correct solution of such problems as designing higher-order functions proposed by the students, or building a 2D-tree. I had to choose between dropping examples and taking shortcuts, and I took shortcuts. (When taking a shortcut, I identified each design step I wished to skip, and I asked students' permission to skip it.) You may need to make similar compromises.

Laboratory experiences and assisted programming At Tufts, instruction is limited to 150 minutes of lecture per week, plus a 75-minute lab. A lab accommodates up to 22 students and is supervised by a staff of two or three undergraduate assistants, plus a "lab runner," who is typically a doctoral student. My class was limited to 40 students, so I needed only two labs, which I ran myself—primarily so I could observe students at work.

In lab, I tried to replicate the *assisted programming* model described by Bieniusa et al. (2008): students are given a set of small programming exercises, of which they are expected to finish half. Students worked in pairs, and I asked them, at the end of each lab, to write what they had done and what they learned. Although personal observation told me more, the self-assessments helped me judge students' learning and address issues in subsequent lectures. And self-assessments scale in a way that personal observation doesn't.

My labs presented many of the same issues described by Bieniusa et al., especially the construction of exercises with a suitable number of problems of suitable difficulty. My most popular labs were those that posed many small problems. Examples included a list lab that asked for one data definition and ten functions, and a higher-order functions lab that asked for ten functions and the results of several function applications. My least popular labs were those that posed a single problem broken down into many pieces. Examples included a lab to convert any S-expression into a sequence of atoms (and back again); a lab to build a game of whack-a-mole; and a lab to build an interactive map of the northeast United States, highlighting the hospital nearest the mouse cursor. No student completed any of these labs, so students did not enjoy the early successes that so help their motivation and learning (Ambrose et al. 2010, Chapter 3).

Other instructors report being challenged to develop good labs that work in 90 or 120 minutes. A 75-minute lab is even more challenging. If possible, arrange for a longer lab.

4. Working with the languages, libraries and tools

In this section I explain what I learned about DrRacket, the teaching languages, and the teaching libraries.

4.1 Using the teaching languages with DrRacket

For over fifteen years I have taught programming languages using little languages (Kamin 1990; Ramsey 2016). With this experience as background, I cannot praise the Racket teaching languages highly enough. The language design is lapidary. I was especially impressed that functions in Beginning Student Language may not have local variables. At first I thought this restriction was crazy, but after observing students at work, I see that not only is the language simplified,[7] but without local variables, students are nudged to create helper functions—a notorious point of difficulty for beginning students.

Including `check-expect` is a masterstroke. Even if you use only the first edition of the textbook, you must teach `check-expect`, because it is so beautifully integrated with DrRacket. Clicking Run runs all tests, and DrRacket shows untested code in red on a reverse-video background. After seeing this feature demonstrated in one or two early lectures, almost all students routinely submitted code with complete "statement" coverage. They submitted untested code only in assignments that were substantially incomplete. Why? Probably because *every time you compile, DrRacket runs your tests and tells you about coverage.* When my fellow instructors and I compare programming environments, we agree that easy, routine, automatic testing and coverage analysis is DrRacket's most important benefit.

4.2 Teaching with world programs and the universe library

The teaching languages come with purely functional `image` and `universe` libraries, which can be used to create interactive graphical applications as well as distributed applications (Felleisen et al. 2009). Interactive applications are called "world programs," and my students wrote lots of them. (We did no distributed computing.) A world program is built around a single higher-order function, `big-bang`,[8] which has a polymorphic type. The unspecified, universally quantified type is called the *world state.*[9] Client code provides a function to render a world state as an image, as well as pure functions that respond to mouse and keyboard events, or even to the passage of time, by mapping world states to world states. The design of world programs is discussed briefly by Felleisen et al. (2009) and at length in the second edition of *How to Design Programs.* My summary guide is reproduced in Web Appendix E.

[7] A first-order language with local variables must explain how local definitions (which may not include first-class functions) differ from top-level definitions (which do include first-class functions). Intermediate Student Language, in which all functions are first-class, needs only one, simple, uniform account of the meaning of a local definition.

[8] Actually, `big-bang` is a syntactic form, but you don't need to know this.

[9] Felleisen et al. explain world programs using units (modules), but an explanation using polymorphism and type variables also works.

World programs impressed me very favorably: `big-bang` is both powerful and simple, and creating satisfying interactive programs is easy. But world programs have more intellectual depth than I realized, and I made some mistakes (Section 5.4 below). I trace my mistakes to a shallow understanding of the `universe` library; I was too willing to take at face value the idea that the purpose of the library is to enable students to "construct a program that is like the applications they use on their computers" (Felleisen et al. 2009). I now believe the library serves broader and deeper purposes:

- The library provides a simple space in which students can develop and practice the skill of "look at the world; see data; define a representation in the computer."
- The library provides a safe, guided environment in which students can design *programs*, not just functions.
- The library exposes students to the power of data abstraction (over the world state).
- The library provides flexibility for students to choose different representations of a world state and to design the event handlers required by `big-bang`. This kind of flexibility, and the control students have over their choices, enhance motivation and learning (Ambrose et al. 2010, Chapter 3).

Pleasing students with lifelike applications is all very well, but world programs are important because of their other purposes. In the future, the aspects I will emphasize most are the skill of modeling the world in the computer, and the practice in designing programs, not just functions.

4.3 What to expect from the programming environment

Except for the help and menu system, I found the student-facing part of DrRacket as good as advertised. Almost all of my students were instantly productive using the Beginning Student Language. The help and menu system does present a problem: as far as I can tell, students are expected to deal with the same help and menu system that fully fledged Racket programmers use. Most students were willing to ignore menu items they didn't understand, but almost all of my students tried to use the help system and found themselves reading documentation for full Racket—especially library documentation. This documentation, with its idiosyncratic notation for function signatures, was difficult even for my teaching assistants.

The instructor-facing part of DrRacket surprised me. I was expecting mature, well-documented, stable production software. I got mature, well-documented, evolving *research* software. Once I adjusted my expectations, I got along fine, but I hit a couple of pain points worth knowing about. Because I hope these pain points will soon disappear, I have relegated the details to Web Appendix D.3.

One pain point is not going to disappear: if you write libraries, you are expected to use full Racket. If, like me, you've learned only up to Intermediate Student Language, full Racket presents some problems: it's not just bigger; it's different. I tripped over differences in definitions of structure types and in meanings of numeric literals. Luckily, Matthew Flatt suggested a great compromise: use Intermediate Student Language plus full Racket's `provide` form. To get `provide`, you need only a small file written in full Racket. You import that file (using `require`), use `provide` to export your public names, then write the rest of your library in Intermediate Student Language.

One final caution: it is all too easy for a student to use DrRacket's menus to import the wrong library ("teachpack") by mistake—a mistake that both students and teaching assistants found hard to diagnose. Insist that your students import libraries only by using `require` in their source code. Using `require` makes manifest what libraries have been imported, and as a bonus, it puts your own libraries on the same footing as built-in libraries.

5. Rookie mistakes and what I learned from them

People love to do things well, but we learn more from our mistakes. I asked other instructors to help me learn from their mistakes, but those who made beginner's mistakes did not share them. Shriram Krishnamurthi did identify two common mistakes: failing to get complete buy-in from teaching assistants, and allowing experienced students to disrupt or undermine a class. What follows is an account of my own most significant mistakes—the ones from which I learned the most, and the ones I most wish I had avoided.

5.1 Misdirected effort in preparation and planning

I began preparing my course by trying to identify learning outcomes, in more detail than I present in Section 2 above. I read the textbook painstakingly and took detailed notes. This work turned out to have been a poor use of my time. I later skimmed the book *quickly* and made a high-level summary. The summary, which splits the material into six broad tiers and articulates a simple learning goal for each tier, helped me far more than my detailed notes. It still does not contain what my colleagues in education would consider proper learning objectives, but in hopes that it may also help you, I have reproduced it as Web Appendix B.

I worked on the course with seven students who had studied functional programming with me. None of us had used Racket or its teaching languages; what we had used was a dialect of Scheme called μScheme, which is a bit smaller than Racket's Intermediate Student Language. We did not try to learn the teaching languages in advance, which was a good decision: we picked them up quickly and easily.

We spent our preparation time on potential homework assignments. Because our departmental culture encourages "projects," which are big, open-ended assignments intended to provide scope for significant design choices (Web Appendix C), we focused almost exclusively on project ideas. We especially wanted projects that would meet our departmental goals of establishing connections to real-world technology, to real-world data, or to students' interests outside of computer science. In the light of experience, our focus was misdirected.

- In almost every week of a course in *Program by Design*, students learn a new way to organize data. Unfortunately, coming up with projects that organize data in sufficiently diverse ways was beyond our abilities. Almost every one of our project ideas required a list of structures, and for many ideas, a list of structures was sufficient. But in *Program by Design*, before students are ready to work with a list of structures, they have to spend a month learning simpler forms of data. They then have only a week or two in which lists of structures are on topic, after which they move on to other forms of data. Even after much effort, we couldn't imagine a set of projects that would fit a course in *Program by Design*.
- In *Program by Design*, students learn so much technique that there isn't *room* for a lot of projects. In a 13-week course, even though I chose not to teach mutation, I felt that I had only about $3\frac{1}{2}$ weeks in which I could give students a project that was not driven by a technical learning objective. I was able to use only one of those weeks for a project. (I used another week to remediate difficulties with templates, and I used the remaining week and a half to help my students prepare a learning portfolio, which served them in lieu of a final examination.)

My staff and I also looked for problem domains that could serve as unifying themes for multiple labs and homeworks. We settled on two themes: probability and GPS navigation. I knew probability was a stretch, but I wanted to deliver a project that has repeatedly been popular in our first course: write a naïve Bayesian classifier that identifies the natural language in which a web page is written. I was more confident in GPS navigation: I felt that it would provide a more interesting introduction to numeric computation than the ancient, boring Fahrenheit/Centigrade conversions, and I felt it would lead up to interactive mapping applications. But neither of the two themes worked out as well as I had hoped.

- We didn't have time to take probability seriously. We started well enough by having students estimate and measure some real-world probabilities, using log odds. We then ignored probability for ten weeks, and in the eleventh week, I bombed students with a few dense pages of probabilistic notation and Bayesian reasoning, so they could build classifiers. I don't believe they retained anything.
- We did better with GPS navigation, but I underestimated my students' discomfort with sines and cosines. Not only did my students find sines and cosines intimidating, but sines and cosines use "inexact" (floating-point) arithmetic, which I could otherwise have delayed or avoided. Many students struggled to write simple functions on GPS coordinates, which took them far more time and effort than I ever imagined.

These two problem domains may or may not have been poor choices, but my real blunder was more fundamental. I was warped by my youthful experiences with C and Pascal, and without thinking, I assumed that problems for beginners should use *numbers*. Numbers have their benefits—students can draw on their school experience to develop examples and tests that are independent of their code—but Beginning Student Language also includes a first-class *image* type. This type comes with a lovely algebra of operations, and it even enjoys special support in DrRacket's read-eval-print loop! Or if I hadn't thought of images, as a longtime Haskell and ML programmer I should definitely have thought of *strings*.[10] I promise future students that their very first experiences of computing will include examples that draw pictures and say things, not just examples that compute numbers. Bloch (2010) agrees.

What else did I learn from my mistakes in course planning?

- I found room for only one or two things beyond basic functional programming. The textbook suggests mutation, but I chose instead to take an extended look at tree structures (1D- and 2D-trees) and to use a novel final assessment (learning portfolios).
- I believe in projects,[11] but when I teach the course again, I will identify *one* project and have students build it in pieces throughout the term. I might try a simple web browser or perhaps a browser for some other kind of database. I would consider a game like Scrabble, which would provide practice in data structures and in designing world programs, but my department is cautious about games (Web Appendix C).

5.2 Miscalibrated homework

My most embarrassing mistake was to assign a problem I thought was simple without first having completed the *entire* design process myself. I asked students to write three functions on GPS positions: distance, bearing, and projection. I had previously implemented the functions, and I knew that the function descriptions and codes were simple. I also knew that some of the trigonometry was subtle, so I prepared my students thoroughly for the trigonometric calculations. I thought that was enough.

I was wrong: I badly misjudged the cost of developing functional examples and unit tests. When I finally finished my reference solution, the code itself, even with liberal use of helper functions, took only 24 lines of Beginning Student Language. But to test it properly, I had to define at least another half a dozen functions, and the full solution contained 226 nonblank lines of code, tests, and documentation. The assignment turned out to be about three times as much work as I had meant to ask for, and I was lucky my students did not desert *en masse*.

5.3 Misunderstood templates

As a beginner, I was a little too eager to construct function templates by leaping at the elimination form for one of the argument types, as described in Section 2.3 above. I had learned from the book that when you get a value of sum or product type, you take it apart using a conditional or a set of selector functions. But there's always another choice: you can leave an argument alone, not inspect it or take it apart, but simply pass it to another function. I didn't teach my students this choice early enough. The possibility, however, can be taught from the very beginning; indeed, values of atomic type can *only* be passed to other functions.

Midway through the term, I tried to correct my mistake by introducing a new word for an uninspected value: *sealed*. The decision about whether to leave arguments sealed comes into play in the book's section on processing multiple pieces of complex data, but I wish I had introduced it earlier. Delaying may have contributed to my students' difficulties with templates and to my own difficulties in teaching function composition.

5.4 My world-state disaster

When I introduced world programs to my students, I made my biggest mistake of the term. I wanted to show them an interactive graphics program that did something interesting, and they had learned about structures but not yet about lists. I somehow got the idea of a program that would drop a disk on the screen at every mouse click, potentially filling the screen with disks. No lists? No problem! I chose as my world state an *image* containing all the dropped disks. Had I been *trying* to sabotage myself, I could not have chosen a worse example. For weeks, my students conflated world states with images, and when asked to write new world programs, they struggled mightily. To get everybody sorted out on the difference between an image and a world state took my teaching assistants a month of hard work. Next time I introduce world programs, I will begin with a simple state containing just one disk which can change position.

6. Open problems

During the semester, I identified a number of teaching problems that I have not yet solved. Some problems require Racket programming that is beyond my skills; some require a depth of understanding that I have not yet developed; and some require time, effort, and in-class experimentation that I have not yet been able to invest. I begin with easier problems and move to more difficult ones.

6.1 Making data examples first-class

In Section 3.1 above, in Step 1B (data examples), I enumerate the ways in which data examples are second-class citizens, not supported by the teaching languages or by DrRacket. All the problems

[10] Although the first edition of *How to Design Programs* uses LISP symbols almost exclusively, the second edition uses strings, and there is a fine string library.

[11] An anonymous reviewer suggests that in conventional courses, projects are necessary because the cognitive and syntactic overhead of industrial languages is so great that problems with small solutions rarely provide much intellectual challenge. By contrast, the reviewer finds the Racket teaching languages expressive enough, with little enough overhead, that even problems with 20-line solutions can present significant intellectual challenges.

my students had could be addressed by adding a syntactic form like this one:

```
(check-eval expression)
```

where *expression* is the data example. The semantics I intend is that DrRacket accumulates the expressions and then evaluates them, like the expressions in a `check-expect`, after all definitions are in scope. DrRacket could then report something like "All 7 data examples built!"

This `check-eval` proposal, which says simply "I have some data," does not please the experts. Experts have, however, shown significant interest in more ambitious proposals, all of which say "I have some data *of a particular class*." But the experts do not agree on how a class of data should be formally specified. One specification language, *contracts* (Findler and Felleisen 2002), has grown into a large and important part of full Racket. Another specification language, *signatures* (Crestani and Sperber 2010), has been used successfully with beginning students. These languages will do well for instructors who have the skill and inclination to go beyond *How to Design Programs*. But as long as the book teaches students to write function signatures that are informal and unchecked, I hope a place can be found for a data-example form in which the class of data is also informal and unchecked.

6.2 Enabling templates to persist and be reviewed

DrRacket does not provide enough support for function templates. The teaching languages do include forms such as `...` and `....`, which can be used to *write* templates. But DrRacket does not recognize these forms as special: it complains that they are untested code. Untested code is anathema, and DrRacket's complaints push students to turn templates into code as soon as possible. And once a template has been turned into code, it is gone forever.

Because templates disappear, a student cannot review a template to see if it makes sense in the context of a given signature and data definition, and a student cannot compare a template with a function definition to see if the two are consistent. Bad templates account for almost all the times my students wrote horrible code or went off the rails entirely. And students don't see them! As an experienced functional programmer, I can look at a function and imagine the template from which it was derived, and I can identify problems that stem from the template in my imagination. But such acts of critical imagination are too much to expect of beginning students.

Every other step of the original design process (data description, data examples, function description, functional examples, code, and tests) leaves behind a visible artifact that can be assessed. Templates should leave footprints, too. It might be enough to extend DrRacket with a new syntactic form, perhaps called `define-template`, which would define a new species of function. Such a "template function" would undergo the same static checks as a regular function, would be required to contain the `...` form or related forms, would be expected not to be tested, and could coexist with a true function of the same name. Template functions would play many roles:

- Most important, template functions would provide scaffolding to help students define ordinary functions that are consistent with the definitions of the data those functions consume.
- During the "review and refactor" step, template functions would make it possible for students to answer two crucial questions: Is the template consistent with the signature and the data definition? And is the function definition consistent with the template? When the template itself is invisible, as at present, these questions are too difficult for my students to answer.
- Template functions would help my teaching staff communicate with students during laboratories and office hours; my staff could ask to see a template function and then could ask students the same two questions about consistency.
- Finally, explicit template functions would help my staff and me assess students' code and provide better feedback.

It is also possible that DrRacket could check to see if a function's definition is consistent with its template. For example, DrRacket could check if a definition could be obtained from its template by replacing each ellipsis with a term. I am not confident that such a check would provide much additional value—I think the important property of a function template is that it be *present*—but it's an experimental question. The real value that I am confident of is that explicit, persistent templates would help my students apply design recipes correctly. If I could change only one thing about DrRacket, making templates explicit and persistent would have the biggest effect on my students' learning.

6.3 Developing the "review and refactor" step

I plan to teach an explicit "review and refactor" step not only to unify some disparate instructions and activities that are distributed throughout *How to Design Programs*, but also to show students that mature designers don't just write good code; they improve code by refactoring. To identify review and refactoring activities and to match them to levels of learning and development, much work remains to be done. As a first step, here are some suggested activities, starting with those suitable for very beginning students:

- Check signatures for arity problems, references to unqualified "lists" or "structures," and other faults. (Crestani and Sperber (2010) observe that this activity can be profitably automated by adding formal signatures to a teaching language.)
- Check functional examples to be sure every choice of input is represented.
- Check functional examples to be sure every choice of *output* is represented. This activity is especially valuable for functions returning Booleans.
- Examine code for violations of the template approach, especially the "confused conditionals" and the "stubborn" sums or structures described in Section 3.1.
- Look for duplicate or near-duplicate codes; if you can identify parameters to abstract over, replace them with calls to a single, new function.
- Look for functions that have similar purpose statements (specifications) and consume the same kind of data. Identify and eliminate redundancies.
- Look for groups of similar data definitions; if you can identify type parameters to abstract over, replace them with instances of a single, new, parametric data definition.
- Look for functions that take one or more arguments of sum, product, and arrow types. Identify which arguments are "inspected" (by `cond` or selectors) and which are "sealed" (ignored or passed to other functions). Decide if the decision to inspect or seal makes sense or if the code would be improved by deciding differently. Especially, look for arguments that are inspected but could be sealed.
- Rewrite or eliminate conditionals in which one case can subsume others.
- Look for recursive functions that consume lists and can be expressed using standard higher-order list functions.

- Look for uses of `foldl` and `foldr` that can be rewritten using `map` or `filter`.
- Look for recursive functions with similar structures, and replace them with new higher-order functions.
- Review type signatures of polymorphic functions. For each type variable, try substituting different actual types, such as image, Boolean, and list of number. Verify that *after* substitution, each signature accurately describes the types of data that you expect to flow into and out of the function.

6.4 Developing better guidance for conditionals

How should students design conditionals? What role(s) should `else` play? When we review a conditional expression, how do we tell if it's good or bad? How can a *student* tell if a conditional expression is good or bad? I can answer only in two situations:

- An experienced Haskell or ML programmer knows that pattern matching in `case` expressions is most easily understood when patterns are non-overlapping, so the behavior of the program is independent of the order in which the cases appear. Each case can be understood in isolation, without considering the others. The corresponding principle in the Racket teaching languages is that when `cond` is used to choose among alternatives in a sum type, each alternative should be identified by an appropriate predicate. For example, a function that consumes a list `xs` should use the predicates `(empty? xs)` and `(cons? xs)`; it should not use `else`. However, in the first edition of *How to Design Programs*, students will see `else` used more often than "`(cons? xs)`." In the second edition, "`(cons? xs)`" is used more often.
- When a `cond` uses just two predicates, they are nontrivial, and they are complements, use `else`.[12] For example, this code from a student would be clearer with `else`:

```
(cond [(look-across? tree close x y) ...]
      [(not (look-across? tree close x y)) ...])
```

Beyond these two situations, I don't know what to tell my students. And while I myself can usually look at a conditional and distinguish good from bad, I don't know how to teach graders to do it.

6.5 Assessing students' programs

The open problem that most affected my students' learning was that I found no clear, principled basis on which to assign grades. My staff and I got bogged down with grading, to a point where we could not give students timely feedback on their work—and without such feedback, students learn less and are less confident. My staff and I got bogged down because although we knew the big question we wanted to answer—whether our students were practicing systematic design—we could not figure out how, or on what scale, to evaluate systematic design.

Many instructors use a system of points. For example, Mitch Wand uses a detailed rubric graded on a 50-point scale and containing over 65 potential deductions. Unfortunately, this rubric is designed for beginning master's students, and it assumes an in-person code review. I did not understand the principles used to create the rubric and so could not adapt it for my situation. Also, just as instructors in Germany have special concerns about plagiarism (Bieniusa et al. 2008), I, like many other instructors in America, have concerns about wrangling with students over points.

[12] The second edition muddies these waters further by adding `if` to the Beginning Student Language. However, the 2013 draft uses over eight times fewer `if`s than `cond`s, and I plan to ignore them.

As a promising alternative to a points system, the education literature recommends that we identify *primary traits* to look for in students' work, and that we evaluate each trait on a scale with three to five choices (Stevens and Levi 2005; Walvoord and Anderson 2011). I have used primary traits successfully in our third and fourth courses. In principle, these courses use the same five-point scale that the NSF uses to grade proposals: Excellent, Very Good, Good, Fair, and Poor. In practice, the two extreme grades are rarely used and are easy to identify; "normal" work is graded on a three-point scale of Very Good (meets all expectations, equivalent to an American A), Good (does not meet all expectations but shows evidence of quality and significant learning), and Fair (the lowest passing grade).[13]

To apply this scale to a course, the instructor must characterize traits of work that is Very Good, Good, or Fair. But my staff and I were able to characterize only Very Good and Fair work:

- Very Good work may contain flaws, but it shows evidence throughout of having been developed using the design process.
- Fair work shows a *systemic* failure to apply the appropriate design recipe. For example, a solution would be graded Fair if every function's purpose statement merely restated the information given the function's signature.

We were not able to develop criteria by which to place students' work *between* Very Good (developed according to a design recipe) and Fair (systemic failure of design). And we are not comfortable grading on a two-point scale.

An ideal analysis of primary traits characterizes what is observed about each trait for each level of performance. But a partial analysis, in which only the highest levels of performance are characterized, can also be useful. For instance, Jordan Johnson has developed a list of 27 characteristics of exemplary work in *Program by Design*. To assign a grade, Johnson counts how often these characteristics appear, on a scale of Always, Usually, Sometimes, Seldom, and Never. He reports good results, but his classes are small—at most 14 students each. In my class of 40 students, we tried to replicate the "counting" approach for a just a few characteristics on a couple of homework assignments, with a coarser scale. But our graders reported that even a little counting was time-consuming and stressful, and I felt that the counts did not really characterize the quality of students' work. For students, I expect Johnson's characteristics would make a fine checklist, but for graders, the counting approach is too expensive and does not lead to an obvious grade.

Another alternative is to base grades on a program's functional correctness, perhaps as determined by testing. In *Program by Design*, test results are less important than systematic design, but students do wish to be rewarded for producing "working" code. Automated testing finds bugs effectively (Claessen and Hughes 2000; Crestani and Sperber 2010). But automated tests require well-specified interfaces, and an essential aspect of *Program by Design* is that the interfaces are designed by the *students*, not the instructor. Were I to specify interfaces for students to implement, I would be doing much of the design work that I want them to learn to do.[14]

Bieniusa et al. (2008) use a "semi-automatic" tool that checks a student's program and assigns a preliminary "score." But the tool appears to require interfaces to be specified. And unfortunately,

[13] At the extremes, Excellent work exceeds expectations and impresses the course staff (an American A-plus). Poor work shows evidence of serious deficiencies, typically by being substantially incomplete (a failing grade).

[14] I have developed prototype software that *discovers* students' interface designs by probing their code, but it relies on compile-time type checking.

Bieniusa et al. do not discuss the set of possible scores, algorithms by which scores are assigned, principles on which such algorithms are based, or instructions given to the teaching assistant who converts the preliminary score to a final score.

A principled grading method that lies outside the context of *Program by Design* is described by Edwards (2003): students submit both code and tests, and the submission is scored by multiplying three fractions: the fraction of the student's tests that are consistent with the problem statement, the fraction of the student's tests that the student's code passes, and the fraction of the *instructor's* code *covered* by the student's tests. Like other testing approaches, this approach limits students' freedom to design.

Program by Design's method enables yet another approach, with which we can assess functional correctness without limiting students' freedom to design: we assess correctness by reading purpose statements and unit tests (functional examples). DrRacket tells us which code has actually been executed. If a function's purpose statement is clear, the code has been tested, and the tests seem sufficient to validate the purpose statement, the function is deemed correct. This approach gives students the freedom to design interfaces, but compared with automated approaches, it is significantly more expensive.

7. Conclusion

Principled course design focuses not on material but on students: what they can do, and how we know they can do it (Wiggins and McTighe 2005). *How to Design Programs* is a great source of material, and prior work (Bieniusa et al. 2008; Crestani and Sperber 2010; Sperber and Crestani 2012) tells us a great deal about how to teach it. This paper adds to that work, showing some significant mistakes to avoid, and telling us more about students: what they learn to do, and where they do and don't struggle in learning to do it. Plenty of problems are still open, of which the most difficult is assessing whether students can do what we think they can do: we need reliable, cost-effective ways of knowing when and to what degree students are really programming by design.

Acknowledgments

For help with the manuscript, Stephen Bloch, Matthias Felleisen, Andrew Gallant, Shriram Krishnamurthi, Ben Shapiro, Mike Sperber, Aaron Tietz, Mitch Wand, and Jayme Woogerd.

For their thoughtful reviews, and especially their observations about the pedagogical value of programming with numbers, the anonymous referees. And for an unusually wide-ranging and thorough review, Referee 1.

For analysis of senior surveys and data about Tufts faculty, Dawn Terkla and Lauren Conoscenti.

For help preparing the way, Sam Guyer, Ben Hescott, Kathleen Fisher, and Carla Brodley.

For preliminary planning and for learning portfolios, Ariel Hamlin.

For educational matters, Annie Soisson and Donna Qualters. And for pointers to even more education papers, Ben Shapiro.

For help teaching, in addition to those named in the text, many members of the `plt-edu` mailing list, including Stephen Bloch, Matthew Flatt, Gregor Kiczales, Shriram Krishnamurthi, Viera Proulx, and Mitch Wand. Especially Stephen and Viera.

For help above and beyond the call of duty, provided to me and to my staff, Matthias Felleisen.

For making it happen, the students and staff of COMP 50, Fall 2013.

References

Harold Abelson and Gerald Jay Sussman. 1985. *Structure and Interpretation of Computer Programs*. McGraw-Hill, New York.

Susan A. Ambrose, Michael W. Bridges, Michele DiPietro, Marsha C. Lovett, Marie K. Norman, and Richard E. Mayer. 2010. *How Learning Works: Seven Research-Based Principles for Smart Teaching*. Jossey-Bass higher and adult education series. Wiley.

Annette Bieniusa, Markus Degen, Phillip Heidegger, Peter Thiemann, Stefan Wehr, Martin Gasbichler, Michael Sperber, Marcus Crestani, Herbert Klaeren, and Eric Knauel. 2008. HtDP and DMdA in the battlefield: A case study in first-year programming instruction. In *FDPE '08: Proceedings of the 2008 International Workshop on Functional and Declarative Programming in Education*, pages 1–12, New York, NY. ACM.

Richard Bird and Philip Wadler. 1988. *Introduction to Functional Programming*. Prentice Hall, New York.

Stephen Bloch. 2010. *Picturing Programs: An Introduction to Computer Programming*. College Publications (Kings College London).

Frederick P. Brooks, Jr. 1975. *The Mythical Man-Month*. Addison Wesley, Reading, MA.

Hugh Burkhardt and Alan H Schoenfeld. 2003. Improving educational research: Toward a more useful, more influential, and better-funded enterprise. *Educational Researcher*, 32(9):3–14.

Koen Claessen and John Hughes. 2000 (September). QuickCheck: a lightweight tool for random testing of Haskell programs. *Proceedings of the Fifth ACM SIGPLAN International Conference on Functional Programming (ICFP'00)*, in *SIGPLAN Notices*, 35(9):268–279.

Marcus Crestani and Michael Sperber. 2010 (September). Experience Report: Growing programming languages for beginning students. *Proceedings of the Fifteenth ACM SIGPLAN International Conference on Functional Programming (ICFP'10)*, in *SIGPLAN Notices*, 45(9):229–234.

Stephen H. Edwards. 2003 (September). Improving student performance by evaluating how well students test their own programs. *Journal on Educational Resources in Computing*, 3(3).

Matthias Felleisen, Robert Bruce Findler, Matthew Flatt, and Shriram Krishnamurthi. 2001. *How to Design Programs: An Introduction to Programming and Computing*. MIT Press, Cambridge, MA, first edition.

Matthias Felleisen, Robert Bruce Findler, Matthew Flatt, and Shriram Krishnamurthi. 2004a. The structure and interpretation of the Computer Science curriculum. *Journal of Functional Programming*, 14(4):365–378.

Matthias Felleisen, Robert Bruce Findler, Matthew Flatt, and Shriram Krishnamurthi. 2004b. The TeachScheme! project: Computing and programming for every student. *Computer Science Education*, 14(1):55–77.

Matthias Felleisen, Robert Bruce Findler, Matthew Flatt, and Shriram Krishnamurthi. 2009 (August). A functional I/O system or, fun for freshman kids. *Proceedings of the Fourteenth ACM SIGPLAN International Conference on Functional Programming (ICFP'09)*, in *SIGPLAN Notices*, 44(9):47–58.

Robert Bruce Findler, John Clements, Cormac Flanagan, Matthew Flatt, Shriram Krishnamurthi, Paul Steckler, and Matthias Felleisen. 2002. DrScheme: A programming environment for Scheme. *Journal of Functional Programming*, 12(2):159–182.

Robert Bruce Findler and Matthias Felleisen. 2002 (September). Contracts for higher-order functions. *Proceedings of the Seventh ACM SIGPLAN International Conference on Functional Programming (ICFP'02),* in *SIGPLAN Notices*, 37(9):48–59.

David R. Hanson. 1996. *C Interfaces and Implementations*. Addison Wesley.

John Hughes. 1989 (April). Why functional programming matters. *The Computer Journal*, 32(2):98–107.

Michael A. Jackson. 1975. *Principles of Program Design*. Academic Press, London.

Samuel N. Kamin. 1990. *Programming Languages: An Interpreter-Based Approach*. Addison-Wesley, Reading, MA.

John McCarthy. 1960 (April). Recursive functions of symbolic expressions and their computation by machine, part I. *Communications of the ACM*, 3(4):184–195.

Bertrand Meyer. 1997. *Object-Oriented Software Construction*. Prentice-Hall, Englewood Cliffs, NJ, second edition.

Norman Ramsey. 2016. *Programming Languages: Build, Prove, and Compare*. Cambridge University Press. Forthcoming.

Emmanuel Schanzer, Kathi Fisler, and Shriram Krishnamurthi. 2013. Bootstrap: Going beyond programming in after-school computer science. In *SPLASH-E (Education track of OOPSLA/SPLASH)*.

Michael Sperber and Marcus Crestani. 2012. Form over function—teaching beginners how to construct programs. In *Scheme and Functional Programming 2012*. At press time, the workshop proceedings had not yet been published, but the paper could be found at `schemeworkshop.org`.

Guy Lewis Steele, Jr. 1990. *Common LISP: The Language*. Digital Press, Newton, Mass., 2nd edition.

Danelle D. Stevens and Antonia Levi. 2005. *Introduction to Rubrics: An Assessment Tool to Save Grading Time, Convey Effective Feedback, and Promote Student Learning*. Stylus.

Gerald Jay Sussman and Guy Lewis Steele, Jr. 1975 (December). Scheme: An interpreter for extended lambda calculus. MIT AI Memo No. 349, reprinted in *Higher-Order and Symbolic Computation* 11(4):405–439, Dec 1998.

Barbara E. Walvoord and Virginia Johnson Anderson. 2011. *Effective Grading: A Tool for Learning and Assessment in College*. Wiley.

Grant P. Wiggins and Jay McTighe. 2005. *Understanding by Design*. ACSD, Alexandria, VA, second edition.

A. Teaching experience

My teaching experience includes a track record of creating required programming courses that have long-term impact. One measure of this impact is our university-wide survey of graduating students, which asks them about highlights of their four years at Tufts. Students identify up to three faculty or staff who had a "significant impact" on their development, and they identify one course that exemplifies "what a truly excellent college course should be."

In aggregate, students surveyed in 2012 and 2013 were taught by 700 to 750 faculty, of whom they named 300 to 500 on the surveys. In 2012, 16 graduating students named me as having a significant impact on their development, and 11 named one of my courses as an exemplar of excellence. In 2013 the numbers were 16 and 18, respectively. (Students named both the third and fourth courses in our programming sequence.) The responses to my teaching place me, among the 40% to 70% of our faculty who are named on the surveys, in the 98th, 98th, 95th, and 99th percentiles.

Supplemental material

A technical-report version of this paper is accompanied by additional appendices, which are referred to in the text as Web Appendix B through Web Appendix E. These appendices have not been peer-reviewed.

SML# in Industry: A Practical ERP System Development

Atsushi Ohori *, Katsuhiro Ueno* †

Tohoku University

{ohori, katsu}@riec.tohoku.ac.jp

Kazunori Hoshi, Shinji Nozaki, Takashi Sato, Tasuku Makabe, Yuki Ito

NEC Solution Innovetors, Ltd. ‡

{k-hoshi, s-nozaki}@wh.jp.nec.com, t-sato@yk.jp.nec.com

{t-makabe, yu-ito}@wr.jp.nec.com

Abstract

This paper reports on our industry-academia project of using a functional language in business software production. The general motivation behind the project is our ultimate goal of adopting an ML-style higher-order typed functional language in a wide range of ordinary software development in industry. To probe the feasibility and identify various practical problems and needs, we have conducted a 15 month pilot project for developing an enterprise resource planning (ERP) system in SML#. The project has successfully completed as we have planned, demonstrating the feasibility of SML#. In particular, seamless integration of SQL and direct C language interface are shown to be useful in reliable and efficient development of a data intensive business application. During the program development, we have found several useful functional programming patterns and a number of possible extensions of an ML-style language with records. This paper reports on the project details and the lessons learned from the project.

Categories and Subject Descriptors D.3.2 [*Language Classifications*]: Applicative (Functional) Programming

Keywords Standard ML; Business Application; Database Programming; Record Polymorphism

1. Introduction

Advantages of ML-style polymorphic languages have been widely recognized in academia. Higher-order functions allow programmers to write elaborate code in a concise and declarative manner. Polymorphic typing and a sophisticated module system enhance the reliability of the system through static type checking and data abstraction. Despite these advantages, ML-style languages have not yet been widely used in industry. Among major software companies in Japan, for example, very little is known about ML and there is virtually no experience in using ML in software production. As a developer of an ML-style language SML# [13], we find this situation unfortunate. As a software company, we also find an ML-style language as a significant potential in enhancing the productivity and reliability in our ordinary software production. Declarative programming, static type inference, signature checking, safe and scalable module system should all have significant positive impact not only in symbolic computation such as theorem provers and compilers but also in ordinary software development such as inventory management, management accounting, and resource planning.

Based on these general observations, NEC Solution Innovetors, Ltd. and Tohoku University have started joint research aiming at establishing a programming environment of SML# for general software development. SML# is a new ML-style language being developed at Tohoku University [13]. In addition to its conformance with the Definition of Standard ML [8], it supports several practically useful features including: seamless integration SQL (the standard database query language), direct C language interface, concurrent GC and native multithreading support on multicore CPU. Among them, seamless SQL integration and direct C language interface should be particularly useful in data intensive business software development.

As the first step in this endeavor, we have conducted a 15 month pilot project to develop an enterprise resource planning (ERP) system in SML#, which will be used in NEC Solution Innovetors, Ltd. to manage the company's projects and related resources. The goal of this project is to probe the feasibility of SML# and to identify various practical problems and needs in using SML# for ordinary software development in industry. As we shall explain in the next section, an ERP system is chosen by considering this goal. The system development has successfully completed, and the ERP system is currently under evaluation with the actual databases containing the company's project, personnel and accounting information. Although we do not have statistical measurement of the productivity of using SML# at this moment, the development has been completed as we planned with the expected productivity. The SML# features of the seamless database integration and direct C library interface have indeed been shown to be useful.

In addition to the completed ERP system, we have obtained project management skills in designing and developing business applications in ML. As a software development project using a new language in a company, we had to manage a number of problems including programming education, software quality control, and design method. After sorting out these problems, the program development has been smoothly done with a satisfactory result. During the development, we have found several useful polymorphic pro-

* Atsushi Ohori and Katsuhiro Ueno have been partially supported by Grant-in-aid for scientific research (B), grant no:25280019.

† Katsuhiro Ueno has also been partially supported by Grant-in-aid for scientific research (young investigator B), grant no:24700021.

‡ On April 1st, 2014, NEC Software Tohoku, Ltd. became a part of NEC Solution Innovators, Ltd.

ICFP '14, September 1–6, 2014, Gothenburg, Sweden.
Copyright © 2014 ACM 978-1-4503-2873-9 /14/09...$15.00.
http://dx.doi.org/10.1145/2628136.2628164

gramming idioms that can serve as *functional design patterns* for data intensive business software development in ML. Another important assets we have acquired through this project are the insights toward improving ML-style languages. Experience with database programming revealed the needs and interesting research issues concerning flexible manipulation of records in a polymorphic language. These lessons learned from our project should also be useful for anyone who plans to adopt an ML-style language in industry.

The rest of the paper is organized as follows. Section 2 describes the overview of the system we have developed and miscellaneous problems we have tackled in carrying out the project. Section 3 describes the system architecture and the details of the development. Section 4 discusses evaluation of the project management and new findings through the project. Section 5 discusses the lessons learned through the project and suggests future improvement of ML-style languages. Section 6 reports the current status and initial evaluation of the developed system. Section 7 concludes the paper with a brief description of our future plan.

2. The Project Overview

This section outlines the system we have developed, and discusses miscellaneous problems we have overcome out in carrying out the project.

2.1 The target ERP system

We have set our goal to develop an ERP system that has the following functionality.

1. It reports the current status of each software project in the company based on the company database which are updated frequently.
2. It simulates the future costs and expected profits of existing and planned projects under a given set of parameters on resources entered by the operator.

There have been growing needs among managers and executives in the company for accurate estimate of each project status at any given time, which is not easily available in the currently used system. So an ERP system having these functionalities is itself a highly desired system in the company. In addition, this target system is appropriate for our purpose of probing the feasibility and identifies various practical problems in using SML#. Firstly, it represents a typical business application involving extensive database accesses, various business logic programming, and report generation. Secondly, since we do not have much previous experience in developing a similar system, the development must contain an entire software development process: requirement identification, system architecture selection, system design, program development, testing and evaluation. Finally, through the use of the developed system in NEC Solution Innovetors, Ltd., we can evaluate the system's maintainability and extensibility as well as its performance and overall quality.

2.2 Miscellaneous issues in carrying out the project

To carry out the first software development project using ML in the company, we had to sort out a number of problems before starting the program development. We list some of them below.

- Programming education.

  Since none of the software engineers in NEC Solution Innovetors, Ltd. had previous experience in ML, we have set up an education course on ML programming and the related techniques. We have designed and given a 6 day intensive course, covering ML programming basics, SML# features, system programming, and an example system development.

- Acquiring domain knowledge.

  As stated earlier, we do not have much previous experience in an ERP system development. So we have studied the basics of management accounting, and have analyzed the company's accounting principles and resources. Sharing these domain knowledge has been crucial for our combined development team to understand, analyze and review the program code.

- Software quality control.

  The software development must conforms to the ordinary quality standard set by the company. This requires to make documents for: requirement definition, primary design, functional design, program design, and test design. Since there is no standard method available for ML, we had adopted the existing standards for most of the cases and have adjusted during the project . For example, we have adapted class diagram with ML-style signatures for program design.

- Design method.

  We had to develop and share a design method for the system, i.e. how to analyze the problem and how to represent it as a programming system. For this purpose, again, we have found very little resources for ML-based system development. As a compromising starting point, we have adopted the model-view-controller approach [6], and have tried to refine their components for ML based system. One positive outcome of this effort is *abstract model construction* we shall present in Section 4.1.

Once we had sorted out these problems, program development has been largely smooth.

3. The ERP System

This section describes the architecture design and the details of the system development.

3.1 The system architecture

To design the overall architecture of this system, we regard the ERP system as a web application and decompose the system into its major components by adopting the model-view-controller architecture. We then design the system by elaborating each component. The following are the final structure of the system.

- **The Model.** This part consists of SML# modules realizing the services the ERP system offers, including current status reporting and a several forms of simulations. The set of modules are organized into the following two layers.

  1. *Persistent data (raw models).* Most of the data are stored in a large relational database system serving through SQL Server. Figure 1 shows a simplified ER diagram of the database schema. In the actual database, table names and column names are represented in Japanese and they are directly handled by SML# programs. It contains the current status of company's various resources, including projects, employees, contracts and orders and is updated frequently. This database is directly accessed through SML# SQL integration [12]. In addition, the system reads data files in CVS and TVS formats, containing semi-stable data such as the current labor costs for each rank of employees, and the budgets of the current half year term.

     These data are represented as a set of ML modules and are regarded as *raw models* used by the *abstract models* described below.

  2. *Abstract models.* They are modules that realize the required services such as status reporting and several form of simu-

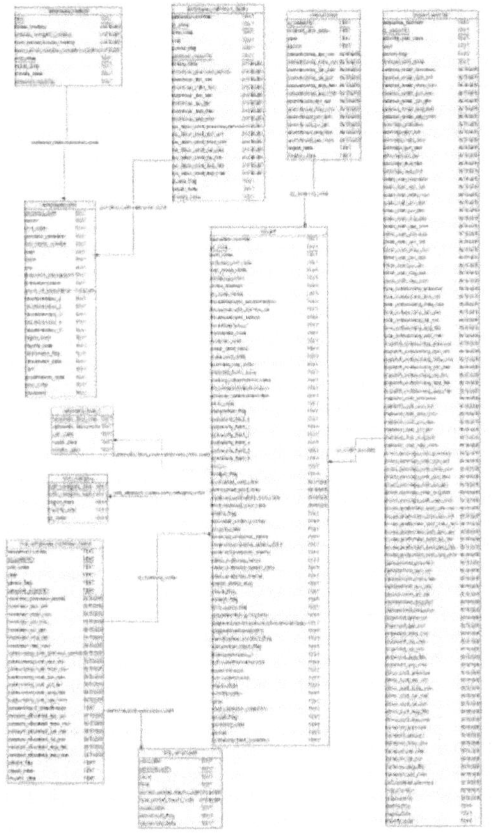

Figure 1. A Simplified ER Diagram of the Database

lations. They are implemented by ML programs using raw models.

This two-layered organization is our new design patterns that refines conventional MVC pattern, which we describe in details in Section 4.1,

- **The Controller.** A set of functions that are called from the dispatcher function to perform appropriate action according to the user request. The dispatcher function is called from `main` function of the web application framework described below, and performs the following loop.
  - get a user request,
  - initialize the time,
  - analyze the user request and call the corresponding controller function,
  - generate a view and return a response to the user.
- **The View.** This part consists of a set of ClearSilver template files for various report formats. These files are manipulated by the SML# ClearSilver binding described below.
- **Libraries**
  - Web Server Framework. A simple framework written in SML# that provides datatypes for requests, responses and forms, and the sever function

    ```
    main : (request -> response) -> unit
    ```
  - Common Libraries including those for CVS and TVS file parsers, time and date format conversions.

```
_require "basis.smi"
_require "./form.smi"
_require "./Log.smi"
_require "./Exception.smi"
_require "./Fcgi.smi"
structure Server =
struct
  datatype method = GET | POST
  type request = ...
  type response = ...
  val main : (request -> response) -> unit
  val uriOf : string list -> string
end
```

Figure 2. Interface File Example : Web Server Framework

  - Global functions for system configuration and logging.
  - External (third party) Libraries
    - FastCGI for web server framework. C API (`FCGI_getchar` etc) are directly imported through SML# C FFI.
    - JSON parser. We have used Standard ML of New Jersey's implementation.
    - ClearSilver HTML Template System. We write a simple C stub functions and import them through SML# C FFI.
    - JavaScript Libraries: Bootstrap, Prototype, jQuery, ccchart.

3.2 The development details

The development has been done in two stages: the prototype development and the development of the system version 1. About 30% of prototype codes are re-used, and the rest are re-written in the version 1 system. Most coding has been done by NEC Solution Innovetors, Ltd. Tohoku University has developed the web server framework and provided the necessary language extensions and supports. To achieve industry strength ML coding, we have held weekly meeting for code review and re-factoring. This has been quite effective in enhancing the quality of the system and boosting ML programming skills of the project members.

ML components have been developed using the separate compilation feature of SML#. For each major module, we first decide the initial interface by writing an interface file of SML#. As an example, Figure 2 shows the interface file of the web server framework. Using these interface files, we have developed each component separately. For each SML# source file, SML# separate compiler produces an object file in the standard ELF format. SML# object files, C object files and libraries are then linked together by SML#, which is invoked through the Unix `make` system. This model works effectively among our team.

The developed system consists of about 25 k lines of code excluding third-party libraries, among which 12 k lines are written in SML#. The code size details are given in the following table.

type	files	total size (k lines)
SML# interface file	61	2.1
SML# source file	61	9.7
ClearSilver template	17	3.5
c source file	1	0.09
html files	10	5.4
css files	11	1.2
js files	6	2.4

The following table shows the summary of the production costs.

Figure 3. Information Window of the System

type	activities	man-hour
prototype	education & analysis	320
	design	320
	coding and test	1120
version 1	education & analysis	640
	design	320
	coding and test	1280

A new member has joined at the start of version 1 system. The relatively high education cost is inevitable for this project that adopts a new language and new method. Considering this and the fact that we have developed an entirely new system from scratch with problem analysis and prototype developing, we regard the development of the project efficient, and the overall development quite satisfactory.

As we shall report in Section 6, the developed system is currently under evaluation. Overall, the system shows expected behavior. Figures 3 shows a simulation window.

4. Evaluation of the Project and New Findings

As we shall discuss in detail in the next section, we have found several needs of improvements of an ML-style functional language, but the overall development has been quite satisfactory. We have confirmed that functional programming and SML# features have contributed to the productivity of the project, as we have expected. We have also found and developed some useful programming patterns for data intensive business applications. In this section, we discuss some of them below.

4.1 Abstract model construction that refines MVC pattern

We started the system design by adopting the popular MVC pattern, where the notion of models represent data with a set of procedures. In a simple web application such as a system to display a picture associated to some key, a model naturally corresponds to persistent data stored in a database system. The required procedures are retrieving, updating, and deleting the designated data element. In this simple situation, a database can be properly abstracted through object-relational mapping. However, in a typical business application such as the one we have developed, large and complex data are stored in a relational database as a highly normalized (in the sense of relational database theory [7]) set of flat relations. For example, the company database we had to deal with in this project (whose outline is shown in Figure 1) has 15 tables, each has 4 to 103 columns. The total number of columns is 395. To retrieve a data for each user request, we have to make complicated database joins among a subset of 15 tables, taking account of the database schema design, and to project the results on some particular columns. User responses are then computed from the retrieved column values. We do not think that a database consisting of 15 tables with 395 columns is exceptionally large. For such a large relational database with highly normalized schema, it is very difficult to make an object relational mapping that can deal with various user requests.

```
fun findEmployeeNameByCode employeeCode =
  let
    infix andAlso ==
    val r = SQL.fetchOne
      (_sqleval
        (let
           open SQL
         in
           _sql db =>
             select #e.NAME as employeeName
             from #db.M_PDBS as e
             where (#e.PCD == (toSQL employeeCode))
         end)
        (DBConnector.conn ()))
  in
    #employeeName r
  end
```

Figure 4. SQL integration used in abstract model construction

The seamless integration of SQL in an ML-style language achieved by SML# provides an ideal solution to this problem. In SML#, database queries (SQL commands) are polymorphically typed ordinary ML expressions denoting a list of records. It is then a routine matter to use higher-order functions and to construct a desired data structure on top of whatever complex record structures returned by a query expression. We conceptually regard this layer of computation, *abstract model construction*, which refines the usual MVC pattern, i.e. the conventional *model* M in MVC pattern is refined to two layers of *raw models* of databases and *abstract models* constructed by higher-order functions on top of raw models.

Figure 4 shows a fragment of a simple function that is used in abstract model construction, where we replace the actual Japanese column names with simple labels. We note that `_sql db => select ...` is an expression having a polymorphic type, and not an ad-hoc embedding. See [12] for the details. This property guarantees complete static typechecking through ML's polymorphic type inference. This feature completely relieves problematic runtime query failure due to schema mismatch. Considering the size of databases and complexity of SQL queries used, this property should otherwise be difficult to obtain. Seamless SQL integration in SML# enables the programmer to develop required abstract models through easy, declarative, and type safe programming. This is the most contributing factor in productivity of our development.

4.2 Data intensive programming with record polymorphism

Record polymorphism of SML# provides a powerful mechanism for modular programming in data intensive application development. As we mentioned, database query results contain labeled records with a large number of fields. For example, a frequently appearing typical type in our system contains 35 fields. Each module processes only some subset of the fields. To organize a system consisting of a number of such modules in a modular and type safe way, record polymorphism plays a central role. For example, a utility function that filters out low-ranked software projects has the following interface type

```
val excludeE : ['a#{rank:rank}. 'a list -> 'a list]
```

which represents the precise polymorphism and type constraint this utility function has.

In addition to writing various utility functions through record polymorphism, we have also found several *functional design patterns* that have general usefulness. Here we show a typical one below. In our system, we generate result HTML files through ClearSilver templates. This is done by filling each hole in a template with specific values. In order to organize this process in a modular and type safe way, we find the following pattern using polymorphic record update, which we present below. This pattern has not yet fully exploited in the current system; we plan to re-factor the system with this pattern in near future. Suppose we have two attributes A and B and that they are independently computed by two functions fillA and fillB. This is a simplified model of decomposing the template filling task into a set of independent modules. In an actual situation, {A, B} becomes a set of sets of attributes. This situation is cleanly represented by the following design pattern. We represent each field of type τ as τ option, where NONE indicates a non-filled hole and SOME v indicates the hole filled with v. The function fillA is then implemented as a function of the form

```
fun fillA (x as {A = NONE, ...}) =
      let val v = computing a value to be filled in A
      in x # {A = v}
      end
  | fillA (x as {A = SOME _, ...}) =
      raise AlreadyFilled
```

where x # {A = v} is polymorphic record update operation which creates a new record from x by modifying the field A. This function has the following polymorphic type.

```
fillA : ['a#{A: τ option}. 'a -> 'a]
```

This type precisely represents the fact that fillA operates only on field A and that it can compose with any function that operates on any other fields. fillB has a similar structure. A template package is defined as a module containing the following

```
val init = {A=NONE, B=NONE}
fun check (x as {A=SOME _, B= SOME _}) = x
  | check _ = raise ThereAreMissingField
fun fill F = check (F init)
```

where init represents the empty template, and fill invokes hole filling function F and dynamically ensures that all the fields are filled through function check. The controller to dispatch fillA and fillB can then be implemented as

```
fun dispatch AB () = fill (fillB o fillA)
```

by composing fillA and fillB functions.

This record pattern scales to set of subsets of fields and is generally helpful in compositional development of a component having multiple attributes/aspects.

4.3 Development with best-of-breed components

In a large system development in industry, selecting best-of-breed components from available choices is essential. The direct C interface of SML# has greatly contributed to this practice in the project. As we show in Section 3, we have used several external libraries such as FastCGI and ClearSilver. Figure 5 shows a fragment of FastCGI module written and used in the project. In this code, FCGI_··· is a C function provided by the FCGI package. With this feature, we can directly import a library package almost instantly as far as the package provides a C API. SML#'s separate compilation system links the referenced packages. Through this mechanism, the programmer can select best suited packages from a rich collection of library packages with C API.

```
structure FCGI =
struct
  exception IO of string
  val accept = _import "FCGI_Accept" : () -> int
  val finish = _import "FCGI_Finish" : () -> ()
  val setExitStatus =
      _import "FCGI_SetExitStatus" : int -> ()
  val FCGI_getchar =
      _import "FCGI_getchar" : () -> int
  fun getchar () =
      SOME (chr (FCGI_getchar ()))
      handle Chr => NONE
   ...
end
```

Figure 5. FCGI binding through SML# C FFI

5. Insights Towards Better Record Programming

Manipulation of record structures is one of the central aspects in our ERP system. This should be true for many data-intensive business applications. In textbook examples, records are rather small and are typically used as parameters to a function or a datatype constructor. In business applications using databases, however, we frequently deal with records with a large number of fields. Experience with record programming in our project have given us various invaluable insights towards extending and improving record programming primitives in SML# and ML-style functional languages. In this section, we discuss some important ones.

5.1 Uniform operations on a set of fields.

A record often contains a set of related fields such as labor cost fields of all the months. We have often encountered cases of writing similar or same code for each such field. Such a program would become much more concise and maintainable if the language supports uniform operations such as map and fold for a set of record fields. Using first-class polymorphic field selectors, this can already be achieved in SML# to some extent. For example, summing up a given list F of fields in a record X can be coded as follows.

```
foldr (fn (f,S) =>(f X + S)) 0 F
```

For example, in SML#, we can write the following function

```
fn X => foldr (fn (f,S) =>(f X + S)) 0 [#jan, #feb]
  : ['a#{feb: int, jan: int}. 'a -> int]
```

that adds up jan and feb fields in a given record. This polymorphic idiom is itself useful for cases where fields are accumulated to a single value. However, we often encounter the cases where each field of one record is accumulated to the same or corresponding field in another record. To deal with this situation, it is desirable for the language to contain a mechanism to treat labels as first-class entities so that we can write, for example, the code of the form:

```
fn (X,Y) =>
   foldr (fn (L,Y) => Y # {L = #L X + #L Y})
         Y [<jan>, <feb>]
```

This pseudo code would increment each of jan and feb fields in Y record with the corresponding field in X record. <jan> and <feb> are hypothetical "label literals" which are bound to L and used as a label. This mechanism would significantly improve database programming. At this moment, we do not know whether or not such extension is possible. We regard this an interesting future work on ML-style languages with records.

It has been suggested to us that "Fieldslib" of Camlp4 [14] provides first class labels through type-directed code generation using the language module system. We note however that the functionality we want is the ability to abstract a polymorphic pattern that access multiple records and creates new records according to a given set of labels. In a language where record types must be declared and field access are monomorphic, even addressing the problem of flexible and modular manipulation of record structure is difficult. We also note that, as shown above, field access functions in SML# are already first-class polymorphic functions, on which we can map and fold.

5.2 Type-safe dynamic views on records.

Another insight we have gained through our database programming is the usefulness of customized "views" on a large flat record. In a relational database schema, each table contains a normalized flat record. For those relational schema, we often encountered cases where some fields are properties of an entity determined by a key stored in another field. In such case, we have to write codes that transform a flat record into a nested record. Although there is no difficulty, writing each such code is tedious and makes the entire program lengthy. Since the code is determined by the source record type and the target record type, language support to provide a view that automatically generates those code from types is highly desirable. We believe that previous results on functional type isomorphism [1, 5] can be used to integrate such a mechanism in SML# and other ML-like languages with records.

Another observation we have during database programming in this project is that such a view should also support uniform treatment of implicitly enforced *non-null* constraint. In a relational schema, each field can contain the so called "null value" (unless otherwise explicitly specified as *non-null*). In our SQL integration, a field with null value is represented as an option type. However, this modeling is over strict; in may cases non-null constraint is omitted and context information such as some value in some field determines that theses fields are restricted to be non-null values. In such case, a view mechanism that dynamically checks and converts τ `option` to τ would be quite useful. The programmer then invokes a view only once when he/she knows that some set of fields are non-null. This mechanism would free the programmer from tedious burden of checking the case of `NONE` and writing error handing code. Again we believe this mechanism can be incorporated based on existing research on type isomorphisms mentioned above.

5.3 Natural join in a programming language

The pattern for template filling we have shown in Section 4.2 works reasonably well but is not ideal. It uses `NONE` of an option type to represent non-filled hole. A better approach would be to join locally computed set of attributes together to obtain a complete set of attributes to be filled in a template. Let τ to be the set of attributes required for a template. Since τ usually consists of a large set of attribute fields, we would like to decompose it into a set $\{\tau_1, \ldots, \tau_n\}$, each of which is independently computed. In relational databases, this problem corresponds to decomposing a large relation τ into a set of relations $\{\tau_1, \ldots, \tau_n\}$. The desired relation is obtained by joining the set of component relations. In the relational model, this natural join operation is restricted to flat relations, but can be generalized to a term algebra containing records and sets [2, 9]. Using the notions developed in those works, we can regard this decomposition as an equation

$$\tau_1 \sqcup \cdots \sqcup \tau_n = \tau$$

where $A \sqcup B$ is the least upper bound of two structures A and B. In our setting, we can think of this as an operation that recursively joins nested records. For example.

$$\begin{aligned} &\{\texttt{id:int,proj:}\{\texttt{name:string}\}\} \\ \sqcup\ &\{\texttt{id:int,proj:}\{\texttt{rank:int}\}\} \\ =\ &\{\texttt{id:int, proj:}\{\texttt{name:string,rank:int}\}\} \end{aligned}$$

Using this notion, the template filling example can be better represented as follows.

We independently write functions to compute partial values

```
val fill₁ : unit -> τ₁
...
val fillₙ : unit -> τₙ
```

each of which generates a piece of information as a nested record τ_i. The template module can be

```
fun fill (F:τ) = ...
```

which simply takes all the necessary information and fills the template completely. Its type safety is straightforwardly specified by the type constraint of nested record type τ. Dispatching the set $\texttt{fill}_1$, ..., $\texttt{fill}_n$ of hole filling methods can be done

```
fill (Join (fill₁ (), ..., fillₙ ()))
```

where `Join` is a nested application of a polymorphic nested record joining function `_join` having the constrained type of the form:

```
_join : 'a * 'b -> 'c where 'c = 'a ⊔ 'b
```

This solution is much more robust and modular since the completeness and consistence of the information needed to fill all the template holes are represented and checked by the type system.

Although the current SML# does not support this operation, the necessary type theoretical machinery has been well established in [3, 10] and a language having this operation has been proposed [11]. A preliminary extension to the SML# type system has been done. In the extension, the following code can be written

```
val fn (x,y) => _join(x,y);
  : ['a#{}, 'b#{}, 'c#{}('a,'b). 'a * 'b -> 'c]
```

where `'c#{}('a,'b)` represents the least upper bound constraint. Currently, this extension is only for typing natural join of SQL commands, and does not support runtime execution. We hope that with further development of the implementation method, we can support user-level natural joins on nested records.

Another possible approach to this problem would be to provide those elaborate record operations through language independent query [4]. It remains to be investigated how language independent query can be uniformly integrated in a host language polymorphic type system.

6. Initial Evaluation of the Developed System

Our industry-academia project of developing the ERP system has been completed at the end of March 2014. The current status of the system and our plan of its deployment are the following.

1. After the completion, the system has been put into a trial use in a department of NEC Solution Innovetors, Ltd., where the development team belongs. The department consists of about 60 engineers.
2. The trial use have continued in the department for a few months. During this period, we have improved and polished the system.
3. After the improvement, the company plans to start using the system in the division consisting of 5 departments for thorough

evaluation of the system's functionality and usability. This evaluation will be completed before September 2014.

4. After September 2014, the company plans to deploy the system in the entire Tohoku branch of NEC Solution Innovetors, Ltd.

This current plan is almost exact scenario we had drawn up at the start of the project in December 2013. At that time, the Tohoku branch of NEC Solution Innovetors, Ltd. was an independent company located in Tohoku, called NEC Software Tohoku, Ltd., which was merged into NEC Solution Innovetors, Ltd. in April, 2014.

The steps 1 and 2 of the above deployment process have progressed as we expected, and we have a positive perspective of completing the entire deployment process as planned. In particular, improvement of the system has been smoothly done. We have so far found several problems and shortcomings of the system. Some major ones include the following.

- Long system start-up time. The system start-up time was much longer than we expected. Our analysis showed that this delay was due to redundant database connection calls and redundant calls to a date computation function.
- Insufficient treatment of incomplete database states. One main goal of the system is to obtain real-time status of each project. To achieve this, the system uses the data stored in the company database, which is continuously updated. It is then inevitable that some data such as workloads of some project is partially filled, with some missing values. Such incomplete database states showed anomalous results.
- Insufficient problem analysis and design. At the time of designing the system, we analyzed the company's business model and constructed our internal data model by extending the existing one for real-time status reporting. During the evaluation, we found that certain financial data in the company are only meaning full at the end of each month, and due to this, the system behaved anomalously in its few functions.

We have successfully improved all the problems so far found. All the improvements have been done mostly by the company team. For long initialization time, we have reused an established database connection and have factored out date computation, resulting in significant reduction of the start-up time. For the incomplete database states, we have added codes to check the anomalous value, to warn the operator and to solicit the operator for missing values. We have also improved our internal model so that the system estimates those values that are only available at the end of each month. These improvements have been done quite smoothly and efficiently without much help of the academic team. This experience confirms our confidence in maintaining and extending functional codes written in SML#.

7. Conclusions and Future Plan

We have reported on our project of developing an enterprise resource planning (ERP) System using a functional programming language SML#. This project is our initial attempt to establish a programming environment for an ML-style higher-order typed functional language in wide range of ordinary software development in industry. The development project has successfully completed as we have planned, demonstrating the feasibility of SML# in software production in industry. Evaluation of the project has confirmed the usefulness of the seamless SQL integration and direct C interface of SML#. By defining an abstract model layers on top of database access through higher-order functions, the ERP system has been easily structured in a natural and type-safe manner. The project has also given invaluable insights on possible future extensions to an ML-style language for data intensive business application developments, including uniform operations on record fields, type-safe dynamic views on records, and introduction of natural join on nested records.

This is our initial attempt toward establishing a functional programming environment for our general software development in industry, and a number of challenging issues remain to be investigated before a functional language such as SML# can become a mainstream production language. Here we only mention one of them which is, we believe, the most important one. Throughout the project, which has been mainly carried out in NEC Solution Innovetors, Ltd., a major software company in Japan, we have frequently encountered a difficulty of analyzing a problem and making a basic program design for each programming task. This has been mainly due to the lack of common abstraction concepts in breaking down a problem into programming component in a functional language. To improve this situation, we have identified and shared several patterns during the project both in coerce and fine grain. The notion of abstract model construction on database access we reported in Section 4.1 and the polymorphic record update pattern in Section 4.2 are typical examples. Collecting such useful functional programming patterns and sharing them with industry will be of great help in disseminating functional languages in industry. As one of important future work of our academia-industry collaboration, we would like to collect such patterns, and ultimately to establish functional programming methodology that is readily usable in industry.

Acknowledgments

We thank the anonymous reviewers for helpful comments and suggestions for improving the presentation of the paper.

References

[1] G. Barthe. A computational view of implicit coercions in type theory. *Mathematical. Structures in Comp. Sci.*, 15(5):839–874, 2005.

[2] P. Buneman, A. Jung, and A. Ohori. Using powerdomains to generalize relational databases. *Theoretical Computer Science*, 91(1):23–56, 1991.

[3] P. Buneman and A. Ohori. Polymorphism and type inference in database programming. *ACM Transactions on Database Systems*, 21(1):30–74, 1996.

[4] J. Cheney. S. Lindley, and P. Wadler. A practical theory of language-integrated query. In *Proc. ACM International Conference on Functional Programming*, 403–416, 2013.

[5] R. Di Cosmo. A short survey of isomorphisms of types. *Mathematical. Structures in Comp. Sci.*, 15(5):825–838, 2005.

[6] G. E. Krasner and S. T. Pope. A cookbook for using the model-view controller user interface paradigm in smalltalk-80. *J. Object Oriented Program.*, 1(3):26–49, 1988.

[7] D. Maier. *The Theory of Relational Databases.* Computer Science Press, 1983.

[8] R. Milner, M. Tofte, and R. Harper. *The Definition of Standard ML.* The MIT Press, 1990.

[9] A. Ohori. Semantics of types for database objects. *Theoretical Computer Science*, 76:53–91, 1990.

[10] A. Ohori and P. Buneman. Type inference in a database programming language. In *Proc. ACM Conference on LISP and Functional Programming*, pages 174–183, 1988.

[11] A. Ohori, P. Buneman, and V. Breazu-Tannen. Database programming in Machiavelli – a polymorphic language with static type inference. In *Proc. the ACM SIGMOD conference*, pages 46–57, 1989.

[12] A. Ohori and K. Ueno. Making Standard ML a practical database programming language. In *Proc. ACM ICFP*, pages 307–319, 2011.

[13] SML#. http://www.riec.tohoku.ac.jp/smlsharp/, 2006 – 2014.

[14] Fieldslib. https://github.com/janestreet/fieldslib

Lem: Reusable Engineering of Real-world Semantics

Dominic P. Mulligan
University of Cambridge
dominic.p.mulligan@gmail.com

Scott Owens
University of Kent
s.a.owens@kent.ac.uk

Kathryn E. Gray
University of Cambridge
kathryn.gray@cl.cam.ac.uk

Tom Ridge
University of Leicester
tr61@le.ac.uk

Peter Sewell
University of Cambridge
peter.sewell@cl.cam.ac.uk

Abstract

Recent years have seen remarkable successes in *rigorous engineering*: using mathematically rigorous semantic models (not just idealised calculi) of real-world processors, programming languages, protocols, and security mechanisms, for testing, proof, analysis, and design. Building these models is challenging, requiring experimentation, dialogue with vendors or standards bodies, and validation; their scale adds engineering issues akin to those of programming to the task of writing clear and usable mathematics. But language and tool support for specification is lacking. Proof assistants can be used but bring their own difficulties, and a model produced in one, perhaps requiring many person-years effort and maintained over an extended period, cannot be used by those familiar with another.

We introduce Lem, a language for engineering *reusable* large-scale semantic models. The Lem design takes inspiration both from functional programming languages and from proof assistants, and Lem definitions are translatable into OCaml for testing, Coq, HOL4, and Isabelle/HOL for proof, and LaTeX and HTML for presentation. This requires a delicate balance of expressiveness, careful library design, and implementation of transformations – akin to compilation, but subject to the constraint of producing usable and human-readable code for each target. Lem's effectiveness is demonstrated by its use in practice.

Keywords Lem; real-world semantics; specification language; proof assistants

Categories and Subject Descriptors F.3.1 [*Logics and Meanings of Programs*]: Specifying and Verifying and Reasoning about Programs—Specification techniques; D.2.1 [*Software Engineering*]: Requirements/Specifications—Specification languages and Tools; D.2.4 [*Software Engineering*]: Formal methods and Correctness Proofs

ICFP '14, September 1–6, 2014, Gothenburg, Sweden.

http://dx.doi.org/10.1145/2628136.2628143

1. Introduction

Recent years have seen a rise in *rigorous engineering*: research projects making essential use of mathematically rigorous semantic models or specifications of key computational abstractions, such as processor architectures, programming languages, protocols, and security enforcement mechanisms. These models are used in many different ways: to elucidate the behaviour of an existing real-world abstraction, as oracles to test implementations against, as the underlying assumptions or goals of verification by mechanised interactive proof, as an explicit basis for program analysis, and as a medium for design. We set the context for our work by first recalling a few representative examples. Experimental semantics research, exploring existing real-world abstractions by a combination of empirical investigation and standards formalisation, has addressed the TCP/IP protocols [6], the sequential and concurrent behaviour of x86, Power, and ARM multiprocessors [10, 11, 30, 32], JavaScript [7, 27], the (sequential) C standard [9], and the concurrency model of C/C++11 [3]; these typically require models that can be used as oracles to decide whether some experimentally observed behaviour is permitted in the model, or to enumerate all the model-permitted behaviour. Verification work using mechanised interactive proof has produced verified compilers [19, 36, 40], verified operating system kernels [17], and verified secure fault isolation [24], each based on rigorous models of the underlying processor or language and of the abstraction the verified system aims to provide. Static and dynamic analysis must either build in implicit assumptions or be explicitly based on such a model, e.g. for binary analysis w.r.t. processor architectures [20].

This is a remarkable success story, contrasting with the state a decade ago when semantics was largely restricted to small idealised calculi: the above all involve models of (identified aspects of) real-world computer systems. But it raises its own problems. Constructing a substantial model is a major undertaking:

- one needs to understand the system being modelled in detail, often with experimental investigation of a de facto standard that has not been clearly specified even in prose;
- one has to deal with large-scale specifications, more like modest-scale programs (1–10k lines of specification) than the page or two of pencil-and-paper mathematics of a small calculus, with all the engineering and readability issues that entails; and
- models need extensive experimental validation, to establish confidence (in the absence of full formal verification down to the gate level) that they are correct models of reality; they need theoretical validation, e.g. by proofs of sanity properties showing that they are internally consistent; and they need social validation, discussion with the relevant vendors, standards committees, or community to

ensure that they capture the right intent (especially for specifications that are looser than any particular implementation).

But language and tool support for such modelling and specification activities is lacking. As we discuss below, there has been no language that is specifically designed for the task, making model development more awkward than it should be, and, more importantly, *reuse* of models in different contexts is challenging and rarely achieved. For example, the above-cited works independently developed no less than six partial models of x86 instruction behaviour and two of JavaScript, and the literature contains yet more. For a small application-specific model this is not a problem, but where model development and validation may take person-years of effort such duplication of effort is not viable. The best one could do at present to make a model reusable in multiple provers would often be ad hoc porting (with scripts and hand-editing), but that is highly error prone, and at odds with the fact that these models must be maintained and developed over time.

Our thesis is that, as the subject matures and rigorous engineering becomes more widespread, the community needs to amortise this effort, establishing a collection of models of the basic abstractions, those processor architectures, programming languages and protocols that are relatively stable interfaces that computer systems depend on. These should be comprehensive and well-tested, and they have to be made available in multiple forms to enable their use for many different purposes by different groups. This should lead to a virtuous circle: the prospect of reuse motivating more complete modelling and validation, and this enabling new research that would be impossible without substantial models.

In this paper we work towards this goal. Our main contribution is the design and implementation of a modelling and specification language, Lem, to support the engineering of reusable large-scale semantic models.

Related work To explain the distinctive features of Lem we first consider the alternatives. In some cases one can use a conventional typed functional programming language (such as Haskell, OCaml, or SML) to express a model as a pure functional reference implementation or test oracle. This gives the advantages of a mature and familiar programming language, but it does not give a basis for proofs about the model, and one often needs more logical expressiveness, especially for loose specifications. In particular, one often needs good support for sets and higher-order logic, inductive relation definitions, and a clearer understanding of when one is in the fragment of the language with a direct mathematical interpretation. For reasoning, one typically turns to a proof assistant such as ACL2, Agda, Coq, HOL4, Isabelle/HOL, Matita, PVS, or Twelf. These provide very powerful proof tooling but are hard to master, and their definition languages have accreted functionality over time rather than being designed top-down as modelling/specification languages; inevitably introducing various idiosyncrasies to the language.

More seriously, the community suffers from *proof-assistant lock-in*: the difficulty in becoming fluent in their use means that very few people can use more than one effectively, and the field is partitioned into schools around each. Indeed, even within some of our own projects we have had to use multiple provers due to differing local expertise. The differences between the tools mean that it is a major and error-prone task to port even the definition of a model from one to another, rarely attempted even where much effort has gone into model development. Sometimes this is for fundamental reasons: for example, definitions which make essential use of the dependent types of Coq may be hard or impossible to practically port to HOL4 or Isabelle/HOL. However, many of the examples cited above are logically undemanding: they have no need of dependent types, the differences between classical and constructive reasoning are not particularly relevant, and there is often little or no object-language variable binding. In such cases, where a model is basically expressible in the intersection of the definition languages of several proof assistants, it should in principle be possible to port definitions; the challenge is one of robustly translating between the source languages, definition styles, and libraries. This is made particularly hard by the sensitivity of proof assistants to whether definitions are *idiomatic*: given two logically equivalent definitions, one may be much more amenable than the other to machine-assisted proof or executable code generation in a particular prover.

Previous work has established connections between different provers at the level of their internal logics [1, 12–15, 39]. These enable results proved in one system to be made available in another, but they do not provide usable *source definitions*. Between provers and programming languages, all the provers mentioned above support some kind of code generation; the other direction is less developed, though Haskabelle [28] provides a mapping from a fragment of Haskell to Isabelle source.

There are, of course, also many other specification tools, often with extensively engineered support for particular kinds of specification. For some examples in current use (this is by no means exhaustive) we mention ASF+SDF [35], K [29], and Maude [23] (all of which support some form of term rewriting), Ott [33] (for inductive relations over inductive syntax), and PLT Redex [16] (for reduction semantics); other tools target SMT and first-order problems. These all have advantages in their particular domains, but they are tackling rather different problems to Lem (with its focus on specification portable across multiple provers), and they lack the definitional expressiveness of higher-order logic and inductively defined relations. The need for both of these in a range of our large-scale specifications is what motivated us to develop Lem, and the choice of a language expressive enough for them but not so rich (e.g. with general dependent types) that it cannot be translated to multiple targets is central to Lem's design.

Contribution Lem aims to combine the ease-of-use and uniform language design of programming languages with the logical expressiveness required for specification of the established proof assistants. Most importantly, it aims to support *portable* specifications, that can be used in multiple provers (it is not itself a proof tool). Spelling out our contribution in more detail:

A language of executable mathematics Lem is oriented towards (though not restricted to) executable definitions; the executable fragment of Lem can be translated into OCaml code to use as a test oracle for experimental validation, or for model exploration.

Support for multiple proof-assistant targets Lem definitions can be translated to proof-assistant definitions for Coq, HOL4, and Isabelle/HOL, to support interactive proof. The language design involves a delicate balance of expressiveness: expressive enough for a range of large-scale modelling tasks, but restricted enough to make it translatable into usable definitions in the various proof-assistant targets, as idiomatically as we can achieve by automatic translation (reasonably well for HOL4 and Isabelle/HOL; somewhat less so for Coq). These translations are related to, but interestingly different from, conventional programming-language implementation techniques; for example in the translations of equality and pattern matching. Perhaps surprisingly, in some cases it is best to translate into mathematically different code in different targets. The design and implementation choices that make this and the next point possible are described in §3.

Human-readable output It is also important to make the proof assistant generated definitions *human-readable*: Lem preserves the source structure and comments where it can (modulo the tension with generating idiomatic code), and it uses the same machinery to give the user control of layout for generation of production-quality LaTeX that can be used directly in papers and documentation, avoiding the error-prone and tedious manual typesetting of definitions for publication that can be necessary for some proof assistants. Lem can also generate simple HTML.

Programming-language engineering The language is designed using best-practice programming-language techniques, taking advantage of the opportunity to do a coherent design without the backwards-compatibility issues faced by proof assistants that have been extended over many years. The syntax and type system of Lem itself are specified using the Ott tool [33], which helped make the design regular (without odd corner cases); it should be easy to use by those familiar with typed functional languages such as OCaml, Haskell, or SML. Lem appears to the user much like a compiler: there is no need to learn a complex interface, and the implementation provides prompt feedback (e.g. for type errors) to the user, so that one can do type-based development and refactoring of specifications in the style of development in a typed programming language.

Library design A specification language needs a good standard library just as much as a programming language does. In §4 we describe the Lem library support and, more challenging, how it has to be related to the differing prover libraries.

Substantial usage Lem has been developed since 2010 and its effectiveness is demonstrated by a number of applications, with both academic and industrial impact. We begin in §2 by recalling those, to explain more clearly what it is (and is not) good for, and discuss one in more detail in §5. Some of the motivation behind Lem, and its initial implementation, was first presented in a short "Rough Diamond" paper [26]. Lem and its documentation are available (under a BSD license from a Bitbucket repository) from `http://www.cl.cam.ac.uk/~pes20/lem/`.

2. Lem in practice

To explain more concretely the kind of specification work that Lem is aimed at, and to demonstrate its practical effectiveness as a tool for large-scale specification, we describe the main Lem developments produced to date. These underlie multiple academic publications (six in POPL, PLDI, and CAV) and have had industrial impact, in clarifying the IBM Power and ARM concurrency behaviour, on the C/C++11 ISO standard concurrency semantics, and on the compilation scheme of the latter to Power and ARM. For each development we give the number of non-comment lines of specification (LoS) and the Lem targets used, and comment on the mathematical style of the specification.

Sarkar et al. [30] describe an operational model (3008 LoS) for the relaxed-memory behaviour of IBM Power and ARM multiprocessors. The executable Lem-generated OCaml code forms the kernel of the `ppcmem` tool (`http://www.cl.cam.ac.uk/~pes20/ppcmem`) for exhaustive and interactive exploration of the model on examples; that and the generated LaTeX supported experimental validation and extensive discussion with an IBM architect during model development; and the generated Coq has been used for some modest experiments with mechanised proof (unpublished). This model uses a combination of mathematical styles. For specifying the multiprocessor memory subsystem it has an abstract machine built over sets, relations, and lists of memory events, while the thread semantics involves abstract syntax trees of assembly and micro-operation instructions. These each define labelled transition systems (LTSs), which are combined with an inductive-relation top-level parallel composition.

Batty et al. [3] describe an axiomatic memory model and various sub-models (1517 LoS) for concurrency in the C/C++11 standards. The Lem-generated OCaml and HTML form the kernel of the `cppmem` tool, again with a web interface for interactive and exhaustive exploration of the model on examples (`http://svr-pes20-cppmem.cl.cam.ac.uk/cppmem/`); that and the generated LaTeX supported discussion with the ISO standards committee to develop the model and improve the standard, and `cppmem` has been used by some GCC and Linux developers and within ARM. The generated HOL4 code has been used for mechanised proof of metatheory, and the generated Coq and Isabelle code have also been used for proof experiments. The bulk of this development comprises predicates over candidate executions, represented as sets of events with various order relations; we describe it in more detail in § 5.

Batty et al. [4, 31] describe extensions to the above Power and C/C++11 models and correctness proofs for a compilation scheme from C/C++11 concurrency primitives to Power concurrency primitives; these are hand proofs but with lemmas expressed in Lem (931 LoS); this is a useful middle ground between LaTeX and fully mechanised proofs.

Mador-Haim et al. [21] describe an axiomatic memory model for Power and mappings between that and the operational model above (1155 LoS), again with hand proofs; the generated OCaml code was used to test equivalence of the two models on examples and the generated LaTeX to define the model in the paper.

The specification of the de facto standard of the TCP/IP network protocols and the Sockets API by Bishop et al. [6] was originally expressed in HOL4 and has now been ported to Lem (6681 LoS). The style is essentially pure higher-order functional programming, but with sets and maps, a relational monad, inductive relations, and logic. The port to Lem was essentially straightforward except that the original specification made heavy use of HOL4's advanced features for user-defined syntax, while Lem has a more uniform but more restricted syntax; these had to be manually unpicked.

The Ott definition of $\text{OCaml}_{\text{light}}$ by Owens [25], originally used to generate HOL4, has been adapted to generate Lem (3133 LoS in Lem, from 4253 lines of Ott source). $\text{OCaml}_{\text{light}}$ uses a typical mathematical style for a typed functional programming language semantics, with inductive relations specifying a type system and small-step operational semantics. Lem's inductive relation support was general enough to support a direct and automatic translation from Ott. This development is of a different character than the others in that here we are translating *into* Lem, showing its potential to be used as a general purpose front-end for domain-specific tools (here Ott) that target multiple provers.

Kumar et al. [18] describe CakeML (`http://cakeml.org`), a mechanically verified ML system above x86-64 machine code. The source language definition (AST, type checking, and small- and big-step operational semantics), compiler, and some additional machinery are written in Lem (4897 LoS); the generated HOL4 code is used for proofs. The operational semantics of CakeML and the low-level CakeML bytecode, and the CakeML type system are given as inductively defined relations. The compiler is specified as a collection of recursive functions, in a typical functional programming style. Furthermore, the semantics and type system rely heavily on helper functions. This is in marked contrast with the $\text{OCaml}_{\text{light}}$ semantics which was almost entirely relational. It was convenient when doing the proofs for helper (partial) functions (e.g., environment lookup) to be specified as functions rather than relations. Besides relations, functions, and datatype definitions, CakeML uses the Lem list, finite map, and string libraries. The Lem sources are in the `compiler`, `bytecode`, `semantics`, and `translator` subdirectories of the repository.

Ongoing work describes a model for a substantial part of the C programming language (8274 LoS), largely in a functional style over an inductively defined abstract syntax. This initially used only the OCaml target but has recently been adapted to also generate Coq (which has been used for significant proofs); the effort involved was nontrivial but remains small (weeks vs years) in comparison to the time required to develop the model.

Models extracted from Lem to proof assistant and OCaml code are typically of a similar size to the original specification. For example, the C/C++11 concurrency model constitutes 2409 LoS, whereas the OCaml, HOL4 4 and Coq extractions are 2673, 2768 and 2249 lines in length, respectively. LaTeX code generated from the same model is roughly twice the length of the original specification.

Together, these developments demonstrate that Lem is expressive enough for a range of modelling tasks, spanning processor architectures, C and ML-like programming languages, and network protocols, and that it compiles to usable executable code for model exploration and usable definitions in multiple provers for proof. Anecdotally, our experience is that it is reasonably easy to use (analogous to a functional programming language) and that Lem models are malleable: in developing a model, one can largely focus on the domain being modelled rather than issues of expressing the model in Lem, and models can be easily changed as they are developed. Our impression so far is that adding a new target to a specification is usually easy or (at worst) like the last example above, but it is possible that to get a truly idiomatic version in a new target one may need to hand-rewrite substantial parts of the specification in that target, and prove equivalence to the Lem-generated versions. For an intricate specification, embodying much development and validation effort, even that may be preferable to the alternative of hand-rewriting the whole. More experience is needed to see which is normally the case.

Lem is a general-purpose specification language but not, of course, an all-purpose one. It does not aim to support specifications with elaborate dependently typed hierarchies of mathematical structures. It has a straightforward syntax (again similar to that of a functional programming language), without support for rich user-defined syntax. The executable code Lem generates is designed to have a clear relationship to the source and has sufficient performance to support exploration of models on the intricate but small examples that (e.g.) arise as concurrency test cases; it is not aimed at producing performance-optimised code. Lem complements the Ott tool [33]: Ott supports arbitrary context-free user-defined syntax and inductive relations; this is a good fit for high-level programming language and calculus semantics but the lack of the more general types, functions and library support of Lem makes it awkward to use for modelling the lower-level systems and languages described above. Lem can serve as an intermediate language for other tools that produce definitions of types, functions, or inductive relations, and we have refactored Ott (which originally produced source code for Coq, HOL4, and Isabelle/HOL directly) to produce Lem definitions, leaving Lem to handle the prover-specific idiosyncrasies.

3. Design for portable specification

Aiming to support a range of specification tasks, Lem does not build in any domain-specific assumptions on the form of specification permitted: it is a general language of type, higher-order function, and inductive relation definitions.

The language is intended to be as expressive and straightforward as possible given this generality; it avoids novel or exotic features that would give it a steep learning curve, or render translations into the various targets infeasible. From functional programming languages we take pure higher-order functions, general recursion, recursive algebraic datatypes, records $\langle| \cdot |\rangle$, lists $[\cdot]$, pattern matching, parametric polymorphism, a simple type class mechanism for overloading, and a simple module system. To these we add logical constructs familiar in provers: universal and existential quantification, sets $\{\cdot\}$ (including set comprehensions), relations, finite maps, inductive relation definitions, and lemma statements.

The concrete syntax for types, patterns, expressions, top-level declarations and definitions are broadly standard, as one can see in the excerpts in Fig. 1. For types, patterns, expressions, and definitions Lem's grammar largely follows OCaml for the common constructs (the main exceptions being prefix type applications, curried constructors, and records using $\langle| \cdot |\rangle$, to allow $\{\cdot\}$ for sets, more sophisticated control of opening of modules via `open import`, and the addition of inductive relation and type class and instances declarations). Lem also adds a series of top-level commands, via the `declare` syntax, to let the user tune how Lem definitions are mapped into the various targets (by declaring target representations and controlling notation, renaming, inlining, and type classes), to generate witness types and executable functions from inductive relations, and for assertions; we describe all these below.

Although most of Lem's features should be unsurprising at first sight, their detailed design must carefully manage tradeoffs between Lem's expressiveness and usability as specification language, and the need to generate usable code for the various target languages and provers. In this section, we first describe the basic architecture of the Lem implementation, and then describe the design issues and our solutions for each of these seemingly simple features – including polymorphism, equality, partiality, sets, and inductive relations. In the next section (§4), we will describe Lem's library definition mechanism, and explain how it connects the Lem standard library to the widely varying standard libraries of the targets.

3.1 System architecture

Lem is written in OCaml, and it follows the architecture of a traditional compiler invoked from the command line, with conventional lexing and parsing of source files into an untyped AST, followed by type inference (in the style of Milner's Algorithm W) into a typed AST. The OCaml type declarations for the untyped AST are automatically extracted from the formal definition of Lem's syntax by Ott [33], to help keep the Lem implementation and formal specification in agreement. Its parser and lexer are implemented using `ocamlyacc` and `ocamllex`.

To produce output for a particular target, the typed AST is then transformed, compiling away features that the target does not support (transforming away type classes via dictionary passing, compiling away unsupported pattern matching forms, etc.). Special idiosyncrasies of the target may require additional clean-up (e.g., variable name clashes, extra required parentheses, different infix operator syntax); then the resulting AST is printed in the target's source syntax. The individual transformations are reused in different combinations for the different targets, as required, and the implementation checks that they preserve typing, greatly easing debugging of Lem itself.

Lem has about 29 000 lines of OCaml code. This compactness makes it easy to understand and adapt. The library is extensive in comparison to the code size: there are about 7700 lines of Lem libraries, together with 1800 lines of OCaml, 1200 lines of Isabelle/HOL, 500 lines of Coq and 300 lines of HOL4.

3.2 Whitespace preservation and refactoring support

Unlike a compiler or proof assistant, Lem's front end preserves all of the comments, whitespace, and line breaks in the source files. Lem attempts to format its output using the formatting of the input, rather than a pretty printing algorithm, in order to give the user fine-grained control of the output layout. Of course, this is not always possible when the input had to undergo significant transformation, such as the pattern match compilation or dictionary passing translation discussed below. In these cases, we use a standard pretty-printing algorithm for the affected expressions, but can at least keep all of the comments from the input. Crucially, the LaTeX backend does not perform such transformations, and so the user has control over the typesetting of their specifications, including linebreaks and indentation.

Types

$typ ::= \_ \mid \alpha \mid typ_1 \rightarrow typ_2 \mid typ_1 \times \ldots. \times typ_n \mid id\ typ_1 \mathbin{..} typ_n \mid backtick\_string\ typ_1 \mathbin{..} typ_n \mid (typ)$

Patterns

$pat ::= \_ \mid (pat\ \mathbf{as}\ x) \mid (pat : typ) \mid id\ pat_1 \mathbin{..} pat_n \mid \langle| fpat_1; \ldots; fpat_n\ ;^? |\rangle \mid (pat_1, \ldots., pat_n) \mid [pat_1; \mathbin{..}; pat_n\ ;^?] \mid (pat) \mid pat_1 :: pat_2$
$\mid x + num \mid lit$

Expressions

$lit ::= \mathbf{true} \mid \mathbf{false} \mid num \mid hex \mid bin \mid string \mid ()$

$exp ::= id \mid backtick\_string \mid \mathbf{fun}\ psexp \mid \mathbf{function}\ |^?\ pexp_1 | \ldots | pexp_n\ \mathbf{end} \mid exp_1\ exp_2 \mid exp_1\ ix\ exp_2 \mid \langle| fexps |\rangle \mid \langle| exp\ \mathbf{with}\ fexps |\rangle$
$\mid exp.id \mid \mathbf{match}\ exp\ \mathbf{with}\ |^?\ pexp_1 | \ldots | pexp_n\ \mathbf{end} \mid (exp : typ) \mid \mathbf{let}\ letbind\ \mathbf{in}\ exp \mid (exp_1, \ldots., exp_n) \mid [exp_1; \mathbin{..}; exp_n\ ;^?] \mid (exp)$
$\mid \mathbf{begin}\ exp\ \mathbf{end} \mid \mathbf{if}\ exp_1\ \mathbf{then}\ exp_2\ \mathbf{else}\ exp_3 \mid exp_1 :: exp_2 \mid lit \mid \{exp_1 | exp_2\} \mid \{exp_1 | \mathbf{forall}\ qbind_1 \mathbin{..} qbind_n | exp_2\}$
$\mid \{exp_1; \mathbin{..}; exp_n\ ;^?\} \mid q\ qbind_1 \ldots qbind_n.exp \mid [exp_1 | \mathbf{forall}\ qbind_1 \mathbin{..} qbind_n | exp_2] \mid \mathbf{do}\ id\ pat_1 \leftarrow exp_1; \mathbin{..} pat_n \leftarrow exp_n;\ \mathbf{in}\ exp\ \mathbf{end}$

$psexp ::= pat_1 \ldots pat_n \rightarrow exp$

$qbind ::= x \mid (pat\ \mathbf{IN}\ exp) \mid (pat\ \mathbf{MEM}\ exp)$

$q ::= \mathbf{forall} \mid \mathbf{exists}$

Declarations

$target ::= \mathbf{hol} \mid \mathbf{isabelle} \mid \mathbf{ocaml} \mid \mathbf{coq} \mid \mathbf{tex} \mid \mathbf{html} \mid \mathbf{lem}$

$lemma\_decl ::= \mathbf{lemma}\ x : exp$

$component ::= \mathbf{module} \mid \mathbf{function} \mid \mathbf{type} \mid \mathbf{field}$

$target\_rep\_rhs ::= \mathbf{infix}\ fixity\_decl\ backtick\_string \mid exp \mid typ \mid$

$target\_rep\_lhs ::= target\_rep\ component\ id\ x_1 \mathbin{..} x_n \mid target\_rep\ component\ id\ tnvars$

$declare\_def ::=$
$\mid \mathbf{declare}\ compile\_message\ id = string$
$\mid \mathbf{declare\ rename\ module} = x\ target\_modules\_opt$
$\mid \mathbf{declare\ rename}\ component\ id = x$
$\mid \mathbf{declare}\ ascii\_rep\ component\ id = backtick\_string$
$\mid \mathbf{declare}\ target\ target\_rep\ target\_rep\_lhs = target\_rep\_rhs$
$\mid \mathbf{declare}\ set\_flag\ x_1 = x_2$
$\mid \mathbf{declare}\ termination\_argument\ id = termination\_setting$
$\mid \mathbf{declare}\ pattern\_match\ exhaustivity\_setting\ id\ tnvars = [id_1; \ldots; id_n\ ;^?]\ elim\_opt$

Definitions

$val\_def ::= \mathbf{let}\ letbind \mid \mathbf{let\ rec}\ funcl_1\ \mathbf{and} \ldots \mathbf{and}\ funcl_n \mid \mathbf{let\ inline}\ letbind$

$def ::=$
$\mid \mathbf{module}\ x = \mathbf{struct}\ defs\ \mathbf{end}$ (* module definition*)
$\mid \mathbf{module}\ x = id$ (* module alias *)
$\mid open\_import\ id_1 \ldots id_n \mid open\_import\ backtick\_string_1 \ldots backtick\_string_n$ (* import and/or open of modules *)
$\mid class\_decl(x\ tnvar)\ \mathbf{val}\ x_1\ ascii\_opt_1 : typ_{1\ 1} \ldots \mathbf{val}\ x_n\ ascii\_opt_n : typ_{n\ n}\ \mathbf{end}$ (* typeclass definitions *)
$\mid instance\_decl\ instschm\ val\_def_{1\ 1} \ldots val\_def_{n\ n}\ \mathbf{end}$ (* typeclass instantiations *)
$\mid \mathbf{type}\ td_1\ \mathbf{and} \ldots \mathbf{and}\ td_n$ (* type definition *)
$\mid \mathbf{val}\ x\ ascii\_opt : typschm$ (* value type constraint *)
$\mid val\_def$ (* value definition *)
$\mid \mathbf{indreln}\ indreln\_name_1\ \mathbf{and} \ldots \mathbf{and}\ indreln\_name_i\ rule_1\ \mathbf{and} \ldots \mathbf{and}\ rule_n$ (* inductively defined relations *)
$\mid \mathbf{lemma}\ x : exp$ (* lemma statement *)
$\mid declare\_def$ (* target-behaviour declaration *)

Lem source files

$defs ::= def_1\ ;;^?_1 \mathbin{..} def_n\ ;;^?_n$

Figure 1. Lem Syntax Excerpts

Since Lem preserves comments, whitespace and linebreaks, it can reproduce its input exactly. This means that Lem can also be used as a refactoring tool for its own input. A special refactoring backend is able to rename functions and types, remove or add function arguments, move definitions to different modules and much more. For example, including

```
declare {lem} target_rep function f = 'g'
```

in a source file and then running the file through Lem will produce a new source file with all occurrences of the function `f` renamed to `g`. Via a similar mechanism, one may add or remove parameters to functions, rename types, fields, and so on, or inline function calls with their definition.

Whitespace preservation also means that a standard OCaml profiling tool can be used for coverage analysis of a *specification*, identifying the parts of a Lem specification that are exercised by a particular set of tests run in a semantics exploration tool (with kernel generated from the specification): the generated OCaml is close enough to the Lem source that one can usually easily relate one to the other.

3.3 Polymorphism and dependency

Parametric polymorphism is essential in our specifications – most obviously, for the library functions over lists, sets, and suchlike, and for functions over user-defined polymorphic inductive types. But, as is well-known in the higher-order-logic context, let-polymorphism (the implicit generalisation of types to type-schemes in nested **let** bindings) makes higher-order logic unsound (see Section 5 of [8]). Accordingly, Lem supports top-level parametric polymorphism, but type generalisation is restricted to (module) top-level definitions, as in HOL4 and Isabelle/HOL, but diverging from the Hindley-Milner-style polymorphism found in ML-like programming languages. We have not found this to be limiting in practice, and Vytiniotis et al. [37, §4.3] provide empirical evidence that let-polymorphism is rarely used in practical Haskell programming.

More sophisticated type-language features, such as System F-style polymorphism, dependent types, and subtyping, are also not included in Lem, because these would be unduly difficult or impossible to support in many of our chosen targets. However, we do support *ad hoc* polymorphism with type classes.

3.4 Equality and type classes

There are substantial differences in the treatment of equality in our different targets. In the two implementations of higher-order logic, Isabelle/HOL and HOL4, there is a 'pervasive' equality constant $=$, at type $\alpha \to \alpha \to$ `bool`. OCaml features a similarly typed equality constant, but it is only usable for non-function types (raising an exception otherwise). Further, this OCaml polymorphic equality is structural, and does not take into account equivalence relations between data types. For abstract types such as sets (implemented in the Lem translation to OCaml as ordered balanced binary trees) one needs to use an equality function specific to sets that compares sets based on their elements, rather than their low-level representation in memory, and that function must have access to the order relation used to build the trees. We could introduce specific equalities at each type, for example `setEq` at type $\forall\alpha.\ (\alpha \to \alpha \to$ `bool`$) \to$ `set` $\alpha \to$ `set` $\alpha \to$ `bool`. However, this would force the user to supply the equality function on elements of the set by hand (a task that should be automated), and break the uniformity of the treatment of equality within the language. Lem includes type classes to solve both of these problems.

The Lem `Eq` type class has the following form:

```
class (Eq α)
  val (=) ['isEqual'] : α → α → bool
  val (<>) ['isInequal'] : α → α → bool
end
```

This type class introduces two methods, equality `=`, and inequality `<>` (together with alphanumeric alternative names). The type class may be instantiated at any type by providing implementations for the equality and inequality methods at that type. For OCaml, Coq, Isabelle/HOL and HOL4, the Lem translation introduces explicit dictionary passing to handle the general case of type classes and their constraints. But there are three situations in which introducing dictionary passing would lead to non-idiomatic code and obstruct use of the extensive proof automation facilities of the provers.

First, for the backends with a general polymorphic boolean equality, Isabelle/HOL and HOL4, we wish to map the Lem overloaded equality constant to that native equality constant. We achieve this with a general inlining method:

```
let inline {hol;isabelle} (=)  =
  unsafe_structural_equality
```

This inlining effectively 'turns off' the equality type class for HOL4 and Isabelle/HOL. Since all methods are implemented without using the type-class mechanism, the class (and the associated dictionary passing) is not generated for these backends. Here `unsafe_structural_equality`, intended to be used by library authors only, is mapped to the native equality constants in the Isabelle/HOL and HOL4 backends. It is also mapped to the pervasive (but restricted as above, hence the '`unsafe`') equality function in the OCaml backend.

Secondly, sometimes we want to use a method only for certain backends. With the normal Lem standard library, Lem sets are represented in Coq and OCaml as ordered, balanced binary trees and therefore an order on their elements needs to be provided. This is achieved via a Lem type class `SetType`. However, the HOL4 and Isabelle/HOL sets do not require an order, so using the type class mechanism naïvely would lead to non-idiomatic HOL4 and Isabelle/HOL code by generating unnecessary dictionary arguments. By restricting class-methods to certain backends, this problem can be solved:

```
class ( SetType α )
  val {ocaml;coq} setElemCompare:  α → α → ordering
end
```

Lem's type-checker ensures that the method `setElemCompare` is only used in the Coq and OCaml backends, with the type class being safely eliminated for all other backends.

Thirdly, we wish to avoid introducing dictionary passing where all occurrences of a type class can be statically resolved, for example for the Lem type-class `Numeral`, used for overloading numeral syntax for multiple number types. This type class is declared as *inline*. All occurrences must be resolved, and all methods of an inlined type-class are replaced (inlined) with their instantiations.

Using type classes for equality in Lem also works around another issue in the Coq backend. In Coq the types `bool` and `Prop` (technically a *sort*) are distinct, with 'propositional equality' having type $\forall\alpha.\ \alpha \to \alpha \to$ `Prop`. It is generally impossible in Coq, without additional axioms, to produce an equality constant of type $\forall\alpha.\ \alpha \to \alpha \to$ `bool`. Rather, 'boolean equalities' are given at specific types, such as `nateq` of type $\mathbb{N} \to \mathbb{N} \to$ `bool` and `booleq` of type `bool` $\to$ `bool` $\to$ `bool`, and so on. Lem, following Isabelle/HOL and HOL4, identifies boolean-typed expressions and propositions, or formulae. This poses a problem with extraction to Coq, as innocuous Lem code—e.g. `if 4 = 5 then true else false`—becomes problematic if we try to extract an equality constant in Lem to Coq's propositional equality constant, as case analysis over `Prop` is not permitted. Boolean equality is therefore needed, and type classes are used to handle this uniformly. We return to `bool` and `Prop` in §3.13.

In principle, it should be straightforward for Lem to automatically generate the appropriate instance declarations for its basic library type classes (`Eq`, `Ord`, `SetType`, and `MapKeyType`) for most user-defined types, analogous to Haskell's `deriving` mechanism. Unfortunately that is not currently implemented, and a default instantiation mechanism is used instead, where a type class instance, usually supplied in the Lem library, may be marked as the 'default' instance to select if no over-riding instance is provided by the user. This means the user must take care to give non-default instantiations (with the correct equality or comparison function) in some places, e.g., for the OCaml backend, for types which both contain an abstract type and are used as set elements.

Compared to Haskell's type class system, Lem's is intentionally less expressive: our goal is to support simple overloaded operators and to solve the above-mentioned issues dealing with the subtle differences between our target systems, not to enable generic and polytypic programming. In particular, Lem does not support constructor classes (type classes with type variables at a higher kind than $*$), default implementations of methods, or backchaining search for instances, nor does it support more recent extensions: multi-parameter type classes, functional dependencies, and so on.

Our implementation already has much of the underlying infrastructure needed for some extensions: instances at compound types, multi-parameter classes, default methods, and other features that would make type classes more convenient to use, and these should be easy to implement in the future. However, constructor classes and the like pose more significant technical challenges, because their dictionary-passing translations are not naturally typeable in the systems of ML-style polymorphism of our OCaml and HOL4 targets and Lem itself. One possible design choice would be to support them, but only at statically known types (i.e., where dictionaries are not required).

3.5 Module system and 'do' notation

Lem has a simple module system designed to support the organisation of large-scale specifications into multiple files, and to allow the reuse of specification libraries (including Lem's standard library itself) across developments. It does not include the *programming-in-the-large* features of advanced PL module/component systems, such as enforced abstraction or parameterisation, because those are primarily useful in code bases that are orders of magnitude larger than even large specifications. Our larger developments each comprise between 10 and 40 non-library Lem files.

The module system is based on a restricted subset of OCaml's module system: modules contain sequences of definitions, and modules can be defined at the top level (but not inside of expressions). Definitions inside of a module are accessed from outside either through the `open` declaration, or by explicitly spelling out the module path (with dot notation). There are no signatures or functors.

Lem supports a Haskell-like do notation for specifications that involve monads. Unlike Haskell, Lem's type class system is not powerful enough to infer which monad is being used (since a monad is a type constructor rather than a type). Instead, each `do` expression is annotated with a module name that defines the relevant bind and return operations.

3.6 Pattern matching

The usefulness of pattern matching is well-established in functional programming languages, and it is even more valuable in a specification language like Lem because it supports high level, abstract and clear code. But the support for pattern matching varies significantly between the different backends we target. For example, record patterns are supported by OCaml and (recently) Coq, but not by HOL4 or Isabelle/HOL; `as`-patterns are supported by OCaml and Coq, but not by Isabelle/HOL or HOL4; and idiomatic HOL4, Isabelle/HOL and Coq code uses pattern matching on natural numbers (using zero and the successor function as constructors), whereas this is not supported by OCaml. Besides differences in explicit pattern match expressions, there are also differences in how one can use patterns elsewhere. Anonymous functions in OCaml allow arbitrary patterns as arguments, but in HOL4, Isabelle/HOL and Coq only tuples of variables are allowed. The situation is similar for `let`-expressions and patterns occurring in restricted quantifications. Beyond these local syntactic properties, there are also important semantic differences: Isabelle/HOL supports non-exhaustive pattern matches, but no redundant rows; Coq requires pattern matches to be exhaustive and prohibits redundant rows; OCaml allows both redundant and non-exhaustive pattern matches; and HOL4 allows non-exhaustive pattern matches but redundant rows only at certain places.

We take the opportunity in the Lem language design to provide more general pattern matching, combining the facilities of each target, and compile those general patterns away where necessary. This compilation mostly follows a simple, standard approach, essentially switching on the outermost constructor symbols ([2]) in order to compile pattern matches to decision trees, implemented efficiently following ideas from [22]. But in contrast to the normal PL situation, where one wants to compile away pattern matching altogether, for Lem to produce idiomatic and human-readable code, we have to *preserve* as much of the original structure as possible; Lem needs sophisticated models of the capabilities of each backend in order to compile only the unsupported features and preserve as much of the original structure as possible.

For example, consider the following Lem record pattern match:

```
type t = ⟨| f1: nat; f2: bool |⟩

let test_fun x = match x with
  | Nothing ⇒ 0
  | Just ⟨| f2 = true |⟩ ⇒ 1
  | Just ⟨| f1 = 0 |⟩ ⇒ (1 : nat)
  | Just ⟨| f1 = x |⟩ ⇒ x + 2
end
```

OCaml supports all these pattern forms, so the resulting OCaml code looks very similar to the input; pattern compilation is not needed. In contrast, HOL4 does not support record patterns, and compiling them away – while preserving as much of the structure as possible – leads to the following HOL4 result:

```
val _ = Define ‘test_fun x = case x of
    NONE   ⇒ 0
  | SOME t ⇒ (case (t.f2, t.f1) of
        (T,_) ⇒ 1
      | (_,0) ⇒ (1 : num)
      | (_,_) ⇒ let x = t.f1 in x + 2)’;
```

Our implementation also supports a mechanism similar to view patterns [38]. This feature allows users to write more abstract, higher-level specifications. For example, consider the type of sets. Functional programmers might be tempted to use the `choose` function to get the unique element out of a set known by the programmer to be a singleton. However, `choose` requires the axiom of choice in Coq, and its result is undefined for empty sets and underspecified for sets with more than one element. A solution is using a case-split for sets:

```
let set_case s c_empty c_sing c_else =
  if (null s) then c_empty else
  if (size s = 1) then c_sing (choose s) else
  c_else
```

This `set_case` can be implemented in all backends and is even executable. Lem's view-pattern feature allows setting it up together with `empty` and `singleton` for pattern matching.

```
declare pattern_match inexhaustive
  set 'a = [ empty; singleton ] set_case
```

This setup provides easily readable syntax, as below:

```
let set_test s : nat =
  match (s : set nat) with
    | empty ⇒ 0
    | singleton (x + 3) ⇒ 2
    | singleton _ ⇒ 1
    | _ ⇒ 3
  end
```

3.7 Partial pattern matches

Programming languages typically permit non-exhaustive or partial pattern matches, with a dynamic exception or error if a match fails at runtime. This supports two use cases: (a) where the programmer knows that the match will never actually fail, because of some invariant (e.g. that a list is nonempty) that may not be expressible in the language's type system, and (b) where the intended control flow includes paths where an exception is raised and handled.

Proof assistants are more restrictive to retain soundness. For (a), in the HOL4 and Isabelle/HOL logics the Hilbert choice operator lets one construct an arbitrary unknown default value at any type, but in Coq all matches must be total (though the Coq type system can capture complex invariants). None of the three support (b) directly, as that would require a deeply embedded exception monad.

Lem permits partial matches, to support (a), and the Lem library also exports a `failwith` constant which is intended to signal 'catastrophic' failure with some user-supplied error message which may be used at any type. For OCaml partial matches are mapped directly onto similarly partial matches (any `Match_failure` exceptions can be handled by wrappers around the Lem-generated code, but not within that code). Lem can be configured with a flag at compile time to eliminate match branches that contain only `failwith` in favour of a partial match. For HOL4 and Isabelle/HOL partial matches are mapped to syntactically partial matches that ultimately use the Hilbert choice operator, which is appropriate in cases where the match can never fail. For Coq, the story is more complex. Given a partial match at a concrete type, e.g.

```
match (m: maybe bool) with
  | Just j ⇒ j
end
```

that lacks a case for the `Nothing` constructor of the `maybe` type and whose result type is the concrete `bool`, we generate the following:

```
match (m: maybe bool) with
  | Just j ⇒ j
  | _ ⇒ bool_default
```

Here `bool_default` is a *default value*. Default values for base types are provided in an external harness file and Lem automatically generates default values for all user-defined types during generation of Coq code. Again this is suitable in cases where the user knows that the result of that branch is irrelevant.

Partial matches with a polymorphic result type are more problematic (though in practice we have not found many cases where they arise), e.g.

```
match (m: maybe β) with
  | Just j ⇒ j
end
```

We could use a type class with a default-value method, at the cost of introducing dictionary passing for that into the generated Coq for any definition which hereditarily involves a partial polymorphic match. Instead, on the assumption that the user would usually prefer to adapt their specification to avoid this, at present we translate into a complete Coq match

```
match (m: maybe β) with
  | Just j ⇒ j
  | _       ⇒ DAEMON (* From <position>. *)
end
```

that introduces a placeholder marking a point in the source specification that needs to be addressed, and a warning or error is issued. Here, `DAEMON` is a constant of type $\forall\alpha.\alpha$—the type of logical falsity. This lets one build the remaining development but its presence as an axiom makes Coq's logic inconsistent, so one would aim to remove all such usages.

Lem itself has no operational semantics, its meaning being defined by the translations to the various targets. It is pure in the sense that it has no I/O or store effects, but in general the use of partial pattern matches and their compilation using exceptions in the OCaml backend can make the OCaml evaluation order observable in generated OCaml code (and there is a similar issue for nontermination). However, if partial matches are only used for (a) above, with missing cases only in places that are unreachable under any evaluation order (and if one uses only Lem functions that are robustly terminating in the same sense), then the target evaluation order should be irrelevant.

3.8 General recursion vs total functions

Functional languages typically allow general recursion, whereas proof assistants generally require some kind of termination proof for all recursive functions in order to maintain the soundness of their logic. For example, the function `let rec f x = not (f x)` will diverge in OCaml when called, but would introduce an unsoundness to a proof assistant. Defining a recursive function in Coq, HOL4 or Isabelle/HOL therefore requires the user, often assisted by the proof assistant itself but in quite different ways, to supply evidence that the function terminates on all inputs. Lem permits general recursion but with hooks to invoke the backend's various automatic termination provers, where they exist, e.g.:

```
declare termination_argument my_rec_function = automatic
```

If that does not suffice, for the HOL4 and Isabelle/HOL backends Lem can defer termination proofs, letting the user provide them manually later (see §3.11).

Currently, the Coq backend extracts recursive functions to a `Fixpoint` definition using Sozeau's `Program` facility [34]. In practice, we have only encountered one recursive function that Coq's automated proof tools failed to establish as terminating and had to be rewritten by hand within Lem. However, as with HOL4 and Isabelle/HOL, `Program` allows the user to defer termination proofs, and therefore a strategy of defering such proofs to the user to be filled in manually later could also be adopted for the Coq backend.

Both facilities are used in CakeML, where simple functions (e.g., `stackshift` in `compiler/toBytecode.lem`) declare an automatic termination argument. More complex ones that HOL cannot automatically prove termination for (e.g., the mutually recursive `exp_to_Cexp` of the same file) are proved in a separate HOL file (e.g. `compiler/compilerTerminationScript.sml`).

3.9 Per-target representation differences

One might imagine that a portable specification should necessarily map onto mathematically equivalent definitions in the different targets, but this turns out not to be the case: there is a tension between it and the need to generate idiomatic code.

For example, in OCaml the standard type for numbers is `int`, 31- or 63-bit signed integers, while our proof assistant targets use unbounded natural numbers as their standard type. In each target common functions like the list `length` function use that target's local standard number type, so either Lem has to add wrappers to such functions or map the same Lem type to different mathematical constructs in different targets.

We give the user the choice, providing a Lem type `nat` which is translated to the standard number type of the targets (for use where the user knows the differences are irrelevant, e.g. when using numbers just as unique identifiers) and a Lem type `natural` which always maps to unbounded naturals. Similarly we provide `int` and `integer`. We provide conversion functions between the different number types; polymorphic numeral constants and polymorphic arithmetic functions make switching between number types easy.

The choice of set representations is more involved. Since Lem is geared towards executability, one might want to model only finite sets, and in practice users are often only concerned with finite structures, e.g. as arising in finite executions of the models described in §2. On the other hand, potentially infinite sets are very common and very useful for specifications and more convenient to work with in some provers. Similar questions occur with quantification. Only bounded quantification is easily executable, but unbounded quantification is often useful for specifications. Lem permits unbounded quantification and infinite sets, but only for the HOL4 and Isabelle/HOL targets; for OCaml and Coq the library currently only provides finite sets and bounded quantification. In future we will provide alternatives as for `nat` and `natural` above.

Having decided on finite or infinite sets, there remains a nontrivial choice of the best target representation. OCaml has a set implementation in its standard library, but with a functorised interface to supply an order on elements; we use a library with a polymorphic interface instead. For Isabelle/HOL and HOL4 the idiomatic potentially infinite sets are used. Isabelle/HOL also has several interesting alternative ones with improved executability, but they are supplied with an order via Isabelle/HOL's type-class mechanism which would require the user to supply potentially nontrivial proof. For Coq, there is no single idiomatic set library: FSets provides a module-oriented implementation, the Collections wrapper around this library uses type classes, and one can also represent sets as functions into `bool` or `Prop` ('ensembles'). They all also require an order, or at least a decidable equality relation, which would have to be provided via Coq's type-class mechanism. We add a simple finite-set library, leaving additional Lem libraries to map Lem sets to other Coq representations as future work.

Associative maps have similar issues to sets. Lem translates maps to Lem-specific finite map implementations in OCaml and Coq and into the idiomatic map types for HOL4 and Isabelle/HOL, which are finite maps and infinite maps respectively.

The binary relation type is closely related to sets and therefore also has similar design issues: relations can be seen as sets of pairs or as binary predicates. Both Isabelle/HOL and HOL4 provide dedicated libraries for both representations, and Lem currently maps only to the set representations.

3.10 Naming, notation and namespace issues

The namespaces and the sets of pre-defined identifiers and reserved keywords differ in each backend. For example, `op` is a reserved word in Isabelle/HOL but not in Coq. Without reserving every reserved word and every pre-defined identifier in each of our backends in Lem, we must implement a renaming mechanism to avoid name clashes post extraction.

Lem has a simple model of the namespaces and a list of the reserved words of each target. If a reserved word for the backend in question is encountered, Lem will automatically rename the constant and issue a warning. For example,

```
let op f g = ...
```

is automatically renamed to `op0`, or some other globally fresh name, when extracting to Isabelle/HOL. All occurrences of this constant are also suitably renamed. A warning is issued on the command line to notify users of the renaming. The user can also manually control renaming. For instance, placing

```
declare {isa} rename function op = isaop
```

in a Lem source file will rename `op` to `isaop` during extraction to Isabelle/HOL.

Note that Lem provides fine-grained control over how various syntactic components are renamed. The command above instructs Lem to rename only the *function* `op`, leaving the names of any shadowing record fields, modules or types fixed. Replacing the `function` keyword in the command above with `type` or `field`, for example, would allow the user to rename those components instead. This mechanism allows us to avoid auto-generated names, making Lem generate stable, predictable output even in the presence of name clashes, whilst also allowing the renaming of constants to follow the conventions of a particular backend, facilitating the generation of idiomatic backend code.

The Lem renaming mechanism respects target-specific differences in scoping. For example,

```
let op op = ...
```

features a function `op` taking a parameter called `op`. For some backends, this is problematic, and so the two should be renamed apart there, but not otherwise. In our running example, the function `op` will be renamed to `isaop` and the argument `op` to `op0` to avoid clashes with the Isabelle/HOL keyword. Lem correctly renames the name of the parameter apart from all constants present in the context.

3.11 Assertions, lemmata, and auxiliary outputs

Lem is intended to translate into target output that can be directly used, without manual editing by the user: Lem definitions generate target definitions which can be fully automatically checked. However, Lem can also generate aids for the user in additional *auxiliary* files, intended to be copied and manually edited by the user as necessary. For example, when defining a complicated recursive function in Lem, HOL4 and Isabelle/HOL can leave the termination proof to the user. Lem generates in the auxiliary file a template for its termination proof which the user can flesh out.

Lem also supports *assertions*, *lemmas* and *theorems*. Assertions are executable, for automated testing of simple properties. For OCaml they generate code in an auxiliary file that runs automated unit tests. For the theorem prover backends, they generate proof obligations, which are attempted to be discharged automatically. Lemmas and theorems are non-executable; they add proof obligations to auxiliary files. Simple, low-level lemmas can also be used for testing: often the resulting proof obligations can be automatically discharged. Exporting complicated lemmas and theorems might be beneficial as well. For example, Isabelle/HOL provides highly automated, powerful tools, and by exporting a lemma to Isabelle/HOL, this powerful machinery is easily accessible even by users not familiar with Isabelle. The following Lem lemma:

```
lemma unzip_zip:
  ∀l1 l2. unzip (zip l1 l2) = (l1, l2)
```

is translated to the Isabelle/HOL code:

```
lemma unzip_zip:
  "∀l1 l2. list_unzip (zip l1 l2) = (l1, l2)"
(* try *) by auto
```

The automated proof attempt by the `auto` method fails. If the user then uncomments `try`, various automated methods are run to either prove the lemma or find a counterexample. These methods include running external SMT and first order provers, internal natural deduction tools, and a sophisticated counterexample generator. In this example, Isabelle/HOL quickly finds a counterexample:

```
Nitpick found a counterexample for card 'a = 2 and card 'b = 2:
  Skolem constants: l1 = [a1], l2 = []
```

In general, tools like the counterexample generator Nitpick work well with Lem-generated Isabelle/HOL code, because Lem is tailored toward executability and this executability is (as far as possible) preserved by the translation to Isabelle/HOL. Therefore, non-trivial counterexamples can often be found automatically.

3.12 Inductive relations

Specifications often involve inductively defined relations, such as type systems or evaluation relations defined as the smallest relations satisfying a collection of rules. Lem provides an *inductive relations* mechanism for this purpose.

The following Lem definition (generated by Ott from a similar definition expressed over a calculus syntax) captures the reduction relation of the call-by-value λ-calculus:

```
indreln [reduce: term → term → bool]
  ax_app: ∀ x t1 v2.
    (is_val_of_term v2) ⟹
      reduce (T_app (T_lam x t1) v2) (subst v2 x t1)
and
  ctx_app_fun: ∀ t1 t t1'.
    (reduce t1 t1') ⟹
      reduce (T_app t1 t) (T_app t1' t)
and
  ctx_app_arg: ∀ v t1 t1'.
    (is_val_of_term v) ∧ (reduce t1 t1') ⟹
      reduce (T_app v t1) (T_app v t1')
```

Here, reduce is introduced as a relation—Lem relations are essentially functions into bool—between AST terms. In this case, the reduce relation is defined via three clauses. Within a clause, the full power of the Lem language is available, rather than a purely relational subset, as in Prolog. For instance, is_val_of_term and subst are functions, rather than relations. One may also define mutually recursive inductive relations.

The Isabelle/HOL, HOL4 and Coq backends support inductive relations, and we map Lem inductive relations into the native inductive relations of these backends.

However, inductive relations are not naturally expressible in our OCaml backend. We therefore implement a compilation process, compiling a Lem inductive relation into a function that searches for derivations. The compilation process is given a *mode* by the user, a description of which components of the relation are to be treated as 'inputs' and which are to be treated as 'outputs'. This compilation scheme is similar to one implemented within the Isabelle/HOL proof assistant, as implemented by Berghofer et al. [5] (there verified within Isabelle/HOL).

We go further than the Isabelle/HOL compilation scheme in automatically generating *witness types*, which encode a derivation tree for a given inductive relation. The functions generated by the compilation scheme can return witnesses, and additional functions check whether an element of the witness type belongs to the relation. These witnesses may also be produced externally, e.g. by a typechecker implementation that one wants to test, using the Lem-generated checker functions, against its definition. The generated types and functions are themselves defined in Lem and added to the Lem typing context, and therefore can be used by later Lem definitions and translated to any of the Lem targets.

For example, the following syntax instructs Lem to generate a reduction function for reduce, naming it onestep:

```
[reduce:  term  → term → bool
 onestep: input → output ]
```

The mode annotation on onestep instructs the compilation machinery to consider the first component of reduce as an input, and the second an output. Additional annotations can indicate that the function returns multiple results, that there must be a unique return value, or to generate a witness for the relation. Generated functions that are partial are treated in the same way as partial pattern matches. For non-deterministic rules, the generation searches exhaustively and, according to the annotation, either returns a list of elements in the relation or a single one (or is undefined).

To generate witness types and witness-checking functions, one can write:

```
[reduce : term → term → bool
 witness type r_witness; check check_r;]
```

This generates a witness type for the reduce relation:

```
type r_witness =
| Ctx_app_arg_witness of term × term × term × r_witness
| Ctx_app_fun_witness of term × term × term × r_witness
| Ax_app_witness of string × term × term
```

Instrumenting an interpreter or type-checker to produce such witnesses should be straightforward. Doing that, and also scaling this code generation up to make it work well on practical examples, is in progress.

3.13 Prop and bool in the Coq backend

As mentioned in our discussion of equality and type classes in Lem, Coq maintains a distinction between a *sort* of propositions, Prop, and a *type* of boolean-valued expressions, *bool*. Lem, similarly to Isabelle/HOL and HOL4, collapses these two notions into a single type, bool. This mismatch between the languages causes difficulties, most notably in how we handle equality, as we have seen, but also in how we handle inductive relations and lemmata.

Take, as an example, the following Lem inductive relation[1]:

```
indreln [even: nat → bool]
    even_zero: true ⟹ even 0
and even_plus: ∀n. even n ⟹ even (n + 2)
```

This is translated to an ordinary Coq inductive type residing in Prop (as all inductive types in Coq must reside in a sort):

```
Inductive even: nat → Prop :=
  | even_zero: true → even 0
  | even_plus: ∀n, even n → even (n + 2).
```

Here the premises of the introduction rules of the inductive relation (for example, true in even_zero) are of boolean type, whereas they need to inhabit Prop. We use a Coq coercion from the Coq bool type into Prop to circumvent this problem: a function of type bool → Prop declared as a coercion automatically lifts a boolean expression into Prop. A similar problem occurs with lemma statements, which reside in bool in Lem but must reside in Prop in Coq.

However, problems persist elsewhere. Case analysis in Prop is restricted in Coq, and one may only perform case analysis on a term of type Prop if the resulting type of the term obtained from the analysis is also of type Prop. However, Lem allows one to perform case analyses with if- and case-expressions on expressions which reside in Prop in the generated code. For example, Lem allows users to perform a case analysis on inductive relations:

```
let odd n = if even n then false else true
```

[1] Here, the true premise in even_zero is unnecessary from a purely logical viewpoint but Lem's parser currently requires every clause in an inductive relation definition to have a premise.

In the generated Coq code, the term `even n` has type `Prop` when it is expected to have type `bool` due to its position in the `if`-expression. There are four possibilities here:

1. Make this an error in Lem. However for backends like Isabelle/HOL and HOL4 the definition above is completely innocuous and rejecting it would be too restrictive.
2. Make use of Coq's generalised `if-then-else` notation (supporting any inductive type with exactly two constructors), include the `sumbool` type usually used to capture decidability, and attempt to automatically show decidability for inductive types such as `even` above. The above would then be translated to:

   ```
   let odd n = if even_dec n then false else true
   ```

   where `even_dec` is a decidability theorem of type $\forall n.\ \{\text{even}\ n\} + \{\neg\ \text{even}\ n\}$. However, this approach becomes much more involved if we use inductive relations in more complex ways within Lem, for example, in a list of booleans: `[4 < 5, even 4, false]`, or in some other complex expression, and it is not clear how well it will scale.
3. Enrich Lem's type system to identify a computational sublanguage, at the cost of significant complication.
4. Admit classical axioms—known to be consistent with Coq's logic—and collapse `Prop` into `bool`.

We ultimately adopt the last alternative, with a function `bool_of_Prop` of type `Prop` $\rightarrow$ `bool`, wrapping this function around any propositional term that is being used in a way where a boolean-typed term is expected. The admission of classical axioms to collapse `Prop` into `bool` is a matter of taste. Some large Coq developments happily assume classical axioms, others stay firmly within the existing constructive logic provided by Coq. We feel, however, that not restricting the Lem source language to accommodate every nuance exhibited by the backends is worth the admission of these axioms, though to what extent they affect the computational behaviour and automation and proof search tactics of Coq will require further experimentation to fully resolve.

4. Library mechanisms and design

Library design The Lem distribution supplies a default set of types and functions in its library, focussed on specification. Collections such as lists, sets and maps, basic data types such as disjoint sums, optional types, booleans and tuples, useful combinators on functions, and a library for working with relations are all included.

Specific function names and types exposed to the Lem user by the library are adopted from the Haskell standard library where possible. This is a well-designed library with a focus on purity. We also wish to provide flexibility in the specific choice of *backend* libraries function names and types in the Lem library are mapped to. Often, picking one library over another involves a trade-off between competing factors, with no clear winner. We therefore made it possible for users to change and extend the library as they see fit, including replacing it wholesale. Lem library files are standard source files, their only distinguishing feature being their inclusion in the Lem distribution. No 'prelude' or 'pervasive' environment is automatically loaded during Lem compilation.

Lem aims to accommodate both programming languages and proof assistants as backends. Further, we aim to support users who wish to target a subset of these backends, or all of them, favouring neither one nor the other. As a result, the Lem library must be suitably flexible in its design. Our design philosophy in the library is *permit partiality and under-specification, but isolate them.* We bifurcate the library into two sets of modules: the 'main' and 'extra' modules. The main hierarchy of files contain total, terminating functions that we believe are well-specified enough to be portable across all backends. Totality of pattern matching is guaranteed by Lem, which can be configured to produce a compile error upon encountering an incomplete pattern match, whereas termination is established by inspection, and running the generated library code through the proof assistant backends, which implement their own termination checking. All other functions are placed in the extra modules. For example, the library file `function.lem` includes various useful combinators such as `flip` and `const`. The `function_extra.lem` file, on the other hand, contains the constant `THE` with type $\forall\alpha.\ (\alpha \rightarrow$ `bool`$) \rightarrow$ `maybe` α, inexpressible in Coq. This design means there is always a conscious decision made on the part of the user to import functionality that assumes choice or exhibits partiality into their development.

Technical mechanisms Proof assistants provide a large body of facts about data types such as lists and numbers. Often, these facts are bundled together into simplification procedures for use in proof automation. In line with our goal of producing idiomatic backend code, we would like to map data types and functions in our Lem source to their corresponding implementations in the proof assistant, rather than generate our own copies, so that those facts and simplification procedures can be used. To this end, Lem features an array of tools for binding Lem functions and types to existing functions and types in the backends. For example

```
declare ocaml target_rep type set = 'Pset.set'
```

declares that Lem sets should be represented in OCaml by the existing OCaml-type `PSet.set`. Similarly, constants and functions can also be mapped to existing target representations:

```
val snoc : ∀α. α → list α → list α
let snoc e l = l ⊕ [e]
declare hol target_rep function snoc = 'SNOC'
let inline {isabelle;coq} snoc e l = l ⊕ [e]
```

Here, we introduce a Lem constant `snoc` and provide a Lem definition for it. For the HOL4 backend, `snoc` is mapped to the `SNOC` function from the HOL4 list-library. Coq and Isabelle/HOL do not provide their own native constants and this operation is expressed idiomatically using list concatenation. Lem's inlining mechanism replaces all occurrences of the `snoc` constant with the append of a singleton list in the generated Isabelle/HOL and Coq code. Finally, for all other backends that Lem supports (i.e. OCaml in the example), a default implementation of the function is generated. Note no inlining occurs here—the call to `snoc` is preserved, with the resulting OCaml code looking similar to the Lem source code.

The Lem target-representation and inlining mechanisms are powerful enough to 'smooth over' inconsistencies between the backends. For instance, folds over lists display a surprising variety in the order in which arguments are expected. Our mechanisms allow us to provide a consistent interface within Lem for functions such as these whilst mapping to idiomatic backend code:

```
declare hol   target_rep function foldr = 'FOLDR'
declare ocaml target_rep function foldr f b l =
  'List.fold_right' f l b
```

Target representations can also declare a constant as infix for certain backends. For example, the set-membership constant is mapped as follows:

```
declare ocaml target_rep function member = 'Pset.mem'
declare hol   target_rep function member = infix 'IN'
declare html  target_rep function member = infix '&isin;'
```

This function is prefix for OCaml but infix for HOL4. We could also provide additional associativity and binding strength information about infix constants in order to avoid generating superfluous parenthesis. Note that the user can also provide HTML and LaTeX target representations and that target representations are not restricted to valid Lem identifiers.

Unit testing through lemmata The Lem library attempts to clarify the semantics of each function by providing a definition, even if there are target-specific representations for all targets. Moreover, assertions and lemma statements can be used to describe the supposed behaviour of library files. As described in §3.11, assertions are executable tests used for unit testing. They generate executable testing code for OCaml. For the theorem prover backends they generate proof obligations which are (mostly) closed automatically by the prover's computation mechanisms. Lemmata are non-executable tests. They are ignored by the OCaml backend, while the theorem prover backends generate proof obligations that need to be discharged manually by the user. For the `snoc` example, the library contains the following assertions and lemmata:

```
assert snoc_1 : snoc (2:nat) [] = [2]
assert snoc_2 : snoc (2:nat) [3;4] = [3;4;2]
lemma snoc_length :
  ∀e l. length (snoc e l) = succ (length l)
```

If both a definition and a target-specific representation are present, Lem automatically generates a lemma that the target representation satisfies the definition. For example, the following lemma is automatically generated for the HOL4 backend:

```
lemma snoc_def_lemma: ∀l e. (l ⊕ [e]) = (SNOC e l)
```

Whilst we do not aim to completely describe the semantics of every function in the Lem library with assertions and lemmata, we believe this peppering of executable checks and proof obligations provides some assurance that each of the bindings in the respective backends has the intended semantics.

5. Example

In this section we show excerpts from one of our major Lem developments, the C/C++11 axiomatic concurrency model of Batty et al., highlighting especially where any target-specific features of Lem were necessary. The complete specification is around 2500 lines of Lem source (1500 non-comment), defining several related models. The generated OCaml forms the kernel of our `cppmem` tool, with a web interface (also using the HTML) for interactive and exhaustive exploration of the model on small examples, the generated LaTeX is used in papers and C/C++11 standards committee working notes, and the generated HOL4 code is the basis for mechanised proofs. The generated Coq and Isabelle code has also been used for (relatively minor) proof experiments.

The specification begins by opening standard Lem libraries:

```
open import Pervasives
```

and then proceeds by defining the types of action identifiers, C/C++11 memory orders, and the memory actions of the model. Action identifiers are taken to be strings for convenience in the `cppmem` user interface; for the meta-theory we just need a type with a decidable equality and infinitely many inhabitants.

```
type aid = string

type memory_order =
  | NA       | Seq_cst   | Relaxed   | Release
  | Acquire  | Consume   | Acq_rel

type action =
  | Load  of aid × tid × memory_order × location × cvalue
  | Store of aid × tid × memory_order × location × cvalue
  | Fence of aid × tid × memory_order
  | ...
```

In the usual 'axiomatic memory model' style, the model is expressed as predicates over a notion of *candidate execution*, comprising a set of actions and various relations over them that describe one execution which might or might not be permitted by the model. Some of those are collected in the following record type:

```
type pre_execution =
  <| actions : set (action);
     threads : set (tid);
     lk      : location → location_kind;
     sb      : set (action × action) ;
     asw     : set (action × action) ;
     dd      : set (action × action) ;
  |>
```

For the HOL4 meta-theory, we want to consider possibly infinite candidate executions, therefore the representation of Lem sets as the usual idiomatic-HOL4 characteristic functions is appropriate. In the OCaml tool, we will only deal with finite candidate executions, and so the idiomatic, ordered balanced binary tree representation is appropriate there. The sets used here all contain only elements of concrete types (for which the OCaml pervasive comparison will be correct), so no user instantiation of the `SetType` type class is required.

The specification continues with some routine functions defined by pattern matching, for example:

```
let is_at_non_atomic_location lk a =
  match loc_of a with
  | Just l  ⇒ (lk l = Non_Atomic)
  | Nothing ⇒ false
  end
```

The bulk of the specification consists of definitions of derived relations and predicates over candidate executions. For example, given a set of actions and a *happens-before* relation `hb`, the following picks out the write-read pairs in `hb` for which the write is a *visible side effect* (in the terms of the C/C++11 standards) for the read. It uses a Lem set comprehension, ranging over the supplied `hb` (which will be known and finite at execution time in the generated OCaml). The body of the comprehension uses standard propositional logic and an existential quantifier, here bounded by the set of actions.

```
let visible_side_effect_set actions hb =
  { (a,b) | forall ((a,b) IN hb) |
    is_write a && is_read b && (loc_of a = loc_of b) &&
    not ( exists (c IN actions). not (c IN {a;b}) &&
        is_write c && (loc_of c = loc_of b) &&
        (a,c) IN hb && (c,b) IN hb) }
```

The Lem-typeset version of this definition can be used simply by including

```
\LEMvisibleSideEffectSet
```

in a LaTeX source file (after including the Lem-generated definitions with `\usepackage{lem}` and `\include{Cmm-inc}`), to give:

let $\mathit{visible\_side\_effect\_set}\ \mathit{actions}\ \mathit{hb}\ =$
$\{\ (a,\ b)\ |\ \forall\ (a,\ b) \in \mathit{hb}\ |$
is_write $a \wedge$ is_read $b \wedge$ (loc_of a = loc_of b) $\wedge$
$\neg\ (\ \exists\ c \in \mathit{actions}.\ \neg\ (c \in \{a,\ b\}) \wedge$
is_write $c \wedge$ (loc_of c = loc_of b) $\wedge$
$(a,\ c) \in \mathit{hb} \wedge (c,\ b) \in \mathit{hb})\ \}$

Note the preservation of line breaks and indentation, giving fine control of the typeset layout. The generated HOL4 in this case is almost a direct transcription of the Lem source, as HOL4 supports similar set comprehension forms. The generated OCaml is somewhat more complex, using `Pset` library folds, membership tests, and set constructors, all with a suitable comparison function.

These excerpts are representative of typical Lem usage: mathematically straightforward higher-order logic definitions, with the real content in the details of exactly what the defined relations and predicates say. Though this development does not use inductively defined relations or recursively defined data types and functions extensively, others do, in a straightforward manner. In the previous sections we discussed many aspects of the Lem design that make it possible to generate code for all the targets in general, but it is common for only a few of those to be in play at once.

For this development the only target-specific definitions are as follows. First, there are those encapsulated in the Lem libraries used: `Basic_classes`, `Bool`, `Maybe`, `Num`, `Set`, `List`, and `Relation` (this development does not use `Tuple`, `Either`, `Function`, `Map`, `String`, `Word`, or `Sorting`, or any of the 'extra' libraries).

We give a general Lem definition for a predicate `strict_total_order_over` but in the HOL4 backend we bind it to the equivalent HOL4 standard library definition:

```
declare hol target_rep function strict_total_order_over
  = 'strict_linear_order'
```

For Coq we define one measure function in Lem that is used in a hand proof of the termination of a recursive evaluation function over a type of trees of lists of named predicates:

```
type named_predicate_tree =
  | Leaf of (complete_execution → bool)
  | Node of list (string × named_predicate_tree)
```

To handle infinitary executions in the meta-theory, the definitions include assumptions that certain relations of a candidate execution, e.g. the coherence order, have finite prefixes. This is given a Lem definition for Isabelle/HOL, mapped to a HOL4 standard library function (in the same manner as above), and mapped to just a constant true for OCaml and Coq, which are both dealing only with the finitary case (using the default Lem set representations in each).

Then there are a number of definitions which are used only in the meta-theory, not in the tool, for which we do not produce OCaml output. This includes the top-level definition of each model (the 15 `behaviour` predicates), which are parameterised on a thread-local semantics (whereas in the tool we use a fixed thread-local semantics). The meta-theory also uses a receptiveness assumption and 11 other auxiliaries.

The amount of target-specific code needed in other developments is similarly small. For example, in CakeML there are 10 HOL4-specific source lines, introducing 5 HOL4 library functions that are not in the Lem library.

This C/C++11 development is also typical in that it is the product of a considerable investment of effort (multiple person-years by several people, of dialogue with the standards committee, experimentation, and proof) and that it is a specification that we need to maintain over an extended period of time. Manually propagating changes from versions in one target to another would have been prohibitive.

The Lem design is focussed on the reuse of a specification in multiple targets, not on reuse of parts of one specification in another, but the latter is also an important question. In particular, here the metatheory by Batty is over the model as above, but for a different purpose we have recently extended the model, adding new constructors of the `action` type and corresponding new function and predicate clauses. At present we do this (while avoiding forking the main specification file) by ad hoc means, but ideally one might want a mixin-style module composition.

6. Conclusion

Lem provides a new alternative for building large-scale semantic models and specifications, combining the uniform language design and ease of use of a good programming language with the definitional expressiveness provided by a theorem prover, and supporting *portable* definitions. It is more general-purpose than existing specification languages like K, Ott, or PLT Redex. Using Lem inevitably imposes some restrictions compared with working natively in a single prover but offers some advantages even in that case, and for modelling/specification exercises where the model creation and validation effort is large, the prospect of portability is compelling. It is demonstrably flexible enough to naturally specify a wide range of large-scale models while also allowing users to use their preferred tools for proof. That said, it is not perfect (of course), and we would like to revisit some aspects of the design with the benefit of hindsight: the type class mechanism, bool vs prop, multiple prover set representations, and inductive relation code generation.

Lem is a higher-order, typed, functional language, as are all of the backends that Lem currently targets. We anticipate that targeting new languages that fall into this pattern, for example Haskell, SML or Matita, would be straightforward.

Lem's syntax and type system are formally defined, but its logical semantics is defined by the translations into the targets. We attempt no formal guarantee that the result of translating into one target has the same mathematical meaning as that of translating into another, and indeed sometimes they intentionally do not (§3.9). Even when intuitively they do, stating and proving that fact would require creating, as a starting point, formal models of the semantics of the various targets, including Coq's underlying type system, Isabelle's datatype package, HOL's inductive relations package, etc. That would be worthwhile and challenging, but ours here is a first, pragmatic, goal: to support the working specifier.

Acknowledgments

We thank Thomas Tuerk for his contributions to many aspects of Lem, Thomas Williams for his work on the Lem inductive relations package, Ohad Kammar for his work on model porting, and all the users of Lem for their feedback. We acknowledge funding from EPSRC grants EP/H005633 (Leadership Fellowship, Sewell) and EP/K008528 (REMS Programme Grant).

References

[1] A. Asperti, C. Sacerdoti Coen, E. Tassi, and S. Zacchiroli. User interaction with the Matita proof assistant. *J. Autom. Reason.*, 2006.

[2] L. Augustsson. Compiling pattern matching. In *Functional Programming Languages and Computer Architecture*, LNCS 201. 1985. ISBN 978-3-540-15975-9. . URL http://dx.doi.org/10.1007/3-540-15975-4_48.

[3] M. Batty, S. Owens, S. Sarkar, P. Sewell, and T. Weber. Mathematizing C++ concurrency. In *Proc. POPL*, 2011.

[4] M. Batty, K. Memarian, S. Owens, S. Sarkar, and P. Sewell. Clarifying and compiling C/C++ concurrency: from C++11 to POWER. In *Proc. POPL*, 2012.

[5] S. Berghofer, L. Bulwahn, and F. Haftmann. Turning inductive into equational specifications. In *Proc. TPHOLs*, 2009.

[6] S. Bishop, M. Fairbairn, M. Norrish, P. Sewell, M. Smith, and K. Wansbrough. Rigorous specification and conformance testing techniques for network protocols, as applied to TCP, UDP, and Sockets. In *Proc. SIGCOMM*, 2005.

[7] M. Bodin, A. Charguéraud, D. Filaretti, P. Gardner, S. Maffeis, D. Naudziuniene, A. Schmitt, and G. Smith. A trusted mechanised JavaScript specification. In *Proc. POPL*, 2014.

[8] T. Coquand. An analysis of girard's paradox. In *Logic in Computer Science*, 1986.

[9] C. Ellison and G. Rosu. An executable formal semantics of C with applications. In *Proc. POPL*, 2012.

[10] A. C. J. Fox and M. O. Myreen. A trustworthy monadic formalization of the ARMv7 instruction set architecture. In *Proc. ITP*, 2010.

[11] S. Goel, W. A. H. Jr., and M. Kaufmann. Abstract Stobjs and their application to ISA modeling. In *Proc. ACL2 Workshop*, 2013.

[12] M. J. C. Gordon, J. Reynolds, W. A. H. Jr., and M. Kaufmann. An integration of HOL and ACL2. In *Proc. FMCAD*, 2006.

[13] J. Hurd. The OpenTheory standard theory library. In *NASA Formal Methods*, LNCS 6617, 2011.

[14] C. Kaliszyk and A. Krauss. Scalable LCF-Style proof translation. In *Proc. ITP*, LNCS 7998, 2013.

[15] C. Keller and B. Werner. Importing HOL Light into Coq. In *Proc. ITP*, LNCS 6172, 2010. ISBN 3-642-14051-3, 978-3-642-14051-8. . URL http://dx.doi.org/10.1007/978-3-642-14052-5_22.

[16] C. Klein, J. Clements, C. Dimoulas, C. Eastlund, M. Felleisen, M. Flatt, J. A. McCarthy, J. Rafkind, S. Tobin-Hochstadt, and R. B. Findler. Run your research: on the effectiveness of lightweight mechanization. In *Proc. POPL*, 2012. ISBN 978-1-4503-1083-3.

[17] G. Klein, K. Elphinstone, G. Heiser, J. Andronick, D. Cock, P. Derrin, D. Elkaduwe, K. Engelhardt, R. Kolanski, M. Norrish, T. Sewell, H. Tuch, and S. Winwood. seL4: formal verification of an OS kernel. In *Proc. SOSP*, 2009.

[18] R. Kumar, M. O. Myreen, M. Norrish, and S. Owens. CakeML: A Verified Implementation of ML. In *Proc. POPL*, 2014.

[19] X. Leroy. A formally verified compiler back-end. *Journal of Automated Reasoning*, 43(4):363–446, 2009.

[20] J. Lim and T. Reps. TSL: A system for generating abstract interpreters and its application to machine-code analysis. *TOPLAS*, 35(1), 2013.

[21] S. Mador-Haim, L. Maranget, S. Sarkar, K. Memarian, J. Alglave, S. Owens, R. Alur, M. M. K. Martin, P. Sewell, and D. Williams. An axiomatic memory model for POWER multiprocessors. In *CAV*, 2012.

[22] L. Maranget. Compiling pattern matching to good decision trees. In *Proc. Workshop on ML*, 2008. ISBN 978-1-60558-062-3. . URL http://doi.acm.org/10.1145/1411304.1411311.

[23] J. Meseguer. Twenty years of rewriting logic. In *Proc. WRLA*, WRLA'10, 2010.

[24] G. Morrisett, G. Tan, J. Tassarotti, J.-B. Tristan, and E. Gan. RockSalt: better, faster, stronger SFI for the x86. In *Proc. PLDI*, 2012.

[25] S. Owens. A sound semantics for OCaml light. In *Proc. ESOP, LNCS 4960*, 2008.

[26] S. Owens, P. Böhm, F. Zappa Nardelli, and P. Sewell. Lem: A lightweight tool for heavyweight semantics. In *Proc. ITP, LNCS 6898*, pages 363–369, 2011. "Rough Diamond" section.

[27] J. G. Politz, M. J. Carroll, B. S. Lerner, J. Pombrio, and S. Krishnamurthi. A tested semantics for getters, setters, and eval in JavaScript. In *Proc. DSL*, 2012.

[28] T. Rittweiler and F. Haftmann. Haskabelle — converting Haskell source files to Isabelle/HOL theories. http://isabelle.in.tum.de/haskabelle.html.

[29] G. Roşu and T. F. Şerbănuţă. An overview of the K semantic framework. *J. Logic and Algebraic Programming*, 79(6):397–434, 2010.

[30] S. Sarkar, P. Sewell, J. Alglave, L. Maranget, and D. Williams. Understanding POWER multiprocessors. In *Proc. PLDI*, 2011.

[31] S. Sarkar, K. Memarian, S. Owens, M. Batty, P. Sewell, L. Maranget, J. Alglave, and D. Williams. Synchronising C/C++ and POWER. In *Proc. PLDI*, 2012.

[32] P. Sewell, S. Sarkar, S. Owens, F. Zappa Nardelli, and M. O. Myreen. x86-TSO: A rigorous and usable programmer's model for x86 multiprocessors. *C. ACM*, 53(7):89–97, 2010.

[33] P. Sewell, F. Zappa Nardelli, S. Owens, G. Peskine, T. Ridge, S. Sarkar, and R. Strniša. Ott: Effective tool support for the working semanticist. *J. Funct. Program.*, 20(1):71–122, 2010. ISSN 0956-7968.

[34] M. Sozeau. Subset coercions in Coq. In *TYPES*, volume 4502 of *Lecture Notes in Computer Science*, pages 237–252, 2007.

[35] M. G. J. van den Brand, A. Deursen, J. Heering, H. A. d. Jong, M. Jonge, T. Kuipers, P. Klint, L. Moonen, P. A. Olivier, J. Scheerder, J. J. Vinju, E. Visser, and J. Visser. The ASF+SDF meta-environment: A component-based language development environment. In *Proc. LDTA, ENTCS 44*, 2001.

[36] J. Ševčík, V. Vafeiadis, F. Zappa Nardelli, S. Jagannathan, and P. Sewell. CompCertTSO: A verified compiler for relaxed-memory concurrency. *J. ACM*, 60(3):22:1–22:50, June 2013. ISSN 0004-5411. . URL http://doi.acm.org/10.1145/2487241.2487248.

[37] D. Vytiniotis, S. L. P. Jones, T. Schrijvers, and M. Sulzmann. OutsideIn(X) modular type inference with local assumptions. *J. Funct. Program.*, 21(4-5):333–412, 2011.

[38] P. Wadler. Views: a way for pattern matching to cohabit with data abstraction. In *Proc. POPL*, 1987. ISBN 0-89791-215-2. . URL http://doi.acm.org/10.1145/41625.41653.

[39] F. Wiedijk. Encoding the HOL Light logic in Coq, 2007. Note.

[40] J. Zhao, S. Nagarakatte, M. M. K. Martin, and S. Zdancewic. Formalizing the LLVM intermediate representation for verified program transformations. In *Proc. POPL*, 2012.

Safe Zero-cost Coercions for Haskell

Joachim Breitner
Karlsruhe Institute of Technology
breitner@kit.edu

Richard A. Eisenberg
University of Pennsylvania
eir@cis.upenn.edu

Simon Peyton Jones
Microsoft Research
simonpj@microsoft.com

Stephanie Weirich
University of Pennsylvania
sweirich@cis.upenn.edu

Abstract

Generative type abstractions – present in Haskell, OCaml, and other languages – are useful concepts to help prevent programmer errors. They serve to create new types that are distinct at compile time but share a run-time representation with some base type. We present a new mechanism that allows for zero-cost conversions between generative type abstractions and their representations, even when such types are deeply nested. We prove type safety in the presence of these conversions and have implemented our work in GHC.

Categories and Subject Descriptors D.3.3 [*Programming Languages*]: Language Constructs and Features—abstract data types; F.3.3 [*Logics and Meanings of Programs*]: Studies of Program Constructs—Type structure

Keywords Haskell; Coercion; Type class; Newtype deriving

1. Introduction

Modular languages support *generative type abstraction*, the ability for programmers to define application-specific types, and rely on the type system to distinguish between these new types and their underlying representations. Type abstraction is a powerful tool for programmers, enabling both flexibility (implementors can change representations) and security (implementors can maintain invariants about representations). Typed languages provide these mechanisms with zero run-time cost – there should be no performance penalty for creating abstractions – using mechanisms such as ML's module system [MTHM97] and Haskell's **newtype** declaration [Mar10].

For example, a Haskell programmer might create an abstract type for HTML data, representing them as Strings (Figure 1). Although String values use the same patterns of bits in memory as HTML values, the two types are distinct. That is, a String will not be accepted by a function expecting an HTML. The constructor Mk converts a String to an HTML (see function text), while using Mk in a pattern converts in the other direction (see function unMk). By exporting the type HTML, but not its data constructor, module Html ensures that the type HTML is *abstract* – clients cannot make arbitrary strings into HTML – and thereby prevent cross-site scripting attacks.

```
module Html( HTML, text, unMk, ... ) where
  newtype HTML = Mk String
  unMk :: HTML → String
  unMk (Mk s) = s
  text :: String → HTML
  text s = Mk (escapeSpecialCharacters s)
```

Figure 1. An abstraction for HTML values

Using **newtype** for abstraction in Haskell has always suffered from an embarrassing difficulty. Suppose in the module Html, the programmer wants to break HTML data into a list of lines:

```
linesH :: HTML → [HTML]
linesH h = map Mk (lines (unMk h))
```

To get the resulting [HTML] we are forced to map Mk over the list. Operationally, this map is the identity function – the run-time representation of [String] is identical to [HTML] – *but it will carry a run-time cost nevertheless*. The optimiser in the Glasgow Haskell Compiler (GHC) is powerless to fix the problem, because it works over a *typed* intermediate language; the Mk constructor changes the type of its operand, and hence cannot be optimised away. There is nothing that the programmer can do to prevent this run-time cost. What has become of the claim of zero-overhead abstraction?

In this paper we describe a robust, simple mechanism that programmers can use to solve this problem, making the following contributions:

- We describe the design of *safe coercions* (Section 2), which introduces the function

  ```
  coerce :: Coercible a b ⇒ a → b
  ```

  and a new type class Coercible. This function performs a zero-cost conversion between two types a and b that have the same representation. The crucial question becomes

ICFP '14, September 1–6, 2014, Gothenburg, Sweden.

ACM 978-1-4503-2873-9 /14/09...$15.00.
http://dx.doi.org/10.1145/10.1145/2628136.2628141

what instances of Coercible exist? We give a simple but non-obvious strategy (Sections 2.1–2.2), expressed largely in the familiar language of Haskell type classes.

- We formalise Coercible by translation into GHC's intermediate language System FC, augmented with the concept of *roles* (Section 2.2), adapted from prior work [WVPZ11]. Our new contribution is a significant simplification of the roles idea in System FC; we formalise this simpler system and give the usual proofs of preservation and progress in Section 4.
- Adding safe coercions to the source language raises new issues for abstract types, and for the coherence of type elaboration. We articulate the issues, and introduce *role annotations* to solve them (Section 3).
- It would be too onerous to insist on programmer-supplied role annotations for every type, so we give a *role inference algorithm* in Section 5.
- To support our claim of practical utility, we have implemented the whole scheme in GHC (Section 6), and evaluated it against thousands of Haskell libraries (Section 9).

Our work finally resolves a notorious and long-standing bug in GHC (#1496), which concerns the interaction of newtype coercions with type families (Section 7). While earlier work [WVPZ11] was motivated by the same bug, it was too complicated to implement. Our new approach finds a sweet spot, offering a considerably simpler system in exchange for a minor loss of expressiveness (Sections 8 and 10).

As this work demonstrates, the interactions between type abstraction and advanced type system features, such as type families and GADTs, are subtle. The ability to create and enforce zero-cost type abstraction is not unique to Haskell – notably the ML module system also provides this capability, and more. As a result, OCaml developers are now grappling with similar difficulties. We discuss the connection between roles and OCaml's variance annotations (Section 8), as well as other related work.

2. The design and interface of Coercible

We begin by focusing exclusively on the programmer's-eye-view of safe coercions. We need no new syntax; rather, the programmer simply sees a new API, provided in just two declarations:

```
class Coercible a b
coerce :: Coercible a b ⇒ a → b
```

The type class Coercible is abstract, i.e. its methods are not visible. It differs from other type classes in a few minor points: The user cannot create manual instances; instances are automatically generated by the compiler; and the visibility of instances is conditional. Generally, users can think of it as a normal type class, which is a nice property of the design.

The key principle is this: *If two types* s *and* t *are related by* Coercible s t*, then* s *and* t *have bit-for-bit identical run-time representations.* Moreover, as you can see from the type of coerce, if Coercible s t holds then coerce can convert a value of type s to one of type t. And that's it!

The crucial question, to which we devote the rest of this section and the next, becomes this: exactly when does Coercible s t hold? To whet your appetite consider these declarations:

```
newtype Age      = MkAge Int
newtype AgeRange = MkAR (Int,Int)
newtype BigAge   = MkBig Age
```

GHC generates the following instances of Coercible:

(1) **instance** Coercible a a

(2) For every **newtype** NT x = MkNT (T x), the instances

```
instance Coercible (T x) b ⇒ Coercible (NT x) b
instance Coercible a (T x) ⇒ Coercible a (NT x)
```

which are visible if and only if the constructor MkNT is in scope.

(3) For every type constructor TC r p n, where
   - r stands for TC's parameters at role representational,
   - p for those at role phantom and
   - n for those at role nominal,

   the instance

```
instance Coercible r1 r2 ⇒
        Coercible (TC r1 p1 n) (TC r2 p2 n)
```

Figure 2. Coercible instances

Here are some coercions that hold, so that a single call to coerce suffices to convert between the two types:

- Coercible Int Age: we can coerce from Int to Age at zero cost; this is simply the MkAge constructor.
- Coercible Age Int: and the reverse; this is pattern matching on MkAge.
- Coercible [Age] [Int]: lifting the coercion over lists.
- Coercible (Either Int Age) (Either Int Int): lifting the coercion over Either.
- Coercible (Either Int Age) (Either Age Int): this is more complicated, because first argument of Either must be coerced in one direction, and the second in the other.
- Coercible (Int → Age) (Age → Int): all this works over function arrows too.
- Coercible (Age, Age) AgeRange: we have to unwrap the pair of Ages and then wrap with MkAR.
- Coercible [BigAge] [Int]: two levels of coercion.

In the rest of this section we will describe how Coercible constraints are solved or, equivalently, which instances of Coercible exist. (See Figure 2 for a concise summary.)

2.1 Coercing newtypes

Since Coercible relates a newtype with its base type, we need Coercible instance declarations for every such newtype. The naive **instance** Coercible Int Age does not work well, for reasons explained in the box on page 3, so instead we generate *two* instances for each newtype:

```
instance Coercible a Int ⇒ Coercible a Age  — (A1)
instance Coercible Int b ⇒ Coercible Age b  — (A2)

instance Coercible a Age ⇒ Coercible a BigAge  — (B1)
instance Coercible Age b ⇒ Coercible BigAge b  — (B2)

instance Coercible a AgeRange ⇒ Coercible a (Int,Int)
instance Coercible AgeRange b ⇒ Coercible (Int,Int) b
```

Notice that each instance unwraps just one layer of the newtype, so we call them the "unwrapping instances".

If we now want to solve, say, a constraint Coercible s Age, for any type s, we can use (A1) to reduce it to the simpler goal Coercible s Int. A more complicated, two-layer coercion Coercible BigAge Int is readily reduced, in two such steps, to Coercible Int Int. All we need now is for GHC to have a built-in witness of reflexivity, expressing that any type has the same run-time representation as itself:

```
instance Coercible a a
```

This simple scheme allows coercions that involve arbitrary levels of wrapping or unwrapping, in either direction, with a single call to coerce. The solution path is not fully determined, but that does not matter. For example, here are two ways to solve Coercible BigAge Age:

	Coercible BigAge Age	
⟶	Coercible BigAge Int	— By (A1)
⟶	Coercible Age Int	— By (B2)
⟶	Coercible Int Int	— By (A2)
⟶	*solved*	— By reflexivity

	Coercible BigAge Age	
⟶	Coercible Age Age	— By (B2)
⟶	*solved*	— By reflexivity

Since Coercible constraints have no run-time behaviour (unlike normal type class constraints), we have no concerns about incoherence; any solution will do.

The newtype-unwrapping instances (i.e., (2) in Figure 2) are available *only if the corresponding newtype data constructor* (Mk in our current example) *is in scope*; this is required to preserve abstraction, as we explain in Section 3.1.

2.2 Coercing parameters of type constructors

As Figure 2 shows, as well as the unwrapping instances for a **newtype**, we also generate one instance for each type constructor, including data types, newtypes the function type, and built-in data types like tuples. We call this instance the "lifting instance" for the type, because it lifts coercions through the type. The shape of the instance depends on the so-called *roles* of the type constructor. Each type parameter of a type constructor has a role, determined by the way in which the parameter is used in the definition of the type constructor. In practice, the roles of a declared data type are determined by a role inference algorithm (Section 5) and can be modified by role annotations (Section 3.1). Once defined, the roles of a type constructor are the same in every scope, regardless of whether the concrete definition of that type is available in that scope.

Roles, a development of earlier work [WVPZ11] (Section 8), are a new concept for the programmer. In the following subsections, we discuss how the three possible roles, *representational*, *phantom* and *nominal*, ensure that lifting instances do not violate type safety by allowing coercions between types with different run-time representations.

2.2.1 Coercing representational type parameters

The most common role is *representational*. It is the role that is assigned to the type parameters of ordinary newtypes and data types like Maybe, the list type and Either. The Coercible instances for these type constructors are:

```
instance Coercible a b ⇒ Coercible (Maybe a) (Maybe b)
instance Coercible a b ⇒ Coercible [a] [b]
instance (Coercible a1 b1, Coercible a2 b2)
        ⇒ Coercible (Either a1 a2) (Either b1 b2)
```

Why a single instance is not enough

Why do we create two instances for every newtype, rather than just the single declaration

```
instance Coercible Int Age
```

to witness the fact that Int and Age have the same run-time representation?

That would indeed allow us to convert from Int to Age, using coerce, but what about the reverse direction? We then might need a second function

```
uncoerce :: Coercible a b ⇒ b → a
```

although it would be tiresome for the programmer to remember which one to call. Alternatively, perhaps GHC should generate *two* instances:

```
instance Coercible Int Age
instance Coercible Age Int
```

But how would we get from BigAge to Int? We could try this:

```
down :: BigAge → Int
down x = coerce (coerce x)
```

Our intent here is that each invocation of coerce unwraps one "layer" of newtype. But this is not good, because the type inference engine cannot figure out which type to use for the result of the inner coerce. To make the code typecheck we would have to add a type signature:

```
down :: BigAge → Int
down x = coerce (coerce x :: Age)
```

Not very nice. Moreover we would prefer to do all this with a *single* call to coerce, implying that Coercible BigAge Int must hold. That might make us consider adding the instance declaration

```
instance (Coercible a b, Coercible b c) ⇒ Coercible a c
```

to express the transitivity of Coercible. But now the problem of the un-specified intermediate type b re-appears, and cannot be solved with a type signature.

All of these problems are nicely solved using the instances in Figure 2.

These instances are just as you would expect: for example, the type Maybe t1 and Maybe t2 have the same run-time representation if and only if t1 and t2 have the same representation.

Most primitive type constructors also have representational roles for their arguments. For example, the domain and co-domain of arrow types are representational, giving rise to the following Coercible instance:

```
instance (Coercible a1 b1, Coercible a2 b2)
        ⇒ Coercible (a1 → a2) (b1 → b2)
```

Likewise, the type IORef has a representational parameter, so expressions of type IORef Int can be converted to type IORef Age for zero cost (and outside of the IO monad).

Returning to the introduction, we can use these instances to write linesH very directly, thus:

```
linesH :: HTML → [HTML]
linesH = coerce lines
```

In this case, the call to coerce gives rise to a constraint Coercible (String → [String]) (HTML → [HTML]), which gets simplified to Coercible String HTML using the instances for arrow and list types. Then the instance for the newtype HTML reduces it to Coercible String String, which is solved by the reflexive instance.

2.2.2 Coercing phantom type parameters

A type parameter has a *phantom* role if it does not occur in the definition of the type, or if it does, then only as a phantom parameter of another type constructor. For example, these declarations

```
data Phantom b = Phantom
data NestedPhantom b = L [Phantom b] | SomethingElse
```

both have parameter b at a phantom role.

When do the types Phantom t1 and Phantom t2 have the same run-time representation? Always! Therefore, we have the instances

```
instance Coercible (Phantom a) (Phantom b)
instance Coercible (NestedPhantom a) (NestedPhantom b)
```

and coerce can be used to change the phantom parameter arbitrarily.

2.2.3 Coercing nominal type parameters

In contrast, the *nominal* role induces the strictest preconditions for Coercible instances. This role is assigned to a parameter that possibly affects the run-time representation of a type, commonly because it is passed to a type function. For example, consider the following code

```
type family EncData a where
  EncData String = (ByteString, Encoding)
  EncData HTML = ByteString

data Encoding = ...
data EncText a = MkET (EncData a)
```

Even though we have Coercible HTML String, it would be wrong to derive the instance Coercible (EncText HTML) (EncText String), because these two types have quite different run-time representations! Therefore, there are no instances that change a nominal parameter of a type constructor.

All parameters of a type or data *family* have nominal role, because they could be inspected by the type family instances. For similar reasons, the non-uniform parameters to GADTs are also required to be nominal.

2.2.4 Coercing multiple type parameters

A type constructor can have multiple type parameters, each at a different role. In that case, an appropriate constraint for each type parameter is used:

```
data Params r p n = Con1 (Maybe r) | Con2 (EncData n)
```

yields the instance

```
instance Coercible r1 r2
        ⇒ Coercible (Params r1 p1 n) (Params r2 p2 n)
```

This instance expresses that the representational type parameters may change if there is a Coercible instance for them; the phantom type parameters may change arbitrarily; and the nominal type parameters must stay the same.

3. Abstraction and coherence

The purpose of the HTML type from the introduction is to prevent accidentally mixing up unescaped strings and HTML fragments. Rejecting programs that make this mistake is not a matter of type safety as traditionally construed, but rather of preserving a desired abstraction.

While the previous section described how the Coercible instances ensure that uses of coerce are type safe, this section discusses two other properties: *abstraction* and *class coherence*.

3.1 Preserving abstraction

When the constructors of a type are in scope then we can write code semantically equivalent to coerce by hand (although it might be less efficient). In this situation, the use of coerce should definitely be allowed. However, when the constructors are not in scope, it turns out that we sometimes want the lifting instance, and sometimes we do *not* want it.

The newtype unwrapping instance is directly controlled by the visibility of the constructor and can be used if and only if this is in scope. (See Section 2.1 for how this is accomplished.) For example, since the author of module Html did not export Mk, a client does not see the unwrapping instances for HTML, and the abstraction is preserved.

However, we permit the use of the coercion lifting instance for a type constructor even when the data constructors are not available. For example, built-in types like IORef or the function type (→) do not even have constructors that can be in scope. Nevertheless, coercing from IORef HTML to IORef String and from HTML → HTML to String → String should be allowed.

Therefore the rule for the lifting instance is that it can be used independent of the visibility of constructors. Instead, its form – what coercions it allows – is controlled by the roles of the type constructor's parameters.

Library authors can control the roles assigned to type constructors using *role annotations*. In many cases, the role inferred by the type checker is sufficient, even for abstract types. Consider a library for non-empty lists:

```
module NonEmptyListLib( NE, singleton, ... ) where
  data NE a = MkNE [a]
  singleton :: a → NE a
  ...etc...
```

The type must be exported abstractly; otherwise, the non-empty property can be broken by its users. Nevertheless lifting a coercion through NE, i.e. coercing NE HTML to NE String, should be allowed. Therefore, the role of NE's parameter should be representational. In this case, the library author does not have to actively set it: As it is the most permissive type-safe role, the role inference algorithm (Section 5.2) already chooses representational.

However, sometimes library authors must restrict the usage of the lifting coercion to ensure that the invariants of their abstract types can be preserved. For example, consider the data type Map k v, which implements an efficient finite map from keys of type k to values of type v, using an internal representation based on a balanced tree, something like this:

```
data Map k v = Leaf | Node k v (Map k v) (Map k v)
```

It would be disastrous if the user were allowed to coerce from (Map Age v) to (Map Int v), because a valid tree with regard to the ordering of Age might be completely bogus when using the ordering of Int.

To prevent that difficulty, the author specifies

```
type role Map nominal representational
```

As explained in Section 2.2, we now have the desirable and useful lifting instance

```
instance Coercible a b ⇒ Coercible (Map k a) (Map k b)
```

which allows the coercion from Map k HTML to Map k String.

Note that in the declaration of Map the parameters k and v are used in exactly the same way, so this distinction cannot be made by the compiler; it can only be specified by the programmer. However, the compiler ensures that programmer-specified role annotations cannot subvert the type system: if the annotation specifies an unsafe role, the compiler will reject the program.

3.2 Preserving class coherence

Another property of Haskell, independent of type-safety, is the coherence of type classes. There should only ever be one class instance for a particular class and type. We call this desirable property *coherence*. Without extra checks, Coercible could be used to create incoherence.

Consider this (non-Haskell98) data type, which reifies a Show instance as a value:

```
data HowToShow a where
  MkHTS :: Show a ⇒ HowToShow a

showH :: HowToShow a → a → String
showH MkHTS x = show x
```

Here showH pattern-matches on a HowToShow value, and uses the instance stored inside it to obtain the show method. If we are not careful, the following code would break the coherence of the Show type class:

```
instance Show HTML where
  show (Mk s) = "HTML:" ++ show s

stringShow :: HowToShow String
stringShow = MkHTS
htmlShow :: HowToShow HTML
htmlShow = MkHTS
badShow :: HowToShow HTML
badShow = coerce stringShow

λ> showH stringShow "Hello"
"Hello"
λ> showH htmlShow (Mk "Hello")
"HTML:Hello"
λ> showH badShow (Mk "Hello")
"Hello"
```

In the final example we were applying show to a value of type HTML, but the Show instance for String (coerced to (Show HTML)) was used.

To avoid this confusion, the parameters of a type class are all assigned a *nominal* role by default. Accordingly, the parameter of HowToShow is also assigned a nominal role by default, preventing the coercion between (HowToShow HTML) and (HowToShow String).

Metavariables:

x	term	α, β	type	c	coercion
C	axiom	D	data type	N	newtype
F	type family	K	data constructor		

e	$::= \lambda c{:}\phi.e \mid e\,\gamma \mid e \triangleright \gamma \mid \cdots$	terms
τ, σ	$::= \alpha \mid \tau_1\,\tau_2 \mid \forall\alpha{:}\kappa.\tau \mid H \mid F(\overline{\tau})$	types
κ	$::= \star \mid \kappa_1 \to \kappa_2$	kinds
H	$::= (\to) \mid (\Rightarrow) \mid (\sim^{\kappa}_{\rho}) \mid T$	type constants
T	$::= D \mid N$	algebraic data types
ϕ	$::= \tau \sim^{\kappa}_{\rho} \sigma$	proposition
γ, η	$::=$	coercions
	$\mid \langle\tau\rangle \mid \langle\tau,\sigma\rangle_{\mathsf{P}} \mid \mathbf{sym}\,\gamma \mid \gamma_1 ; \gamma_2$	equivalence
	$\mid H(\overline{\gamma}) \mid F(\overline{\gamma}) \mid \gamma_1\,\gamma_2 \mid \forall\alpha{:}\kappa.\gamma$	congruence
	$\mid c \mid C(\overline{\tau})$	assumptions
	$\mid \mathbf{nth}^i\,\gamma \mid \mathbf{left}\,\gamma \mid \mathbf{right}\,\gamma \mid \gamma@\tau$	decomposition
	$\mid \mathbf{sub}\,\gamma$	sub-roling
ρ	$::= \mathsf{N} \mid \mathsf{R} \mid \mathsf{P}$	roles
Γ	$::= \varnothing \mid \Gamma, \alpha{:}\kappa \mid \Gamma, c{:}\phi \mid \Gamma, x{:}\tau$	typing contexts
Ω	$::= \varnothing \mid \Omega, \alpha{:}\rho$	role contexts

Figure 3. An excerpt of the grammar of System FC

4. Ensuring type safety: System FC with roles

Haskell is a large and complicated language. How do we know that the ideas sketched above in source-language terms are actually sound? What, precisely, do roles mean, and when precisely are two types equal? In this section we answer these questions for GHC's small, statically-typed intermediate language, GHC Core. Every Haskell program is translated into Core, and we can typecheck Core to reassure ourselves that the (large, complicated) front end accepts only good programs.

Core is an implementation of a calculus called System FC, itself an extension of the classical Girard/Reynolds System F. The version of FC that we develop in this paper derives from much prior work.[1] However, for clarity we give a self-contained description of the system and do not assume familiarity with previous versions.

Figure 3 gives the syntax of System FC. The starting point is an entirely conventional lambda calculus in the style of System F. We therefore elide most of the syntax of terms e, giving the typing judgement for terms in the extended version of this paper [BEPW14] . Types τ are also conventional, except that we add (saturated) type-family applications $F(\overline{\tau})$, to reflect their addition to source Haskell [CKP05, CKPM05]. Types are classified by kinds κ in the usual way; the kinding judgement $\Gamma \vdash \tau : \kappa$ on types is conventional and appears in the extended version of this paper. To avoid clutter we use only monomorphic kinds, but it is easy to add kind polymorphism along the lines of [YWC+12], and our implementation does so.

[1] Several versions of System FC are described in published work. Some of these variants have had decorations to the FC name, such as FC_2 or $F_C^{\uparrow}$. We do not make these distinctions in the present work, referring instead to all of these systems – in fact, one evolving system – as "FC".

4.1 Roles and casts

FC's distinctive feature is a type-safe cast ($e \triangleright \gamma$) (Figure 3), which uses a *coercion* γ to cast a term from one type to another. A coercion γ is a witness or proof of the equality of two types. Coercions are classified by the judgement

$$\Gamma \vdash \gamma : \tau \sim^{\kappa}_{\rho} \sigma$$

given in Figure 4, and pronounced "in type environment Γ the coercion γ witnesses that the types τ and σ both have kind κ, and are equal at role ρ". The notion of being "equal at role ρ" is the important feature of this paper; it is a development of earlier work, as Section 8 describes. There are precisely three roles (see Figure 3), written N, R, and P, with the following meaning:

Nominal equality, written $\sim_{\mathsf{N}}$, is the equality that the type checker reasons about. When a Haskell programmer says that two Haskell types are the "same", we mean that the types are nominally equal. Thus, we can say that $\mathsf{Int} \sim_{\mathsf{N}} \mathsf{Int}$. Type families introduce new nominal equalities. So, if we have **type instance** F Int = Bool, then $\mathsf{F\ Int} \sim_{\mathsf{N}} \mathsf{Bool}$.

Representational equality, written $\sim_{\mathsf{R}}$, holds between two types that share the same run-time representation. Because all types that are nominally equal also share the same representation, nominal equality is a subset of representational equality. Continuing the example from the introduction, $\mathsf{HTML} \sim_{\mathsf{R}} \mathsf{String}$.

Phantom equality, written $\sim_{\mathsf{P}}$, holds between any two types, whatsoever. It may seem odd that we produce and consume proofs of this "equality", but doing so keeps the system uniform and easier to reason about. The idea of phantom equality is new in this work, and it allows for zero-cost conversions among types with phantom parameters.

We can now give the typing judgement for type-safe cast:

$$\frac{\Gamma \vdash e : \tau_1 \qquad \Gamma \vdash \gamma : \tau_1 \sim_{\mathsf{R}} \tau_2}{\Gamma \vdash e \triangleright \gamma : \tau_2}\ \textsc{Tm\_Cast}$$

The coercion γ must be a proof of *representational* equality, as witnessed by the R subscript to the result of the coercion typing premise. This makes good sense: we can treat an expression of one type τ_1 as an expression of some other type τ_2 if and only if those types share a representation.

4.2 Coercions

Coercions (Figure 3) and their typing rules (Figure 4) are the heart of System FC. The basic typing judgement for coercions is $\Gamma \vdash \gamma : \tau \sim^{\kappa}_{\rho} \sigma$. When this judgement holds, it is easy to prove that τ and σ must have the same kind κ. However, kinds are not very relevant to the focus of this work, and so we often omit the kind annotation in our presentation. It can always be recovered by using the (syntax-directed) kinding judgement on types.

We can understand the typing rules in Figure 4, by thinking about the equalities that they define.

4.2.1 Nominal implies representational

If we have a proof that two types are nominally equal, then they are certainly representationally equal. This intuition is expressed by the **sub** operator, and the rule Co_Sub.

$\boxed{\Gamma \vdash \gamma : \phi}$

$$\frac{\Gamma \vdash \tau : \kappa}{\Gamma \vdash \langle\tau\rangle : \tau \sim_{\mathsf{N}} \tau}\ \textsc{Co\_Refl}$$

$$\frac{\Gamma \vdash \gamma : \sigma \sim_{\rho} \tau}{\Gamma \vdash \mathbf{sym}\,\gamma : \tau \sim_{\rho} \sigma}\ \textsc{Co\_Sym}$$

$$\frac{\Gamma \vdash \gamma_1 : \tau_1 \sim_{\rho} \tau_2 \qquad \Gamma \vdash \gamma_2 : \tau_2 \sim_{\rho} \tau_3}{\Gamma \vdash \gamma_1 \fatsemi \gamma_2 : \tau_1 \sim_{\rho} \tau_3}\ \textsc{Co\_Trans}$$

$$\frac{\overline{\Gamma \vdash \gamma : \tau \sim_{\rho} \sigma} \qquad \overline{\rho} \text{ is a prefix of } \mathit{roles}(H) \qquad \Gamma \vdash H\overline{\tau} : \kappa \qquad \Gamma \vdash H\overline{\sigma} : \kappa}{\Gamma \vdash H(\overline{\gamma}) : H\overline{\tau} \sim_{\mathsf{R}} H\overline{\sigma}}\ \textsc{Co\_TyConApp}$$

$$\frac{\overline{\Gamma \vdash \gamma : \tau \sim_{\mathsf{N}} \sigma} \qquad \Gamma \vdash F(\overline{\tau}) : \kappa \qquad \Gamma \vdash F(\overline{\sigma}) : \kappa}{\Gamma \vdash F(\overline{\gamma}) : F(\overline{\tau}) \sim_{\mathsf{N}} F(\overline{\sigma})}\ \textsc{Co\_TyFam}$$

$$\frac{\Gamma \vdash \gamma_1 : \tau_1 \sim_{\rho} \sigma_1 \qquad \Gamma \vdash \gamma_2 : \tau_2 \sim_{\mathsf{N}} \sigma_2 \qquad \Gamma \vdash \tau_1\,\tau_2 : \kappa \qquad \Gamma \vdash \sigma_1\,\sigma_2 : \kappa}{\Gamma \vdash \gamma_1\,\gamma_2 : \tau_1\,\tau_2 \sim_{\rho} \sigma_1\,\sigma_2}\ \textsc{Co\_App}$$

$$\frac{\Gamma, \alpha{:}\kappa \vdash \gamma : \tau \sim_{\rho} \sigma}{\Gamma \vdash \forall\alpha{:}\kappa.\gamma : \forall\alpha{:}\kappa.\tau \sim_{\rho} \forall\alpha{:}\kappa.\sigma}\ \textsc{Co\_ForAll}$$

$$\frac{\Gamma \vdash \tau : \kappa \qquad \Gamma \vdash \sigma : \kappa}{\Gamma \vdash \langle\tau,\sigma\rangle_{\mathsf{P}} : \tau \sim_{\mathsf{P}} \sigma}\ \textsc{Co\_Phantom}$$

$$\frac{c{:}\tau \sim_{\rho} \sigma \in \Gamma}{\Gamma \vdash c : \tau \sim_{\rho} \sigma}\ \textsc{Co\_Var}$$

$$\frac{C : [\overline{\alpha{:}\kappa}].\sigma_1 \sim_{\rho} \sigma_2 \qquad \overline{\Gamma \vdash \tau : \kappa}}{\Gamma \vdash C(\overline{\tau}) : \sigma_1[\overline{\tau/\alpha}] \sim_{\rho} \sigma_2[\overline{\tau/\alpha}]}\ \textsc{Co\_Axiom}$$

$$\frac{\Gamma \vdash \gamma : H\overline{\tau} \sim_{\mathsf{R}} H\overline{\sigma} \qquad \overline{\rho} \text{ is a prefix of } \mathit{roles}(H) \qquad H \text{ is not a } \mathbf{newtype}}{\Gamma \vdash \mathbf{nth}^{i}\,\gamma : \tau_i \sim_{\rho_i} \sigma_i}\ \textsc{Co\_Nth}$$

$$\frac{\Gamma \vdash \gamma : \tau_1\,\tau_2 \sim_{\mathsf{N}} \sigma_1\,\sigma_2 \qquad \Gamma \vdash \tau_1 : \kappa \qquad \Gamma \vdash \sigma_1 : \kappa}{\Gamma \vdash \mathbf{left}\,\gamma : \tau_1 \sim_{\mathsf{N}} \sigma_1}\ \textsc{Co\_Left}$$

$$\frac{\Gamma \vdash \gamma : \tau_1\,\tau_2 \sim_{\mathsf{N}} \sigma_1\,\sigma_2 \qquad \Gamma \vdash \tau_2 : \kappa \qquad \Gamma \vdash \sigma_2 : \kappa}{\Gamma \vdash \mathbf{right}\,\gamma : \tau_2 \sim_{\mathsf{N}} \sigma_2}\ \textsc{Co\_Right}$$

$$\frac{\Gamma \vdash \gamma : \forall\alpha{:}\kappa.\tau_1 \sim_{\rho} \forall\alpha{:}\kappa.\sigma_1 \qquad \Gamma \vdash \tau : \kappa}{\Gamma \vdash \gamma@\tau : \tau_1[\tau/\alpha] \sim_{\rho} \sigma_1[\tau/\alpha]}\ \textsc{Co\_Inst}$$

$$\frac{\Gamma \vdash \gamma : \tau \sim_{\mathsf{N}} \sigma}{\Gamma \vdash \mathbf{sub}\,\gamma : \tau \sim_{\mathsf{R}} \sigma}\ \textsc{Co\_Sub}$$

Figure 4. Formation rules for coercions

4.2.2 Equality is an equivalence relation

Equality is an equivalence relation at all three roles. Symmetry (rule CO_SYM) and transitivity (CO_TRANS) work for any role ρ. Reflexivity is more interesting: CO_REFL is a proof of nominal equality only. From this we can easily get representational reflexivity using **sub**. But what does "phantom" reflexivity mean? It is a proof term that any two types τ and σ are equal at role P, and we need a new coercion form to express that, written as $\langle\tau,\sigma\rangle_{\mathsf{P}}$ (rule CO_PHANTOM).

4.2.3 Axioms for equality

Each newtype declaration, and each type-family instance, gives rise to an FC *axiom*; newtypes give rise to representational axioms, and type-family instances give rise to nominal axioms.[2] For example, the declarations

```
newtype HTML = Mk String
type family F [a] = Maybe a
```

produce the axioms

$$C_1 : \mathsf{HTML} \sim_{\mathsf{R}} \mathsf{String}$$
$$C_2 : [\alpha{:}\star].\mathsf{F}\,([\alpha]) \sim_{\mathsf{N}} \mathsf{Maybe}\,\alpha$$

Axiom C_1 states that HTML is *representationally* equal to String (since they are distinct types, but share a common representation), while C_2 states that $F([\sigma])$ is *nominally* equal to Maybe σ (meaning that the two are considered to be the same type by the type checker). In C_2, the notation "$[\alpha{:}\star]$." binds α in the types being equated. Uses of these axioms are governed by the rule CO_AXIOM. Axioms must always appear fully applied, and we assume that they live in a global context, separate from the local context Γ.

4.2.4 Equality can be abstracted

Just as one can abstract over types and values in System F, one can also abstract over equality proofs in FC. To this end, FC terms (Figure 3) include coercion abstraction $\lambda c{:}\phi.e$ and application $e\,\gamma$. These are the introduction and elimination forms for the coercion-abstraction arrow ($\Rightarrow$), just as ordinary value abstraction and application are the introduction and elimination forms for ordinary arrow ($\rightarrow$) (see the extended version of this paper).

A coercion abstraction binds a coercion variable $c{:}\phi$. These variables can occur only in coercions; see the entirely conventional rule CO_VAR. Coercion variables can also be bound in the patterns of a **case** expression, which supports the implementation of generalised algebraic data types (GADTs).

4.2.5 Equality is congruent

Several rules witness that, ignoring roles, equality is *congruent* – for example, if $\sigma \sim_\rho \tau$ then Maybe $\sigma \sim_\rho$ Maybe τ. However, the roles in these rules deserve some study, as they are the key to understanding the whole system.

Congruence of type application Before diving into the rules themselves, it is helpful to consider some examples of how we want congruence and roles to interact. Let's consider the definitions in Figure 5. With these definitions in hand, what equalities should be derivable? (Recall the intuitive meanings of the different roles in Section 4.1.)

```
newtype HTML = Mk String

type family F a
type instance F String = Int
type instance F HTML = Bool

data T a = MkT (F a)
```

Figure 5. Congruence and roles example code

1. Should Maybe HTML $\sim_{\mathsf{R}}$ Maybe String hold?
   Yes, it should. The type parameter to Maybe has a representational role, so it makes sense that two Maybes built out of representationally equal types should be representationally equal.
2. Should Maybe HTML $\sim_{\mathsf{N}}$ Maybe String hold?
   Certainly not. These two types are entirely distinct to Haskell programmers and its type checker.
3. Should T HTML $\sim_{\mathsf{R}}$ T String hold?
   Certainly not. We can see, by unfolding the definition for T, that the representations of the two types are different.
4. Should α HTML $\sim_{\mathsf{R}}$ α String hold, for a type variable α?
   It depends on the instantiation of α! If α becomes Maybe, then "yes"; if α becomes T, then "no". Since we may be abstracting over α, we do not know which of the two will happen, so we take the conservative stance and say that α HTML $\sim_{\mathsf{R}}$ α String does *not* hold.

This last point is critical. The alternative is to express α's argument roles in its kind, but that leads to a much more complicated system; see related work in Section 8. A distinguishing feature of this paper is the substantial simplification we obtain by attributing roles only to the arguments to type constants (H, in the grammar), and not to abstracted type variables. We thereby lose a little expressiveness, but we have not found that to be a big problem in practice. See Section 8.1 for an example of an easily fixed problem case.

To support both (1) and (4) requires two coercion forms and corresponding typing rules:

- The coercion form $H(\overline{\gamma})$ has an explicit type constant at its head. This form always proves a representational equality, and it requires input coercions of the roles designated by the roles of H's parameters (rule CO_TYCONAPP). The *roles* function gives the list of roles assigned to H's parameters, as explained in Section 2.2. We allow $\overline{\rho}$ to be a prefix of *roles*(H) to accommodate partially-applied type constants.
- The coercion form $\gamma_1\,\gamma_2$ does not have an explicit type constant, so we must use the conservative treatment of roles discussed above. Rule CO_APP therefore requires γ_2 to be a nominal coercion, though the role of γ_1 carries through to $\gamma_1\,\gamma_2$.

What if we wish to prove a nominal equality such as Maybe (F String) $\sim_{\mathsf{N}}$ Maybe Int? We can't use the $H(\overline{\gamma})$ form, which proves only representational equality, but we can use the $\gamma_1\,\gamma_2$ form. The leftmost coercion would just be $\langle$Maybe$\rangle$.

Congruence of type family application Rule CO_TYFAM proves the equality of two type-family applications. It requires nominal coercions among all the arguments. Why? Because type families can inspect their (type) arguments and branch on them. We would not want to be able to prove any equality between F String and F HTML.

Congruence of polymorphic types The rule CO_FORALL works for any role ρ; polymorphism and roles do not interact.

[2] For simplicity, we are restricting ourselves to *open* type families. Closed type families [EVPW14] are readily accommodated.

4.2.6 Equality can be decomposed

If we have a proof of $\mathsf{Maybe}\,\sigma \sim_\rho \mathsf{Maybe}\,\tau$, should we be able to get a proof of $\sigma \sim_\rho \tau$, by decomposing the equality? Yes, in this case, but we must be careful here as well.

Rule CO_NTH is almost an inverse to CO_TYCONAPP. The difference is that CO_NTH prohibits decomposing equalities among newtypes. Why? Because **nth** witnesses injectivity and newtypes are not injective! For example, consider these definitions:

```
data Phant a = MkPhant
newtype App a b = MkApp (a b)
```

Here, $roles(\mathsf{App}) = \mathsf{R}, \mathsf{N}$. (The roles are inferred during compilation; see Section 5.) Yet, we can see the following chain of equalities:

$$\mathsf{App\ Phant\ Int} \sim_{\mathsf{R}} \mathsf{Phant\ Int} \sim_{\mathsf{R}} \mathsf{Phant\ Bool} \sim_{\mathsf{R}} \mathsf{App\ Phant\ Bool}$$

By transitivity, we can derive a coercion γ witnessing

$$\mathsf{App\ Phant\ Int} \sim_{\mathsf{R}} \mathsf{App\ Phant\ Bool}$$

If we could use $\mathbf{nth}^2$ on γ, we would get $\mathsf{Int} \sim_{\mathsf{N}} \mathsf{Bool}$: disaster! We eliminate this possibility by preventing **nth** on newtypes.

The rules CO_LEFT and CO_RIGHT are almost inverses to CO_APP. The difference is that both CO_LEFT and CO_RIGHT require and produce only nominal coercions. We need a new newtype to see why this must be so:

```
newtype EitherInt a = MkEI (Either a Int)
```

This definition yields an axiom showing that, for all a, $\mathsf{EitherInt\ a} \sim_{\mathsf{R}} (\mathsf{Either\ a\ Int})$. Suppose we could apply **left** and **right** to coercions formed from this axiom. Using **left** would get us a proof of $\mathsf{EitherInt} \sim_{\mathsf{R}} (\mathsf{Either\ a})$, which could then be used to show, say, $(\mathsf{Either\ Char}) \sim_{\mathsf{R}} (\mathsf{Either\ Bool})$ and then (using **nth**) $\mathsf{Char} \sim_{\mathsf{N}} \mathsf{Bool}$. Using **right** would get us a proof of $\mathsf{a} \sim_{\mathsf{R}} \mathsf{Int}$, for *any* a. These are both clearly disastrous. So, we forbid using these coercion formers on representational coercions.[3]

Thankfully, polymorphism and roles play well together, and the CO_INST rule (inverse to CO_FORALL) shows quite straightforwardly that, if two polytypes are equal, then so are the instantiated types.

There is no decomposition form for type family applications: knowing that $F(\overline{\tau})$ is equal to $F(\overline{\sigma})$ tells us nothing whatsoever about the relationship between $\overline{\tau}$ and $\overline{\sigma}$.

4.3 Role attribution for type constants

In System FC we assume an unwritten global environment of top-level constants: data types, type families, axioms, and so on. For a data type H, for example, this environment will give the kind of H, the types of H's data constructors, and the roles of H's parameters. Clearly this global environment must be internally consistent. For example, a data constructor K must return a value of type $D\,\overline{\tau}$ where D is a data type; K's type must be well-kinded, and that kind must be consistent with D's kind.

[3] We note in passing that the forms **left** and **right** are present merely to increase expressivity. They are not needed anywhere in the metatheory to prove type soundness. Though originally part of FC, they were omitted in previous versions [WVPZ11] and even in the implementation. Haskell users then found that some desirable program were no longer type-checking. Thus, these forms were reintroduced.

$\boxed{\overline{\rho} \models H}$ "$\overline{\rho}$ are appropriate roles for H."

$$\frac{\begin{array}{l}\forall \overline{\alpha}, \overline{\beta}, \overline{\sigma} \text{ s.t. } K : \forall \overline{\alpha{:}\kappa}.\forall \overline{\beta{:}\kappa'}.\overline{\phi} \Rightarrow \overline{\sigma} \to D\,\overline{\alpha} : \\ \quad \forall \tau \text{ s.t. } \tau \in \overline{\sigma} \vee \tau \in \overline{\phi} : \\ \quad \overline{\alpha{:}\rho}, \overline{\beta{:}\mathsf{N}} \vdash \tau : \mathsf{R}\end{array}}{\overline{\rho} \models D} \quad \text{ROLES\_DATA}$$

$$\frac{C : [\overline{\alpha{:}\kappa}].N\,\overline{\alpha} \sim_{\mathsf{R}} \sigma \qquad \overline{\alpha{:}\rho} \vdash \sigma : \mathsf{R}}{\overline{\rho} \models N} \quad \text{ROLES\_NEWTYPE}$$

$$\frac{}{\mathsf{R}, \mathsf{R} \models (\to)} \qquad \frac{}{\mathsf{R}, \mathsf{R} \models (\Rightarrow)} \qquad \frac{}{\rho, \rho \models (\sim_\rho)}$$

$\boxed{\Omega \vdash \tau : \rho}$ "Assuming Ω, τ can be used at role ρ."

$$\frac{\alpha{:}\rho' \in \Omega \qquad \rho' \leq \rho}{\Omega \vdash \alpha : \rho} \quad \text{RTY\_VAR}$$

$$\frac{\begin{array}{l}\overline{\rho} \text{ is a prefix of } roles(H) \\ \overline{\Omega \vdash \tau : \rho}\end{array}}{\Omega \vdash H\,\overline{\tau} : \mathsf{R}} \quad \text{RTY\_TYCONAPP}$$

$$\frac{}{\Omega \vdash H : \mathsf{N}} \quad \text{RTY\_TYCON}$$

$$\frac{\Omega \vdash \tau : \rho \qquad \Omega \vdash \sigma : \mathsf{N}}{\Omega \vdash \tau\,\sigma : \rho} \quad \text{RTY\_APP}$$

$$\frac{\Omega, \alpha{:}\mathsf{N} \vdash \tau : \rho}{\Omega \vdash \forall \alpha{:}\kappa.\tau : \rho} \quad \text{RTY\_FORALL}$$

$$\frac{\overline{\Omega \vdash \tau : \mathsf{N}}}{\Omega \vdash F(\overline{\tau}) : \rho} \quad \text{RTY\_TYFAM}$$

$$\frac{}{\Omega \vdash \tau : \mathsf{P}} \quad \text{RTY\_PHANTOM}$$

$\boxed{\rho_1 \leq \rho_2}$ "ρ_1 is a sub-role of ρ_2."

$$\frac{}{\mathsf{N} \leq \rho} \qquad \frac{}{\rho \leq \mathsf{P}} \qquad \frac{}{\rho \leq \rho}$$

Figure 6. Rules asserting a correct assignment of roles to data types

All of this is standard except for roles. It is essential that the roles of D's parameters, $roles(D)$, are consistent with D's definition. For example, it would be utterly wrong for the global environment to claim that $roles(\mathsf{Maybe}) = P$, because then we could prove that $\mathsf{Maybe\,Int} \sim_{\mathsf{R}} \mathsf{Maybe\,Bool}$ using CO_TYCONAPP.

We use the judgement $\overline{\rho} \models H$, to mean "$\overline{\rho}$ are suitable roles for the parameters of H", and in our proof of type safety, we assume that $roles(H) \models H$ for all H. The rules for this judgement and two auxiliary judgements appear in Figure 6. Note that this judgement defines a *relation* between roles and data types. Our role inference algorithm (Section 5) determines the most permissible roles for this relation, but often other, less permissive roles, such as those specified by role annotations, are also included by this relation.

Start with ROLES_NEWTYPE. Recall that a newtype declaration for N gives rise to an axiom $C : [\overline{\alpha{:}\kappa}].N\,\overline{\alpha} \sim_{\mathsf{R}} \sigma$. The rule says that roles $\overline{\rho}$ are acceptable for N if each parameter α_i is used in σ in a way consistent with ρ_i, expressed using the auxiliary judgement $\overline{\alpha{:}\rho} \vdash \sigma : \mathsf{R}$.

The key auxiliary judgement $\Omega \vdash \tau : \rho$ checks that the type variables in τ are used in a way consistent with their roles specified in Ω, when considered at role ρ. More precisely, if $\alpha{:}\rho' \in \Omega$ and if $\sigma_1 \sim_{\rho'} \sigma_2$ then $\tau[\sigma_1/\alpha] \sim_\rho \tau[\sigma_2/\alpha]$. Unlike in many typing judgements, the role ρ (as well as Ω) is an *input* to this judgement, not an output. With this in mind, the rules for the auxiliary judgement are straightforward. For example, RTY_TYFAM says that the argument types of a type family application are used at nominal role. The variable rule, RTY_VAR, allows a variable to be assigned a more restrictive role (via the sub-role judgement) than required, which is needed both for multiple occurrences of the same variable, and to account for role signatures. Note that rules RTY_TYCONAPP and RTY_APP overlap – this judgement is not syntax-directed.

Returning to our original judgement $\overline{\rho} \models H$, ROLES_DATA deals with algebraic data types D, by checking roles in each of its data constructors K. The type of a constructor is parameterised by universal type variables $\overline{\alpha}$, existential type variables $\overline{\beta}$, coercions (with types $\overline{\phi}$), and term-level arguments (with types $\overline{\sigma}$). For each constructor, we must examine each proposition ϕ and each term-level argument type σ, checking to make sure that each is used at a representational role. Why check for a representational role specifically? Because *roles* is used in CO_TYCONAPP, which produces a representational coercion. In other words, we must make sure that each term-level argument appears at a representational role within the type of each constructor K for CO_TYCONAPP to be sound.

Finally $(\rightarrow)$ and $(\Rightarrow)$ have representational roles: functions care about representational equality but never branch on the nominal identity of a type. (For example, functions always treat HTML and String identically.) We also see that the roles of the arguments to an equality proposition match the role of the proposition. This fact comes from the congruence of the respective equality relations.

These definitions lead to a powerful theorem:

Theorem (Roles assignments are flexible). *If $\overline{\rho} \models H$, where H is a data type or newtype, and $\overline{\rho}'$ is such that $\rho_i' \leq \rho_i$ (for $\rho_i \in \overline{\rho}$ and $\rho_i' \in \overline{\rho}'$), then $\overline{\rho}' \models H$.*

Proof. Straightforward induction on $\Omega \vdash \tau : \rho$. □

This theorem states that, given a sound role assignment for H, any more restrictive role assignment is also sound. This property of our system here is one of its distinguishing characteristics from our prior work on roles – see Section 10 for discussion.

4.4 Metatheory

The preceding discussion gave several non-obvious examples where admitting *too many* coercions would lead to unsoundness. However, we must have *enough* coercions to allow us to make progress when evaluating a program. (We do not have space to elaborate, but a key example is the use of **nth** in rule S_KPUSH, presented in the extended version of this paper.) Happily, we can be confident that we have enough coercions, but not too many, because we prove the usual progress and preservation theorems for System FC. The structure of the proofs follows broadly that in previous work, such as [WVPZ11] or [YWC+12].

A key step in the proof of progress is to prove *consistency*; that is, that no coercion can exist between, say, Int and Bool. This is done by defining a non-deterministic, role-directed rewrite relation on types and showing that the rewrite system is confluent and preserves type constants (other than newtypes) appearing in the heads of types. We then prove that, if a coercion exists between two types τ_1 and τ_2, these two types both rewrite to a type σ. We conclude then that τ_1 and τ_2, if headed by a non-newtype type constant, must be headed by the same such constant.

Alas, the rewrite relation is *not* confluent! The non-linear patterns allowed in type families (that is, with a repeated variable on the left-hand side), combined with non-termination, break the confluence property (previous work gives full details [EVPW14]). However, losing confluence does not necessarily threaten consistency – it just threatens the particular proof technique we use. However, a more powerful proof appears to be an open problem in the term rewriting community.[4] For the purposes of our proof we dodge this difficulty by restricting type families to have only linear patterns, thus leading to confluence; consistency of the full system remains an open problem.

The full proof of type safety appears in the extended version of this paper; it exhibits no new proof techniques.

5. Roles on type constructors

In System FC we assume that, for every type constant H, the global enviroment specifies *roles*(H), the roles of H's parameters. However, there is some flexibility about this role assignment; the only requirement for type soundness is that *roles*$(H) \models H$.

In GHC, the roles of a type constructor are determined first by any role annotations provided by the programmer. If these are missing, the type checker calculates the default roles using the inference algorithm described below.

5.1 Role inference

A type constructor's roles are assigned depending on its nature:

- Primitive type constructors like $(\rightarrow)$ and $(\sim_\rho^\kappa)$ have predefined roles (Figure 6).
- Type families (Section 2.2.3) and type classes (Section 3.2) have nominal roles for all parameters.
- For a **data** type or **newtype** T GHC *infers* the roles for T's type parameters, possibly modified by role annotations (Section 3.1).

The role inference algorithm is quite straightforward. At a high level, it simply starts with the role information of the built-in constants $(\rightarrow)$, $(\Rightarrow)$, and $(\sim_\rho)$, and propagates the roles until it finds a fixpoint. In the description of the algorithm, we assume a mutable environment; *roles*(H) pulls a list of roles from this environment. Only after the algorithm is complete will *roles*$(H) \models H$ hold.

1. Populate *roles*(T) (for all T) with user-supplied annotations; omitted role annotations default to phantom. (See Section 5.2 for discussion about this choice of default.)
2. For every data type D, every constructor for that data type K, and every coercion type and term-level argument type σ to that constructor: run walk(D, σ).
3. For every newtype N with representation type σ, run walk(N, σ).
4. If the role of any parameter to any type constant changed in the previous steps, go to step 2.

[4] Specifically, we believe that a positive answer to open problem #79 of the Rewriting Techniques and Applications (RTA) conference would lead to a proof of consistency; see http://www.win.tue.nl/rtaloop/problems/79.html.

5. For every T, check *roles*(T) against a user-supplied annotation, if any. If these disagree, reject the program. Otherwise, *roles*(T) $\models T$ holds.

The procedure walk(T, σ) is defined as follows, matching from top to bottom:

walk(T, α) := mark the α parameter to T as R.
walk($T, H\,\overline{\tau}$) := let $\overline{\rho} = roles(H)$;
 for every i, $0 < i \leq \mathsf{length}\,(\overline{\tau})$:
 if $\rho_i = \mathsf{N}$, then
 mark all variables free in τ_i as N;
 else if $\rho_i = \mathsf{R}$, then walk(T, τ_i).
walk($T, \tau_1\,\tau_2$) := walk(T, τ_1);
 mark all variables free in τ_2 as N.
walk($T, F(\overline{\tau})$) := mark all variables free in the $\overline{\tau}$ as N.
walk($T, \forall\,\beta{:}\kappa.\tau$) := walk($T, \tau$).

When marking, we must follow these two rules:

1. If a variable to be marked does not appear as a type-level argument to the data type T in question, ignore it.
2. Never allow a variable previously marked N to be marked R. If such a mark is requested, ignore it.

The first rule above deals with existential and local ($\forall$-bound) type variables, and the second one deals with the case where a variable is used both in a nominal and in a representational context. In this case, we wish the variable to be marked N, not R.

Theorem. *The role inference algorithm always terminates.*

Theorem (Role inference is sound). *After running the role inference algorithm, roles*(H) $\models H$ *will hold for all H.*

Theorem (Role inference is optimal). *After running the role inference algorithm, any loosening of roles (a change from* ρ *to* ρ', *where* $\rho \leq \rho'$ *and* $\rho \neq \rho'$*) would violate roles*(H) $\models H$.

Proofs of these theorems appear in the extended version of this paper.

5.2 The role of role inference

According to the specification of sound role assignments in Figure 6, a type constructor H can potentially have several different sound role assignments. For example, assigning Maybe's parameter to have a representational role is type-safe, but assigning a nominal role would be, too. Note that nominal roles are always sound for data types, according to the definition in Figure 6. However, as we saw in the description of the role inference algorithm, we choose default roles for data types to be as permissive as possible – in other words, the default role for a data type constructor parameter starts at phantom and only change when constrained by the algorithm. Here, we discuss this design decision and its consequences.

What if we had no role inference whatsoever and required programmers to annotate every data type? In this case, the burden on programmers seems drastic and migration to this system overwhelming, requiring all existing data type declarations to be annotated with roles.

Alternatively, we could specify that all unnanotated roles default to nominal (thus removing the need for role inference). This choice would lead to greater abstraction safety by default – we would not have to worry that the implementor of Map is unaware of roles and forgets a critical role annotation.

However, we choose to use the most permissive roles by default for several reasons. First, for convenience: this choice increases the availability of coerce (as only those types with annotations would be Coercible otherwise), and it supports backward compatibility with the Generalized Newtype Deriving (GND) feature (see Section 7).

Furthermore, our choice of using phantom as the default also means that the majority of programmers do not need to learn about roles. They will not need role annotations in their code. Users of coerce will need to consider roles, as will library implementors who use class-based invariants (see Section 3.1). Other users are unaffected by roles and will not be burdened by them.

Our choices in the design of the role system, and the default of phantom in particular, has generated vigorous debate.[5] This discussion is healthy for the Haskell community. The difficulty with abstraction is not new: with GND, it has always been possible to lift coercions through data types, potentially violating their class-based invariants. The features described in this paper make this subversion both more convenient (through the use of coerce) and, more importantly, now preventable (through the use of role annotations).

6. Implementing Coercible

We have described the source-language view of Coercible (Sections 2, 3), and System FC, the intermediate language into which the source language is elaborated (Section 4). In this section we link the two by describing how the source-language use of Coercible is translated into Core.

6.1 Coercible and coerce

When the compiler transforms Haskell to Core, type classes become ordinary types and type class constraints turn into ordinary value arguments [WB89]. In particular, type classes typically become simple product types with one field per method.

The same holds for the type class Coercible a b, which has one method, namely the witness of representational equality a $\sim_\mathsf{R}$ b. As that type cannot be expressed in Haskell, the actual definition of Coercible is built in:

```
data Coercible a b = MkCoercible (a ~R b)
```

The definition of coerce, which is also only possible in Core, pattern-matches on MkCoercible to get hold of the equality witness, and then uses Core's primitive cast operation:

```
coerce :: forall α β. Coercible α β → α → β
coerce = Λ α β. λ (c :: Coercible α β) (x :: α). case c of
  MkCoercible eq → x ▷ eq
```

Since type applications are explicit in Core, coerce now takes four arguments: the types to cast from and to, the coercion witness, and finally the value to cast.

The data type Coercible also serves to *box* the primitive, unboxed type $\sim_\mathsf{R}$, just as Int serves to box the primitive, unboxed type Int#:

```
data Int = I# Int#
```

All boxed types are represented uniformly by a heap pointer. In GHC all constraints (such as Eq a or Coercible a b) are boxed, so that they can be treated uniformly, and even polymorphically [YWC+12]. In contrast, an unboxed type is rep-

[5] To read some of this debate, see the thread beginning with this post: http://www.haskell.org/pipermail/libraries/2014-March/022321.html

resented by a non-pointer bit field, such as a 32 or 64-bit int in the case of Int# [PL91].

A witness of (unboxed) type $\sim_R$ carries no information: we never actually inspect an equality proof at run-time. So the type $\sim_R$ can be represented by a *zero-width* bit-field – that is, by nothing at all. This implementation trick, of boxing a zero-bit witness, is exactly analogous to the wrapping of boxed nominal equalities used to implement deferred type errors [VPMa12].

Since Coercible is a regular data type, you might worry about bogus programs like this, which uses recursion to construct an unsound witness co whose value is bottom:

```
looksUnsound :: forall α β. α → β
looksUnsound = \α β x →
  let co :: Coercible α β = co in
  coerce α β co x
```

However, since coerce evaluates the Coercible argument (see the definition of coerce above), looksUnsound will simply diverge. Again, this follows the behaviour of deferred type errors [VPMa12].

In uses of coerce, the Coercible argument will be constructed from the instances which, as described below (Section 6.4), are guaranteed to be acyclic. The usual simplification machinery of GHC then ensures that these are inlined, causing the **case** to cancel with the MkCoercible constructor, leaving only the cast x ▷ eq, which is operationally free.

6.2 On-demand instance generation

The language of Section 2 suggests that we generate Haskell instance declarations for Coercible, based on type declarations. Although this is a useful way to explain the design to a programmer (who is already familiar with type classes and instance declarations), GHC's implementation is much simpler and more direct.

Rather than generate and compile instance declarations, the constraint solver treats Coercible constraints specially: to solve a Coercible constraint, the solver uses the rules of Section 2 directly to decompose the constraint into simpler sub-goals. This approach makes it easy to implement the non-standard visibility rules of Coercible instances (see Section 3.1), by simply not applying the newtype-unwrapping rule if the constructor is not in scope.

6.3 The higher rank instance

Consider this declaration, whose constructor uses a higher-rank type:

```
newtype Sel = MkSel (forall a. [a] → a)
```

We would expect its newtype-unwrapping instance to take the form

```
instance Coercible (forall a. [a] → a) b ⇒ Coercible Sel b
instance Coercible a (forall a. [a] → a) ⇒ Coercible a Sel
```

These declarations are illegal in source Haskell, even with all GHC extensions enabled. Nevertheless, we can generate internally and work with them in the solver just fine. This leads to constraints of the form

```
Coercible (forall a. s) (forall b. t)
```

which need special support in the solver. It already supports solving (nominal) type equalities of the form (**forall** a. s) $\sim$ (**forall** b. t), by generating a fresh type variable c and solving s[c/a] $\sim$ t[c/b]. We generalised this functionality to handle representational type equalities as well.

6.4 Preventing circular reasoning and diverging instances

For most type classes, like Show, it is perfectly fine (and useful) to use a not-yet solved type class constraint to solve another, even though this can lead to cycles [LP05]. Consider the following code and execution:

```
newtype Fix a = MkFix (a (Fix a))
deriving instance Show (a (Fix a)) ⇒ Show (Fix a)

λ> show (MkFix (Just (MkFix (Just (MkFix Nothing)))))
"MkFix (Just (MkFix (Just (MkFix Nothing))))"
```

There are two Show instances at work: one for Show (Maybe a), which uses the instance of Show a; and one for Show (Fix a), which uses the the instance Show (a (Fix a)). Plugging them together to solve Show (Fix Maybe), we see that this instance calls, by way of Show (Maybe (Fix Maybe)), itself. Nevertheless, the result is perfectly well-behaved and indeed terminates.

But with Coercible, such circular reasoning would be problematic; we could then seemingly write the bogus function looksUnsoundH:

```
newtype Id a = MkId a
c1 :: a → Fix Id
c1 = coerce
c2 :: Fix Id → b
c2 = coerce
looksUnsoundH :: a → b
looksUnsoundH = c2 ∘ c1
```

With the usual constraint solving, this code would type check: to solve the constraint Coercible a (Fix Id), we need to solve Coercible a (Id (Fix Id)), which requires Coercible a (Fix Id). This is a constraint we already looked at, so the constraint solver would normally consider all required constraints solved and accept the program.

Fortunately, there is no soundness problem here. Circular constraint-solving leads to a recursive definition of the Coercible constraints, exactly like the (Core) looksUnsound in Section 6.1, and looksUnsoundH will diverge just like looksUnsound. Nevertheless, unlike normal type classes, a recursive definition of Coercible is *never* useful, so it is more helpful to reject it statically. GHC therefore uses the existing depth-counter of the solver to spot and reject recursion of Coercible constraints.

6.5 Coercible and rewrite rules

What if a client of module Html writes this?

```
....( map unMk hs)...
```

She cannot use coerce because HTML is an abstract type, so the type system would (rightly) reject an attempt to use coerce (Section 3.1). However, since HTML is a newtype, one might hope that GHC's optimiser would transform (map unMk) to coerce. The optimiser must respect type soundness, but (by design) it does not respect abstraction boundaries: dissolving abstractions is one key to high performance.

The correctness of transforming (map unMk) to coerce depends on a theorem about map, which a compiler can hardly be expected to identify and prove all by itself. Fortunately GHC already comes with a mechanism that allows a library author to specify *rewrite rules* for their code [PTH01]. The author takes the proof obligation that the rewrite is semantics-preserving, while GHC simply applies the rewrite whenever possible. In this case the programmer could write

```
{-# RULES "map/co" map coerce = coerce #-}
```

In our example, the programmer wrote (map unMk). The definition unMk in module Html does not mention coerce, but both produce the same System FC code (a cast). So via cross-module inlining (more dissolution of abstraction boundaries) unMk will be inlined, transforming the call to the equivalent of (map coerce), and that in turn fires the rewrite rule. Indeed even a nested call like map (map unMk) will also be turned into a single call of coerce by this same process applied twice.

The bottom line is this: the author of a map-like function someMap can accompany someMap with a RULE, and thereby optimise calls of someMap that do nothing into a simple call to coerce.

Could we dispense with a user-visible coerce function altogether, instead using map-like functions and RULEs as above? No: doing so would replace the zero-cost guarantee with best-effort optimisation; it would burden the author of every map-like function with the obligation to write a suitable RULE; it would be much less convenient to use in deeply-nested cases; and there might simply *be* no suitable map-like function available.

7. Generalized Newtype Deriving done right

As mentioned before, **newtype** is a great tool to make programs more likely to be correct, by having the type checker enforce certain invariants or abstractions. But newtypes can also lead to tedious boilerplate. Assume the programmer needs an instance of the type class Monoid for her type HTML. The underlying type String already comes with a suitable instance for Monoid. Nevertheless, she has to write quite a bit of code to convert that instance into one for HTML:

```
instance Monoid HTML where
  mempty = Mk mempty
  mappend (Mk a) (Mk b) = Mk (mappend a b)
  mconcat xs = Mk (mconcat (map unMk xs))
```

Note that this definition is not only verbose, but also non-trivial, as invocations of Mk and unMk have to be put in the right places, possibly via some higher order functions like map – all just to say "just use the underlying instance"!

This task is greatly simplified with Coercible: Instead of wrapping and unwrapping arguments and results, she can directly coerce the method of the base type's instance itself:

```
instance Monoid HTML where
  mempty = coerce (mempty :: String)
  mappend = coerce (mappend :: String → String → String)
  mconcat = coerce (mconcat :: [String] → String)
```

The code is pure boilerplate: apply coerce to the method, instantiated at the base type by a type signature. And because it is boilerplate, the compiler can do it for her; all she has to do is to declare which instances of the base type should be lifted to the new type by listing them in the **deriving** clause:

```
newtype HTML = Mk String deriving Monoid
```

This is not a new feature: GHC has provided this *Generalized Newtype Deriving* (GND) for many years. But, the implementation was "magic" – GND would produce code that a user could not write herself. Now, the feature can be explained easily and fully via coerce.

Furthermore, GND was previously unsound [WVPZ11]. When combined with other extensions of GHC, such as type families [CKP05, CKPM05] or GADTs [CH03], GND could be exploited to completely break the type system: Figure 7 shows how this notorious bug can allow any type to be coerced to any other. The clause "**deriving** (UnsafeCast b)" is the bogus use of GND, and now will generate the instance

```
instance UnsafeCast b c ⇒ UnsafeCast b (Id2 c) where
  unsafe = coerce (unsafe :: c → Discern c b)
```

which will rightly be rejected because Discern's first parameter has a nominal role. Indeed, preventing abuse of GND was the entire subject of the previous work [WVPZ11] the current paper is based on.

Similarly, it was possible to use GND to break invariants of abstract data types. The addition of coerce makes it yet easier to break such abstractions. As discussed in Section 3.1, these abuses can now be prevented via role annotations.

```
newtype Id1 a = MkId1 a
newtype Id2 a = MkId2 (Id1 a) deriving (UnsafeCast b)

type family Discern a b
type instance Discern (Id1 a) b = a
type instance Discern (Id2 a) b = b

class UnsafeCast to from where
  unsafe :: from → Discern from to

instance UnsafeCast b (Id1 a) where
  unsafe (MkId1 x) = x

unsafeCoerce :: a → b
unsafeCoerce x = unsafe (MkId2 (MkId1 x))
```

Figure 7. The above implementation of unsafeCoerce compiles (with appropriate flags) in GHC 7.6.3 but does not in GHC 7.8.1.

8. Related work

Prior work discusses the relationship between roles in FC and languages with generativity and abstraction, type-indexed constructs, and universes in dependent type theory. We do not repeat that discussion here. Instead we use this section to clarify the relationship between this paper and [WVPZ11], as well as make connections to other systems.

8.1 Prior version of roles

The idea of *roles* was initially developed in [WVPZ11] as a solution to the Generalized Newtype Deriving problem. That work introduces the equality relations $\sim_R$ and $\sim_N$ (called "type equality" and "code equality" resp. in [WVPZ11]). However, the system presented in [WVPZ11] was quite invasive: it required annotating every sub-tree of every kind with a role. Kinds in GHC are already quite complicated because of kind polymorphism, and a new form of role-annotated kinds would be more complex still.

In this paper, we present a substantially simplified version of the roles system of [WVPZ11], requiring role information only on the parameters to data types. Our new design keeps roles and kinds modularly separate, so that roles can be handled almost entirely separately (both intellectually and in the implementation) from kinds. The key simplification is to "assume the worst" about higher-kinded parameters, by assuming that their arguments are all nominal. In exchange we give up some expressiveness; specifically, we give up the ability to abstract over type constructors with non-nominal argument roles (see Section 10).

Furthermore, the observation that it is sound to "assume the worst" and use parameterised types with less permissive roles opens the door to role annotations. In this work, programmers are allowed to deliberately specify less permissive roles, giving them the ability to preserve type abstractions.

Surprisingly, this flexibility means that our version of roles actually *increases* expressiveness compared to [WVPZ11] in some places. In [WVPZ11] a role is part of a type's kind, so a type expecting a higher-kinded argument (such as Monad) would also have to specify the roles expected by its argument. Therefore if Monad is applicable to Maybe, it would not also be applicable to a type T whose parameter has a nominal role. In the current work, however, there is no problem because Maybe and T have the same kind.

Besides the simplification discussed above, this paper makes two other changes to the specification of roles presented in [WVPZ11].

- The treatment of the phantom role is entirely novel; the rule CO_PHANTOM has no analogue in prior work.
- The coercion formation rules (Figure 4) are refactored so that the role on the coercion is an *output* of the (syntax-directed) judgement instead of an input. This is motivated by the implementation (which does not know the role at which coercions should be checked) and requires the addition of the CO_SUB rule.

There are, of course, other minor differences between this system and [WVPZ11] in keeping with the evolution of System FC. The main significant change, unrelated to roles, is the re-introduction of **left** and **right** coercions; see Section 4.2.6.

One important non-difference relates to the linear-pattern requirement. Section 4.4 describes that our language is restricted to have only *linear* patterns in its type families. (GHC, on the other hand, allows non-linear patterns as well.) This restriction exists in the language in [WVPZ11] as well. Section 4.2.2 of [WVPZ11] defines so-called Good contexts as having certain properties. Condition 1 in this definition subtly implies that all type families have linear patterns – if a type family had a non-linear pattern, it would be impossible, in general, to establish this condition. The fact that the definition of Good implies linear patterns came as a surprise, further explored in [EVPW14]. The language described in the present paper clarifies this restriction, but it is not a new restriction.

Finally, because this system has been implemented in GHC, this paper discusses more details related to compilation from source Haskell. In particular, the role inference algorithm of Section 5 is a new contribution of this work.

8.2 OCaml and variance annotations

The interactions between sub-typing, type abstraction, and various type system extensions such as GADTs and parameter constraints also appear in the OCaml language. In that context, *variance annotations* act like roles; they ensure that subtype coercions between compatible types are safe. For example, the type α `list` of immutable lists is covariant in the parameter α: if $\sigma \leq \tau$ then σ `list` $\leq$ τ `list`. Variances form a lattice, with *invariant*, the most restrictive, at the bottom; *covariant* and *contravariant* incomparable; and *bivariant* at the top, allowing sub-typing in both directions. It is tempting to identify invariant with nominal and bivariant with phantom, but the exact connection is unclear. Scherer and Rémy [SR13] show that GADT parameters are not always invariant.

Exploration of the interactions between type abstraction, GADTs, and other features have recently revealed a soundness issue in OCaml[6] that has been confirmed to date back several years. Garrigue discusses these issues [Gar13]. His proposed solution is to "assume that nothing is known about abstract types when they are used in parameter constraints and GADT return types" – akin to assigning nominal roles. However, this solution is too conservative, and in practice the OCaml 4.01 compiler relies on no fewer than *six* flags to describe the variance of type parameters. However, lacking anything equivalent to Core and its tractable metatheory, the OCaml developers cannot demonstrate the soundness of their solution in the way that we have done here.

What is clear, however, is that generative type abstraction interacts in interesting and non-trivial ways with type equality and sub-typing. Roles and type-safe coercion solve an immediate practical problem in Haskell, but we believe that the ideas have broader applicability in advanced type systems.

9. Roles in Practice

We have described a mechanism to allow safe coercions among distinct types, and we have reimplemented GHC's previously unsafe GeneralizedNewtypeDeriving extension in terms of these safe coercions. Naturally, this change causes some code that was previously accepted to be rejected. Given that Haskell has a large user base and a good deal of production code, how does this change affect the community?

Advance testing During the development of this feature, we tested it against several popular Haskell packages available through Hackage, an online Haskell open-source distribution site. These tests were all encouraging and did not find any instances of hard-to-repair code in the wild.

Compiling all of Hackage As of 30 September 2013, 3,234 packages on Hackage compiled with GHC 7.6.3, the last released version without roles. The development version of GHC at that time included roles. A total of only four packages failed to compile directly due to GND failure.[7] Of these, three of the failures were legitimate – the use of GND was indeed unsafe. For example, one case involved coercing a type variable passed into a type family; the author implicitly assumed that a newtype and its representation type were always considered equivalent with respect to the type family. Only one package failed to compile because of the gap in expressiveness between the roles in [WVPZ11] and those here. No other Hackage package depends on this one, indicating it is not a key part of the Haskell open-source fabric. See Section 10 for discussion of the failure.

These data were gathered almost two months after the implementation of roles was pushed into the development version of GHC, so active maintainers may have made changes to their packages before the study took place. Indeed, we are aware of a few packages that needed manual updates. In these cases, instances previously derived using GND had to be written by hand, but quite straightforwardly.

[6] http://caml.inria.fr/mantis/view.php?id=5985

[7] These data come from Bryan O'Sullivan's work, described here: http://www.haskell.org/pipermail/ghc-devs/2013-September/002693.html That posting includes 3 additional GND failures; these were due to an implementation bug, since fixed.

10. Future directions

As of the date of writing (May 2014), roles seem not to have caused an undue burden to the community. The first release candidate for GHC 7.8 was released on 3 February 2014, followed by the full release on 9 April, and package authors have been updating their work to be compatible for some time. The authors of this paper are unaware of any major problems that Haskellers have had in updating existing code, despite hundreds of packages being available for GHC 7.8.[8]

However, we are aware that some users wish to use roles in higher-order scenarios that are currently impossible. We focus on one such scenario, as it is representative of all examples we have seen, including the package that did not compile when testing all of Hackage (Section 9).

Imagine adding the join method to the Monad class, as follows:

```
class Monad m where
  ...
  join :: forall a. m (m a) → m a
```

With this definition, GND would still work in many cases. For example, if we define

```
newtype M a = Mk (Maybe a)
  deriving Monad
```

GND will work without a problem. We would need to show Coercible (Maybe (Maybe a) → Maybe a) (M (M a) → M a), which is straightforward.

More complicated constructions run into trouble, though. Take this definition, written to restrict a monad's interface:

```
newtype Restr m a = Mk (m a)
  deriving Monad
```

To perform GND in this scenario, we must prove Coercible (m (m a) → m a) (Restr m (Restr m a) → Restr m a). In solving for this constraint, we eventually simplify to Coercible (m (m a)) (m (Restr m a). At this point, we are stuck, because we do not have any information about the role of m's parameter, so we must assume it is nominal. The GND feature is thus not available here. Similar problems arise when trying to use GND on monad transformers, a relatively common idiom.

How would this scenario play out under the system proposed in [WVPZ11]? This particular problem wouldn't exist – m's kind could have the right roles – but a different problem would. A type's kind also stores its roles in [WVPZ11]. This means that Monad instances could be defined only for types that expect a representational parameter. Yet, it is sometimes convenient to define a Monad instance for a data type whose parameter is properly assigned a nominal role. The fact that the system described in this paper can accept Monad instances both for types with representational parameters and nominal parameters is a direct consequence of the *Role assignments are flexible* theorem (Section 4.3), which does not hold of the system in [WVPZ11].

Looking forward, there is a proposal to indeed add join to Monad, and so we want to be able to allow the use of GND on this enhanced Monad class. We have started to formulate solutions to this problem and have hope that we can overcome this barrier without modifications to the core language.

[8] Package authors have the option of specifying which compilers their package is known to work with. Of the 555 packages listed as working with one of the GHC 7.6 versions, 183 also are listed as compatible with GHC 7.8. These packages include 43 that use the GND extension.

11. Conclusion

Our focus has been on Haskell, for the sake of concreteness, but we believe that this work is important beyond the Haskell community. Any language that offers *both* generative type abstraction *and* type-level computation must deal with their interaction, and those interactions are extremely subtle. We have described one sound and tractable way to combine the two, including the source language changes, type inference, core calculus, and metatheory. In doing so we have given a concrete foundation for others to build upon.

Acknowledgments

Thanks to Antal Spector-Zabusky for contributing to this version of FC; and to Edward Kmett and Dimitrios Vytiniotis for discussion and feedback. This material is based upon work supported by the National Science Foundation under grant nos. CCF-1116620 and CCF-1319880. The first author was supported by the Deutsche Telekom Stiftung.

References

[BEPW14] Joachim Breitner, Richard A. Eisenberg, Simon Peyton Jones, and Stephanie Weirich, *Safe zero-cost coercions for Haskell (extended version)*, Tech. Report MS-CIS-14-07, University of Pennsylvania, 2014.

[CH03] James Cheney and Ralf Hinze, *First-class phantom types*, Tech. report, Cornell University, 2003.

[CKP05] Manuel M. T. Chakravarty, Gabriele Keller, and Simon Peyton Jones, *Associated type synonyms*, ICFP, ACM, 2005, pp. 241–253.

[CKPM05] Manuel M. T. Chakravarty, Gabriele Keller, Simon Peyton Jones, and Simon Marlow, *Associated types with class*, POPL, ACM, 2005, pp. 1–13.

[EVPW14] Richard A. Eisenberg, Dimitrios Vytiniotis, Simon Peyton Jones, and Stephanie Weirich, *Closed type families with overlapping equations*, POPL, ACM, 2014, pp. 671–683.

[Gar13] Jacques Garrigue, *On variance, injectivity, and abstraction*, OCaml Meeting, Boston., September 2013.

[LP05] Ralf Lämmel and Simon Peyton Jones, *Scrap your boilerplate with class: Extensible generic functions*, ICFP, 2005.

[Mar10] Simon Marlow (editor), *Haskell 2010 language report*, 2010.

[MTHM97] Robin Milner, Mads Tofte, Robert Harper, and David MacQueen, *The definition of Standard ML (revised)*, 1997.

[PL91] Simon Peyton Jones and J Launchbury, *Unboxed values as first class citizens*, FPCA, LNCS, vol. 523, 1991, pp. 636–666.

[PTH01] Simon Peyton Jones, Andrew Tolmach, and Tony Hoare, *Playing by the rules: rewriting as a practical optimisation technique in GHC*, Haskell Workshop, 2001, pp. 203–233.

[SR13] Gabriel Scherer and Didier Rémy, *GADTs meet subtyping*, ESOP, 2013, pp. 554–573.

[VPMa12] Dimitrios Vytiniotis, Simon Peyton Jones, and José Pedro Magalhães, *Equality proofs and deferred type errors: A compiler pearl*, ICFP, ACM, 2012, pp. 341–352.

[WB89] Philip Wadler and Stephen Blott, *How to make ad-hoc polymorphism less ad-hoc*, POPL, ACM, 1989, pp. 60–76.

[WVPZ11] Stephanie Weirich, Dimitrios Vytiniotis, Simon Peyton Jones, and Steve Zdancewic, *Generative type abstraction and type-level computation*, POPL, ACM, 2011, pp. 227–240.

[YWC+12] Brent A. Yorgey, Stephanie Weirich, Julien Cretin, Simon Peyton Jones, Dimitrios Vytiniotis, and José Pedro Magalhães, *Giving Haskell a promotion*, TLDI, ACM, 2012, pp. 53–66.

Hindley-Milner Elaboration in Applicative Style

Functional pearl

François Pottier
INRIA
Francois.Pottier@inria.fr

Abstract

Type inference—the problem of determining whether a program is well-typed—is well-understood. In contrast, elaboration—the task of constructing an explicitly-typed representation of the program—seems to have received relatively little attention, even though, in a non-local type inference system, it is non-trivial. We show that the constraint-based presentation of Hindley-Milner type inference can be extended to deal with elaboration, while preserving its elegance. This involves introducing a new notion of "constraint with a value", which forms an applicative functor.

Categories and Subject Descriptors D.1.1 [*Programming Techniques*]: Applicative (Functional) Programming; F.3.3 [*Logics and Meanings of Programs*]: Studies of Program Constructs—Type structure

Keywords Type inference; elaboration; polymorphism; constraints

1. Prologue

It was a bright morning. The Advisor was idle, when his newest student suddenly entered the room. "I need your help," she began. "I am supposed to test my type-preserving compiler for ML21," the Student continued, "but I can't conduct any experiments because I don't know how to connect the compiler with the front-end."

"Hmm," the Advisor thought. This experimental compiler was supposed to translate an *explicitly-typed* presentation of ML21 all the way down to typed assembly language. The stumbling block was that the parser produced abstract syntax for an *implicitly-typed* presentation of ML21, and neither student nor advisor had so far given much thought to the issue of converting one presentation to the other. After all, it was just good old Hindley-Milner type inference [15], wasn't it?

"So," the Student pressed. "Suppose the term t carries no type annotations. How do I determine whether t admits the type τ? And if it does, which type-annotated term t' should I produce?"

The Advisor sighed. Such effrontery! At least, the problem had been stated in a clear manner. He expounded: "Let us consider just simply-typed λ-calculus, to begin with. The answers to your questions are very simple." On the whiteboard, he wrote:

- If t is a function $\lambda x.u$, then, for some types τ_1 and τ_2,
  - the types τ and $\tau_1 \rightarrow \tau_2$ should be equal,
  - assuming that the type of x is τ_1, u should have type τ_2,

  and t' should be the type-annotated abstraction $\lambda x : \tau_1.u'$.
- If t is an application $t_1\ t_2$, then, for some type τ_2,
  - t_1 should have type $\tau_2 \rightarrow \tau$,
  - t_2 should have type τ_2,

  and t' should be $t'_1\ t'_2$.
- If t is a variable x, and if the type of x is θ, then
  - the types τ and θ should be equal,

  and t' should be x.

"There is your algorithm," the Advisor declared, setting the pen down and motioning towards the door. "It *can't* be any more complicated than this."

"This is a declarative specification," the Student thought. "It is not quite obvious whether an executable algorithm could be written in this style." It then occurred to her that the Advisor had not addressed the most challenging part of the question. "Wait," she said. "What about polymorphism?"

The Advisor pondered. He was not quite sure, offhand, how to extend this description with Hindley-Milner polymorphism.

"Let's see," he thought. So far, he had been implicitly thinking in terms of constraints $C ::= \mathsf{true} \mid C \wedge C \mid \tau = \tau \mid \exists\alpha.C$ [25]. When he wrote "the types τ and θ should be equal", he had in mind an equality constraint $\tau = \theta$. When he wrote "for some type τ_2," he had in mind an existentially quantified constraint $\exists\alpha_2.\ldots$ (and he rather conveniently ignored the distinction between the type variable α_2 and the type τ_2 that he was really after). When he wrote "t has type τ", he had in mind a constraint, which, once t and τ are given, can be systematically constructed: on the whiteboard was a recursive description of this constraint generation process.

Now, one way of understanding Hindley-Milner polymorphism is to construct the predicate $\lambda\alpha.(t \text{ has type } \alpha)$. This is a constraint, parameterized over one type variable; in other words, a *constraint abstraction* [7]. A key theorem is that every satisfiable constraint abstraction $\lambda\alpha.C$ can be transformed to an equivalent canonical form, $\lambda\alpha.\exists\vec{\beta}.(\alpha = \theta)$, for suitably chosen type variables $\vec{\beta}$ and type θ. In traditional parlance, this canonical form is usually known as a *type scheme* [8] and written $\forall\vec{\beta}.\theta$. A type that satisfies the predicate $\lambda\alpha.\exists\vec{\beta}.(\alpha = \theta)$ is usually referred to as an *instance* of the type scheme $\forall\vec{\beta}.\theta$. The existence of such canonical forms for constraint abstractions is the *principal type scheme* property [8, 2].

"Jolly good," the Advisor resumed. "Let me amend the case of variables as follows."

ICFP '14, September 1–6, 2014, Gothenburg, Sweden.
Copyright is held by the owner/author(s). Publication rights licensed to ACM.
ACM 978-1-4503-2873-9/14/09...$15.00.
http://dx.doi.org/10.1145/2628136.2628145

- If t is x, and if the type scheme of x is $\forall\vec{\beta}.\theta$, then
  - for some vector $\vec{\tau}$, the types τ and $[\vec{\tau}/\vec{\beta}]\theta$ should be equal,

  and t' should be the type application $x\ \vec{\tau}$.

"And let me add a new case for let bindings." Somewhat more hesitantly, he wrote:

- If t is let $x = t_1$ in t_2, then:
  - the constraint abstraction "$\lambda\alpha.(t_1$ has type $\alpha)$" should have some canonical form $\forall\vec{\beta}.\theta$,
  - assuming that the type scheme of x is $\forall\vec{\beta}.\theta$, the term t_2 should have type τ,

  and t' should be let $x = \Lambda\vec{\beta}.t'_1$ in t'_2.

"There you are now." The Advisor seemed relieved. Apparently he had been able to write something plausible.

"This looks reasonably pretty, but is really still quite fuzzy," the Student thought. "For one thing, which type variables are supposed, or not supposed, to occur in the term t'? Is it clear that Λ-abstracting the type variables $\vec{\beta}$ in t'_1 is the right thing to do?" Indeed, the Advisor's specification would turn out to be incorrect or misleading (§B). "And," the Student thought, "it is now even less obvious how this description could be turned into executable code without compromising its elegance."

As if divining her thought, the Advisor added: "ML21 is a large language, whose design is not fixed. It is quite important that the elaboration code be as simple as possible, so as to evolve easily. Split it into a constraint generator, along the lines of the whiteboard specification, and a constraint solver. The generator will be specific of ML21, but will be easy to adapt when the language evolves. The solver will be independent of ML21."

The Student shrugged imperceptibly. Such amazing confidence! Her advisor was a constraint buff. He probably thought constraints could save the world!

2. Constraints: a recap

The Student was well schooled, and knew most of what had been spelled out on the whiteboard. Why didn't her advisor's answer fully address her concerns?

Type inference in the simply-typed case can be reduced to solving a conjunction of type equations [25], or in other words, to solving constraints of the form $C ::= \mathsf{true} \mid C \wedge C \mid \tau = \tau \mid \exists\alpha.C$. In its simplest formulation, the problem is to determine whether the equations (or the constraint) are satisfiable. In a more demanding formulation, the problem is to compute a most general unifier of the equations, or in other words, to bring the constraint into an equivalent solved form. These problems are collectively known as *first-order unification*. They are solved in quasi-linear time by Huet's first-order unification algorithm [9], which relies on Tarjan's efficient union-find data structure [23].

Type inference with Hindley-Milner polymorphism can also be considered a constraint solving problem, for a suitably extended constraint language [7, 19]:

$$\begin{array}{rcl} \tau & ::= & \alpha \mid \tau \to \tau \mid \ldots \\ C & ::= & \mathsf{true} \mid C \wedge C \mid \tau = \tau \mid \exists\alpha.C \\ & \mid & \mathsf{let}\ x = \lambda\alpha.C\ \mathsf{in}\ C \\ & \mid & x\ \tau \end{array}$$

The extension is quite simple. The let construct binds the variable x to the constraint abstraction $\lambda\alpha.C$. The instantiation construct $x\ \tau$ applies the constraint abstraction denoted by x to the type τ. One way of defining or explaining the meaning of these constructs is to expand them away via the following substitution law:

$$\mathsf{let}\ x = \lambda\alpha.C_1\ \mathsf{in}\ C_2 \quad \equiv \quad \exists\alpha.C_1 \wedge [\lambda\alpha.C_1/x]C_2$$

That is, the let constraint on the left-hand side is equivalent to (a) requiring that there exist at least one value of α for which C_1 holds; and (b) replacing[1] every reference to x in C_2 with a copy of the constraint abstraction $\lambda\alpha.C_1$.

According to the accepted wisdom, as repeated by the Advisor, one should write a constraint generator, which maps an unannotated term t to a constraint C, and a constraint solver, mapping a constraint C to a "satisfiable" or "unsatisfiable" answer. By composing the generator and the solver, one can determine whether t is well-typed.

In greater detail, the constraint generator takes the form of a recursive function that maps a term t and a type τ to a constraint $[\![t : \tau]\!]$, which informally means "t has type τ". It can be defined as follows [19]:

$$\begin{array}{rcl} [\![x : \tau]\!] & = & x\ \tau \\ [\![\lambda x.u : \tau]\!] & = & \exists\alpha_1\alpha_2.\left(\begin{array}{l} \tau = \alpha_1 \to \alpha_2\ \wedge \\ \mathsf{def}\ x = \alpha_1\ \mathsf{in}\ [\![u : \alpha_2]\!] \end{array}\right) \\ [\![t_1\ t_2 : \tau]\!] & = & \exists\alpha.([\![t_1 : \alpha \to \tau]\!] \wedge [\![t_2 : \alpha]\!]) \\ [\![\mathsf{let}\ x = t_1\ \mathsf{in}\ t_2 : \tau]\!] & = & \mathsf{let}\ x = \lambda\alpha.[\![t_1 : \alpha]\!]\ \mathsf{in}\ [\![t_2 : \tau]\!] \end{array}$$

There, def $x = \tau$ in c is a short-hand for let $x = \lambda\alpha.(\alpha = \tau)$ in c. A variable x that occurs free in the term t also occurs free in the constraint $[\![t : \tau]\!]$, where it now stands for a constraint abstraction. It is convenient to keep the name x, since the term t and the constraint $[\![t : \tau]\!]$ have the same binding structure.

This resembles the Advisor's whiteboard specification, but solves only the *type inference* problem, that is, the problem of determining whether a program is well-typed. It does not solve the *elaboration* problem, that is, the problem of constructing an explicitly-typed representation of the program. If the solver returns only a Boolean answer, how does one construct a type-annotated term t'? How does one obtain the necessary type information? A "satisfiable" or "unsatisfiable" answer is not nearly enough.

One may object that a solver should not just produce a Boolean answer, but also transform a constraint C into an equivalent solved form. However, if the term t is closed, then the constraint $[\![t : \alpha]\!]$ has just one free type variable, namely α. This implies that a solved form of $[\![t : \alpha]\!]$ cannot constrain any type variables other than α. Such a solved form could be, for instance, $\alpha = unit$, which tells us that t has type *unit*, but does not tell us how to construct t', which presumably must contain many type annotations.

A more promising idea, or a better formulation of this idea, would be to let the solver produce a satisfiability witness W, whose shape is dictated by the shape of C. (This could be implemented simply by annotating the constraint with extra information.) One would then write an elaboration function, mapping t and W to an explicitly-typed term t'.

Certainly, this approach is workable: the solution advocated in this paper can be viewed as a nicely-packaged version of it. If implemented plainly in the manner suggested above, however, it seems unsatisfactory. For one thing, the elaboration function expects two arguments, namely a term t and a witness W, and must deconstruct them in a "synchronous" manner, keeping careful track of the correlation between them. This is unpleasant[2]. Furthermore, in this approach, the type inference and elaboration process is split

[1] Technically, one defines $[\lambda\alpha.C/x](x\ \tau)$ as $[\tau/\alpha]C$; that is, the β-redex $(\lambda\alpha.C)\ \tau$ is reduced on the fly as part of the substitution.

[2] Rémy and Yakobowski's elaboration of eMLF into xMLF [21] merges the syntax of terms, constraints, and witnesses. Similarly, Gundry suggests "identifying the syntactic and linguistic contexts" [6, §2.4]. If one follows them, then the constraint C carries more information than the term t, and the witness W in turn carries more information than C. This means that the elaboration phase does not have to be a function of two arguments: it maps

in three phases, namely constraint generation, constraint solving, and elaboration. Only the second phase is independent of the programming language at hand. The first and last phases are not. For our Student, this means that, at every evolution of ML21, two places in the code have to be consistently updated. This is not as elegant as we (or the Student's exacting advisor) would like.

In summary, the traditional presentation of type inference as a constraint solving problem seems to fall a little short of offering an elegant solution to the elaboration problem.

3. Constraints with a value

The fundamental reason why there must be three separate phases (namely generation, solving, elaboration) is that constraint solving is a non-local process. In a constraint of the form $(\exists\alpha.C_1)\wedge C_2$, for instance, the final value of α cannot be determined by inspecting just C_1: the solver must inspect also C_2. In other words, when looking at a constraint of the form $\exists\alpha.C$, the final value of α cannot be determined by examining C alone: this value can be influenced by the surrounding context. Thus, one must wait until constraint solving is finished before one can query the solver about the value of α. One cannot query it and obtain an answer right away.

Yet, the pseudo-code on the whiteboard (§1) seems to be written *as if* this was possible. It wishes for some type τ to exist, subject to certain constraints, then goes on and uses τ in the construction of the term t'. In other words, even though phases 1 and 3 (that is, generation and elaboration) must be separately *executed,* we wish to *express* them together. This is the key reason why this pseudo-code seems concise, compositional, and maintainable (i.e., when ML21 evolves, only one piece of code must be updated).

Fortunately, one *can* give precise, executable meaning to the Advisor's style of expression. This is what the Student discovered and worked out, confirming that his Advisor was on the right track, even though he most likely did not have a very clear idea of the difficulties involved.

Described in high-level, declarative terms, what is desired is a language of "constraints with a value", that is, constraints that not only impose certain requirements on their free type variables, but also (provided these requirements are met) produce a result. Here, this result is an explicitly-typed term. In general, though, it could be anything. The language of constraints-with-a-value can (and should) be independent of the nature of the values that are computed. For any type α of the meta-language[3], we would like to be able to construct "α-constraints", that is, constraints which (once satisfied) produce a result of type α.

Described in lower-level, operational terms, one wishes to bring together the code of phase 1, which builds a constraint, and the code of phase 3, which (by exploiting the information provided by the solver) produces a result. So, one could think of an "α-constraint" as a pair of (a) a raw constraint (which can be submitted to the solver) and (b) a function which (after the solver has finished) computes a value of type α. Our OCaml implementation (§4) is based on this representation.

We propose the following syntax of constraints-with-a-value:

$$\begin{array}{rl} C ::= & \\ & \mid \mathsf{true} \mid C \wedge C \mid \tau = \tau \mid \exists\alpha.C \\ & \mid \mathsf{let}\ x = \lambda\alpha.C\ \mathsf{in}\ C \\ & \mid x\ \tau \\ & \mid \mathit{map}\ f\ C \end{array}$$

This syntax is identical to that of raw constraints (§2), with one addition. A new construct appears: *map* f C, where f is a meta-language function. The intention is that this constraint is satisfied when C is satisfied, and if the constraint C produces some value V, then *map* f C produces the value $f\ V$.

The other constructs retain their previous logical meaning, and in addition, acquire a new meaning as producers of meta-language values. At this point, let us give only an informal description of the value that each construct produces. Things are made more precise when we present the high-level interface of the OCaml library (§4.3). Furthermore, to the mathematically inclined reader, an appendix (§A) offers a formal definition of the meaning of constraints-with-a-value, that is, when they are satisfied, and what value they produce. This allows us to specify what the OCaml code is supposed to compute.

As usual, a conjunction $C_1 \wedge C_2$ is satisfied if and only if C_1 and C_2 are satisfied. In addition, if C_1 and C_2 respectively produce the values V_1 and V_2, then the conjunction $C_1 \wedge C_2$ produces the pair (V_1, V_2).

The constraints true and $\tau_1 = \tau_2$ produce a unit value.

Existential quantification is more interesting. If C produces the value V, then $\exists\alpha.C$ produces the pair (T, V), where T is the witness, that is, the value that must be assigned to the type variable α in order to satisfy the constraint C. (We write T for a "decoded type". This notion is clarified in §4, from an OCaml programmer's point of view, and in §A, from a more formal point of view.) The type T may have free "decoded type variables", which we write a. The reader may wonder where and how these variables are supposed to be introduced. This is answered below in the discussion of let constraints.

An instantiation constraint $x\ \tau$ produces a vector $\vec{T}$ of decoded types. These are again witnesses: they indicate how to the type scheme associated with x must be instantiated in order to obtain the type τ.

A constraint of the form let $x = \lambda\alpha.C_1$ in C_2 produces a tuple of three values:

1. The canonical form of the constraint abstraction $\lambda\alpha.C_1$. In other words, this is the type scheme that was inferred for x, and that was associated with x while solving C_2. It is a "decoded type scheme", of the form $\forall\vec{b}.T$.
2. A value of the form $\Lambda\vec{a}.V_1$, if V_1 is the value produced by C_1.
3. The value V_2 produced by C_2.

In order to understand the binder "$\Lambda\vec{a}$" in the second item, one must note that, in general, the value V_1 may have free decoded type variables. For instance, if C_1 begins with an existential quantifier $\exists\alpha.\ldots$, then V_1 is a pair $(T,\ldots)$, where the decoded type T may have free decoded type variables. By introducing the binder "$\Lambda\vec{a}$", the solver is telling the user that, at this particular place, the type variables $\vec{a}$ should be introduced. (In the OCaml code, the solver separately returns $\vec{a}$ and V_1, and the user is responsible for building an appropriate abstraction.)

The reader may wonder whether there should be a connection between the vectors $\vec{a}$ and $\vec{b}$. The short answer is, in general, $\vec{b}$ is a subset of $\vec{a}$. This is discussed in detail in the appendices (§A, §B).

4. Solving constraints with a value

We have implemented our proposal as an OCaml library, whose code is available online [17]. It is organized in two layers. The low-level layer (§4.2) solves a raw constraint, exports information via write-once references, and offers facilities to decode this information. The high-level layer (§4.3) hides many of these low-level details. It allows the client to construct constraints-with-a-value and offers a single function *solve*; nothing else is needed.

just W to t'. A disadvantage of this approach, though, is that the syntax of constraints is no longer independent of the programming language at hand.

[3] In our implementation (§4, §5), the meta-language is OCaml.

```
module type TEVAR = sig
  type tevar
  val compare: tevar → tevar → int
end
```

Figure 1. Term variables

```
module type STRUCTURE = sig
  type α structure
  val map: (α → β) → α structure → β structure
  val iter: (α → unit) → α structure → unit
  val fold: (α → β → β) → α structure → β → β
  exception Iter2
  val iter2: (α → β → unit) → α structure → β structure → unit
end
```

Figure 2. Shallow structure of types

```
module type OUTPUT = sig
  type tyvar = int
  type α structure
  type ty
  val variable: tyvar → ty
  val structure: ty structure → ty
  val mu: tyvar → ty → ty
  type scheme = tyvar list × ty
end
```

Figure 3. Decoded representation of types

4.1 Parameters

The low-level and high-level solvers are functors, parameterized over three arguments.

The first argument (Figure 1) provides the type *tevar* of term variables. This type must be equipped with a total ordering.

The second argument (Figure 2) provides a type α *structure*, which defines the first-order universe over which type variables are interpreted. A value of type α *structure* is a shallow type: it represents an application of a constructor (say, arrow, or product) to a suitable number of arguments of type α. It must be equipped with a *map* function (as well as *iter* and *fold*, which in principle can be derived from *map*) and with $iter_2$, which is expected to fail if its arguments exhibit distinct constructors.

The last argument (Figure 3) provides the types *tyvar* and *ty* of decoded type variables and decoded types. For simplicity, the definition of *tyvar* is fixed: it is just *int*. That is, a decoded type variable is represented as an integer name. The type *ty* is the client's representation of types. It must be able to express type variables (the function *variable* is an injection of *tyvar* into *ty*) as well as types built by applying a constructor to other types (the function *structure* is an injection of *ty structure* into *ty*).

The type *ty* must also come with a function *mu*, which allows constructing recursive types. If *a* is a type variable and *t* represents an arbitrary type, then *mu a t* should represent the recursive type $\mu a.t$. This feature is required for two reasons: (a) the solver optionally supports recursive types, in the style of `ocaml -rectypes`; and (b) even if this option is disabled, the types carried by the solver exceptions *Unify* and *Cycle* (Figure 5) can be cyclic.

The last line of Figure 3 specifies that a decoded type scheme is represented as a pair of a list of type variables (the universal quantifiers) and a type (the body).

```
module Make
  (X : TEVAR)
  (S : STRUCTURE)
  (O : OUTPUT with type α structure = α S.structure)
: sig
  open X
  open S
  open O
  type variable
  val fresh: variable structure option → variable

  type ischeme
  type rawco =
  | CTrue
  | CConj of rawco × rawco
  | CEq of variable × variable
  | CExist of variable × rawco
  | CInstance of tevar × variable × variable list WriteOnceRef.t
  | CDef of tevar × variable × rawco
  | CLet of (tevar × variable × ischeme WriteOnceRef.t) list
        × rawco
        × rawco
        × variable list WriteOnceRef.t

  exception Unbound of tevar
  exception Unify of variable × variable
  exception Cycle of variable
  val solve: bool → rawco → unit

  val decode_variable: variable → tyvar
  type decoder = variable → ty
  val new_decoder: bool → decoder
  val decode_scheme: decoder → ischeme → scheme
end
```

Figure 4. The solver's low-level interface

4.2 Low-level interface

As the low-level layer is not a contribution of this paper, we describe it rather briefly. The reader who would like to know more may consult its code online [17]. Its interface appears in Figure 4.

The types *variable* and *ischeme* are abstract. They are the solver's internal representations of type variables and type schemes. Here, a type variable can be thought of as a vertex in the graph maintained by the first-order unification algorithm. The function *fresh* allows the client to create new vertices. It can be applied to *None* or to *Some t*, where *t* is a shallow type. In the former case, the new vertex can be thought of as a fresh unification variable; in the latter case, it can be thought of as standing for the type *t*.

The type *rawco* is the type of raw constraints. Their syntax is as previously described (§2), except that *CLet* allows binding several term variables at once, a feature that we do not describe in this paper. A couple of low-level aspects will be later hidden in the high-level interface, so we do not describe them in detail:

- In *CExist* (*v*, *c*), the type variable *v* must be fresh and unique. A similar requirement bears on the type variables carried by *CLet*.
- *CInstance* and *CLet* carry write-once references (i.e., references to an option), which must be fresh (uninitialized) and unique. The solver sets these references[4].

[4] Instead of setting write-once references, the solver could build a witness, a copy of the constraint that carries more information. That would be somewhat more verbose and less efficient, though. Since these details are ultimately hidden, we prefer to rely on side effects.

The function *solve* expects a closed constraint and determines whether it is satisfiable. The Boolean parameter indicates whether recursive types, in the style of `ocaml -rectypes`, are legal.

If the constraint is unsatisfiable, an exception is raised. The exception *Unify* (v_1, v_2) means that the type variables v_1 and v_2 cannot be unified; the exception *Cycle* v means that a cycle in the type structure has been detected, which the type variable v participates in.

If the constraint is satisfiable, the solver produces no result, but annotates the constraint by setting the write-once references embedded in it.

The type information that is made available to the client, either via the exceptions *Unify* and *Cycle* or via the write-once references, consists of values of type *variable* and *ischeme*. These are abstract types: we do not wish to expose the internal data structures used by the solver. Thus, the solver must also offer facilities for decoding this information, that is, for converting it to values of type *tyvar*, *ty*, etc. These decoding functions are supposed to be used only after the constraint solving phase is finished.

The function *decode_variable* decodes a type variable. As noted earlier, the type *tyvar* is just *int*: a type variable is decoded to its unique integer identifier.

The function *new_decoder* constructs a new type decoder, that is, a function of type *variable* $\rightarrow$ *ty*. (The Boolean parameter tells whether the decoder should be prepared to support cyclic types.) This decoder has persistent state. Indeed, decoding consists in traversing the graph constructed by the unification algorithm and turning it into what appears to be a tree (a value of type *ty*) but is really a DAG. The decoder internally keeps track of the visited vertices and their decoded form (i.e., it maintains a mapping of *variable* to *ty*), so that the overall cost of decoding remains linear in the size of the graph[5].

We lack space to describe the implementation of the low-level solver, and it is, anyway, beside the point of the paper. Let us just emphasize that it is is modular: (a) at the lowest layer lies Tarjan's efficient union-find algorithm [23]; (b) above it, one finds Huet's first-order unification algorithm [9]; (c) then comes the treatment of generalization and instantiation, which exploits Rémy's integer ranks [20, 12, 11] to efficiently determine which type variables must be generalized; (d) the last layer interprets the syntax of constraints. The solver meets McAllester asymptotic time bound [12]: under the assumption that all of the type schemes that are ever constructed have bounded size, its time complexity is $O(nk)$, where n is the size of the constraint and k is the left-nesting depth of *CLet* nodes.

4.3 High-level interface

The solver's high-level interface appears in Figure 5. It abstracts away several details of raw constraints, including the transmission of information from solver to client via write-once references and the need to decode types. In short, it provides: (a) an abstract type α *co* of constraints that produce a value of type α; (b) a number of ways of constructing such constraints; and (c) a single function, *solve*, that solves and evaluates such a constraint and (if successful) produces a final result of type α.

The type α *co* is internally defined as follows:

```
type α co =
  rawco × (env → α)
```

That is, a constraint-with-a-value is a pair of a raw constraint *rc* and a continuation *k*, which is intended to be invoked after the constraint solving phase is over, and is expected to produce a result of type α. The continuation receives an environment which, in the current implementation, contains just a type decoder:

```
type env =
  decoder
```

If one wished to implement α *co* in a purely functional style, one would certainly come up with a different definition of α *co*. Perhaps something along the lines of *rawco* $\times$ (*witness* $\rightarrow \alpha$ *m*), where *witness* is the type of the satisfiability witness produced by the low-level solver (no more write-once references!) and α *m* is a suitable monad, so as to allow threading the state of the type decoder through the elaboration phase. Perhaps one might also wish to use a dependent type, or a GADT, to encode the fact that the shape of the witness is dictated by the shape of the raw constraint. We use OCaml's imperative features because we can, but the point is, the end user does not need to know; the abstraction that we offer is independent of these details, and is not inherently imperative.

The combinators (*pure*, ..., let_1) allow building constraints-with-a-value. Most of them produce a little bit of the underlying raw constraint, together with an appropriate continuation. The only exception is *map*, which installs a continuation but does not affect the underlying raw constraint.

The constraint *pure a* is always satisfied and produces the value *a*. It is defined as follows:

```
let pure a =
  CTrue,
  fun env → a
```

If c_1 and c_2 are constraints of types α *co* and β *co*, then c_1 ^& c_2 is a constraint of type $(\alpha \times \beta)$ *co*. It represents the conjunction of the underlying raw constraints, and produces a pair of the results produced by c_1 and c_2.

```
let (^&) (rc1, k1) (rc2, k2) =
  CConj (rc1, rc2),
  fun env → (k1 env, k2 env)
```

```
module Make
  (X : TEVAR)
  (S : STRUCTURE)
  (O : OUTPUT with type α structure = α S.structure)
: sig
  open X
  open S
  open O
  type variable

  type α co
  val pure: α → α co
  val (^&): α co → β co → (α × β) co
  val map: (α → β) → α co → β co
  val (--): variable → variable → unit co
  val (---): variable → variable structure → unit co
  val exist: (variable → α co) → (ty × α) co
  val instance: tevar → variable → ty list co
  val def: tevar → variable → α co → α co
  val let1: tevar → (variable → α co) → β co →
            (scheme × tyvar list × α × β) co

  exception Unbound of tevar
  exception Unify of ty × ty
  exception Cycle of ty
  val solve: bool → α co → α
end
```

Figure 5. The solver's high-level interface

[5] This is true when support for cyclic types is disabled. When it is enabled, one must place μ binders in a correct manner, and this seems to prevent the use of persistent state. We conjecture that the unary μ is too impoverished a construct: it does not allow describing arbitrary cyclic graphs without a potential explosion in size.

If c is a constraint of type α *co* and if the user-supplied function f maps α to β, then *map* f c is a constraint of type β *co*. Its logical meaning is the same as that of c.

```
let map f (rc, k) =
  rc,
  fun env → f (k env)
```

Equipped with the combinators *pure*, ^&, and *map*, the type constructor *co* is an applicative functor. More specifically, it is an instance of McBride and Paterson's type class *Monoidal* [13, §7]. Furthermore, the combinator ^& is commutative, that is, it enjoys the following law:

$$c_1 \mathbin{\char`^\&} c_2 \equiv map\ swap\ (c_2 \mathbin{\char`^\&} c_1)$$

where *swap* (a_2, a_1) is (a_1, a_2). This law holds because *CConj* is commutative; the order in which the members of a conjunction are considered by the solver does not influence the final result.

It is worth noting that *co* is not a monad, as there is no sensible way of defining a *bind* operation of type α *co* $\rightarrow$ ($\alpha \rightarrow \beta$ *co*) $\rightarrow \beta$ *co*. In an attempt to define *bind* (rc_1, k_1) f_2, one would like to construct a raw conjunction *CConj* (rc_1, rc_2). In order to obtain rc_2, one must invoke f_2, and in order to do that, one needs a value of type α, which must be produced by k_1. But the continuation k_1 must not be invoked until the raw constraint rc_1 has been solved. In summary, a constraint-with-a-value is a pair of a static component (the raw constraint) and a dynamic component (the continuation), and this precludes a definition of *bind*. This phenomenon, which was observed in Swierstra and Duponcheel's LL(1) parser combinators [22], was one of the motivations that led to the recognition of arrows [10] and applicative functors [13] as useful abstractions.

Although we do not have *bind*, we have *map*. When one builds a constraint *map* f c, one is assured that the function f will be run after the constraint solving phase is finished. In particular, f is run after c has been solved. We emphasize this by defining a version of *map* with reversed argument order:

```
let (<$$>) a f =
  map f a
```

The combinators -- and --- construct equations, i.e., unification constraints. The constraint v_1 -- v_2 imposes an equality between the variables v_1 and v_2, and produces a unit value. Its definition is straightforward:

```
let (--) v1 v2 =
  CEq (v1, v2),
  fun env → ()
```

The constraint v_1 --- t_2 is also an equation, whose second member is a shallow type.

The next combinator, *exist*, builds an existentially quantified constraint $\exists\alpha.C$. Its argument is a user-defined function f which, once supplied with a fresh type variable α, must construct C. It is defined as follows:

```
let exist f =
  let v = fresh None in
  let rc, k = f v in
  CExist (v, rc),
  fun env →
    let decode = env in
    (decode v, k env)
```

At constraint construction time, we create a fresh variable v and pass it to the client by invoking f v. This produces a constraint, i.e., a pair of a raw constraint *rc* and a continuation k. We can then construct the raw constraint *CExist* (v, rc). We define a new continuation, which constructs a pair of the decoded value of v and the value produced by k. As a result, the constraint *exist* f has type ($ty \times \alpha$) *co*: it produces a pair whose first component is a decoded type. The process of decoding types has been made transparent to the client.

The combinator *instance* constructs an instantiation constraint x v, where x is a term variable and v is a type variable. The type of *instance* x v is *ty list co*: this constraint produces a vector of decoded types, so as to indicate how the type scheme associated with x was instantiated. This combinator is implemented as follows:

```
let instance x v =
  let witnesses = WriteOnceRef.create() in
  CInstance (x, v, witnesses),
  fun env →
    let decode = env in
    List.map decode (WriteOnceRef.get witnesses)
```

At constraint construction time, we create an empty write-once reference, *witnesses*, and construct the raw constraint *CInstance* (x, v, *witnesses*), which carries a pointer to this write-once reference. During the constraint solving phase, this reference is written by the solver, so that, when the continuation is invoked, we may read the reference and decode the list of types that it contains. Thus, the transmission of information from the solver to the client via write-once references has been made transparent.

The last combinator, let_1, builds a let constraint. It should be applied to three arguments, namely: (a) a term variable x; (b) a user-supplied function f_1, which denotes a constraint abstraction $\lambda\alpha.c_1$ (i.e., when applied to a fresh type variable α, this function constructs the constraint c_1); (c) a constraint c_2. We omit its code, which is in the same style as that of *instance* above. As promised earlier (§3), this constraint produces the following results:

- A decoded type scheme, $\forall\vec{b}.T$, of type *scheme*. It can be viewed as the canonical form of the constraint abstraction $\lambda\alpha.c_1$. This type scheme has been associated with x while solving c_2. We guarantee that $\vec{b}$ is a subset of $\vec{a}$ (see §A and §B for details).
- A vector of decoded type variables $\vec{a}$, of type *tyvar list*, and a value V_1, of type α, produced by c_1. The type variables $\vec{a}$ may occur in V_1. The user is responsible for somehow binding them in V_1, so as to obtain the value referred to as "$\Lambda\vec{a}.V_1$" in §3.
- A value V_2, produced by c_2, of type β.

The function *solve* takes a constraint of type α *co* to a result of type α. If the constraint is unsatisfiable, then the exception that is raised (*Unify* or *Cycle*) carries a decoded type, so that (once again) the decoding process is transparent. Thus, in the implementation, we redefine *Unify* and *Cycle*:

```
exception Unify of O.ty × O.ty
exception Cycle of O.ty
```

and implement *solve* as follows:

```
let solve rectypes (rc, k) =
  begin try
    Lo.solve rectypes rc
  with
  | Lo.Unify (v1, v2) →
      let decode = new_decoder true in
      raise (Unify (decode v1, decode v2))
  | Lo.Cycle v →
      let decode = new_decoder true in
      raise (Cycle (decode v))
  end;
  let decode = new_decoder rectypes in
  let env = decode in
  k env
```

The computation is in two phases. First, the low-level solver, *Lo.solve*, is applied to the raw constraint *rc*. Then, elaboration

```
type tevar = string
type term =
  | Var of tevar
  | Abs of tevar × term
  | App of term × term
  | Let of tevar × term × term
```

Figure 6. Syntax of the untyped calculus (ML)

```
type (α, β) typ =
  | TyVar of α
  | TyArrow of (α, β) typ × (α, β) typ
  | TyProduct of (α, β) typ × (α, β) typ
  | TyForall of β × (α, β) typ
  | TyMu of β × (α, β) typ
type tyvar = int
type nominal_type = (tyvar, tyvar) typ
type tevar = string
type (α, β) term =
  | Var of tevar
  | Abs of tevar × (α, β) typ × (α, β) term
  | App of (α, β) term × (α, β) term
  | Let of tevar × (α, β) term × (α, β) term
  | TyAbs of β × (α, β) term
  | TyApp of (α, β) term × (α, β) typ
type nominal_term = (tyvar, tyvar) term

let ftyabs vs t =
  List.fold_right (fun v t → TyAbs (v, t)) vs t
let ftyapp t tys =
  List.fold_left (fun t ty → TyApp (t, ty)) t tys
```

Figure 7. Syntax of the typed calculus (F)

takes place: the continuation k is invoked. It is passed a fresh type decoder, which has persistent state[6], so that (as announced earlier) the overall cost of decoding is linear.

If the raw constraint *rc* is found to be unsatisfiable, the exception raised by the low-level solver (*Lo.Unify* or *Lo.Cycle*) is caught; its arguments are decoded, and an exception (*Unify* or *Cycle*) is raised again. The decoder that is used for this purpose must support recursive types, even if *rectypes* is *false*. Obviously, the argument carried by *Cycle* is a vertex that participates in a cycle! Perhaps more surprisingly, the arguments carried by *Unify* may participate in cycles too, as the occurs check is performed late (i.e., only at *CLet* constraints) and in a piece-wise manner (i.e., only on the so-called "young generation").

The high-level solver has asymptotic complexity $O(nk)$, like the low-level solver. Indeed, the cost of constructing and invoking continuations is $O(n)$, and the cost of decoding is linear in the total number of type variables ever created, that is, $O(nk)$.

5. Elaborating ML into System F

We now show how to perform elaboration for an untyped calculus ("ML", shown in Figure 6) and translate it to an explicitly-typed form ("F", shown in Figure 7). The code (Figure 8) is a formal and rather faithful rendition of the Advisor's pseudo-code (§1).

5.1 Representations of type variables and binders

In both calculi, the representation of term variables is nominal. (Here, they are just strings. One could use unique integers instead.) The representation of type variables in System F is not fixed: the syntax is parametric in α (a type variable occurrence) and β (a type variable binding site). A nominal representation is obtained by instantiating α and β with *tyvar* (which is defined as *int*, so a type variable is represented by a unique integer identifier), whereas de Bruijn's representation (not shown) is obtained by instantiating α with *int* (a de Bruijn index) and β with *unit*.

In the following, we construct type-annotated terms under a nominal representation. This is natural, because the constraint solver internally represents type variables as mutable objects with unique identity, and presents them to us as unique integers. One may later perform a conversion to de Bruijn's representation, which is perhaps more traditional for use in a System F type-checker.

[6] Provided *rectypes* is *false* (§4.2).

```
let rec hastype (t : ML.term) (w : variable) : F.nominal_term co
= match t with
  | ML.Var x →
      instance x w <$$> fun tys →
      F.ftyapp (F.Var x) tys
  | ML.Abs (x, u) →
      exist (fun v1 →
        exist (fun v2 →
          w --- arrow v1 v2 ^&
          def x v1 (hastype u v2)
        )
      ) <$$> fun (ty1, (ty2, ((), u'))) →
      F.Abs (x, ty1, u')
  | ML.App (t1, t2) →
      exist (fun v →
        lift hastype t1 (arrow v w) ^&
        hastype t2 v
      ) <$$> fun (ty, (t1', t2')) →
      F.App (t1', t2')
  | ML.Let (x, t, u) →
      let1 x (hastype t)
        (hastype u w)
      <$$> fun ((b, _), a, t', u') →
      F.Let (x, F.ftyabs a t',
      F.Let (x, coerce a b (F.Var x),
      u'))
```

Figure 8. Type inference and translation of ML to F

5.2 Translation

Thanks to the high-level solver interface, type inference for ML and elaboration of ML into F are performed in what appears to be one pass. The code is simple and compositional: it takes the form of a single recursive function, *hastype*. This function maps an ML term t and a unification variable w to a constraint of type *F.nominal_term co*. This constraint describes, at the same time, a raw constraint (what is a necessary and sufficient condition for the term t to have type w?) and a process by which (if the raw constraint is satisfied) a term of System F is constructed.

The function *hastype* appears in Figure 8. Most of it should be clear, since it corresponds to the whiteboard specification of §1. Let us explain just a few points.

The auxiliary function *lift* (not shown) transforms a function of type $\alpha \rightarrow$ *variable* $\rightarrow \beta$ *co* into one of type $\alpha \rightarrow$ *variable structure* $\rightarrow \beta$ *co*. It can be defined in terms of *map*, *exist*, and ---. Thus, whereas the second argument of *hastype* is a type variable, the second argument of *lift hastype* is a shallow type. This offers a convenient notation in the case of *ML.App*.

In the case of *ML.Let*, the partial application *hastype t* is quite literally a constraint abstraction! The construct *ML.Let* is translated to *F.Let*. (One could encode *F.Let* as a β-redex, at the cost of extra type annotations.) The type variables a are explicitly Λ-abstracted in the term t', as explained in the description of let_1 (§4.3).

In the next-to-last line of Figure 8, the variable x is re-bound to an application of a certain coercion to x, which is constructed by the function call *coerce a b (F.Var x)*. This coercion has no effect when the vectors of type variables a and b are equal. The case where they differ is discussed in the appendix (§B).

6. Conclusion

What have we achieved? We have started with a language of "raw" constraints (§2) that can express the type inference problem in a concise and elegant manner. Its syntax is simple. Yet, it requires a non-trivial and non-local constraint solving procedure, involving first-order unification as well as generalization and instantiation. We have argued that it does not solve the elaboration problem. A "satisfiable" or "unsatisfiable" answer is not enough, and asking the solver to produce more information typically results in a low-level interface (§4.2) that does not directly allow us to express elaboration in an elegant manner. The key contribution of this paper is a high-level solver interface (§4.3) that allows (and forces) the user to tie together the constraint generation phase and the elaboration phase, resulting in concise and elegant code (§5). The high-level interface offers one key abstraction, namely the type α *co* of "constraints with a value". Its meaning can be specified in a declarative manner (§A). It is an applicative functor, which suggests that it is a natural way of structuring an elaboration algorithm that has the side effect of emitting and solving a constraint. The high-level interface can be modularly constructed above the low-level solver, without knowledge of how the latter is implemented, provided the low-level solver produces some form of satisfiability witness.

The idea of "constraints with a value" is not specific of the Hindley-Milner setting. It is in principle applicable and useful in other settings where constraint solving is non-local. For instance, elaboration in programming languages with dependent types and implicit arguments [6], which typically relies on higher-order pattern unification [14], could perhaps benefit from this approach.

The constraint language is small, but powerful. As one scales up to a real-world programming language in the style of ML, the constraint language should not need to grow much. The current library [17] already offers a combinator *letn* for defining a constraint abstraction with n entry points; this allows dealing with ML's "let $p = t_1$ in t_2", which simultaneously performs generalization and pattern matching. Two simple extensions would be universal quantification in constraints [18, §1.10], which allows dealing with "rigid", user-provided type annotations, and rows [19, §10.8], which allow dealing with structural object types in the style of OCaml. The value restriction requires no extension to the library, but the relaxed value restriction [3] would require one: the solver would have to be made aware of the variance of every type constructor. Higher-rank polymorphism [4, 16], polymorphism in the style of MLF [21], and GADTs [24, 5] would require other extensions, which we have not considered.

The current library has limited support for reporting type errors, in the form of the exceptions *Cycle* and *Unify*. The unification algorithm is transactional. Equations are submitted to it one by one, and each submission either succeeds and updates the algorithm's current state, or fails and has no effect. This means that the types carried by the exception *Unify* reflect the state of the solver just before the problematic equation was encountered. The library could easily be extended with support for embedding source code locations (of a user-specified type) in constraints. This should allow displaying type error messages of roughly the same quality as those of the OCaml type-checker. A more ambitious treatment of type errors might require a different constraint solver, which hopefully would offer the same interface as the present one, so that the elaboration code need not be duplicated.

Our claim that the elaboration of ML into System F has complexity $O(nk)$ (§4.3) must be taken with a grain of salt. In our current implementation, this is true because elaboration does not produce a System F *term*: it actually constructs a System F *DAG*, with sharing in the type annotations. Displaying this DAG in a naive manner, or converting it in a naive way to another representation, such as de Bruijn's representation, causes an increase in size, which in the worst case could be exponential. One could address this issue by extending System F with a local type abbreviation construct, of the form let $a = T$ in t, where a is a type variable and T is a type. The elaboration algorithm would emit this construct at let nodes. (The low-level and high-level solver interfaces would have to be adapted. The solver would publish, at every let node, a set of local type definitions.) All type annotations (at λ-abstractions and at type applications) would then be reduced to type variables. This could be an interesting avenue for research, as this extension of System F might enjoy significantly faster type-checking.

References

[1] Julien Cretin and Didier Rémy. On the power of coercion abstraction. In *Principles of Programming Languages (POPL)*, pages 361–372, 2012.

[2] Luis Damas and Robin Milner. Principal type-schemes for functional programs. In *Principles of Programming Languages (POPL)*, pages 207–212, 1982.

[3] Jacques Garrigue. Relaxing the value restriction. In *Functional and Logic Programming*, volume 2998 of *Lecture Notes in Computer Science*, pages 196–213. Springer, 2004.

[4] Jacques Garrigue and Didier Rémy. Extending ML with semi-explicit higher-order polymorphism. *Information and Computation*, 155(1):134–169, 1999.

[5] Jacques Garrigue and Didier Rémy. Ambivalent types for principal type inference with GADTs. In *Asian Symposium on Programming Languages and Systems (APLAS)*, 2013.

[6] Adam Gundry. *Type Inference, Haskell and Dependent Types*. PhD thesis, University of Strathclyde, 2013.

[7] Jörgen Gustavsson and Josef Svenningsson. Constraint abstractions. In *Symposium on Programs as Data Objects*, volume 2053 of *Lecture Notes in Computer Science*. Springer, 2001.

[8] J. Roger Hindley. The principal type-scheme of an object in combinatory logic. *Transactions of the American Mathematical Society*, 146:29–60, 1969.

[9] Gérard Huet. *Résolution d'équations dans des langages d'ordre 1, 2, . . ., ω*. PhD thesis, Université Paris 7, 1976.

[10] John Hughes. Generalising monads to arrows. *Science of Computer Programming*, 37(1–3):67–111, 2000.

[11] George Kuan and David MacQueen. Efficient type inference using ranked type variables. In *ACM Workshop on ML*, pages 3–14, 2007.

[12] David McAllester. A logical algorithm for ML type inference. In *Rewriting Techniques and Applications (RTA)*, volume 2706 of *Lecture Notes in Computer Science*, pages 436–451. Springer, 2003.

[13] Conor McBride and Ross Paterson. Applicative programming with effects. *Journal of Functional Programming*, 18(1):1–13, 2008.

[14] Dale Miller. Unification under a mixed prefix. *Journal of Symbolic Computation*, 14(4):321–358, 1992.

[15] Robin Milner. A theory of type polymorphism in programming. *Journal of Computer and System Sciences*, 17(3):348–375, 1978.

[16] Simon Peyton Jones, Dimitrios Vytiniotis, Stephanie Weirich, and Mark Shields. Practical type inference for arbitrary-rank types. *Journal of Functional Programming*, 17(1):1–82, 2007.

[17] François Pottier. Inferno: a library for Hindley-Milner type inference and elaboration, February 2014. http://gallium.inria.fr/~fpottier/inferno/inferno.tar.gz.

[18] François Pottier and Didier Rémy. The essence of ML type inference. Draft of an extended version. Unpublished, 2003.

[19] François Pottier and Didier Rémy. The essence of ML type inference. In Benjamin C. Pierce, editor, *Advanced Topics in Types and Programming Languages*, chapter 10, pages 389–489. MIT Press, 2005.

[20] Didier Rémy. Extending ML type system with a sorted equational theory. Technical Report 1766, INRIA, 1992.

[21] Didier Rémy and Boris Yakobowski. A Church-style intermediate language for MLF. *Theoretical Computer Science*, 435(1):77–105, 2012.

[22] S. Doaitse Swierstra and Luc Duponcheel. Deterministic, error-correcting combinator parsers. In *Advanced Functional Programming*, volume 1129 of *Lecture Notes in Computer Science*, pages 184–207. Springer, 1996.

[23] Robert Endre Tarjan. Efficiency of a good but not linear set union algorithm. *Journal of the ACM*, 22(2):215–225, 1975.

[24] Dimitrios Vytiniotis, Simon L. Peyton Jones, Tom Schrijvers, and Martin Sulzmann. OutsideIn(X): Modular type inference with local assumptions. *Journal of Functional Programming*, 21(4–5):333–412, 2011.

[25] Mitchell Wand. A simple algorithm and proof for type inference. *Fundamenta Informaticæ*, 10:115–122, 1987.

A. Semantics of constraints with a value

In order to clarify the definition that follows, we must distinguish two namespaces of type variables. In the syntax of constraints (§2, §3), we have been using α to denote a type variable. Such a variable may appear in a type τ and in a constraint C. It represents a type to be determined; one could refer to it informally as a "unification variable". In contrast, the explicitly-typed terms that we wish to construct also contain type variables, but those do not stand for types to be determined; they are type constants, so to speak. For the sake of clarity, we use distinct meta-variables, namely a and b, to denote them, and we write T for a first-order type built on them:

$$T ::= a \mid T \to T \mid \ldots$$

We refer to a as a "decoded" type variable and to T as a "decoded" type. In the following, we write ϕ for a partial mapping of the type variables α to decoded types T. The application of ϕ to a type τ produces a decoded type T.

We wish to define when a constraint C may produce a value V, where V denotes a value of the meta-language. (In §5, the values that we build are OCaml representations of System F terms.) We do not wish to fix the syntax of values, as it is under the user's control. We assume that it includes: (a) tuples of arbitrary arity, (b) decoded type schemes, and (c) a way of binding a vector $\vec{a}$ in a value V:

$$V ::= (V, \ldots, V) \mid \forall\vec{a}.T \mid \Lambda\vec{a}.V \mid \ldots$$

In order to define when a constraint C may produce a value V, we need a judgement of at least two arguments, namely C and V. In order to indicate which term variables x and which decoded type variables a are in scope, we add a third argument, namely an environment E, whose structure is as follows:

$$E ::= \emptyset \mid E, x : \forall\vec{a}.T \mid E, a$$

(This is essentially an ML type environment.)

Finally, to keep track of the values assigned to unification variables, we add a fourth and last argument, namely a substitution ϕ. Thus, we define a judgement of the following form:

$$E; \phi \vdash C \leadsto V$$

$$E;\phi \vdash \mathsf{true} \leadsto () \qquad \frac{E;\phi \vdash C_1 \leadsto V_1 \quad E;\phi \vdash C_2 \leadsto V_2}{E;\phi \vdash C_1 \wedge C_2 \leadsto (V_1, V_2)}$$

$$\frac{\phi(\tau_1) = \phi(\tau_2)}{E;\phi \vdash \tau_1 = \tau_2 \leadsto ()} \qquad \frac{E \vdash T \text{ ok} \quad E;\phi[\alpha \mapsto T] \vdash C \leadsto V}{E;\phi \vdash \exists\alpha.C \leadsto (T, V)}$$

$$\frac{E(x) = \forall\vec{a}.T \quad \phi(\tau) = [\vec{T}/\vec{a}]T}{E;\phi \vdash x\ \tau \leadsto \vec{T}} \qquad \frac{E;\phi \vdash C \leadsto V}{E;\phi \vdash \mathit{map}\ f\ C \leadsto f\ V}$$

$$\frac{\begin{array}{c} E, \vec{b} \vdash T \text{ ok} \quad \vec{b} \subseteq \vec{a} \\ E, \vec{a}; \phi[\alpha \mapsto T] \vdash C_1 \leadsto V_1 \\ E, x : \forall\vec{b}.T; \phi \vdash C_2 \leadsto V_2 \end{array}}{E;\phi \vdash \mathsf{let}\ x = \lambda\alpha.C_1\ \mathsf{in}\ C_2 \leadsto (\forall\vec{b}.T, \Lambda\vec{a}.V_1, V_2)}$$

Figure 9. Semantics of constraints with a value

where the free term variables of C are in the domain of E and the free type variables of C are in the domain of ϕ. This judgement means that *in the context E, the constraint C is satisfied by ϕ and produces the value V*.

The definition of this judgement appears in Figure 9.

The meaning of truth and conjunction is straightforward. The constraint true produces the empty tuple $()$, while a conjunction $C_1 \wedge C_2$ produces a pair (V_1, V_2), as announced earlier.

Quite obviously, an equation $\tau_1 = \tau_2$ is satisfied by ϕ only if the decoded types $\phi(\tau_1)$ and $\phi(\tau_2)$ are equal. Such an equation produces the empty tuple $()$.

The rule for existential quantification states that the constraint $\exists\alpha.C$ is satisfied iff there exists an assignment of α that satisfies C. More precisely, ϕ satisfies $\exists\alpha.C$ iff there exists a decoded type T such that $\phi[\alpha \mapsto T]$ satisfies C. This is a non-deterministic specification, not an executable algorithm, so the witness T is "magically" chosen. (The first premise requires the free type variables of T to be in the domain of E.) Finally, the rule states that if C produces the value V, then $\exists\alpha.C$ produces the pair (T, V). This means that the end user has access to the witness T.

An instantiation constraint $x\ \tau$ is satisfied by ϕ iff the decoded type $\phi(\tau)$ is an instance of the type scheme associated with x. The first premise looks up this type scheme, say $\forall\vec{a}.T$, in E. The second premise checks that the instance relation holds: that is, for some vector $\vec{T}$, the decoded types $\phi(\tau)$ and $[\vec{T}/\vec{a}]T$ are equal. The vector $\vec{T}$ is again "magically" chosen. Finally, this constraint produces the value $\vec{T}$. This means that the end user has access to the witnesses $\vec{T}$.

The constraint *map* f C is satisfied iff C is satisfied. If C produces V, then *map* f C produces $f\ V$. This allows the end user to transform, or post-process, the value produced by a constraint.

For the moment, let us read the rule that describes the constraint let $x = \lambda\alpha.C_1$ in C_2 as if the vector $\vec{b}$ was equal to $\vec{a}$. We explain why they might differ in §B.

The rule's third premise requires that C_1 be satisfied by mapping α to T, in a context extended with a number of new type variables $\vec{a}$. This means that every instance of the type scheme $\forall\vec{a}.T$ satisfies the constraint abstraction $\lambda\alpha.C_1$. Again, $\vec{a}$ and T are "magically" chosen. The last premise requires that, under the assumption that x is associated with the type scheme $\forall\vec{a}.T$, the constraint C_2 be satisfied.

The conclusion states that, if C_1 and C_2 respectively produce the values V_1 and V_2, then the constraint let $x = \lambda\alpha.C_1$ in C_2 produces the triple $(\forall\vec{a}.T, \Lambda\vec{a}.V_1, V_2)$. The first component of this triple is the type scheme that has been associated with x while examining C_2. The second component is V_1, in which the "new" type variables $\vec{a}$ have been made anonymous, so as ensure that "if $E; \phi \vdash C \leadsto V$ holds, then the free type variables of V are in the domain of E". The last component is just V_2.

Our proposed definition of the judgement $E; \phi \vdash C \leadsto V$ should be taken with a grain of salt, as we have not conducted any proofs about it. One might wish to prove that it is in agreement with the semantics of raw constraints, as defined by Rémy and the present author [19, p. 414].

The judgement $E; \phi \vdash C \leadsto V$ can be used to express the specification of the constraint solver. Let C be a closed constraint. The solver is correct: if the solver, applied to C, succeeds and produces a value V, then the judgement $\emptyset; \emptyset \vdash C \leadsto V$ holds, i.e., C is satisfiable and V can be viewed as a correct description of the solution. The solver is complete: if there exists a value V such that $\emptyset; \emptyset \vdash C \leadsto V$ holds, then the solver, applied to C, succeeds and produces a value V'[7].

B. On redundant quantifiers

B.1 The issue

The last rule of Figure 9, read in the special case where $\vec{b}$ is $\vec{a}$, states that such the constraint let $x = \lambda\alpha.C_1$ in C_2 produces a triple of the form $(\Lambda\vec{a}.V_1, \forall\vec{a}.T, V_2)$. We pointed out earlier (§A) that abstracting the type variables $\vec{a}$ in the value V_1 is necessary, as all of these variables may appear in V_1. However, it could happen that some of these variables do not occur in the type T, which means that the type scheme $\forall\vec{a}.T$ exhibits redundant quantifiers.

In other words, simplifying the last rule of Figure 9 by forcing a coincidence between $\vec{b}$ and $\vec{a}$ would make good sense, but would lead to an inefficiency.

For instance, consider the ML term:

$$\mathsf{let}\ u = (\lambda f.())\ (\lambda x.x)\ \mathsf{in}\ \ldots$$

The left-hand side of the let construct applies a constant function, which always returns the unit value, to the identity function. Thus, intuitively, it seems that the type scheme assigned to the variable u should be just *unit*. However, if one constructs the contraint-with-a-value that describes this term (as per Figure 8) and if one applies the rules of Figure 9 in the most general manner possible, so as to determine what value this constraint produces, one finds that, at the let construct, one must introduce a type variable a, which stands for the type of x. In this case, the vector $\vec{a}$ consists of just a. The value V_1 is the explicitly-typed version of the function application, that is:

$$(\lambda f : a \to a.())\ (\lambda x : a.x)$$

The type T of this term is just *unit*. We see that the binder "Λa" in $\Lambda a.V_1$ is essential, since a occurs in V_1, whereas the binder "$\forall a$" in $\forall a.T$ is redundant, since a does not occur in T. The translation of our ML term in System F is as follows:

$$\mathsf{let}\ u = \Lambda a.(\lambda f : a \to a.())\ (\lambda x : a.x)\ \mathsf{in}\ \ldots$$

The type of u in System F is $\forall a.unit$ (which is not the same as *unit*). In the right-hand side $(\ldots)$, every use of u must be wrapped in a type application, which instantiates the quantifier a. But, one may ask, what will a be instantiated with? Well, naturally, with another type variable, which itself will later give rise to another redundant quantifier, and so on. Redundant quantifiers accumulate and multiply!

This is slightly unsatisfactory. In fact, formally, this may well violate our claim that the constraint solver has good complexity under the assumption that "type schemes have bounded size" [12]. Indeed, a plausible clarification of McAllester's hypothesis is that "all type schemes ever inferred, once deprived of their redundant quantifiers, have bounded size", and that does *not* imply that "all type schemes ever inferred, in the absence of redundant quantifier elimination, have bounded size".

B.2 A solution

We address this issue by allowing the vectors $\vec{b}$ and $\vec{a}$ to differ in the last rule of Figure 9. In general, $\vec{b}$ is a subset of $\vec{a}$ (second premise) that the variables in $\vec{b}$ may occur in T while those in $\vec{a} \setminus \vec{b}$ definitely do not occur in T (first premise). All of the variables $\vec{a}$ are needed to express the solution of C_1 (third premise), hence all of them may appear in the value V_1. Thus, one must abstract over $\vec{a}$ in the value V_1. But the solver examines the constraint C_2 under the assumption that x has type scheme $\forall\vec{b}.T$, where the redundant quantifiers have been removed (last premise).

We can now explain in what way the Advisor's informal code (§1) was misleading. In the Advisor's discourse, $\forall\vec{\beta}.\theta$ is supposed to be a canonical form of a (raw) constraint abstraction, or in other words, a principal type scheme. Certainly it is permitted to assume that it does not have any redundant quantifiers. So, $\vec{\beta}$ there corresponds to $\vec{b}$ here. When the Advisor suggested Λ-abstracting over $\vec{\beta}$, he was wrong. This is not enough: one must Λ-abstract over $\vec{a}$, or one ends up with dangling type variables.

Naturally, the potential mismatch between $\vec{a}$ and $\vec{b}$ means that one must be careful in the construction of an explicitly-typed term. When viewed as ML type schemes, $\forall\vec{a}.T$ and $\forall\vec{b}.T$ are usually considered equivalent; yet, when viewed as System F types, they most definitely are not.

For this reason, it does not make sense to translate the ML term "let $x = t_1$ in t_2" to the System F term "let $x = \Lambda\vec{a}.t'_1$ in t'_2". The subterm $\Lambda\vec{a}.t'_1$ has type $\forall\vec{a}.T$, but the subterm t'_2 is constructed under the assumption that x has type $\forall\vec{b}.T$. Thus, one must adjust the type of x, by inserting an explicit coercion:

$$\mathsf{let}\ x = \Lambda\vec{a}.t'_1\ \mathsf{in}\ \mathsf{let}\ x = (x : \forall\vec{a}.T :> \forall\vec{b}.T)\ \mathsf{in}\ t'_2$$

This coercion is not a primitive construct in System F. It can be encoded via a suitable series of type abstractions and applications. The function *coerce* used at the end of Figure 8 (whose definition is omittted) performs this task. This function can be made to run in time linear in the size of $\vec{a}$ and can be made to produce no code at all if the lists $\vec{a}$ and $\vec{b}$ are equal.

The need to introduce a coercion may seem inelegant or curious. In fact, it is a phenomenon that becomes more plainly obvious as the source language grows. For instance, several real-world languages of the ML family have a construct that simultaneously performs pattern matching and generalization, such as "let $(x, y) = t$ in u". It is clear that the quantifiers of the type scheme of x (resp. y) are in general a subset of the quantifiers that appear in the most general type scheme of the term t. Furthermore, upon closer investigation, one discovers that the type of the translated term t' is of the form $\forall\vec{\alpha}.(\tau_1 \times \tau_2)$, whereas deconstructing a pair in System F requires a term of type $(\forall\vec{\alpha}_1.\tau_1) \times (\forall\vec{\alpha}_2.\tau_2)$. Thus, a coercion is required in order to push the universal quantifiers into the pair and get rid, within each component, of the redundant quantifiers. In System F, such a coercion can be encoded, at the cost of an η-expansion. In an extension of System F with primitive erasable coercions, such as Cretin and Rémy's [1], this cost is avoided.

[7] We cannot require V' to be V, because the judgement $E; \phi \vdash C \leadsto V$ is non-deterministic: when E and C are fixed, there may be multiple choices of ϕ and V such that the judgement holds. In practice, a reasonable constraint solver always computes a most general solution ϕ and the value V that corresponds to it. One might wish to build this guarantee into the statement of completeness.

Settable and Non-Interfering Signal Functions for FRP

How a First-Order Switch is More Than Enough

Daniel Winograd-Cort
Yale University
dwc@cs.yale.edu

Paul Hudak
Yale University
paul.hudak@yale.edu

Abstract

Functional Reactive Programming (FRP) provides a method for programming continuous, reactive systems by utilizing *signal functions* that, abstractly, transform continuous input signals into continuous output signals. These signals may also be *streams of events*, and indeed, by allowing signal functions themselves to be the values carried by these events (in essence, signals of signal functions), one can conveniently make discrete changes in program behavior by "switching" into and out of these signal functions. This higher-order notion of switching is common among many FRP systems, in particular those based on arrows, such as Yampa.

Although convenient, the power of switching is often an overkill and can pose problems for certain types of program optimization (such as *causal commutative arrows* [14]), as it causes the structure of the program to change dynamically at run-time. Without a notion of just-in-time compilation or related idea, which itself is beset with problems, such optimizations are not possible at compile time.

This paper introduces two new ideas that obviate, in a predominance of cases, the need for switching. The first is a *non-interference law* for arrows with choice that allows an arrowized FRP program to dynamically alter its own structure (within statically limited bounds) as well as abandon unused streams. The other idea is a notion of a *settable signal function* that allows a signal function to capture its present state and later be restarted from some previous state. With these two features, canonical uses of higher-order switchers can be replaced with a suitable first-order design, thus enabling a broader range of static optimizations.

Categories and Subject Descriptors D.3.3 [*Programming Languages*]: Language Constructs and Features

Keywords Functional Reactive Programming; Arrows; Arrow-Choice; Switch

1. Introduction

Functional Reactive Programming (FRP) is based on the idea of programming with *signals*, or time-varying values. Signals can be continuous, in which case they are defined for every moment in time, or they can be discrete event streams, in which case they are defined at particular moments. The FRP model allows one to essentially define behaviors for these streams, using signal functions that react as the streams change over time.

A problem with classic FRP systems (such as Fran [6]) is their propensity toward space and time leaks [15]. One method for addressing these leaks is by using *arrows* [12, 13] in so called *arrowized* FRP (AFRP), which has been used in *Yampa* [3, 11] (for animation, robotics, GUI design, and more), *Nettle* [18] (for networking), and *Euterpea* [10] (for audio processing and sound synthesis). In AFRP, instead of treating the signal as a first class value, one treats the *signal function* as the core component. The arrow structure then allows the signal functions to be composed quite naturally.

Furthermore, the arrow abstraction lends itself well to aggressive optimizations. An arrow's structure must be defined statically, and once defined, it cannot be altered mid-computation. Therefore, regardless of what data the signals contain, the arrow's overall behavior is fixed. For example, CCA [14] relies on this restriction to optimize an FRP program and often improve its performance in GHC by an order of magnitude.

1.1 Switch

One problem with arrows is that they do not naturally have the full capabilities that classic FRP provides. As mentioned, an arrow's structure must be fixed at compile-time, but classic FRP provides behavior-switching mechanisms. Thus, arrows are typically augmented with a higher-order *switch* operator to recover this ability.

Switching allows a program to accept and utilize a stream of signal functions, thus allowing for higher-order signal function expression in which the program can update its own structure during execution. Additionally, in the realm of signal functions, a higher-order ability like this provides the only means of starting and stopping signals mid-computation, which is often a necessity for good performance. For instance, new signal functions can be provided at runtime and "switched on" to augment the current behavior of a program. Likewise, given an event that a certain signal is no longer needed, the program can "switch off" the portion of itself that is computing values for that signal, thus preventing unneeded computations from being performed. In fact, arrows with switch are as powerful as *ArrowApply* arrows, which are equivalent to monads [12].

Unfortunately, this power comes at a cost: the inherent higher-order nature of switch that allows it to run arbitrary signal functions from a stream makes certain compile-time optimizations and static guarantees much more difficult or even impossible. For example, arrows with switch cannot undergo the CCA optimizations. Likewise, in the realm of embedded systems, where static code is required due to strict time and resource constraints, switch can be an intolerable hole in a static guarantee.

ICFP '14, September 1–6, 2014, Gothenburg, Sweden.
Copyright is held by the owner/author(s). Publication rights licensed to ACM.
ACM 978-1-4503-2873-9 /14/09...$15.00.
http://dx.doi.org/10.1145/2628136.2628140

1.2 An Alternative to Switch

The motivation of this research is to ask whether switch is really necessary. Most FRP programmers would be reluctant to give it up – indeed, some FRP programs would be inexpressible with just first-order arrows – but perhaps there is an operator that is powerful enough to replace switch in most cases while still being weak enough to allow for CCA-like optimizations. In order to consider this, we first must examine more closely exactly what switching provides.

Switch allows one to express two fundamental behaviors that are otherwise impossible with just arrows. First, it provides a way for signal functions to dynamically start and stop mid-computation, which is useful not just for expressing certain programs but also for obtaining high performance. Second, it allows for higher-order signal expression, essentially providing a way to flatten a stream of streams into a single stream or insert a dynamic signal function into the arrow structure itself.

The first of these effects is similar to what is provided by *arrow choice*, which allows an arrow to choose between statically defined branches based on a dynamic argument. However, although the streaming argument will only be processed by one branch of an arrow choice conditional, every effect from the arrows from every branch will be executed. This means that arrow choice cannot be used to entirely suspend a branch in the way that switch can suspend a "switched out" signal function.

To address this, we can modify arrow choice by adding a new law in order to make it *non-interfering*. Non-interfering choice asserts that effects from only one branch of the choice will happen, and so if one branch is taken, it is as if the other does not exist.

Technically, non-interfering choice allows us only to pause signal functions and not actually start or stop them. For this reason, we additionally provide a method for making an arrow *settable*: a settable arrow's state can be saved, reloaded, and even reset.

Combining settability with non-interfering choice gives us the full power of the first effect of switch. That is, we can "start" a signal function by using choice and then resetting its state, and we can "stop" a signal function by indefinitely pausing it.

Interestingly, non-interfering choice allows for another unforeseen benefit: arrowized recursion. Because only one branch's effects can take place, we can do a form of recursion that allows behaviors that were previously only possible with switch. Combining this with settability allows for some surprising power.

1.3 Contributions

In this paper, we aim to show that switch is not essential to AFRP and that many powerful FRP programs that were previously believed to require switch may not actually need it. Indeed, we will take a number of example programs that utilize various forms of switchers in standard ways and show that our system is just as expressive. With this conclusion, we hope that we can open the doors to new and improved optimization techniques for arrows; we begin this process by demonstrating an extension to the CCA optimization that takes non-interfering choice and settability into account.

In the next section we will discuss arrows in general along with some details about the switch operators that we will be comparing our work against. Following that, we will make cases for both non-interfering choice and settability in Sections 3 and 4, in which we will show leading examples and present our first-order solutions. In Section 5, we will culminate our examples with a parallel choice example in the music domain that will bring together all of the topics so far discussed. From there, we will move into some implementation details, first describing our implementation of settability in Section 6 and then detailing an optimization for non-interfering choice in Section 7. Finally, we will present a brief, concluding discussion of the differences between our work here and switch in general as well as a comparison of this work to related work in Sections 8 and 9.

$$
\begin{array}{rl}
\mathit{arr} & :: (\alpha \to \beta) \to (\alpha \leadsto \beta) \\
\mathit{first} & :: (\alpha \leadsto \beta) \to ((\alpha,\gamma) \leadsto (\beta,\gamma)) \\
(\ggg) & :: (\alpha \leadsto \beta) \to (\beta \leadsto \gamma) \to (\alpha \leadsto \gamma) \\
(|||) & :: (\alpha \leadsto \gamma) \to (\beta \leadsto \gamma) \to ((\alpha+\beta) \leadsto \gamma) \\
\mathit{loop} & :: ((\gamma,\alpha) \leadsto (\gamma,\beta)) \to (\alpha \leadsto \beta) \\
\mathit{delay} & :: \beta \to (\beta \leadsto \beta)
\end{array}
$$

Figure 1. The types of the arrow operators.

2. Arrows

2.1 Signal Processing

Programming with AFRP is a lot like expressing signal processing diagrams. Where signal processing diagrams have lines, AFRP has *signals*, and where diagrams have boxes that act on those lines, AFRP has *signal functions*. These signals can represent either continuously-defined time-varying values or streams of discrete events.

Because AFRP is based on arrows, we can use Paterson's *arrow syntax* [17] to make programming with it easier. For example, we can turn this simple signal processing diagram:

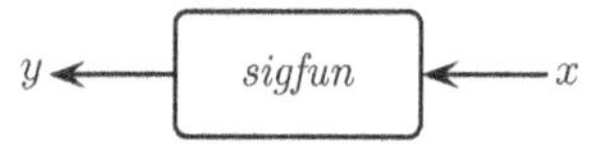

into just as simple a code snippet:

$$y \leftarrow \mathit{sigfun} \prec x$$

In this example, *sigfun* is a signal function that takes the input stream x and produces the output stream y.

For this paper, we will use Haskell's arrow syntax and operators to express code examples. Thus, the above code fragment cannot appear alone, but instead must be part of a **proc** construct. The expression in the middle must be a signal function, whose type we write as $\alpha \leadsto \beta$ for some types α and β. The expression on the right may be any well-typed expression with type α, and the expression on the left must be a variable or pattern of type β.

The purpose of the arrow notation is to allow the programmer to manipulate the instantaneous values of the signals. For example, the following is a definition for *sigfun* that integrates a signal and adds one to the output:

$$
\begin{array}{l}
\mathit{sigfun} = \mathbf{proc}\ x \to \mathbf{do} \\
\quad y \leftarrow \mathit{integral} \prec x \\
\quad \mathit{returnA} \prec y+1
\end{array}
$$

The notation "**proc** $x \to$ **do** ..." introduces a signal function, binding the name x to the instantaneous values of the input. The second line sends the input signal into an integrator, whose output is named y. Finally, we add one to the value and feed it into the signal function *returnA*, that returns the result. The last line of this notation has no binding component – instead, whatever value is produced in the last line is returned in total.

Of course, one can use arrows without Haskell's arrow syntax. Arrows are made up of three basic operators: construction (*arr*), partial application (*first*), and composition ($\ggg$). Furthermore, we extend our arrows with choice ($|||$) [12] to allow dynamic control flow, looping (*loop*) [17] to allow value-level recursion, and delay (*delay*). The types of these operators are shown in Figure 1.

For example, the signal function *sigfun* defined earlier can be written without arrow syntax as follows:

$$sigfun = integral \ggg arr\ (\lambda y.\ y+1)$$

Note that *returnA* is defined simply as *arr id*, which is why it is used for clarity to return values in the last line of arrow syntax but is omitted from the above definition of *sigfun*. We will also use the function $constA :: \beta \rightarrow (\alpha \rightsquigarrow \beta)$ in this paper, which takes one static argument and returns a signal function that ignores its input stream and returns a constant stream of the given value.

Events and Event Streams

The classical interpretation of a signal of type α is that it is a function from time to α defined for all points in time. We call this a *continuous* signal. However, we frequently require the ability to define a signal that has values at only discrete points in time and is undefined elsewhere. These so-called *event streams* are represented by encapsulating the signal's type with an option type. For this paper, we will use the following:

$$\textbf{data}\ Event\ \alpha = Event\ \alpha \mid NoEvent$$

Note that we are overloading the name *Event* such that it is both the general type as well as the constructor for an event. Thus, if a signal has type *Event* α, then we know that it is defined when it provides an *Event* and undefined when it provides *NoEvent*.

In this paper, we will make use of the fact that *Event* is a functor in the obvious way and freely *fmap* functions over *Event* values.

2.2 State via loop and delay

A key component of FRP systems (AFRP included) is the ability to perform stateful computation. For example, Yampa includes the *integral* function that integrates its input signal, a process impossible without some form of internal state.

Although stateful signal functions can be achieved in a variety of ways, we follow Liu et al. [14] in the use of a *delay*[1] operator along with *loop*. In this model, we use the loop as a feedback mechanism, allowing an auxiliary output containing the state to be fed back as an input, and we use the delay to prevent an infinite feedback loop. Indeed, Liu et al. [14] even demonstrate that *integral* can be defined using this method:

$$\begin{aligned}&integral = \textbf{proc}\ x \rightarrow \textbf{do}\\ &\quad \textbf{rec}\ v \leftarrow delay\ 0 \prec v + dt * x\\ &\quad returnA \prec v\end{aligned}$$

Note here that the **rec** keyword in arrow syntax invokes the *loop* operator and that we assume *dt* is a global time step.

2.3 Switch

As discussed in the introduction, the ability to dynamically *switch* one signal function for another during the execution of a program is a staple of most FRP systems. Considering that one of our primary goals is to show an alternative to switching, we will here describe switch's capabilities.

The idea of switching was introduced along with the earliest models of FRP [6]. These non-arrowized FRP implementations had the ability to sequence periods of signal function execution, a process that is inherently monadic in nature. However, the move to the arrow abstraction would not allow this behavior, and to prevent any loss in expressiveness, Hudak et al. [11] introduced the *switch* function in Yampa.

Actually, Yampa includes some 14 different variations on the switch function ranging from the simplest switch to the recursive, parallel, batch-input, delayed switch. We will briefly examine three of these switchers.

Switch

The most basic switch function has the following type:

$$\begin{aligned}switch :: &(\alpha \rightsquigarrow (\beta, Event\ \gamma))\\ &\rightarrow (\gamma \rightarrow (\alpha \rightsquigarrow \beta))\\ &\rightarrow (\alpha \rightsquigarrow \beta)\end{aligned}$$

The first argument is the initial signal function that the result will behave as. When that signal function produces an event, the switch will use the data from that event along with its second argument to produce a new signal function. From then on, it will behave as that new signal function.

Recursive Switch

A slightly more advanced version of switching allows for the signal function to be switched out more than once:

$$\begin{aligned}rSwitch :: &(\alpha \rightsquigarrow \beta)\\ &\rightarrow ((\alpha, Event\ (\alpha \rightsquigarrow \beta)) \rightsquigarrow \beta)\end{aligned}$$

Here, the resulting signal function takes an event stream of signal functions along with the stream of input α values. When the event stream contains an event, it switches into the signal function contained in the event.

Parallel Switch

The parallel version of switch is significantly more intimidating from its type signature but also quite powerful:

$$\begin{aligned}&pSwitch :: Functor\ col\\ &\quad \Rightarrow col\ (\alpha \rightsquigarrow \beta)\\ &\quad \rightarrow ((\alpha, col\ \beta) \rightsquigarrow Event\ \gamma)\\ &\quad \rightarrow (col\ (\alpha \rightsquigarrow \beta) \rightarrow \gamma \rightarrow (\alpha \rightsquigarrow col\ \beta))\\ &\quad \rightarrow (\alpha \rightsquigarrow col\ \beta)\end{aligned}$$

The parallel switcher works on *collections* of signal functions, where a collection must be a *Functor*. First, it is given an initial collection of signal functions to run and a signal function that produces update events. The third argument takes the current collection of signal functions and the value from an event in order to produce a new collection of signal functions. In total, *pSwitch* will run every signal function in its collection and produce as output a collection of their results.

Note that any one of these versions of switch is strong enough to implement the others. The reason for Yampa's many varieties of switch is not due to power differences, but rather due to ease of use. That is, for example, using *switch* to do an operation that requires *rSwitch* is tedious, so both varieties are provided.

3. A Case for Non-Interfering Choice

We will begin this section by exploring one of the main uses of switchers: as a method to allow the dynamic starting and stopping of signal functions. We will present our first-order alternative and then demonstrate it in a few practical settings.

3.1 Pausable Signal Functions

At a basic level, switch is often used to improve performance of an AFRP program. Without switch, signal functions will last forever, and this typically means that they will compute future values indefinitely. Using switch, one can "turn off" signal functions that are not currently necessary and even turn them back on if they are required again in the future.

For example, consider the scenario where we would like to integrate a stream only when a certain condition holds. Naïvely, we can write the following program:

[1] Note that in [14], this operator is referred to as *init*.

$$
\begin{array}{l}
\textit{integralWhen}_{Naive} :: (\textit{Double}, \textit{Bool}) \rightsquigarrow \textit{Double} \\
\textit{integralWhen}_{Naive} = \textbf{proc}\ (i, b) \rightarrow \textbf{do} \\
\quad v \leftarrow \textit{integral} \prec i \\
\quad v_{prev} \leftarrow \textit{delay}\ 0 \prec v \\
\quad \textbf{let}\ v_{\Delta} = v - v_{prev} \\
\quad \textbf{rec}\ \textit{result} \leftarrow \textit{delay}\ 0 \prec \textbf{if}\ b\ \textbf{then}\ \textit{result} + v_{\Delta}\ \textbf{else}\ \textit{result} \\
\quad \textit{returnA} \prec \textit{result}
\end{array}
$$

This program will only update the result when the boolean is *True*, but it is still unsatisfying that the integral is being computed at all when it is not being used. If integral were instead a costly signal function and the boolean were usually *False*, this could be seriously problematic to performance.

In cases like this, switch can be employed to prevent the integral from running when it is not needed:

$$
\begin{array}{l}
\textit{integralWhen}_{Switch} :: (\textit{Double}, \textit{Event Bool}) \rightsquigarrow \textit{Double} \\
\textit{integralWhen}_{Switch} = \textbf{proc}\ (i, e_b) \rightarrow \textbf{do} \\
\quad \textbf{rec}\ v \leftarrow \textit{rSwitch}\ (\textit{constA}\ 0) \prec (i, \\
\qquad\qquad \textit{fmap}\ (\lambda b \rightarrow \textbf{if}\ b \\
\qquad\qquad\qquad \textbf{then}\ (\textit{integral} \ggg \textit{arr}\ (+v)) \\
\qquad\qquad\qquad \textbf{else}\ \ (\textit{constA}\ v))\ e_b) \\
\quad \textit{returnA} \prec v
\end{array}
$$

For this version, we modified the type to make it more amenable to switching by converting the streaming boolean value to an event stream that will send events only when the stream would change from *True* to *False* or back. Internally, we use the *rSwitch* function that we introduced in Section 2.3 to switch between *integral* and a constant function. Each time we switch into *integral*, it is fresh and has no history from the last time we were using *integral*, so we additionally compose it with $arr\ (+v)$ so it can maintain its history.

3.2 Non-interfering Choice

Although the above example is a fairly common use for switch, careful examination of the problem reveals that switch is far more powerful that necessary. That is, while switch allows us to dynamically incorporate new signal functions into the running computation, here, we are simply making a *choice* of whether to run a component signal function based on a dynamic value. Our solution to this problem will thus be built around arrow choice, so we will begin by examining it more closely.

The general choice operator we use ($|||$ in Figure 1) can actually be built from a simpler component:

$$\textit{left} :: (\alpha \rightsquigarrow \beta) \rightarrow ((\alpha + \gamma) \rightsquigarrow (\beta + \gamma))$$

where *left f* calls *f* when the input signal contains *Left* values and acts as the identity function otherwise. With the *left* function, we can also define an analogous *right* function and then use the two together to define $|||$.

Choice also comes with a set of laws that we show in Figure 2. For us, the most notable law is the *exchange* law, which acts as a weak form of commutativity between *left* functions and *right* functions. One may ask why choice does not demand full commutativity (i.e. $\textit{left}\ f \ggg \textit{right}\ g = \textit{right}\ g \ggg \textit{left}\ f$), and in the context of signal processing, this question is very sensible. After all, it seems intuitively obvious that either the *left* function or the *right* function will run, but in no case will both run. However, because arrows can have effects regardless of their dynamic inputs, and the compositional order of these effects can alter the program itself, choice is weakened. It is precisely this leniency that makes switching necessary in cases such as the above example.

Extension	$\textit{left}\ (\textit{arr}\ f)$	$=$	$\textit{arr}\ (\textit{left}\ f)$
Functor	$\textit{left}\ (f \ggg g)$	$=$	$\textit{left}\ f \ggg \textit{left}\ g$
Exchange	$\textit{left}\ f \ggg \textit{arr}\ (\textit{right}\ g)$	$=$	$\textit{arr}\ (\textit{right}\ g) \ggg \textit{left}\ f$
Unit	$f \ggg \textit{arr Left}$	$=$	$\textit{arr Left} \ggg \textit{left}\ f$
Assoc.	$\textit{left}\ (\textit{left}\ f) \ggg \textit{arr}\ \textit{assoc}_+$	$=$	$\textit{arr}\ \textit{assoc}_+ \ggg \textit{left}\ f$

$$
\begin{array}{ll}
\textit{assoc}_+\ (\textit{Left}\ (\textit{Left}\ x)) & = \textit{Left}\ x \\
\textit{assoc}_+\ (\textit{Left}\ (\textit{Right}\ y)) & = \textit{Right}\ (\textit{Left}\ y) \\
\textit{assoc}_+\ (\textit{Right}\ z) & = \textit{Right}\ (\textit{Right}\ z)
\end{array}
$$

Non-interference $\quad \textit{arr Right} \ggg \textit{left}\ f\ =\ \textit{arr Right}$

Figure 2. The standard laws for arrow choice with our new non-interference law below.

In order to give choice the extra power it needs to be an adequate replacement for switch, we strengthen the *exchange* law into the more powerful:

$$\text{Non-interference} \qquad \textit{arr Right} \ggg \textit{left}\ f\ =\ \textit{arr Right}$$

Indeed, *non-interference* implies exchange and even commutativity as it is stronger than either (see Appendix A for details). It states that once the streaming value is tagged as a *Right* value, then it will not be applicable to *left f*, and so it should behave as if the *left f* is not even there. Thus, by including the non-interference law for choice, we assert that either signal functions cannot have static effects or that the choice operation has the power to dynamically choose which effects to perform.

3.3 Pausable Signal Functions Revisited

With non-interfering choice in our arsenal, we can define a new version of *integralWhen* in an even more intuitive and straightforward way:

$$
\begin{array}{l}
\textit{integralWhen}_{Choice} :: (\textit{Double}, \textit{Bool}) \rightsquigarrow \textit{Double} \\
\textit{integralWhen}_{Choice} = \textbf{proc}\ (i, b) \rightarrow \textbf{do} \\
\quad \textbf{rec}\ v \leftarrow \textbf{if}\ b\ \textbf{then}\ \textit{integral} \prec i \\
\qquad\qquad\qquad \textbf{else}\ \ \textit{returnA} \prec v \\
\quad \textit{returnA} \prec v
\end{array}
$$

Because we are not actually switching out of the *integral* signal function, it will retain its state internally. When it is executed, it will calculate and add the latest delta of integral, and otherwise, it will simply wait.

3.4 A Single First-Order Switch

The most basic switching operation is to non-recursively switch out one signal function for another dynamically. For example, we could write a simple guessing game that accepted an event stream of guesses, and when the correct answer was provided, it would switch into a signal function that ignored its input and declared that the game was over:

$$
\begin{array}{l}
\textit{guess} :: \textit{Event Int} \rightsquigarrow () \\
\textit{guess} = \textit{switch}\ (\textit{arr}\ f)\ (\lambda\ t \rightarrow \textit{label}\ t) \\
\quad \textbf{where}\ \ f\ (\textit{Event}\ i) | (i == 3) = ((), \textit{Event}\ \text{"You Win!"}) \\
\qquad\qquad\ f\ \_ \qquad\qquad\qquad\ = ((), \textit{NoEvent})
\end{array}
$$

where *label* is a signal function widget that ignores its streaming input and displays the text it was given as its static argument. Note that we are using the plain, non-recursive, non-parallel version of switch that we presented in Section 2.3. In *guess*, when the event containing 3 is processed, the string "You win!" is given to the label, and the guessing is switched out for that label.

For this example again, switch is too strong. Notice that the argument given to the switched-in signal function is not itself a

$$
\begin{aligned}
&runNTimes :: Int \to (\alpha \leadsto \beta) \to ([\alpha] \leadsto [\beta])\\
&runNTimes\ 0\ \_ \ = constA\ [\,]\\
&runNTimes\ n\ sf = \mathbf{proc}\ (b : bs) \to \mathbf{do}\\
&\quad c \leftarrow sf \prec b\\
&\quad cs \leftarrow runNTimes\ (n-1)\ sf \prec bs\\
&\quad returnA \prec (c : cs)
\end{aligned}
$$

Figure 3. The implementation of *runNTimes* using structural recursion.

$$
\begin{aligned}
&runDynamic :: (\alpha \leadsto \beta) \to ([\alpha] \leadsto [\beta])\\
&runDynamic\ sf = \mathbf{proc}\ lst \to \mathbf{do}\\
&\quad \mathbf{case}\ lst\ \mathbf{of}\\
&\quad\quad [\,] \qquad\ \to returnA \prec [\,]\\
&\quad\quad (b : bs) \to \mathbf{do}\ c \leftarrow sf \prec b\\
&\quad\quad\quad\quad\quad\quad cs \leftarrow runDynamic\ sf \prec bs\\
&\quad\quad\quad\quad\quad\quad returnA \prec (c : cs)
\end{aligned}
$$

Figure 4. The implementation of the choice-based *runDynamic* function using arrowized recursion.

signal function. In fact, it's just a constant! We can rewrite this with non-interfering choice:

$$
\begin{aligned}
&guess_{choice} :: Int \leadsto ()\\
&guess_{choice} = \mathbf{proc}\ i \to \mathbf{do}\\
&\quad \mathbf{rec}\ haveWon \leftarrow delay\ False \prec haveWon\ ||\ (i == 3)\\
&\quad \mathbf{if}\ haveWon\ \mathbf{then}\ label\ \text{“You Win!”} \prec ()\\
&\quad\quad\quad\quad\quad\quad \mathbf{else}\ \ returnA \prec ()
\end{aligned}
$$

Note that we changed the input stream to a continuous stream as opposed to an event stream simply to make the example clearer.

Reacting to dynamic events

The above versions of *guess* are quite primitive, and although we use switching in the first one, we are far from using its full power. We can make the example slightly more complex by adding an additional component to the input such that the program is actually reactive:

$$
\begin{aligned}
&guess' :: Event\ (Int, String) \leadsto ()\\
&guess' = switch\ (arr\ f)\ (\lambda\ t \to label\ t)\\
&\quad \mathbf{where}\ f\ (Event\ (i,s))|(i == 3) = ((),\ Event\ s)\\
&\quad\quad\quad\quad f\ \_ \qquad\qquad\qquad\quad\ = ((),\ NoEvent)
\end{aligned}
$$

In *guess'*, the text to put in the label is no longer static and instead is part of the guess event, and in its current form, switching is a necessity as it is the only way to provide the dynamically streaming string to the static *label* function. However, we could once again lift the need for switching if we could redesign the label to instead take an *impulse*. An impulse is a one time event that initializes a signal function, so in this case, the type for *label* would change from $String \to (\alpha \leadsto ())$ to $(Event\ String) \leadsto ()$.

With an impulse driven label widget, we can once again convert the *guess'* function to a switch-free alternative:

$$
\begin{aligned}
&guess'_{choice} :: (Int, String) \leadsto ()\\
&guess'_{choice} = \mathbf{proc}\ (i,s) \to \mathbf{do}\\
&\quad \mathbf{rec}\ haveWon \leftarrow delay\ False \prec haveWon\ ||\ (i == 3)\\
&\quad \mathbf{let}\ imp = \mathbf{if}\ not\ haveWon\ \&\&\ i == 3\\
&\quad\quad\quad\quad\quad \mathbf{then}\ Event\ s\ \mathbf{else}\ NoEvent\\
&\quad \mathbf{if}\ haveWon\ \mathbf{then}\ label \prec imp\\
&\quad\quad\quad\quad\quad \mathbf{else}\ \ returnA \prec ()
\end{aligned}
$$

3.5 Arrowized Recursion

As we have shown in the previous two examples, there is a direct usage for non-interfering choice, but the non-interference law also gives us a less obvious benefit. By restricting the arrow effects to only one branch, we open the door to the possibility of a new kind of recursion.

Typically, arrows can perform recursive behaviors in one of two ways. First, arrows can use the *loop* functionality to perform a value level recursion, or a sort of fix point recursion. After all, one of the laws for *loop* is:

$$loop\ (arr\ f) = arr\ (\lambda\ b \to fst\ (fix\ (\lambda(c,d) \to f\ (b,d))))$$

Second, there is *structural* recursion. Structural recursion happens when the host language's recursion is used to create an arrow in a recursive way. For instance, we might have a function like:

$$runNTimes :: Int \to (\alpha \leadsto \beta) \to ([\alpha] \leadsto [\beta])$$

When defining this function, we use Haskell's conditional syntax to recur on the value of the first argument: while it is greater than zero, we run the signal function and recur, and when it is equal to zero, we return a constant stream of the empty list. We show a definition of *runNTimes* using this form of recursion in Figure 3.

A key frustration with structural recursion is that the recursive argument is static as opposed to streaming. Thus, structural recursion is often performed in tandem with higher-order switching to allow a streaming value to be used in place of the static argument.

With, non-interfering choice, we extend arrows with a new kind of recursion that we call *arrowized* recursion. Arrowized recursion is very similar to structural recursion except that instead of using the host language's conditional, we use arrow choice. Ordinarily, this would be impossible: because all branches of an arrow choice must be executed for their effects, if one were recursive, then it would cause an infinite loop. However, non-interference gets around this by restricting arrow effects dynamically.

Thus, with arrowized recursion, we can write a function similar to the above *runNTimes* but that needs no static argument to perform its recursion. In fact, we can make the input stream of lists the recursive argument and eliminate the need for an "N" altogether. We call this function *runDynamic* and show it in Figure 4.

3.6 Dynamic GUI

One power of switch, showcased particularly in *Fruit* [2], is the ability to allow a dynamic number of signal functions to execute. That is, by default, arrows have a fixed structure, and the streaming values moving through an AFRP program cannot affect that structure. However, switch allows one to dynamically alter the arrow at runtime based on the streaming values.

For example, one may desire a GUI that gathers the names of an unknown group of people. If the size of the group were fixed or at least known at compile time, then this is achievable trivially with arrows, but if the size is a parameter that is filled in by the user of the GUI, then standard arrows are stymied. One approach is to use a switching mechanism.

For this example, we will assume a few GUI widgets:

$$
\begin{aligned}
&label &&:: String \to (() \leadsto ())\\
&getInteger &&:: () \leadsto Int\\
&getIntegerE &&:: () \leadsto Event\ Int\\
&getName &&:: () \leadsto String
\end{aligned}
$$

Note that we have both a regular and event-based version of *getInteger*: the event-based one, which produces an event each time the value changes, is useful for our example with switch, and we will use the regular one with choice.

We can use these widgets in combination with the *rSwitch* function to make our GUI:

```
getNames :: () ⇝ [String]
getNames = proc () → do
  _ ← label "How many people?" ≺ ()
  e_n ← getIntegerE ≺ ()
  rSwitch (constA [ ]) ≺ (repeat (),
      fmap (λ n → runNTimes n getName) e_n)
```

where the *runNTimes* function is the one we discussed in the previous subsection (that uses structural recursion to run the given signal function the given number of times, as shown in Figure 3).

The above definition of *getNames*, although correct, is using the higher order nature of switch when it is not truly necessary. Switching gives the power to substitute in any new signal function for the currently running one, but here, the nature of the new signal function is already known: it will be some number of *getName* widgets. Because this fact is known at compile time, we can use arrowized recursion instead to create a simpler, switch-free GUI.

```
getNames :: () ⇝ [String]
getNames = proc () → do
  _ ← label "How many people?" ≺ ()
  n ← getInteger ≺ ()
  runDynamic getName ≺ replicate n ()
```

Because *runDynamic* uses arrow choice to do arrowized recursion, we do not need to use any switching.

4. A Case for Settability

In this section, we will explore a second main use of switchers: the ability to start a signal function mid-computation with no prior state. Once again, we will begin with a simple yet canonical example before describing our first-order alternative and some further usage examples.

4.1 Restartable Computation

Although pausing signal functions is useful (as in the *integralWhen* example of Sections 3.1 and 3.3), there are times when we really do want to restart a signal function, resetting its state to its initial defaults. In fact, with switching, this is even easier than pausing considering that switch naturally starts its new signal function from the beginning.

For instance, let us consider the scenario where we would like to take the integral of a stream, but at any moment, we may be given an event that indicates that we should reset the integral's accumulation to its initial default. With switch, this is actually trivial: we simply lift the *integral* function into the resetting event, and send everything into a recursive switcher:

```
integralReset_Switch :: (Double, Event ()) ⇝ Double
integralReset_Switch = proc (i, e) → do
  rSwitch integral ≺ (i, fmap (const integral) e)
```

Without switch, this seems like a tough problem, and nothing about non-interfering choice lends any help.

One idea is to try to simulate the behavior of a restart without actually touching *integral* itself. That is, because the function we are lifting is just an integral, we could take a snapshot of its output at the restarting moment and then continuously subtract that value from future outputs:

```
integralReset_Basic :: (Double, Event ()) ⇝ Double
integralReset_Basic = proc (i, e) → do
  o ← integral ≺ i
  rec k ← delay 0 ≺ k'
      let k' = if isEvent e then o else k
  returnA ≺ o − k
```

Although this is a valid solution to this particular situation, it is a technique that does not scale well to more complicated problems.

4.2 Settability

At this point, the idea of lifting a signal function into the event stream, as we did in $integralReset_{Switch}$ above, should seem unnecessary. Indeed, we are not even switching into some dynamically given new signal function but rather just using a new instance of the same signal function again. Rather than switching, our first-order approach is to develop a notion of signal function *settability*, or a way to change the internal state of a signal function at arbitrary points.

Because we are dealing with state, we will begin with an even more primitive example and examine the *delay* operator directly. At first glance, it seems to suffer from the same problem as *integral* – the *delay* will always output old values, so what can we do to reset it? However, modifying it to be resettable requires only the addition of a single input event stream:

```
resettableDelay :: β → ((β, Event ()) ⇝ β)
resettableDelay i = proc (b, e) → do
  out ← delay i ≺ b
  returnA ≺ case e of
    NoEvent → out
    Event () → i
```

Whenever *resettableDelay* is given an event, it will immediately output its initial value again, essentially behaving as if it has only just started. In fact, we can take this one step further and construct a version of *delay* that can be set to any value of our choosing:

```
settableDelay :: β → ((β, Event (Maybe β)) ⇝ β)
settableDelay i = proc (b, e) → do
  out ← delay i ≺ b
  returnA ≺ case e of
    NoEvent       → out
    Event Nothing → i
    Event (Just s) → s
```

With *settableDelay*, the event stream can potentially carry a new value to set the internal state, and if there is no value, we perform a reset. It may seem superfluous to have an event of an option, but adding the ability to set the state does not make resetting the state obsolete.

A fortuitous bonus to this function is that, in addition to being able to set the state, we can also capture the current state. That is, because the input stream is necessarily setting the new current state, it can also be made to provide it directly. Thus, we can use *settableDelay* to both "store" and "load" state.

General Settability

Although a settable version of *delay* may be useful on its own, it would be much more useful to have any arbitrary signal function be settable. However, this would require manually changing every internal *delay* operator to its settable alternative and then properly routing the state-setting events to the appropriate places. Additionally, if capturing the state at a given moment were important, all of the inputs to the *delay* functions would also need to be grouped and appropriately routed to the output. This would be exceptionally cumbersome and not at all feasible. What we want is a function like:

```
settable :: (α ⇝ β) → ((α, Event State) ⇝ (β, State))
```

that will automatically take a signal function and allow us to both pass in an optional new state as well as save its current state.

This *settable* function should hold to certain principles of behavior. For example, if it is never provided with a state, then it

$settable :: (\alpha \rightsquigarrow \beta) \rightarrow ((\alpha, Event\ State) \rightsquigarrow (\beta, State))$

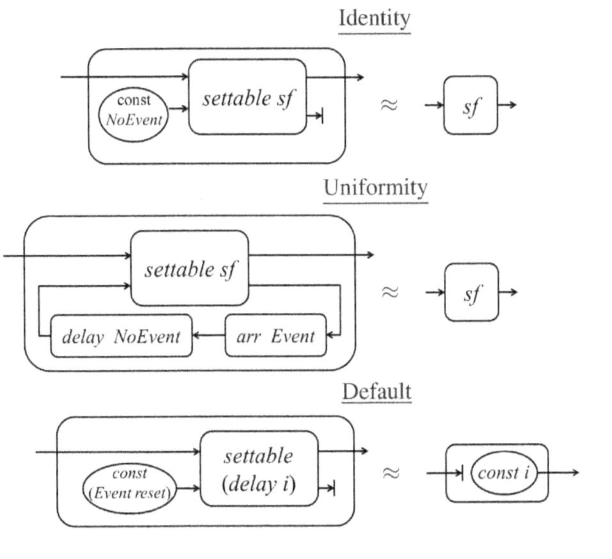

Figure 5. The *settable* function and its laws.

should do nothing. Similarly, if the state it produces is used to set it, then there should be no observable difference in behavior. Additionally, there should be a particular value of *State* that acts as a *reset* (in our *settableDelay* function from earlier, this was *Event Nothing*). Thus, if one were to feed a constant stream of reset states, the output would always use the default values. We declare these principles as laws of behavior for *settable* and show them diagrammatically in Figure 5.

In fact, with an appropriate code transformation, any arrow can be extended with a *settable* function. We will explore the details of this transformation in Section 6, but for now, it suffices to state that it is possible and available in our examples.

4.3 Restartable Computation Revisited

With the *settable* function, defining *integralReset* is just as trivial as with switch:

```
integralReset :: (Double, Event ()) ⇝ Double
integralReset = proc (i, e) → do
  (v, s) ← settable integral ⤙ (i, fmap (const reset) e)
  returnA ⤙ v
```

Rather than lifting a dynamic signal function to the signal level just to be activated by switch as we did previously, we lift only a reset signal. The difference in the amount of code between this function and $integralReset_{switch}$ is negligible (it basically comes down to ignoring the state output of the settable signal function), but the conceptual difference is quite important: rather than needing to stop a currently running signal function to replace it with a new, fresh instance of itself, it is possible to refresh it while leaving it active.

4.4 Freezing and Duplicating

This *settable* function has applications beyond just resetting arbitrary, stateful signal functions. By separating the state from the signal function, we are essentially separating the current behavior from the structure. That is, the *settable* function gives us the power to *freeze* signal functions.

Typically freezing a signal function is thought of as a higher-order operation achievable only with a switch operator. Specifically, freezing is the process of stopping a running signal function mid-execution and providing it as a piece of data to reuse. Later, it can be resumed by using a switcher to reintegrate it into the structure of the program.

Rather than providing a copy of itself, a function made settable will provide a stream of its *essence* (i.e. its current state), which can then be reinserted at any time later. Thus, we gain the ability to freeze and resume without actually resorting to switch.

```
gui :: () ⇝ ()
gui = proc () → do
  e_dup ← button "Duplicate pane?" ⤙ ()
  e_del ← button "Delete pane?" ⤙ ()
  i ← choosePane ⤙ ()
  rec stateLst ← delay [reset] ⤙ stateLst_new
      ((), state_new) ← settable drawing ⤙ ((), stateLst !! i)
      let stateLst_new = case (e_dup, e_del) of
            (Event (), _) → set i stateLst state_new ++ [state_new]
            (NoEvent, Event ()) → delete i stateLst
            _ → set i stateLst state_new
  returnA ⤙ ()
```

Figure 6. The implementation of the GUI from Section 4.4.

Example

For this example, we will construct a GUI for drawing. The main window will feature a drawing pane, but the user will be able to create new panes and switch between them. When a new pane is created, it is automatically populated with a copy of whatever is currently on the current pane.

For this example, we will assume a few widgets:

```
drawing    :: () ⇝ ()
choosePane :: () ⇝ Int
button     :: String → (() ⇝ Event ())
```

The *drawing* widget is a stateful, effectful widget that provides a canvas and allows the user to draw; the *choosePane* widget returns an *Int* stream that represents the currently selected pane; and the *button* widget takes a static label and produces an event stream that indicates when the button is depressed.

With these widgets, we can create the GUI we described (shown in Figure 6). The state for the GUI is kept as a list of drawing states, initialized in the sixth line as a one element list containing a *reset* state. This initial list describes a GUI with a single pane that has a blank drawing canvas. When a user wishes to duplicate the current pane, the current state is added to the list allowing the GUI to "save" the original pane while providing a duplicate state for the new one. The key here is that instead of keeping track of different instances of the signal function, each with its own state, we keep track of multiple states themselves and use them with a single signal function.

We omit a version of this GUI that utilizes switching because it is surprisingly complicated, and it is not particularly necessary to contrast it with the GUI we present in Figure 6.

5. An Alternative to *pSwitch*

Here, we will pull together the ideas of both settability and non-interfering choice that we have highlighted in the previous sections to present a high power yet first-order version of a parallel switcher.

As we mentioned in Section 2.3, parallel switchers allow for whole collections of signal functions to be managed and switched in or out at once. One example of the usefulness of this kind of switcher can be seen in the musical realm where one might have a program that plays music with software "instruments" that are actually themselves signal functions. The music is given as a sequence of "On" and "Off" events, where the "On" events provide the instrument to play and some initializing data about what note to play, and the "Off" events tell which instrument to stop:

$$\textbf{data}\ NoteEvt = NoteOn\ UID\ Instr\ InitData \mid NoteOff\ UID\ Instr$$

$$\textbf{type}\ Instr = InitData \to (() \rightsquigarrow Sound)$$

$$sumSound :: [Sound] \rightsquigarrow Sound$$

Note that the *UID* type is a unique identifier that is used to connect a given *NoteOn* event with its *NoteOff* counterpart, and the *Sound* data type represents the sound that an instrument produces. The *sumSound* signal function is for summing dynamic lists of sounds together.

Although we will use the same *pSwitch* that we introduced in Section 2.3, for clarity, we will show its type signature again, this time with a few of the type variables instantiated for our example.

$$\begin{aligned} pSwitch :: &[UID, () \rightsquigarrow \beta] \\ &\to (() \rightsquigarrow Event\ \gamma) \\ &\to ([UID, () \rightsquigarrow \beta] \to \gamma \to [UID, () \rightsquigarrow \beta]) \\ &\to (() \rightsquigarrow [\beta]) \end{aligned}$$

For our collection, we use a mapping of *UID* to signal function (which we implement as a list for simplicity), and we set α to $()$.

For this musical example, the initial list of signal functions will be empty, the events to change that list will be *NoteEvt*s, and the function will use the *NoteEvt* data to add or remove signal functions from the list as necessary:

$$\begin{aligned} &maestro :: (() \rightsquigarrow Event\ [NoteEvt]) \to (() \rightsquigarrow Sound) \\ &maestro\ music = pSwitch\ [\,]\ music\ f \ggg sumSound \\ &\quad \textbf{where}\ f\ lst\ [\,] = lst \\ &\qquad f\ lst\ (NoteOn\ u\ i\ imp : rst) = f\ ((u, i\ imp) : lst)\ rst \\ &\qquad f\ lst\ (NoteOff\ u\ i : rst) = f\ (filter\ ((\neq u)\ .\ fst)\ lst)\ rst \end{aligned}$$

In order to remove our reliance on switch, we need to make a few small changes to the layout of the problem. First, as we did in Section 3.4, we will need to change the instruments from functions that take a "static" initializing argument to functions that take that argument as an impulse. Second, we need to know statically what the different signal functions are, so we make use of a finite data type and add one layer of indirection:

$$\textbf{data}\ Instr = Trumpet \mid FHorn \mid Trombone \mid Tuba$$

$$\textbf{type}\ Instrument = Event\ InitData \rightsquigarrow Sound$$

$$toInstrument :: Instr \to Instrument$$

Because the *Instr* type is finite, we know exactly which *Instrument* signal functions can possibly be called. This is critical because choice is not actually higher order. Fortunately, in most situations where parallel switching is used, the possibilities of signal functions are known statically, so a transformation like this one is not difficult.

With these changes made, we can utilize the *pChoice* function. The idea behind *pChoice* is that as long as we know the possible signal functions that we may use, we can run each one a dynamic number of times. So, rather than keep a dynamic list of signal functions, we keep a static list of signal functions and a dynamic list of signal function *states*. We then use a combination of structural and arrowized recursion: structural recursion to provide access to each possible signal function and arrowized recursion to allow a dynamic number of runs per possibility.

The type of *pChoice* is:

$$\begin{aligned} pChoice :: Eq\ key \Rightarrow &[(key, Event\ \alpha \rightsquigarrow \beta)] \to \\ &([(key, (UID, Event\ \alpha))] \rightsquigarrow [\beta]) \end{aligned}$$

and as it is somewhat complicated, we leave its implementation and a more detailed description of its inner-functioning to Appendix B.

We can use *pChoice* to reimplement our music program without switch:

$$\begin{aligned} &maestro :: [NoteEvt] \rightsquigarrow Sound \\ &maestro = arr\ (map\ f) \ggg pChoice\ lst \ggg sumSound \\ &\quad \textbf{where}\ lst = map\ (\lambda\ i \to (i, toInstrument\ i))\ allInstrs \\ &\qquad f\ (NoteOn\ u\ i\ imp) = (i, (u, Event\ imp)) \\ &\qquad f\ (NoteOff\ u\ i) \quad\ = (i, (u, NoEvent)) \end{aligned}$$

where *allInstrs* is a complete list of all of the *Instr*s that might be played. In fact, one notable difference between this version of *maestro* and the switch-based alternative from earlier is this *allInstrs* list: the reason that we can write this program at all is because *allInstrs* can be defined statically.

6. Implementing Settability

As we mentioned in Section 4.2, we can achieve settability of any arrow with a code transformation. Here, we will provide a detailed description of the transformation process before presenting Haskell code that implements it.

6.1 Design

In essence, the idea of settability is the idea of having access to the internal state of an arrow. Thus, as we discussed previously, it is encapsulated by a function like:

$$settable :: (\alpha \rightsquigarrow \beta) \to ((\alpha, Event\ State) \rightsquigarrow (\beta, State))$$

that will automatically take a signal function and allow us to both pass in an optional new state as well as save its current state. However, in order to achieve this, we will need to rewrite the underlying arrow to support this behavior. Therefore, we will describe a recursive transformation that will provide settable capabilities to ordinary arrows.

Intuitively, this settability transformation is a simple process of routing state update information in through the various arrow combinators so that it can be easily accessed by any internal delay operators and then routing current state data back out through the combinators to the level of the *settable* call. For each combinator, there is a transformation that achieves exactly this goal; we show circuit diagrams for these transformations in Figure 7 and describe them in detail below. Note that we use the notation $\underline{sf}$ to denote the signal function *sf* after having been transformed, and we assume that the *Event State* input stream and *State* output stream are always the lower input and output.

- We will begin at the lowest level by examining the *delay* operator itself. In Section 4.2, we showed a design for a settable version of delay, but we need to modify it just slightly in order for it to be general enough for our *settable* transformation: in addition to taking in an *Event State* stream, it also needs to emit its current *State* as a stream. This is rather trivial as its current state is identical to its own input stream, but this is important to the transformation as a whole. Thus, our circuit diagram shows the input stream both being sent to the embedded *delay* operator as well as being duplicated to the *State* output, and the output is determined by a case analysis of the *Event State* input with data from the *delay*'s output.
- The simplest transformation is that of the *arr* operator, which has no state and should essentially remain unaffected. In this

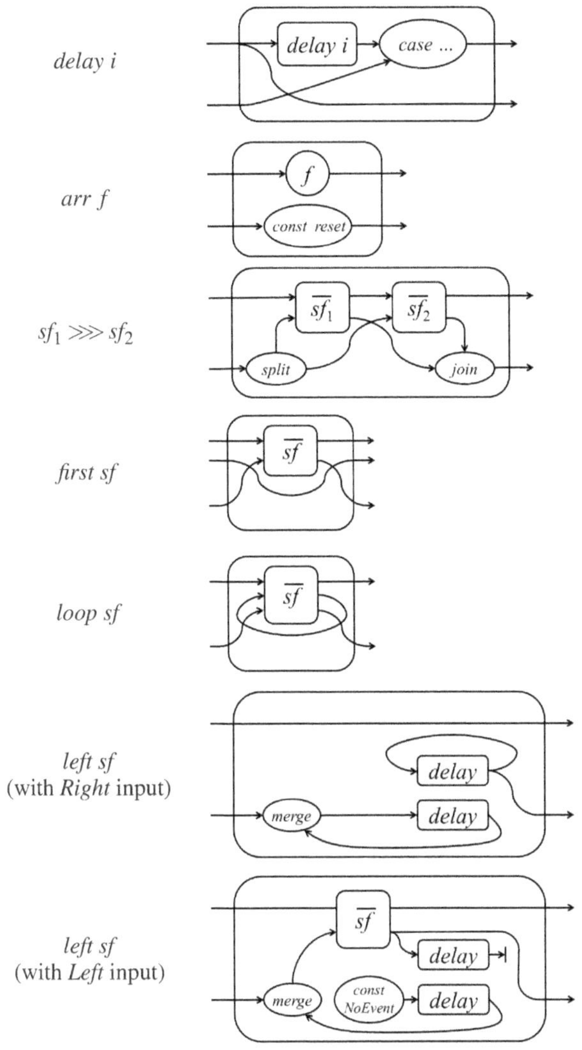

Figure 7. The circuit diagrams showing the settability transformations for the various arrow combinators.

case, we ignore the input *Event State* and return a constant stream of the null, or *reset*, state.

- The composition of two functions is a little more interesting. Each of the two composed signal functions may have state, so we need to split the incoming *Event State* into two pieces and pass the first to the first signal function and the second to the second. We gather the resulting states together and join them into a single output state.
- Applying a partial application (*first*) is a simple matter of rerouting the state data and the unused input stream properly.
- Looping is handled similarly to partial application with a simple rerouting of streams.
- The most complicated transformation is for our non-interfering choice's *left* operator. This is because there are two difficult questions that we must address in designing this transformation. First, in the case of an input *Right* value, the embedded signal function is not executed, so where can we get a *State* value for the output *State* stream? And second, again in the case of an input *Right* value, if we are given an *Event State* that requires updating the embedded signal function, how can we get that event where it needs to go? The way to address both of these questions is to allow the transformed choice operator to contain some internal state, which we achieve with *loop* and *delay*.

  Furthermore, in an effort to clarify the behavior of the transformed choice, we provide two diagrams to describe its behavior: one that shows how it behaves when given a *Right* value and the other for when it is given a *Left* value. The *delays* are shared between both diagrams: the upper *delay* should be assumed to be initialized with a *NoEvent* value and the lower with a null, or *reset*, state value. The *merge* function is a standard overwriting event merge that favors the left (newly incoming) event in the case of two events.

  When given a *Right* input, the input stream is identical to the output stream. The *Event State* input is merged with the stored *Event State* and stored once again, thus updating the store with any new setting events. The output *State* is the stored one.

  When given a *Left* input, we will execute the embedded signal function. We still merge the *Event State* input with the stored one, but the result goes directly into the embedded signal function, and the store is instead updated with a *NoEvent*, indicating that there are no past *Event States* waiting to be delivered. The output of the transformed, embedded signal function, both the streaming *Left* value as well as the output *State*, become the output of the overall transformed signal function, but the output *State* is also stored for potential future use. The stored *State* value is discarded outright as it is now obsolete.

6.2 Haskell Implementation

Rather than relying on Haskell's rewrite rules or Template Haskell, we can perform the entire transformation with only type classes. Our method involves creating a wrapper for a generic arrow that itself instantiates the arrow classes. Then, any code that is an arbitrary arrow could just as well be this wrapper.

Thus, our goal will be to concretely define our types and then instantiate the arrow classes using them.

Data Types

The first type we must choose a concrete representation for is the *State* data type. Although we could use Haskell's type families and other features to make a type-safe solution, its complexity would detract from the point. Therefore, to keep the types simple, we will make use of Haskell's *Dynamic* data type to store arbitrary state information from individual *delay* functions.[2] Also, rather than use an auxiliary option type to represent a default state or an absence of state (as we did in the *settableDelay* function in Section 4.2), we will build this directly into the type.

We show the definition of the *State* data type along with the few helper functions we need in Figure 8. Note that because *NoState* represents an absence of state information, trying to split it returns a similar lack of information.

With the *State* type defined, we next build our wrapper for a general arrow:

$$\textbf{data}\ SA\ (\leadsto)\ \alpha\ \beta = SA\ ((\alpha, Event\ State) \leadsto (\beta, State))$$

Already, we can see that this *SA* data type is merely hiding the extra piping that will be required to store and load the state.

[2] Technically, using *Dynamic* in this way enforces a *Typeable* restriction to the types of the individual state components, but this is of little consequence.

$$
\begin{aligned}
\textbf{data}\ \mathit{State}\ &=\ \mathit{NoState}\\
&\mid\ \mathit{DState\ Dynamic}\\
&\mid\ \mathit{PairState\ State\ State}
\end{aligned}
$$

$$\mathit{reset} = \mathit{NoState}$$

$$
\begin{aligned}
&\mathit{split} :: \mathit{Event\ State} \rightarrow (\mathit{Event\ State}, \mathit{Event\ State})\\
&\mathit{split\ NoEvent} = (\mathit{NoEvent}, \mathit{NoEvent})\\
&\mathit{split}\ (\mathit{Event\ NoState}) = (\mathit{Event\ NoState}, \mathit{Event\ NoState})\\
&\mathit{split}\ (\mathit{Event}\ (\mathit{PairState}\ l\ r)) = (\mathit{Event}\ l, \mathit{Event}\ r)
\end{aligned}
$$

$$
\begin{aligned}
&\mathit{join} :: \mathit{State} \rightarrow \mathit{State} \rightarrow \mathit{State}\\
&\mathit{join}\ l\ r = \mathit{PairState}\ l\ r
\end{aligned}
$$

$$
\begin{aligned}
&\mathit{merge} :: \mathit{Event} \rightarrow \mathit{Event} \rightarrow \mathit{Event}\\
&\mathit{merge\ NoEvent}\ \ e = e\\
&\mathit{merge}\ e\ \ \_ = e
\end{aligned}
$$

Figure 8. The *State* data type and its two accessor functions.

Instantiating Arrow

Next, we show how $SA\ (\rightsquigarrow)$ can instantiate the arrow operators themselves. If it can, then any program written using the arrow operators could just as well be written for the generic arrow $(\rightsquigarrow)$ as for $SA\ (\rightsquigarrow)$. Thus, this instantiation will essentially provide a method to perform a code transformation to allow any arrow to behave as if it could be made settable. In fact, it will not even matter if this instantiation actually obeys the arrow laws; because the arrow it is built atop does, we can always strip off the wrapper and be left with an arrow that does satisfy the laws. The implementations are shown in Figure 9.

The implementations follow directly from the circuit diagrams from Figure 7, and thus we will omit any further description of how they function.

Settable

It feels like we could make an $SA\ (\rightsquigarrow)$ settable merely by removing the *SA* wrapper – after all, the underlying arrow will be of the appropriate type. However, this approach limits modularity by forcing the input and output arrows of the *settable* function to be different. Therefore, we instead write a *settable* function for *SA* directly:

$$
\begin{aligned}
&\mathit{settable}\ (\mathit{SA}\ f) = \mathit{SA}\ \$\ \textbf{proc}\ ((b,e_s),e_s') \rightarrow \textbf{do}\\
&\quad (c,s) \leftarrow f \prec (b, \mathit{merge}\ e_s\ e_s')\\
&\quad \mathit{returnA} \prec ((c,s),s)
\end{aligned}
$$

This *settable* function is straightforward with one exception. If there is already a state-update event that is propagating a new state (shown here as e_s'), and the settable signal function is also given a state-update event (e_s), which one takes precedence? In fact, the new one must take precedence in order to guarantee the laws we set out in Figure 5.

7. Optimizations

Providing such an expressive, first-order alternative to the higher-order switch function is a boon for optimizations as it allows the arrow structure to be fully determinable at compile time. For instance, Causal Commutative Arrows (CCAs) are a particular subclass of arrows that have been shown to be highly optimizable [14], but they are restricted to be only first-order. As a demonstration of the optimization capabilities of our work, we extend the Haskell CCA transformation to include non-interfering choice and show the promising results. We begin with a brief overview of CCAs.

$$\mathit{arr}\ f = \mathit{SA}\ \$\ \mathit{arr}\ (\lambda\ (b,\_) \rightarrow (f\ b, \mathit{NoState}))$$

$$
\begin{aligned}
&\mathit{first}\ (\mathit{SA}\ f) = \mathit{SA}\ \$\ \textbf{proc}\ ((b,d),e_s) \rightarrow \textbf{do}\\
&\quad (c,s) \leftarrow f \prec (b,e_s)\\
&\quad \mathit{returnA} \prec ((c,d),s)
\end{aligned}
$$

$$
\begin{aligned}
&(\mathit{SA}\ f) \ggg (\mathit{SA}\ g) = \mathit{SA}\ \$\ \textbf{proc}\ (b,e_s) \rightarrow \textbf{do}\\
&\quad \textbf{let}\ (e_l,e_r) = \mathit{split}\ e_s\\
&\quad (c,s_l) \leftarrow f \prec (b,\ e_l)\\
&\quad (d,s_r) \leftarrow g \prec (c,\ e_r)\\
&\quad \mathit{returnA} \prec (d,\ \mathit{join}\ s_l\ s_r)
\end{aligned}
$$

$$
\begin{aligned}
&\mathit{loop}\ (\mathit{SA}\ f) = \mathit{SA}\ \$\ \textbf{proc}\ (b,e_s) \rightarrow \textbf{do}\\
&\quad \textbf{rec}\ ((c,d),s) \leftarrow f \prec ((b,d),e_s)\\
&\quad \mathit{returnA} \prec (c,s)
\end{aligned}
$$

$$
\begin{aligned}
&\mathit{delay}\ i = \mathit{SA}\ \$\ \textbf{proc}\ (s_{new},e_s) \rightarrow \textbf{do}\\
&\quad s_{old} \leftarrow \mathit{delay}\ i \prec s_{new}\\
&\quad \mathit{returnA} \prec (f\ s_{old}\ e_s, \mathit{DState}\ (\mathit{toDyn}\ s_{new}))\\
&\ \ \textbf{where}\ f\ s\ \mathit{NoEvent} = s\\
&\qquad\quad f\ \_\ (\mathit{Event\ NoState}) = i\\
&\qquad\quad f\ \_\ (\mathit{Event}\ (\mathit{DState}\ d)) = \mathit{fromDyn}\ d
\end{aligned}
$$

$$
\begin{aligned}
&\mathit{left}\ \sim\!(\mathit{SA}\ f) = \mathit{SA}\ \$\ \textbf{proc}\ (bd,e_s) \rightarrow \textbf{do}\\
&\quad \textbf{rec}\ (s_{old},e_{old}) \leftarrow \mathit{delay}\ (\mathit{NoState},\ \mathit{NoEvent}) \prec (s_{now},e_{next})\\
&\qquad \textbf{let}\ e_{now} = \mathit{merge}\ e_s\ e_{old}\\
&\qquad (s_{now},e_{next},cd) \leftarrow \textbf{case}\ bd\ \textbf{of}\\
&\qquad\quad \mathit{Left}\ b \rightarrow \textbf{do}\\
&\qquad\qquad (c,s) \leftarrow f \prec (b,e_{now})\\
&\qquad\qquad \mathit{returnA} \prec (s,\mathit{NoEvent},\mathit{Left}\ c)\\
&\qquad\quad \mathit{Right}\ d \rightarrow \mathit{returnA} \prec (s_{old},e_{now},\mathit{Right}\ d)\\
&\quad \mathit{returnA} \prec (cd,s_{now})
\end{aligned}
$$

Figure 9. *SA* implementations of the Arrow class functions.

7.1 Causal Commutative Arrows

Causal Commutative Arrows are arrows that have two additional laws: a commutativity law that essentially states that signal function effects can be reordered at will, and a product law that governs the behavior of the causal operator (the *init* or *delay* operator). With these two laws at their disposal, Liu et al. [14] describe a transformation that allows an arrow to be reduced to a normal form, which they call the Causal Commutative Normal Form (CCNF), and then even stream fused into a standard function. The authors demonstrate that GHC can then aggressively optimize this, yielding performance increases of orders of magnitude.

The CCA transformation is of particular interest to us as it is what we will be extending to add support for non-interfering choice, but first, we must describe the CCNF. The CCNF of an arrow is either of the form:

$$\mathit{arr}\ f$$

or

$$\mathit{loop}\ (\mathit{arr}\ f \ggg \mathit{second}\ (\mathit{delay}\ i))$$

where f is a pure function and i is a state. We can express these more simply by calling them *Arr* f and *LoopD* $i\ f$. The transformation, then, is the process of reducing an arrow built with the arrow operators into one of these two forms. It is a recursive transformation that applies a set of reduction rules until the normal form is produced.

For instance, if the transformation comes across an arrow of the form *first sf*, then it will recursively reduce *sf* and then choose one of the following two rules based on the result:

$$\begin{array}{rcl} \textit{first}\ (\textit{Arr}\ f) & \mapsto & \textit{Arr}\ (f \times \textit{id}) \\ \textit{first}\ (\textit{LoopD}\ i\ f) & \mapsto & \textit{LoopD}\ i\ (\textit{juggle}\ .\ (f \times \textit{id})\ .\ \textit{juggle}) \end{array}$$

where *juggle* is a pure helper function to reorder the inputs and outputs as necessary.

7.2 Extending CCA

CCAs already have a mechanism for dealing with choice, and at first glance, it appears to work with non-interfering choice too. However, it is the arrowized recursion that non-interfering choice allows, and not the choice operator directly, that actually poses a problem for the CCA transformation.

As is, the CCA transformation does not support recursion. Of course, as we mentioned when we introduced arrowized recursion in Section 3.5, arrows themselves are not guaranteed to support it, so its absense is perfectly sensible as it serves no purpose without non-interfering choice. However, the absense of recursion support is *not* due to inability – indeed, we can add that functionality in a straightforward manner.

Intuitively, the presense of arrowized recursion will present us with the following two scenarios:

$$\textit{Arr}\ f = \textit{Arr}\ (g\ f)$$

$$\textit{LoopD}\ i\ f = \textit{LoopD}\ (j\ i)\ (g\ f)$$

In the first case, we find that a signal function of the form *Arr f* is defined based on that same function f, and the second is the same except for both f and its state i. However, because f and g (and j) are pure functions, this is a trivial relation to solve: indeed the solution to the first form is as simple as applying a fix point operator:

$$f = \textit{fix}\ g$$

The second form is slightly more complicated as it requires the use of a coinductive data type for i. We would need a data type such as:

$$\textbf{data}\ \textit{StateCCA}\ k = S\ (k\ (\textit{StateCCA}\ k))$$

and with it, we can solve for i and f:

$$\begin{array}{l} i = s \quad \textbf{where}\ s = S\ (j\ s) \\ f = \textit{fix}\ g \end{array}$$

7.3 Haskell Implementation

We model the Haskell implementation off of the original CCA transformation design. We use Template Haskell along with a clever use of the Arrow type classes to perform a preprocessing step on only the arrowized components. Thus, rather than try to interfere with Haskell's native recursion support, we introduce a new type class to capture it only where we need it:

$$\begin{array}{l} \textbf{class}\ \textit{ArrowFix}\ (\rightsquigarrow)\ \textbf{where} \\ \quad \textit{afix} :: (b \rightsquigarrow c \rightarrow b \rightsquigarrow c) \rightarrow b \rightsquigarrow c \end{array}$$

The *ArrowFix* type class introduces the *afix* function that acts as a fix point function particularly for arrowized recursion. In practice, we could merely define *afix* to be equivalent to the regular fix point operator, but we will make better use of it for the transformation.

Specifically, when the recursive transformation encounters an arrow of the form *afix f*, the first thing it will do is to produce a fresh, unique "hole". The hole (which we represent with $\bullet$) is a special internal data structure that acts like *Arr* or *LoopD* except that instead of holding the function f and state i, it keeps track of the modifying functions g and j. That is, if the hole is an *Arr* form, then we know that we will eventually come to a scenario such as

$$\textit{Arr}\ f = \textit{Arr}\ (g\ f)$$

Name	GHC	arrowp	CCNF	Stream
Dynamic Counters	1.0	1.66	10.91	12.73
Chained Adder	1.0	1.91	4.06	4.29
Chained Integral	1.0	2.17	13.27	15.40

Figure 10. Performance Ratio (higher is better)

and since f is unknown and will be deduced via the fix point operation, the hole instead keeps track of g. Applying this hole as the argument to f and then recursively running the transformation will reduce the result to one of the two forms we identified in the previous subsection, which we have already shown can be solved easily.

To facilitate this, we create a second set of transformation rules that are nearly identical to the original except that they expect an additional argument. For instance, if the transformation comes across a partial application of a hole, then it will follow one of the following two rules:

$$\begin{array}{rcl} \textit{first}\ (\bullet_{\textit{Arr}}\ g) & \mapsto & \bullet_{\textit{Arr}}\ (\lambda\ f \rightarrow (g\ f \times \textit{id})) \\ \textit{first}\ (\bullet_{\textit{LoopD}}\ j\ g) & \mapsto & \bullet_{\textit{LoopD}}\ j\ (\lambda\ f \rightarrow \\ & & \quad (\textit{juggle}\ .\ (g\ f \times \textit{id})\ .\ \textit{juggle})) \end{array}$$

Note the similarities between this and the description for the non-hole version at the end of Section 7.1. They are almost identical except for the fact that the hole's arguments are functions of functions.

Coinductive State

We mentioned in the previous subsection that taking a fix point of the state i would require a coinductive data type, but we make no mention of that. Indeed, because Haskell makes it difficult to dynamically create new types and adding that behavior to the existing CCA Template Haskell transformation would involve completely rewriting it, we instead utilize Haskell's *Dynamic* data type as an all-purpose coinductive wrapper. Although not the most elegant solution, it gets the job done.

7.4 Performance Results

We followed the same procedure for performance testing that Liu et al. [14] use. That is, for each program, we:

1. Compiled with GHC, which has a built-in translator for arrow syntax.
2. Translated the arrow syntax to arrow combinators using Paterson's *arrowp* pre-processor [17] and then compiled with GHC.
3. Normalized into CCNF combinators and compiled with GHC.
4. Normalized into CCNF combinators, rewrote in terms of streams, and compiled with GHC using stream fusion.

The three benchmark programs we used are based on the examples from this paper but are simplified. The first uses the *runDynamic* function to run multiple stateful counters at the same time. The second and third use a function similar to *runDynamic* that runs a signal function multiple times but chains the output from one run to the input of the next, essentially linking them together. For the second, we link together a basic, stateless adder, and for the third, we link an integral function.

The programs were compiled and run on an Intel Core i7 machine with GHC version 7.6.3, using the −O2 optimization. The results are shown in Figure 10, where the numbers represent normalized speedup ratios.

In general, the results show a similarly dramatic performance improvement compared with standard CCA. Notably, the performance of the chained adder, although improved in CCNF, does not show nearly the speedup that the others show. We believe this is because the chained adder has no internal state whatsoever, making the pre-processed performance better.

8. Other effects of switching from switch

As stated earlier, arrows with switch are fundamentally more powerful than those without. Thus, it was never our goal to demonstrate that non-interfering choice and state settability could provide the tools to replace switch outright, but rather that switch's power is often underutilized, and in those cases, switch can be replaced.

8.1 First order

The primary and most important difference between switch and non-interfering choice is that switch is truly higher order while choice is not. This means that while programs with switch can accept streams of signal functions and then run those signal functions, programs with only choice cannot.

8.2 Memory Use

One of the main reasons to use switch in a program is to improve performance. Rather than run a signal function when its results are not being used, we can switch it off, reducing unneeded computation. Signal functions that have been switched out will never be restarted and so can be garbage collected to free memory.

With non-interfering choice, we can similarly stop a signal function, but because it might be restarted, it cannot be garbage collected. Rather, once started, it will remain in memory forever. This is a fundamental reason for demonstrating state settability of signal functions: a signal function that is waiting in memory can have its state re-set so that it can behave as a fresh instance of itself. Thus, with proper management of state, we should never be creating new signal functions while others are left for dead but stranded in memory. Therefore, though our system will always use at least as much memory as a version with switch and often times more, it should be capped by the maximum amount of memory that a comparable switch-based version would use at any one time.

9. Related Work

The idea of using continuous modeling for dynamic, reactive behavior (now usually referred to as "functional reactive programming," or FRP) is due to Elliott, beginning with early work on TBAG, a C++ based model for animation [7]. Subsequent work on Fran ("functional reactive animation") embedded the ideas in Haskell [6, 9], and other embeddings were explored in [5].

After the Arrow framework was proposed by Hughes [12], it was quickly adopted for use in FRP in the GUI language Fruit [1, 2], which also introduced the first arrowized switch function (before then, higher-order signals were dealt with by a function typically called *until*). The design of Yampa [3, 11] built off of this and expanded the idea of switching into fourteen distinct switch operators.

As mentioned, Liu et al. [14] proposed causal commutative arrows, which provide an optimization strategy for first-order arrowized FRP, but which cannot handle higher-order switching. Additionally, some work has minimally explored a restricted form of switch [19], although there is no evidence that this provides any actionable benefits. Patai [16] presents an alternative approach of embracing the higher-order mentality and shows a method for dealing with higher-order streams directly and efficiently using a monadic interface.

Other attempts at optimizing FRP (such as Reactive [8] and Elm [4]) have focused on avoiding recomputation of values when unnecessary. Reactive additionally uses deterministic concurrency for even better performance.

Acknowledgments

This research was supported by a gift from Microsoft Research and a grant from the National Science Foundation (CCF-1302327). We would also like to thank our referees for their comments and suggestions.

References

[1] A. Courtney. *Modelling User Interfaces in a Functional Language*. PhD thesis, Department of Computer Science, Yale University, May 2004.

[2] A. Courtney and C. Elliott. Genuinely functional user interfaces. In *2001 Haskell Workshop*, September 2001.

[3] A. Courtney, H. Nilsson, and J. Peterson. The Yampa arcade. In *Haskell Workshop*, Haskell '03, pages 7–18. ACM, August 2003.

[4] E. Czaplicki and S. Chong. Asynchronous functional reactive programming for GUIs. In *PLDI*, pages 411–422, 2013.

[5] C. Elliott. Functional implementations of continuous modeled animation. In *Proceedings of PLILP/ALP '98*. Springer-Verlag, 1998.

[6] C. Elliott and P. Hudak. Functional reactive animation. In *International Conference on Functional Programming*, pages 263–273. ACM, June 1997.

[7] C. Elliott, G. Schechter, R. Yeung, and S. Abi-Ezzi. TBAG: A high level framework for interactive, animated 3D graphics applications. In *21st Conference on Computer Graphics and Interactive Techniques*, pages 421–434. ACM, July 1994.

[8] C. M. Elliott. Push-pull functional reactive programming. In *Proceedings of the 2Nd ACM SIGPLAN Symposium on Haskell*, Haskell '09, pages 25–36, New York, NY, USA, September 2009. ACM.

[9] P. Hudak. *The Haskell School of Expression – Learning Functional Programming through Multimedia*. Cambridge University Press, New York, NY, 2000.

[10] P. Hudak. *The Haskell School of Music – From Signals to Symphonies*. (Version 2.6), January 2014.

[11] P. Hudak, A. Courtney, H. Nilsson, and J. Peterson. Arrows, robots, and functional reactive programming. In *Summer School on Advanced Functional Programming 2002, Oxford University*, volume 2638 of *Lecture Notes in Computer Science*, pages 159–187. Springer-Verlag, August 2003.

[12] J. Hughes. Generalising monads to arrows. *Science of Computer Programming*, 37(1–3):67–111, May 2000.

[13] S. Lindley, P. Wadler, and J. Yallop. The arrow calculus. *Journal of Functional Programming*, 20(1):51–69, January 2010.

[14] H. Liu, E. Cheng, and P. Hudak. Causal commutative arrows. *Journal of Functional Programming*, 21(4–5):467–496, September 2011.

[15] P. Liu and P. Hudak. Plugging a space leak with an arrow. *Electronic Notes in Theoretical Computer Science*, 193(1):29–45, November 2007.

[16] G. Patai. Efficient and compositional higher-order streams. In *Proceedings of the 19th International Conference on Functional and Constraint Logic Programming*, WFLP'10, pages 137–154, Berlin, Heidelberg, 2011. Springer-Verlag.

[17] R. Paterson. A new notation for arrows. In *Sixth International Conference on Functional Programming*, pages 229–240. ACM, September 2001.

[18] A. Voellmy and P. Hudak. Nettle: Taking the sting out of programming network routers. In *Practical Aspects of Declarative Languages*, volume 6539 of *Lecture Notes in Computer Science*. Springer-Verlag, January 2011.

[19] D. Winograd-Cort and P. Hudak. Wormholes: Introducing Effects to FRP. In *Haskell Symposium*, pages 91–103. ACM, September 2012.

A. Proof That Non-Interference Implies Commutativity (and Exchange)

Theorem (Commutativity).

$$right\ f \ggg left\ g = left\ g \ggg right\ f$$

Proof. This proof is straightforward. We will begin by assuming *Right* inputs only, and thus we can modify our assertion to:

$$arr\ Right \ggg right\ f \ggg left\ g = arr\ Right \ggg left\ g \ggg right\ f$$

Starting with the left hand side,

$$\begin{aligned}
& arr\ Right \ggg right\ f \ggg left\ g \\
= \ & \{ \text{Unit backwards} \} \\
& f \ggg arr\ Right \ggg left\ g \\
= \ & \{ \text{Non-Interference} \} \\
& f \ggg arr\ Right \\
= \ & \{ \text{Unit} \} \\
& arr\ Right \ggg right\ f \\
= \ & \{ \text{Non-Interference backwards} \} \\
& arr\ Right \ggg left\ g \ggg right\ f
\end{aligned}$$

For *Left* input values, the proof works in exactly the same way except that we must use non-interference's mirror:

$$arr\ Left \ggg right\ f = arr\ Left$$

which follows directly from non-interference and the definition of *right*. □

B. Choice-Based Implementations of First-Order Switch

Although using non-interfering choice and settability allows for a different paradigm for designing FRP programs, we can also use these tools to implement operators that are similar to the classic switchers. We show two such implementations in this appendix.

B.1 Standard Switch

The standard *switch* function can be implemented with non-interfering choice in a straightforward manner:

```
switch_choice :: (α ⇝ (β, Event γ)) → ((Event γ, α) ⇝ β)
      → (α ⇝ β)
switch_choice sf1 sf2 = proc a → do
  onOne ← delay True ≺ not onTwo
  (b, et) ← if onOne then sf1 ≺ a
                     else returnA ≺ (undefined, NoEvent)
  let onTwo = (isEvent et) || (not onOne)
  if onTwo then sf2 ≺ (et, a)
           else returnA ≺ b
```

Here, we keep track of two internal state variables called *onOne* and *onTwo* that indicate whether we should be running the first or the second signal function. When the first produces an event, we set *onOne* to *False* so that we stop running it, and we set *onTwo* to *True*. Then, we pass the impulse generated from the first signal function to the second one, and for the future, the impulse stream contains only *NoEvent* values.

```
pChoice :: Eq key ⇒ [(key, Event α ⇝ β)] →
           ([(key, (UID, Event α))] ⇝ [β])
pChoice [ ] = constA [ ]
pChoice ((key, sf) : rst) = proc es → do
  rec states ← delay [ ] ≺ states_new
      let es_this = map snd $ filter ((== key) . fst) es
          states_inp = update states es_this
      output ← runDynamic (first (settable sf)) ≺ states_inp
      let states_new = map (λ ((_, s), uid) →
                         ((NoEvent, Event s), uid)) output
  rs ← pChoice rst ≺ es
  returnA ≺ (map (fst . fst) output) ++ rs

 where update :: [((Event α, Event State), UID)]
           → [(UID, Event α)]
           → [((Event α, Event State), UID)]
       update s [ ] = s
       update s ((uid, NoEvent) : rst) =
                 update (filter ((≠ uid) . snd) s) rst
       update s ((uid, i) : rst) =
                 update (((i, Event reset), uid) : s) rst
```

Figure 11. The implementation of *pChoice*.

B.2 Parallel Switch

The *pChoice* function is somewhat more complicated and is shown in Figure 11. *pChoice* takes a mapping of keys to signal functions (implemented here as a list for simplicity) as its static argument. For each element of this static list, we keep a dynamic list of states (the *states* variable in the figure). We check the input events for any that are keyed to the signal function we are currently processing and update the state list accordingly (by either adding or removing elements), and then we run the signal function for each state and recur. Note that the static signal functions are all impulse driven; thus, when new states are first added to the state list (which is done in the *update* helper function), they are given an impulse event, but otherwise, they are given *NoEvent* (i.e. in the definition of $states_{new}$). This restriction to strictly impulse driven signal functions is not fundamental – indeed, we could write a version of *pChoice* that accepts signal functions that also take a streaming input – but making it more generic would needlessly complicate this already dense definition.

It is also worth noting that there is a subtle difference in performance between *pChoice* and *pSwitch*. When the finite data type is large but rarely used, *pSwitch* may outperform *pChoice* because *pChoice* still has to iterate through its entire static list on each step while *pSwitch*'s dynamic list will be just the relevant signal functions. That said, their performance should be comparable when the finite data type is small compared to the number of currently running signal functions.

Functional Programming for Dynamic and Large Data with Self-Adjusting Computation

Yan Chen
Max Planck Institute for Software Systems
chenyan@mpi-sws.org

Umut A. Acar
Carnegie Mellon University
and INRIA
umut@cs.cmu.edu

Kanat Tangwongsan
Mahidol University International College
kanat.tan@mahidol.ac.th

Abstract

Combining type theory, language design, and empirical work, we present techniques for computing with large and dynamically changing datasets. Based on lambda calculus, our techniques are suitable for expressing a diverse set of algorithms on large datasets and, via self-adjusting computation, enable computations to respond automatically to changes in their data. To improve the scalability of self-adjusting computation, we present a type system for precise dependency tracking that minimizes the time and space for storing dependency metadata. The type system eliminates an important assumption of prior work that can lead to recording spurious dependencies. We present a type-directed translation algorithm that generates correct self-adjusting programs without relying on this assumption. We then show a probabilistic-chunking technique to further decrease space usage by controlling the fundamental space-time tradeoff in self-adjusting computation. We implement and evaluate these techniques, showing promising results on challenging benchmarks involving large graphs.

Categories and Subject Descriptors D.1.1 [*Programming Techniques*]: Applicative (Functional) Programming; F.3.3 [*Logics and Meanings of Programs*]: Studies of Program Constructs

Keywords Self-adjusting computation; information-flow type system; granularity control; incremental graph algorithms; performance

1. Introduction

Recent advances in the ability to collect, store, and process large amounts of information, often represented in the form of graphs, have led to a plethora of research on "big data." In addition to being large, such datasets are *diverse*, arising in many domains ranging from scientific applications to social networks, and *dynamic*, meaning they change gradually over time. For example, a social-network graph changes as users join and leave, or as they change their set of friends. Prior research on languages and programming systems for big-data applications has two important limitations:

- Due to their diversity, big-data applications benefit from expressive programming languages. Yet existing work offers domain-specific languages and systems such as "MapReduce" [20] with limited expressiveness that not only restrict the set of problems that can be solved but also how efficiently they can be solved (by limiting the algorithms that can be implemented).
- Even though big data applications often require operating on dynamically changing datasets, many existing languages and systems provide for a batch model of computation, where the data is assumed to be static or unchanging.

In this paper, we show that, when combined with the right set of techniques, functional programming can help overcome both of these limitations. First, as an expressive, general purpose programming model, functional programming enables efficient implementations of a broad range of algorithms for big data. Second, since functional programming is consistent with self-adjusting computation [1, 6, 15–17], it can also enable programs to respond efficiently to changing data provided that a major limitation of self-adjusting computation—space usage—can be overcome.

Self-adjusting computation [1, 6, 15–17] refers to a technique for compiling batch programs into programs that can automatically respond to changes to their data. The idea behind self-adjusting computation is to establish a space-time tradeoff so that the results of prior computations can be reused when computing the result for a different but similar input. Self-adjusting computation achieves this by representing the execution of a program as a higher-order graph data structure called a *dynamic dependency graph*, which records certain dependencies in the computation, and by using a *change-propagation algorithm* to update this graph and the computation. In a nutshell, change propagation identifies and rebuilds (via re-execution) only the parts of the computation that are affected by the changes. Unfortunately, existing approaches to self-adjusting computation require a significant amount of memory to store the dynamic dependency graph. For example, on a modest input of 10^7 integers, a self-adjusting version of merge sort uses approximately 100x more space than its batch counterpart. Such demands for space can limit its applicability to relatively small problem sizes.

This paper presents two techniques for improving space usage of self-adjusting computation. The first technique reduces space usage by improving the precision of dependency tracking that self-adjusting computation relies on. The second technique enables programmers to control the space-time tradeoff fundamental to self-adjusting computation. Our first technique relies on a type system for precisely tracking dependencies and a type-directed translation algorithm that can generate correct and efficient self-adjusting programs. Our second technique is a probabilistic chunking scheme for coarsening the granularity at which dependencies are tracked without disproportionately degrading the update performance.

Our starting point is the recent work on type-based automatic incrementalization [15–17]. That work enables translating batch programs into self-adjusting programs that can efficiently respond to incremental changes. The idea behind the approach is to use a type inference algorithm to infer all *changeable data*, which

ICFP '14, September 1–6, 2014, Gothenburg, Sweden.

http://dx.doi.org/10.1145/2628136.2628150

change over time, and track only their dependencies. Unfortunately, the type inference algorithm can identify non-changeable data as changeable, causing redundant dependencies to be recorded. The reason for this is the modal type system that all previous work on self-adjusting computation relies on [6]. That modal type system ensures a crucial property, that all relevant dependencies are tracked, but at the cost of being conservative and disallowing changeable data from being nested inside non-changeable data, which leads to redundant dependencies.

We solve this problem by designing a more refined type systems (Section 3) and a translation algorithm (Section 6) that can correctly translate source programs (Section 4) into a lower-level target language (Section 5). Our source-level type system is an information-flow type system that enables precise dependency tracking. This type system break an important assumption of prior work, allowing changeable data to be nested inside non-changeable data. We present a translation algorithm that nevertheless produces correct self-adjusting executables by emitting target code written in a destination-passing style. To provide the flexibility needed for operation on changeables without creating redundant dependencies, the target language is imperative but relies on a type and effect system [52] for correctness, guaranteeing that all dependencies are tracked. We prove that the translation generates well-typed and sound target code, consistent with the source typing, and thus guarantees the correctness of the resulting self-adjusting code in the target language.

When combined with an important facility in self-adjusting computation—the ability to control the granularity of dependency tracking by selectively tracking dependencies—precise dependency tracking offers a powerful mechanism to control the space-time tradeoff fundamental to self-adjusting computation. By tracking dependencies at the level of (large) blocks of data, rather than individual data items, the programmer can further reduce space consumption. As we describe, however, this straightforward idea can lead to disproportionately slow updates (Section 7), because it can cause a small change to propagate to many blocks. We overcome this problem by presenting a *probabilistic blocking* technique. This technique divides the data into blocks in a probabilistic way, ensuring that small changes affect a small number of blocks.

We implement the proposed techniques in Standard ML and present an empirical evaluation by considering several list primitives, sorting algorithms, and more challenging algorithms for large graphs such as PageRank, graph connectivity, and approximate social-circle size. These problems, which are highly unstructured, put our techniques through a serious test. Our empirical evaluation leads to the following conclusions.

- Expressive languages such as lambda calculus augmented with simple type annotations, instead of domain-specific languages such as MapReduce, can lead to large (e.g. 50-100x) improvements in time and space efficiency.
- The type system for precise dependency tracking can significantly reduce space and time requirements (e.g., approximately by 2x and 6x respectively for MapReduce applications).
- Our techniques for controlling the space-time tradeoff for list data structures can reduce memory consumption effectively while only proportionally slowing down updates.
- Our techniques can enable responding significantly faster (e.g., several orders of magnitude or more) to both small and aggregate changes while moderately increasing memory usage compared to the familiar batch model of computation.

2. Background and Overview

Using a simple list-partitioning function, we illustrate the self-adjusting computation framework, outline two limitations of previous approaches, and describe how we resolve them.

2.1 Background and List Partition

Figure 1 shows SML code for a list-partition function `partition f l`, which applies f to each element x of l, from left to right, and returns a pair (pos, neg) where pos is the list of elements for which f evaluated to true, and neg is the list of those for which $f\ x$ evaluated to false. The elements of pos and neg retain the same relative order from l. Ignoring the annotation $\mathbb{C}$, this is the same function from the SML basis library, which takes $\Theta(n)$ time for a list of size n.

Self-adjusting computation enables the programmer to develop efficient incremental programs by annotating the code for the non-incremental or batch programs. The key language construct is a *modifiable (reference)*, which stores a *changeable* value that may change over time [6]. The runtime system of a self-adjusting language track dependencies on modifiables in a dynamic dependency graph, enabling efficient *change propagation* when the data changes in small amounts.

Developing a self-adjusting program can involve significant changes to the batch program. Recent work [15–17] proposes a type-directed approach for automatically deriving self-adjusting programs via simple type annotations. For example, given the code in the leftmost column of Figure 1 and the annotation $\mathbb{C}$ (the second line) that marks the tail of the list changeable, the compiler automatically derives the code in the middle figure.

These type annotations, broadly referred to as *level types*, partition all data types into stable and changeable *levels*. Programmers only need to annotate the types of changeable data with $\mathbb{C}$; all other types remain stable, meaning they cannot be changed later on. For example, $\mathbf{int}^{\mathbb{S}}$ is a stable integer, $\mathbf{int}^{\mathbb{C}}$ is a changeable integer and $\mathbf{int}^{\mathbb{S}}\ \mathbf{list}^{\mathbb{C}}$ is a changeable list of stable integers. This list allows insertion and deletion but each individual element cannot be altered.

In the translated code (Figure 1, middle), changeable data are stored in modifiables: a changeable `int` becomes an `int` **mod**. Given the self-adjusting list-partition function, we can run it in much the same way as running the batch version. After a complete first run, we can change any or all of the changeable data and update the output by performing change propagation. As an example, consider inserting an element into the input list and performing change propagation. This will trigger the execution of computation on the newly inserted elements without recomputing the whole list. It is straightforward to show that change propagation takes $\Theta(1)$ time for a single insertion.

2.2 Limitation 1: Redundant Dependencies

The problem. As with all other prior work on self-adjusting computation (e.g. [1]) that relies on a type system to eliminate difficult correctness problem (in change propagation), recent work [15–17] uses a modal type system to guarantee properties important to the correctness of self-adjusting computation—all changeables are initialized and all their dependencies are tracked. This type system can be conservative and disallow changeable data to be nested inside changeable data. For example, in list partition, the type system forces the return the type to be changeable, i.e., the type (α `list` **mod** * α `list` **mod**) **mod**. This type is conservative; the outer modifiable (**mod**) is unnecessary as any observable change can be performed without it. By requiring the outer modifiable, the type system causes redundant dependencies to be recorded. In this simple example, this can nearly double the space usage while also degrading performance (likely as much as an order of magnitude).

```
1  fun partition f l
2    : (α list^C * α list^C) =
3
4    case l of
5      nil ⇒ (nil, nil)
6
7    | h::t ⇒
8       let val (a,b) = partition f t
9
10
11
12      in if f h then (h::a, b)
13
14         else (a, h::b)
15
16      end
```

```
fun partition f l
  : (α list mod * α list mod) mod =
 read l as l' in
  case l' of
   nil ⇒ write (mod (write nil),
               mod (write nil))
  | h::t ⇒
   let val pair = mod (partition f t)

   in if f h then read pair as (a,b) in
        write (mod (write h::a), b)
      else read pair as (a,b) in
        write (a, mod (write h::b))
   end
```

```
fun partition f l (l00,l01)
  : (α list mod * α list mod) =
 let val () = read l as l' in
   case l' of
     nil ⇒ (write (l00,nil);
           write (l01,nil))
   | h::t ⇒
     let val (a,b) = let
         val (l00,l01) = (mod nil, mod nil)
         in partition f t (l00,l01)
         end
     in if f h then (write (l00, h::a);
          read b as b' in write (l01, b'))
        else (read a as a' in write (l00, a');
            write (l01, h::b))
     end
 in (l00,l01) end
```

Figure 1. The list partition function: ordinary (left), self-adjusting (center), and with destination passing (right).

Our solution. We can circumvent this problem by using unsafe, imperative operations. For our running example, `partition` can be rewritten as shown in Figure 1(right), in a destination passing style. The code takes an input list and two destinations, which are recorded separately. Without restrictions of the modal type system, it can return (α `list` **mod** * α `list` **mod**), as desired.

A major problem with this approach, however, is correctness: a simple mistake in using the imperative constructs can lead to errors in change propagation that are extremely difficult to identify. We therefore would like to derive the efficient, imperative version automatically from its purely functional version. There are three main challenges to such translation. (1) The source language has to identify which data is written to which part of the aggregate data types. (2) All changeable data should be placed into modifiables and all their dependencies should be tracked. (3) The target language must verify that self-adjusting constructs are used correctly to ensure correctness of change propagation.

To address the first challenge, we enrich an information-flow type to check dependencies among different components of the changeable pairs. We introduce *labels* ρ into the changeable level annotations, denoted as $\mathbb{C}_\rho$. The label serves as an identifier for modifiables. For each function of type $\tau_1 \rightarrow \tau_2$, we give labels for the return type τ_2. The information flow type system then infers the dependencies for each label in the function body. These labels decide which data goes into which modifiable in the translated code.

To address the second challenge, the translation algorithm takes the inferred labels from the source program, and conducts a type directed translation to generate self-adjusting programs in *destination passing style*. Specifically, the labels in the function return type are translated into destinations (modifiables) in the target language, and expressions that have labeled level types are translated into explicit write into their corresponding modifiables. Finally, we wrap the destinations into the appropriate type and return the value.

As an example, consider how we derive the imperative self-adjusting program for list partition, starting from the purely functional implementation on the leftmost column of Figure 1. First, we mark the return type of the partition function as $(\alpha\ \texttt{list}^{\mathbb{C}_{00}} * \alpha\ \texttt{list}^{\mathbb{C}_{01}})^{\mathbb{S}}$, which indicates the return has two destinations l_{00} and l_{01}, and the translated function will take, besides the original arguments f and l, two modifiables l_{00} and l_{01} as arguments. Then an information flow type system infers that the expression `(h::a,b)` on line 12 of Figure 1 (left) has type $(\alpha\ \texttt{list}^{\mathbb{C}_{00}} * \alpha\ \texttt{list}^{\mathbb{C}_{01}})^{\mathbb{S}}$. Using these label information, the compiler generates a target expression **write** `(l00,h::a)`; **write** `(l01,b)`. Finally, the translated function returns the destination as a pair `(l00,l01)`. Figure 1 (right) shows the translated code for list partition using our translation.

To address the third challenge, we design a new type system for the imperative target language. The type system distinguishes the modifiable as fresh modifiables and finalized modifiables. The typing rules enforce that all modifiables are finalized before reading, and the function fills in all the destinations, no matter which control branch the program is taken. We further prove that following the translation rules, we generate target programs that are of the appropriate type, and are type safe.

2.3 Limitation 2: Dependency Metadata.

The problem. Even with precise dependency tracking, self-adjusting programs can require large amounts of memory, making them difficult to scale to large inputs. One culprit is the dynamic dependency graph that stores operations on modifiables. For example, the list partition function contains about n **read** operations. Our experiments show, for example, that self-adjusting list partition requires 41x more memory than its batch counterpart. In principle, there is a way around this: simply treat blocks of data as a changeable unit instead of treating each unit as a changeable. However, it turns out to be difficult to make this work because doing so can disproportionately degrade performance.

At a very high level, self-adjusting computation may be seen as a technique for establishing a trade-off between space and time. By storing the dependency metadata, the technique enables responding to small changes to data significantly faster by identifying and recomputing only the parts of the computation affected by the changes. It is natural to wonder whether it would be possible to control this trade-off so that, for example, a $1/B$-th fraction (for some B) of the dependency metadata is stored at the expense of an increased update time, hopefully by no more than a factor of B.

Our solution. To see how we might solve this problem, consider the following simple idea: partition the data into equal-sized blocks and treat each of these blocks as a unit of changeable computation at which dependencies are tracked. This intuitive idea is indeed simple and natural to implement. But there is a fundamental problem: fixed-size chunking is highly sensitive to small changes to the input. As a simple example, consider inserting or deleting a single element to a list of blocks. Such a change will cascade to all blocks in the list, preventing much of the prior computation from being reused. Even "in-place" changes, which the reader may feel would not cause this problem, are in fact unacceptable because they do not compose. Consider, for example, the output to the `filter` function, which takes an input list and outputs only elements for which a certain predicate evaluates to true. Modifying an input element in-place may drop or add an element to the output list, which can create a

Levels $\delta ::= \mathbb{S} \mid \mathbb{C}_\rho \mid \alpha$

Types $\tau ::= \mathbf{int}^\delta \mid (\tau_1 \times \tau_2)^\delta \mid (\tau_1 + \tau_2)^\delta \mid (\tau_1 \to \tau_2)^\delta$

Constraints $C, D ::= \mathbf{true} \mid \mathbf{false} \mid \alpha = \beta \mid \alpha \leq \beta \mid \delta \lhd \tau \mid \rho_1 = \rho_2$

Figure 2. Levels, types and constraints

ripple effect to all the blocks. The main challenge in these examples lies in making sure the blocks remain stable under changes.

We solve these problems by eliminating the intrinsic dependency between block boundaries and the data itself. More precisely, we propose a *probabilistic chunking scheme* that decides block boundaries using a (random) hash function independently of the structure of the data rather than deterministically. Using this technique, we are able to reduce size of the dependency metadata by a factor B in expectation by chunking the data into blocks of expected size B while taking only about a factor of B hit in the update time.

3. Fine-grained Information Flow Types

In this section, we derive a type system for self-adjusting computation that can identify precisely which part of the data, down to individual attributes of a record or tuple, is changeable. In particular, we extend the surface type system from previous work to track fine-grained dependencies in the surface language.

The formalism rests on a simple insight that *data that depends on changeable data must itself be changeable*, similar to situations in information-flow type systems, where "secret" (high-security) data is infectious; therefore, any data that depends on secret data itself must be secret.

To track dependency precisely, we distinguish different changeable data further by giving them unique labels. Our types include a lattice of *(security) levels*: stable and changeable with labels. We generally follow the approach and notation of Chen et al. [15, 17] except that we need not have a mode on function types.

Levels. *Levels* $\mathbb{S}$ *(stable)* and $\mathbb{C}_\rho$ *(changeable)* have a partial order:

$$\frac{}{\mathbb{S} \leq \mathbb{S}} \qquad \frac{}{\mathbb{C}_\rho \leq \mathbb{C}_\rho} \qquad \frac{}{\mathbb{S} \leq \mathbb{C}_\rho} \qquad \frac{}{\mathbb{C}_{1\rho} \leq \mathbb{C}_{0\rho}}$$

Stable levels are lower than changeable; changeable levels with different labels are generally incomparable. Here, labels are used to distinguish different changeable data in the program. We also assume that labels with prefix 1 are lower than labels with prefix 0. This allows changeable data to flow into their corresponding destinations (labeled with prefix 0). We will discuss the subsumption in Section 4.

Types. Types consist of integers tagged with their levels, products, sums and arrow (function) types with an associated level, as shown in Figure 2. The label ρ associated with each changeable level denotes fine-grained dependencies among changeables: two changeables with the same label have a dependency between them.

Labels. Labels are identifiers for changeable data. To facilitate translation into a destination-passing style, we use particular binary-encoded labels that identify each label with its destination. This binary encoding works in concert with the relation $\tau \downarrow_\rho \mathcal{D}; \mathcal{L}$, in Figure 3, which recursively determines the labels with respect to a prefix ρ, where the type of the destinations and the destination names are stored in $\mathcal{D}$ and $\mathcal{L}$, respectively. For stable product, rule (#prodS), we label it based on the structure of the product. Specifically, we append 0 if the changeable level is on the left part of a product, and we append 1 if the changeable level is on the right part of a product. For changeable level types, we require that the outer level label is ρ. The relation does not restrict the inner labels. For stable level integers, sums and arrows, we do not look into the type structure, the inner changeable types can be labeled arbitrarily. As an example,

$$\frac{}{\mathbf{int}^{\mathbb{S}} \downarrow_\rho \emptyset; \emptyset}\ (\#\text{intS}) \qquad \frac{}{\mathbf{int}^{\mathbb{C}_\rho} \downarrow_\rho \{\mathbf{int}\}; \{l_\rho\}}\ (\#\text{intC})$$

$$\frac{}{(\tau_1 + \tau_2)^{\mathbb{S}} \downarrow_\rho \emptyset; \emptyset}\ (\#\text{sumS}) \qquad \frac{}{(\tau_1 \to \tau_2)^{\mathbb{S}} \downarrow_\rho \emptyset; \emptyset}\ (\#\text{funS})$$

$$\frac{\tau_1 \downarrow_{\rho 0} \mathcal{D}; \mathcal{L} \qquad \tau_2 \downarrow_{\rho 1} \mathcal{D}'; \mathcal{L}'}{(\tau_1 \times \tau_2)^{\mathbb{S}} \downarrow_\rho \mathcal{D} \cup \mathcal{D}'; \mathcal{L} \cup \mathcal{L}'}\ (\#\text{prodS})$$

$$\frac{}{(\tau_1 \times \tau_2)^{\mathbb{C}_\rho} \downarrow_\rho \{(\tau_1 \times \tau_2)\}; \{l_\rho\}}\ (\#\text{prodC})$$

$$\frac{}{(\tau_1 + \tau_2)^{\mathbb{C}_\rho} \downarrow_\rho \{(\tau_1 + \tau_2)\}; \{l_\rho\}}\ (\#\text{sumC})$$

$$\frac{}{(\tau_1 \to \tau_2)^{\mathbb{C}_\rho} \downarrow_\rho \{(\tau_1 \to \tau_2)\}; \{l_\rho\}}\ (\#\text{funC})$$

Figure 3. Labeling changeable types

$$[\![\mathbf{int}^\delta]\!] = \delta \qquad [\![(\tau_1 + \tau_2)^\delta]\!] = \delta$$
$$[\![(\tau_1 \times \tau_2)^\delta]\!] = \delta \qquad [\![(\tau_1 \to \tau_2)^\delta]\!] = \delta$$

$$\mathbf{int}^{\delta_1} \doteq \mathbf{int}^{\delta_2} \qquad (\tau_1 + \tau_2)^{\delta_1} \doteq (\tau_1 + \tau_2)^{\delta_2}$$
$$(\tau_1 \times \tau_2)^{\delta_1} \doteq (\tau_1 \times \tau_2)^{\delta_2} \qquad (\tau_1 \to \tau_2)^{\delta_1} \doteq (\tau_1 \to \tau_2)^{\delta_2}$$

Figure 6. Outer level of types, and equality up to outer levels

Values $v ::= n \mid x \mid (v_1, v_2) \mid \mathbf{inl}\ v \mid \mathbf{inr}\ v \mid \mathbf{fun}\ f(x) = e$

Expr.'s $e ::= v \mid \oplus(x_1, x_2) \mid \mathbf{fst}\ x \mid \mathbf{snd}\ x \mid \mathbf{case}\ x\ \mathbf{of}\ \{x_1 \Rightarrow e_1\ ,\ x_2 \Rightarrow e_2\} \mid \mathbf{apply}(x_1, x_2) \mid \mathbf{let}\ x = e_1\ \mathbf{in}\ e_2$

Figure 7. Abstract syntax of the source language

$\tau = \left(\mathbf{int}^{\mathbb{C}_{00}} \times \left(\mathbf{int}^{\mathbb{C}_{111}} + \mathbf{int}^{\mathbb{S}}\right)^{\mathbb{C}_{01}}\right)^{\mathbb{S}}$ is a valid label for $\tau \downarrow_0 \mathcal{D}; \mathcal{L}$. The type for the destinations are $\mathcal{D} = \{\mathbf{int}, \left(\mathbf{int}^{\mathbb{C}_{111}} + \mathbf{int}^{\mathbb{S}}\right)\}$, and the destination names are $\mathcal{L} = \{l_{00}, l_{01}\}$.

Subtyping. Figure 4 shows the subtyping relation $\tau <: \tau'$, which is standard except for the levels. It requires that the outer level of the subtype is smaller than the outer level of the supertype.

Levels and types. We need relations between levels and types to ensure certain invariants. A type τ is *higher than* δ, written $\delta \lhd \tau$, if the outer level of the type is at least δ. In other words, δ is a lower bound of the outer level of τ. For products with outer stable levels, we check if each component is higher than δ. Note that we do not check the component of a stable sum type. Figure 5 defines this relation.

We define an outer-level operation $[\![\tau]\!]$ that derives the outer level of a type in Figure 6). Finally, two types τ_1 and τ_2 are *equal up to their outer levels*, written $\tau_1 \doteq \tau_2$, if $\tau_1 = \tau_2$ or they differ only in their outer levels.

4. Source Language

Abstract syntax. Figure 7 shows the syntax for our source language, a purely functional language with integers (as base types), products, and sums. The expressions consist of values (integers, pairs, tagged values, and recursive functions), projections, case expressions, function applications, and let bindings. For convenience, we consider only expressions in A-normal form, which names in-

$$\frac{\delta \le \delta'}{\mathbf{int}^{\delta} <: \mathbf{int}^{\delta'}}\ (\text{subInt}) \quad \frac{\tau_1 <: \tau_1' \quad \tau_2 <: \tau_2' \quad \delta \le \delta'}{(\tau_1 \times \tau_2)^{\delta} <: (\tau_1' \times \tau_2')^{\delta'}}\ (\text{subProd}) \quad \frac{\tau_1 <: \tau_1' \quad \tau_2 <: \tau_2' \quad \delta \le \delta'}{(\tau_1 + \tau_2)^{\delta} <: (\tau_1' + \tau_2')^{\delta'}}\ (\text{subSum}) \quad \frac{\delta \le \delta' \quad \tau_1' <: \tau_1 \quad \tau_2 <: \tau_2'}{(\tau_1 \to \tau_2)^{\delta} <: (\tau_1' \to \tau_2')^{\delta'}}\ (\text{subArr})$$

Figure 4. Subtyping

$$\frac{\delta \le \delta'}{\delta \lhd \mathbf{int}^{\delta'}}\ (\lhd\text{-Int}) \quad \frac{\delta \le \delta'}{\delta \lhd (\tau_1 \times \tau_2)^{\delta'}}\ (\lhd\text{-Prod}) \quad \frac{\delta \lhd \tau_1 \quad \delta \lhd \tau_2}{\delta \lhd (\tau_1 \times \tau_2)^{\mathbb{S}}}\ (\lhd\text{-InnerProd}) \quad \frac{\delta \le \delta'}{\delta \lhd (\tau_1 \to \tau_2)^{\delta'}}\ (\lhd\text{-Arrow}) \quad \frac{\delta \le \delta'}{\delta \lhd (\tau_1 + \tau_2)^{\delta'}}\ (\lhd\text{-Sum})$$

Figure 5. Lower bound of a type

$\boxed{C;\mathcal{P};\Gamma \vdash e : \tau}$ Under constraint C, label set $\mathcal{P}$ and source typing environment Γ, source expression e has type τ

$$\frac{}{C;\mathcal{P};\Gamma \vdash n : \mathbf{int}^{\mathbb{S}}}\ (\text{SInt}) \quad \frac{\Gamma(x) = \tau}{C;\mathcal{P};\Gamma \vdash x : \tau}\ (\text{SVar})$$

$$\frac{C;\mathcal{P};\Gamma \vdash v_1 : \tau_1 \qquad C;\mathcal{P};\Gamma \vdash v_2 : \tau_2}{C;\mathcal{P};\Gamma \vdash (v_1, v_2) : (\tau_1 \times \tau_2)^{\mathbb{S}}}\ (\text{SPair})$$

$$\frac{C;\mathcal{P};\Gamma \vdash v : \tau_1}{C;\mathcal{P};\Gamma \vdash \mathbf{inl}\ v : (\tau_1 + \tau_2)^{\mathbb{S}}}\ (\text{SSum}) \quad \frac{C;\mathcal{P};\Gamma \vdash x : (\tau_1 \times \tau_2)^{\delta}}{C;\mathcal{P};\Gamma \vdash \mathbf{fst}\ x : \tau_1}\ (\text{SFst})$$

$$\frac{\begin{array}{c} C;\{1\rho\};\Gamma, x : \tau_1, f : (\tau_1 \to \tau_2)^{\mathbb{S}} \vdash e : \tau_2 \\ [\![\tau_1]\!] = \mathbb{C}_{1\rho} \qquad C \Vdash \tau_2 \downarrow_0 \mathcal{D}; \mathcal{L} \end{array}}{C;\mathcal{P}';\Gamma \vdash (\mathbf{fun}\ f(x) = e) : (\tau_1 \to \tau_2)^{\mathbb{S}}}\ (\text{SFun})$$

$$\frac{\begin{array}{l} C;\mathcal{P};\Gamma \vdash x_1 : \mathbf{int}^{\delta_1} \\ C;\mathcal{P};\Gamma \vdash x_2 : \mathbf{int}^{\delta_2} \quad C \Vdash \delta_1 = \delta_2 \quad \oplus : \mathbf{int} \times \mathbf{int} \to \mathbf{int} \end{array}}{C;\mathcal{P};\Gamma \vdash \oplus(x_1, x_2) : \mathbf{int}^{\delta_1}}\ (\text{SPrim})$$

$$\frac{\begin{array}{ll} C;\mathcal{P};\Gamma \vdash e_1 : \tau' & C \Vdash \tau' <: \tau'' \quad [\![\tau'']\!] = \mathbb{C}_{\rho} \\ C;\mathcal{P} \cup \{\rho\};\Gamma, x : \tau'' \vdash e_2 : \tau & C \Vdash \tau' \doteq \tau'' \quad C \Vdash \rho \notin \mathcal{P} \end{array}}{C;\mathcal{P};\Gamma \vdash \mathbf{let}\ x = e_1\ \mathbf{in}\ e_2 : \tau}\ (\text{SLet})$$

$$\frac{\begin{array}{c} C;\mathcal{P};\Gamma \vdash x_1 : (\tau_1 \to \tau_2)^{\delta} \\ C;\mathcal{P};\Gamma \vdash x_2 : \tau_1 \qquad C \Vdash \delta \lhd \tau_2 \end{array}}{C;\mathcal{P};\Gamma \vdash \mathbf{apply}(x_1, x_2) : \tau_2}\ (\text{SApp})$$

$$\frac{\begin{array}{ll} C;\mathcal{P};\Gamma \vdash x : (\tau_1 + \tau_2)^{\delta} & C;\mathcal{P};\Gamma, x_1 : \tau_1 \vdash e_1 : \tau \\ C \Vdash \delta \lhd \tau & C;\mathcal{P};\Gamma, x_2 : \tau_2 \vdash e_2 : \tau \end{array}}{C;\mathcal{P};\Gamma \vdash \mathbf{case}\ x\ \mathbf{of}\ \{x_1 \Rightarrow e_1\ ,\ x_2 \Rightarrow e_2\} : \tau}\ (\text{SCase})$$

Figure 8. Typing rules for source language

termediate results. A-normal form simplifies some technical issues, while maintaining expressiveness.

Constraint-based type system. The type system has the fine-grained level-decorated types and constraints (Figure 2) as was described in Section 3. After discussing the rules themselves, we will look at type inference.

The typing judgment $C;\mathcal{P};\Gamma \vdash e : \tau$ has a constraint C, a label set $\mathcal{P}$ (storing used label names) and typing environment Γ, and infers type τ for expression e. Our work extends the type system in Chen et al. [15, 17] with labels. Although most of the typing rules remain the same, there are two major differences: (1) The source typing judgment no longer has a mode; (2) Our generalization has a label set in the typing rules to make sure the labels inside a function are unique. Furthermore, our generalization of changeable levels with labels does not affect inferring level polymorphic types. To simplify the presentation, we assume the source language presented here is level monomorphic.

The typing rules for variables (SVar), integers (SInt), pairs (SPair), sums (SSum), primitive operations (SPrim), and projections (SFst) are standard. (We omit the symmetric rules for **inr** v and **snd** x.) To type a function (SFun), we type the body specified by the function type $(\tau_1 \to \tau_2)^{\delta}$. The changeable types in the return type will translate to destinations when translating in the target language. To facilitate the translation, we need to fix the destination labels in the return type via $\tau_2 \downarrow_0 \mathcal{D}; \mathcal{L}$, where we assume destination labels all have prefix 0. We also assume that non-destination labels, e.g. labels for changeable input, have prefix 1. Note that these labels are only in a function scope, labels in different functions do not need to be unique. We omit the simpler rule for $[\![\tau_1]\!] = \mathbb{S}$.

Like in previous work, we allow subsumption only at let binding (SLet), e.g. from a bound expression e_1 of subtype $\mathbf{int}^{\mathbb{S}}$ to an assumption $x : \mathbf{int}^{\mathbb{C}_{\rho}}$. Note that when binding an expression into a variable with a changeable level, the label ρ must be either unique or one of the labels from the destination. The subtype allows changeable labels with prefix 1 to be "promoted" as labels with prefix 0. This restriction makes sure the input data can flow to destinations, and the information flow type system tracks dependency correctly. We omit the simpler rule for $[\![\tau'']\!] = \mathbb{S}$. As in previous work, we restrict that we subsume only when the subtype and supertype are equal up to their outer levels. This simplifies the translation, with no loss of expressiveness: to handle "deep" subsumption, such as $(\mathbf{int}^{\mathbb{S}} \to \mathbf{int}^{\mathbb{S}})^{\mathbb{S}} <: (\mathbf{int}^{\mathbb{S}} \to \mathbf{int}^{\mathbb{C}_{\rho}})^{\mathbb{C}_{\rho'}}$, we can insert *coercions* into the source program before typing it with these rules. (This process could easily be automated.)

A function application (SApp) requires that the result of the function must be higher than the function's level: if a function is itself changeable $(\tau_1 \to \tau_2)^{\mathbb{C}_{\rho}}$, then it could be replaced by another function and thus the result of this application must be changeable. Due to **let**-subsumption, checking this in (SFun) alone is not enough. Similarly, in rule (SCase) for typing a case expression, we ensure that the level of the result τ must also be higher than δ: if the scrutinee changes, we may take the other branch, requiring a changeable result.

Constraints and type inference. Our rules and constraints fall within the HM(X) framework [44], permitting inference of principal types via constraint solving. Although our type system requires explicit labels for changeable levels, these labels can be inferred automatically. The user does not need to provide explicit labels when programming in the surface language. In all, we extend the type system with fine-grained dependency tracking without any burden on the programmer.

5. Target Language

Abstract syntax. The target language (Figure 9) is an imperative self-adjusting language with modifiables. In addition to integers,

$$
\begin{array}{lrcl}
\textit{Types} & \underline{\tau} & ::= & \textbf{unit} \mid \textbf{int} \mid \underline{\tau}\ \textbf{mod} \mid \square\,\underline{\tau} \mid \underline{\tau}_1 \times \underline{\tau}_2 \mid \\
 & & & \underline{\tau}_1 + \underline{\tau}_2 \mid \underline{\tau}_1 \underset{\mathcal{D}}{\rightarrow} \underline{\tau}_2 \\
\textit{Dest. Types} & \mathcal{D} & ::= & \left\{\underline{\tau}_1, \cdots, \underline{\tau}_n\right\} \\
\textit{Labels} & \mathcal{L} & ::= & \{l_1, \cdots, l_n\} \\
\textit{Variables} & x & ::= & y \mid l_i \\
\textit{Typing Env.} & \Gamma & ::= & \cdot \mid \Gamma, x : \underline{\tau} \\
\textit{Values} & v & ::= & n \mid x \mid \ell \mid (v_1, v_2) \mid \textbf{inl}\ v \mid \textbf{inr}\ v \mid \\
 & & & \textbf{fun}^{\mathcal{L}}\ f(x) = e \\
\textit{Expressions} & e & ::= & v \mid \oplus(x_1, x_2) \mid \textbf{fst}\ x \mid \textbf{snd}\ x \mid \\
 & & & \textbf{apply}^{\mathcal{L}}(x_1, x_2) \mid \textbf{let}\ x = e_1\ \textbf{in}\ e_2 \mid \\
 & & & \textbf{case}\ x\ \textbf{of}\ \{x_1 \Rightarrow e_1\ ,\ x_2 \Rightarrow e_2\} \mid \\
 & & & \textbf{mod}\ v \mid \textbf{read}\ x\ \textbf{as}\ y\ \textbf{in}\ e \mid \textbf{write}(x_1, x_2)
\end{array}
$$

Figure 9. Types and expressions in the target language

units, products, sums, the target type system makes a distinction between fresh modifiable types $\square$ **int** (modifiables that are freshly allocated) and finalized modifiable types **int mod** (modifiables that are written after the allocation). The function type $\underline{\tau}_1 \underset{\mathcal{D}}{\rightarrow} \underline{\tau}_2$ contains an ordered set of destination types $\mathcal{D}$, indicating the type of the destinations of the function.

The variables consist of labels l_i and ordinary variables y, which are drawn from different syntactically categories. The label variable l_i is used as bindings for destinations.

The values of the language consist of integers, variables, locations ℓ (which appear only at runtime), pairs, tagged values, and functions. Each function $\textbf{fun}^{\mathcal{L}}\ f(x) = e$ takes an ordered label set $\mathcal{L}$, which contains a set of destination modifiables l_i that should be filled in before the function returns. An empty $\mathcal{L}$ indicates the function returns all stable values, and therefore takes no destination.

The expression $\textbf{apply}^{\mathcal{L}}(x_1, x_2)$ applies a function while supplying a set of destination modifiables $\mathcal{L}$. The **mod** v construct creates a new fresh modifiable $\square\,\underline{\tau}$ with an initial value v. The **read** expression binds the contents of a modifiable x to a variable y and evaluates the body of the **read**. The **write** constructor imperatively updates a modifiable x_1 with value x_2. The **write** operator can update both modifiables in destination labels $\mathcal{L}$ and modifiables created by **mod**.

Static semantics. The typing rules in Figure 10 follow the structure of the expressions. Rules (TLoc), (TInt), (TVar), (TPair), (TSum), (TFst), (TPrim) are standard. Given an initial value x of type $\underline{\tau}$, rule (TAlloc) creates a fresh modifiable of type $\square\,\underline{\tau}$. Note that the type system guarantees that this initial value x will never be read. The reason for providing the an initial value is to determine the type of the modifiable, and making the type system sound. Rule (TWrite) writes a value x_2 of type $\underline{\tau}$ into a modifiable x_1, when x_1 is a fresh modifiable of type $\square\,\underline{\tau}$, and produces a new typing environment substituting the type of x_1 into an finalized modifiable type $\underline{\tau}$ **mod**. Note that Rule (TWrite) only allows writing into a fresh modifiable, thus guarantees that each modifiable can be written only once. Intuitively, **mod** and **write** separates the process of creating a value in a purely functional language into two steps: the creation of location and initialization. This separation is critical for writing programs in destination passing style. Rule (TRead) enforces that the programmer can only read a modifiable when it has been already written, that is the type of the modifiable should be $\underline{\tau}$ **mod**.

Rule (TLet) takes the produced new typing environment from the let binding, and uses it to check e_2. This allows the type system to keep track of the effects of **write** in the let binding. To ensure the correct usage of self-adjusting constructs, rule (TCase) enforces a conservative restriction that both the result type and the produced typing environment for each branch should be the same. This means that each branch should write to the same set of modifiables. If a modifiable x is finalized in one branch, the other branch should also finalize the same modifiable.

$\boxed{\Lambda; \Gamma \vdash e : \underline{\tau} \dashv \Gamma'}$ Under store typing Λ and target typing environment Γ, target expression e has target type $\underline{\tau}$, and produces a typing environment Γ'

$$\frac{\Lambda(\ell) = \underline{\tau}}{\Lambda; \Gamma \vdash \ell : \underline{\tau} \dashv \Gamma}\ (\text{TLoc}) \qquad \frac{}{\Lambda; \Gamma \vdash n : \textbf{int} \dashv \Gamma}\ (\text{TInt})$$

$$\frac{\Gamma(x) = \underline{\tau}}{\Lambda; \Gamma \vdash x : \underline{\tau} \dashv \Gamma}\ (\text{TVar}) \qquad \frac{\Lambda; \Gamma \vdash v : \underline{\tau} \dashv \Gamma}{\Lambda; \Gamma \vdash \textbf{mod}\ v : \square\,\underline{\tau} \dashv \Gamma}\ (\text{TAlloc})$$

$$\frac{\Lambda; \Gamma \vdash x_2 : \underline{\tau} \dashv \Gamma}{\Lambda; \Gamma, x_1 : \square\,\underline{\tau} \vdash \textbf{write}(x_1, x_2) : \textbf{unit} \dashv \Gamma, x_1 : \underline{\tau}\ \textbf{mod}}\ (\text{TWrite})$$

$$\frac{\Lambda; \Gamma \vdash x_1 : \underline{\tau}_1\ \textbf{mod} \dashv \Gamma \qquad \Lambda; \Gamma, x : \underline{\tau}_1 \vdash e_2 : \underline{\tau}_2 \dashv \Gamma'}{\Lambda; \Gamma \vdash \textbf{read}\ x_1\ \textbf{as}\ x\ \textbf{in}\ e_2 : \textbf{unit} \dashv \Gamma'}\ (\text{TRead})$$

$$\frac{\Lambda; \Gamma \vdash v_1 : \underline{\tau}_1 \dashv \Gamma \qquad \Lambda; \Gamma \vdash v_2 : \underline{\tau}_2 \dashv \Gamma}{\Lambda; \Gamma \vdash (v_1, v_2) : \underline{\tau}_1 \times \underline{\tau}_2 \dashv \Gamma}\ (\text{TPair})$$

$$\frac{\begin{array}{c}\mathcal{L} = \{l_1, \cdots, l_n\} \quad \mathcal{D} = \{\underline{\tau}'_1, \cdots, \underline{\tau}'_n\} \quad \underline{\tau}_1 \neq \square\,\underline{\tau}' \\ \Gamma_d(l_i) = \cdot, l_1 : \square\,\underline{\tau}'_1, \cdots, l_n : \square\,\underline{\tau}'_n \\ For\, i = 1, \cdots, n \quad \Gamma'(l_i) = \underline{\tau}'_i\ \textbf{mod} \\ \Lambda; \Gamma, x : \underline{\tau}_1, f : (\underline{\tau}_1 \underset{\mathcal{D}}{\rightarrow} \underline{\tau}_2), \Gamma_d \vdash e : \underline{\tau}_2 \dashv \Gamma'\end{array}}{\Lambda; \Gamma \vdash \textbf{fun}^{\mathcal{L}}\ f(x) = e : (\underline{\tau}_1 \underset{\mathcal{D}}{\rightarrow} \underline{\tau}_2) \dashv \Gamma}\ (\text{TFun})$$

$$\frac{\Lambda; \Gamma \vdash v : \underline{\tau}_1 \dashv \Gamma}{\Lambda; \Gamma \vdash \textbf{inl}\ v : \underline{\tau}_1 + \underline{\tau}_2 \dashv \Gamma}\ (\text{TSum}) \qquad \frac{\Lambda; \Gamma \vdash x : \underline{\tau}_1 \times \underline{\tau}_2 \dashv \Gamma}{\Lambda; \Gamma \vdash \textbf{fst}\ x : \underline{\tau}_1 \dashv \Gamma}\ (\text{TFst})$$

$$\frac{\begin{array}{l}\Lambda; \Gamma \vdash x_1 : \textbf{int} \dashv \Gamma \\ \Lambda; \Gamma \vdash x_2 : \textbf{int} \dashv \Gamma \qquad \vdash \oplus : \textbf{int} \times \textbf{int} \rightarrow \textbf{int}\end{array}}{\Lambda; \Gamma \vdash \oplus(x_1, x_2) : \textbf{int} \dashv \Gamma}\ (\text{TPrim})$$

$$\frac{\Lambda; \Gamma \vdash e_1 : \underline{\tau} \dashv \Gamma' \qquad \Lambda; \Gamma', x : \underline{\tau} \vdash e_2 : \underline{\tau}' \dashv \Gamma''}{\Lambda; \Gamma \vdash \textbf{let}\ x = e_1\ \textbf{in}\ e_2 : \underline{\tau}' \dashv \Gamma''}\ (\text{TLet})$$

$$\frac{\begin{array}{c}\mathcal{L} = \{l_1, \cdots, l_n\} \qquad \mathcal{D} = \{\underline{\tau}'_1, \cdots, \underline{\tau}'_n\} \\ For\, i = 1, \cdots, n \quad \Gamma(l_i) = \square\,\underline{\tau}'_i \quad \Gamma'(l_i) = \underline{\tau}'_i\ \textbf{mod} \\ \Lambda; \Gamma \vdash x_1 : (\underline{\tau}_1 \underset{\mathcal{D}}{\rightarrow} \underline{\tau}_2) \dashv \Gamma \qquad \Lambda; \Gamma \vdash x_2 : \underline{\tau}_1 \dashv \Gamma\end{array}}{\Lambda; \Gamma \vdash \textbf{apply}^{\mathcal{L}}(x_1, x_2) : \underline{\tau}_2 \dashv \Gamma'}\ (\text{TApp})$$

$$\frac{\Lambda; \Gamma \vdash x : \underline{\tau}_1 + \underline{\tau}_2 \dashv \Gamma \qquad \begin{array}{l}\Lambda; \Gamma, x_1 : \underline{\tau}_1 \vdash e_1 : \underline{\tau} \dashv \Gamma' \\ \Lambda; \Gamma, x_2 : \underline{\tau}_2 \vdash e_2 : \underline{\tau} \dashv \Gamma'\end{array}}{\Lambda; \Gamma \vdash \textbf{case}\ x\ \textbf{of}\ \{x_1 \Rightarrow e_1\ ,\ x_2 \Rightarrow e_2\} : \underline{\tau} \dashv \Gamma'}\ (\text{TCase})$$

Figure 10. Typing rules of the target language

Rule (TFun) defines the typing requirement for a function: (1) the destination types $\mathcal{D}$ are fresh modifiables, and the argument type should not contains fresh modifiable. Intuitively, the function arguments are partitions into two parts: destinations and ordinary arguments; (2) the body of the function e has to finalize all the destination modifiables presented in $\mathcal{L}$. This requirement can be achieved by either explicitly **write**'ing into modifiables in $\mathcal{L}$, or by passing these modifiables into another function that takes the responsibility to write an actual value to them. Although all the modifiables in $\mathcal{L}$ should be finalized, other modifiables created inside the function body may be fresh, as long as there is no read of those modifiables in the function body.

Rule (TApp) applies a function with fresh modifiables $\mathcal{L}$. The type of these modifiables should be the same as the destination types $\mathcal{D}$ as presented in the function type. The typing rule produces a new

$$
\begin{array}{rcl}
\|\mathbf{int}^{\mathbb{S}}\| & = & \mathbf{int} \\
\|(\tau_1 \to \tau_2)^{\mathbb{S}}\| & = & \|\tau_1\| \underset{\|\mathcal{D}\|}{\to} \|\tau_2\| \quad (\tau_2 \downarrow_0 \mathcal{D}; \mathcal{L}) \\
\|(\tau_1 \times \tau_2)^{\mathbb{S}}\| & = & \|\tau_1\| \times \|\tau_2\| \\
\|(\tau_1 + \tau_2)^{\mathbb{S}}\| & = & \|\tau_1\| + \|\tau_2\| \\
\|\tau\| & = & \| |\tau|^{\mathbb{S}} \| \, \mathbf{mod} \quad ([\![\tau]\!] = \mathbb{C}_\rho)
\end{array}
$$

$$
\begin{array}{ll}
\|\cdot\| = \cdot & \|\tau\|_\phi = \|[\phi]\tau\| \\
\|\Gamma, x : \tau\| = \|\Gamma\|, x : \|\tau\| & \|\Gamma\|_\phi = \|[\phi]\Gamma\|
\end{array}
$$

Figure 11. Translations $\|\tau\|$ of types and typing environments

typing environment that guarantees that all the supplied destination modifiables are finalized after the function application.

Dynamic semantics. The dynamic semantics of our target language matches that of Acar et al [4] after two syntactical changes: $\mathbf{fun}^{\mathcal{L}}\ f(x) = e$ is represented as $\mathbf{fun}\ f(x) = \lambda\mathcal{L}.e$, and $\mathbf{apply}^{\mathcal{L}}(x_1, x_2)$ is represented as $(x_1\ x_2)\ \mathcal{L}$.

6. Translation

This section gives a high-level overview of the translation from the source language to the target self-adjusting language. To ensure type safety, we translate types and expressions together using a type-directed translation. Since the source and the target languages have different type systems, an expression $e : \tau$ cannot be translated to a target expression e' of type τ, the type also has to be translated, producing some $e' : \underline{\tau}'$ where $\underline{\tau}'$ is a target type that *corresponds to* τ. We therefore developed the translation of expressions and types together, along with the proof that the desired property holds. To understand how to translate expressions, it is helpful to first understand how we translate types.

6.1 Translating types.

Figure 11 defines the translation of types from the source language's types into the target types. We also use it to translate the types in the typing environment Γ. We define $\|\tau\|$ as the translation of types from the source language into the target types. We also use it for translating the types in the typing environment Γ. For integers, sums, and products with stable levels, we simply erase the level notation $\mathbb{S}$, and apply the function recursively into the type structure. For arrow types, we need to derive the destination types. In the source typing, we fix the destination type labels by $\tau_2 \downarrow_0 \mathcal{D}; \mathcal{L}$, where $\mathcal{D}$ stores the source type for the destinations. Therefore, the destination types for the target arrow function will be $\|\mathcal{D}\|$.

For source types with changeable levels, the target type will be modifiables. Since the source language is purely functional, the final result will always be a finalized modifiable τ **mod**. Here, we define a *stabilization* function $|\tau|^{\mathbb{S}}$ for changeable source types, which changes the outer level of τ from changeable into stable. Formally, we define the function as,

$$|\tau|^{\mathbb{S}} = \tau', \text{where } [\![\tau]\!] = \mathbb{C}_\rho, [\![\tau']\!] = \mathbb{S} \text{ and } \tau \doteq \tau'$$

Then, the target type for a changeable level source type τ will be $\| |\tau|^{\mathbb{S}}\ \mathbf{mod} \|$.

6.2 Translating Expressions

We define the translation of expressions as a set of type-directed rules. Given (1) a derivation of $C; \mathcal{P}; \Gamma \vdash e : \tau$ in the constraint-based typing system and (2) a satisfying assignment ϕ for C, it is always possible to produce a correctly-typed target expression e_t (see Theorem 6.1 below). The environment Γ in the translation rules is a source-typing environment and must have no free level variables. Given an environment Γ from the constraint typing, we apply the satisfying assignment ϕ to eliminate its free level variables before

$\boxed{\Gamma \vdash e : \tau \hookrightarrow e'}$ Under closed source typing environment Γ, source expression e is translated at type τ to target expression e'

$$\frac{}{\Gamma \vdash n : \mathbf{int}^{\mathbb{S}} \hookrightarrow n}\ (\text{Int}) \qquad \frac{\Gamma(x) = \tau}{\Gamma \vdash x : \tau \hookrightarrow x}\ (\text{Var})$$

$$\frac{\Gamma \vdash v_1 : \tau_1 \hookrightarrow v_1' \qquad \Gamma \vdash v_2 : \tau_2 \hookrightarrow v_2'}{\Gamma \vdash (v_1, v_2) : (\tau_1 \times \tau_2)^{\mathbb{S}} \hookrightarrow (v_1', v_2')}\ (\text{Pair})$$

$$\frac{\Gamma, x : \tau_1, f : (\tau_1 \to \tau_2)^{\mathbb{S}} \vdash e : \tau_2 \rightsquigarrow e' \qquad \tau_2 \downarrow_0 \mathcal{D}; \mathcal{L}}{\Gamma \vdash \mathbf{fun}\ f(x) = e : (\tau_1 \to \tau_2)^{\mathbb{S}} \hookrightarrow \mathbf{fun}^{\mathcal{L}}\ f(x) = e'}\ (\text{Fun})$$

$$\frac{\Gamma \vdash v : \tau_1 \hookrightarrow v'}{\Gamma \vdash \mathbf{inl}\ v : (\tau_1 + \tau_2)^{\mathbb{S}} \hookrightarrow \mathbf{inl}\ v'}\ (\text{Sum}) \qquad \frac{\Gamma \vdash x : (\tau_1 \times \tau_2)^{\mathbb{S}} \hookrightarrow \underline{x}}{\Gamma \vdash \mathbf{fst}\ x : \tau_1 \hookrightarrow \mathbf{fst}\ \underline{x}}\ (\text{Fst})$$

$$\frac{\Gamma \vdash x_1 : \mathbf{int}^{\mathbb{S}} \hookrightarrow \underline{x_1} \qquad \Gamma \vdash x_2 : \mathbf{int}^{\mathbb{S}} \hookrightarrow \underline{x_2}}{\Gamma \vdash \oplus(x_1, x_2) : \mathbf{int}^{\delta} \hookrightarrow \oplus(\underline{x_1}, \underline{x_2})}\ (\text{Prim})$$

$$\frac{\begin{array}{c}\Gamma \vdash x_1 : (\tau_1 \to \tau_2)^{\mathbb{S}} \hookrightarrow \underline{x_1} \\ \Gamma \vdash x_2 : \tau_1 \hookrightarrow \underline{x_2} \qquad \tau_2 \downarrow_0 \mathcal{D}; \mathcal{L}\end{array}}{\begin{array}{l}\Gamma \vdash \quad \mathbf{apply}(x_1, x_2) : \tau_2 \\ \quad \hookrightarrow \mathbf{let}\ \{l_i = \mathbf{mod}\ (\tau_i'|_v)\}_{l_i \in \mathcal{L}}^{\tau_i' \in \mathcal{D}}\ \mathbf{in}\ \mathbf{apply}^{\mathcal{L}}(\underline{x_1}, \underline{x_2})\end{array}}\ (\text{App})$$

$$\frac{\Gamma \vdash x : (\tau_1 + \tau_2)^{\mathbb{S}} \hookrightarrow \underline{x} \qquad \begin{array}{c}\Gamma, x_1 : \tau_1 \vdash e_1 : \tau \hookrightarrow e_1' \\ \Gamma, x_2 : \tau_2 \vdash e_2 : \tau \hookrightarrow e_2'\end{array}}{\begin{array}{l}\Gamma \vdash \quad \mathbf{case}\ x\ \mathbf{of}\ \{x_1 \Rightarrow e_1\ ,\ x_2 \Rightarrow e_2\} : \tau \\ \quad \hookrightarrow \mathbf{case}\ \underline{x}\ \mathbf{of}\ \{x_1 \Rightarrow e_1'\ ,\ x_2 \Rightarrow e_2'\}\end{array}}\ (\text{Case})$$

$$\frac{\Gamma \vdash e_1 : \tau' \hookrightarrow e_1' \qquad \Gamma, x : \tau' \vdash e_2 : \tau \hookrightarrow e_2'}{\Gamma \vdash \mathbf{let}\ x = e_1\ \mathbf{in}\ e_2 : \tau \hookrightarrow \mathbf{let}\ x = e_1'\ \mathbf{in}\ e_2'}\ (\text{Let})$$

$$\frac{\Gamma \vdash e : \tau \hookrightarrow e' \qquad [\![\tau]\!] = \mathbb{C}_{1\rho} \qquad \tau|_v = v}{\Gamma \vdash e : \tau \hookrightarrow \mathbf{let}\ l_{1\rho} = \mathbf{mod}\ v\ \mathbf{in}\ e'}\ (\text{Mod})$$

$$\frac{\Gamma \vdash e : \tau' \hookrightarrow e' \qquad [\![\tau]\!] = \mathbb{C}_{1\rho} \qquad |\tau|^{\mathbb{S}} = \tau' \qquad \tau|_v = v}{\Gamma \vdash e : \tau \hookrightarrow \mathbf{let}\ l_{1\rho} = \mathbf{mod}\ v\ \mathbf{in}\ e'}\ (\text{Lift})$$

$$\frac{\Gamma \vdash e : \tau \hookrightarrow e' \qquad [\![\tau]\!] = \mathbb{C}_\rho}{\Gamma \vdash e : \tau \hookrightarrow \mathbf{let}\ () = \mathbf{write}(l_\rho, e')\ \mathbf{in}\ l_\rho}\ (\text{Write})$$

$$\frac{\begin{array}{ll}\Gamma \vdash e \leadsto (x \gg x' : \tau' \vdash e') & [\![\tau']\!] = \mathbb{C}_\rho \\ \Gamma, x' : |\tau'|^{\mathbb{S}} \vdash e' : \tau \hookrightarrow e'' & \Gamma \vdash x : \tau' \hookrightarrow \underline{x}\end{array}}{\Gamma \vdash e : \tau \hookrightarrow \mathbf{read}\ \underline{x}\ \mathbf{as}\ x'\ \mathbf{in}\ e''}\ (\text{Read})$$

Figure 12. Translation for destination passing style

using it in the translation $[\phi]\Gamma$. With the environment closed, we need not refer to C.

Our rules are nondeterministic, avoiding the need to "decorate" them with context-sensitive details.

Direct rules. The rules (Int), (Var), (Pair), (Sum), (Fst) and (Prim) follows the structure of the expression, and directly translate the expressions.

Changeable rules. The rules (Lift), (Mod), and (Write) translate expressions with outer level changeable $\mathbb{C}_\rho$. Given a translation of e to some pure expression e', rule (Write) translates e into an imperative **write** expression that writes e' into modifiable l_ρ.

For expressions with non-destination changeable levels, that is the label ρ has a 1 as the prefix, we need to create a modifiable first. Rules (Lift) and (Mod) achieves this goal. (Mod) is the simpler of the two: if e translates to e' at type τ, then e translates to the **mod** expression at type τ. To get an initial value for the modifiable, we define a function $\tau|_v$ that takes a source type τ and returns any

$\boxed{\Gamma \vdash e \leadsto (x \gg x' : \tau \vdash e')}$ Under source typing Γ, renaming the "head" x in e to $x' : \tau$ yields expression e'

$$\frac{\Gamma \vdash x : \tau}{\Gamma \vdash x \leadsto (x \gg x' : \tau \vdash x')}\ \text{(LVar)} \qquad \frac{\Gamma \vdash x : \tau}{\Gamma \vdash \mathbf{fst}\ x \leadsto (x \gg x' : \tau \vdash \mathbf{fst}\ x')}\ \text{(LFst)}$$

$$\frac{\Gamma \vdash x_1 : \tau}{\Gamma \vdash \oplus(x_1, x_2) \leadsto (x_1 \gg x_1' : \tau \vdash \oplus(x_1', x_2))}\ \text{(LPrimop1)}$$

$$\frac{\Gamma \vdash x_1 : \tau}{\Gamma \vdash \mathbf{apply}(x_1, x_2) \leadsto (x_1 \gg x' : \tau \vdash \mathbf{apply}(x', x_2))}\ \text{(LApply)}$$

$$\frac{\Gamma \vdash x : \tau}{\begin{array}{l}\Gamma \vdash \mathbf{case}\ x\ \mathbf{of}\ \{x_1 \Rightarrow e_1\ ,\ x_2 \Rightarrow e_2\} \\ \quad \leadsto (x \gg x' : \tau \vdash \mathbf{case}\ x'\ \mathbf{of}\ \{x_1 \Rightarrow e_1\ ,\ x_2 \Rightarrow e_2\})\end{array}}\ \text{(LCase)}$$

Figure 13. Renaming the variable to be read

value v of that type. Note that the initial value is only a placeholder, and will never be read, so the choice of the value is not important. In (Lift), the expression is translated not at the given type τ but at its *stabilized* $|\tau|^{\mathbb{S}}$, capturing the "shallow subsumption" in the constraint typing rules (SLet): a bound expression of type $\tau_0^{\mathbb{S}}$ can be translated at type $\tau_0^{\mathbb{S}}$ to e', and then "promoted" to type $\tau_0^{\mathbb{C}_p}$ by placing it inside a modifiable l_p.

Reading from changeable data. To use an expression of changeable type in a context where a stable value is needed—such as passing some $x : \mathbf{int}^{\mathbb{C}}$ to a function expecting $\mathbf{int}^{\mathbb{S}}$—the (Read) rule generates a target expression that reads the value out of $x : \mathbf{int}^{\mathbb{C}}$ into a variable $x' : \mathbf{int}^{\mathbb{S}}$. The variable-renaming judgment $\Gamma \vdash e \leadsto (x \gg x' : \tau \vdash e')$ takes the expression e, finds a variable x about to be used, and yields an expression e' with that occurrence replaced by x'. For example, $\Gamma \vdash \mathbf{case}\ x\ \mathbf{of}\ \ldots \leadsto (x \gg x' : \tau \vdash \mathbf{case}\ x'\ \mathbf{of}\ \ldots)$. This judgment is derivable only for variable, **apply**, **case**, **fst**, and $\oplus$. For $\oplus(x_1, x_2)$, we need to read both variables; we omit the symmetric rules for reading the second variable. The rules are given in Figure 13.

$\boxed{\Gamma \vdash e : \tau \rightsquigarrow e'}$ Under closed source typing environment Γ, function body e is translated at type τ to target expression e' with destination returns.

$$\frac{\Gamma \vdash v_1 : \tau_1 \rightsquigarrow v_1' \qquad \Gamma \vdash v_2 : \tau_2 \rightsquigarrow v_2'}{\Gamma \vdash (v_1, v_2) : (\tau_1 \times \tau_2)^{\mathbb{S}} \rightsquigarrow (v_1', v_2')}\ \text{(RPair)}$$

$$\frac{\Gamma, x_1 : \tau_1 \vdash e_1 : \tau \rightsquigarrow e_1'}{\Gamma \vdash \mathbf{case}\ x\ \mathbf{of}\ \{x_1 \Rightarrow e_1\ ,\ x_2 \Rightarrow e_2\} : \tau \rightsquigarrow e_1'}\ \text{(RCase)}$$

$$\frac{[\![\tau]\!] = \mathbb{C}_\rho}{\Gamma \vdash e : \tau \rightsquigarrow l_\rho}\ \text{(RMod)} \qquad \frac{\Gamma \vdash e : \tau \hookrightarrow e'}{\Gamma \vdash e : \tau \rightsquigarrow e'}\ \text{(RTrans)}$$

$$\frac{\begin{array}{ll}\Gamma \vdash e_1 : \tau' \hookrightarrow e_1' & \Gamma \vdash e_2 : \tau' \hookrightarrow e_2' \\ \Gamma, x : \tau' \vdash e_2 : \tau \rightsquigarrow ret & e_2 \neq \mathbf{let}\ x' = e_1'\ \mathbf{in}\ e_2'\end{array}}{\begin{array}{l}\Gamma \vdash \mathbf{let}\ x = e_1\ \mathbf{in}\ e_2 : \tau \rightsquigarrow \mathbf{let}\ x = e_1'\ \mathbf{in} \\ \qquad\qquad\qquad\qquad\qquad \mathbf{let}\ \_ = e_2'\ \mathbf{in}\ ret\end{array}}\ \text{(RLet)}$$

Figure 14. Deriving destination return

Function and application rules. Since the self-adjusting primitives are imperative, an expression with outer changeable levels will be translated into a target expression that returns unit. To recover the type of the function return for the target language, we need to wrap the destinations, so that the function returns the correct type. Figure 14 shows the rules for translating the function body and wrapping the destinations. For a tuple expression (RPair), the translation returns the destination for each component. For a case expression (RCase), it is enough to return destinations from one of the branches since the source typing rule (SCase) guarantees that both branches will write to the same destinations. When the expression has a outer changeable level $\mathbb{C}_\rho$, rule (RMod) returns its modifiable variable l_ρ. For let bindings, rule (RLet) translates all the bindings in the usual way and derive destinations for the expressions in the tail position. For all other expressions, the translation simply switches to the ordinary translation rules in Figure 12. For example, expression $(1, x) : \left(\mathbf{int}^{\mathbb{S}} \times \mathbf{int}^{\mathbb{C}_{01}}\right)^{\mathbb{S}}$ will be translated to $(1, l_{01})$ by applying rules (RProd) (RTrans) (Int) (RMod).

When applying functions $\mathbf{apply}(x_1, x_2)$, rule (App) first creates a set of fresh modifiable destinations using **mod** , then supply both the destination set $\mathcal{L}$ and argument x_2 to function x_1. Note that although the destination names l_i may overlap with the current function destination names, these variables are only locally scoped, the application of the function will return a new value, which contains the supplied destinations $\mathcal{L}$, but they are never mentioned outside of the function application.

The translation rules are guided only by local information—the structure of types and terms. This locality is key to simplifying the algorithm and the implementation but it often generates code with redundant operations. For example, the translation rules can generate expressions like $\mathbf{read}\ x\ \mathbf{as}\ x'\ \mathbf{in}\ \mathbf{write}(l_\rho, x')$, which is equivalent to x. We can easily apply rewriting rules to get rid of these redundant operations after the translation.

Translation correctness. Given a constraint-based source typing derivation and assignment ϕ for some term e, there are translations from e to (1) a target expression e_t and (2) a destination return expression e_r, with appropriate target types:

Theorem 6.1. *If $C; \mathcal{P}; \Gamma \vdash e : \tau$, and ϕ is a satisfying assignment for C, then*

(1) there exists e_t and Γ' such that $[\phi]\Gamma \vdash e : [\phi]\tau \hookrightarrow e_t$, and $\cdot; \|\Gamma\|_\phi \vdash e_t : \|\tau\|_\phi \dashv \Gamma'$,

(2) there exists e_r and Γ' such that $[\phi]\Gamma \vdash e : [\phi]\tau \rightsquigarrow e_r$, and $\cdot; \|\Gamma\|_\phi \vdash e_r : \|\tau\|_\phi \dashv \Gamma'$.

The proof is by induction on the height of the given derivation of $C; \mathcal{P}; \Gamma \vdash e : \tau$. The proof relies on a substitution lemma for (SLet) case. We present the full proof in the appendix [14].

7. Probabilistic Chunking

Precise dependency tracking saves space by eliminating redundant dependencies. But even then, the dependency metadata required can still be large, preventing scaling to large datasets. In this section, we show how to reduce the size of dependency metadata further by controlling the granularity of dependency tracking, crucially in a way that does not affect performance disproportionately.

The basic idea is to track dependencies at the granularity of a *block* of items. This idea is straightforward to implement: simply place blocks of data into modifiables (e.g., store an array of integers as a block instead of just one number). As such, if any data in a block changes, the computation that depends on that block must be rerun. While this saves space, the key question for performance is therefore: *how to chunk data into blocks without disproportionately affecting the update time?*

For fast updates, our chunking strategy must ensure that a small change to the input remains small and local, without affecting many other blocks. The simple strategy of chunking into fixed-size blocks does not work. To see why, consider the example in Figure 15 (left half), where a list containing numbers 1 through 16, missing 2, is chunked into equal-sized blocks of 4. The trouble begins when we insert 2 into the list between 1 and 3. With fixed-size chunking, all the blocks will change because the insertion shifts the position of all block boundaries by one. As a result, when tracking dependencies

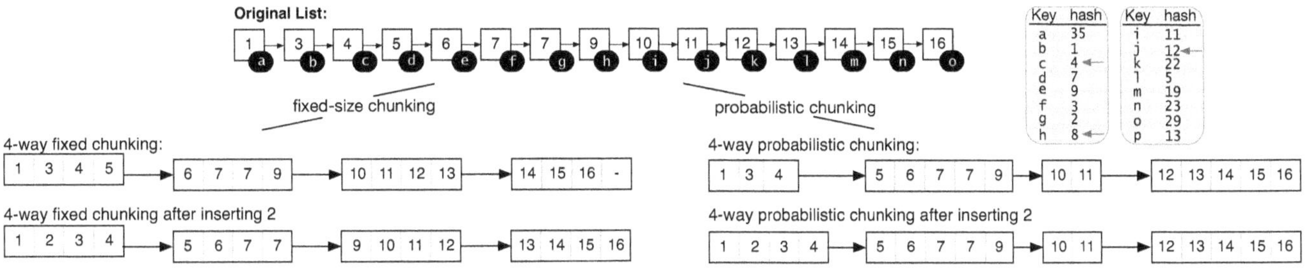

Figure 15. Fixed-size chunking versus probabilistic chunking: with block size $B = 4$. Next to each data cell in the original list (top) is a unique identifier (location). The hash values of these identifiers (used in probabilistic chunking) are shown in the table, with values divisible by $B = 4$ marked with an arrow.

at the level of blocks, we cannot reuse any prior computations and will essentially recompute the result anew.

We propose a *probabilistic chunking scheme* (PCS), which decouples locations of block boundaries from the data contents and absolute positions in the list while allowing users to control the block size probabilistically. Using randomization, we are able to prevent small (even adversarial) changes from spreading to the rest of the computation. Similar probabilistic chunking schemes have been proposed in other work but differently, they aim at discovering similarities across pieces of data (see, e.g., [43, 53] and the references therein) rather than creating independence between the data and how it is chunked as we do here.

PCS takes a target block size B and determines block boundaries by hashing the location or the unique identifier of each data item and declaring it a block boundary if the hash is divisible by B. Figure 15 (right) illustrates how this works. Consider, again, a list holding numbers from 1 to 16, missing 2, with their location identifiers (a, b, ...) shown next to them. PCS chunks this into blocks of *expected* size $B = 4$ by applying a random hash function to each item. For this example, the hash values are given in a table on the right of the figure; hash values divisible by 4 are marked with an arrow. PCS declares block boundaries where the hash value is 0 mod $B = 4$, thereby selecting 1 in 4 elements to be on the boundary. This means finishing the blocks at 4, 9, and 11, as shown.

To understand what happens when the input changes, consider inserting 2 (with location identifier p) between 1 and 3. Because the hash value of p is 13, it is not on the boundary. This is the common case as there is only a $1/B$-th probability that a random hash value is divisible by B. As a result, only the block $[\![1, 3, 4]\!]$, where 2 is added, is affected. If, however, 2 happened to be a boundary element, we would only have two new blocks (inserting 2 splits an existing block into two). Either way, the rest of the list remains unaffected, enabling computation that depended on other blocks to be reused. Deletion is symmetric.

To conclude, by chunking a dataset into size-B blocks, probabilistic chunking reduces the dependency metadata by a factor of B in expectation. Furthermore, by keeping changes small and local, probabilistic chunking ensures maximum reuse of existing computations. Change propagation works analogously to the non-block version, except that if a block changes, work on the whole block must be redone, thus often increasing the update time by B folds.

8. Evaluation

We performed extensive empirical evaluation on a range of benchmarks, including standard benchmarks from prior work, as well as new, more involved benchmarks on social network graphs. We report selected results in this section. All our experiments were performed on a 2GHz Intel Xeon with 1 TB memory running Linux. Our implementation is single-threaded and therefore uses only one core. The code was compiled with MLton version 20100608 with flags to measure maximum live memory usage.

8.1 Benchmarks and Measurements

We have completed an implementation of the target language as a Standard ML (SML) library. The implementation follows the formalism except for the following: (1) it treats both fresh and finalized modifiable types as a single $\underline{\tau}$ **mod** type; (2) for function $\mathbf{fun}^{\mathcal{L}}\ f(x) = e$, it includes destination labels as part of the function argument, so the function is represented as `fun f(x) = fn` $\mathcal{L}$ `=>` `e`. Accordingly, the arrow type $(\underline{\tau}_1 \xrightarrow[\mathcal{D}]{} \underline{\tau}_2)$ is represented as $\underline{\tau}_1 \to \underline{\tau}' \to \underline{\tau}_2$, where $\underline{\tau}' = \underline{\tau}_1' \ \mathbf{mod} \times \cdots \times \underline{\tau}_n' \ \mathbf{mod}$ and $\mathcal{D} = \{\underline{\tau}_1', \cdots, \underline{\tau}_n'\}$.

Since our approach provides for an expressive language (any pure SML program can be made self-adjusting), we can implement a variety of domain-specific languages and algorithms. For the evaluation, we implemented the following:

- a *blocked list* abstract data type that uses our probabilistic chunking algorithm (Section 7),
- a sparse matrix abstract data type,
- as implementation of the MapReduce framework [20] that uses the blocked lists,
- several list operations and the merge sort algorithm,
- more sophisticated algorithms on graphs, which use the sparse-matrix data type to represent graphs, where a row of the matrix represents a vertex in the compressed sparse row format, including only the nonzero entries.

In our graph benchmarks, we control the space-time trade-off by treating a block of 100 nonzero elements as a single changeable unit. For the graphs used, this block size is quite natural, as it corresponds roughly to the average degree of a node (the degree ranges between 20 and 200 depending on the graph).

For each benchmark, we implemented a *batch* version—an optimized implementation that operates on unchanging inputs—and a *self-adjusting* version by using techniques proposed in this paper. We compare these versions by considering a mix of synthetic and real-world data, and by considering different forms of changes ranging from small *unit changes* (e.g., insertion/deletion of one item) to *aggregate changes* consisting of many unit changes (e.g., insertion/deletion of 1000 items). We describe specific datasets employed and changes performed in the description of each experiment.

8.2 Block Lists and Sorting

Using our block list representation, we implemented batch and self-adjusting versions of several standard list primitives such as `map`, `partition`, and `reduce` as well as the merge sort algorithm `msort`. In the evaluation, all benchmarks operate on integers: `map` applies $f(i) = i \div 2$ to each element; `partition` partitions its input based on the parity of each element; `reduce` computes the sum of the list modular 100; and `msort` implements merge sort.

Table 1 reports our measurements at fixed input sizes 10^7. For each benchmark, we consider three different versions: (1) a batch version (written with the `-batch` suffix); (2) a self-adjusting version *without* the chunking scheme (the first row below batch); (3) the self-adjusting version with different block sizes ($B = 3, 10, \ldots$). We report the block size used (B); the time to run from scratch (denoted by "Run") in seconds; the average time for a change propagation after one insertion/deletion from the input list (denoted by "Prop.") in milliseconds. Note that for batch versions, the propagation time (i.e., a rerun) is the same as a complete from-scratch run. We calculate the *speedup* as the ratio of the time for a run from-scratch to average propagation, i.e., the performance improvement obtained by the self-adjusting version with respect to the batch version of the same benchmark. "Memory" column shows the maximum memory footprint. The experiments show that as the block size increases, both the self-adjusting (from-scratch) run time and memory decreases, confirming that larger blocks generate fewer dependencies. As block size increases, time for change propagation does also, but in proportion with the block size. (From $B = 3$ to $B = 10$, propagation time decreases, because the benefit for processing more elements per block exceeds the overhead for accessing the blocks).

Benchmark	B	Run (s)	Prop. (ms)	Speedup	Memory
map-batch	1	0.497	497	1	344M
map	1	11.21	0.001	497000	7G
	3	16.86	0.012	41416	10G
	10	5.726	0.009	55222	3G
	100	1.796	0.048	10354	1479M
	1000	1.370	0.635	783	1192M
	10000	1.347	9.498	52	1168M
partition-batch	1	0.557	557	1	344M
partition	1	10.42	0.015	37133	8G
	3	20.06	0.033	16878	14G
	10	6.736	0.028	19892	3G
	100	1.920	0.049	11367	1508M
	1000	1.420	0.823	677	1159M
	10000	1.417	11.71	47	1124M
reduce-batch	1	0.330	330	1	344M
reduce	1	9.529	0.064	5156	5G
	3	13.39	0.129	2558	6G
	10	4.230	0.085	3882	1317M
	100	0.990	0.083	3976	592M
	1000	0.627	0.075	4400	420M
	10000	0.593	0.244	1352	327M
msort-batch	1	12.82	12820	1	1.3G
msort	1	676.4	0.956	13410	121G
	3	725.0	1.479	8668	157G
	10	204.4	1.012	12668	44G
	100	52.00	3.033	4227	10G
	1000	43.80	22.36	573	9G
	10000	35.35	119.7	107	8G

Table 1. Blocked lists and sorting: time and space with varying block sizes on fixed input sizes of 10^7.

In terms of memory usage, the version *without* block lists ($B = 1$) requires 15–100x more memory than the batch version. Block lists significantly reduce the memory footprint. For example, with block size B = 100, the benchmarks require at most 7x more memory than the batch version, while still providing 4000–10000x speedup. In our experiments, we confirm that probabilistic chunking (Section 7) is essential for performance—when using fixed-size chunking, merge sort does not yield noticeable improvements.

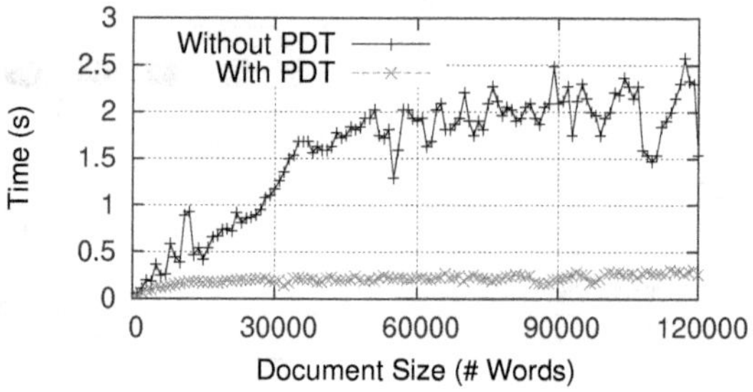

Figure 16. Run time (seconds) of incremental word count.

Benchmark	Source	Input Size	Prop. (s)	Speedup	Memory
PR-Batch	Orkut	3×10^6 vertices	7	1	3G
PageRank		1×10^8 edges	0.021	333	36G
PR-Batch	LiveJournal-1	4×10^6 vertices	18	1	5G
PageRank		3×10^7 edges	0.023	783	61G
PR-Batch	Twitter-1	3×10^7 vertices	137	1	50G
PageRank		7×10^8 edges	0.254	539	495G
Conn-Batch	LiveJournal-2	1×10^6 vertices	105	1	4G
Connectivity		8×10^6 edges	0.531	198	140G
SC-Batch	Twitter-2	1×10^5 vertices	8	1	2G
Social Circle		2×10^6 edges	0.079	101	34G

Table 2. Incremental sparse graphs: time and space.

8.3 Word Count

A standard microbenchmark for big-data applications is word count, which maintains the frequency of each word in a document. Using our MapReduce library (run with block size 1,000), we implemented a batch version and a self-adjusting version of this benchmark, which can update the frequencies as the document changes over time.

We use this benchmark to illustrate, in isolation, the impact of our precise dependency tracking mechanism. To this end, we implemented two versions of word count: one using prior art [16] (which contains redundant dependencies) and the other using the techniques presented in this paper. We use a publicly available Wikipedia dataset[1] and simulate evolution of the document by dividing it into blocks and incrementally adding these blocks to the existing text; the whole text has about 120,000 words.

Figure 16 shows the time to insert 1,000 words at a time into the existing corpus, where the horizontal axis shows the corpus size at the time of insertion. Note that the two curves differ only in whether the new precise dependency tracking is used. Overall, both incremental versions appear to have a logarithmic trend because in this case, both the shuffle and reduce phases require $\Theta(\log n)$ time for a single-entry update, where n is the number of input words. Importantly, with precise dependency tracking (PDT), the update time is around 6x faster than without. In terms of memory consumption, PDT is 2.4x more space efficient. Compared to a batch run, PDT is ~ 100x faster for a corpus of size 100K words or larger (since we change 1000 words/update, this is essentially optimal).

8.4 PageRank: Two Implementations

Another important big data benchmark is the PageRank algorithm, which computes the page rank of a vertex (site) in a graph (network). This algorithm can be implemented in several ways. For example, a domain specific language such as MapReduce can be (and often is) used even though it is known that for this algorithm, the shuffle step required by MapReduce is not needed. We implemented the

[1] Wikipedia dataset: `http://wiki.dbpedia.org/`

PageRank algorithm in two ways: once using our MapReduce library and once using a direct implementation, which takes advantage of the expressive power of our framework. Both implementations use the same block size of 100 for the underlying block-list data type. The second implementation is an iterative algorithm, which performs sparse matrix-vector multiplication at each step, until convergence.

In both implementations, we use floating-point numbers to represent PageRank values. Due to the imprecision in equality check for floating point numbers, we set three parameters to control the precision of our computation: 1) the iteration convergence threshold $\mathtt{con}_\varepsilon$; 2) the equality threshold for page rank values $\mathtt{eq}_\varepsilon$, i.e. if a page rank value does not change for more than $\mathtt{eq}_\varepsilon$, we will not recompute the value; 3) the equality threshold for verifying the correctness of the result $\mathtt{verify}_\varepsilon$. For all our experiments, we set $\mathtt{con}_\varepsilon = 1 \times 10^{-6}$, and $\mathtt{eq}_\varepsilon = 1 \times 10^{-8}$. For each change, we also perform a batch run to ensure the correctness of the result. All our experiments guarantee that $\mathtt{verify}_\varepsilon \le 1 \times 10^{-5}$.

Our experiments with PageRank show that MapReduce based implementation does not scale for incremental computation, because it requires massive amounts of memory, consuming 80GB of memory even for a small downsampled Twitter graph with 3×10^3 vertices and 10^4 edges. After careful profiling, we found that this is due to the shuffle step performed by MapReduce, which is not needed for the PageRank algorithm. This is an example where a domain-specific approach such as MapReduce is too restrictive for an efficient implementation.

Our second implementation, which uses the expressive power of functional programming, performs well. Compared to the MapReduce-based version, it requires 0.88GB memory on the same graph, nearly 100-fold less, and the update time is 50x faster on average.[2] We are thus able to use the second implementation on relatively large graphs. Table 2 shows a summary of our findings. For these experiments, we divide the edges into groups of 1,000 edges starting with the first vertex and consider each of them in turn: for each group, we measure the time to complete the following steps: 1) delete all the edges from the group, 2) update the result, 3) reintroduce the edges, and 4) update the result. Since the average degree per vertex is approximately 100, each aggregate change affects approximately 10 vertices, which can then propagate to other vertices. (Since the vertices are ordered arbitrarily, this aggregate change can be viewed as inserting/deleting 10 arbitrarily chosen vertices).

Our PageRank implementation delivers significant speedups at the cost of approximately 10x more memory with different graphs including the datasets Orkut[3], LiveJournal[4] and Twitter graph[5]. For example on the Twitter datasets (labeled Twitter-1) with 30M vertices and 700M edges, our PageRank implementation reaches an average speedup of more than 500x compared to the batch version, at the cost of 10x more memory. Detailed measurements for the first 100 groups, as shown in Figure 17(left), show that for most trials, speedups usually approximate 4 orders of magnitude.

8.5 Incremental graph connectivity

Connectivity, which indicates the existence of a path between two vertices, is a central graph problem with many applications. Our incremental graph connectivity benchmark computes a label $\ell(v) \in \mathbb{Z}_+$ for every node v of an undirected graph such that two nodes u and v have the same label (i.e. $\ell(u) = \ell(v)$) if and only if u and v are connected. We use a randomized version of Kang et al.'s algorithm [36] that starts with random initial labels for improved incremental efficiency. The algorithm is iterative; in each iteration the label of each vertex is replaced with the minimum of its labels and those of its neighbors. We evaluate the efficiency of the algorithm under dynamic changes by for each vertex, deleting that vertex, updating the result, and reintroducing the vertex. We test the benchmark on an undirected graph from LiveJournal with 1M nodes and 8M edges. Our findings for 100 randomly selected vertices are shown in Figure 17(center); cumulative (average) measurements are shown in 2. Since deleting a vertex can cause widespread changes in connectivity, affecting many vertices, we expect this benchmark to be significantly more expensive than PageRank. Indeed, each change is more expensive than in PageRank but we still obtain speedups of as much as 200x.

8.6 Incremental social circles

An important quantity in social networks is the size of the circle of influence of a member of the network. Using advances in streaming algorithms, our final benchmark estimates for each vertex v, the number of vertices reachable from v within 2 hops (i.e., how many friends and friends of friends a person has). Our implementation is similar to Kang et al.'s [35], which maintains for each node 10 Flajolet-Martin sketches (each a 32-bit word). The technique can be naturally extended to compute the number of nodes reachable from a starting point within k hops ($k > 2$). To evaluate this benchmark, we use a down-sampled Twitter graph (Twitter-2) with 100K nodes and 2M edges. The experiment divides the edges into groups of 20 edges and considers each of these groups in turn: for each group, we measure the time to complete the following steps: delete the edges from the group, update social-circle sizes, reintroduce the edges, and update the social-circle sizes. The findings for 100 groups are shown in Figure 17(right); cumulative (average) measurements are shown in 2 in the last row. Our incremental version is approximately 100x faster than batch for most trials.

9. Related Work

Incremental computation techniques have been extensively studied in several areas of computer science. Much of this research focuses on time efficiency rather than space efficiency. In addition, there is relatively little (if any) work on providing control over the space-time tradeoff fundamental to essentially any incremental-computation technique. We discussed closely related work in the introduction (Section 1). In this section, we present a brief overview of some of the more remotely related work.

Algorithmic Solutions. Research in the algorithms community focuses primarily on devising *dynamic algorithms* or *dynamic data structures* for individual problems. There have been hundreds of papers with several excellent surveys reviewing the work (e.g., [23, 47]. Dynamic algorithms enable computing a desired property while allowing modifications to the input (e.g., inserting/deleting elements). These algorithms are often carefully designed to exploit problem-specific structures and are therefore highly efficient. But they can be quite complex and difficult to design, analyze, and implement even for problems that are simple in the batch model where no changes to data are allowed. While dynamic algorithms can, in principle, be used with large datasets, space consumption is a major problem [22]. Bader et al. [48] present techniques for implementing certain dynamic graphs algorithms for large graphs.

Language-Based Approaches. Motivated by the difficulty in designing and implementing ad hoc dynamic algorithms, the programming languages community works on developing general-purpose, language-based solutions to incremental computation. This research has lead to the development of many approaches [21, 27, 46, 47],

[2] This performance gap increases with the input size, so this is quite a conservative number.

[3] Orkut dataset: `http://snap.stanford.edu/data/com-Orkut.html`

[4] LiveJournal dataset: `http://snap.stanford.edu/data/com-LiveJournal.html`

[5] Twitter dataset:`http://an.kaist.ac.kr/traces/WWW2010.html`

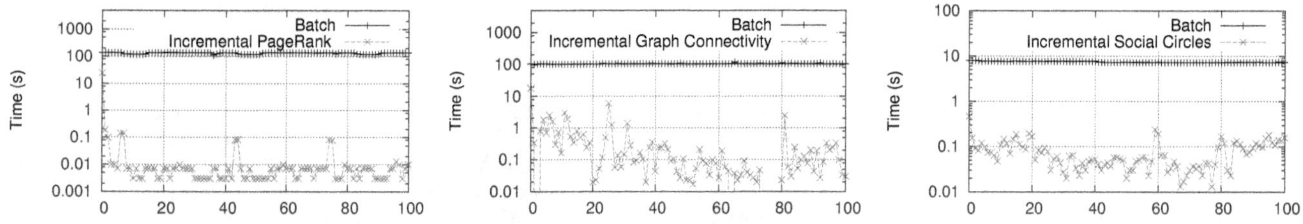

Figure 17. (left) PageRank: 100 trials (x-axis) of deleting 1,000 edges; (center) Connectivity: 100 trials of deleting a vertex; (right) Approximate social-circle size: 100 trials of deleting 20 edges. *Note: y-axis is in log-scale.*

including static dependency graphs [21], memoization [46], and partial evaluation [27]. Recent advances on self-adjusting computation [1, 6] builds on this prior work to offer techniques for efficient incremental computation expressed in a general-purpose purely functional and imperative languages. Variants of self-adjusting computation has been implemented in SML [1], Haskell [12], C [30], and OCaml [31]. The techniques have been applied to a number of problems in a relatively diverse set of domains including motion simulation [2, 5], dynamic computational geometry [7, 8], and machine learning [3, 51].

In more recent work, researchers proposed improvements on the power of underlying self-adjusting computation techniques. Hammer et al proposed techniques for demand-driven self-adjusting computation, where updates may be delayed until they are demanded [31]. Another line of research realized an interesting duality between incremental and parallel computation—both benefit from identifying independent computations—and proposed techniques for parallel self-adjusting computation. Some earlier work considered techniques for performing efficient parallel updates in the context of a lambda calculus extended with fork-join style parallelism [29]. Follow-up work considered the technique in the context of a more sophisticated problem showing both theoretical and empirical results of its effectiveness [7]. Burckhardt et al consider a more powerful language based on concurrent-revisions, provide techniques for parallel change propagation for programs written in this language, and perform an experimental evaluation. Their evaluation shows relatively broad effectiveness in a challenging set of benchmarks [11].

Systems. There are several systems for big data computations such as MapReduce [20], Dryad [32], Pregel [40], GraphLab [39], and Dremel [41]. While these systems allow for computing with large datasets, they are primarily aimed at supporting the batch model of computation, where data does not change, and consider domain-specific languages such as flat data-parallel algorithms and certain graph algorithms.

Data flow systems like MapReduce and Dryad have been extended with support for incremental computation. MapReduce Online [18] can react efficiently to additional input records. Nectar [28] caches the intermediate results of DryadLINQ programs and generates programs that can re-use results from this cache. Prior work on Incoop applies the principles of self-adjusting computation to the big data setting but only in the context of MapReduce, a domain-specific language, by extending Hadoop to operate on dynamic datasets [10]. In addition, Incoop supports an asymptotically suboptimal change-propagation algorithm. Naiad [42] enables incremental computation on dynamic datasets in programs written with a specific set of data-flow primitives. In Naiad, dynamic updates cannot alter the dependency structure of the computation. Naiad is thus closely related to earlier work on incremental computation with static dependency graphs [21, 56]. Percolator [45] is Google's proprietary system that enables a more general programming model but requires programming in an event-based model with call-backs (notifications), a very low level of abstraction. While domain specific, these systems can all run in parallel and on multiple machines. The work that we presented here assumes sequential computation.

Functional Reactive Programming. More remotely related work includes functional reactive programming. Elliott and Hudak [26] introduced functional reactive programming (FRP) to provide primitives for operating on time-varying values. While greatly expressive, Elliott and Hudak's proposal turned out to be difficult to implement safely and efficiently, leading to much follow-up work on refinements such as real-time FRP [54], event-driven FRP [55], arrowized FRP [38], which restrict the set of acceptable FRP programs by using syntax and types to make possible efficient implementation. More recent approaches to FRP based on temporal logics include those of Sculthorpe and Nilsson [49], Jeffrey [33], Jeltsch [34], and Krishnaswami [37].

Much of the work on FRP can be viewed as a generalization of synchronous dataflow languages [9, 13] to handle richer computations where the dataflow graph can accept certain changes between steps. One limitation of the synchronous approach to reactive programming is that one step cannot be started before the previous one finishes. This leads to a range of other practical difficulties, such as the choice of the right frequency (or step size) for updates [19, 50]. Czaplicki and Chong propose techniques for asynchronous execution that allow certain computations to span multiple time steps [19].

While it appears likely that FRP programs would benefit from the efficiency improvements of incremental updates, much of the aforementioned work does not provide support for incremental updates. One exception is the recent work of Demetrescu et al, which provides the programmer with techniques for writing incremental update functions in (imperative) reactive programs [24]. Another exception is Donham's Froc [25], which provides support for FRP based on a data-driven implementation using self-adjusting computation.

10. Conclusion

We present techniques for improving the scalability of automatic incrementalization techniques based on self-adjusting computation. These techniques enable expressing big-data applications in a functional language and rely on 1) an information-flow type systems and translation algorithm for tracking dependencies precisely, and 2) a probabilistic chunking technique for controlling the fundamental space-time trade-off that self-adjusting computation offers. Our results are encouraging, leading to important improvements over prior work, and delivering significant speedups over batch computation at the cost of moderate space overheads. Our results also show that functional programming can be significantly more effective than domain-specific languages such as MapReduce. In future work, we plan to parallelize these techniques, which would enable scaling to larger problems that require multiple computers. Parallelization seems fundamentally feasible because functional programming is inherently compatible with parallel computing.

Acknowledgements

This research is partially supported by the National Science Foundation under grant number CCF-1320563 and by the European Research Council under grant number ERC-2012-StG-308246.

References

[1] U. A. Acar, G. E. Blelloch, and R. Harper. Adaptive functional programming. *ACM Trans. Prog. Lang. Sys.*, 28(6):990–1034, 2006.

[2] U. A. Acar, G. E. Blelloch, K. Tangwongsan, and J. L. Vittes. Kinetic algorithms via self-adjusting computation. In *Proceedings of the 14th Annual European Symposium on Algorithms*, pages 636–647, Sept. 2006.

[3] U. A. Acar, A. Ihler, R. Mettu, and O. Sümer. Adaptive Bayesian inference. In *Neural Information Processing Systems (NIPS)*, 2007.

[4] U. A. Acar, A. Ahmed, and M. Blume. Imperative self-adjusting computation. In *Proceedings of the 25th Annual ACM Symposium on Principles of Programming Languages*, 2008.

[5] U. A. Acar, G. E. Blelloch, K. Tangwongsan, and D. Türkoğlu. Robust kinetic convex hulls in 3D. In *Proceedings of the 16th Annual European Symposium on Algorithms*, Sept. 2008.

[6] U. A. Acar, G. E. Blelloch, M. Blume, R. Harper, and K. Tangwongsan. An experimental analysis of self-adjusting computation. *ACM Trans. Prog. Lang. Sys.*, 32(1):3:1–53, 2009.

[7] U. A. Acar, A. Cotter, B. Hudson, and D. Türkoğlu. Parallelism in dynamic well-spaced point sets. In *Proceedings of the 23rd ACM Symposium on Parallelism in Algorithms and Architectures*, 2011.

[8] U. A. Acar, A. Cotter, B. Hudson, and D. Türkoğlu. Dynamic well-spaced point sets. *Journal of Computational Geometry: Theory and Applications*, 2013.

[9] G. Berry and G. Gonthier. The esterel synchronous programming language: design, semantics, implementation. *Sci. Comput. Program.*, 19(2):87–152, Nov. 1992. ISSN 0167-6423.

[10] P. Bhatotia, A. Wieder, R. Rodrigues, U. A. Acar, and R. Pasquini. Incoop: MapReduce for incremental computations. In *ACM Symposium on Cloud Computing*, 2011.

[11] S. Burckhardt, D. Leijen, C. Sadowski, J. Yi, and T. Ball. Two for the price of one: A model for parallel and incremental computation. In *ACM SIGPLAN Conference on Object-Oriented Programming, Systems, Languages, and Applications*, 2011.

[12] M. Carlsson. Monads for incremental computing. In *International Conference on Functional Programming*, pages 26–35, 2002.

[13] P. Caspi, D. Pilaud, N. Halbwachs, and J. A. Plaice. Lustre: a declarative language for real-time programming. In *Proceedings of the 14th ACM SIGACT-SIGPLAN symposium on Principles of programming languages*, POPL '87, pages 178–188, 1987. ISBN 0-89791-215-2.

[14] Y. Chen, U. A. Acar, and K. Tangwongsan. Appendix to functional programming for dynamic and large data with self-adjusting computation. URL `http://www.mpi-sws.org/~chenyan/papers/icfp14-appendix.pdf`.

[15] Y. Chen, J. Dunfield, M. A. Hammer, and U. A. Acar. Implicit self-adjusting computation for purely functional programs. In *Int'l Conference on Functional Programming (ICFP '11)*, pages 129–141, Sept. 2011.

[16] Y. Chen, J. Dunfield, and U. A. Acar. Type-directed automatic incrementalization. In *ACM SIGPLAN Conference on Programming Language Design and Implementation (PLDI)*, Jun 2012.

[17] Y. Chen, J. Dunfield, M. A. Hammer, and U. A. Acar. Implicit self-adjusting computation for purely functional programs. *Journal of Functional Programming*, 24:56–112, 1 2014. ISSN 1469-7653.

[18] T. Condie, N. Conway, P. Alvaro, J. M. Hellerstein, K. Elmeleegy, and R. Sears. Mapreduce online. In *Proc. 7th Symposium on Networked systems design and implementation (NSDI'10)*.

[19] E. Czaplicki and S. Chong. Asynchronous functional reactive programming for guis. In *Proceedings of the 34th ACM SIGPLAN conference on Programming language design and implementation*, PLDI '13, pages 411–422, 2013. ISBN 978-1-4503-2014-6.

[20] J. Dean and S. Ghemawat. MapReduce: simplified data processing on large clusters. *Communications of the ACM*, 51(1):107–113, 2008.

[21] A. Demers, T. Reps, and T. Teitelbaum. Incremental evaluation of attribute grammars with application to syntax-directed editors. In *Principles of Programming Languages*, pages 105–116, 1981.

[22] C. Demetrescu, S. Emiliozzi, and G. F. Italiano. Experimental analysis of dynamic all pairs shortest path algorithms. In *ACM-SIAM Symposium on Discrete Algorithms (SODA)*, pages 369–378, 2004.

[23] C. Demetrescu, I. Finocchi, and G. Italiano. *Handbook on Data Structures and Applications*, chapter 36: Dynamic Graphs. CRC Press, 2005.

[24] C. Demetrescu, I. Finocchi, and A. Ribichini. Reactive imperative programming with dataflow constraints. In *Proceedings of ACM SIGPLAN Conference on Object-Oriented Programming, Systems, Languages, and Applications (OOPSLA)*, 2011.

[25] J. Donham. Froc: a library for functional reactive programming in ocaml, 2010. URL `http://jaked.github.com/froc`.

[26] C. Elliott and P. Hudak. Functional reactive animation. In *Proceedings of the second ACM SIGPLAN International Conference on Functional Programming*, pages 263–273. ACM, 1997.

[27] J. Field and T. Teitelbaum. Incremental reduction in the lambda calculus. In *ACM Conference on LISP and Functional Programming*, pages 307–322, 1990.

[28] P. K. Gunda, L. Ravindranath, C. A. Thekkath, Y. Yu, and L. Zhuang. Nectar: Automatic management of data and computation in data centers. In *OSDI'10*.

[29] M. Hammer, U. A. Acar, M. Rajagopalan, and A. Ghuloum. A proposal for parallel self-adjusting computation. In *DAMP '07: Declarative Aspects of Multicore Programming*, 2007.

[30] M. A. Hammer, U. A. Acar, and Y. Chen. CEAL: a C-based language for self-adjusting computation. In *ACM SIGPLAN Conference on Programming Language Design and Implementation*, 2009.

[31] M. A. Hammer, K. Y. Phang, M. Hicks, and J. S. Foster. Adapton: Composable, demand-driven incremental computation. In *Proceedings of the 35th ACM SIGPLAN Conference on Programming Language Design and Implementation*, PLDI '14, pages 156–166, 2014. ISBN 978-1-4503-2784-8.

[32] M. Isard, M. Budiu, Y. Yu, A. Birrell, and D. Fetterly. Dryad: distributed data-parallel programs from sequential building blocks. *SIGOPS Oper. Syst. Rev.*, 41(3):59–72, Mar. 2007. ISSN 0163-5980.

[33] A. Jeffrey. LTL types FRP: linear-time temporal logic propositions as types, proofs as functional reactive programs. In *PLPV '12: Proceedings of the sixth workshop on Programming languages meets program verification*, pages 49–60, 2012. ISBN 978-1-4503-1125-0.

[34] W. Jeltsch. Temporal logic with "until", functional reactive programming with processes, and concrete process categories. In *Proceedings of the 7th Workshop on Programming Languages Meets Program Verification*, PLPV '13, pages 69–78, 2013. ISBN 978-1-4503-1860-0.

[35] U. Kang, C. E. Tsourakakis, A. P. Appel, C. Faloutsos, and J. Leskovec. Hadi: Mining radii of large graphs. *TKDD*, 5(2):8, 2011.

[36] U. Kang, C. E. Tsourakakis, and C. Faloutsos. Pegasus: mining peta-scale graphs. *Knowl. Inf. Syst.*, 27(2):303–325, 2011.

[37] N. R. Krishnaswami. Higher-order functional reactive programming without spacetime leaks. *SIGPLAN Not.*, 48(9):221–232, Sept. 2013. ISSN 0362-1340.

[38] H. Liu, E. Cheng, and P. Hudak. Causal commutative arrows and their optimization. In *Proceedings of the 14th ACM SIGPLAN international conference on Functional programming*, ICFP '09, pages 35–46, 2009. ISBN 978-1-60558-332-7.

[39] Y. Low, D. Bickson, J. Gonzalez, C. Guestrin, A. Kyrola, and J. M. Hellerstein. Distributed GraphLab: a framework for machine learning and data mining in the cloud. *VLDB Endow.*, 5(8):716–727, Apr. 2012.

[40] G. Malewicz, M. H. Austern, A. J. Bik, J. C. Dehnert, I. Horn, N. Leiser, and G. Czajkowski. Pregel: a system for large-scale graph processing. In *Proceedings of the 2010 ACM SIGMOD International Conference on Management of data*, SIGMOD '10, pages 135–146, 2010.

[41] S. Melnik, A. Gubarev, J. J. Long, G. Romer, S. Shivakumar, M. Tolton, and T. Vassilakis. Dremel: interactive analysis of web-scale datasets. *Commun. ACM*, 54(6):114–123, June 2011. ISSN 0001-0782.

[42] D. G. Murray, F. McSherry, R. Isaacs, M. Isard, P. Barham, and M. Abadi. Naiad: A timely dataflow system. In *Proc. of SOSP*, pages 439–455, 2013.

[43] A. Muthitacharoen, B. Chen, and D. Mazières. A low-bandwidth network file system. In *SOSP*, pages 174–187, 2001.

[44] M. Odersky, M. Sulzmann, and M. Wehr. Type inference with constrained types. *Theory and Practice of Object Systems*, 5(1):35–55, 1999.

[45] D. Peng and F. Dabek. Large-scale incremental processing using distributed transactions and notifications. In *Proc. 9th Symposium on Operating Systems Design and Implementation (OSDI'10)*, 2010.

[46] W. Pugh and T. Teitelbaum. Incremental computation via function caching. In *Principles of Programming Languages*, pages 315–328, 1989.

[47] G. Ramalingam and T. Reps. A categorized bibliography on incremental computation. In *Principles of Programming Languages*, pages 502–510, 1993.

[48] E. J. Riedy, H. Meyerhenke, D. A. Bader, D. Ediger, and T. G. Mattson. Analysis of streaming social networks and graphs on multicore architectures. In *ICASSP*, pages 5337–5340, 2012.

[49] N. Sculthorpe and H. Nilsson. Keeping calm in the face of change. *Higher Order Symbol. Comput.*, 23(2):227–271, June 2010. ISSN 1388-3690.

[50] N. Sculthorpe and H. Nilsson. Safe functional reactive programming through dependent types. *SIGPLAN Not.*, 44(9):23–34, Aug. 2009. ISSN 0362-1340.

[51] O. Sümer, U. A. Acar, A. Ihler, and R. Mettu. Adaptive exact inference in graphical models. *Journal of Machine Learning*, 8:180–186, 2011.

[52] J.-P. Talpin and P. Jouvelot. The type and effect discipline. *Inf. Comput.*, 111(2):245–296, June 1994. ISSN 0890-5401.

[53] K. Tangwongsan, H. Pucha, D. G. Andersen, and M. Kaminsky. Efficient similarity estimation for systems exploiting data redundancy. In *INFOCOM*, pages 1487–1495, 2010.

[54] Z. Wan, W. Taha, and P. Hudak. Real-time FRP. *SIGPLAN Not.*, 36 (10):146–156, 2001.

[55] Z. Wan, W. Taha, and P. Hudak. Event-driven FRP. In *Proceedings of the 4th International Symposium on Practical Aspects of Declarative Languages*, PADL '02, pages 155–172, 2002.

[56] D. M. Yellin and R. E. Strom. INC: a language for incremental computations. *ACM Transactions on Programming Languages and Systems*, 13(2):211–236, Apr. 1991.

Depending on Types

Stephanie Weirich
University of Pennsylvania
Philadelphia, PA, USA
sweirich@cis.upenn.edu

Abstract

Is Haskell a dependently typed programming language? Should it be? GHC's many type-system features, such as Generalized Algebraic Datatypes (GADTs), datatype promotion, multiparameter type classes, and type families, give programmers the ability to encode domain-specific invariants in their types. Clever Haskell programmers have used these features to enhance the reasoning capabilities of static type checking. But really, how far have we come? Could we do more?

In this talk, I will discuss dependently typed programming in Haskell, through examples, analysis and comparisons with modern full-spectrum dependently typed languages, such as Coq, Agda and Idris. What sorts of dependently typed programming can be done in Haskell now? What could GHC learn from these languages? Conversely, what lessons can GHC offer in return?

This material is based upon work supported by the National Science Foundation under grants CCF-1116620 and CCF-1319880.

ACM Classification: F.3.3 Studies of Program Constructs (Type Systems) ; D.1.1 Applicative (Functional) Programming

Author Keywords: Dependent types; Haskell

Bio

Stephanie Weirich is an Associate Professor at the University of Pennsylvania. Her research centers on programming languages, type theory and machine-assisted reasoning. In particular, she studies generic programming, metaprogramming, dependent type systems, and type inference in the context of functional programming languages. She is currently an Editor of the Journal of Functional Programming and served as the program chair for ICFP in 2010 and the Haskell Symposium in 2009.

ICFP14, September 1–6, 2014, Gothenburg, Sweden.
ACM 978-1-4503-2873-9/14/09.
http://dx.doi.org/10.1145/2628136.2631168

Homotopical Patch Theory

Carlo Angiuli *
Carnegie Mellon University
cangiuli@cs.cmu.edu

Edward Morehouse *
Carnegie Mellon University
edmo@cs.cmu.edu

Daniel R. Licata
Wesleyan University
dlicata@wesleyan.edu

Robert Harper *
Carnegie Mellon University
rwh@cs.cmu.edu

Abstract

Homotopy type theory is an extension of Martin-Löf type theory, based on a correspondence with homotopy theory and higher category theory. In homotopy type theory, the propositional equality type becomes proof-relevant, and corresponds to paths in a space. This allows for a new class of datatypes, called higher inductive types, which are specified by constructors not only for points but also for paths. In this paper, we consider a programming application of higher inductive types. Version control systems such as Darcs are based on the notion of patches—syntactic representations of edits to a repository. We show how patch theory can be developed in homotopy type theory. Our formulation separates formal theories of patches from their interpretation as edits to repositories. A patch theory is presented as a higher inductive type. Models of a patch theory are given by maps out of that type, which, being functors, automatically preserve the structure of patches. Several standard tools of homotopy theory come into play, demonstrating the use of these methods in a practical programming context.

Categories and Subject Descriptors F.3.3 [*Logics and Meanings of Programs*]: Studies of Program Constructs—Type Structure

General Terms Languages, Theory

1. Introduction

Martin-Löf's intensional type theory (MLTT) is the basis of proof assistants such as Agda [29] and Coq [9]. Homotopy type theory is an extension of MLTT based on a correspondence with homotopy theory and higher category theory [4, 11, 13, 14, 24, 36–38]. In homotopy theory, one studies topological spaces by way of their points, paths (between points), homotopies (paths or continuous deformations between paths), homotopies between homotopies (paths between paths between paths), and so on. In type theory, a space corresponds to a type A. Points of a space correspond to elements $a, b : A$. Paths in a space are represented by elements of the identity type (propositional equality), which we notate $p : a =_A b$. Homotopies between paths p and q correspond to elements of the iterated identity type $p =_{a=_A b} q$. The rules for the identity type allow one to define the operations on paths that are considered in homotopy theory. These include identity paths $\mathsf{refl} : a = a$ (reflexivity of equality), inverse paths $!\,p : b = a$ when $p : a = b$ (symmetry of equality), and composition of paths $q \circ p : a = c$ when $p : a = b$ and $q : b = c$ (transitivity of equality), as well as homotopies relating these operations (for example, $\mathsf{refl} \circ p = p$), and homotopies relating those homotopies, etc. This correspondence has suggested several extensions to type theory. One is Voevodsky's *univalence axiom* [17, 37], which describes the path structure of the universe (the type of small types). Another is *higher inductive types* [25, 26, 32], a new class of datatypes specified by constructors not only for points but also for paths. Higher inductive types were originally introduced to permit basic topological spaces such as circles and spheres to be defined in type theory, and have had significant applications in a line of work on using homotopy type theory to give computer-checked proofs in homotopy theory [19, 20, 23, 35].

The computational interpretation of homotopy type theory as a programming language is a subject of active research, though some special cases have been solved, and work in progress is promising [5, 6, 22, 33]. The main lesson of this work is that, in homotopy type theory, proofs of equality have computational content, and can influence how a program runs. This suggests investigating whether there are programming applications of computationally relevant equality proofs. Some preliminary applications have been investigated. For example, Licata and Harper [21] apply ideas related to homotopy type theory to modeling variable binding. Altenkirch [2] shows that containers [1] in homotopy type theory can be used to represent more data structures than in MLTT, such as sets and bags. However, at present, the programming side is less well-developed than the mathematical applications.

In this paper, we present an example of using higher inductive types in programming. The example we consider is *patch theory* [7, 10, 15, 16, 28, 31], inspired by the version control system Darcs [31]. Intuitively, a patch is a syntactic representation of a function that changes a repository. A patch ("delete file f") applies in certain repository contexts (where the file f exists), and results in another repository context (where the file f no longer exists)—so the contexts act as types for patches. Patches are closed under

* This research was sponsored in part by the National Science Foundation under grant number CCF-1116703. The views and conclusions contained in this document are those of the author and should not be interpreted as representing the official policies, either expressed or implied, of any sponsoring institution, the U.S. government or any other entity.

ICFP '14, September 1–6, 2014, Gothenburg, Sweden.

ACM 978-1-4503-2873-9/14/09...$15.00.
http://dx.doi.org/10.1145/2628136.2628158

identity (a no-op), composition (sequencing), and perhaps inverses (undo) — which is present in some formulations of patch theory but not others. These satisfy certain general laws—composition is associative; inverses cancel. Moreover, there are domain-specific patch laws about the basic patches ("the order of edits to independent lines of a file can be swapped"). The *semantics* of a patch explains how to apply it to change a repository. Several syntactic transformations on patches are considered, such as merging, which reconciles divergent edits to a repository, and cherry-picking, which selects a subset of changes to merge. The semantics and syntactic transformations are required to satisfy certain laws, such as the fact that applying a composition of patches has the same effect as the composition of applying the patches (facilitating optimization), and that merging is a symmetric operation, so that independently computed merges agree (facilitating collaboration).

Building on this work, we develop patch theory in the context of homotopy type theory, using paths to represent aspects of patch theory. Specifically, we represent *patches as paths* — making use of the proof-relevant notion of equality in homotopy type theory — and we represent the laws that patches and transformations must satisfy as paths-between-paths. We make an explicit distinction between patch theories[1] and models. A patch theory is presented by a higher inductive type, where the points of the type are repository contexts, the paths in the type are patches, and the paths between paths are patch laws. This presentation of a patch theory consists of only the basic patches ("add / remove files") and laws about them. Identity, inverse, and composition operations are provided by the higher inductive type, and automatically satisfy the desired laws.

Models of a patch theory are represented as functions from the higher inductive type representing it. Because functions in homotopy type theory are always functorial, such models are a *functorial semantics* in the sense of Lawvere [18]. These models depend crucially on the proof-relevance of paths, assigning proofs of equalities a computational meaning as functions acting on repositories. Functoriality implies that a model must respect identity, inverses, and composition (e.g. sending composition of patches to composition of functions) and validate the patch laws. So a patch theory is a formal object, a particular higher inductive type, and the theory is realized by a formal object, a mapping into another type. One syntactic theory of patches can have many different models, e.g. ones that maintain different metadata. Syntactic transformations on patches, such as patch optimization or merging, can be implemented as functions on paths. Some of these operations can be defined directly in a functorial way, whereas others require developing a derived recursion principle for patches.

Our work shows what standard homotopy-theoretic tools mean in a practical programming setting. For example, our first example of a patch theory is actually the circle. Defining the semantics of patch theories uses a programming technique derived from homotopy-theoretic examples. The derived recursion principle for patches is analogous to calculations of homotopy groups in homotopy theory. We hope that this paper will make higher inductive types more accessible to the functional programming community, so that programmers can begin to consider applications of them.

Homotopy type theory is still under development, and one of our goals in this paper is to provide a worked example that can motivate future work on it. First, we use an informal concrete syntax for higher inductive types and pattern-matching functions on them; this is similar to the informal type theory used in the Homotopy Type Theory book [35], but with a more programming-oriented notation. Our development using this syntax could be translated to Agda or Coq, using techniques to simulate higher inductives, but we have not yet implemented the examples in this paper in a proof assistant. Second, because a full interpretation of homotopy type theory as a programming language is work in progress, we do not have a formal operational semantics that we can use to run the programs in this paper. However, we will speculate on how we expect these specific programs to run, based on existing work on this topic [5, 6, 22, 33]. One interesting issue that arises is that several of the examples in the paper are functions into contractible types, which are types with exactly one inhabitant up to homotopy. Thus, up to paths/propositional equality, such a function can return any element of the type. However, based on existing work on the computational interpretation, we expect that the functions we define will in fact compute the elements we intend them to, illustrating how computation is finer than paths.

In Section 2, we provide a brief introduction to homotopy type theory and higher inductive types. In Section 3, we review patch theory, and describe our approach to representing it in homotopy type theory. In Sections 4, 5, and 6, we discuss three successively more complex patch languages.

2. Basics of Homotopy Type Theory

We review some basic definitions; see [35] for more details.

2.1 Paths

In type theory, there are two notions of equality. *Definitional equality* is a proof-irrelevant judgement relating two terms. It is a congruence containing operational steps like β-reduction (`(`λ `x.e) e'` is definitionally equal to `[e'/x]e`). Uses of definitional equality are not marked in the proof term or program: if `e` has type τ, then `e` also has any other type τ' that is definitionally equal to τ. On the other hand, *propositional equality* is a proof-relevant *type* relating two terms; it is often also called the *identity type*, which we write `e = e'`. Uses of propositional equality *are* explicitly marked in the program: if `e` has type τ and `p` is an element of the identity type $\tau = \tau'$, then `coe p e` has type τ'.

In homotopy type theory, elements of the identity type are used to model a notion of *paths in a space* or *morphisms in a groupoid*. Using the identity type, specified by its introduction rule, reflexivity, and elimination rule, known as path induction or J, one can define path operations including a constant path `refl` (witnessing the reflexivity of equality); composition of paths `q ∘ p` (witnessing the transitivity of equality)[2], and the inverse of a path `! p` (witnessing the symmetry of equality). Moreover, there are *paths between paths*, or *homotopies*, which are represented by proofs of equality in identity types. For example, there are homotopies expressing that the path operations satisfy the group(oid) laws:

```
refl ∘ p = p = p ∘ refl
(r ∘ q) ∘ p = r ∘ (q ∘ p)
(! p ∘ p) = refl = (p ∘ ! p)
```

Any simply-typed function `f : A → B` determines a function

```
ap f : x = y → f(x) = f(y)
```

that takes paths $x =_A y$ to paths $f(x) =_B f(y)$. Logically, this expresses that propositional equality is a congruence; homotopically, it expresses that any function has an **a**ction on **p**aths; and categorically, it expresses that functions are *functors*, preserving the path structure of types. `ap f` preserves the path operations, in the sense that there are homotopies

[1] There is an unfortunate terminological coincidence here: "Patch theory" means "the study of patches," just as "group theory" is the study of groups. "A patch theory" means "a specific language of patches," just as "a theory in first-order logic" is a specific collection of terms and formulae.

[2] Composition is in function-composition, or applicative, order, `(q:y=z) ∘ (p:x=y) : x=z`.

```
ap f (refl(x)) = refl(f x)
ap f (! p) = ! (ap f p)
ap f (q ∘ p) = (ap f q) ∘ (ap f p)
```

For a family of types `B : A → Type` and a dependent function `f : (x : A) → B(x)`, there is a function

```
apd : (p : x = y) → PathOver B p (f x) (f y)
```

`PathOver B p b1 b2` represents a path in the dependent type `B` between `b1 : B(a1)` and `b2 : B(a2)` correlated by a path `p : a1 = a2`. Logically, it is a kind of heterogeneous equality [27]; categorically, it is a path in the total space of the fibration determined by the type family. For `apd`, this kind of heterogeneous equality is necessary because `f x : B(x)` whereas `f y : B(y)`.

2.2 n-types

A type `A` is a *set*, or 0-type, iff any two parallel paths in `A` are equal—for any two elements `m,n:A`, and any two proofs `p,q : m = n`, there is a path `p = q`. Similarly, a type is a 1-type iff any two paths between parallel paths are equal. A type is a *mere proposition*, or (-1)-type, iff any two elements are equal. A type is *contractible* iff it is a mere proposition and moreover it has an element.

2.3 Univalence

Writing `Type` for a type of (small) types, Voevodsky's *univalence axiom* states that, for sets `A` and `B`, the paths $A =_{Type} B$ are given by bijections between `A` and `B`.[3] That is, define `Bijection A B` to be the type of quadruples

```
(f : A → B, g : B → A,
 p : (x : A) → g (f x) = x, q : (y : B) → f (g y) = y)
```

consisting of two functions that are mutually inverse up to paths. Then one consequence of univalence is that there is a function

```
ua : Bijection A B → A = B
```

which says that a bijection between `A` and `B` determines a path between `A` and `B`. The force of this is to stipulate that *all constructions respect bijection*; for example, if `C[X]` is a parametrized type (e.g. `C` could be `List`, `Tree`, `Monoid`, etc.), then given a bijection `b : Bijection A B`, we have

```
ap C (ua b) : C[A] = C[B]
```

which is a bijection between `C[A]` and `C[B]`. In plain MLTT, one would need to spell out how a bijection between types lifts to a bijection on lists or monoids over those types; with univalence, this lifting is given by a new generic program in the form of `ap`. This generic program is one of the sources of computational applications of homotopy type theory.

We can define the identity, inverse, and composition of bijections directly (focusing on the underlying functions, and writing `f2 . f1` for `(λ x -> f2(f1(x)))`:

```
reflb : Bijection A A
reflb = ((\ x -> x), (\ x -> x) , ...)

!b : Bijection A B → Bijection B A
!b (f,g,p,q) = (g,f,q,p)

_ob_ : Bijection B C → Bijection A B → Bijection A C
(f2,g2,p2,q2) ob (f1,g1,p1,q1) = (f2 . f1, g1 . g2, ...)
```

Applying path operations to univalence is homotopic to applying the corresponding operations to bijections:

```
ua reflb = refl
! (ua b) = ua (!b b)
ua b2 ∘ ua b1 = ua (b2 ob b1)
```

[3] For types that are not sets, univalence requires a notion of *equivalence* that generalizes bijection. However, here we will only use it for sets.

When `p : A = B`, we write `coe p : A → B` for the function, defined by identity type elimination, that "coerces" along the path `p`. `coe` is functorial, in the sense that

```
coe refl x = x
coe (q ∘ p) x = coe q (coe p x)
```

`coe p` is a bijection, with inverse `coe !p`; we write `coe-biject p : Bijection A B` when `p : A = B`. The univalence axiom additionally asserts that there is a computation rule

```
coe (ua (f,g,p,q)) x = f(x)
```

That is, coercing along a path constructed by univalence applies the given bijection. Because `! (ua (f,g,p,q)) = ua (!b (f,g,p,q))`, we also have that

```
coe (! (ua (f,g,p,q))) x = g x
```

Because of these rules, in the presence of univalence, paths can have non-trivial computational content. A bijection `(f,g,p,q)` determines a path `ua(f,g,p,q)`, and coercing along this path applies `f`. Thus, two different bijections `(f,g,p,q)` and `(f',g',p',q')` determine two paths `ua(f,...)` and `ua(f',...)` that behave differently when coerced along.

2.4 Higher Inductive Types

Ordinary inductive types are specified by *generators*; for example, the natural numbers have generators zero and successor: `zero : Nat` and `succ : Nat → Nat`. *Higher-dimensional inductive types* (or just *higher inductive types*) [25, 26, 32] generalize inductive types by allowing generators not only for points (terms), but also for paths. For example, one might draw the circle like this:

This drawing has a single point, and a single non-identity loop from this base point to itself. This translates to a higher inductive type with two generators:

```
space Circle : Type where
  -- point constructor:
  base : Circle
  -- path constructor:
  loop : base = base
```

`base` constructs an element of the inductive type (taking no arguments, just like `zero : Nat`). `loop` generates a path on the circle, which is an element of the identity type $\texttt{base} =_{\texttt{Circle}} \texttt{base}$—think of this as "going around the circle once clockwise". The paths of higher inductive types are constructed from generators, such as `loop`, using the path operations described above. The intuition is that `refl` stands still at the base point, whereas `loop ∘ loop` goes around the circle twice clockwise, and `! loop` goes around the circle once counter-clockwise.

2.4.1 Circle Recursion

The fact that the type of natural numbers is *inductively* generated by zero and successor is encoded in its elimination rule, primitive recursion. Primitive recursion says that to define a function `f : Nat → X`, it suffices to map the generators into `X`, giving `x0 : X` and `x1 : X → X`. Then the function `f` satisfies the equations

```
f zero = x0
f (succ n) = x1(f n)
```

Similarly, the circle is inductively generated by `base` and `loop`, so to define a function from the circle into some other type, it suffices to map these generators into that type, which means giving a point and a loop in that type. That is, to define a function `f : Circle → X`, it suffices to give `b' : X` and `l' : b' =`$_X$ `b'`.

For an inductive type, the β-reduction rules state that applying the elimination rule to a generator computes to the corresponding branch. Thus, by analogy, the computation rules for the circle should say that, for a function `f : Circle → X` that is defined by giving `b'` and `l'`,

```
f base = b'
f loop = l'      -- does not typecheck!
```

The second equation does not quite make sense, because `f` is a function `Circle → X` but `loop` is a *path* on the circle. Therefore we use `ap` (defined above) to denote `f`'s action on paths:

```
ap f loop = l'
```

This computation rule preserves types because its left-hand side is a proof of `f base = f base`, which by the first computation rule equals `b' = b'`, which is the type of `l'`.

EXAMPLE 2.1. As a first example, we write a function to "reverse" a path on the circle—to send the path that goes around the circle n times clockwise to the path that goes around the circle n times counter-clockwise, and vice versa. Because a path on the circle is represented by the identity type `base = base`, we seek a function

```
revPath : (base = base) → (base = base)
```

such that, for example, `revPath (loop ∘ loop) = ! loop ∘ ! loop` and `revPath (! loop ∘ ! loop) = loop ∘ loop`. We could define this function by `revpath p = ! p`, but because the goal is to illustrate circle recursion, we instead give an equivalent definition that analyzes `p`.

To define this function using circle recursion, we need to rephrase the problem as constructing a function `Circle → X` for some type `X`. The key idea is to define a function `rev : Circle → Circle` and then to define `revPath` to be `ap rev`. That is, to define a function on the *paths* of the circle, we define a function on the circle itself, whose action on paths is the desired function. In this case, we define

```
rev : Circle → Circle
rev base = base
ap rev loop = ! loop

revPath p = ap rev p
```

One technical issue about higher inductive types is whether the computation rule `ap f loop = l'` is a definitional equality or a path/propositional equality. Current models and implementations justify only the latter, so we will take it to be a propositional equality. When we illustrate how programs run in this paper, we will do it by giving a sequence of propositional equalities relating a program to a value, so the rule still functions as a "computation" step—as do the rules mentioned above, which state that ap behaves homomorphically on paths built from the group operations. For example, one can calculate

```
  revPath (loop ∘ loop)
= ap rev (loop ∘ loop)
= (ap rev loop) ∘ (ap rev loop)
= ! loop ∘ ! loop
```

Just as the recursion principle for the natural numbers can be generalized to an induction principle, the full form of the circle elimination rule is a principle of "circle induction": to define a dependent function `f : (x : Circle) → C(x)`, it suffices to give `b' : C(base)` and `l' : PathOver C loop b' b'`. We refer the reader to [23, 35] for topological intuition.

3. General Patch Theory

Patch theory [7, 10, 12, 15, 16, 28] provides a general framework for describing properties of version control systems, which allows us to specify the behavior of patches under operations such as composing, reverting and merging. Here, we formulate patch theory in the context of homotopy type theory. This allows us to separate the purely algebraic aspects of a version control system (the laws that it must obey) from its implementation details (how repositories and patches are represented). We refer to a particular algebraic characterization of a version control system as a theory of version control, or a *patch theory*; and to an implementation that obeys the laws of such a theory as a *model* of that theory.

In a patch theory, each patch comes equipped with specified domain and codomain *contexts*, representing respectively, the repository states on which a patch is applicable, and the states resulting from such an application. For example, a patch that deletes a file is applicable only to states in which the file exists, and results in a state in which it does not. In addition, patches respect certain laws that relate sequences of patches to equivalent sequences of patches—equivalent, in the sense that the two sequences have the same effect on the state of a repository.

3.1 Patch Theories as Higher Inductive Types

Homotopy type theory allows us to present a patch theory as a higher inductive type whose structure encodes both generic aspects of version control (such as the behavior of patches under composition) as well as the aspects particular to the given theory, specifying the basic patches available and the specialized laws that these patches obey. An advantage of this approach is that in homotopy type theory functions are functors that necessarily preserve the path structure of a type, so that any function we define out of the higher inductive type representing a patch theory must validate all the laws of that theory, and thus determines a model for it. An additional benefit of this approach is that the metatheory of homotopy type theory itself enforces the groupoid laws, so that we need not specify the behavior of patches and patch laws under composition—i.e. that all compositions are associative, unital and respect inverses—this all comes for free from the groupoid structure of higher inductive types. In the following sections we will present several examples of patch theories encoded as higher inductive types, together with interpretations for them as functors to a universe of sets.

When encoding a patch theory as a higher inductive type, patch contexts are represented as points of the type. Patches are represented as paths between the representations of their domain and codomain contexts, with the path operations refl, $q \circ p$ and $!p$ representing a no-op patch, patch composition, and undo, respectively. Encoding patches as paths in a higher inductive type imposes the requirement that they have inverses, as opposed to just retractions. As one would expect, applying the inverse of a patch after applying the patch itself ($!p \circ p$) undoes the effect of the patch. But it is also possible to apply the inverse patch first ($p \circ !p$), to an appropriate repository state, and this composition should also be equivalent to doing nothing. This forces us to use some care when defining contexts and patches. In some cases we use inverse patches directly in our theory, while in others they end up getting in the way and we must work around them.

Patch laws are represented as 2-dimensional paths between paths. Patch laws are helpful for reasoning about syntactic transformations on patches, such as an optimizer, which should compute a patch equivalent to the one it is given, or a merge, which, given two divergent edits, computes a pair of patches that reconciles them.

3.2 Merging

At a minimum, merging is an operation that takes a pair of diverging patches or *span*, (f_1, f_2), and returns a pair of converging patches or *cospan*, (g_1, g_2), which is a *reconciliation* of the span in the sense that

$$merge(f_1, f_2) = (g_1, g_2) \Longrightarrow g_1 \circ f_1 = g_2 \circ f_2 :$$

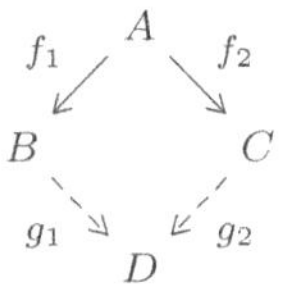

In order to support distributed version control systems, we will further require that the merge operation be *symmetric*,

$$merge(f_1, f_2) = (g_1, g_2) \Longrightarrow merge(f_2, f_1) = (g_2, g_1)$$

so that your reconciliation of my changes with your changes agrees with my reconciliation of your changes with my changes.

Depending on the circumstances, we may wish to impose other laws on merge as well. For example, in the patch theory underlying the distributed revision control system Darcs[12, 31], the merge operation is required to respect patch inverses in the sense that,

$$merge(f_1, f_2) = (g_1, g_2) \Longrightarrow merge(g_1, !f_1) = (!g_2, f_2)$$

A symmetric reconciliation with this property is equivalent to—indeed, the categorical mate of—an operation known as *pseudo-commutation*, which is the primitive operation in terms of which the other operations of Darcs' patch theory are defined.

It is always possible to define a total merge function, since for any span we may give $merge(f_1, f_2) = (!f_1, !f_2)$, the reconciliation that undoes both changes. This can be used to signal a *merge conflict*, a situation in which we are unable to automatically reconcile the competing changes in a sensible way, and for which human intervention is required.

It is important to realize that a merge function that is a symmetric reconciliation need not respect the groupoid structure of a higher inductive type. For example, we may define merge recursively by *tiling*, that is, define

```
merge (g ∘ f , h) = (h'' , g' ∘ f')
  where
    (h' , f') = merge (f , h)
    (h'' , g') = merge (g , h')
```

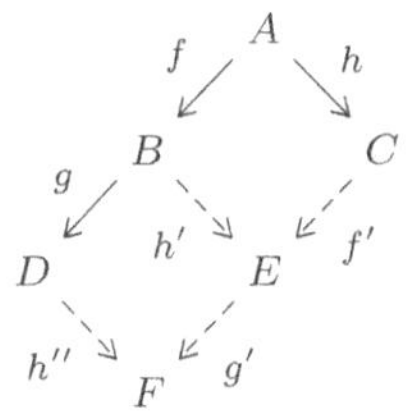

If we define merging a patch with a no-op and merging a patch with itself by

```
merge (f , refl) = (refl , f)
merge (f , f) = (refl , refl)
```

then under the assumption that `f` conflicts with `h`, merging `(!f ∘ f , h)` by tiling results in a conflict, whereas first performing the composition yields `(h , refl)`.

Nevertheless, we may still define merge recursively by quotienting syntactic paths by the groupoid and domain-specific patch laws, and choosing a canonical representative for each class. For example, in a theory without any domain-specific laws, we may normalize `(z ∘ (refl ∘ y)) ∘ ((x ∘ !w) ∘ w)` to `z ∘ y ∘ x`, with a canonical association. In the presence of domain-specific laws, these would need to be taken into account as well. We will make use of this technique in section 6.

Next, we present several examples of patch theories as higher inductive types. We show how to implement their semantics, and additionally some examples of patch optimization and merging, to illustrate syntactic transformations.

4. An Elementary Patch Theory

First, we define a very simple language of patches, to illustrate the basic technique: we take the repository to be a single integer, and the patches to be adding or subtracting some number n from it. Because all patches apply to any repository state, we need only a single patch context, which we call `num`. Patches will then be represented as paths `num = num`, which represents the fact that every patch can be applied to context `num` and results in context `num`. Suppose we have a patch `add1` that represents adding 1 to the repository. Then, because paths can be constructed from identity, inverses, and composition, we also have paths `refl`, which represents adding 0, and `add1 ∘ add1`, which represents adding 2, and `! add1`, which represents subtracting 1, and so on. In fact, the patches adding n for any integer n are *generated* by `add1`, because the integers are the free group on one generator. This motivates the following higher inductive definition of this simple Repository and its patches:

```
space R : Type where
  -- point constructor (patch context):
  num  : R
  --  path constructor (basic patch):
  add1 : num = num
```

This is, of course, just a renaming of the circle!

REMARK 4.1. By presenting it using a higher inductive type, the patch theory automatically includes identity, inverses, and composition. Without higher inductive types, one would need syntax constructors for identity, composition, and inverses; e.g. using a datatype as follows:

```
data Patch where
  add1 : Patch
  id  : Patch
  compose : Patch → Patch → Patch
  inv : Patch → Patch
```

Then, to achieve the correct equational theory of patches, one would need to impose the group laws on this type; this could be done using a quotient type [8] to assert that

```
assoc : compose r (compose q p) = compose (compose r q) p
invr : compose p (inv p) = id
invl : compose (inv p) p = id
unitr : compose p id = p
unitl : compose id p = p
```

By representing a patch theory as a higher inductive type, the group operations and laws are provided by the ambient type theory, so the definition need not include these boilerplate constructors. □

4.1 Interpreter

Next, we define an interpreter, which explains how to apply a patch to a repository. Because the intended semantics is that the repository is an integer, we would like to interpret the repository context `num` as the type `Int` of integers. Because patches are invertible, we would like to interpret each patch as an element of the type `Bijection Int Int`.

REMARK 4.2. To build intuition, consider writing the interpreter "by hand", for the quotient type `Patch` defined in Remark 4.1, which includes constructors for identity, inverse, and composition. We would first define:

```
interp : Patch → Bijection Int Int
interp add1 = successor
interp id = reflb
interp (compose p2 p1) = interp p2 ∘b interp p1
interp (inv p) = !b (interp p)
```

where `successor : Bijection Int Int` is the bijection given by `(\ x → x + 1, \ x → x - 1, ...)` Then, to show that this definition is well-defined on the quotient of patches by the group laws, we would need to do a proof with 5 cases for the 5 group laws, where in each case we appeal to the inductive hypotheses and the corresponding group law for bijections. □

Returning to our higher-inductive representation of patches, we define the interpreter using the recursion principle for R, which is of course the same as circle recursion, as discussed in Section 2. We want to interpret each point of R, which represents a repository context, as the type of repositories in that context, and each path as a bijection between the corresponding types. In this case, that means we would like to interpret `num` as `Int` and `add1` as the successor bijection. R-recursion says that to define a function `f : R → X`, it suffices to find a point `x0 : X` and a loop `p : x0 = x0`. Thus, we can represent the interpretation by a function `R → Type`, because a point of `Type` is a type, and a loop in `Type` is, by univalence, the same as a bijection! This motivates the following definition:

```
I : R → Type
I num = Int
ap I add1 = ua (successor)

interp : (num = num) → Bijection Int Int
interp p = coe-biject (ap I p)
```

Up to propositional equality, this definition satisfies the defining equations of `interp` as defined in Remark 4.2. First, we can calculate that `interp add1 = successor`,

```
  interp add1
= coe-biject (ap I add1)      [definition]
= coe-biject (ua successor)  [ap I on add1]
= successor                  [coe on ua successor]
```

using the computation rules for `ap I` on `add` (from higher inductive elimination) and `coe` on `ua b` (from univalence).[4]

Moreover, `interp` takes path operations to the corresponding operations on bijections, because it is defined via `ap`, and `ap` preserves the path operations. For example,

```
  interp (q ∘ p)
= coe-biject (ap I (q ∘ p))
= coe-biject (ap I q ∘ ap I p)   [ap on ∘]
= coe-biject (ap I q) ∘b (coe-biject (ap I p))
= interp q ∘b interp p
```

`interp refl = reflb` and `interp (! p) = !b (interp b)` are similar. That is, the semantics is functorial.

For example, if we apply[5] a patch `add1 ∘ !add1` to a repository whose contents are 0, we have

```
  (interp (add1 ∘ ! add1)) 0
= ((interp add1) ∘b interp (! add1)) 0
= ((interp add1) ∘b !b (interp add1)) 0
= (successor ∘b !b successor) 0
= successor (!b successor 0)
= successor -1
= 0
```

Comparing this definition of `interp` with Remark 4.2, we see that the recursion principle for the higher-inductive representation of patches provides an elegant way to express the semantics of a patch theory, where much of the code in Remark 4.2 is provided "for free". We needed to give only the key case for `add1`, and not the inductive cases for the group operations—the semantics of the basic patches is automatically lifted functorially to the patch operations. Moreover, we did not need to prove that bijections satisfy the group laws—this fact is necessary for the univalence axiom to make sense, so it is effectively part of the metatheory of homotopy type theory, rather than of our program. This example illustrates that *univalence can be used to extract computational content from a path*, by mapping the path into a path in the universe, which by univalence can be given by a bijection.

Because R is the circle, one may wonder about the topological meaning of this interpreter. In fact, the type family `I` defined here is called the *universal cover of the circle*, and is discussed further in [23, 35]. `interp` computes what is called the *winding number* of a path on the circle, which can be thought of as a normal form that counts how many times that path goes around the circle, after "detours" such as `loop ∘ ! loop` have been reduced.

It is also worth noting that, although we were thinking of `num` as an integer and `add1` as successor, there is nothing forcing this interpretation of the syntax: we can give a sound interpretation `I` in any type with a bijection on it. For example,

```
I' : R → Type
I' num = Bool
ap I' add1 = ua notb
```

where `notb : Bijection Bool Bool = (not , not , ...)`. That is, we interpret the patches in `Bool` instead of `Int`, and we interpret `add1` as adding 1 modulo 2. This semantics satisfies additional equations that are not reflected in the theory, such as

```
ap I' add1 ∘ ap I' add1 = ua (notb ∘b notb) = refl
```

In the next section we show how to augment a patch theory with equations such as these—but doing so would of course rule out the previous semantics in `Int`, because adding 1 to an integer is not self-inverse. The equational theory of R is *complete* for the interpretation as `Int`, which in homotopy theory is known as the fact that the fundamental group of the circle is $\mathbb{Z}$ (see [23, 35]). The idea that we can have multiple models of a patch theory (`I` and `I'`) will be exploited in Section 6, when we give a "logging" interpretation that produces a data representation of what happens when a patch is evaluated.

4.2 Merge

Next we implement a merge operation, which satisfies the laws discussed in Section 3. Writing `Patch` for `doc = doc`, and specializing the interface to the setting where we have only one context, we need to implement the following:

```
merge : Patch × Patch → Patch × Patch
reconcile : (f1 f2 g1 g2 : Patch)
          → merge (f1 , f2) = (g1 , g2)
          → g1 ∘ f1 = g2 ∘ f2
symmetric : (f1 f2 g1 g2 : Patch)
          → merge (f1 , f2) = (g1 , g2)
          → merge (f2 , f1) = (g2 , g1)
```

In this simple setting, any two patches commute, essentially because addition is commutative. Thus, we define

```
merge(f1 , f2) = (f2 , f1)
```

For `symmetric`, because `g1 = f2` and `g2 = f1`, we need to show that `merge (f2,f1) = (f1,f2)`, which is true by definition.

For `reconcile`, we need to prove that `f2 ∘ f1 = f1 ∘ f2`, for any two loops `num = num` on the circle—the group of loops on the circle is abelian. It is not immediately obvious how to do

[4] We also use that fact that two bijections are equal iff their underlying functions are equal, because inverses are unique up to homotopy.

[5] We elide the projection from `Bijection A B` to `A → B`.

this, because homotopy type theory does not provide a direct induction principle for the loops in a type. That is, there is no built-in elimination rule that allows one to, for example, analyze a loop `f` as either `add1`, or the identity, or an inverse, or a composition—because such a case-analysis would additionally need to respect all equations on paths, which differ from type to type. Instead, such induction principles for paths are *proved* for each type from the basic induction principles for the higher inductive types—roughly analogously to how, for the natural numbers, course-of-values (or strong) induction is derived from mathematical induction. Moreover, proving these induction principles is sometimes a significant mathematical theorem. In homotopy theory, it is called calculating the homotopy groups of a space, and even for spaces as simple as the spheres some homotopy groups are unknown. However, we have developed some techniques for calculating homotopy groups in type theory [19, 20, 23, 35], which can be applied here.

For this particular example, the calculation has already be done: we know that the fundamental group of the circle is $\mathbb{Z}$. Specifically, we know that the type `num = num` of loops at `num`, which we use to represent patches, is in bijection with `Int`. That is, the integers give canonical representatives ("add x, for $x \in \mathbb{Z}$") for equivalence classes of patches in the above patch theory, considered modulo the group laws. This is proved by giving functions back and forth that compose to the identity. The function `encode : num=num → Int` is exactly `λ p → interp p 0`, for `interp p` as defined above. The function `repeat : Int → num=num` is defined by induction on the `Int`, viewing `Int` as a datatype with three constructors, 0; `+ n` (where `n` itself is positive) representing positive `n`; and `- n` (where `n` itself is positive) representing negative `n`.

```
repeat 0 = refl
repeat (+ n) = add1 ∘ add1 ∘ ... ∘ add1 [n times]
repeat (- n) = !add1 ∘ !add1 ∘ ... ∘ !add1 [n times]
```

The proof that `encode` and `repeat` are mutually inverse is described in [23, 35]. Moreover, they define a group homomorphism, which means that `repeat (x + y) = repeat x ∘ repeat y`.

The bijection between `num=num` and `Int` induces a derived induction principle, which says that to prove `P(p)` for all paths `p:num=num`, it suffices to prove `P(repeat n)` for all integers `n`—any patch can be viewed as `repeat n` for some `n`. Applying this (twice) to the goal `f2 ∘ f1 = f1 ∘ f2`, it suffices to show

```
repeat x ∘ repeat y = repeat y ∘ repeat x
```

This is proved as follows:

```
  repeat x ∘ repeat y
= repeat (x + y) [group homomorphism]
= repeat (y + x) [commutativity of addition]
= repeat y ∘ repeat x
```

Thus, for this language of patches, the correctness of merge follows from the fact that the fundamental group of the circle is $\mathbb{Z}$—our first example of a software correctness proof being a corollary of a theorem in homotopy theory!

One further point to note is that, in this example, we were able to *define* merge without converting paths to integers, while to prove the reconciliation property we needed to reason inductively, using canonical representatives of group-law-equivalence-classes. This is because all patches commute, so we can define `merge(x,y) = (y,x)` without analyzing the structure of patches. In more interesting settings, such as Section 6, we will need to make use of canonical representatives to define the merge function itself. To illustrate this, we can give an alternate definition of merge, which uses a helper function `merge''` that recursively swaps two integers; writing the code in this way illustrates the general technique of defining merge by choosing canonical representatives for paths and using induction on these representatives.

```
merge'(p,q) =
  let (a,b) = merge''(encode p, encode q)
   in (repeat a , repeat b)

merge'' : Int × Int → Int × Int
merge''(+ (1+x) , - (1+y)) =
  let (a , b) = merge'' (+ x , - y)
   in (a-1 , b+1)
...
```

The function `merge'` is defined by converting the given paths `p` and `q` (which are considered up to the group laws, such as associativity) to chosen representatives, integers. Paths that are equal according to the group laws are sent to equal representatives; e.g. both `(add1 ∘ add1) ∘ add1` and `add1 ∘ (add1 ∘ add1)` are sent to 3. We may then compose this choice of representatives with any function we want — including functions that do not themselves respect the group laws, as merge in general might not (see Section 3) — and the overall composite still respects the group laws. In this case, we compose with a function `merge''` that case-analyzes the given integers, and recursively "merges" the two numbers with cases such as the one given above. This case copies a positive successor on the left to a positive successor on the right, and a negative successor on the right to a negative successor on the left—think of it as merging "add 1 and then do x" with "subtract 1 and then do y" by merging `x` and `y` and then moving the "add 1" to the right and the "subtract 1" to the left. For this patch theory, all primitive patches commute, but this form of case analysis gives the opportunity to detect conflicting patches. Finally, once `merge''` has computed the merge of two chosen representatives, `merge'` calls `repeat` to convert the resulting integers back to paths. One can prove by induction that `merge''(x,y) = (y,x)`; and `encode` and `repeat` are mutually inverse, so `merge'` agrees with the original definition of `merge`.

5. A Patch Theory with Laws

In this section, we consider a slightly more complex patch theory, to illustrate how patch laws are handled. In the intended semantics of this theory, the repository consists of one document with a fixed number `n` of lines, and there is one basic patch, which modifies the string at a particular line. To fit this into a framework of bijections, we take the patch `s1 ↔ s2 @ i` to mean "permute `s1` and `s2` at position `i`". That is, applying this patch replaces line `i` with `s2` if it is `s1`, or with `s1` if it is `s2`, or leaves it unchanged otherwise. We impose some equational laws on this patch—e.g., edits at independent lines commute. We consider an interpretation function `I` and a simple patch optimizer; we do not consider merge in this section, because we discuss it for the more general language in Section 6.

5.1 Definition of Patches

This patch theory is represented by the following higher inductive type:

```
space R : Type where
  -- point constructor (patch context):
  doc : R
  -- path constructor (basic patch):
  _↔_@_ : (s1 s2 : String) (i : Fin n) → (doc = doc)
  -- path-between-path constructors (patch laws):
  indep : (s t u v : String) (i j : Fin n) → (i ≠ j) →
            (s ↔ t @ i) ∘ (u ↔ v @ j)
          = (u ↔ v @ j) ∘ (s ↔ t @ i)
  noop : (s : String) (i : Fin n) s ↔ s @ i = refl
```

`doc` should be thought of as a document with `n` lines (for some `n` fixed throughout this section). The path constructor `s1 ↔ s2 @ i` represents the basic patch, swapping `s1` and `s2` at line number `i`. `Fin n` is the type of natural numbers less than `n`, which we interpret here as line numbers in an n-line document (where we start numbering at 0).

For this language there are some non-trivial patch laws, which are represented by giving generators for *paths between paths*; we show two as an example. The equation `noop` states that swapping `s` with `s` is the identity for all `s`; this is useful for justifying a simple optimizer, which optimizes away the two string comparisons that executing `s ↔ s @ i` would require. The equation `indep` states that edits to independent lines commute; this is useful for defining `merge` (`x ≠ y` is the negation of `x = y`, i.e. `(x = y) → void`).

Because `R` is our first example of a type with both paths and paths between paths, we go over its recursion and induction principles in detail. To define a function `f : R → X`, it suffices to give

```
doc'   : X
swap'  : (s1 s2 : String) (i : Fin n) → doc' = doc'
indep' : (s t u v : String) (i j : Fin n) → i ≠ j
       → swap' s t i ∘ swap' u v j
       = swap' u v j ∘ swap' s t i
noop'  : (s : String) (i : Fin n)
       → swap' s s i = refl
```

and then we have the following computation rules

```
f(doc) = doc'
β1 : ap f (s ↔ t @ i) = swap' s t i
β21 : PathOver (x . x = refl) β1
                (ap (ap f) (noop s i))
                (noop' s i)
β22 : PathOver (x,y. x ∘ y = y ∘ x) (β1, β1)
                (ap (ap f) (indep s t u v i j neq))
                (indep' s t u v i j neq)
```

The first computation rule is in fact a definitional equality, while the second is a path. The well-typedness of the third computation rule, which says roughly that `ap (ap f) (noop s i)` equals `(noop' s i)`, depends on the second computation rule, $\beta 1$. This is because `ap (ap f) (noop s i)` has type `ap f (s ↔ s @ i) = ap f refl`, but `noop'` has type `swap' s s i = refl`. While `ap f refl` is definitionally equal to `refl`, `ap f (s ↔ s @ i)` is only propositionally equal to `swap' s s i` by $\beta 1$. Thus, we use the `PathOver` type state them, which allows for a heterogeneous equality. We will use clausal function notation for maps out of `R`, but keep in mind that the types of the right-hand sides of the equations are those of `doc'` and `swap'` and `indep'` and `noop'` above, which (in the latter two cases) are only propositionally equal to the types of the left-hand sides.

The induction principle for `R` states that to define a function `f : (x : R) → C(x)`, it suffices to give

- `c' : C(doc)`
- `s' : PathOver C (s1 ↔ s2 @ i) c' c'`
- A 2-dimensional path over a path as the image of `indep`.
- A 2-dimensional path over a path as the image of `noop`.

We omit the details of the final two, which are not used below.

5.2 Interpreter

Because patches are represented by the type `doc = doc`, the interpreter for patches is a function

```
interp : (doc = doc)
       → Bijection (Vec String n) (Vec String n)
```

As above, we generalize this to an interpretation of the whole patch theory `R`, and define a function `I : R → Type` such that

```
interp p = coe-biject (ap I p)
```

To interpret the basic patch `s1 ↔ s2 @ i`, we need a corresponding bijection that permutes two strings at a position in a length-n vector of strings, represented by the type `Vec String n`.

```
permute : (String × String) → String → String
permute (s1,s2) s | String.equals (s1,s) = s2
permute (s1,s2) s | String.equals (s2,s) = s1
permute (s1,s2) s | _ = s

applyat : (A → A) → Fin n → Vec A n → Vec A n
applyat f i <x1,...xn> = <x1,...,f xi,...,xn>

swapat : (String × String) → Fin n
       → Bijection (Vec A n) (Vec A n)
swapat (s1,s2) i = (applyat (permute (s1,s2)) i, ...)
```

The interpretation `I` is defined as follows:

```
I : R → Type
I doc = Vec String n
ap I (s1 ↔ s2 @ i) = ua (swapat (s1,s2) i)
ap (ap I) (indep s t u v i j i≠j) =
  GOAL0 : ua(swapat(s,t) i) ∘ ua(swapat(u,v) j)
        = ua(swapat(u,v) j) ∘ ua(swapat(s,t) i)
ap (ap I) (noop s i) = GOAL1 : ua(swapat(s,s) i) = refl
```

We interpret `doc` as `Vec String n`. The image of `s1 ↔ s2 @ i` must be a path in `Type` between `I(doc)` and `I(doc)`—i.e. between `Vec String n` and itself. For this, we choose the bijection `swapat (s1,s2) i`, packed up as a path in the universe using the univalence axiom. The metavariables `GOAL0` and `GOAL1` represent *goals*, that is, terms that must still be provided before the proof/program is complete. The image of `indep` and `noop` are the goals `GOAL0` and `GOAL1`, with the types written out above—which say that we need to validate the patch laws for the interpretation. These goals can be solved by equational properties of bijections, combined with the rules about the interaction of univalence with identity and composition described in Section 2. For example, `GOAL1` is solved by observing that `swapat(s,s) i` is the the identity bijection, and then using the fact that `ua reflb = refl`. `GOAL0` is solved by turning both sides into a composition of bijections using the fact that `ua b2 ∘ ua b1 = ua (b2 ∘b b1)` , and then proving the corresponding fact about `swapat`:

```
swapat-independent :
  (i ≠ j) → (swapat (s,t) i) ∘b (swapat (u,v) j)
          = (swapat (u,v) j) ∘b (swapat (s,t) i)
```

As above, we do not need to give cases for the group operations or prove the group laws—these come for free, from functoriality.

5.3 Optimizer

To illustrate using the patch laws, we write a simple optimizer

```
optimize : (p : doc = doc) → Σ (q : doc = doc). p = q
```

The type of `optimize` says that it takes a patch `p` and produces a patch `q` that behaves the same, according to the patch laws, as `p`. The goal is to optimize `s ↔ s @ i` to `refl`, saving ourselves two unnecessary string comparisons when the patch is applied. The optimizer requires analyzing the syntax of patches.

We show two definitions of `optimize`, to illustrate some different aspects of programming in homotopy type theory.

Program then prove. In this definition, we first write a function `optimize1 : doc=doc → doc=doc`, and then prove that this function returns a path that is equal, according to the patch laws, to its input. The idea is to apply the following function `opt0` to each patch `s1 ↔ s2 @ i`:

```
opt0 : String → String → Fin n → doc=doc
opt0 s1 s2 i = if String.equals s1 s2
```

```
            then refl
            else (s1 ↔ s2 @ i)
```

To define `optimize1`, we generalize the problem to defining a function `opt1` that acts on all of R, and then derive `optimize1` as its action on paths (the same technique as reversing the circle in Section 2.1). This is defined as follows:

```
opt1 : R → R
opt1 doc = doc
ap opt1 (s1 ↔ s2 @ i) = opt0 s1 s2 i
ap (ap opt1) (noop s i) =
  GOAL0 : opt0 s s i = refl
ap (ap opt1) (indep s t u v i j i≠j) =
  GOAL1 : opt0 s1 s2 i ∘ opt0 s3 s4 j
        = opt0 s3 s4 j ∘ opt0 s1 s2 i
```

We map `doc` to `doc`, and apply `opt0` to `s1 ↔ s2 @ i`. However, to complete the definition, we must show that the optimization respects the patch laws, via the goals `GOAL0` and `GOAL1` whose types are given above. The goal `GOAL0` is true because `String.equals s s` will be true, so, after case-analysis, `refl` proves that `opt1 s s i = refl`. The goal `GOAL1` requires case-analyzing both `String.equals s1 s2` and `String.equals s3 s4`. If both are true, the goal reduces to `refl ∘ refl = refl ∘ refl`, which is true by `refl`. If the former but not the latter is true, the goal reduces to `refl ∘ s3 ↔ s4 @ j = s3 ↔ s4 @ j ∘ refl`, which is true by unit laws. The third case is symmetric. Finally, if neither are true, then the goal holds by `indep`.

Next, we prove this optimization correct using R-induction:

```
opt1-correct : (x : R) → x = opt1 x
opt1-correct doc = refl
apd opt1-correct (s1 ↔ s2 @ i) =
  GOAL0 : PathOver (x. x = opt1 x) (s1 ↔ s2 @ i) refl refl
apd (apd opt1-correct) (noop s i) = GOAL0
apd (apd opt1-correct) (indep s t u v i j i≠j) = GOAL1
```

In the case for `doc`, we need to give a path `doc = opt1 doc`, but `opt1 doc` is `doc`, so we give `refl`. In the case for `s1 ↔ s2 @ i`, the induction principle requires an element of the type listed above. It turns out that, by rules for `PathOver`, this type is equivalent to

```
s1 ↔ s2 @ i = opt0 s1 s2 i
```

So this is where we prove that `opt0` preserves the meaning of a patch. This requires two cases: when `s1` is equal to `s2`, we use `noop`; when it is not, we use `refl`.

The remaining two cases require proving that *this proof of correctness of* ***opt*** respects the patch laws. In each case, the goal asks us to prove the equality of two proofs of equality of patches. That is, the goal has the form

$$f_1 =_{p =_{\mathtt{doc}=\mathtt{doc}} q} f_2$$

where p and q are two patches, and f_1 and f_2 are two proofs that these two patches are equal—which homotopically can be thought of as paths-between-paths, or, in more geometrically evocative terminology, as *faces* between *edges*.

One might think that such a goal would be trivial, because f_1 and f_2 are representing proofs that two patches are equal according to the patch laws, and we think of patch equality as a proof-irrelevant relation. But for the definition we have given above, there is nothing that actually forces any two such faces to be identified. For example, we can compose `indep i≠j ∘ indep j≠i`, a proof that `(s ↔ t @ i) ∘ (u ↔ v @ j)` is equal to itself, but there is no reason that this proof, which swaps twice, is necessarily the identity. Thus, although we have not considered any applications of this so far, we could potentially consider proof-relevant identifications between patches—proof-relevant patch laws. If we wished to do so, then these goals would need to be proven.

However, if we do not wish to consider proof-relevant patch equations, we *can* make these goals trivial by a technique called *truncation* [35, Chapter 7]. In this case, this means adding another constructor to R of type

```
-- path-between-path-between-path constructor
   (all proofs of patch laws are equal)
trunc : (x y : R) (p q : x = y) (f1 f2 : p = q)
        → f1 = f2
```

This constructor adds a path between any two faces `f1` and `f2`—which allows the above goals to be solved. The price for truncating is that functions defined by R-recursion/induction are only permitted when the result is also a 1-type. Fortunately, we can still define `opt1` with this restriction (because R is a 1-type), as well as `opt1-correct` (because paths in a 1-type are a 0-type, and therefore a 1-type) and the function `I` used for `interp` (because it interprets the point of R as a set, and the collection of all sets is a 1-type). Thus, truncating R would be an appropriate and helpful modification in this case.

Program and prove. An alternative, which requires neither truncation nor proving any equations between faces, is to simultaneously implement the optimizer, and prove that it returns a patch equal to its input. To define

```
optimize : (p : doc = doc) → Σ (q : doc = doc). p = q
```

we need to define a function on all of R, and derive `optimize` via its action on paths. However, `optimize` is dependently typed, and `ap f` for a simply-typed function `f` never has such a dependent type. Thus, we define a dependently typed function and use the dependent form of `ap`, `apd`. Specifically, we define

```
opt : (x : R) → Σ (y : R). y = x
```

This type has the same shape as the type of `optimize` above, except it is at the level of the *points* of R rather than the paths. Its action on paths has the following type:

```
apd opt (p : doc = doc) :
  PathOver (x. Σy:R. y = x) p (opt doc) (opt doc)
```

When the family B is known, the type `PathOver B p b1 b2` can be "reduced" (via propositional equalities) to another type. In the case where B is `x.Σ (y:R.y = x)`, as above, the rules for path-over-a-path in Σ-types, constant families, and path types, yield an identification `e` as follows:[6]

```
e :   PathOver (x. Σy:R. y = x) p (doc,refl) (doc,refl)
    = Σ (q : doc = doc). p = q
```

Thus, if we define `opt` such that

```
opt doc = (doc , refl)
```

then

[6] This is because a path over a path in a Σ-type is a path-over-a-path in each component (the second over the first), because a path-over-a-path in a constant family `x.R` is just a path in R, and a path-over-a-path in the identity type is a square in the underlying type—specifically, `PathOver (x,y. y = x) (p,q) (refl,refl)` is a square

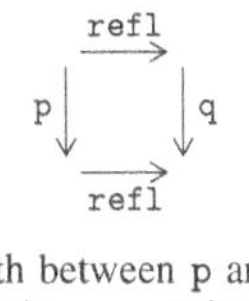

which is the same as a path between `p` and `q` (this is what motivates the choice of `(doc,refl)` and `(doc,refl)` as the endpoints of the path-over-a-path).

```
apd opt (p : doc = doc) :
  PathOver (x. Σy:R. y = x) p (doc , refl) (doc , refl)
```

and we can define `optimize` by composing this with `e`:

```
optimize : (p : doc = doc) → Σ (q : doc = doc). p = q
optimize p = coe (! e) (apd opt p)
```

This reduces the problem to defining `opt`, which we do as follows:

```
opt doc = (doc, refl)
opt (s1 ↔ s2 @ i) = coe e
                    (if String.equals s1 s2
                     then (refl , noop s1 i)
                     else (s1 ↔ s2 @ i , refl))
ap (ap opt) _ = <contractibility>
```

We set `opt doc = (doc , refl)`, as motivated above. For the second clause, we need a

```
PathOver (x. Σy:R. y = x) p (doc , refl) (doc , refl)
```

By `e`, it suffices to give a

```
Σ (q : doc = doc). (s1 ↔ s2 @ i) = q
```

Thus, this is where we put the key step that we wanted to make, which is optimizing `s1 ↔ s2 @ i` to `refl` when the strings are equal, and leaving the patch unchanged otherwise—and pairing each with a proof that it is equal to `s1 ↔ s2 @ i`.

For each of the `noop` and `indep` cases, we need to give a face between two specific paths between two specific points in the type `Σ y:R. y = x` (for some `x`). However, the type `Σ y:R.x = y` is in fact *contractible*—it is equivalent to `unit`. Intuitively, any pair `(y,p)` can be continuously deformed to `(x,refl)` by sliding `y` along `p`; see [35, Lemma 3.11.8]. The identity types of any contractible type are mere propositions, so any two paths are connected by a face. Thus, because we formulated the problem as mapping into a contractible type, the remaining goals are trivial.

This definition of `opt`, consisting of only the three cases given above, is shorter than our previous attempt. Moreover, for comparison, suppose we instead wrote this optimizer for a datatype of patches that included identity, inverses, and composition as constructors (analogous to the one in Remark 4.1). Then, in addition to giving the key case for optimizing `s1 ↔ s2 @ i`, we would need to give inductive cases describing how the optimizer acts on identity, inverses, and composition. Here, because the optimizer can be defined as a group homomorphism, we need to give only the "interesting" case; the inductive cases are provided by the framework.

Singleton Types and Computation Because the type `Σ(y:A).x = y` is contractible, we can think of it as a *singleton type*, written `S(x)`. It consists of "everything in `A` that is equal to `x`," or, more precisely, a point in `A` with a path to `x`. One may well wonder what is the point of writing a function into a contractible type? Using the singleton notation we have

```
optimize : (p : doc = doc) → S(p).
```

Because `S(p)` is contractible, and hence equivalent to `unit`, isn't this just a triviality? The answer is "no" because even if two elements of a type are connected by a path (and hence cannot be distinguished by any other operation of type theory), the type nevertheless has meaningful computational content in that we may observe its output when it is run and thereby make distinctions that are obscured within the theory.

Thus, even though the `optimize` function that we wrote above is equal (i.e., homotopic) to the function that simply returns `p` itself—or, indeed, any other function with that type—we expect, based on work on the computational interpretation of homotopy type theory, that it will in fact compute appropriately—e.g. `optimize (s ↔ s @ i)` will in fact return `refl` because of the way it is programmed. This is consistent with prior experience with, for example, function extensionality in type theory [3]. A higher-order computation will compute a *particular* function, not any function with the same graph; computation does not respect extensional equality of functions.

6. A Patch Theory With Richer Contexts

In the previous section we considered patches of the form `s1 ↔ s2 @ i`, which naturally induce total bijections on the type of `n`-line documents. In Section 5, we exploited this fact to model these patches as paths in a higher inductive type, using univalence to map them to bijections on `Vec String n`. Now we will consider a richer language of patches—inserting a string `s` as the `l`th line in a file (`ADD s@l`), and removing the `l`th line of a file (`RM l`).These patches only make sense in certain situations. For example, the only patch applicable to an empty file is `ADD s@0`; to the resulting file we may apply one of `ADD s'@0`, `ADD s'@1`, or `RM 0`, which respectively add `s'` before or after `s`, or deletes `s`.

A suitable patch theory must express such constraints on composition using contexts. More than one context is required, because not all patches are composable with one another. For example, it makes sense to classify repositories by the number of lines they contain so that removal from an empty file is ruled inadmissible by the patch theory. This may be achieved by defining the contexts (the points of `R`) to be of the form `doc n`, where `n` is of type `Nat`. The patch that adds a line is, generally in `n`, a path in `R` witnessing `doc n = doc n+1`. Similarly, the patch that deletes a line is a path in `R` witnessing `doc n+1 = doc n`. Although this formulation expresses necessary constraints on the use of the primitive patches, it fails to admit the obvious interpretation of `doc n` as the type of `n`-line files, `Vec n String`. The difficulty is that the type theory demands that the interpretation respect paths, and we have `doc n = doc n+1` in `R`, yet the types `Vec n String` and `Vec n+1 String` are not bijective, and hence are not equated by univalence.

To motivate what follows, let us observe that we may expect there to be an "initial" context describing the empty repository, the initial state of a repository. Because there is only one empty repository, the empty file, we would expect the interpretation of the initial context to be a contractible type whose element is the empty file. Moreover, we would expect there to be a path from the initial context to every other context, based on the idea that it should be possible to reach every repository state by some sequence of patches. Thus, every context would be equal to the initial context, and by functoriality and univalence all contexts must be modeled by a contractible type.

Given that the interpretation of a context should be a type containing repository files as elements, its contractibility, together with univalence, suggest that each context be modeled by the *singleton type*, `S(file)`, containing *only* the file in question. But if the meaning of a context is to be such a singleton, the context must essentially determine the contents of the repository. The obvious way to achieve this is to consider contexts of the form `doc n file`, where `n` is, as before, the number of lines, and `file` is a file of that length, an element of `Vec n String`. The patch `ADD s@l` would then be a path `doc n file = doc n+1 file'`, where `file'` is the result of adding `s` at line `l` in `file`, and similarly for `RM l`. We can interpret `doc n file` as `S(file)` functorially, because any two singletons, being contractible, are equivalent types, and hence equal by univalence.

The trouble with this formulation is that it intermixes the abstract theory of patches with its concrete realization as a file. Although we reject it as a solution, it does suggest another, more satisfactory, formulation. The main idea is that the contexts need only *determine* the contents of the repository, not literally contain them, in order to construct the singletons model. This is achieved by indexing contexts by *patch histories*, which are sequences of composable patches applicable to files of a given length. With respect to any particular realization of patches, a history applicable to the empty file uniquely determines the resulting file's contents. As an added benefit, histories also reify sequences of patches in a way which facilitates certain operations on repositories, such as moving forward or backward in time.

Patch contexts may be understood as types for patches, limiting how they may be composed, and we expect these to be erasable at run-time. This will require us to compute views of identity types that are more amenable to computation, similarly to the way in which we used the characterization of the loop space of the circle in Section 4.

6.1 Definition of Patches

Let `History m n` be the type of patch histories (sequences of patches) applicable to `m`-line files which result in `n`-line files. We will define `History m n` as a quotient higher inductive type to equate sequences of patches which result in the same changes to a file. For example, two additions in sequence can be commuted if the line numbers are shifted.

```
space History : Nat → Nat → Type where
  -- point constructors:
  [] : History m m
  ADD_@_::_ : {m n : Nat} (s : String) (l : Fin n+1) →
              History m n → History m n+1
  RM_::_    : {m n : Nat} (l : Fin n+1) →
              History m n+1 → History m n
  -- path constructors:
  ADD-ADD-< : {m n : Nat} (l1 : Fin n+1) (l2 : Fin n+2)
    (s1 s2 : String) (h : History m n) → l1 < l2 →
    (ADD s2 @ l2 :: ADD s1 @ l1 :: h)
      = (ADD s1 @ l1 :: ADD s2 @ (l2-1) :: h)
  ADD-ADD-≥ : {n : Nat} (l1 : Fin n+1) (l2 : Fin n+2)
    (s1 s2 : String) (h : History m n) → l1 ≥ l2 →
    (ADD s2 @ l2 :: ADD s1 @ l1 :: h)
      = (ADD s1 @ l1+1) :: ADD s2 @ l2 :: h)
```

(For the sake of clarity we have omitted some coercions between different `Fin` types.) To simplify the code in the remainder of this section, we have omitted the paths commuting ADD-RM, RM-ADD, and RM-RM, which can be defined in exactly the same way.

Histories applicable to the empty file (elements of `History 0 n`) uniquely identify files because the history can be "replayed" from the start. These *complete histories* will serve as the patch contexts in this language—the domain of a patch is a complete history identifying a file to which the patch is applicable, and the codomain is the domain history extended by the patch which was just applied.

```
space R : Type where
  -- point constructor:
  doc : {n : Nat} → History 0 n → R
  -- path constructors:
  addP : {n : Nat} (s : String) (l : Fin n+1)
         (h : History 0 n) → doc h = doc (ADD s@l :: h)
  rmP  : {n : Nat} (l : Fin n+1)
         (h : History 0 n+1) → doc h = doc (RM l :: h)
```

Next, we would like to insert faces equating commuting sequences of patches, but our definition of histories means that no differing sequences of paths will ever be parallel! For example, when `l1 < l2`, the two paths

```
addP s2 l2 ∘ addP s1 l1
  : h = ADD s2@l2 :: ADD s1@l1 :: h
addP s1 l1 ∘ addP s2 (l2-1)
  : h = ADD s1@l1 :: ADD s2@(l2-1) :: h
```

ought to be "equal" as patches, but it does not even make type sense to state this equation. We rely on the fact that histories are quotiented by the same commutation laws—that is, we already equated those exact elements of `History 0 n` with the path `ADD-ADD-<`. Therefore, we can stipulate that the above two paths are equal *over* the `ADD-ADD-<` equation from `History 0 n`, with respect to the type family `x.h = x`. Thus the faces of `R` are defined as follows:

```
addP-addP-< : {n : Nat} (l1 : Fin n+1) (l2 : Fin n+2)
  (s1 s2 : String) (h : History 0 n) → l1 < l2 →
  PathOver (x.doc h = doc x) ADD-ADD-<
    (addP s2 l2 ∘ addP s1 l1)
    (addP s1 l1 ∘ addP s2 (l2-1))

addP-addP-≥ : {n : Nat} (l1 : Fin n+1) (l2 : Fin n+2)
  (s1 s2 : String) (h : History 0 n) → l1 ≥ l2 →
  PathOver (x.doc h = doc x) ADD-ADD-≥
    (addP s2 l2 ∘ addP s1 l1)
    (addP s1 (l1+1) ∘ addP s2 l2)
```

6.2 Interpreter

Assume we have functions `add` and `rm` which implement our patches on concrete vectors of `Strings`.

```
add : {n : Nat} (s : String) (l : Fin n+1)
      → Vec String n → Vec String n+1
rm  : {n : Nat} (l : Fin n+1)
      → Vec String n+1 → Vec String n
```

We want to define a function `I : R → Type` which models, or interprets, points of `R` (complete histories) as types, and paths of `R` (patches) as bijections between those types. Then we can define `interp p = coe-biject (ap I p)` and obtain

```
interp : {n1 n2 : Nat} {h1 : History 0 n1}
         {h2 : History 0 n2} → (doc h1 = doc h2)
         → Bijection (I (doc h1)) (I (doc h2))
```

with the idea that `interp (addP s l h)` should in some sense be `add s l`, and `interp (rmP l h)` should be `rm l`.

The type of `interp` has gotten more complex than before, because there are now many patch contexts, instead of the single `doc`. As a result, we must choose the interpretation of each `doc h` into the type universe.

As we discussed at the beginning of this section, we cannot simply interpret `doc h` as `Vec String n`, because these types are not bijective. Instead, we will essentially interpret `doc h` as the exact file which arises from applying the patches in `h`. That is, we will record in its type exactly which file is described by this history, rather than simply regarding it as a plain text file.

We can specialize any function `f : A → B` to a function between singleton types, as follows:

```
tosingleton : (f : A → B) → {M : A} → S(M) → S(f M)
tosingleton f (x,p) = (f x, ap f p)
```

Because singleton types are contractible (contain exactly one point, and have trivial higher structure), every function between singleton types is automatically a bijection. Call this fact `single-biject`. Then we can define the interpretation

```
I : R → Type

I (doc h) = S(replay h)
ap I (addP s l h) =
  ua (single-biject (tosingleton (add s l)))
ap I (rmP l h) = ua (single-biject (tosingleton (rm l)))
apd' (ap I) (addP-addP-< l1 l2 s1 s2 h p) =
  <replay respects this patch law>
apd' (ap I) (addP-addP-≥ l1 l2 s1 s2 h p) =
  <replay respects this patch law>
```

where `apd'` is a function which gives the action of a function on a `PathOver` (we omit the details, since they will not be used below), and `replay` is a function which steps through a complete history to compute the file specified by that history:

```
replay : {n : Nat} → History 0 n → Vec String n

replay [] = []
replay (ADD s @ l :: h) = add s l (replay h)
replay (RM l :: h) = rm l (replay h)

ap replay (ADD-ADD-< l1 l2 s1 s2 h pf) =
  GOAL0 : add s2 l2 (add s1 l1 (replay h))
        = add s1 l1 (add s2 (l2-1) (replay h))
ap replay (ADD-ADD-≥ l1 l2 s1 s2 h pf) =
  GOAL1 : add s2 l2 (add s1 l1 (replay h))
        = add s1 l1+1 (add s2 l2 (replay h))
```

Because histories are quotiented by the commutation laws, we must prove in `GOAL0` and `GOAL1` that `replay` sends equal histories to equal files, which amounts to showing that `add` satisfies the same laws as `ADD`.

The implementation of `replay` is needed during typechecking of the definition of `ap I (addP s l h)`, which must be in `Bijection S(replay h) S(replay (ADD s @ l :: h))`. By unrolling the definition of `replay`, the latter type is `S(add s l (replay h))`.

6.3 Logs

The interpreter above suggests that one may implement a version control system in homotopy type theory by storing sequences of patches as paths, and repositories as vectors of strings. A repository can be updated by running `interp` on a new patch. Note that, although the types of the paths include histories which redundantly encode the patch data, these types are only needed to compute the singleton type of the file data, which is not needed at runtime; the file data itself is computed only from the patches themselves. Thus, it would be sensible to discard the histories at runtime, through some erasure mechanism.

Another feature we might like to implement is the ability to print out an explicit representation, or *log*, of all the patches that have been applied to the repository. Logs can't be generated directly from the changes induced by patches on the repository, because we cannot inspect the intensions of functions `S(file) → S(file')`.

Instead, just as we computed changes on repositories by interpreting points of `R` as singleton files, we can compute the changes induced on *histories* through an alternate interpretation of points of `R` as singleton histories:

```
I' : R → Type

I' (doc h) = S(h)
ap I' (addP s l h) =
  ua (single-biject (tosingleton (\ h → ADD s@l :: h))
ap I' (rmP l h) =
  ua (single-biject (tosingleton (\ h → RM l :: h)))
apd' (ap I') (addP-addP-< l1 l2 s1 s2 h p) =
  ADD-ADD-< l1 l2 s1 s2 h p
apd' (ap I') (addP-addP-≥ l1 l2 s1 s2 h p) =
  ADD-ADD-≥ l1 l2 s1 s2 h p

interpH : doc h = doc h' → S(h) → S(h')
interpH p = coe (ap I' p)
```

Then `interpH` takes a patch `p`, which updates the repository history `h`, to the history `h'` which results from applying the patch `p`. As with `interp`, this function computes updates to the repository representation without relying on the endpoints (contexts)—this shows that we could recover a history from a patch (and an initial history), if we were to erase histories at run-time.

`I'` is a good example of the benefit of functorial semantics—both `I` and `I'` are models of the patch theory `R`, and the natural functoriality of functions in homotopy type theory ensures that both validate all the patch laws of the theory.

6.4 Merge

In Section 3, we said that `merge` takes any pair of diverging patches to a pair of converging patches that reconciles them. Our definition of `merge` in Section 4 accepted arbitrary pairs of patches, because that patch theory had a single context `num`.

Now that we have history-indexed patches, we might expect `merge` to take a pair `(doc h = doc h1) × (doc h = doc h2)` and, if a merge is possible, produce a pair `(doc h1 = doc h')` `× (doc h2 = doc h')`. However, as discussed in Section 3, even though some divergent patches are impossible to reconcile automatically—for example, given `addP s 0` and `addP s' 0`, we have no reason to favor either `[s,s']` or `[s',s]` over the other—we can produce a valid merge that simply undoes both edits. Therefore merge can be a total function that always returns a pair of patches `(doc h1 = doc h') × (doc h2 = doc h')`. A user-friendly system might recognize when merge undoes the edits, indicating a merge conflict, and prompt for manual intervention.

Defining such a function requires a "view" or derived recursion principle for these types, as we illustrated in Section 4.2. The `History` type characterizes the "forward-pointing" paths in `R` as sequences of composable primitive patches `ADD` and `RM`, modulo patch laws. But to define such a `merge` we would also need a characterization of, for example, the type of the path `!(rmP l' h)`,

```
doc {n} (RM l' :: h) = doc {n+1} h
```

The type `History n n+1` does not characterize this type, because the only elements of `History n n+1` lengthen the history `h` (by prepending sequences of `ADD`s and `RM`s), while this path shortens it. In other words, a history contains only compositions of primitive patches, and not their inverses. On the other hand, a merge involving inverse paths is not sensible in this patch theory. Although `!(rmP l' h)` and `addP s l (RM l' :: h)` have a common domain of `doc (RM l' :: h)`, the former is not part of the patch theory we are studying; instead, it was imposed by the natural symmetry of identity types.

We can avoid these undesirable inverses by restricting merge to divergent paths with shared domain `doc []`. This ensures that a patch `p` to be merged can be mapped to a complete history `interpH p []`. Users of a version control system will always encounter compositions of generating patches starting from the empty file, so this restriction does not come up in practice.

```
merge : {n1 n2 : Nat}
        {h1 : History 0 n1} {h2 : History 0 n2}
        (doc [] = doc h1) → (doc [] = doc h2) →
        Σ(n' : Nat). Σ(h' : History 0 n').
          (doc h1 = doc h') × (doc h2 = doc h')
```

Because this `merge` is more intricate than the one considered in Section 4, we will convert the input paths to complete histories using `interpH`, then define a function `mergeH` which computes merges of complete histories, and convert the resulting histories back into paths.

To reconcile two divergent complete histories, we define the notion that a history `h2` has `h1` as a prefix (or `h2` *extends* `h1`):

```
Extension : {n1 n2 : Nat} → History 0 n1
          → History 0 n2 → Type
Extension h1 h2 = Σ(s : History n1 n2). h1 ++ s = h2
```

Here, `++ : History n1 n2 → History n2 n3 → History n1 n3` appends two histories. Then, if we have a pair of complete histories `h1,h2`, we reconcile them by returning a history `h'` which extends both `h1` and `h2`. The suffixes of `h1` and `h2` yielding `h'` are the pair of converging patches produced by the merge.

```
mergeH : {n n1 n2 : Nat}
         (h1 : History 0 n1) (h2 : History 0 n2) →
         Σ(n' : Nat). Σ(h' : History 0 n').
           Extension h1 h' × Extension h2 h'
```

Once we have defined `mergeH`, we can convert its output back to paths. A complete history can be transformed into a path `doc [] = doc h` by repeated concatenation:

```
toPath : {n : Nat} (h : History 0 n) → doc [] = doc h
toPath [] = refl
toPath (ADD s@l :: h') = addP s l ∘ toPath h'
toPath (RM l :: h') = rmP l ∘ toPath h'
```

To turn an `Extension h h'` into a path, we need only travel from `doc h` to `doc []` and back to `doc h'`:

```
extToPath : {n n' : Nat}
            {h : History 0 n} {h' : History 0 n'} →
            Extension h h' → doc h = doc h'
extToPath _ = (toPath h') ∘ !(toPath h)
```

`extToPath` completely ignores the extension itself; intuitively, this is possible because extensions are more informative than paths, since the former contain only compositions of generators.

Combining these ingredients, we define `merge` as:

```
merge p1 p2 =
  let (n',(h',(e1,e2))) =
    mergeH (interpH p1 []) (interpH p2 [])
    in (n', (h', (extToPath e1, extToPath e2)))
```

This shows that `merge` reduces to `mergeH`. We have not yet defined `mergeH`, but we can reduce it to defining a merge on simple text files. Because `History 0 n` is quotiented by patch laws, we must show that `mergeH` sends equal histories to equal results. One way to handle this is to choose a representative for each equivalence class of histories, and then compute on these representatives. Here, we can use the function `replay` to convert each `History 0 n` to its file contents in `Vec n String`. Then, we could define a merge function directly on files (perhaps using existing algorithms), and then compute extensions of the input histories which result in that those files. Such a `mergeH` would necessarily respect the patch laws because `replay` does.

7. Related Work

Several prior category-theoretic analyses of version control have been considered. Jacobson [16] interprets patches in inverse semigroups, where they are essentially partial bijections. Mimram and Di Giusto [28] analyze merging as a pushout, which provides a canonical merge for every pair of patches, including a primitive representation of merge conflicts. Houston [15] also discusses merge as pushout, and a duality with exceptions. Our contribution, relative to these analyses, is to present patch theory in a categorical setting that is also a programming formalism, so it directly leads to an implementation. These analyses consider settings where not all maps are invertible. In homotopy type theory all identity types are symmetric, and to fit patch theories into this symmetric setting, we either considered a language where all patches were naturally total bijections on any repository (Section 4 and 5), or used types to restrict patches to repositories where they are bijections (Section 6).

Dagit [10] presents an approach to proving some invariants of a version control implementation using advanced features of Haskell's type system. Camp (Commute And Merge Patches) [7] is an experimental version control system based on Darcs; the Camp project aims to prove the correctness of its patch theory in Coq. We have not yet mechanized the programs described here, but our work provides another possible path to formalization.

Swierstra and Löh [34] explore the use of separation logic [30] for specifying the behavior of patches. In Section 6, we took repository contexts to be patch histories, but it would be interesting to consider using separation logic formulas to describe histories, which would allow for small-footprint specifications of patches.

8. Conclusion

Inspired by the patch theory of Darcs [12], which emphasizes the groupoid structure of patches, we have explored the formulation of patch theory within the framework of homotopy type theory. Patch theories are given as higher inductive definitions in which we specify generators for the points (path contexts), 1-dimensional paths (patches), and 2-dimensional paths (patch laws). The groupoid laws come "for free", and so need not be specified explicitly. An idealized implementation of a patch theory is given by a function mapping the patch theory into a univalent universe of sets and bijections. The sets are concrete repositories and the bijections are the actual actions of the patches on repositories. The mapping is intrinsically functorial, and hence must respect the intrinsic groupoid structure, but is given by the elimination principle for higher-inductive types, which demands that patches be realized by bijections satisfying the patch laws.

Besides these general structural considerations, some homotopy-theoretic concepts play a role in the development. In particular the "encode/decode" functions used to characterize identity types [23, 35] here become an implementation technique. For example, to define the merge of a span of patches (that is, a pair of paths with a common domain), we first pass to a concrete representation of paths, define the merge on the representation, and then pass back to a reconciliation, a cospan of patches (a pair of patches with common codomain) in the identity type. Other interpretations of a patch theory are definable in a similar manner, providing operations, such as logging, of practical interest for revision control.

There is much more to be done. Most importantly, the development of the merge operation in Section 6 is incomplete, because we have not proved the required properties of it. There we define `merge` using a partial characterization of the identity type of `R` as complete histories. Defining functions in either direction is sufficient to pass between these two representations, but not to prove properties of `merge` via properties of `mergeH`, such as the merge laws. For this, a more precise characterization is needed, namely an inductive type which is *equivalent* to the identity type, as $\mathbb{Z}$ is to the identity type of the circle. We leave this to future work.

More broadly, the computational interpretation of homotopy type theory must be developed further, including a fuller understanding of the interplay between definitional equality, propositional equality, and computation, and an understanding of what type erasure would mean in that setting. This includes developing a fuller understanding of "sub-homotopical" computation, meaning the mapping into contractible types.

One aspect of the homotopical framework that we have found limiting is the requirement that paths be symmetric (have inverses). In Darcs, inverses are used to define merging in terms of the elegant concept of pseudocommutation. But demanding inverses, rather than just retractions representing "undo" operations, is both conceptually questionable and practically problematic. We worked around the presence of inverses by refining contexts using patch histories, and using histories it was possible to define merge directly on only "forward" patches, rather than using inverses and pseudocommutation. Despite efforts, we were unable to formulate pseudocommutation in our setting, because to do so seems to require a complete characterization of the space of spans of patches. One direction for future work is to study this problem using the tools of homotopy theory to characterize such spans in a way that is amenable to our purposes. Another is to develop a type theory with non-symmetric paths (as suggested by [21]) grounded in directed homotopy theory, where we could formulate theories of partial patches without refining their contexts, which might simplify the development in Section 6.

Acknowledgments We thank the participants of the 2013 IFIP WG 2.8 meeting for helpful conversations about this work, and the anonymous reviewers for their helpful feedback on this article.

References

[1] M. Abbott, T. Altenkirch, and N. Ghani. Containers: constructing strictly positive types. *Theoretic Computer Science*, 342(1):3–27, 2005.

[2] T. Altenkirch. Containers in homotopy type theory. Talk at Mathematical Structures of Computation, Lyon, 2014.

[3] T. Altenkirch, C. McBride, and W. Swierstra. Observational equality, now. In *Programming Languages meets Program Verification Workshop*, 2007.

[4] S. Awodey and M. Warren. Homotopy theoretic models of identity types. *Mathematical Proceedings of the Cambridge Philosophical Society*, 2009.

[5] B. Barras, T. Coquand, and S. Huber. A generalization of Takeuti–Gandy interpretation. To appear in *Mathematical Structures in Computer Science*, 2013.

[6] M. Bezem, T. Coquand, and S. Huber. A model of type theory in cubical sets. Preprint, September 2013.

[7] Camp Project. `http://projects.haskell.org/camp/`, 2010.

[8] R. L. Constable, S. F. Allen, H. M. Bromley, W. R. Cleaveland, J. F. Cremer, R. W. Harper, D. J. Howe, T. B. Knoblock, N. P. Mendler, P. Panangaden, J. T. Sasaki, and S. F. Smith. *Implementing Mathematics with the NuPRL Proof Development System.* Prentice Hall, 1986.

[9] Coq Development Team. *The Coq Proof Assistant Reference Manual, version 8.2.* INRIA, 2009. Available from `http://coq.inria.fr/`.

[10] J. Dagit. Type-correct changes—a safe approach to version control implementation. MS Thesis, 2009.

[11] N. Gambino and R. Garner. The identity type weak factorisation system. *Theoretical Computer Science*, 409(3):94–109, 2008.

[12] Ganesh Sittampalam et al. Some properties of darcs patch theory. Available from `http://urchin.earth.li/darcs/ganesh/darcs-patch-theory/theory/formal.pdf`, 2005.

[13] R. Garner. Two-dimensional models of type theory. *Mathematical. Structures in Computer Science*, 19(4):687–736, 2009.

[14] M. Hofmann and T. Streicher. The groupoid interpretation of type theory. In *Twenty-five years of constructive type theory*. Oxford University Press, 1998.

[15] R. Houston. On editing text. `http://bosker.wordpress.com/2012/05/10/on-editing-text/`, 2012.

[16] J. Jacobson. A formalization of darcs patch theory using inverse semigroups. Available from `ftp://ftp.math.ucla.edu/pub/camreport/cam09-83.pdf`, 2009.

[17] C. Kapulkin, P. L. Lumsdaine, and V. Voevodsky. The simplicial model of univalent foundations. arXiv:1211.2851, 2012.

[18] F. W. Lawvere. *Functorial Semantics of Algebraic Theories and Some Algebraic Problems in the context of Functorial Semantics of Algebraic Theories*. PhD thesis, Columbia University, 1963.

[19] D. R. Licata and G. Brunerie. $\pi_n(S^n)$ in homotopy type theory. In *Certified Programs and Proofs*, 2013.

[20] D. R. Licata and E. Finster. Eilenberg–MacLane spaces in homotopy type theory. Draft available from `http://dlicata.web.wesleyan.edu/pubs.html`, 2014.

[21] D. R. Licata and R. Harper. 2-dimensional directed type theory. In *Mathematical Foundations of Programming Semantics (MFPS)*, 2011.

[22] D. R. Licata and R. Harper. Canonicity for 2-dimensional type theory. In *ACM SIGPLAN-SIGACT Symposium on Principles of Programming Languages*, 2012.

[23] D. R. Licata and M. Shulman. Calculating the fundamental group of the circle in homotopy type theory. In *IEEE Symposium on Logic in Computer Science*, 2013.

[24] P. L. Lumsdaine. Weak ω-categories from intensional type theory. In *International Conference on Typed Lambda Calculi and Applications*, 2009.

[25] P. L. Lumsdaine. Higher inductive types: a tour of the menagerie. `http://homotopytypetheory.org/2011/04/24/higher-inductive-types-a-tour-of-the-menagerie/`, April 2011.

[26] P. L. Lumsdaine and M. Shulman. Higher inductive types. In preparation, 2013.

[27] C. McBride. *Dependently Typed Functional Programs and Their Proofs*. PhD thesis, University of Edinburgh, 2000.

[28] S. Mimram and C. Di Giusto. A categorical theory of patches. *Electronic Notes in Theoretic Computer Science*, 298:283–307, 2013.

[29] U. Norell. *Towards a practical programming language based on dependent type theory*. PhD thesis, Chalmers University of Technology, 2007.

[30] J. C. Reynolds. Separation logic: A logic for shared mutable data structures. In *IEEE Symposium on Logic in Computer Science*, 2002.

[31] D. Roundy. Darcs: Distributed version management in haskell. In *ACM SIGPLAN Workshop on Haskell*. ACM, 2005.

[32] M. Shulman. Homotopy type theory VI: higher inductive types. `http://golem.ph.utexas.edu/category/2011/04/homotopy_type_theory_vi.html`, April 2011.

[33] M. Shulman. Univalence for inverse diagrams, oplax limits, and gluing, and homotopy canonicity. arXiv:1203.3253, 2013.

[34] W. Swierstra and A. Löh. The semantics of version control. Available from `http://www.staff.science.uu.nl/~swier004/`, 2014.

[35] The Univalent Foundations Program, Institute for Advanced Study. *Homotopy Type Theory: Univalent Foundations Of Mathematics*. Available from `homotopytypetheory.org/book`, 2013.

[36] B. van den Berg and R. Garner. Types are weak ω-groupoids. *Proceedings of the London Mathematical Society*, 102(2):370–394, 2011.

[37] V. Voevodsky. Univalent foundations of mathematics. Invited talk at WoLLIC 2011 18th Workshop on Logic, Language, Information and Computation, 2011.

[38] M. A. Warren. *Homotopy theoretic aspects of constructive type theory*. PhD thesis, Carnegie Mellon University, 2008.

Pattern Matching Without K

Jesper Cockx Dominique Devriese Frank Piessens
iMinds-DistriNet, KU Leuven, 3001 Leuven, Belgium.
firstname.lastname@cs.kuleuven.be

Abstract

Dependent pattern matching is an intuitive way to write programs and proofs in dependently typed languages. It is reminiscent of both pattern matching in functional languages and case analysis in on-paper mathematics. However, in general it is incompatible with new type theories such as homotopy type theory (HoTT). As a consequence, proofs in such theories are typically harder to write and to understand. The source of this incompatibility is the reliance of dependent pattern matching on the so-called K axiom – also known as the uniqueness of identity proofs – which is inadmissible in HoTT. The Agda language supports an experimental criterion to detect definitions by pattern matching that make use of the K axiom, but so far it lacked a formal correctness proof.

In this paper, we propose a new criterion for dependent pattern matching without K, and prove it correct by a translation to eliminators in the style of Goguen et al. (2006). Our criterion both allows more good definitions than existing proposals, and solves a previously undetected problem in the criterion offered by Agda. It has been implemented in Agda and is the first to be supported by a formal proof. Thus it brings the benefits of dependent pattern matching to contexts where we cannot assume K, such as HoTT. It also points the way to new forms of dependent pattern matching, for example on higher inductive types.

Categories and Subject Descriptors F.3.3 [*Logics and Meanings of Programs*]: Studies of Program Constructs – functional constructs, program and recursion schemes; D.3.3 [*Programming Languages*]: Language Constructs and Features – data types and structures, patterns, recursion

Keywords Dependent Pattern Matching, K Axiom, Homotopy Type Theory, Agda

1. Introduction

The case for dependent pattern matching. Dependent pattern matching (Coquand 1992) is a technique for writing functions in languages based on dependent type theory, such as Agda (Norell 2007), Coq (Sozeau 2010), and Idris (Brady 2013). It allows us to define functions in a style similar to functional programming languages such as Haskell, by giving a number of equalities called *clauses*. For example, the function $\texttt{half} : \mathbb{N} \to \mathbb{N}$ can be defined as

$$\begin{array}{llcl} \texttt{half} : & \mathbb{N} & \to & \mathbb{N} \\ \texttt{half} & \texttt{zero} & = & \texttt{zero} \\ \texttt{half} & (\texttt{suc}\,\texttt{zero}) & = & \texttt{zero} \\ \texttt{half} & (\texttt{suc}\,(\texttt{suc}\,k)) & = & \texttt{suc}\,(\texttt{half}\,k) \end{array} \quad (1)$$

Note that pattern matching combines two powerful programming features, namely *case analysis* and *recursion*.

Additionally, dependent pattern matching can be used to write *proofs* (in the form of dependently typed functions). For example, we can prove the transitivity of the propositional equality $x \equiv y$ (Martin-Löf 1984) by pattern matching on its only constructor $\texttt{refl}$ of type $x \equiv x$:

$$\begin{array}{l} \texttt{trans} : (x\ y\ z : A) \to x \equiv y \to y \equiv z \to x \equiv z \\ \texttt{trans}\ x\ \lfloor x \rfloor\ \lfloor x \rfloor\ \texttt{refl}\ \texttt{refl} = \texttt{refl} \end{array} \quad (2)$$

Inaccessible patterns, like $\lfloor x \rfloor$ in this example, witness the fact that only one type-correct argument can be in that position. Indeed, matching on a proof of $x \equiv y$ with $\texttt{refl} : x \equiv x$ forces x and y to be the same. Another example is the proof $\texttt{cong}$ that any function maps equal arguments to equal results:

$$\begin{array}{l} \texttt{cong} : (f : A \to B)(x\ y : A) \to x \equiv y \to f\ x \equiv f\ y \\ \texttt{cong}\ f\ x\ \lfloor x \rfloor\ \texttt{refl} = \texttt{refl} \end{array} \quad (3)$$

Proofs by dependent pattern matching are typically much shorter and more readable than ones that use the classical *datatype eliminators* associated with each inductive family. For example, let $\leq$ be the usual ordering on $\mathbb{N}$ defined as an inductive family (Dybjer 1991) defined by the two constructors $\texttt{lz}$ and $\texttt{ls}$:

$$\begin{array}{l} \texttt{lz} : (n : \mathbb{N}) \to \texttt{zero} \leq n \\ \texttt{ls} : (m\ n : \mathbb{N}) \to m \leq n \to \texttt{suc}\ m \leq \texttt{suc}\ n \end{array} \quad (4)$$

We can prove antisymmetry of this relation by pattern matching as follows:

$$\begin{array}{l} \texttt{antisym} : (m\ n : \mathbb{N}) \to m \leq n \to n \leq m \to m \equiv n \\ \texttt{antisym}\ \lfloor\texttt{zero}\rfloor\ \lfloor\texttt{zero}\rfloor\ (\texttt{lz}\ \lfloor\texttt{zero}\rfloor)\ (\texttt{lz}\ \lfloor\texttt{zero}\rfloor) = \\ \qquad \texttt{refl} \\ \texttt{antisym}\ \lfloor\texttt{suc}\ m\rfloor\ \lfloor\texttt{suc}\ n\rfloor\ (\texttt{ls}\ m\ n\ x)\ (\texttt{ls}\ \lfloor n\rfloor\ \lfloor m\rfloor\ y) = \\ \qquad \texttt{cong}\ \texttt{suc}\ (\texttt{antisym}\ m\ n\ x\ y) \end{array} \quad (5)$$

Pattern matching allows us to skip the two cases where one of the arguments is $\texttt{lz}\ n$ and the other is $\texttt{ls}\ n'\ m'$ because $\texttt{zero}$ can never be of the form $\texttt{suc}\ m'$ (this is called the **conflict** rule). In the second clause, m' (the first argument of the second $\texttt{ls}$) was replaced by $\lfloor n \rfloor$ because $\texttt{suc}\ m'$ and $\texttt{suc}\ n$ were forced to be equal, and similarly n' (its second argument) is replaced by $\lfloor m \rfloor$ (this is called the **injectivity** rule).

Desugaring pattern matching. In a dependent type theory with inductive families but without pattern matching, functions have to be written using *datatype eliminators*. They will be defined

ICFP '14, September 1–6, 2014, Gothenburg, Sweden.
Copyright © 2014 ACM 978-1-4503-2873-9 /14/09... $15.00.
http://dx.doi.org/10.1145/2628136.2628139

$$
\begin{aligned}
&\texttt{antisym} : (m\ n : \mathbb{N}) \to m \le n \to n \le m \to m \equiv n \\
&\texttt{antisym} = \texttt{elim}_{\le}\ (\lambda m; n; \_ .\ n \le m \to m \equiv n) \\
&\quad (\lambda n; e.\ \texttt{elim}_{\le}\ (\lambda n; m; \_ .\ m \equiv \texttt{zero} \to m \equiv n) \\
&\qquad (\lambda n; e.\ e) \\
&\qquad (\lambda k; l; \_; \_; e.\ \texttt{elim}_{\bot} (\lambda \_ .\ \texttt{suc}\ l \equiv \texttt{suc}\ k) \\
&\qquad\quad (\texttt{noConf}_{\mathbb{N}}\ (\texttt{suc}\ l)\ \texttt{zero}\ e)) \\
&\qquad n\ \texttt{zero}\ e\ \texttt{refl}) \\
&\quad (\lambda m; n; \_; H; q.\ \texttt{cong}\ \texttt{suc} \\
&\qquad (H \\
&\qquad\quad (\texttt{elim}_{\le}\ (\lambda k; l; \_ .\ k \equiv \texttt{suc}\ n \to l \equiv \texttt{suc}\ m \to n \le m) \\
&\qquad\qquad (\lambda \_; e; \_ .\ \texttt{elim}_{\bot}\ (\lambda \_ .\ n \le m) \\
&\qquad\qquad\quad (\texttt{noConf}_{\mathbb{N}}\ \texttt{zero}\ (\texttt{suc}\ n)\ e)) \\
&\qquad\qquad (\lambda k; l; e; \_; x; y.\ \texttt{subst}\ (\lambda n.\ n \le m) \\
&\qquad\qquad\quad (\texttt{noConf}_{\mathbb{N}}\ (\texttt{suc}\ k)\ (\texttt{suc}\ n)\ x) \\
&\qquad\qquad\quad (\texttt{subst}\ (\lambda m.\ k \le m) \\
&\qquad\qquad\qquad (\texttt{noConf}_{\mathbb{N}}\ (\texttt{suc}\ l)\ (\texttt{suc}\ m)\ y)\ e)) \\
&\qquad\qquad (\texttt{suc}\ n)\ (\texttt{suc}\ m)\ y\ \texttt{refl}\ \texttt{refl})))
\end{aligned}
$$

Figure 1. This proof of the antisymmetry of $\le$ is more complex than the proof by pattern matching (5) because it uses only the standard datatype eliminators (see Section 3.1) and the "no confusion" property of the natural numbers. No confusion can be constructed from the eliminator for $\mathbb{N}$ as well (see Section 3.4).

formally in Section 3.1, but Figure 1 already gives an alternative definition of `antisym` as an example using eliminators only. All the equational reasoning that was done automatically in the definition by pattern matching now has to be done explicitly. The proof with eliminators also requires considerable cleverness for the construction of the *motive* (McBride 2002) of each eliminator, while this is done automatically in the definition by pattern matching. So it is clearly preferable to use pattern matching for this proof.

As shown by Goguen et al. (2006), *all* definitions by dependent pattern matching can be translated to ones that only use eliminators. However, for this translation they depend on the so-called K axiom. Coquand (1992) already observed that pattern matching allows proving this K axiom:

$$
\begin{aligned}
&\mathrm{K} : (P : a \equiv a \to \texttt{Set}) \to \\
&\qquad (p : P\ \texttt{refl})(e : a \equiv a) \to P\ e \\
&\mathrm{K}\quad P\ p\ \texttt{refl} = p
\end{aligned}
\tag{6}
$$

The K axiom is equivalent with the *uniqueness of identity proofs* principle (UIP), which states that any two proofs of $x \equiv y$ must be equal. As observed by Hofmann and Streicher (1994), the K axiom does not follow from the standard rules of type theory, but it is compatible with them.

So far, none of the examples we gave needs the K axiom for the translation to eliminators (except for the definition of K itself). For the next example, remember that in type theory there is no strict boundary between types and terms, so we can form equations between types as well, for example `Bool` $\equiv$ `Bool`. Given such an equation between types, we can coerce terms of the first type to the other using the function `coerce` : $A \equiv B \to A \to B$ (which can be constructed by pattern matching). Now we can use pattern matching to prove that coercing `true` by any proof of `Bool` $\equiv$ `Bool` results in `true`:

$$
\begin{aligned}
&\texttt{coerce-id} : (e : \texttt{Bool} \equiv \texttt{Bool}) \to \texttt{coerce}\ e\ \texttt{true} \equiv \texttt{true} \\
&\texttt{coerce-id}\ \texttt{refl} = \texttt{refl}
\end{aligned}
\tag{7}
$$

This can be desugared to

$$
\texttt{coerce-id} = \lambda e.\ \mathrm{K}\ (\lambda e.\ \texttt{coerce}\ e\ \texttt{true} \equiv \texttt{true})\ \texttt{refl}\ e \tag{8}
$$

The K axiom is necessary to deal with reflexive equations such as `Bool` $\equiv$ `Bool` in this example.

Pattern matching in HoTT. An emerging field within dependent type theory is *homotopy type theory* (HoTT) (The Univalent Foundations Program 2013). It gives a new interpretation of terms of type $x \equiv y$ as *paths* from x to y. Many basic constructions in HoTT can be written very elegantly using pattern matching, for example `trans` (2) corresponds to the composition of two paths, and `cong` (3) can be interpreted as a proof that all functions in HoTT are continuous (in a certain sense).

One of the core elements of HoTT is the *univalence axiom.* This axiom states roughly that any two isomorphic types can be identified, i.e. if there is a function $f : A \to B$ which has both a left and a right inverse, then it gives us a proof `ua` f of $A \equiv B$. Moreover, this proof satisfies `coerce` (`ua` f) $x = f\ x$. Univalence captures the common mathematical practice of informal reasoning "up to isomorphism" in a nice and formalized way. It also has a number of useful consequences, such as *functional extensionality.*

However, the univalence axiom is *incompatible* with dependent pattern matching. For example, we can construct a function `swap` : `Bool` $\to$ `Bool` such that `swap true` $=$ `false` and vice versa. This function is its own inverse, so by univalence it gives us a proof `ua swap` of `Bool` $\equiv$ `Bool` such that coercing `true` along this proof results in `false`. Together with the proof `coerce-id` (7), this leads to a proof of the absurdity `true` $\equiv$ `false`. This has forced people working on HoTT to avoid using pattern matching or risk unsoundness.

Avoiding K. The source of the incompatibility between univalence and dependent pattern matching is that pattern matching relies on the K axiom. If we could somehow restrict definitions by pattern matching so that we could translate them to type theory with eliminators but without the K axiom, then we would be able to use pattern matching in HoTT. One attempt to achieve this is an option in Agda called –without-K (Norell et al. 2012). When enabled, Agda attempts to detect definitions by pattern matching that make use of the K axiom by means of a syntactic check. In theory, this option should allow people to use pattern matching in a safe way when it is undesirable to assume K. However, the option has been criticized many times, for being too restrictive (Sicard-Ramírez 2013), for having unclear semantics (Reed 2013), and for containing errors (Altenkirch 2012; Cockx 2014). These errors allowed one to prove (weaker versions of) the K axiom. While errors are typically fixed quickly after being found, this situation really calls for a more in-depth investigation of dependent pattern matching without K.

Contributions.

- We present a new criterion that describes what kind of definitions by pattern matching are still allowed if we do not assume K. This criterion is strictly more general than previous attempts.
- We give a formal proof that definitions by pattern matching satisfying this criterion are conservative over standard type theory by translating them to eliminators in the style of Goguen et al. (2006), but *without* relying on the K axiom.
- Our criterion has been implemented as a patch to Agda. We test it on a body of examples in order to show its adequacy, soundness, and generality. As of Agda version 2.4.0 (released

on June 5, 2014), our implementation replaces the old version of –without-K.

- Finally, we give an idea how to make pattern matching without K even less restrictive by analyzing which types satisfy K without assuming it as an axiom. Future work is still needed to make this analysis more robust.

Overview. The rest of this paper is organized as follows. In section 2, we describe our criterion for pattern matching without K and compare our implementation with the current one in Agda. Section 3 contains the main technical contribution of this paper: a proof that definitions by pattern matching satisfying our criterion can be translated to eliminators without using K. In section 4, we discuss how pattern matching without K can be made less restrictive. Finally, we discuss related work in section 5.

Supplementary material for this paper can be found online at `http://people.cs.kuleuven.be/~jesper.cockx/Without-K/`. This page contains the implementation of our criterion in Agda, Agda files containing the examples given in this paper, and Agda files illustrating parts of the proof in Section 3.

2. The criterion

A definition by pattern matching can be thought of as given by a number of case splits on the arguments. For example, the function $\texttt{half} : \mathbb{N} \to \mathbb{N}$ in Definition 1 is defined by first doing a case split on the argument $n : \mathbb{N}$ – giving us two cases $n = \texttt{zero}$ and $n = \texttt{suc}\ m$ – and then another case split on m. For definitions like this one, each case split corresponds exactly to one application of the standard eliminator for $\mathbb{N}$, hence the K axiom is not needed.

Things get more complicated for an inductive family (Dybjer 1991) such as $\texttt{Fin}\ n$, the canonical finite set of n elements, or $m \leq n$, the type of proofs that m is smaller than or equal to n. When splitting on a type from an inductive family, we need to apply *unification* in order to determine the possible cases. This unification algorithm depends crucially on the K axiom, so we have to restrict it in order to remove this dependence.

In this section, we first describe the unification algorithm used by Goguen et al. (2006). Next, we describe our restricted unification algorithm that does not depend on K. We also compare our criterion with the syntactic criterion for pattern matching without K in Agda. Finally, we give a short evaluation of our implementation.

2.1 Case splitting by unification of the indices

When checking a definition by pattern matching, we must decide which constructors can be used to construct a term of a particular type, and under which constraints. For example, consider the inductive family $m \leq n$ with constructors `lz` and `ls` as given in Definition 4. Suppose we want to do a case split on a variable of type $k \leq k$, then we have to decide for what kind of arguments the two constructors give a result of the form $k \leq k$. In the case of `lz`, this is when both k and the argument n are equal to `zero`, while for `ls`, this is when the two arguments m and n are equal and $k = \texttt{suc}\ n$.

In general, suppose we are case splitting on a variable $x : \texttt{D}\ \bar{u}$ where D is an inductive family with indices $\bar{u}$ (we consider D to already be applied to its parameters, if any). Suppose D has constructors $\texttt{c}_i$ with return type $\texttt{D}\ \bar{v}_i$ for $i = 1, \ldots, k$, then we have to *unify* $\bar{u}$ with each of the $\bar{v}_i$. Unification is the process of searching for *unifiers*, i.e. substitutions σ such that $\bar{u}\sigma = \bar{v}_i\sigma$. A unification problem is represented as a list of equations $u_1 = v_{i1}, \ldots, u_n = v_{in}$, and the following five unification transitions are used to simplify the problem step by step:

Deletion: $x = x, \Theta \Rightarrow \Theta$

Solution: $x = t, \Theta \Rightarrow \Theta[x \mapsto t]$ (if x is not free in t)

Injectivity: $\texttt{c}\ \bar{s} = \texttt{c}\ \bar{t}, \Theta \Rightarrow \bar{s} = \bar{t}, \Theta$

Conflict: $\texttt{c}_1\ \bar{s} = \texttt{c}_2\ \bar{t}, \Theta \Rightarrow \bot$ (if $\texttt{c}_1 \neq \texttt{c}_2$)

Cycle: $x = \texttt{c}\ \bar{p}[x], \Theta \Rightarrow \bot$ (if $x \prec \texttt{c}\ \bar{p}[x]$)

Exhaustively applying these rules whenever they are applicable terminates by the usual argument (Jouannaud and Kirchner 1990), with three possible outcomes:

Positive success: All equations have been solved, yielding a most general unifier σ.

Negative success: Either the **conflict** or the **cycle** rule applies, meaning that there exist no unifiers.

Failure: An equation is reached for which no transition applies, meaning that the problem is too hard to be solved (by this unification algorithm).

This algorithm is complete for *constructor forms*: if both $\bar{u}$ and $\bar{v}$ are built from constructors and variables only, then unification will never result in a failure.

Case splitting succeeds if unification of $\bar{u}$ with each of the $\bar{v}_i$ succeeds (either positively or negatively). If all of them succeed negatively, we replace x by an *absurd pattern* $\emptyset$, marking that case splitting resulted in zero cases.[1] If on the other hand at least one of them succeeds positively, we get the same number of new cases where x has been replaced by $\texttt{c}_i\ \bar{y}$ and $\bar{y} : \Delta_i$ are fresh variables. To each of these cases, we then apply the substitution σ_i constructed by unification. For example, a function $f : (k : \mathbb{N}) \to k \leq k \to P\ k$ can be defined by the following patterns:

$$\begin{aligned} &f\ \lfloor \texttt{zero} \rfloor\ (\texttt{lz}\ \lfloor \texttt{zero} \rfloor) = \ldots \\ &f\ \lfloor \texttt{suc}\ n \rfloor\ (\texttt{ls}\ n; \lfloor n \rfloor) = \ldots \end{aligned} \tag{9}$$

Here, $\lfloor \ldots \rfloor$ marks an inaccessible pattern: it is not part of a case split, but rather computed by unification. The substitution σ_i is also applied to the result type: in the first clause, the right-hand side should have type $P\ \texttt{zero}$, while in the second one it should have type $P\ (\texttt{suc}\ n)$.

2.2 Restricting the unification rules

Our criterion for pattern matching without K works by limiting the unification algorithm in two ways:

- It is not allowed to use the **deletion** step.
- When applying the **injectivity** step on the equation $c\ \bar{s} = c\ \bar{t}$ where $c\ \bar{s}, c\ \bar{t} : D\ \bar{u}$, the indices $\bar{u}$ should be *self-unifiable*, i.e. unification of $\bar{u}$ with itself should succeed positively (while still adhering to these two restrictions).

This inevitably means that unification will fail more often. However, if unification results in a success (a positive or negative one) then we know that the original rules would have given the same result. Where the original algorithm was complete for constructor forms, our modified version is only complete for *linear* constructor forms (i.e. ones where each variable occurs only once).

As a first example, our criterion allows the definition of the standard J-eliminator for the propositional equality (also known as the principle of *based path induction* in HoTT) by pattern matching:

$$\begin{aligned} &\texttt{J} : (P : (b : A) \to a \equiv b \to \texttt{Set}) \to \\ &\qquad (p : P\ a\ \texttt{refl})(b : A)(e : a \equiv b) \to P\ b\ e \\ &\texttt{J}\ \ P\ p\ \lfloor a \rfloor\ \texttt{refl} = p \end{aligned} \tag{10}$$

The unification problem for the case split on $e : a \equiv b$ with the constructor $\texttt{refl} : a \equiv a$ is given by $b = a$. Unification succeeds positively after one **solution** step, with the most general unifier

[1] The reason for replacing x by an absurd pattern instead of removing the pattern entirely, is to keep coverage checking decidable (Goguen et al. 2006).

$[b \mapsto a]$ as the result. Likewise, the definitions of trans (2), cong (3), and antisym (5) in the introduction are also accepted.

In contrast, the definition of K by pattern matching is not allowed, as case splitting on the argument of type $a \equiv a$ produces a unification problem $a = a$, which fails without the **deletion** step of the unification algorithm.

$$\begin{aligned} &\mathrm{K} : (P : a \equiv a \rightarrow \mathtt{Set}) \rightarrow \\ &\quad (p : P\,\mathtt{refl})(e : a \equiv a) \rightarrow P\; e \\ &\mathrm{K}\quad P\; p\;\mathtt{refl} = p \end{aligned} \tag{11}$$

This already explains the need for the first restriction to the unification algorithm. As an example of why the second restriction is needed, consider the following weaker variant of K:

$$\begin{aligned} &\mathtt{weakK} : (P : \mathtt{refl} \equiv_{a \equiv a} \mathtt{refl} \rightarrow \mathtt{Set}) \rightarrow \\ &\quad (p : P\,\mathtt{refl})(e : \mathtt{refl} \equiv_{a \equiv a} \mathtt{refl}) \rightarrow P\; e \\ &\mathtt{weakK}\quad P\; p\;\mathtt{refl} = p \end{aligned} \tag{12}$$

Like the regular K, this weakK does not follow from the standard rules of type theory and is incompatible with univalence (Kraus and Sattler 2013). However, since refl is a constructor without any arguments, it would be accepted if we did not have the second restriction.

2.3 Comparison with the syntactic criterion

So far, the only credible proposal of a criterion for pattern matching without K was the syntactic criterion used by Agda. So how does our criterion compare to it? One reason to prefer our criterion is that it is more amenable to the correctness proof given in Section 3. But we should also compare their generality, i.e. what kind of definitions are still allowed by each. The criterion currently used in Agda for pattern matching without K is specified as follows:

> If the flag is activated, then Agda only accepts certain case-splits. If the type of the variable to be split is D pars ixs, where D is a data (or record) type, pars stands for the parameters, and ixs the indices, then the following requirements must be satisfied:
>
> - The indices ixs must be applications of constructors (or literals) to distinct variables. Constructors are usually not applied to parameters, but for the purposes of this check constructor parameters are treated as other arguments.
> - These distinct variables must not be free in pars.

This criterion implies that the **deletion** rule is never used during unification. To see why this is true, note that it guarantees that all unification problems generated by pattern matching are of the form $\bar{u} = \bar{v}_i$ where $\bar{u}$ consists of constructors applied to free variables and each variable occurs only once in $\bar{u}$. Moreover, since new constructors introduced by case splitting are applied to fresh variables, the variables in $\bar{u}$ are not free in $\bar{v}_i$. Both the **solution** and the **injectivity** step preserve these three properties, hence we will never reach an equation of the form $x = x$.

On the other hand, the syntactic criterion does not imply that the indices are self-unifiable when applying the **injectivity** rule. But this is actually a bug in the syntactic criterion, allowing one to prove a weaker version of the K axiom (Cockx 2014). So the fact that our criterion is more restrictive in this case is actually a good thing.

Apart from that issue, our criterion is in fact strictly more general than the syntactic one. For example, the syntactic criterion allows us to pattern match with refl on an argument of type $k + l \equiv m$ (where $k, l, m : \mathbb{N}$ are previous arguments), but not on an argument of type $m \equiv k + l$. This asymmetry is created by a technical detail in the standard definition of propositional equality as an inductive family: the first argument is a parameter (so it can be anything), while the second one is an index (so it must consist of constructors applied to free variables). In contrast, our criterion allows both variants because we look at the unifications that are performed instead of syntactical artefacts like the distinction between a parameter and an index. Similarly, Agda's syntactic criterion does not allow us to pattern match on an argument of type $n \leq n$ because the variable n occurs twice. But this turns out to be over-conservative, as evidenced by the fact that it is allowed by our criterion.

Another advantage of our criterion is that unlike the syntactic criterion, it does not put any requirements on the datatype parameters. This is very useful when we need injectivity of a constructor of a parametrized data type. For example, the syntactic criterion does not allow case splitting on an argument of type $x :: xs \equiv y :: ys$ where :: is the list constructor, since the type A of x and y is a parameter and the constructor :: is considered to be applied to this parameter. Our criterion has no such problems.

Unfortunately, our criterion still has some limitations. For example, when working with the $\leq$ relation on finite sets $\mathtt{Fin}\; n$, we cannot pattern match on an argument of type $i \leq i$ where $i : \mathtt{Fin}\; n$. This is because unification gets stuck on the problem $\mathtt{fs}\; n\; x = \mathtt{fs}\; n\; y$, where the **deletion** rule is needed to remove the equation $n = n$. However, this definition is also refused by the syntactic criterion. In Section 4, we discuss a possible solution to this problem.

2.4 Implementation and evaluation

Our new criterion for pattern matching without K has been implemented as a patch to Agda. We used it with a number of Agda programs in order to test it for adequacy, soundness, and generality.

Adequacy. In order to test the adequacy of our approach, we tested it on a number of small examples that should be definable without K, such as the functions half (1), trans (2), cong (3), and antisym (5) from the introduction. We also tested it on a body of Agda code related to propositional equality and HoTT by Danielsson (2013), which was written with Agda's current –without-K flag in mind. All these examples are accepted without problems.

Soundness. To test the soundness of our criterion, we also tested it on a number of variations on the K axiom and weaker versions of it. For example, when we try to define K as in Definition 11, we get the following error message:

> Cannot eliminate reflexive equation $x = x$ of type A because K has been disabled (when checking that the pattern refl has type $x \equiv x$).

Pattern matching with refl on a proof of $\mathtt{Bool} \equiv \mathtt{Bool}$ is also prohibited by our check. Similarly, the elimination rule for heterogeneous equality given by McBride (2000) (which is equivalent with K) is rejected, as are the weaker versions of K given by Altenkirch (2012) and Cockx (2014).

Generality. Finally, to test the generality of our approach, we gave it some definitions that are rejected by Agda's syntactic criterion, but do not actually rely on the K axiom. For example, definitions involving case splitting on types such as $m \leq m$, $k \equiv l + m$, and $x \equiv f\; y$ are accepted. Another notable advantage of our criterion is that adding parameters to a data type will never change the validity of a definition by pattern matching. This is especially useful in Agda since module parameters are also considered to be parameters of the datatypes defined inside that module (Norell 2007, chapter 4). So with the syntactic criterion, moving a definition to another module can cause an error, but with our criterion this is no longer the case.

3. Eliminating pattern matching without K

In this section, we show that definitions by dependent pattern matching satisfying our criterion can be translated to type theory with universes and inductive families, without using the K axiom.

Our proof follows the same general outline as the proof by Goguen et al. (2006), but there are two important differences:

- We work with the homogeneous propositional equality instead of the heterogeneous version. The reason is that the elimination rule they use for the heterogeneous equality is equivalent with K (McBride 2000), something we wish to avoid. Using the homogeneous equality also means that we have to work a little harder to express equality between two sequences of terms in the same telescope.
- Working with the homogeneous equality leads us very naturally to upgraded versions of the unification transitions given by Goguen et al. (2006), where the return type is dependent on the equality proof. The construction of these upgraded transitions will make clear why the two restrictions to the unification algorithm given in Section 2.2 are really needed.

The general idea of the proof is as follows. First, the definition by pattern matching is translated to a case tree. This translation is described in detail by Norell (2007), and we will not repeat it here. Each leaf node of the case tree corresponds to a clause $\mathtt{f}\ \bar{p} = e$, i.e. it defines $\mathtt{f}$ on arguments that match the pattern $\bar{p}$, and each internal node corresponds to a case split of $\bar{p}$ on some variable $x : \mathtt{D}\ \bar{u}$ into patterns $\bar{p}_1, \ldots, \bar{p}_n$. If we can assemble the definitions of $\mathtt{f}\ \bar{p}_1, \ldots, f\ \bar{p}_n$ into a definition of $\mathtt{f}\ \bar{p}$, then we can work backwards from the leaf nodes towards the root, ultimately obtaining a definition of $\mathtt{f}$ on arbitrary variables.

So we need to know how to assemble the definitions of $\mathtt{f}\ \bar{p}_1, \ldots, \mathtt{f}\ \bar{p}_n$ into a definition of $\mathtt{f}\ \bar{p}$. This assembly proceeds in two steps. First we apply a technique called *basic* $\mathtt{case}_\mathtt{D}$*-analysis at* $\bar{u}; x$. This splits the problem into one subproblem for each constructor c_i of $\mathtt{D}$, and gives us proofs of the equations $\bar{u} = \bar{v}_i$ and $x = \mathtt{c}\ \bar{y}$. The second step is to apply *specialization by unification*, simplifying these equations step by step. The unification transitions make sure that we do not have to fill in anything for a negative success. So finally, we fill in the translated definition of $\mathtt{f}\ \bar{p}_i$ for each positive success.

In general there can be recursive calls to the function $\mathtt{f}$ in each clause $\mathtt{f}\ \bar{p} = e$. These recursive calls are required to be structurally recursive on some argument $x : \mathtt{D}\ \bar{u}$ of $\mathtt{f}$. It is important for the proof that the type of x in Δ is already a data type, not just the type of x in each of the clauses separately. This allows us to use well-founded recursion on $\mathtt{D}$ to obtain an inductive hypothesis H, asserting that $\mathtt{f}$ is already defined on arguments structurally smaller than x. This inductive hypothesis is then used to replace the recursive calls to $\mathtt{f}$ in e.

The challenge is then to construct all these techniques (case analysis, specialization by unification, and structural recursion) as terms *internal to type theory*. Before we begin this construction, we repeat some standard definitions from type theory (Section 3.1) and dependent pattern matching (Section 3.2). We continue by showing how the homogeneous propositional equality can be used to express equality of sequences (Section 3.3). We then recall some standard equipment for inductive datatypes given by McBride et al. (2006): case analysis, structural recursion, no confusion, and acyclicity, of which the latter two are slightly adapted to work with the homogeneous equality (Section 3.4). No confusion and acyclicity are subsequently used to construct the unification transitions as terms inside type theory (Section 3.5). Finally, all these tools are brought together for the translation of case trees to eliminators (Section 3.6).

3.1 Type theory

As our version of type theory, we use Luo's Unified Theory of Dependent Types (UTT) with dependent products, inductive families, and universes (Luo 1994). We omit the meta-level logical framework and the impredicative universe of propositions because they are not needed for our current work. The formal rules of the version of UTT we use are summarized in Fig. 2.

$$\frac{}{\epsilon\ \textbf{valid}}\ \text{(Ctx-empty)}$$

$$\frac{\Gamma \vdash A : \mathtt{Set}_i \qquad x \notin FV(\Gamma)}{\Gamma(x : A)\ \textbf{valid}}\ \text{(Ctx-ext)}$$

$$\frac{\Gamma\ \textbf{valid} \qquad x : A \in \Gamma}{\Gamma \vdash x : A}\ \text{(Var)}$$

$$\frac{\Gamma \vdash t : A_1 \qquad \Gamma \vdash A_1 = A_2 : \mathtt{Set}_i}{\Gamma \vdash t : A_2}\ \text{(=Ty)}$$

$$\frac{\Gamma\ \textbf{valid}}{\Gamma \vdash \mathtt{Set}_i : \mathtt{Set}_{i+1}}\ \text{(Set)}$$

$$\frac{\Gamma \vdash A : \mathtt{Set}_i \qquad \Gamma(x : A) \vdash B : \mathtt{Set}_j}{\Gamma \vdash (x : A) \to B : \mathtt{Set}_{\max(i,j)}}\ (\Pi)$$

$$\frac{\Gamma(x : A) \vdash t : B}{\Gamma \vdash \lambda x.\, t : (x : A) \to B}\ (\lambda)$$

$$\frac{\Gamma \vdash f : (x : A) \to B \qquad \Gamma \vdash t : A}{\Gamma \vdash f\ t : B[x \mapsto t]}\ \text{(App)}$$

$$\frac{\Gamma(x : A) \vdash t : B \qquad \Gamma \vdash s : A}{(\lambda x.\, t)\ s = t[x \mapsto s] : B[x \mapsto s]}\ (\beta)$$

$$\frac{\Gamma \vdash f : (x : A) \to B \qquad x \notin FV(f)}{\lambda x.\, f\ x = f : (x : A) \to B}\ (\eta)$$

+ reflexivity, symmetry, transitivity and congruence rules for =

Figure 2. The core formal rules of UTT, including dependent function types $(x : A) \to B$, an infinite hierarchy of universes $\mathtt{Set}_0, \mathtt{Set}_1, \mathtt{Set}_2, \ldots$, and $\beta\eta$-equality.

Contexts and substitutions. We use Greek capitals $\Gamma, \Delta, \ldots$ for contexts, capitals $T, U, \ldots$ for types, and small letters $t, u, \ldots$ for terms. A list of terms is indicated by a bar above the letter, for example $\bar{t}$. Contexts double as the type of such a list of terms, also called a *telescope*, so we can write for example $\bar{t} : \Gamma$ where $\Gamma = (m : \mathbb{N})(p : m \equiv \mathtt{zero})$ and $\bar{t} = \mathtt{zero}; \mathtt{refl}$. Note that the empty context ϵ is inhabited by the empty list (). The simultaneous substitution of the terms $\bar{t}$ for the variables in the context Γ is written as $[\Gamma \mapsto \bar{t}]$. We denote substitutions by small Greek letters $\sigma, \tau, \ldots$

Elimination operators. For any telescope Ξ, we define a Ξ-*elimination operator* (McBride 2002) to be any function with a type of the form

$$\begin{aligned}&(P : \Xi \to \mathtt{Set}_i) \to \\ &(m_1 : \Delta_1 \to P\ \bar{s}_1) \ldots (m_n : \Delta_n \to P\ \bar{s}_n) \to \\ &(\bar{t} : \Xi) \to P\ \bar{t}\end{aligned} \tag{13}$$

We call Ξ the *target*, P the *motive*, and $m_1, \ldots, m_n$ the *methods* of the elimination operator. The reader may think of a Ξ-elimination operator as a way to transform a problem into a set of subproblems. In the type shown above, the original problem is to construct a result of type $P\ \bar{t}$ when given an arbitrary list of values $\bar{t}$ in the telescope Ξ. This original problem is transformed into n sub-problems given by each of the methods: the ith subproblem is to construct a result of type $P\ \bar{s}_i$ when given an arbitrary value satisfying telescope

Δ_i. The elimination operator's type can be read as a function that transforms solutions for the sub-problems into a solution for the original problem.

Inductive families. Inductive families (Dybjer 1991) are (dependent) types inductively defined by a number of *constructors*, for example $\mathbb{N}$ is defined by the constructors $\texttt{zero} : \mathbb{N}$ and $\texttt{suc} : \mathbb{N} \to \mathbb{N}$. Inductive families can also have *parameters* and *indices*, for example $\texttt{Vec}\ A\ n$ is an inductive family with one parameter $A : \texttt{Set}$, one index $n : \mathbb{N}$, and two constructors $\texttt{nil} : \texttt{Vec}\ A\ \texttt{zero}$ and $\texttt{cons} : (n : \mathbb{N}) \to A \to \texttt{Vec}\ A\ n \to \texttt{Vec}\ A\ (\texttt{suc}\ n)$. Each inductive family comes equipped with a *datatype eliminator*, for example the eliminator for $\mathbb{N}$ is

$$\begin{aligned} \texttt{elim}_{\mathbb{N}} : &(P : \mathbb{N} \to \texttt{Set}_i) \to (m_{\texttt{zero}} : P\ \texttt{zero}) \to \\ &(m_{\texttt{suc}} : (n : \mathbb{N}) \to P\ n \to P\ (\texttt{suc}\ n)) \to \\ &(n : \mathbb{N}) \to P\ n \end{aligned} \tag{14}$$

In general, let $\texttt{D}$ be an inductive family. Since everything we do in this paper is parametric in the datatype parameters of $\texttt{D}$, we consider $\texttt{D}$ to be already applied to (arbitrary) parameters. So $\texttt{D}$ is defined by the telescope Ξ of the indices and the constructors

$$\texttt{c}_i : \Delta_i \to (\Phi_{i1} \to \texttt{D}\ \bar{v}_{i1}) \to \ldots \to (\Phi_{in_i} \to \texttt{D}\ \bar{v}_{in_i}) \to \texttt{D}\ \bar{u}_i \tag{15}$$

for $i = 1, \ldots, k$. We write $\bar{\texttt{D}}$ for the telescope $(\bar{u} : \Xi)(x : \texttt{D}\ \bar{u})$. The standard eliminator for $\texttt{D}$ is a $\bar{\texttt{D}}$-elimination operator with methods $m_1, \ldots, m_k$ where

$$\begin{aligned} m_i : &(\bar{t} : \Delta_i) \to \\ &\quad (x_1 : \Phi_{i1} \to \texttt{D}\ \bar{v}_{i1}) \ldots (x_{n_i} : \Phi_{in_i} \to \texttt{D}\ \bar{v}_{in_i}) \to \\ &\quad (h_1 : (\bar{s}_1 : \Phi_{i1}) \to P\ \bar{v}_{i1}\ (x_1\ \bar{s}_1)) \to \ldots \to \\ &\quad (h_{n_i} : (\bar{s}_{n_i} : \Phi_{in_i}) \to P\ \bar{v}_{in_i}\ (x_{n_i}\ \bar{s}_{n_i})) \to \\ &\quad P\ \bar{u}_i\ (\texttt{c}_i\ \bar{t}\ x_1 \ldots x_{n_i}) \end{aligned} \tag{16}$$

i.e. it is of the form

$$\begin{aligned} \texttt{elim}_{\texttt{D}} : &(P : \bar{\texttt{D}} \to \texttt{Set}_i)(m_1 : \ldots) \ldots (m_k : \ldots) \to \\ &(\bar{x} : \bar{\texttt{D}}) \to P\ \bar{x} \end{aligned} \tag{17}$$

where the types of $m_1, \ldots, m_k$ are as given above.

Definitional and propositional equality. In (intensional) type theory, there are two distinct notions of equality. On the one hand, two terms s and t are *definitionally equal* (or *convertible*) if we can derive $\Gamma \vdash s = t : T$, i.e. if s and t are equal up to $\beta\eta$-conversion. On the other hand, two terms s and t are *propositionally equal* if we can prove their equality, i.e. if we can give a term of type $s \equiv t$. Propositional equality was introduced by Martin-Löf (1984). In UTT, it can be defined as an inductive family with two parameters $A : \texttt{Set}_i$ and $a : A$, one index $b : A$, and one constructor $\texttt{refl} : a \equiv a$. The standard eliminator for this datatype is exactly the J rule (10). Substitution by a propositional equality $\texttt{subst} : (P : A \to \texttt{Set}_i) \to x \equiv y \to P\ x \to P\ y$ can readily be defined from J by dropping the dependence of P on the equality proof in the type of J. In the style of HoTT, we write e_* for $\texttt{subst}\ P\ e$ when P is clear from the context.

3.2 Definitions by pattern matching

A definition by pattern matching of a function $\texttt{f}$ consists of a number of equalities called *clauses*, which are of the form $\texttt{f}\ \bar{p} = t$ where $\bar{p}$ is a list of patterns and t is a term called the *right-hand side*. A *pattern* is a term or a list of terms that is built from only (fully applied) constructors and (non-applied) variables, which we call the pattern variables. In dependent pattern matching, patterns can also contain *inaccessible patterns*, which can occur when there is only one type-correct term possible in a given position. Like Norell (2007), we mark inaccessible patterns as $\lfloor t \rfloor$. For example, let $\texttt{Square}\ n$ be an inductive family with one index $n : \mathbb{N}$ and one constructor $\texttt{sq} : (m : \mathbb{N}) \to \texttt{Square}\ m^2$. Then $\lfloor m^2 \rfloor\ (\texttt{sq}\ m)$ is a pattern of type $(n : \mathbb{N})(p : \texttt{Square}\ n)$. Any other pattern $\lfloor t \rfloor\ (\texttt{sq}\ m)$ would be ill-typed, so the use of an inaccessible pattern is justified. We also define an operation $\lceil \bar{p} \rceil$ taking a pattern $\bar{p}$ back to its underlying term.

$$\underline{n} \begin{cases} \texttt{zero} \mapsto \texttt{zero} \\ (\texttt{suc}\ \underline{m}) \begin{cases} \texttt{suc zero} \mapsto \texttt{zero} \\ \texttt{suc}\ (\texttt{suc}\ k) \mapsto \texttt{suc}\ (\texttt{half}\ k) \end{cases} \end{cases}$$

Figure 3. A representation of the function half by a case tree. At each internal node, the variable on which the case split is performed is underlined.

$$\frac{}{t_i \prec \texttt{c}\ t_1 \ldots t_n} \qquad \frac{f \prec t}{f\ s \prec t} \qquad \frac{r \prec s \qquad s \prec t}{r \prec t}$$

Figure 4. The structural order $\prec$ is used to check termination (Goguen et al. 2006).

Case Trees. A definition by pattern matching consists of one or more case splits. We represent these case splits by a *case tree*. The nodes of a case tree for a function $\texttt{f} : \Delta \to T$ are labeled by patterns of type Δ, where the label of the root node consists of variables only. Each internal node of a case tree corresponds to a case split, while each leaf node corresponds to a clause of the definition. An example of a case tree is given in Figure 3.

Using case trees has a number of advantages. First, the patterns at the leaves of a case tree always form a covering, hence case trees guarantee completeness. Secondly, they give an efficient method to evaluate functions defined by pattern matching. Thirdly and most importantly for our purposes, each internal node in a case tree corresponds exactly to the application of an eliminator for an inductive family, so constructing a case tree is a useful first step in the translation of dependent pattern matching to pure type theory as demonstrated by Goguen et al. (2006).

Structural recursion. In order to guarantee termination, functions are required to be *structurally recursive*. This means that the arguments of recursive calls should be *structurally smaller* than the pattern on the left-hand side. The structural order $\prec$ is defined in Figure 4 . For functions with multiple arguments, the function should be structurally recursive on one of its arguments, i.e. there should be some k such that $s_k \prec p_k$ for each clause $\texttt{f}\ \bar{p} = t$ and each recursive call $\texttt{f}\ \bar{s}$ in t.

3.3 Homogeneous telescopic equality

There is a reason why it is hard to see where exactly the K axiom is used in the translation from pattern matching to eliminators by Goguen et al. (2006): they do not use the axiom directly, but instead depend on the heterogeneous propositional equality. The heterogeneous equality allows the formation of equalities between terms of different types, but still only allows a proof when the types are in fact the same. This heterogeneous equality is convenient for expressing equality between sequences of data in a given telescope. Unfortunately, the elimination rule for this heterogeneous equality proposed by McBride is equivalent with the K axiom (McBride 2000). Heterogeneous equality (and its elimination rule) is used almost everywhere in the translation, making it impossible to see where the K axiom is really needed. So instead we work with the *homogeneous* propositional equality and the standard J eliminator.

Working with homogeneous equality also means we have to work a little harder to express equality of two sequences of terms in the same telescope. We define telescopic equality $\bar{s} \equiv \bar{t}$ inductively on the length of the telescope as follows:

$$\begin{array}{rcccl} () & \equiv & () & := & \epsilon \\ s;\bar{s} & \equiv & t;\bar{t} & := & (e : s \equiv t)(\bar{e} : e_* \ \bar{s} \equiv \bar{t}) \end{array} \quad (18)$$

where $e_* \ (s_1;\ldots;s_n) := (e_* \ s_1;\ldots;e_* \ s_n)$. Note that the substitution e_* is needed to make the equation between $\bar{s}$ and $\bar{t}$ again homogeneous. Telescopic inequality is defined by $\bar{s} \not\equiv \bar{t} := \bar{s} \equiv \bar{t} \to \bot$. For each $\bar{t} : \Delta$, we define $\overline{\texttt{refl}} : \bar{t} \equiv \bar{t}$ as $\texttt{refl};\ldots;\texttt{refl}$. We also have the telescopic eliminator

$$\begin{array}{l} \bar{\mathrm{J}} : (P : (\bar{s} : \Delta) \to \bar{r} \equiv \bar{s} \to \mathtt{Set}_i) \\ \quad P \ \bar{r} \ \overline{\texttt{refl}} \to (\bar{s} : \Delta) \to (\bar{e} : \bar{r} \equiv \bar{s}) \to P \ \bar{s} \ \bar{e} \end{array} \quad (19)$$

It is defined by eliminating the equations $\bar{e}$ from left to right using J. Each elimination of an equation $e_i : r_i \equiv s_i$ fills in `refl` for all occurrences of e_i, allowing the next equations to reduce and in particular ensuring that the following equation is of the correct form. Telescopic substitution $\overline{\texttt{subst}}$ is defined by dropping the dependence of P on $\bar{r} \equiv \bar{s}$ in the definition of $\bar{\mathrm{J}}$. Again, we write $\bar{e}_*$ for $\overline{\texttt{subst}} \ P \ \bar{e}$ when P is clear from the context. A formalization of homogeneous telescopic equality and the constructions in this section can be found in the file `TelescopicEquality.agda` in the supplementary material.

3.4 A few homogeneous constructions on constructors

McBride et al. (2006) developed tools for working with inductive families of datatypes: case analysis, recursion, no confusion (subsuming both injectivity and disjointness), and acyclicity. In this section, we present these rules adapted to work with homogeneous instead of heterogeneous equality. We refer to the appendix for the actual construction of these tools, as the differences with the work of McBride et al. are minor and rather technical. A computer-checked version of these constructions for some concrete data types (binary trees, dependent sums, finite sets, the identity type, and indexed containers) can be found in the file `ConstructionsOnConstructors.agda` in the supplementary material. For the rest of this section, let $\mathtt{D} : \Xi \to \mathtt{Set}_i$ be an inductive family.

Case analysis $\mathtt{case}_{\mathtt{D}}$ is a weakened version of the standard eliminator $\mathtt{elim}_{\mathtt{D}}$ that we get by dropping the inductive hypotheses of the methods. For example, $\mathtt{case}_{\mathbb{N}}$ has type

$$\begin{array}{l} (P : \mathbb{N} \to \mathtt{Set}_i) \to (m_{\mathsf{zero}} : P \ \mathtt{zero}) \to \\ (m_{\mathsf{suc}} : (n : \mathbb{N}) \to P \ (\mathtt{suc} \ n)) \to (n : \mathbb{N}) \to P \ n \end{array} \quad (20)$$

Recursion is given in two levels. First, for $x : \mathtt{D} \ \bar{u}$, $\mathtt{Below}_{\mathtt{D}} \ P \ \bar{u} \ x$ is a tuple type that is inhabited whenever $P \ \bar{v} \ y$ holds for all $y : \mathtt{D} \ \bar{v}$ which are structurally smaller than $x : \mathtt{D} \ \bar{u}$. For example for $\mathbb{N}$, we have $\mathtt{Below}_{\mathbb{N}} \ P \ \mathtt{zero} = \top$ (the unit type) and $\mathtt{Below}_{\mathbb{N}} \ P \ (\mathtt{suc} \ n) = \mathtt{Below}_{\mathbb{N}} \ P \ n \times P \ n$. Secondly, the helper function $\mathtt{below}_{\mathtt{D}}$ constructs this tuple:

$$\begin{array}{l} \mathtt{below}_{\mathtt{D}} : (P : (\bar{x} : \bar{\mathtt{D}}) \to \mathtt{Set}_i) \to \\ \quad ((\bar{x} : \bar{\mathtt{D}}) \to \mathtt{Below}_{\mathtt{D}} \ P \ \bar{x} \to P \ \bar{x}) \to \\ \quad (\bar{x} : \bar{\mathtt{D}}) \to \mathtt{Below}_{\mathtt{D}} \ P \ \bar{x} \end{array} \quad (21)$$

Finally,

$$\begin{array}{l} \mathtt{rec}_{\mathtt{D}} : (P : (\bar{x} : \bar{\mathtt{D}}) \to \mathtt{Set}_i) \to \\ \quad ((\bar{x} : \bar{\mathtt{D}}) \to \mathtt{Below}_{\mathtt{D}} \ P \ \bar{x} \to P \ \bar{x}) \to \\ \quad (\bar{x} : \bar{\mathtt{D}}) \to P \ \bar{x} \end{array} \quad (22)$$

is used for well-founded recursion over values of type D.

No confusion is also given in two levels. First, $\mathtt{NoConfusion}_{\mathtt{D}} : \bar{\mathtt{D}} \to \bar{\mathtt{D}} \to \mathtt{Set}_d$ is a type such that

$$\begin{array}{l} \mathtt{NoConfusion}_{\mathtt{D}} \ (\bar{u}; c \ \bar{s}) \ (\bar{v}; c \ \bar{t}) = \bar{s} \equiv \bar{t} \\ \mathtt{NoConfusion}_{\mathtt{D}} \ (\bar{u}; c \ \bar{s}) \ (\bar{v}; c' \ \bar{t}) = \bot \ (\text{when } c \neq c') \end{array} \quad (23)$$

Secondly, we construct

$$\mathtt{noConf}_{\mathtt{D}} : (\bar{x} \ \bar{y} : \bar{\mathtt{D}}) \to \bar{x} \equiv \bar{y} \to \mathtt{NoConfusion}_{\mathtt{D}} \ \bar{x} \ \bar{y} \quad (24)$$

We also construct an inverse

$$\mathtt{noConf}_{\mathtt{D}}^{-1} : (\bar{x} \ \bar{y} : \bar{\mathtt{D}}) \to \mathtt{NoConfusion}_{\mathtt{D}} \ \bar{x} \ \bar{y} \to \bar{x} \equiv \bar{y} \quad (25)$$

and give a proof $\mathtt{isLeftInv}_{\mathtt{D}}$ that $(\mathtt{noConf}_{\mathtt{D}}^{-1} \ \bar{x} \ \bar{y}) \circ (\mathtt{noConf} \ \bar{x} \ \bar{y})$ is the identity on $\bar{x} \equiv \bar{y}$.[2] The need for this inverse will become clear when we construct the unification transitions in Section 3.5.

Acyclicity is yet again given in two levels. First, $\bar{x} \not< \bar{y}$ is defined as a tuple type stating that $\bar{x} : \bar{\mathtt{D}}$ is not structurally smaller than $\bar{y} : \bar{\mathtt{D}}$. For example, $x \not< 2 = (x \not\equiv 0) \times (x \not\equiv 1)$. Secondly, $\mathtt{noCycle}_{\mathtt{D}} : (\bar{x} \ \bar{y} : \bar{\mathtt{D}}) \to \bar{x} \equiv \bar{y} \to \bar{x} \not< \bar{y}$ states that no term can be structurally smaller than itself.

Basic analysis. Note that $\mathtt{elim}_{\mathtt{D}}$, $\mathtt{case}_{\mathtt{D}}$, and $\mathtt{rec}_{\mathtt{D}}$ are all $\bar{\mathtt{D}}$-elimination operators, i.e. for a motive $P : \bar{\mathtt{D}} \to \mathtt{Set}_j$ they return something of type $(\bar{u} : \Xi)(x : \mathtt{D} \ \bar{u}) \to P \ (\bar{u}; x)$. However, we often need a return type where the indices $\bar{u}$ of x are more specialized, for example to construct a function of type $(k : \mathbb{N})(y : k \leq \mathtt{zero}) \to \mathtt{zero} \equiv k$. McBride (2002) solves this problem by adding the constraints on the indices as additional arguments to the motive P, and filling in $\overline{\texttt{refl}}$ as soon as the constraints are satisfied. This technique is called *basic analysis*. In the example above, the basic $\mathtt{case}_{\leq}$-analysis of $\mathtt{zero} \equiv k$ at $k; \mathtt{zero}; y$ has type

$$\begin{array}{l} (m_1 : (m : \mathbb{N})(k : \mathbb{N})(y : k \leq \mathtt{zero}) \to \\ \quad (\mathtt{zero}; m; \mathtt{lz} \ m) \equiv (k; \mathtt{zero}; y) \to \mathtt{zero} \equiv k) \to \\ (m_2 : (m \ n : \mathbb{N})(x : m \leq n)(k : \mathbb{N})(y : k \leq \mathtt{zero}) \to \\ \quad (\mathtt{suc} \ m; \mathtt{suc} \ n; \mathtt{ls} \ m \ n \ x) \equiv (k; \mathtt{zero}; y) \to \mathtt{zero} \equiv k) \to \\ (k : \mathbb{N})(y : k \leq \mathtt{zero}) \to \mathtt{zero} \equiv k \end{array} \quad (26)$$

Note that applying $\mathtt{case}_{\leq}$ directly to $y : k \leq \mathtt{zero}$ would lead to loss of the information that the second index of y is `zero`, thus leaving us unable to provide m_1 and m_2.

In general, let `elim` be any Ξ-elimination operator, and suppose we want to construct a function of type $\Delta \to \Phi$ by applying this eliminator to $\bar{t}$ where $\Delta \vdash \bar{t} : \Xi$. Then we apply `elim` to the motive $\lambda(\bar{s} : \Xi).\ \Delta \to \bar{s} \equiv \bar{t} \to \Phi$. Filling in $\bar{t}$ for $\bar{s}$ and $\overline{\texttt{refl}}$ for the proof of $\bar{s} \equiv \bar{t}$ gives us the *basic* `elim`*-analysis of* Φ *at* $\bar{t}$:

$$\begin{array}{l} \lambda m_1;\ldots;m_n;\bar{x}. \\ \quad \mathtt{elim} \ (\lambda \bar{s}.\ \Delta \to \bar{s} \equiv \bar{t} \to \Phi) \ m_1 \ \ldots \ m_n \ \bar{t} \ \bar{x} \ \overline{\texttt{refl}} \end{array} \quad (27)$$

which is of type

$$\begin{array}{l} (m_1 : \Delta_1 \Delta \to \bar{s}_1 \equiv \bar{t} \to \Phi) \to \ldots \to \\ (m_n : \Delta_n \Delta \to \bar{s}_n \equiv \bar{t} \to \Phi) \to \Delta \to \Phi \end{array} \quad (28)$$

Basic analysis will be used thoughout the proof: once with $\mathtt{rec}_{\mathtt{D}}$ for structural recursion, and once with $\mathtt{case}_{\mathtt{D}}$ for each case split.

3.5 Unification without K

In order to translate a node of the case tree to the application of an eliminator, we need terms that give an account of the unification

[2] We could also prove that $(\mathtt{noConf}_{\mathtt{D}} \ \bar{x} \ \bar{y}) \circ (\mathtt{noConf}_{\mathtt{D}}^{-1} \ \bar{x} \ \bar{y})$ is the identity on $\mathtt{NoConfusion}_{\mathtt{D}} \ \bar{x} \ \bar{y}$, thus establishing that $\mathtt{noConf}_{\mathtt{D}} \ \bar{x} \ \bar{y}$ is an equivalence. However, this is not needed for the present work.

$$
\begin{aligned}
&\mathtt{solution} : (\Phi : (x : A)(e : x_0 \equiv x) \to \mathtt{Set}_i) \to \\
&\quad (m : \Phi\; x_0\; \mathtt{refl}) \to \\
&\quad (x : A)(e : x_0 \equiv x) \to \Phi\; x\; e \\
&\mathtt{solution}\;\; \Phi\; m\; x\; e = \mathrm{J}\; A\; x_0\; \Phi\; m\; x\; e
\end{aligned}
$$

$$
\begin{aligned}
&\mathtt{injectivity} : (\Phi : (\bar{e} : \bar{u}_s; \mathtt{c}\; \bar{s} \equiv \bar{u}_t; \mathtt{c}\; \bar{t}) \to \mathtt{Set}_i) \to \\
&\quad (m : (\bar{e} : \bar{s} \equiv \bar{t}) \\
&\qquad \to \Phi\; (\mathtt{noConf}_{\mathtt{D}}{}^{-1}\; (\bar{u}_s; \mathtt{c}\; \bar{s})\; (\bar{u}_t; \mathtt{c}\; \bar{t})\; \bar{e})) \to \\
&\quad (\bar{e} : \bar{u}_s; \mathtt{c}\; \bar{s} \equiv \bar{u}_t; \mathtt{c}\; \bar{t}) \to \Phi\; \bar{e} \\
&\mathtt{injectivity}\;\; \Phi\; m\; \bar{e} = (\mathtt{isLeftInv}_{\mathtt{D}}\; (\bar{u}_s; \mathtt{c}\; \bar{s})\; (\bar{u}_t; \mathtt{c}\; \bar{t})\; \bar{e})_* \\
&\quad (m\; (\mathtt{noConf}_{\mathtt{D}}\; (\bar{u}_s; \mathtt{c}\; \bar{s})\; (\bar{u}_t; \mathtt{c}\; \bar{t})\; \bar{e}))
\end{aligned}
$$

$$
\begin{aligned}
&\mathtt{conflict} : (\Phi : (\bar{e} : \bar{u}_s; \mathtt{c}_1\; \bar{s} \equiv \bar{u}_t; \mathtt{c}_2\; \bar{t}) \to \mathtt{Set}_i) \to \\
&\quad (\bar{e} : \bar{u}_s; \mathtt{c}_1\; \bar{s} \equiv \bar{u}_t; \mathtt{c}_2\; \bar{t}) \to \Phi\; \bar{e} \\
&\mathtt{conflict}\;\; \Phi\; \bar{e} = \mathtt{elim}_{\bot}\; (\lambda\_.\; \Phi\; \bar{e}) \\
&\qquad (\mathtt{noConf}_{\mathtt{D}}\; (\bar{u}_s; \mathtt{c}_1\; \bar{s})\; (\bar{u}_t; \mathtt{c}_2\; \bar{t})\; \bar{e})
\end{aligned}
$$

$$
\begin{aligned}
&\mathtt{cycle} : (\Phi : (\bar{e} : \bar{u}; x \equiv \bar{v}; \mathtt{c}\; \bar{s}[x]) \to \mathtt{Set}_i) \to \\
&\quad (\bar{e} : \bar{u}; x \equiv \bar{v}; \mathtt{c}\; \bar{s}[x]) \to \Phi\; \bar{e} \\
&\mathtt{cycle}\;\; \Phi\; \bar{e} = \mathtt{elim}_{\bot}\; (\lambda\_.\; \Phi\; e) \\
&\qquad (\pi\; (\mathtt{noCycle}_{\mathtt{D}}\; (\bar{u}; x)\; (\bar{v}; \mathtt{c}\; \bar{s}[x])\; \bar{e})\; \overline{\mathtt{refl}}) \\
&\qquad (\text{where } \pi : \bar{u}; x \not< \bar{v}; \mathtt{c}\; \bar{s}[x] \to \bar{u}; x \not\equiv \bar{u}; x)
\end{aligned}
$$

Figure 5. The unification transitions represented as type-theoretic terms. Compared to the transitions given by Goguen et al. (2006), these work with the homogeneous equality and Φ has an additional dependence on the equality proof. While these unification transitions are the most general ones we can construct, they are *not* the ones that we use for case splitting in practice. Rather, `injectivity`, `conflict`, and `cycle` are replaced by their more specialized variants `injectivity'` (33), `conflict'` (34), and `cycle'` (35).

process inside of type theory itself. In order to do this, we use the "no confusion" and "no cycle" properties from the previous section. The unification transitions are given in Figure 5. A computer-checked construction of them for some concrete data types can be found in the file **`Unification.agda`** in the supplementary material. Compared to Goguen et al. (2006), working with homogeneous equality leads us very naturally to upgraded unification transitions which are dependent on the equality proof. For example, consider a context $\Xi = (a : A)(b : B\; a)$ and a Ξ-elimination operator `elim`. Basic `elim`-analysis requires us to construct methods of type $\Delta \to a; b \equiv a'; b' \to T$, or if we expand the definition of telescopic equality:

$$\Delta \to (e_a : a \equiv a') \to (e_a)_*\; b \equiv b' \to T \tag{29}$$

The motive for eliminating $a \equiv a'$ is $(e_a)_*\; b \equiv b' \to T$, which depends on the proof e_a. So the dependence of Φ on the equality proofs is caused by the need to use substitution in the definition of homogeneous telescopic equality. Intuitively, it is not surprising that not assuming UIP leads us to consider identity proofs relevant!

The first thing we want to point out about Figure 5 is the lack of a `deletion` transition. The non-dependent version of `deletion` given by Goguen et al. (2006) has type

$$(\Phi : \mathtt{Set}_i) \to (m : \Phi) \to (e : x_0 \equiv x_0) \to \Phi \tag{30}$$

which can be constructed without K but would be quite useless in our situation because Φ cannot depend on e. In contrast, a dependent `deletion` rule would look like

$$
\begin{aligned}
\mathtt{deletion} : (\Phi : (e : x_0 \equiv x_0) \to \mathtt{Set}_i) \to& \\
(m : \Phi\; \mathtt{refl}) \to& \\
(e : x_0 \equiv x_0) \to \Phi\; e&
\end{aligned}
\tag{31}
$$

which is exactly the K axiom. This is the reason for the first restriction on the unification algorithm in our criterion, namely that the **deletion** rule cannot be used.

A second point of interest in Figure 5 is the type of Φ in the `injectivity` function: it is indexed over the equality proof of the indices $\bar{u}_s$ and $\bar{u}_t$ as well as the equality proof of $\mathtt{c}\; \bar{s}$ and $\mathtt{c}\; \bar{t}$. But this does not correspond exactly to the **injectivity** rule from Section 2.1. Rather, we need a more specialized version of `injectivity` where the indices $\bar{u}_s$ and $\bar{u}_t$ are already definitionally equal:

$$
\begin{aligned}
\mathtt{injectivity}_{\mathtt{bad}} : (\Phi : (e : \mathtt{c}\; \bar{s} \equiv \mathtt{c}\; \bar{t}) \to \mathtt{Set}_i) \to& \\
(m : (\bar{e} : \bar{s} \equiv \bar{t}) \to \Phi\; ???)) \to& \\
(e : \mathtt{c}\; \bar{s} \equiv \mathtt{c}\; \bar{t}) \to \Phi\; e&
\end{aligned}
\tag{32}
$$

However, unlike `injectivity` such a function can *not* be constructed from $\mathtt{noConf}_{\mathtt{D}}$. This is because in order to fill in the question marks, we need a function $g : \bar{s} \equiv \bar{t} \to \mathtt{c}\; \bar{s} \equiv \mathtt{c}\; \bar{t}$ such that we can prove $g\; (\mathtt{noConf}_{\mathtt{D}}\; (\bar{u}_s; \mathtt{c}\; \bar{s})\; (\bar{u}_t; \mathtt{c}\; \bar{t})\; \overline{\mathtt{refl}}\; e) \equiv e$ for arbitrary e, but no such g can be found. In fact, wrongly using this transition caused a bug in Agda's –without-K option, allowing one to prove a weaker version of the K axiom (Cockx 2014).

What we *can* construct from $\mathtt{noConf}_{\mathtt{D}}$ is the following:

$$
\begin{aligned}
\mathtt{injectivity'} : (\Phi : (\bar{e} : \bar{u}; \mathtt{c}\; \bar{s} \equiv \bar{u}; \mathtt{c}\; \bar{t}) \to \mathtt{Set}_i) \to& \\
(m : (\bar{e} : \bar{s} \equiv \bar{t}) \to& \\
\Phi\; (\mathtt{noConf}_{\mathtt{D}}{}^{-1}\; (\bar{u}; \mathtt{c}\; \bar{s})\; (\bar{u}; \mathtt{c}\; \bar{t})\; \bar{e})) \to& \\
(e : \mathtt{c}\; \bar{s} \equiv \mathtt{c}\; \bar{t}) \to \Phi\; \overline{\mathtt{refl}}\; e&
\end{aligned}
\tag{33}
$$

This rule is simply a specialized version of the `injectivity` rule in Figure 5. However, there is still a problem with this rule. Suppose we want to use it to construct a function of type $(e : \mathtt{c}\; \bar{s} \equiv \mathtt{c}\; \bar{t}) \to \Phi'\; e$ where $\Phi' : \mathtt{c}\; \bar{s} \equiv \mathtt{c}\; \bar{t} \to \mathtt{Set}_i$, and we want to apply `injectivity'`. Then we need to find $\Phi : \bar{u}; \mathtt{c}\; \bar{s} \equiv \bar{u}; \mathtt{c}\; \bar{t} \to \mathtt{Set}_i$ such that $\Phi\; \overline{\mathtt{refl}}\; e = \Phi'\; e$ for arbitrary $e : \mathtt{c}\; \bar{s} \equiv \mathtt{c}\; \bar{t}$. This is problematic because we cannot eliminate the equations $\bar{u} \equiv \bar{u}$ in general without using the K axiom. This is the reason for the second restriction on the unification algorithm in our criterion, namely that the indices $\bar{u}$ should be *self-unifiable*. This condition guarantees that we can construct Φ from Φ' by applying the unification transitions used in the self-unification of $\bar{u}$ by applying *specialization by unification* (see below).

At first sight, the **conflict** and **cycle** rule suffer from the same problem as the **injectivity** rule because their motive Φ depends on the proof of $\bar{u}_s \equiv \bar{u}_t$ as well. However, in these cases the problem can be solved because both `conflict` and `cycle` factor through the empty type $\bot$. To illustrate this, suppose we want to construct a function of type $(e : \mathtt{c}_1\; \bar{s} \equiv \mathtt{c}_2\; \bar{t}) \to \Phi'\; e$. First we apply `conflict` with $\Phi = \lambda \bar{e}.\; \bot$, giving us a function of type $(\bar{e} : \bar{u}; \mathtt{c}_1\; \bar{s} \equiv \bar{u}; \mathtt{c}_2\; \bar{t}) \to \bot$. Filling in $\overline{\mathtt{refl}}$ for the equations $\bar{u} \equiv \bar{u}$ gives us $(e : \mathtt{c}_1\; \bar{s} \equiv \mathtt{c}_2\; \bar{t}) \to \bot$. Now by $\bot$-elimination, we also get a function $(e : \mathtt{c}_1\; \bar{s} \equiv \mathtt{c}_2\; \bar{t}) \to \Phi'\; e$. This gives us the following rule:

$$
\begin{aligned}
\mathtt{conflict'} : (\Phi : (e : \mathtt{c}_1\; \bar{s} \equiv \mathtt{c}_2\; \bar{t}) \to \mathtt{Set}_i) \to& \\
(e : \mathtt{c}_1\; \bar{s} \equiv \mathtt{c}_2\; \bar{t}) \to \Phi\; e&
\end{aligned}
\tag{34}
$$

Analogously we can construct a function

$$
\begin{aligned}
\mathtt{cycle'} : (\Phi : (e : x \equiv \mathtt{c}\; \bar{s}[x]) \to \mathtt{Set}_i) \to& \\
(e : x \equiv \mathtt{c}\; \bar{s}[x]) \to \Phi\; \bar{e}&
\end{aligned}
\tag{35}
$$

In our proof, we will use the primed variants `injectivity'`, `conflict'`, and `cycle'`.

Specialization by unification. Given any type of the form $\Delta \to \bar{u} \equiv \bar{v} \to T$ (for example the types of $m_1, \ldots, m_n$ in the basic $\mathtt{case_D}$-analysis), we may seek to construct an inhabitant of this type, called a *specializer*, by exhaustively iterating the unification transitions as applicable. In case of a positive success, a specializer is found, given some $m : \Delta' \to T\sigma$ where $\sigma : \Delta' \to \Delta$ is a substitution. In the case of a negative success, a specializer is found without any additional assumptions.

The `solution` rule removes one variable from Δ, while `injectivity'` keeps it the same. Hence in the case of a positive success we have $\Delta' \subseteq \Delta$, and σ is idempotent. So for any $\bar{t} : \Delta$, we can define an inverse $\sigma^{-1}[\bar{t}] : \Delta'$ by selecting the variables of Δ' from Δ. If specialization by unification delivers a specializer s satisfying

$$(m : \Delta'.T\sigma) \vdash s : \Delta \to \bar{u} \equiv \bar{v} \to T \quad (36)$$

and $\bar{t} : \Delta$ is such that $\bar{u}[\Delta \mapsto \bar{t}] = \bar{v}[\Delta \mapsto \bar{t}]$, then we have $s\ \bar{t}\ \overline{\mathtt{refl}} \leadsto m\ \sigma^{-1}[\bar{t}]$. It is clear why this holds for `solution`, it also holds for `injectivity'` since both $\underline{\mathtt{noConf}}$ and $\mathtt{isLeftInv}$ map $\overline{\mathtt{refl}}$ to $\overline{\mathtt{refl}}$, hence $\mathtt{injectivity'}\ \Phi\ m\ \overline{\mathtt{refl}} \leadsto m\ \mathtt{refl}$.

3.6 From case trees to eliminators

Now we use the tools described in the previous sections to translate a function $\mathtt{f} : (\bar{t} : \Delta) \to T$ given by a structurally recursive case tree to another one $\mathtt{f'} : (\bar{t} : \Delta) \to T$ constructed from eliminators only. As a running example, let $\mathtt{f} = \mathtt{antisym}$ from Definition (5). For this example, we have $\Delta = (m\ n : \mathbb{N})(x : m \leq n)(y : n \leq m)$ and $T = m \equiv n$. Define $\{e\}_{\mathtt{f}}^{\mathtt{f'}}$ by replacing all occurrences of `f` by `f'` in e. Then we have moreover that `f'` satisfies $\mathtt{f'}\ \bar{t} \leadsto^* \{u\}_{\mathtt{f}}^{\mathtt{f'}}$ whenever $\mathtt{f}\ \bar{t} \leadsto u$, i.e. it has the same reduction behaviour as `f`.

Without loss of generality, let `f` be structurally recursive on some $t_j : \mathtt{D}\ \bar{v}$, the jth variable in Δ. In our example, `antisym` is structurally recursive all four arguments, so we arbitrarily choose to do structural recursion on $x : m \leq n$. The basic $\mathtt{rec_D}$-analysis of T at $\bar{v}; t_j$ is

$$\lambda m^s; \bar{t}.\ \mathtt{rec_D}\ P\ m^s\ (\bar{v}; t_j)\ \bar{t}\ \overline{\mathtt{refl}} \quad (37)$$

which has type

$$\begin{aligned}&(m^s : (\bar{x} : \bar{\mathtt{D}}) \to \mathtt{Below_D}\ P\ \bar{x} \to P\ \bar{x}) \to \\ &(\bar{t} : \Delta) \to T\end{aligned} \quad (38)$$

where $P = \lambda \bar{x}.\ (\bar{t} : \Delta) \to \bar{x} \equiv \bar{v}; t_j \to T$. In our example, we have $P = \lambda m'; n'; x'.\ \Delta \to (m'; n'; x') \equiv (m; n; x) \to m \equiv n$.

Suppose we have an $m : (\bar{t} : \Delta) \to \mathtt{Below_D}\ P\ (\bar{v}; t_j) \to T$, then we construct $m^s : (\bar{x} : \bar{\mathtt{D}}) \to \mathtt{Below_D}\ P\ \bar{x} \to (\bar{t} : \Delta) \to \bar{x} \equiv \bar{v}; t_j \to T$ by applying the telescopic equality eliminator $\bar{\mathtt{J}}$ on the equations $\bar{x} \equiv \bar{v}; t_j$. More precisely, m^s is defined as

$$\lambda \bar{x}; H; \bar{t}; \bar{e}.\ \bar{\mathtt{J}}\ (\lambda \bar{x}; \bar{e}.\ \mathtt{Below_D}\ P\ \bar{x} \to T)\ (m\ \bar{t})\ (\mathtt{sym}\ \bar{e})\ H \quad (39)$$

where $\mathtt{sym} : \bar{x} \equiv \bar{y} \to \bar{y} \equiv \bar{x}$. For any $\bar{t} : \Delta$, we have

$$m^s\ (\bar{v}; t_j)\ H\ \bar{t}\ \overline{\mathtt{refl}} \leadsto m\ \bar{t}\ H \quad (40)$$

We will define `f'` as

$$\lambda \bar{t}.\ \mathtt{rec_D}\ P\ m^s\ (\bar{v}; t_j)\ \bar{t}\ \overline{\mathtt{refl}} : (\bar{t} : \Delta) \to T \quad (41)$$

once we have constructed a suitable m. Note that m may make 'recursive calls' to `f'` on arguments structurally smaller than t_j using its argument of type $\mathtt{Below_D}\ P\ (\bar{v}; t_j)$. Also note that

$$\begin{aligned}\mathtt{f'}\ \bar{t} &\leadsto^* \mathtt{rec_D}\ P\ m^s\ (\bar{v}; t_j)\ \bar{t}\ \overline{\mathtt{refl}} \\ &\leadsto^* m^s\ (\bar{v}; t_j)\ (\mathtt{below_D}\ P\ m^s\ (\bar{v}; t_j))\ \bar{t}\ \overline{\mathtt{refl}} \\ &\leadsto^* m\ \bar{t}\ (\mathtt{below_D}\ P\ m^s\ (\bar{v}; t_j))\end{aligned} \quad (42)$$

In order to construct m, we proceed by induction on the structure of `f`'s case tree. So suppose that we have arrived at some node with label $\bar{p}$ where $\bar{p}$ has pattern variables from a context Θ and we wish to construct $m : \Theta \to \mathtt{Below_D}\ P\ (\bar{v}; t_j)\tau \to T\tau$ where $\tau = [\Delta \mapsto \lceil \bar{p} \rceil]$. Note that we have $\Theta = \Delta$ at the root node. There are three cases:

Internal node. In this case, the context is split on some variable y where $\Theta = \Theta_1(y : \mathtt{D'}\ \bar{v}_y)\Theta_2$ and `D'` is an inductive family. The basic $\mathtt{case_{D'}}$-analysis of $\mathtt{Below_D}\ P\ (\bar{v}; t_j)\tau \to T\tau$ at $\bar{v}_y; y$ has type

$$\begin{aligned}&\ldots \to \\ &(m_{\mathtt{c}} : (\bar{s} : \Delta_{\mathtt{c}}) \to \Theta \to \bar{u}_s; \mathtt{c}\ \bar{s} \equiv \bar{v}_y; y \to \\ &\quad \mathtt{Below_D}\ P\ (\bar{v}; t_j)\tau \to T\tau) \to \\ &\ldots \to \\ &\Theta \to \mathtt{Below_D}\ P\ (\bar{v}; t_j)\tau \to T\tau\end{aligned} \quad (43)$$

where there is one method $m_{\mathtt{c}}$ for each constructor `c` of `D'`. In our example, the first case split is on $x : m \leq n$, and the basic $\mathtt{case}_{\leq}$-analysis has type

$$\begin{aligned}&(m_{\mathtt{lz}} : (k\ m\ n : \mathbb{N})(x : m \leq n)(y : n \leq m) \to \\ &\quad (\mathtt{zero}; k; \mathtt{lz}\ k) \equiv (m; n; x) \to \\ &\quad \mathtt{Below}\ P\ m\ n\ x \to m \equiv n) \\ &(m_{\mathtt{ls}} : (k\ l : \mathbb{N})(u : k \leq l) \to \\ &\quad (m\ n : \mathbb{N})(x : m \leq n)(y : n \leq m) \to \\ &\quad (\mathtt{suc}\ k; \mathtt{suc}\ l; \mathtt{ls}\ k\ l\ u) \equiv (m; n; x) \to \\ &\quad \mathtt{Below}\ P\ m\ n\ x \to m \equiv n) \\ &(m\ n : \mathbb{N})(x : m \leq n)(y : n \leq m) \to \\ &\mathtt{Below}\ P\ m\ n\ x \to m \equiv n\end{aligned} \quad (44)$$

To construct the methods $m_{\mathtt{c}}$, we apply specialization by unification on the equations $\bar{u}_s; \mathtt{c}\ \bar{s} \equiv \bar{v}_y; y$, which we know will succeed by definition of a valid case tree. For the method $m_{\mathtt{lz}}$ above, the first step is to apply `solution` to the equation $\mathtt{zero} \equiv m$, simplifying the goal type to

$$\begin{aligned}m'_{\mathtt{lz}} &: (k\ n : \mathbb{N})(x : \mathtt{zero} \leq n)(y : n \leq \mathtt{zero}) \to \\ &\quad (k; \mathtt{lz}\ k) \equiv (n; x) \to \\ &\quad \mathtt{Below}\ P\ \mathtt{zero}\ n\ x \to \mathtt{zero} \equiv n\end{aligned} \quad (45)$$

As another example, later on `conflict` is applied to the equation $\mathtt{suc}\ l \equiv \mathtt{zero}$ to construct a function

$$\begin{aligned}m_{\mathtt{lz;ls}} &: (k\ l : \mathbb{N})(u : k \leq l)(y : \mathtt{suc}\ k \leq \mathtt{zero}) \\ &\quad (\mathtt{suc}\ l; \mathtt{ls}\ k\ l\ u) \equiv (\mathtt{zero}; y) \to \\ &\quad \mathtt{Below}_{\leq}\ P\ \mathtt{zero}\ (\mathtt{suc}\ k)\ (\mathtt{lz}\ (\mathtt{suc}\ k)) \to \\ &\quad \mathtt{zero} \equiv \mathtt{suc}\ k\end{aligned} \quad (46)$$

For each `c` with positive success, we have to deliver a

$$m'_{\mathtt{c}} : \Theta' \to \mathtt{Below_D}\ P\ (\bar{v}; t_j)\tau\sigma \to T\tau\sigma \quad (47)$$

where $\sigma : \Theta' \to \Delta_{\mathtt{c}}\Theta$ is the substitution found by unification. But the inductive hypothesis for the subtree corresponding to the constructor `c` gives us exactly such a function. For $m_{\mathtt{lz}}$, the goal type becomes

$$\begin{aligned}m'''_{\mathtt{lz}} &: (k : \mathbb{N})(y : k \leq \mathtt{zero}) \to \\ &\quad \mathtt{Below}\ P\ \mathtt{zero}\ k\ (\mathtt{lz}\ k) \to \mathtt{zero} \equiv k\end{aligned} \quad (48)$$

after applying `solution` two more times, at which point we proceed with another case split on y.

For any $\bar{t}_1; \mathtt{c}\ \bar{s}; \bar{t}_2 : \Theta_1(y : \mathtt{D'}\ \bar{v}_y)\Theta_2$, we have

$$\begin{aligned} m\ (\bar{t}_1; \mathtt{c}\ \bar{s}; \bar{t}_2) &\rightsquigarrow^* m_\mathtt{c}\ \bar{s}\ (\bar{t}_1; \mathtt{c}\ \bar{s}; \bar{t}_2)\ \overline{\mathtt{refl}} \\ &\rightsquigarrow^* m'_\mathtt{c}\ \sigma^{-1}[\bar{s}; \bar{t}_1; \mathtt{c}\ \bar{s}; \bar{t}_2] \end{aligned} \tag{49}$$

Empty node. We follow the same construction as in the previous case, noting that all unifications will succeed negatively, hence no methods $m_\mathtt{c}$ are needed. Absurd clauses have no right-hand side, so they describe no reduction behaviour.

Leaf node. At each leaf node, we have the right-hand side $\Delta_i \vdash e_i : T\tau$. We wish to instantiate $m_i = \lambda\bar{s}; H.\ e_i$, but e_i may still contain recursive calls to `f`. In our example, the goal type for the second leaf node is

$$\begin{aligned} &m_2 : (k\ l : \mathbb{N})(u : k \leq l)(v : l \leq k) \to \\ &\quad \mathtt{Below}_{\leq}\ P\ (\mathtt{suc}\ k)\ (\mathtt{suc}\ l)\ (\mathtt{ls}\ k\ l\ u) \to \\ &\quad \mathtt{suc}\ k \equiv \mathtt{suc}\ l \end{aligned} \tag{50}$$

and the right-hand side is $\mathtt{cong\ suc}\ (\mathtt{antisym}\ k\ l\ u\ v)$. We first have to replace these recursive calls by appropriate calls to $H : \mathtt{Below}_\mathtt{D}\ P\ (\bar{v}; t_j)\tau$. So consider a recursive call $\mathtt{f}\ \bar{r}$ in e_i. Since `f` is structurally recursive, we have $r_j \prec \lceil p_{ij} \rceil$ where $r_j : D\ \bar{w}$. By construction of $\mathtt{Below}_\mathtt{D}$, we have a projection π such that $\pi\ H : (\bar{t} : \Delta) \to \bar{w}; r_j \equiv \bar{v}; t_j \to T$. Hence we can define e'_i by replacing $\mathtt{f}\ \bar{r}$ by $\pi\ H\ \bar{r}\ \overline{\mathtt{refl}} : T[\Delta \mapsto \bar{r}]$ in e_i, and take $m_i = \lambda\bar{s}; H.\ e'_i$. For `antisym`, we have

$$\begin{aligned} &\pi_1\ H : (m\ n : \mathbb{N})(x : m \leq n)(y : n \leq m) \to \\ &\quad (k; l; u) \equiv (m; n; x) \to m \equiv n \end{aligned} \tag{51}$$

so we replace the recursive call $\mathtt{antisym}\ k\ l\ u\ v$ by $\pi_1\ H\ k\ l\ u\ v\ \overline{\mathtt{refl}}$.

When we fill in $H = \mathtt{below}_\mathtt{D}\ P\ m^s\ (\bar{v}; t_j)$, we get

$$\begin{aligned} &\pi\ (\mathtt{below}_\mathtt{D}\ P\ m^s\ (\bar{v}; t_j))\ \bar{r}\ \overline{\mathtt{refl}} \\ &\quad \rightsquigarrow^* m^s\ (\bar{w}; r_j)\ (\mathtt{below}_\mathtt{D}\ P\ m^s\ (\bar{w}; r_j))\ \bar{r}\ \overline{\mathtt{refl}} \\ &\quad \rightsquigarrow^* m\ \bar{r}\ (\mathtt{below}_\mathtt{D}\ P\ m^s\ (\bar{w}; r_j)) = \mathtt{f'}\ \bar{r} \end{aligned} \tag{52}$$

By induction, we now have the required $m : (\bar{t} : \Delta) \to \mathtt{Below}_\mathtt{D}\ P\ \bar{v}\ x \to T$, thus finishing the construction of `f'`.

For each clause

$$\mathtt{f}\ \bar{p}_i = e_i \tag{53}$$

with pattern variables $\bar{s} : \Delta_i$ at a leaf node of `f`'s case tree, we have

$$\begin{aligned} \mathtt{f'}\ \lceil \bar{p}_i \rceil &\rightsquigarrow^* m\ \lceil \bar{p}_i \rceil\ (\mathtt{below}_\mathtt{D}\ P\ m^s\ \bar{u}\ \lceil p_{ij} \rceil) \\ &\rightsquigarrow^* m_\mathtt{c}\ \ldots\ \text{(working our way down the case tree)} \\ &\rightsquigarrow^* m_i\ \bar{s}\ (\mathtt{below}_\mathtt{D}\ P\ m^s\ \bar{u}\ \lceil p_{ij} \rceil) \\ &\rightsquigarrow^* e'_i[H \mapsto \mathtt{below}_\mathtt{D}\ P\ m^s\ \bar{u}\ \lceil p_{ij} \rceil] \\ &\rightsquigarrow^* \{e_i\}_\mathtt{f}^{\mathtt{f'}} \end{aligned} \tag{54}$$

Hence we can conclude that whenever $\mathtt{f}\ \bar{t} \rightsquigarrow u$, we also have $\mathtt{f'}\ \bar{t} \rightsquigarrow^* \{u\}_\mathtt{f}^{\mathtt{f'}}$, as we wanted to prove.

4. Making pattern matching without K less restrictive

In Section 2.3, we remarked that our criterion was more general than the syntactic one. However, it still has some problems of its own. Suppose for example we are working with the inequality $\leq$ indexed over finite sets $\mathtt{Fin}\ n$, and we try to unify two successors in the same finite set. The problem $\mathtt{fs}\ n\ x = \mathtt{fs}\ n\ y$ requires solving $n = n$, but then we get stuck because we cannot use **deletion**. It can be proven that K is not really needed for this example, so the criterion is still overly conservative. We now discuss a possible solution to handle cases like this one.

$$\begin{aligned} &\mathrm{K}_\mathbb{N} : (n : \mathbb{N})(P : n \equiv n \to \mathtt{Set}) \to \\ &\qquad P\ \mathtt{refl} \to (e : n \equiv n) \to P\ e \\ &\mathrm{K}_\mathbb{N}\quad \mathtt{zero}\ P\ p\ \mathtt{refl} = p \\ &\mathrm{K}_\mathbb{N}\quad (\mathtt{suc}\ n)\ P\ p\ e = \mathtt{subst}\ P\ (\mathtt{add\text{-}drop}\ e) \\ &\qquad\qquad\qquad (\mathrm{K}_\mathbb{N}\ n\ (P \circ \mathtt{add})\ p\ (\mathtt{drop}\ e)) \end{aligned}$$

where

$$\begin{aligned} &\mathtt{add} &&: n \equiv n \to \mathtt{suc}\ n \equiv \mathtt{suc}\ n \\ &\mathtt{add} &&= \mathtt{noConf}_\mathbb{N}{}^{-1}\ (\mathtt{suc}\ n)\ (\mathtt{suc}\ n) \\ &\mathtt{drop} &&: \mathtt{suc}\ n \equiv \mathtt{suc}\ n \to n \equiv n \\ &\mathtt{drop} &&= \mathtt{noConf}_\mathbb{N}\ (\mathtt{suc}\ n)\ (\mathtt{suc}\ n) \\ &\mathtt{add\text{-}drop} &&: (e : \mathtt{suc}\ n \equiv \mathtt{suc}\ n) \to \mathtt{add}\ (\mathtt{drop}\ e) \equiv e \\ &\mathtt{add\text{-}drop} &&= \mathtt{isLeftInv}_\mathbb{N}\ (\mathtt{suc}\ n)\ (\mathtt{suc}\ n) \end{aligned}$$

Figure 6. A proof that the type $\mathbb{N}$ of natural numbers satisfies K, using dependent pattern matching with our criterion. The match on `refl` in the first clause passes our criterion because the unification problem is `zero` = `zero`, which can be solved by **injectivity**. The recursive call to $\mathrm{K}_\mathbb{N}$ in the second clause is permitted because the first argument decreases from $\mathtt{suc}\ n$ to n. We use the functions `noConf`, $\mathtt{noConf}^{-1}$ and `isLeftInv` constructed from eliminators in the appendix, but we could define these functions using pattern matching as well.

Looking back at the construction of the unification transitions in Section 3.5, we disallowed using **deletion** on an equation $x = x$ because *in general* this requires assuming K. However, for certain types of x, K can actually be proven without assuming it as an axiom. These types are called *(homotopy) sets* in HoTT. For example, $\mathbb{N}$ is a set (see Figure 6 for a proof of this fact), so it would be fine to use **deletion** on $n = n$ when $n : \mathbb{N}$. This would already solve the problem described above.

The question then remains how to detect which types are sets and which are not. One possible solution is to require the user to prove K manually for a particular type, and then use this proof during unification by means of a typeclass-like system such as given by Devriese and Piessens (2011).

A nicer, but probably also harder approach is to try to detect sets automatically. This problem is very hard in general, but we could at least try to detect easy cases like $\mathbb{N}$, using Hedberg's theorem or a generalization of it (Kraus et al. 2013). Hedberg's theorem states that if a type A has decidable equality, then it is a set. In particular, if D is a simple (non-indexed) data type such that each constructor is of the form $c : \Delta_c \to D \to \ldots \to D \to D$ where all of the types in Δ_c have decidable equality, then D itself also has decidable equality, hence it is a set by Hedberg's theorem. For example, this can be used to see that $\mathbb{N}$ is a set. This criterion can be used to reintroduce the **deletion** step of the unification algorithm on a more limited basis, namely to delete an equation $x = x$ only if the type of x can be seen to be a set based on the criterion.

5. Related work

Most implementations of dependent pattern matching in the style of Coquand (1992) do this by assuming the K axiom. Examples include Agda (when –without-K is not enabled), Idris (Brady 2013), and the Equations package for Coq (Sozeau 2010).

Coq also support a more primitive notion of pattern matching via the `match` construct in Gallina (The Coq development team 2012).

The full version of this construct is

$$\begin{array}{l} \texttt{match } e \texttt{ as } x \texttt{ in } D\ \bar{u} \texttt{ return } P \texttt{ with} \\ \quad \mid c_1\ \bar{y}_1 \Rightarrow e_1 \\ \quad \mid \ldots \\ \quad \mid c_n\ \bar{y}_n \Rightarrow e_n \\ \texttt{end} \end{array} \tag{55}$$

In the language of this paper, this corresponds to

$$\texttt{case}_{\texttt{D}}\ (\lambda\bar{u}; x.\ P)\ (\lambda\bar{y}_1.\ e_1)\ \ldots\ (\lambda\bar{y}_n.\ e_n)\ e \tag{56}$$

Coq also allows skipping the parts labeled by `as`, `in`, and `return`, in which case it will attempt to construct the motive P automatically.

Note that the motive P must be fully generalized over the indices $\bar{u}$, ensuring that no unification is necessary. Hence this kind of matching also prevents us from proving K. However, it is more low-level than the kind of pattern matching described in this paper, because it requires the user to give each case split explicitly, and does not perform any unification.

An unpublished first version of dependent pattern matching by McBride (1998) also used homogeneous equality with telescopic substitution and hence a proof-relevant unification algorithm. Similar to our present work, he observes that the innocent-looking **deletion** rule turns into the rather less innocent K. However, the published version of this work uses the heterogeneous equality, thus making it rely on K.

6. Conclusion and future work

Dependent pattern matching is an important tool for writing dependently typed functions and proofs in a readable way, but so far it needed the K axiom to function. What this paper shows, is that there is no need to throw away the baby with the bath water: by carefully analysing where K is used, we can give a restricted formulation of dependent pattern matching that does not need it. We hope that this is enough to convince the HoTT community that pattern matching does not require K *an sich*, and maybe even helps in the creation of a practical language based on HoTT.

One thing we noticed during the writing of this proof is how easily a small mistake can have grave impact on the soundness. For example, it was only after a long time that we realized just disabling **deletion** was not enough, but that the **injectivity** rule also subtly depends on K. To increase our confidence, we should make the type checker of our languages perform the translation from pattern matching to a core calculus in practice. This is already done in the Equations package for Coq by Sozeau (2010), but they still need the K axiom for the translation. It would be interesting to see if our criterion could be integrated into this approach. Another very appealing idea is to write a compiler for dependent pattern matching inside the type theory by means of *datatype-generic programming* as described by Dagand (2013).

Our criterion makes it possible to do pattern matching on *regular* inductive families without assuming K. But HoTT also introduces the concept of *higher inductive types*, which can have nontrivial identity proofs between their constructors. This implies that in general they do not satisfy the injectivity, disjointness, or acyclicity properties. Luckily, the proof given in this paper is entirely *parametric* in the actual unification transitions that are used. So in order to allow pattern matching in a context with higher inductive types, we should just limit the unification algorithm further. Our present paper gives a glimpse of how a theory of pattern matching with higher inductive types might look like, but future research will have to show how much of the original pattern matching algorithm can be salvaged.

Acknowledgments

This research is partially funded by the Research Fund KU Leuven, and by the Research Foundation - Flanders under grant number G004321N. Jesper Cockx and Dominique Devriese both hold a Ph.D. fellowship of the Research Foundation - Flanders (FWO).

References

T. Altenkirch. Without-K problem, 2012. URL `https://lists.chalmers.se/pipermail/agda/2012/004104.html`. On the Agda mailing list.

E. Brady. Idris, a general purpose dependently typed programming language: Design and implementation. *Journal of Functional Programming*, 23(5), 2013.

J. Cockx. Yet another way Agda –without-K is incompatible with univalence, 2014. URL `https://lists.chalmers.se/pipermail/agda/2014/006367.html`. On the Agda mailing list.

T. Coquand. Pattern matching with dependent types. In *Types for proofs and programs*, 1992.

P.-E. Dagand. *A cosmology of datatypes: reusability and dependent types*. PhD thesis, University of Strathclyde, 2013.

N. A. Danielsson. Experiments related to equality, 2013. URL `http://www.cse.chalmers.se/~nad/repos/equality/`. Agda code.

D. Devriese and F. Piessens. On the bright side of type classes: instance arguments in Agda. *ACM SIGPLAN International Conference on Functional Programming (ICFP)*, pages 143–155, 2011.

P. Dybjer. Inductive sets and families in Martin-Löf's type theory and their set-theoretic semantics. In *Proceedings of the first workshop on Logical frameworks*, 1991.

H. Goguen, C. McBride, and J. McKinna. Eliminating dependent pattern matching. In *Algebra, Meaning, and Computation*. 2006.

M. Hofmann and T. Streicher. The groupoid model refutes uniqueness of identity proofs. In *Logic in Computer Science*, pages 208–212, 1994.

J.-P. Jouannaud and C. Kirchner. *Solving equations in abstract algebras: A rule-based survey of unification*. 1990.

N. Kraus and C. Sattler. On the hierarchy of univalent universes: U(n) is not n-truncated. *arXiv preprint arXiv:1311.4002*, 2013.

N. Kraus, M. Escardó, T. Coquand, and T. Altenkirch. Generalizations of Hedberg's theorem. In *Typed Lambda Calculi and Applications*, pages 173–188. Springer, 2013.

Z. Luo. *Computation and reasoning: a type theory for computer science*, volume 11 of *International Series of Monographs on Computer Science*. 1994.

P. Martin-Löf. *Intuitionistic type theory*. Number 1 in Studies in Proof Theory. 1984.

C. McBride. Towards dependent pattern matching in lego. TYPES meeting, 1998.

C. McBride. *Dependently typed functional programs and their proofs*. PhD thesis, University of Edinburgh, 2000.

C. McBride. Elimination with a motive. In *Types for proofs and programs*, 2002.

C. McBride, H. Goguen, and J. McKinna. A few constructions on constructors. In *Types for Proofs and Programs*, 2006.

U. Norell. *Towards a practical programming language based on dependent type theory*. PhD thesis, Chalmers University of Technology, 2007.

U. Norell, A. Abel, and N. A. Danielsson. Release notes for Agda 2 version 2.3.2, 2012. URL `http://wiki.portal.chalmers.se/agda/pmwiki.php?n=Main.Version-2-3-2`.

J. Reed. Another possible without-K problem, 2013. URL `https://lists.chalmers.se/pipermail/agda/2013/005578.html`. On the Agda mailing list.

A. Sicard-Ramírez. –without-K option too restrictive?, 2013. URL `https://lists.chalmers.se/pipermail/agda/2013/005407.html`. On the Agda mailing list.

M. Sozeau. Equations: A dependent pattern-matching compiler. In *Interactive theorem proving*, 2010.

The Coq development team. *The Coq proof assistant reference manual.* LogiCal Project, 2012. URL http://coq.inria.fr. Version 8.4.

The Univalent Foundations Program. *Homotopy Type Theory: Univalent Foundations of Mathematics.* http://homotopytypetheory.org/book, Institute for Advanced Study, 2013.

A. A few homogeneous constructions on constructors

Case Analysis. $\mathtt{case}_\mathtt{D}$ is given by dropping the inductive hypotheses from the eliminator, i.e. it is itself a $\bar{\mathtt{D}}$-elimination operator with methods

$$\begin{aligned} m_i : (\bar{t} : \Delta_i) \to \\ (x_1 : \Phi_{i1} \to D\ \bar{v}_{i1})\ \ldots\ (x_{n_i} : \Phi_{in_i} \to D\ \bar{v}_{in_i}) \to \\ P\ \bar{u}_i\ (\mathtt{c_i}\ \bar{t}\ x_1\ \ldots\ x_{n_i}) \end{aligned} \tag{57}$$

for $i = 1, \ldots k$.

Recursion. In order to define $\mathtt{Below}_\mathtt{D}\ P$, we apply the eliminator $\mathtt{elim}_\mathtt{D}$ to the motive $\Phi = \lambda\ \_.\ \mathtt{Set}_i$. For the method m_i corresponding to the constructor $\mathtt{c_i}$ we give the following:

$$\begin{aligned} m_i = \lambda\bar{t}; x_1; \ldots; x_{n_i}; h_1; \ldots; h_{n_i}. \\ (\Phi_{i1} \to h_1\ \Phi_{i1} \times P\ \bar{v}_{i1}\ (x_1\ \Phi_{i1})) \times \ldots \\ \times (\Phi_{in_i} \to h_{n_i}\ \Phi_{in_i} \times P\ \bar{v}_{in_i}\ (x_{n_i}\ \Phi_{in_i})) \end{aligned} \tag{58}$$

i.e. $\mathtt{Below}_\mathtt{D}\ P\ x$ is a tuple asserting $P\ y$ for all y structurally smaller than x. Next, to define $\mathtt{below}_\mathtt{D}\ P\ p$, we apply $\mathtt{elim}_\mathtt{D}$ with the motive $\mathtt{Below}_\mathtt{D}\ P$. We give the following for the method m_i:

$$\begin{aligned} m_i = \lambda\bar{t}; x_1; \ldots; x_{n_i}; h_1; \ldots; h_{n_i}. \\ (\lambda\Phi_{i1}.\ h_1\ \Phi_{i1},\ p\ \bar{v}_{i1}\ x_1\ (h_1\ \Phi_{i1})),\ \ldots, \\ (\lambda\Phi_{in_i}.\ h_{n_i}\ \Phi_{in_i},\ p\ \bar{v}_{in_i}\ x_{n_i}\ (h_{n_i}\ \Phi_{in_i})) \end{aligned} \tag{59}$$

Finally, we define $\mathtt{rec}_\mathtt{D}\ P\ p\ \bar{\mathtt{D}} := p\ \bar{\mathtt{D}}\ (\mathtt{below}_\mathtt{D}\ P\ p\ \bar{\mathtt{D}})$.

No Confusion. First, we define $\mathtt{NoConfusion}_\mathtt{D}\ \bar{a}\ \bar{b}$ by applying $\mathtt{case}_\mathtt{D}$ with the motive $\lambda\ \_.\ \mathtt{Set}_i$ on $\bar{a}$. For each method $m_i\ \bar{x}$, we apply $\mathtt{case}_\mathtt{D}$ again with the same motive, but this time on $\bar{b}$. This gives us k^2 methods m_{ij} to fill in, one for each pair of constructors. On the diagonal (where $i = j$) we define $m_{ii} = \lambda\bar{x}; \bar{x}'.\ \bar{x} \equiv \bar{x}'$, and if $i \neq j$ we simply give $m_{ij} = \lambda\bar{x}; \bar{x}'.\ \bot$ (the empty type). Next, we define $\mathtt{noConf}_\mathtt{D}\ \bar{a}\ \bar{b}$. By telescopic substitution $\overline{\mathtt{subst}}$ with motive $\mathtt{NoConfusion}_\mathtt{D}\ \bar{a}$, it is sufficient to give a function of type $(\bar{a} : \bar{\mathtt{D}}) \to \mathtt{NoConfusion}_\mathtt{D}\ \bar{a}\ \bar{a}$. But this can be done using $\mathtt{case}_\mathtt{D}$ with motive $\lambda\ \bar{a}.\ \mathtt{NoConfusion}_\mathtt{D}\ \bar{a}\ \bar{a}$: for each method $m_i\ \bar{x}$ we can fill in $\overline{\mathtt{refl}}$.

For the inverse $\mathtt{noConf}_\mathtt{D}{}^{-1}\ \bar{a}\ \bar{b}$, we need to do a little more work. First, we apply $\mathtt{case}_\mathtt{D}$ twice as in the definition of $\mathtt{NoConfusion}_\mathtt{D}$. Now we are left to give methods

$$\begin{aligned} m_{ij} : \mathtt{NoConfusion}_\mathtt{D}\ (\bar{u}_i; \mathtt{c_i}\ \bar{x})\ (\bar{u}'_j; \mathtt{c_j}\ \bar{x}') \to \\ \bar{u}_i\ (\mathtt{c_i}\ \bar{x}) \equiv \bar{u}'_j\ (\mathtt{c_j}\ \bar{x}') \end{aligned} \tag{60}$$

When $i \neq j$, this is easy: we get an element of type $\bot$ from $\mathtt{NoConfusion}_\mathtt{D}$, from which we can conclude anything. On the diagonal (where $i = j$) we get a proof of $\bar{x} \equiv \bar{x}'$. Applying $\overline{\mathtt{subst}}$ to this equality leaves us the goal $\bar{u}'_j\ (\mathtt{c_j}\ \bar{x}') \equiv \bar{u}'_j\ (\mathtt{c_j}\ \bar{x}')$, which we can fill in with $\overline{\mathtt{refl}}$. Finally, we prove that this is indeed a (left) inverse by constructing a function of type

$$(\bar{a}\ \bar{b} : \bar{\mathtt{D}})(\bar{e} : \bar{a} \equiv \bar{b}) \to \mathtt{noConf}_\mathtt{D}{}^{-1}\ \bar{a}\ \bar{b}\ (\mathtt{noConf}_\mathtt{D}\ \bar{a}\ \bar{b}\ \bar{e}) \equiv \bar{e} \tag{61}$$

By $\bar{\mathrm{J}}$, it is sufficient to give a function of type

$$(\bar{a} : \bar{\mathtt{D}}) \to \mathtt{noConf}_\mathtt{D}{}^{-1}\ \bar{a}\ \bar{a}\ (\mathtt{noConf}_\mathtt{D}\ \bar{a}\ \bar{a}\ \overline{\mathtt{refl}}) \equiv \overline{\mathtt{refl}} \tag{62}$$

But this we can do by applying $\mathtt{case}_\mathtt{D}$ with methods $m_i\ \bar{x} = \overline{\mathtt{refl}}$.

Acyclicity. The relation $\not<$ is defined using $\mathtt{Below}_\mathtt{D}$: $\bar{a} \not< \bar{b} := \mathtt{Below}_\mathtt{D}\ (\lambda\bar{b}'.\ \bar{a} \not\equiv \bar{b}')\ \bar{b}$. We also define $\bar{a} \not\leq \bar{b} := \bar{a} \not< \bar{b} \times \bar{a} \not\equiv \bar{b}$. If $x : \mathtt{D}\ \bar{u}$ and $y : \mathtt{D}\ \bar{v}$ then we often write $x \not< y$ and $x \not\leq y$ instead of $\bar{u}; x \not< \bar{v}; y$ and $\bar{u}; x \not\leq \bar{v}; y$ to avoid having to write too much clutter. Note that $x \not< \mathtt{c_i}\ \Delta_i\ x_1\ \ldots\ x_{n_i} = (\Phi_{i1} \to x \not\leq x_1\ \Phi_{i1}) \times \ldots \times (\Phi_{in_i} \to x \not\leq x_{n_i}\ \Phi_{in_i})$ by definition of $\mathtt{Below}_\mathtt{D}$ and $\not\leq$. Now to construct $\mathtt{noCycle}_\mathtt{D}$, we start by eliminating the equation $\bar{a} \equiv \bar{b}$ using $\bar{\mathrm{J}}$, which leaves us the goal $(\bar{a} : \bar{\mathtt{D}}) \to \bar{a} \not< \bar{a}$. Next we apply $\mathtt{elim}_\mathtt{D}$ with motive $\lambda\bar{a}.\ \bar{a} \not< \bar{a}$, producing for each constructor $\mathtt{c_i} : \Delta_i \to (\Phi_{i1} \to \mathtt{D}\ \bar{v}_{i1}) \to \ldots \to (\Phi_{in_i} \to \mathtt{D}\ \bar{v}_{in_i}) \to \mathtt{D}\ \bar{u}_i$ the subgoal $(\bar{t} : \Delta_i) \to (x_1 : \Phi_{i1} \to \mathtt{D}\ \bar{v}_{i1})\ \ldots\ (x_{n_i} : \Phi_{in_i} \to \mathtt{D}\ \bar{v}_{in_i}) \to (h_1 : \Phi_{i1} \to x_1\ \Phi_{i1} \not< x_1\ \Phi_{i1})\ \ldots\ (h_{n_i} : \Phi_{in_i} \to x_{n_i}\ \Phi_{in_i} \not< x_{n_i}\ \Phi_{in_i}) \to \mathtt{c_i}\ \bar{t}\ x_1\ \ldots\ x_{n_i} \not< \mathtt{c_i}\ \bar{t}\ x_1\ \ldots\ x_{n_i}$. In order to continue, we first define the auxiliary types $\mathtt{Step_{ij}} : \Delta_i \to (x_1 : \Phi_{i1} \to \mathtt{D}\ \bar{v}_{i1})\ \ldots\ (x_{n_i} : \Phi_{in_i} \to \mathtt{D}\ \bar{v}_{in_i}) \to \Phi_{ij} \to \bar{\mathtt{D}} \to \mathtt{Set}_d$ for $i = 1, \ldots, k$ and $j = 1, \ldots, n_i$ as follows:

$$\begin{aligned} \mathtt{Step_{ij}}\ \bar{t}\ x_1\ \ldots\ x_{n_i}\ \Phi_{ij}\ (\bar{u}; b) = \\ (x_j\ \Phi_{ij}) \not< b \to (\mathtt{c_i}\ \bar{t}\ x_1\ \ldots\ x_{n_i}) \not\leq b \end{aligned} \tag{63}$$

Now suppose that we can construct $\mathtt{step_{ij}} : (\bar{t} : \Delta_i) \to (x_1 : \Phi_{i1} \to \mathtt{D}\ \bar{v}_{i1})\ \ldots\ (x_{n_i} : \Phi_{in_i} \to \mathtt{D}\ \bar{v}_{in_i}) \to \Phi_{ij} \to (\bar{a} : \bar{\mathtt{D}}) \to \mathtt{Step_{ij}}\ \bar{t}\ x_1\ \ldots\ x_{n_i}\ \Phi_{ij}\ \bar{a}$. Then we can solve the subgoal by filling in

$$\begin{aligned} &\lambda\bar{t}; \bar{x}; \bar{h}. \\ &\quad (\lambda\Phi_{i1}.\ \mathtt{step_{i1}}\ \bar{t}\ \bar{x}\ \Phi_{i1}\ \bar{v}_{i1}\ (x_1\ \Phi_{i1})\ (h_1\ \Phi_{i1})), \\ &\quad \ldots, \\ &\quad (\lambda\Phi_{in_i}.\ \mathtt{step_{in_i}}\ \bar{t}\ \bar{x}\ \Phi_{in_i}\ \bar{v}_{in_i}\ (x_{n_i}\ \Phi_{in_i})\ (h_{n_i}\ \Phi_{in_i})) \end{aligned} \tag{64}$$

So we only need to construct the $\mathtt{step_{ij}}$. The construction of $\mathtt{step_{ij}}\ \bar{t}\ x_1\ \ldots\ x_{n_i}\ \Phi_{ij} : (\bar{a} : \bar{\mathtt{D}}) \to \mathtt{Step_{ij}}\ \bar{t}\ x_1\ \ldots\ x_{n_i}\ \Phi_{ij}\ \bar{a}$ proceeds by applying $\mathtt{elim}_\mathtt{D}$ with motive $\mathtt{Step_{ij}}\ \bar{t}\ x_1\ \ldots\ x_{n_i}\ \Phi_{ij}$. The new subgoals are of the form

$$\begin{aligned} &(\bar{t}' : \Delta'_p)(x'_1 : \Phi'_{p1} \to \mathtt{D}\ \bar{v}'_{p1})\ \ldots\ (x'_{n_p} : \Phi'_{pn_p} \to \mathtt{D}\ \bar{v}'_{pn_p}) \to \\ &\quad (h_1 : (\bar{s}'_1 : \Phi'_{p1}) \to \mathtt{Step_{ij}}\ \bar{t}\ \bar{x}\ \Phi_{ij}\ \bar{v}'_{p1}\ (x'_1\ \bar{s}'_1))\ \ldots \\ &\quad (h_{n_p} : (\bar{s}'_{n_p} : \Phi'_{pn_p}) \to \mathtt{Step_{ij}}\ \bar{t}\ \bar{x}\ \Phi_{ij}\ \bar{v}'_{pn_p}\ (x'_{n_p}\ \bar{s}'_{n_p})) \to \\ &\quad \mathtt{Step_{ij}}\ \bar{t}\ \bar{x}\ \Phi_{ij}\ \bar{u}'_p\ (\mathtt{c_p}\ \bar{t}'\ \bar{x}') \end{aligned} \tag{65}$$

We solve them by giving:

$$\lambda\bar{t}'; x'_1; \ldots; x'_{n_p}; h_1; \ldots; h_{n_p}; H.\ \alpha, \beta \tag{66}$$

where we still have to construct

$$\alpha : \mathtt{c_i}\ \bar{t}\ x_1\ \ldots\ x_{n_i} \not< \mathtt{c_p}\ \bar{t}'\ x'_1\ \ldots\ x'_{n_p} \tag{67}$$

and

$$\beta : \mathtt{c_i}\ \bar{t}\ x_1\ \ldots\ x_{n_i} \not\equiv \mathtt{c_p}\ \bar{t}'\ x'_1\ \ldots\ x'_{n_p} \tag{68}$$

For any $\bar{s} : \Phi_{ij}$, we have $H : x_j\ \bar{s} \not< \mathtt{c_p}\ \Delta'_p\ x'_1\ \ldots\ x'_{n_p}$ or, by definition of $\not<$, $H = (H_1, \ldots, H_{n_p})$ where $H_q : (\bar{s}' : \Phi'_{pq}) \to x_j\ \bar{s} \not\leq x'_q\ \bar{s}'$. The construction of α reduces to the construction of components $\alpha_q : \Phi'_{pq} \to \mathtt{c_i}\ \bar{t}\ x_1\ \ldots\ x_{n_i} \not\leq x'_q\ \Phi'_{pq}$. But these we can give as $\alpha_q = \lambda\bar{s}'.\ h_q\ (\pi_1\ (H_p\ \bar{s}'))$ (where π_1 is projection onto the first component). For constructing β, we assume $\mathtt{c_i}\ \bar{t}\ x_1\ \ldots\ x_{n_i} \equiv \mathtt{c_p}\ \bar{t}'\ x'_1\ \ldots\ x'_{n_p}$ and derive an element of $\bot$. By $\mathtt{noConf}_\mathtt{D}$, it suffices to consider the case where $i = p$, $\Delta_i = \Delta'_i$, and $x_1; \ldots; x_{n_i} = x'_1, \ldots, x'_{n_i}$. But then we have $H_j\ \bar{s} : x_j\ \bar{s} \not\leq x_j\ \bar{s}$, hence $\pi_2\ (H_j\ \Phi_{ij})\ \overline{\mathtt{refl}} : \bot$. This finishes the construction of $\mathtt{noCycle}_\mathtt{D}$.

Refinement Types For Haskell

Niki Vazou Eric L. Seidel Ranjit Jhala
UC San Diego

Dimitrios Vytiniotis Simon Peyton-Jones
Microsoft Research

Abstract

SMT-based checking of refinement types for call-by-value languages is a well-studied subject. Unfortunately, the classical translation of refinement types to verification conditions is unsound under lazy evaluation. When checking an expression, such systems implicitly assume that all the free variables in the expression are bound to *values*. This property is trivially guaranteed by eager, but does not hold under lazy, evaluation. Thus, to be sound and precise, a refinement type system for Haskell and the corresponding verification conditions must take into account *which subset of* binders actually reduces to values. We present a stratified type system that labels binders as potentially diverging or not, and that (circularly) uses refinement types to verify the labeling. We have implemented our system in LIQUIDHASKELL and present an experimental evaluation of our approach on more than 10,000 lines of widely used Haskell libraries. We show that LIQUIDHASKELL is able to prove 96% of all recursive functions terminating, while requiring a modest 1.7 lines of termination-annotations per 100 lines of code.

1. Introduction

Refinement types encode invariants by composing types with SMT-decidable refinement predicates [27, 37], generalizing Floyd-Hoare Logic (*e.g.* EscJava [14]) for functional languages. For example

```
type Pos = {v:Int | v >  0}
type Nat = {v:Int | v >= 0}
```

are the basic type `Int` refined with logical predicates that state that "the values" `v` described by the type are respectively strictly positive and non-negative. We encode *pre-* and *post*-conditions (contracts) using refined function types like

```
div :: n:Nat -> d:Pos -> {v:Nat | v <= n}
```

which states that the function `div` *requires* inputs that are respectively non-negative and positive, and *ensures* that the output is less than the first input `n`. If a program containing `div` statically type-checks, we can rest assured that executing the program will not lead to any unpleasant divide-by-zero errors. By combining types and SMT based validity checking, refinement types have automated the verification of programs with recursive datatypes, higher-order functions, and polymorphism. Several groups have used refinements to statically verify properties ranging from simple array safety [26, 37] to functional correctness of data structures [20], security protocols [4], and compiler correctness [31].

ICFP '14, September 1–6, 2014, Gothenburg, Sweden.

http://dx.doi.org/10.1145/2628136.2628161

Given the remarkable effectiveness of the technique, we embarked on the project of developing a refinement type based verifier for Haskell. The previous systems were all developed for eager, *call-by-value* languages, but we presumed that the order of evaluation would surely prove irrelevant, and that the soundness guarantees would translate to Haskell's lazy, *call-by-need* regime.

We were wrong. Our first contribution is to show that standard refinement systems crucially rely on a property of eager languages: when analyzing any term, one can assume that *all* the free variables appearing in the term are bound to *values*. This property lets us check each term in an environment where the free variables are logically constrained according to their refinements. Unfortunately, this property does not hold for lazy evaluation, where free variables can be lazily substituted with arbitrary (potentially diverging) expressions, which breaks soundness (§2).

The two natural paths towards soundness are blocked by challenging problems. The first path is to *conservatively ignore* free variables except those that are guaranteed to be values *e.g.* by pattern matching, `seq` or strictness annotations. While sound, this leads to a drastic loss of precision. The second path is to *explicitly* reason about divergence within the refinement logic. This would be sound and precise – however it is far from obvious to us how to re-use and extend existing SMT machinery for this purpose. (§8)

Our second contribution is a novel approach that enables sound and precise checking with existing SMT solvers, using a *stratified* type system that labels binders as potentially diverging or not (§4). While previous stratified systems [10] would suffice for soundness, we show how to recover precision by using refinement types to develop a notion of *terminating fixpoint* combinators that allows the type system to automatically verify that a wide variety of recursive functions actually terminate (§5).

Our third contribution is an extensive empirical evaluation of our approach on more than 10,000 lines of widely used complex Haskell libraries. We have implemented our approach in LIQUIDHASKELL, an SMT based verifier for Haskell. LIQUIDHASKELL is able to prove 96% of all recursive functions terminating, requiring a modest 1.7 lines of termination annotations per 100 lines of code, thereby enabling the sound, precise, and automated verification of functional correctness properties of real-world Haskell code (§6).

2. Overview

We start with an overview of our contributions. After recapitulating the basics of refinement types we illustrate why the classical approach based on verification conditions (VCs) is unsound due to lazy evaluation. Next, we step back to understand precisely how the VCs arise from refinement subtyping, and how subtyping is different under eager and lazy evaluation. In particular, we demonstrate that under lazy, but *not* eager, evaluation, the refinement type system, and hence the VCs, must account for divergence. Consequently, we develop a type system that accounts for divergence in a modular and syntactic fashion, and illustrate its use via several small examples. Finally, we show how a refinement-based termination analysis can be used to improve precision, yielding a highly effective SMT-based verifier for Haskell.

2.1 Standard Refinement Types: From Subtyping to VC

First, let us see how standard refinement type systems [21, 26] will use the refinement type aliases `Pos` and `Nat` and the specification for `div` from §1 to *accept* `good` and *reject* `bad`. We use the syntax of Figure 1, where r is a *refinement expression*, or just *refinement* for short. We will vary the expressiveness of the language of refinements in different parts of the paper.

```
good     :: Nat -> Nat -> Int
good x y = let z = y + 1 in x `div` z

bad      :: Nat -> Nat -> Int
bad x y  = x `div` y
```

Refinement Subtyping To analyze the body of `bad`, the refinement type system will check that the second parameter `y` has type `Pos` at the call to `div`; formally, that the actual parameter `y` is a *subtype* of the type of `div`'s second input, via a subtyping query:

$$\begin{matrix}\mathtt{x}{:}\{\mathtt{x}{:}\mathtt{Int} \mid \mathtt{x} \geq 0\}, \\ \mathtt{y}{:}\{\mathtt{y}{:}\mathtt{Int} \mid \mathtt{y} \geq 0\}\end{matrix} \vdash \{\mathtt{y}{:}\mathtt{Int} \mid \mathtt{y} \geq 0\} \preceq \{\mathtt{v}{:}\mathtt{Int} \mid \mathtt{v} > 0\}$$

We use the Abbreviations of Figure 1 to simplify the syntax of the queries. So the above query simplifies to:

$$\mathtt{x}{:}\{\mathtt{x} \geq 0\},\ \mathtt{y}{:}\{\mathtt{y} \geq 0\} \vdash \{\mathtt{v} \geq 0\} \preceq \{\mathtt{v} > 0\}$$

Verification Conditions To discharge the above subtyping query, a refinement type system generates a *verification condition* (VC), a logical formula that stipulates that under the assumptions corresponding to the environment bindings, the refinement in the subtype *implies* the refinement in the super-type. We use the translation $(\!| \cdot |\!)$ shown in Figure 1 to reduce a subtyping query to a verification condition. The translation of a basic type into logic is the refinement of the type. The translation of an environment is the conjunction of its bindings. Finally, the translation of a binding $x{:}\tau$ is the embedding of τ guarded by a predicate denoting that "x is a value". For now, let us ignore this guard and see how the subtyping query for `bad` reduces to the *classical* VC:

$$(\mathtt{x} \geq 0) \wedge (\mathtt{y} \geq 0)\ \Rightarrow\ (\mathtt{v} \geq 0) \Rightarrow (\mathtt{v} > 0)$$

Refinement type systems are carefully engineered (§4) so that (*unlike* with full dependent types) the logic of refinements *precludes* arbitrary functions and only includes formulas from efficiently decidable logics, *e.g.* the quantifier-free logic of linear arithmetic and uninterpreted functions (QF-EUFLIA). Thus, VCs like the above can be efficiently validated by SMT solvers [11]. In this case, the solver will reject the above VC as *invalid* meaning the implication, and hence, the relevant subtyping requirement does not hold. So the refinement type system will *reject* `bad`.

On the other hand, a refinement system *accepts* `good`. Here, `+`'s type exactly captures its behaviour into the logic:

```
(+) :: x:Int -> y:Int -> {v:Int | v = x + y}
```

Thus, we can conclude that the divisor `z` is a positive number. The subtyping query for the argument to `div` is

$$\begin{matrix}\mathtt{x}{:}\{\mathtt{x} \geq 0\}, \mathtt{y}{:}\{\mathtt{y} \geq 0\}, \\ \mathtt{z}{:}\{\mathtt{z} = \mathtt{y}+1\}\end{matrix} \vdash \{\mathtt{v} = \mathtt{y}+1\} \preceq \{\mathtt{v} > 0\}$$

which reduces to the *valid* VC

$$\begin{matrix}(\mathtt{x} \geq 0) \wedge (\mathtt{y} \geq 0) \wedge \\ (\mathtt{z} = \mathtt{y}+1)\end{matrix} \Rightarrow (\mathtt{v} = \mathtt{y}+1) \Rightarrow (\mathtt{v} > 0)$$

Refinements	r	$::=$	$\ldots$ varies $\ldots$
Basic Types	b	$::=$	$\{v{:}\mathtt{Int} \mid r\} \mid \ldots$
Types	τ	$::=$	$b \mid x{:}\tau \rightarrow \tau$
Environment	Γ	$::=$	$\emptyset \mid x{:}\tau, \Gamma$
Subtyping			$\Gamma \vdash \tau_1 \preceq \tau_2$
Abbreviations			
$x{:}\{r\}$		$\doteq$	$x{:}\{x{:}\mathtt{Int} \mid r\}$
$\{x \mid r\}$		$\doteq$	$\{x{:}\mathtt{Int} \mid r\}$
$\{r\}$		$\doteq$	$\{v{:}\mathtt{Int} \mid r\}$
$\{x{:}\{y{:}\mathtt{Int} \mid r_y\} \mid r_x\}$		$\doteq$	$\{x{:}\mathtt{Int} \mid r_x \wedge r_y\,[x/y]\}$
Translation			
$(\!\|\Gamma \vdash b_1 \preceq b_2\|\!)$		$\doteq$	$(\!\|\Gamma\|\!) \Rightarrow (\!\|b_1\|\!) \Rightarrow (\!\|b_2\|\!)$
$(\!\|\{x{:}\mathtt{Int} \mid r\}\|\!)$		$\doteq$	r
$(\!\|x{:}\{v{:}\mathtt{Int} \mid r\}\|\!)$		$\doteq$	"x is a value" $\Rightarrow r\,[x/v]$
$(\!\|x{:}(y{:}\tau_y \rightarrow \tau)\|\!)$		$\doteq$	**true**
$(\!\|x_1{:}\tau_1, \ldots, x_n{:}\tau_n\|\!)$		$\doteq$	$(\!\|x_1{:}\tau_1\|\!) \wedge \ldots \wedge (\!\|x_n{:}\tau_n\|\!)$

Figure 1. Notation: Types, Subtyping & VCs

2.2 Lazy Evaluation Makes VCs Unsound

To generate the classical VC, we ignored the "x is a value" guard that appears in the embedding of a binding $(\!|x{:}\tau|\!)$ (Figure 1). Under lazy evaluation, ignoring this "is a value" guard can lead to unsoundness. Consider

```
diverge   :: Int -> {v:Int | false}
diverge n = diverge n
```

The output type captures the *post-condition* that the function returns an `Int` satisfying `false`. This counter-intuitive specification states, in essence, that the function *does not terminate*, *i.e.* does not return *any* value. Any standard refinement type checker (or Floyd-Hoare verifier like Dafny[1]) will verify the given signature for `diverge` via the classical method of inductively *assuming* the signature holds for `diverge` and then *guaranteeing* the signature [16, 23]. Next, consider the call to `div` in `explode`:

```
explode   :: Int -> Int
explode x = let {n = diverge 1; y = 0}
            in  x `div` y
```

To analyze `explode`, the refinement type system will check that `y` has type `Pos` at the call to `div`, *i.e.* will check that

$$\mathtt{n}{:}\{\mathtt{false}\},\ \mathtt{y}{:}\{\mathtt{y} = 0\} \vdash \{\mathtt{v} = 0\} \preceq \{\mathtt{v} > 0\} \qquad (1)$$

In the subtyping environment `n` is bound to the type corresponding to the *output* type of `diverge`, and `y` is bound to the singleton type stating `y` equals `0`. In this environment, we must prove that actual parameter's type – *i.e.* that of `y` – is a subtype of `Pos`. The subtyping, using the embedding of Figure 1 and ignoring the "is a value" guard, reduces to the VC:

$$\mathtt{false} \wedge \mathtt{y} = 0\ \Rightarrow (\mathtt{v} = 0) \Rightarrow (\mathtt{v} > 0) \qquad (2)$$

The SMT solver proves this VC valid by using the contradiction in the antecedent, thereby unsoundly proving the call to `div` safe!

Eager vs. Lazy Verification Conditions At this point, we pause to emphasize that the problem lies in the fact that the classical

[1] http://rise4fun.com/Dafny/wVGc

technique for encoding subtyping (or generally, Hoare's "rule of consequence" [16]) with VCs is *unsound under lazy evaluation.* To see this, observe that the VC (2) is perfectly *sound* under eager (strict, call-by-value) evaluation. In the eager setting, the program is safe in that `div` is never called with the divisor `0`, as it is not called at all! The inconsistent antecedent in the VC logically encodes the fact that, under eager evaluation, the call to `div` is *dead code.* Of course, this conclusion is spurious under Haskell's lazy semantics. As `n` is not required, the program will dive headlong into evaluating the `div` and hence crash, rendering the VC meaningless.

The Problem is Laziness Readers familar with fully dependently typed languages like Cayenne [1], Agda [24], Coq [5], or Idris [7], may be tempted to attribute the unsoundness to the presence of arbitrary recursion and hence non-termination (*e.g.* `diverge`). While it *is* possible to define a sound semantics for dependent types that mention potentially non-terminating expressions [21], it is not clear how to reconcile such semantics with decidable type checking.

Refinement type systems avoid this situation by carefully restricting types so that they do not contain arbitrary terms (even through substitution), but rather only terms from restricted logics that preclude arbitrary user-defined functions [13, 31, 37]. Very much like previous work, we enforce the same restriction with a *well-formedness condition* on refinements (WF-BASE-D in Fig. 6).

However, we show that this restriction *is plainly not sufficient for soundness* when laziness is combined with non-termination, as binders can be bound to diverging expressions. Unsurprisingly, in a strongly normalizing language the question of lazy or strict semantics is irrelevant for soundness, and hence an "easy" way to solve the problem would be to completely eliminate non-termination and rely on the soundness of previous refinement or dependent type systems! Instead, we show here how to recover soundness for a lazy language *without* imposing such a drastic requirement.

2.3 Semantics, Subtyping & Verification Conditions

To understand the problem, let us take a step back to get a clear view of the relationship between the operational semantics, subtyping, and verification conditions. We use the formulation of evaluation-order independent refinement subtyping developed for λ^H [21] in which refinements r are *arbitrary* expressions e from the source language. We define a denotation for types and use it to define subtyping declaratively.

Denotations of Types and Environments Recall the type `Pos` defined as `{v:Int | 0 < v}`. Intuitively, `Pos` denotes the *set of* `Int` expressions which evaluate to values greater than `0`. We formalize this intuition by defining the denotation of a type as:

$$[\![\{x{:}\tau \mid r\}]\!] \doteq \{e \mid \emptyset \vdash e : \tau,\ \text{if } e \hookrightarrow^* w \text{ then } r\,[w/x] \hookrightarrow^* \texttt{true}\}$$

That is, the type denotes the set of expressions e that have the corresponding base type τ which *diverge or* reduce to values that make the refinement `true`. The guard $e \hookrightarrow^* w$ is crucially required to prove soundness in the presence of recursion. Thus, quoting [21], "refinement types specify partial and not total correctness".

An *environment* Γ is a sequence of type bindings, and a *closing substitution* θ is a sequence of expression bindings:

$$\Gamma \doteq x_1{:}\tau_1, \ldots x_n{:}\tau_n \qquad \theta \doteq x_1 \mapsto e_1, \ldots, x_n \mapsto e_n$$

Thus, we define the denotation of Γ as the set of substitutions:

$$[\![\Gamma]\!] \doteq \{\theta \mid \forall x{:}\tau \in \Gamma.\theta(x) \in [\![\theta(\tau)]\!]\}$$

Declarative Subtyping Equipped with interpretations for types and environments, we define the *declarative subtyping* $\preceq$-BASE (over basic types b, shown in Figure 1) to be containment between the types' denotations:

$$\frac{\forall \theta \in [\![\Gamma]\!].\ [\![\theta(\{v{:}B \mid r_1\})]\!] \subseteq [\![\theta(\{v{:}B \mid r_2\})]\!]}{\Gamma \vdash \{v{:}B \mid r_1\} \preceq \{v{:}B \mid r_2\}}\ \preceq\text{-BASE}$$

Let us revisit the `explode` example from §2.2; recall that the function is safe under eager evaluation but unsafe under lazy evaluation. Let us see how the declarative subtyping allows us to reject in the one case and accept in the other.

Declarative Subtyping with Lazy Evaluation Let us revisit the query (1) to see whether it holds under the declarative subtyping rule $\preceq$-BASE. The denotation containment

$$\forall \theta \in [\![\texttt{n}{:}\{\texttt{false}\},\ \texttt{y}{:}\{\texttt{y} = \texttt{0}\}]\!].[\![\theta\ \{\texttt{v} = \texttt{0}\}]\!] \subseteq [\![\theta\ \{\texttt{v} > \texttt{0}\}]\!] \quad (3)$$

does not hold. To see why, consider a θ that maps n to any diverging expression of type `Int` and y to the value 0. Then, $0 \in [\![\theta\ \{\texttt{v} = \texttt{0}\}]\!]$ but $0 \notin [\![\theta\ \{\texttt{v} > \texttt{0}\}]\!]$, thereby showing that the denotation containment does not hold.

Declarative Subtyping with Eager Evaluation Since denotational containment (3) does not hold, λ^H cannot verify `explode` under eager evaluation. However, Belo *et al.* [3] note that under eager (call-by-value) evaluation, each binder in the environment is only added *after* the previous binders have been reduced to *values.* Hence, under eager evaluation we can *restrict the range* of the closing substitutions to values (as opposed to expressions). Let us reconsider (3) in this new light: there *is no value* that we can map `n` to, so the set of denotations of the environment is empty. Hence, the containment (3) vacuously holds under eager evaluation, which proves the program safe. Belo's observation is implicitly used by refinement types for eager languages to prove that the standard (*i.e.* under call-by-value) reduction from subtyping to VC is sound.

Algorithmic Subtyping via Verification Conditions The above subtyping ($\preceq$-BASE) rule allows us to prove preservation and progress [21] but quantifies over evaluation of arbitrary expressions, and so is undecidable. To make checking *algorithmic* we approximate the denotational containment using *verification conditions* (VCs), formulas drawn from a decidable logic, that are valid only if the undecidable containment holds. As we have seen, the classical VC is sound only under eager evaluation. Next, let us use the distinctions between lazy and eager declarative subtyping, to obtain both sound and decidable VCs for the lazy setting.

Step 1: Restricting Refinements To Decidable Logics Given that in λ^H refinements can be *arbitrary* expressions, the first step towards obtaining a VC, regardless of evaluation order, is to restrict the refinements to a *decidable* logic. We choose the quantifier free logic of equality, uninterpreted functions and linear arithmetic (QF-EUFLIA). We design our typing rules to ensure that for any valid derivation, all the refinements belong in this restricted language.

Step 2: Translating Containment into VCs Our goal is to encode the denotation containment antecedent of $\preceq$-BASE

$$\forall \theta \in [\![\Gamma]\!].\ [\![\theta(\{v{:}B \mid r_1\})]\!] \subseteq [\![\theta(\{v{:}B \mid r_2\})]\!] \quad (4)$$

as a logical formula, that is valid *only when* the above holds. Intuitively, we can think of the closing substitutions θ as corresponding to *assignments*$(\!|\theta|\!)$ of variables X of the VC. We use the variable x to approximate denotational containment by stating that if x belongs to the type $\{v{:}B \mid r_1\}$ then x belongs to the type $\{v{:}B \mid r_2\}$:

$$\forall X \in dom(\Gamma), x.(\!|\Gamma|\!) \Rightarrow (\!|x{:}\{v{:}B \mid r_1\}|\!) \Rightarrow (\!|x{:}\{v{:}B \mid r_2\}|\!)$$

where $(\!|\Gamma|\!)$ and $(\!|x{:}\tau|\!)$ are respectively the translation of the environment and bindings into logical formulas that are only satisfied by assignments $(\!|\theta|\!)$ as shown in Figure 1. Using the translation of bindings, and by renaming x to v, we rewrite the the condition as

$$\begin{aligned}\forall X \in dom(\Gamma), v.(\!|\Gamma|\!) &\Rightarrow (\text{“}v \text{ is a value”} \Rightarrow r_1)\\ &\Rightarrow (\text{“}v \text{ is a value”} \Rightarrow r_2)\end{aligned}$$

Type refinements are carefully chosen to belong to the decidable logical sublanguage QF-EUFLIA, thus we directly translate type refinements into the logic. Thus, what is left is to translate into logic the environment and the "is a value" guards. We postpone translation of the guards as we approximate the above formula by a *stronger*, *i.e.* sound with respect to 4, VC that just omits the guards:

$$\forall X \in dom(\Gamma), v.(\!|\Gamma|\!) \Rightarrow r_1 \Rightarrow r_2$$

To translate environments, we conjoin their bindings' translations:

$$(\!| x_1{:}\tau_1, \ldots, x_n{:}\tau_n |\!) \doteq (\!| x_1{:}\tau_1 |\!) \wedge \ldots \wedge (\!| x_n{:}\tau_n |\!)$$

However, since types denote *partial correctness*, the translations must also explicitly account for possible divergence:

$$(\!| x{:}\{v{:}\texttt{Int} \mid r\} |\!) \doteq \text{"}x \text{ is a value"} \Rightarrow r\,[x/v]$$

That is, we *cannot* assume that each x satisfies its refinement r; we must *guard* that assumption with a predicate stating that x is bound to a value (not a diverging term.)

The crucial question is: *how* can one discharge these guards to conclude that x indeed satisfies r? One natural route is to enrich the refinement logic with a predicate that states that "x is a value", and then use the SMT solver to *explicitly* reason about this predicate and hence, divergence. Unfortunately, we show in §8, that such predicates lead to three-valued logics, which fall outside the scope of the efficiently decidable theories supported by current solvers. Hence, this route is problematic if we want to use existing SMT machinery to build automated verifiers for Haskell.

2.4 Our Answer: Implicit Reasoning About Divergence

One way forward is to *implicitly* reason about divergence by *eliminating* the "x is a value" guards (*i.e. value guards*) from the VCs.

Implicit Reasoning: Eager Evaluation Under eager evaluation the domain of the closing substitutions can be restricted to values [3]. Thus, we can trivially eliminate the value guards, as they are guaranteed to hold by virtue of the evaluation order. Returning to `explode`, we see that after eliminating the value guards, we get the VC (2) which is, therefore, sound under eager evaluation.

Implicit Reasoning: Lazy Evaluation However, with lazy evaluation, we cannot just eliminate the value guards, as the closing substitutions are not restricted to just values. Our solution is to take this reasoning out of the hands of the SMT logic and place it in the hands of a *stratified type system*. We use a non-deterministic β-reduction (formally defined in §3) to label each type as: A Div-type, written τ, which are the default types given to binders that *may diverge*, or, a Wnf-type, written $\tau^{\downarrow}$, which are given to binders that are guaranteed to reduce, in a finite number of steps, to *Haskell values* in Weak Head Normal Form (WHNF). Up to now we only discussed `Int` basic types, but our theory supports user-defined algebraic data types. An expression like `0 : repeat 0` is an infinite Haskell value. As we shall discuss, such infinite values cannot be represented in the logic. To distinguish infinite from finite values, we use a Fin-type, written $\tau^{\Downarrow}$, to label binders of expressions that are guaranteed to reduce to *finite values* with no redexes. This stratification lets us generate VCs that are sound for lazy evaluation. Let B be a basic labelled type. The key piece is the translation of environment bindings:

$$(\!| x{:}\{v{:}B \mid r\} |\!) \doteq \begin{cases} \texttt{true}, & \text{if } B \text{ is a Div type} \\ r\,[x/v]\,, & \text{otherwise} \end{cases}$$

That is, if the binder may diverge, we simply *omit* any constraints for it in the VC, and otherwise the translation directly states (*i.e.* without the value guard) that the refinement holds. Returning to `explode`, the subtyping query (1) yields the *invalid* VC

$$\texttt{true} \Rightarrow \texttt{v} = 0 \Rightarrow \texttt{v} > 0$$

and so `explode` is soundly rejected under lazy evaluation.

As binders appear in refinements, and binders may refer to potentially infinite computations (*e.g.* `[0..]`), we must ensure that refinements are well defined (*i.e.* do not diverge). We achieve this via stratification itself, *i.e.* by ensuring that all refinements have type $\texttt{Bool}^{\Downarrow}$. By Corollary 1, this suffices to ensure that all the refinements are indeed well-defined and converge.

2.5 Verification With Stratified Types

While it is reassuring that the lazy VC soundly *rejects* unsafe programs like `explode`, we now demonstrate by example that it usefully *accepts* safe programs. First, we show how the basic system – all terms have Div types – allows us to prove "partial correctness" properties without requiring termination. Second, we show how to extend the basic system by using Haskell's pattern matching semantics to assign the pattern match scrutinees Wnf types, thereby increasing the expressiveness of the verifier. Third, we show how to further improve the precision and usability of the system by using a termination checker to assign various terms Fin types. Fourth, we close the loop, by illustrating how the termination checker can itself be realized using refinement types. Finally, we use the termination checker to ensure that all refinements are well-defined (*i.e.* do converge.)

Example: VCs and Partial Correctness The first example illustrates how, unlike Curry-Howard based systems, refinement types *do not require* termination. That is, we retain the Floyd-Hoare notion of "partial correctness", and can verify programs where *all* terms have Div-types. Consider `ex1` which uses the result of `collatz` as a divisor.

```
ex1   :: Int -> Int
ex1 n = let x = collatz n in 10 `div` x

collatz :: Int -> {v:Int | v = 1}
collatz n
  | n == 1    = 1
  | even n    = collatz (n / 2)
  | otherwise = collatz (3*n + 1)
```

The jury is still out on *whether* the `collatz` function terminates, but it is easy to verify that its output is a Div `Int` equal to `1`. At the call to `div` the parameter `x` has the output type of `collatz`, yielding the subtyping query:

$$\texttt{x}{:}\{\texttt{v}{:}\texttt{Int} \mid \texttt{v} = 1\} \vdash \{\texttt{v} = 1\} \preceq \{\texttt{v} > 0\}$$

where the sub-type is just the type of `x`. As `Int` is a Div type, the above reduces to the VC ($\texttt{true} \Rightarrow \texttt{v} = 1 \Rightarrow \texttt{v} > 0$) which the SMT solver proves valid, thereby verifying `ex1`.

Example: Improving Precision By Forcing Evaluation If all binders in the environment have Div-types then, effectively, the verifier can make *no* assumptions about the context in which a term evaluates, which leads to a drastic loss of precision. Consider:

```
ex2 = let {x = 1; y = inc x} in 10 `div` y

inc :: z:Int -> {v:Int | v > z }
inc = \z -> z + 1
```

The call to `div` in `ex2` is obviously safe, but the system would reject it, as the call yields the subtyping query:

$$\texttt{x}{:}\{\texttt{x}{:}\texttt{Int} \mid \texttt{x} = 1\},\ \texttt{y}{:}\{\texttt{y}{:}\texttt{Int} \mid \texttt{y} > \texttt{x}\} \vdash \{\texttt{v} > \texttt{x}\} \preceq \{\texttt{v} > 0\}$$

Which, as `x` is a Div type, reduces to the invalid VC

$$\texttt{true} \Rightarrow \texttt{v} > \texttt{x} \Rightarrow \texttt{v} > 0$$

We could solve the problem by forcing evaluation of `x`. In Haskell the `seq` operator or a bang-pattern can be used to force evaluation. In our system the same effect is achieved by the **`case-of`** primitive:

inside each case the matched binder is guaranteed to be a Haskell value in WHNF. This intuition is formalized by the typing rule (T-CASE-D), which checks each case after assuming the scrutinee and the match binder have Wnf types.

If we force `x`'s evaluation, using the case primitive, the call to `div` yields the subtyping query:

$$\begin{matrix}\mathtt{x}{:}\{\mathtt{x}{:}\mathtt{Int}^{\downarrow} \mid \mathtt{x} = 1\} \\ \mathtt{y}{:}\{\mathtt{y}{:}\mathtt{Int} \mid \mathtt{y} > \mathtt{x}\}\end{matrix} \vdash \{\mathtt{v} > \mathtt{x}\} \preceq \{\mathtt{v} > 0\} \tag{5}$$

As x is Wnf, we accept `ex2` by proving the validity of the VC

$$\mathtt{x} = 1 \Rightarrow \mathtt{v} > \mathtt{x} \Rightarrow \mathtt{v} > 0 \tag{6}$$

Example: Improving Precision By Termination While forcing evaluation allows us to ensure that certain environment binders have non-Div types, it requires program rewriting using case-splitting or the `seq` operator which leads to non-idiomatic code.

Instead, our next key optimization is based on the observation that in practice, *most terms don't diverge*. Thus, we can use a termination analysis to aggressively assign terminating expressions Fin types, which lets us strengthen the environment assumptions needed to prove the VCs. For example, in the `ex2` example the term `1` obviously terminates. Hence, we type `x` as $\mathtt{Int}^{\Downarrow}$, yielding the subtyping query for `div` application:

$$\begin{matrix}\mathtt{x}{:}\{\mathtt{x}{:}\mathtt{Int}^{\Downarrow} \mid \mathtt{x} = 1\} \\ \mathtt{y}{:}\{\mathtt{y}{:}\mathtt{Int} \mid \mathtt{y} > \mathtt{x}\}\end{matrix} \vdash \{\mathtt{v} > \mathtt{x}\} \preceq \{\mathtt{v} > 0\} \tag{7}$$

As x is Fin, we accept `ex2` by proving the validity of the VC

$$\mathtt{x} = 1 \Rightarrow \mathtt{v} > \mathtt{x} \Rightarrow \mathtt{v} > 0 \tag{8}$$

Example: Verifying Termination With Refinements While it is straightforward to conclude that the term `1` does not diverge, how do we do so in general? For example:

```
ex4 = let {x = f 9; y = inc x} in 10 `div` y

f   :: Nat -> {v:Int | v = 1}
f n = if n == 0 then 1 else f (n-1)
```

We check the call to `div` via subtyping query (7) and VC (8), which requires us to prove that `f` terminates on *all* $\mathtt{Nat}^{\Downarrow}$ inputs.

We solve this problem by showing how refinement types may themselves be used to prove termination, by following the classical recipe of proving termination via decreasing metrics [32] as embodied in sized types [17, 36]. The key idea is to show that each recursive call is made with arguments of a *strictly smaller* size, where the size is itself a well founded metric, *e.g.* a natural number.

We formalize this intuition by type checking recursive procedures in a termination-weakened environment where the procedure itself may only be called with arguments that are strictly smaller than the current parameter (using terminating fixpoints of §4.2.) For example, to prove `f` terminates, we check its body in an environment

$$\mathtt{n} : \mathtt{Nat}^{\Downarrow} \qquad \mathtt{f} : \{\mathtt{n}'{:}\mathtt{Nat}^{\Downarrow} \mid \mathtt{n}' < \mathtt{n}\} \to \{\mathtt{v} = 1\}$$

where we have weakened the type of f to stipulate that it *only* be (recursively) called with Nat values $\mathtt{n}'$ that are *strictly less than* the (current) parameter n. The argument of f exactly captures these constraints, as using the Abbreviations of Figure 1 the argument of f is expanded to $\{\mathtt{n}'{:}\mathtt{Int}^{\Downarrow} \mid \mathtt{n}' < \mathtt{n} \wedge \mathtt{n}' >= 0\}$. The body type-checks as the recursive call generates the valid VC

$$0 \leq \mathtt{n} \wedge \neg(0 = \mathtt{n}) \Rightarrow \mathtt{v} = \mathtt{n} - 1 \Rightarrow (0 \leq \mathtt{v} < \mathtt{n})$$

Example: Diverging Refinements In this final example we discuss why refinements should always converge and how we statically ensure convergence. Consider the invalid specification

```
diverge 0 :: {v:Int | v = 12}
```

Definition			
	def	$::=$	$\mathtt{measure}\ f :: \tau$ $eq_1 \ldots eq_n$
Equation			
	eq	$::=$	$f\ (D\ \overline{x}) = r$
Equation to Type			
$(\!| f\ (D\ \overline{x}) = r |\!)$		$\doteq$	$D :: \overline{x{:}\tau} \to \{\mathtt{v}{:}\tau \mid f\ \mathtt{v} = r\}$

Figure 2. Syntax of Measures

that states that the value of a diverging integer is `12`. The above specification should be rejected, as the refinement $\mathtt{v} = 12$ does not evaluate to **true** ($\mathtt{diverge}\ 0 = 12 \not\hookrightarrow^* \mathbf{true}$), instead it diverges.

We want to check the validity of the formula $\mathtt{v} = 12$ under a model that maps v to the diverging integer **diverge** 0. Any system that decides this formula to be true will be unsound, *i.e.* the VCs will not soundly approximate subtyping. For similar reasons, the system should not decide that this formula is false. To reason about diverging refinements one needs three valued logic, where logical formulas can be solved to true, false, or diverging. Since we want to discharge VC using SMT solvers that currently do not support three valued reasoning, we exclude diverging refinements from types. To do so, we restrict = to finite integers

$$= :: \mathtt{Int}^{\Downarrow} \to \mathtt{Int}^{\Downarrow} \to \mathtt{Bool}^{\Downarrow}$$

and we say that $\{v{:}B \mid r\}$ is well-formed *iff* r has a $\mathtt{Bool}^{\Downarrow}$ type (Corollary 1). Thus the initial invalid specification will be rejected as non well-formed.

2.6 Measures: From Integers to Data Types

So far, all our examples have used only integer and boolean expressions in refinements. To describe properties of algebraic data types, we use *measures*, introduced in prior work on Liquid Types [20]. Measures are inductively defined functions that can be used in refinements, and provide an efficient way to axiomatize properties of data types. For example, `emp` determines whether a list is empty:

```
measure emp   :: [Int] -> Bool
  emp []      = true
  emp (x:xs)  = false
```

The syntax for measures deliberately looks like Haskell, but it is *far* more restricted, and should really be considered as a separate language. A measure has exactly one argument, and is defined by a list of equations, each of which has a simple pattern on the left hand side (see Figure 2). The right-hand side of the equation is a refinement expression r. Measure definitions are typechecked in the usual way; we omit the typing rules which are standard. (Our metatheory does not support type polymorphism, so in this paper we simply reason about lists of integers; however, our implementation supports polymorphism.)

Denotational semantics The denotational semantics of types in λ^H in §2.3 is readily extended to support measures. In λ^H a refinement r is an arbitrary expression, and calls to a measure are evaluated in the usual way by pattern matching. For example, with the above definition of `emp` it is straightforward to show that

$$[1, 2, 3] :: \{\mathtt{v}{:}[\mathtt{Int}] \mid \mathtt{not}\ (\mathtt{emp}\ \mathtt{v})\} \tag{9}$$

as the refinement `not (emp ([1, 2, 3]))` evaluates to **true**.

Measures as Axioms How can we reason about invocations of measures in the decidable logic of VCs? A natural approach is to treat a measure like `emp` as an uninterpreted function, and add logical axioms that capture its behaviour. This looks easy: each equation of the measure definition corresponds to an axiom, thus:

$$\texttt{emp}\ [] = \texttt{true}$$
$$\forall \texttt{x}, \texttt{xs}.\ \texttt{emp}\ (\texttt{x} : \texttt{xs}) = \texttt{false}$$

Under these axioms the judgement 9 is indeed valid.

Measures as Refinements in Types of Data Constructors Axiomatizing measures is *precise*; that is, the axioms exactly capture the meaning of measures. Alas, axioms render SMT solvers *inefficient*, and render the VC mechanism *unpredictable*, as one must rely on various brittle syntactic matching and instantiation heuristics [12].

Instead, we use a different approach that is *both* precise *and* efficient. The key idea is this: *instead of translating each measure equation into an axiom, we translate each equation into a refined type for the corresponding data constructor* [20]. This translation is given in Figure 2. For example, the definition of the measure `emp` yields the following refined types for the list data constructors:

$$[]\ ::\ \{\texttt{v}{:}[\texttt{Int}] \mid \texttt{emp}\ \texttt{v} = \texttt{true}\}$$
$$:\ ::\ \texttt{x}{:}\texttt{Int} \to \texttt{xs}{:}[\texttt{Int}] \to \{\texttt{v}{:}[\texttt{Int}] \mid \texttt{emp}\ \texttt{v} = \texttt{false}\}$$

These types ensure that: (1) each time a list value is *constructed*, its type carries the appropriate emptiness information. Thus our system is able to statically decide that (9) is valid, and, (2) each time a list value is *matched*, the appropriate emptiness information is used to improve precision of pattern matching, as we see next.

Using Measures As an example, we use the measure `emp` to provide an appropriate type for the `head` function:

```
head    :: {v:[Int] | not (emp v)} -> Int
head xs = case xs of
            (x:_) -> x
            []    -> error "yikes"

error   :: {v:String | false} -> a
error   = undefined
```

`head` is safe as its input type stipulates that it will only be called with lists that are *not* `[]`, and so `error "..."` is dead code. The call to `error` generates the subtyping query

$$\begin{array}{l}\texttt{xs}{:}\{\texttt{xs}{:}[\texttt{Int}]^{\downarrow} \mid \neg(\texttt{emp}\ \texttt{xs})\} \\ \texttt{b}{:}\{\texttt{b}{:}[\texttt{Int}]^{\downarrow} \mid (\texttt{emp}\ \texttt{xs}) = \texttt{true}\}\end{array} \vdash \{\texttt{true}\} \preceq \{\texttt{false}\}$$

The match-binder `b` holds the result of the match [30]. In the `[]` case, we assign it the refinement of the type of `[]` which is $(\texttt{emp xs}) = \texttt{true}$. Since the call is done inside a **`case-of`** expressions both `xs` and `b` are guaranteed to be in WHNF, thus they have Wnf types.

The verifier *accepts* the program as the above subtyping reduces to the valid VC

$$\neg(\texttt{emp xs}) \wedge ((\texttt{emp xs}) = \texttt{true}) \Rightarrow \texttt{true} \Rightarrow \texttt{false}$$

Consequently, our system can naturally support idiomatic Haskell, *e.g.* taking the `head` of an infinite list:

```
ex x     = head (repeat x)

repeat   :: Int -> {v:[Int] | not (emp v)}
repeat y = y : repeat y
```

Multiple Measures If a type has multiple measures, we simply refine each data constructor's type with the *conjunction* of the refinements from each measure. For example, consider a measure that computes the length of a list:

```
measure len  :: [Int] -> Int
  len ([])   = 0
  len (x:xs) = 1 + len xs
```

Constants	c	$::=$	$0, 1, -1, \ldots \mid \texttt{true}, \texttt{false}$
		$\mid$	$+, -, \ldots \mid =, <, \ldots \mid \texttt{crash}$
Values	w	$::=$	$c \mid \lambda x.e \mid D\,\overline{e}$
Expressions	e	$::=$	$w \mid x \mid e\ e \mid \texttt{let}\ x = e\ \texttt{in}\ e$
		$\mid$	$\texttt{case}\ x = e\ \texttt{of}\ \{D\,\overline{x} \to e\}$
Refinements	r	$::=$	e
Basic Types	B	$::=$	$\texttt{Int} \mid \texttt{Bool} \mid \texttt{T}$
Types	τ	$::=$	$\{v{:}B \mid r\} \mid x{:}\tau \to \tau$
Contexts	C	$::=$	$\bullet \mid C\ e \mid c\ C \mid D\,\overline{e}\,C\,\overline{e}$
		$\mid$	$\texttt{case}\ x = C\ \texttt{of}\ \{D\,\overline{y} \to e\}$

Reduction $\boxed{e \hookrightarrow e}$

$$\begin{array}{rcll} C[e] & \hookrightarrow & C[e'] & \text{if } e \hookrightarrow e' \\ c\ v & \hookrightarrow & \delta(c, v) & \\ (\lambda x.e)\ e_x & \hookrightarrow & e\,[e_x/x] & \\ \texttt{let}\ x = e_x\ \texttt{in}\ e & \hookrightarrow & e\,[e_x/x] & \\ \texttt{case}\ x = D_j\,\overline{e}\ \texttt{of}\ \{D_i\,\overline{y_i} \to e_i\} & \hookrightarrow & e_j\,[D_j\,\overline{e}/x]\,[\overline{e}/\overline{y_j}] & \end{array}$$

Figure 3. λ^U: Syntax and Operational Semantics

Using the translation of Figure 2, we extract the following types for list's data constructors.

$$[]\ ::\ \{\texttt{v}{:}[\texttt{Int}] \mid \texttt{len}\ \texttt{v} = 0\}$$
$$:\ ::\ \texttt{x}{:}\texttt{Int} \to \texttt{xs}{:}[\texttt{Int}] \to \{\texttt{v}{:}[\texttt{Int}] \mid \texttt{len}\ \texttt{v} = 1 + (\texttt{len}\ \texttt{xs})\}$$

The final types for list data constructors will be the conjunction of the refinements from `len` and `emp`:

$$[]\ ::\ \{\texttt{v}{:}[\texttt{Int}] \mid \texttt{emp}\ \texttt{v} = \texttt{true} \wedge \texttt{len}\ \texttt{v} = 0\}$$
$$:\ ::\ \texttt{x}{:}\texttt{Int} \to \texttt{xs}{:}[\texttt{Int}] \to$$
$$\{\texttt{v}{:}[\texttt{Int}] \mid \texttt{emp}\ \texttt{v} = \texttt{false} \wedge \texttt{len}\ \texttt{v} = 1 + (\texttt{len}\ \texttt{xs})\}$$

3. Declarative Typing: λ^U

Next, we formalize our stratified refinement type system, in two steps. First, in this section, we present a core calculus λ^U, with a general β-reduction semantics. We describe the syntax, operational semantics, and sound but undecidable declarative typing rules for λ^U. Second, in §4, we describe QF-EUFLIA, a subset of λ^U that forms a decidable logic of refinements, and use it to obtain λ^D with decidable SMT-based algorithmic typing.

3.1 Syntax

Figure 3 summarizes the syntax of λ^U, which is essentially the calculus λ^H [21] *without* the dynamic checking features (like casts), but *with* the addition of data constructors. In λ^U, as in λ^H, refinement expressions r are not drawn from a decidable logical sublanguage, but can be arbitrary expressions e (hence $r ::= e$ in Figure 3). This choice allows us to prove preservation and progress, but renders typechecking undecidable.

Constants The primitive constants of λ^U include **true**, **false**, 0, 1, -1, *etc.*, and arithmetic and logical operators like $+$, $-$, $\leq$, $/$, $\wedge$, $\neg$. In addition, we include a special *untypable* constant **crash** that models "going wrong". Primitive operations return a **crash** when invoked with inputs outside their domain, *e.g.* when $/$ is invoked with 0 as the divisor, or when **assert** is applied to **false**.

Data Constructors We encode data constructors as special constants. Each data type has an arity $\mathsf{Arity}(T)$ that represents the exact number of data constructors that return a value of type T. For example the data type [Int], which represents lists of integers, has two data constructors: [] and :, *i.e.* has arity 2.

Values & Expressions The values of λ^U include constants, λ-abstractions $\lambda x.e$, and fully applied data constructors D that wrap expressions. The expressions of λ^U include values, as well as variables x, applications $e\ e$, and the `case` and `let` expressions.

3.2 Operational Semantics

Figure 3 summarizes the small step contextual β-reduction semantics for λ^U. Note that we allow for reductions under data constructors, and thus, values may be further reduced. We write $e \hookrightarrow^j e'$ if there exist $e_1, \ldots, e_j$ such that e is e_1, e' is e_j and $\forall i, j, 1 \leq i < j$, we have $e_i \hookrightarrow e_{i+1}$. We write $e \hookrightarrow^* e'$ if there exists some (finite) j such that $e \hookrightarrow^j e'$.

Constants Application of a constant requires the argument be reduced to a value; in a single step the expression is reduced to the output of the primitive constant operation. For example, consider $=$, the primitive equality operator on integers. We have $\delta(=, n) \doteq =_n$ where $\delta(=_n, m)$ equals `true` iff m is the same as n.

3.3 Types

λ^U types include basic types, which are *refined* with predicates, and dependent function types. *Basic types* B comprise integers, booleans, and a family of data-types T (representing lists, trees *etc.*.) For example the data type [Int] represents lists of integers. We refine basic types with predicates (boolean valued expressions e) to obtain *basic refinement types* $\{v{:}B \mid e\}$. Finally, we have dependent *function types* $x{:}\tau_x \rightarrow \tau$ where the input x has the type τ_x and the output τ may refer to the input binder x.

Notation We write B to abbreviate $\{v{:}B \mid \mathtt{true}\}$, and $\tau_x \rightarrow \tau$ to abbreviate $x{:}\tau_x \rightarrow \tau$ if x does not appear in τ. We use _ for unused binders. We write $\{v{:}\mathtt{nat}^l \mid r\}$ to abbreviate $\{v{:}\mathtt{Int}^l \mid 0 \leq v \wedge r\}$.

Denotations Each type τ *denotes* a set of expressions $[\![\tau]\!]$, that are defined via the dynamic semantics [21]. Let $\lfloor\tau\rfloor$ be the type we get if we erase all refinements from τ and $e{:}\lfloor\tau\rfloor$ be the standard typing relation for the typed lambda calculus. Then, we define the denotation of types as:

$$[\![\{x{:}B \mid r\}]\!] \doteq \{e \mid e{:}B, \text{ if } e \hookrightarrow^* w \text{ then } r\,[w/x] \hookrightarrow^* \mathtt{true}\}$$
$$[\![x{:}\tau_x \rightarrow \tau]\!] \doteq \{e \mid e{:}\lfloor\tau_x \rightarrow \tau\rfloor, \forall e_x \in [\![\tau_x]\!].\ e\ e_x \in [\![\tau\,[e_x/x]]\!]\}$$

Constants For each constant c we define its type $\mathsf{Ty}(c)$ such that $c \in [\![\mathsf{Ty}(c)]\!]$. For example,

$$\begin{array}{lcl} \mathsf{Ty}(3) & \doteq & \{\mathtt{v}{:}\mathtt{Int} \mid \mathtt{v} = 3\} \\ \mathsf{Ty}(+) & \doteq & \mathtt{x}{:}\mathtt{Int} \rightarrow \mathtt{y}{:}\mathtt{Int} \rightarrow \{\mathtt{v}{:}\mathtt{Int} \mid \mathtt{v} = \mathtt{x} + \mathtt{y}\} \\ \mathsf{Ty}(/) & \doteq & \mathtt{Int} \rightarrow \{\mathtt{v}{:}\mathtt{Int} \mid \mathtt{v} > 0\} \rightarrow \mathtt{Int} \\ \mathsf{Ty}(\mathtt{error}_\tau) & \doteq & \{\mathtt{v}{:}\mathtt{Int} \mid \mathtt{false}\} \rightarrow \tau \end{array}$$

So, by definition we get the constant typing lemma

Lemma 1. *[Constant Typing] Every constant* $c \in [\![\mathsf{Ty}(c)]\!]$.

Thus, if $\mathsf{Ty}(c) \doteq x{:}\tau_x \rightarrow \tau$, then for every value $w \in [\![\tau_x]\!]$, we require that $\delta(c, w) \in [\![\tau\,[w/x]]\!]$. For every value $w \notin [\![\tau_x]\!]$, it suffices to define $\delta(c, w)$ as `crash`, a special untyped value.

Data Constructors The types of data constructor constants are refined with predicates that track the semantics of the *measures* associated with the data type. For example, as discussed in §2.6 we use emp to refine the list data constructors' types:

$$\begin{array}{lcl} \mathsf{Ty}([]) & \doteq & \{\mathtt{v}{:}[\mathtt{Int}] \mid \mathtt{emp\ v}\} \\ \mathsf{Ty}(:) & \doteq & \mathtt{Int} \rightarrow [\mathtt{Int}] \rightarrow \{\mathtt{v}{:}[\mathtt{Int}] \mid \neg(\mathtt{emp\ v})\} \end{array}$$

By construction it is easy to prove that Lemma 1 holds for data constructors. For example, `emp []` goes to `true`.

Well-Formedness $\boxed{\Gamma \vdash_U \tau}$

$$\frac{\Gamma, v{:}B \vdash_U r : \mathtt{Bool}}{\Gamma \vdash_U \{v{:}B \mid r\}}\ \text{WF-BASE}$$

$$\frac{\Gamma \vdash_U \tau_x \quad \Gamma, x{:}\tau_x \vdash_U \tau}{\Gamma \vdash_U x{:}\tau_x \rightarrow \tau}\ \text{WF-FUN}$$

Subtyping $\boxed{\Gamma \vdash_U \tau_1 \preceq \tau_2}$

$$\frac{\forall \theta \in [\![\Gamma]\!].[\![\theta(\{v{:}B \mid r_1\})]\!] \subseteq [\![\theta(\{v{:}B \mid r_2\})]\!]}{\Gamma \vdash_U \{v{:}B \mid r_1\} \preceq \{v{:}B \mid r_2\}}\ \preceq\text{-BASE}$$

$$\frac{\Gamma \vdash_U \tau_x' \preceq \tau_x \quad \Gamma, x{:}\tau_x' \vdash_U \tau \preceq \tau'}{\Gamma \vdash_U x{:}\tau_x \rightarrow \tau \preceq x{:}\tau_x' \rightarrow \tau'}\ \preceq\text{-FUN}$$

Typing $\boxed{\Gamma \vdash_U e : \tau}$

$$\frac{(x, \tau) \in \Gamma}{\Gamma \vdash_U x : \tau}\ \text{T-VAR} \qquad \frac{}{\Gamma \vdash_U c : \mathsf{Ty}(c)}\ \text{T-CON}$$

$$\frac{\Gamma \vdash_U e : \tau' \quad \Gamma \vdash_U \tau' \preceq \tau \quad \Gamma \vdash_U \tau}{\Gamma \vdash_U e : \tau}\ \text{T-SUB}$$

$$\frac{\Gamma, x{:}\tau_x \vdash_U e : \tau \quad \Gamma \vdash_U \tau_x}{\Gamma \vdash_U \lambda x.e : (x{:}\tau_x \rightarrow \tau)}\ \text{T-FUN}$$

$$\frac{\Gamma \vdash_U e_1 : (x{:}\tau_x \rightarrow \tau) \quad \Gamma \vdash_U e_2 : \tau_x}{\Gamma \vdash_U e_1\ e_2 : \tau\,[e_2/x]}\ \text{T-APP}$$

$$\frac{\Gamma \vdash_U e_x : \tau_x \quad \Gamma, x{:}\tau_x \vdash_U e : \tau \quad \Gamma \vdash_U \tau}{\Gamma \vdash_U \mathtt{let}\ x = e_x\ \mathtt{in}\ e : \tau}\ \text{T-LET}$$

$$\frac{\begin{array}{c}\Gamma \vdash_U e : \{v{:}T \mid r\} \qquad \Gamma \vdash_U \tau \\ \forall i. \mathsf{Ty}(D_i) = \overline{y_j{:}\tau_j} \rightarrow \{v{:}T \mid r_i\} \\ \Gamma, \overline{y_j{:}\tau_j}, x{:}\{v{:}T \mid r \wedge r_i\} \vdash_U e_i : \tau\end{array}}{\Gamma \vdash_U \mathtt{case}\ x = e\ \mathtt{of}\ \{D_i\ \overline{y_j} \rightarrow e_i\} : \tau}\ \text{T-CASE}$$

Figure 4. Type-checking for λ^U

3.4 Type Checking

Next, we present the type-checking judgments and rules of λ^U.

Environments and Closing Substitutions A *type environment* Γ is a sequence of type bindings $x_1{:}\tau_1, \ldots, x_n{:}\tau_n$. An environment denotes a set of *closing substitutions* θ which are sequences of expression bindings: $x_1 \mapsto e_1, \ldots, x_n \mapsto e_n$ such that:

$$[\![\Gamma]\!] \doteq \{\theta \mid \forall x{:}\tau \in \Gamma. \theta(x) \in [\![\theta(\tau)]\!]\}$$

Judgments We use environments to define three kinds of rules: Well-formedness, Subtyping, and Typing [4, 21]. A judgment $\Gamma \vdash_U \tau$ states that the refinement type τ is well-formed in the environment Γ. Intuitively, the type τ is well-formed if all the refinements in τ are `Bool`-typed in Γ. A judgment $\Gamma \vdash_U \tau_1 \preceq \tau_2$ states that the type τ_1 is a subtype of τ_2 in the environment Γ. Informally, τ_1 is a subtype of τ_2 if, when the free variables of τ_1 and τ_2 are bound to expressions described by Γ, the denotation of τ_1 is *contained in* the denotation of τ_2. Subtyping of basic types reduces to denotational containment checking. That is, for any closing substitution θ in the denotation of Γ, for every expression e, if $e \in [\![\theta(\tau_1)]\!]$ then $e \in [\![\theta(\tau_2)]\!]$. A judgment $\Gamma \vdash_U e : \tau$ states that the expression e has the type τ in the environment Γ. That is, when the free variables in e are bound to expressions described by Γ, the expression e will evaluate to a value described by τ.

Expressions, *Values*, *Constants*, *Basic types*: see Figure 3

Types	τ	$::=$	$\{v{:}B \mid r\} \mid \{v{:}B^l \mid r\}$
		$\mid$	$x{:}\tau \rightarrow \tau$
Labels	l	$::=$	$\downarrow \mid \Downarrow$
Refinements	r	$::=$	p
Predicates	p	$::=$	$p = p \mid p < p \mid p \wedge p \mid \neg p$
		$\mid$	$n \mid x \mid f\,\overline{p} \mid p \oplus p$
		$\mid$	$\texttt{true} \mid \texttt{false}$
Measures	f, g, h		
Operators	$\oplus$	$::=$	$+ \mid - \mid \ldots$
Integers	n	$::=$	$0 \mid 1 \mid -1 \mid \ldots$
Domain	d	$::=$	$n \mid c_w \mid D\,\overline{d} \mid \texttt{true} \mid \texttt{false}$
Model	σ	$::=$	$x_1 \mapsto d_1, \ldots, x_n \mapsto d_n$
Lifted Values	$w^\perp$	$::=$	$c \mid \lambda x.e \mid D\,\overline{w^\perp} \mid \perp$

Figure 5. Syntax of λ^D

Soundness Following λ^H [21], we use the (undecidable) $\preceq$-BASE to show that each step of evaluation preserves typing, and that if an expression is not a value, then it can be further evaluated:

- **Preservation:** If $\emptyset \vdash_U e : \tau$ and $e \hookrightarrow e'$, then $\emptyset \vdash_U e' : \tau$.
- **Progress:** If $\emptyset \vdash_U e : \tau$ and $e \neq w$, then $e \hookrightarrow e'$.

We combine the above to prove that evaluation preserves typing, and that a well typed term will not `crash`.

Theorem 1. *[Soundness of λ^U]*

- ***Type-Preservation:*** *If $\emptyset \vdash_U e : \tau$, $e \hookrightarrow^* w$ then $\emptyset \vdash_U w : \tau$.*
- ***Crash-Freedom:*** *If $\emptyset \vdash_U e : \tau$ then $e \not\hookrightarrow^*$* `crash`.

We prove the above following the overall recipe of [21]. Crash-freedom follows from type-preservation and as `crash` has no type. The Substitution Lemma, in particular, follows from a connection between the typing relation and type denotations:

Lemma 2. *[Denotation Typing] If $\emptyset \vdash_U e : \tau$ then $e \in [\![\tau]\!]$.*

4. Algorithmic Typing: λ^D

While λ^U is sound, it cannot be *implemented* thanks to the undecidable denotational containment rule $\preceq$-BASE (Figure 4). Next, we go from λ^U to λ^D, a core calculus with sound, SMT-based algorithmic type-checking in four steps. First, we show how to restrict the language of refinements to an SMT-decidable sub-language QF-EUFLIA (§4.1). Second, we *stratify* the types to specify whether their inhabitants may diverge, must reduce to values, or must reduce to finite values (§4.2). Third, we show how to *enforce* the stratification by encoding recursion using special fixpoint combinator constants (§4.2). Finally, we show how to use QF-EUFLIA and the stratification to approximate the undecidable $\preceq$-BASE with a decidable verification condition $\preceq$-BASE-D, thereby obtaining the algorithmic system λ^D (§4.3).

4.1 Refinement Logic: QF-EUFLIA

Figure 5 summarizes the syntax of λ^D. Refinements r are now predicates p, drawn from QF-EUFLIA, the decidable logic of equality, uninterpreted functions and linear arithmetic [22]. Predicates p include linear arithmetic constraints, function application where function symbols correspond to measures (as described in §2.6), and boolean combinations of sub-predicates.

All rules as in Figure 4 except as follows:

Well-Formedness $\boxed{\Gamma \vdash_D \tau}$

$$\frac{\Gamma, v{:}B \vdash_D p : \texttt{Bool}^{\Downarrow}}{\Gamma \vdash_D \{v{:}B \mid p\}}\ \text{WF-BASE-D}$$

Subtyping $\boxed{\Gamma \vdash_D \tau_1 \preceq \tau_2}$

$$\frac{(\!|\Gamma, v : B|\!) \Rightarrow (\!|p_1|\!) \Rightarrow (\!|p_2|\!) \text{ is valid}}{\Gamma \vdash_D \{v{:}B \mid p_1\} \preceq \{v{:}B \mid p_2\}}\ \preceq\text{-BASE-D}$$

Typing $\boxed{\Gamma \vdash_D e : \tau}$

$$\frac{\Gamma \vdash_D e_1 : (x{:}\tau_x \rightarrow \tau) \qquad \Gamma \vdash_D y : \tau_x}{\Gamma \vdash_D e_1\, y : \tau\,[y/x]}\ \text{T-APP-D}$$

$$\frac{\begin{array}{c} l \not\in \{\Downarrow, \downarrow\} \Rightarrow \tau \text{ is Div} \\ \Gamma \vdash_D e : \{v{:}T^l \mid r\} \qquad \Gamma \vdash_D \tau \\ \forall i. \mathsf{Ty}(D_i) = \overline{y_j \tau_j} \rightarrow \{v{:}T \mid r_i\} \\ \Gamma, \overline{y_j{:}\tau_j}, x{:}\{v{:}T^{\downarrow} \mid r \wedge r_i\} \vdash_D e_i : \tau \end{array}}{\Gamma \vdash_D \texttt{case}\ x = e\ \texttt{of}\ \{D_i\ \overline{y_j} \rightarrow e_i\} : \tau}\ \text{T-CASE-D}$$

Figure 6. Typechecking for λ^D

Well-Formedness For a predicate to be well-formed it should be boolean and arithmetic operators should be applied to integer terms, measures should be applied to appropriate arguments (*i.e.* `emp` is applied to `[Int]`), and equality or inequality to basic (integer or boolean) terms. Furthermore, we require that refinements, and thus measures, always evaluate to a value. We capture these requirements by assigning appropriate types to operators and measure functions, after which we require that each refinement r has type $\texttt{Bool}^{\Downarrow}$ (rule WF-BASE-D in Figure 6).

Assignments Figure 5 defines the elements d of the domain $\mathcal{D}$ of integers, booleans, and data constructors that wrap elements from $\mathcal{D}$. The domain $\mathcal{D}$ also contains a constant c_w for each value w of λ^U that does not otherwise belong in $\mathcal{D}$ (*e.g.* functions or other primitives). An *assignment* σ is a map from variables to $\mathcal{D}$.

Satisfiability & Validity We interpret boolean predicates in the logic over the domain $\mathcal{D}$. We write $\sigma \models p$ if σ is a model of p. We omit the formal definition for space. A predicate p is *satisfiable* if there *exists* $\sigma \models p$. A predicate p is *valid* if *for all* assignments $\sigma \models p$.

Connecting Evaluation and Logic To prove soundness, we need to formally connect the notion of logical models with the evaluation of a refinement to `true`. We do this in several steps, briefly outlined for brevity. First, we introduce a primitive *bottom expression* $\perp$ that can have *any* Div type, but does not evaluate. Second, we define *lifted values* $w^\perp$ (Figure 5), which are values that contain $\perp$. Third, we define *lifted substitutions* $\theta^\perp$, which are mappings from variables to lifted values. Finally, we show how to *embed* a lifted substitution $\theta^\perp$ into a *set of* assignments $(\!|\theta^\perp|\!)$ where, intuitively speaking, each $\perp$ is replaced by some arbitrarily chosen element of $\mathcal{D}$. Now, we can connect evaluation and logical satisfaction:

Theorem 2. *If $\emptyset \vdash_D \theta^\perp(p) : \texttt{Bool}^{\Downarrow}$, then*

$$\theta^\perp(p) \hookrightarrow^* \texttt{true} \text{ iff } \forall \sigma \in (\!|\theta^\perp|\!).\sigma \models p$$

Restricting Refinements to Predicates Our goal is to restrict $\preceq$-BASE so that only predicates from the decidable logic QF-EUFLIA (not arbitrary expressions) appear in implications $(\!|\Gamma|\!) \Rightarrow \{v{:}b \mid p_1\} \Rightarrow \{v{:}b \mid p_2\}$. Towards this goal, as shown in Figures 5 and 6, we restrict the syntax and well-formedness of types to contain only predicates, and we convert the program to ANF after which we can restrict the application rule T-APP-D to applications to variables, which ensures that refinements remain within the logic after substitution [26]. Recall, that this is not enough to ensure that refinements do converge, as under lazy evaluation, even binders can refer to potentially divergent values.

4.2 Stratified Types

The typing rules for λ^D are given in Figure 6. Instead of *explicitly* reasoning about divergence or strictness in the refinement logic, which leads to significant theoretical and practical problems, as discussed in §8, we choose to reason *implicitly* about divergence within the type system. Thus, the second critical step in our path to λ^D is the stratification of types into those inhabited by potentially diverging terms, terms that only reduce to values, and terms which reduce to finite values. Furthermore, the stratification crucially allows us to prove Theorem 2, which requires that refinements do not diverge (*e.g.* by computing the length of an infinite list) by ensuring that inductively defined measures are only applied to finite values. Next, we describe how we stratify types with labels, and then type the various constants, in particular the fixpoint combinators, to enforce stratification.

Labels We specify stratification using two *labels* for types. The label $\downarrow$ (resp. $\Downarrow$) is assigned to types given to expressions that reduce (using β-reduction as defined in Figure 3) to a value w (resp. *finite* value, *i.e.* an element of the inductively defined $\mathcal{D}$). Formally,

$$\textbf{\textit{Wnf types}}\quad [\![\{v{:}B^{\downarrow} \mid r\}]\!] \doteq [\![\{v{:}B \mid r\}]\!] \cap \{e \mid e \hookrightarrow^{*} w\} \quad (10)$$

$$\textbf{\textit{Fin types}}\quad [\![\{v{:}B^{\Downarrow} \mid r\}]\!] \doteq [\![\{v{:}B \mid r\}]\!] \cap \{e \mid e \hookrightarrow^{*} d\} \quad (11)$$

Unlabelled types are assigned to expressions that may diverge. Note that for any B and refinement r we have

$$[\![\{v{:}B^{\Downarrow} \mid r\}]\!] \subseteq [\![\{v{:}B^{\downarrow} \mid r\}]\!] \subseteq [\![\{v{:}B \mid r\}]\!]$$

The first two sets are *equal* for `Int` and `Bool`, and *unequal* for (lazily) constructed data types T. We need not stratify function types (*i.e.* they are Div types) as binders with function types do not appear inside the VC, and are not applied to measures.

Enforcing Stratification We enforce stratification in two steps. First, the T-CASE-D rule uses the operational semantics of case-of to type-check each case in an environment where the scrutinee x is assumed to have a Wnf type. All the other rules, not mentioned in Figure 6, remain the same as in Figure 4. Second, we create stratified variants for the primitive constants and *separate* fixpoint combinator constants for (arbitary, potentially non-terminating) recursion (`fix`) and bounded recursion (`tfix`).

Stratified Primitives First, we restrict the primitive operators whose output types are refined with logical operators, so they are only invoked on finite arguments (so that the corresponding refinements are guaranteed to not diverge).

$$\begin{aligned}
\mathsf{Ty}(n) &\doteq \{v{:}\mathtt{Int}^{\Downarrow} \mid v = n\}\\
\mathsf{Ty}(=) &\doteq x{:}B^{\Downarrow} \rightarrow y{:}B^{\Downarrow} \rightarrow \{v{:}\mathtt{Bool}^{\Downarrow} \mid v \Leftrightarrow x = y\}\\
\mathsf{Ty}(+) &\doteq x{:}\mathtt{Int}^{\Downarrow} \rightarrow y{:}\mathtt{Int}^{\Downarrow} \rightarrow \{v{:}\mathtt{Int}^{\Downarrow} \mid v = x + y\}\\
\mathsf{Ty}(\wedge) &\doteq x{:}\mathtt{Bool}^{\Downarrow} \rightarrow y{:}\mathtt{Bool}^{\Downarrow} \rightarrow \{v{:}\mathtt{Bool}^{\Downarrow} \mid v \Leftrightarrow x \wedge y\}
\end{aligned}$$

It is easy to prove that the above primitives respect their stratification labels, *i.e.* belong in the denotations of their types.

Note that the above types are restricted in that they can only be applied to finite arguments. In future work, we could address this issue with unrefined versions of primitive types that soundly allow operation on arbitrary arguments. For example, with the current type for $+$, addition of potentially diverging expressions is rejected. Thus, we could define an unrefined signature

$$\mathsf{Ty}(+) \doteq x{:}\mathtt{Int} \rightarrow y{:}\mathtt{Int} \rightarrow \mathtt{Int}$$

and allow the two types of $+$ to co-exist (as an intersection type), where the type checker would choose the precise refined type if and only if both of $+$'s arguments are finite.

Diverging Fixpoints **($\mathtt{fix}_\tau$)** Next, note that the only place where divergence enters the picture is through the fixpoint combinators used to encode recursion. For any function or basic type $\tau \doteq \tau_1 \rightarrow \ldots \rightarrow \tau_n$, we define the *result* to be the type τ_n.

For each τ whose result is a Div type, there is a *diverging fixpoint* combinator $\mathtt{fix}_\tau$, such that

$$\begin{aligned}
\delta(\mathtt{fix}_\tau, f) &\doteq f\,(\mathtt{fix}_\tau\, f)\\
\mathsf{Ty}(\mathtt{fix}_\tau) &\doteq (\tau \rightarrow \tau) \rightarrow \tau
\end{aligned}$$

i.e., $\mathtt{fix}_\tau$ yields recursive functions of type τ. Of course, $\mathtt{fix}_\tau$ belongs in the denotation of its type [25] *only if* the result type is a Div type (and *not* when the result is a Wnf or Fin type). Thus, we restrict diverging fixpoints to functions with Div result types.

Indexed Fixpoints **($\mathtt{tfix}^n_\tau$)** For each type τ whose result is a Fin type, we have a family of *indexed* fixpoints combinators $\mathtt{tfix}^n_\tau$:

$$\begin{aligned}
\delta(\mathtt{tfix}^n_\tau, f) &\doteq \lambda m. f\; m\; (\mathtt{tfix}^m_\tau\; f)\\
\mathsf{Ty}(\mathtt{tfix}^n_\tau) &\doteq (n{:}\mathtt{nat}^{\Downarrow} \rightarrow \tau_n \rightarrow \tau) \rightarrow \tau_n\\
\text{where, } \tau_n &\doteq \{v{:}\mathtt{nat}^{\Downarrow} \mid v < n\} \rightarrow \tau
\end{aligned}$$

τ_n is a *weakened* version of τ that can only be invoked on inputs *smaller* than n. Thus, we enforce termination by requiring that $\mathtt{tfix}^n_\tau$ is *only* called with m that are *strictly smaller than* n. As the indices are well-founded `nat`s, evaluation will terminate.

Terminating Fixpoints **($\mathtt{tfix}_\tau$)** Finally, we use the indexed combinators to define the *terminating* fixpoint combinator $\mathtt{tfix}_\tau$ as:

$$\begin{aligned}
\delta(\mathtt{tfix}_\tau, f) &\doteq \lambda n. f\; n\; (\mathtt{tfix}^n_\tau\; f)\\
\mathsf{Ty}(\mathtt{tfix}_\tau) &\doteq (n{:}\mathtt{nat}^{\Downarrow} \rightarrow \tau_n \rightarrow \tau) \rightarrow \mathtt{nat}^{\Downarrow} \rightarrow \tau
\end{aligned}$$

Thus, the top-level call to the recursive function requires a $\mathtt{nat}^{\Downarrow}$ parameter n that acts as a *starting* index, after which, all "recursive" calls are to combinators with *smaller* indices, ensuring termination.

Example: Factorial Consider the factorial function:

$$\mathtt{fac} \doteq \lambda n.\lambda f.\mathtt{case}\ \_ = (n = 0)\ \mathtt{of} \left\{ \begin{array}{l} \mathtt{true} \rightarrow 1 \\ \_ \rightarrow n \times f(n-1) \end{array} \right\}$$

Let $\tau \doteq \mathtt{nat}^{\Downarrow}$. We prove termination by typing

$$\emptyset \vdash_D \mathtt{tfix}_\tau\ \mathtt{fac} : \mathtt{nat}^{\Downarrow} \rightarrow \tau$$

To understand *why*, note that $\mathtt{tfix}^n_\tau$ is only called with arguments strictly smaller than n

$$\begin{aligned}
\mathtt{tfix}_\tau\ \mathtt{fac}\ n &\hookrightarrow^{*} \mathtt{fac}\ n\ (\mathtt{tfix}^n_\tau\ \mathtt{fac})\\
&\hookrightarrow^{*} n \times (\mathtt{tfix}^n_\tau\ \mathtt{fac}\ (n-1))\\
&\hookrightarrow^{*} n \times (\mathtt{fac}\ (n-1)\ (\mathtt{tfix}^{n-1}_\tau\ \mathtt{fac}))\\
&\hookrightarrow^{*} n \times n-1 \times (\mathtt{tfix}^{n-1}_\tau\ \mathtt{fac}\ (n-2))\\
&\hookrightarrow^{*} n \times n-1 \times \ldots \times (\mathtt{tfix}^{1}_\tau\ \mathtt{fac}\ 0)\\
&\hookrightarrow^{*} n \times n-1 \times \ldots \times (\mathtt{fac}\ 0\ (\mathtt{tfix}^{0}_\tau\ \mathtt{fac}))\\
&\hookrightarrow^{*} n \times n-1 \times \ldots \times 1
\end{aligned}$$

Soundness of Stratification To formally *prove* that stratification is soundly enforced, it suffices to prove that the Denotation Lemma 2 holds for λ^D. This, in turn, boils down to proving that each (stratified) constant belongs in its type's denotation, *i.e.* each $c \in [\![\mathsf{Ty}(c)]\!]$ or that the Lemma 1 holds for λ^D. The crucial part of the above is proving that the indexed and terminating fixpoints inhabit their types' denotations.

Theorem 3. *[Fixpoint Typing]*

- $\mathtt{fix}_\tau \in [\![\mathsf{Ty}(\mathtt{fix}_\tau)]\!]$,
- $\forall n.\mathtt{tfix}^n_\tau \in [\![\mathsf{Ty}(\mathtt{tfix}^n_\tau)]\!]$,
- $\mathtt{tfix}_\tau \in [\![\mathsf{Ty}(\mathtt{tfix}_\tau)]\!]$.

With the above we can prove soundness of Stratification as a corollary Denotation Lemma 2, given the interpretations of the stratified types.

Corollary 1. *[Soundness of Stratification]*

1. If $\emptyset \vdash_D e : \tau^{\Downarrow}$, then evaluation of e is finite.
2. If $\emptyset \vdash_D e : \tau^{\downarrow}$, then e reduces to WHNF.
3. If $\emptyset \vdash_D e : \{v{:}\tau \mid p\}$, then p cannot diverge.

Finally, as a direct implication the well-formedness rule WF-BASE-D we conclude 3, *i.e.* that refinements cannot diverge.

4.3 Verification With Stratified Types

We put the pieces together to obtain an algorithmic implication rule $\preceq$-BASE-D instead of the undecidable $\preceq$-BASE (from Figure 4). Intuitively, each closing substitution θ corresponds to a set of logical assignments $(\!|\theta|\!)$. Thus, we will translate Γ into logical formula $(\!|\Gamma|\!)$ and denotation inclusion into logical implication such that:

- $\theta \in [\![\Gamma]\!]$ iff all $\sigma \in (\!|\theta|\!)$ satisfy $(\!|\Gamma|\!)$, and
- $\theta\{v{:}B \mid p_1\} \subseteq \theta\{v{:}B \mid p_2\}$ iff all $\sigma \in (\!|\theta|\!)$ satisfy $p_1 \Rightarrow p_2$.

Translating Refinements & Environments To translate environments into logical formulas, recall that $\theta \in [\![\Gamma]\!]$ iff for each $x{:}\tau \in \Gamma$, we have $\theta(x) \in [\![\theta(\tau)]\!]$. Thus,

$$(\!|x_1{:}\tau_1, \ldots, x_n{:}\tau_n|\!) \doteq (\!|x_1{:}\tau_1|\!) \wedge \ldots \wedge (\!|x_n{:}\tau_n|\!)$$

How should we translate a single binding? Since a binding denotes

$$[\![\{x{:}B \mid p\}]\!] \doteq \{e \mid \text{if } e \hookrightarrow^* w \text{ then } p\,[w/x] \hookrightarrow^* \mathtt{true}\}$$

a direct translation would require a logical value predicate $\mathsf{Val}(x)$, which we could use to obtain the logical translation

$$(\!|\{x{:}B \mid p\}|\!) \doteq \neg\mathsf{Val}(x) \vee p$$

This translation poses several theoretical and practical problems that preclude the use of existing SMT solvers (as detailed in §8). However, our stratification guarantees (cf. (10), (11)) that labeled types reduces to values, and so we can simply conservatively translate the Div and labeled (Wnf, Fin) bindings as:

$$(\!|\{x{:}B \mid p\}|\!) \doteq \mathtt{true} \qquad (\!|\{x{:}B^l \mid p\}|\!) \doteq p$$

Soundness We prove soundness by showing that the decidable implication $\preceq$-BASE-D approximates the undecidable $\preceq$-BASE.

Theorem 4. *If $(\!|\Gamma|\!) \Rightarrow p_1 \Rightarrow p_2$ is valid then*

$$\Gamma \vdash_U \{v{:}B \mid p_1\} \preceq \{v{:}B \mid p_2\}$$

To prove the above, let $VC \doteq (\!|\Gamma|\!) \Rightarrow p_1 \Rightarrow p_2$. We prove that if the VC is valid then $\Gamma \vdash_U \{v{:}b \mid p_1\} \preceq \{v{:}b \mid p_2\}$. This fact relies crucially on a notion of *tracking evaluation* which allows us to reduce a closing substitution θ to a lifted substitution $\theta^\perp$, written $\theta \hookrightarrow^*_\perp \theta^\perp$, after which we prove:

Lemma 3. *[Lifting] $\theta(e) \hookrightarrow^* c$ iff $\exists\theta \hookrightarrow^*_\perp \theta^\perp$ s.t. $\theta^\perp(e) \hookrightarrow^* c$.*

We combine the Lifting Lemma and the equivalence Theorem 2 to prove that the validity of the VC demonstrates the denotational containment $\forall\theta \in [\![\Gamma]\!].[\![\theta(\{v{:}B \mid p_1\})]\!] \subseteq [\![\theta(\{v{:}B \mid p_2\})]\!]$. The soundness of algorithmic typing follows from Theorems 4 and 1:

Theorem 5. *[Soundness of λ^D]*

- ***Approximation:*** *If $\emptyset \vdash_D e : \tau$ then $\emptyset \vdash_U e : \tau$.*
- ***Crash-Freedom:*** *If $\emptyset \vdash_D e : \tau$ then $e \not\hookrightarrow^* \mathtt{crash}$.*

5. Implementation: LIQUIDHASKELL

We have implemented λ^D in LIQUIDHASKELL (§2). Next, we describe the key steps in the transition from λ^D to Haskell.

5.1 Termination

Haskell's recursive functions of type $\mathtt{nat}^{\Downarrow} \to \tau$ are represented, in GHC's Core [30] as $\mathtt{let\ rec}\ f = \lambda n.e$ which is operationally equivalent to $\mathtt{let}\ f = \mathtt{tfix}_\tau\ (\lambda n.\lambda f.e)$. Given the type of $\mathtt{tfix}_\tau$, checking that f has type $\mathtt{nat}^{\Downarrow} \to \tau$ reduces to checking e in a *termination-weakened environment* where

$$f : \{v{:}\mathtt{nat}^{\Downarrow} \mid v < n\} \to \tau$$

Thus, LIQUIDHASKELL proves termination just as λ^D does: by checking the body in the above environment, where the recursive binder is called with `nat` inputs that are strictly smaller than n.

Default Metric For example, LIQUIDHASKELL proves that

```
fac n = if n == 0 then 1 else n * fac (n-1)
```

has type $\mathtt{nat}^{\Downarrow} \to \mathtt{nat}^{\Downarrow}$ by typechecking the body of `fac` in a termination-weakened environment `fac` : $\{\mathtt{v{:}nat}^{\Downarrow} \mid \mathtt{v} < \mathtt{n}\} \to \mathtt{nat}^{\Downarrow}$ The recursive call generates the subtyping query:

$$\mathtt{n}{:}\{0 \le \mathtt{n}\}, \neg(\mathtt{n} = 0) \vdash_D \{\mathtt{v} = \mathtt{n} - 1\} \preceq \{0 \le \mathtt{v} \wedge \mathtt{v} < \mathtt{n}\}$$

Which reduces to the valid VC

$$0 \le \mathtt{n} \wedge \neg(\mathtt{n} = 0) \Rightarrow (\mathtt{v} = \mathtt{n} - 1) \Rightarrow (0 \le \mathtt{v} \wedge \mathtt{v} < \mathtt{n})$$

proving that `fac` terminates, in essence because the *first parameter* forms a *well-founded decreasing metric*.

Refinements Enable Termination Consider Euclid's GCD:

```
gcd :: a:Nat -> {v:Nat | v < a} -> Nat
gcd a 0 = a
gcd a b = gcd b (a `mod` b)
```

Here, the first parameter is decreasing, but this requires the fact that the second parameter is smaller than the first and that `mod` returns results smaller than its second parameter. Both facts are easily expressed as refinements, but elude non-extensible checkers [15].

Explicit Termination Metrics The indexed-fixpoint combinator technique is easily extended to cases where some parameter *other* than the first is the well-founded metric. For example, consider:

```
tfac     :: Nat -> n:Nat -> Nat / [n]
tfac x n | n == 0    = x
         | otherwise = tfac (n*x) (n-1)
```

We specify that the *last parameter* is decreasing by using an explicit termination metric `/ [n]` in the type. LIQUIDHASKELL *desugars* the termination metric into a new `nat`-valued *ghost parameter* `d` whose value is always equal to the termination metric `n`:

```
tfac :: d:Nat -> Nat -> {n:Nat | d = n} -> Nat
tfac d x n | n == 0    = x
           | otherwise = tfac (n-1) (n*x) (n-1)
```

Type checking, as before, checks the body in an environment where the first argument of `tfac` is weakened, *i.e.*, requires proving `d > n-1`. So, the system needs to know that the ghost argument `d` represents the decreasing metric. We capture this information in the type signature of `tfac` where the *last* argument exactly specifies that `d` is the termination metric `n`, *i.e.*, `d = n`. Note that since the termination metric can depend on any argument, it is important to refine the last argument, so that all arguments are in scope, with the fact that d is the termination metric.

To generalize, desugaring of termination metrics proceeds as follows. Let f be a recursive function with parameters $\overline{x}$, and termination metric $\mu(\overline{x})$. Then LIQUIDHASKELL will

- add a **nat**-valued ghost first parameter d in the definition of f,
- weaken the last argument of f with the refinement $d = \mu(\overline{x})$,
- at each recursive call of $f\ \overline{e}$, apply $\mu(\overline{e})$ as the first argument.

Explicit Termination Expressions Let us now apply the previous technique in a function where none of the parameters themselves decrease across recursive calls, but there is some *expression* that forms the decreasing metric. Consider range lo hi, which returns the list of Ints from lo to hi: We generalize the explicit metric specification to *expressions* like hi-lo. LIQUIDHASKELL *desugars* the expression into a new **nat**-valued *ghost parameter* whose value is always equal to hi-lo, that is:

```
range :: lo:Nat -> {hi:Nat | hi >= lo} -> [Nat]
       / [hi-lo]
range lo hi | lo < hi = lo : range (lo + 1) hi
            | _       = []
```

Here, neither parameter is decreasing (indeed, the first one is *increasing*) but hi-lo decreases across each call. We generalize the explicit metric specification to *expressions* like hi-lo. LIQUIDHASKELL *desugars* the expression into a new **nat**-valued *ghost parameter* whose value is always equal to hi-lo, that is:

```
range lo hi = go (hi-lo) lo hi
  where
    go :: d:Nat -> lo:Nat
       -> {hi:Nat | d = hi - lo} -> [Nat]
    go d lo hi
     | lo < hi = l : go (hi-(lo+1)) (lo+1) hi
     | _       = []
```

After which, it proves go terminating, by showing that the first argument d is a **nat** that decreases across each recursive call.

Recursion over Data Types The above strategy generalizes easily to functions that recurse over (finite) data structures like arrays, lists, and trees. In these cases, we simply use *measures* to project the structure onto **nat**, thereby reducing the verification to the previously seen cases. For each user defined type, *e.g.*

```
data L [sz] a = N | C a (L a)
```

we can define a *measure*

```
measure sz  :: L a -> Nat
  sz (C x xs) = 1 + (sz xs)
  sz N        = 0
```

and use it as the decreasing metric to prove that map terminates:

```
map :: (a -> b) -> xs:L a -> L b / [sz xs]
map f (C x xs) = C (f x) (map f xs)
map f N        = N
```

Generalized Metrics Over Datatypes Finally, in many functions there is no single argument whose (measure) provably decreases. For example, consider:

```
merge :: xs:_ -> ys:_ -> _ / [sz xs + sz ys]
merge (C x xs) (C y ys)
  | x < y     = x `C` (merge xs  (y `C` ys))
  | otherwise = y `C` (merge (x `C` xs)  ys)
```

from the homonymous sorting routine. Here, neither parameter decreases, but the *sum* of their sizes does. As before LIQUIDHASKELL desugars the decreasing expression into a ghost parameter and thereby proves termination (assuming, of course, that the inputs were finite lists, *i.e.* $L^{\Downarrow}\ a$.)

Automation: Default Size Measures Structural recursion on the first argument is a common pattern in Haskell code. LIQUIDHASKELL automates termination proofs for this common case, by allowing users to specify a *size measure* for each data type, (*e.g.* sz for L a). Now, if *no* termination metric is given, by default LIQUIDHASKELL assumes that the *first* argument whose type has an associated size measure decreases. Thus, in the above, we need not specify metrics for fac or gcd or map as the size measure is automatically used to prove termination. This simple heuristic allows us to automatically prove 67% of recursive functions terminating.

5.2 Non-termination

By default, LIQUIDHASKELL checks that every function is terminating. We show in §6 that this is in fact the overwhelmingly common case in practice. However, annotating a function as **lazy** deactivates LIQUIDHASKELL's termination check (and marks the result as a Div type). This allows us to check functions that are non-terminating, and allows LIQUIDHASKELL to prove safety properties of programs that manipulate *infinite* data, such as streams, which arise idiomatically with Haskell's lazy semantics. For example, consider the classic repeat function:

```
repeat x = x `C` repeat x
```

We cannot use the **tfix** combinators to represent this kind of recursion, and hence, use the non-terminating **fix** combinator instead.

Let us see how we can use refinements to statically distinguish between finite and infinite streams. The direct, *global* route of using an inductively defined measure to describe infinite lists is unavailable as such a measure, and hence, the corresponding refinement would be non-terminating. Instead, we describe infinite lists in *local* fashion, by stating that each *tail* is non-empty.

Step 1: Abstract Refinements We can parametrize a datatype with abstract refinements that relate sub-parts of the structure [33]. For example, we parameterize the list type as:

```
data L a <p :: L a -> Prop>
  = N | C a {v: L<p> a | (p v)}
```

which parameterizes the list with a refinement p which holds *for each* tail of the list, *i.e.* holds for each of the second arguments to the C constructor in each sub-list.

Step 2: Measuring Emptiness Now, we can write a measure that states when a list is *empty*

```
measure emp   :: L a -> Prop
  emp N        = true
  emp (C x xs) = false
```

As described in §4, LIQUIDHASKELL translates the abstract refinements and measures into refined types for N and C.

Step 3: Specification & Verification Finally, we can use the abstract refinements and measures to write a type alias describing a refined version of L a representing infinite streams:

```
type Stream a =
  {xs: L <{\v -> not(emp v)}> a | not(emp xs)}
```

We can now type repeat as:

```
lazy repeat :: a -> Stream a
repeat x     = x `C` repeat x
```

The **lazy** keyword *deactivates* termination checking, and marks the output as a Div type. Even more interestingly, we can prove safety properties of infinite lists, for example:

```
take            :: Nat -> Stream a -> L a
take 0 _        = N
take n (C x xs) = x `C` take (n-1) xs
take _ N        = error "never happens"
```

LIQUIDHASKELL proves, similar to the `head` example from §2, that we never match a `N` when the input is a `Stream`.

Finite vs. Infinite Lists Thus, the combination of refinements and labels allows our stratified type system to specify and verify whether a list is finite or infinite. Note that: $L^{\Downarrow}\ a$ represents *finite* lists *i.e.* those produced using the (inductive) terminating fixpoint combinators, $L^{\downarrow}\ a$ represents (potentially) infinite lists which are guaranteed to reduce to values, *i.e.* non-diverging computations that yield finite or infinite lists, and $L\ a$ represents computations that may diverge or produce a finite or infinite list.

6. Evaluation

Our goal is to build a practical and effective SMT & refinement type-based verifier for Haskell. We have shown that lazy evaluation requires the verifier to reason about divergence; we have proposed an approach for implicitly reasoning about divergence by eagerly proving termination, thereby optimizing the precision of the verifier. Next, we describe an experimental evaluation of our approach that uses LIQUIDHASKELL to prove termination and functional correctness properties of a suite of widely used Haskell libraries totaling more than 10KLOC. Our evaluation seeks to determine whether our approach is *suitable* for a lazy language (*i.e.* do most Haskell functions terminate?), *precise* enough to capture the termination reasons (*i.e.* is LIQUIDHASKELL able to prove that most functions terminate?), *usable* without placing an unreasonably high burden on the user in the form of explicit termination annotations, and *effective* enough to enable the verification of functional correctness properties. For brevity, we omit a description of the properties other than termination, please see [34] for details.

Implementation LIQUIDHASKELL takes as input: (1) A Haskell *source* file, (2) Refinement type *specifications*, including refined datatype definitions, measures, predicate and type aliases, and function signatures, and (3) Predicate fragments called *qualifiers* which are used to infer refinement types using the abstract interpretation framework of Liquid Typing [26]. The verifier returns as output, SAFE or UNSAFE, depending on whether the code meets the specifications or not, and, importantly for debugging the code (or specification!) the inferred types for all sub-expressions.

Benchmarks As benchmarks, we used the following libraries: `GHC.List` and `Data.List`, which together implement many standard list operations, `Data.Set.Splay`, which implements an splay functional set, `Data.Map.Base`, which implements a functional map, `Vector-Algorithms`, which includes a suite of "imperative" array-based sorting algorithms, `Bytestring`, a library for manipulating byte arrays, and `Text`, a library for high-performance Unicode text processing. These benchmarks represent a wide spectrum of idiomatic Haskell codes: the first three are widely used libraries based on recursive data structures, the fourth and fifth perform subtle, low-level arithmetic manipulation of array indices and pointers, and the last is a rich, high-level library with sophisticated application-specific invariants, well outside the scope of even Haskell's expressive type system. Thus, this suite provides a diverse and challenging test-bed for evaluating LIQUIDHASKELL.

Results Table 1 summarizes our experiments, which covered 39 modules totaling 10,209 non-comment lines of source code. The results were collected on a machine with an Intel Xeon X5600 and 32GB of RAM (no benchmark required more than 1GB). Timing data was for runs that performed full verification of safety and functional correctness properties in addition to termination.

- *Suitable:* Our approach of eagerly proving termination is in fact, *highly* suitable: of the 504 recursive functions, only 12 functions were *actually* non-terminating (*i.e.* non-inductive). That is, 97.6% of recursive functions are inductively defined.

Module	LOC	Fun	Rec	Div	Hint	Time
`GHC.List`	309	66	34	5	0	14
`Data.List`	504	97	50	2	6	11
`Data.Map.Base`	1396	180	94	0	12	175
`Data.Set.Splay`	149	35	17	0	7	26
`Bytestring`	3505	569	154	8	73	285
`Vector-Algorithms`	1218	99	31	0	31	85
`Text`	3128	493	124	5	44	481
Total	10209	1539	504	20	173	1080

Table 1. A quantitative evaluation of our experiments. **LOC** is the number of non-comment lines of source code as reported by `sloccount`. **Fun** is the total number of functions in the library. **Rec** is the number of recursive functions. **Div** is the number of functions marked as potentially non-terminating. **Hint** is the number of termination hints, in the form of *termination expressions*, given to LIQUIDHASKELL. **Time** is the time, in seconds, required to run LIQUIDHASKELL.

- *Precise:* Our approach is extremely precise, as refinements provide auxiliary invariants and extensibility that is crucial for proving termination. We successfully *prove* that 96.0% of recursive functions terminate.
- *Usable:* Our approach is highly usable and only places a modest annotation burden on the user. The default metric, namely the first parameter with an associated size measure, suffices to automatically prove 65.7% of recursive functions terminating. Thus, only 34.3% require explicit termination metric, totaling about 1.7 witnesses (about 1 line each) per 100 lines of code.
- *Effective:* Our approach is extremely effective at improving the precision of the overall verifier (by allowing the VC to use facts about binders that provably reduce to values.) Without the termination optimization, *i.e.* by only using information for matched-binders (thus in WHNF), LIQUIDHASKELL reports 1,395 unique functional correctness warnings – about 1 per 7 lines. With termination information, this number goes to zero.

7. Related Work

Next we situate our work with closely related lines of research.

Dependent Types are the basis of many verifiers, or more generally, proof assistants. In this setting arbitrary terms may appear inside types, so to prevent logical inconsistencies, and enable the checking of type equivalence, all terms must terminate. "Full" dependently typed systems like Coq [5], Agda [24], and Idris [7] typically use *structural* checks where recursion is allowed on sub-terms of ADTs to ensure that *all* terms terminate. We differ in that, since the refinement logic is restricted, we do not require that all functions terminate, and hence, we can prove properties of possibly diverging functions like `collatz` as well as lazy functions like `repeat`. Recent languages like Aura [18] and Zombie [9] allow general recursion, but constrain the logic to a terminating sublanguage, as we do, to avoid reasoning about divergence in the logic. In contrast to us, the above systems crucially assume *call-by-value* semantics to ensure that binders are bound to values, *i.e.* cannot diverge.

Refinement Types are a form of dependent types where invariants are encoded via a combination of types and predicates from a restricted *SMT-decidable* logic [4, 13, 27, 37]. The restriction makes it safe to support arbitrary recursion, which has hitherto never been a problem for refinement types. However, we show that this is because all the above systems implicitly assume that all free variables are bound to values, which is only guaranteed under CBV and, as we have seen, leads to unsoundness under lazy evaluation.

Tracking Divergent Computations The notion of type stratification to track potentially diverging computations dates to at least [10] which uses $\bar{\tau}$ to encode diverging terms, and types **`fix`** as $(\bar{\tau} \rightarrow \bar{\tau}) \rightarrow \bar{\tau})$. More recently, [8] tracks diverging computations within a *partiality monad*. Unlike the above, we use refinements to obtain terminating fixpoints (`tfix`), which let us prove the vast majority (of sub-expressions) in real world libraries as non-diverging, avoiding the restructuring that would be required by the partiality monad.

Termination Analyses Various authors have proposed techniques to verify termination of recursive functions, either using the "size-change principle" [19, 28], or by annotating types with size indices and verifying that the arguments of recursive calls have smaller indices [2, 17]. Our use of refinements to encode terminating fixpoints is most closely related to [36], but this work also crucially assumes CBV semantics for soundness.

AProVE [15] implements a powerful, fully-automatic termination analysis for Haskell based on term-rewriting. While we could use an external analysis like AProVE, we have found that encoding the termination proof via refinements provided advantages that are crucial in large, real-world code bases. Specifically, refinements let us (1) prove termination over a subset (not all) of inputs; many functions (*e.g.* `fac`) terminate only on `Nat` inputs and not all `Int` s, (2) encode pre-conditions, post-conditions, and auxiliary invariants that are essential for proving termination, (*e.g.* `gcd`), (3) easily specify non-standard decreasing metrics and prove termination, (*e.g.* `range`). In each case, the code could be (significantly) *rewritten* to be amenable to AProVE but this defeats the purpose of an automatic checker. Finally, none of the above analyses have been empirically evaluated on large and complex real-world libraries.

Static Contract Checkers like ESCJava [14] are a classical way of verifying correctness through assertions and pre- and post-conditions. Side-effects like modifications of global variables are a well known issue for static checkers for imperative languages; the standard approach is to use an effect analysis to determine the "modifies clause" *i.e.* the set of globals modified by a procedure. Similarly, one can view our approach as implicitly computing the non-termination effects. [38] describes a static contract checker for Haskell that uses symbolic execution to unroll procedures upto some fixed depth, yielding weaker "bounded" soundness guarantees. Similarly, Zeno [29] is an automatic Haskell prover that combines unrolling with heuristics for rewriting and proof-search. Based on rewriting, it is sound but "Zeno might loop forever" when faced with non-termination. Finally, the Halo [35] contract checker encodes Haskell programs into first-order logic by directly modeling the code's denotational semantics, again, requiring heuristics for instantiating axioms describing functions' behavior. Halo's translation of Haskell programs directly encodes constructors as uninterpreted functions, axiomatized to be injective (as the denotational semantics requires). This heavyweight encoding is more precise than predicate abstraction but leads to model-theoretic problems (outlined in the Halo paper) and affects the efficiency of the encoding when scaling to larger programs (see also 8, paragraph B) in the lack of specialized decisions procedures. Unlike any of the above, our type-based approach does not rely on heuristics for unrolling recursive procedures, or instantiating axioms. Instead we are based on decidable SMT validity checking and abstract interpretation [26] which makes the tool predictable and the overall workflow scale to the verification of large, real-world code bases.

8. Conclusions & Future Work

Our goal is to use the recent advances in SMT solving to build automated refinement type-based verifiers for Haskell. In this paper, we have made the following advances towards the goal. First, we demonstrated how the classical technique for generating VCs from refinement subtyping queries is unsound under lazy evaluation. Second, we have presented a solution that addresses the unsoundness by stratifying types into those that are inhabited by terms that may diverge, those that must reduce to Haskell values, and those that must reduce to finite values, and have shown how refinement types may themselves be used to soundly verify the stratification. Third, we have developed an implementation of our technique in LIQUIDHASKELL and have evaluated the tool on a large corpus comprising 10KLOC of widely used Haskell libraries. Our experiments empirically demonstrate the practical effectiveness of our approach: using refinement types, we were able to prove 96% of recursive functions as terminating, and to crucially use this information to prove a variety of functional correctness properties.

Limitations While our approach is demonstrably effective *in practice*, it relies critically on proving termination, which, while independently useful, is not wholly satisfying *in theory*, as adding divergence shouldn't *break* a safety proof. Our system can prove a program safe, but if the program is modified by making some functions non-deterministically diverge, then, we may no longer be able to prove safety. Thus, in future work, it would be valuable to explore *other* ways to reconcile laziness and refinement typing. We outline some routes and the challenging obstacles along them.

A. Convert Lazy To Eager Evaluation One alternative might be to translate the program from lazy to eager evaluation, for example, to replace every (thunk) e with an abstraction $\lambda().e$, and every use of a lazy value x with an application x (). After this, we could simply assume eager evaluation, and so the usual refinement type systems could be used to verify Haskell. Alas, no. While sound, this translation doesn't solve the problem of reasoning about divergence. A dependent function type $x{:}\texttt{Int} \rightarrow \{v{:}\texttt{Int} \mid v > x\}$ would be transformed to $x{:}(() \rightarrow \texttt{Int}) \rightarrow \{v{:}\texttt{Int} \mid v > x\ ()\}$ The transformed type is problematic as it uses arbitrary function applications in the refinement logic! The type is only sensible if x () provably reduces to a value, bringing us back to square one.

B. Explicit Reasoning about Divergence Another alternative is to enrich the refinement logic with a *value predicate* $\mathsf{Val}(x)$ that is true when "x is a value" and use the SMT solver to *explicitly* reason about divergence. (Note that $\mathsf{Val}(x)$ is equivalent to introducing a $\perp$ constant denoting divergence, and writing $(x \neq \perp)$.) Unfortunately, this $\mathsf{Val}(x)$ predicate takes the VCs outside the scope of the standard efficiently decidable logics supported by SMT solvers. To see why, recall the subtyping query from `good` in §2. With explicit value predicates, this subtyping reduces to the VC:

$$\begin{matrix}(\mathsf{Val}(x) \Rightarrow x \geq 0) \\ (\mathsf{Val}(y) \Rightarrow y \geq 0)\end{matrix} \Rightarrow (v = y + 1) \Rightarrow (v > 0) \qquad (12)$$

To prove the above valid, we require the knowledge that $(v = y+1)$ implies that y is a value, *i.e.* that $\mathsf{Val}(y)$ holds. This fact, while obvious to a *human* reader, is outside the decidable theories of linear arithmetic of the existing SMT solvers. Thus, existing solvers would be unable to prove (12) valid, causing us to reject `good`.

Possible Fix: Explicit Reasoning With Axioms? One possible fix for the above would be to specify a collection of *axioms* that characterize how the value predicate behaves with respect to the other theory operators. For example, we might specify axioms like:

$$\forall x, y, z.(x = y + z) \Rightarrow (\mathsf{Val}(x) \wedge \mathsf{Val}(y) \wedge \mathsf{Val}(z))$$
$$\forall x, y.(x < y) \Rightarrow (\mathsf{Val}(x) \wedge \mathsf{Val}(y))$$

etc.. However, this is a non-solution for several reasons. First, it is not clear what a complete set of axioms is. Second, there is the well known loss of predictable checking that arises when using axioms, as one must rely on various brittle, syntactic matching and instantiation heuristics [12]. It is unclear how well these heuristics will work with the sophisticated linear programming-based algorithms used to decide arithmetic theories. Thus, proper support for value predicates could require significant changes to existing decision procedures, making it impossible to use existing SMT solvers.

Possible Fix: Explicit Reasoning With Types? Another possible fix would be to encode the behavior of the value predicates within the refinement types for different operators, after which the predicate itself could be treated as an *uninterpreted function* in the refinement logic [6]. For instance, we could type the primitives:

```
(+)  :: x:Int -> y:Int
     -> {v | v  =  x + y && Val x && Val y}
(<)  :: x:Int -> y:Int
     -> {v | v <=> x < y && Val x && Val y}
```

While this approach requires *no* changes to the SMT machinery, it makes specifications complex and verbose. We cannot just add the value predicates to the primitives' specifications. Consider

```
choose b x y = if b then x+1 else y+2
```

To reason about the output of `choose` we must type it as:

```
choose :: Bool -> x:Int -> y:Int
       -> {v|(v > x && Val x)||(v > y && Val y)}
```

Thus, the value predicates will pervasively clutter all signatures with strictness information, making the system unpleasant to use.

Divergence Requires 3-Valued Logic Finally, for either "fix", the value predicate poses a model-theoretic problem: what is the meaning of $\mathsf{Val}(x)$? One sensible approach is to extend the universe with a family of *distinct* $\bot$ constants, such that $\mathsf{Val}(\bot)$ is false. These constants lead inevitably into a three-valued logic (in order to give meaning to formulas like $\bot = \bot$). Thus, even if we were to find a way to reason with the value predicate via axioms or types, we would have to ensure that we properly handled the 3-valued logic within existing 2-valued SMT solvers.

Future Work Thus, in future work it would be worthwhile to address the above technical and usability problems to enable explicit reasoning with the value predicate. This explicit system would be *more expressive* than our stratified approach, *e.g.* would let us check `let x = collatz 10 in 12 `div` x+1` by encoding strictness inside the logic. Nevertheless, we suspect such a verifier would use stratification to eliminate the value predicate in the common case. At any rate, until these hurdles are crossed, we can take comfort in stratified refinement types and can just *eagerly* use termination to prove safety for *lazy* languages.

Acknowledgements

We thank Kenneth Knowles, Kenneth L. McMillan, Andrey Rybalchenko, Philip Wadler, and the reviewers for their excellent suggestions and feedback. This work was supported by NSF grants CNS-0964702, CNS-1223850, CCF-1218344, CCF-1018672, and a generous gift from Microsoft Research.

References

[1] L. Augustsson. Cayenne - a language with dependent types. In *ICFP*, 1998.

[2] G. Barthe, M. J. Frade, E. Giménez, L. Pinto, and T. Uustalu. Type-based termination of recursive definitions. *Mathematical Structures in Computer Science*, 2004.

[3] J. F. Belo, M. Greenberg, A. Igarashi, and B. C. Pierce. Polymorphic contracts. In *ESOP*, 2011.

[4] J. Bengtson, K. Bhargavan, C. Fournet, A. D. Gordon, and S. Maffeis. Refinement types for secure implementations. *ACM TOPLAS*, 2011.

[5] Y. Bertot and P. Castéran. *Coq'Art: The Calculus of Inductive Constructions*. Springer Verlag, 2004.

[6] A. Bradley and Z. Manna. *The Calculus of Computation: Decision Procedures With Application To Verification*. Springer-Verlag, 2007.

[7] E. Brady. Idris: general purpose programming with dependent types. In *PLPV*, 2013.

[8] V. Capretta. General recursion via coinductive types. *Logical Methods in Computer Science*, 2005.

[9] C. Casinghino, V. Sjöberg, and S. Weirich. Combining proofs and programs in a dependently typed language. In *POPL*, 2014.

[10] R. L. Constable and S. F. Smith. Partial objects in constructive type theory. In *LICS*, 1987.

[11] L. de Moura and N. Bjørner. Z3: An efficient SMT solver. 2008.

[12] D. Detlefs, G. Nelson, and J. B. Saxe. Simplify: a theorem prover for program checking. *J. ACM*, 2005.

[13] J. Dunfield. Refined typechecking with Stardust. In *PLPV*, 2007.

[14] C. Flanagan, K.R.M. Leino, M. Lillibridge, G. Nelson, J. B. Saxe, and R. Stata. Extended static checking for Java. In *PLDI*, 2002.

[15] J. Giesl, M. Raffelsieper, P. Schneider-Kamp, S. Swiderski, and R. Thiemann. Automated termination proofs for Haskell by term rewriting. *TPLS*, 2011.

[16] C. A. R. Hoare. Procedures and parameters: An axiomatic approach. In *Symposium on Semantics of Algorithmic Languages*. 1971.

[17] J. Hughes, L. Pareto, and A. Sabry. Proving the correctness of reactive systems using sized types. In *POPL*, 1996.

[18] L. Jia, J. A. Vaughan, K. Mazurak, J. Zhao, L. Zarko, J. Schorr, and S. Zdancewic. Aura: a programming language for authorization and audit. In *ICFP*, 2008.

[19] N. D. Jones and N. Bohr. Termination analysis of the untyped lamba-calculus. In *RTA*, 2004.

[20] M. Kawaguchi, P. Rondon, and R. Jhala. Type-based data structure verification. In *PLDI*, 2009.

[21] K.W. Knowles and C. Flanagan. Hybrid type checking. *ACM TOPLAS*, 2010.

[22] G. Nelson. Techniques for program verification. Technical Report CSL81-10, Xerox Palo Alto Research Center, 1981.

[23] T. Nipkow. Hoare logics for recursive procedures and unbounded nondeterminism. In *CSL*, 2002.

[24] U. Norell. *Towards a practical programming language based on dependent type theory*. PhD thesis, Chalmers, 2007.

[25] S. R. Della Rocca and L. Paolini. *The Parametric Lambda Calculus, A Metamodel for Computation*. 2004.

[26] P. Rondon, M. Kawaguchi, and R. Jhala. Liquid Types. In *PLDI*, 2008.

[27] J. Rushby, S. Owre, and N. Shankar. Subtypes for specifications: Predicate subtyping in pvs. *IEEE TSE*, 1998.

[28] D. Sereni and N.D. Jones. Termination analysis of higher-order functional programs. In *APLAS*, 2005.

[29] W. Sonnex, S. Drossopoulou, and S. Eisenbach. Zeno: An automated prover for properties of recursive data structures. In *TACAS*, 2012.

[30] M. Sulzmann, M. M. T. Chakravarty, S. L. Peyton-Jones, and K. Donnelly. System F with type equality coercions. In *TLDI*, 2007.

[31] N. Swamy, J. Chen, C. Fournet, P-Y. Strub, K. Bhargavan, and J. Yang. Secure distributed programming with value-dependent types. In *ICFP*, 2011.

[32] A. M. Turing. On computable numbers, with an application to the eintscheidungsproblem. In *LMS*, 1936.

[33] N. Vazou, P. Rondon, and R. Jhala. Abstract refinement types. In *ESOP*, 2013.

[34] N. Vazou, E. L. Seidel, and R. Jhala. Liquidhaskell: Experience with refinement types in the real world. In *Haskell Symposium*, 2014.

[35] D. Vytiniotis, S.L. Peyton-Jones, K. Claessen, and D. Rosén. Halo: haskell to logic through denotational semantics. In *POPL*, 2013.

[36] H. Xi. Dependent types for program termination verification. In *LICS*, 2001.

[37] H. Xi and F. Pfenning. Eliminating array bound checking through dependent types. In *PLDI*, 1998.

[38] D. N. Xu, S. L. Peyton-Jones, and K. Claessen. Static contract checking for haskell. In *POPL*, 2009.

A Theory of Gradual Effect Systems

Felipe Bañados Schwerter *
PLEIAD Lab
Computer Science Department (DCC)
University of Chile
fbanados@dcc.uchile.cl

Ronald Garcia †
Software Practices Lab
Department of Computer Science
University of British Columbia
rxg@cs.ubc.ca

Éric Tanter ‡
PLEIAD Lab
Computer Science Department (DCC)
University of Chile
etanter@dcc.uchile.cl

Abstract

Effect systems have the potential to help software developers, but their practical adoption has been very limited. We conjecture that this limited adoption is due in part to the difficulty of transitioning from a system where effects are implicit and unrestricted to a system with a static effect discipline, which must settle for conservative checking in order to be decidable. To address this hindrance, we develop a theory of gradual effect checking, which makes it possible to incrementally annotate and statically check effects, while still rejecting statically inconsistent programs. We extend the generic type-and-effect framework of Marino and Millstein with a notion of unknown effects, which turns out to be significantly more subtle than unknown types in traditional gradual typing. We appeal to abstract interpretation to develop and validate the concepts of gradual effect checking. We also demonstrate how an effect system formulated in Marino and Millstein's framework can be automatically extended to support gradual checking.

Categories and Subject Descriptors D.3.1 [*Software*]: Programming Languages—Formal Definitions and Theory

Keywords Type-and-effect systems; gradual typing; abstract interpretation

1. Introduction

Type-and-effect systems allow static reasoning about the computational effects of programs. Effect systems were originally introduced to safely support mutable variables in functional languages [11], but more recently, effect systems have been developed for a variety of effect domains, e.g., I/O, exceptions, locking, atomicity, confinement, and purity [1–3, 12, 13, 17, 18].

To abstract from specific effect domains and account for effect systems in general, Marino and Millstein (M&M) developed a generic effect system [15]. In their framework, effect systems are seen as granting and checking privileges. Genericity is obtained by parameterizing the type system and runtime semantics of a language with two operations, called *adjust* and *check*, which respectively specify how the set of held privileges is adjusted and checked during type checking. A particular effect system is instantiated by providing a syntax for effects and a definition of the check and adjust operations. They demonstrate that several effect systems from the literature can be formulated as instantiations of the generic framework.

The generic effect system underlies the design of the Scala effect checker plugin, which extends the M&M framework with a form of effect polymorphism [17]. Several specific effect systems for this plugin include IO effects, exceptions, and more recently, state effects [18].

Despite their obvious advantages in terms of static reasoning, the adoption of effect systems has been rather limited in practice. While effect polymorphism supports the definition of higher-order functions that are polymorphic in the effects of their arguments (e.g., *map*), writing fully-annotated effectful programs is complex, and is hardly ever done.[1]

We conjecture that an important reason for the limited adoption of effect systems is the difficulty of transitioning from a system where effects are implicit and unrestricted to a system with a fully static effect discipline. Another explanation is that effect systems are necessarily conservative and therefore occasionally reject valid programs. We follow the line of work on *gradual* verification of program properties (e.g., gradual typing [22, 23], gradual ownership types [21], gradual typestate [10, 26]), and develop a theory of gradual effect systems. Our contributions are as follows:

- We shed light on the meaning of gradual effect checking, and its fundamental differences from traditional gradual typing, by formulating it in the framework of abstract interpretation [4]. Abstract interpretation allows us to clearly and precisely specify otherwise informal design intentions about gradual effect systems. Key notions like the meaning of unknown effects, consistent privilege sets, and consistent containment between them, are defined in terms of abstraction and concretization operations.
- We extend the generic effect system of Marino and Millstein into a generic framework for gradual effects. As with gradual typing, our approach relies on a translation to an internal language with explicit checks and casts. The nature of these checks and casts is, however, quite different. We prove the type safety of the internal language and the preservation of typability by the translation.
- We demonstrate how an effect system formulated in the M&M framework can be immediately extended to support gradual

* Funded by CONICYT-PCHA/Magíster Nacional/2013-22130167
† Partially funded by an NSERC discovery grant
‡ Partially funded by FONDECYT project 1110051

ICFP '14, September 1–6, 2014, Gothenburg, Sweden.
Copyright © 2014 ACM 978-1-4503-2873-9/14/09...$15.00.
http://dx.doi.org/10.1145/2628136.2628149

[1] Pure functional languages like Haskell and Clean are notable exceptions.

checking by lifting existing adjust and check functions to the gradual setting.

- We present a concrete instantiation of the generic framework to gradually check exceptions. The resulting system is compact and provides a tangible and self-contained example of gradual effect checking.

We believe this work can help effect system developers extend their designs with support for gradual checking, thereby facilitating their adoption.

2. Background and Motivation

In this section, we introduce the idea of static effect checking, and give an intuition for how gradual effect checking is related. We finish with a brief introduction to the M&M generic framework for specifying type-and-effect systems.

2.1 Effect Systems

Effect systems classify the computational effects that an expression performs when evaluated. To illustrate this idea, consider a simple functional language with integers, booleans, and references. We focus on three mutable state effects: `alloc`, `read` and `write`.

A value such as 7 or $(\lambda x : \mathtt{Int} \,.\, x)$ has no effect; neither does an arithmetic expression whose sub-expressions have no effect, such as $7 + 12$. Conversely, creating a reference such as $\mathtt{ref}\ 6$ has type `Ref Int` and effect `alloc`. Similarly, an assignment expression such as $x := 2$ has type `Unit` and effect `write`, and dereferencing a reference $!x$ has the type of the reference content, and effect `read`.

Since functions are values they have no effects, but they may perform effects when applied. To modularly check effects, then, function types are annotated with the effects of the function body. For instance, the function f:

$$f = \lambda x : \mathtt{Ref\ Int} \,.\, !\, x$$

has type $(\mathtt{Ref\ Int}) \xrightarrow{\{\mathtt{read}\}} \mathtt{Int}$ because a `read` effect happens during the application of the function. Note that the effect may not happen during some applications of a function, for instance (assuming $y : \mathtt{Bool}$ is in scope):

$$g = \lambda x : \mathtt{Ref\ Int} \,.\, \mathtt{if}\ y\ \mathtt{then}\ x := 3; 0\ \mathtt{else}\ 1$$

has type $(\mathtt{Ref\ Int}) \xrightarrow{\{\mathtt{write}\}} \mathtt{Int}$ because its applications *may* perform a `write` effect.

Of course, an expression can induce more than one effect, hence the use of *effect sets* in the annotations. Though the language does not define any notion of subtyping on types themselves, effect sets leads to a natural notion of subtyping [25]. Consider the following higher-order function:

$$h : ((\mathtt{Ref\ Int}) \xrightarrow{\{\mathtt{read},\mathtt{alloc}\}} \mathtt{Int}) \xrightarrow{\dots} \mathtt{Int}$$

This function restricts the effects of its function argument to $\{\mathtt{read}, \mathtt{alloc}\}$. Intuitively, it is valid to apply h to f, whose effect set is $\{\mathtt{read}\}$, because that would not violate the expectations of h. In other words:

$$(\mathtt{Ref\ Int}) \xrightarrow{\{\mathtt{read}\}} \mathtt{Int} <: (\mathtt{Ref\ Int}) \xrightarrow{\{\mathtt{read},\mathtt{alloc}\}} \mathtt{Int}$$

because the effects of the former are a subset of the latter. Conversely, it is invalid to apply h to g.

From effects to privileges. Following Marino and Millstein [15], we interpret effect systems in terms of *privilege checking*: to each effectful operation corresponds a privilege required to perform it. For instance, we can view `alloc`, `read` and `write` as the privileges required to respectively allocate, dereference and assign a reference. In this framework, the function type $(\mathtt{Ref\ Int}) \xrightarrow{\{\mathtt{read}\}} \mathtt{Int}$ is interpreted as the type of a function that *requires* the `read` privilege in order to be applied. Effect checking ensures that sufficient privileges have been granted to perform effectful operations.

2.2 Towards Gradual Effect Checking

Programming in the presence of a statically checked discipline brings stronger guarantees about the behavior of programs, but doing so is demanding. In addition, one is limited by the fact that the checker is conservative. Recently, several practical effect systems have been applied to existing libraries, and the empirical findings highlight the need to occasionally bypass static effect checking [12, 17].

For instance, the JavaUI effect system [12], which prevents non-UI threads from accessing UI objects or invoking UI-thread-only methods, cannot be used to verify libraries that dynamically check which thread they are running on and adapt their behavior accordingly. As explained by the authors, the patterns of dynamic checks they found in existing code go beyond simple if-then-else statements and so cannot be handled simply by specializing the static type system. While JavaUI lives with this limitation, the Scala effect plugin [17] has recently been updated with an `@unchecked` annotation to simply turn off effect checking locally. The use of this annotation however breaks the guarantees offered by the effect system, since there are no associated runtime checks.

In the realm of standard type systems, gradual typing [23] is a promising approach that alleviates the complexity and conservativeness issues by integrating static and dynamic checking seamlessly and safely. The appeal of gradual typing has inspired the development of gradual approaches to a variety of type disciplines, including objects [14, 22, 24], ownership types [21], typestates [10, 26], and information flow typing [6].

This paper develops gradual effect checking, following the core design principles that are common to all gradual checking approaches: *(a)* The same language can support both fully static and fully dynamic checking of program properties. *(b)* The programmer has fine grained control over the static-to-dynamic spectrum. *(c)* The gradual checker statically rejects programs on the basis that they surely go wrong; programs that *may* go right are accepted statically, but subject to dynamic checking. *(d)* Runtime checks are minimized based on static information. *(e)* Violations of properties are detected as runtime errors—there are no stuck programs.

2.3 Gradual Effects in Action

Recall the function g defined in Sec. 2.1, which requires $\{\mathtt{write}\}$ privileges. The program $h\ g$ is rejected because h only accepts functions that require $\{\mathtt{read}, \mathtt{alloc}\}$ privileges. Even if the programmer knows that for a particular use of g, the `if` condition y is false—and thus needs no `write` privilege after all—the program is rejected.

In direct analogy to the unknown type ? introduced by Siek and Taha [23] for gradual typing, we introduce *statically unknown privileges*, denoted ¿, to our language. One can ascribe unknown privileges to any expression e, using the notation $e :: ¿$. For instance, if g is defined as:

$$g = \lambda x : \mathtt{Ref\ Int} \,.\, \mathtt{if}\ y\ \mathtt{then}\ (x := 3; 0) :: ¿\ \mathtt{else}\ 1$$

then it is given the type $(\mathtt{Ref\ Int}) \xrightarrow{\{¿\}} \mathtt{Int}$. The application $h\ g$ is now statically accepted by the gradual effect system. At runtime, if only the `else` branch is ever executed, then no error occurs. If, on the other hand, the programmer wrongly assumed that g would not require the `write` privilege and the `then` branch is executed, an effect error is raised, preventing the assignment to x.

The ascription expression $e :: ¿$ introduces dynamic checking semantics. Statically, it *hides* the privileges required by e from the surrounding context, and allows the subexpressions of e to attempt effectful operations. At runtime, checks occur to ensure that the static privileges that e requires are available as needed.

One can partially expose (and hence dynamically check) required privileges by ascribing specific privileges in addition to $¿$. For instance, $e :: \{\texttt{read}, ¿\}$ statically reveals that e requires the `read` privilege, but hides other potential requirements.[2]

The static-to-dynamic spectrum We have illustrated the use of gradual effect checking from the point of view of "softening static checking"—introducing islands of dynamicity in an otherwise static verification process. Gradual verification is about supporting both ends of the static-to-dynamic spectrum as well as any middle ground. We now discuss gradual effect checking from the point of view of "hardening dynamic checking"—introducing static checks in an otherwise dynamic verification process.

A fully-dynamic effectful program corresponds to a gradually-typed program without any effect-related annotations in which all effectful operations are wrapped by a $:: ¿$ ascription.[3] Static checking trivially succeeds because all expressions hide their required privileges. Forbidden effects will only be detected at runtime. Then, the programmer can progressively introduce static privilege annotations (function argument types, ascriptions) and remove $:: ¿$ ascriptions, statically revealing required privileges. The static checker may reject the program if inconsistencies are detected, or it may accept the program and runtime errors may occur. As more static information is revealed, fewer dynamic checks are required. The effect discipline is hardened.

2.4 Generic Effect Systems

To avoid re-inventing gradual effects for each possible effect discipline, we build on the generic effect framework Marino and Millstein (M&M) [15], which we briefly describe in this section.

The M&M effect framework defines a parameterized typing judgment $\Phi; \Gamma; \Sigma \vdash e : T$. It checks an expression under a set of privileges Φ, representing the effects that are allowed during the evaluation of the expression e. For instance, here is the generic typing rule for functions:

$$\text{T-Fun}\ \frac{\Phi_1; \Gamma, x : T_1; \Sigma \vdash e : T_2}{\Phi; \Gamma; \Sigma \vdash (\lambda x : T_1 \,.\, e)_\varepsilon : \{\varepsilon\}(T_1 \xrightarrow{\Phi_1} T_2)}$$

Since a function needs no specific permissions, any privilege set Φ will do. The function body itself may require privileges Φ_1 and these are used to annotate the function type. We explain the tag ε shortly.

A given privilege discipline (mutable state, exceptions, etc.) is instantiated by defining two operations, a *check* predicate and an *adjust* function. The check predicate is used to determine whether the current privileges are sufficient to evaluate non-value expression forms. To achieve genericity, the check predicate $\textbf{check}_C$ is indexed by *check contexts* C, which represent the non-value expression forms. The adjust function is used to evolve the available privileges while evaluating the subexpressions of a given expression form. This function takes the current privileges and returns the privileges used to check the considered subexpression. To achieve genericity, the adjust function $\textbf{adjust}_A$ is indexed by *adjust contexts* A, which represent the immediate context around a given subexpression.

To increase its overall expressiveness, the framework also incorporates a notion of *tags* ε, which represent auxiliary static information for an effect discipline (e.g. abstract locations). Expressions that create new values, like constants and lambdas, are indexed with tags. The check and adjust contexts contain *tag sets* π so that $\textbf{check}_C$ and $\textbf{adjust}_A$ can leverage static information about the values of subexpressions. To facilitate abstract value-tracking, type constructors are annotated with tagsets, so types take the form $T \equiv \pi\rho$. For more precise control, effect disciplines can associate tags to privileges e.g., $\texttt{read}(\varepsilon_1)$, $\texttt{read}(\varepsilon_2)$, etc.[4]

For example, a check predicate for controlling mutable state is defined as follows:

$$\begin{aligned} \textbf{check}_{!\pi}(\Phi) &\iff \texttt{read} \in \Phi \\ \textbf{check}_{\texttt{ref}\,\pi}(\Phi) &\iff \texttt{alloc} \in \Phi \\ \textbf{check}_{\pi_1 := \pi_2}(\Phi) &\iff \texttt{write} \in \Phi \\ \textbf{check}_C(\Phi) &\text{ holds for all other } C \end{aligned}$$

In this case, only state-manipulating expression forms have interesting check predicates, which simply require the corresponding privilege; the rest always hold.

Since the assignment expression involves evaluating two subexpressions (the reference and the new value), there are two adjust contexts. The $\downarrow := \uparrow$ context, which corresponds to evaluating the reference to be assigned, and the $\pi := \downarrow$ context, which corresponds to evaluating the assigned value. The $\downarrow$ denotes the subexpression for which privileges should be adjusted. The tagset π represents statically known information about any subexpressions that would be evaluated before the current expression. The $\uparrow$ denotes a subexpression that would be evaluated after the current expression.

For certain disciplines, like mutable state, the adjust function is simply the identity for every context. But one could, for example, require that all subexpressions assigned to references must be effect-free by defining adjust as follows:

$$\begin{aligned} \textbf{adjust}_{\pi := \downarrow}(\Phi) &= \emptyset \\ \textbf{adjust}_A(\Phi) &= \Phi \text{ otherwise} \end{aligned}$$

All typing rules in the generic system use check and adjust to enforce the intended effect discipline. For instance, here is the typing rule for assignment:

$$\text{T-Asgn}\ \frac{\begin{array}{c} \textbf{adjust}_{\downarrow := \uparrow}(\Phi); \Gamma; \Sigma \vdash e_1 : \pi_1 \texttt{Ref}\ T_1 \\ \textbf{adjust}_{\pi_1 := \downarrow}(\Phi); \Gamma; \Sigma \vdash e_2 : \pi_2\rho_2 \\ \textbf{check}_{\pi_1 := \pi_2}(\Phi) \qquad \pi_2\rho_2 <: T_1 \end{array}}{\Phi; \Gamma; \Sigma \vdash (e_1 := e_2)_\varepsilon : \{\varepsilon\}\texttt{Unit}}$$

The subexpressions e_1 and e_2 are typed using adjusted privilege sets. Their corresponding types have associated tagsets π_i that are used to adjust and check privileges. Note that in accord with left-to-right evaluation, $\textbf{adjust}_{\pi_1 := \downarrow}$ knows which tags are associated with typing e_1. Finally, $\textbf{check}_{\pi_1 := \pi_2}$ verifies that assignment is allowed with the given permissions and the subexpression tag sets. Subtyping is used here only to account for inclusion of privilege sets between function types.

[2] In a static effect system, an effect ascription $e :: \{\texttt{read}\}$ is directly analogous to a type ascription [16]. Static effect ascriptions were introduced by Gifford and Lucassen [11].

[3] This corresponds to the translation of terms from the untyped λ-calculus to the gradually-typed λ-calculus, which lifts all functions to the $? \to ?$ type to introduce runtime checks [23].

[4] Gradual effects are compatible with effect systems that do not need tags. See Sec. 5.

For maximum flexibility, the framework imposes only two constraints on the definitions of **check** and **adjust**:

Property 1 (Privilege Monotonicity).

- *If* $\Phi_1 \subseteq \Phi_2$ *then* $\mathbf{check}_C(\Phi_1) \implies \mathbf{check}_C(\Phi_2)$*;*
- *If* $\Phi_1 \subseteq \Phi_2$ *then* $\mathbf{adjust}_A(\Phi_1) \subseteq \mathbf{adjust}_A(\Phi_2)$.

Property 2 (Tag Monotonicity).

- *If* $C_1 \sqsubseteq C_2$ *then* $\mathbf{check}_{C_2}(\Phi) \implies \mathbf{check}_{C_1}(\Phi)$*;*
- *If* $A_1 \sqsubseteq A_2$ *then* $\mathbf{adjust}_{A_2}(\Phi) \subseteq \mathbf{adjust}_{A_1}(\Phi)$.

Privilege monotonicity captures the idea that once an expression has sufficient privileges to run, one can always safely add more. This corresponds to effect subsumption in many particular effect systems. In contrast, tag monotonicity captures the idea that more tags implies more uncertainty about the source of a runtime value. The $\sqsubseteq$ relation holds when contexts have the same structure and the tagsets of the first context are subsets of the corresponding tagsets of the second context. For example, $\mathtt{ref}\,\pi_1 \sqsubseteq \mathtt{ref}\,\pi_2$ if and only if $\pi_1 \subseteq \pi_2$. In summary, **check** and **adjust** are order-preserving with respect to privileges and order-reversing with respect to tags.

The framework can be instantiated with any pair of check and adjust functions that satisfy both privilege and tag monotonicity. The resulting type system is safe with respect to the corresponding runtime semantics: no runtime privilege check fails, so no program gets stuck.

3. Gradual Effects as an Abstract Interpretation

In this section we present a formal analysis of gradual effects, guided by the design principles presented in Sec. 2.2. We use abstract interpretation [4] to define our notion of unknown effects, and find that as a result the formal definitions capture our stated design intentions, and that the resulting framework for gradual effects is quite generic and highly reusable.

3.1 The Challenge of Gradual Effects

The central concept underlying gradual effects is the idea of *unknown privileges*, ¿. This concept was inspired by the notion of unknown type ? introduced by Siek and Taha [23], but this concept is not as straightforward to understand and formalize.

First, gradual types reflect the tree structure of type names. Siek and Taha treat gradual types as trees with unknown leafs. Two types are deemed consistent whenever their known parts match up exactly. For instance, the types $? \to$ `Int` and `Bool` $\to\ ?$ are consistent because their $\to$ constructors line up: ? is consistent with any type structure. In contrast, privilege sets are unordered collections of individual effects, so a structure-based definition of consistency is not as immediately apparent.

Second, under gradual typing, the unknown type always stands for one type, so casts always associate an unknown type with one other concrete type. On the contrary, the unknown privileges annotation ¿ stands for any number of privileges: zero, one, or many.

Third, simple types are related to the final value of a computation. In contrast, privileges are related to the dynamic extent of an expression as it produces a final value. As such, defining what it means to gradually check privileges involves tracking steps of computation, rather than wrapping a final value with type information.

Finally, as we have seen in Sec. 2.1, effect systems naturally induce a notion of subtyping, which must be accounted for in a gradual effect system. In general, subtyping characterizes *substitutability*: which expressions or values can be substituted for others, based on static properties. In prior work, Siek and Taha demonstrate how structural subtyping and gradual typing can be combined [22], but the criteria for substitutability differ substantially between structural types and effects, so it is not straightforward to adapt Siek and Taha's design to suit gradual effects.

Our initial attempts to adapt gradual typing to gradual effects met with these challenges. We found abstract interpretation to be an informative and effective framework in which to specify and develop gradual effects. The rest of this section develops the notion of unknown effect privileges and consistent privilege sets. The rest of the paper then uses the framework as needed to introduce concepts and formalize gradual effect checking.

3.2 Fundamental Concepts

This subsection conceives gradual effects as an instance of abstract interpretation. We do not assume any prior familiarity with abstract interpretation: we build up the relevant concepts as needed.

For purpose of discussion, consider again the effect privileges for mutable state from Sec. 2.1:

$$\Phi \in \mathbf{PrivSet} = \mathcal{P}(\{\mathtt{read}, \mathtt{write}, \mathtt{alloc}\})$$
$$\Xi \in \mathbf{CPrivSet} = \mathcal{P}(\{\mathtt{read}, \mathtt{write}, \mathtt{alloc}, ¿\})$$

We already understand privilege sets Φ, but we want a clear understanding of what consistent privilege sets Ξ—privilege sets that may have unknown effects—really mean. Consider the following two consistent privilege sets:

$$\Xi_1 = \{\mathtt{read}\} \qquad \Xi_2 = \{\mathtt{read}, ¿\}$$

The set Ξ_1 is completely static: it refers exactly to the set of privileges $\{\mathtt{read}\}$. The set Ξ_2 on the other hand is gradual: it refers to the `read` privilege, but leaves open the possibility of other privileges. In this case, the ¿ stands for several possibilities: no additional privileges, the `write` privilege alone, the `alloc` privilege alone, or both `write` and `alloc`.

Thus, each consistent privilege set stands for some set of possible privilege sets. To formalize this interpretation, we introduce a *concretization* function γ, which maps a consistent privilege set Ξ to the concrete set of privilege sets that it stands for.[5]

Definition 1 (Concretization). *Let* $\gamma : \mathbf{CPrivSet} \to \mathcal{P}(\mathbf{PrivSet})$ *be defined as follows:*

$$\gamma(\Xi) = \begin{cases} \{\Xi\} & ¿ \notin \Xi \\ \{(\Xi \setminus \{¿\}) \cup \Phi \mid \Phi \in \mathbf{PrivSet}\} & \textit{otherwise}\ . \end{cases}$$

Reconsidering our two example consistent privilege sets, we find that

$$\gamma(\Xi_1) = \{\{\mathtt{read}\}\}$$
$$\gamma(\Xi_2) = \left\{ \begin{array}{l} \{\mathtt{read}, \mathtt{write}\}, \{\mathtt{read}, \mathtt{alloc}\}, \\ \{\mathtt{read}\}, \{\mathtt{read}, \mathtt{alloc}, \mathtt{write}\} \end{array} \right\}$$

Since each consistent privilege set stands for a number of possible concrete privilege sets, we say that a particular privilege set Φ is *represented* by a consistent privilege set Ξ if $\Phi \in \gamma(\Xi)$.

If we consider these two resulting sets of privilege sets, it is immediately clear that Ξ_1 is more restrictive about what privilege sets it represents (only one), while Ξ_2 subsumes Ξ_1 in that it also represents $\{\mathtt{read}\}$, as well as some others. Thus, Ξ_1 is strictly more *precise* than Ξ_2, and so γ induces a *precision relation* between different consistent privilege sets.

Definition 2 (Precision). Ξ_1 *is less imprecise (i.e. more precise) than* Ξ_2*, notation* $\Xi_1 \sqsubseteq \Xi_2$*, if and only if* $\gamma(\Xi_1) \subseteq \gamma(\Xi_2)$

Precision formalizes the idea that some consistent privilege sets imply more information about the privilege sets that they represent

[5] We introduce an *abstraction* function α in Sec. 3.4

than others. For instance, $\{\texttt{read}\}$ is strictly more precise than $\{\texttt{read}, ¿\}$ because $\{\texttt{read}\} \sqsubseteq \{\texttt{read}, ¿\}$ but not vice-versa.

3.3 Lifting Predicates to Consistent Privilege Sets

Now that we have established a formal correspondence between consistent privilege sets and concrete privilege sets, we can systematically adapt our understanding of the latter to the former.

Recall the $\mathbf{check}_C$ predicates of the generic effect framework (Sec. 2.4), which determine if a particular effect set fulfills the requirements of some effectful operator. Gradual checking implies that checking a consistent privilege set succeeds so long as checking its runtime representative could *plausibly* succeed. We formalize this as a notion of *consistent checking*.

Definition 3 (Consistent Checking). *Let* $\mathbf{check}_C$ *be a predicate on privilege sets. Then we define a corresponding* consistent check *predicate* $\widetilde{\mathbf{check}}_C$ *on consistent privilege sets as follows:*

$$\widetilde{\mathbf{check}}_C(\Xi) \iff \mathbf{check}_C(\Phi) \textit{ for } \text{some } \Phi \in \gamma(\Xi).$$

Under some circumstances, however, we must be sure that a consistent privilege set *definitely* has the necessary privileges to pass a check. For this purpose we introduce a notion of *strict checking*.

Definition 4 (Strict Checking). *Let* $\mathbf{check}_C$ *be a predicate on privilege sets. Then we define a corresponding* strict check *predicate* ***strict-check***$_C$ *on consistent privilege sets as follows:*

$$\textit{\textbf{strict-check}}_C(\Xi) \iff \mathbf{check}_C(\Phi) \textit{ for } \text{all } \Phi \in \gamma(\Xi).$$

By defining both consistent checking and strict checking in terms of representative sets, our formalizations are both intuitive and independent of the underlying $\mathbf{check}_C$ predicate. Furthermore, these definitions can be recast directly over consistent privilege sets once we settle on a particular $\mathbf{check}_C$ predicate (cf. Sec. 5).

3.4 Lifting Functions to Consistent Privilege Sets

In addition to predicates on consistent privilege sets, we must also define functions on them. For instance, the M&M framework is parameterized over a family of adjust functions $\mathbf{adjust}_A : \mathbf{PrivSet} \rightarrow \mathbf{PrivSet}$, which alter the set of available effect privileges (Sec. 2.4). Using abstract interpretation, we lift these to *consistent* adjust functions $\widetilde{\mathbf{adjust}}_A : \mathbf{CPrivSet} \rightarrow \mathbf{CPrivSet}$. To do so we must first complete the abstract interpretation framework.

Consider our two example consistent privilege sets. Each represents some set of privilege sets, so we expect that adjusting a consistent privilege set should be related to adjusting the corresponding concrete privilege sets. The key insight is that adjusting a consistent privilege set should correspond somehow to adjusting each individual privilege set in its represented collection. For example $\widetilde{\mathbf{adjust}}_A(\{\texttt{read}, \texttt{alloc}\})$ should be related to the set $\{\mathbf{adjust}_A(\{\texttt{read}, \texttt{alloc}\})\}$, and $\widetilde{\mathbf{adjust}}_A(\{\texttt{read}, ¿\})$ should be related to the following set:

$$\left\{\begin{array}{l}\mathbf{adjust}_A(\{\texttt{read}, \texttt{write}\}), \mathbf{adjust}_A(\{\texttt{read}, \texttt{alloc}\}), \\ \mathbf{adjust}_A(\{\texttt{read}\}), \mathbf{adjust}_A(\{\texttt{read}, \texttt{alloc}, \texttt{write}\})\end{array}\right\}$$

To formalize these relationships, we need an *abstraction* function $\alpha : \mathcal{P}(\mathbf{PrivSet}) \rightarrow \mathbf{CPrivSet}$ that maps collections of privilege sets back to corresponding consistent privilege sets. For such a function to make sense, it must at least be *sound*.

Proposition 1 (Soundness). $\Upsilon \subseteq \gamma(\alpha(\Upsilon))$ *for all* $\Upsilon \in \mathcal{P}(\mathbf{PrivSet})$.

Soundness implies that the corresponding consistent privilege set $\alpha(\Upsilon)$ represents at least as many privilege sets as the original collection Υ. A simple and sound definition of α is $\alpha(\Upsilon) = \{¿\}$. This definition is terrible, though, because it needlessly loses information. For instance, $\alpha(\gamma(\Xi_1)) = \{¿\}$, and since $\{¿\}$ represents every possible privilege set, that mapping loses all the information in the original set. At the least, we would like $\alpha(\gamma(\Xi_1)) = \Xi_1$.

Our actual definition of α is far better than the one proposed above:

Definition 5 (Abstraction). *Let* $\alpha : \mathcal{P}(\mathbf{PrivSet}) \rightarrow \mathbf{CPrivSet}$ *be defined as follows*[6]*:*

$$\alpha(\Upsilon) = \begin{cases} \Phi & \Upsilon = \{\Phi\} \\ (\bigcap \Upsilon) \cup \{¿\} & \textit{otherwise.} \end{cases}$$

In words, abstraction preserves the common concrete privileges, and adds unknown privileges to the resulting consistent set if needed. As required, this abstraction function α is sound.

Even better though, given our interpretation of consistent privilege sets, this α is the best possible one.

Proposition 2 (Optimality). *Suppose* $\Upsilon \subseteq \gamma(\Xi)$. *Then* $\alpha(\Upsilon) \sqsubseteq \Xi$.

Optimality ensures that α gives us not only a sound consistent privilege set, but also the most precise one[7]. In our particular case, optimality implies that $\alpha(\gamma(\Xi)) = \Xi$ for all Ξ but one: $\alpha(\gamma(\{\texttt{read}, \texttt{write}, \texttt{alloc}, ¿\})) = \{\texttt{read}, \texttt{write}, \texttt{alloc}\}$. Both consistent privilege sets represent the same thing.

Using α and γ, we can lift any function f on privilege sets to a function on consistent privilege sets. In particular, we lift the generic adjust functions:

Definition 6 (Consistent Adjust).
Let $\widetilde{\mathbf{adjust}}_A : \mathbf{CPrivSet} \rightarrow \mathbf{CPrivSet}$ *be defined as follows:*

$$\widetilde{\mathbf{adjust}}_A(\Xi) = \alpha\left(\{\mathbf{adjust}_A(\Phi) \mid \Phi \in \gamma(\Xi)\}\right).$$

The $\widetilde{\mathbf{adjust}}$ function reflects all of the information that can be retained when conceptually adjusting all the sets represented by some consistent privilege set.

The $\widetilde{\mathbf{check}}$ and $\widetilde{\mathbf{adjust}}$ operators are critical to our generic presentation of gradual effects. Both definitions are independent of the underlying concrete definitions of **check** and **adjust**. As we show through the rest of the paper, in fact, the abstract interpretation framework presented here time and again provides a clear and effective way to conceive and formalize concepts that we need for gradual effect checking.

4. A Generic Framework for Gradual Effects

In this section we present a generic framework for gradual effect systems. As is standard for gradual checking, the framework includes a source language that supports unknown annotations, an internal language that introduces runtime checks, and a type-directed translation from the former to the latter.

4.1 The Source Language

The core language (Fig. 1) is a simply-typed functional language with a unit value, mutable state, and effect ascriptions $e :: \Xi$. The language is parameterized on some finite set of effect privileges **Priv**, as well as a set of tags **Tag**. The **Priv** set is the basis for consistent privileges **CPriv**, privilege sets **PrivSet**, and consistent privilege sets **CPrivSet**. The **Tag** set is the basis for tag sets **TagSet**. Each type constructor is annotated with a tag set, so types are

[6] For simplicity, we assume Υ is not empty, since $\alpha(\emptyset) = \bot$ plays no role in our development.

[7] Abstract interpretation literature expresses this in part by saying that α and γ form a *Galois connection*[5].

$$\phi \in \textbf{Priv}, \quad \xi \in \textbf{CPriv} = \textbf{Priv} \cup \{¿\}$$
$$\Phi \in \textbf{PrivSet} = \mathcal{P}(\textbf{Priv}), \quad \Xi \in \textbf{CPrivSet} = \mathcal{P}(\textbf{CPriv})$$
$$\varepsilon \in \mathsf{Tags} \;.\; \pi \in \mathcal{P}(\mathsf{Tags})$$

$$\begin{array}{rcll}
w & ::= & \texttt{unit} \mid \lambda x\colon T\,.\,e \mid l & \text{Prevalues} \\
v & ::= & w_\varepsilon & \text{Values} \\
e & ::= & x \mid v \mid e\;e \mid e :: \Xi & \text{Terms} \\
 & & \mid (\texttt{ref}\;e)_\varepsilon \mid\; !e \mid (e := e)_\varepsilon & \\
T & ::= & \pi\,\rho & \text{Types} \\
\rho & ::= & \texttt{Unit} \mid T \xrightarrow{\Xi} T \mid \texttt{Ref}\;T & \text{PreTypes} \\
A & ::= & \downarrow\uparrow \;\mid \pi\downarrow \mid \texttt{ref}\downarrow \;\mid\; !\downarrow & \text{Adjust Contexts} \\
 & & \mid\; \downarrow:=\uparrow \;\mid\; \pi :=\downarrow & \\
C & ::= & \pi\,\pi \mid \texttt{ref}\;\pi \mid\; !\pi \mid \pi := \pi & \text{Check Contexts}
\end{array}$$

Figure 1. Syntax of the source language

annotated deeply. Each value-creating expression is annotated with a tag so that effect systems can abstractly track values. The type of a function carries a consistent privilege set Ξ that characterizes the privileges required to execute the function body.

The source language also specifies a set of adjust contexts A and check contexts C. Each adjust context is determined by an evaluation context frame f (Sec. 4.2). They index $\widetilde{\textbf{adjust}}_A$ to determine how privileges are altered when evaluating in a particular context. Similarly, the check contexts correspond to program operations like function application. They index $\widetilde{\textbf{check}}_C$ to determine which privileges are needed to perform the operation.

Fig. 2 presents the type system. The judgment $\Xi; \Gamma; \Sigma \vdash e : T$ means that the expression e has type T in the lexical environment Γ and store typing Σ, when provided with the privileges Ξ. Based on the judgment, e is free to perform any of the effectful operations denoted by the privileges in Ξ. If the consistent privilege set contains the unknown privileges ¿, then e might also try any other effectful operation, but at runtime a check for the necessary privileges is performed.

Each type rule extends the standard formulation with operations to account for effects. All notions of gradual checking are encapsulated in consistent effect sets Ξ and operations on them. The [T-Fn] rule associates some sufficient set of privileges with the body of the function. In practice we can deduce a minimal set to avoid spurious checks.

The [T-App] rule illustrates the structure of the non-value typing rules. It enhances the M&M typing rule for function application (similar to [T-Asgn] in Sec. 2.4) to support gradual effects. In particular, each privilege check from the original rule is replaced with a *consistent* counterpart: consistent predicates succeed as long as the consistent privilege sets represent some plausible concrete privilege set, and consistent functions represent information about what is possible in their resulting consistent set. $\widetilde{\textbf{adjust}}$ and $\widetilde{\textbf{check}}$ are defined in Sec. 3, and we use the same techniques introduced there to lift effect subtyping to a notion of *consistent subtyping*. To do so, we first lift traditional privilege set containment to *consistent containment*:

Definition 7 (Consistent Containment). Ξ_1 *is* consistently contained *in* Ξ_2, *notation* $\Xi_1 \mathrel{\widetilde{\sqsubseteq}} \Xi_2$ *if and only if* $\Phi_1 \subseteq \Phi_2$ *for* some $\Phi_1 \in \gamma(\Phi_1)$ *and* $\Phi_2 \in \gamma(\Xi_2)$[8].

[8] We give $\widetilde{\sqsubseteq}$ a simple direct characterization in Sec. 4.2.

$$\boxed{\Xi; \Gamma; \Sigma \vdash e\colon T}$$

$$\text{T-Fn}\;\frac{\Xi_1; \Gamma, x\colon T_1; \Sigma \vdash e\colon T_2}{\Xi; \Gamma; \Sigma \vdash (\lambda x\colon T_1\,.\,e)_\varepsilon : \{\varepsilon\}T_1 \xrightarrow{\Xi_1} T_2}$$

$$\text{T-Unit}\;\frac{}{\Xi; \Gamma; \Sigma \vdash \texttt{unit}_\varepsilon : \{\varepsilon\}\texttt{Unit}}$$

$$\text{T-Loc}\;\frac{\Sigma(l) = T}{\Xi; \Gamma; \Sigma \vdash l_\varepsilon\colon \{\varepsilon\}\texttt{Ref}\;T} \qquad \text{T-Var}\;\frac{\Gamma(x) = T}{\Xi; \Gamma; \Sigma \vdash x\colon T}$$

$$\text{T-App}\;\frac{\begin{array}{c}\widetilde{\textbf{adjust}}_{\downarrow\uparrow}(\Xi)\,; \Gamma; \Sigma \vdash e_1\colon \pi_1(T_1 \xrightarrow{\Xi_1} T_3) \\ \widetilde{\textbf{adjust}}_{\pi_1\downarrow}(\Xi)\,; \Gamma; \Sigma \vdash e_2\colon \pi_2\rho_2 \\ \pi_1(T_1 \xrightarrow{\Xi_1} T_3) \lesssim \pi_1(\pi_2\rho_2 \xrightarrow{\Xi} T_3) \quad \widetilde{\textbf{check}}_{\pi_1\pi_2}(\Xi)\end{array}}{\Xi; \Gamma; \Sigma \vdash e_1\;e_2\colon T_3}$$

$$\text{T-Eff}\;\frac{\Xi_1; \Gamma; \Sigma \vdash e\colon T \quad \Xi_1 \mathrel{\widetilde{\sqsubseteq}} \Xi}{\Xi; \Gamma; \Sigma \vdash (e :: \Xi_1) : T}$$

$$\text{T-Ref}\;\frac{\begin{array}{c}\widetilde{\textbf{adjust}}_{\texttt{ref}\downarrow}(\Xi)\,; \Gamma; \Sigma \vdash e\colon \pi\rho \\ \widetilde{\textbf{check}}_{\texttt{ref}\;\pi}(\Xi)\end{array}}{\Xi; \Gamma; \Sigma \vdash (\texttt{ref}\;e)_\varepsilon : \{\varepsilon\}\texttt{Ref}\;\pi\rho}$$

$$\text{T-Deref}\;\frac{\begin{array}{c}\widetilde{\textbf{adjust}}_{!\downarrow}(\Xi)\,; \Gamma; \Sigma \vdash e\colon \pi\texttt{Ref}\;T \\ \widetilde{\textbf{check}}_{!\pi}(\Xi)\end{array}}{\Xi; \Gamma; \Sigma \vdash !e\colon T}$$

$$\text{T-Asgn}\;\frac{\begin{array}{c}\widetilde{\textbf{adjust}}_{\downarrow:=\uparrow}(\Xi)\,; \Gamma; \Sigma \vdash e_1\colon \pi_1\texttt{Ref}\;T_1 \\ \widetilde{\textbf{adjust}}_{\pi_1:=\downarrow}(\Xi)\,; \Gamma; \Sigma \vdash e_2\colon \pi_2\rho_2 \\ \widetilde{\textbf{check}}_{\pi_1:=\pi_2}(\Xi) \qquad \pi_2\rho_2 \lesssim T_1\end{array}}{\Xi; \Gamma; \Sigma \vdash (e_1 := e_2)_\varepsilon : \{\varepsilon\}\texttt{Unit}}$$

Figure 2. Type system for the source language

Consistent containment means that privilege set containment may hold unless we guarantee that it cannot. Of course, this claim must sometimes be protected with a runtime check in the internal language, as discussed further in the next section. Consistent subtyping $\lesssim$ is defined by replacing the privilege subset premise of traditional effect subtyping with consistent containment.

$$\frac{\pi_1 \subseteq \pi_2}{\pi_1\rho \lesssim \pi_2\rho} \qquad \frac{\begin{array}{cc}T_3 \lesssim T_1 & T_2 \lesssim T_4 \\ \pi_1 \subseteq \pi_2 & \Xi_1 \mathrel{\widetilde{\sqsubseteq}} \Xi_2\end{array}}{\pi_1 T_1 \xrightarrow{\Xi_1} T_2 \lesssim \pi_2 T_3 \xrightarrow{\Xi_2} T_4}$$

This relation expresses plausible substitutability. Consistent containment is not transitive, and as a result neither is consistent subtyping. This property is directly analogous to consistent subtyping for gradual object systems [22].

All other rules in the type system can be characterized as consistent liftings of the corresponding M&M rules. Each uses $\widetilde{\textbf{adjust}}_A$ to type subexpressions, and $\widetilde{\textbf{check}}_C$ to check privileges.

Finally, [T-Eff] reflects the consistent counterpart of static effect ascriptions, which do not appear in the M&M system. The rule requires that the ascribed consistent privileges be consistently contained in the current consistent privileges. Ascribing ¿ delays some privilege checks to runtime, as discussed next.

4.2 The Internal Language

The semantics of the source language is given by a type-directed translation to an internal language that makes runtime checks ex-

$$
\begin{array}{llll}
e & ::= & \ldots \mid \mathsf{Error} \mid \langle T \Leftarrow T \rangle e & \text{Terms} \\
 & & \mid \mathtt{has}\ \Phi\ e \mid \mathtt{restrict}\ \Xi\ e & \\
f & ::= & \square\, e \mid v\, \square \mid (\mathtt{ref}\ \square)_{\varepsilon} & \text{Frames} \\
 & & \mid !\square \mid (\square := e)_{\varepsilon} \mid (w_{\varepsilon} := \square)_{\varepsilon} & \\
g & ::= & f \mid \langle T_2 \Leftarrow T_1 \rangle \square \mid \mathtt{has}\ \Phi\ \square & \text{Error Frames} \\
 & & \mid \mathtt{restrict}\ \Xi\ \square &
\end{array}
$$

Figure 3. Syntax of the internal language

$\boxed{\Xi; \Gamma; \Sigma \vdash e : T}$

$$
\text{IT-App}\ \frac{\begin{array}{c}\widetilde{\mathbf{adjust}}_{\downarrow\uparrow}(\Xi)\,; \Gamma; \Sigma \vdash e_1 : \pi_1(T_1 \xrightarrow{\Xi_1} T_3) \\ \widetilde{\mathbf{adjust}}_{\pi_1\downarrow}(\Xi)\,; \Gamma; \Sigma \vdash e_2 : \pi_2\rho_2 \\ \textbf{\textit{strict-check}}_{\pi_1\pi_2}(\Xi) \qquad \pi_1 T_1 \xrightarrow{\Xi_1} T_3 <: \pi_1\pi_2\rho_2 \xrightarrow{\Xi} T_3\end{array}}{\Xi; \Gamma; \Sigma \vdash e_1\, e_2 : T_3}
$$

$$
\text{IT-Cast}\ \frac{\Xi; \Gamma; \Sigma \vdash e : T_0 \qquad T_0 <: T_1 \qquad T_1 \lesssim T_2}{\Xi; \Gamma; \Sigma \vdash \langle T_2 \Leftarrow T_1 \rangle e : T_2}
$$

$$
\text{IT-Has}\ \frac{(\Phi \cup \Xi); \Gamma; \Sigma \vdash e : T}{\Xi; \Gamma; \Sigma \vdash \mathtt{has}\ \Phi\ e : T} \qquad \text{IT-Error}\ \frac{}{\Xi; \Gamma; \Sigma \vdash \mathsf{Error} : T}
$$

$$
\text{IT-Rst}\ \frac{\Xi_1; \Gamma; \Sigma \vdash e : T \qquad \Xi_1 \leq \Xi}{\Xi; \Gamma; \Sigma \vdash \mathtt{restrict}\ \Xi_1\ e : T}
$$

$$
\text{IT-Ref}\ \frac{\begin{array}{c}\widetilde{\mathbf{adjust}}_{\mathtt{ref}\,\downarrow}(\Xi)\,; \Gamma; \Sigma \vdash e : \pi\rho \\ \textbf{\textit{strict-check}}_{\mathtt{ref}\ \pi}(\Xi)\end{array}}{\Xi; \Gamma; \Sigma \vdash (\mathtt{ref}\ e)_{\varepsilon} : \{\varepsilon\}\mathtt{Ref}\ \pi\rho}
$$

$$
\text{IT-Deref}\ \frac{\begin{array}{c}\widetilde{\mathbf{adjust}}_{!\downarrow}(\Xi)\,; \Gamma; \Sigma \vdash e : \pi\mathtt{Ref}\ T \\ \textbf{\textit{strict-check}}_{!\pi}(\Xi)\end{array}}{\Xi; \Gamma; \Sigma \vdash !e : T}
$$

$$
\text{IT-Asgn}\ \frac{\begin{array}{c}\widetilde{\mathbf{adjust}}_{\downarrow:=\uparrow}(\Xi)\,; \Gamma; \Sigma \vdash e_1 : \pi_1\mathtt{Ref}\ T_1 \\ \widetilde{\mathbf{adjust}}_{\pi_1:=\downarrow}(\Xi)\,; \Gamma; \Sigma \vdash e_2 : \pi_2\rho_2 \\ \textbf{\textit{strict-check}}_{\pi_1:=\pi_2}(\Xi) \qquad \pi_2\rho_2 <: T_1\end{array}}{\Xi; \Gamma; \Sigma \vdash (e_1 := e_2)_{\varepsilon} : \{\varepsilon\}\mathtt{Unit}}
$$

Figure 4. Typing rules for the internal language

plicit. This section presents the internal language. The translation is presented in Sec. 4.3.

Fig. 3 presents the syntax of the internal language. It extends the source language with explicit features for managing runtime effect checks. The Error construct indicates that a runtime effect check failed, and aborts the rest of the computation. Casts $\langle T \Leftarrow T \rangle e$ express type coercions between consistent types. The `has` operation checks for the availability of particular effect privileges at runtime. The `restrict` operation restricts the privileges available while evaluating its subexpression.

Frames represent evaluation contexts in our small-step semantics. By using frames, we present a system with structural semantics like the M&M framework while defining fewer evaluation rules as in a reduction semantics.

Static semantics The type system of the internal language (Fig. 4) mostly extends the surface language type system, with a few critical differences. First, recall that type rules for source language operators, like function application [T-App], verify effects based on *consistent* checking: so long as some representative privilege set is checkable, the expression is accepted. In contrast, the internal language introduces new typing rules for these operators, like [IT-App] (changes highlighted in gray).

In the internal language, effectful operations *must* have enough privileges to be performed: plausibility is not sufficient anymore. As we see in the next section, consistent checks from source programs are either resolved statically or rely on runtime privilege checks to guarantee satisfaction before reaching an effectful operation. For this reason, uses of $\widetilde{\textbf{check}}$ are replaced with ***strict-check*** (Sec. 3.3, Def. 4). Consistent subtyping $\lesssim$ is replaced with a notion of subtyping $<:$ that is based on ordinary set containment for consistent privilege sets and tags:

$$
\frac{\pi_1 \subseteq \pi_2}{\pi_1\rho <: \pi_2\rho} \qquad \frac{\begin{array}{cc} T_3 <: T_1 & T_2 <: T_4 \\ \pi_1 \subseteq \pi_2 & \Xi_1 \subseteq \Xi_2 \end{array}}{\pi_1 T_1 \xrightarrow{\Xi_1} T_2 <: \pi_2 T_3 \xrightarrow{\Xi_2} T_4}
$$

The intuition is that an expression that can be typed with a given set of consistent permissions should still be typable if additional permissions become available. We formalize this intuition below.

In addition to ordinary set containment, the internal language depends on a stronger notion of containment that focuses on statically known permissions. A consistent privilege set represents some number of concrete privilege sets, each containing some different privileges, but most consistent privilege sets have some reliable information. For instance, any set represented by $\Xi = \{\mathtt{read}, ?\}$ may have a variety of privileges, but any such set will surely contain the `read` privilege. We formalize this idea in terms of concretization as the *static part* of a consistent privilege set.

Definition 8 (Static Part). *The* static part *of a consistent privilege set,* $|\cdot|$: **CPrivSet** $\to$ **PrivSet** *is defined as*

$$
|\Xi| = \bigcap \gamma(\Xi).
$$

The definition directly embodies the intuition of "all reliable information," but this operation also has a simple direct characterization: $|\Xi| = \Xi \setminus \{¿\}$.[9]

Using the notion of static part, we define the concept of *static containment* for consistent privilege sets.

Definition 9 (Static Containment). Ξ_1 *is* statically contained *in* Ξ_2, *notation* $\Xi_1 \leq \Xi_2$, *if and only if* $|\Xi_1| \subseteq |\Xi_2|$.

The intuition behind static containment is that an expression can be safely used in any context that is guaranteed to provide at least its statically-known privilege requirements.

We need static containment to help us characterize effect subsumption in the internal language. Privilege subsumption says that if Φ is sufficient to type e, then so can any larger set Φ' [25]. To establish this, we must consider properties of both ***strict-check*** and $\widetilde{\textbf{adjust}}$. Conveniently, ***strict-check*** is monotonic with respect to consistent privilege set containment.

Lemma 3.
If ***strict-check***$_C(\Xi_1)$ *and* $\Xi_1 \subseteq \Xi_2$ *then* ***strict-check***$_C(\Xi_2)$.

To the contrary, though, $\widetilde{\textbf{adjust}}$ is not monotonic with respect to set containment on consistent privilege sets. Instead, it *is* monotonic with respect to static containment.

Lemma 4. *If* $\Xi_1 \leq \Xi_2$ *then* $\widetilde{\textbf{adjust}}_C(\Xi_1) \leq \widetilde{\textbf{adjust}}_C(\Xi_2)$

We exploit this to establish effect subsumption.

[9] The γ-based definition is useful for proving Strong Effect Subsumption (Prop. 5 below).

$$\text{E-Ref}\;\frac{\textbf{check}_{\texttt{ref}\ \{\varepsilon_1\}}(\Phi) \qquad l \notin \mathrm{dom}\,(\mu)}{\Phi \vdash (\texttt{ref}\ w_{\varepsilon_1})_{\varepsilon_2} \mid \mu \rightarrow l_{\varepsilon_2} \mid \mu[l \mapsto w_{\varepsilon_1}]} \qquad \text{E-Asgn}\;\frac{\textbf{check}_{\{\varepsilon_1\}:=\{\varepsilon_2\}}(\Phi)}{\Phi \vdash (l_{\varepsilon_1} := w_{\varepsilon_2})_{\varepsilon} \mid \mu \rightarrow \textbf{unit}_{\varepsilon} \mid \mu[l \mapsto w_{\varepsilon_2}]}$$

$$\text{E-Deref}\;\frac{\textbf{check}_{!\{\varepsilon\}}(\Phi) \qquad \mu(l) = v}{\Phi \vdash !l_{\varepsilon} \mid \mu \rightarrow v \mid \mu} \qquad \text{E-Frame}\;\frac{\textbf{adjust}_{A(f)}(\Phi) \vdash e \mid \mu \rightarrow e' \mid \mu'}{\Phi \vdash f[e] \mid \mu \rightarrow f[e'] \mid \mu'} \qquad \text{E-Error}\;\frac{}{\Phi \vdash g[\mathsf{Error}] \mid \mu \rightarrow \mathsf{Error} \mid \mu}$$

$$\text{E-Has-T}\;\frac{\Phi' \subseteq \Phi \qquad \Phi \vdash e \mid \mu \rightarrow e' \mid \mu'}{\Phi \vdash \texttt{has}\ \Phi'\ e \mid \mu \rightarrow \texttt{has}\ \Phi'\ e' \mid \mu'} \qquad \text{E-Has-V}\;\frac{}{\Phi \vdash \texttt{has}\ \Phi'\ v \mid \mu \rightarrow v \mid \mu} \qquad \text{E-Has-F}\;\frac{\Phi' \not\subseteq \Phi}{\Phi \vdash \texttt{has}\ \Phi'\ e \mid \mu \rightarrow \mathsf{Error} \mid \mu}$$

$$\text{E-Rst-V}\;\frac{}{\Phi \vdash \texttt{restrict}\ \Xi\ v \mid \mu \rightarrow v \mid \mu} \qquad \text{E-Rst}\;\frac{\Phi'' = \max\{\Phi' \in \gamma(\Xi) \mid \Phi' \subseteq \Phi\} \qquad \Phi'' \vdash e \mid \mu \rightarrow e' \mid \mu'}{\Phi \vdash \texttt{restrict}\ \Xi\ e \mid \mu \rightarrow \texttt{restrict}\ \Xi\ e' \mid \mu'}$$

$$\text{E-App}\;\frac{\textbf{check}_{\{\varepsilon_1\}\{\varepsilon_2\}}(\Phi)}{\Phi \vdash (\lambda x\colon T_1\,.\,e)_{\varepsilon_1}\ w_{\varepsilon_2} \mid \mu \rightarrow [{}^{w_{\varepsilon_2}}/x]\,e \mid \mu} \qquad \text{E-Cast-Frame}\;\frac{\Phi \vdash e \mid \mu \rightarrow e' \mid \mu'}{\Phi \vdash \langle T_2 \Leftarrow T_1\rangle e \mid \mu \rightarrow \langle T_2 \Leftarrow T_1\rangle e' \mid \mu'} \qquad \text{E-Cast-Id}\;\frac{\varepsilon \in \pi_1 \qquad \pi_1 \subseteq \pi_2}{\Phi \vdash \langle \pi_2\rho \Leftarrow \pi_1\rho\rangle w_{\varepsilon} \mid \mu \rightarrow w_{\varepsilon} \mid \mu}$$

$$\text{E-Cast-Fn}\;\frac{\varepsilon \in \pi_1 \qquad \pi_1 \subseteq \pi_2}{\Phi \vdash \langle \pi_2 T_{21} \xrightarrow{\Xi_2} T_{22} \Leftarrow \pi_1 T_{11} \xrightarrow{\Xi_1} T_{12}\rangle\,(\lambda x\colon T_{11}\,.\,e)_{\varepsilon} \mid \mu \rightarrow (\lambda x\colon T_{21}\,.\,\langle T_{22} \Leftarrow T_{12}\rangle \texttt{restrict}\ \Xi_2\ \texttt{has}\ (|\Xi_1| \setminus |\Xi_2|)\ [{}^{(\langle T_{11} \Leftarrow T_{21}\rangle x)}/x]\,e)_{\varepsilon} \mid \mu}$$

Figure 5. Small-step semantics of the internal language

Proposition 5 (Strong Effect Subsumption).
If $\Xi_1; \Gamma; \Sigma \vdash e\colon T$ *and* $\Xi_1 \leq \Xi_2$*, then* $\Xi_2; \Gamma; \Sigma \vdash e\colon T$.

Proof. By induction over the typing derivations $\Xi_1; \Gamma; \Sigma \vdash e\colon T$. □

Corollary 6 (Effect Subsumption).
If $\Xi_1; \Gamma; \Sigma \vdash e\colon T$ *and* $\Xi_1 \subseteq \Xi_2$*, then* $\Xi_2; \Gamma; \Sigma \vdash e\colon T$.

Proof. Set containment implies static containment. □

We now turn to the new syntactic forms of the internal language. Casts represent explicit dynamic checks for consistent subtyping relationships. The `has` operator checks if the privileges in Φ are currently available. Its subexpression e is typed using the consistent set that is extended statically with Φ.[10]

The `restrict` operator constrains its subexpression to be typable in a consistent privilege set that is statically-contained in the current set. Since ¿ does not play a role in static containment, the set Ξ_1 can introduce dynamism that was not present in Ξ. As we will see when we translate source programs, this is key to how ascription can introduce more dynamism into a program.

As it happens, we can use notions from this section to simply characterize notions that we, for reasons of conceptual clarity, defined using the concretization function and collections of plausible privilege sets. The concretization-based definitions clearly formalize our intentions, but these new extensionally equivalent characterizations are well suited to efficient implementation.

First, we can characterize consistent containment as an extension of static containment, and strict checking as simply checking the statically known part of a consistent privilege set.

Proposition 7.

1. $\Xi_1 \mathrel{\underset{\sim}{\sqsubseteq}} \Xi_2$ *if and only if* $\Xi_1 \subseteq \Xi_2$ *or* ¿ $\in \Xi_2$.
2. ***strict-check***$_C(\Xi)$ *if and only if* $\textbf{check}_C(|\Xi|)$.

[10] Note that $\Phi \cup \Xi$ is the same as lifting the function $f(\Phi') = \Phi \cup \Phi'$, and $\Phi \mathrel{\underset{\sim}{\sqsubseteq}} \Xi$ is the same as lifting the predicate $P(\Phi') = \Phi \subseteq \Phi'$.

Furthermore, we can characterize consistent checking based on whether the consistent privilege set in question contains unknown privileges.

Proposition 8.

1. *If* ¿ $\in \Xi$ *then* $\widetilde{\textbf{check}}_C(\Xi)$ *if and only if* $\textbf{check}_C(\textbf{PrivSet})$.
2. *If* ¿ $\notin \Xi$ *then* $\widetilde{\textbf{check}}_C(\Xi)$ *if and only if* $\textbf{check}_C(\Xi)$.

Dynamic semantics Fig. 5 presents the evaluation rules of the internal language. The judgment $\Phi \vdash e \mid \mu \rightarrow e' \mid \mu'$ means that under the privilege set Φ and store μ, the expression e takes a step to e' and μ'. Effectful constructs consult Φ to determine whether they have sufficient privileges to proceed.

The `has` expression checks dynamically for privileges. If the privileges in Φ are available, then execution may proceed: if not, then an Error is thrown. Note that in a real implementation, `has` only needs to check for privileges once: the semantics keeps `has` around only to support our type safety proof.

The `restrict` expression restricts the privileges available in the dynamic extent of the current subexpression. The intuition is as follows. Ξ represents any number of privilege sets. At least one of those sets must be contained in Φ or the program gets stuck: `restrict` cannot add new privileges. So `restrict` limits its subexpression to the largest subset of currently available privileges that Ξ can represent. In practice, this means that if Ξ is fully static, then Ξ represents only one subset Φ' of Φ and the subexpression can only use those privileges. If ¿ $\in \Xi$, then Ξ can represent *all* of Φ, so the privilege set is not restricted at all. This property of `restrict` enables ascription to support dynamic privileges.

Since function application is controlled under some effect disciplines, the [E-App] rule is guarded by the $\textbf{check}_{\text{app}}$ predicate inherited from the M&M framework. If this check fails, then the program is stuck. More generally, any effectful operation added to the framework is guarded by such a check. These checks are needed to give intensional meaning to our type safety theorem: if programs never get stuck, then any effectful operation that is encountered must have the proper privileges to run. This implies that either the permissions were statically inferred by the type checker, or the operation is guarded by a `has` expression, which throws an Error if needed privileges are not available. It also means that thanks to type safety, an actual implementation would not need *any* of the $\mathbf{check}_C$ checks: the `has` checks suffice. This supports the pay-as-you-go principle of gradual checking.

Higher-order casts incrementally verify at runtime that consistent subtyping really implies privilege set containment. In particular they guard function calls. First, they restrict the set of available privileges to detect privilege inconsistencies in the function body. Then, they check the resulting privilege set for the minimal privileges needed to validate the containment relationship. Intuitively, we only need to check for the statically determined permissions that are not already accounted for.

To illustrate, consider the following example: $\{\texttt{read}, \texttt{alloc}\} \mathrel{\widetilde{\sqsubseteq}} \{\texttt{read}, ¿\}$ because `alloc` *could* be in a representative of $\{\texttt{read}, ¿\}$, but $\{\texttt{read}, \texttt{alloc}\} \not\sqsubseteq \{\texttt{read}, ¿\}$ since that is not definitely true. Thus, to be sure at runtime, we must check for $|\{\texttt{read}, \texttt{alloc}\}| \setminus |\{\texttt{read}, ¿\}| = \{\texttt{alloc}\}$. Note that the rule [E-Cast-Fn] uses the standard approach to higher-order casts due to Findler and Felleisen [8]. As a formalization convenience, the rule uses substitution directly rather than function application so as to protect the implementation internals from effect checks and adjustments. In practice the internal language would simply use function application without checking or adjusting privileges.

Type safety We prove type safety in the style of Wright and Felleisen [27]. Program execution begins with a closed term e as well as an initial privilege set Φ. The initial program must be well typed and the privilege set must be represented by the consistent privilege set Ξ used to type the program. Under these conditions, the program will not get stuck.

Our statements of Progress and Preservation introduce the representation restrictions between consistent privilege sets and the privilege sets used as contexts for evaluation. These restrictions can be summarized in that typing ensures that evaluation does not get stuck in any particular context represented statically.[11]

Theorem 9 (Progress). *Suppose $\Xi; \emptyset; \Sigma \vdash e : T$. Then either e is a value v, an* Error, *or $\Phi \vdash e \mid \mu \to e' \mid \mu'$ for all privilege sets $\Phi \in \gamma(\Xi)$ and for any store μ such that $\emptyset \mid \Sigma \vdash \mu$.*

Proof. By structural induction over derivations of $\Xi; \emptyset; \Sigma \vdash e : T$. □

Theorem 10 (Preservation). *If $\Xi; \Gamma; \Sigma \vdash e : T$, and $\Phi \vdash e \mid \mu \to e' \mid \mu'$ for $\Phi \in \gamma(\Xi)$ and $\Gamma \mid \Sigma \vdash \mu$, then $\Gamma \mid \Sigma' \vdash \mu'$ and $\Xi; \Gamma; \Sigma' \vdash e' : T'$ for some $T' <: T$ and $\Sigma' \supseteq \Sigma$.*

Proof. By structural induction over the typing derivation. Preservation of types under substitution for values (required for [E-App]) and for identifiers (required for [E-Cast-Fn]) follows as a standard proof since neither performs effects. □

4.3 Translating Source Programs to the Internal Language

Fig. 6 presents the type-directed translation of source programs to the internal language (the interesting parts have been highlighted). The translation uses static type and effect information from the source program to determine where runtime checks are needed in the corresponding internal language program. In particular, any consistent check, containment, or subtyping that is not also a strict check, static containment, or static subtyping, respectively, must be guarded by a `has` expression (for checks and containments) or a cast (for subtypings).

Recall from Sec. 4.2 that the `has` expression checks if some particular privileges are available at runtime. The translation system determines for each program point which privileges (if any)

[11] We also proved soundness for a minimal system with neither tags nor state.

$$\boxed{\Xi; \Gamma; \Sigma \vdash e \Rightarrow e : T}$$

$$\text{C-Fn}\ \frac{\Xi_1; \Gamma, x : T_1; \Sigma \vdash e \Rightarrow e' : T_2}{\Xi; \Gamma; \Sigma \vdash (\lambda x : T_1 \,.\, e)_\varepsilon \Rightarrow (\lambda x : T_1 \,.\, e')_\varepsilon : \{\varepsilon\}T_1 \xrightarrow{\Xi_1} T_2}$$

$$\text{C-Unit}\ \frac{}{\Xi; \Gamma; \Sigma \vdash \texttt{unit}_\varepsilon \Rightarrow \texttt{unit}_\varepsilon : \{\varepsilon\}\texttt{Unit}}$$

$$\text{C-Var}\ \frac{\Gamma(x) = T}{\Xi; \Gamma; \Sigma \vdash x \Rightarrow x : T}$$

$$\text{C-Loc}\ \frac{\Sigma(l) = T}{\Xi; \Gamma; \Sigma \vdash l_\varepsilon \Rightarrow l_\varepsilon : \{\varepsilon\}\texttt{Ref}\ T}$$

$$\text{C-App}\ \frac{\begin{array}{c} \widetilde{\mathbf{adjust}}_{\downarrow\uparrow}(\Xi)\,; \Gamma; \Sigma \vdash e_1 \Rightarrow e_1' : \pi_1(T_1 \xrightarrow{\Xi_1} T_3) \\ \widetilde{\mathbf{adjust}}_{\pi_1\downarrow}(\Xi)\,; \Gamma; \Sigma \vdash e_2 \Rightarrow e_2' : \pi_2\rho_2 \\ e''_1 = (\ \langle\langle \pi_1(\pi_2\rho_2 \xrightarrow{\Xi} T_3) \Leftarrow \pi_1(T_1 \xrightarrow{\Xi_1} T_3)\rangle\rangle\ e_1') \\ \pi_1(T_1 \xrightarrow{\Xi_1} T_3) \lesssim \pi_1(\pi_2\rho_2 \xrightarrow{\Xi} T_3) \\ \widetilde{\mathbf{check}}_{\pi_1\pi_2}(\Xi) \qquad \Phi = \Delta_{\pi_1\pi_2}(\Xi) \end{array}}{\Xi; \Gamma; \Sigma \vdash e_1\ e_2 \Rightarrow \textit{insert-has?}(\Phi, e''_1\ e_2') : T_3}$$

$$\text{C-Eff}\ \frac{\Xi_1; \Gamma; \Sigma \vdash e \Rightarrow e' : T \qquad \Xi_1 \mathrel{\widetilde{\sqsubseteq}} \Xi \qquad \Phi = (|\Xi_1| \setminus |\Xi|)}{\Xi; \Gamma; \Sigma \vdash (e :: \Xi_1) \Rightarrow \textit{insert-has?}(\Phi, \texttt{restrict}\ \Xi_1\ e') : T}$$

$$\text{C-Ref}\ \frac{\begin{array}{c} \widetilde{\mathbf{adjust}}_{\texttt{ref}\,\downarrow}(\Xi)\,; \Gamma; \Sigma \vdash e \Rightarrow e' : \pi\rho \\ \widetilde{\mathbf{check}}_{\texttt{ref}\ \pi}(\Xi) \qquad \Phi = \Delta_{\texttt{ref}\ \pi}(\Xi) \end{array}}{\Xi; \Gamma; \Sigma \vdash (\texttt{ref}\ e)_\varepsilon \Rightarrow \textit{insert-has?}(\Phi, (\texttt{ref}\ e')_\varepsilon) : \{\varepsilon\}\texttt{Ref}\ \pi\rho}$$

$$\text{C-Deref}\ \frac{\begin{array}{c} \widetilde{\mathbf{adjust}}_{!\downarrow}(\Xi)\,; \Gamma; \Sigma \vdash e \Rightarrow e' : \pi\texttt{Ref}\ T \\ \widetilde{\mathbf{check}}_{!\pi}(\Xi) \qquad \Phi = \Delta_{!\pi}(\Xi) \end{array}}{\Xi; \Gamma; \Sigma \vdash !e \Rightarrow \textit{insert-has?}(\Phi, !e') : T}$$

$$\text{C-Asgn}\ \frac{\begin{array}{c} \widetilde{\mathbf{adjust}}_{\downarrow:=\uparrow}(\Xi)\,; \Gamma; \Sigma \vdash e_1 \Rightarrow e_1' : \pi_1\texttt{Ref}\ T_1 \\ \widetilde{\mathbf{adjust}}_{\pi_1:=\downarrow}(\Xi)\,; \Gamma; \Sigma \vdash e_2 \Rightarrow e_2' : \pi_2\rho_2 \\ \widetilde{\mathbf{check}}_{\pi_1:=\pi_2}(\Xi) \qquad \pi_2\rho_2 \lesssim T_1 \qquad \Phi = \Delta_{\pi_1:=\pi_2}(\Xi) \end{array}}{\Xi; \Gamma; \Sigma \vdash (e_1 := e_2)_\varepsilon \Rightarrow \textit{insert-has?}(\Phi, (e_1' := e_2')_\varepsilon) : \{\varepsilon\}\texttt{Unit}}$$

Figure 6. Translation of source programs to the internal language

must be checked. Since the generic framework imposes only privilege and tag monotonicity restrictions on the **check** and **adjust** functions, deducing these checks can be subtle.

Consider a hypothetical check predicate for a mutable state effect discipline:

$$\mathbf{check}_C(\Phi) \iff \texttt{read} \in \Phi \text{ or } \texttt{write} \in \Phi.$$

Though strange here, an effect discipline that is satisfied by one of two possible privileges is generally plausible, and in fact satisfies the monotonicity restrictions. When, say, the consistent check $\widetilde{\mathbf{check}}_C(\{¿\})$ succeeds in some program, which privileges should be checked at runtime?

The key insight is that the internal language program must check for all privileges that can produce a minimal satisfying privilege set.

In the case of the above example, we must conservatively check for *both* **read** and **write**. However, we do not need to check for any privileges that are already known to be statically available.

We formalize this general idea as follows. First, since we do not want to require and check for any more permissions than needed, we only consider all possible *minimal* privilege sets that satisfy the check. We isolate the minimal privilege sets using the *mins* function:

$$mins(\Upsilon) = \{\Phi \in \Upsilon \mid \forall \Phi' \in \Upsilon . \Phi' \not\subset \Phi\}.$$

Given some consistent privilege set Ξ, we identify all of its plausible privilege sets that satisfy a particular check, and select only the minimal ones. In many cases there is a unique minimal set, but as above, there may not.[12] To finish, we coalesce this collection of minimal privileges, and remove any that are already statically known to be available based on Ξ. These steps are combined in the following function.

Definition 10 (Minimal Privilege Check). *Let C be some checking context. Then define Δ_C :* **CPrivSet** $\rightarrow$ **PrivSet** *as follows:*

$$\Delta_C(\Xi) = \left(\bigcup mins(\{\Phi \in \gamma(\Xi) \mid \mathbf{check}_C(\Phi)\})\right) \setminus |\Xi|$$

The Δ_C function transforms a given consistent privilege set into the minimal conservative set of additional privileges needed to safely pass the $\mathbf{check}_C$ function. For instance, the [C-App] translation rule uses it to guard a function application, if need be, with a runtime privilege check. These checks are introduced by the *insert-has?* metafunction.

$$\textit{insert-has?}(\Phi, e) = \begin{cases} e & \text{if } \Phi = \emptyset \\ \texttt{has}\ \Phi\ e & \text{otherwise} \end{cases}$$

Note that the metafunction only inserts a check if needed. This supports the pay-as-you-go principle of gradual checking.

Since [C-App] also appeals to consistent subtyping, a cast may be introduced in the translation as well. For this, we appeal to a cast insertion metafunction:

$$\langle\langle T_2 \Leftarrow T_1 \rangle\rangle e = \begin{cases} e & \text{if } T_1 <: T_2 \\ \langle T_2 \Leftarrow T_1 \rangle e & \text{otherwise.} \end{cases}$$

Once again, casts are only inserted when static subtyping does not already hold.

The [C-Eff] rule translates effect ascription in the source language to the **restrict** form in the internal language. If more privileges are needed to ensure static containment between Ξ_1 and Ξ, then translation inserts a runtime **has** check to bridge the gap.[13]

Crucially, the translation system preserves typing.

Theorem 11 (Translation preserves typing). *If $\Xi; \Gamma; \Sigma \vdash e \Rightarrow e' : T$ in the source language then $\Xi; \Gamma; \Sigma \vdash e' : T$ in the internal language.*

Proof. By structural induction over the translation derivation rules. The proof relies on the fact that $\Delta_C(\Xi)$ introduces enough runtime checks (via *insert-has?*) that any related ***strict-check***$_C(\Xi)$ predicate is sure to succeed at runtime, so those rules do not get stuck. The instance of *insert-has?* in the [C-Eff] rule plays the same role there. □

[12] One could retain precision by extending our abstraction to support *disjunctions* of consistent effect sets, at the cost of increased complexity in the translation and type system.

[13] The formula for Φ is analogous to the Δ_C operation for $\mathbf{check}_C$.

$$\begin{array}{llll}
e & ::= & \ldots \mid \texttt{raise}\ s_T(e) & \text{Terms} \\
 & & \mid \texttt{try}\ e\ \texttt{handle}\ s_T(x)\ .\ e & \\
f & ::= & f' \mid \texttt{try}\ \square\ \texttt{handle}\ s_T\ e & \text{Source Frames} \\
f' & ::= & \textit{(Original Source Frames)} & \text{Propagating Frames} \\
 & & \mid \texttt{raise}\ s_T(\square) & \\
C & ::= & \ldots \mid \texttt{raise}\ s_T(\pi) & \text{Check Contexts} \\
 & & \mid \texttt{try}\ \pi\ \texttt{handle}\ s_T\ \uparrow & \\
A & ::= & \ldots \mid \texttt{raise}\ s_T(\downarrow) & \text{Adjust Contexts} \\
 & & \mid \texttt{try}\ \downarrow\ \texttt{handle}\ s_T\ \uparrow &
\end{array}$$

Figure 7. Syntax for a Gradual Effect System with Exceptions

$$\text{E-Raise-Frame}\ \frac{\mathbf{check}_{\texttt{raise}\ s_T(\{\bullet\})}(\Phi)}{\Phi \vdash f'[\texttt{raise}\ s_T(v)] \mid \mu \rightarrow \texttt{raise}\ s_T(v) \mid \mu}$$

$$\text{E-Try-V}\ \frac{\mathbf{check}_{\texttt{try}\ \{\bullet\}\ \texttt{handle}\ s_T \uparrow}(\Phi)}{\Phi \vdash \texttt{try}\ v\ \texttt{handle}\ s_T(x).e \mid \mu \rightarrow v \mid \mu}$$

$$\text{E-Try-T}\ \frac{\mathbf{check}_{\texttt{try}\ \emptyset\ \texttt{handle}\ s_T \uparrow}(\Phi)}{\Phi \vdash \texttt{try raise}\ s_T(v)\ \texttt{handle}\ s_T(x).e \mid \mu \rightarrow [v/x]\,e \mid \mu e}$$

E-Try-F

$$\frac{\mathbf{check}_{\texttt{raise}\ s_{T_1}(\{\bullet\})}(\Phi)}{\Phi \vdash \texttt{try raise}\ s_{T_1}(v)\ \texttt{handle}\ s_{T_2}(x).e \mid \mu \rightarrow \texttt{raise}\ s_{T_1}(v) \mid \mu}$$

Figure 8. Evaluation rules added to the operational semantics for a system with exceptions

5. Example: Gradual Effects for Exceptions

In this section we show how to use our framework to define systems with richer language features. We extend the language with exception handling and introduce an effect discipline that verifies that every raised exception is caught by some handler. We introduce new syntax; privilege and tag domains; adjust and check operations and contexts; and typing, translation, and evaluation rules. Note that the example system is general enough to allow different effect disciplines for exceptions.

The language introduces an infinite set of exception constructors s_T, which are indexed on the type T of argument that they carry as a payload. An exception is triggered by the **raise** $s_T(e)$ expression, which indicates that the expression e should be evaluated to a value of type T, wrapped in the exception constructor, and raised. An exception handler, **try** e_1 **handle** $s_T(x).e_2$, attempts to evaluate the expression e_1. If successful, its result is returned; if e_1 raises a s_T exception, it binds the payload to x and evaluates e_2.

We also introduce new adjust and check contexts. These contexts are used to parameterize different effect disciplines over the same constructs. They are used by the **adjust** and **check** functions in the operational semantics, by the type system and the translation algorithm. Following M&M, we define a new check context for each new redex and a new adjust context for each new evaluation frame.

Fig. 8 presents the semantics for exceptions in our system. Exceptions propagate out of evaluation frames by rule [E-Raise-Frame] until they are caught by a matching handler. Since handlers are also evaluation frames, we must distinguish the rest of the evaluation frames from handlers. As presented in Fig. 7, we call non-handler frames "Propagating Frames".

A **try** handler first reduces the guarded expression. If it is a value, the exception handler is discarded through rule [E-Try-V]. If

$$\frac{\widetilde{\textbf{adjust}}_{\texttt{raise}\ s_T(\downarrow)}(\Xi)\,;\Gamma;\Sigma \vdash e\colon T \qquad \widetilde{\textbf{check}}_{\texttt{raise}\ s_T(\{\bullet\})}(\Xi)}{\Xi;\Gamma;\Sigma \vdash \texttt{raise}\ s_T(e)\colon T'}$$

$$\frac{\widetilde{\textbf{adjust}}_{\texttt{try}\ \downarrow\texttt{handle}\ s_T\uparrow}(\Xi)\,;\Gamma;\Sigma \vdash e_1\colon T_1 \qquad \Xi;\Gamma,x\colon T;\Sigma \vdash e_2\colon T_2 \quad T_2 \lesssim T_1 \qquad \widetilde{\textbf{check}}_{\texttt{try}\ \{\bullet\}\texttt{handle}\ s_T\uparrow}(\Xi)}{\Xi;\Gamma;\Sigma \vdash \texttt{try}\ e_1\ \texttt{handle}\ s_T(x).e_2\colon T_1}$$

Figure 9. Source language typing rules for exceptions

the guarded expression reduces to an exception whose constructor matches the handler, rule [E-Try-T] substitutes the payload value in the handling expression. If the constructor does not match the handler, the exception is propagated by rule [E-Try-F], and the handler discarded.

Rule [E-Try-T] uses $\emptyset$ in the check context instead of a tagset because the guarded expression produced an exception instead of a value. The type system does not relate the type of the exception payload to the type of the guarded expression, so when **check** is evaluated it cannot access tag information related to the guarded expression. We followed the most conservative strategy for this case. Thanks to the tag monotonicity property, we know that **check** holds with $\emptyset$ if it holds for any particular π because $\texttt{try}\ \emptyset\ \texttt{handle}\ s_T\uparrow\ \sqsubseteq \texttt{try}\ \pi\ \texttt{handle}\ s_T\uparrow$.

The new source language typing rules are presented in Figure 9. The corresponding typing rules for the internal language follow the same pattern as for rules in the general framework: $\widetilde{\textbf{check}}$ is replaced by ***strict-check*** and $\lesssim$ is replaced by $<:$. In the translation system, the rules introduce Δ_C and *insert-has?*.

As presented so far, our gradual effect system with exceptions does not enforce any particular effect discipline. To do so, we need to define both a domain for privileges and concrete **check** and **adjust** functions. We instantiate privileges **Priv** to be the exception constructors (of the form s_T), and provide the following definitions for **check** and **adjust**, which capture the standard effect discipline for exceptions:

$$\textbf{check}_{\texttt{raise}\ s_T(\pi)}(\Phi) \iff s_T \in \Phi$$
$$\textbf{check}_C(\Phi) \text{ holds for all other } C$$

$$\textbf{adjust}_{\texttt{try}\ \downarrow\ \texttt{handle}\ s_T\ \uparrow}(\Phi) = \Phi \cup \{s_T\}$$
$$\textbf{adjust}_A(\Phi) = \Phi \text{ otherwise}$$

Note that this effect discipline does not require tags, so technically we use a singleton set for the universe of tags ($\varepsilon \in \{\bullet\}$). In practice the tags can be removed altogether.

Implementation With a concrete effect discipline, an instance of the general effect system can be specialized to produce concrete operational semantics, type system and translation algorithm rules, inlining the calls to **check** and **adjust**. Figure 10 presents specialized translation rules for the concrete discipline we have chosen. These rules directly incorporate the semantics of the *insert-has?* function, separating its two cases across two separate translation rules. Since the only non-trivial check context in the effect discipline is $\texttt{raise}\ s_T(\pi)$, we provide separate rules only for `raise` using the feasible values for $\Delta_{\texttt{raise}\ s_T(\pi)}$ in each case ($\emptyset$ or $\{s_T\}$).

Illustration By making the exception checking discipline gradual, we achieve a more expressive language. Consider the following function, which also uses conditionals and arithmetic expressions:

$$\frac{\Xi;\Gamma;\Sigma \vdash e \Rightarrow e'\colon T_1 \qquad \{s_{T_1}\} \subseteq \Xi}{\Xi;\Gamma;\Sigma \vdash \texttt{raise}\ s_{T_1}(e) \Rightarrow \texttt{raise}\ s_{T_1}(e')\colon T_2}$$

$$\frac{\Xi;\Gamma;\Sigma \vdash e \Rightarrow e'\colon T_1 \qquad \{s_{T_1}\} \not\subseteq \Xi \quad \{s_{T_1}\} \mathrel{\widetilde{\sqsubseteq}} \Xi}{\Xi;\Gamma;\Sigma \vdash \texttt{raise}\ s_{T_1}(e) \Rightarrow \texttt{has}\ \{s_{T_1}\}\ \texttt{raise}\ s_{T_1}(e')\colon T_2}$$

$$\frac{\Xi \cup \{s_T\};\Gamma;\Sigma \vdash e_1 \Rightarrow e_1'\colon T_1 \qquad \Xi;\Gamma,x\colon T;\Sigma \vdash e_2 \Rightarrow e_2'\colon T_2 \quad T_2 <: T_1 \qquad e' = \texttt{try}\ e_1'\ \texttt{handle}\ s_T(x).e_2'}{\Xi;\Gamma;\Sigma \vdash \texttt{try}\ e_1\ \texttt{handle}\ s_T(x).e_2 \Rightarrow e'\colon T_1}$$

Figure 10. Implementation version of the translation rules for a system with exceptions

$$\begin{array}{ll}\textbf{let} & squared = \lambda f\colon \texttt{Int} \xrightarrow{\Xi} \texttt{Int}\,.\,(\lambda x\colon \texttt{Int}\,.\,(f(x*x)) :: \emptyset) \\ & positive = \lambda x\colon \texttt{Int}\,.\,\texttt{if}\ x \geq 0\ \texttt{then}\ x\ \texttt{else}\ \texttt{raise}\ s_{\texttt{Int}}(x) \\ & \textbf{in}\ (squared\ positive)\end{array}$$

A key property of the *positive* function is that it never raises an exception when applied to a non-negative argument. On the other hand, function *squared* always calls f with $x * x$ as an argument, which is never negative. We therefore know that the function produced by evaluating $(squared\ positive)$ never raises an exception, so we would like to type it as $\texttt{Int} \xrightarrow{\emptyset} \texttt{Int}$. A static effect system is too restrictive to do so, but a gradual effect system provides the flexibility to assign the desired type to the function.

The *squared* function's parameter is declared to have type $\texttt{Int} \xrightarrow{\Xi} \texttt{Int}$, for some Ξ. Without gradual effects, the only options for Ξ are either $\Xi = \emptyset$, in which case the type system will reject the application$(squared\ positive)$ because the argument requires too many privileges, or $\{s_{\texttt{Int}}\} \subseteq \Xi$, which means the returned function cannot be typed as $\texttt{Int} \xrightarrow{\emptyset} \texttt{Int}$.

In the gradual exception system, we can annotate function *positive* to hide its side effects, delaying privilege checking to runtime, and annotate function *squared* to allow functions that may throw exceptions, as in the following:

$$\begin{array}{l}\textbf{let}\, squared = \lambda f\colon \texttt{Int} \xrightarrow{\{¿\}} \texttt{Int}\,.\,(\lambda x\colon \texttt{Int}\,.\,(f(x*x)) :: \emptyset) \\ \quad positive = \lambda x\colon \texttt{Int}\,.\,(\texttt{if}\ x \geq 0\ \texttt{then}\ x\ \texttt{else}\ \texttt{raise}\ s_{\texttt{Int}}(x)) :: \{¿\} \\ \quad \textbf{in}\ (squared\ positive)\end{array}$$

The translation algorithm then produces the following program in the intermediate language:

$$\begin{array}{lll}\textbf{let}\ squared & = & \lambda\, f\colon \texttt{Int} \xrightarrow{\{¿\}} \texttt{Int}. \\ & & \lambda\, x\colon \texttt{Int}. \\ & & \quad \texttt{restrict}\ \emptyset \\ & & \quad (((\langle \texttt{Int} \xrightarrow{\emptyset} \texttt{Int} \Leftarrow \texttt{Int} \xrightarrow{\{¿\}} \texttt{Int}\rangle f)(x*x))) \\ \quad positive & = & \lambda\, x\colon \texttt{Int}. \\ & & \quad \texttt{restrict}\ \{¿\} \\ & & \quad \texttt{if}\ x \geq 0 \\ & & \quad \texttt{then}\ x \\ & & \quad \texttt{else}\ \texttt{has}\ \{s_{\texttt{Int}}\}\ \texttt{raise}\ s_{\texttt{Int}}(x) \\ \textbf{in}\ (squared\ positive) & & \end{array}$$

In this program, application $(squared\ positive)$ can be typed as $\texttt{Int} \xrightarrow{\emptyset} \texttt{Int}$, as desired. Given the properties of integer numbers, the `else` branch in the body of *positive* will never be executed. The higher-order cast for f in the body of *squared* never fails because rule [E-Cast-Fn] only introduces $\texttt{restrict}\ \emptyset\ \texttt{has}\ \emptyset$checks.

Effect errors are not exceptions Gradual Effects for Exceptions is more expressive than simply raising uncaught exceptions. Triggering an Error instead of propagating the exception prevents the system from following implicit exceptional control flows, where an outer handler catches an exception that was locally forbidden. The following example demonstrates how this behavior can affect evaluation of a program:

let $positive = \lambda x\colon \texttt{Int}\,.\,(\texttt{if}\ x \geq 0\ \texttt{then}\ x\ \texttt{else raise}\ s_{\texttt{Int}}(x)) :: \{¿\}$
$nonzero = \lambda x\colon \texttt{Int}\,.\ \texttt{if}\ x = 0\ \texttt{raise}\ s_{\texttt{Int}}\ (x)\ \texttt{else}\ x$
in `try`
$nonzero\ ((positive\ -1) :: \emptyset)$
`handle` $s_{\texttt{Int}}(x)$
`print` "0 is an invalid argument"

The handler in the **let** body is designed to catch the exceptions thrown by the body of *nonzero*. To this end, the code uses an effect ascription to ensure that the argument to *nonzero* does not throw any exception.

At the same time, the program reuses the *positive* function introduced in the previous example, but applies the function to a negative number. Given this incorrect argument, *positive* attempts to raise an exception. An effect ascription to the $\emptyset$ privilege set forces the application to not raise any exception at all. This inconsistent behavior is caught at runtime by the gradual effect discipline.

We purposely used the same label for exceptions in *positive* and in *nonzero*. If the system simply threw the uncaught exception in *positive*, the handler would take control even though it was not designed for that exception. Instead, since *positive* has no exception raising privileges, the system triggers an Error just before it would have thrown the exception. Evaluation thus terminates without control ever reaching the exception handler, which was designed for failures of *nonzero* only.

6. Related Work

In the realm of effect systems, the most closely related work is the generic framework of Marino and Millstein [15], which we have extensively discussed in this paper, because we build upon it to formulate gradual effect checking in a generic setting.

Rytz *et al.* [17] develop a notion of lightweight effect polymorphism, which lets functions be polymorphic in the effects of their higher-order arguments. The formulation is also generic like the M&M framework, although there are more technical differences; most notably, the system is formulated to infer effects instead of checking privileges. An implementation of the generic polymorphic framework has been developed for Scala, originally only with IO and exceptions as effects. More recently, a purity analysis has been integrated in the compiler plugin [18]. The effect system has been applied to a number of Scala libraries. Interestingly, Rytz *et al.* report cases where they suffer from the conservativeness of the effect analysis, similar to the example of Sec. 2. To address this, Rytz recently introduced an `@unchecked` annotation. Although it is called a cast, it is an "unsafe cast", since no dynamic checking is associated to it; i.e. it is just a mechanism to bypass static checking. We believe our work on gradual effect checking could be of direct practical use in Scala, and intend to pursue that route.

While there is a long history in the area of combining static and dynamic checking, the gradual typing approach of Siek and Taha [23] has been particularly successful and triggered many developments. Its main contribution was to identify the notion of consistency as a key to support the full spectrum of static-to-dynamic typing. Originally developed for functional languages, it has been extended in several directions, including structural objects [22] and generics [14]. Most directly related to this work is the application of the gradual typing principles to other typing disciplines, such as ownership types, typestates, and information flow typing.

Wolff *et al.* [26] develop gradual typestate checking. Typestates reflect the changing states of objects in their types. To support flexible aliasing in the face of state change, the language provides access permissions to support rely-guarantee reasoning about aliases, and state guarantees, which preserve type information for distinct aliases of shared objects.

Sergey and Clarke propose gradual ownership types [21]. Like gradual typestates, gradual ownership expresses and dynamically tracks heap properties. While typestate focuses on objects changing state, ownership controls the flow of object references.

Disney and Flanagan [6] explore the idea of gradual security with a gradual information flow type system. Data can be marked as confidential, and the runtime system ensures that it is not leaked. This dynamically-checked discipline is moved towards the static end of the spectrum by introducing security labels on types.

Extensions to contract systems for higher-order functions [9], such as computational contracts [19, 20] and temporal contracts [7], have the ability to monitor for the occurrence of specific (sequences of) execution events, in particular effectful operations. These approaches rely on full runtime monitoring; it is not clear if they could be reconciled with the pay-as-you-go model of gradual checking.

As far as we know, none of the existing approaches to gradual checking relies on abstract interpretation to develop an account of uncertainty. While it remains to be studied, it seems that the abstract interpretation approach we follow here could be used to investigate existing and as-yet unexplored notions of gradual checking.

7. Conclusion

The primary contribution of this paper is a framework for developing gradually checked effect systems for any number of effect systems that can be couched in the M&M framework. Using our approach, one can systematically transform a static effect discipline into one that supports full static checking, full dynamic checking, and any intermediate blend. We believe that gradual effect checking can facilitate the process of migrating programs toward a statically checked effect discipline, as well as bringing dynamic effect checks to languages that have no such checks whatsoever, and leaving wiggle room for programs that can only partially fit an effect discipline. To empirically evaluate this claim, we intend to implement our framework in the Scala language, and extend it to support the effect features that the language already provides.

Initially, we relied on the principles of gradual checking and our intuitions to guide the design, but found it challenging to develop and validate our concepts. We found abstract interpretation to be an effective framework in which to develop and validate our intuitions. Using it we were able to generically define the idea of consistent functions and predicates, as well as explain and define auxiliary concepts such as strict checking and static containment. We believe that, in addition to gradual effects, other gradual checking notions could be fruitfully investigated in this framework. In particular, we intend to extend our system to support full gradual type-and-effect systems, which depend on gradual effects as an initial step, and define blame tracking for effect casts.

References

[1] M. Abadi, C. Flanagan, and S. N. Freund. Types for safe locking: Static race detection for Java. *ACM Transactions on Programming Languages and Systems*, 28(2):207–255, 2006.

[2] M. Abadi, A. Birrell, T. Harris, and M. Isard. Semantics of transactional memory and automatic mutual exclusion. In *Proceedings of the 35th ACM SIGPLAN-SIGACT Symposium on Principles of Programming Languages (POPL 2008)*, pages 63–74, San Francisco, CA, USA, Jan. 2008. ACM Press.

[3] N. Benton and P. Buchlovsky. Semantics of an effect analysis for exceptions. In *Proceedings of the 2007 ACM SIGPLAN International*

Workshop on Types in Languages Design and Implementation (TLDI 07), pages 15–26, New York, NY, USA, 2007. ACM.

[4] P. Cousot and R. Cousot. Abstract interpretation: A unified lattice model for static analysis of programs by construction or approximation of fixpoints. In *Conference Record of the 4th ACM Symposium on Principles of Programming Languages (POPL 77)*, pages 238–252, Los Angeles, CA, USA, Jan. 1977. ACM Press.

[5] P. Cousot and R. Cousot. Systematic design of program analysis frameworks. In *Proceedings of the 6th ACM SIGACT-SIGPLAN Symposium on Principles of Programming Languages (POPL 79)*, pages 269–282, New York, NY, USA, 1979. ACM.

[6] T. Disney and C. Flanagan. Gradual information flow typing. In *International Workshop on Scripts to Programs*, 2011.

[7] T. Disney, C. Flanagan, and J. McCarthy. Temporal higher-order contracts. In *Proceedings of the 16th ACM SIGPLAN Conference on Functional Programming (ICFP 2011)*, pages 176–188, Tokyo, Japan, Sept. 2011. ACM Press.

[8] R. B. Findler and M. Felleisen. Contracts for higher-order functions. In *Proceedings of the 7th ACM SIGPLAN International Conference on Functional Programming*, pages 48–59, Pittsburgh, PA, USA, October 2002. ACM Press.

[9] R. B. Findler and M. Felleisen. Contracts for higher-order functions. In *Proceedings of the 7th ACM SIGPLAN International Conference on Functional Programming (ICFP 2002)*, pages 48–59, Pittsburgh, PA, USA, 2002. ACM Press.

[10] R. Garcia, É. Tanter, R. Wolff, and J. Aldrich. Foundations of typestate-oriented programming. *ACM Transactions on Programming Languages and Systems*, 2014. To appear.

[11] D. K. Gifford and J. M. Lucassen. Integrating functional and imperative programming. In *Proceedings of the 1986 ACM Conference on Lisp and Functional Programming*, pages 28–38, Cambridge, MA, USA, Aug. 1986. ACM Press.

[12] C. S. Gordon, W. Dietl, M. D. Ernst, and D. Grossman. JavaUI: Effects for controlling UI object access. In G. Castagna, editor, *Proceedings of the 27th European Conference on Object-oriented Programming (ECOOP 2013)*, volume 7920 of *Lecture Notes in Computer Science*, pages 179–204, Montpellier, France, July 2013. Springer-Verlag.

[13] J. Gosling, B. Joy, G. Steele, and G. Bracha. *The Java Language Specification, Third Edition*. Addison-Wesley, 2003.

[14] L. Ina and A. Igarashi. Gradual typing for generics. In *Proceedings of the 26th ACM SIGPLAN Conference on Object-Oriented Programming Systems, Languages and Applications (OOPSLA 2011)*, pages 609–624, Portland, Oregon, USA, Oct. 2011. ACM Press.

[15] D. Marino and T. Millstein. A generic type-and-effect system. In *Proceedings of the ACM SIGPLAN International Workshop on Types in Language Design and Implementation*, pages 39–50, 2009.

[16] B. C. Pierce. *Types and programming languages*. MIT Press, Cambridge, MA, USA, 2002. ISBN 0-262-16209-1.

[17] L. Rytz, M. Odersky, and P. Haller. Lightweight polymorphic effects. In J. Noble, editor, *Proceedings of the 26th European Conference on Object-oriented Programming (ECOOP 2012)*, volume 7313 of *Lecture Notes in Computer Science*, pages 258–282, Beijing, China, June 2012. Springer-Verlag.

[18] L. Rytz, N. Amin, and M. Odersky. A flow-insensitive, modular effect system for purity. In *Proceedings of the Workshop on Formal Techniques for Java-like Programs*, 2013. Article No.: 4.

[19] C. Scholliers, É. Tanter, and W. De Meuter. Computational contracts. In *Scheme and Functional Programming Workshop*, 2011.

[20] C. Scholliers, É. Tanter, and W. De Meuter. Computational contracts. *Science of Computer Programming (To Appear)*, Oct. 2013. URL `http://dx.doi.org/10.1016/j.scico.2013.09.005`.

[21] I. Sergey and D. Clarke. Gradual ownership types. In H. Seidl, editor, *Proceedings of the 21st European Symposium on Programming Languages and Systems (ESOP 2012)*, volume 7211 of *Lecture Notes in Computer Science*, pages 579–599, Tallinn, Estonia, 2012. Springer-Verlag.

[22] J. Siek and W. Taha. Gradual typing for objects. In E. Ernst, editor, *Proceedings of the 21st European Conference on Object-oriented Programming (ECOOP 2007)*, number 4609 in Lecture Notes in Computer Science, pages 2–27, Berlin, Germany, July 2007. Springer-Verlag.

[23] J. G. Siek and W. Taha. Gradual typing for functional languages. In *Proceedings of the Scheme and Functional Programming Workshop*, pages 81–92, Sept. 2006.

[24] A. Takikawa, T. S. Strickland, C. Dimoulas, S. Tobin-Hochstadt, and M. Felleisen. Gradual typing for first-class classes. In *Proceedings of the 27th ACM SIGPLAN Conference on Object-Oriented Programming Systems, Languages and Applications (OOPSLA 2012)*, pages 793–810, Tucson, AZ, USA, Oct. 2012. ACM Press.

[25] Y. M. Tang and P. Jouvelot. Effect systems with subtyping. In *Proceedings of the 1995 ACM SIGPLAN Symposium on Partial Evaluation and Semantics-based Program Manipulation (PEPM 95)*, pages 45–53, New York, NY, USA, 1995. ACM. ISBN 0-89791-720-0.

[26] R. Wolff, R. Garcia, É. Tanter, and J. Aldrich. Gradual typestate. In M. Mezini, editor, *Proceedings of the 25th European Conference on Object-oriented Programming (ECOOP 2011)*, volume 6813 of *Lecture Notes in Computer Science*, pages 459–483, Lancaster, UK, July 2011. Springer-Verlag.

[27] A. K. Wright and M. Felleisen. A syntactic approach to type soundness. *Journal of Information and Computation*, 115(1):38–94, Nov. 1994.

How to Keep Your Neighbours in Order

Conor McBride
University of Strathclyde
Conor.McBride@strath.ac.uk

Abstract

I present a datatype-generic treatment of recursive container types whose elements are guaranteed to be stored in increasing order, with the ordering invariant rolled out systematically. Intervals, lists and binary search trees are instances of the generic treatment. On the journey to this treatment, I report a variety of failed experiments and the transferable learning experiences they triggered. I demonstrate that a *total* element ordering is enough to deliver insertion and flattening algorithms, and show that (with care about the formulation of the types) the implementations remain as usual. Agda's *instance arguments* and *pattern synonyms* maximize the proof search done by the typechecker and minimize the appearance of proofs in program text, often eradicating them entirely. Generalizing to indexed recursive container types, invariants such as *size* and *balance* can be expressed in addition to *ordering*. By way of example, I implement insertion and deletion for 2-3 trees, ensuring both order and balance by the discipline of type checking.

Categories and Subject Descriptors D.1.1 [*Programming Techniques*]: Applicative (Functional) Programming; D.3.3 [*Language Constructs and Features*]: Data types and structures

Keywords dependent types; Agda; ordering; balancing; sorting

1. Introduction

It has taken years to see what was under my nose. I have been experimenting with ordered container structures for a *long* time [12]: how to keep lists ordered, how to keep binary search trees ordered, how to flatten the latter to the former. Recently, the pattern common to the structures and methods I had often found effective became clear to me. Let me tell you about it. Patterns are, of course, underarticulated abstractions. Correspondingly, let us construct a *universe* of container-like datatypes ensuring that elements are in increasing order, good for intervals, ordered lists, binary search trees, and more besides.

This paper is a literate Agda development, available online at `https://github.com/pigworker/Pivotal`. As well as contributing

- a datatype-generic treatment of ordering invariants and operations which respect them
- a technique for hiding proofs from program texts
- a precise implementation of insertion and deletion for 2-3 trees

I take the time to explore the design space, reporting a selection of the wrong turnings and false dawns I encountered on my journey to these results. I try to extrapolate transferable design principles, so that others in future may suffer less than I.

2. How to Hide the Truth

If we intend to enforce invariants, we shall need to mix a little bit of logic in with our types and a little bit of proof in with our programming. It is worth taking some trouble to set up our logical apparatus to maximize the effort we can get from the computer and to minimize the textual cost of proofs. We should prefer to encounter logic only when it is dangerously absent!

Our basic tools are the types representing falsity and truth by virtue of their number of inhabitants:

```
data 0 : Set where                       -- no constructors!
record 1 : Set where constructor ⟨⟩     -- no fields!
```

Dependent types allow us to compute sets from data. E.g., we can represent evidence for the truth of some Boolean expression which we might have tested.

```
data 2 : Set where tt ff : 2
So : 2 → Set
So tt = 1
So ff = 0
```

A set P which evaluates to 0 or to 1 might be considered 'propositional' in that we are unlikely to want to *distinguish* its inhabitants. We might even prefer not even to *see* its inhabitants. I define a wrapper type for propositions whose purpose is to hide proofs.

```
record ⌜_⌝ (P : Set) : Set where
  constructor !
  field {{prf}} : P
```

Agda uses braces to indicate that an argument or field is to be suppressed by default in program texts and inferred somehow by the typechecker. Single-braced variables are solved by unification, in the tradition of Milner [16]. Doubled braces indicate *instance arguments*, inferred by *contextual search*: if just one hypothesis can take the place of an instance argument, it is silently filled in, allowing us a tiny bit of proof automation [6]. If an inhabitant of ⌜So b⌝ is required, we may write ! to indicate that we expect the truth of b to be known.

Careful positioning of instance arguments seeds the context with useful information. We may hypothesize over them quietly,

```
_⇒_ : Set → Set → Set
P ⇒ T = {{p : P}} → T
infixr 3 _⇒_
```

and support forward reasoning with a 'therefore' operator.

ICFP '14, September 1–6, 2014, Gothenburg, Sweden.

http://dx.doi.org/10.1145/2628136.2628163

```
_∴_ : ∀{P T} → ⌜P⌝ → (P ⇒ T) → T
! ∴ t = t
```

This apparatus can give the traditional conditional a subtly more informative type, thus:

```
¬ : 2 → 2; ¬ tt = ff; ¬ ff = tt
if_then_else_ :
  ∀{X} b → (So b ⇒ X) → (So (¬ b) ⇒ X) → X
if tt then t else f = t
if ff then t else f = f
infix 1 if_then_else_
```

If ever there is a proof of 0 in the context, we should be able to ask for anything we want. Let us define

```
magic : {X : Set} → 0 ⇒ X
magic {{()}}
```

using Agda's *absurd pattern* to mark the impossible instance argument which shows that no value need be returned. E.g., if tt then ff else magic : 2.

Instance arguments are not a perfect fit for proof search: they were intended as a cheap alternative to type classes, hence the requirement for exactly one candidate instance. For proofs we might prefer to be less fussy about redundancy, but we shall manage perfectly well for the purposes of this paper.

3. Barking Up the Wrong Search Trees

David Turner [17] notes that whilst *quicksort* is often cited as a program which defies structural recursion, it performs the same sorting algorithm (although not with the same memory usage pattern) as building a binary search tree and then flattening it. The irony is completed by noting that the latter sorting algorithm is the archetype of structural recursion in Rod Burstall's development of the concept [4]. Binary search trees have empty leaves and nodes labelled with elements which act like *pivots* in quicksort: the left subtree stores elements which precede the pivot, the right subtree elements which follow it. Surely this invariant is crying out to be a dependent type! Let us search for a type for search trees.

We could, of course, define binary search trees as ordinary node-labelled trees with parameter P giving the type of pivots:

```
data Tree : Set where
  leaf : Tree;   node : Tree → P → Tree → Tree
```

We might then define the invariant as a predicate IsBST : Tree → Set, implement insertion in our usual way, and prove separately that our program maintains the invariant. However, the joy of dependently typed programming is that refining the types of the data themselves can often alleviate or obviate the burden of proof. Let us try to bake the invariant in.

What should the type of a subtree tell us? If we want to check the invariant at a given node, we shall need some information about the subtrees which we might expect comes from their type. We require that the elements left of the pivot precede it, so we could require the whole set of those elements represented somehow, but of course, for any order worthy of the name, it suffices to check only the largest. Similarly, we shall need to know the smallest element of the right subtree. It would seem that we need the type of a search tree to tell us its extreme elements (or that it is empty).

```
data STRange : Set where
  ∅ : STRange;      _–_ : P → P → STRange
infix 9 _–_
```

From checking the invariant to enforcing it. Assuming we can test the order on P with some $le : P \to P \to 2$, we could write a recursive function to check whether a Tree is a valid search tree and compute its range if it has one. Of course, we must account for the possibility of invalidity, so let us admit failure in the customary manner.

```
data Maybe (X : Set) : Set where
  yes : X → Maybe X;      no : Maybe X
_?⟩_ : ∀{X} → 2 → Maybe X → Maybe X
b ?⟩ mx = if b then mx else no
infixr 4 _?⟩_
```

The guarding operator ?⟩ allows us to attach a Boolean test. We may now validate the range of a Tree.

```
valid : Tree → Maybe STRange
valid leaf = yes ∅
valid (node l p r) with valid l | valid r
... | yes ∅       | yes ∅       = yes (p – p)
... | yes ∅       | yes (c – d) = le p c ?⟩ yes (p – d)
... | yes (a – b) | yes ∅       = le b p ?⟩ yes (a – p)
... | yes (a – b) | yes (c – d)
    = le b p ?⟩ le p c ?⟩ yes (a – d)
... | _           | _           = no
```

As valid is a *fold* over the structure of Tree, we can follow my colleagues Bob Atkey, Neil Ghani and Patricia Johann in computing the *partial refinement* [2] of Tree which valid induces. We seek a type BST : STRange → Set such that BST $r \cong \{t$: Tree | valid t = yes $r\}$ and we find it by refining the type of each constructor of Tree with the check performed by the corresponding case of valid, assuming that the subtrees yielded valid ranges. We can calculate the conditions to check and the means to compute the output range if successful.

```
lOK : STRange → P → 2
lOK ∅       p = tt
lOK (_ – u) p = le u p

rOK : P → STRange → 2
rOK p ∅       = tt
rOK p (l – _) = le p l

outRan : STRange → P → STRange → STRange
outRan ∅       p ∅       = p – p
outRan ∅       p (_ – u) = p – u
outRan (l – _) p ∅       = l – p
outRan (l – _) _ (_ – u) = l – u
```

We thus obtain the following refinement from Tree to BST:

```
data BST : STRange → Set where
  leaf : BST ∅
  node : ∀{l r} → BST l → (p : P) → BST r →
    So (lOK l p) ⇒ So (rOK p r) ⇒ BST (outRan l p r)
```

Attempting to implement insertion. Now that each binary search tree tells us its type, can we implement insertion? Rod Burstall's implementation is as follows

```
insert : P → Tree → Tree
insert y leaf            = node leaf y leaf
insert y (node lt p rt) =
  if le y p then node (insert y lt) p rt
            else  node lt p (insert y rt)
```

but we shall have to try a little harder to give a type to insert, as we must somehow negotiate the ranges. If we are inserting a new extremum, then the range will be wider afterwards than before.

```
insRan : STRange → P → STRange
insRan ∅       y = y − y
insRan (l − u) y =
  if le y l then y − u else if le u y then l − y else l − u
```

So, we have the right type for our data and for our program. Surely the implementation will go like clockwork!

```
insert : ∀{r} y → BST r → BST (insRan r y)
insert y leaf          = node leaf y leaf
insert y (node lt p rt) =
  if le y p then (node (insert y lt) p rt)
            else (node lt p (insert y rt))
```

The leaf case checks easily, but alas for node! We have lt : BST l and rt : BST r for some ranges l and r. The then branch delivers a BST (outRan (insRan l y) p r), but the type required is BST (insRan (outRan l p r) y), so we need some theorem-proving to fix the types, let alone to discharge the obligation So (IOK (insRan l y) p). We could plough on with proof and, coughing, push this definition through, but tough work ought to make us ponder if we might have thought askew.

We have defined a datatype which is logically correct but which is pragmatically disastrous. Is it thus inevitable that all datatype definitions which enforce the ordering invariant will be pragmatically disastrous? Or are there lessons we can learn about dependently typed programming that will help us to do better?

4. Why Measure When You Can Require?

Last section, we got the wrong answer because we asked the wrong question: "What should the type of a subtree tell us?" somewhat presupposes that information bubbles outward from subtrees to the nodes which contain them. In Milner's tradition, we are used to synthesizing the type of a thing. Moreover, the very syntax of **data** declarations treats the index delivered from each constructor as an output. It seems natural to treat datatype indices as measures of the data. That is all very well for the length of a vector, but when the measurement is intricate, as when computing a search tree's extrema, programming becomes vexed by the need for theorems about the measuring functions. The presence of 'green slime'—defined functions in the return types of constructors—is a danger sign.

We can take an alternative view of types, not as synthesized measurements of data, bubbled outward, but as checked *requirements* of data, pushed *inward*. To enforce the invariant, let us rather ask "What should we tell the type of a subtree?".

The elements of the left subtree must precede the pivot in the order; those of the right must follow it. Correspondingly, our requirements on a subtree amount to an *interval* in which its elements must fall. As any element can find a place somewhere in a search tree, we shall need to consider unbounded intervals also. We can extend any type with top and bottom elements as follows.

```
data _⊤⊥ (P : Set) : Set where
  ⊤ : P⊤⊥; # : P → P⊤⊥; ⊥ : P⊤⊥
```

and extend the order accordingly:

```
_⊤⊥ : ∀{P} → (P → P → 2) → P⊤⊥ → P⊤⊥ → 2
le⊤⊥ _    ⊤    = tt
le⊤⊥ (#x) (#y) = le x y
le⊤⊥ ⊥    _    = tt
le⊤⊥ _    _    = ff
```

We can now index search trees by a pair of *loose bounds*, not measuring the range of the contents exactly, but constraining it sufficiently. At each node, we can require that the pivot falls in the interval, then use the pivot to bound the subtrees.

```
data BST (l u : P⊤⊥) : Set where
  leaf  : BST l u
  pnode : (p : P) → BST l (#p) → BST (#p) u →
    So (le⊤⊥ l (#p)) ⇒ So (le⊤⊥ (#p) u) ⇒ BST l u
```

In doing so, we eliminate all the 'green slime' from the indices of the type. The leaf constructor now has many types, indicating all its elements satisfy any requirements. We also gain BST ⊥ ⊤ as the general type of binary search trees for P. Unfortunately, we have been forced to make the pivot value p, the first argument to pnode, as the type of the subtrees now depends on it. Luckily, Agda now supports *pattern synonyms*, allowing linear macros to abbreviate both patterns on the left and pattern-like expressions on the right [1]. We may fix up the picture:

```
pattern node lp p pu = pnode p lp pu
```

Can we implement insert for this definition? We can certainly give it a rather cleaner type. When we insert a new element into the left subtree of a node, we must ensure that it precedes the pivot: that is, we expect insertion to *preserve* the bounds of the subtree, and we should already know that the new element falls within them.

```
insert : ∀{l u} y → BST l u →
  So (le⊤⊥ l (#y)) ⇒ So (le⊤⊥ (#y) u) ⇒ BST l u
insert y leaf          = node leaf y leaf
insert y (node lt p rt) =
  if le y p then node (insert y lt) p rt
            else node lt p ( insert y rt )
```

We have no need to repair type errors by theorem proving, and most of our proof obligations follow directly from our assumptions. The recursive call in the then branch requires a proof of So (le y p), but that is just the evidence delivered by our evidence-transmitting conditional. However, the else case snatches defeat from the jaws of victory: the recursive call needs a proof of So (le p y), but all we have is a proof of So (¬ (le y p)). For any given total ordering, we should be able to fix this mismatch up by proving a theorem, but this is still more work than I enjoy. The trouble is that we couched our definition in terms of the truth of bits computed in a particular way, rather than the ordering *relation*. Let us now tidy up this detail.

5. One Way Or The Other

We can recast our definition in terms of relations—families of sets Rel P indexed by pairs.

```
Rel : Set → Set₁
Rel P = P × P → Set
```

giving us types which directly make statements about elements of P, rather than about bits.

I must, of course, say how such pairs are defined: the habit of dependently typed programmers is to obtain them as the degenerate case of dependent pairs: let us have them.

```
record Σ (S : Set) (T : S → Set) : Set where
  constructor _,_
  field
    π₁ : S
    π₂ : T π₁
open Σ
_×_ : Set → Set → Set
S × T = Σ S λ _ → T
infixr 5 _×_ _,_
```

Now, suppose we have some 'less or equal' ordering L : Rel P. Let us have natural numbers by way of example,

```
data ℕ : Set where 0 : ℕ; s : ℕ → ℕ
Lℕ : Rel ℕ
Lℕ (x, y) = x ≤ y where
  _≤_ : ℕ → ℕ → Set
  0   ≤ y   = 1
  s x ≤ 0   = 0
  s x ≤ s y = x ≤ y
```

The information we shall need is exactly the totality of L: for any given x and y, L must hold *One Way Or The Other*, as captured by the disjoint sum type, OWOTO $L\ (x, y)$, defined as follows:

```
data _+_ (S T : Set) : Set where
  ◁ : S → S + T;    ▷ : T → S + T
infixr 4 _+_

OWOTO : ∀{P} (L : Rel P) → Rel P
OWOTO L (x, y) = ⌜L (x, y)⌝ + ⌜L (y, x)⌝

pattern le = ◁ !
pattern ge = ▷ !
```

I have used pattern synonyms to restore the impression that we are just working with a Boolean type, but the ! serves to unpack evidence when we test and to pack it when we inform. We shall usually be able to keep silent about ordering evidence, even from the point of its introduction. For ℕ, let us have

```
owoto : ∀x y → OWOTO Lℕ (x, y)
owoto 0     y     = le
owoto (s x) 0     = ge
owoto (s x) (s y) = owoto x y
```

Note that we speak only of the crucial bit of information. Moreover, we especially benefit from type-level computation in the step case: OWOTO Lℕ (s x , s y) is the very same type as OWOTO Lℕ (x, y).

Any ordering relation on elements lifts readily to bounds: I have overloaded the notation for lifting in the typesetting of this paper, but sadly not in the Agda source code. Let us take the opportunity to add propositional wrapping, to help us hide ordering proofs.

```
_⊤⊥ ⌜_⌝ : ∀{P} → Rel P → Rel P⊤⊥
L⊤⊥ (_ , ⊤)    = 1
L⊤⊥ (#x, #y)   = L (x, y)
L⊤⊥ (⊥ , _)    = 1
L⊤⊥ (_ , _)    = 0
⌜L⌝ xy = ⌜L⊤⊥ xy⌝
```

The type $\ulcorner L \urcorner\ (x, y)$ thus represents ordering evidence on bounds with matching and construction by !, unaccompanied.

6. Equipment for Relations and Other Families

Before we get back to work in earnest, let us build a few tools for working with relations and other such indexed type families: a relation is a family which happens to be indexed by a pair. We shall have need of pointwise truth and falsity.

```
0̇ 1̇ : {I : Set} → I → Set
0̇ i = 0
1̇ i = 1
```

We shall also need to lift disjunction, conjunction and implication to to their pointwise counterparts.

```
_+̇_ _×̇_ _→̇_ : {I : Set} →
  (I → Set) → (I → Set) → I → Set
(S +̇ T) i = S i + T i
(S ×̇ T) i = S i × T i
(S →̇ T) i = S i → T i
infixr 3 _+̇_; infixr 4 _×̇_; infixr 2 _→̇_
```

Pointwise implication will be useful for writing *index-respecting* functions, e.g., bounds-preserving operations. It is useful to be able to state that something holds at every index (i.e., 'always works').

```
[_] : {I : Set} → (I → Set) → Set
[F] = ∀{i} → F i
```

With this apparatus, we can quite often talk about indexed things without mentioning the indices, resulting in code which almost looks like its simply typed counterpart. You can check that for any S and T, ◁ : $[S \mathbin{\dot\to} S \mathbin{\dot+} T]$ and so forth.

7. Working with Bounded Sets

It will be useful to consider sets indexed by bounds in the same framework as relations on bounds: *propositions-as-types* means we have been doing this from the start! Useful combinator on such sets is the *pivoted pair*, $S \mathbin{\dot\wedge} T$, indicating that some pivot value p exists, with S holding before p and T afterwards. A pattern synonym arranges the order neatly.

```
_∧̇_ : ∀{P} → Rel P⊤⊥ → Rel P⊤⊥ → Rel P⊤⊥
_∧̇_ {P} S T (l, u) = Σ P λ p → S (l, #p) × T (#p, u)
pattern _‘_‘_ s p t = p, s, t
infixr 5 _‘_‘_
```

Immediately, we can define an *interval* to be the type of an element proven to lie within given bounds.

```
_• : ∀{P} (L : Rel P) → Rel P⊤⊥
L• = ⌜L⌝ ∧̇ ⌜L⌝
pattern _° p = !‘ p ‘!
```

With habitual tidiness, a pattern synonym conceals the evidence.

Let us then parametrize over some

```
owoto : ∀x y → OWOTO L (x, y)
```

and reorganise our development.

```
data BST (lu : P⊤⊥ × P⊤⊥) : Set where
  leaf  : BST lu
  pnode : ((⌜L⌝ ×̇ BST) ∧̇ (⌜L⌝ ×̇ BST) →̇ BST) lu
pattern node lt p rt = pnode (p, (!, lt), (!, rt))
```

Reassuringly, the standard undergraduate error, arising from thinking about *doing* rather than *being*, is now ill typed.

```
insert : [L• →̇ BST →̇ BST]
insert y° leaf            = node leaf y leaf
insert y° (node lt p rt) with owoto y p
... | le = (insert y° lt)
... | ge = (insert y° rt)
```

However, once we remember to restore the unchanged parts of the tree, we achieve victory, at last!

```
insert : [L• →̇ BST →̇ BST]
insert y° leaf            = node leaf y leaf
insert y° (node lt p rt) with owoto y p
... | le = node (insert y° lt) p rt
... | ge = node lt p (insert y° rt)
```

The evidence generated by testing *owoto y p* is just what is needed to access the appropriate subtree. We have found a method which seems to work! But do not write home yet.

8. The Importance of Local Knowledge

Our current representation of an ordered tree with n elements contains $2n$ pieces of ordering evidence, which is $n-1$ too many. We should need only $n+1$ proofs, relating the lower bound to the least element, then comparing neighbours all the way along to the greatest element (one per element, so far) which must then fall below the upper bound (so, one more). As things stand, the pivot at the root is known to be greater than every element in the right spine of its left subtree and less than every element in the left spine of its right subtree. If the tree was built by iterated insertion, these comparisons will surely have happened, but that does not mean we should retain the information.

Suppose, for example, that we want to rotate a tree, perhaps to keep it balanced, then we have a little local difficulty:

```
rotR : [BST ∸> BST]
rotR (node (node lt m mt) p rt)
  = node lt m (node mt p rt)
rotR t = t
```

Agda rejects the outer node of the rotated tree for lack of evidence. I expand the pattern synonyms to show what is missing.

```
rotR : [BST ∸> BST]
rotR (pnode
  ((! {{lp}}, pnode ((! {{lm}}, lt), m, (! {{mp}}, mt)))
  , p, (! {{pu}}, rt))) = pnode ((! {{lm}}, lt), m,
  (! {{ ?0 }}, pnode ((! {{mp}}, mt), p, (! {{pu}}, rt))))
rotR t = t
```

We can discard the non-local ordering evidence $lp : L_{\perp}^{\top}(l, \# p)$, but now we need the non-local $?_0 : L_{\perp}^{\top}(\# m, u)$ that we lack. Of course, we can prove this goal from mp and pu if L is transitive, but if we want to make less work, we should rather not demand non-local ordering evidence in the first place.

Looking back at the type of node, note that the indices at which we demand *ordering* are the same as the indices at which we demand *subtrees*. If we strengthen the invariant on trees to ensure that there is a sequence of ordering steps from the lower to the upper bound, we could dispense with the sometimes non-local evidence stored in nodes, at the cost of a new constraint for leaf.

```
data BST (lu : P⊥⊤ × P⊥⊤) : Set where
  pleaf : (⌜L⌝ ∸> BST) lu
  pnode : (BST ∧̇ BST ∸> BST) lu
pattern leaf         = pleaf !
pattern node lt p rt = pnode (lt, p, rt)
```

Indeed, a binary tree with n nodes will have $n+1$ leaves. An in-order traversal of a binary tree is a strict alternation, leaf-node-leaf-...-node-leaf, making a leaf the ideal place to keep the evidence that neighbouring nodes are in order! Insertion remains easy.

```
insert : [L• ∸> BST ∸> BST]
insert y° leaf = node leaf y leaf
insert y° (node lt p rt) with owoto y p
... | le = node (insert y° lt) p rt
... | ge = node lt p (insert y° rt)
```

Rotation becomes very easy: the above code now typechecks, with no leaves in sight, so no proofs to rearrange!

```
rotR : [BST ∸> BST]
rotR (node (node lt m mt) p rt)
  = node lt m (node mt p rt)
rotR t = t
```

We have arrived at a neat way to keep a search tree in order, storing pivot elements at nodes and proofs in leaves. Phew!

But it is only the end of the beginning. To complete our sorting algorithm, we need to flatten binary search trees to ordered *lists*. Are we due another long story about the discovery of a good definition of the latter? Fortunately not! The key idea is that an ordered list is just a particularly badly balanced binary search tree, where every left subtree is a leaf. We can nail that down in short order, just by inlining leaf's data in the left subtree of node, yielding a sensible cons.

```
data OList (lu : P⊥⊤ × P⊥⊤) : Set where
  nil  : (⌜L⌝ ∸> OList) lu
  cons : (⌜L⌝ ∧̇ OList ∸> OList) lu
```

These are exactly the ordered lists Sam Lindley and I defined in Haskell [11], but now we can see where the definition comes from.

By figuring out how to build ordered binary search trees, we have actually discovered how to build quite a variety of in-order data structures. We simply need to show how the data are built from particular patterns of BST components. So, rather than flattening binary search trees, let us pursue a generic account of in-order datatypes, then flatten them *all*.

9. Jansson and Jeuring's PolyP Universe

If we want to see how to make the treatment of ordered container structures systematic, we shall need some datatype-generic account of recursive types with places for elements. A compelling starting point is the 'PolyP' system of Patrik Jansson and Johan Jeuring [8], which we can bottle as a universe—a system of codes for types—in Agda, as follows:

```
data JJ : Set where
  'R 'P '1 : JJ
  _'+_ _'×_ : JJ → JJ → JJ
infixr 4 _'+_
infixr 5 _'×_
```

The 'R stands for 'recursive substructure' and the 'P stands for 'parameter'—the type of elements stored in the container. Given meanings for these, we interpret a code in JJ as a set.

```
⟦_⟧JJ : JJ → Set → Set → Set
⟦'R⟧JJ       R P = R
⟦'P⟧JJ       R P = P
⟦'1⟧JJ       R P = 1
⟦S '+ T⟧JJ R P = ⟦S⟧JJ R P + ⟦T⟧JJ R P
⟦S '× T⟧JJ R P = ⟦S⟧JJ R P × ⟦T⟧JJ R P
```

When we 'tie the knot' in $\mu_{JJ}\ F\ P$, we replace F's 'Ps by some actual P and its 'Rs by recursive uses of $\mu_{JJ}\ F\ P$.

```
data μJJ (F : JJ) (P : Set) : Set where
  ⟨_⟩ : ⟦F⟧JJ (μJJ F P) P → μJJ F P
```

Being finitary and first-order, all of the containers encoded by JJ are *traversable* in the sense defined by Ross Paterson and myself [14]. We shall need to introduce the interface for Applicative functors

```
record Applicative (H : Set → Set) : Set₁ where
  field
    pure : ∀{X} → X → H X
    ap   : ∀{S T} → H (S → T) → H S → H T
open Applicative
```

and then abstract over Applicative to compute the datatype generic treatment of traverse.

```
traverse : ∀{H F A B} → Applicative H →
  (A → H B) → μJJ F A → H (μJJ F B)
traverse {H} {F} {A} {B} AH h t = go ‘R t where
  pu = pure AH; _⊛_ = ap AH
  go : ∀G →
    ⟦ G ⟧JJ (μJJ F A) A → H (⟦ G ⟧JJ (μJJ F B) B)
  go ‘R        ⟨ t ⟩    = pu ⟨_⟩ ⊛ go F t
  go ‘P        a        = h a
  go ‘1        ⟨⟩       = pu ⟨⟩
  go (S ‘+ T) (◁ s)    = pu ◁ ⊛ go S s
  go (S ‘+ T) (▷ t)    = pu ▷ ⊛ go T t
  go (S ‘× T) (s, t)   = (pu _,_ ⊛ go S s) ⊛ go T t
```

We can specialise traverse to standard functorial map by choosing the identity functor.

```
idApp : Applicative (λ X → X)
idApp = record {pure = id; ap = id}
map : ∀{F A B} →
  (A → B) → μJJ F A → μJJ F B
map = traverse idApp
```

We can equally well specialise traverse to a monoidal crush by choosing a constant functor.

```
record Monoid (X : Set) : Set where
  field
    neutral : X
    combine : X → X → X
  monApp : Applicative (λ _ → X)
  monApp = record
    {pure = λ _ → neutral; ap = combine}
  crush : ∀{P F} → (P → X) → μJJ F P → X
  crush = traverse {B = 0} monApp
open Monoid
```

Perversely, the fact that the constant functor discards the return value type, B in traverse's type signature, results in the absence of constraints on B in the definition of crush, and hence the need to give B explicitly. I choose 0 merely to emphasize that B-values are not involved.

Endofunctions on a given set form a monoid with respect to composition, which allows us a generic foldr-style operation.

```
compMon : ∀{X} → Monoid (X → X)
compMon = record
  {neutral = id; combine = λ f g → f ∘ g}
foldr : ∀{F A B} →
  (A → B → B) → B → μJJ F A → B
foldr f b t = crush compMon f t b
```

We can use foldr to build up Bs from any structure containing As, given a way to 'insert' an A into a B, and an 'empty' B to start with. Let us check that our generic machinery is fit for purpose.

10. The Simple Orderable Subuniverse of JJ

The quicksort algorithm divides a sorting problem in two by partitioning about a selected *pivot* element the remaining data. Rendered as the process of building then flattening a binary search tree [4], the pivot element clearly marks the upper bound of the lower subtree and the lower bound of the upper subtree, giving exactly the information required to guide insertion.

We can require the presence of pivots between substructures by combining the parameter ‘P and pairing ‘× constructs of the PolyP universe into a single pivoting construct, ‘∧, with two substructures and a pivot in between. We thus acquire the simple orderable universe, SO, a subset of JJ picked out as the image of a function, ⟦_⟧SO. Now, ‘P stands also for pivot!

```
data SO : Set where
  ‘R ‘1   : SO
  _‘+_ _‘∧_ : SO → SO → SO
infixr 5 _‘∧_
⟦_⟧SO : SO → JJ
⟦ ‘R ⟧SO      = ‘R
⟦ ‘1 ⟧SO      = ‘1
⟦ S ‘+ T ⟧SO  = ⟦ S ⟧SO ‘+ ⟦ T ⟧SO
⟦ S ‘∧ T ⟧SO  = ⟦ S ⟧SO ‘× ‘P ‘× ⟦ T ⟧SO
μSO : SO → Set → Set
μSO F P = μJJ ⟦ F ⟧SO P
```

Let us give SO codes for structures we often order and bound:

```
‘List ‘Tree ‘Interval : SO
‘List     = ‘1 ‘+ (‘1 ‘∧ ‘R)
‘Tree     = ‘1 ‘+ (‘R ‘∧ ‘R)
‘Interval = ‘1 ‘∧ ‘1
```

Every data structure described by SO is a regulated variety of node-labelled binary trees. Let us check that we can turn anything into a tree, preserving the substructure relationship. The method[1] is to introduce a helper function, go, whose type separates G, the structure of the top node, from F the structure of recursive subnodes, allowing us to take the top node apart: we kick off with $G = F$.

```
tree : ∀{P F} → μSO F P → μSO ‘Tree P
tree {P} {F} ⟨ f ⟩ = go F f where
  go : ∀G → ⟦ ⟦ G ⟧SO ⟧JJ (μSO F P) P → μSO ‘Tree P
  go ‘R        f          = tree f
  go ‘1        ⟨⟩         = ⟨ ◁ ⟨⟩ ⟩
  go (S ‘+ T) (◁ s)      = go S s
  go (S ‘+ T) (▷ t)      = go T t
  go (S ‘∧ T) (s, p, t)  = ⟨ ▷ (go S s, p, go T t) ⟩
```

All tree does is strip out the ◁s and ▷s corresponding to the structural choices offered by the input type and instead label the void leaves ◁ and the pivoted nodes ▷. Note well that a singleton tree has void leaves as its left and right substructures, and hence that the inorder traversal is a strict alternation of leaves and pivots, beginning with the leaf at the end of the left spine and ending with the leaf at the end of the right spine. As our tree function preserves the leaf/pivot structure of its input, we learn that *every* datatype we can define in SO stores such an alternation of leaves and pivots.

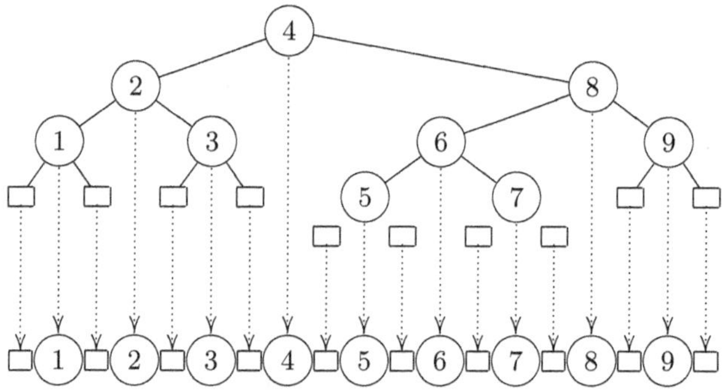

We are now in a position to roll out the "loose bounds" method to the whole of the SO universe. We need to ensure that each pivot

[1] If you try constructing the division operator as a primitive recursive function, this method will teach itself to you.

is in order with its neighbours and with the outer bounds, and the alternating leaf/pivot structure gives us just what we need: let us store the ordering evidence at the leaves!

```
⟦_⟧≤SO : SO → ∀{P} → Rel P⊤⊥ → Rel P → Rel P⊤⊥
⟦ 'R ⟧≤SO        R L = R
⟦ '1 ⟧≤SO        R L = ⌜L⌝
⟦ S '+ T ⟧≤SO R L = ⟦ S ⟧≤SO R L ∔ ⟦ T ⟧≤SO R L
⟦ S '∧ T ⟧≤SO R L = ⟦ S ⟧≤SO R L ∧̇ ⟦ T ⟧≤SO R L

data μ≤SO (F : SO) {P : Set} (L : Rel P)
          (lu : P⊤⊥ × P⊤⊥) : Set where
  ⟨_⟩ : ⟦ F ⟧≤SO (μ≤SO F L) L lu → μ≤SO F L lu
```

We have shifted from sets to relations, in that our types are indexed by lower and upper bounds. The leaves demand evidence that the bounds are in order, whilst the nodes require the pivot first, then use it to bound the substructures appropriately.

Meanwhile, the need in nodes to bound the left substructure's type with the pivot value disrupts the left-to-right spatial ordering of the data, but we can apply a little cosmetic treatment, thanks to the availability of pattern synonyms.

With these two devices available, let us check that we can still turn any ordered data into an ordered tree, writing $L^{\Delta}\ (l, u)$ for $\mu^{\leq}_{\mathsf{SO}}$ 'Tree $L\ (l, u)$, and redefining intervals accordingly.

```
_Δ _• : ∀{P} → Rel P → Rel P⊤⊥
LΔ = μ≤SO 'Tree     L
pattern leaf         = ⟨◁ !⟩
pattern node lp p pu = ⟨▷ (lp ‚ p ‚ pu)⟩

L• = μ≤SO 'Interval L
pattern _° p = ⟨(p ‚ ! ‚ !)⟩

tree : ∀{P F} {L : Rel P} → [μ≤SO F L ∸> LΔ]
tree {P} {F} {L} ⟨f⟩ = go F f where
  go : ∀G → [⟦ G ⟧≤SO (μ≤SO F L) L ∸> LΔ]
  go 'R        f       = tree f
  go '1        !       = leaf
  go (S '+ T) (◁ s)    = go S s
  go (S '+ T) (▷ t)    = go T t
  go (S '∧ T) (s ‚ p ‚ t) = node (go S s) p (go T t)
```

We have acquired a collection of orderable datatypes which all amount to specific patterns of node-labelled binary trees: an interval is a singleton node; a list is a right spine. All share the treelike structure which ensures that pivots alternate with leaves bearing the evidence the pivots are correctly placed with respect to their immediate neighbours.

Let us check that we are where we were, so to speak. Hence we can rebuild our binary search tree insertion for an element in the corresponding interval:

```
insert : [L• ∸> LΔ ∸> LΔ]
insert y° leaf           = node leaf y leaf
insert y° (node lt p rt) with owoto y p
... | le = node (insert y° lt) p rt
... | ge = node lt p (insert y° rt)
```

The constraints on the inserted element are readily expressed via our 'Interval type, but at no point need we ever name the ordering evidence involved. The *owoto* test brings just enough new evidence into scope that all proof obligations on the right-hand side can be discharged by search of assumptions. We can now make a search tree from any input container.

```
makeTree : ∀{F} → μJJ F P → LΔ (⊥, ⊤)
makeTree = foldr (λ p → insert p°) leaf
```

11. Digression: Merging Monoidally

Let us name our family of ordered lists L^{+}, as the leaves form a nonempty chain of $\ulcorner L \urcorner$ ordering evidence.

```
_+ : ∀{P} → Rel P → Rel P⊤⊥
L+ = μ≤SO 'List L
pattern []          = ⟨◁ !⟩
pattern _::_ x xs   = ⟨▷ (x ‚ ! ‚ xs)⟩
infixr 6 _::_
```

The next section addresses the issue of how to *flatten* ordered structures to ordered lists, but let us first consider how to *merge* them. Merging sorts differ from flattening sorts in that order is introduced when 'conquering' rather than 'dividing'.

We can be sure that whenever two ordered lists share lower and upper bounds, they can be merged within the same bounds. Again, let us assume a type P of pivots, with *owoto* witnessing the totality of order L. The familiar definition of merge typechecks but falls just outside the class of lexicographic recursions accepted by Agda's termination checker. I have locally expanded pattern synonyms to dig out the concealed evidence which causes the trouble.

```
merge : [L+ ∸> L+ ∸> L+]
merge []   ys    = ys
merge xs   []    = xs
merge ⟨▷ (! {{_}}) ‚ x ‚ xs⟩ (y :: ys) with owoto x y
... | le = x :: merge xs (y // ys)
... | ge = y :: merge ⟨▷ ((! {{_}}) ‚ x ‚ xs)⟩ ys
```

In one step case, the first list gets smaller, but in the other, where we decrease the second list, the first does not remain the same: it contains fresh evidence that x is above the tighter lower bound, y. Separating the recursion on the second list is sufficient to show that both recursions are structural.

```
merge : [L+ ∸> L+ ∸> L+]
merge        []        = id
merge {l, u} (x :: xs) = go where
  go : ∀{l} {{_ : L⊤⊥ (l, #x)}} → (L+ ∸> L+) (l, u)
  go []          = x :: xs
  go (y :: ys) with owoto x y
  ... | le = x :: merge xs (y :: ys)
  ... | ge = y :: go ys
```

The helper function go inserts x at its rightful place in the second list, then resumes merging with xs.

Merging equips ordered lists with monoidal structure.

```
olMon : ∀{lu} → L⊤⊥ lu ⇒ Monoid (L+ lu)
olMon = record {neutral = []; combine = merge}
```

An immediate consequence is that we gain a family of sorting algorithms which amount to depth-first merging of a given intermediate data structure, making a singleton from each pivot.

```
mergeJJ : ∀{F} → μJJ F P → L+ (⊥, ⊤)
mergeJJ = crush olMon λ p → p :: []
```

The instance of mergeJJ for *lists* is exactly *insertion* sort: at each cons, the singleton list of the head is merged with the sorted tail. To obtain an efficient mergeSort, we should arrange the inputs as a leaf-labelled binary tree.

```
'qLTree : JJ
'qLTree = ('1 '+ 'P) '+ 'R '× 'R
```

As ever, pattern synonyms prove invaluable for restoring readability.

```
pattern none     = ⟨◁ (◁ ⟨⟩)⟩
pattern one p    = ⟨◁ (▷ p)⟩
pattern fork l r = ⟨▷ (l, r)⟩
```

We can add each successive elements to the tree with a twisting insertion, placing the new element at the bottom of the left spine, but swapping the subtrees at each layer along the way to ensure fair distribution.

```
twistIn : P → μJJ ‘qLTree P → μJJ ‘qLTree P
twistIn p none       = one p
twistIn p (one q)    = fork (one p) (one q)
twistIn p (fork l r) = fork (twistIn p r) l
```

If we notice that twistIn maps elements to endofunctions on trees, we can build up trees by a monoidal crush, obtaining an efficient generic sort for any container in the JJ universe.

```
mergeSort : ∀{F} → μJJ F P → L⁺ (⊥,⊤)
mergeSort = mergeJJ ∘ foldr twistIn none
```

12. Flattening With Concatenation

Several sorting algorithms amount to building an ordered intermediate structure, then flattening it to an ordered list. As all of our orderable structures amount to trees, it suffices to flatten trees to lists. Let us take the usual naïve approach as our starting point. In Haskell, we might write

```
flatten Leaf         = []
flatten (Node l p r) = flatten l ++ p : flatten r
```

so let us try to do the same in Agda with ordered lists. We shall need concatenation, so let us try to join lists with a shared bound p in the middle.

```
infixr 8 _++_
_++_ : ∀{P} {L : Rel P} {l p u} →
  L⁺ (l,p) → L⁺ (p,u) → L⁺ (l,u)
[]        ++ ys = ys
(x :: xs) ++ ys = x :: xs ++ ys
```

The ‘cons’ case goes without a hitch, but there is trouble at ‘nil’. We have $ys : \mu^{\le}_{SO}$ ‘List $L\ (p, u)$ and we know $L^{\top}_{\bot}\ (l, p)$, but we need to return a $\mu^{\le}_{SO}$ ‘List $L\ (l, u)$.

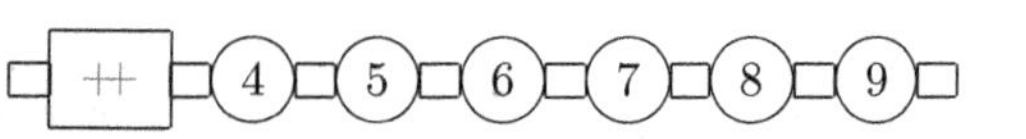

“The trouble is easy to fix,” one might confidently assert, whilst secretly thinking, “What a nuisance!”. We can readily write a helper function which unpacks ys, and whether it is nil or cons, extends its leftmost order evidence by transitivity. And this really is a nuisance, because, thus far, we have not required transitivity to keep our code well typed: all order evidence has stood between neighbouring elements. Here, we have two pieces of ordering evidence which we must join, because we have nothing to put in between them. Then, the penny drops. Looking back at the code for flatten, observe that p is the pivot and the whole plan is to put it between the lists. You can’t always get what you want, but you can get what you need.

```
sandwich : ∀{P} {L : Rel P} → [(L⁺ ∧̇ L⁺) →̇ L⁺]
sandwich ([]      ‚p‚ ys) = p :: ys
sandwich (x :: xs ‚p‚ ys) = x :: sandwich (xs ‚p‚ ys)
```

We are now ready to flatten trees, thence any ordered structure:

```
flatten : ∀{P} {L : Rel P} → [L^Δ →̇ L⁺]
flatten leaf         = []
flatten (node l p r) = sandwich (flatten l ‚p‚ flatten r)

flatten≤SO : ∀{P} {L : Rel P} {F} → [μ≤SO F L →̇ L⁺]
flatten≤SO = flatten ∘ tree
```

For a little extra speed we might fuse that composition, but it seems frivolous to do so as the benefit is outweighed by the quadratic penalty of left-nested concatenation. The standard remedy applies: we can introduce an accumulator [18], but our experience with ++ should alert us to the possibility that it may require some thought.

13. Faster Flattening, Generically

We may define flatten generically, and introduce an accumulator yielding a combined flatten-and-append which works right-to-left, growing the result with successive conses. But what should be the bounds of the accumulator? If we have not learned our lesson, we might be tempted by

```
flapp : ∀{F P} {L : Rel P} {l p u} →
  μ≤SO F L (l,p) → L⁺ (p,u) → L⁺ (l,u)
```

but again we face the question of what to do when we reach a leaf. We should not need transitivity to rearrange a tree of ordered neighbours into a sequence. We can adopt the previous remedy of inserting the element p in the middle, but we shall then need to think about where p will come from in the first instance, for example when flattening an empty structure.

```
flapp : ∀{F P} {L : Rel P} G →
  [⟦ G ⟧≤SO (μ≤SO F L) L ∧̇ L⁺ →̇ L⁺]
flapp {F} ‘R      (⟨t⟩        ‚p‚ ys) = flapp F (t‚p‚ys)
flapp ‘1          (!          ‚p‚ ys) = p :: ys
flapp (S ‘+ T) (◁ s           ‚p‚ ys) = flapp S (s‚p‚ys)
flapp (S ‘+ T) (▷ t           ‚p‚ ys) = flapp T (t‚p‚ys)
flapp (S ‘∧ T) ((s‚p′‚t)‚p‚ys)
  = flapp S (s‚p′‚flapp T (t‚p‚ys))
```

To finish the job, we need to work our way down the right spine of the input in search of its rightmost element, which initialises p.

```
flatten : ∀{F P} {L : Rel P} → [μ≤SO F L →̇ L⁺]
flatten {F} {P} {L} {l,u} ⟨t⟩ = go F t where
  go : ∀{l} G → ⟦ G ⟧≤SO (μ≤SO F L) L (l,u) → L⁺ (l,u)
  go ‘R          t         = flatten t
  go ‘1          !         = []
  go (S ‘+ T) (◁ s)        = go S s
  go (S ‘+ T) (▷ t)        = go T t
  go (S ‘∧ T) (s‚p‚t)      = flapp S (s‚p‚go T t)
```

This is effective, but it is more complicated than I should like. It is basically the same function twice, in two different modes, depending on what is to be affixed *after* the rightmost order evidence in the structure being flattened: either a pivot-and-tail in the case of flapp, or nothing in the case of flatten. The problem is one of parity: the thing we must affix to one odd-length leaf-node-leaf alternation to get another is an even-length node-leaf alternation. Correspondingly, it is hard to express the type of the accumulator cleanly. Once again, I begin to suspect that this is a difficult thing to do because it is the wrong thing to do. How can we reframe the problem, so that we work only with odd-length leaf-delimited data?

14. A Replacement for Concatenation

My mathematical mentor, Tom Körner, is fond of remarking “A mathematician is someone who knows that 0 is 0 + 0”. It is often difficult to recognize the structure you need when the problem in front of you is a degenerate case of it. If we think again about concatenation, we might realise that it does not amount to *affixing* one list to another, but rather *replacing* the 'nil' of the first list with the whole of the second. We might then notice that the *monoidal* structure of lists is in fact degenerate *monadic* structure.

Any syntax has a monadic structure, where 'return' embeds variables as terms and 'bind' is substitution. Quite apart from their 'prioritised choice' monadic structure, lists are the terms of a degenerate syntax with one variable (called 'nil') and only unary operators ('cons' with a choice of element). Correspondingly, they have this substitution structure: substituting nil gives concatenation, and the monad laws are the monoid laws.

Given this clue, let us consider concatenation and flattening in terms of *replacing* the rightmost leaf by a list, rather than affixing more data to it. We replace the list to append with a function which maps the contents of the rightmost leaf—some order evidence—to its replacement. The type looks more like that of 'bind' than 'append', because in some sense it is!

```
infixr 8 _++_
RepL : ∀{P} → Rel P → Rel P^⊤_⊥
RepL L (n, u) = ∀{m} → L^⊤_⊥ (m, n) ⇒ L^+ (m, u)
_++_ : ∀{P}{L : Rel P}{l n u} →
  L^+ (l, n) → RepL L (n, u) → L^+ (l, u)
[]        ++ ys = ys
(x :: xs) ++ ys = x :: xs ++ ys
```

Careful use of instance arguments leaves all the manipulation of evidence to the machine. In the [] case, *ys* is silently instantiated with exactly the evidence exposed in the [] pattern on the left.

Let us now deploy the same technique for flatten.

```
flapp : ∀{P}{L : Rel P}{F}{l n u} →
  μ≤SO F L (l, n) → RepL L (n, u) → L^+ (l, u)
flapp {P}{L}{F}{u = u} t ys = go ‘R t ys where
  go : ∀{l n} G → ⟦ G ⟧≤SO (μ≤SO F L) L (l, n) →
          RepL L (n, u) → L^+ (l, u)
  go ‘R        ⟨ t ⟩     ys = go F t ys
  go ‘1        !         ys = ys
  go (S ‘+ T)  (◁ s)     ys = go S s ys
  go (S ‘+ T)  (▷ t)     ys = go T t ys
  go (S ‘∧ T)  (s , p , t) ys = go S s (p :: go T t ys)
flatten : ∀{P}{L : Rel P}{F} → [μ≤SO F L →̇ L^+]
flatten t = flapp t []
```

15. An Indexed Universe of Orderable Data

Ordering is not the only invariant we might want to enforce on orderable data structures. We might have other properties in mind, such as size, or balancing invariants. It is straightforward to extend our simple universe to allow general indexing as well as orderability. We can extend our simple orderable universe SO to an indexed orderable universe IO, just by marking each recursive position with an index, then computing the code for each node as a function of its index. We may add a ‘0 code to rule out some cases as illegal.

```
data IO (I : Set) : Set where
  ‘R        : I → IO I
  ‘0 ‘1     : IO I
  _‘+_ _‘∧_ : IO I → IO I → IO I
```

When interpreting such a code, we now require the family of relations which sit in recursive positions, one for each element of the index set, I. However, the interpretation function is not concerned with indexing the overall node. The function mapping each index to the code for the appropriate node structure appears only when we tie the recursive knot.

```
⟦_⟧≤IO : ∀{I P} → IO I →
         (I → Rel P^⊤_⊥) → Rel P → Rel P^⊤_⊥
⟦ ‘R i ⟧≤IO     R L = R i
⟦ ‘0 ⟧≤IO       R L = λ _ → 0
⟦ ‘1 ⟧≤IO       R L = ⌜L⌝
⟦ S ‘+ T ⟧≤IO   R L = ⟦ S ⟧≤IO R L +̇ ⟦ T ⟧≤IO R L
⟦ S ‘∧ T ⟧≤IO   R L = ⟦ S ⟧≤IO R L ∧̇ ⟦ T ⟧≤IO R L
data μ≤IO {I P : Set} (F : I → IO I) (L : Rel P)
          (i : I) (lu : P^⊤_⊥ × P^⊤_⊥) : Set where
  ⟨_⟩ : ⟦ F i ⟧≤IO (μ≤IO F L) L lu → μ≤IO F L i lu
```

We recover all our existing data structures by trivial indexing.

```
‘List ‘Tree ‘Interval : 1 → IO 1
‘List     _ = ‘1 ‘+ (‘1 ‘∧ ‘R ⟨⟩)
‘Tree     _ = ‘1 ‘+ (‘R ⟨⟩ ‘∧ ‘R ⟨⟩)
‘Interval _ = ‘1 ‘∧ ‘1
```

We also lift our existing type-forming abbreviations:

```
_^+ _^Δ _^• : ∀{P} → Rel P → Rel P^⊤_⊥
L^+ = μ≤IO ‘List     L ⟨⟩
L^Δ = μ≤IO ‘Tree     L ⟨⟩
L^• = μ≤IO ‘Interval L ⟨⟩
```

However, we may also make profitable use of indexing: here are ordered *vectors*.

```
‘Vec : ℕ → IO ℕ
‘Vec 0     = ‘1
‘Vec (s n) = ‘1 ‘∧ ‘R n
```

Note that we need no choice of constructor or storage of length information: the index determines the shape. If we want, say, even-length tuples, we can use ‘0 to rule out the odd cases.

```
‘Even : ℕ → IO ℕ
‘Even 0         = ‘1
‘Even (s 0)     = ‘0
‘Even (s (s n)) = ‘1 ‘∧ ‘1 ‘∧ ‘R n
```

We could achieve a still more flexible notion of data structure by allowing a general Σ-type rather than our binary ‘+, but we have what we need for finitary data structures with computable conditions on indices.

The tree operation carries over unproblematically, with more indexed input but plain output.

```
tree : ∀{I P F}{L : Rel P}{i : I} →
  [μ≤IO F L i →̇ L^Δ]
```

Similarly, flatten works (efficiently) just as before.

```
flatten : ∀{I P F}{L : Rel P}{i : I} →
  [μ≤IO F L i →̇ L^+]
```

We now have a universe of indexed orderable data structures with efficient flattening. Let us put it to work.

16. Balanced 2-3 Trees

To ensure a logarithmic access time for search trees, we can keep them balanced. Maintaining balance as close to perfect as possible is rather fiddly, but we can gain enough balance by allowing a little redundancy. A standard way to achieve this is to insist on uniform height, but allow internal nodes to have either one pivot and two subtrees, or two pivots and three subtrees. We may readily encode these *2-3 trees* and give pattern synonyms for the three kinds of structure. This approach is much like that of *red-black* (effectively,

2-3-4) trees, for which typesafe balancing has a tradition going back to Hongwei Xi and Stefan Kahrs [9, 19].

As with 'Vec, case analysis on the index, now representing height, tells us whether we are at a leaf or an internal node.

```
'Tree23 : ℕ → IO ℕ
'Tree23 0      = '1
'Tree23 (s h)  = 'R h '∧ ('R h '+ ('R h '∧ 'R h))

_²³ : ∀{P} (L : Rel P) → ℕ → Rel P⊤⊥
L²³ = μ≤IO 'Tree23 L

pattern no₀                = ⟨!⟩
pattern no₂ lt p rt        = ⟨p, lt,◁ rt⟩
pattern no₃ lt p mt q rt   = ⟨p, lt,▷ (q, mt, rt)⟩
```

When we map a 2-3 tree of height n back to binary trees, we get a tree whose left spine has length n and whose right spine has a length between n and $2n$.

Insertion is quite similar to binary search tree insertion, except that it can have the impact of increasing height. The worst that can happen is that the resulting tree is too tall but has just one pivot at the root. Indeed, we need this extra wiggle room immediately for the base case!

```
ins23 : ∀h {lu} → L• lu → L²³ h lu →
          L²³ h lu +
          Σ P λ p → L²³ h (π₁ lu, #p) × L²³ h (#p, π₂ lu)
ins23 0 y° no₀ = ▷ (⟨!⟩, y, ⟨!⟩)
```

In the step case, we must find our way to the appropriate subtree by suitable use of comparison.

```
ins23 (s h) y° ⟨lt, p, rest⟩          with owoto y p
ins23 (s h) y° ⟨lt, p, rest⟩          | le = ?0
ins23 (s h) y° (no₂ lt p rt)          | ge = ?1
ins23 (s h) y° (no₃ lt p mt q rt)     | ge with owoto y q
ins23 (s h) y° (no₃ lt p mt q rt)     | ge | le = ?2
ins23 (s h) y° (no₃ lt p mt q rt)     | ge | ge = ?3
```

Our $?_0$ covers the case where the new element belongs in the left subtree of either a 2- or 3-node; $?_1$ handles the right subtree of a 2-node; $?_2$ and $?_3$ handle middle and right subtrees of a 3-node after a further comparison. Note that we inspect *rest* only after we have checked the result of the first comparison, making real use of the way the **with** construct brings more data to the case analysis but keeps the existing patterns open to further refinement, a need foreseen by the construct's designers [13].

Once we have identified the appropriate subtree, we can make the recursive call. If we are lucky, the result will plug straight back into the same hole. Here is the case for the left subtree.

```
ins23 (s h) y° ⟨lt, p, rest⟩ | le
  with ins23 h y° lt
ins23 (s h) y° ⟨lt, p, rest⟩ | le
  | ◁ lt' = ◁ ⟨lt', p, rest⟩
```

However, if we are unlucky, the result of the recursive call is too big. If the top node was a 2-node, we can accommodate the extra data by returning a 3-node. Otherwise, we must rebalance and pass the 'too big' problem upward. Again, we gain from delaying the inspection of *rest* until we are sure reconfiguration will be needed.

```
ins23 (s h) y° (no₂ lt p rt)        | le
  | ▷ (llt, r, lrt) = ◁ (no₃ llt r lrt p rt)
ins23 (s h) y° (no₃ lt p mt q rt)   | le
  | ▷ (llt, r, lrt) = ▷ (no₂ llt r lrt, p, no₂ mt q rt)
```

For the $?_1$ problems, the top 2-node can always accept the result of the recursive call somehow, and the choice offered by the return type conveniently matches the node-arity choice, right of the pivot. For completeness, I give the middle ($?_2$) and right ($?_3$) cases for 3-nodes, but it works just as on the left.

```
ins23 (s h) y° (no₃ lt p mt q rt) | ge | le
  with ins23 h y° mt
ins23 (s h) y° (no₃ lt p mt q rt) | ge | le
  | ◁ mt'             = ◁ (no₃ lt p mt' q rt)
ins23 (s h) y° (no₃ lt p mt q rt) | ge | le
  | ▷ (mlt, r, mrt)   = ▷ (no₂ lt p mlt, r, no₂ mrt q rt)
ins23 (s h) y° (no₃ lt p mt q rt) | ge | ge
  with ins23 h y° rt
ins23 (s h) y° (no₃ lt p mt q rt) | ge | ge
  | ◁ rt'             = ◁ (no₃ lt p mt q rt')
ins23 (s h) y° (no₃ lt p mt q rt) | ge | ge
  | ▷ (rlt, r, rrt)   = ▷ (no₂ lt p mt, q, no₂ rlt r rrt)
```

Pleasingly, the task of constructing suitable return values in each of these cases is facilitated by Agda's type directed search gadget, *Agsy* [10]. There are but two valid outputs constructible from the pieces available: the original tree reconstituted, and the correct output.

To complete the efficient sorting algorithm based on 2-3 trees, we can use a Σ-type to hide the height data, giving us a type which admits iterative construction.

```
Tree23 = Σ ℕ λ h → L²³ h (⊥, ⊤)

insert : P → Tree23 → Tree23
insert p (h, t) with ins23 h p° t
... | ◁ t'            = h , t'
... | ▷ (lt, r, rt)   = s h, no₂ lt r rt

sort : ∀{F} → μJJ F P → L⁺ (⊥, ⊤)
sort = flatten ∘ π₂ ∘ foldr insert (0, no₀)
```

17. Deletion from 2-3 Trees

Might is right: the omission of *deletion* from treatments of balanced search trees is always a little unfortunate [15]. Deletion is a significant additional challenge because we can lose a key from the *middle* of the tree, not just from the *fringe* of nodes whose children are leaves. Insertion acts always to extend the fringe, so the problem is only to bubble an anomaly up from the fringe to the root. Fortunately, just as nodes and leaves alternate in the traversal of a tree, so do middle nodes and fringe nodes: whenever we need to delete a middle node, it always has a neighbour at the fringe which we can move into the gap, leaving us once more with the task of bubbling a problem up from the fringe.

Our situation is further complicated by the need to restore the neighbourhood ordering invariant when one key is removed. At last, we shall need our ordering to be transitive. We shall also need a decidable equality on keys.

```
data _≡_ {X : Set} (x : X) : X → Set where
  ⟨⟩ : x ≡ x
infix 6 _≡_

trans : ∀{x} y {z} → L (x, y) ⇒ L (y, z) ⇒ ⌜L (x, z)⌝

eq? : (x y : P) → x ≡ y + (x ≡ y → 0)
```

Correspondingly, a small amount of theorem proving is indicated, ironically, to show that it is sound to throw information about local ordering away.

Transitivity for bounds. Transitivity we may readily lift to bounds with a key in the middle:

```
pattern via p = p,!,!

trans⊥⊤ : [(⌜L⌝ ∧̇ ⌜L⌝) →̇ ⌜L⌝]
trans⊥⊤ {_ ,⊤} _        = !
trans⊥⊤ {⊥ ,⊥} _        = !
trans⊥⊤ {⊥ ,#u} _       = !
trans⊥⊤ {⊤ ,_} (via _)  = magic
trans⊥⊤ {#l ,#u} (via p) = trans p ∴ !
trans⊥⊤ {#l ,⊥} (via _) = magic
```

What is the type of deletion? When we remove an element from a 2-3 tree of height n, the tree will often stay the same height, but there will be situations in which it must get shorter, becoming a 3-node or a leaf, as appropriate.

```
Del²³ Short²³ : ℕ → Rel P⊥⊤
Del²³   h lu    = Short²³ h lu + L²³ h lu
Short²³ 0 lu    = 0
Short²³ (s h) lu = L²³ h lu
```

The task of deletion has three phases: finding the key to delete; moving the problem to the fringe; plugging a short tree into a tall hole. The first of these will be done by our main function,

```
del²³ : ∀{h} → [L• →̇ L²³ h →̇ Del²³ h]
```

and the second by extracting the extreme right key from a nonempty left subtree,

```
extr : ∀{h} → [L²³ (s h) →̇ (Del²³ (s h) ∧̇ L⊥⊤)]
```

recovering the (possily short) remainder of the tree and the evidence that the key is below the upper bound (which will be the deleted key). Both of these operations will need to reconstruct trees with one short subtree, so let us build 'smart constructors' for just that purpose, then return to the main problem.

Rebalancing reconstructors. If we try to reconstruct a 2-node with a possibly-short subtree, we might be lucky enough to deliver a 2-node, or we might come up short. We certainly will not deliver a 3-node of full height and it helps to reflect that in the type. Shortness can be balanced out if we are adjacent to a 3-node, but if we have only a 2-node, we must give a short answer.

```
Re2 : ℕ → Rel P⊥⊤
Re2 h = Short²³ (s h) +̇ (L²³ h ∧̇ L²³ h)
d2t : ∀{h} → [(Del²³ h ∧̇ L²³ h) →̇ Re2 h]
d2t {h}   (▷ lp,p,pu)             = ▷ (lp,p,pu)
d2t {0}   (◁ (),p,pu)
d2t {s h} (◁ lp,p,no₂ pq q qu)    = ◁ (no₃ lp p pq q qu)
d2t {s h} (◁ lp,p,no₃ pq q qr r ru)
  = ▷ (no₂ lp p pq,q,no₂ qr r ru)
t2d : ∀{h} → [(L²³ h ∧̇ Del²³ h) →̇ Re2 h]
t2d {h}   (lp,p,▷ pu)             = ▷ (lp,p,pu)
t2d {0}   (lp,p,◁ ())
t2d {s h} (no₂ ln n np,p,◁ pu)    = ◁ (no₃ ln n np p pu)
t2d {s h} (no₃ lm m mn n np,p,◁ pu)
  = ▷ (no₂ lm m mn,n,no₂ np p pu)
rd : ∀{h} → [Re2 h →̇ Del²³ (s h)]
rd (◁ s)           = (◁ s)
rd (▷ (lp,p,pu))   = ▷ (no₂ lp p pu)
```

The adaptor rd allows us to throw away the knowledge that the full height reconstruction must be a 2-node if we do not need it, but the extra detail allows us to use 2-node reconstructors in the course of 3-node reconstruction. To reconstruct a 3-node with one possibly-short subtree, rebuild a 2-node containing the suspect, and then restore the extra subtree. We thus need to implement the latter.

```
r3t : ∀{h} → [(Re2 h ∧̇ L²³ h) →̇ Del²³ (s h)]
r3t (▷ (lm,m,mp),p,pu) = ▷ (no₃ lm m mp p pu)
r3t (◁ lp,p,pu)        = ▷ (no₂ lp p pu)
t3r : ∀{h} → [(L²³ h ∧̇ Re2 h) →̇ Del²³ (s h)]
t3r (lp,p,▷ (pq,q,qu)) = ▷ (no₃ lp p pq q qu)
t3r (lp,p,◁ pu)        = ▷ (no₂ lp p pu)
```

Cutting out the extreme right. We may now implement extr, grabbing the rightmost key from a tree. I use

```
pattern _△_ lr r = r,lr,!
```

to keep the extracted element on the right and hide the ordering proofs.

```
extr : ∀{h} → [L²³ (s h) →̇ (Del²³ (s h) ∧̇ ⌜L⌝)]
extr {0} (no₂ lr r no₀)        = ◁ lr △ r
extr {0} (no₃ lp p pr r no₀)   = ▷ (no₂ lp p pr) △ r
extr {s h} (no₂ lp p pu)       with extr pu
... | pr △ r = rd (t2d (lp,p,pr)) △ r
extr {s h} (no₃ lp p pq q qu)  with extr qu
... | qr △ r = t3r (lp,p,t2d (pq,q,qr)) △ r
```

To delete the pivot key from between two trees, we extract the rightmost key from the left tree, then weaken the bound on the right tree (traversing its left spine only). Again, we are sure that if the height remains the same, we shall deliver a 2-node.

```
delp : ∀{h} → [(L²³ h ∧̇ L²³ h) →̇ Re2 h]
delp {0} {lu} (no₀,p,no₀) = trans⊥⊤ {lu} (via p) ∴ ◁ no₀
delp {s h}    (lp,p,pu) with extr lp
... | lr △ r = d2t (lr,r,weak pu) where
  weak : ∀{h u} → L²³ h (#p,u) → L²³ h (#r,u)
  weak {0} {u} no₀ = trans⊥⊤ {#r,u} (via p) ∴ no₀
  weak {s h} ⟨pq,q,qu⟩ = ⟨weak pq,q,qu⟩
```

A remark on weakenings. It may seem regrettable that we have to write weak, which is manifestly an obfuscated identity function, and programmers who do not wish the ordering guarantees are entitled not to pay and not to receive. If we took an extrinsic approach to managing these invariants, weak would still be present, but it would just be the proof of the proposition that you can lower a lower bound that you know for a tree. Consequently, the truly regrettable thing about weak is not that it is written but that it is *executed*. The 'colored' analysis of Bernardy and Moulin offers a suitable method to ensure that the weakening operation belongs to code which is erased at run time [3]. An alternative might be a notion of 'propositional subtyping', allowing us to establish coercions between types which are guaranteed erasable at runtime because all they do is fix up indexing and the associated content-free proof objects.

The completion of deletion. Now that we can remove a key, we need only find the key to remove. I have chosen to delete the topmost occurrence of the given key, and to return the tree unscathed if the key does not occur at all.

As with insertion, the discipline of indexing by bounds and height is quite sufficient to ensure in silence that rebalancing works as required. Indeed, no further explicit proof effort is needed: once delp reestablishes the local ordering invariant around the deleted element, the rest of the ordering evidence stays intact from input to output.

```
del^23 : ∀{h} → [L• ⇾ L^23 h ⇾ Del^23 h]
del^23 {0} _     no0                  = ▷ no0
del^23 {s h} y°  ⟨lp, p, pu⟩           with eq? y p
del^23 {s h} .p° (no2 lp p pu)         | ◁ ⟨⟩
  = rd (delp (lp, p, pu))
del^23 {s h} .p° (no3 lp p pq q qu)    | ◁ ⟨⟩
  = r3t (delp (lp, p, pq), q, qu)
del^23 {s h} y°  ⟨lp, p, pu⟩           | ▷ _ with owoto y p
del^23 {s h} y°  (no2 lp p pu)         | ▷ _ | le
  = rd (d2t (del^23 y° lp, p, pu))
del^23 {s h} y°  (no2 lp p pu)         | ▷ _ | ge
  = rd (t2d (lp, p, del^23 y° pu))
del^23 {s h} y°  (no3 lp p pq q qu)    | ▷ _ | le
  = r3t (d2t (del^23 y° lp, p, pq), q, qu)
del^23 {s h} y°  (no3 lp p pq q qu)    | ▷ _ | ge with eq? y q
del^23 {s h} .q° (no3 lp p pq q qu)    | ▷ _ | ge | ◁ ⟨⟩
  = t3r (lp, p, delp (pq, q, qu))
... | ▷ _ with owoto y q
... | le = r3t (t2d (lp, p, del^23 y° pq), q, qu)
... | ge = t3r (lp, p, t2d (pq, q, del^23 y° qu))
```

At no point did we need to construct trees with the invariant broken. Rather, we chose types which expressed with precision the range of possible imbalances arising locally from a deletion. It is exactly this precision which allowed us to build and justify the rebalancing reconstruction operators we reused so effectively to avoid an explosion of cases.

18. Discussion

We have seen *intrinsic* dependently typed programming at work. Internalizing ordering and balancing invariants to our datatypes, we discovered not an explosion of proof obligations, but rather that unremarkable programs check at richer types because they *accountably* do the testing which justifies their choices.

Of course, to make the programs fit neatly into the types, we must take care of how we craft the latter. I will not pretend for one moment that the good definition is the first to occur to me, and it is certainly the case that one is not automatically talented at designing dependent types, even when one is an experienced programmer in Haskell or ML. There is a new skill to learn. Hopefully, by taking the time to explore the design space for ordering invariants, I have exposed some transferable lessons. In particular, we must overcome our type inference training and learn to see types as pushing requirements inwards, as well as pulling guarantees out.

It is positive progress that work is shifting from the program definitions to the type definitions, cashing out in our tools as considerable mechanical assistance in program construction. A precise type structures its space of possible programs so tightly that an ineractive editor can often offer us a small choice of plausible alternatives, usually including the thing we want. It is exhilarating being drawn to one's code by the strong currents of a good design. But that happens only in the last iteration: we are just as efficiently dashed against the rocks by a bad design, and the best tool to support recovery remains, literally, the drawing board. We should give more thought to machine-assisted exploration.

A real pleasure to me in doing this work was the realisation that I not only had 'a good idea for ordered lists' and 'a good idea for ordered trees', but that they were the *same* idea, and moreover that I could implement the idea in a datatype-generic manner. The key underpinning technology is first-class datatype description. By the end of the paper, we had just one main datatype $\mu^{\leq}_{IO}$, whose sole role was to 'tie the knot' in a recursive node structure determined by a computable code. The resulting raw data are strewn with artefacts of the encoding, but pattern synonyms do a remarkably good job of recovering the appearance of bespoke constructors whenever we work specifically to one encoded datatype.

Indeed, there is clearly room for even more datatype-generic technology in the developments given here. On the one hand, the business of finding the substructure in which a key belongs, whether for insertion or deletion, is crying out for a generic construction of Gérard Huet's 'zippers' [7]. Moreover, the treatment of ordered structures as variations on the theme of the binary search tree demands consideration in the framework of 'ornaments', as studied by Pierre-Évariste Dagand and others [5]. Intuitively, it seems likely that the IO universe corresponds closely to the ornaments on node-labelled binary trees which add only finitely many bits (because IO has '+ rather than a general Σ). Of course, one node of a $\mu^{\leq}_{IO}$ type corresponds to a region of nodes in a tree: perhaps ornaments, too, should be extended to allow the unrolling of recursive structure.

Having developed a story about ordering invariants to the extent that our favourite sorting algorithms silently establish them, we still do not have total correctness intrinsically. *What about permutation?* It has always maddened me that the insertion and flattening operations manifestly construct their output by rearranging their input: the proof that sorting permutes should thus be *by inspection*. Experiments suggest that many sorting algorithms can be expressed in a domain specific language whose type system is linear for keys. We should be able to establish a general purpose permutation invariant for this language, once and for all, by a logical relations argument. We are used to making sense of programs, but it is we who make the sense, not the programs. It is time we made programs make their own sense.

Acknowledgements. I should like to thank my father for filling my childhood with the joy of precision in programming. His sad and sudden death somewhat disrupted my writing schedule, so I am grateful to Manuel Chakravarty and Lisa Tolles for their forbearance and support. Thanks are due also to Amanda Clare and colleagues for arranging emergency electricity by the sea.

References

[1] William Aitken and John Reppy. Abstract value constructors. Technical Report TR 92-1290, Cornell University, 1992.

[2] Robert Atkey, Patricia Johann, and Neil Ghani. Refining inductive types. *Logical Methods in Computer Science*, 8(2), 2012.

[3] Jean-Philippe Bernardy and Guilhem Moulin. Type-theory in color. In Greg Morrisett and Tarmo Uustalu, editors, *ICFP*, pages 61–72. ACM, 2013. ISBN 978-1-4503-2326-0.

[4] Rod Burstall. Proving properties of programs by structural induction. *Computer Journal*, 12(1):41–48, 1969.

[5] Pierre-Évariste Dagand and Conor McBride. Transporting functions across ornaments. In Peter Thiemann and Robby Bruce Findler, editors, *ICFP*, pages 103–114. ACM, 2012. ISBN 978-1-4503-1054-3.

[6] Dominique Devriese and Frank Piessens. On the bright side of type classes: instance arguments in Agda. In Manuel M. T. Chakravarty, Zhenjiang Hu, and Olivier Danvy, editors, *ICFP*, pages 143–155. ACM, 2011. ISBN 978-1-4503-0865-6.

[7] Gérard P. Huet. The zipper. *J. Funct. Program.*, 7(5):549–554, 1997.

[8] Patrik Jansson and Johan Jeuring. PolyP - a polytypic programming language. In Peter Lee, Fritz Henglein, and Neil D. Jones, editors, *POPL*, pages 470–482. ACM Press, 1997. ISBN 0-89791-853-3.

[9] Stefan Kahrs. Red-black trees with types. *J. Funct. Program.*, 11(4): 425–432, 2001.

[10] Fredrik Lindblad and Marcin Benke. A Tool for Automated Theorem Proving in Agda. In Jean-Christophe Filliâtre, Christine Paulin-Mohring, and Benjamin Werner, editors, *TYPES*, volume 3839 of *Lec-*

ture Notes in Computer Science, pages 154–169. Springer, 2004. ISBN 3-540-31428-8.

[11] Sam Lindley and Conor McBride. Hasochism: the pleasure and pain of dependently typed haskell programming. In Chung-chieh Shan, editor, *Haskell*, pages 81–92. ACM, 2013. ISBN 978-1-4503-2383-3.

[12] Conor McBride. A Case For Dependent Families. LFCS Theory Seminar, Edinburgh, 2000. URL http://strictlypositive.org/a-case/.

[13] Conor McBride and James McKinna. The view from the left. *J. Funct. Program.*, 14(1):69–111, 2004.

[14] Conor McBride and Ross Paterson. Applicative programming with effects. *J. Funct. Program.*, 18(1):1–13, 2008.

[15] Matthew Might. The missing method: Deleting from Okasaki's red-black trees. Blog post, 2010. http://matt.might.net/articles/red-black-delete/.

[16] Robin Milner. A theory of type polymorphism in programming. *J. Comput. Syst. Sci.*, 17(3):348–375, 1978.

[17] David Turner. Elementary strong functional programming. 1987. URL http://sblp2004.ic.uff.br/papers/turner.pdf.

[18] Philip Wadler. The concatenate vanishes. Technical report, 1987.

[19] Hongwei Xi. Dependently Typed Data Structures. In *Proceedings of Workshop of Algorithmic Aspects of Advanced Programming Languages (WAAAPL '99)*, pages 17–32, Paris, September 1999.

A Relational Framework for Higher-Order Shape Analysis

Gowtham Kaki Suresh Jagannathan
Purdue University
{gkaki,suresh}@cs.purdue.edu

Abstract

We propose the integration of a relational specification framework within a dependent type system capable of verifying complex invariants over the shapes of algebraic datatypes. Our approach is based on the observation that structural properties of such datatypes can often be naturally expressed as inductively-defined *relations* over the recursive structure evident in their definitions. By interpreting constructor applications (abstractly) in a relational domain, we can define expressive relational abstractions for a variety of complex data structures, whose structural and shape invariants can be automatically verified. Our specification language also allows for definitions of *parametric* relations for polymorphic data types that enable highly composable specifications and naturally generalizes to higher-order polymorphic functions.

We describe an algorithm that translates relational specifications into a decidable fragment of first-order logic that can be efficiently discharged by an SMT solver. We have implemented these ideas in a type checker called CATALYST that is incorporated within the MLton SML compiler. Experimental results and case studies indicate that our verification strategy is both practical and effective.

Categories and Subject Descriptors D.3.2 [*Language Classifications*]: Applicative (Functional) Languages; F.3.1 [*Logics and Meanings of Programs*]: Specifying and Verifying and Reasoning about Programs; D.2.4 [*Software Engineering*]: Software/Program Verification

Keywords Relational Specifications; Inductive Relations; Parametric Relations; Dependent Types; Decidability; Standard ML

1. Introduction

Dependent types are well-studied vehicles capable of expressing rich program invariants. A prototypical example is the type of a list that is indexed by a natural number denoting its length. Length-indexed lists can be written in several mainstream languages that support some form of dependent typing, including GHC Haskell [24], F* [21, 23], and OCaml [16]. For example, the following Haskell signatures specify how the length of the result list for `append` and `rev` relate to their arguments:

```
append :: List a n -> List a m -> List a (Plus n m)
rev    :: List a n -> List a n
```

While length-indexed lists capture stronger invariants over `append`, and `rev` than possible with just simple types, they still underspecify the intended behavior of these operations. For example, a correctly written `append` function must additionally preserve the order of its input lists; a function that incorrectly produces an output list that is a permutation of its inputs would nonetheless satisfy `append`'s type as written above. Similarly, the identity function would clearly satisfy the type given for `rev`; a type that fully captures `rev`'s behavior would also have to specify that the order of elements in `rev`'s output list is the inverse of the order of its input. Is it possible to ascribe such expressive types to capture these kinds of important shape properties, which can nonetheless be easily stated, and efficiently checked?

One approach is to directly state desired behavior in type refinements, as in the following signature:

$$\texttt{rev : } \{\texttt{l : 'a list}\} \longrightarrow \{\nu\texttt{: 'a list | } \nu \texttt{ = rev'(l)}\}$$

Here, `rev'` represents some reference implementation of `rev`. Checking `rev`'s implementation against this refinement is tantamount to proving the equivalence of `rev` and `rev'`. Given the undecidability of the general problem, expecting these types to be machine checkable would require the definition of `rev'` to closely resemble `rev`'s. For all but the most trivial of definitions, this approach is unlikely to be fruitful. An alternative approach is to define `rev` within a theorem prover, and directly assert and prove properties on it - for example, that `rev` is involutive. Although modern theorem provers support rich theories over datatypes like lists, this strategy nonetheless requires that the program be fully described in logic, and reasoned about by the solver in its entirety. Thus, defining `rev` in this way also requires an equational definition of `append`, assuming the former is defined in terms of the latter. For non-trivial programs, this may require equipping provers with arbitrarily complex theories, whose combination may not be decidable. Such a methodology also does not obviously address our original goal of specifying `rev`'s functional correctness, independent of its definition; note that in the case of `rev`, involution does not imply functional correctness. Clearly, the challenges in building suitably typed definitions that let us reason about interesting shape properties of a data structure are substantial.

Nonetheless, the way the length of a list is tracked using its length-indexed type offers a useful hint about how we can reason about its shape. Akin to the `Nat` domain that indexes a list type with a length abstraction, we need an appropriate abstract domain that we can use to help us reason about a list's shape properties. For instance, in the case of list reversal, the abstract domain should allow us to structurally reason about the order of elements in the input and output lists. A useful interpretation of a list order that satisfies this requirement would be one that relates every element in a list with every another element based on an ordering predicate (e.g., *occurs-before* or *occurs-after*). By defining an exhaustive enumeration of the set of all such pairs under this ordering, we can effectively specify the total order of all elements in the list. More precisely, observe that the notion of order can be broken down to the level of a binary relation over elements in the list, with the

ICFP '14, September 1–6, 2014, Gothenburg, Sweden.
Copyright © 2014 ACM 978-1-4503-2873-9 /14/09... $15.00.
http://dx.doi.org/10.1145/10.1145/2628136.2628159

transitive closure of such a relation effectively serving as a faithful representation.

For example, consider a relation R_{ob} that relates a list to a pair if the first element in the pair *occurs before* the second in the list. For a concrete list `l=[x1,x2,x3]` , the relation's closure R^*_{ob} would be:

$$\{\langle \mathtt{l}, \langle \mathtt{x1}, \mathtt{x2}\rangle\rangle, \langle \mathtt{l}, \langle \mathtt{x1}, \mathtt{x3}\rangle\rangle, \langle \mathtt{l}, \langle \mathtt{x2}, \mathtt{x3}\rangle\rangle\}$$ [1]

Conversely, an *occurs-after* (R_{oa}) relation serves as the semantic inverse of *occurs-before*; given these two relations, we can specify the following type for `rev`:

$\mathtt{rev} : \{ \mathtt{l} : \text{'a list}\} \longrightarrow \{\nu: \text{'a list} \mid R^*_{ob}(\mathtt{l}) = R^*_{oa}(\nu)\}$

Since $R^*_{ob}(\mathtt{l})$ represents the set of pairs whose elements exhibit the *occurs-before* property in the input list, and $R^*_{oa}(\nu)$ represents the set of pairs whose elements exhibit the *occurs-after* property in the output list, the above specification effectively asserts that for every pair of elements x and y in the input list `l`, if x occurs before y in `l`, then x has to occur after y in the result list ν.

This property succinctly captures the fact that the result list is the same as the original list in reverse order without appealing to the operational definition of how the result list is constructed from the input. By using a relational domain to reason about the shape of the list, we avoid having to construct a statically checkable reference implementation of `rev`.

We refer to operators like R_{ob} and R_{oa} as *structural relations* because they explicitly describe structural properties of a data structure. Such relations can be used as appropriate abstract domains to reason about the shapes of structures generated by constructor applications in algebraic data types. Given that relations naturally translate to sets of tuples, standard set operations such as union and cross-product are typically sufficient to build useful relational abstractions from any concrete domain. This simplicity makes relational specifications highly amenable for automatic verification.

The type of `rev` given above captures its functional behavior by referring to the order of elements in its argument and result lists. However, the notion of order as a relation between elements of the list is not always sufficient. For example, consider the function,

$$\mathtt{dup} : \text{'a list} \rightarrow \text{('a*'a) list}$$

that duplicates the elements in its input list. An invariant that we can expect of any correct implementation is that the order of left components of pairs in the output list is the same as the order of its right components, and both are equal to the order of elements in the input list. Clearly, our definitions of R_{ob} and R_{oa} as relations over elements in a list are insufficient to express the order of individual components of pairs in a list of pairs. How do we construct general definitions that let us capture ordering invariants over different kinds of lists without generating distinct relations for each kind?

We address this issue by allowing structural relations defined over a polymorphic data type to be parameterized by relations over type variables in the data type. For instance, the R_{ob} relation defined over a `'a list` can be parameterized by a polymorphic relation R over `'a`. Instead of directly relating the order of two elements x and y in a polymorphic list, a parametric *occurs-before* relation generically relates the ordering of $R(x)$ and $R(y)$; R's specific instantiation would draw from the set of relations defined over the data type that instantiates the type variable (`'a`). In the case of `dup`, R_{ob} could be instantiated with relations like R_{fst} and R_{snd} that project the first and second elements of the pairs in `dup`'s output list. The ability to parameterize relations in this way allows structural relations to be used seamlessly with higher-order polymorphic functions, and enables composable specifications over defined relations.

In this paper, we present an automated verification framework integrated within a refinement type system to express and check specifications of the kind given above. We describe a specification language based on relational algebra to define and compose structural relations for any algebraic data type. These definitions are only as complex as the data type definition itself in the sense that it is possible to construct equivalent relational definitions directly *superimposed* on the data type. Relations thus defined, including their automatically generated inductive variants, can be used to specify shape invariants and other relational properties. Our typechecking procedure verifies specifications by interpreting constructor applications as set operations within these abstract relational domains. Typechecking in our system is decidable, a result which follows from the completeness of encoding our specification language in a decidable logic.

The paper makes the following contributions:

1. We present a rich specification language for expressing refinements that are given in terms of relational expressions and familiar relational algebraic operations. The language is equipped with pattern-matching operations over constructors of algebraic data types, thus allowing the definition of useful shape properties in terms of relational constraints.
2. To allow relational refinements to express shape properties over complex data structures, and to be effective in defining such properties on higher-order programs, we allow the inductive relations found in type refinements to be parameterized over other inductively defined relations. While the semantics of a relationally parametric specification can be understood intuitively in second-order logic, we show that it can be equivalently encoded in a decidable fragment of first-order logic, leading to a practical and efficient type-checking algorithm.
3. We present a formalization of our ideas, including a static semantics, meta-theory that establishes the soundness of well-typed programs, a translation mechanism that maps well-typed relational expressions and refinements to a decidable many-sorted first-order logic, and a decidability result that justifies the translation scheme.
4. We describe an implementation of these ideas in a type checker called CATALYST that is incorporated within the MLton Standard ML compiler, and demonstrate the utility of these ideas through a series of examples, including a detailed case study that automatically verifies the correctness of α-conversion and capture-avoiding substitution operations of the untyped lambda calculus, whose types are expressed using relational expressions.

The remainder of the paper is structured as follows. In the next section, we present additional motivation and examples for our ideas. Sec. 3 formalizes the syntax and static semantics of relational refinements in the context of a simply-typed core language. Sec. 4 extends the formalization to support parametric refinements within a polymorphic core language. Our formalization also presents a translation scheme from relational refinements to a decidable first-order logic. Details about the implementation are given in Sec. 5. Sec. 6 presents a case study. Secs. 7, 8 and 9 present related work, directions for future work, and conclusions, respectively.

[1] Given a relation $R = \{\langle x, y_1\rangle, \langle x, y_2\rangle, \ldots, \langle x, y_n\rangle\}$ where x is an instance of some datatype, and the y_i are tuples that capture some shape property of interest, we write $R(x)$ as shorthand for $\{y_1, y_2, \ldots, y_n\}$. Thus,

$$R^*_{ob}(\mathtt{l}) = \{\langle \mathtt{x1}, \mathtt{x2}\rangle, \langle \mathtt{x1}, \mathtt{x3}\rangle, \langle \mathtt{x2}, \mathtt{x3}\rangle\}$$

2. Structural Relations

Our specification language is primarily the language of relational expressions composed using familiar relational algebraic operators. This language is additionally equipped with pattern matching over constructors of algebraic types to define shape properties in terms of these expressions. A number of built-in polymorphic relations are provided, the most important of which are listed below:

$$\begin{array}{lcl} R_{id}\ (\texttt{x}) & = & \{\langle\texttt{x}\rangle\} \\ R_{dup}\ (\texttt{x}) & = & \{\langle\texttt{x},\texttt{x}\rangle\} \\ R_{notEq_k}\ (\texttt{x}) & = & \{\langle\texttt{x}\rangle\} - \{\langle\texttt{k}\rangle\} \\ R_{eq_k}\ (\texttt{x}) & = & \{\langle\texttt{x}\rangle\} - (\{\langle\texttt{x}\rangle\} - \{\langle\texttt{k}\rangle\}) \end{array}$$

R_{id} is the identity relation, R_{dup} is a relation that associates a value with a pair that duplicates that value, R_{notEq_k} is a relation indexed by a constant `k` (of some base type) that relates `x` to itself, provided `x` is not equal to `k`, and R_{eq_k} is defined similarly, except it relates `x` to itself exactly when `x` is equal to `k`. Apart from the relations defined above, the language also includes the primitive relation $\emptyset$ that denotes the empty set.

To see how new structural relations can be built using relational operators, primitive relations, and pattern-match syntax, consider the specification of the *list-head* relation that relates a list to its head element:

$$\begin{array}{lll} \textbf{relation}\ R_{hd}\ (\texttt{x::xs}) & = & \{\langle\texttt{x}\rangle\} \\ \quad\mid R_{hd}\ \texttt{[]} & = & \emptyset \end{array}$$

For a concrete list `l`, R_{hd}(`l`) produces the set of unary tuples whose elements are in the *head* relation with `l`. This set is clearly a singleton when the list is non-empty and empty otherwise. The above definition states that for any list pattern constructed using "::" whose head is represented by pattern variable `x` and whose tail is represented by pattern variable `xs`, (1) $\langle \texttt{x} :: \texttt{xs}, \texttt{x}\rangle \in R_{hd}$, and (2) there does not exist an `x'` such that $\texttt{x}' \neq \texttt{x}$ and $\langle \texttt{x} :: \texttt{xs}, \texttt{x}'\rangle \in R_{hd}$. The declarative syntax of the kind shown above is the primary means of defining structural relations in our system.

2.1 Relational Composition

Simple structural relations such as R_{hd} have fixed cardinality , i.e., they have a fixed number of tuples regardless of the concrete size of the data structure on which they are defined. However, practical verification problems require relations over algebraic datatypes to have cardinality comparable to the size of the data structure, which may be recursive.

For example, the problem of verifying that an implementation of `rev` reverses the ordering of its input requires specifying a *membership* relation (R_{mem}) that relates a list `l` to every element in `l` (regardless of `l`'s size). This relation would allow us to define an ordering property such as *occurs-before* or *occurs-after* on precisely those elements that comprise `rev`'s input and output lists. A recursive definition of R_{mem} looks like [2]:

$$R_{mem}\ (\texttt{x} :: \texttt{xs}) = \{\langle\texttt{x}\rangle\} \cup R_{mem}\ (\texttt{xs})$$

We can equivalently express R_{mem} as an *inductive extension* of the head relation R_{hd} defined above. Suppose R is a structural relation that relates a list l of type `'a list` with elements v of type `'a`. Then, the inductive extension of R (written R^*) is the least relation that satisfies the following conditions:

- if $\langle l, v\rangle \in R$, then $\langle l, v\rangle \in R^*$
- if $l = x :: xs$ and $\langle xs, v\rangle \in R$ then $\langle l, v\rangle \in R^*$

[2] In some our examples, we elide the case for the empty list, which defaults to the empty set.

Thus, $R_{mem} = R^*_{hd}$. We can think of the induction operator as a controlled abstraction for structural recursion. Based on the recursive structure of an algebraic data type, sophisticated inductive definitions can be generated from simple structural relations defined for that data type.

Equipped with R_{mem}, we can now precisely define the *occurs-before* relation defined earlier. Because R_{ob} relates a list to a pair whose first element is the head of the list, and whose second element is a member of its tail, it can be expressed in terms of R_{mem} thus:

$$\textbf{relation}\ R_{ob}\ (\texttt{x} :: \texttt{xs}) = \{\langle\texttt{x}\rangle\} \times R_{mem}\ (\texttt{xs})$$

The transitive closure of this relation R^*_{ob} expresses the *occurs-before* property on every element in the list. The *occurs-after* relation can be defined similarly:

$$\textbf{relation}\ R_{oa}\ (\texttt{x} :: \texttt{xs}) = R_{mem}\ (\texttt{xs}) \times \{\langle\texttt{x}\rangle\}$$

2.2 Parametric Relations

Consider how we might specify a `zip` function over lists, with the following type:

$$\texttt{zip} : \texttt{'a list} \rightarrow \texttt{'b list} \rightarrow (\texttt{'a * 'b})\ \texttt{list}$$

Any correct implementation of `zip` must guarantee that the elements of the output list are pairs of elements drawn from both argument lists. The R_{mem} relation defined above provides much of the functionality we require to specify this invariant; intuitively, the specification should indicate that the first (resp. second) element of every pair in the output list is in a membership relation with `zip`'s first (resp. second) argument. Unfortunately, as currently defined, R_{mem} operates directly on the pair elements of the output, not the pair's individual components. What we require is a mechanism that allows R_{mem} to assert the membership property on the pair's components (rather than the pair directly).

To do this, we allow structural relations to be *parameterized* over other relations. In the case of `zip`, the parameterized membership relation can be instantiated with the appropriate relationally-defined projections on a pair type. Concretely, given new parameterized definitions of R_{hd} and R_{mem}, and related auxiliary relations:

$$\begin{array}{lll} \textbf{relation}\ (R_{hd}\ R)\ (\texttt{x::xs}) & = & R\ (\texttt{x}) \\ \quad\mid (R_{hd}\ R)\ \texttt{[]} & = & \emptyset \\ \textbf{relation}\ (R_{mem}\ R) & = & (R_{hd}\ R)^* \\ \textbf{relation}\ R_{fst}\ (\texttt{x,y}) & = & \{\langle\texttt{x}\rangle\} \\ \textbf{relation}\ R_{snd}\ (\texttt{x,y}) & = & \{\langle\texttt{y}\rangle\} \end{array}$$

`zip` can now be assigned the following type that faithfully captures the membership relation between its input lists and its output:[3]

$$\begin{array}{l} \texttt{zip} : \texttt{l}_1 \rightarrow \texttt{l}_2 \rightarrow \\ \quad \{\ \nu \mid ((R_{mem}\ R_{fst})\ \nu) = ((R_{mem}\ R_{id})\ \texttt{l}_1) \\ \quad\quad \wedge ((R_{mem}\ R_{snd})\ \nu) = ((R_{mem}\ R_{id})\ \texttt{l}_2)\ \} \end{array}$$

Similarly, we can define parametric versions of R_{ob} and R_{oa}:

$$\begin{array}{lll} \textbf{relation}\ (R_{ob}\ R)\ (\texttt{x:xs}) & = & R\ (\texttt{x}) \times ((R_{mem}\ R)\ \texttt{xs}) \\ \textbf{relation}\ (R_{oa}\ R)\ (\texttt{x:xs}) & = & ((R_{mem}\ R)\ \texttt{xs}) \times R\ (\texttt{x}) \end{array}$$

Using this parametric version of R_{ob}, the `dup` function described in the previous section can now be specified thus:

$$\begin{array}{l} \texttt{dup} : \texttt{l} \rightarrow \{\ \nu \mid ((R_{ob}\ R_{fst})^*\ \nu) = ((R_{ob}\ R_{id})^*\ \texttt{l}) \\ \quad\quad \wedge ((R_{ob}\ R_{snd})^*\ \nu) = ((R_{ob}\ R_{id})^*\ \texttt{l})\ \} \end{array}$$

[3] We drop ML types from dependent type specifications when obvious from context.

2.3 Parametric Dependent Types

Our specification language also allows dependent types to be parameterized over relations used in type refinements. In the spirit of type variables, we use relation variables to denote parameterized relations in a type. To illustrate why such parameterization is useful, consider the following signature for `foldl`:

$$
\begin{array}{l}
('R_{bm})\ \texttt{foldl} : \\
\quad \{\texttt{l} : \texttt{'a list}\} \to \{\texttt{b} : \texttt{'b}\} \to \\
\quad\quad (\{\texttt{f}: \{\texttt{x} : \texttt{'a}\} \to \{\texttt{acc} : \texttt{'b}\} \to \\
\quad\quad\quad \{\texttt{z} : \texttt{'b} \mid 'R_{bm}(\texttt{z}) = \{\langle \texttt{x} \rangle\} \cup 'R_{bm}(\texttt{acc})\}\}) \to \\
\quad \{\nu \mid 'R_{bm}(\nu) = R_{mem}(\texttt{l}) \cup 'R_{bm}(\texttt{b})\}
\end{array}
$$

This type relates membership properties on `foldl`'s input list, expressed in terms of a non-parametric R_{mem} relation, to an abstract notion of membership over its result type (`'b`) captured using a relation variable ($'R_{bm}$). This signature constrains `foldl` to produce a result for which a membership property is a sensible notion. For instance, if `foldl` were applied to arguments in which `b` was of some list type (e.g., `[]`) because it is used as a list transform operator, then $'R_{bm}$ could be trivially instantiated with R_{mem}. However, allowing types to be parameterized over relation variables enable richer properties to be expressed. For example, consider the function `makeTree` that uses `foldl` to generate a binary tree using function `treeInsert` (not shown):

```
datatype 'a tree = Leaf
                 | Tree of 'a * ('a Tree) * ('a Tree)
```

$$
\begin{array}{l}
\texttt{relation}\ R_{thd}\ \texttt{Leaf}\ = \emptyset \\
\quad\quad \mid R_{thd}\ (\texttt{Tree}\ (\texttt{x},\texttt{t}_1,\texttt{t}_2)) = \{\langle \texttt{x} \rangle\} \\
\texttt{relation}\ R_{tmem} = R^*_{thd}
\end{array}
$$

$$
\begin{array}{l}
\texttt{makeTree} : \{\texttt{l} : \texttt{'a list}\} \to \\
\quad\quad \{\nu : \texttt{'a tree} \mid R_{tmem}(\nu) = R_{mem}(\texttt{l})\} \\
\texttt{val makeTree = fn l =>} \\
\quad \texttt{foldl}\ (R_{tmem})\ \texttt{l Leaf treeInsert}
\end{array}
$$

Function `makeTree` uses `foldl` by first instantiating the relation variable $'R_{bm}$ in the type of `foldl` to R_{tmem}. The resultant type of `foldl` requires its higher-order argument to construct a tree using members of its tree argument (`acc`), and the list element (`x`) to which it is applied. In return, `foldl` guarantees to produce a tree, which contains all the members of its list argument. It should be noted that a correct implementation of `treeInsert` will have the required type of `foldl`'s higher-order argument, after instantiating $'R_{bm}$ to R_{tmem}. Thus, the application of `foldl` in the above example typechecks, producing the required invariant of `makeTree`.

`Foldl`'s type can also be parameterized over an abstract notion of membership for type variable `'a`, captured by another relation variable ($'R_{am}$) to state a more general membership invariant. Concretely, this requires that the tuple ($\{\langle \texttt{x} \rangle\}$) in the type refinement of higher-order argument (`f`) be replaced with $'R_{am}(\texttt{x})$), and the non-parametric R_{mem} relation in the result type refinement be substituted with a parametric ($R_{mem}\ 'R_{am}$) relation. In cases when there does not exist any useful notion of membership for types that instantiate `'a` and `'b`, relation variables $'R_{am}$ and R_{bm} can be instantiated with $\emptyset$ to yield tautological type refinements.

An alternative type for `foldl` could relate the order of elements in the argument list to some order of the result. The intuition is as follows: suppose the result type (`'b`) has some notion of order captured by a relation such that the result of `foldl`'s higher-order argument (`f`) has a refinement given in terms of this relation; i.e., it says something about how the order relation of its result (`z`) relates to its arguments (`x` and `acc`). But, `x` comes from the list being folded, and `f` is applied over elements of this list in a pre-defined order. Therefore, we can express invariants that relate the order of the input list to the order of the result type, given that we know the order in which `f` is applied over the list. The type of `foldl` that tries to match the abstract order ($'R_{bo}$) on the result type (`'b`) to an occurs-after order on the input list is shown below. For brevity, we avoid reproducing membership invariants from the type of `foldl` from the previous example, using ellipses in their place:

$$
\begin{array}{l}
('R_{bm}, 'R_{bo})\ \texttt{foldl} : \{\texttt{l} : \texttt{'a list}\} \to \{\texttt{b} : \texttt{'b}\} \to \\
\quad (\{\texttt{f} : \{\texttt{x} : \texttt{'a}\} \to \{\texttt{acc} : \texttt{'b}\} \to \\
\quad\quad \{\texttt{z} \mid 'R_{bo}(\texttt{z}) = (\{\langle \texttt{x} \rangle\} \times 'R_{bm}(\texttt{acc})) \cup \\
\quad\quad\quad 'R_{bo}(\texttt{acc}) \wedge ...\}) \to \\
\quad \{\nu \mid 'R_{bo}(\nu) = R^*_{oa}(\texttt{l}) \cup 'R_{bo}(\texttt{b})) \cup \\
\quad\quad ((R_{mem}(\texttt{l})) \times 'R_{bm}(\texttt{b})) \wedge ...\}
\end{array}
$$

An implementation of `rev` that uses `foldl` is given below:

$$
\begin{array}{l}
\texttt{rev} : \{\texttt{l} : \texttt{'a list}\} \to \{\nu : \texttt{'a list} \mid R^*_{ob}(\nu) = R^*_{oa}(l)\} \\
\texttt{val Cons = fn x => fn xs => x::xs} \\
\texttt{val rev = fn l => foldl}\ (R_{mem}, R^*_{ob})\ \texttt{l [] Cons}
\end{array}
$$

Our type checker successfully typechecks the above program, given the standard definition of `foldl`. Note that, due to the difference in the order in which the higher-order argument is applied over the input list, the type of `foldr` will be necessarily different from `foldl`. Consequently, using `foldr` instead of `foldl` in the above program fails type checking, as would be expected.

Calculus λ_R

x, y, z, ν	$\in$	*variables*	n $\in$ *integers*		
c	::=	Cons ∣ Nil ∣ n		*constants*
v	::=	$x \mid \lambda(x : \tau).\, e \mid c \mid \textsf{Cons}\, v \mid \textsf{Cons}\, v\, v$		*value*
e	::=	$v \mid e\ v \mid$ `let` $x = e$ `in` $e \mid$ `match` v `with` $\textsf{Cons}\, x\, y \Rightarrow e\, \textsf{else}\, e$		*expression*
T	::=	int ∣ intlist		*datatypes*
τ	::=	$\{\nu : T \mid \phi\} \mid x : \tau \to \tau$		*dep. types*

Specification Language

R	$\in$	*relation names*	
r	::=	$R(v) \mid r \cup r \mid r \times r$	*relational exp.*
ϕ	::=	$r = r \mid r \subseteq r \mid \phi \wedge \phi \mid \phi \vee \phi \mid true$	*type refinement*
Δ_R	::=	$\langle R, \tau_R, \textsf{Cons}\, x\, y \Rightarrow r \mid \textsf{Nil} \Rightarrow r \rangle \mid \langle R, \tau_R, R^* \rangle$	*relation def.*
θ	::=	$T \mid T * \theta$	*tuple sort*
τ_R	::=	$\textsf{intlist} :\to \{\theta\} \mid \textsf{int} :\to \{\theta\}$	*relation sort*

Figure 1: Language

3. Core language

3.1 Syntax

We formalize our ideas using a core calculus (λ_R) shown in Fig. 1, an A-normalized extension of the simply-typed lambda calculus. The language supports a primitive type (int), a recursive data type (intlist), along with dependent base and function types. Because the mechanisms and syntax to define and elaborate recursive data types are kept separate from the core, λ_R is only provided with two constructors, Nil and Cons used to build lists. The language has a standard call-by-value operational semantics, details of which can be found in an accompanying technical report [10].[4]

Dependent type refinements (ϕ) in λ_R are assertions over relational expressions (r); these expressions, which are themselves

[4] Proofs for all lemmas and theorems given in this paper are also provided in the report.

Sort Checking Specification Language $\boxed{\Gamma \vdash r :: \{\theta\}, \quad \Gamma \vdash R :: T :\to \{\theta\}}$

S-REL

$$\frac{R \triangleq \langle \mathsf{Nil} \Rightarrow r_1,\ \mathsf{Cons}\, x\, y \Rightarrow r_2\rangle \quad \cdot \vdash r1 :: \{\theta\} \quad \cdot, x : \mathsf{int}, y : \mathsf{intlist} \vdash r2 :: \{\theta\}}{\cdot \vdash R :: \mathsf{intlist} :\to \{\theta\}}$$

S-REL-STAR

$$\frac{R_1 \triangleq R_2^* \quad \cdot \vdash R_2 :: \tau_R}{\cdot \vdash R_1 :: \tau_R}$$

S-APP

$$\frac{\|\Gamma\| \Vdash v : T \quad \cdot \vdash R :: T :\to \{\theta\}}{\Gamma \vdash R(v) :: \{\theta\}}$$

S-REL-ID

$$\frac{}{\cdot \vdash R_{id} :: \mathsf{int} :\to \{\mathsf{int}\}}$$

S-UNION

$$\frac{\Gamma \vdash r_1 :: \{\theta\} \quad \Gamma \vdash r_2 :: \{\theta\}}{\Gamma \vdash r_1 \cup r_2 :: \{\theta\}}$$

S-CROSS

$$\frac{\Gamma \vdash r_1 :: \{\theta_1\} \quad \Gamma \vdash r_2 :: \{\theta_2\}}{\Gamma \vdash r_1 \times r_2 :: \{\theta_1 * \theta_2\}}$$

Well-Formedness $\boxed{\Gamma \vdash \phi, \quad \Gamma \vdash \tau}$

WF-RPRED

$$\frac{\odot \in \{=, \subset\} \quad \Gamma \vdash r_1 :: \{\theta\} \quad \Gamma \vdash r_2 :: \{\theta\}}{\Gamma \vdash r_1 \odot r_2}$$

WF-REF

$$\frac{\odot \in \{\wedge, \vee\} \quad \Gamma \vdash \phi_1 \quad \Gamma \vdash \phi_2}{\Gamma \vdash \phi_1 \odot \phi_2}$$

WF-BASE

$$\frac{\Gamma, \nu : T \vdash \phi}{\Gamma \vdash \{\nu : T \mid \phi\}}$$

WF-FUN

$$\frac{\Gamma \vdash \tau_1 \quad \Gamma, x : \tau_1 \vdash \tau_2}{\Gamma \vdash x : \tau_1 \to \tau_2}$$

Subtyping $\boxed{\Gamma \vdash \tau_1 <: \tau_2}$

SUBT-BASE

$$\frac{\Gamma \vdash \{\nu : T \mid \phi_1\} \quad \Gamma \vdash \{\nu : T \mid \phi_2\} \quad [\![\Gamma_R]\!] \models [\![\Gamma, \nu : T]\!] \Rightarrow [\![\phi_1]\!] \Rightarrow [\![\phi_2]\!]}{\Gamma \vdash \{\nu : T \mid \phi_1\} <: \{\nu : T \mid \phi_2\}}$$

SUBT-ARROW

$$\frac{\Gamma \vdash \tau_{21} <: \tau_{11} \quad \Gamma, x : \tau_{21} \vdash \tau_{12} <: \tau_{22}}{\Gamma \vdash (x : \tau_{11}) \to \tau_{12} <: (x : \tau_{21}) \to \tau_{22}}$$

Type Checking Expression Language $\boxed{\Gamma \vdash e : \tau}$

T-VAR

$$\frac{(x : \tau) \in \Gamma}{\Gamma \vdash x : \tau}$$

T-ABS

$$\frac{\Gamma \vdash \tau_1 \quad \Gamma, x : \tau_1 \vdash e : \tau_2}{\Gamma \vdash \lambda(x : \tau_1).e : (x : \tau_1) \to \tau_2}$$

T-MATCH

$$\frac{\begin{array}{c}\Gamma \vdash v : \mathsf{intlist} \quad \Gamma \vdash \mathsf{Nil} : \{\nu : \mathsf{intlist} \mid \phi_n\} \\ \Gamma \vdash \mathsf{Cons} : x : \mathsf{int} \to y : \mathsf{intlist} \to \{\nu : \mathsf{intlist} \mid \phi_c\} \\ \Gamma_c = x : \mathsf{int}, y : \mathsf{intlist},\ [v/\nu]\,\phi_c \quad \Gamma_n = [v/\nu]\,\phi_n \\ \Gamma \vdash \tau \quad \Gamma, \Gamma_c \vdash e1 : \tau \quad \Gamma, \Gamma_n \vdash e2 : \tau\end{array}}{\Gamma \vdash \mathtt{match}\ v\ \mathtt{with}\ \mathsf{Cons}\, x\, y \Rightarrow e_1\ \mathtt{else}\ e_2 : \tau}$$

T-CONST

$$\frac{\cdot \vdash ty(c)}{\Gamma \vdash c : ty(c)}$$

T-SUB

$$\frac{\Gamma \vdash e : \tau_1 \quad \Gamma \vdash \tau_1 <: \tau_2}{\Gamma \vdash e : \tau_2}$$

T-APP

$$\frac{\Gamma \vdash e : (x : \tau_1) \to \tau_2 \quad \Gamma \vdash v : \tau_1}{\Gamma \vdash e\ v : [v/x]\tau_2}$$

T-LET

$$\frac{\Gamma \vdash e_1 : \tau_1 \quad \Gamma, x : \tau_1 \vdash e_2 : \tau_2 \quad \Gamma \vdash \tau_2}{\Gamma \vdash \mathtt{let}\ x = e_1\ \mathtt{in}\ e_2 : \tau_2}$$

Figure 3: Static semantics of λ_R

typed, constitute the syntactic class of expressions in our specification language. We refer to the types of relational expressions as *sorts*, in order to distinguish them from λ_R types. We write $r :: s$ to denote that a relational expression r has sort s. A structural relation is a triple, consisting of a unique relation name, its sort, and its definition as (a) a pattern-match sequence that relates constructors of an algebraic data type to a relation expression, or (b) an inductive extension of an existing relation, captured using the closure operator (*). We write $R \triangleq \delta$ to denote that a relation R has a (pattern-match or inductive) definition δ.

A structural relation maps a value to a set of tuples (θ). We use ":$\to$" to distinguish such maps from the mapping expressed by dependent function types. For example, the notation:

$$R_{ob} :: \mathsf{intlist}\ :\to\ \{\mathsf{int}\ *\ \mathsf{int}\}$$

indicates that the sort of relation R_{ob} is a map from integer lists to pairs. As reflected by the syntactic class of relation sorts (τ_R), the domain of a λ_R relation is either intlist or int. For the purposes of the formalization, we assume the existence of a single primitive relation R_{id} whose sort is $\mathtt{int}\ :\to\ \{\mathtt{int}\}$ that defines an identity relation on integers.

3.2 Sorts, Types and Well-formedness

Fig. 3 defines rules to check sorts of structural relations and relational expressions, establish well-formedness conditions of type refinements, and type-check expressions. The judgments defined by these rules make use of environment Γ, defined as follows:

$$\Gamma ::= \cdot \mid \Gamma, x : \tau \mid \Gamma, \phi$$

Environments are ordered sets of assertions that make up a typing context. Assertions are either (a) type bindings for variables, or (b) type refinements that reflect branch conditions collected from `match` expressions. We assume that any variable is bound only once in Γ.

Structural relations are sort checked under an empty type environment. The rule S-REL type checks a relation definition by ensuring that relational expressions associated with the constructors that comprise the definition all have the same sort. The rule S-REL-

MSFOL

$$
\begin{array}{lcl@{\qquad}lcl}
x & \in & \lambda_R \ \textit{variable} & i,k,j & \in & \textit{bound variable} \\
R & \in & \textit{uninterpreted relation} & A & \in & \textit{uninterpreted sort}
\end{array}
$$

$$
\begin{array}{lcll}
\phi^F & ::= & v \mid v = v \mid \phi^F\ \phi^F \mid \phi^F \Leftrightarrow \phi^F & \textit{quantifier} - \textit{free} \\
 & \mid & \phi^F \Rightarrow \phi^F \mid \phi^F \vee \phi^F \mid \phi^F \wedge \phi^F & \textit{proposition} \\
 & \mid & v : \tau^F & \\
\phi^L & ::= & \forall (k : T^F).\, \phi^L \mid \phi^F \mid \phi^L \wedge \phi^L & \textit{quantified} \\
 & \mid & \phi^L \vee \phi^L & \textit{proposition} \\
v & ::= & x \mid k \mid j \mid R & \textit{variable} \\
T^F & ::= & A \mid \textit{bool} & \textit{sort} \\
\tau^F & ::= & \textit{bool} \mid T^F \to \tau^F & \textit{sort of } \phi^F
\end{array}
$$

Auxiliary Definitions

$$
\begin{array}{lcl}
\mathcal{F} & : & T \to A \\
\mathit{Inst} & : & \phi^L \times v \to \phi^L \\
\mathit{Inst}(\forall (k : T^F).\phi^L,\ y) & = & [y/k]\phi^L \\
\eta_{wrap} & : & \phi^F \times \tau^F \to \phi^L \\
\eta_{wrap}(\phi^F, T^F \to \tau^F) & = & \forall (k : T^F).\eta_{wrap}(\phi^F\ k, \tau^F) \\
\eta_{wrap}(\phi^F, \textit{bool}) & = & \phi^F
\end{array}
$$

Semantics of Relational Expressions $\boxed{[\![r]\!]}$

$$
\begin{array}{lcl}
[\![R(\mathsf{Cons}\, v_1\, v_2)]\!] & = & [\![\Sigma_R(R)(\mathsf{Cons}\, v_1\, v_2)]\!] \\
[\![R(\mathsf{Nil})]\!] & = & [\![\Sigma_R(R)(\mathsf{Nil})]\!] \\
[\![T]\!] & = & \mathcal{F}(T) \\
[\![\{T\}]\!] & = & [\![T]\!] \to \textit{bool} \\
[\![\{T * \theta\}]\!] & = & [\![T]\!] \to [\![\{\theta\}]\!] \\
[\![T :\to \{\theta\}]\!] & = & [\![T]\!] \to [\![\{\theta\}]\!] \\
[\![R_{id}]\!] & = & \forall (j : [\![\,\mathtt{int}\,]\!]). \\
 & & \quad \forall (k : [\![\,\mathtt{int}\,]\!]).j = k
\end{array}
$$

$$
\begin{array}{lcl}
[\![R]\!] & = & \eta_{wrap}(R, [\![\Gamma_R(R)]\!]) \\
[\![R(x)]\!] & = & \mathit{Inst}([\![R]\!], x) \\
[\![r_1 \cup r_2]\!] & = & \gamma_{\sqcup}([\![r_1]\!], \vee, [\![r_2]\!]) \\
[\![r_1 \times r_2]\!] & = & \gamma_{\bowtie}([\![r_1]\!], \wedge, [\![r_2]\!]) \\
\gamma_{\sqcup}(\forall (k : T^F).\, e_1, \odot, \forall (k : T^F).\, e_2) & = & \forall (k : T^F).\, \gamma_{\sqcup}(e_1, \odot, e_2) \\
\gamma_{\sqcup}(\phi_1^F, \odot, \phi_2^F) & = & \phi_1^F \odot \phi_2^F \\
\gamma_{\bowtie}(\forall \overline{j : T_j^F}.\, \phi_1^F, \odot, \forall \overline{k : T_k^F}.\, \phi_1^F) & = & \forall (\overline{j : T_j^F}).\, \forall (\overline{k : T_k^F}).\, \phi_1^F \odot \phi_2^F
\end{array}
$$

Semantics of Type Refinements $\boxed{[\![\phi]\!]}$

$$
\begin{array}{lcl@{\qquad}lcl}
[\![\phi_1 \wedge \phi_2]\!] & = & [\![\phi_1]\!] \wedge [\![\phi_2]\!] & [\![r_1 = r_2]\!] & = & \gamma_{\sqcup}([\![r_1]\!], \Leftrightarrow, [\![r_2]\!]) \\
[\![\phi_1 \vee \phi_2]\!] & = & [\![\phi_1]\!] \vee [\![\phi_2]\!] & [\![r_1 \subseteq r_2]\!] & = & \gamma_{\sqcup}([\![r_1]\!], \Rightarrow, [\![r_2]\!])
\end{array}
$$

Figure 4: Semantics of Specification Language

STAR captures the fact that an inductive extension of a relation has the same type as the relation itself. The rule S-APP sort checks relation applications by ensuring that the argument to the relation has the required simple (non-dependent) type. The rule makes use of a simple typing judgment ($\Vdash$) under a *refinement erased* Γ (denoted $\|\Gamma\|$) for this purpose. Rules for simple typing judgments are straightforward, and are elided here; the full set of rules can be found in the accompanying technical report [10].

Refinement erasure on a dependent base type (τ) sets its type refinement to $true$, effectively erasing the refinement to yield a simple type. For function types, erasure is defined recursively:

$$\|\{\nu : T \mid \phi\}\| \;=\; T \qquad \|(x : \tau_1) \to \tau_2\| \;=\; \|\tau_1\| \to \|\tau_2\|$$

Refinement erasure for type environments performs erasure over all type bindings within the environment, in addition to erasing all recorded branch conditions. For an empty environment, refinement erasure is an identity.

$$
\begin{array}{lcl@{\qquad}lcl}
\|\Gamma,\, x : \tau\| & = & \|\Gamma\|,\, x : \|\tau\| & \|\Gamma,\, \phi\| & = & \|\Gamma\| \\
\|\cdot\| & = & \cdot & & &
\end{array}
$$

The dependent type checking rules for λ_R expressions are mostly standard, except for T-CONST and T-MATCH. The rule T-CONST makes use of a function ty that maps a constant c to a type ($ty(c)$), which remains its type under any Γ. The function ty is defined below:

$$
\begin{array}{lcl}
\forall i \in \mathbb{Z},\ ty(i) & = & \mathsf{int} \\
ty(\mathsf{Nil}) & = & \{\nu : \mathsf{intlist} \mid \phi_n\} \\
ty(\mathsf{Cons}) & = & x : \mathsf{int} \to y : \mathsf{intlist} \to \{\nu : \mathsf{intlist} \mid \phi_c\}
\end{array}
$$

The type refinements of Nil (ϕ_n) and Cons (ϕ_c) in the T-MATCH rule are conjunctive aggregations of Nil and Cons cases (resp.) of all structural relation definitions found within a program. To help us precisely define ϕ_n and ϕ_c, we assume the presence of (a) a globally-defined finite map (Σ_R) that maps relation names to their pattern-match definitions, and (b) a finite ordered map Γ_R that maps relation names to their sorts. We implicitly parameterize our typing judgment over Σ_R (i.e., our $\vdash$ is actually $\vdash_{\langle \Sigma_R, \Gamma_R \rangle}$). Inductive relations defined using the closure operator are assumed to be unfolded to pattern-match definitions before being bound in Σ_R:

$$\frac{R \triangleq R_2^* \quad \Sigma_R(R_2) = \langle \mathsf{Nil} \Rightarrow r_1,\ \mathsf{Cons}\, x\, y \Rightarrow r_2 \rangle}{\Sigma_R(R) = \langle \mathsf{Nil} \Rightarrow r_1,\ \mathsf{Cons}\, x\, y \Rightarrow r_2 \cup R(y) \rangle}$$

For the sake of presentation, we treat the pattern-match definition of a structural relation as a map from constructor patterns to relational expressions. Consequently, when $\Sigma_R(R) = \langle \mathsf{Nil} \Rightarrow r_1,\ \mathsf{Cons}\, x\, y \Rightarrow r_2 \cup R(y) \rangle$, the notation $\Sigma_R(R)(\mathsf{Nil})$ denotes r_1, and $\Sigma_R(R)(\mathsf{Cons}\, x\, y)$ denotes r_2. With help of Σ_R, we now define ϕ_n, and ϕ_c as:

$$
\begin{array}{lcl}
\phi_n & = & \bigwedge_{R \in dom(\Sigma_R)} R(\nu) = \Sigma_R(R)(\mathsf{Nil}) \\
\phi_c & = & \bigwedge_{R \in dom(\Sigma_R)} R(\nu) = \Sigma_R(R)(\mathsf{Cons}\, x\, y)
\end{array}
$$

For instance, consider a case where Σ_R has only one element (R) in its domain:

$$\Sigma_R = [R \mapsto \langle \mathsf{Nil} \Rightarrow R_{id}(0) \mid \mathsf{Cons}\, x\, y \Rightarrow R_{id}(x) \rangle]$$

The type of Nil and Cons in such case is as following:

$$
\begin{array}{lcl}
ty(\mathsf{Nil}) & = & \{\nu : \mathsf{intlist} \mid R(\nu) = R_{id}(0)\} \\
ty(\mathsf{Cons}) & = & x : \mathsf{int} \to y : \mathsf{intlist} \to \{\nu : \mathsf{intlist} \mid R(\nu) = R_{id}(x)\}
\end{array}
$$

The T-MATCH rule type checks each branch of the `match` expression under an environment that records the corresponding branch condition. Additionally, the type environment for the Cons branch is also extended with the types of matched pattern variables (x and y). The branch condition for the Cons (alternatively, Nil) case is obtained by substituting the test value (v) for the bound variable (ν) in the type refinement of Cons (Nil). Intuitively, the branch condition of Cons (alternatively, Nil) captures the fact that the value v was obtained by applying the constructor Cons (Nil); therefore, it should satisfy the invariant of Cons (Nil). For instance, consider the `match` expression:

$$\mathtt{match}\ z\ \mathtt{with}\ \mathsf{Cons}\ x\ y \Rightarrow e_1\ \mathtt{else}\ e_2$$

where Cons has type[5]

$$\text{Cons} : x{:}\text{int} \to y{:}\text{intlist} \to \{\nu : \text{intlist} \mid R_{mem}(\nu) = R_{id}(x) \cup R_{mem}(y)\}$$

Expression e_1 is type-checked under the extended environment:

$$\Gamma, x{:}\{\nu{:}\text{int} \mid \mathit{true}\}, xs{:}\{\nu{:}\text{intlist} \mid \mathit{true}\}, R_{mem}(z) = R_{id}(x) \cup R_{mem}(y)$$

The subtyping rules allow us to propagate dependent type information, and relate the subtype judgment to a notion of semantic entailment ($\models$) in logic. The cornerstone of subtyping is the subtyping judgment between base dependent types defined by the rule SUBT-BASE. The rule refers to the map Γ_R that provides sorts for relations occurring free in type refinements. Intuitively, the rule asserts dependent type τ_1 to be a subtype of τ_2, if and only if:

- Their base types match, and,
- Given a logical system L, and interpretations of type environment (Γ, $\nu : T$) and the type refinement ϕ_1 (of τ_1) in L, the following implication holds in L:

$$[\![\Gamma, \nu : T]\!] \Rightarrow [\![\phi_1]\!] \Rightarrow [\![\phi_2]\!]$$

The context under which the implication has to be valid ($[\![\Gamma_R]\!]$, is the interpretation of sort bindings of relations in L.

The soundness of λ_R's type system is defined with respect to a reduction relation ($\longrightarrow$) that specifies the langauge's operational semantics:

THEOREM 3.1. **(Type Safety)** *if* $\cdot \vdash e : \tau$, *then either* e *is a value, or there exists an* e' *such that* $e \longrightarrow e'$ *and* $\cdot \vdash e' : \tau$.

3.3 Semantics of the Specification Language

The semantics of our specification language is defined via a translation from well-typed relational expressions and well-formed type refinements to quantified propositions of many-sorted first-order logic (MSFOL).

Many-sorted first-order logic extends first-order logic (FOL) with sorts (types) for variables. For our purpose, we only consider the extension with Booleans and uninterpreted sorts, i.e., sorts that, unlike `int`, do not have an attached interpretation. Ground terms, or quantifier-free formulas, of MSFOL are drawn from propositional logic with equality and n-ary uninterpreted functions.

Our MSFOL semantics make use of the Σ_R map defined previously. For perspicuity, we introduce the following syntactic sugar:

$$\Sigma_R(R)(\text{Cons}\, v_1\, v_2) = [v_2/y]\,[v_1/x]\,\Sigma_R(R)(\text{Cons}\, x\, y)$$

Further, we also assume a finite ordered map Γ_R that maps structural relations to their sorts. That is, for all R such that $\cdot \vdash R :: \tau_R$, we have that $\Gamma_R(R) = \tau_R$.

Fig. 4 describes the MSFOL semantics of λ_R's specification language. The semantics is operational in the sense that it describes an algorithm to compile assertions in λ_R type refinements to formulas in MSFOL. Our semantics are parameterized over an auxiliary function ($\mathcal{F}$) that maps λ_R datatypes to uninterpreted sorts in MSFOL. The specific uninterpreted sorts types map to are not relevant here. However, $\mathcal{F}$ has to be a total function over λ_R datatypes. Note that despite treating interpreted types (eg: intlist and int) as uninterpreted sorts in the underlying logic, the exercise of ascribing a semantics to the type refinement language is complete. This is because the interpretation of any type is the collection of operations allowed on that type, and our type refinement language does not contain operations that are specific to values of any specific type.

[5] In our examples, we assign the same names to formal and actual arguments for convenience.

Relations translate to uninterpreted functions with a Boolean co-domain in MSFOL. We choose to curry sorts of uninterpreted functions representing relations (R) to simplify the semantics. The auxiliary function η_{wrap} wraps an uninterpreted function under a quantified formula; this can be construed as an eta-equivalent abstraction of an uninterpreted function in prenex quantified logic. As an example, suppose we have

$$R :: \text{intlist} :\to \{\text{int}\}$$

That is, Γ_R maps R to intlist $:\to \{\text{int}\}$. Assume that: $[\![\text{int}]\!] = A_0$ and $[\![\text{intlist}]\!] = A_1$. Now,

$$\begin{aligned}
[\![R]\!] \;=\; & \eta_{wrap}(R, \Gamma_R(R)) \\
& \eta_{wrap}(R, [\![\text{intlist} :\to \{\text{int}\}]\!]) \\
& \eta_{wrap}(R, [\![\text{intlist}]\!] \to [\![\{\text{int}\}]\!]) \\
& \eta_{wrap}(R, A_1 \to A_0 \to \mathit{bool}) \\
& \forall(k : A_1).\eta_{wrap}(R\,k, A_0 \to \mathit{bool}) \\
& \forall(k : A_1).\forall(j : A_0).\eta_{wrap}(R\,k\,j, \mathit{bool}) \\
& \forall(k : A_1).\forall(j : A_0).R\,k\,j
\end{aligned}$$

Auxiliary function *Inst* instantiates a prenex-quantified formula. We employ the standard interpretation of set union and cross product operations, when sets are represented using prenex-quantified propositions:

$$\begin{aligned}
\forall\overline{x}.\phi_1 \;\cup\; \forall\overline{x}.\phi_2 &= \forall\overline{x}.(\phi_1 \vee \phi_2) \\
\forall\overline{x}.\phi_1 \;\times\; \forall\overline{y}.\phi_2 &= \forall\overline{x}.\forall\overline{y}.(\phi_1 \wedge \phi_2)
\end{aligned}$$

Our semantics use syntactic rewrite functions - $\gamma_{\sqcup}$ and $\gamma_{\bowtie}$, to perform this translation, and to move quantification to prenex position when composing quantified formulas using logical connectives.

To demonstrate the compilation process, we consider the following λ_R assertion:

$$R_{ob}(\mathtt{1}) \;\mathtt{=}\; R_{id}(\mathtt{x}) \times R_{mem}(\mathtt{xs})$$

involving *membership* and *occurs-before* relations for integer lists:

$$\begin{aligned}
R_{mem} &:: \text{intlist} :\to \{\text{int}\} \\
R_{ob} &:: \text{intlist} :\to \{\text{int*int}\}
\end{aligned}$$

The series of steps that compile the assertion to an MSFOL formula, which captures the semantics of the assertion, are shown in Fig. 5.[6] The example assumes that $\mathcal{F}$ maps `int` to sort A_0, and `intlist` to sort A_1.

The semantics of types and type refinements given Fig. 4 can be lifted in a straightforward way to the level of type environments (Γ):

$$\begin{aligned}
[\![\Gamma, x : \{\nu : T \mid \phi\}]\!] &= [\![\Gamma]\!] \Rightarrow x : [\![T]\!] \Rightarrow [\![[x/\nu]\phi]\!] \\
[\![\Gamma, \phi]\!] &= [\![\Gamma]\!] \Rightarrow [\![\phi]\!] \\
[\![\cdot]\!] &= \mathit{true}
\end{aligned}$$

The interpretation of relation sort environment (Γ_R) is a set of assertions over MSFOL sorts of uninterpreted relations:

$$\begin{aligned}
[\![\Gamma_R, R :: \tau_R]\!] &= [\![\Gamma_R]\!] \cup \{R : [\![\tau_R]\!]\} \\
[\![\cdot]\!] &= \{\}
\end{aligned}$$

The following lemma states that the translation to MSFOL is complete for a well-formed type refinement:

LEMMA 3.2. (Completeness of semantics) *For all* ϕ, Γ, *if* $\Gamma \vdash \phi$, *then there exists an MSFOL proposition* ϕ^L *such that* $[\![\phi]\!] = \phi^L$.

[6] We focus only on the underlined part of the assertion as compilation stack increases. We switch back to showing complete assertion when all sub-parts are reduced. The digit before the dot in a step number indicates this switch.

$$
\begin{array}{rr}
[\![\mathtt{R}_{ob}(\mathtt{l}) = \mathtt{R}_{id}(\mathtt{x}) \times \mathtt{R}_{mem}(\mathtt{xs})]\!] & (1.1)\\
\gamma_{\sqcup}(\underline{[\![\mathtt{R}_{ob}(\mathtt{l})]\!]},\ \Leftrightarrow,\ [\![\mathtt{R}_{id}(\mathtt{x}) \times \mathtt{R}_{mem}(\mathtt{xs})]\!]) & (1.2)\\
\mathit{Inst}[\![\mathtt{R}_{ob}]\!]\ l & (2.1)\\
\mathit{Inst}(\ \forall(\mathtt{i} : [\![\mathtt{intlist}]\!]).\forall(\mathtt{j} : [\![\mathtt{int}]\!]). & (2.2)\\
\forall(\mathtt{k} : [\![\mathtt{int}]\!]).(\mathtt{Rob\ i\ j\ k})\ )\ \mathtt{x} & \\
\mathit{Inst}\,(\forall(\mathtt{i} : \mathtt{A_1}).\forall(\mathtt{j} : \mathtt{A_0}).\forall(\mathtt{k} : \mathtt{A_0}).(\mathtt{Rob\ i\ j\ k}))\ \mathtt{x} & (2.3)\\
(\forall(\mathtt{j} : \mathtt{A_0}).\forall(\mathtt{k} : \mathtt{A_0}).(\mathtt{Rob\ x\ j\ k})) & (2.4)\\
\gamma_{\sqcup}([\![\mathtt{R}_{ob}(\mathtt{l})]\!],\ \Leftrightarrow,\ \underline{[\![\mathtt{R}_{id}(\mathtt{x}) \times \mathtt{R}_{mem}(\mathtt{xs})]\!]}) & (1.2)\\
\gamma_{\bowtie}(\underline{[\![\mathtt{R}_{id}(\mathtt{x})]\!]},\ \wedge,\ [\![\mathtt{R}_{mem}(\mathtt{xs})]\!]) & (3.1)\\
\mathit{Inst}\,(\forall(\mathtt{i} : [\![\mathtt{int}]\!].\forall(\mathtt{j} : [\![\mathtt{int}]\!]).(\mathtt{i} = \mathtt{j}))\ \mathtt{x} & (4.1)\\
\forall(\mathtt{j} : \mathtt{A_0}).(\mathtt{x} = \mathtt{j}) & (4.2)\\
\gamma_{\bowtie}([\![\mathtt{R}_{id}(\mathtt{x})]\!],\ \wedge,\ \underline{[\![\mathtt{R}_{mem}(\mathtt{xs})]\!]}) & (3.1)\\
(\forall(\mathtt{k} : \mathtt{A_0})(\mathtt{Rmem\ xs\ k})) & (5.1)\\
\gamma_{\bowtie}(\ \forall(\mathtt{j} : \mathtt{A_0}).(\mathtt{x} = \mathtt{j})\ ,\ \wedge,\ (\forall(\mathtt{k} : \mathtt{A_0})(\mathtt{Rmem\ xs\ k}))\ ) & (3.2)\\
\forall(\mathtt{j} : \mathtt{A_0}).\forall(\mathtt{k} : \mathtt{A_0}).(\mathtt{x} = \mathtt{j}) \wedge (\mathtt{Rmem\ xs\ k}) & (3.3)\\
\gamma_{\sqcup}(\ (\forall(\mathtt{j} : \mathtt{A_0}).\forall(\mathtt{k} : \mathtt{A_0}).(\mathtt{Rob\ x\ j\ k}))\ ,\ \Leftrightarrow, & (1.3)\\
\forall(\mathtt{j} : \mathtt{A_0}).\forall(\mathtt{k} : \mathtt{A_0}).(\mathtt{x} = \mathtt{j}) \wedge (\mathtt{Rmem\ xs\ k})\ ) & \\
\forall(\mathtt{j} : \mathtt{A_0}).\forall(\mathtt{k} : \mathtt{A_0}).(\mathtt{Rob\ l\ j\ k}) \Leftrightarrow (\mathtt{x} = \mathtt{j}) \wedge (\mathtt{Rmem\ xs\ k}) & (1.4)
\end{array}
$$

Figure 5: Compiling a λ_R assertion to MSFOL

3.4 Decidability of λ_R Type Checking

The subtyping judgment in our core language (λ_R) relies on the semantic entailment judgment of MSFOL. The premise of SUBT-BASE contains the following:

$$[\![\Gamma_R]\!] \models [\![\Gamma, \nu : T]\!] \Rightarrow [\![\phi_1]\!] \Rightarrow [\![\phi_2]\!]$$

Consequently, decidability of type checking in λ_R reduces to decidability of semantic entailment in MSFOL. Although semantic entailment is undecidable for full first-order logic, our subset of MSFOL is a carefully chosen decidable fragment. This fragment, known as Effectively Propositional (EPR) first-order logic, or Bernay-Schönfinkel-Ramsey (BSR) logic, consists of prenex quantified propositions with uninterpreted relations and equality. Off-the-shelf SMT solvers (e.g., Z3) are equipped with efficient decision procedures for EPR logic [19], making type checking in λ_R a practical exercise.

THEOREM 3.3. (**Decidability**) *Type checking in λ_R is decidable.*

Proof Follows from Lemma 3.2 and decidability proof of EPR logic. ∎

4. Parametricity

4.1 Syntax

We now extend our core language (λ_R) with parametric polymorphism, and the specification language with parametric relations - relations parameterized over other relations . We refer to the extended calculus as $\lambda_{\forall R}$. Figure 6 shows the type and specification language of $\lambda_{\forall R}$. We have elided $\lambda_{\forall R}$'s expression language in the interest of space. Unmodified syntactic forms of λ_R are also elided.

The only algebraic data type in $\lambda_{\forall R}$ is a polymorphic list, which is the domain for structural relations. Consequently, structural relations have sort schemes (σ_R), akin to type schemes (σ) of the term language. For example, the non-parametric head relation (R_{hd}) from Section 2, when defined over a polymorphic `'a list` will have sort scheme, $\forall$ `'a. 'a list` $:\!\rightarrow$ `'a`. The specification language also contains an expression ($\mathcal{R}\,T$) to instantiate a generalized type variable in parametric relation sorts.

A parametric relation generalizes a structural relation, just as a polymorphic list generalizes a monomorphic one. Our syntax

Calculus $\lambda_{\forall R}$

t	$\in$	*tuple − sort variables*	$x, y, k \in$	*variables*
$'a$, $'b$	$\in$	*type variables*		
T	$::=$	$'a \mid 'a\,\mathtt{list} \mid \mathsf{int}$		*datatypes*
τ	$::=$	$\{\nu : T \mid \Phi\} \mid (x : \tau) \rightarrow \tau$		*dependent type*
δ	$::=$	$\forall t.\forall(R :: 'a :\!\rightarrow t).\ \delta \mid \tau$		*parametric dep. type*
σ	$::=$	$\forall 'a.\ \sigma \mid \delta$		*type scheme*

Specification Language

Φ	$::=$	$\rho = \rho \mid \rho \subseteq \rho \mid \Phi \wedge \Phi \mid true$	*type refinement*
ρ	$::=$	$\mathcal{R}(x) \mid \rho \cup \rho \mid \rho \times \rho$	*rel. expression*
$\mathcal{R}$	$::=$	$\mathcal{R}\,T \mid \mathcal{R}\,\theta\,\mathcal{R} \mid R$	*instantiation*
θ	$::=$	$t \mid t * \theta \mid T * \theta \mid T$	*tuple sort*
τ_R	$::=$	$\forall t.\ ('a :\!\rightarrow t) :\!\rightarrow ('a\,\mathtt{list} :\!\rightarrow \theta)$	*relation sort*
	$\mid$	$'a\,\mathtt{list} :\!\rightarrow \theta$	
σ_R	$::=$	$\forall 'a.\ \tau_R \mid \tau_R$	*sort scheme*
Δ_R	$::=$	$\langle R,\ R_p,\ \sigma_R,\ \mathsf{Cons}\,x\,y \Rightarrow r \mid \mathsf{Nil} \Rightarrow r \rangle$	*rel. definition*
	$\mid$	$\langle R,\ R_p,\ \sigma_R,\ \mathcal{R}^* \rangle$	

Figure 6: $\lambda_{\forall R}$ - Language with parametric relations

and semantics for parametric relations are based on this correspondence. Since the `list` type constructor takes only one type argument, structural relations in $\lambda_{\forall R}$ are parameterized over one relational parameter. The domain of a relational parameter to a structural relation over a `'a list` should be `'a`. When the type variable in `'a list` is instantiated with, e.g., `'b list`, the parameter of a parametric relation over `'a list` can be instantiated with a structural relation over `'b list`. For instance, the relational parameter R in the parametric membership relation (R_{mem} R), defined in Sec. 2, can be instantiated with the non-parametric head relation, R_{hd}[7], after instantiating `'a` in its sort scheme with a `'b list`. The resulting relation can now be applied to a list of lists (i.e., a `'b list list`) to denote the set of head elements in the constituent lists.

The definition (Δ_R) of a parametric relation is a tuple containing its name (R), the name of its relational parameter (R_p), its sort scheme (σ_R), and its definition. A parametric relation definition very often does not place constraints over the co-domain of its relational parameter. For instance, consider the parametric R_{hd} relation over `'a list` reproduced from Section 2:

```
relation (R_hd R) (x::xs) = R(x)
       | (R_hd R) []      = ∅
```

R_{hd} requires that the domain of its parameter be `'a`, but it places no restriction on the co-domain of R. In order to have a truly parametric definition of R_{hd}, it is essential that we let the relational parameter have an unrestricted co-domain. Therefore, we let tuple-sort variables (t) be used in tuple sorts (θ). Such a variable can be instantiated with a tuple sort, such as int*int.

In order to use a parametric relation in a type refinement, its relational parameter has to be instantiated. Polymorphism in $\lambda_{\forall R}$ is predicative so parameterization over relations in $\lambda_{\forall R}$ is also predicative. An *instantiated* parametric relation is equivalent to a non-parametric relation; it can be *applied* to a variable of the term language, and can also be used to instantiate other parametric relations.

[7] A note on notation: We use (R_{mem} R) and (R_{hd} R) to denote parametric membership and head relations, resp. We continue to use R_{mem} and R_{hd} to denote their non-parametric versions. We use qualifiers "parametric" and "non-parametric" to disambiguate.

r	$::=$	$R(x) \mid r \times r$	
F_R	$::=$	$\lambda(\overline{x:T}).\, r$	*transformer*
e_b	$::=$	$\texttt{bind}\,(R(x), F_R)$	*bind expression*
E_b	$::=$	$\lambda(x:T).\,\texttt{bind}\,(R(x), F_R)$	*bind abstraction*
ψ	$::=$	$R = E_b$	*bind equation*
Σ^b_R	$::=$	$\lambda R.\, E_b$	*bind definition*

Figure 7: Bind Syntax

To extend the generality of parametric relations to dependent types of the term language, we lift the parameterization over relations from the level of type refinements to the level of types. We refer to dependent types parameterized over relations as *parametric dependent types* (δ). An example of a parametric dependent type is the type of `foldl` from Section 2. Another example is the type of map shown below:

$$('R_1,\ 'R_2)\ \texttt{map}\ :$$
$$\texttt{l} \to (\texttt{f} : \texttt{x} \to \{\nu \mid {'R_2}(\nu) = {'R_1}(\texttt{x})\}) \to$$
$$\{\nu \mid ((R_{ob}\ {'R_2})^*\ \nu) = ((R_{ob}\ {'R_1})^*\ \texttt{l})\}$$

4.2 Sort and Type Checking

Rules to check sorts of relational expressions and well-formedness of type refinements (Φ) in $\lambda_{\forall R}$ are straightforward extensions of similar rules for λ_R and are omitted here. Sort-checking a parametric relation definition reduces to sort-checking a non-parametric relation definition under an environment extended with the sort of its relational parameter. Checking the sort of a relation instantiation is the same as checking the sort of a function application in other typed calculi, such as System F, as are rules to type-check generalization and instantiation expressions.

4.3 Semantics of Parametric Relations

Before we describe our semantics for parametric relations, we present a few auxiliary definitions:

Ground Relations. A ground relation of a parametric relation (R) is a non-parametric relation obtained by instantiating the relational parameter with the identity R_{id} relation in its definition. Since we require the co-domain of the relational parameter to be a tuple-sort variable (t), an instantiation of the parameter with R_{id} is always sort-safe. Therefore, there exists a ground relation for every parametric relation in $\lambda_{\forall R}$.

Transformer Expression. A transformer expression (F_R) is a λ_R relational expression under a binder that binds a tuple of variables. A transformer expression is expected to transform the tuple to a set of tuples through a cross-product combination of relation applications. The sort of a transformer application is a map (under ':$\to$') from tuple-sort (θ_1) to a set sort ($\{\theta_2\}$). An example of a transformer expression of sort `'a` $:\to$ $\{$ `'a*'a` $\}$ is the *reflexive transformer*:

$$\lambda x.\, R_{id}(x) \times R_{id}(x)$$

Bind Expressions. Consider an operator that accepts a relation application and a transformer expression (F_R), applies F_R over every tuple in the set representing a relation application, and subsequently folds the resulting set of sets using set union. Such an operator has following sort:

$$\forall t_1, t_2.\{t_1\} :\to (t_1 :\to \{t_2\}) :\to \{t_2\}$$

We name the operator `bind`, after set monadic bind. The syntax of bind expressions is given in Fig. 7. For brevity, we exclude sort annotations on bind expressions (F_R) and bind abstractions (E_b) in our examples.

By *binding* a relation application with a transformer expression, a bind expression effectively creates a new relation. For instance, given a list `l` with type `'a list`, the bind expression that binds $R_{mem}(l)$ with a reflexive transformer is as following:

$$\texttt{bind}\,(R_{mem}(l),\ \lambda x.R_{id}(x)\times\ R_{id}(x))$$

The result of evaluating this expression is the set of reflexive pairs of elements in the list, which is equivalent to instantiating R_{mem} with R_{dup}:

$$(R_{mem}\ R_{dup})(l)\ =\ \texttt{bind}\,(R_{mem}(l),\ \lambda\, x.R_{id}(x)\times\ R_{id}(x))$$

Here, equality is interpreted as equality of sets on both sides. Since the semantics of a relation application is the set of tuples, the above equation defines the semantics of $(R_{mem}\ R_{dup})$ in terms of its ground relation R_{mem}. Indeed, a parametric R_{mem} relation (call it R^{π}_{mem}) can be defined equivalently in terms of its non-parametric variant as:

$$R^{\pi}_{mem}\ \equiv \lambda\, R.\lambda l.\ \texttt{bind}\,(R_{mem}(l),\ \lambda x.R(x))$$

We refer to the above definition as the *bind definition* of parametric R_{mem} relation. Every well-sorted parametric structural relation definition in $\lambda_{\forall R}$ can be transformed to a bind definition that is extensionally equal, i.e., both produce the same set of tuples for every instantiation, and subsequent application. Therefore, the pattern-match syntax used to define parametric relations is simply syntactic sugar over its underlying bind definition.

4.3.1 Elaboration to Bind Definition

Elaborating a parametric relation definition to a bind definition requires that we construct its ground relation, and a transformer expression (F_R). A ground relation definition is derived by instantiating its parametric definition with R_{id}, as stated previously. Constructing a transformer expression is equally simple - one only needs to examine the co-domain tuple sort of the parametric relation, which is also the co-domain tuple sort of the transformer expression (from the type of `bind`). A sort variable in the tuple sort is interpreted as application of its parameter relation, an asterisk in the sort translates to a cross-product, and a $\lambda_{\forall R}$ type in the tuple sort translates to application of R_{id}. For instance, consider a hypothetical parametric relation R_x with the following sort:

$$R_x\ ::\ \forall t.\ (\text{int} :\to \{t\}) :\to (\text{int list} :\to \{\text{int} * t * t\})$$

We let R denote the relational parameter of R_x. The ground relation of R_x (call it $R_{x'}$) is the instantiated parametric relation ($R_x\ R_{id}$), which has the sort $\text{int list} :\to \{\text{int} * \text{int} * \text{int}\}$. From the type of `bind`, we know that the sort of the required transformer expression (F_R) is $(\text{int}{*}\text{int}{*}\text{int}) :\to \{\text{int}{*}t{*}t\}$. Recalling that F_R is a lambda bound relational expression, which is a cross product combination of relation applications (Fig. 7), we observe that the only possible solution for F_R is:

$$\lambda(x,y,z).R_{id}(x)\times R(y)\times R(z)$$

Consequently, we derive the following bind definition of R_x:

$$\lambda R.\lambda l.\texttt{bind}(R_{x'}(l),\ \lambda(x,y,z).\ R_{id}(x)\times R(y)\times R(z))$$

4.3.2 Bind Equations

By substituting parametric relations with their bind definitions, every instantiation of a parametric relation can be reduced to a bind abstraction (E_b in Figure 7), which, like any non-parametric structural relation in $\lambda_{\forall R}$, is a map from a `'a list` to a set of tuples. Therefore, an instantiated parametric relation can be treated as a new non-parametric relation that is defined using `bind`. For example, $(R_{mem}\ R_{dup})$ can be treated as a new non-parametric relation R_1, defined in terms of `bind`:

Semantics of Bind Equations $\boxed{[\![\psi]\!]}$

$$\begin{array}{rcl}
[\![R_2 = \lambda(x:T_1).\, \mathtt{bind}\,(R_1(x), \lambda(\overline{k:T_2}).\, r)]\!] & = & \forall(x:[\![T_1]\!]).\, \gamma_{\Rightarrow}([\![R_1(x)]\!],\, \forall(\overline{(k:[\![T_2]\!]}).[\![r]\!],\, [\![R_2(x)]\!]) \\
& \wedge & \forall(x:[\![T_1]\!]).\, \gamma_{\Leftarrow}([\![R_1(x)]\!],\, \forall(\overline{k:[\![T_2]\!]}).[\![r]\!],\, [\![R_2(x)]\!]) \\
\gamma_{\Rightarrow}(\forall(\overline{k:T_1^F}).\phi_1^F,\, \forall(\overline{k:T_1^F}).\forall(\overline{j:T_2^F}).\phi_2^F,\, \nu^F) & = & \forall(\overline{k:T_1^F}).\forall(\overline{j:T_2^F}).\, \phi_1^F \wedge \phi_2^F \Rightarrow \nu^F\, \overline{j} \\
\gamma_{\Leftarrow}(\forall(\overline{k:T_1^F}).\phi_1^F,\, \forall(\overline{k:T_1^F}).\forall(\overline{j:T_2^F}).\phi_2^F,\, \nu^F) & = & \forall(\overline{j:T_2^F}).\exists(\overline{k:T_1^F}).\, \nu^F\, \overline{j} \Rightarrow \phi_1^F \wedge \phi_2^F
\end{array}$$

Figure 8: Semantics of bind equations for parametric relations in $\lambda_{\forall R}$

$$R_1 = \lambda l.\,\mathtt{bind}\,(R_{mem}(l),\ \lambda x.R_{id}(x) \times\ R_{id}(x))$$

By rigorously defining the semantics of *bind equations* as above, we can effectively capture the semantics of any instantiation of a parametric relation in terms of its ground relation. This is the insight that allows us to use parametric relations seamlessly in type refinements. For instance, the bind semantics for $(R_{mem}\ R_{dup})$ lets us prove the following implication, which could potentially arise during subtype checking:

$$((R_{mem}\ R_{dup})\ l_1) = ((R_{mem}\ R_{dup})\ l_2) \\ \Rightarrow R_{mem}(l_1) = R_{mem}(l_2)$$

The formal semantics of bind equations, which also define an algorithm to compile bind equations to MSFOL formulas, is described in Fig. 8. Under our semantics, the bind equation for $(R_{mem}\ R_{dup})$ is interpreted as a conjunction of following first-order formulas (elaborated for clarity):

- If $\langle x \rangle \in R_{mem}(l)$, and $\langle y \rangle \in R_{id}(x) \times R_{id}(x)$, then $\langle y \rangle \in ((R_{mem}\ R_{dup})\ l)$.
- If $\langle y \rangle \in ((R_{mem}\ R_{dup})\ l)$, then there must exist x such that $\langle x \rangle \in R_{mem}(l)$ and $\langle y \rangle \in R_{id}(x) \times R_{id}(x)$.

Since sets have no other notion associated with them other than membership, the above first-order assertions *completely* describe $((R_{mem}\ R_{dup})\, l)$ in terms of $(R_{mem}\ l)$.

4.4 Decidability of Type Checking

Type refinements (Φ) in $\lambda_{\forall R}$ can be elaborated to a conjunction of bind equations representing semantics of instantiated relations, and a λ_R type refinement (ϕ). Consequently, we have the following result:

THEOREM 4.1. **(Decidability)** *Type checking in $\lambda_{\forall R}$ is decidable.*

Proof Follows from the decidability proof of EPR logic, to which bind equations are compiled, and the decidability result (Theorem 3.3) for λ_R. ∎

5. Implementation

We have implemented our specification language and verification procedure as an extended type-checking pass (called CATALYST) in MLton [15], a whole-program optimizing compiler for Standard ML (SML).[8] The input to our system is CoreML, an A-normalized intermediate representation with pattern-matching, but with all SML module constructs elaborated and removed. SML programs are annotated with relational specifications, defined in terms of relational dependent types that decorate function signatures, along with definitions of parameterized structural relations over the program's datatypes. The type system is a conservative extension of SML's, so all programs that are well-typed under CATALYST are well-typed SML programs. Our type-checking and verification process closely follows the description given in the previous sections. Verification conditions, representing the consequent of the SUBT-BASE type-checking rule (Fig. 3) are compiled to a first-order formula, as described in Sections 3 and 4, and checked for validity (satisfiability of its negation) using the Z3 SMT solver.

To be practically useful, our implementation extends the formal system described thus far in three important ways:

Primitive Relations. We provide a general framework to add new primitive relations that allows the class of relational expressions to be extended by permitting relational expressions to be abstracted in prenex form. The framework only needs to be seeded with the single primitive relation R_{id}. For example, R_{notEq_k} can be defined as the following primitive relation:

$$R_{notEq} = \lambda k.\, \lambda x.\, R_{id}(x) - R_{id}(k)$$

Similarly, R_{eq_k} can be defined as:

$$R_{eq} = \lambda k.\, \lambda x.\, R_{id}(x) - (R_{id}(x) - R_{id}(k))$$

Both R_{notEq} and R_{eq} can be ascribed colon-arrow sorts, similar to structural relations. Once defined, a primitive relation can be used freely in type refinements. For example, the relation yielded by evaluating $(R_{notEq}\ \mathtt{c})$ can be used to instantiate the parametric R_{mem} relation to define the set of all elements in a list that are not equal to some constant `c`.

Base Predicates: Consider the obvious relation refinement for the polymorphic identity function:

$$\mathtt{id}\ :\ \mathtt{x} \rightarrow \{\mathtt{v}\ \mid\ R_{id}(\mathtt{v})\ =\ R_{id}(\mathtt{x})\ \}$$

The type refinement used here is an unintuitive way of expressing the simple fact that `id` returns its argument. To avoid such needless verbosity, we admit non-relational assertions (called *base predicates*), drawn from propositional logic with equality, to our specification language; these predicates may be freely composed in type refinements using logical connectives.

Inference and Annotation Burden: Our implementation infers sorts for structural relations, and relational parameters in dependent types. Our term language and specification language have distinct sort instantiation expressions. We also infer appropriate tuple-sort instantiations by unification. Therefore, neither the ML program, nor the specification needs to be annotated with sorts.

The type checking algorithm performs bi-directional type checking [18], and needs annotations only for recursive function definitions. For all other expressions, CATALYST synthesizes a suitable dependent type. For example, types from different branches of ML `case` expressions are unified using a logical disjunction. Generating a suitable type for a `let` expression requires that we use an existential quantifier in type refinements, which is skolemized while encoding the VC in MSFOL. Notably, we do not expose any quantifiers in our specification language.

[8] The source code for the implementation as well as a Web interface to the system is available online from: *https://github.com/tycon/catalyst.*

```
datatype color = R | B
datatype 'a tree = E | T of color * 'a tree
                        * 'a * 'a tree
fun balance (t:'a tree) : 'a tree = case t of
    T (B,T (R,T (R,a,x,b),y,c),z,d) =>
            T (R,T (B,a,x,b),y,T (B,c,z,d))
  | T (B,T (R,a,x,T (R,b,y,c)),z,d) =>
            T (R,T (B,a,x,b),y,T (B,c,z,d))
  | T (B,a,x,T (R,T (R,b,y,c),z,d)) =>
            T (R,T (B,a,x,b),y,T (B,c,z,d))
  | T (B,a,x,T (R,b,y,T (R,c,z,d))) =>
            T (R,T (B,a,x,b),y,T (B,c,z,d))
  | _ => t
```

(a) balance

```
(* Tree head (root) relation *)
relation R_thd (T(c,l,n,r)) = {(n)};
(* Tree membership relation *)
relation R_tmem = R*_thd;
(* Total-order relation among tree members *)
relation R_to (T (c,l,n,r)) = R_tmem(l) × {(n)}
                             ∪ {(n)} × R_tmem(r)
                             ∪ R_tmem(l) × R_tmem(r);
(*
 * "balance" preserves the total-order among members
 * of the tree
 *)
balance : t → {t' | R*_to(t') = R*_to(t)};
```

(b) Relational specification of balance

Figure 9: Red-Black Tree Example

For non-recursive function applications, although it is possible to infer instantiation annotations for parametric relations with the help of an expensive fixpoint computation that generates an exhaustive list of all possible instantiations, CATALYST relies on manual annotations for parameter instantiations to avoid this cost. An example of such annotation is shown in Fig. 10c (the `contains` function).

5.1 Experiments

We have investigated the automatic verification of expressive shape invariants using CATALYST on a number of programs, including:

1. List library functions, such as as `concat`, `rev`, `revAppend`, `foldl`, `foldr`, `zip`, `unzip` etc. (some of these specifications have been discussed in Sec. 2 and 4), and
2. Okasaki's red-black tree [17] library functions, such as `balance`, multiple order traversal functions, and `mirrorImage`.
3. Compiler transformations over MLton's SSA (Static Single Assignment) intermediate representation.

For several of these benchmarks (especially those in (1) and (2)), CATALYST was able to successfully verify specifications to the extent of full functional correctness. Excluding the time take by the MLton compiler to elaborate and type check these Standard ML programs, none of our benchmarks take more than 0.2s to verify; this time includes A-Normalization, specification elaboration, VC generation, and SMT solving through Z3.

Red-Black Tree. The specification of the red-black tree `balance` function, shown in Fig. 9b, illustrates the kind of specifications that were automatically verified by CATALYST in our experiments. The specification asserts that the `balance` function on red-black trees (Fig. 9a) preserves a *total-order* among members of the tree. The non-inductive *total-order* relation (R_{to} in Fig. 9b) is defined in terms of the tree *membership* relation (R_{tmem}) described in Sec. 2.3, and relates (a) elements in the left sub-tree to the root element, (b) root to the elements in the right sub-tree, and (c) elements in the left sub-tree to those in right. The inductive *total-order* relation (R^*_{to}) on a red-black tree, obtained by closing the R_{to} relation over the tree, relates every pair of elements in the tree that are *in-order*. Consequently, the specification of the `balance` function effectively asserts that in-order traversal over an unbalanced red-black tree, and in-order traversal on its balanced version, return the same sequence of elements.

CATALYST can verify full functional correctness of standard tree traversal functions that return a list of elements. The relational specifications for such functions essentially relate different order relations on the input tree to an *occurs-before* order of the result list. For instance, a function `inOrder` that performs in-order traversal on a red-black tree (t) returns a list (l) such that its inductive *occurs-before* relation is the same as that of t's inductive *total-order* relation:

$$\texttt{inOrder : t} \rightarrow \{\mathrm{l} \mid R^*_{ob}(\mathrm{l}) = R^*_{to}(\mathrm{t})\}$$

SSA. An important intermediate representation used in MLton is a variant of SSA that is operated upon by a number of optimization passes. After each such pass, MLton checks the well-formedness of the output by checking, for example, that variable definitions dominate variable uses in the SSA dominator tree. Because MLton performs this check after every optimization pass, compile times can suffer, especially as program size scales. A potential application of CATALYST is to statically typecheck the integrity of SSA optimization passes, thereby eliminating this overhead.

A program in SSA form is represented as a tree of basic blocks, where each block consists of a set of straight-line instructions (e.g., definitions, assignments, primitive applications). The specification of an SSA program makes use of several inductive relations: R_{du}, the *def-use* relation, R_{ud}, the *use-def* relation, and $R_{use\text{-}refl}$, the reflective variant of R_{use}, the *use* relation, that collects all variables used on the right-hand side of an assignment. The *def-use* relation relates a *def*, i.e., a variable that is defined using an assignment statement, to all *use*s that are dominated by the definition. Conversely, R_{ud} relates a *use* to all *def*s that it dominates. With these definitions, we can express the type of an SSA tree thus:

$$\texttt{type ssa\_tree} = \{\nu : \texttt{block tree} \mid R_{use\text{-}refl}(\nu) \subseteq R_{du}(\nu) \wedge R_{use\text{-}refl}(\nu) \cap R_{ud}(\nu) = \emptyset\}$$

This type captures the two essential structural properties of SSA: (1) every use of a variable must be dominated by its definition; and (2) no definition of a variable is ever dominated by its use. Verifying that a transformation pass over the SSA IR has the type:

$$\texttt{ssa\_tree} \rightarrow \texttt{ssa\_tree}$$

is tantamount to proving the transformation preserves the salient SSA invariant that definitions always dominate uses.

6. Case Study

An SML implementation of the untyped lambda calculus is shown in Fig. 11. The implementation makes use of auxiliary functions, such as `filter` and `contains`, directly, and `exists` through `contains`. By the virtue of being compositional, our verification process relies on expressive relational types of these auxiliary functions, which can nevertheless be verified by CATALYST. We present them below:

exists. Consider the higher-order `exists` function over lists shown in Fig. 10a; dependent type signatures are elided for brevity.

```
fun exists f l = case l of
  [] => false
| x::xs =>
  let
    val v1 = exists f xs
    val v2 = f x
  in
    v1 orelse v2
  end
```

(a) exists

```
fun filter f l = case l of
  [] => []
| x::xs =>
  let
    val xs' = filter f xs
  in
    if f x then x::xs'
          else xs'
  end
```

(b) filter

```
fun contains l str =
  let
    val isStr = fn x => x=str
    (* Instantiate the implicit
     * relational parameter in type
     * of "exists" with (REq str) *)
    val hasStr = exists (REq str)
          isStr l
  in
    hasStr
  end
```

(c) contains

Figure 10: Examples

ML Program

```
datatype exp =     Var of string
                 | App of exp*exp
                 | Abs of string*exp

fun freeVars e = case e of
    Var id => [id]
  | App (e1,e2) =>
      concat [freeVars e1, freeVars e2]
  | Abs (id,e') => filter (RNeq id)
      (fn fv => not (fv = id)) (freeVars e')

fun alphaConvert e = case e of
    Abs (id,e') =>
    let
      val fv_e' = freeVars e'
      val id' = createNewName fv_e' id
    in
      Abs(id',subst(Var id',id,e'))
    end
  | _ => raise Error
and subst e1 id e2  = case e2 of
    Var id' => if id = id'
      then e1 else e2
  | App(e21,e22) =>
    let
      val e21' = subst e1 id e21,
      val e22' = subst e1 id e22
    in
      App (e21',e22')
    end
  | Abs(id',e2') => if id' = id then e2 else
    let
      val fv_e1 = freeVars e1
    in
      if contains fv_e1 id'
      then subst e1 id (alphaConvert e2)
      else Abs(id',subst e1 id e2')
    end
```

Relational Specification

```
relation R_fv (Var x) = {(x)}
       | R_fv (App (e1,e2)) = R_fv(e1) ∪ R_fv(e2)
       | R_fv (Abs (id,e)) = R_fv(e) - {(id)};

createNewName : fvs → id → {v | not (v = id) ∧ not ({(v)} ⊆ Rmem(fvs))};
freeVars : e → {l | Rmem(l) = R_fv(e)};
alphaConvert : e → {ex | R_fv(ex) = R_fv(e)};
subst : e1 → id → e2 →
        {ex | if ({(id)} ⊆ R_fv(e2)) then R_fv(ex) = (R_fv(e2) - {(id)}) ∪ R_fv(e1) else R_fv(ex) = R_fv(e2)};
```

Figure 11: SML implementation and specification of the untyped lambda calculus.

A type that captures the semantics of exists, irrespective of its implementation, should assert that exists returns true if and only if its higher-order argument returns true for some member of the list. We express the invariant as the following type:

$$\begin{array}{l}(\texttt{'}R\ \texttt{exists})\ :\\ \quad \texttt{l} \rightarrow (\texttt{f}\ :\ \texttt{x} \rightarrow \{\nu \mid \nu = \texttt{true} \Leftrightarrow \texttt{'}R(\texttt{x}) \neq \emptyset\}) \rightarrow\\ \quad \{\nu \mid \nu = \texttt{true} \Leftrightarrow ((R_{mem}\ \texttt{'}R)\ \nu) \neq \emptyset\}\end{array}$$

The interpretation of the type is as follows: Let there be a relation $'R$ such that f returns true if and only if relation $'R(\texttt{x})$ is not the empty set for f's argument x. Then, exists returns true if and only if relation R is not the empty set for some element in list.

filter. A parametric dependent type for filter, shown in Fig. 10b is given below:

$$\begin{array}{l}(\texttt{'}R\ \texttt{filter})\ :\\ \quad \texttt{l} \rightarrow \texttt{f}\ :\ \texttt{x} \rightarrow \{\nu \mid \nu = \texttt{false} \Rightarrow \texttt{'}R(\texttt{x}) = \emptyset\\ \qquad\qquad\qquad\quad \wedge\ \nu = \texttt{true} \Rightarrow \texttt{'}R(\texttt{x}) = R_{id}(\texttt{x})\} \rightarrow\\ \quad \{\nu \mid R_{mem}(\nu) = ((R_{mem}\ \texttt{'}R)\ \texttt{l})\}\end{array}$$

The intuition behind this type is same as that of exists. Filter retains only those elements for which its higher-order argument returns true.

contains. Consider the definition of the contains function shown in Fig. 10c that uses exists to check for the existence of a constant string str in a list l. Since the higher-order function passed to exists is:

```
val isStr = fn x => x=str
```

the relational dependent type of isStr is:

$$\texttt{isStr}\ :\ \texttt{x} \rightarrow \{\nu \mid R_{eq_{str}}(\nu) \neq \emptyset\}$$

This clearly suggests that the relational parameter of exists has to be instantiated with $R_{eq_{str}}$. Having made this observation, we stress that no type annotation is required for isStr, as it is a non-recursive function.

Observe that the call to exists from contains includes explicit parameter instantiation. The resultant type of hasStr is:

$$\texttt{hasStr}\ :\ \{\nu \mid \nu = \texttt{true} \Leftrightarrow ((R_{mem}\ R_{eq_{str}})\ \texttt{l}) \neq \emptyset\}$$

The type refinement for `hasStr` indicates that `hasStr` is `true` if and only if the set of all elements of list `l` that are equal to `str` is not empty. Due to the equivalence of its first-order encoding to that of the following assertion:

$$\{\nu\texttt{=true} \Leftrightarrow R_{id}(\texttt{s}) \subseteq R_{mem}(\texttt{l})\},$$

the implementation of `contains` type-checks against the type:

$$\texttt{l} \rightarrow \texttt{str} \rightarrow \{\nu \mid \nu \texttt{ = true} \Leftrightarrow R_{id}(\texttt{str}) \subseteq R_{mem}(\texttt{l})\}$$

6.1 α-conversion

The substitution operation (`subst`) substitutes a free variable (`id`) in an expression (`e2`) with another expression (`e1`). Function `alphaConvert` consistently renames occurrences of the bound variable in an abstraction expression. Observe that `subst` and `alphaConvert` are mutually recursive definitions. Both functions make use of `freeVars` , which returns a list of an expression's free variables.

It is widely agreed that substitution and α-conversion operations on lambda calculus terms are quite tricky to define correctly [6, 26]. Some of the behaviors exhibited by incorrect implementations include (a) α-conversion renames a free variable, or fails to rename a bound variable; (b) substitution fails to substitute free occurrences of the variable (`id`), or substitutes a bound occurrence of the variable; or (c) substitution is not capture-avoiding, i.e., substituting `e1` for `id` in `e2` captures variables of `e1` , which are otherwise free.

The relational specification of substitution and α conversion is given in the bottom-half of Fig. 11.[9] Note that one need not expose notions of capture-avoidance, or other such intricacies, to write down the specification, which is given in terms of a new structural relation R_{fv} that relates an expression of the calculus to its free variables. Function `freeVars` returns a list, whose members are free variables of its input expression. Its type represents this fact.

CATALYST successfully verifies the implementation against its specification. Alternate (incorrect) implementations such as those that fail to perform the capture-avoiding check on line 35, or the free variable check on line 31 trigger a type error. Conversely, note that, despite enforcing strong invariants, the relational specifications for `subst` and `alphaConvert` do not constrain how these functions are realized in ML. For instance, an implementation of `subst` that proactively renames bound variables in `e2` before substitution is successfully verified against the same specification.

7. Related Work

Type systems of mainstream functional languages, such as GHC Haskell and OCaml, support a basic form of dependent typing [12, 13] using GADTs [27]. At a high level, a structural relation of a data type is similar to a GADT insofar as it corresponds to an index that tracks an inductively definable relation over the data type. However, unlike the indexed type systems of Haskell and OCaml, where types are kept separate from terms, ours is a dependent type system. In this sense, our type system is similar to the refinement based dependent type system of F* [23]. Type refinements in F* are drawn from unrestricted (higher-order) logic extended with theories, whereas our specification language for ML programs is an abstraction over first-order logic that was tailor-made for equational and relational reasoning. The expressivity gained by allowing unrestricted type refinements in F* comes at the cost of decidability of type checking.

Structural relations, in their operational manifestation, can be compared to the structurally recursive *measures* of liquid types [11, 25] where the co-domain is always a set. Parametric structural relations may be viewed as generalizing such measures to higher-order measures. Relationally parametric dependent types can be compared to liquid types with abstract refinements [25], which let liquid types parameterize over type refinements (Boolean predicates). Once applied to a value, an abstract refinement becomes a concrete refinement, which can only be used to refine a type. On the other hand, a relational parameter can be treated just as any other relation in our type refinements, including being passed as an argument to other parametric relations. We require this generality to reason about shape invariants of higher-order catamorphisms such as `map` and `foldr` . For example, using only abstract refinements, it is not possible to verify that projecting a list of pairs using `map` and `fst` preserves ordering, or that an implementation of list `append` that uses `foldr` is correct.

Measures are an example of structurally recursive abstraction functions that map an algebraic data type to an abstract domain, such as natural numbers or sets. Suter *et al.* [22] describe decision procedures for the theory of algebraic data types extended with abstraction functions to decidable abstract domains. Our encoding does not require such extensions since a structural relation directly translates to an uninterpreted relation in first-order logic. Our encoding also supports parametric relations, which would otherwise require higher-order abstraction functions.

Imperative shape analyses have previously used relations to capture some inductive properties [5], and to describe memory configurations [9]. However, their applicability has been limited owing to destructive updates and pointer manipulations in imperative programs. In [14], Might describes a shape analysis of closures in higher-order programs. Our type system is capable of describing some notion of control flow for higher-order functions; e.g., the order in which the higher-order argument of `foldl` is applied over the list. However, inductive relations are conspicuous by their absence in functional program analysis, despite the fact that such programs are highly amenable for inductive reasoning. To the best of our knowledge, our type system is the first to use inductive relations for performing shape analysis on functional programs.

Logical relations have been used extensively to reason about contextual equivalence [1, 7]. Whereas a logical relation relates two terms of a (possibly recursive) type, a structural relation relates a term of an algebraic type to its constituent values. Parametric logical relations have also been used to reason about contextual equivalence for effectful programs [2–4]. In these efforts, a binary logical relation that relates effectful expressions is parameterized by a relation that relates their states. In contrast, a parametric structural relation is a structural relation over a polymorphic data type, that is parameterized by relations over type variables in the data type. While the primary purpose of structural relations is to enable specification and static verification, there is a possibility of sufficiently equipping our framework to reason about invariance of arbitrary relations, which is the key to reasoning about contextual equivalence. This is a possible avenue for future research.

Henglein [8] describes a domain-specific language to define ordering relations for composite data types such as lists and trees. However, the notion of order explored is the domain order used to compare two elements of same domain, such as a lexicographic order. In contrast, the order relation in our system describes relative ordering of elements in a composite data type.

8. Future Work

Due to the undecidability of program equivalence in general, it is impossible for any specification language that is based on a decidable logic to completely specify functional correctness of all possible ML programs. The expressivity of our specification language is inherently bound by the limits imposed by our choice of the un-

[9] We introduce some syntactic sugar in defining type refinements. For example, the branch expression (`if` ϕ `then` ϕ_1 `else` ϕ_2) in a type refinement translates to $((\phi \wedge \phi_1) \vee (\neg\phi \wedge \phi_2))$.

derlying decidable first-order logic. Confinement to relational and equational theory means that it is not possible to express properties that rely on specific theories, such as arithmetic. For instance, it is not possible to write a relational specification that asserts that the result of folding over a list of integers with `(op +)` is the sum of all integers in the list. Further, we restrict ourselves to (parametric) structural relations over (polymorphic) inductive datatypes in this work. With this restriction, it may not be possible to express shape related properties over arbitrary non-inductive datatypes. For example, it is currently not possible to assert that in a random access array, an element at a smaller index *occurs-before* an element at a larger index. Nevertheless, these drawbacks can be mitigated by (a) admitting relations without requiring their equational definitions, and (b) extending our specification language with theory-specific artifacts (especially, from the theory of arithmetic) in such a way that the combination remains decidable. We intend to explore both these extensions as part of future work.

One noticeable limitation of our current system is the lack of a general type inference mechanism. Given that relational specifications which make use of parametric relations to express rich invariants are non-trivial, and can be quite verbose, writing such specifications sometimes requires considerable manual effort. While providing higher level abstractions in the specification language can mitigate the problem by enabling the programmer to reason directly at the level of properties, rather than at the level of relations, the approach can be substantiated with a lightweight type inference mechanism based on refinement templates [20] to reduce the burden of manual annotation. The integration of such mechanisms within CATALYST is another avenue we anticipate pursuing.

9. Conclusions

This paper presents a relational specification language integrated with a dependent type system that is expressive enough to state structural invariants on functions over algebraic data types, often to the extent of full-functional correctness. We describe how parametric relations can be used to enable compositional verification in the presence of parametric polymorphism and higher-order functions. We additionally provide a translation mechanism to a decidable fragment of first-order logic that enables practical type checking. Experimental results based on an implementation (CATALYST) of these ideas justify the applicability of our approach.

Acknowledgments

We thank Matt Might, Ranjit Jhala, and the anonymous reviewers for their detailed comments and suggestions. This work is supported by the National Science Foundation under grants CCF-1216613 and CCF-1318227.

References

[1] A. Ahmed. Step-Indexed Syntactic Logical Relations for Recursive and Quantified Types. In *ESOP'06*, pages 69–83, 2006.

[2] N. Benton and B. Leperchey. Relational Reasoning in a Nominal Semantics for Storage. In *TLCA*, pages 86–101, 2005.

[3] N. Benton, A. Kennedy, M. Hofmann, and L. Beringer. Reading, Writing and Relations: Towards Extensional Semantics for Effect Analyses. In *APLAS*, pages 114–130, 2006.

[4] N. Benton, A. Kennedy, L. Beringer, and M. Hofmann. Relational Semantics for Effect-based Program Transformations: Higher-order Store. In *PPDP*, pages 301–312, 2009.

[5] B.-Y. E. Chang and X. Rival. Relational Inductive Shape Analysis. In *POPL*, pages 247–260, 2008.

[6] A. Charguraud. The Locally Nameless Representation. *Journal of Automated Reasoning*, 49(3):363–408, 2012. ISSN 0168-7433.

[7] D. Dreyer, A. Ahmed, and L. Birkedal. Logical Step-Indexed Logical Relations. In *LICS'09*, pages 71–80, 2009.

[8] F. Henglein. Generic Top-down Discrimination for Sorting and Partitioning in Linear Time*. *J. Funct. Program.*, pages 300–374, 2012.

[9] B. Jeannet, A. Loginov, T. Reps, and M. Sagiv. A relational approach to interprocedural shape analysis. *ACM Trans. Program. Lang. Syst.*, 32(2), Feb. 2010.

[10] G. Kaki and S. Jagannathan. A Relational Framework for Higher-Order Shape Analysis. Technical Report TR-14-002, Purdue University, 2014. URL `http://docs.lib.purdue.edu/cstech/1772/`.

[11] M. Kawaguchi, P. Rondon, and R. Jhala. Type-based Data Structure Verification. In *PLDI*, pages 304–315, 2009.

[12] S. Lindley and C. McBride. Hasochism: The Pleasure and Pain of Dependently Typed Haskell Programming. In *Haskell Symposium*, pages 81–92, 2013.

[13] C. McBride. Faking it: Simulating dependent types in Haskell. *J. Funct. Program.*, 12(5):375–392, July 2002.

[14] M. Might. Shape Analysis in the Absence of Pointers and Structure. In *VMCAI*, pages 263–278, 2010.

[15] MLton. `http://mlton.org/`.

[16] Objective Caml. `http://ocaml.org/`.

[17] C. Okasaki. *Purely Functional Data Structures*. Cambridge University Press, New York, NY, USA, 1998.

[18] B. C. Pierce and D. N. Turner. Local Type Inference. *ACM Trans. Program. Lang. Syst.*, 22(1), Jan. 2000.

[19] R. Piskac, L. de Moura, and N. Bjørner. Deciding Effectively Propositional Logic with Equality. Technical Report MSR-TR-2008-181.

[20] P. M. Rondon, M. Kawaguchi, and R. Jhala. Liquid Types. In *PLDI*, pages 159–169, 2008.

[21] P.-Y. Strub, N. Swamy, C. Fournet, and J. Chen. Self-Certification: Bootstrapping Certified Typecheckers in F* with Coq. In *POPL*, pages 571–584, 2012.

[22] P. Suter, M. Dotta, and V. Kuncak. Decision Procedures for Algebraic Data Types with Abstractions. In *POPL*, pages 199–210, 2010.

[23] N. Swamy, J. Chen, C. Fournet, P.-Y. Strub, K. Bhargavan, and J. Yang. Secure distributed programming with value-dependent types. In *ICFP*, pages 266–278, 2011.

[24] The Glasgow Haskell Compiler. `https://www.haskell.org/ghc/`.

[25] N. Vazou, P. M. Rondon, and R. Jhala. Abstract Refinement Types. In *ESOP*, pages 209–228, 2013.

[26] S. Weirich, B. A. Yorgey, and T. Sheard. Binders Unbound. In *ICFP*, pages 333–345, 2011.

[27] H. Xi, C. Chen, and G. Chen. Guarded Recursive Datatype Constructors. In *POPL*, pages 224–235, 2003.

There is no Fork: an Abstraction for Efficient, Concurrent, and Concise Data Access

Simon Marlow
Facebook
smarlow@fb.com

Louis Brandy
Facebook
ldbrandy@fb.com

Jonathan Coens
Facebook
jon.coens@fb.com

Jon Purdy
Facebook
jonp@fb.com

Abstract

We describe a new programming idiom for concurrency, based on Applicative Functors, where concurrency is implicit in the Applicative `<*>` operator. The result is that concurrent programs can be written in a natural applicative style, and they retain a high degree of clarity and modularity while executing with maximal concurrency. This idiom is particularly useful for programming against external data sources, where the application code is written without the use of explicit concurrency constructs, while the implementation is able to batch together multiple requests for data from the same source, and fetch data from multiple sources concurrently. Our abstraction uses a cache to ensure that multiple requests for the same data return the same result, which frees the programmer from having to arrange to fetch data only once, which in turn leads to greater modularity.

While it is generally applicable, our technique was designed with a particular application in mind: an internal service at Facebook that identifies particular types of content and takes actions based on it. Our application has a large body of business logic that fetches data from several different external sources. The framework described in this paper enables the business logic to execute efficiently by automatically fetching data concurrently; we present some preliminary results.

Keywords Haskell; concurrency; applicative; monad; data-fetching; distributed

1. Introduction

Consider the problem of building a network service that encapsulates business logic behind an API; a special case of this being a web-based application. Services of this kind often need to efficiently obtain and process data from a heterogeneous set of external sources. In the case of a web application, the service usually needs to access at least databases, and possibly other application-specific services that make up the distributed architecture of the system.

The *business logic* in this setting is the code that determines, for each request made using this service, what data to deliver as the result. In the case of a web application, the input is an HTTP request, and the output is a web page. Our goal is to have clear and concise business logic, uncluttered by performance-related details. In particular the programmer should not need to be concerned with accessing external data efficiently. However, one particular problem often arises that creates a tension between conciseness and efficiency in this setting: accessing multiple remote data sources efficiently requires *concurrency*, and that normally requires the programmer to intervene and program the concurrency explicitly.

When the business logic is only concerned with *reading* data from external sources and not *writing*, the programmer doesn't care about the order in which data accesses happen, since there are no side-effects that could make the result different when the order changes. So in this case the programmer would be entirely happy with not having to specify either ordering or concurrency, and letting the system perform data access in the most efficient way possible. In this paper we present an embedded domain-specific language (EDSL), written in Haskell, that facilitates this style of programming, while automatically extracting and exploiting any concurrency inherent in the program.

Our contributions can be summarised as follows:

- We present an `Applicative` abstraction that allows implicit concurrency to be extracted from computations written with a combination of `Monad` and `Applicative`. This is an extension of the idea of concurrency monads [10], using Applicative `<*>` as a way to introduce concurrency (Section 4). We then develop the idea into an abstraction that supports concurrent access to remote data (Section 5), and failure (Section 8).
- We show how to add a *cache* to the framework (Section 6). The cache memoises the results of previous data fetches, which provides not only performance benefits, but also consistency in the face of changes to the external data.
- We show that it isn't necessary for the programmer to use `Applicative` operators in order to benefit from concurrency in our framework, for two reasons: first, bulk monadic operations such as maps and filters use `Applicative` internally, which provides a lot of the benefit of `Applicative` concurrency for almost zero effort (Section 5.5), and secondly we can automatically translate code written using monadic style into `Applicative` in certain cases (Section 7).
- We have implemented this system at Facebook in a back-end service that contains over 200,000 lines of business logic. We present some preliminary results showing that our system running with production data efficiently optimises the data accesses. When running without our automatic concurrency, typical latencies were 51% longer (Section 9).

While our work is mostly focused on a setting in which all the operations of the DSL are data reads, we consider how to incorporate side-effecting operations in Section 9.3. Section 10 compares our design with other concurrent programming models.

ICFP '14, September 1–6, 2014, Gothenburg, Sweden.

ACM 978-1-4503-2873-9/14/09.
http://dx.doi.org/10.1145/2628136.2628144

2. Motivation

To motivate the design, we will present two use cases. The first is a typical web application, which needs to render a web page based on data fetched from one or more external sources. The second is a real-world use case from Facebook: a rule-engine for detecting certain types of content and taking actions based on it.

2.1 Example: rendering a blog

In this example we'll look at some code to render a blog, focusing on the part of the application that fetches and processes the data from the external data source (e.g. a database). The blog web page will consist of two panes:

- The main pane shows the most recent posts to the blog in date order.
- The side pane contains two sub-panes:
  - a list of the posts with the most page views ("popular posts"),
  - a list of topics and the number of posts in each topic.

Assuming a set of operations to fetch the necessary data, and a set of functions to actually render the HTML, the task is to write the code to collect the necessary data and call the rendering functions for each of the separate parts of the page. The goal is to write code that has two properties:

- It should be *modular*, so that new sections on the page can be added and removed without disturbing the rest of the code.
- It should execute *efficiently*, but without the programmer having to implement optimisations manually. In particular, we should be fetching as much data concurrently as possible.

Our framework allows both of these goals to be met; the code will be both maximally modular and maximally efficient (in terms of overlapping and batching external requests for data).

The example requires a bit of setup. First, some types:

```
data PostId        -- identifies a post
data Date          -- a calendar date
data PostContent   -- the content of a post

data PostInfo = PostInfo
  { postId    :: PostId
  , postDate  :: Date
  , postTopic :: String
  }
```

A post on the blog is represented by two types: `PostInfo` and `PostContent`. `PostInfo` contains the metadata about the post: the date it was created, and its topic. The actual content of the post is represented by the abstract `PostContent` type.

Posts have an identifier that allows them to be fetched from the database, namely `PostId`. For the purposes of this example we will assume the simplest storage model possible: the storage performs no computation at all, so all sorting, joining, and so forth must be done by the client.

Our computation will be done in a monad called `Fetch`. The implementation of `Fetch` will be given later, but for this example all we need to know is that `Fetch` has instances of `Monad`, `Functor` and `Applicative`, and has the following operations for fetching data:

```
getPostIds     :: Fetch [PostId]
getPostInfo    :: PostId -> Fetch PostInfo
getPostContent :: PostId -> Fetch PostContent
getPostViews   :: PostId -> Fetch Int
```

`getPostIds` returns the identifiers of all the posts, `getPostInfo` retrieves the metadata about a particular post, `getPostContent` fetches the content of a post, and finally `getPostViews` returns a count of the number of page views for a post. Each of these operations needs to retrieve the data from some external source, perhaps one or more databases. Furthermore a database might be highly distributed, so there is no expectation that any two requests will be served by the same machine.

We assume a set of rendering functions, including.

```
renderPosts :: [(PostInfo,PostContent)] -> Html
renderPage  :: Html -> Html -> Html
```

`renderPosts` takes a set of posts and returns the corresponding HTML. Note that we need both the `PostInfo` and the `PostContent` to render a post. The `renderPage` function constructs the whole page given the HTML for the side pane and the main pane. We'll see various other functions beginning with `render`; the implementations of these functions aren't important for the example.

Now that the background is set, we can move on to the actual code of the example. We'll start at the top and work down; here is the top-level function, `blog`:

```
blog :: Fetch Html
blog = renderPage <$> leftPane <*> mainPane
```

`blog` generates a web page by calling `leftPane` and `mainPane` to generate the two panes, and then calling `renderPage` to put the results together. Note that we're using the `Applicative` combinators `<$>` and `<*>` to construct the expression: `leftPane` and `mainPane` are both `Fetch` operations because they will need to fetch data.

To make the main pane, we need to fetch all the information about the posts, sort them into date order, and then take the first few (say 5) to pass to `renderPosts`:

```
mainPane :: Fetch Html
mainPane = do
  posts <- getAllPostsInfo
  let ordered =
        take 5 $
        sortBy (flip (comparing postDate)) posts
  content <- mapM (getPostContent . postId) ordered
  return $ renderPosts (zip ordered content)
```

Here `getAllPostsInfo` is an auxiliary function, defined as follows:

```
getAllPostsInfo :: Fetch [PostInfo]
getAllPostsInfo = mapM getPostInfo =<< getPostIds
```

As you might expect, to fetch all the `PostInfo`s we have to first fetch all the `PostId`s with `getPostIds`, and then fetch each `PostInfo` with `getPostInfo`.

The left pane consists of two sub-panes, so in order to construct the left pane we must render the sub-panes and put the result together by calling another rendering function, `renderSidePane`:

```
leftPane :: Fetch Html
leftPane = renderSidePane <$> popularPosts <*> topics
```

Next we'll look at the `popularPosts` sub-pane. In order to define this we'll need an auxiliary function, `getPostDetails`, which fetches both the `PostInfo` and the `PostContent` for a post:

```
getPostDetails :: PostId
               -> Fetch (PostInfo, PostContent)
getPostDetails pid =
 (,) <$> getPostInfo pid <*> getPostContent pid
```

Here is the code for popularPosts:

```
popularPosts :: Fetch Html
popularPosts = do
  pids <- getPostIds
  views <- mapM getPostViews pids
  let ordered =
        take 5 $ map fst $
        sortBy (flip (comparing snd))
               (zip pids views)
  content <- mapM getPostDetails ordered
  return $ renderPostList content
```

First we get the list of PostIds, and then the number of page views for each of these. The number of page views are used to sort the list; the value ordered is a list of the top five PostIds by page views. We can use this list to fetch the information about the posts that we need to render, by calling getPostDetails for each one, and finally the result is passed to renderPostList to render the list of popular posts.

Next the code for rendering the menu of topics:

```
topics :: Fetch Html
topics = do
  posts <- getAllPostsInfo
  let topiccounts =
        Map.fromListWith (+)
          [ (postTopic p, 1) | p <- posts ]
  return $ renderTopics topiccounts
```

Creating the list of topics is a matter of calculating a mapping from topic to the number of posts in that topic from the list of PostInfos, and then passing that to renderTopics to render it.

This completes the code for the example. The code clearly expresses the functionality of the application, with no concession to performance. Yet we want it to execute efficiently too; there are two ways in which our framework will automatically improve the efficiency when this code is executed:

- **Concurrency**. A lot of the data fetching can be done concurrently. For example:
  - every time we use mapM with a data-fetching operation, there is an opportunity for concurrency.
  - we can compute mainPane and leftPane at the same time, and within leftPane we can compute popularPosts and topics at the same time.

  Our goal is to exploit all this inherent concurrency without the programmer having to lift a finger. The framework we will describe in this paper does exactly that: with the code as written, the data will be fetched in the pattern shown in Figure 1. The dotted lines indicate a *round* of data-fetching, where all the items in a round are fetched concurrently. There are three rounds:
  - getPostIds (needed by all three panes)
  - getPostInfo for all posts (needed by mainPane and topics), and getPostViews for all posts (needed by popularPosts).
  - getPostContent for each of the posts displayed in the main pane, and getPostInfo and getPostContent for each of the posts displayed in popularPosts.
- **Caching**. We made no explicit attempt to fetch each piece of data only once. For example, we are calling getPostIds three times. Remember the goal is to be *modular*: there is no global knowledge about what data is needed by each part of the page.

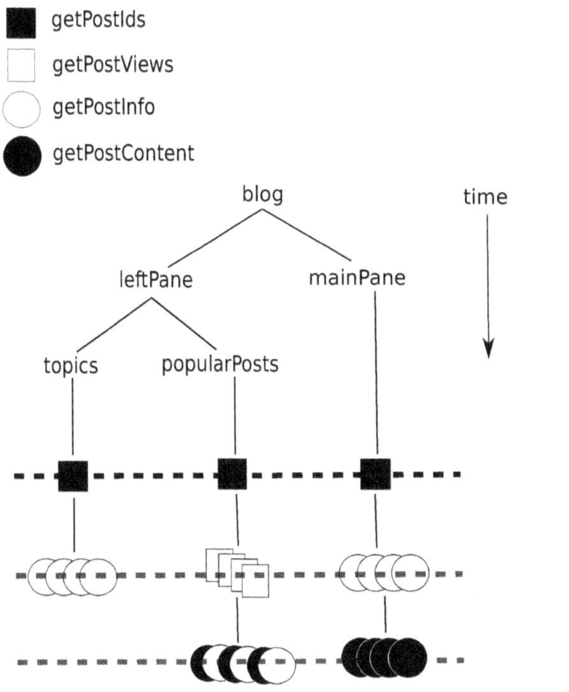

Figure 1. Data fetching in the blog example

Furthermore, even though we could reasonably predict that we need getPostIds in several places and so do it once up front, it is much harder to predict which getPostContent calls will be made: the main pane displays the five most recent posts, and the side pane displays the five most popular posts. There might well be overlap between these two sets, but to write the code to fetch the minimal set of PostContent would require destroying the modularity.

Our system uses caching to avoid fetching the same data multiple times, which lets the programmer keep the modularity in their code without worrying about duplicate data fetching. Furthermore, as we describe in Section 6, caching has important benefits beyond the obvious performance gains.

2.2 Example: a data-rich DSL

Our second use-case is a service inside the Facebook infrastructure that identifies spam, malware, and other types of undesirable content [11]. Every action that creates an item of content on the site results in a request to this service, and it is the job of the service to return a result indicating whether the content should be allowed or rejected[1]. The service runs on many machines, and each instance of the service runs the same set of business logic, which is typically modified many times per day.

As an example of the kind of calculations that our business logic needs to perform, consider this hypothetical expression fragment:

```
length (intersect (friendsOf x) (friendsOf y))
```

length is the usual list length operation, intersect takes the intersection of two lists, and friendsOf is a function that returns the list of friends of a user:

```
friendsOf :: UserId -> [UserId]
```

[1] This is a huge simplification, but will suffice for this paper.

The value of this expression is the number of friends that x and y have in common; this value tends to be a useful quantity in our business logic and is often computed.

This code fragment is an example of how we would like the business logic to look: clear, concise, and without any mention of implementation details.

Now, the `friendsOf` function needs to access a remote database in order to return its result. So if we were to implement this directly in Haskell, even if we hide the remote data access behind a pure API like `friendsOf`, when we run the program it will make two requests for data in series: first to fetch the friends of x, and then to fetch the friends of y. We ought to do far better than this: not only could we do these two requests concurrently, but in fact the database serving these requests (TAO, [14]) supports submitting several requests as a single batch, so we could submit both requests in a single unit.

The question is, how could we modify our language such that it supports an implementation that submits these two requests concurrently? The problem is not just one of exploring simple expressions like this; in general we might have to wait for the results of some data accesses before we can evaluate more of the expression. Consider this:

```
let
   numCommonFriends =
     length (intersect (friendsOf x) (friendsOf y))
in
if numCommonFriends < 2 && daysRegistered x < 30
   then ...
   else ...
```

Here `daysRegistered` returns the number of days that a user has been registered on the site.

So now, assuming that we want a lazy `&&` such that if the left side is `False` we don't evaluate the right side at all, then we cannot fetch the data for `daysRegistered` until we have the results of the two `friendsOf` calls.

Scaling this up, when we consider computing the result of a request that involves running a large amount of business logic, in general at any given time there might be many requests for data that could be submitted concurrently. Having fetched the results of those requests, the computation can proceed further, possibly along multiple paths, until it gets blocked again on a new set of data fetches.

Our solution is to build an abstraction using `Applicative` and `Monad` to support concurrent data access, which we describe in the next few sections. We will return in Section 5.3 to see how our DSL looks when built on top of the framework.

3. Concurrency monads

A concurrency monad embodies the fundamental notion of a computation that can pause and be resumed. The concurrency monad will be the foundation of the abstractions we develop in this paper. Here is its type:

```
data Fetch a = Done a | Blocked (Fetch a)
```

An operation of type `Fetch a` has either completed and delivered a value a, indicated by `Done`, or it is blocked (or paused), indicated by `Blocked`. The argument to `Blocked` is the computation to run to continue, of type `Fetch a`.

For reference, we give the definitions of the `Functor` and `Monad` type classes in Figure 2. The instances of `Functor` and `Monad` for `Fetch` are as follows:

```
class Functor f where
  fmap :: (a -> b) -> f a -> f b

class Functor f => Applicative f where
  pure  :: a -> f a
  (<*>) :: f (a -> b) -> f a -> f b

class Monad f where
  return :: a -> f a
  (>>=) :: f a -> (a -> f b) -> f b

ap :: (Monad m) => m (a -> b) -> m a -> m b
ap mf mx = do f <- mf; x <- mx; return (f x)
```

Figure 2. Definitions of `Functor`, `Applicative`, `Monad`, and `ap`

```
instance Functor Fetch where
  fmap f (Done x) = Done (f x)
  fmap f (Blocked c) = Blocked (fmap f c)

instance Monad Fetch where
  return = Done

  Done a    >>= k = k a
  Blocked c >>= k = Blocked (c >>= k)
```

In general, a computation in this monad will be a sequence of `Blocked` constructors ending in a `Done` with the return value. This is the essence of (cooperative) concurrency: for example, one could implement a simple round-robin scheduler to interleave multiple tasks by keeping track of a queue of blocked tasks, running the task at the front of the queue until it blocks again, and then returning it to the end of the queue.

Our monad isn't very useful yet. There are two key pieces missing: a way to introduce concurrency into a computation, and a way for a computation to say what data it is waiting for when it blocks. We will present these elaborations respectively in the next two sections. Following that, we will return to our motivating examples and show how the `Fetch` framework enables efficient and modular data-fetching.

4. Applicative concurrency

Concurrency monads have occurred in the literature several times. Scholz [10] originally introduced a concurrency monad based on a continuation monad, and then Claessen [2] used this as the basis for his Poor Man's Concurrency Monad. This idea was used by Li and Zdancewic [5] to implement scalable network services. A slightly different formulation but with similar functionality was dubbed the *resumption monad* by Harrison [4]. The resumption monad formulation was used in describing the semantics of concurrency by Swierstra and Altenkirch [12]. Our `Fetch` monad follows the resumption monad formulation. It is also worth noting that this idea is an instance of a *free monad* [1].

All these previous formulations of concurrency monads used some kind of *fork* operation to explicitly indicate when to create a new thread of control. In contrast, in this paper *there is no fork*. The concurrency will be implicit in the structure of the computations we write using this abstraction. To make it possible to build computations that contain implicit concurrency, we need to make `Fetch` an Applicative Functor [7]. For reference, the definition of the `Applicative` class is given in Figure 2 (omitting the `*>` and `<*` operators, which are not important for this paper).

Applicative Functors are a class of functors that may have effects that compose using the `<*>` operator. Morally, the class of Applicative Functors sits between Functors and Monads: every Monad is an Applicative Functor, but the reverse is not true. For historical reasons, `Applicative` is not currently a superclass of `Monad` in Haskell, although this is expected to change in the future.

An `Applicative` instance can be given for any `Monad`, simply by making `pure = return` and `<*> = ap` (Figure 2). However, for `Fetch` we want a custom `Applicative` instance that takes advantage of the fact that the arguments to `<*>` are independent, and uses this to introduce concurrency:

```
instance Applicative Fetch where
  pure = return

  Done g    <*> Done y    = Done (g y)
  Done g    <*> Blocked c = Blocked (g <$> c)
  Blocked c <*> Done y    = Blocked (c <*> Done y)
  Blocked c <*> Blocked d = Blocked (c <*> d)
```

This is the key piece of our design: when computations in `Fetch` are composed using the `<*>` operator, *both* arguments of `<*>` can be explored to search for `Blocked` computations, which creates the possibility that a computation may be blocked on multiple things simultaneously. This is in contrast to the monadic bind operator, `>>=`, which does not admit exploration of both arguments, because the right hand side cannot be evaluated without the result from the left.

For comparison, if we used `<*> = ap`, the standard definition for a `Monad`, we would get the following (refactored slightly):

```
instance Applicative Fetch where
  pure = return

  Done f    <*> x = f <$> x
  Blocked c <*> x = Blocked (c <*> x)
```

Note how only the first argument of `<*>` is inspected. The difference between these two will become clear if we consider an example: `Blocked (Done (+1)) <*> Blocked (Done 1)`. Under our `Applicative` instance this evaluates to:

```
 Blocked (Done (+1) <*> Done 1)
==>
 Blocked (Done (1 + 1))
```

whereas under the standard `Applicative` instance, the same example would evaluate to:

```
 Blocked (Done (+1) <*> Blocked (Done 1))
==>
 Blocked ((+1) <$> Blocked (Done 1))
==>
 Blocked (Blocked ((+1) <$> Done 1))
==>
 Blocked (Blocked (Done (1 + 1)))
```

If `Blocked` indicates a set of remote data fetches that must be performed (we'll see how this happens in the next section), then with our `Applicative` instance we only have to stop and fetch data once, whereas the standard instance has two layers of `Blocked`, so we would stop twice.

Now that we have established the basic idea, we need to elaborate it to do something useful; namely to perform multiple requests for data simultaneously.

5. Fetching data

In order to fetch some data, we need a primitive that takes a description of the data to fetch, and returns the data itself. We will call this operation `dataFetch`:

```
dataFetch :: Request a -> Fetch a
```

where `Request` is an application-specific type that specifies requests; a value of type `Request a` is an instruction that the system can use to fetch a value of type `a`. For now the `Request` type is a concrete but unspecified type; we will show how to instantiate this for our blog example in Section 5.2, and we outline how to abstract the framework over the request type in Section 9.

How can we implement `dataFetch`? One idea is to elaborate the `Blocked` constructor to include a request:

```
data Fetch a
  = Done a
  | forall r . Blocked (Request r) (r -> Fetch a)
```

This works for a single request, but quickly runs into trouble when we want to block on *multiple* requests because it becomes hard to maintain the connections between multiple result types `r` and their continuations.

We solve this problem by storing results in mutable references. This requires two changes. First we encapsulate the request and the place to store the result in an existentially quantified `BlockedRequest` type:

```
data BlockedRequest =
  forall a . BlockedRequest (Request a)
                            (IORef (FetchStatus a))
```

(a `forall` outside the constructor definition is Haskell's syntax for an existentially-quantified type variable). `IORef` is Haskell's mutable reference type, which supports the following operations for creation, reading and writing respectively:

```
newIORef   :: a -> IO (IORef a)
readIORef  :: IORef a -> IO a
writeIORef :: IORef a -> a -> IO ()
```

The `FetchStatus` type is defined as follows:

```
data FetchStatus a
  = NotFetched
  | FetchSuccess a
```

Before the result is available, the `IORef` contains `NotFetched`. When the result is available, it contains `FetchSuccess`. As we will see later, using an `IORef` here also makes it easier to add caching to the framework.

The use of `IORef` requires that we layer our monad on top of the `IO` monad. In practice this isn't a drawback, because the `IO` monad is necessary in order to perform the actual data fetching, so it will be available when executing a computation in the `Fetch` monad anyway. The `IO` monad will not be exposed to user code.

Considering that we will need computations that can block on multiple requests, our monad now also needs to collect the set of `BlockedRequest` associated with a blocked computation. A list would work for this purpose, but it suffers from performance problems due to nested appends, so instead we will use Haskell's `Seq` type, which supports logarithmic-time append.

With these two modifications (adding `IO` and attaching `Seq BlockedRequest` to the `Blocked` constructor), the monad now looks like this:

```
data Result a
  = Done a
  | Blocked (Seq BlockedRequest) (Fetch a)

newtype Fetch a = Fetch { unFetch :: IO (Result a) }
```

```
instance Applicative Fetch where
  pure = return

  Fetch f <*> Fetch x = Fetch $ do
    f' <- f
    x' <- x
    case (f',x') of
      (Done g,        Done y       ) -> return (Done (g y))
      (Done g,        Blocked br c ) -> return (Blocked br (g <$> c))
      (Blocked br c,  Done y       ) -> return (Blocked br (c <*> return y))
      (Blocked br1 c, Blocked br2 d) -> return (Blocked (br1 <> br2) (c <*> d))
```

Figure 3. Applicative instance for `Fetch`

```
instance Monad Fetch where
  return a = Fetch $ return (Done a)

  Fetch m >>= k = Fetch $ do
    r <- m
    case r of
      Done a       -> unFetch (k a)
      Blocked br c -> return (Blocked br (c >>= k))
```

and the `Applicative` instance is given in Figure 3. Note that in the case where both arguments to `<*>` are `Blocked`, we must combine the sets of blocked requests from each side.

Finally we are in a position to implement `dataFetch`:

```
dataFetch :: Request a -> Fetch a
dataFetch request = Fetch $ do
  box <- newIORef NotFetched                  -- (1)
  let br = BlockedRequest request box         -- (2)
  let cont = Fetch $ do                       -- (3)
        FetchSuccess a <- readIORef box       -- (4)
        return (Done a)                       -- (5)
  return (Blocked (singleton br) cont)        -- (6)
```

Where:

- Line 1 creates a new `IORef` to store the result, initially containing `NotFetched`.
- Line 2 creates a `BlockedRequest` for this request.
- Lines 3–5 define the continuation, which reads the result from the `IORef` and returns it in the monad. Note that the contents of the `IORef` is assumed to be `FetchSuccess a` when the continuation is executed. It is an internal error of the framework if this is not true, so we don't attempt to handle the error condition here.
- Line 6: `dataFetch` returns `Blocked` in the monad, including the `BlockedRequest`.

5.1 Running a computation

We've defined the `Fetch` type and its `Monad` and `Applicative` instances, but we also need a way to *run* a `Fetch` computation. Clearly the details of how we actually fetch data are application-specific, but there's a standard pattern for running a computation that works in all settings.

The application-specific data-fetching can be abstracted as a function `fetch`:

```
fetch :: [BlockedRequest] -> IO ()
```

The job of `fetch` is to fill in the `IORef` in each `BlockedRequest` with the data fetched. Ideally, `fetch` will take full advantage of concurrency where possible, and will batch together requests for data from the same source. For example, multiple HTTP requests could be handled by a pool of connections where each connection processes a pipelined batch of requests. Our actual implementation at Facebook has several data sources, corresponding to various internal services in the Facebook infrastructure. Most have asynchronous APIs but some are synchronous, and several of them support batched requests. We can fetch data from all of them concurrently.

Given `fetch`, the basic scheme for running a `Fetch` computation is as follows:

```
runFetch :: Fetch a -> IO a
runFetch (Fetch h) = do
  r <- h
  case r of
    Done a -> return a
    Blocked br cont -> do
      fetch (toList br)
      runFetch cont
```

This works as follows. First, we run the `Fetch` computation. If the result was `Done`, then we are finished; return the result. If the result was `Blocked`, then fetch the data by calling `fetch`, and then run the continuation from the `Blocked` constructor by recursively invoking `runFetch`.

The overall effect is to run the computation in stages that we call *rounds*. In each round `runFetch` performs as much computation as possible and then performs all the data fetching concurrently. This process is repeated until the computation returns `Done`.

By performing as much computation as possible we maximise the amount of data fetching we can perform concurrently. This makes good use of our network resources, by providing the maximum chance that we can batch multiple requests to the same data source, but it might not be the optimal scheme from a latency perspective; we consider alternatives in Section 11.

Our design does not impose a particular concurrency strategy on the data sources. The implementation of `fetch` has complete freedom to use the most appropriate strategy for executing the requests it is given. Typically that will involve a combination of batching requests to individual data sources, and performing requests to multiple data sources concurrently with each other using Haskell's existing concurrency mechanisms.

5.2 Example: blog

In this section we will instantiate our framework for the blog example described in Section 2.1, and show how it delivers automatic concurrency.

First, we need to define the `Request` type. Requests are parameterised by their result type, and since there will be multiple requests with different result types, a `Request` must be a GADT [9]. Here is the `Request` type for our blog example:

```
data Request a where
  FetchPosts        :: Request [PostId]
  FetchPostInfo     :: PostId -> Request PostInfo
  FetchPostContent  :: PostId -> Request PostContent
  FetchPostViews    :: PostId -> Request Int
```

Next we need to provide implementations for the data-fetching operations (`getPostIds` etc.), which are simply calls to `dataFetch` passing the appropriate `Request`:

```
getPostIds     = dataFetch FetchPosts
getPostInfo    = dataFetch . FetchPostInfo
getPostContent = dataFetch . FetchPostContent
getPostViews   = dataFetch . FetchPostViews
```

Now, if we provide a dummy implementation of `fetch` that simulates a remote data source and prints out requests as they are made[2], we do indeed find that the requests are made in three rounds as described in Section 2.1. A real implementation of `fetch` would perform the requests in each round concurrently.

5.3 Example: Haxl

In Section 2.2 we introduced our motivation for designing the applicative concurrency abstraction. Our implementation is called `Haxl`, and we will describe it in more detail in Section 9.1. Here, we briefly return to the original example to show how to implement it using `Fetch`.

The example we used was this expression:

```
length (intersect (friendsOf x) (friendsOf y))
```

How does this look when used with our `Fetch` monad? Any operation that may fetch data must be a `Fetch` operation, hence

```
friendsOf :: UserId -> Fetch [UserId]
```

while `length` and `intersect` are the usual pure functions. So to write the expression as a whole we need to lift the pure operations into the `Applicative` world, like so:

```
length <$> intersect' (friendsOf x) (friendsOf y)
  where intersect' = liftA2 intersect
```

This is just one way we could write it, there are many other equivalent alternatives. As we shall see in Section 7, it is also acceptable to use the plain do-notation, together with a source-to-source transformation that turns do-notation into `Applicative` operations:

```
do a <- friendsOf x
   b <- friendsOf y
   return (length (intersect a b))
```

In fact, this is the style we advocate for users of our DSL.

5.4 Semantics of Fetch

It's worth pondering on the implications of what we have done here. Arguably we broke the rules: while the `Applicative` laws do hold for `Fetch`, the documentation for `Applicative` also states that if a type is also a `Monad`, then its `Applicative` instance should satisfy `pure = return` and `<*> = ap`. This is clearly not the case for our `Applicative` instance. But in some sense, our intentions are pure: the goal is for code written using `Applicative` to execute more efficiently, not for it to give a different answer than when written using `Monad`.

Our justification for this `Applicative` instance is based on more than its literal definition. We intend `dataFetch` to have certain properties: it should not be observable to the programmer writing code using `Fetch` whether their `dataFetch` calls were performed concurrently or sequentially, or indeed in which order they were performed, the results should be the same. Therefore, `dataFetch` should not have any observable side-effects—all our requests must be read-only. To the user of `Fetch` it is *as if* the `Applicative` instance is the default `<*> = ap`, except that the code runs more efficiently, and for this to be the case we must restrict ourselves to read-only requests (although we return to this question and consider side-effects again in Section 9.3).

Life is not quite that simple, however, since we are reading data from the outside world, and the data may change between calls to `dataFetch`. The programmer might be able to observe a change in the data and hence observe an ordering of `dataFetch` operations. Our approach is to close this loophole as far as we can: in Section 6 we add a cache to the system, which will ensure that identical requests always return the same result within a single run of `Fetch`. Technically we can argue that `runFetch` is in the `IO` monad and therefore we are justified in making a non-deterministic choice for the ordering of `dataFetch` operations, but in practice we find that for the majority of applications this technicality is not important: we just write code as if we are working against a snapshot of the external data.

If we actually did have access to an unchanging snapshot of the remote data, then we could make a strong claim of determinism for the programming model. Of course that's not generally possible when there are multiple data sources in use, although certain individual data sources do support access to a fixed snapshot of their data; one example is Datomic[3].

5.5 Bulk operations: mapM and sequence

In our example blog code we used the combinators `mapM` and `sequence` to perform bulk operations. As things stand in Haskell today, these functions are defined using monadic bind, for example `sequence` is defined in the Haskell 2010 Report as

```
sequence :: Monad m => [m a] -> m [a]
sequence =  foldr mcons (return [])
 where mcons p q = do x <- p; y <- q; return (x:y)
```

Unfortunately, because this uses monadic bind rather than Applicative `<*>`, in our framework it will serialise the operations rather than perform them concurrently. Fortunately `sequence` doesn't require monadic bind; `Applicative` is sufficient [7], and indeed the the `Data.Traversable` module provides an equivalent that uses `Applicative`: `sequenceA`. Similarly, `traverse` is the `Applicative` equivalent of `mapM`. Nevertheless, Haskell programmers tend to be less familiar with the `Applicative` equivalents, so in our EDSL library we map `sequence` to `sequenceA` and `mapM` to `traverse`, so that client code can use these well-known operations and obtain automatic concurrency.

In due course when `Applicative` is made a superclass of `Monad`, the `Applicative` versions of these functions will become the defaults, and our workaround can be removed without changing the client code or its performance.

6. Adding a cache

In Section 2.1 we identified two ways that the framework can provide automatic performance benefits for the application. So far we have demonstrated the first, namely exploiting implicit concurrency. In this section we turn our attention to the second: avoiding duplicate requests for data.

[2] Sample code is available at `https://github.com/simonmar/haxl-icfp14-sample-code`

[3] `http://www.datomic.com/`

The solution is not surprising, namely to add caching. However, as we shall see, the presence of a cache provides some rather nice benefits in addition to the obvious performance improvements.

Recall that data is fetched using `dataFetch`:

```
dataFetch :: Request a -> Fetch a
```

Caching amounts to memoising this operation, such that the second time it is called with a request that has been previously issued, it returns the result from the original request. Not only do we gain performance by not repeating identical data-fetches, as mentioned in Section 5.4 the programmer can rely on identical requests returning the same results, which provides consistency within a single `Fetch` computation in the face of data that might be changing.

We also gain the ability to do some source-to-source transformations. For example, common subexpression elimination:

```
  do x <- N; M
==>
  do x <- N; M[return x/N]
```

Where `M` and `N` stand for arbitrary `Fetch` expressions, This holds provided `dataFetch` is the only way to do I/O in our framework, and all `dataFetch` requests are cached.

6.1 Implementing the cache

Let's consider how to add a cache to the system. In order to store a mapping from requests to results, we need the following API:

```
data DataCache

lookup :: Request a -> DataCache -> Maybe a
insert :: Request a -> a -> DataCache -> DataCache
```

If we want to use an existing efficient map implementation, we cannot implement this API directly because its type-correctness relies on the correctness of the map implementation, and the `Eq` and `Ord` instances for `Request`. But if we trust these, Haskell provides an unsafe back-door, `unsafeCoerce`, that lets us convey this promise to the type system. The use of unsafe features to implement a purely functional API is common practice in Haskell; often the motivation is performance, but here it is the need to maintain a link between two types in the type system.

A possible implementation is as follows:

```
newtype DataCache =
  DataCache (forall a . HashMap (Request a) a)
```

The contents of a `DataCache` is a mapping that, for all types `a`, maps things of type `Request a` to things of type `a`. The invariant we require is that a key of type `Request a` is either not present in the mapping, or maps to a value of type `a`. We will enforce the invariant when an element is inserted into the `Map`, and assume it when an element is extracted. If the `Map` is correctly implemented, then our assumption is valid.

Note that we use a `HashMap` rather than a plain `Map`. This is because `Map` requires the key type to be an instance of the `Ord` class, but `Ord` cannot be defined for all `Request a` because it would entail comparing keys of different types. On the other hand, `HashMap` requires `Eq` and `Hashable`, both of which can be straightforwardly defined for `Request a`, the former using a standalone deriving declaration:

```
deriving instance Eq (Request a)
```

and the latter with a hand-written `Hashable` instance (see the sample code[4]).

[4] `https://github.com/simonmar/haxl-icfp14-sample-code`

Looking up in the cache is simply a `lookup` in the `Map`:

```
lookup :: Request a -> DataCache -> Maybe a
lookup key (DataCache m) = Map.lookup key m
```

This works because we have already declared that the `Map` in a `DataCache` works for all types `a`. The `insert` operation is where we have to make a promise to the type system:

```
insert :: Request a -> a -> DataCache -> DataCache
insert key val (DataCache m) =
  DataCache $ unsafeCoerce (Map.insert key val m)
```

We can insert a key/value pair into the `Map` without any difficulty. However, that results in a `Map` instantiated at a *particular* type `a` (the type of `val` passed to `insert`), so in order to get back a `Map` that works for any `a` we need to apply `unsafeCoerce`. The `unsafeCoerce` function has this type:

```
unsafeCoerce :: forall a b . a -> b
```

Therefore, applying `unsafeCoerce` to the `Map` allows it to be generalised to the type required by `DataCache`.

Now we have a cache that can store a type-safe mapping from requests to results. We will need to plumb this around the `Monad` to pass it to each call to `dataFetch` so that we can check the cache for a previous result. However, this won't be enough: consider what happens when we make two identical requests in the same *round*: there won't be a cached result, but nevertheless we want to ensure that we only make a single request and use the same result for both `dataFetch` calls. Indeed, this happens several times in our blog example: the first round issues three calls to `getPostIds`, for example.

In `dataFetch` we need to distinguish three different cases:

1. The request has not been encountered before: we need to create a `BlockedRequest`, and block.
2. The request has already been fetched: we can return the cached result and continue.
3. The request has been encountered in the current round but not yet fetched: we need to block, but not create a new `BlockedRequest` since it will already have been added to the set of requests to fetch elsewhere.

The key idea is that in the third case we can share the `IORef (FetchStatus a)` from the `BlockedRequest` that was created the first time the request was encountered. Hence, all calls to `dataFetch` for a given request will automatically share the same result. How can we find the `IORef` for a request? *We store it in the cache.*

So instead of storing only results in our `DataCache`, we need to store `IORef (FetchStatus a)`. This lets us distinguish the three cases above:

1. The request is not in the `DataCache`.
2. The request is in the `DataCache`, and the `IORef` contains `FetchSuccess a`.
3. The request is in the `DataCache`, and the `IORef` contains `NotFetched`.

This implies that we must add an item to the cache as soon as the request is issued; we don't wait until the result is available. Filling in the details, our `DataCache` now has the following API:

```
data DataCache

lookup :: Request a -> DataCache
       -> Maybe (IORef (FetchStatus a))
```

```
dataFetch :: Request a -> Fetch a
dataFetch req = Fetch $ \ref -> do
  cache <- readIORef ref
  case lookup req cache of
    Nothing -> do
      box <- newIORef NotFetched
      writeIORef ref (insert req box cache)
      let br = BlockedRequest req box
      return (Blocked (singleton br) (cont box))
    Just box -> do
      r <- readIORef box
      case r of
        FetchSuccess result ->
          return (Done result)
        NotFetched ->
          return (Blocked Seq.empty (cont box))
 where
  cont box = Fetch $ \ref -> do
    FetchSuccess a <- readIORef box
    return (Done a)
```

Figure 4. `dataFetch` implementation with caching

```
insert :: Request a -> IORef (FetchStatus a)
       -> DataCache -> DataCache
```

(the implementation is the same). The cache itself needs to be stored in an `IORef` and passed around in the monad; `Fetch` now has this definition:

```
newtype Fetch a = Fetch {
  unFetch :: IORef DataCache -> IO (Result a) }
```

The alterations to the `Monad` and `Applicative` instances are straightforward, so we omit them here.

The definition of `dataFetch` is given in Figure 4, The three cases identified earlier are dealt with in that order:

1. If the request is not in the cache, then we create a new `IORef` for the result (initially containing `NotFetched`) and add that to the cache. Then we create a `BlockedRequest`, and return `Blocked` in the monad, with a continuation that will read the result from the `IORef` we created.
2. If the request is in the cache, then we check the contents of the `IORef`. If it contains `FetchSuccess result`, then we have a cached result, and `dataFetch` returns `Done` immediately (it doesn't block).
3. If the contents of the `IORef` is `NotFetched`, then we return `Blocked`, but with an empty set of `BlockedRequests`, and a continuation that will read the result from the `IORef`.

6.2 Cache Persistence and Replaying

Within a single `runFetch`, the cache only accumulates information, and never discards it. In the use-cases we have described, this is not a problem: requests to a network-based service typically take a short period of time to deliver the result, after which we can discard the cache. During a computation we don't want to discard any cached data, because the programmer might rely on the cache for consistency.

We have found that the cache provides other benefits in addition to the ones already described:

- at the end of a `Fetch` computation, the cache is a complete record of all the requests that were made, and the data that was fetched. Re-running the computation with the fully populated cache is guaranteed to give the same result, and will not fetch any data. So by persisting the cache, we can replay computations for the purposes of fault diagnosis or profiling. When the external data is changing rapidly, being able to reliably reproduce past executions is extremely valuable.
- We can store things in the cache that are not technically remote data fetches, but nevertheless we want to have a single deterministic value for. For example, in our implementation we cache the current time: within a `Fetch` computation the current time is a constant. We can also memoise whole `Fetch` computations by storing their results in the cache.

7. Automatic Applicative

Our `Fetch` abstraction requires the programmer to use the operations of `Applicative` in order to benefit from concurrency. While these operations are concise and expressive, many programmers are more comfortable with monadic notation and prefer to use it even when `Applicative` is available. Furthermore, we don't want to penalise code that uses monadic style: it should be automatically concurrent too. Our monad is commutative, so we are free to re-order operations at will, including replacing serial `>>=` with concurrent `<*>`.

In general, the transformation we want to apply is this:

```
  do p <- A; q <- B; ...
==> {- if no variable of p is a free variable of B -}
  do (p,q) <- (,) <$> A <*> B
```

for patterns `p` and `q` and expressions `A` and `B`. The transformation can be applied recursively, so that long sequences of independent statements in do-notation can be automatically replaced by `Applicative` notation.

At the time of writing, the transformation is proposed but not implemented in GHC; it is our intention to implement it as an optional extension (because it is not necessarily valid for every `Applicative` instance). In our `Haxl` implementation we currently apply this transformation as part of the automatic translation of our existing DSL into Haskell.

8. Exceptions

Handling failure is an important part of a framework that is designed to retrieve data from external sources. We have found that it is important for the application programmer to be able to handle failure, particularly transient failures that occur due to network problems or outages in external services. In these cases the programmer typically wants to choose between having the whole computation fail, or substituting a conservative default value in place of the data requested.

We need to consider failure in two ways: first, the way in which exceptions propagate in the monad, and second, how failure is handled at the data-fetching layer. We'll deal with these in order.

8.1 Exceptions in Fetch

First, we add explicit exception support to our monad. We need to add one constructor to the `Result` type, `Throw`, which represents a thrown exception:

```
data Result a
  = Done a
  | Blocked (Seq BlockedRequest) (Fetch a)
  | Throw SomeException
```

The `SomeException` type is from Haskell's `Control.Exception` library and represents an arbitrary exception [6]. To throw an exception we need to convert it to a SomeException and return it with Throw:

```
throw :: Exception e => e -> Fetch a
throw e = Fetch $ \_ ->
  return (Throw (toException e))
```

The Monad instance for Fetch with the Throw constructor is as follows:

```
instance Monad Fetch where
  return a = Fetch $ \ref -> return (Done a)

  Fetch m >>= k = Fetch $ \ref -> do
    r <- m ref
    case r of
      Done a         -> unFetch (k a) ref
      Blocked br c -> return (Blocked br (c >>= k))
      Throw e        -> return (Throw e)
```

and Figure 5 gives the Applicative instance. It is straightforward except for one case: in <*>, where the left side returns Blocked and the right side returns Throw, we *must not propagate the exception yet*, and instead we must return a Blocked computation. The reason is that we don't yet know whether the left side will throw an exception when it becomes unblocked; if it does throw an exception, then that is the exception that the computation as a whole should throw, and not the exception from the right argument of <*>. If we were to throw the exception from the right argument of <*> immediately, the result would be non-determinism: the exception that gets thrown depends on whether the left argument blocks.

We also need a catch function:

```
catch :: Exception e
      => Fetch a -> (e -> Fetch a) -> Fetch a

catch (Fetch h) handler = Fetch $ \ref -> do
  r <- h ref
  case r of
    Done a -> return (Done a)
    Blocked br c ->
      return (Blocked br (catch c handler))
    Throw e -> case fromException e of
      Just e' -> unFetch (handler e') ref
      Nothing -> return (Throw e)
```

As with catch in the IO monad, our catch catches only exceptions of the type expected by the handler (the second argument to catch). The function fromException returns Just e' if the exception can be coerced to the appropriate type, or Nothing otherwise. The interesting case from our perspective is the Blocked case, where we construct the continuation by wrapping a call to catch around the inner continuation.

8.2 Exceptions in dataFetch

When a failure occurs in a data fetching operation, it must be thrown as an exception to the caller of dataFetch. We need to program this propagation explicitly, because the data is being fetched in the top-level runFetch loop, outside the context of the Fetch computation that called dataFetch.

We propagate an exception in the same way that we communicate the result of the data fetch: via the IORef that stores the result. So we modify the FetchStatus type to include the possibility that the fetch failed with an exception:

```
data FetchStatus a
  = NotFetched
  | FetchSuccess a
  | FetchFailure SomeException
```

and we also modify dataFetch to turn a FetchFailure into a Throw after the fetch has executed (these modifications are straightforward, so we omit the code here).

This is all the support we need for exceptions. There is one pitfall: we found in our real implementation that some care is needed in the implementation of a data source to ensure that an exception is properly reported as a FetchFailure and not just thrown by the data source; the latter causes the whole Fetch computation to be aborted, since the exception is thrown during the call to fetch in runFetch.

9. Implementation and evaluation

The basics of our use-case at Facebook were introduced in Section 2.2. Essentially it is a network-based service that is used to detect and eliminate spam, malware, and other undesirable content on Facebook. There are about 600 different kinds of request, all implemented by a body of Haskell code of approximately 200,000 lines; this was automatically translated into Haskell from our previous in-house DSL, FXL.

The system can be viewed as a rule-engine, where rules are Fetch computations. Each request runs a large set of rules and aggregates the results from all the rules. Rules are often (but not always) short, and most of them fetch some external data. In our system we run all the rules for a request using sequence; this has the effect of executing all the rules concurrently.

We will give an outline of our implementation in the next section, and then present some preliminary results.

9.1 Implementation

In the earlier description, the implementation of the Fetch monad depended on the Request type, because the monad carries around a DataCache that stores Requests, and the dataFetch operation takes a Request as an argument. This is straightforward but somewhat inconvenient, because we want to have the flexibility to add new data sources in a modular way, without modifying a single shared Request type. Furthermore, we want to be able to build and test data sources independently of each other, and to test the framework against "mock" versions of the data sources that don't fetch data over the wire.

To gain this flexibility, in our implementation we abstracted the core framework over the data sources and request types. Space limitations preclude a full description of this, but the basic idea is to use Haskell's Typeable class so that we can store requests of arbitrary type in the cache. The dataFetch operation has this type:

```
dataFetch :: (DataSource req, Request req a)
          => req a -> Fetch a
```

where Request is a package of constraints including Typeable, and DataSource is defined like this:

```
class DataSource req where
  fetch :: [BlockedFetch req] -> PerformFetch

data PerformFetch
  = SyncFetch  (IO ())
  | AsyncFetch (IO () -> IO ())
```

A data source is coupled to the type of requests that it serves, so for each request type there must be an instance of DataSource that defines how those requests are fetched. The fetch method takes

```
instance Applicative Fetch where
  pure = return

  Fetch f <*> Fetch x = Fetch $ \ref -> do
    f' <- f ref
    x' <- x ref
    case (f',x') of
      (Done g,        Done y       ) -> return (Done (g y))
      (Done g,        Blocked br c ) -> return (Blocked br (g <$> c))
      (Done g,        Throw e      ) -> return (Throw e)
      (Blocked br c,  Done y       ) -> return (Blocked br (c <*> return y))
      (Blocked br1 c, Blocked br2 d) -> return (Blocked (br1 <> br2) (c <*> d))
      (Blocked br c,  Throw e      ) -> return (Blocked br (c <*> throw e))
      (Throw e,       _            ) -> return (Throw e)
```

Figure 5. Applicative instance for `Fetch` with exceptions

a list of `BlockedRequests` containing requests that belong to this data source (the `BlockedRequest` type is now parameterised by the type of the request that it contains). The job of `fetch` is to fetch the data for those requests; it can do that synchronously or asynchronously, indicated by the `PerformFetch` type. An `AsyncFetch` is a function that takes as an argument the `IO` operation to perform *while the data is being fetched*. The idea is that when fetching data from multiple sources we wrap all the asynchronous fetches around a sequence of the synchronous fetches:

```
scheduleFetches :: [PerformFetch] -> IO ()
scheduleFetches fetches = asyncs syncs
 where
  asyncs = foldr (.) id [f | AsyncFetch f <- fetches]
  syncs  = sequence_ [io | SyncFetch io <- fetches]
```

In our implementation, most data sources are asynchronous. Maximal concurrency is achieved when at most one data source in a given round is synchronous, which is the case for the vast majority of our fetching rounds. When there are multiple synchronous data sources we could achieve more concurrency by using Haskell's own concurrency mechanisms; this is something we intend to explore in the future.

9.2 Results

To evaluate how well our system exploits concurrency, we ran a random sample of 10,000 actual requests for a single common request type. We measured the number of data fetches performed by each request (not including those that were served from the cache), the number of *rounds* (batches of fetches performed concurrently), and the total end-to-end processing time of each request. Figure 6 gives the results, in the form of histograms of the number of requests against fetches, rounds, and total time (latency). Note that the number of requests on the Y-axis is a log scale. In the histogram of fetches, the buckets are 5 wide, so for example the first bar represents the number of requests with 10–15 data fetches (there were no requests that performed fewer than 10 fetches). The histogram of rounds has integral buckets, and the time histogram has buckets of 20ms.

Figure 7 gives the 50th (median), 95th, and 99th percentiles, and the maximum value, for each of fetches, rounds, and time. Note that the figures for each column were calculated by sorting the requests by fetches, rounds, and time respectively. It is not necessarily the case that the request that performed the maximum number of fetches is the same request that took the maximum number of rounds or the longest time.

We can see that 95% of our 10,000 requests require at most 4 rounds of fetching (median 3), 95% perform at most 27 data fetches (median 18), and 95% run in at most 26.3ms (median 9.5ms). There is a long tail, however, with some requests requiring more than 2000 data fetches. A few requests took an inordinately long time to run (the longest was 2.2s), and this turned out to be because one particular data fetch to another service took a long time.

The second table in Figure 7 shows for comparison what happens when we disable concurrency—this was achieved by making `(<*>) = ap`, so that `<*>` no longer batches together the fetches from both of its arguments (caching was still enabled, however). We can see that the number of rounds is equal to the number of fetches, as expected. The experiments were run against production data, so there are minor differences in the number of fetches between the two runs in Figure 7, but we can see that the effect on total runtime is significant, increasing the median time for a request by 51%. One extreme example is the request that required 2793 fetches, which increased from 220ms to 1.3s with concurrency disabled. Concurrency had no effect on the pathological data fetches, so the maximum time was unchanged at 2.2s.

9.2.1 Discussion

We have shown that the automatic concurrency provided by our framework has a sizeable impact on latency for requests in our system, but is it enough? Our existing FXL-based system performs similar data-fetching optimisations, but it does so using a special-purpose interpreter, whereas our Haskell version is implemented in libraries without modifying the language implementation.

Our workload is primarily I/O bound, so although Haskell is far faster than FXL at raw compute workloads, this has little effect on comparisons between our two systems. Thus we believe that executing data fetches concurrently is the most important factor affecting performance, and if the Haskell system were less able to exploit concurrency that would hinder its performance in these benchmarks. At the time of writing we have only preliminary measurements, but performance of the two systems does appears to be broadly similar, and we have spent very little time optimising the Haskell system so far.

It is also worth noting that the current workload is I/O bound partly because compute-heavy tasks have historically been offloaded to C++ code rather than written in FXL, because using FXL would have been too slow. In the Haskell version of our system we have reimplemented some of this functionality natively in Haskell, because its performance is more than adequate for compute tasks, and the Haskell code is significantly cleaner and safer. We believe that being able to implement compute tasks directly in Haskell will empower the users of our DSL to solve problems that they couldn't previously solve without adding C++ primitives to the language implementation.

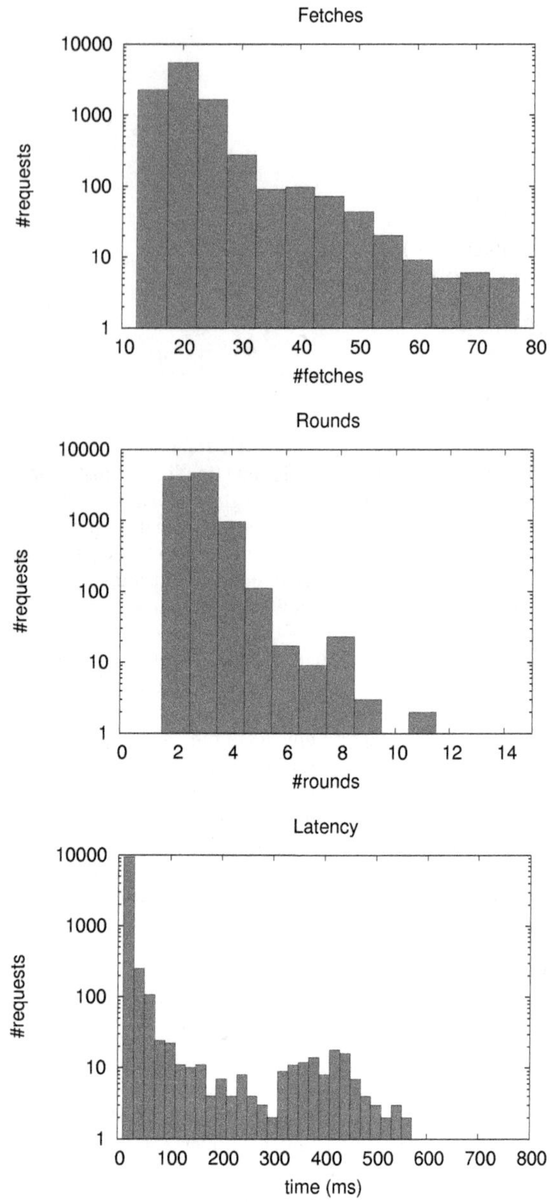

Figure 6. Results

Concurrency	Fetches	Rounds	Time (ms)
50%	18	3	9.5
95%	27	4	26.3
99%	47	5	356.5
Max	2793	11	2200.0

No concurrency	Fetches	Rounds	Time (ms)
50%	17	17	14.4
95%	27	27	36.1
99%	46	46	381.4
Max	2792	2792	2200.0

Figure 7. Summary results, with and without concurrency

9.3 Using Applicative Concurrency with Side-effects

As described, our framework has no side-effects except for reading, for good reason: operations in `Fetch` may take place in any order (Section 5.4). However, side-effects are important. For example, a web application needs to take actions based on user input, and it might need to generate some statistics that get stored. Our implementation at Facebook has various side effects, including storing values in a separate `memcache` service, and incrementing shared counters.

One safe way to perform side effects is to return them from `runFetch`, and perform them afterwards. Indeed, this is exactly the way that side effects are typically performed when using Software Transactional Memory (`STM`) in Haskell.

Sometimes it is convenient to allow side-effects as part of the `Fetch` computation itself. This is fine as long as it is *not possible to observe the side-effect with a* `Fetch` *operation*, which would expose the ordering of operations to the user. But this is quite flexible: we can, for example, have a write-only instance of `Fetch` that allows write operations to benefit from concurrency (obviously, the cache is not necessary for this), or we can have side-effects that cannot be observed, such as accumulating statistics.

10. Comparison and related work

Probably the closest relatives to the `Fetch` framework are the family of *async* programming models that have been enjoying popularity recently in several languages: F# [13], C#, OCaml [15], Scala [3], and Clojure[5].

A common trait of these programming models is that they are based on a concurrency-monad-like substrate; they behave like lightweight threads with cooperative scheduling. When a computation is suspended, its continuation is saved and re-executed later. These frameworks are typically good for scheduling large numbers of concurrent I/O tasks, because they have lower overhead than the heavyweight threads of their parent languages.

In contrast with the `Fetch` framework, the async style has an explicit fork operation, in the form of an asynchronous method call that returns an object that can later be queried for the result. For example, in C# a typical sequence looks like this:

```
Task<int> a = getData();
int y = doSomethingElse();
int x = await a;
```

The goal in this pattern is to perform `getData()` concurrently with `doSomethingElse()`. The effects of `getData()` will be interleaved with those of `doSomethingElse()`, although the degree of non-determinism is tempered somewhat by the use of cooperative scheduling.

Ignoring non-determinism, in our system this could be written

```
do [x,y] <- sequence [getData,doSomethingElse]
   ...
```

making it clear that `getData` and `doSomethingElse` are executed together.

A similar style is available in F# and C# using `Async.Parallel` and `Task.WhenAll` respectively; so it seems that in practice there are few differences between the asynchronous programming models provided by these languages and our `Fetch` monad. However, we believe the differences are important:

- In the asynchronous programming models, concurrency is achieved using special-purpose operations, whereas in our approach existing standard idioms like `sequence` and `mapM` become concurrent automatically by virtue of the `Applicative`

[5] `http://clojure.github.io/core.async/`

instance that we are using. Programmers don't need to learn a new concurrency library; they just use data-fetching operations together with the tools they already know for structuring code, and concurrency comes for free.

- Our system has a built-in cache, which is important for modularity, as we described in Section 2.1.

Explicit blocking (as in `await` above) is often shunned in the asynchronous programming models; instead it is recommended to attach callback methods to the results, like this (in Scala):

```
val future = getData();
future map(x => x + 1);
```

This has the advantage that we don't have to block on the result of the future in order to operate on it, which allows the system to exploit more concurrency. However, the programming style is somewhat indirect; in our system, this would be written

```
do x <- getData; return (x+1)
```

Reactive programming models [8] add another dimension to asynchronous programming, where instead of a single result being returned, there is a stream of results. This is a separate problem space from the one we are addressing in this paper.

11. Further work

The method for taking advantage of concurrency described in Section 4 is fairly simplistic: we run as much computation as possible, and then perform all the data fetching concurrently, repeating these two steps as many times as necessary to complete the computation. There are two ways we could overlap the computation phase with the data-fetching phase:

- As soon as we have the result of any data fetch, we can start running the corresponding blocked part(s) of the computation.
- We might want to emit some requests before we have finished exploring the whole computation. This potentially reduces concurrency but might also reduce latency.

We intend to investigate these in future work.

Acknowledgements

We would like to thank Richard Eisenberg for providing helpful feedback on an early draft of this paper.

References

[1] S. Awodey. *Category Theory*, volume 49 of *Oxford Logic Guides*. Oxford University Press, 2006.

[2] K. Claessen. A poor man's concurrency monad. *J. Funct. Program.*, 9(3):313–323, May 1999.

[3] M. Eriksen. Your server as a function. In *Proceedings of the Seventh Workshop on Programming Languages and Operating Systems*, PLOS '13, pages 5:1–5:7. ACM, 2013. ISBN 978-1-4503-2460-1.

[4] W. L. Harrison. Cheap (but functional) threads. Submitted for publication, `http://people.cs.missouri.edu/~harrisonwl/drafts/CheapThreads.pdf`.

[5] P. Li and S. Zdancewic. Combining events and threads for scalable network services implementation and evaluation of monadic, application-level concurrency primitives. In *Proceedings of the 2007 ACM SIGPLAN Conference on Programming Language Design and Implementation*, PLDI '07, pages 189–199, 2007.

[6] S. Marlow. An extensible dynamically-typed hierarchy of exceptions. In *Proceedings of the 2006 ACM SIGPLAN Workshop on Haskell*, Haskell '06, pages 96–106, 2006.

[7] C. Mcbride and R. Paterson. Applicative programming with effects. *J. Funct. Program.*, 18(1):1–13, Jan. 2008. ISSN 0956-7968.

[8] E. Meijer. Reactive extensions (Rx): Curing your asynchronous programming blues. In *ACM SIGPLAN Commercial Users of Functional Programming*, CUFP '10, pages 11:1–11:1. ACM, 2010.

[9] S. Peyton Jones, D. Vytiniotis, S. Weirich, and G. Washburn. Simple unification-based type inference for GADTs. In *Proceedings of the Eleventh ACM SIGPLAN International Conference on Functional Programming*, ICFP '06, pages 50–61. ACM, 2006.

[10] E. Scholz. A concurrency monad based on constructor primitives, or, being first-class is not enough. Technical report, Universität Berlin, 1995.

[11] T. Stein, E. Chen, and K. Mangla. Facebook immune system. In *Proceedings of the 4th Workshop on Social Network Systems*, SNS '11, pages 8:1–8:8. ACM, 2011.

[12] W. Swierstra and T. Altenkirch. Beauty in the beast. In *Proceedings of the ACM SIGPLAN Workshop on Haskell Workshop*, Haskell '07, pages 25–36, 2007. ISBN 978-1-59593-674-5.

[13] D. Syme, T. Petricek, and D. Lomov. The F# asynchronous programming model. In *Practical Aspects of Declarative Languages*, volume 6539 of *Lecture Notes in Computer Science*, pages 175–189. Springer Berlin Heidelberg, 2011.

[14] V. Venkataramani, Z. Amsden, N. Bronson, G. Cabrera III, P. Chakka, P. Dimov, H. Ding, J. Ferris, A. Giardullo, J. Hoon, S. Kulkarni, N. Lawrence, M. Marchukov, D. Petrov, and L. Puzar. TAO: How facebook serves the social graph. In *Proceedings of the 2012 ACM SIGMOD International Conference on Management of Data*, SIGMOD '12, pages 791–792, 2012.

[15] J. Vouillon. Lwt: A cooperative thread library. In *Proceedings of the 2008 ACM SIGPLAN Workshop on ML*, ML '08, pages 3–12. ACM, 2008.

Folding Domain-Specific Languages: Deep and Shallow Embeddings

(Functional Pearl)

Jeremy Gibbons   Nicolas Wu

Department of Computer Science, University of Oxford

{jeremy.gibbons,nicolas.wu}@cs.ox.ac.uk

Abstract

A domain-specific language can be implemented by embedding within a general-purpose host language. This embedding may be *deep* or *shallow*, depending on whether terms in the language construct syntactic or semantic representations. The deep and shallow styles are closely related, and intimately connected to folds; in this paper, we explore that connection.

1. Introduction

General-purpose programming languages (GPLs) are great for generality. But this very generality can count against them: it may take a lot of programming to establish a suitable context for a particular domain; and the programmer may end up being spoilt for choice with the options available to her—especially if she is a domain specialist rather than primarily a software engineer. This tension motivates many years of work on techniques to support the development of *domain-specific languages* (DSLs) such as VHDL, SQL and PostScript: languages specialized for a particular domain, incorporating the contextual assumptions of that domain and guiding the programmer specifically towards programs suitable for that domain.

There are two main approaches to DSLs. *Standalone* DSLs provide their own custom syntax and semantics, and standard compilation techniques are used to translate or interpret programs written in the DSL for execution. Standalone DSLs can be designed for maximal convenience to their intended users. But the exercise can be a significant undertaking for the implementer, involving an entirely separate ecosystem—compiler, editor, debugger, and so on—and typically also much reinvention of standard language features such as local definitions, conditionals, and iteration.

The alternative approach is to *embed* the DSL within a host GPL, essentially as a collection of definitions written in the host language. All the existing facilities and infrastructure of the host environment can be appropriated for the DSL, and familiarity with the syntactic conventions and tools of the host language can be carried over to the DSL. Whereas the standalone approach is the most common one within object-oriented circles [10], the embedded approach is typically favoured by functional programmers [18]. It seems that core FP features such as algebraic datatypes and higher-order functions are extremely helpful in defining embedded DSLs; conversely, it has been said [23] that language-oriented tasks such as DSLs are the killer application for FP.

Amongst embedded DSLs, there are two further refinements. With a *deep embedding*, terms in the DSL are implemented simply to construct an abstract syntax tree (AST), which is subsequently transformed for optimization and traversed for evaluation. With a *shallow embedding*, terms in the DSL are implemented directly by their semantics, bypassing the intermediate AST and its traversal. The names 'deep' and 'shallow' seem to have originated in the work of Boulton and colleagues on embedding hardware description languages in theorem provers for the purposes of verification [6]. Boulton's motivation for the names was that a deep embedding preserves the syntactic representation of a term, "whereas in a shallow embedding [the syntax] is just a surface layer that is easily blown away by rewriting" [5]. It turns out that deep and shallow embeddings are closely related, and intimately connected to folds; our purpose in this paper is to explore that connection.

ICFP '14, September 1–6, 2014, Gothenburg, Sweden.

http://dx.doi.org/10.1145/2628136.2628138

2. Embedding DSLs

We start by looking a little closer at deep and shallow embeddings. Consider a very simple language of arithmetic expressions, involving integer constants and addition:

$$\begin{array}{l}\textbf{type}\ \mathit{Expr}_1 = \ldots\\ \mathit{lit}\ \ :: \mathit{Integer} \qquad\qquad \to \mathit{Expr}_1\\ \mathit{add} :: \mathit{Expr}_1 \to \mathit{Expr}_1 \to \mathit{Expr}_1\end{array}$$

The expression $(3+4)+5$ is represented in the DSL by the term $\mathit{add}\ (\mathit{add}\ (\mathit{lit}\ 3)\ (\mathit{lit}\ 4))\ (\mathit{lit}\ 5)$.

As a deeply embedded DSL, the two operations *lit* and *add* are encoded directly as constructors of an algebraic datatype:

$$\begin{array}{l}\textbf{data}\ \mathit{Expr}_2 :: * \ \textbf{where}\\ \quad \mathit{Lit}\ \ :: \mathit{Integer} \qquad\qquad \to \mathit{Expr}_2\\ \quad \mathit{Add} :: \mathit{Expr}_2 \to \mathit{Expr}_2 \to \mathit{Expr}_2\\ \mathit{lit}\ n \quad\ = \mathit{Lit}\ n\\ \mathit{add}\ x\ y = \mathit{Add}\ x\ y\end{array}$$

(We have used Haskell's 'generalized algebraic datatype' notation, in order to make the types of the constructors *Lit* and *Add* explicit; but we are not using the generality of GADTs here, and the old-fashioned way would have worked too.) Observations of terms in the DSL are defined as functions over the algebraic datatype. For example, here is how to evaluate an expression:

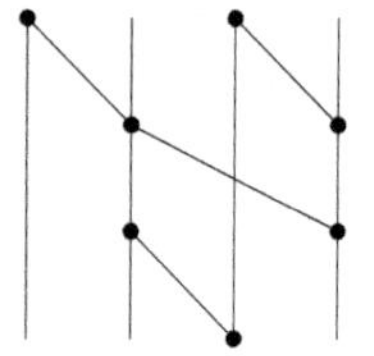

Figure 1. The Brent–Kung parallel prefix circuit of width 4

$eval_2 :: Expr_2 \rightarrow Integer$
$eval_2\ (Lit\ n) \quad = n$
$eval_2\ (Add\ x\ y) = eval_2\ x + eval_2\ y$

This might be used as follows:

$> eval_2\ (Add\ (Add\ (Lit\ 3)\ (Lit\ 4))\ (Lit\ 5))$
12

In other words, a deep embedding consists of a representation of the abstract syntax as an algebraic datatype, together with some functions that assign semantics to that syntax by traversing the algebraic datatype.

A shallow embedding eschews the algebraic datatype, and hence the explicit representation of the abstract syntax of the language; instead, the language is defined directly in terms of its semantics. For example, if the semantics is to be evaluation, then we could define:

type $Expr_3 = Integer$

$lit\ n \quad = n$
$add\ x\ y = x + y$

$eval_3 :: Expr_3 \rightarrow Integer$
$eval_3\ n = n$

This might be used as follows:

$> eval_3\ (add\ (add\ (lit\ 3)\ (lit\ 4))\ (lit\ 5))$
12

We have used subscripts to distinguish different representations of morally 'the same' functions ($eval_2$ and $eval_3$) and types ($Expr_2$ and $Expr_3$). We will continue that convention throughout the paper.

One might see the deep and shallow embeddings as duals, in a variety of senses. For one sense, the language constructs *Lit* and *Add* in the deep embedding do none of the work, leaving this entirely to the observation function *eval*; in contrast, in the shallow embedding, the language constructs *lit* and *add* do all the work, and the observer $eval_3$ is simply the identity function.

For a second sense, it is trivial to add a second observer such as pretty-printing to the deep embedding—just define another function alongside *eval*—but awkward to add a new construct such as multiplication: doing so entails revisiting the definitions of all existing observers to add an additional clause. In contrast, adding a construct to the shallow embedding—alongside *lit* and *add*—is trivial, but the obvious way of introducing an additional observer entails completely revising the semantics by changing the definitions of all existing constructs. This is precisely the tension underlying the *expression problem* [22, 29], so named for precisely this example.

The types of *lit* and *add* in the shallow embedding coincide with those of *Lit* and *Add* in the deep embedding; moreover, the definitions of *lit* and *add* in the shallow embedding correspond to the 'actions' in each clause of the definition of the observer in the deep embedding. The shallow embedding presents a *compositional* semantics for the language, since the semantics of a composite term is explicitly composed from the semantics of its components. Indeed, it is only such compositional semantics that can be captured in a shallow embedding; it is possible to define a more sophisticated non-compositional semantics as an interpretation of a deep embedding, but not possible to represent that semantics directly via a shallow embedding.

Figure 2. Identity circuit *identity* 4 and fan circuit *fan* 4 of width 4

However, there is no duality in the categorical sense of reversing arrows. Although deep and shallow embeddings have been called the 'initial' and 'final' approaches [8], in fact the two approaches are equivalent, and both correspond to initial algebras; Carette *et al.* say only that they use the term 'final' "because we represent each object term not by its abstract syntax but by its denotation in a semantic algebra", and they are not concerned with final coalgebras.

3. Scans

The expression language above is very simple—perhaps too simple to serve as a convincing vehicle for discussion. As a more interesting example of a DSL, we turn to a language for parallel prefix circuits [13], which crop up in a number of different applications—carry-lookahead adders, parallel sorting, and stream compaction, to name but a few. Given an associative binary operator $\bullet$, a prefix computation of width $n > 0$ takes a sequence $x_1, x_2, ..., x_n$ of inputs and produces the sequence $x_1, x_1 \bullet x_2, ..., x_1 \bullet x_2 \bullet \cdots \bullet x_n$ of outputs. A parallel prefix circuit performs this computation in parallel, in a fixed format independent of the input values x_i.

An example of such a circuit is depicted in Figure 1. This circuit diagram should be read as follows. The inputs are fed in at the top, and the outputs fall out at the bottom. Each node (the blobs in the diagram) represents a local computation, combining the values on each of its input wires using $\bullet$, in left-to-right order, and providing copies of the result on each of its output wires. It is an instructive exercise to check that this circuit does indeed take x_1, x_2, x_3, x_4 to $x_1, x_1 \bullet x_2, x_1 \bullet x_2 \bullet x_3, x_1 \bullet x_2 \bullet x_3 \bullet x_4$.

Such circuits can be constructed using the following operators:

type $Size = Int$ -- positive
type $Circuit_1 = ...$

$identity :: Size \rightarrow Circuit_1$
$fan \quad :: Size \rightarrow Circuit_1$
$above \quad :: Circuit_1 \rightarrow Circuit_1 \rightarrow Circuit_1$
$beside \quad :: Circuit_1 \rightarrow Circuit_1 \rightarrow Circuit_1$
$stretch \quad :: [Size] \rightarrow Circuit_1 \rightarrow Circuit_1$

The most basic building block is the identity circuit, *identity n*, which creates a circuit consisting of *n* parallel wires that copy input to output. The other primitive is the fan circuit; *fan n* takes *n* inputs, and adds its first input to each of the others. We only consider non-empty circuits, so *n* must be positive in both cases. Instances of *identity* and *fan* of width 4 are shown in Figure 2.

Then there are three combinators for circuits. The series or vertical composition, *above c d*, takes two circuits *c* and *d* of the same width, and connects the outputs of *c* to the inputs of *d*. The parallel or horizontal composition, *beside c d*, places *c* beside *d*, leaving them unconnected; there are no width constraints on *c* and *d*. Figure 3 shows a 2-fan beside a 1-identity, a 1-identity beside a 2-fan, and the first of these above the second (note that they both have width 3); this yields the "serial" parallel prefix circuit of width 3.

Finally, the stretch combinator, *stretch ws c*, takes a non-empty list of positive widths $ws = [w_1, ..., w_n]$ of length *n*, and a circuit *c* of width *n*, and "stretches" *c* out to width *sum ws* by interleaving some additional wires. Of the first bundle of w_1 inputs, the last is routed to the first input of *c* and the rest pass straight through; of

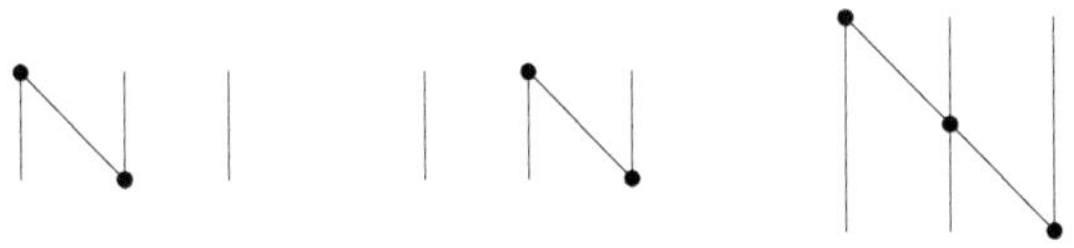

Figure 3. The construction of a parallel prefix circuit of width 3

the next bundle of w_2 inputs, the last is routed to the second input of *c* and the rest pass straight through; and so on. (Note that each bundle width w_i must be positive.) For example, Figure 4 shows a 3-fan stretched out to width 8, in bundles of $[3,2,3]$.

So one possible construction of the Brent–Kung parallel prefix circuit in Figure 1 is

```
(fan 2 `beside` fan 2) `above`
stretch [2,2] (fan 2) `above`
(identity 1 `beside` fan 2 `beside` identity 1)
```

The general Brent–Kung construction [7] is given recursively. The general pattern is a row of 2-fans, possibly with an extra wire in the case of odd width; then a Brent–Kung circuit of half the width, stretched out by a factor of two; then another row of 2-fans, shifted one place to the right.

```
brentkung :: Size → Circuit1
brentkung 1 = identity 1
brentkung w
  = (row (replicate u (fan 2)) `pad` w) `above`
    (stretch (replicate u 2) (brentkung u) `pad` w) `above`
    (row (identity 1 : replicate v (fan 2)) `pad` (w − 1))
  where (u, v)   = (w `div` 2, (w − 1) `div` 2)
        c `pad` w = if even w then c else c `beside` identity 1
        row       = foldr1 beside
```

The Brent–Kung circuit of width 16 is shown in Figure 5. Note one major benefit of defining *Circuit* as an embedded rather than a standalone DSL: we can exploit for free host language constructions such as *replicate* and *foldr1*, rather than having to reinvent them within the DSL.

As a deeply embedded DSL, circuits can be captured by the following algebraic datatype:

```
data Circuit2 :: * where
  Identity :: Size →                       Circuit2
  Fan      :: Size →                       Circuit2
  Above    :: Circuit2 → Circuit2 → Circuit2
  Beside   :: Circuit2 → Circuit2 → Circuit2
  Stretch  :: [Size] → Circuit2 →   Circuit2
```

It is, of course, straightforward to define functions to manipulate this representation. Here is one, which computes the width of a circuit:

```
type Width = Int
width2 :: Circuit2 → Width
width2 (Identity w)   = w
width2 (Fan w)        = w
width2 (Above x y)    = width2 x
width2 (Beside x y)   = width2 x + width2 y
width2 (Stretch ws x) = sum ws
```

Note that $width_2$ is compositional: it is a fold over the abstract syntax of $Circuit_2$s. That makes it a suitable semantics for a shallow embedding. That is, we could represent circuits directly by their widths, as follows:

```
type Circuit3 = Width
identity w   = w
```

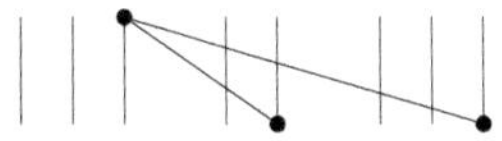

Figure 4. A 3-fan stretched out by widths $[3,2,3]$

```
fan w        = w
above x y    = x
beside x y   = x + y
stretch ws x = sum ws
width3 :: Circuit3 → Width
width3 = id
```

Clearly, width is a rather uninteresting semantics to give to circuits. But what other kinds of semantics will fit the pattern of compositionality, and so be suitable for a shallow embedding? In order to explore that question, we need to look a bit more closely at folds and their variations.

4. Folds

Folds are the natural pattern of computation induced by inductively defined algebraic datatypes. We consider here just polynomial algebraic datatypes, namely those with one or more constructors, each constructor taking zero or more arguments to the datatype being defined, and each argument either having a fixed type independent of the datatype, or being a recursive occurrence of the datatype itself. For example, the polynomial algebraic datatype $Circuit_2$ above has five constructors; *Identity* and *Fan* each take one argument of the fixed type *Size*; *Above* and *Beside* take two arguments, both recursive occurrences; *Stretch* takes two arguments, one of which is the fixed type $[Size]$, and the other is a recursive argument. Thus, we rule out contravariant recursion, polymorphic datatypes, higher kinds, and other such esoterica. For simplicity, we also ignore DSLs with binding constructs, which complicate matters significantly; for more on this, see [1, 8].

The general case is captured by a shape—also called a base or pattern functor—which is an instance of the *Functor* type class:

```
class Functor f where
  fmap :: (a → b) → (f a → f b)
```

For $Circuit_2$, the shape is given by *CircuitF* as follows, where the parameter *x* marks the recursive spots:

```
data CircuitF :: * → * where
  IdentityF :: Size →         CircuitF x
  FanF      :: Size →         CircuitF x
  AboveF    :: x → x →        CircuitF x
  BesideF   :: x → x →        CircuitF x
  StretchF  :: [Size] → x →   CircuitF x
instance Functor CircuitF where
  fmap f (IdentityF w)     = IdentityF w
  fmap f (FanF w)          = FanF w
  fmap f (AboveF x1 x2)    = AboveF (f x1) (f x2)
  fmap f (BesideF x1 x2)   = BesideF (f x1) (f x2)
  fmap f (StretchF ws x)   = StretchF ws (f x)
```

We can use this shape functor as the basis of an alternative definition of the algebraic datatype $Circuit_2$:

```
data Circuit4 = In (CircuitF Circuit4)
```

Now, an algebra for a functor *f* consists of a type *a* and a function taking an *f*-structure of *a*-values to an *a*-value. For the functor *CircuitF*, this is:

```
type CircuitAlg a = CircuitF a → a
```

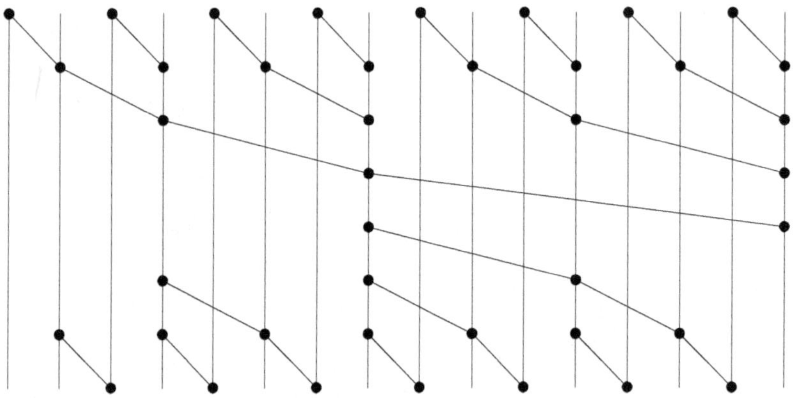

Figure 5. The Brent–Kung parallel prefix circuit of width 16

Such an algebra is precisely the information needed to fold a data structure:

$$\mathit{foldC} :: \mathit{CircuitAlg}\ a \rightarrow \mathit{Circuit}_4 \rightarrow a$$
$$\mathit{foldC}\ h\ (\mathit{In}\ x) = h\ (\mathit{fmap}\ (\mathit{foldC}\ h)\ x)$$

For example, *width* is a fold for the deeply embedded DSL of shape *CircuitF*, and is determined by the following algebra:

$$\begin{aligned}
&\mathit{widthAlg} :: \mathit{CircuitAlg}\ \mathit{Width}\\
&\mathit{widthAlg}\ (\mathit{IdentityF}\ w) &&= w\\
&\mathit{widthAlg}\ (\mathit{FanF}\ w) &&= w\\
&\mathit{widthAlg}\ (\mathit{AboveF}\ x\ y) &&= x\\
&\mathit{widthAlg}\ (\mathit{BesideF}\ x\ y) &&= x + y\\
&\mathit{widthAlg}\ (\mathit{StretchF}\ ws\ x) &&= \mathit{sum}\ ws
\end{aligned}$$

$$\begin{aligned}
&\mathit{width}_4 :: \mathit{Circuit}_4 \rightarrow \mathit{Width}\\
&\mathit{width}_4 = \mathit{foldC}\ \mathit{widthAlg}
\end{aligned}$$

So a compositional observation function for the deep embedding, such as width_4, is precisely a fold using such an the algebra. We know a lot about folds, and this tells us a lot about embedded DSLs. We discuss these consequences next.

4.1 Multiple interpretations

As mentioned above, the deep embedding smoothly supports additional observations. For example, suppose that we also wanted to find the depth of our circuits. No problem—we can just define another observation function.

$$\textbf{type}\ \mathit{Depth} = \mathit{Int}$$

$$\begin{aligned}
&\mathit{depthAlg} :: \mathit{CircuitAlg}\ \mathit{Depth}\\
&\mathit{depthAlg}\ (\mathit{IdentityF}\ w) &&= 0\\
&\mathit{depthAlg}\ (\mathit{FanF}\ w) &&= 1\\
&\mathit{depthAlg}\ (\mathit{AboveF}\ x\ y) &&= x + y\\
&\mathit{depthAlg}\ (\mathit{BesideF}\ x\ y) &&= x\ \text{`}\mathit{max}\text{`}\ y\\
&\mathit{depthAlg}\ (\mathit{StretchF}\ ws\ x) &&= x
\end{aligned}$$

$$\begin{aligned}
&\mathit{depth}_4 :: \mathit{Circuit}_4 \rightarrow \mathit{Depth}\\
&\mathit{depth}_4 = \mathit{foldC}\ \mathit{depthAlg}
\end{aligned}$$

But what about with a shallow embedding? With this approach, circuits can only have a single semantics, so how do we accommodate finding both the width and the depth of a circuit? It's not much more difficult than with a deep embedding; we simply make the semantics a pair, providing both interpretations simultaneously.

$$\textbf{type}\ \mathit{Circuit}_5 = (\mathit{Width}, \mathit{Depth})$$

Now the observation functions width_5 and depth_5 become projections, rather than just the identity function.

$$\begin{aligned}
&\mathit{width}_5 :: \mathit{Circuit}_5 \rightarrow \mathit{Width}\\
&\mathit{width}_5 = \mathit{fst}
\end{aligned}$$

$$\begin{aligned}
&\mathit{depth}_5 :: \mathit{Circuit}_5 \rightarrow \mathit{Depth}\\
&\mathit{depth}_5 = \mathit{snd}
\end{aligned}$$

The individual operations can be defined much as before, just by projecting the relevant components out of the pair:

$$\begin{aligned}
&\mathit{wdAlg} :: \mathit{CircuitAlg}\ \mathit{Circuit}_5\\
&\mathit{wdAlg}\ (\mathit{IdentityF}\ w) &&= (w, 0)\\
&\mathit{wdAlg}\ (\mathit{FanF}\ w) &&= (w, 1)\\
&\mathit{wdAlg}\ (\mathit{AboveF}\ x\ y) &&= (\mathit{width}_5\ x, \mathit{depth}_5\ x + \mathit{depth}_5\ y)\\
&\mathit{wdAlg}\ (\mathit{BesideF}\ x\ y) &&= (\mathit{width}_5\ x + \mathit{width}_5\ y,\\
& &&\quad\ \mathit{depth}_5\ x\ \text{`}\mathit{max}\text{`}\ \mathit{depth}_5\ y)\\
&\mathit{wdAlg}\ (\mathit{StretchF}\ ws\ x) &&= (\mathit{sum}\ ws, \mathit{depth}_5\ x)
\end{aligned}$$

This algebra is the essence of the shallow embedding; for example,

$$\mathit{identity}_5\ w = \mathit{wdAlg}\ (\mathit{IdentityF}\ w)$$

and so on. Of course, this works better under lazy than under eager evaluation: if only one of the two interpretations of an expression is needed, only that one is evaluated. And it's rather clumsy from a modularity perspective; we will return to this point later.

Seen from the fold perspective, this step is no surprise: the 'banana split law' [9] tells us that tupling two independent folds gives another fold, so multiple interpretations can be provided in the shallow embedding nearly as easily as in the deep embedding.

4.2 Dependent interpretations

A shallow embedding supports only compositional interpretations, whereas a deep embedding provides full access to the AST and hence also non-compositional manipulations. Here, 'compositionality' of an interpretation means that the interpretation of a whole may be determined solely from the interpretations of its parts; it is both a valuable property for reasoning and a significant limitation to expressivity. Not all interpretations are of this form; sometimes a 'primary' interpretation of the whole depends also on 'secondary' interpretations of its parts.

For example, whether a circuit is well formed depends on the widths of its constituent parts. Given that we have an untyped (or rather, 'unsized') model of circuits, we might capture this property in a separate function *wellSized*:

$$\textbf{type}\ \mathit{WellSized} = \mathit{Bool}$$

$$\begin{aligned}
&\mathit{wellSized} :: \mathit{Circuit}_2 \rightarrow \mathit{WellSized}\\
&\mathit{wellSized}\ (\mathit{Identity}\ w) &&= \mathit{True}\\
&\mathit{wellSized}\ (\mathit{Fan}\ w) &&= \mathit{True}
\end{aligned}$$

$$
\begin{aligned}
&\textit{wellSized}\ (\textit{Above}\ x\ y) &&= \textit{wellSized}\ x \wedge \textit{wellSized}\ y \\
& &&\quad \wedge\ \textit{width}\ x \equiv \textit{width}\ y \\
&\textit{wellSized}\ (\textit{Beside}\ x\ y) &&= \textit{wellSized}\ x \wedge \textit{wellSized}\ y \\
&\textit{wellSized}\ (\textit{Stretch}\ \textit{ws}\ x) &&= \textit{wellSized}\ x \wedge \textit{length}\ \textit{ws} \equiv \textit{width}\ x
\end{aligned}
$$

This is a non-compositional interpretation of the abstract syntax, because *wellSized* sometimes depends on the *width* of subcircuits as well as their recursive image under *wellSized*. In other words, *wellSized* is not a fold, and there is no corresponding *CircuitAlg*.

What can we do about such non-compositional interpretations in the shallow embedding? Again, fold theory comes to the rescue: *wellSized* and *width* together form a *mutumorphism* [9]—that is, two mutually dependent folds—and the tuple of these two functions again forms a fold. (In fact, this is a special case, a *zygomorphism* [9], since the dependency is only one-way. Simpler still, we have seen another special case in the banana split above, where neither of the two folds depends on the other.)

$$
\begin{aligned}
&\textbf{type}\ \textit{Circuit}_6 = (\textit{WellSized}, \textit{Width}) \\
&\textit{wswAlg} :: \textit{CircuitAlg}\ \textit{Circuit}_6 \\
&\textit{wswAlg}\ (\textit{IdentityF}\ w) &&= (\textit{True}, w) \\
&\textit{wswAlg}\ (\textit{FanF}\ w) &&= (\textit{True}, w) \\
&\textit{wswAlg}\ (\textit{AboveF}\ x\ y) &&= (\textit{fst}\ x \wedge \textit{fst}\ y \wedge \textit{snd}\ x \equiv \textit{snd}\ y, \textit{snd}\ x) \\
&\textit{wswAlg}\ (\textit{BesideF}\ x\ y) &&= (\textit{fst}\ x \wedge \textit{fst}\ y, \textit{snd}\ x + \textit{snd}\ y) \\
&\textit{wswAlg}\ (\textit{StretchF}\ \textit{ws}\ x) &&= (\textit{fst}\ x \wedge \textit{length}\ \textit{ws} \equiv \textit{snd}\ x, \textit{sum}\ \textit{ws})
\end{aligned}
$$

So although $\textit{wellSized} = \textit{fst} \circ \textit{foldC}\ \textit{wswAlg}$ is not a fold, it is manifestly clear that *foldC wswAlg* is. Tupling functions in this way is analogous to strengthening the invariant of an imperative loop to record additional information [19], and is a standard trick in program calculation [17].

Another example of a dependent interpretation is provided by what Hinze [13] calls the *standard model* of the circuit: its interpretation as a computation. As discussed in the introduction, this is defined in terms of an associative binary operator $(\bullet)$, which we capture by the following type class:

$$
\begin{aligned}
&\textbf{class}\ \textit{Semigroup}\ s\ \textbf{where} \\
&\quad (\bullet) :: s \to s \to s \quad \text{-- } \bullet \text{ is associative}
\end{aligned}
$$

The interpretation *apply* interprets a circuit of width *n* as a function operating on lists of length *n*:

$$
\begin{aligned}
&\textit{apply} :: \textit{Semigroup}\ a \Rightarrow \textit{Circuit}_2 \to [a] \to [a] \\
&\textit{apply}\ (\textit{Identity}\ w)\ \ \textit{xs} &&= \textit{xs} \\
&\textit{apply}\ (\textit{Fan}\ w)\ \ (x : \textit{xs}) &&= x : \textit{map}\ (x\bullet)\ \textit{xs} \\
&\textit{apply}\ (\textit{Above}\ c\ d)\ \ \textit{xs} &&= \textit{apply}\ d\ (\textit{apply}\ c\ \textit{xs}) \\
&\textit{apply}\ (\textit{Beside}\ c\ d)\ \ \textit{xs} &&= \textit{apply}\ c\ \textit{ys} +\!\!+ \textit{apply}\ d\ \textit{zs} \\
&\quad \textbf{where}\ (\textit{ys}, \textit{zs}) = \textit{splitAt}\ (\textit{width}\ c)\ \textit{xs} \\
&\textit{apply}\ (\textit{Stretch}\ \textit{ws}\ c)\ \textit{xs} &&= \textit{concat} \\
&\quad (\textit{zipWith}\ \textit{snoc}\ (\textit{map}\ \textit{init}\ \textit{xss})\ (\textit{apply}\ c\ (\textit{map}\ \textit{last}\ \textit{xss}))) \\
&\quad \textbf{where}\ \textit{xss} = \textit{bundle}\ \textit{ws}\ \textit{xs}
\end{aligned}
$$

Here, *snoc* is 'cons' backwards,

$$\textit{snoc}\ \textit{ys}\ z = \textit{ys} +\!\!+ [z]$$

and *bundle ws xs* groups the list *xs* into bundles of widths *ws*, assuming that $\textit{sum}\ \textit{ws} \equiv \textit{length}\ \textit{xs}$:

$$
\begin{aligned}
&\textit{bundle} :: \textit{Integral}\ i \Rightarrow [i] \to [a] \to [[a]] \\
&\textit{bundle}\ [\,]\ \ \ [\,] = [\,] \\
&\textit{bundle}\ (w : \textit{ws})\ \textit{xs} = \textit{ys} : \textit{bundle}\ \textit{ws}\ \textit{zs} \\
&\quad \textbf{where}\ (\textit{ys}, \textit{zs}) = \textit{splitAt}\ w\ \textit{xs}
\end{aligned}
$$

The *apply* interpretation is another zygomorphism, because in the *Beside* case *apply* depends on *width c* as well as *apply c* and *apply d*. And indeed, Hinze's 'standard model' [13] comprises both the list transformer and the width, tupled together.

4.3 Context-sensitive interpretations

Consider generating a circuit layout from a circuit description, for example as the first step in expressing the circuit in a hardware description language such as VHDL—or, for that matter, for producing the diagrams in this paper. The essence of the translation is to determine the connections between vertical wires. Note that each circuit can be thought of as a sequence of layers, and connections only go from one layer to the next (and only rightwards, too). So it suffices to generate a list of layers, where each layer is a collection of pairs (i,j) denoting a connection from wire i on this layer to wire j on the next. The ordering of the pairs on each layer is not significant. We count from 0. For example, the Brent–Kung circuit of size 4 given in Figure 1 has the following connections:

$$[[(0,1),(2,3)],\ [(1,3)],\ [(1,2)]]$$

That is, there are three layers; the first layer has connections from wire 0 to wire 1 and from wire 2 to wire 3; the second a single connection from wire 1 to wire 3; and the third a single connection from wire 1 to wire 2.

$$
\begin{aligned}
&\textbf{type}\ \textit{Layout} = [[(\textit{Size}, \textit{Size})]] \\
&\textit{layout} :: \textit{Circuit}_2 \to \textit{Layout} \\
&\textit{layout}\ (\textit{Identity}\ w) &&= [\,] \\
&\textit{layout}\ (\textit{Fan}\ w) &&= [[(0,j) \mid j \leftarrow [1\,..\,w-1]]] \\
&\textit{layout}\ (\textit{Above}\ c\ d) &&= \textit{layout}\ c +\!\!+ \textit{layout}\ d \\
&\textit{layout}\ (\textit{Beside}\ c\ d) &&= \textit{lzw}\ (+\!\!+)\ (\textit{layout}\ c) \\
& &&\qquad (\textit{shift}\ (\textit{width}\ c)\ (\textit{layout}\ d)) \\
&\textit{layout}\ (\textit{Stretch}\ \textit{ws}\ c) &&= \textit{map}\ (\textit{map}\ (\textit{connect}\ \textit{ws}))\ (\textit{layout}\ c) \\
&\textit{shift}\ w &&= \textit{map}\ (\textit{map}\ (\textit{pmap}\ (w+))) \\
&\textit{connect}\ \textit{ws} &&= \textit{pmap}\ (\textit{pred} \circ ((\textit{scanl1}\ (+)\ \textit{ws})!!))
\end{aligned}
$$

Here, *pmap* is the map function for homogeneous pairs:

$$
\begin{aligned}
&\textit{pmap} :: (a \to b) \to (a,a) \to (b,b) \\
&\textit{pmap}\ f\ (x,y) = (f\ x, f\ y)
\end{aligned}
$$

The function *lzw* is 'long zip with' [12], which zips two lists together and returns a result as long as the longer argument. The binary operator is used to combine corresponding elements; if one list is shorter then the remaining elements of the other are simply copied.

$$
\begin{aligned}
&\textit{lzw} :: (a \to a \to a) \to [a] \to [a] \to [a] \\
&\textit{lzw}\ f\ [\,]\ \ \ \textit{ys} &&= \textit{ys} \\
&\textit{lzw}\ f\ \textit{xs}\ \ \ [\,] &&= \textit{xs} \\
&\textit{lzw}\ f\ (x : \textit{xs})\ (y : \textit{ys}) &&= f\ x\ y : \textit{lzw}\ f\ \textit{xs}\ \textit{ys}
\end{aligned}
$$

The *layout* interpretation is yet another zygomorphism, because *layout* (*Beside c d*) depends on *width c* as well as *layout c* and *layout d*. In fact, in general we need the width of the circuit anyway in order to determine the layout, in case the rightmost wire is not connected to the others. So the techniques discussed above will allow us to express the layout as a shallow embedding, whose essence is as follows:

$$
\begin{aligned}
&\textit{lwAlg} :: \textit{CircuitAlg}\ (\textit{Layout}, \textit{Width}) \\
&\textit{lwAlg}\ (\textit{IdentityF}\ w) &&= ([\,], w) \\
&\textit{lwAlg}\ (\textit{FanF}\ w) &&= ([[(0,j) \mid j \leftarrow [1\,..\,w-1]]], w) \\
&\textit{lwAlg}\ (\textit{AboveF}\ c\ d) &&= (l_1 +\!\!+ l_2, w_2) \\
&\quad \textbf{where}\ (l_1, w_1) = c; (l_2, w_2) = d \\
&\textit{lwAlg}\ (\textit{BesideF}\ c\ d) &&= (\textit{lzw}\ (+\!\!+)\ l_1\ (\textit{shift}\ w_1\ l_2), w_1 + w_2) \\
&\quad \textbf{where}\ (l_1, w_1) = c; (l_2, w_2) = d \\
&\textit{lwAlg}\ (\textit{StretchF}\ \textit{ws}\ (l, w)) &&= (\textit{map}\ (\textit{map}\ (\textit{connect}\ \textit{ws}))\ l, \textit{sum}\ \textit{ws})
\end{aligned}
$$

But even having achieved this, there is room for improvement. In the *Beside* and *Stretch* clauses, sublayouts are postprocessed using *shift* and *map* (*map* (*connect ws*)) respectively. It would be more efficient to do this processing via an *accumulating parameter* [3] instead. In this case, a transformation on wire indices suffices as the accumulating parameter ('*tlayout*' stands for 'transformed *layout*'):

```
tlayout :: (Size → Size) → Circuit2 → Layout
tlayout f c = map (map (pmap f)) (layout c)
```

Of course, *layout* = *tlayout id*, and it is a straightforward exercise to synthesize the following more efficient definition of *tlayout*:

```
tlayout :: (Size → Size) → Circuit2 → Layout
tlayout f (Identity w)   = []
tlayout f (Fan w)        = [[(f 0, f j) | j ← [1 .. w − 1]]]
tlayout f (Above c d)    = tlayout f c ++ tlayout f d
tlayout f (Beside c d)   = lzw (++) (tlayout f c)
                                    (tlayout ((w+) ∘ f) d)
  where w = width c
tlayout f (Stretch ws c) = tlayout (pred ∘ (vs!!) ∘ f) c
  where vs = scanl1 (+) ws
```

And how does this work out with a shallow embedding? Note that *tlayout f* is no longer a fold, because the accumulating parameter changes in some recursive calls. One might say that *tlayout* is a context-sensitive layout function, and the context may vary in recursive calls. But standard fold technology comes to the rescue once more: *tlayout* may not be a fold, but *flip tlayout* is—specifically, an accumulating fold.

```
tlwAlg :: CircuitAlg ((Size → Size) → Layout, Width)
tlwAlg (IdentityF w)    = (λf → [], w)
tlwAlg (FanF w)         = (λf → [[(f 0, f j) | j ← [1 .. w − 1]]], w)
tlwAlg (AboveF c d)     = (λf → fst c f ++ fst d f, snd c)
tlwAlg (BesideF c d)    = (λf → lzw (++) (fst c f)
                                    (fst d ((snd c+) ∘ f)),
                           snd c + snd d)
tlwAlg (StretchF ws c)  = (λf → fst c (pred ∘ (vs!!) ∘ f), sum ws)
  where vs = scanl1 (+) ws
```

The alert reader may have noted another source of inefficiency in *layout*, namely the uses of ++ and *lzw* (++) in the *Above* and *Beside* cases. These too can be removed, by introducing two more accumulating parameters, giving:

```
ulayout :: (Size → Size) → Layout → Layout →
           Circuit2 → Layout
ulayout f l l' c = (lzw (++) (map (map (pmap f)) (layout c)) l) ++ l'
```

(now '*ulayout*' stands for 'ultimate *layout*'). From this specification we can synthesize a definition that takes linear time in the 'size' of the circuit, for a reasonable definition of 'size'. We leave the details as an exercise.

In fact, the standard interpretation *apply* given above is really another accumulating fold, in disguise. Rather than reading the type

```
apply :: Semigroup a ⇒ Circuit2 → [a] → [a]
```

as defining an interpretation of circuits as list transformers of type *Semigroup a* ⇒ ([*a*] → [*a*]), one can read it as defining a context-dependent interpretation as an output list of type *Semigroup a* ⇒ [*a*], dependent on some input list of the same type. The interpretation is implemented in terms of an accumulating parameter; this is initially the input list, but it 'accumulates' by attrition via *splitAt* and *map last* ∘ *bundle ws* as the evaluation proceeds.

4.4 Parametrized interpretations

We saw in Section 4.1 that it is not difficult to provide multiple interpretations with a shallow embedding, by constructing a tuple as the semantics of an expression and projecting the desired interpretation from the tuple. But this is still a bit clumsy: it entails revising existing code each time a new interpretation is added, and wide tuples generally lack good language support [24].

But as we have also seen, all compositional interpretations conform to a common pattern: they are folds. So we can provide a shallow embedding as precisely that pattern—that is, in terms of a single *parametrized* interpretation, which is a higher-order value representing the fold.

```
newtype Circuit7 = C7 {unC7 :: ∀a . CircuitAlg a → a}
identity7 w   = C7 (λh → h (IdentityF w))
fan7 w        = C7 (λh → h (FanF w))
above7 x y    = C7 (λh → h (AboveF (unC7 x h) (unC7 y h)))
beside7 x y   = C7 (λh → h (BesideF (unC7 x h) (unC7 y h)))
stretch7 ws x = C7 (λh → h (StretchF ws (unC7 x h)))
```

(We need the **newtype** instead of a plain **type** synonym because of the quantified type.) This shallow encoding subsumes all others; it specializes to *depth* and *width*, and of course to any other fold:

```
width7 :: Circuit7 → Width
width7 circuit = unC7 circuit widthAlg

depth7 :: Circuit7 → Depth
depth7 circuit = unC7 circuit depthAlg
```

In fact, the shallow embedding provides a universal generic interpretation as the *Church encoding* [14] of the AST—or more precisely, because it is typed, the *Böhm–Berarducci encoding* [4].

Universality is witnessed by the observation that it is possible to recover the deep embedding from this one 'mother of all shallow embeddings' [8]:

```
deep :: Circuit7 → Circuit4
deep circuit = unC7 circuit In
```

(So it turns out that the syntax of the DSL is not really as ephemeral in a shallow embedding as Boulton's choice of terms [6] suggests.) And conversely, one can map from the deep embedding to the parametrized shallow embedding, and thence to any other shallow embedding:

```
shallow :: Circuit4 → Circuit7
shallow = foldC shallowAlg

shallowAlg :: CircuitAlg Circuit7
shallowAlg (IdentityF w)   = identity7 w
shallowAlg (FanF w)        = fan7 w
shallowAlg (AboveF c d)    = above7 c d
shallowAlg (BesideF c d)   = beside7 c d
shallowAlg (StretchF ws c) = stretch7 ws c
```

Moreover, *deep* and *shallow* are each other's inverses, assuming parametricity [28].

4.5 Implicitly parametrized interpretations

The shallow embedding in Section 4.4 involves explicitly passing an algebra with which to interpret terms. That parameter may be passed implicitly instead, if it can be determined from the type of the interpretation. In Haskell, this can be done by defining a suitable type class:

```
class Circuit8 circuit where
  identity8 :: Size →                       circuit
  fan8      :: Size →                       circuit
  above8    :: circuit → circuit →          circuit
  beside8   :: circuit → circuit →          circuit
  stretch8  :: [Size] → circuit →           circuit
```

To specify a particular interpretation, one defines an instance of the type class for the type of that interpretation. For example, here is the specification of the 'width' interpretation:

```
newtype Width8 = Width {unWidth :: Int}
```

$$
\begin{array}{l}
\textbf{instance } \mathit{Circuit}_8\ \mathit{Width}_8 \textbf{ where}\\
\quad \mathit{identity}_8\ w \quad = \mathit{Width}\ w\\
\quad \mathit{fan}_8\ w \quad = \mathit{Width}\ w\\
\quad \mathit{above}_8\ x\ y \quad = x\\
\quad \mathit{beside}_8\ x\ y \quad = \mathit{Width}\ (\mathit{unWidth}\ x + \mathit{unWidth}\ y)\\
\quad \mathit{stretch}_8\ ws\ x = \mathit{Width}\ (\mathit{sum}\ ws)
\end{array}
$$

The **newtype** wrapper is often needed to allow multiple interpretations over the same underlying type; for example, we can provide both 'width' and 'depth' interpretations over integers:

$$
\begin{array}{l}
\textbf{newtype } \mathit{Depth}_8 = \mathit{Depth}\ \{\mathit{unDepth} :: \mathit{Int}\}\\
\textbf{instance } \mathit{Circuit}_8\ \mathit{Depth}_8 \textbf{ where}\\
\quad \mathit{identity}_8\ w \quad = \mathit{Depth}\ 0\\
\quad \mathit{fan}_8\ w \quad = \mathit{Depth}\ 1\\
\quad \mathit{above}_8\ x\ y \quad = \mathit{Depth}\ (\mathit{unDepth}\ x + \mathit{unDepth}\ y)\\
\quad \mathit{beside}_8\ x\ y \quad = \mathit{Depth}\ (\mathit{unDepth}\ x\ \text{`}\mathit{max}\text{`}\ \mathit{unDepth}\ y)\\
\quad \mathit{stretch}_8\ ws\ x = x
\end{array}
$$

Some of the wrapping and unwrapping of Width_8 and Depth_8 values could be avoided by installing these types as instances of the *Num* and *Ord* type classes; this can even be done automatically in GHC, by exploiting the 'Generalized Newtype Deriving' extension.

The conventional implementation of type classes [30] involves constructing a *dictionary* for each type in the type class, and generating code that selects and passes the appropriate dictionary as an additional parameter to each overloaded member function ($\mathit{identity}_8, \mathit{fan}_8$ etc). For an instance c of the type class $\mathit{Circuit}_8$, the dictionary type is equivalent to *CircuitAlg c*. Indeed, we might have defined instead

$$
\begin{array}{l}
\textbf{class } \mathit{Circuit}_9\ c \textbf{ where}\\
\quad \mathit{alg} :: \mathit{CircuitAlg}\ c\\
\textbf{instance } \mathit{Circuit}_9\ \mathit{Width}_8 \textbf{ where}\\
\quad \mathit{alg} = \mathit{Width} \circ \mathit{widthAlg} \circ \mathit{fmap}\ \mathit{unWidth}
\end{array}
$$

so that the dictionary type is literally a *CircuitAlg c*: the Böhm–Berarducci and type-class approaches are really very similar.

4.6 Intermediate interpretations

Good practice in the design of embedded DSLs is to distinguish between a minimal 'core' language and a more useful 'everyday' language [26]. The former is more convenient for the language designer, but the latter more convenient for the language user. This apparent tension can be resolved by defining the additional constructs in the everyday language by translation to the core language.

For example, the *identity* construct in our DSL of circuits is redundant: *identity* 1 is morally equivalent to *fan* 1, and for any other width *n*, we can construct a circuit equivalent to *identity n* by placing *n* copies of *identity* 1 side by side (or alternatively, as *stretch* $[n]$ (*identity* 1)). One might therefore identify a simpler datatype

$$
\begin{array}{llll}
\multicolumn{4}{l}{\textbf{data } \mathit{CoreCircuit} :: * \textbf{ where}}\\
\quad \mathit{CFan} & :: \mathit{Size} \to & & \mathit{CoreCircuit}\\
\quad \mathit{CAbove} & :: \mathit{CoreCircuit} \to & \mathit{CoreCircuit} \to & \mathit{CoreCircuit}\\
\quad \mathit{CBeside} & :: \mathit{CoreCircuit} \to & \mathit{CoreCircuit} \to & \mathit{CoreCircuit}\\
\quad \mathit{CStretch} & :: [\mathit{Size}] \to & \mathit{CoreCircuit} \to & \mathit{CoreCircuit}
\end{array}
$$

and use it as the carrier of a shallow embedding for the everyday language. The everyday constructs that correspond to core constructs are represented directly; the derived constructs are defined by translation.

$$
\begin{array}{l}
\textbf{type } \mathit{Circuit}_{10} = \mathit{CoreCircuit}\\
\mathit{coreAlg} :: \mathit{CircuitAlg}\ \mathit{Circuit}_{10}\\
\mathit{coreAlg}\ (\mathit{IdentityF}\ w) \quad = \mathit{foldr1}\ \mathit{CBeside}\ (\mathit{replicate}\ w\ (\mathit{CFan}\ 1))\\
\mathit{coreAlg}\ (\mathit{FanF}\ w) \quad = \mathit{CFan}\ w\\
\mathit{coreAlg}\ (\mathit{AboveF}\ x\ y) \quad = \mathit{CAbove}\ x\ y\\
\mathit{coreAlg}\ (\mathit{BesideF}\ x\ y) \quad = \mathit{CBeside}\ x\ y\\
\mathit{coreAlg}\ (\mathit{StretchF}\ ws\ x) = \mathit{CStretch}\ ws\ x
\end{array}
$$

One might see this as a shallow embedding, with the carrier *CoreCircuit* itself the deep embedding of a different, smaller language; the core constructs are implemented directly as constructors of *CoreCircuit*, and non-core constructs as a kind of 'smart constructor'.

This suggests that 'deep' and 'shallow' do not form a dichotomy, but rather are two extreme points on a scale of embedding depth. Augustsson [2] discusses representations of intermediate depth, in which some constructs have deep embeddings and some shallow. In particular, for a language with a 'semantics' in the form of generated assembly code, the deeply embedded constructs will persist as generated code, whereas those with shallow embeddings will get translated away at 'compile time'. Augustsson calls these *neritic* embeddings, after the region of the sea between the shore and the edge of the continental shelf.

4.7 Modular interpretations

The previous section explored cutting down the grammar of circuits by eliminating a constructor. Conversely, one might extend the grammar by adding constructors. Indeed, in addition to the 'left stretch' combinator we have used, Hinze [13] also provides a 'right stretch' combinator, which connects the first rather than the last wire of each bundle to the inner circuit. This is not needed in the core language, because it can be built out of existing components:

$$
\mathit{rstretch}\ (ws +\!\!+ [w+1])\ c = \mathit{stretch}\ (1 : ws)\ c\ \text{`}\mathit{beside}\text{`}\ \mathit{identity}\ w
$$

So one might extend the grammar of the everyday language, as embodied in the functor *CircuitF* or the type class $\mathit{Circuit}_8$, to incorporate this additional operator, but still use *CoreCircuit* as the actual representation.

Alternatively, one might hope for a modular technique for assembling embedded languages and their interpretations from parts, so that it is straightforward to add additional constructors like 'right stretch'. Swierstra's *datatypes à la carte* machinery [27] provides precisely such a thing, going some way towards addressing the expression problem discussed in Section 2.

The key idea is to represent each constructor separately:

$$
\begin{array}{lll}
\textbf{data } \mathit{Identity}_{11}\ c = \mathit{Identity}_{11}\ \mathit{Size} & \textbf{deriving } \mathit{Functor}\\
\textbf{data } \mathit{Fan}_{11}\ c \quad = \mathit{Fan}_{11}\ \mathit{Size} & \textbf{deriving } \mathit{Functor}\\
\textbf{data } \mathit{Above}_{11}\ c \quad = \mathit{Above}_{11}\ c\ c & \textbf{deriving } \mathit{Functor}\\
\textbf{data } \mathit{Beside}_{11}\ c \quad = \mathit{Beside}_{11}\ c\ c & \textbf{deriving } \mathit{Functor}\\
\textbf{data } \mathit{Stretch}_{11}\ c \quad = \mathit{Stretch}_{11}\ [\mathit{Size}]\ c & \textbf{deriving } \mathit{Functor}
\end{array}
$$

with a right-associating 'sum' operator for combining them:

$$
\begin{array}{l}
\textbf{data } (f :+: g)\ e = \mathit{Inl}\ (f\ e) \mid \mathit{Inr}\ (g\ e) \textbf{ deriving } \mathit{Functor}\\
\textbf{infixr} :+:
\end{array}
$$

One can assemble a functor from these components and make a deep embedding from it. For example, the sum of functors $\mathit{CircuitF}_{11}$ is equivalent to *CircuitF* from the start of Section 4, and its fixpoint $\mathit{Circuit}_{11}$ to $\mathit{Circuit}_4$:

$$
\begin{array}{l}
\textbf{type } \mathit{CircuitF}_{11} = \mathit{Identity}_{11} :+: \mathit{Fan}_{11} :+: \mathit{Above}_{11} :+:\\
\qquad\qquad\qquad \mathit{Beside}_{11} :+: \mathit{Stretch}_{11}\\
\textbf{data } \mathit{Fix}\ f = \mathit{In}\ (f\ (\mathit{Fix}\ f))\\
\textbf{type } \mathit{Circuit}_{11} = \mathit{Fix}\ \mathit{CircuitF}_{11}
\end{array}
$$

This works, but it is rather clumsy. In particular, an expression of type $\mathit{Circuit}_{11}$ involves a mess of *Inl*, *Inr* and *In* constructors, as seen in this rendition of the circuit in Figure 4:

```
stretchfan :: Circuit11
stretchfan = In (Inr (Inr (Inr (Inr (Stretch11 [3,2,3] (
               In (Inr (Inl (Fan11 3)))))))))
```

Fortunately, there is an obvious way of injecting payloads into sum types in this fashion, which we can express through a simple notion of subtyping between functors, witnessed by an injection:

```
class (Functor f, Functor g) => f :≺: g where
  inj :: f a -> g a
```

Subtyping is reflexive, and summands are subtypes of their sum:

```
instance Functor f => f :≺: f where
  inj = id
instance (Functor f, Functor g) => f :≺: (f :+: g) where
  inj = Inl
instance (Functor f, Functor g, Functor h, f :≺: g) =>
           f :≺: (h :+: g) where
  inj = Inr ∘ inj
```

Note that these type class instances overlap, going beyond Haskell 98; nevertheless, as Swierstra explains, provided that sums are associated to the right this should not cause any problems.

Now we can define smart constructors that inject in this 'obvious' way:

```
identity11 :: (Identity11 :≺: f) => Width -> Fix f
identity11 w = In (inj (Identity11 w))
fan11 :: (Fan11 :≺: f) => Width -> Fix f
fan11 w = In (inj (Fan11 w))
above11 :: (Above11 :≺: f) => Fix f -> Fix f -> Fix f
above11 x y = In (inj (Above11 x y))
beside11 :: (Beside11 :≺: f) => Fix f -> Fix f -> Fix f
beside11 x y = In (inj (Beside11 x y))
stretch11 :: (Stretch11 :≺: f) => [Width] -> Fix f -> Fix f
stretch11 ws x = In (inj (Stretch11 ws x))
```

and the mess of injections can be inferred instead:

```
stretchfan :: (Fan11 :≺: f, Stretch11 :≺: f) => Fix f
stretchfan = stretch11 [3,2,3] (fan11 3)
```

Crucially, this technique also leaves the precise choice of grammar open; all that is required is for the grammar to provide fan and stretch constructors, and we can capture that dependence in the flexible declared type for *stretchfan*.

Interpretations can be similarly modularized. Of course, we expect them to be folds:

```
fold :: Functor f => (f a -> a) -> Fix f -> a
fold h (In x) = h (fmap (fold h) x)
```

In order to accommodate open datatypes, we define interpretations in pieces. We declare a type class of those constructors supporting a given interpretation:

```
class Functor f => WidthAlg f where
  widthAlg11 :: f Width -> Width
```

Interpretations lift through sums in the obvious way:

```
instance (WidthAlg f, WidthAlg g) => WidthAlg (f :+: g) where
  widthAlg11 (Inl x) = widthAlg11 x
  widthAlg11 (Inr y) = widthAlg11 y
```

Then we provide instances for each of the relevant constructors. For example, if we only ever wanted to compute the width of circuits expressed in terms of the fan and stretch constructors, we need only define those two instances:

```
instance WidthAlg Fan11 where
  widthAlg11 (Fan11 w) = w
instance WidthAlg Stretch11 where
  widthAlg11 (Stretch11 ws x) = sum ws
```

For example, this width function works for the flexibly typed circuit *stretchfan* above:

```
width11 :: WidthAlg f => Fix f -> Width
width11 = fold widthAlg11
```

—although the circuit does need to be given a specific type first:

```
> width11 (stretchfan :: Circuit11)
8
```

These algebra fragments together constitute the essence of an implicitly parametrized shallow embedding.

But the main benefit of the *à la carte* approach is that it is easy to add new constructors. We just need to add the datatype constructor as a functor, and provide a smart constructor:

```
data RStretch11 c = RStretch11 [Size] c deriving Functor
rstretch11 :: (RStretch11 :≺: f) => [Width] -> Fix f -> Fix f
rstretch11 ws x = In (inj (RStretch11 ws x))
```

Now the circuit in Figure 4 can be expressed using right stretch instead of left stretch:

```
rstretchfan :: (Identity11 :≺: f, Fan11 :≺: f, Beside11 :≺: f,
                RStretch11 :≺: f) => Fix f
rstretchfan = beside11 (identity11 2)
                       (rstretch11 [2,3,1] (fan11 3))
```

When adding new constructors such as $RStretch_{11}$, it is tempting to provide an instance for each of the interpretations of interest, such as *WidthAlg*. However, this is an unnecessary duplication of effort when $rstretch_{11}$ can itself be simulated out of existing components. We might instead write a function that *handles* the $RStretch_{11}$ constructor:

```
handle :: (Stretch11 :≺: f, Beside11 :≺: f, Identity11 :≺: f) =>
            Fix (RStretch11 :+: f) -> Fix f
handle (In (Inl (RStretch11 ws c))) =
  stretch11 (1 : ws') (handle c) `beside11` identity11 w
  where (ws', w) = (init ws, last ws - 1)
handle (In (Inr other)) = In (fmap handle other)
```

Here, we recursively translate all instances of $RStretch_{11}$ into other constructors. This technique is at the heart of the effects and handlers approach [21], although the setting there uses the free monad rather than *Fix*. With this in place, we can first handle all of the $RStretch_{11}$ constructors before passing the result on to an interpretation function such as $width_{11}$ that need not deal with $RStretch_{11}$s. This method of interpreting only a core fragment of syntax might not be optimally efficient, but of course we still leave open the possibility of providing a specialized instance if that is an issue.

5. Discussion

The essential observation made here—that *shallow embeddings correspond to the algebras of folds over the abstract syntax captured by a deep embedding*—is surely not new. For example, it was probably known to Reynolds [25], who contrasted deep embeddings ('user defined types') and shallow ('procedural data structures'), and observed that the former were free algebras; but he didn't explicitly discuss anything corresponding to folds.

It is also implicit in the *finally tagless* approach [8], which uses a shallow embedding and observes that 'this representation makes it trivial to implement a primitive recursive function over object terms', providing an interface that such functions should implement; but this comment is made rather in passing, and their focus is mainly on staging and partial evaluation. The observation is more explicit in Kiselyov's lecture notes on the finally tagless approach [20], which go into more detail on compositionality; he makes the connection to "denotational semantics, which is required to be compositional", and observes that "making context explicit turns seemingly non-compositional operations compositional". The finally tagless approach also covers DSLs with binding constructs, which we have ignored here.

Neither is it a new observation that algebraic datatypes (such as $Circuit_4$) and their Böhm–Berarducci encodings (such as $Circuit_7$) are equivalent. And of course, none of this is specific in any way to the *Circuit* DSL; a datatype-generic version of the story can be told, by abstracting away from the shape functor *CircuitF*—the reader may enjoy working out the details.

Nevertheless, the observation that shallow embeddings correspond to the algebras of folds over deep embeddings seems not to be widely appreciated; at least, we have been unable to find an explicit statement to this effect, either in the DSL literature or elsewhere. And it makes a nice application of folds: many results about folds evidently have interesting statements about shallow embeddings as corollaries. The three generalizations of folds (banana split, mutumorphisms, and accumulating parameters) exploited in Section 4 are all special cases of *adjoint fold* [15, 16]; perhaps other adjoint folds yield other interesting insights about shallow embeddings?

Acknowledgements

This paper arose from ideas discussed at the Summer School on Domain Specific Languages in Cluj-Napoca in July 2013 [11]; JG thanks the organizers for the invitation to lecture there. José Pedro Magalhães, Ralf Hinze, Jacques Carette, James McKinna, and the anonymous reviewers all made helpful comments, and Oleg Kiselyov gave many constructive criticisms and much inspiration, for which we are very grateful. This work has been funded by EPSRC grant number EP/J010995/1, on Unifying Theories of Generic Programming.

References

[1] Robert Atkey, Sam Lindley, and Jeremy Yallop. Unembedding domain-specific languages. In *Haskell Symposium*, pages 37–48. ACM, 2009.

[2] Lennart Augustsson. Making EDSLs fly. In *TechMesh*, London, December 2012. Video at `http://vimeo.com/73223479`.

[3] Richard S. Bird. The promotion and accumulation strategies in transformational programming. *ACM Transactions on Programming Languages and Systems*, 6(4):487–504, October 1984. Addendum in TOPLAS 7(3):490–492, July 1985.

[4] Corrado Böhm and Alessandro Berarducci. Automatic synthesis of typed λ-programs on term algebras. *Theoretical Computer Science*, 39:135–154, 1985.

[5] Richard Boulton. Personal communication, 10th February 2014.

[6] Richard Boulton, Andrew Gordon, Mike Gordon, John Harrison, John Herbert, and John Van Tassel. Experience with embedding hardware description languages in HOL. In Victoria Stavridou, Thomas F. Melham, and Raymond T. Boute, editors, *IFIP TC10/WG 10.2 International Conference on Theorem Provers in Circuit Design: Theory, Practice and Experience*, pages 129–156. North-Holland/Elsevier, 1992.

[7] Richard P. Brent and Hsiang-Tsung Kung. The chip complexity of binary arithmetic. In *Symposium on Theory of Computing*, pages 190–200. ACM, 1980.

[8] Jacques Carette, Oleg Kiselyov, and Chung-chieh Shan. Finally tagless, partially evaluated: Tagless staged interpreters for simpler typed languages. *Journal of Functional Programming*, 19(5):509–543, 2009.

[9] Maarten M. Fokkinga. Tupling and mutumorphisms. *The Squiggolist*, 1(4):81–82, June 1990.

[10] Martin Fowler. *Domain-Specific Languages*. Addison-Wesley, 2011.

[11] Jeremy Gibbons. Functional programming for domain-specific languages. In Viktória Zsók, editor, *Central European Functional Programming Summer School*, volume 8606 of *Lecture Notes in Computer Science*, pages 1–27. Springer, 2014. To appear.

[12] Jeremy Gibbons and Geraint Jones. The under-appreciated unfold. In *International Conference on Functional Programming*, pages 273–279, Baltimore, Maryland, September 1998.

[13] Ralf Hinze. An algebra of scans. In *Mathematics of Program Construction*, volume 3125 of *Lecture Notes in Computer Science*, pages 186–210. Springer, 2004.

[14] Ralf Hinze. Church numerals, twice! *Journal of Functional Programming*, 15(1), 2005.

[15] Ralf Hinze. Adjoint folds and unfolds: An extended study. *Science of Computer Programming*, 78(11):2108–2159, 2013.

[16] Ralf Hinze, Nicolas Wu, and Jeremy Gibbons. Unifying structured recursion schemes. In *International Conference on Functional Programming*, pages 209–220, Boston, Massachusetts, September 2013.

[17] Zhenjiang Hu, Hideya Iwasaki, and Masato Takeichi. Formal derivation of efficient parallel programs by construction of list homomorphisms. *ACM Transactions on Programming Languages and Systems*, 19(3):444–461, 1997.

[18] Paul Hudak. Building domain-specific embedded languages. *ACM Computing Surveys*, 28(4), 1996.

[19] Anne Kaldewaij. *Programming: The Derivation of Algorithms*. Prentice Hall, 1990.

[20] Oleg Kiselyov. Typed tagless final interpreters. In Jeremy Gibbons, editor, *Generic and Indexed Programming*, volume 7470 of *Lecture Notes in Computer Science*, pages 130–174. Springer, 2012.

[21] Oleg Kiselyov, Amr Sabry, and Cameron Swords. Extensible effects: An alternative to monad transformers. In *Haskell Symposium*, pages 59–70. ACM, 2013.

[22] Shriram Krishnamurthi, Matthias Felleisen, and Daniel P. Friedman. Synthesizing object-oriented and functional design to promote re-use. In *European Conference on Object-Oriented Programming*, volume 1445 of *Lecture Notes in Computer Science*, pages 91–113. Springer, 1998.

[23] Ehud Lamm. CUFP write-up. Blog post, `http://lambda-the-ultimate.org/node/2572`, December 2007.

[24] Ralf Lämmel, Joost Visser, and Jan Kort. Dealing with large bananas. In Johan Jeuring, editor, *Workshop on Generic Programming*, volume Technical Report UU-CS-2000-19. Universiteit Utrecht, 2000.

[25] John Reynolds. User-defined types and procedural data structures as complementary approaches to data abstraction. In Stephen A. Schuman, editor, *New Directions in Algorithmic Languages*, pages 157–168, 1975.

[26] Josef Svenningsson and Emil Axelsson. Combining deep and shallow embedding for embedded domain-specific languages. In *Trends in Functional Programming 2012*, volume 7829 of *Lecture Notes in Computer Science*, pages 21–36, 2013.

[27] Wouter Swierstra. Datatypes à la carte. *Journal of Functional Programming*, 18(4):423–436, 2008.

[28] Philip Wadler. Theorems for free! In *Functional Programming Languages and Computer Architecture*, pages 347–359. ACM, 1989.

[29] Philip Wadler. The expression problem. Java Genericity Mailing list, November 1998. `http://homepages.inf.ed.ac.uk/wadler/papers/expression/expression.txt`.

[30] Philip Wadler and Stephen Blott. How to make ad-hoc polymorphism less ad hoc. In *Principles of Programming Languages*, pages 60–76. ACM, 1989.

Krivine Nets

A semantic foundation for distributed execution

Olle Fredriksson Dan R. Ghica
University of Birmingham

Abstract

We define a new approach to compilation to distributed architectures based on networks of abstract machines. Using it we can implement a generalised and fully transparent form of Remote Procedure Call that supports calling higher-order functions across node boundaries, without sending actual code. Our starting point is the classic Krivine machine, which implements reduction for untyped call-by-name PCF. We successively add the features that we need for distributed execution and show the correctness of each addition. Then we construct a two-level operational semantics, where the high level is a network of communicating machines, and the low level is given by local machine transitions. Using these networks, we arrive at our final system, the *Krivine Net*. We show that Krivine Nets give a correct distributed implementation of the Krivine machine, which preserves both termination and non-termination properties. All the technical results have been formalised and proved correct in AGDA. We also implement a prototype compiler which we compare with previous distributing compilers based on Girard's Geometry of Interaction and on Game Semantics.

Categories and Subject Descriptors D.3.1 [*Programming Languages*]: Formal Definitions and Theory—semantics; D.3.2 [*Programming Languages*]: Language Classifications—concurrent, distributed, and parallel languages; F.1.1 [*Computation by Abstract Devices*]: models of computation

Keywords abstract machines; distributed execution; simulation relation; Agda

1. Seamless distribution

There are two extreme views of programming languages. At one extreme we have the *machine-oriented* view, where the programming language is construed as the medium through which a programmer instructs a computer to perform certain operations. The other extremal view is *mathematical-logical* in which the programming language is a medium of expressing abstract computational concepts such as algorithms or data structures. Historically, the first programming languages were, by necessity, machine-oriented, but algorithmic (i.e. mathematical-logical) machine independent languages appeared soon after (FORTRAN, LISP, ALGOL, etc.). The case for machine independent programming has been made, quite successfully, a long time ago.

ICFP'14, September 1–6, 2014, Gothenburg, Sweden.

ACM 978-1-4503-2873-9/14/09...$15.00.
http://dx.doi.org/10.1145/2628136.2628152

Machine independence means that programs can just be recompiled to run on different devices with similar architectures. *Architecture independence* pushes this idea even further to devices with *different* architectures, such as conventional CPUs, distributed systems, GPUs and reconfigurable hardware. In a series of papers [12–14] we have examined the possibility of lifting machine independence to architecture independence in the context of distributed computing. The reason is that in distributed computing the *deployment* of a program is often reflected at the level of source code. For example, these two ERLANG programs:

```
c(A_pid)-> receive X -> A_pid ! X*X end, c(A_pid).
main()->
  C_pid = spawn(f, c, [self()]), C_pid ! 3,
  receive X -> C_pid ! 4, receive Y -> X+Y end
end.
```

and

```
c()-> receive {Pid, X} -> Pid ! X*X end, c().
b(A_pid, C_pid)-> receive
    request0 -> C_pid ! {self(), 3},
                receive X -> A_pid ! X end;
    request1 -> C_pid ! {self(), 4},
                receive X -> A_pid ! X end end,
  b(A_pid, C_pid).
main()->
  C_pid = spawn(f, c, []),
  B_pid = spawn(f, b, [self(), C_pid]),
  B_pid ! request0, receive X ->
  B_pid ! request1, receive Y -> X+Y end end.
```

perform the same function, which in a computation on a single node we may write as `let f = λx. x * x in f 3 + f 4`, except that the deployment is different. The first program is distributed on two nodes whereas the second is distributed on three nodes. Our proposal is as follows:

> *The program should not need to specify details of the runtime deployment pattern.*

This means that communication and process management should largely disappear from the source code, as they are the means by which deployment patterns are implemented. To explain our metaphor, they are the *seam* which we aim to eliminate. For example, the deployment pattern could be indicated using a configuration file or pragma-like code annotations assigning nodes to arbitrary sub-terms of the program:

```
let f = (λx. x * x)@C in (f 3 + f 4)@B
```

We would like the invocations of `f` in the program to semantically work exactly like a local function call even though the function is located on the node `C` and invoked from node `B`. The compiler should automatically handle the communication for us by for triggering a small exchange of messages between the two nodes: For example, node `B` would start by sending a message to `C`, requesting the evaluation of `f` and providing the location of the argument and where to return to.

At this early stage we make no claims that our approach is a practical alternative to established distributed programming methodologies, but we believe that there should be room for exploring machine (or architecture) independent, purely algorithmic, languages in the context of distributed computing. Our approach is in contrast to communication-oriented idioms such as MPI and ERLANG. It is also philosophically different to *domain specific languages* for distributed computing, which expose communication but use concepts associated with high-level programming languages such as *types* [17] to avoid certain classes of errors. The closest to our approach are *remote procedure calls*, so our research programme can be reformulated as an answer to the question:

> *Can remote procedure calls be incorporated transparently, correctly and efficiently into the programming language?*

1.1 Contribution

In this paper we present an extension of the classic Krivine abstract machine for the call-by-name lambda calculus [19] for seamless distributed computing. Our previous work gave a compilation technique [13] based on the Geometry of Interaction (GOI) token abstract machine [23] and another one [14] based on game semantics (GAMC) [15]. They both achieve seamless distribution but have certain apparent unavoidable inefficiencies. The GOI-based compilation has the potential to be locally efficient but has a possibly insurmountable communication overhead, whereas the games-based compiler communicates efficiently but requires very high computational overhead on each node. The current approach, which we are also exploring for the SECD machine and call-by-value [12], combines the best of both worlds: it communicates efficiently by keeping the size of the message within a small fixed bound and it executes efficiently on each node. In fact, the compilation scheme degenerates to that of the conventional Krivine machine if the whole program is deployed on a single node. An additional advantage which this current technique offers is that, unlike the exotic GOI and games-based approaches, it is in some technical sense standard so that it can interface trivially with legacy code which was compiled to the Krivine machine.

Because the formal definitions of the formalism of *Krivine Nets* which we propose can be in places fairly intricate we adopt a fully formal approach, expressing all the definitions and the correctness proofs in the dependently-typed programming language AGDA [27]. This allows us to present technical results with a high degree of confidence and to remove all proof details, which can be found elsewhere [1], from the paper. In this paper we can focus on the exposition. The reader is not assumed to know AGDA in order to read the paper, which is self-contained, but a good knowledge of the language is required in order to understand the correctness proofs.

2. The Krivine machine

We are compiling the untyped applied call-by-name lambda calculus, i.e. a lambda calculus with constants. For the sake of a concrete yet simple presentation we assume that the only data is natural numbers, and the constants are numeric literals, arithmetic operators and if-then-else. Informally, the grammar of the language is

$$M ::= x \mid \lambda x.M \mid MM \mid \text{if } M \text{ then } M \text{ else } M \mid n \mid M \oplus M \mid M@A.$$

Formally, we define the data-type of *terms* with the following constructors:

```
data Term : ⋆ where
  λ_  : Term → Term
  _$_ : (t t' : Term) → Term
  var : ℕ → Term
  lit : ℕ → Term
  op  : (f : ℕ → ℕ → ℕ) (t t' : Term) → Term
  if0_then_else_ : (b t f : Term) → Term
  _@_ : Term → Node → Term
```

Above, $\star$ is the "type of types". We are using the De Bruijn index notation, so abstraction (**λ_**) is a unary operator and each variable (**var**) is a natural number. The value of the index denotes the number of binders between the variable and its binder. Function application (**_$_**, an *infix* operator) is an explicit constructor, for clarity. Numeric literals (**lit**) and branching (**if0_then_else_**) are obvious, noting that the constructor for the latter is a *mixfix operator*. Binary arithmetic operators (**op**) take three arguments: the function giving the operation and two terms.

We also introduce syntactic support in the language (**_@_**, another infix operator) for specifying node assignments for *closed* sub-terms. This is done strictly for simplicity. Node assignment could be otherwise specified, e.g. using a separate configuration file, but it would needlessly complicate the presentation. Node assignment is a "compiler pragma" and has no bearing on observational properties of the programming languages. The requirement that node assignment is specified for closed terms only keeps the presentation as simple as possible. This apparent restriction can be easily overcome using lambda lifting.

EXAMPLE 1. *The term* $(\lambda x.\lambda y.y + x)\,3\,4$ *is represented as*

```
termExample : Term
termExample = λ (λ (var 0 +' var 1)) $ lit 3 $ lit 4
  where _+'_ = op _+_
```

The Krivine machine is the standard abstract machine for call-by-name. It has three components: code, environment and stack. The stack and the environment contain *thunks*, which are closures representing unevaluated function arguments. The evaluations are delayed until the values are needed. For the pure lambda calculus, the Krivine machine uses three instructions:

POPARG pop an argument from the stack and add it to the environment.

PUSHARG push a thunk for some code given as argument.

VAR look up the argument in the environment and start evaluation.

For the applied lambda calculus the machine becomes more complex because arithmetic operations are strict, so extra mechanisms are required to force the evaluation of arguments.

Formally, we define closures and environments by mutual recursion:

```
mutual
  Closure = Term × Env
  data EnvEl : ⋆ where
    clos : Closure → EnvEl
  Env = List EnvEl
```

The constructor **clos** that takes a *Closure* into an environment element *EnvEl* is only needed for formal reasons, to prevent the AGDA type-checker from reporting a circular definition.

Stacks and configurations are:

$$
\begin{array}{lll}
\text{data } \mathit{StackElem} : \star \text{ where} & & \\
\quad \mathbf{arg} : \mathit{Closure} & & \rightarrow \mathit{StackElem} \\
\quad \mathbf{if0} : \mathit{Closure} & \rightarrow \mathit{Closure} & \rightarrow \mathit{StackElem} \\
\quad \mathbf{op}_2 : (\mathbb{N} \rightarrow \mathbb{N} \rightarrow \mathbb{N}) & \rightarrow \mathit{Closure} & \rightarrow \mathit{StackElem} \\
\quad \mathbf{op}_1 : (\mathbb{N} \rightarrow \mathbb{N}) & & \rightarrow \mathit{StackElem} \\
\mathit{Stack} = \mathit{List\ StackElem} & & \\
\mathit{Config} = \mathit{Term} \times \mathit{Env} \times \mathit{Stack} & &
\end{array}
$$

The generic stack elements (for function arguments) are constructed using **arg**, whereas **if0**, $\mathbf{op}_2$, $\mathbf{op}_1$ are used by the constants.

The signature of the Krivine machine is given as a data-type, defining a *Rel*ation on *Config*urations of the Krivine machine:

$$\text{data } \_ \longrightarrow_{\mathcal{K}} \_ : \mathit{Rel\ Config\ Config} \text{ where}$$

The relation type $\mathit{Rel}\ A\ B$ is defined to be $A \rightarrow B \rightarrow \star$, so two elements a and b are R-related exactly when $R\ a\ b$ is inhabited, given $R : \mathit{Rel}\ A\ B$. Each rule, i.e. each instruction of the machine, will thus correspond to a constructor. We explain the formal definition of each rule.

$$
\begin{array}{l}
\mathbf{POPARG} : \{t : \mathit{Term}\}\ \{e : \mathit{Env}\}\ \{c : \mathit{Closure}\}\ \{s : \mathit{Stack}\} \rightarrow \\
\quad (\boldsymbol{\lambda}\ t, e, \mathbf{arg}\ c :: s) \longrightarrow_{\mathcal{K}} (t, \mathbf{clos}\ c :: e, s)
\end{array}
$$

POPARG handles abstractions $\boldsymbol{\lambda}\ t$ by moving the top of the stack $\mathbf{arg}\ c$ into the first position of the environment e. The constructors **arg**, **clos** are needed for type-checking and would be omitted in an informal presentation. The constructor arguments (t, e, c, s) are implicit, indicated syntactically in AGDA by curly brackets.

$$
\begin{array}{l}
\mathbf{PUSHARG} : \{t\ t' : \mathit{Term}\}\ \{e : \mathit{Env}\}\ \{s : \mathit{Stack}\} \rightarrow \\
\quad ((t\ \$\ t'), e, s) \longrightarrow_{\mathcal{K}} (t, e, \mathbf{arg}\ (t', e) :: s)
\end{array}
$$

PUSHARG handles application $t\ \$\ t'$ by creating a new closure $\mathbf{arg}\ (t', e)$ and pushing it onto the stack, then carrying on with the execution of the function body t.

$$
\begin{array}{l}
\mathbf{VAR} : \{n : \mathbb{N}\}\ \{e\ e' : \mathit{Env}\}\ \{t : \mathit{Term}\}\ \{s : \mathit{Stack}\} \rightarrow \\
\quad \mathit{lookup}\ n\ e \equiv \mathbf{just}\ (\mathbf{clos}\ (t, e')) \rightarrow \\
\quad (\mathbf{var}\ n, e, s) \longrightarrow_{\mathcal{K}} (t, e', s)
\end{array}
$$

In AGDA the $\equiv$ operator denotes *propositional* equality, which necessitates a proof, whereas $=$ is used to introduce new definitions. The **VAR** rule looks up the variable n in the current environment e and, if successful, retrieves the closure at that position (t, e') and proceeds to execute from it, with the current stack.

Because this is an applied lambda calculus we need additional operations for conditionals and operators. Here we omit the types of the implicit arguments since they can be inferred:

$$
\begin{array}{l}
\mathbf{COND} : \forall\ \{b\ t\ f\ e\ s\} \rightarrow \\
\quad (\mathbf{if0}\ b\ \mathbf{then}\ t\ \mathbf{else}\ f, e, s) \longrightarrow_{\mathcal{K}} (b, e, \mathbf{if0}\ (t, e)\ (f, e) :: s) \\
\mathbf{COND\text{-}0} : \forall\ \{e\ t\ e'\ f\ s\} \rightarrow \\
\quad (\mathbf{lit}\ 0, e, \mathbf{if0}\ (t, e')\ f :: s) \longrightarrow_{\mathcal{K}} (t, e', s) \\
\mathbf{COND\text{-}suc} : \forall\ \{n\ e\ t\ f\ e'\ s\} \rightarrow \\
\quad (\mathbf{lit}\ (1 + n), e, \mathbf{if0}\ t\ (f, e') :: s) \longrightarrow_{\mathcal{K}} (f, e', s) \\
\mathbf{OP} : \forall\ \{f\ t\ t'\ e\ s\} \rightarrow \\
\quad (\mathbf{op}\ f\ t\ t', e, s) \longrightarrow_{\mathcal{K}} (t, e, \mathbf{op}_2\ f\ (t', e) :: s) \\
\mathbf{OP}_2 : \forall\ \{n\ e\ f\ t\ e'\ s\} \rightarrow \\
\quad (\mathbf{lit}\ n, e, \mathbf{op}_2\ f\ (t, e') :: s) \longrightarrow_{\mathcal{K}} (t, e', \mathbf{op}_1\ (f\ n) :: s) \\
\mathbf{OP}_1 : \forall\ \{n\ e\ f\ s\} \rightarrow \\
\quad (\mathbf{lit}\ n, e, \mathbf{op}_1\ f :: s) \longrightarrow_{\mathcal{K}} (\mathbf{lit}\ (f\ n), [\,], s)
\end{array}
$$

EXAMPLE 2. *We can see the Krivine machine at work in this simple example. The term in Ex. 1 has the following execution trace, written informally as follows:*

$$
\begin{array}{l}
((\boldsymbol{\lambda}\ (\boldsymbol{\lambda}\ \_+\_\ 0\ 1)\ \$\ 3\ \$\ 4), [\,], [\,]) \\
\quad \longrightarrow \langle\ \mathbf{PUSHARG}\ \rangle \\
((\boldsymbol{\lambda}\ (\boldsymbol{\lambda}\ \_+\_\ 0\ 1)\ \$\ 3), [\,], [(4, [\,])]) \\
\quad \longrightarrow \langle\ \mathbf{PUSHARG}\ \rangle \\
(\boldsymbol{\lambda}\ (\boldsymbol{\lambda}\ \_+\_\ 0\ 1), [\,], [(3, [\,]), (4, [\,])]) \\
\quad \longrightarrow \langle\ \mathbf{POPARG}\ \rangle \\
(\boldsymbol{\lambda}\ \_+\_\ 0\ 1, [(3, [\,])], [(4, [\,])]) \\
\quad \longrightarrow \langle\ \mathbf{POPARG}\ \rangle \\
(\_+\_\ 0\ 1, [(4, [\,]), (3, [\,])], [\,]) \\
\quad \longrightarrow \langle\ \mathbf{OP}\ \rangle \\
(0, [(4, [\,]), (3, [\,])], [\mathbf{op}_2\ \_+\_\ (1, [(4, [\,]), (3, [\,])])]) \\
\quad \longrightarrow \langle\ \mathbf{VAR\ refl}\ \rangle \\
(4, [\,], [\mathbf{op}_2\ \_+\_\ (1, [(4, [\,]), (3, [\,])])]) \\
\quad \longrightarrow \langle\ \mathbf{OP}_2\ \rangle \\
(1, [(4, [\,]), (3, [\,])], [\mathbf{op}_1\ (\_+\_\ 4)]) \\
\quad \longrightarrow \langle\ \mathbf{VAR\ refl}\ \rangle \\
(3, [\,], [\mathbf{op}_1\ (\_+\_\ 4)]) \\
\quad \longrightarrow \langle\ \mathbf{OP}_1\ \rangle \\
(7, [\,], [\,])
\end{array}
$$

In the above we have omitted the constructors **op**, **var**, **arg**, *etc. for brevity.*

Finally, we include a (degenerate) instruction for remote execution:

$$\mathbf{REMOTE} : \forall\ \{t\ i\ e\ s\} \rightarrow (t\ @\ i, e, s) \longrightarrow_{\mathcal{K}} (t, [\,], s)$$

This instruction is included strictly so that the _@_ construct for node assignment does not trigger a runtime error, but it is effectively a *no-op*: it simply erases the environment e, since node assignment is meant to be applied only to closed terms. In the following section we will define the distributed Krivine machine, where the **REMOTE** instruction is meaningful.

3. Krivine nets

3.1 The machine

We now extend the Krivine machine so that it supports an arbitrary pattern of distribution by letting several instances of the extended machine run in a network. We call these machines *DKrivine* machines and they form *Krivine Nets*. The DKrivine machines extend the Krivine machines conservatively by adding new features. Each such machine is identified as a *node* in the network and has a dedicated heap. A pointer into a heap may be tagged with a node identifier, case in which it is a *remote pointer*, which can now be stored in the environment along with local closures. The stack may now have as a bottom element a remote pointer indicating the existence of a *remote stack extension*, i.e. the fact that the information which logically belongs to this stack is physically located on a different node. Finally, the configuration of the Krivine machine is now called a *thread* indicating that its execution can be dynamically started and halted. Internally, the heap structure is used for storing persistent data that needs to out-live the runtime of a thread. The new formal definitions are as follows:

$$
\begin{array}{l}
\mathit{RPtr} = \mathit{Ptr} \times \mathit{Node} \\
\mathit{ContPtr} = \mathit{RPtr}
\end{array}
$$

$$
\begin{array}{lll}
\text{data } \mathit{EnvElem} : \star \text{ where} & & \\
\quad \mathbf{local} : \mathit{Closure} \rightarrow & & \mathit{EnvElem} \\
\quad \mathbf{remote} : \mathit{ContPtr} \rightarrow \mathbb{N} \rightarrow \mathit{EnvElem} & &
\end{array}
$$

$$
\begin{array}{lcl}
\mathit{Stack} & = & \mathit{List\ StackElem} \times \mathit{Maybe}\ (\mathit{ContPtr} \times \mathbb{N} \times \mathbb{N}) \\
\mathit{ContHeap} & = & \mathit{Heap\ Stack} \\
\mathit{Thread} & = & \mathit{Term} \times \mathit{Env} \times \mathit{Stack} \\
\mathit{Machine} & = & \mathit{Maybe\ Thread} \times \mathit{ContHeap}
\end{array}
$$

The definitions are straightforward, except for the **remote** environment element and the definition of stacks which require explanation. A remote *ContPtr* is a pointer to a continuation stack, and the constructor **remote** takes an additional natural number argument indicating the offset in that continuation stack where the referred closure is stored. As stated, the stack now possibly includes a remote stack extension. This extension is to be thought of as being located at the bottom of the local stack, and consists of a *ContPtr* pointing into the heap of a remote node holding the stack, and two natural numbers that form the current node's *view* of that stack. The second number is the offset into the remote stack that the view starts from, and the first number stores how many consecutive arguments there are on on it.

Because DKrivine machines are networked they exchange messages, which fall into three categories, formalised as constructors for the *Msg* datatype:

REMOTE A message with this tag initiates remote evaluation, formally defined as

$$\textbf{REMOTE} : \mathit{Term} \to \mathit{Node} \to \mathit{ContPtr} \to \mathbb{N} \to \mathit{Msg}$$

The message consists of a *Term*, a destination *Node* identifier, a *ContPtr* to the sender's current continuation stack and a natural number indicating how many arguments are on that stack.

The design decision to make a *Term* part of the message structure is for simplicity of formalisation only. In the actual implementation only a *code pointer* needs to be sent to the node, which already has the required code available. The mechanism through which compiled code arrives at each node is handled by a *distributed program loader* (see e.g. [11]) which is part of the runtime system and, as such, beyond the scope of this work. It should be obvious that distributed program loading is possible in principle here because all code is static and available at compile-time.

RETURN These messages are sent when computation has terminated and reached a literal, and the value must be returned to the node that has initiated the computation. The formal definition is:

$$\textbf{RETURN} : \mathit{ContPtr} \to \mathbb{N} \to \mathbb{N} \to \mathit{Msg}$$

The message contains a *ContPtr* to the remote stack of the machine that is receiving the message, the natural number calculated and another number indicating to the receiving machine how many arguments can be now discarded from the stack, corresponding to the offset of sending node's view of the stack.

VAR is a message used to access remotely located variables. It consists of a remote *ContPtr*, an offset into the remote continuation stack, a local continuation stack and the number of arguments on it.

$$\textbf{VAR} : \mathit{ContPtr} \to \mathbb{N} \to \mathit{ContPtr} \to \mathbb{N} \to \mathit{Msg}$$

We need to send the continuation stack of the calling node (like in the **REMOTE** rule) because the remote variable may refer to a function, in which case the arguments are supplied by the calling node, or it may be part of an operation on the calling node, in which case the resulting number needs to be returned there once it has been calculated.

Deliberate in the design of the Krivine nets is the need to minimise message exchange. To achieve this, machines do not send remote "pop" messages for manipulating remote stack extensions, but perform this operation locally. When a node sends a pointer to a new continuation stack it also sends the number of arguments that are on that stack, so that the receiving node can pop arguments from its local view of that stack.

We can now start describing the transitions of the DKrivine machine. The signature of the transition relation is:

$$\begin{array}{l}\mathsf{data}\ \_\vdash\!\longrightarrow_{\mathcal{DK}}\langle\_\rangle\_\ (i : \mathit{Node}) :\\ \quad \mathit{Machine} \to \mathit{Tagged\ Msg} \to \mathit{Machine} \to \star\end{array}$$

DKrivine transitions are parameterised by the current node identifier and map a *Machine* state and a *Tagged Msg* into a new *Machine* state. The tag applied to the message indicates whether the message is sent, received or absent (i.e. a *silent* transition):

$$\begin{array}{ll}\multicolumn{2}{l}{\mathsf{data}\ \mathit{Tagged}\ (\mathit{Msg} : \star) : \star\ \mathsf{where}}\\ \boldsymbol{\tau} & : \mathit{Tagged\ Msg}\\ \textbf{send} & : \mathit{Msg} \to \mathit{Tagged\ Msg}\\ \textbf{receive} & : \mathit{Msg} \to \mathit{Tagged\ Msg}\end{array}$$

All the old rules are present, but now expressed in the presence of the continuation heap.

$$\begin{array}{l}\textbf{POPARG} : \forall \{t\ e\ c\ s\ r\ ch\} \to\\ \quad i \vdash (\textbf{just}\ (\boldsymbol{\lambda}\ t, e, \textbf{arg}\ c :: s, r), ch) \ \longrightarrow_{\mathcal{DK}} \langle \boldsymbol{\tau} \rangle\\ \quad (\textbf{just}\ (t, \textbf{local}\ c :: e, s, r), ch)\end{array}$$

Compared to the **POPARG** rule of the original machine, the only differences are the tag on the configuration (**just** ...), which expresses the fact that the DKrivine thread is running, and the continuation heap *ch* which remains constant during the application of this rule. The environment element constructor **local** now emphasises that the variable is local. Because the transition involves only one node it is $\boldsymbol{\tau}$, i.e. no messages are exchanged.

The other old transition rules are embedded into the DKrivine machine in a similar way. They are all silent and the continuation heap *ch* stays unchanged:

$$\begin{array}{l}\textbf{PUSHARG} : \forall \{t\ t'\ e\ s\ r\ ch\} \to\\ \quad i \vdash (\textbf{just}\ ((t\ \$\ t'), e, s, r), ch) \ \longrightarrow_{\mathcal{DK}} \langle \boldsymbol{\tau} \rangle\\ \quad (\textbf{just}\ (t, e, \textbf{arg}\ (t', e) :: s, r), ch)\\ \textbf{VAR} : \forall \{n\ e\ s\ r\ ch\ t\ e'\} \to\\ \quad \mathit{lookup}\ n\ e \equiv \textbf{just}\ (\textbf{local}\ (t, e')) \to\\ \quad i \vdash (\textbf{just}\ (\textbf{var}\ n, e, s, r), ch) \ \longrightarrow_{\mathcal{DK}} \langle \boldsymbol{\tau} \rangle\\ \quad (\textbf{just}\ (t, e', s, r), ch)\\ \textbf{COND} : \forall \{b\ t\ f\ e\ s\ r\ ch\} \to\\ \quad i \vdash (\textbf{just}\ (\textbf{if0}\ b\ \textbf{then}\ t\ \textbf{else} f, e, s, r), ch) \ \longrightarrow_{\mathcal{DK}} \langle \boldsymbol{\tau} \rangle\\ \quad (\textbf{just}\ (b, e, \textbf{if0}\ (t, e)\ (f, e) :: s, r), ch)\\ \textbf{COND-0} : \forall \{e\ t\ e'\ f\ s\ r\ ch\} \to\\ \quad i \vdash (\textbf{just}\ (\textbf{lit}\ 0, e, \textbf{if0}\ (t, e')\ f :: s, r), ch) \ \longrightarrow_{\mathcal{DK}} \langle \boldsymbol{\tau} \rangle\\ \quad (\textbf{just}\ (t, e', s, r), ch)\\ \textbf{COND-suc} : \forall \{n\ e\ t\ e'\ f\ s\ r\ ch\} \to\\ \quad i \vdash (\textbf{just}\ (\textbf{lit}\ (1 +\ n), e, \textbf{if0}\ t\ (f, e') :: s, r), ch) \ \longrightarrow_{\mathcal{DK}} \langle \boldsymbol{\tau} \rangle\\ \quad (\textbf{just}\ (f, e', s, r), ch)\\ \textbf{OP} : \forall \{f\ t\ t'\ e\ s\ r\ ch\} \to\\ \quad i \vdash (\textbf{just}\ (\textbf{op} f\ t\ t', e, s, r), ch) \ \longrightarrow_{\mathcal{DK}} \langle \boldsymbol{\tau} \rangle\\ \quad (\textbf{just}\ (t, e, \textbf{op}_2\ f\ (t', e) :: s, r), ch)\\ \textbf{OP}_2 : \forall \{n\ e\ f\ t\ e'\ s\ r\ ch\} \to\\ \quad i \vdash (\textbf{just}\ (\textbf{lit}\ n, e, \textbf{op}_2\ f\ (t, e') :: s, r), ch) \ \longrightarrow_{\mathcal{DK}} \langle \boldsymbol{\tau} \rangle\\ \quad (\textbf{just}\ (t, e', \textbf{op}_1\ (f\ n) :: s, r), ch)\\ \textbf{OP}_1 : \forall \{n\ e\ f\ s\ r\ ch\} \to\\ \quad i \vdash (\textbf{just}\ (\textbf{lit}\ n, e, \textbf{op}_1\ f :: s, r), ch) \ \longrightarrow_{\mathcal{DK}} \langle \boldsymbol{\tau} \rangle\\ \quad (\textbf{just}\ (\textbf{lit}\ (f\ n), [\,], s, r), ch)\end{array}$$

The **REMOTE** execution rule is now meaningful, and it has a **send** and a **receive** version:

$$\begin{array}{l}\textbf{REMOTE-send} : \forall \{t\ i'\ e\ s\ ch\} \to\\ \quad \mathsf{let}\ (ch', kp) = i \vdash ch \rhd s\ \mathsf{in}\\ \quad i \vdash (\textbf{just}\ (t\ @\ i', e, s), ch)\\ \qquad \longrightarrow_{\mathcal{DK}} \langle \textbf{send}\ (\textbf{REMOTE}\ t\ i'\ kp\ (\mathit{num\text{-}args}\ s)) \rangle\\ \quad (\textbf{nothing}, ch')\end{array}$$

The operation $i \vdash ch \rhd s$ signifies allocating at node i in heap ch a new pointer pointing at stack s, and it returns a pair of the updated heap ch' and the newly allocated remote pointer kp. The remote-execution directive $t\ @\ i'$ is carried out by sending a **REMOTE** message to i' consisting of the (pointer to) code t, the destination i', the local continuation-stack pointer kp and the number of arguments on it. After sending the remote execution message the thread halts, i.e. its state is **nothing**.

The function that calculates the number of arguments on the stack is quite subtle and we give its formal expression below:

$$\begin{array}{lll}
\textit{num-args} : \textit{Stack} & & \rightarrow \mathbb{N} \\
\textit{num-args}\ ([\,] & , \textbf{nothing}) & = \textit{0} \\
\textit{num-args}\ ([\,] & , \textbf{just}\ (_, n, _)) & = n \\
\textit{num-args}\ (\textbf{arg}\ _ :: s & , r) & = \textit{1} + \textit{num-args}\ (s, r) \\
\textit{num-args}\ (\textbf{if0}\ _\ _ :: _ & , _) & = \textit{0} \\
\textit{num-args}\ (\textbf{op}_2\ _\ _ :: _ & , _) & = \textit{0} \\
\textit{num-args}\ (\textbf{op}_1\ _ :: _ & , _) & = \textit{0}
\end{array}$$

The function returns the number of arguments at the top of the stack, but it takes into account the possibility that some arguments are local and some arguments are remote. Recall that the remote pointer that we store at the bottom of the stack, pointing to the remote stack extension, also has a natural number *numargs* expressing how many arguments are stored remotely. This is an important optimisation because it makes it possible for this function to be evaluated *locally*, without querying the remote machine where the stack extension is physically located.

The counterpart **REMOTE-receive** rule is:

$$\begin{array}{l}
\textbf{REMOTE-receive} : \forall \{ch\ t\ kp\ numargs\} \rightarrow \\
\quad i \vdash (\textbf{nothing}, ch) \\
\qquad \longrightarrow_{\mathcal{DK}} \langle \textbf{receive}\ (\textbf{REMOTE}\ t\ i\ kp\ numargs) \rangle \\
\qquad (\textbf{just}\ (t, [\,], [\,], \textbf{just}\ (kp, numargs, 0)), ch)
\end{array}$$

The thread on node i is halted when it receives the **REMOTE** execution message, with the same contents as above. The code t becomes the currently executed code, in an empty environment (t is, as we explained before, closed) and empty stack remotely extended by kp to the originating machine stack.

Additionally, some of the original rules now have *send* and *receive* counterparts to handle the situation when remote variables or continuations need to be processed. Remarkably, it is possible to avoid sending messages when popping a remote argument, and we can get by with the following new instruction:

$$\begin{array}{l}
\textbf{POPARG-remote} : \forall \{t\ e\ kp\ args\ m\ ch\} \rightarrow \\
\quad i \vdash (\textbf{just}\ (\boldsymbol{\lambda}\ t, e, [\,], \textbf{just}\ (kp, 1 +\ args, m)), ch) \\
\qquad \longrightarrow_{\mathcal{DK}} \langle \tau \rangle \\
\qquad (\textbf{just}\ (t, \textbf{remote}\ kp\ m :: e, [\,], \textbf{just}\ (kp, args, 1 +\ m)), ch)
\end{array}$$

Note that this is a silent (τ) transition. A machine does not really "pop" the arguments of a remote stack extension but changes its view of this remote stack. This avoids instituting a whole class of messages for stack management and it also gives a more robust stack management framework in which stacks, along with heaps and any other data structures involved, are only changed *locally*.

This rule is triggered when a **POPARG** action encounters a local empty stack, which means that the remote stack extension needs to be used. Just like in the case of a local **POPARG**, the environment is updated, but this time with the remote pointer kp which has its offset set at m. The offset in the view of the remote stack extension is updated (to $1 +\ m$) to reflect the fact that another argument has been "popped".

The rules that need genuine remote counterparts are **VAR**, for accessing remote variables, and **RETURN**, for returning a literal from a remote computation.

$$\begin{array}{l}
\textbf{VAR-send} : \forall \{n\ e\ s\ rkp\ index\ ch\} \rightarrow \\
\quad lookup\ n\ e \equiv \textbf{just}\ (\textbf{remote}\ rkp\ index) \rightarrow \\
\quad \text{let}\ (ch', kp)\ =\ i \vdash ch \rhd s\ \text{in} \\
\quad i \vdash (\textbf{just}\ (\textbf{var}\ n, e, s), ch) \\
\qquad \longrightarrow_{\mathcal{DK}} \langle \textbf{send}\ (\textbf{VAR}\ rkp\ index\ kp\ (\textit{num-args}\ s)) \rangle \\
\qquad (\textbf{nothing}, ch')
\end{array}$$

The rule is triggered when the machine detects a **remote** pointer in its environment e. Just like in the case of the **REMOTE** instruction, the current continuation stack is saved in the continuation heap of the machine i, at address kp. The machine then sends a **VAR**-tagged message onto the network, with the structure discussed before, and halts, i.e. its thread is **nothing**. Note that the left-hand-side of the transition triggered by the **VAR-send** rule is almost the same as that of the local **VAR** rule.

Upon receiving a **VAR** message, a (halted) machine executes the **VAR-receive** instruction:

$$\begin{array}{l}
\textbf{VAR-receive} : \forall \{ch\ kp\ s\ n\ rkp\ m\ el\} \rightarrow \\
\quad ch\ !\ kp \equiv \textbf{just}\ s \rightarrow \\
\quad \textit{stack-index}\ s\ n \equiv \textbf{just}\ el \rightarrow \\
\quad i \vdash (\textbf{nothing}, ch) \\
\qquad \longrightarrow_{\mathcal{DK}} \langle \textbf{receive}\ (\textbf{VAR}\ (kp, i)\ n\ rkp\ m) \rangle \\
\qquad (\textbf{just}\ (\textbf{var}\ 0, el :: [\,], [\,], \textbf{just}\ (rkp, m, 0)), ch)
\end{array}$$

The right-hand-side of the **VAR-receive** rule introduces a new variable **var** *0*, perhaps surprisingly. In order to avoid having special cases where the retrieved variable index is itself either local or remote, we create the dummy variable **var** *0* referring to the variable pointed-to by the received **VAR** message. This is what the $\textit{stack-index} : \textit{Stack} \rightarrow \mathbb{N} \rightarrow \textit{Maybe EnvElem}$ function, invoked on the stack that kp points to, achieves. If the stack element at index n in the stack is a local argument, then it returns that closure as a **local** environment element. If the element at index n refers to an argument on the remote stack extension, it returns a corresponding **remote** environment element. Afterwards we can use the existing local **VAR** or **VAR-send** rules depending on whether the variable is local or remote also to this node.

$$\begin{array}{l}
\textbf{RETURN-send} : \forall \{n\ e\ kp\ m\ ch\} \rightarrow \\
\quad i \vdash (\textbf{just}\ (\textbf{lit}\ n, e, [\,], \textbf{just}\ (kp, 0, m)), ch) \\
\qquad \longrightarrow_{\mathcal{DK}} \langle \textbf{send}\ (\textbf{RETURN}\ kp\ n\ m) \rangle \\
\qquad (\textbf{nothing}, ch) \\
\textbf{RETURN-receive} : \forall \{ch\ kp\ s\ s'\ n\ m\} \rightarrow \\
\quad ch\ !\ kp \equiv \textbf{just}\ s \rightarrow \textit{drop-stack}\ s\ m \equiv \textbf{just}\ s' \rightarrow \\
\quad i \vdash (\textbf{nothing}, ch) \\
\qquad \longrightarrow_{\mathcal{DK}} \langle \textbf{receive}\ (\textbf{RETURN}\ (kp, i)\ n\ m) \rangle \\
\qquad (\textbf{just}\ (\textbf{lit}\ n, [\,], s'), ch)
\end{array}$$

Finally, the **RETURN-send** and **RETURN-receive** rules are triggered when a machine has reached a literal and has a remote stack extension without any arguments, implying that the remote stack is either empty (i.e. it is located at the root node of the whole execution) or it has a continuation requiring a natural number literal. In both cases we want to send the literal back to the node where the stack is located. The one thing to notice is that the message includes the number m to be used by the receiver to drop the correct number of elements from the top of the stack. This is handled by the *drop-stack* function, defined as follows:

$$\begin{array}{lll}
\textit{drop-stack} : \textit{Stack} \rightarrow \mathbb{N} \rightarrow \textit{Maybe Stack} & & \\
\textit{drop-stack}\ (s, r) & 0 & = \textbf{just}\ (s, r) \\
\textit{drop-stack}\ ([\,], \textbf{just}\ (_, 0, _))\ (1 +\ _) & & = \textbf{nothing} \\
\textit{drop-stack}\ ([\,], \textbf{just}\ (kp, 1 +\ n, m))\ (1 +\ i) & & = \\
\quad \textit{drop-stack}\ ([\,], \textbf{just}\ (kp, n, 1 +\ m))\ i & & \\
\textit{drop-stack}\ ([\,], \textbf{nothing}) & (1 +\ _) & = \textbf{nothing} \\
\textit{drop-stack}\ (\textbf{arg}\ _ :: s, r) & (1 +\ i) & = \textit{drop-stack}\ (s, r)\ i \\
\textit{drop-stack}\ (_ :: _, _) & (1 +\ _) & = \textbf{nothing}
\end{array}$$

As in the case of *num-args* the function may change the local view of a remote stack extension, without requiring further message exchanges between nodes. If not enough arguments are on the stack the function returns **nothing**, which should not happen during a normal execution since we take care to keep the stack views consistent.

3.2 The network

We consider two kinds of networks, either based on synchronous message passing (blocking send) or asynchronous message passing (non-blocking send). The two definitions are:

$$\begin{array}{lll}
\mathcal{S}\mathcal{N}et & = & \textit{Node} \rightarrow \textit{Machine} \\
\mathcal{A}s\mathcal{N}et & = & (\textit{Node} \rightarrow \textit{Machine}) \times \textit{List Msg}
\end{array}$$

The way we model the asynchronous network is inspired by the Chemical Abstract Machine (CHAM) [3]. The network is, in addition to a family of machines indexed by *Node* identifiers, a global multiset of messages *List Msg* in which sent messages

```
data _⟶S_ (nodes : SNet) : SNet → ⋆ where
  silent-step : ∀ {i m'} → (i ⊢ nodes i ⟶ ⟨τ⟩ m') → nodes ⟶S update nodes i m'

  comm-step : ∀ {s r msg sender' receiver'} →
    let nodes' = update nodes s sender' in
    (s ⊢ nodes s ⟶ ⟨send msg⟩ sender') → (r ⊢ nodes' r ⟶ ⟨receive msg⟩ receiver') → nodes ⟶S update nodes' r receiver'

data _⟶As_ : AsNet → AsNet → ⋆ where
  step : ∀ {nodes} msgsl msgsr {tmsg m' i} →
    let (msgin, msgout) = detag tmsg in
    (i ⊢ nodes i ⟶ ⟨tmsg⟩ m') → (nodes, msgsl ++ msgin ++ msgsr) ⟶As (update nodes i m', msgsl ++ msgout ++ msgsr)
```

Figure 1. Network transitions

are placed, and from which received messages are retrieved. The formal definitions are given in Fig. 1.

In the *SNet* messages are passed directly between machines. Network transitions are either a **silent-step** when a node makes a τ transition, or **comm-step** when two nodes exchange information. The *AsNet* only has a generic **step**, because no synchronisation is needed. A machine on a node may take a τ step or a communication step, case in which a message is placed or removed from the global set of messages. The function *detag* figures out what messages a node is sending and receiving, allowing one rule for all three cases, as at most one of *msgin* and *msgout* in the rule is non-empty:

```
detag : {A : ⋆} → Tagged A → List A × List A
detag τ           = [] , []
detag (send x)    = [] , [x]
detag (receive x) = [x], []
```

Another helper function used in the definitions is *update*, which updates the state of a node in the network. It is the usual function update, commonly written as $(f \mid x \mapsto y)$, here relying on the assumption that the set of node identifiers has decidable equality ($\_\stackrel{?}{=}\_$). It is formally defined as:

```
update : {A : ⋆} → (Node → A) → Node → A → Node → A
update nodes n m n' with n' ≟ n
update nodes n m n'    | yes _ = m
update nodes n m n'    | no _  = nodes n'
```

In AGDA, the with keyword introduces patterns additional to the arguments in a function definition.

The definition of network transitions is parameterised by a machine transition relation $\_ \vdash \_ \longrightarrow \langle\_\rangle \_$, which is subsequently instantiated to $\longrightarrow_{\mathcal{DK}}$, and initialised by starting from a designated node *i* with code *t* and all other constituents empty.

```
open import Network Node _≟_ _⊢⟶DK ⟨_⟩_ public
initial-networkS : Term → Node → SNet
initial-networkS t i =
  update (λ i' → (nothing, ∅)) i (just (t, [], [], nothing), ∅)
initial-networkAs : Term → Node → AsNet
initial-networkAs c i = initial-networkS c i, []
```

It is immediate to show that a *SNet* can be represented by the more expressive *AsNet*. This is the function mapping a *Sync* transition to an *Async* one by placing, then removing, the message in the global message pool (here $\_^{+}$ takes the transitive closure of a relation, constructed with list-like notation):

```
Sync-to-Async⁺ : ∀ {a b} → (a     ⟶S b) →
                           (a, []) ⟶⁺As (b, [])
Sync-to-Async⁺ (silent-step s)    = [step [] [] s]
Sync-to-Async⁺ (comm-step s₁ s₂)  = step [] [] s₁ :: [step [] [] s₂]
```

The other direction is not as trivial, and is formalised by the following lemma, stating that whenever some DKrivine machines can make an *Async* transition with the global pool of messages remaining the same (empty, for simplicity), the same transition could be made in a *SNet*:

```
Async⁺-to-Sync⁺ : ∀ {nodes nodes'} i →
                  all nodes except i are inactive →
                  ((nodes, []) ⟶⁺As (nodes', [])) →
                  nodes        ⟶⁺S  nodes'
Async⁺-to-Sync⁺ = Async⁺-to-Sync⁺-lemma refl refl
```

The proof is an immediate application of a more complex lemma which is omitted from this presentation. In contrast to the *Sync-to-Async*$^{+}$ embedding, this embedding is specific to DKrivine machines. More precisely, two properties of these machines make this possible: The first one is that the DKrivine machines halt after each message **send** and **receive** only from halting states. The second one is that they are deterministic. Intuitively, it is fairly clear that the two styles of communication are equivalent under these circumstances.

These two results about Krivine Nets are interesting because they show that we do not need to commit to a synchronous or asynchronous network of DKrivine machines since they are equivalent. We may therefore use whichever is more convenient for correctness proofs in the knowledge that the properties we prove transfer immediately to the other one.

3.3 Example

Let us compare briefly the execution of a rather simple term,

$$((\lambda f.\lambda x.f\ x)@B)(\lambda y.y)\ 0$$

on a single machine and on a distributed machine. The program is located on (the default) node *A*, except for $\lambda f.\lambda x.f\ x$ which is on node *B*. This program is similar to our introductory example in that it does a remote function call, and additionally shows that higher-order remote function calls are also possible.

As we discussed earlier, the Krivine machine ignores the @ construct (the **REMOTE** rule is a no-op), producing the execution trace **PUSHARG**; **PUSHARG**; **REMOTE**; **POPARG**; **POPARG**; **PUSHARG**; **VAR**; **POPARG**; **VAR**; **VAR**, which leaves the machine in state (**lit** *0*, [], []).

The Krivine Net of two nodes produces the following trace (informally, indicating machine state only when interesting). Node *A* starts with **PUSHARG**; **PUSHARG**; **REMOTE-send**, which produces message

REMOTE (**λ** (**λ** (**var** *1* **$** **var** *0*))) *B* (ptr_1, A) *2*

where ptr_1 points to the stack ([(**λ var** *0*, []), (*0*, [])], **nothing**).

Node *B* receives the message and executes **REMOTE-receive**; **POPARG-remote**; **POPARG-remote**; **PUSHARG**; **VAR-send**, which produces message **VAR** (ptr_1, A) *0* (ptr_2, B) *1*, where ptr_2 points to the stack

[(**var** *0*, [**remote** (ptr_1, A) *1*, **remote** (ptr_1, A) *0*])], **just** $((ptr_1, A), 0, 2)$

Note that the two traces are essentially the same, except for the **REMOTE** rule becoming meaningful. As we explained before, the **POPARG-remote** rule only changes the local view of the remote stack extension and generates no communication overhead. Also note that the stack at ptr_2 extends remotely to the stack at ptr_1 and uses it in its own stored closures.

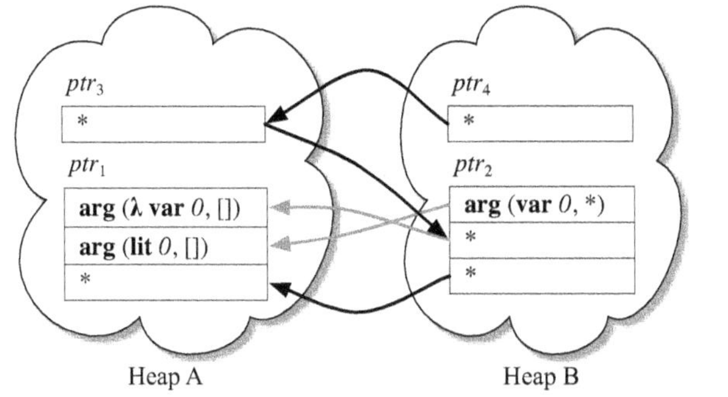

Figure 2. Final heap

The rest of the dialogue is as follows:

Node A : **VAR-receive**; **VAR**; **POPARG-remote**; **VAR-send**
Node B : **VAR-receive**; **VAR**; **VAR-send**
Node A : **VAR-receive**; **VAR**; **RETURN-send**
Node B : **RETURN-receive**; **RETURN-send**
Node A : **RETURN-receive**; **RETURN-send**
Node B : **RETURN-receive**; **RETURN-send**
Node A : **RETURN-receive**

Compared to the Krivine trace, the **VAR** instructions is here broken into a **send** and **receive** version if the requested variable is remote. There is also the additional **VAR** rule needed to avoid a case statement on whether a variable is local or remote. The **RETURN** instructions are new, required to forward computed values to the caller.

After the execution, the heaps of the two nodes are:

$$
\begin{aligned}
A \ :\ & \{ptr_1 \mapsto ([\mathbf{arg}\ (\lambda\ \mathbf{var}\ 0, []); \mathbf{arg}\ (\mathbf{lit}\ 0, [])], \mathbf{nothing}),\\
& \ ptr_3 \mapsto ([], \mathbf{just}\ ((ptr_2, B), 0, 1))\}\\
B \ :\ & \{ptr_2 \mapsto ([\mathbf{arg}\ (\mathbf{var}\ 0, [\mathbf{remote}\ (ptr_1, A)\ 1; \mathbf{remote}\ (ptr_1, A)\ 0])],\\
& \qquad \mathbf{just}\ ((ptr_1, A), 0, 2)),\\
& \ ptr_4 \mapsto ([], \mathbf{just}\ ((ptr_3, A), 0, 0))\}
\end{aligned}
$$

A graphical representation of the final heap is in Fig. 2, with stack extension pointers in black and remote variables in grey.

Unlike the Krivine machine, the Krivine Nets will result in non-empty heaps (*garbage*) in the individual DKrivine machines. We will discuss how to deal with this in the conclusion.

4. Correctness

We prove the correctness of the DKrivine Net by exhibiting a simulation between the conventional Krivine machine and a Krivine Net. The simulation is then used to prove the following *Soundness theorems*:

$$
\begin{aligned}
\textit{termination-agrees}_{\mathcal{S}} \ :\ & \forall\ \textit{cfg nodes}\ n \to R_{\mathcal{S}}\ \textit{cfg nodes} \to\\
& \textit{cfg} \downarrow_{\mathcal{K}} \mathbf{lit}\ n \to \textit{nodes} \downarrow_{\mathcal{S}} \mathbf{lit}\ n\\
\textit{divergence-agrees}_{\mathcal{S}} \ :\ & \forall\ \textit{cfg nodes} \to R_{\mathcal{S}}\ \textit{cfg nodes} \to\\
& \textit{cfg} \uparrow_{\mathcal{K}} \to \textit{nodes} \uparrow_{\mathcal{S}}
\end{aligned}
$$

The termination theorem states that for any Krivine machine configuration *cfg* and any Krivine Net configuration *nodes*, if we have a *simulation relation* $R_{\mathcal{S}}$ between them then for any literal *n*, if the Krivine machine starting from *cfg* produces the literal *n*, then the Krivine Net starting from configuration *nodes* produces the same. Note that we are using *Sync* nets, because they are more convenient and because *Async* nets can be reduced to *Sync* nets in the case of Krivine Nets, as discussed in Sec. 3.2. The divergence theorem makes a similar point about non-termination: from related states, if the Krivine machine diverges then the Krivine Net diverges.

4.1 The simulation relation

The most important ingredient of the correctness proof is defining and exhibiting the appropriate simulation relation. At the top level, the relation between the Krivine machine and Krivine Nets configurations is defined formally as follows:

$$
\begin{aligned}
& R_{\mathcal{S}}\ :\ \textit{Rel Config SNet}\\
& R_{\mathcal{S}}\ \textit{cfg nodes}\ =\ \exists\ \lambda\ i \to\\
& \quad \textit{all nodes except i are inactive} \times\\
& \quad R_{\textit{Machine}}\ (\textit{proj}_2 \circ \textit{nodes})\ \textit{cfg}\ (\textit{proj}_1\ (\textit{nodes}\ i))
\end{aligned}
$$

In AGDA notation the existential statement $\exists i.P(i)$ is written $\exists\ \lambda\ i \to P\ i$. The predicate *all_except_are_* is defined as

$$
\textit{all f except x are P}\ =\ \forall\ x' \to x' \not\equiv x \to P\ (f\ x')
$$

and *inactive node* holds when the thread of *node* is **nothing**. A simulation between machine and net configurations exists only when precisely one node *i* is active in the net. The machine at that node ($\textit{proj}_1$ $(\textit{nodes}\ i)$) must be related to the configuration of the Krivine machine through the following machine-simulation relation:

$$
\begin{aligned}
& R_{\textit{Machine}}\ :\ \textit{Heaps} \to \textit{Rel Config (Maybe Thread)}\\
& R_{\textit{Machine}}\ \textit{hs}\ (t_1, e_1, s_1)\ (\mathbf{just}\ (t_2, e_2, s_2))\ =\\
& \quad R_{\textit{Term}}\ t_1\ t_2 \times R_{\textit{Env}}\ \textit{hs}\ e_1\ e_2 \times (\exists\ \lambda\ \textit{rank} \to R_{\textit{Stack}}\ \textit{rank hs}\ s_1\ s_2)\\
& R_{\textit{Machine}}\ \textit{hs}\ (t_1, e_1, s_1)\ \mathbf{nothing}\ =\ \bot
\end{aligned}
$$

The relation is indexed by the distributed heap of the Krivine Net *hs* : *Heaps*, which is the *Node*-indexed family of all the individual heaps. This relation $R_{\textit{Machine}}$ simply distributes the relation further to terms using $R_{\textit{Term}}$, environments using $R_{\textit{Env}}$ and stacks using $R_{\textit{Stack}}$. In order for this to be possible it is required that the DKrivine machine is not halted (**nothing** : *Maybe Thread*).

On terms, the relation $R_{\textit{Term}}$ is just propositional equality, while $R_{\textit{Env}}$ and $R_{\textit{Stack}}$ are more subtle and require a non-trivial proof technique. $R_{\textit{Stack}}$ is similar to a *step-indexed* relation [2] on stacks. It is defined by induction on a natural number *rank* in order to ensure that the cascading remote stack extensions do not have any cycles. Unlike a step-indexed relation, *rank* means that we do exactly *rank* remote-pointer dereferencings in the process of relating two stacks, and $R_{\textit{Stack}}$ requires that this number is known. $R_{\textit{EnvElem}}$, used by $R_{\textit{Env}}$ to relate environment elements, is defined by induction on a *rank* for the same reason.

4.1.1 Relating environments

On environments, the formal definition of the relation is:

$$
\begin{aligned}
& R_{\textit{Env}}\ :\ \textit{Heaps} \to \textit{Rel Krivine.Env DKrivine.Env}\\
& R_{\textit{Env}}\ \textit{hs}\ []\ \qquad\quad []\ \qquad\qquad = \top\\
& R_{\textit{Env}}\ \textit{hs}\ []\ \qquad\quad (x_2 :: e_2)\ = \bot\\
& R_{\textit{Env}}\ \textit{hs}\ (x_1 :: e_1)\ []\ \qquad\quad = \bot\\
& R_{\textit{Env}}\ \textit{hs}\ (x_1 :: e_1)\ (x_2 :: e_2)\ =\\
& \quad (\exists\ \lambda\ \textit{rank} \to R_{\textit{EnvElem}}\ \textit{rank hs}\ x_1\ x_2) \times R_{\textit{Env}}\ \textit{hs}\ e_1\ e_2
\end{aligned}
$$

Empty environments are trivially related, but environments of different shapes cannot be related. If both environments are non-empty then the definition is inductive on the structure of the environment. Environment elements are related by requiring that there exists a *rank* such that they are related by $R_{\textit{EnvElem}}$:

$$
\begin{aligned}
& R_{\textit{EnvElem}}\ :\ \mathbb{N} \to \textit{Heaps} \to \textit{Rel Krivine.EnvElem DKrivine.EnvElem}\\
& R_{\textit{EnvElem}}\ 0 \qquad\qquad\ \textit{hs}\ (\mathbf{clos}\ c_1)\ (\mathbf{local}\ c_2)\ =\ R_{\textit{Closure}}\ \textit{hs}\ c_1\ c_2\\
& R_{\textit{EnvElem}}\ (1 +\ \textit{rank})\ \textit{hs}\ (\mathbf{clos}\ c_1)\ (\mathbf{local}\ c_2)\ =\ \bot\\
& R_{\textit{EnvElem}}\ 0 \qquad\qquad\ \textit{hs}\ (\mathbf{clos}\ c_1)\ (\mathbf{remote}\ \textit{contptr index})\ =\ \bot\\
& R_{\textit{EnvElem}}\ (1 +\ \textit{rank})\ \textit{hs}\ (\mathbf{clos}\ c_1)\ (\mathbf{remote}\ \textit{contptr index})\ =\\
& \quad \textit{stack-ext-pred hs contptr}\\
& \qquad (\lambda\ s_2 \to \exists\ \lambda\ \textit{ee}_2 \to \textit{stack-index}\ s_2\ \textit{index} \equiv \mathbf{just}\ \textit{ee}_2\\
& \qquad\qquad \times R_{\textit{EnvElem}}\ \textit{rank hs}\ (\mathbf{clos}\ c_1)\ \textit{ee}_2)
\end{aligned}
$$

Local closures of the DKrivine machine relate to closures of the Krivine machine ($R_{\textit{Closure}}$) if their terms are equal and their environments are related through $R_{\textit{Env}}$. Relating remote closures (**remote** *contptr index*) of the DKrivine machine to the closures of the Krivine machine (**clos** c_1) is perhaps the most subtle part of the definition. It uses the following helper function which ensures that, given a distributed heap *hs* : *Heaps*, a remote pointer (*ptr*, *loc*) : *ContPtr* and a predicate on distributed stacks *DKrivine.Stack* → ⋆, the pointer points to a stack in the heap of node *loc* such that the predicate holds:

```
stack-ext-pred : Heaps → ContPtr → (DKrivine.Stack → ⋆) → ⋆
stack-ext-pred hs (ptr, loc) P = ∃ λ s → hs loc ! ptr ≡ just s × P s
```

The pointer dereferencing operation is *hs loc* ! *ptr*. The predicate which we use in the definition of $R_{EnvElem}$ is that there exists an element ee_2 in the environment of the DKrivine machine such that it $R_{EnvElem}$ relates to the Krivine closure **clos** c_1 in one less step.

Note that the *rank* has to be *0* to relate local elements, and it has to be 1 + *rank* to relate a remote element. The recursive call is done with the predecessor *rank*, which makes sure that there are exactly *rank* pointers to follow to reach a local closure if we have an element of $R_{EnvElem}$ *rank hs* x_1 x_2.

4.1.2 Relating stacks

Relating stacks is somewhat similar.

```
R_Stack : ℕ → Heaps → Rel Krivine.Stack DKrivine.Stack
R_Stack rank     hs (x₁ :: s₁) ([], nothing) = ⊥
R_Stack rank     hs []         (x₂ :: s₂, r) = ⊥
R_Stack 0        hs []         ([], nothing) = ⊤
R_Stack (1+ rank) hs []        ([], nothing) = ⊥
R_Stack rank     hs (x₁ :: s₁) (x₂ :: s₂, r) =
  R_StackElem hs x₁ x₂ × R_Stack rank hs s₁ (s₂, r)
R_Stack 0        hs s₁ ([], just (contptr, args, drop)) = ⊥
R_Stack (1+ rank) hs s₁ ([], just (contptr, args, drop)) =
  stack-ext-pred hs contptr (λ s₂ →
    ∃ λ ds₂ → drop-stack s₂ drop ≡ just ds₂
        × num-args ds₂ ≡ args × R_Stack rank hs s₁ ds₂)
```

Empty stacks, with no remote extensions, are related if the *rank* is 0, whereas empty and non-empty are not. Two non-empty stacks are related if the elements on top are related by $R_{EnvElem}$ and the remaining stacks are related. The relation is interesting when remote pointer extensions are involved. If there is a remote stack extension but the step index is 0 then it cannot be related to a Krivine stack. If there is a non-zero step index then, using the same helper function *stack-ext-pred*, we require that the sub-stack ds_2 of s_2 obtained by dropping the *drop* arguments required by the remote stack extension pointer **just** (*contptr*, *args*, *drop*) is related to the Krivine stack s_1 using a smaller (by one) index.

Finally, stack elements are related if they have the same head constructor, and the constituents are related:

```
R_StackElem : Heaps → Rel Krivine.StackElem DKrivine.StackElem
R_StackElem hs (arg c₁)     (arg c₂)     = R_Closure hs c₁ c₂
R_StackElem hs (if0 c₁ c₁') (if0 c₂ c₂') = R_Closure hs c₁ c₂ ×
                                           R_Closure hs c₁' c₂'
R_StackElem hs (op₂ f c₁)   (op₂ g c₂)   = f ≡ g ×
                                           R_Closure hs c₁ c₂
R_StackElem hs (op₁ f)      (op₁ g)      = f ≡ g
R_StackElem hs _            _            = ⊥
```

4.2 Proof outline

In order to prove the main property we need to first establish the monotonicity of all the heap-indexed relations relative to heap inclusion: if two configurations, machines, environments, environment elements or stacks are related in a family of heaps *hs* they are also related in any larger family of heaps *hs* $\subseteq_s$ *hs'*. The properties are proved in a module parameterised by the heap inclusion property, and therefore it does not need to be included in each statement – it is a background assumption:

```
module HeapUpdate (hs hs' : Heaps) (inc : hs ⊆ₛ hs') where
  envelem   : ∀ rank el el' → R_EnvElem rank hs el el'
                            → R_EnvElem rank hs' el el'
  env       : ∀ e e' → R_Env hs e e' → R_Env hs' e e'
  stackelem : ∀ el el' → R_StackElem hs el el'
                       → R_StackElem hs' el el'
  stack     : ∀ rank s s' → R_Stack rank hs s s'
                          → R_Stack rank hs' s s'
  machine   : ∀ cfg m → R_Machine hs cfg m
                      → R_Machine hs' cfg m
```

The proofs are largely straightforward, inductively on the structure of the data structure the lemma is concerned with. The key auxiliary property that makes monotonicity of the relations true is the fact that any predicate which relies on heap dereferencing is preserved:

```
s-ext-pred : ∀ contptr {P Q} → (∀ s → P s → Q s) →
  stack-ext-pred hs contptr P → stack-ext-pred hs' contptr Q
```

For example, for environments, environment elements and closures the proofs are mutually recursive, inductive on their structures:

```
closure : ∀ c c' → R_Closure hs c c' → R_Closure hs' c c'
envelem : ∀ rank el el' → R_EnvElem rank hs el el'
  → R_EnvElem rank hs' el el'
envelem 0        (clos c) (local c') Rcc' = closure c c' Rcc'
envelem (1+ rank) (clos c) (local c') Rcc' = Rcc'
envelem 0        (clos c) (remote contptr index) Relel' = Relel'
envelem (1+ rank) (clos c) (remote contptr index) Relel' =
  s-ext-pred contptr f Relel'
  where
    f : ∀ s →
      (∃ λ ee' → stack-index s index ≡ just ee'
        × R_EnvElem rank hs (clos c) ee') →
        ∃ λ ee' → stack-index s index ≡ just ee'
        × R_EnvElem rank hs' (clos c) ee'
    f s (ee', si, Rcee') = ee', si, envelem rank (clos c) ee' Rcee'
env : ∀ e e' → R_Env hs e e' → R_Env hs' e e'
env []       []        Ree'              = Ree'
env []       (x :: e') Ree'              = Ree'
env (x :: e) []        Ree'              = Ree'
env (x :: e) (x' :: e') ((rank, Rxx'), Ree') =
  (rank, envelem rank x x' Rxx'), env e e' Ree'
closure (t, e) (t', e') (Rtt', Ree') = Rtt', env e e' Ree'
```

The soundness theorem *termination-agrees*$_{\mathcal{S}}$ stated at the beginning of this section follows directly from two important lemmas, *simulation*$_{\mathcal{S}}$ and *termination-return*. The former is the main technical result of the paper (soundness is merely a corollary of it) and the latter is used to handle the only non-trivial case of the soundness proof, that of cascading **RETURN** statements at the end of an execution.

The theorem

$$simulation_{\mathcal{S}} : Simulation\ \_ \longrightarrow_{\mathcal{K}} \_\ \_ \longrightarrow^{+}_{\mathcal{S}} \_\ R_{\mathcal{S}}$$

states that $R_{\mathcal{S}}$, discussed in the previous sub-section, is a *Simulation* relation between the $\longrightarrow_{\mathcal{K}}$ and $\longrightarrow^{+}_{\mathcal{S}}$ transition relations. The simulation relation is defined in the standard way, where $\longrightarrow$ and $\longrightarrow'$ are transition relations:

```
Simulation : (_R_ : Rel A B) → ⋆
Simulation _R_ = ∀ a a' b → (a ⟶ a') → a R b →
                 ∃ λ b' → (b ⟶' b') × a' R b'
```

The proof of *simulation*$_{\mathcal{S}}$ is lengthy but largely routine. The non-trivial cases are:

- **RETURN** actions of the DKrivine machines, which are handled by the lemma *simulation-return*:

$$
\begin{array}{l}
\textit{simulation-return} : \forall\ n\ e\ s\ cfg'\ e'\ s'\ i\ nodes\ srank\ conth \to \\
\quad \text{let}\ cfg = (\mathbf{lit}\ n, e, s) \\
\qquad\quad hs = proj_2 \circ nodes \\
\quad \text{in}\ cfg \longrightarrow_{\mathcal{K}} cfg' \to \\
\qquad all\ nodes\ except\ i\ are\ inactive \to \\
\qquad nodes\ i \equiv \mathbf{just}\ (\mathbf{lit}\ n, e', s'), conth \to \\
\qquad R_{Stack}\ srank\ hs\ s\ s' \to \exists\ \lambda\ nodes' \to \\
\qquad\quad nodes \longrightarrow^{+}_{\mathcal{S}} nodes' \times R_{\mathcal{S}}\ cfg'\ nodes'
\end{array}
$$

- **VAR** remote actions of the DKrivine machine, which are handled by the lemma *simulation-var*:

$$
\begin{array}{l}
\textit{simulation-var} : \forall\ t\ e\ s\ n\ e'\ s'\ nodes\ i\ conth\ el \to \\
\quad \text{let}\ hs = proj_2 \circ nodes\ \text{in} \\
\qquad (\exists\ \lambda\ rank \to R_{EnvElem}\ rank\ hs\ (\mathbf{clos}\ (t, e))\ el) \to \\
\qquad (\exists\ \lambda\ rank \to R_{Stack}\ rank\ hs\ s\ s') \to \\
\qquad all\ nodes\ except\ i\ are\ inactive \to \\
\qquad nodes\ i \equiv \mathbf{just}\ (\mathbf{var}\ n, e', s'), conth \to \\
\qquad lookup\ n\ e' \equiv \mathbf{just}\ el \to \\
\qquad \exists\ \lambda\ nodes' \to (nodes \longrightarrow^{+}_{\mathcal{S}} nodes') \times R_{\mathcal{S}}\ (t, e, s)\ nodes'
\end{array}
$$

What is interesting about these two lemmas, which establish the conditions under which the simulation relation is preserved by transitions related to the integer operations and **VAR** rules, is that it requires a different proof technique, induction on the *rank*. This is because the distributed machine may need to perform a cascade of returns (or variable accesses) between different nodes before it reaches a configuration related to that of the Krivine machine, as we saw in the example in Sec. 3.3.

The *termination-return* lemma mentioned earlier uses a similar proof technique (induction on the *rank*); its full statement is:

$$
\begin{array}{l}
\textit{termination-return} : \forall\ n\ e'\ s'\ i\ nodes\ srank\ conth \to \\
\quad \text{let}\ hs = proj_2 \circ nodes \\
\quad\ \text{in}\ all\ nodes\ except\ i\ are\ inactive \to \\
\qquad nodes\ i \equiv \mathbf{just}\ (\mathbf{lit}\ n, e', s'), conth \to \\
\qquad R_{Stack}\ srank\ hs\ [\,]\ s' \to nodes \downarrow_{\mathcal{S}} \mathbf{lit}\ n
\end{array}
$$

The second part of the soundness proof is the agreement on divergence between the Krivine machine and the Krivine net. This proof relies essentially on the fact that a Krivine Net transition is deterministic whenever only one node is active and that the Krivine machine transition's codomain is decidable in the following sense (proofs are omitted):

$$
\begin{array}{l}
\_is\text{-}deterministic\text{-}at\_ : \{A\ B : \star\}\ (R : Rel\ A\ B)\ (x : A) \to \star \\
\_R\_\ is\text{-}deterministic\text{-}at\ a = \forall\ \{b\ b'\} \to a\ R\ b \to a\ R\ b' \to b \equiv b' \\
determinism_{\mathcal{S}} : \forall\ nodes\ i \to all\ nodes\ except\ i\ are\ inactive \to \\
\quad \_ \longrightarrow_{\mathcal{S}} \_\ is\text{-}deterministic\text{-}at\ nodes \\
\_is\text{-}decidable : \{A\ B : \star\}\ (\_R\_ : Rel\ A\ B) \to \star \\
\_R\_\ is\text{-}decidable = \forall\ a \to Dec\ (\exists\ \lambda\ b \to a\ R\ b) \\
decidable_{\mathcal{K}} : \_ \longrightarrow_{\mathcal{K}} \_\ is\text{-}decidable
\end{array}
$$

To conclude this section, we also need to show that initial configurations are related so that we have a starting point for the simulation. This is easy to prove since the environments and stacks are empty:

$$
\textit{initial-related}_{\mathcal{S}} : \forall\ t\ root \to R_{\mathcal{S}}\ (t, [\,], [\,])\ (\textit{initial-network}_{\mathcal{S}}\ t\ root)
$$

5. Proof of concept implementation

We have implemented a prototype compiler for Krivine Nets [1]. Except for the _@_ directive, compilation to Krivine Nets is implemented by using the same standard compilation scheme used to compile to Krivine machines. It is the runtime system of the DKrivine machine that takes into account whether pointers are local or remote and behaves in the correct way. The _@_ directive is translated directly into a predefined **REMOTE** bytecode instruction, which constructs and sends a **REMOTE** message at runtime. As we said, we avoid sending code by grouping fragments of output code that correspond to the same node, and compiling each group as a separate binary. The fragment of code that corresponds to t inside a subterm t @ A is assigned, at compile-time, a global identifier that an invoking node can use to activate t on node A, meaning that no actual code has to be sent at runtime.

The "bytecode" of the Krivine machine is translated into C functions, and message passing is implemented using MPI. The aim is not efficiency as much as simplicity. The compiler is not certified or extracted from the proofs, so we choose an implementation that is, as much as reasonably possible, "clearly correct."

5.1 Comparison with GOI and GAMC

A principled comparison with the GOI and GAMC compilers, which also follow the methodological principles of seamless compilation, is difficult because it cannot be a precise like-for-like comparison. We summarise the differences between the three implementations below.

Krivine Nets and GOI implement call-by-name PCF, but not in the same way. Krivine Nets implement the type-free language and recursion is dealt with using a Y combinator in the source programming language, which is inefficient. On the other hand, the GOI compiler uses a specialised fixpoint constant but it also requires specialised machinery to handle variable contraction. So there are various contingent sources of inefficiencies which straightforward but laborious optimisations could remove.

The GAMC compiler, on the other hand, implements a much larger language: a typed applied CBN lambda calculus with mutable references and concurrency. It is also tidier than the Krivine Net approach, in that it explicitly deallocates useless memory. These features require a significant amount of overhead, some of which already is present in the DKrivine infrastructure but some of which will need to be subsequently added.

However, there are some features that make the comparison of the three compilers meaningful. The first one is that the programs we use are virtually identical and the fact that they all use CBN means no language-level considerations come into play. The second one is that all three compilers are written as representations of the semantic model of the language, with a similar level of disregard for optimisations against a similar level of concern for "obvious" correctness. The third one is that all three target C and MPI, meaning that benchmarks can be run on the same computer.

With these significant caveats in mind we will attempt a rough performance comparison of the three compilers in several ways. Our benchmarks are small programs operating on integers:

`arith`**:** Computing the sum of applying a complicated integer function to the numbers in the sequence $0, \ldots, 299$.

`fib`**:** Computing the 10th Fibonacci number (using the exponential algorithm) 100 times and taking the sum.

`root`**:** Compute the (integer) root of a polynomial using 20 iterations of the bisection method.

Krivine baseline. We take the classic Krivine machine as a reference point and run the compilers in a degenerate single-node mode. This gives a rough measure of the overall overhead of the compiler before communication costs even come into play. In the case of the GOI compiler the overheads are mainly due to the implementation of contraction, whereas in the case of GAMC they are due to the large amount of heap allocation and deallocation. However, note that the discrepancy would be even greater if we had a fixpoint operator in the Krivine machine instead of relying on the term-level Y combinator.

	arith	fib	root
Baseline	100% (0.34s)	100% (0.094s)	100% (0.009s)
GOI	3,042% (10.3s)	2,832% (2.7s)	20,222% (0.18s)
GAMC	765% (2.6s)	395% (0.53s)	356% (0.032s)
DKrivine	131% (0.44s)	141% (0.13s)	233% (0.021s)

Single node baseline. We measure each compiler using its own single-node performance as a reference point and we split the program in two nodes such that a large communication overhead is introduced. We measure it both in terms of relative execution time and in terms of average and maximum size of the messages, in bytes. Note that the overheads are only due to the processing required by the node to send and receive the nodes and not due to network latencies. In order to factor them out we run all the (virtual) MPI nodes on the same physical computer.

The data is shown in Tab. 1 and we can see that the DKrivine compiler is not only faster for local execution, but also has a comparatively small communication overhead. Each time entry in the table is relative to the same compiler's local execution time, and the absolute time is shown in parentheses. We can see that DKrivine is well ahead of the others in terms of absolute execution time. Both GAMC and DKrivine use messages of a bound size, whereas GOI's messages grow, sometimes significantly, during execution. The high overhead across all three compilers for the `root` benchmark is because it does a relatively small amount of local computations before it needs to communicate. We suspect that the high overhead for GOI and GAMC in many benchmarks is also due to the large amount of "bookkeeping" C code that is required, even for simple terms. The way the C compiler optimiser works plays an important role in the performance gap between single node and distribution. When all the code is on the same node the functions are aggressively inlined because they belong to the same binary output. When the code is distributed this is no longer possible. Also, an analysis of the produced code shows that the C optimiser generally struggles with the code for the distributed nodes, because it does not have a view of the whole program.

6. Previous and related work

Programming languages and libraries for distributed and client-server computing (which can be seen as a particularly simple form of distribution) are a vast area of research. Relevant to us are functional programming languages for distributed execution, and several surveys are available [21, 32].

Functional programming languages for distributed systems take different approaches in terms of process and communication management. Languages such as ERLANG, which are meant for system-level development offer a fairly low-level view of distribution in which both process and communication are managed explicitly; this is the language we used for contrasting effect in the introduction. To tame communication some languages in this category use mechanisms imported from process-calculi, such as PICT [33]. Programming languages do not need to be created from scratch to include improved language support for communication. Session types have been used to extend a variety of languages, including functional languages, with better communication primitives [34] or, alternatively, to provide language-independent frameworks for integrating distributed applications, such as SCRIBBLE [1].

Our approach is, however, quite different. We aim to make communication implicit, or *seamless*. In some sense this is already widely used in programming practice, especially in the context of client-server applications, in the form of *remote procedure calls* (RPC) and related technologies such as *Simple Object Access Protocol* (SOAP). What we aim to do is to integrate these approaches into the programming language so that from a programmer perspective there is no distinction between a remote and local call, even at higher order. Perhaps the closest to our aim is Remote Evaluation (REV) [31], another generalisation of RPC, which enables the use of higher-order functions across node boundaries. The main differences between REV and our work is that REV relies on sending unevaluated code. The REV approach evolved into a variety of *mobile code languages* [7] which add several layers of sophistication to this approach, but have evolved in a direction that is not directly relevant to transparent distribution.

The EDEN project [22], an implementation of parallel HASKELL for distributed systems which keeps most communication implicit, is also close to our aims. Another similarity to our work is that the specification of the language is tiered: an operational semantics at the level of the language and an abstract-machine semantics for execution environment, *the Distributed Eden Abstract Machine* (DREAM) [5]. EDEN is not perfectly seamless: a small set of syntactic constructs are used to manage processes explicitly and communication is always performed using head-strict lazy lists. There are significant technical differences between DREAM and Krivine Nets since the DREAM is a mechanism of distribution for the *Spineless Tagless G-machine* [18] whereas we develop the Krivine machine. Also, in terms of emphasis, EDEN is an implementation-focussed project whereas we want to create a firm theoretical foundation on which compilation to distributed platforms can be carried out. Whereas (as far as we know) no soundness results exist for the DREAM, we provide a fully formalised proof.

Other similar implementation-oriented projects are for *tierless client-server computing* such as LINKS [8], where "tierless" has a similar meaning to our use of "seamless". The execution mechanism that LINKS builds on, the client/server calculus [9], is specialised to systems with two nodes, namely client and server. The two nodes are not equal peers: the server is designed to be *stateless* to be able to handle a large number of clients. The work on the client/server calculus also spawned work on a more general parallel abstract machine, LSAM, that handles an arbitrary number of nodes [26]. A predecessor to LSAM, called DML, uses a similar abstract machine but for a richer language [28]. The main difference between these machines and Krivine Nets is that they are based on higher-level machines for call-by-value lambda calculi, that use explicit substitutions and are therefore less straightforward to use as a basis for compilation. In contrast to our work, they also assume synchronous communication models.

Abstract machines for distributed systems have also been studied. In fact, as early as 1980 a formal proposal for standardising distributed computing using an abstract machine model was put forth, although it did not catch on [30]. The DREAM, DML and the LSAM are, as far as we are aware, the only abstract machines for general distributed systems which, like the DKrivine machine, combine conventional execution mechanisms with communication primitives. Abstract machines for communication only have been proposed [16], inspired by the CHAM (which we also take inspiration from, to model the communication network), but they only deal with half the problem when it comes to compiling conventional languages.

Finally, we mention the compilation of conventional programming languages to (possibly) distributed architectures via process calculi, such as PICT [33], which also uses an abstract machine with communication primitives. We have studied techniques based on interaction semantics in prior work, using the Geometry of Interaction [13] or Game Semantics [14]. Although such more exotic approaches can be effective at creating correct and transparent distribution, it seems to be the case that the single-node execution model is bound to be less efficient than that of conventional abstract machines. Without over-emphasising efficiency at this early stage,

[1] `https://www.jboss.org/scribble`

	arith			fib			root		
	time	avg. size	max. size	time	avg. size	max. size	time	avg. size	max size
GOI	114% (11.6s)	107	172	4,017% (3.8s)	302	444	19,422% (1.7s)	717	1,312
GAMC	193% (5.0s)	20	24	1,481% (7.8s)	20	24	22,872% (7.3s)	20	24
DKrivine	140% (0.62s)	32	40	238% (0.32s)	32	40	890% (0.19s)	32	40

Table 1. Benchmarks for distribution overheads

it is also the case that interfacing code compiled using conventional techniques with code compiled using exotic techniques is difficult and leads to problems with interoperability via foreign-function interfaces. To us this is a significant short-coming which the current work seeks to avoid.

7. Conclusion

In this paper we have presented a method of distributing the execution of the Krivine machine into what we call a Krivine Net. This gives us a principled compilation model of the applied CBN lambda calculus to an abstract distributed architecture. Our main results are a rigorous, fully formalised, proof of correctness of the Krivine Net by comparing it to the conventional Krivine machine, and a proof-of-concept compiler which allows us to compare this compilation scheme with alternative methods based on other abstract machines and more exotic semantics such as Geometry of Interaction and Games. Compared to the more implementation-oriented prior work on transparent (or tierless or seamless) compilation to distributed or client-server architectures, our emphasis is on correctness. We believe that our main contribution is a theoretical firm starting point for the principled study of compilation targetting such architectures.

A broader question worth asking is whether this transparent and integrated approach to distributed computing is *practical*. There are two main possible objections:

Performance Some might say that higher-level languages have poorer performance than system-oriented programming language, which makes them impractical. This debate started when Backus proposed FORTRAN as a machine-independent programming language, and has carried on fruitlessly ever since. We believe that the full spectrum of languages, from machine code to the most abstract, are worth investigating seriously. Seamless computing focusses on the latter, somewhat in the extreme, in the belief that the principled study of heterogeneous (not just distributed, but also reconfigurable etc.) compilation techniques will broaden and deepen our understanding of programming languages in general. And, if we are lucky and diligent, it may even yield a practical and very useful programming paradigm.

Control Distributed computing raises certain specific obstacles in the way of using higher-level languages seamlessly, and this leads to more cogent arguments against their use. A distributed architecture is more volatile than a single node because individual nodes may fail, communication links may break and messages may get lost. Because of this, a remote call may fail in ways that a local call may not. Is it reasonable to present them to the programmer as if they are the same thing? We argue that there is a significant class of applications where the answer is *yes*. If the programmer's objectives are algorithmic rather than the development of systems, it does not seem right to burden them with the often onerous task of failure management in a distributed system. Another argument against higher-level languages is that they may hide the details of the program's dataflow and not provide enough control to eliminate bottlenecks. To us it seems that the right way to manage both failure and dataflow issues in distributed *algorithmic* programming requires a separation of concerns. Suitable runtime systems must present a more robust programming interface; MAPREDUCE [10] and CIEL [25] are examples of execution engines with runtime systems that automatically handle configuration and failure management aspects, the latter supporting dynamic dataflow dependencies. If more fine-grained control is required, then separate deployment and configuration policies which are transparent to the programmer should be employed. In general, we believe that the role and the scope of orchestration languages [6] should be greatly expanded to this end.

7.1 Further work

In this paper we largely ignored the finer issues of efficiency. Our aim was to support *in-principle* efficient single-node compilation, which happens when the DKrivine machine executes trivially on a single node as a Krivine machine, and to reduce the communication overhead by sending only small (bounded-size) messages which are necessary. For example, our use of *views* of remote stack extensions avoids the need to send *pop* messages. In the future we would like to examine the possibility of *efficient* compilation on a hunch that this could be a practical programming paradigm for distributed computing. In order to do this several immediate efficiency issues must and can be addressed.

Remote pointers In the RPC literature it is sometimes argued that a shared or virtual address space, which is where our distributed heap of continuation stacks lives, is prohibitively expensive. However, research progress in tagged pointer representation [24] suggests that we can use pointer tags to distinguish between local and remote pointers without even having to dereference them. With such tags we would pay a very low, if any, performance penalty for the local pointers.

Garbage collection The execution of the Krivine Net creates garbage in the machines. Distributed garbage collection can be a serious problem [29], but we have strong reasons to believe that it can be avoided here, because the heap structures that get created are quite simple. Most importantly, there are never circular linked structures, otherwise the relations would not be well founded. This means that a simpler method, reference-counting, can be used [4]. We also know that efficient memory management is possible when compiling CBN functional programming languages to distributed architectures. The GOI compiler is purely stack-based, while the GAMC compiler uses heaps but does explicit deallocations of locations that are no longer needed.

Shortcut forwarding One of the most unpleasant features of the current Krivine Net approach is the excessive forwarding of data, especially on remote **RETURN**. A way to alleviate this issue might be to not create indirections when a node has a stack consisting only of a stack extension at the time of a remote invocation, meaning that the remote node could return directly to the current node's invoker. However, the implementation is complex enough to raise non-trivial issues of correctness and therefore this falls outside the scope of this paper.

We also plan to improve the programming language by adding more expressiveness, such as parallelism, assignable state and algebraic datatypes. Some of these features have been already implemented in a compiler based on game semantics, but we hope they will be more efficient in the current setting. We also aim to enrich the type system to pay more attention to possibly unrealistic patterns of distributions. Type systems such as ML5 [35] can ensure that the interaction between local and remote resource is safe – in our approach all such interactions are *safe*, but some can be extremely inefficient and a type system can issue at least warnings against unreasonable deployments. Finally, another language-level development that could be useful is the principled development of configuration, deployment and, more generally, choreography languages.

Our dream is the eventual development of an end-to-end seamless distributed compiler for a higher-order imperative and parallel functional programming language, along the lines of the COMPCERT project [20]. The formalisation of the correctness of the Krivine Net, relative to the conventional Krivine machine, is the first, but technically the most demanding step.

Acknowledgments

We acknowledge the support of the UK EPSRC and of Microsoft Research. We discussed our project with a large number of people and their feedback was invaluable in steering us in a hopefully reasonable direction: Satnam Singh, Louis Ryan, Pavan Adharapurapu and David Espinosa (Google); Guido van Rossum (Dropbox); Peter Sewell (Cambridge); Simon Peyton-Jones and Nick Benton (Microsoft Research). Lastly, we thank the anonymous reviewers for their insightful comments and criticism.

References

[1] Krivine Nets, proofs and compiler implementation. `https://bitbucket.org/ollef/krivine-nets`. Last accessed: 3 June 2014.

[2] Amal J. Ahmed. Step-indexed syntactic logical relations for recursive and quantified types. In Peter Sestoft, editor, *ESOP*, volume 3924 of *Lecture Notes in Computer Science*, pages 69–83. Springer, 2006.

[3] Gérard Berry and Gérard Boudol. The chemical abstract machine. *Theoretical Computer Science*, 96(1):217 - 248, 1992. Selected Papers of the 2nd Workshop on Concurrency and Compositionality.

[4] D. I. Bevan. Distributed garbage collection using reference counting. In J. W. de Bakker, A. J. Nijman, and Philip C. Treleaven, editors, *PARLE (2)*, volume 259 of *Lecture Notes in Computer Science*, pages 176–187. Springer, 1987.

[5] Silvia Breitinger, Ulrike Klusik, Rita Loogen, Yolanda Ortega-Mallén, and Ricardo Pena. Dream: The distributed eden abstract machine. In Chris Clack, Kevin Hammond, and Antony J. T. Davie, editors, *Implementation of Functional Languages*, volume 1467 of *Lecture Notes in Computer Science*, pages 250–269. Springer, 1997.

[6] Nadia Busi, Roberto Gorrieri, Claudio Guidi, Roberto Lucchi, and Gianluigi Zavattaro. Choreography and orchestration: A synergic approach for system design. In Boualem Benatallah, Fabio Casati, and Paolo Traverso, editors, *ICSOC*, volume 3826 of *Lecture Notes in Computer Science*, pages 228–240. Springer, 2005.

[7] Antonio Carzaniga, Gian Pietro Picco, and Giovanni Vigna. Designing distributed applications with mobile code paradigms. In W. Richards Adrion, Alfonso Fuggetta, Richard N. Taylor, and Anthony I. Wasserman, editors, *ICSE*, pages 22–32. ACM, 1997.

[8] Ezra Cooper, Sam Lindley, Philip Wadler, and Jeremy Yallop. Links: Web programming without tiers. In Frank S. de Boer, Marcello M. Bonsangue, Susanne Graf, and Willem P. de Roever, editors, *FMCO*, volume 4709 of *Lecture Notes in Computer Science*, pages 266–296. Springer, 2006.

[9] Ezra Cooper and Philip Wadler. The RPC calculus. In António Porto and Francisco Javier López-Fraguas, editors, *PPDP*, pages 231–242. ACM, 2009.

[10] Jeffrey Dean and Sanjay Ghemawat. Mapreduce: a flexible data processing tool. *Commun. ACM*, 53(1):72–77, 2010.

[11] Adam Dunkels, Björn Grönvall, and Thiemo Voigt. Contiki - a lightweight and flexible operating system for tiny networked sensors. In *LCN*, pages 455–462. IEEE Computer Society, 2004.

[12] Olle Fredriksson. Distributed call-by-value machines. *CoRR*, abs/1401.5097, 2014.

[13] Olle Fredriksson and Dan R. Ghica. Seamless distributed computing from the geometry of interaction. In Catuscia Palamidessi and Mark Dermot Ryan, editors, *TGC*, volume 8191 of *Lecture Notes in Computer Science*, pages 34–48. Springer, 2012.

[14] Olle Fredriksson and Dan R. Ghica. Abstract machines for game semantics, revisited. In *LICS*, pages 560–569. IEEE Computer Society, 2013.

[15] Dan R. Ghica. Applications of game semantics: From program analysis to hardware synthesis. In *LICS*, pages 17–26. IEEE Computer Society, 2009.

[16] Daniel Hirschkoff, Damien Pous, and Davide Sangiorgi. An efficient abstract machine for safe ambients. *J. Log. Algebr. Program.*, 71(2):114–149, 2007.

[17] Kohei Honda. Session types and distributed computing. In Artur Czumaj, Kurt Mehlhorn, Andrew M. Pitts, and Roger Wattenhofer, editors, *ICALP (2)*, volume 7392 of *Lecture Notes in Computer Science*, page 23. Springer, 2012.

[18] Simon L. Peyton Jones. Implementing lazy functional languages on stock hardware: The spineless tagless g-machine. *J. Funct. Program.*, 2(2):127–202, 1992.

[19] Jean-Louis Krivine. A call-by-name lambda-calculus machine. *Higher-Order and Symbolic Computation*, 20(3):199–207, 2007.

[20] Xavier Leroy. Formal certification of a compiler back-end or: programming a compiler with a proof assistant. In J. Gregory Morrisett and Simon L. Peyton Jones, editors, *POPL*, pages 42–54. ACM, 2006.

[21] Hans-Wolfgang Loidl, Fernando Rubio, Norman Scaife, Kevin Hammond, Susumu Horiguchi, Ulrike Klusik, Rita Loogen, Greg Michaelson, Ricardo Pena, Steffen Priebe, Álvaro J. Rebón Portillo, and Philip W. Trinder. Comparing Parallel Functional Languages: Programming and Performance. *Higher-Order and Symbolic Computation*, 16(3):203–251, 2003.

[22] Rita Loogen, Yolanda Ortega-Mallén, and Ricardo Peña-Marí. Parallel functional programming in eden. *J. Funct. Program.*, 15(3):431–475, 2005.

[23] Ian Mackie. The geometry of interaction machine. In Ron K. Cytron and Peter Lee, editors, *POPL*, pages 198–208. ACM Press, 1995.

[24] Simon Marlow, Alexey Rodriguez Yakushev, and Simon L. Peyton Jones. Faster laziness using dynamic pointer tagging. In Ralf Hinze and Norman Ramsey, editors, *ICFP*, pages 277–288. ACM, 2007.

[25] Derek Gordon Murray, Malte Schwarzkopf, Christopher Smowton, Steven Smith, Anil Madhavapeddy, and Steven Hand. Ciel: A universal execution engine for distributed data-flow computing. In David G. Andersen and Sylvia Ratnasamy, editors, *NSDI*. USENIX Association, 2010.

[26] Kensuke Narita and Shin-ya Nishizaki. A parallel abstract machine for the RPC calculus. In *Informatics Engineering and Information Science*, pages 320–332. Springer, 2011.

[27] Ulf Norell. Dependently typed programming in agda. In Andrew Kennedy and Amal Ahmed, editors, *TLDI*, pages 1–2. ACM, 2009.

[28] Atsushi Ohori and Kazuhiko Kato. Semantics for communication primitives in an polymorphic language. In Mary S. Van Deusen and Bernard Lang, editors, *POPL*, pages 99–112. ACM Press, 1993.

[29] David Plainfossé and Marc Shapiro. A survey of distributed garbage collection techniques. In Henry G. Baker, editor, *IWMM*, volume 986 of *Lecture Notes in Computer Science*, pages 211–249. Springer, 1995.

[30] Sigram Schindler. Standards and protocols: Distributed abstract machine. *Comput. Commun.*, 3(5):208–220, October 1980.

[31] James W. Stamos and David K. Gifford. Remote evaluation. *ACM Trans. Program. Lang. Syst.*, 12(4):537–565, 1990.

[32] Philip W. Trinder, Hans-Wolfgang Loidl, and Robert F. Pointon. Parallel and Distributed Haskells. *J. Funct. Program.*, 12(4&5):469–510, 2002.

[33] David Turner et al. *The polymorphic pi-calculus: Theory and implementation*. PhD thesis, University of Edinburgh. College of Science and Engineering. School of Informatics., 1996.

[34] Vasco Thudichum Vasconcelos, Simon J. Gay, and António Ravara. Type checking a multithreaded functional language with session types. *Theor. Comput. Sci.*, 368(1-2):64–87, 2006.

[35] Tom Murphy VII, Karl Crary, and Robert Harper. Type-safe distributed programming with ML5. In Gilles Barthe and Cédric Fournet, editors, *TGC*, volume 4912 of *Lecture Notes in Computer Science*, pages 108–123. Springer, 2007.

Distilling Abstract Machines

Beniamino Accattoli
Carnegie Mellon University & Università di Bologna
beniamino.accattoli@gmail.com

Pablo Barenbaum
University of Buenos Aires - CONICET
pbarenbaum@dc.uba.ar

Damiano Mazza
CNRS, UMR 7030, LIPN, Université Paris 13, Sorbonne Paris Cité
Damiano.Mazza@lipn.univ-paris13.fr

Abstract

It is well-known that many environment-based abstract machines can be seen as strategies in lambda calculi with explicit substitutions (ES). Recently, graphical syntaxes and linear logic led to the linear substitution calculus (LSC), a new approach to ES that is halfway between small-step calculi and traditional calculi with ES. This paper studies the relationship between the LSC and environment-based abstract machines. While traditional calculi with ES simulate abstract machines, the LSC rather distills them: some transitions are simulated while others vanish, as they map to a notion of structural congruence. The distillation process unveils that abstract machines in fact implement weak linear head reduction, a notion of evaluation having a central role in the theory of linear logic. We show that such a pattern applies uniformly in call-by-name, call-by-value, and call-by-need, catching many machines in the literature. We start by distilling the KAM, the CEK, and a sketch of the ZINC, and then provide simplified versions of the SECD, the lazy KAM, and Sestoft's machine. Along the way we also introduce some new machines with global environments. Moreover, we show that distillation preserves the time complexity of the executions, i.e. the LSC is a complexity-preserving abstraction of abstract machines.

Categories and Subject Descriptors D.1.1 [*Programming Techniques*]: Functional Programming; F.1.1 [*Computation by Abstract Devices*]: Models of Computation; F.3.2 [*Logics and Meaning of Programs*]: Semantics of Programming Languages — Operational Semantics.; F.4.1 [*Mathematical Logic and Formal Languages*]: Mathematical Logic — Lambda Calculus and Related Systems.; I.1.3 [*Symbolic and Algebraic Manipulation*]: Languages and Systems — Evaluation Strategies

Keywords Lambda-calculus, abstract machines, explicit substitutions, linear logic, call-by-need, linear head reduction.

1. Introduction

In the theory of higher-order programming languages, abstract machines and explicit substitutions are two tools used to model the execution of programs on real machines while omitting many details of the actual implementation. Abstract machines can usually be seen as evaluation strategies in calculi of explicit substitutions (see at least [16, 19, 30, 36]), that can in turn be interpreted as cut-elimination strategies in sequent calculi [14].

Another tool providing a fine analysis of higher-order evaluation is linear logic, especially via the new perspectives on cut-elimination provided by *proof nets*, its graphical syntax. Explicit substitutions (ES) have been connected to linear logic by Kesner and co-authors in a sequence of works [26, 32, 33], culminating in the *linear substitution calculus* (LSC), a new formalism with ES behaviorally isomorphic to proof nets (introduced in [6], developed in [1, 3, 4, 7, 10], and bearing similarities with calculi by De Bruijn [25], Nederpelt [42], and Milner [41]). Since linear logic can model all evaluation schemes (call-by-name/value/need) [39], the LSC can express them modularly, by minor variations on rewriting rules and evaluation contexts. In this paper we revisit the relationship between environment-based abstract machines and ES. Traditionally, calculi with ES simulate machines. The LSC, instead, distills them.

A Bird's Eye View. In a simulation, every machine transition is simulated by some steps in the calculus with ES. In a distillation—a concept which we will formally define in the paper—only some of the machine transitions are simulated, while the others are mapped to the structural equivalence of the calculus, a specific trait of the LSC. Such an equivalence has a useful property: it commutes with evaluation, *i.e.* it can be postponed. Thus, the transitions mapped to the structural congruence fade away, without compromising the result of evaluation. Additionally, we show that machine executions and their distilled representation in the LSC have the same asymptotic length, *i.e.* the distillation process preserves the complexity of evaluation. The main point is that the LSC is arguably simpler than abstract machines, and also—as we will show—it can uniformly represent and decompose many different machines in the literature.

Traditional vs Contextual ES. Traditional calculi with ES (see [31] for a survey) implement β-reduction $(\lambda x.t)u \to_\beta t\{x{\leftarrow}u\}$ introducing an annotation (the explicit substitution $[x{\leftarrow}u]$),

$$(\lambda x.t)u \quad \to_{\mathtt{B}} \quad t[x{\leftarrow}u]$$

and percolating it through the term structure,

$$\begin{array}{rcl} (tw)[x{\leftarrow}u] & \to_{@} & t[x{\leftarrow}u]w[x{\leftarrow}u] \\ (\lambda x.t)[y{\leftarrow}u] & \to_{\lambda} & \lambda x.t[y{\leftarrow}u] \end{array} \qquad (1)$$

until they reach variable occurrences on which they finally substitute or get garbage collected,

$$\begin{array}{rcl} x[x{\leftarrow}u] & \to_{\mathtt{var}} & u \\ y[x{\leftarrow}u] & \to_{\neq} & y \end{array}$$

The LSC, instead, is based on a *contextual* view of evaluation and substitution, also known as *substitution at a distance*. The idea is that one can get rid of the rules percolating through the term structure—*i.e.* @ and λ—by introducing contexts C (i.e. terms with

ICFP '14, September 1–6, 2014, Gothenburg, Sweden.

ACM 978-1-4503-2873-9/14/09...$15.00.
http://dx.doi.org/10.1145/2628136.2628154

a hole $\langle\cdot\rangle$) and generalizing the base cases, obtaining just two rules, *linear substitution* (ls) and *garbage collection* (gc):

$$\begin{array}{lll} C\langle x\rangle[x{\leftarrow}u] & \to_{\mathtt{ls}} & C\langle u\rangle[x{\leftarrow}u] \\ t[x{\leftarrow}u] & \to_{\mathtt{gc}} & t \qquad\qquad \text{if } x \notin \mathtt{fv}(t) \end{array}$$

Dually, the rule creating substitutions (B) is generalized to act up to a context of substitutions $[\ldots{\leftarrow}\ldots] := [x_1{\leftarrow}w_1]\ldots[x_k{\leftarrow}w_k]$ obtaining rule dB (B at a distance):

$$(\lambda x.t)[\ldots{\leftarrow}\ldots]u \quad \to_{\mathtt{dB}} \quad t[x{\leftarrow}u][\ldots{\leftarrow}\ldots]$$

Logical Perspective on the LSC. From a sequent calculus point of view, rules @ and λ, corresponding to *commutative* cut-elimination cases, are removed and integrated—via the use of contexts—directly in the definition of the *principal* cases B, var and $\neq$, obtaining the contextual rules dB, ls, and gc. This is analogous, at the level of terms, to the removal of commutative cases provided by proof nets (see [2] for a discussion about commutative cases and proof nets). From a linear logic point of view, $\to_{\mathtt{dB}}$ can be identified with the multiplicative cut-elimination case $\to_{\mathtt{m}}$, while $\to_{\mathtt{ls}}$ and $\to_{\mathtt{gc}}$ correspond to exponential cut-elimination. Actually, garbage collection has a special status, as it can always be postponed. We will then identify exponential cut-elimination $\to_{\mathtt{e}}$ with linear substitution $\to_{\mathtt{ls}}$ alone.

The LSC has a simple meta-theory, and is halfway between traditional calculi with ES—with whom it shares the micro-step dynamics—and λ-calculus—of which it retains most of the simplicity.

Distilling Abstract Machines. Abstract machines implement the traditional approach to ES, by

1. *Weak Evaluation*: forbidding reduction under abstraction (no rule $\to_\lambda$ in (1)),
2. *Evaluation Strategy*: looking for redexes according to some notion of weak evaluation context E,
3. *Context Representation*: using environments e (aka lists of substitutions) and stacks π (lists of terms) to keep track of the current evaluation context.

The LSC factorizes abstract machines. The idea is that one can represent the strategy of a machine by directly plugging the evaluation context in the contextual substitution/exponential rule:

$$E\langle x\rangle[x{\leftarrow}u] \quad \overset{E}{\to}_{\mathtt{e}} \quad E\langle u\rangle[x{\leftarrow}u]$$

factoring out the parts of the machine that just look for the next redex to reduce. By defining $\multimap$ as the closure of $\overset{E}{\to}_{\mathtt{e}}$ and $\to_{\mathtt{m}}$ by evaluation contexts E, one gets a clean representation of the machine strategy.

The mismatch between the two frameworks is in rule $\to_{@}$, that contextually—by nature—cannot be captured. In order to get out of this *cul-de-sac*, the very idea of *simulation* of an abstract machine must be refined. The crucial observation is that the equivalence $\equiv$ induced by $\to_{@} \cup \to_{\mathtt{gc}}$ has the same special status of $\to_{\mathtt{gc}}$, *i.e.* it can be postponed without affecting reduction lengths. More abstractly, $\equiv$ is a *strong bisimulation* with respect to $\multimap$, *i.e.* it verifies (note *one* step to *one* step, and *vice versa*)

$$\begin{array}{ccc} t \multimap r & & t \multimap r \\ \equiv & \Rightarrow \exists q \text{ s.t.} & \equiv \qquad \equiv \\ u & & u \multimap q \end{array}$$

and

$$\begin{array}{ccc} t & & t \multimap r \\ \equiv & \Rightarrow \exists r \text{ s.t.} & \equiv \qquad \equiv \\ u \multimap q & & u \multimap q \end{array}$$

These diagrams allow us to take $\equiv$ as a *structural equivalence* on the language. Indeed, the strong bisimulation property states that the transformation expressed by $\equiv$ is irrelevant with respect to $\multimap$, in particular $\equiv$-equivalent terms have $\multimap$-evaluations of the same length ending in $\equiv$-equivalent terms (and this holds even locally).

Abstract machines then are *distilled*: the logically relevant part of the substitution process is retained by $\multimap$ while both the search of the redex $\to_{@}$ and garbage collection $\to_{\neq}$ are isolated into the equivalence $\equiv$. Essentially, $\multimap$ captures principal cases of cut-elimination while $\equiv$ encapsulate the commutative ones (plus garbage collection, corresponding to principal cut-elimination involving weakenings).

Case Studies. We will analyze along these lines many abstract machines. Some are standard (KAM [34], CEK [28], a sketch of the ZINC [37]), some are new (MAM, MAD), and of others we provide simpler versions (SECD [35], Lazy KAM [19, 24], Sestoft's [44]). The previous explanation is a sketch of the distillation of the KAM, but the approach applies *mutatis mutandis* to all the other machines, encompassing most incarnations of call-by-name, call-by-value, and call-by need evaluation. The main contribution of the paper is indeed a modular *contextual* theory of abstract machines. We start by distilling some standard cases, and then show how the contextual view allows to understand and simplify non-trivial machines as the SECD, the lazy KAM, and Sestoft's abstract machine for call-by-need (deemed SAM). Our analysis enlightens their mechanisms as different and modular encodings of evaluation contexts for the LSC.

Call-by-Need. Along the way, we show that the contextual (or *at a distance*) approach of the LSC naturally leads to simple machines with just one global environment, as the newly introduced MAM (M for Milner). Such a feature is then showed to be a key ingredient of call-by-need machines, by using it to introduce a new and simple call-by-need machine, the MAD (the MAM by-neeD), and then showing how to obtain (simplifications of) the Lazy KAM and the SAM by simple tweaks. Morally, the global environment is a store. The contextual character of the LSC, however, models it naturally, without the need of extending the language with references.

Distillation Preserves Complexity. It is natural to wonder what is lost in the distillation process. What is the asymptotic impact of distilling machine executions into $\multimap$? Does it affect in any way the complexity of evaluation? We will show that *nothing is lost*, as machine executions are only linearly longer than $\multimap$. More precisely, they are *bilinear*, *i.e.* they are linear in 1) the length of $\multimap$, and in 2) the size $|t|$ of the starting term t. In other words, the search of redexes and garbage collection can be safely ignored in quantitative (time) analyses, *i.e.* the LSC and $\multimap$ provide a complexity-preserving abstraction of abstract machines. While in call-by-name and call-by-value such an analysis follows from an easy local property of machine executions, the call-by-need case is subtler, as such a local property does not hold and bilinearity can be established only via a global analysis.

Linear Logic and Weak Linear Head Reduction. Beyond the contextual view, our work also unveils a deep connection between abstract machines and linear logic. The strategies modularly encoding the various machines (generically noted $\multimap$ and parametric in a fixed notion of evaluation contexts) are in fact call-by-name/value/need versions of *weak linear head reduction* (WLHR), a fundamental notion in the theory of linear logic [3, 18, 21, 27, 40]. This insight is originally due to Danos and Regnier, who worked it out for the KAM [20]. Here, we develop it in a simpler and tighter way, modularly lifting it to many other abstract machines.

Call-by-Name. The call-by-name case (catching the KAM and the newly introduced MAM) is in fact special, as our distillation theorem has three immediate corollaries, following from results about WLHR in the literature:

1. *Invariance*: it implies that the length of a KAM/MAM execution is an invariant time cost model (*i.e.* polynomially related to, say, Turing machines, in both directions), given that in [4] the same is shown for WLHR.
2. *Evaluation as Communication*: we implicitly establish a link between the KAM/MAM and the π-calculus, given that the evaluation of a term via WLHR is isomorphic to evaluation via Milner's encoding in the π-calculus [3].
3. *Plotkin's Approach*: our study complements the recent [10], where it is shown that WLHR is a standard strategy of the LSC. The two works together provide the lifting to explicit substitutions of Plotkin's approach of relating a machine (the SECD machine in that case, the KAM/MAM in ours) and a calculus (the call-by-value λ-calculus and the LSC, respectively) via a standardization theorem and a standard strategy [43].

Beyond Abstract Machines. This paper is just an episode—about abstract machines—in a recent feuilleton about complexity analysis of functional languages via linear logic and rewriting theory, starring the LSC. The story continues in [5] and [8]. In [5], the LSC is used to prove that the length of leftmost-outermost β-reduction is an invariant cost-model for λ-calculus (*i.e.* it is a measure polynomially related to evaluation in classic computational models like Turing machines or random access machines), solving a long-standing open problem in the theory of λ-calculus. Instead, [8] studies the asymptotic number of exponential steps (for $\multimap$) in terms of the number of multiplicative steps, in the call-by-name/value/need LSC (that is quadratic for call-by-name and linear for call-by-value/need). Via the results presented here, [8] establishes a polynomial relationship between the exponential and the multiplicative transitions of abstract machines, complementing our work.

Related Work. Beyond the already cited works, Danvy and coauthors have studied abstract machines in a number of works. In some of them, they show how to extract an abstract machine from a functional evaluator via a sequence of transformations (closure conversion, CPS, and defunctionalization) [11, 12, 22]. Such a study is orthogonal in spirit to what we do here. The only point of contact is the *rational deconstruction of the SECD* in [22], that is something that we also do, but in an orthogonal and less accurate way. Another sequence of works studies the relationship between abstract machines and calculi with ES [15, 16, 24], and it is clearly closer to our topic, except that: 1) [15, 16] follow the traditional (rather than the contextual) approach to ES; 2) none of these works deals with complexity analysis nor with linear logic. On the other hand, [16] provides a deeper analysis of Leroy's ZINC machine, as ours does not account for the avoidance of needless closure creations that is a distinct feature of the ZINC, and [24] focuses on the distinction between store-based and storeless call-by-need, a distinction that we address only implicitly (the calculus is storeless, but—as it will be discussed along the paper—it is meant to be implemented with a store). Last, what here we call *commutative transitions* essentially corresponds to what Danvy and Nielsen call *decompose* phase in [23].

The call-by-need calculus we use—that is a contextual reformulation of Maraist, Odersky, and Wadler's calculus [38]—is a novelty of this paper. It is simpler than both Ariola and Felleisen's [13] and Maraist, Odersky, and Wadler's calculi because it does not need any re-association axioms. A similar calculus is used by Danvy and Zerny in [24]. Morally, it is a version with let-bindings (avatars of ES) of Chang and Felleisen's calculus [17]. In [29], Garcia, Lumsdaine and Sabry present a further call-by-need machine, with whom we do not deal with.

Proofs. Some proofs have been omitted for lack of space. They can be found in the longer version [9].

2. Preliminaries on the Linear Substitution Calculus

Terms and Contexts. The language of the *weak linear substitution calculus* (WLSC) is generated by the following grammar:

$$t, u, w, r, q, p \quad ::= \quad x \mid v \mid tu \mid t[x{\leftarrow}u] \qquad\qquad v \quad ::= \lambda x.t$$

The constructor $t[x{\leftarrow}u]$ is called an *explicit substitution* (of u for x in t). The usual (implicit) substitution is instead denoted by $t\{x{\leftarrow}u\}$. Both $\lambda x.t$ and $t[x{\leftarrow}u]$ bind x in t, with the usual notion of α-equivalence. Values, noted v, do not include variables: this is a standard choice in the study of abstract machines, whose impact is analyzed in the companion paper [8].

Contexts are terms with one occurrence of the hole $\langle\cdot\rangle$, an additional constant. We will use many different contexts. The most general ones will be *weak contexts* W (*i.e.* not under abstractions), which are defined by:

$$W, W' \quad ::= \quad \langle\cdot\rangle \mid Wu \mid tW \mid W[x{\leftarrow}u] \mid t[x{\leftarrow}W]$$

The *plugging* $W\langle t\rangle$ (resp. $W\langle W'\rangle$) of a term t (resp. context W') in a context W is defined as $\langle t\rangle := t$ (resp. $\langle W'\rangle := W'$), $(Wt)\langle u\rangle := W\langle u\rangle t$ (resp. $(Wt)\langle W'\rangle := W\langle W'\rangle t$), and so on. The set of free variables of a term t (or context W) is denoted by $\mathtt{fv}(t)$ (resp. $\mathtt{fv}(W)$). Plugging in a context may capture free variables (replacing holes on the left of substitutions). These notions will be silently extended to all the contexts used in the paper.

Rewriting Rules. On the above terms, one may define several variants of the LSC by considering two elementary rewriting rules, *distance-β* ($\mathtt{dB}$) and *linear substitution* ($\mathtt{ls}$), each one coming in two variants, call-by-name and call-by-value (the latter variants being abbreviated by $\mathtt{dBv}$ and $\mathtt{lsv}$), and pairing them in different ways and with respect to different evaluation contexts.

The rewriting rules rely in multiple ways on contexts. We start by defining *substitution contexts*, generated by

$$L \quad ::= \langle\cdot\rangle \mid L[x{\leftarrow}t].$$

A term of the form $L\langle v\rangle$ is an *answer*. Given a family of contexts C, the two variants of the elementary rewriting rules, also called *root rules*, are defined as follows:

$$\begin{array}{rcl} L\langle\lambda x.t\rangle u & \mapsto_{\mathtt{dB}} & L\langle t[x{\leftarrow}u]\rangle \\ L\langle\lambda x.t\rangle L'\langle v\rangle & \mapsto_{\mathtt{dBv}} & L\langle t[x{\leftarrow}L'\langle v\rangle]\rangle \\ C\langle x\rangle[x{\leftarrow}u] & \mapsto_{\mathtt{ls}} & C\langle u\rangle[x{\leftarrow}u] \\ C\langle x\rangle[x{\leftarrow}L\langle v\rangle] & \mapsto_{\mathtt{lsv}} & L\langle C\langle v\rangle[x{\leftarrow}v]\rangle \end{array}$$

In the linear substitution rules, we assume that $x \in \mathtt{fv}(C\langle x\rangle)$, *i.e.*, the context C does not capture the variable x, and we also silently work modulo α-equivalence to avoid variable capture in the rewriting rules. Moreover, we use the notations $\overset{C}{\mapsto}_{\mathtt{ls}}$ and $\overset{C}{\mapsto}_{\mathtt{lsv}}$ to specify the family of contexts used by the rules, with C being the meta-variable ranging over such contexts.

All of the above rules are *at a distance* (or *contextual*) because their definition involves contexts. Distance-β and linear substitution correspond, respectively, to the so-called *multiplicative* and *exponential* rules for cut-elimination in proof nets. The presence of contexts is how locality on proof nets is reflected on terms.

The rewriting rules decompose the usual small-step semantics for λ-calculi, by substituting one occurrence at the time, and only when such an occurrence is in evaluation position. We emphasize this fact saying that we adopt a *micro-step semantics*.

Calculus	Evaluation contexts	$\mapsto_{\mathtt{m}}$	$\mapsto_{\mathtt{e}}$	$\multimap_{\mathtt{m}}$	$\multimap_{\mathtt{e}}$
$\mathtt{Name}$	$H ::= \langle\cdot\rangle \mid Ht \mid H[x{\leftarrow}t]$	$\mapsto_{\mathtt{dB}}$	$\overset{H}{\mapsto}_{\mathtt{ls}}$	$H\langle\mapsto_{\mathtt{dB}}\rangle$	$H\langle\overset{H}{\mapsto}_{\mathtt{ls}}\rangle$
$\mathtt{Value}^{\mathtt{LR}}$	$V ::= \langle\cdot\rangle \mid Vt \mid L\langle v\rangle V \mid V[x{\leftarrow}t]$	$\mapsto_{\mathtt{dBv}}$	$\overset{V}{\mapsto}_{\mathtt{lsv}}$	$V\langle\mapsto_{\mathtt{dB}}\rangle$	$V\langle\overset{V}{\mapsto}_{\mathtt{ls}}\rangle$
$\mathtt{Value}^{\mathtt{RL}}$	$S ::= \langle\cdot\rangle \mid SL\langle v\rangle \mid tS \mid S[x{\leftarrow}t]$	$\mapsto_{\mathtt{dBv}}$	$\overset{S}{\mapsto}_{\mathtt{lsv}}$	$S\langle\mapsto_{\mathtt{dB}}\rangle$	$S\langle\overset{S}{\mapsto}_{\mathtt{ls}}\rangle$
$\mathtt{Need}$	$N ::= \langle\cdot\rangle \mid Nt \mid N[x{\leftarrow}t] \mid N'\langle x\rangle[x{\leftarrow}N]$	$\mapsto_{\mathtt{dB}}$	$\overset{N}{\mapsto}_{\mathtt{lsv}}$	$N\langle\mapsto_{\mathtt{dB}}\rangle$	$N\langle\overset{N}{\mapsto}_{\mathtt{ls}}\rangle$

Table 1. The four linear substitution calculi.

A linear substitution calculus is defined by a choice of root rules, *i.e.*, one of $\mathtt{dB}/\mathtt{dBv}$ and one of $\mathtt{ls}/\mathtt{lsv}$, and a family of *evaluation contexts*. The chosen distance-β (resp. linear substitution) root rule is generically denoted by $\mapsto_{\mathtt{m}}$ (resp. $\mapsto_{\mathtt{e}}$). If E ranges over a fixed notion of evaluation context, the context-closures of the root rules are denoted by $\multimap_{\mathtt{m}} := E\langle\mapsto_{\mathtt{m}}\rangle$ and $\multimap_{\mathtt{e}} := E\langle\mapsto_{\mathtt{e}}\rangle$, where $\mathtt{m}$ (resp. $\mathtt{e}$) stands for *multiplicative* (*exponential*). The rewriting relation defining the calculus is then $\multimap := \multimap_{\mathtt{m}} \cup \multimap_{\mathtt{e}}$.

2.1 Calculi

We consider four calculi, noted $\mathtt{Name}$, $\mathtt{Value}^{\mathtt{LR}}$, $\mathtt{Value}^{\mathtt{RL}}$, and $\mathtt{Need}$, and defined in Tab. 1. They correspond to four standard evaluation strategies for functional languages. We are actually slightly abusing the terminology, because—as we will show—they are *deterministic* calculi and thus should be considered as strategies. Our abuse is motivated by the fact that they are not strategies in the same calculus. The essential property of all these four calculi is that they are deterministic, because they implement a reduction strategy.

Proposition 2.1 (Determinism). *The reduction relations of the four calculi of Tab. 1 are deterministic: in each calculus, if E_1, E_2 are evaluation contexts and if r_1, r_2 are redexes (i.e., terms matching the left hand side of the root rules defining the calculus), $E_1\langle r_1\rangle = E_2\langle r_2\rangle$ implies $E_1 = E_2$ and $r_1 = r_2$, so that there is at most one way to reduce a term, if any.*

Proof. See [9]. □

Call-by-Name (CBN). The evaluation contexts H for $\mathtt{Name}$ (defined in Tab. 1) are called *weak head contexts* and—when paired with micro-step evaluation—implement a strategy known as *weak linear head reduction*. The original presentation of this strategy does not use explicit substitutions [20, 40]. The presentation in use here has already appeared in [3, 10] (see also [1, 4]) as the weak head strategy of the *linear substitution calculus* (which is obtained by considering *all* contexts as evaluation contexts), and it avoids many technicalities of the original one. In particular, its relationship with the KAM is extremely natural, as we will show.

Let us give some examples of evaluation. Let $\delta := \lambda x.(xx)$ and consider the usual diverging term $\Omega := \delta\delta$. In $\mathtt{Name}$ it evaluates—diverging—as follows:

$$\begin{array}{llll} \delta\delta = (\lambda x.(xx))\delta & \multimap_{\mathtt{m}} & (xx)[x{\leftarrow}\delta] & \multimap_{\mathtt{e}} \\ & & (\delta x)[x{\leftarrow}\delta] & \multimap_{\mathtt{m}} \\ & & (yy)[y{\leftarrow}x][x{\leftarrow}\delta] & \multimap_{\mathtt{e}} \\ & & (xy)[y{\leftarrow}x][x{\leftarrow}\delta] & \multimap_{\mathtt{e}} \\ & & (\delta y)[y{\leftarrow}x][x{\leftarrow}\delta] & \multimap_{\mathtt{m}} \\ & & (zz)[z{\leftarrow}y][y{\leftarrow}x][x{\leftarrow}\delta] & \multimap_{\mathtt{e}} \ \ldots \end{array}$$

Observe that according to our definitions both $\lambda x.\Omega$ and $x\Omega$ are $\multimap$-normal for $\mathtt{Name}$, because evaluation does not go under abstractions, nor on the right of a variable (but terms like $x\Omega$ will be forbidden, as we will limit ourselves to closed terms). Now let us show the use of the context L in rule $\multimap_{\mathtt{m}}$. Let $I := \lambda y.y$ and $\tau := (\lambda z.\delta)I$, and consider the following variation over Ω, where rule $\multimap_{\mathtt{m}}$ is applied with $L := \langle\cdot\rangle[z{\leftarrow}I]$:

$$\begin{array}{llll} \tau\tau = ((\lambda z.\delta)I)\tau & \multimap_{\mathtt{m}} & \delta[z{\leftarrow}I]\tau & = \\ & & (\lambda x.(xx))[z{\leftarrow}I]\tau & \multimap_{\mathtt{m}} \\ & & (xx)[x{\leftarrow}\tau][z{\leftarrow}I] & \multimap_{\mathtt{e}} \ \ldots \end{array}$$

Call-by-Value (CBV). For CBV calculi (again see Tab. 1), *left-to-right* ($\mathtt{Value}^{\mathtt{LR}}$) and *right-to-left* ($\mathtt{Value}^{\mathtt{RL}}$) refer to the evaluation order of applications, *i.e.* they correspond to *operator first* and *argument first*, respectively (note the dual notions evaluation contexts V and S). The calculi $\mathtt{Value}^{\mathtt{LR}}$ and $\mathtt{Value}^{\mathtt{RL}}$ can be seen as strategies of a micro-step variant of the *value substitution calculus*, the (small-step) CBV calculus at a distance introduced in [7].

As an example, we consider again the evaluation of Ω. In $\mathtt{Value}^{\mathtt{LR}}$ it goes as follows:

$$\begin{array}{llll} \delta\delta = (\lambda x.(xx))\delta & \multimap_{\mathtt{m}} & (xx)[x{\leftarrow}\delta] & \multimap_{\mathtt{e}} \\ & & (\delta x)[x{\leftarrow}\delta] & \multimap_{\mathtt{e}} \\ & & (\delta\delta)[x{\leftarrow}\delta] & \multimap_{\mathtt{m}} \\ & & (yy)[y{\leftarrow}\delta][x{\leftarrow}\delta] & \multimap_{\mathtt{e}} \\ & & (\delta y)[y{\leftarrow}\delta][x{\leftarrow}\delta] & \multimap_{\mathtt{e}} \ldots \end{array}$$

While in $\mathtt{Value}^{\mathtt{RL}}$ it takes the following form:

$$\begin{array}{llll} \delta\delta = (\lambda x.(xx))\delta & \multimap_{\mathtt{m}} & (xx)[x{\leftarrow}\delta] & \multimap_{\mathtt{e}} \\ & & (x\delta)[x{\leftarrow}\delta] & \multimap_{\mathtt{e}} \\ & & (\delta\delta)[x{\leftarrow}\delta] & \multimap_{\mathtt{m}} \\ & & (yy)[y{\leftarrow}\delta][x{\leftarrow}\delta] & \multimap_{\mathtt{e}} \\ & & (y\delta)[y{\leftarrow}\delta][x{\leftarrow}\delta] & \multimap_{\mathtt{e}} \ldots \end{array}$$

Note that the CBV version of $\multimap_{\mathtt{m}}$ and $\multimap_{\mathtt{e}}$ employ substitution contexts L in a new way. An example of their use is given by the term $\tau\tau$ consider before for CBN. For instance, in $\mathtt{Value}^{\mathtt{LR}}$:

$$\begin{array}{llll} \tau\tau = ((\lambda z.\delta)I)\tau & \multimap_{\mathtt{m}} & \delta[z{\leftarrow}I]\tau & \multimap_{\mathtt{m}} \\ & & \delta[z{\leftarrow}I](\delta[z{\leftarrow}I]) & \multimap_{\mathtt{m}} \\ & & (xx)[x{\leftarrow}\delta[z{\leftarrow}I]][z{\leftarrow}I] & \multimap_{\mathtt{e}} \\ & & (\delta x)[x{\leftarrow}\delta[z{\leftarrow}I]][z{\leftarrow}I] & \ldots \end{array}$$

Call-by-Need (CBNeed). The call-by-need calculus $\mathtt{Need}$ (Tab. 1) is a novelty of this paper, and can be seen either as a version at a distance of the calculi of [13, 38] or as a version with explicit substitution of the one in [17]. It fully exploits the fact that the two variants of the root rules may be combined: the β-rule is CBN, which reflects the fact that, operationally, the strategy is *by name*, but substitution is CBV, which forces arguments to be evaluated before being substituted, reflecting the *by need* content of the strategy. Please note the definition of CBNeed evaluation contexts N in Tab. 1. They extend the weak head contexts for CBN with a clause ($N'\langle x\rangle[x{\leftarrow}N]$) turning them into *hereditarily weak head contexts*. This new clause is how sharing is implemented by the reduction strategy. The general (non-deterministic) calculus is obtained by closing the root rules by *all* contexts, but its study is omitted. What we deal with here can be thought as its standard strategy (stopping on a sort of weak head normal form).

$$
\begin{array}{rcll|rcll}
t[x{\leftarrow}u] & \equiv_{gc} & t & \text{if } x \notin \mathtt{fv}(t) & t[x{\leftarrow}u] & \equiv_{dup} & t_{[y]_x}[x{\leftarrow}u][y{\leftarrow}u] & \\
t[x{\leftarrow}u][y{\leftarrow}w] & \equiv_{com} & t[y{\leftarrow}w][x{\leftarrow}u] & \text{if } y \notin \mathtt{fv}(u) \text{ and } x \notin \mathtt{fv}(w) & (tw)[x{\leftarrow}u] & \equiv_{@} & t[x{\leftarrow}u]w[x{\leftarrow}u] & \\
t[x{\leftarrow}u][y{\leftarrow}w] & \equiv_{[\cdot]} & t[x{\leftarrow}u[y{\leftarrow}w]] & \text{if } y \notin \mathtt{fv}(t) & (tw)[x{\leftarrow}u] & \equiv_{@l} & t[x{\leftarrow}u]w & \text{if } x \notin \mathtt{fv}(w)
\end{array}
$$

Figure 1. Axioms for structural equivalences. In $\equiv_{dup}$, $t_{[y]_x}$ denotes a term obtained from t by renaming some (possibly none) occurrences of x as y.

Let us show, once again, the evaluation of Ω an the impact of hereditarily head contexts. Consider:

$$
\begin{array}{rcll}
\delta\delta = (\lambda x.(xx))\delta & \multimap_{\mathtt{m}} & (xx)[x{\leftarrow}\delta] & \multimap_{\mathtt{e}} \\
 & & (\delta x)[x{\leftarrow}\delta] & \multimap_{\mathtt{m}} \\
 & & (yy)[y{\leftarrow}x][x{\leftarrow}\delta] & \multimap_{\mathtt{e}} \\
 & & (yy)[y{\leftarrow}\delta][x{\leftarrow}\delta] & \multimap_{\mathtt{e}} \\
 & & (\delta y)[y{\leftarrow}\delta][x{\leftarrow}\delta] & \multimap_{\mathtt{m}} \\
 & & (zz)[z{\leftarrow}y][y{\leftarrow}\delta][x{\leftarrow}\delta] & \multimap_{\mathtt{e}} \ \ldots
\end{array}
$$

Note the difference with CBN in the second and fourth $\multimap_{\mathtt{e}}$ steps: the substitution rule replaces variable occurrences in explicit substitutions thanks to hereditarily weak evaluation contexts.

Structural equivalence. Another common feature of the four calculi is that they come with a notion of *structural equivalence*, denoted by $\equiv$. Consider Fig. 1. For CBN and CBV calculi, $\equiv$ is defined as the smallest equivalence relation containing the closure by weak contexts of $=_\alpha \cup \equiv_{gc} \cup \equiv_{dup} \cup \equiv_{@} \cup \equiv_{com} \cup \equiv_{[\cdot]}$ where $=_\alpha$ is α-equivalence. Call-by-need evaluates inside some substitutions (those hereditarily substituting on the head) and thus axioms as $\equiv_{dup}$ and $\equiv_{@}$ are too strong. Therefore, the structural equivalence for call-by-need, noted $\equiv_{\mathtt{Need}}$, is the one generated by $\equiv_{@l} \cup \equiv_{com} \cup \equiv_{[\cdot]}$.

Structural equivalence represents the fact that certain manipulations on explicit substitutions are computationally irrelevant, in the sense that they yield behaviorally equivalent terms. Technically, it is a *strong bisimulation* (the proof is in [9]):

Proposition 2.2 ($\equiv$ is a Strong Bisimulation)**.** *Let $\multimap_{\mathtt{m}}$, $\multimap_{\mathtt{e}}$ and $\equiv$ be the reduction relations and the structural equivalence relation of any of the calculi of Tab. 1, and let $\mathtt{x} \in \{\mathtt{m}, \mathtt{e}\}$. Then, $t \equiv u$ and $t \multimap_{\mathtt{x}} t'$ implies that there exists u' such that $u \multimap_{\mathtt{x}} u'$ and $t' \equiv u'$.*

The essential property of strong bisimulations is that they can be postponed. In fact, it is immediate to prove the following, which holds for all four calculi:

Lemma 2.3 ($\equiv$ Postponement)**.** *If $t \ (\multimap_{\mathtt{m}} \cup \multimap_{\mathtt{e}} \cup \equiv)^* \ u$ then $t \ (\multimap_{\mathtt{m}} \cup \multimap_{\mathtt{e}})^* \equiv u$ and the number of $\multimap_{\mathtt{m}}$ and $\multimap_{\mathtt{e}}$ steps in the two reduction sequences is exactly the same.*

In the simulation theorems for machines with a global environment (see Sect. 7.2 and Sect. 8) we will also use the following commutation property between substitutions and evaluation contexts via the structural equivalence of every evaluation scheme, proved by an easy induction on the actual definition of evaluation contexts.

Lemma 2.4 (ES Commute with Evaluation Contexts via $\equiv$)**.** *For every evaluation scheme let C denote an evaluation context s.t. $x \notin \mathtt{fv}(C)$ and $\equiv$ be its structural equivalence. Then $C\langle t\rangle[x{\leftarrow}u] \equiv C\langle t[x{\leftarrow}u]\rangle$.*

3. Preliminaries on Abstract Machines

Codes. All the abstract machines we will consider execute pure λ-terms. In our syntax, these are nothing but terms *without explicit substitutions*. Moreover, while for calculi we work implicitly modulo α, for machines we will *not* consider terms up to α, as the handling of α-equivalence characterizes different approaches to abstract machines. To stress these facts, we use the metavariables $\overline{t}, \overline{u}, \overline{w}, \overline{r}$ for pure λ-terms (not up to α) and $\overline{v}$ for pure values.

States. A machine state s will have various components, of which the first will always be *the code*, *i.e.* a pure λ-term $\overline{t}$. The others (*environment*, *stack*, *dump*,...) are all considered as lists, whose constructors are the empty list ϵ and the concatenation operator $::$. In fact, even if these components are formalized as lists, they may be intended to be implemented differently, as it will be the case for the machines with global environments (*i.e.* the MAM, the MAD, and its variants).

A state s of a machine is *initial* if its code $\overline{t}$ is closed (*i.e.*, $\mathtt{fv}(\overline{t}) = \varnothing$) and all other components are empty. An *execution* ρ is a sequence of transitions of the machine $s_0 \to^* s$ from an initial state s_0. In that case, we say that s is a *reachable state*, and if $\overline{t}$ is the code of s_0 then $\overline{t}$ is the *initial code* of s.

Invariants. For every machine our study will rely on a lemma about some *dynamic invariants*, *i.e.* some properties of the reachable states that are stable by executions. The lemma is always proved by a straightforward induction on the length of the execution and *the proof is omitted.*

Environments and Closures. There will be two types of machines, those with many *local environments* and those with just one *global environment*. Machines with local environments are based on the mutually recursive definition of *closure* (ranged over by c) and *environment* (e):

$$
c \ ::= \ (\overline{t}, e) \qquad e \ ::= \ \epsilon \mid [x{\leftarrow}c] :: e
$$

Global environments are defined by $E ::= \epsilon \mid [x{\leftarrow}\overline{t}] :: E$, and global environment machines will have just one global closure $(\overline{t}, E)$.

Well-Named and Closed Closures. The explicit treatment of α-equivalence, is based on particular representatives of α-classes defined via the notion of support. The *support* Δ of codes, environments, and closures is defined by:

- $\Delta(\overline{t})$ is the *multi*set of its bound names (*e.g.* $\Delta(\lambda x.\lambda y.\lambda x.(zx)) = [x, x, y]$).
- $\Delta(e)$ is the *multi*set of names captured by e (for example $\Delta([x{\leftarrow}c_1][y{\leftarrow}c_2][x{\leftarrow}c_3]) = [x, x, y]$), and similarly for $\Delta(E)$.
- $\Delta(\overline{t}, e) := \Delta(\overline{t}) + \Delta(e)$ and $\Delta(\overline{t}, E) := \Delta(\overline{t}) + \Delta(E)$.

A code/environment/closure $(\overline{t}, e)$ (resp. (t, E)) is *well-named* if its support $\Delta(\overline{t}, e)$ (resp. $\Delta(\overline{t}, E)$) is a set (*i.e.* a multiset with no repetitions). Moreover, a closure $(\overline{t}, e)$ (resp. (t, E)) is *closed* if $\mathtt{fv}(\overline{t}) \subseteq \Delta(e)$ (resp. $\mathtt{fv}(\overline{t}) \subseteq \Delta(E)$).

4. Distilleries

This section presents an abstract, high-level view of the relationship between abstract machines and linear substitution calculi, via the notion of *distillery* (see Tab. 2 for our pairs calculus/machine).

Definition 4.1. *A distillery $\mathtt{D} = (\mathtt{M}, \mathtt{C}, \equiv, \underline{\cdot})$ is given by:*

1. *An* abstract machine $\mathtt{M}$, *given by*
   (a) *a deterministic labeled transition system $\to$ on states s;*
   (b) *a distinguished class of states deemed* initial, *in bijection with closed λ-terms and from which one obtains the* reachable *states by applying $\to^*$;*
   (c) *a partition of the labels of the transition system $\to$ as:*

- commutative *transitions, noted* $\rightarrow_{\mathtt{c}}$*;*
- principal *transitions, in turn partitioned into*
  - multiplicative *transitions, denoted by* $\rightarrow_{\mathtt{m}}$*;*
  - exponential *transitions, denoted by* $\rightarrow_{\mathtt{e}}$*;*

2. *a* linear substitution calculus $\mathtt{C}$ *given by a pair* $(\multimap_{\mathtt{m}}, \multimap_{\mathtt{e}})$ *of rewriting relations on terms with ES;*
3. *a* structural equivalence $\equiv$ *on terms s.t. it is a strong bisimulation with respect to* $\multimap_{\mathtt{m}}$ *and* $\multimap_{\mathtt{e}}$*;*
4. *a* distillation $\underline{\cdot}$*, i.e. a decoding function from states to terms, s.t. on reachable states:*
   - Commutative*:* $s \rightarrow_{\mathtt{c}} s'$ *implies* $\underline{s} \equiv \underline{s'}$.
   - Multiplicative*:* $s \rightarrow_{\mathtt{m}} s'$ *implies* $\underline{s} \multimap_{\mathtt{m}}\equiv \underline{s'}$*;*
   - Exponential*:* $s \rightarrow_{\mathtt{e}} s'$ *implies* $\underline{s} \multimap_{\mathtt{e}}\equiv \underline{s'}$*;*

Given a distillery, the simulation theorem holds abstractly. Let $|\rho|$ (resp. $|d|$), $|\rho|_m$ (resp. $|d|_m$), $|\rho|_e$ (resp. $|d|_e$), and $|\rho|_p$ denote the number of unspecified, multiplicative, exponential, and principal steps in an execution (resp. derivation).

Theorem 4.2 (Simulation)**.** *Let* $\mathtt{D}$ *be a distillery. Then for every execution* $\rho : s \rightarrow^* s'$ *there is a derivation* $d : \underline{s} \multimap^*\equiv \underline{s'}$ *s.t.* $|\rho|_m = |d|_m$*,* $|\rho|_e = |d|_e$*, and* $|\rho|_p = |d|$.

Proof. By induction on $|\rho|$ and by the properties of the decoding, it follows that there is a derivation $e : \underline{s}(\multimap\equiv)^*\underline{s'}$ s.t. the number $|\rho|_p = |e|$. The witness d for the statement is obtained by applying the postponement of strong bisimulations (Lemma 2.3) to e. □

Reflection. Given a distillery, one would also expect that reduction in the calculus is reflected in the machine. This result in fact requires two additional abstract properties.

Definition 4.3 (Reflective Distillery)**.** *A distillery is* reflective *when:*

Termination: $\rightarrow_{\mathtt{c}}$ terminates *(on reachable states); hence, by determinism, every state* s *has a unique* commutative normal form $\mathtt{nf}_{\mathtt{c}}(s)$*;*

Progress: *if* s *is reachable,* $\mathtt{nf}_{\mathtt{c}}(s) = s$ *and* $\underline{s} \multimap_{\mathtt{x}} t$ *with* $\mathtt{x} \in \{\mathtt{m}, \mathtt{e}\}$*, then there exists* s' *such that* $s \rightarrow_{\mathtt{x}} s'$*, i.e.,* s *is not final.*

Then, we may prove the following reflection of steps in full generality:

Proposition 4.4 (Reflection)**.** *Let* $\mathtt{D}$ *be a reflective distillery,* s *be a reachable state, and* $\mathtt{x} \in \{\mathtt{m}, \mathtt{e}\}$*. Then,* $\underline{s} \multimap_{\mathtt{x}} u$ *implies that there exists a state* s' *s.t.* $\mathtt{nf}_{\mathtt{c}}(s) \rightarrow_{\mathtt{x}} s'$ *and* $\underline{s'} \equiv u$.

In other words, every rewriting step on the calculus can be also performed on the machine, up to commutative transitions.

Proof. The proof is by induction on the number n of transitions leading from s to $\mathtt{nf}_{\mathtt{c}}(s)$.

- *Base case* $n = 0$: by the progress property, we have $s \rightarrow_{\mathtt{x}'} s'$ for some state s' and $\mathtt{x}' \in \{\mathtt{m}, \mathtt{e}\}$. By Theorem 4.2, we have $\underline{s} \multimap_{\mathtt{x}'} u' \equiv \underline{s'}$ and we may conclude because $\mathtt{x}' = \mathtt{x}$ and $u' = u$ by determinism of the calculus (Proposition 2.1).
- *Inductive case* $n > 0$: by hypothesis, we have $s \rightarrow_{\mathtt{c}} s_1$. By Theorem 4.2, $\underline{s} \equiv \underline{s_1}$. The hypothesis and the strong bisimulation property (Proposition 2.2) then give us $\underline{s_1} \multimap_{\mathtt{x}} u_1 \equiv u$. But the induction hypothesis holds for s_1, giving us a state s' such that $\mathtt{nf}_{\mathtt{c}}(s_1) \rightarrow_{\mathtt{x}} s'$ and $\underline{s'} \equiv u_1 \equiv u$. We may now conclude because $\mathtt{nf}_{\mathtt{c}}(s) = \mathtt{nf}_{\mathtt{c}}(s_1)$. □

The reflection can then be extended to a reverse simulation.

Corollary 4.5 (Reverse Simulation)**.** *Let* $\mathtt{D}$ *be a reflective distillery and* s *an initial state. Given a derivation* $d : \underline{s} \multimap^* t$ *there is an execution* $\rho : s \rightarrow^* s'$ *s.t.* $t \equiv \underline{s'}$ *and* $|\rho|_m = |d|_m$*,* $|\rho|_e = |d|_e$*, and* $|\rho|_p = |d|$.

Proof. By induction on the length of d, using Proposition 4.4. □

Calculus	*Abstract Machine*
Name	KAM, MAM
$\mathtt{Value}^{\mathtt{LR}}$	CEK, Split CEK
$\mathtt{Value}^{\mathtt{RL}}$	LAM
Need	(Merged/Pointing) MAD

Table 2. Correspondence between calculi of Tab. 1 and abstract machines.

In the following sections we will introduce abstract machines and distillations for which we will prove that they form reflective distilleries with respect to the calculi of Sect. 2. For each machine we will prove: 1) that the decoding is in fact a distillation, and 2) the progress property. *We will instead assume the termination property,* whose proof is delayed to the quantitative study of the second part of the paper, where we will actually prove stronger results, giving explicit bounds.

5. Call-by-Name: the KAM

The Krivine Abstract Machine (KAM) is the simplest machine studied in the paper. A KAM *state* (s) is made out of a closure and of a *stack* (π):

$$\pi \quad ::= \quad \epsilon \mid c :: \pi \qquad\qquad s \quad ::= \quad (c, \pi)$$

For readability, we will use the notation $\overline{t} \mid e \mid \pi$ for a state (c, π) where $c = (\overline{t}, e)$. The transitions of the KAM then are:

$\overline{tu}$	e	π	$\rightarrow_{\mathtt{c}}$	$\overline{t}$	e	$(\overline{u}, e) :: \pi$
$\lambda x.\overline{t}$	e	$c :: \pi$	$\rightarrow_{\mathtt{m}}$	$\overline{t}$	$[x{\leftarrow}c] :: e$	π
x	e	π	$\rightarrow_{\mathtt{e}}$	$\overline{t}$	e'	π

where $\rightarrow_{\mathtt{e}}$ takes place only if $e = e'' :: [x{\leftarrow}(\overline{t}, e')] :: e'''$.

A key point of our study is that environments and stacks rather immediately become contexts of the LSC, through the following decoding:

$$\underline{\epsilon} := \langle\cdot\rangle \qquad \underline{[x{\leftarrow}c] :: e} := \underline{e}\langle\langle\cdot\rangle[x{\leftarrow}\underline{c}]\rangle$$
$$\underline{(\overline{t}, e)} := \underline{e}\langle\overline{t}\rangle \qquad \underline{c :: \pi} := \underline{\pi}\langle\langle\cdot\rangle\underline{c}\rangle$$
$$\underline{\overline{t} \mid e \mid \pi} := \underline{\pi}\langle\underline{e}\langle\overline{t}\rangle\rangle$$

The decoding satisfies the following static properties, shown by easy inductions on the definition.

Lemma 5.1 (Contextual Decoding)**.** *Let* e *be an environment and* π *be a stack of the KAM. Then* $\underline{e}$ *is a substitution context, and both* $\underline{\pi}$ *and* $\underline{\pi}\langle\underline{e}\rangle$ *are evaluation contexts.*

Next, we need the dynamic invariants of the machine.

Lemma 5.2 (KAM Invariants)**.** *Let* $s = \overline{u} \mid e \mid \pi$ *be a KAM reachable state whose initial code* $\overline{t}$ *is well-named. Then:*

1. Closure*: every closure in* s *is closed;*
2. Subterm*: any code in* s *is a literal subterm of* $\overline{t}$.
3. Name*: any closure* c *in* s *is well-named and its names are names of* $\overline{t}$ *(i.e.* $\Delta(c) \subseteq \mathtt{fv}(\overline{t})$*).*
4. Environment Size*: the length of any environment in* s *is bound by* $|\overline{t}|$.

Abstract Considerations on Concrete Implementations. The name invariant is the abstract property that allows to avoid both α-equivalence and name generation in KAM executions. Note that, by definition of well-named closure, there cannot be repetitions in the support of an environment. Then the length of any environment in any reachable state is bound by the number of distinct names in the initial code $\overline{t}$, *i.e.* with $|\overline{t}|$. This fact is important, as the static bound on the size of environments guarantees that $\rightarrow_{\mathtt{e}}$ and $\rightarrow_{\mathtt{c}}$—the transitions looking-up and copying environments—can be implemented (independently of the chosen concrete representation of terms) in at worst linear time in $|t|$, so that an execution ρ can be implemented in $O(|\rho| \cdot |t|)$. The same will hold for every machine with local environments. In fact, we may turn this into a definition: an abstract machine is *reasonable* if its implementation enjoys the above bilinear bound. In this way, the length of an execution of a reasonable machine provides an accurate estimate of its implementation cost.

The previous considerations are based on the name and environment size invariants. The closure invariant is used in the progress part of the next theorem, and the subterm invariant is used in the quantitative analysis in Sect. 11 (Theorem 11.3), subsuming the termination condition of reflective distilleries.

Theorem 5.3 (KAM Distillation)**.** *$(KAM, \mathtt{Name}, \equiv, \underline{\cdot})$ is a reflective distillery. In particular, on a reachable state s we have:*

1. Commutative*: if $s \rightarrow_{\mathtt{c}} s'$ then $\underline{s} \equiv \underline{s'}$.*
2. Multiplicative*: if $s \rightarrow_{\mathtt{m}} s'$ then $\underline{s} \multimap_{\mathtt{m}} \underline{s'}$;*
3. Exponential*: if $s \rightarrow_{\mathtt{e}} s'$ then $\underline{s} \multimap_{\mathtt{e}}\equiv \underline{s'}$;*

Proof. Properties of the decoding:

1. *Commutative.* We have $\overline{tu} \mid e \mid \pi \rightarrow_{\mathtt{c}} \overline{t} \mid e \mid (\overline{u}, e) :: \pi$, and:

$$\begin{array}{rcl} \underline{\overline{tu} \mid e \mid \pi} & = & \underline{\pi}\langle \underline{e}\langle \overline{tu} \rangle\rangle \\ & \equiv^*_{@} & \underline{\pi}\langle \underline{e}\langle \overline{t} \rangle \underline{e}\langle \overline{u} \rangle\rangle \quad = \quad \underline{\overline{t} \mid e \mid (\overline{u}, e) :: \pi} \end{array}$$

2. *Multiplicative.* $\lambda x.\overline{t} \mid e \mid c :: \pi \rightarrow_{\mathtt{m}} \overline{t} \mid [x{\leftarrow}c] :: e \mid \pi$, and

$$\begin{array}{rcl} \underline{\lambda x.\overline{t} \mid e \mid c :: \pi} & = & \underline{\pi}\langle \underline{e}\langle \lambda x.\overline{t} \rangle \underline{c}\rangle \\ & \multimap_{\mathtt{m}} & \underline{\pi}\langle \underline{e}\langle \overline{t}[x{\leftarrow}\underline{c}]\rangle\rangle \\ & = & \underline{\overline{t} \mid [x{\leftarrow}c] :: e \mid \pi} \end{array}$$

The rewriting step can be applied because by contextual decoding (Lemma 5.1) it takes place in an evaluation context.

3. *Exponential.* $x \mid e' :: [x{\leftarrow}(\overline{t}, e)] :: e'' \mid \pi \rightarrow_{\mathtt{e}} \overline{t} \mid e \mid \pi$, and

$$\begin{array}{rcl} \underline{x \mid e' :: [x{\leftarrow}(\overline{t}, e)] :: e'' \mid \pi} & = & \underline{\pi}\langle \underline{e''}\langle \underline{e'}\langle x \rangle [x{\leftarrow}\underline{e}\langle \overline{t} \rangle]\rangle\rangle \\ & \multimap_{\mathtt{e}} & \underline{\pi}\langle \underline{e''}\langle \underline{e'}\langle \underline{e}\langle \overline{t} \rangle\rangle [x{\leftarrow}\underline{e}\langle \overline{t} \rangle]\rangle\rangle \\ & \equiv^*_{gc} & \underline{\pi}\langle \underline{e}\langle \overline{t} \rangle\rangle \\ & = & \underline{\overline{t} \mid e \mid \pi} \end{array}$$

Note that $e''\langle e'\langle e\langle \overline{t} \rangle\rangle [x{\leftarrow}e\langle \overline{t} \rangle]\rangle \equiv^*_{gc} e\langle \overline{t} \rangle$ holds because $e\langle \overline{t} \rangle$ is closed by point 1 of Lemma 5.2, and so all the substitutions around it can be garbage collected.

Termination. Given by (forthcoming) Theorem 11.3 (future proofs of distillery theorems will omit termination).

Progress. Let $s = \overline{t} \mid e \mid \pi$ be a commutative normal form s.t. $\underline{s} \multimap u$. If $\overline{t}$ is

- *an application* $\overline{uw}$. Then a $\rightarrow_{\mathtt{c}}$ transition applies and s is not a commutative normal form, absurd;
- *an abstraction* $\lambda x.\overline{u}$: if $\pi = \epsilon$ then $\underline{s} = \underline{e}\langle \lambda x.\overline{u} \rangle$, which is $\multimap$-normal, absurd. Hence, a $\rightarrow_{\mathtt{m}}$ transition applies;
- *a variable* x: by point 1 of Lemma 5.2.1, we must have $e = e' :: [x{\leftarrow}c] :: e''$, so a $\rightarrow_{\mathtt{e}}$ transition applies. □

6. Call-by-Value: the CEK and the LAM

Here we deal with two adaptations to CBV of the KAM, namely Felleisen and Friedman's CEK machine [28] (without control operators), and a variant, deemed *Leroy Abstract Machine* (LAM). They differ in how they behave with respect to applications: the CEK implements left-to-right CBV, *i.e.* it first evaluates the function part, the LAM gives instead precedence to arguments, realizing right-to-left CBV. The LAM owes its name to Leroy's ZINC machine [37], that implements right-to-left CBV evaluation. We introduce a new name because the ZINC is a quite more sophisticated machine than the LAM: it has a separate sets of instructions to which terms are compiled, it handles arithmetic expressions, and it avoids needless closure creations in a way that it is not captured by the LAM. We deal with the LAM only to stress the modularity of our contextual approach.

CBV States and Stacks. The states of the CEK and the LAM have the same shape of those of the KAM, *i.e.* they are given by a closure plus a stack. The difference is that they use *CBV stacks*, whose elements are labelled either as *functions* or *arguments*, so that the machine may know whether it is launching the evaluation of an argument or it is at the end of such an evaluation. They are re-defined and decoded as follows (c is a closure):

$$\pi \; ::= \; \epsilon \mid \mathbf{f}(c) :: \pi \mid \mathbf{a}(c) :: \pi \qquad \begin{array}{rcl} \underline{\epsilon} & := & \langle\cdot\rangle \\ \underline{\mathbf{f}(c) :: \pi} & := & \underline{\pi}\langle \underline{c}\langle\cdot\rangle\rangle \\ \underline{\mathbf{a}(c) :: \pi} & := & \underline{\pi}\langle\langle\cdot\rangle \underline{c}\rangle \end{array}$$

The states of both machines are decoded exactly as for the KAM, *i.e.* $\underline{\overline{t} \mid e \mid \pi} := \underline{\pi}\langle \underline{e}\langle \overline{t} \rangle\rangle$.

6.1 Left-to Right Call-by-Value: the CEK machine.

The transitions of the CEK are:

$$\begin{array}{c|c|c|c|c|c|c} \overline{tu} & e & \pi & \rightarrow_{\mathtt{c}_1} & \overline{t} & e & \mathbf{a}(\overline{u}, e) :: \pi \\ \overline{v} & e & \mathbf{a}(\overline{u}, e') :: \pi & \rightarrow_{\mathtt{c}_2} & \overline{u} & e' & \mathbf{f}(\overline{v}, e) :: \pi \\ \overline{v} & e & \mathbf{f}(\lambda x.\overline{t}, e') :: \pi & \rightarrow_{\mathtt{m}} & \overline{t} & [x{\leftarrow}(\overline{v}, e)] :: e' & \pi \\ x & e & \pi & \rightarrow_{\mathtt{e}} & \overline{t} & e' & \pi \end{array}$$

where $\rightarrow_{\mathtt{e}}$ takes place only if $e = e'' :: [x{\leftarrow}(\overline{t}, e')] :: e'''$.

While one can still statically prove that environments decode to substitution contexts, to prove that $\underline{\pi}$ and $\underline{\pi}\langle \underline{e} \rangle$ are evaluation contexts we need the dynamic invariants of the machine.

Lemma 6.1 (CEK Invariants)**.** *Let $s = \overline{u} \mid e \mid \pi$ be a CEK reachable state whose initial code $\overline{t}$ is well-named. Then:*

1. Closure*: every closure in s is closed;*
2. Subterm*: any code in s is a literal subterm of $\overline{t}$;*
3. Value*: any code in e is a value and, for every element of π of the form $\mathbf{f}(\overline{u}, e')$, $\overline{u}$ is a value;*
4. Contextual Decoding*: $\underline{\pi}$ and $\underline{\pi}\langle \underline{e} \rangle$ are left-to-right CBV evaluation contexts.*
5. Name*: any closure c in s is well-named and its names are names of $\overline{t}$ (i.e. $\Delta(c) \subseteq \mathtt{fv}(\overline{t})$).*
6. Environment Size*: the length of any environment in s is bound by $|\overline{t}|$.*

We have everything we need:

Theorem 6.2 (CEK Distillation)**.** *$(CEK, \mathtt{Value}^{\mathtt{LR}}, \equiv, \underline{\cdot})$ is a reflective distillery. In particular, on a reachable state s we have:*

1. Commutative 1*: if $s \rightarrow_{\mathtt{c}_1} s'$ then $\underline{s} \equiv \underline{s'}$;*
2. Commutative 2*: if $s \rightarrow_{\mathtt{c}_2} s'$ then $\underline{s} = \underline{s'}$.*
3. Multiplicative*: if $s \rightarrow_{\mathtt{m}} s'$ then $\underline{s} \multimap_{\mathtt{m}} \underline{s'}$;*
4. Exponential*: if $s \rightarrow_{\mathtt{e}} s'$ then $\underline{s} \multimap_{\mathtt{e}}\equiv \underline{s'}$;*

$\overline{t}\overline{u}$	e	π	D	$\rightarrow_{\mathtt{c}_1}$	$\overline{t}$	e	$(\overline{u},e) :: \pi$	D
$\overline{v}$	e	$(\overline{t},e') :: \pi$	D	$\rightarrow_{\mathtt{c}_2}$	$\overline{t}$	e'	ϵ	$((\overline{v},e),\pi) :: D$
$\overline{v}$	e	ϵ	$((\lambda x.\overline{t},e'),\pi) :: D$	$\rightarrow_{\mathtt{m}}$	$\overline{t}$	$[x{\leftarrow}(\overline{v},e)] :: e'$	π	D
x	$e :: [x{\leftarrow}(\overline{v},e')] :: e''$	π	D	$\rightarrow_{\mathtt{e}}$	$\overline{v}$	e'	π	D

Figure 2. The Split CEK, aka the revisited SECD.

Proof. Properties of the decoding: in the following cases, evaluation will always takes place under a context that by Lemma 6.1.4 will be a left-to-right CBV evaluation context, and similarly structural equivalence will alway be used in a weak context, as it should be.

1. *Commutative 1*. We have $\overline{t}\overline{u} \mid e \mid \pi \rightarrow_{\mathtt{c}_1} \overline{t} \mid e \mid \mathbf{a}(\overline{u},e) :: \pi$:

$$\begin{array}{lcll} \underline{\overline{t}\overline{u} \mid e \mid \pi} & = & \underline{\pi}\langle \underline{e}\langle \overline{t}\overline{u}\rangle\rangle & \equiv_{@}^{*} \\ & & \underline{\pi}\langle \underline{e}\langle \overline{t}\rangle \underline{e}\langle \overline{u}\rangle\rangle & = \quad \underline{\overline{t} \mid e \mid \mathbf{a}(\overline{u},e) :: \pi} \end{array}$$

2. *Commutative 2*. We have $\overline{v} \mid e \mid \mathbf{a}(\overline{u},e') :: \pi \rightarrow_{\mathtt{c}_2} \overline{u} \mid e' \mid \mathbf{f}(\overline{v},e) :: \pi$, and:

$$\begin{array}{lcll} \underline{\overline{v} \mid e \mid \mathbf{a}(\overline{u},e') :: \pi} & = & \underline{\pi}\langle \underline{e}\langle \overline{v}\rangle \underline{e'}\langle \overline{u}\rangle\rangle & = \\ & & \underline{\overline{u} \mid e' \mid \mathbf{f}(\overline{v},e) :: \pi} & \end{array}$$

3. *Multiplicative*. We have $\overline{v} \mid e \mid \mathbf{f}(\lambda x.\overline{t},e') :: \pi \rightarrow_{\mathtt{m}} \overline{u} \mid [x{\leftarrow}(\overline{v},e)] :: e' \mid \pi$, and:

$$\begin{array}{lcll} \underline{\overline{v} \mid e \mid \mathbf{f}(\lambda x.\overline{t},e') :: \pi} & = & \underline{\pi}\langle \underline{e'}\langle \lambda x.\overline{t}\rangle \underline{e}\langle \overline{v}\rangle\rangle & \multimap_{\mathtt{m}} \\ & & \underline{\pi}\langle \underline{e'}\langle \overline{t}[x{\leftarrow}\underline{e}\langle \overline{v}\rangle]\rangle\rangle & = \\ & & \underline{\overline{t} \mid [x{\leftarrow}(\overline{v},e)] :: e' \mid \pi} & \end{array}$$

4. *Exponential*. Let $e = e'' :: [x{\leftarrow}(\overline{t},e')] :: e'''$. We have $x \mid e \mid \pi \rightarrow_{\mathtt{e}} \overline{t} \mid e' \mid \pi$, and:

$$\begin{array}{lcll} \underline{x \mid e \mid \pi} & = & \pi\langle e\langle x\rangle\rangle & = \\ & & \underline{\pi}\langle \underline{e'''}\langle \underline{e''}\langle x\rangle[x{\leftarrow}\underline{e'}\langle \overline{t}\rangle]\rangle\rangle & \multimap_{\mathtt{e}} \\ & & \underline{\pi}\langle \underline{e'''}\langle \underline{e'}\langle \underline{e''}\langle \overline{t}\rangle[x{\leftarrow}\overline{t}]\rangle\rangle\rangle & \equiv_{gc}^{*} \\ & & \underline{\pi}\langle \underline{e'}\langle \overline{t}\rangle\rangle & = \quad \underline{\overline{t} \mid e' \mid \pi} \end{array}$$

   We can apply $\multimap_{\mathtt{e}}$ since by Lemma 6.1.3, $\overline{t}$ is a value. We also use that by Lemma 6.1.1, $\underline{e'}\langle \overline{t}\rangle$ is a closed term to ensure that $\underline{e''}$ and $\underline{e'''}$ can be garbage collected.

Progress. Let $s = \overline{t} \mid e \mid \pi$ be a commutative normal form s.t. $\underline{s} \multimap u$. If $\overline{t}$ is

- *an application* $\overline{u}\overline{w}$. Then a $\rightarrow_{\mathtt{c}_1}$ transition applies and s is not a commutative normal form, absurd;
- *an abstraction* $\overline{v}$: by hypothesis, π cannot be of the form $\mathbf{a}(c) :: \pi'$. Suppose it is equal to ϵ. We would then have $\underline{s} = \underline{e}\langle \overline{v}\rangle$, which is a CBV normal form, because $\underline{e}$ is a substitution context. This would contradict our hypothesis, so π must be of the form $\mathbf{f}(\overline{u},e') :: \pi'$. By point 3 of Lemma 6.1, $\overline{u}$ is an abstraction, hence a $\rightarrow_{\mathtt{m}}$ transition applies;
- *a variable* x: by point 1 of Lemma 6.1, e must be of the form $e' :: [x{\leftarrow}c] :: e''$, so a $\rightarrow_{\mathtt{e}}$ transition applies. □

6.2 Right-to-Left Call-by-Value: the Leroy Abstract Machine

The transitions of the LAM are:

$\overline{t}\overline{u}$	e	π	$\rightarrow_{\mathtt{c}_1}$	$\overline{u}$	e	$\mathbf{f}(\overline{t},e) :: \pi$
$\overline{v}$	e	$\mathbf{f}(\overline{t},e') :: \pi$	$\rightarrow_{\mathtt{c}_2}$	$\overline{t}$	e'	$\mathbf{a}(\overline{v},e) :: \pi$
$\lambda x.\overline{t}$	e	$\mathbf{a}(c) :: \pi$	$\rightarrow_{\mathtt{m}}$	$\overline{t}$	$[x{\leftarrow}c] :: e$	π
x	e	π	$\rightarrow_{\mathtt{e}}$	$\overline{t}$	e'	π

where $\rightarrow_{\mathtt{e}}$ takes place only if $e = e'' :: [x{\leftarrow}(\overline{t},e')] :: e'''$.

We omit all the proofs (that can be found in [9]) because they are minimal variations on those for the CEK.

Lemma 6.3 (LAM Invariants). *Let $s = \overline{u} \mid e \mid \pi$ be a LAM reachable state whose initial code $\overline{t}$ is well-named. Then:*

1. Closure*: every closure in s is closed;*
2. Subterm*: any code in s is a literal subterm of $\overline{t}$;*
3. Value*: any code in e is a value and, for every element of π of the form $\mathbf{a}(\overline{u},e')$, $\overline{u}$ is a value;*
4. Contexts Decoding*: $\underline{\pi}$ and $\underline{\pi}\langle \underline{e}\rangle$ are right-to-left CBV evaluation contexts.*
5. Name*: any closure c in s is well-named and its names are names of $\overline{t}$ (i.e. $\Delta(c) \subseteq \mathtt{fv}(\overline{t})$).*
6. Environment Size*: the length of any environment in s is bound by $|\overline{t}|$.*

Theorem 6.4 (LAM Distillation). *$(LAM, \mathtt{Value}^{\mathtt{RL}}, \equiv, \underline{\cdot})$ is a reflective distillery. In particular, on a reachable state s we have:*

1. Commutative 1*: if $s \rightarrow_{\mathtt{c}_1} s'$ then $\underline{s} \equiv \underline{s'}$;*
2. Commutative 2*: if $s \rightarrow_{\mathtt{c}_2} s'$ then $\underline{s} = \underline{s'}$.*
3. Multiplicative*: if $s \rightarrow_{\mathtt{m}} s'$ then $\underline{s} \multimap_{\mathtt{m}} \underline{s'}$;*
4. Exponential*: if $s \rightarrow_{\mathtt{e}} s'$ then $\underline{s} \multimap_{\mathtt{e}}\equiv \underline{s'}$;*

7. Towards Call-by-Need: the Split CEK and the MAM

In this section we study two further machines:

1. *The Split CEK (SCEK)*, obtained disentangling the two uses of the stack (for arguments and for functions) in the CEK. The split CEK can be seen as a simplification of Landin's SECD machine [35].
2. *The Milner Abstract Machine (MAM)*, that is a variation over the KAM with only one global environment and with just one global closure, what is sometimes called a *heap* or a *store*. Essentially, it unveils the content of distance rules at the machine level.

The ideas at work in these two case studies—both playing with the use of contexts—will be combined in the next section, obtaining a new simple CBNeed machine, the MAD.

7.1 The Split CEK, or Revisiting the SECD Machine

For the CEK machine we proved that the stack, that collects both arguments and functions, decodes to an evaluation context (Lemma 6.1.4). The new CBV machine in Fig. 2, deemed *Split CEK*, has two stacks: one for arguments and one for functions. Both will decode to evaluation contexts.

Note that the evaluation contexts V for the calculus $\mathtt{Value}^{\mathtt{LR}}$:

$$V ::= \langle\cdot\rangle \mid Vt \mid L\langle v\rangle V \mid V[x{\leftarrow}t]$$

have two cases for application. Essentially, when dealing with Vt the machine puts t in a stack for arguments (identical to the stack of the KAM), while in the case $L\langle v\rangle V$ the machine puts the closure (corresponding to) $L\langle v\rangle$ in a stack for functions, called *dump*.

Actually, together with the closure it also has to store the current argument stack, to not mess things up.

Thus, an entry of the function stack is a pair (c, π), where c is a closure $(\overline{v}, e)$, and the three components $\overline{v}$, e, and π together correspond to the evaluation context $\underline{\pi}\langle\underline{e}\langle\overline{v}\langle\cdot\rangle\rangle\rangle$.

Let us explain the idea at the level of the machine. Whenever the code is an abstraction $\overline{v}$ and the argument stack π is non-empty (*i.e.* $\pi = c :: \pi'$), the machine saves the active closure, given by current code $\overline{v}$ and environment e, and the tail of the stack π' by pushing a new entry $((\overline{v}, e), \pi')$ on the dump, and then starts evaluating the first closure c of the stack. The syntax for dumps then is

$$D ::= \epsilon \mid (c, \pi) :: D$$

Every dump decodes to a context according to:

$$\underline{\epsilon} \;:=\; \langle\cdot\rangle \qquad \underline{((\overline{v}, e), \pi) :: D} \;:=\; \underline{D}\langle\underline{\pi}\langle\underline{e}\langle\overline{v}\langle\cdot\rangle\rangle\rangle\rangle$$

Relationship with the SECD. For the acquainted reader, the new stack morally is the *dump* of Landin's SECD machine [35] (but beware that the original definition of the SECD is quite more technical). An in-depth analysis of the SECD machine can be found in Danvy's [22], where it is shown that the SECD implements right-to-left CBV, and not left-to-right CBV as the Split CEK. However, here we are rather interested in showing that *splitting the stack* is a general transformation, modularly captured by distillation and enlightening the dump of the SECD, which may look mysterious at first. It is enough to apply the same transformation to the LAM, getting a *Split LAM*, to get closer to the original SECD. Such an exercise, however, is left to the reader. In Sect. 9 we will instead apply the inverse transformation—merging two stacks into one—to a CBNeed machine.

Distillation. The decoding of terms, environments, closures, and stacks is as for the KAM. The decoding of states is defined as $\underline{\overline{t} \mid e \mid \pi \mid D} := \underline{D}\langle\underline{\pi}\langle\underline{e}\langle\overline{t}\rangle\rangle\rangle$. The proofs for the Split CEK are in [9].

Lemma 7.1 (Split CEK Invariants)**.** *Let $s = \overline{u} \mid e \mid \pi \mid D$ be a Split CEK reachable state whose initial code $\overline{t}$ is well-named. Then:*

1. Closure: *every closure in s is closed;*
2. Subterm: *any code in s is a literal subterm of $\overline{t}$;*
3. Value: *the code of any closure in the dump or in any environment in s is a value;*
4. Contextual Decoding: *$\underline{D}$, $\underline{D}\langle\underline{\pi}\rangle$, and $\underline{D}\langle\underline{\pi}\langle\underline{e}\rangle\rangle$ are left-to-right CBV evaluation context.*
5. Name: *any closure c in s is well-named and its names are names of $\overline{t}$ (i.e. $\Delta(c) \subseteq \mathtt{fv}(\overline{t})$).*
6. Environment Size: *the length of any environment in s is bound by $|\overline{t}|$.*

Theorem 7.2 (Split CEK Distillation)**.** $(\text{Split CEK}, \mathtt{Value}^{\mathtt{LR}}, \equiv, \underline{\cdot})$ *is a reflective distillery. In particular, on a reachable state s we have:*

1. Commutative 1*: if $s \to_{\mathtt{c}_1} s'$ then $\underline{s} \equiv \underline{s'}$;*
2. Commutative 2*: if $s \to_{\mathtt{c}_2} s'$ then $\underline{s} \equiv \underline{s'}$;*
3. Multiplicative*: if $s \to_{\mathtt{m}} s'$ then $\underline{s} \multimap_{\mathtt{m}} \underline{s'}$;*
4. Exponential*: if $s \to_{\mathtt{e}} s'$ then $\underline{s} \multimap_{\mathtt{e}}\equiv \underline{s'}$.*

7.2 Milner Abstract Machine

The LSC suggests the design of a simpler version of the KAM, the *Milner Abstract Machine* (MAM), that avoids the concept of closure. At the language level, the idea is that, by repeatedly applying the axioms $\equiv_{dup}$ and $\equiv_{@}$ of the structural equivalence, explicit substitutions can be folded and brought *outside*. At the machine level, the local environments in the closures are replaced by just one global environment that closes the code and the stack, as well as the global environment itself.

Of course, naively turning to a global environment breaks the well-named invariant of the machine. This point is addressed using an α-renaming and name generation in the variable (or exponential) transition, *i.e.* when substitution takes place.

Here we employ the global environments E of Sect. 3 and we redefine stacks as $\pi ::= \epsilon \mid \overline{t} :: \pi$. A state of the MAM is given by a code $\overline{t}$, a stack π and a global environment E.

The transitions of the MAM are:

$$\begin{array}{c|c|c c c|c|c}
\overline{t}\overline{u} & \pi & E & \to_{\mathtt{c}} & \overline{t} & \overline{u} :: \pi & E \\
\lambda x.\overline{t} & \overline{u} :: \pi & E & \to_{\mathtt{m}} & \overline{t} & \pi & [x{\leftarrow}\overline{u}] :: E \\
x & \pi & E & \to_{\mathtt{e}} & \overline{t}^{\alpha} & \pi & E
\end{array}$$

where $\to_{\mathtt{e}}$ takes place only if $E = E''\langle E'[x{\leftarrow}\overline{t}]\rangle$ and $\overline{t}^{\alpha}$ is a well-named code α-equivalent to $\overline{t}$ and s.t. any bound name in $\overline{t}^{\alpha}$ is fresh with respect to those in π and E.

The decoding of a MAM state $\overline{t} \mid \pi \mid E$ is similar to the decoding of a KAM state, but the stack and the environment context are applied in reverse order (this is why stack and environment in MAM states are swapped with respect to KAM states):

$$\begin{array}{rcl rcl}
\underline{\epsilon} & := & \langle\cdot\rangle & \underline{[x{\leftarrow}\overline{t}] :: E} & := & \underline{E}\langle\langle\cdot\rangle[x{\leftarrow}\overline{t}]\rangle \\
\underline{\overline{t} :: \pi} & := & \underline{\pi}\langle\langle\cdot\rangle\overline{t}\rangle & \underline{\overline{t} \mid \pi \mid E} & := & \underline{E}\langle\underline{\pi}\langle\overline{t}\rangle\rangle
\end{array}$$

To every MAM state $\overline{t} \mid \pi \mid E$ we associate the pair $(\underline{\pi}\langle\overline{t}\rangle, E)$ (note that $\underline{\pi}\langle\overline{t}\rangle$ now is a code, *i.e.* it does not contain explicit substitutions) and call it the *global closure* of the state.

As for the KAM, the decoding of contexts can be done statically, *i.e.* it does not need dynamic invariants.

Lemma 7.3 (Contextual Decoding)**.** *Let E be a global environment and π be a stack of the MAM. Then $\underline{E}$ is a substitution context, and both $\underline{\pi}$ and $\underline{\pi}\langle\underline{E}\rangle$ are evaluation contexts.*

For the dynamic invariants we need a different notion of closed closure.

Definition 7.4. *Given a global environment E and a code $\overline{t}$, we define by mutual induction two predicates* E is closed *and* $(\overline{t}, E)$ is closed *as follows:*

$$\begin{array}{rcl}
 & & \epsilon \textit{ is closed} \\
(\overline{t}, E) \textit{ is closed} & \Longrightarrow & [x{\leftarrow}t] :: E \textit{ is closed} \\
\mathtt{fv}(\overline{t}) \subseteq \Delta(E) \wedge E \textit{ is closed} & \Longrightarrow & (\overline{t}, E) \textit{ is closed}
\end{array}$$

The dynamic invariants are:

Lemma 7.5 (MAM invariants)**.** *Let $s = \overline{u} \mid \pi \mid E$ be a MAM state reached by an execution ρ of initial well-named code $\overline{t}$. Then:*

1. Global Closure: *the global closure $(\underline{\pi}\langle\overline{t}\rangle, E)$ of s is closed;*
2. Subterm: *any code in s is a literal subterm of $\overline{t}$;*
3. Names: *the global closure of s is well-named;*
4. Environment Size: *the length of the global environment in s is bound by $|\rho|_m$.*

Abstract Considerations on Concrete Implementations. Note the new environment size invariant. The bound now depends on the length of the evaluation sequence ρ, not on the size of the initial term $\overline{t}$. If one implements $\to_{\mathtt{e}}$ looking for x in E sequentially, then each $\to_{\mathtt{e}}$ transition has cost $O(|\rho|_m)$, and the cost of implementing ρ is easily seen to become quadratic in $|\rho|$. Therefore—at first sight—the MAM is not a reasonable abstract machine (in the sense of Sect. 5). However, the MAM is meant to be implemented using a representation of codes pointers for variables, so that looking for x in E takes constant time. Then the global environment, even if formalized as a list, should rather be considered as a store.

$\overline{t}\overline{u}$	π	D	E	$\to_{c_1}$	$\overline{t}$	$\overline{u} :: \pi$	D	E
$\lambda x.\overline{t}$	$\overline{u} :: \pi$	D	E	$\to_{\mathtt{m}}$	$\overline{t}$	π	D	$[x \leftarrow \overline{u}] :: E$
x	π	D	$E_1 :: [x \leftarrow \overline{t}] :: E_2$	$\to_{c_2}$	$\overline{t}$	ϵ	$(E_1, x, \pi) :: D$	E_2
$\overline{v}$	ϵ	$(E_1, x, \pi) :: D$	E_2	$\to_{\mathtt{e}}$	$\overline{v}^{\alpha}$	π	D	$E_1 :: [x \leftarrow \overline{v}] :: E_2$

Figure 3. The Milner Abstract machine by-neeD (MAD).

The name invariant is what guarantees that variables can indeed be taken as pointers, as there is no name clash. Note that the cost of a $\to_{\mathtt{e}}$ transition is not constant, as the renaming operation actually makes $\to_{\mathtt{e}}$ linear in $|t|$ (by the subterm invariant). So, assuming a pointer-based representation, ρ can be implemented in time $O(|\rho| \cdot |\overline{t}|)$, as for local machines. In other words, the MAM is a reasonable abstract machine.

Theorem 7.6 (MAM Distillation)**.** *$(MAM, \mathtt{Name}, \equiv, \underline{\cdot})$ is a reflective distillery. In particular, on a reachable state s we have:*

1. Commutative*: if $s \to_{\mathtt{c}} s'$ then $\underline{s} = \underline{s'}$;*
2. Multiplicative*: if $s \to_{\mathtt{m}} s'$ then $\underline{s} \multimap_{\mathtt{m}} \equiv \underline{s'}$;*
3. Exponential*: if $s \to_{\mathtt{e}} s'$ then $\underline{s} \multimap_{\mathtt{e}} =_{\alpha} \underline{s'}$.*

Proof. Properties of the decoding (*progress* is as for the KAM):

1. *Commutative*. In contrast to the KAM, $\to_{\mathtt{c}}$ gives a true identity:

$$\underline{\overline{t}\overline{u} \mid \pi \mid E} \;=\; \underline{E}\langle \underline{\pi}\langle \overline{t}\overline{u}\rangle\rangle \;=\; \underline{\overline{t} \mid \overline{u} :: \pi \mid E}$$

2. *Multiplicative*. Since substitutions and evaluation contexts commute via $\equiv$ (Lemma 2.4), $\to_{\mathtt{m}}$ maps to:

$$\begin{array}{rcll} \underline{\lambda x.\overline{t} \mid \overline{u} :: \pi \mid E} & = & \underline{E}\langle \underline{\pi}\langle (\lambda x.\overline{t})\overline{u}\rangle\rangle & \multimap_{\mathtt{m}} \\ & & \underline{E}\langle \underline{\pi}\langle \overline{t}[x \leftarrow \overline{u}]\rangle\rangle & \equiv_{Lem.2.4} \\ & & \underline{E}\langle \underline{\pi}\langle \overline{t}\rangle [x \leftarrow \overline{u}]\rangle & = \\ & & \underline{\overline{t} \mid \pi \mid [x \leftarrow \overline{u}] :: E} & \end{array}$$

3. *Exponential*. The erasure of part of the environment of the KAM is replaced by an explicit use of α-equivalence:

$$\begin{array}{rcll} \underline{x \mid \pi \mid E :: [x \leftarrow \overline{u}] :: E'} & = & \underline{E'}\langle \underline{E}\langle \underline{\pi}\langle x\rangle\rangle [x \leftarrow \overline{u}]\rangle & \multimap_{\mathtt{e}} \\ & & \underline{E'}\langle \underline{E}\langle \underline{\pi}\langle \overline{u}\rangle\rangle [x \leftarrow \overline{u}]\rangle & =_{\alpha} \\ & & \underline{E'}\langle \underline{E}\langle \underline{\pi}\langle \overline{u}^{\alpha}\rangle\rangle [x \leftarrow \overline{u}]\rangle & = \\ & & \underline{\overline{u}^{\alpha} \mid \pi \mid E :: [x \leftarrow \overline{u}] :: E'} & \end{array}$$

□

Digression about $\equiv$. Note that in the distillation theorem structural equivalence is used only to commute with stacks. The calculus and the machine in fact form a distillery also with respect to the following simpler notion of structural equivalence. Let $\equiv_{\text{MAM}}$ be the smallest equivalence relation generated by the closure by (call-by-name) evaluation contexts of the axiom $\equiv_{@l}$ in Fig. 1 (page 5). The next lemma guarantees that $\equiv_{\text{MAM}}$ is a strong bisimulation (the proof is in [9]), and so $\equiv_{\text{MAM}}$ provides another MAM distillery.

Lemma 7.7. *$\equiv_{MAM}$ is a strong bisimulation with respect to $\multimap$.*

8. Call-by-Need: the MAD and the Merged MAD

In this section we introduce a new abstract machine for CBNeed, deemed *Milner Abstract machine by-neeD* (MAD). The MAD arises very naturally as a reformulation of the `Need` calculus of Sect. 2. The motivations behind the introduction of a new machine are:

1. *Simplicity*: the MAD is arguably simpler than all other CBNeed machines in the literature, in particular its distillation is very natural;
2. *Factorizing the Distillation of the Lazy KAM and of the SAM*: the study of the MAD will be followed by two sections showing how to tweak the MAD in order to obtain (simplifications of) two CBNeed machines in the literature, Cregut's Lazy KAM and Sestoft's machine (here called *SAM*). Expressing the Lazy KAM and the SAM as modifications of the MAD helps understanding their design, their distillation (that would otherwise look very technical), and their relationship;
3. *Simpler Reasoning*: for CBNeed the proof that distillation preserves complexity (in forthcoming Sect. 11) is subtle, and requires a global analysis. The MAD allows to reason on a simple machine. The reasoning is then easily seen to scale up to its modified versions, without having to deal from the start with their complex structure.
4. *Modularity of Our Contextual Theory of Abstract Machines*: the MAD is obtained by applying to the KAM the following two tweaks:
   (a) *Global Environments*: the MAD uses the global environment approach of the MAM to implement memoization;
   (b) *Dump*: the MAD uses the dump-like approach of the Split CEK/SECD to evaluate inside explicit substitutions;

8.1 The MAD

The MAD is shown in Fig. 3. Note that when the code is a variable the transition is now commutative. The idea is that whenever the code is a variable x and the environment has the form $E_1 :: [x \leftarrow \overline{t}] :: E_2$, the machine jumps to evaluate $\overline{t}$ saving the prefix of the environment E_1, the variable x on which it will substitute the result of evaluating $\overline{t}$, and the stack π. This is how hereditarily weak head evaluation context are implemented by the MAD.

Dumps (D) and their decoding are defined by

$$D ::= \epsilon \mid (E, x, \pi) :: D$$

$$\underline{\epsilon} \;:=\; \langle\cdot\rangle \qquad \underline{(E, x, \pi) :: D} \;:=\; \underline{E}\langle \underline{D}\langle \underline{\pi}\langle x\rangle\rangle\rangle [x \leftarrow \langle\cdot\rangle]$$

The decoding of terms, environments, and stacks is defined as for the KAM. The decoding of states is defined by $\underline{\overline{t} \mid \pi \mid D \mid E} := \underline{E}\langle \underline{D}\langle \underline{\pi}\langle \overline{t}\rangle\rangle\rangle$. The decoding of contexts is static:

Lemma 8.1 (Contextual Decoding)**.** *Let D, π, and E be a dump, a stack, and a global environment of the MAD, respectively. Then $\underline{D}$, $\underline{D}\langle\underline{\pi}\rangle$, $\underline{E}\langle\underline{D}\rangle$, and $\underline{E}\langle\underline{D}\langle\underline{\pi}\rangle\rangle$ are CBNeed evaluation contexts.*

Closed closures are defined as for the MAM. Given a state $s = \overline{t} \mid \pi \mid D \mid E_0$ with $D = (E_1, x_1, \pi_1) :: \ldots :: (E_n, x_n, \pi_n)$, its closures are $(\underline{\pi}\langle\overline{t}\rangle, E_0)$ and, for $i \in \{1, \ldots, n\}$,

$$(\underline{\pi_i}\langle x_i\rangle, E_i :: [x_i \leftarrow \underline{\pi_{i-1}}\langle x_{i-1}\rangle] :: \ldots :: [x_1 \leftarrow \underline{\pi}\langle\overline{t}\rangle] :: E_0).$$

The dynamic invariants are:

Lemma 8.2 (MAD invariants)**.** *Let $s = \overline{t} \mid \pi \mid D \mid E_0$ be a MAD reachable state whose initial code $\overline{t}$ is well-named, and s.t. $D = (E_1, x_1, \pi_1) :: \ldots :: (E_n, x_n, \pi_n)$. Then:*

1. Global Closure*: the closures of s are closed;*
2. Subterm*: any code in s is a literal subterm of $\overline{t}$;*
3. Names*: the closures of s are well-named.*

$\overline{t}\overline{u}$	π	E	$\rightarrow_{\mathtt{c}_1}$	$\overline{t}$	$\mathbf{a}(\overline{u}) :: \pi$	E
$\lambda x.\overline{t}$	$\mathbf{a}(\overline{u}) :: \pi$	E	$\rightarrow_{\mathtt{m}}$	$\overline{t}$	π	$[x\leftarrow\overline{u}] :: E$
x	π	$E_1 :: [x\leftarrow\overline{t}] :: E_2$	$\rightarrow_{\mathtt{c}_2}$	$\overline{t}$	$\mathbf{h}(E_1, x) :: \pi$	E_2
$\overline{v}$	$\mathbf{h}(E_1, x) :: \pi$	E_2	$\rightarrow_{\mathtt{e}}$	$\overline{v}^{\alpha}$	π	$E_1 :: [x\leftarrow\overline{v}] :: E_2$

Figure 4. The Merged MAD.

For the properties of the decoding function please note that, as defined in Sect. 2, the structural congruence $\equiv_{\mathtt{Need}}$ for CBNeed is different from before.

Theorem 8.3 (MAD Distillation). $(\mathrm{MAD}, \mathtt{Need}, \equiv_{\mathtt{Need}}, \underline{\cdot})$ *is a reflective distillery. In particular, on a reachable state s we have:*

1. Commutative 1*: if $s \rightarrow_{\mathtt{c}_1} s'$ then $\underline{s} = \underline{s'}$;*
2. Commutative 2*: if $s \rightarrow_{\mathtt{c}_2} s'$ then $\underline{s} = \underline{s'}$;*
3. Multiplicative*: if $s \rightarrow_{\mathtt{m}} s'$ then $\underline{s} \multimap_{\mathtt{m}} \equiv_{\mathtt{Need}} \underline{s'}$;*
4. Exponential*: if $s \rightarrow_{\mathtt{e}} s'$ then $\underline{s} \multimap_{\mathtt{e}} =_{\alpha} \underline{s'}$.*

Proof. 1. *Commutative 1.*

$$\underline{\overline{t}\overline{u} \mid \pi \mid D \mid E} = \underline{E}\langle \underline{D}\langle \underline{\pi}\langle \overline{t}\overline{u}\rangle\rangle\rangle = \underline{\overline{t} \mid \overline{u} :: \pi \mid D \mid E}$$

2. *Commutative 2:*

$$\begin{array}{rcl} \underline{x \mid \pi \mid D \mid E_1 :: [x\leftarrow\overline{t}] :: E_2} & = & \underline{E_2}\langle \underline{E_1}\langle \underline{D}\langle \underline{\pi}\langle x\rangle\rangle\rangle[x\leftarrow\overline{t}]\rangle \\ & = & \underline{\overline{t} \mid \epsilon \mid (E_1, x, \pi) :: D \mid E_2} \end{array}$$

3. *Multiplicative.*

$$\begin{array}{rcll} \underline{\lambda x.\overline{t} \mid \overline{u} :: \pi \mid D \mid E} & = & \underline{E}\langle \underline{D}\langle \underline{\pi}\langle (\lambda x.\overline{t})\,\overline{u}\rangle\rangle\rangle & \multimap_{\mathtt{m}} \\ & & \underline{E}\langle \underline{D}\langle \underline{\pi}\langle \overline{t}[x\leftarrow\overline{u}]\rangle\rangle\rangle & \equiv_{\mathtt{Need}}\ \text{Lem. 2.4} \\ & & \underline{E}\langle \underline{D}\langle \underline{\pi}\langle \overline{t}\rangle\rangle[x\leftarrow\overline{u}]\rangle & = \\ & & \underline{\overline{t} \mid \pi \mid D \mid [x\leftarrow\overline{u}] :: E} & \end{array}$$

Note that to apply Lemma 2.4 we use the global closure invariant, as $\overline{u}$, being on the stack, is closed by E and so $\underline{D}$ does not capture its free variables.

4. *Exponential.*

$$\begin{array}{rcl} \underline{\overline{v} \mid \epsilon \mid (E_1, x, \pi) :: D \mid E_2} & = & \underline{E_2}\langle \underline{E_1}\langle \underline{D}\langle \underline{\pi}\langle x\rangle\rangle\rangle[x\leftarrow\overline{v}]\rangle \\ & \multimap_{\mathtt{e}} & \underline{E_2}\langle \underline{E_1}\langle \underline{D}\langle \underline{\pi}\langle \overline{v}\rangle\rangle\rangle[x\leftarrow\overline{v}]\rangle \\ & =_{\alpha} & \underline{E_2}\langle \underline{E_1}\langle \underline{D}\langle \underline{\pi}\langle \overline{v}^{\alpha}\rangle\rangle\rangle[x\leftarrow\overline{v}]\rangle \\ & = & \underline{\overline{v}^{\alpha} \mid \pi \mid D \mid E_1 :: [x\leftarrow\overline{v}] :: E_2} \end{array}$$

Progress. Let $s = \overline{t} \mid \pi \mid D \mid E$ be a commutative normal form s.t. $\underline{s} \multimap u$. If $\overline{t}$ is

1. *an application $\overline{u}\overline{w}$.* Then a $\rightarrow_{\mathtt{c}_1}$ transition applies and s is not a commutative normal form, absurd;
2. *an abstraction v.* The decoding $\underline{s}$ is of the form $\underline{E}\langle \underline{D}\langle \underline{\pi}\langle v\rangle\rangle\rangle$. The stack π and the dump D cannot both be empty, since then $\underline{s} = \underline{E}\langle v\rangle$ would be normal. So either the stack is empty and a $\rightarrow_{\mathtt{e}}$ transition applies, or the stack is not empty and a $\rightarrow_{\mathtt{m}}$ transition applies;
3. *a variable x.* By Lemma 8.2.1 it must be bound by E, so a $\rightarrow_{\mathtt{c}_2}$ transition applies, and s is not a commutative normal form, absurd. □

Abstract Considerations on Concrete Implementations. Consider transition $\rightarrow_{\mathtt{c}_2}$. Note that the saving of the prefix E_1 in the dump forces to have E implemented as a list, and so to go through E sequentially. This fact goes against the intuition that E is a store (rather than a list), and makes the MAD an unreasonable abstract machine (see the analogous considerations for the KAM and for the MAM). To solve this point, in Sect. 10 we will present the Pointing MAD, a variant of the MAD (akin to Sestoft's machine for CBNeed [44]) that avoids saving E_1 in a dump entry, and restoring the store view of the global environment. The detour is justified as follows:

1. the Pointing MAD is more involved;
2. for the complexity analysis of distillation in Sect. 11 it is easier to reason on the MAD;
3. this issue about concrete implementations is orthogonal to the complexity analysis of the distillation process.

9. The Merged MAD, or Revisiting the Lazy KAM

Splitting the stack of the CEK machine in two we obtained a simpler form of the SECD machine. In this section we apply to the MAD the reverse transformation. The result is a machine, deemed *Merged MAD*, having only one stack and that can be seen as a simpler version of Cregut's lazy KAM [19] (but we are rather inspired by Danvy and Zerny's presentation in [24]).

To distinguish the two kinds of objects on the stack we use a marker, as for the CEK and the LAM. Formally, the syntax for stacks is:

$$\pi ::= \epsilon \mid \mathbf{a}(\overline{t}) :: \pi \mid \mathbf{h}(E, x) :: \pi$$

where $\mathbf{a}(\overline{t})$ denotes a term to be used as an argument (as for the CEK) and $\mathbf{h}(E, x, \pi)$ is morally an entry of the dump of the MAD, where however there is no need to save the current stack. The transitions of the Merged MAD are in Fig. 4.

The decoding is defined as follows

$$\begin{array}{rcl} \underline{\epsilon} & := & \langle\cdot\rangle \\ \underline{[x\leftarrow\overline{t}] :: E} & := & \underline{E}\langle\langle\cdot\rangle[x\leftarrow\overline{t}]\rangle \\ \underline{\mathbf{h}(E, x) :: \pi} & := & \underline{E}\langle\underline{\pi}\langle x\rangle\rangle[x\leftarrow\langle\cdot\rangle] \\ \underline{\mathbf{a}(\overline{t}) :: \pi} & := & \underline{\pi}\langle\langle\cdot\rangle\overline{t}\rangle \\ \underline{\overline{t} \mid \pi \mid E} & := & \underline{E}\langle\underline{\pi}\langle\overline{t}\rangle\rangle \end{array}$$

Lemma 9.1 (Contextual Decoding). *Let π and E be a stack and a global environment of the Merged MAD. Then $\underline{\pi}$ and $\underline{E}\langle\underline{\pi}\rangle$ are CBNeed evaluation contexts.*

The dynamic invariants of the Merged MAD are exactly the same of the MAD, with respect to an analogous set of closures associated to a state (whose exact definition is omitted). The proof of the following theorem—almost identical to that of the MAD—is in [9].

Theorem 9.2 (Merged MAD Distillation). $(\text{Merged MAD}, \mathtt{Need}, \equiv_{\mathtt{Need}}, \underline{\cdot})$ *is a reflective distillery. In particular, on a reachable state s we have:*

1. Commutative 1*: if $s \rightarrow_{\mathtt{c}_1} s'$ then $\underline{s} = \underline{s'}$;*
2. Commutative 2*: if $s \rightarrow_{\mathtt{c}_2} s'$ then $\underline{s} = \underline{s'}$;*
3. Multiplicative*: if $s \rightarrow_{\mathtt{m}} s'$ then $\underline{s} \multimap_{\mathtt{m}} \equiv_{\mathtt{Need}} \underline{s'}$;*
4. Exponential*: if $s \rightarrow_{\mathtt{e}} s'$ then $\underline{s} \multimap_{\mathtt{e}} =_{\alpha} \underline{s'}$.*

$\overline{t}\overline{u}$	π	D	E	$\rightarrow_{\mathtt{c}_1}$	$\overline{t}$	$\overline{u} :: \pi$	D	E
$\lambda x.\overline{t}$	$\overline{u} :: \pi$	ϵ	E	$\rightarrow_{\mathtt{m}_1}$	$\overline{t}$	π	ϵ	$[x \leftarrow \overline{u}] :: E$
$\lambda x.\overline{t}$	$\overline{u} :: \pi$	$(y, \pi') :: D$	$E_1 :: [y \leftarrow \square] :: E_2$	$\rightarrow_{\mathtt{m}_2}$	$\overline{t}$	π	$(y, \pi') :: D$	$E_1 :: [y \leftarrow \square] :: [x \leftarrow \overline{u}] :: E_2$
x	π	D	$E_1 :: [x \leftarrow \overline{t}] :: E_2$	$\rightarrow_{\mathtt{c}_2}$	$\overline{t}$	ϵ	$(x, \pi) :: D$	$E_1 :: [x \leftarrow \square] :: E_2$
$\overline{v}$	ϵ	$(x, \pi) :: D$	$E_1 :: [x \leftarrow \square] :: E_2$	$\rightarrow_{\mathtt{e}}$	$\overline{v}^{\alpha}$	π	D	$E_1 :: [x \leftarrow \overline{v}] :: E_2$

Figure 5. The Pointing MAD.

10. The Pointing MAD, or Revisiting the SAM

In the MAD, the global environment is divided between the environment of the machine and the entries of the dump. On the one hand, this choice makes the decoding very natural. On the other hand, one would like to keep the global environment in just one place, to validate the intuition that it is a store rather than a list, and let the dump only collect variables and stacks. This is what we do here, exploiting the fact that variable names can be taken as pointers (see the *abstract considerations* in Sect. 7.2 and Sect. 8.1).

The new machine, called Pointing MAD, is in Fig. 5, and uses a new dummy constant $\square$ for the substitutions whose variable is in the dump. It also has two multiplicative transitions, that will both distilled into $\multimap_{\mathtt{m}}$, depending on the content of the dump. It can be seen as a simpler version of *Sestoft's Abstract Machine* [44], here called SAM. Dumps and environments are defined by:

$$\begin{array}{rcl} D & ::= & \epsilon \mid (x, \pi) :: D \\ E & ::= & \epsilon \mid [x \leftarrow \overline{t}] :: E \mid [x \leftarrow \square] :: E \end{array}$$

A substitution of the form $[x \leftarrow \square]$ is *dumped*, and we also say that x is dumped.

Note that the variables of the entries in D appear in reverse order with respect to the corresponding substitutions in E. We will show that fact is an invariant, called *duality*.

Definition 10.1 (Duality $E \bot D$). *Duality $E \bot D$ between environments and dumps is defined by*

1. $\epsilon \bot \epsilon$;
2. $E :: [x \leftarrow \overline{t}] \bot D$ *if* $E \bot D$;
3. $E :: [x \leftarrow \square] \bot (x, \pi) :: D$ *if* $E \bot D$.

Note that in a dual pair the environment is always at least as long as the dump. A dual pair $E \bot D$ decodes to a context as follows:

$$\begin{array}{rcl} \underline{(E, \epsilon)} & := & \underline{E} \\ \underline{(E :: [x \leftarrow \square], (x, \pi) :: D)} & := & \underline{(E, D)} \langle \underline{\pi} \langle x \rangle \rangle [x \leftarrow \langle \cdot \rangle] \\ \underline{(E :: [x \leftarrow \overline{t}], (y, \pi) :: D)} & := & \underline{(E, (y, \pi) :: D)} [x \leftarrow \overline{t}] \end{array}$$

The analysis of the Pointing MAD is based on a complex invariant that includes duality plus a generalization of the global closure invariant. We need an auxiliary definition:

Definition 10.2. *Given an environment E, we define its* slice $E \upharpoonleft$ *as the sequence of substitutions after the rightmost dumped substitution. Formally:*

$$\begin{array}{rcl} \epsilon \upharpoonleft & := & \epsilon \\ (E :: [x \leftarrow \overline{t}]) \upharpoonleft & := & E \upharpoonleft :: [x \leftarrow \overline{t}] \\ (E :: [x \leftarrow \square]) \upharpoonleft & := & \epsilon \end{array}$$

Moreover, if an environment E is of the form $E_1 :: [x \leftarrow \square] :: E_2$, we define $E \upharpoonleft_x := E_1 \upharpoonleft :: [x \leftarrow \square] :: E_2$.

The notion of closed closure with global environment (Sect. 7.2) is extended to dummy constants $\square$ as expected.

Lemma 10.3 (Pointing MAD invariants). *Let $s = \overline{t} \mid E \mid \pi \mid D$ be a Pointing MAD reachable state whose initial code $\overline{t}$ is well-named. Then:*

1. Subterm: *any code in s is a literal subterm of $\overline{t}$;*
2. Names: *the global closure of s is well-named.*
3. Dump-Environment Duality:
   (a) $(\underline{\pi} \langle \overline{t} \rangle, E \upharpoonleft)$ *is closed;*
   (b) *for every pair (x, π') in D, $(\underline{\pi'} \langle x \rangle, E \upharpoonleft_x)$ is closed;*
   (c) $E \bot D$ *holds.*
4. Contextual Decoding: $\underline{(E, D)}$ *is a CBNeed evaluation context.*

Proof. See [9]. $\square$

The decoding of a state is defined as $\underline{\overline{t} \mid \pi \mid D \mid E} := \underline{(E, D)} \langle \underline{\pi} \langle \overline{t} \rangle \rangle$.

Theorem 10.4 (Pointing MADDistillation). (Pointing MAD, $\mathtt{Need}$, $\equiv_{\mathtt{Need}}$, $\underline{\cdot}$) *is a reflective distillery. In particular, on a reachable state s we have:*

1. Commutative 1 & 2: *if $s \rightarrow_{\mathtt{c}_1} s'$ or $s \rightarrow_{\mathtt{c}_2} s'$ then $\underline{s} = \underline{s'}$;*
2. Multiplicative 1 & 2: *if $s \rightarrow_{\mathtt{m}_1} s'$ or $s \rightarrow_{\mathtt{m}_2} s'$ then $\underline{s} \multimap_{\mathtt{m}} \equiv_{\mathtt{Need}} \underline{s'}$;*
3. Exponential: *if $s \rightarrow_{\mathtt{e}} s'$ then $\underline{s} \multimap_{\mathtt{e}} =_{\alpha} \underline{s'}$;*

Proof. Properties of the decoding:

1. *Commutative 1.* We have
$$\underline{\overline{t}\,\overline{u} \mid \pi \mid D \mid E} \;=\; \underline{(E, D)} \langle \underline{\pi} \langle \overline{t}\,\overline{u} \rangle \rangle \;=\; \underline{\overline{t} \mid \overline{u} :: \pi \mid D \mid E}$$
2. *Commutative 2.* Note that E_2 has no dumped substitutions, since $E_1 :: [x \leftarrow \square] :: E_2 \bot (x, \pi) :: D$. Then:
$$\begin{array}{ll} \underline{x \mid \pi \mid D \mid E_1 :: [x \leftarrow \overline{t}] :: E_2} & = \\ \underline{E_2} \langle \underline{(E_1, D)} \langle \underline{\pi} \langle x \rangle \rangle [x \leftarrow \overline{t}] \rangle & = \\ \underline{\overline{t} \mid \epsilon \mid (x, \pi) :: D \mid E_1 :: [x \leftarrow \square] :: E_2} & \end{array}$$
3. *Multiplicative 1, empty dump.*
$$\begin{array}{rcll} \underline{\lambda x.\overline{t} \mid \overline{u} :: \pi \mid \epsilon \mid E} & = & \underline{E} \langle \underline{\pi} \langle (\lambda x.\overline{t})\, \overline{u} \rangle \rangle & \multimap_{\mathtt{m}} \\ & & \underline{E} \langle \underline{\pi} \langle \overline{t}[x \leftarrow \overline{u}] \rangle \rangle & \equiv^{*}_{@l} \text{ Lem. 2.4} \\ & & \underline{E} \langle \underline{\pi} \langle \overline{t} \rangle [x \leftarrow \overline{u}] \rangle & = \\ & & \underline{\overline{t} \mid \pi \mid \epsilon \mid [x \leftarrow \overline{u}] :: E} & \end{array}$$
4. *Multiplicative 2, non-empty dump.*
$$\begin{array}{ll} \underline{\lambda x.\overline{t} \mid \overline{u} :: \pi \mid (y, \pi') :: D \mid E_1 :: [y \leftarrow \square] :: E_2} & = \\ \underline{E_2} \langle \underline{(E_1, D)} \langle \underline{\pi'} \langle y \rangle \rangle [y \leftarrow \underline{\pi} \langle (\lambda x.\overline{t})\, \overline{u} \rangle] \rangle & \multimap_{\mathtt{m}} \\ \underline{E_2} \langle \underline{(E_1, D)} \langle \underline{\pi'} \langle y \rangle \rangle [y \leftarrow \underline{\pi} \langle \overline{t}[x \leftarrow \overline{u}] \rangle] \rangle & \equiv_{\mathtt{Need}} \text{ Lem. 2.4} \\ \underline{E_2} \langle \underline{(E_1, D)} \langle \underline{\pi'} \langle y \rangle \rangle [y \leftarrow \underline{\pi} \langle \overline{t} \rangle][x \leftarrow \overline{u}] \rangle & = \\ \underline{\overline{t} \mid \pi \mid (y, \pi') :: D \mid E_1 :: [y \leftarrow \square] :: [x \leftarrow \overline{u}] :: E_2} & \end{array}$$

5. *Exponential.*

$$\begin{array}{ll} \overline{v} \mid \epsilon \mid (x,\pi) :: D \mid E_1 :: [x{\leftarrow}\square] :: E_2 & = \\ \underline{E_2\langle (E_1, D)\langle \pi\langle x\rangle\rangle [x{\leftarrow}v]\rangle} & \multimap_{\mathtt{e}} \\ \underline{E_2\langle (E_1, D)\langle \pi\langle v\rangle\rangle [x{\leftarrow}v]\rangle} & =_\alpha \\ \underline{E_2\langle (E_1, D)\langle \pi\langle v^\alpha\rangle\rangle [x{\leftarrow}v]\rangle} & = \\ \overline{v}^\alpha \mid \pi \mid D \mid E_1 :: [x{\leftarrow}\overline{v}] :: E_2 & \end{array}$$

Progress. Let $s = \overline{t} \mid \pi \mid D \mid E$ be a commutative normal form s.t. $\underline{s} \multimap u$. If $\overline{t}$ is

- *an application* $\overline{uw}$. Then a $\rightarrow_{\mathtt{c}_1}$ transition applies and s is not a commutative normal form, absurd.
- *a variable* x. By the machine invariant, x must be bound by E1. So $E = E_1 :: [x{\leftarrow}\overline{u}] :: E_2$, a $\rightarrow_{\mathtt{c}_2}$ transition applies, and s is not a commutative normal form, absurd.
- *an abstraction* $\overline{v}$. Two cases:
  - *The stack* π *is empty*. The dump D cannot be empty, since if $D = \epsilon$ we have that $\underline{s} = \underline{e\langle \overline{v}\rangle}$ is normal. So $D = (x, \pi') :: D'$. By duality, $E = E_1 :: [x{\leftarrow}\square] :: E_2$ and a $\rightarrow_{\mathtt{e}}$ transition applies;
  - *The stack* π *is non-empty*. If the dump D is empty, the first case of $\rightarrow_{\mathtt{m}}$ applies. If $D = (x, \pi') :: D'$, by duality $E = E_1 :: [x{\leftarrow}\square] :: E_2$ and the second case of $\rightarrow_{\mathtt{m}}$ applies. □

11. Distillation Preserves Complexity

Here, for every abstract machine we bound the number of commutative steps $|\rho|_{\mathtt{c}}$ in an execution ρ in terms of

1. the number of principal steps $|\rho|_p$,
2. the size $|\overline{t}|$ of the initial code $\overline{t}$.

The analysis only concerns the machines, but via the distillation theorems it expresses the length of the machine executions as a linear function of the length of the distilled derivations in the calculi. For every distillery, we will prove that the relationship is linear in both parameters, namely $|\rho|_{\mathtt{c}} = O((|\overline{t}| + 1) \cdot |\rho|_p)$ holds.

Definition 11.1. *Let* M *be a distilled abstract machine and* $\rho : s \rightarrow^* s'$ *be an execution of initial code* $\overline{t}$*.* M *is*

1. ***Globally bilinear*** *if* $|\rho|_{\mathtt{c}} = O((|\overline{t}| + 1) \cdot |\rho|_p)$*.*
2. ***Locally linear*** *if whenever* $s' \rightarrow_{\mathtt{c}}^k s''$ *then* $k = O(|\overline{t}|)$*.*

The next lemma shows that local linearity is a sufficient condition for global bilinearity.

Proposition 11.2 (Locally Linear ⇒ Globally Bilinear). *Let* M *be a locally linear distilled abstract machine, and* ρ *an execution of initial code* $\overline{t}$*. Then* M *is globally bilinear.*

Proof. The execution ρ writes uniquely as $\rightarrow_{\mathtt{c}}^{k_1} \rightarrow_p^{h_1} \ldots \rightarrow_{\mathtt{c}}^{k_m} \rightarrow_p^{h_m}$. By hypothesis $k_i = O(|\overline{t}|)$ for every $i \in \{1, \ldots, m\}$. From $m \leq |\rho|_p$ follows that $|\rho|_{\mathtt{c}} = O(|\overline{t}| \cdot |\rho|_p)$. We conclude with $|\rho| = |\rho|_p + |\rho|_{\mathtt{c}} = |\rho|_p + O(|\overline{t}| \cdot |\rho|_p) = O((|\overline{t}| + 1) \cdot |\rho|_p)$. □

CBN and CBV machines are easily seen to be locally linear, and thus globally bilinear.

Theorem 11.3. *KAM, MAM, CEK, LAM, and the Split CEK are locally linear, and so also globally bilinear.*

Proof. 1. *KAM/MAM.* Immediate: $\rightarrow_{\mathtt{c}}$ reduces the size of the code, that is bounded by $|\overline{t}|$ by the subterm invariant.
2. *CEK.* Consider the following measure for states:

$$\#(\overline{u} \mid e \mid \pi) := \begin{cases} |\overline{u}| + |\overline{w}| & \text{if } \pi = \mathbf{a}(\overline{w}, e') :: \pi' \\ |\overline{u}| & \text{otherwise} \end{cases}$$

By direct inspection of the rules, it can be seen that both $\rightarrow_{\mathtt{c}_1}$ and $\rightarrow_{\mathtt{c}_2}$ transitions decrease the value of $\#$ for CEK states, and so the relation $\rightarrow_{\mathtt{c}_1} \cup \rightarrow_{\mathtt{c}_2}$ terminates (on reachable states). Moreover, both $|\overline{u}|$ and $|\overline{w}|$ are bounded by $|\overline{t}|$ by the subterm invariant (Lemma 6.1.2), and so $k \leq 2 \cdot |\overline{t}| = O(|\overline{t}|)$.
3. *LAM* and *Split CEK*. Similar to Point 2, see [9]. □

CBNeed machines are not locally linear, because a sequence of $\rightarrow_{\mathtt{c}_2}$ steps (remember $\rightarrow_{\mathtt{c}} := \rightarrow_{\mathtt{c}_1} \cup \rightarrow_{\mathtt{c}_2}$) can be as long as the global environment E, that is not bound by $|\overline{t}|$ but only by the number $|\rho|_p$ of preceding principal transitions (as for the MAM). Adapting the previous reasoning to this other bound would only show that globally $|\rho|_{\mathtt{c}}$ is quadratic in $|\rho|_p$, not linear. Luckily, being locally linear is not a necessary condition for global bilinearity. We are in fact going to show that CBNeed machines are globally bilinear. The key observation is that $|\rho|_{\mathtt{c}_2}$ is not only locally but also globally bound by $|\rho|_p$, as the next lemma formalizes.

We treat the MAD. The reasoning for the Merged/Pointing MAD is analogous. Define $|\epsilon| := 0$ and $|(E, x, \pi) :: D| := 1 + |D|$.

Lemma 11.4. *Let* $s = \overline{t} \mid \pi \mid D \mid E$ *be a MAD state, reached by the execution* ρ*. Then*

1. $|\rho|_{\mathtt{c}_2} = |\rho|_e + |D|$.
2. $|E| + |D| \leq |\rho|_m$
3. $|\rho|_{\mathtt{c}_2} \leq |\rho|_e + |\rho|_m = |\rho|_p$

Proof. 1. Immediate, as $\rightarrow_{\mathtt{c}_2}$ is the only transition that pushes elements on D and $\rightarrow_{\mathtt{e}}$ is the only transition that pops them.
2. The only rule that produces substitutions is $\rightarrow_{\mathtt{m}}$. Note that 1) $\rightarrow_{\mathtt{c}_2}$ and $\rightarrow_{\mathtt{e}}$ preserve the global number of substitutions in a state; 2) E and D are made out of substitutions, if one considers every entry (E, x, π) of the dump as a substitution on x (and so the statement follows); 3) the inequality is given by the fact that an entry of the dump stocks an environment (counting for many substitutions).
3. Substitute Point 2 in Point 1. □

Theorem 11.5. *The MAD has globally linear commutations.*

Proof. Let ρ be an execution of initial code $\overline{t}$. Define $\rightarrow_{\neg c_1} := \rightarrow_{\mathtt{e}} \cup \rightarrow_{\mathtt{m}} \cup \rightarrow_{\mathtt{c}_2}$ and note $|\rho|_{\neg c_1}$ the number of its steps in ρ. We estimate $\rightarrow_{\mathtt{c}} := \rightarrow_{\mathtt{c}_1} \cup \rightarrow_{\mathtt{c}_2}$ by studying its components separately. For $\rightarrow_{\mathtt{c}_2}$, Lemma 11.4.3 proves $|\rho|_{\mathtt{c}_2} \leq |\rho|_p = O(|\rho|_p)$. For $\rightarrow_{\mathtt{c}_1}$, as for the KAM, the length of a maximal $\rightarrow_{\mathtt{c}_1}$ subsequence of ρ is bounded by $|\overline{t}|$. The number of $\rightarrow_{\mathtt{c}_1}$ maximal subsequences of ρ is bounded by $|\rho|_{\neg c_1}$, that by Lemma 11.4.3 is linear in $O(|\rho|_p)$. Then $|\rho|_{\mathtt{c}_1} = O(|\overline{t}| \cdot |\rho|_p)$. Summing up,

$$|\rho|_{\mathtt{c}_2} + |\rho|_{\mathtt{c}_1} = O(|\rho|_p) + O(|\overline{t}| \cdot |\rho|_p) = O((|\overline{t}| + 1) \cdot |\rho|_p)$$ □

The analysis presented here is complemented by the study in [8], where the number of exponential steps $\multimap_{\mathtt{e}}$ in a derivation d is shown to be polynomial (actually quadratic in CBN and linear in CBV and CBNeed) in terms of the number of multiplicative steps $\multimap_{\mathtt{m}}$ in d. Given our distillation theorems, the results in [8] equivalently relate the exponential and multiplicative transitions of the abstract machines. This derived analysis of principal transitions is a fruitful by-product of distilling abstract machines in the LSC.

12. Conclusions

The novelty of our study is the use of the linear substitution calculus (LSC) to discriminate between abstract machine transitions: some of them—the principal ones—are simulated, and thus shown to be logically relevant, while the others—the commutative ones—are mapped to the structural congruence and have to be considered as bookkeeping operations. On one hand, the LSC is a sharp tool to study abstract machines. On the other hand, it provides an alternative to abstract machines which is *simpler* while being *conservative* at the level of complexity analysis.

Acknowledgments

A special acknowledgment to Claudio Sacerdoti Coen, for many useful discussions, comments and corrections to the paper. In particular, we owe him the intuition that a global analysis of call-by-need commutative rules may provide a linear bound. This work was partially supported by the ANR projects LOGOI (10-BLAN-0213-02) and COQUAS (ANR-12-JS02-006-01), by the French-Argentinian Laboratory in Computer Science **INFINIS**, the French-Argentinian project **ECOS-Sud** A12E04, the Qatar National Research Fund under grant NPRP 09-1107-1-168.

References

[1] B. Accattoli. An abstract factorization theorem for explicit substitutions. In *RTA*, pages 6–21, 2012.

[2] B. Accattoli. Linear logic and strong normalization. In *RTA*, pages 39–54, 2013.

[3] B. Accattoli. Evaluating functions as processes. In *TERMGRAPH*, pages 41–55, 2013.

[4] B. Accattoli and U. Dal Lago. On the invariance of the unitary cost model for head reduction. In *RTA*, pages 22–37, 2012.

[5] B. Accattoli and U. Dal Lago. Beta Reduction is Invariant, Indeed. Accepted to LICS/CSL 2014, 2014.

[6] B. Accattoli and D. Kesner. The structural λ-calculus. In *CSL*, pages 381–395, 2010.

[7] B. Accattoli and L. Paolini. Call-by-value solvability, revisited. In *FLOPS*, pages 4–16, 2012.

[8] B. Accattoli and C. Sacerdoti Coen. On the Value of Variables. Accepted to WOLLIC 2014, 2014.

[9] B. Accattoli, P. Barenbaum, and D. Mazza. Distilling Abstract Ma chines (Long Version). Available at `http://arxiv.org/abs/1406.2370`, 2014.

[10] B. Accattoli, E. Bonelli, D. Kesner, and C. Lombardi. A nonstandard standardization theorem. In *POPL*, pages 659–670, 2014.

[11] M. S. Ager, D. Biernacki, O. Danvy, and J. Midtgaard. A functional correspondence between evaluators and abstract machines. In *PPDP*, pages 8–19, 2003.

[12] M. S. Ager, O. Danvy, and J. Midtgaard. A functional correspondence between call-by-need evaluators and lazy abstract machines. *Inf. Process. Lett.*, 90(5):223–232, 2004.

[13] Z. M. Ariola and M. Felleisen. The call-by-need lambda calculus. *J. Funct. Program.*, 7(3):265–301, 1997.

[14] Z. M. Ariola, A. Bohannon, and A. Sabry. Sequent calculi and abstract machines. *ACM Trans. Program. Lang. Syst.*, 31(4), 2009.

[15] M. Biernacka and O. Danvy. A syntactic correspondence between context-sensitive calculi and abstract machines. *Theor. Comput. Sci.*, 375(1-3):76–108, 2007.

[16] M. Biernacka and O. Danvy. A concrete framework for environment machines. *ACM Trans. Comput. Log.*, 9(1), 2007.

[17] S. Chang and M. Felleisen. The call-by-need lambda calculus, revisited. In *ESOP*, pages 128–147, 2012.

[18] P. Clairambault. Estimation of the length of interactions in arena game semantics. In *FOSSACS*, pages 335–349, 2011.

[19] P. Crégut. Strongly reducing variants of the Krivine abstract machine. *Higher-Order and Symbolic Computation*, 20(3):209–230, 2007.

[20] V. Danos and L. Regnier. Head linear reduction. Technical report, 2004.

[21] V. Danos, H. Herbelin, and L. Regnier. Game semantics & abstract machines. In *LICS*, pages 394–405, 1996.

[22] O. Danvy. A rational deconstruction of landin's secd machine. In *IFL*, pages 52–71, 2004.

[23] O. Danvy and L. R. Nielsen. Refocusing in reduction semantics. Technical Report RS-04-26, BRICS, 2004.

[24] O. Danvy and I. Zerny. A synthetic operational account of call-by-need evaluation. In *PPDP*, pages 97–108, 2013.

[25] N. G. de Bruijn. Generalizing Automath by Means of a Lambda-Typed Lambda Calculus. In *Mathematical Logic and Theoretical Computer Science*, number 106 in Lecture Notes in Pure and Applied Mathematics, pages 71–92. Marcel Dekker, 1987.

[26] R. Di Cosmo, D. Kesner, and E. Polonovski. Proof nets and explicit substitutions. *Math. Str. in Comput. Sci.*, 13(3):409–450, 2003.

[27] T. Ehrhard and L. Regnier. Böhm trees, Krivine's machine and the Taylor expansion of lambda-terms. In *CiE*, pages 186–197, 2006.

[28] M. Felleisen and D. P. Friedman. Control operators, the SECD-machine, and the lambda-calculus. In *3rd Working Conference on the Formal Description of Programming Concepts*, Aug. 1986.

[29] R. Garcia, A. Lumsdaine, and A. Sabry. Lazy evaluation and delimited control. In *POPL*, pages 153–164, 2009.

[30] T. Hardin and L. Maranget. Functional runtime systems within the lambda-sigma calculus. *J. Funct. Program.*, 8(2):131–176, 1998.

[31] D. Kesner. A theory of explicit substitutions with safe and full composition. *Logical Methods in Computer Science*, 5(3), 2009.

[32] D. Kesner and S. Lengrand. Resource operators for lambda-calculus. *Inf. Comput.*, 205(4):419–473, 2007.

[33] D. Kesner and F. Renaud. The prismoid of resources. In *MFCS*, pages 464–476, 2009.

[34] J.-L. Krivine. A call-by-name lambda-calculus machine. *Higher-Order and Symbolic Computation*, 20(3):199–207, 2007.

[35] P. J. Landin. The Mechanical Evaluation of Expressions. *The Computer Journal*, 6(4):308–320, Jan. 1964. . URL `http://dx.doi.org/10.1093/comjnl/6.4.308`.

[36] F. Lang. Explaining the lazy Krivine machine using explicit substitution and addresses. *Higher-Order and Symbolic Computation*, 20(3):257–270, 2007.

[37] X. Leroy. The ZINC experiment: an economical implementation of the ML language. Technical report 117, INRIA, 1990. URL `http://gallium.inria.fr/ xleroy/publi/ZINC.pdf`.

[38] J. Maraist, M. Odersky, and P. Wadler. The call-by-need lambda calculus. *J. Funct. Program.*, 8(3):275–317, 1998.

[39] J. Maraist, M. Odersky, D. N. Turner, and P. Wadler. Call-by-name, call-by-value, call-by-need and the linear lambda calculus. *Theor. Comput. Sci.*, 228(1-2):175–210, 1999.

[40] G. Mascari and M. Pedicini. Head linear reduction and pure proof net extraction. *Theor. Comput. Sci.*, 135(1):111–137, 1994.

[41] R. Milner. Local bigraphs and confluence: Two conjectures. *Electr. Notes Theor. Comput. Sci.*, 175(3):65–73, 2007.

[42] R. P. Nederpelt. The fine-structure of lambda calculus. Technical Report CSN 92/07, Eindhoven Univ. of Technology, 1992.

[43] G. D. Plotkin. Call-by-name, call-by-value and the lambda-calculus. *Theor. Comput. Sci.*, 1(2):125–159, 1975.

[44] P. Sestoft. Deriving a lazy abstract machine. *J. Funct. Program*, 7(3): 231–264, 1997.

Author Index

www.ingramcontent.com/pod-product-compliance
Lightning Source LLC
Chambersburg PA
CBHW080707220326
41598CB00033B/5336
* 9 7 8 1 4 5 0 3 3 2 6 5 1 *